Human Resource Management:

Positioning for the 21st Century

Sixth Edition

SIXTH EDITION

Human Resource Management:

Positioning for the 21st Century

Randall S. Schuler
NEW YORK UNIVERSITY

Susan E. Jackson
NEW YORK UNIVERSITY

West Publishing Company
MINNEAPOLIS/ST. PAUL
NEW YORK
LOS ANGELES
SAN FRANCISCO

PRODUCTION CREDITS:

Copyeditor Cheryl Drivdahl
Text Design Diane Beasley
Composition Carlisle Communications, Inc.

WEST'S COMMITMENT TO THE ENVIRONMENT

In 1906, West Publishing Company began recycling materials left over from the production of books. This began a tradition of efficient and responsible use of resources. Today, up to 95 percent of our legal books are printed on recycled, acid-free stock. West also recycles nearly 22 million pounds of scrap paper annually—the equivalent of 181,717 trees. Since the 1960s, West has devised ways to capture and recycle waste inks, solvents, oils, and vapors created in the printing process. We also recycle plastics of all kinds, wood, glass, corrugated cardboard, and batteries, and have eliminated the use of styrofoam book packaging. We at West are proud of the longevity and the scope of our commitment to the environment.

Production, Prepress, Printing and Binding by West Publishing Company.

 TEXT IS PRINTED ON 10% POST CONSUMER RECYCLED PAPER    PRINTED WITH SOY INK™

British Library Cataloguing-in-Publication Data. A catalogue record for this book is available from the British Library.

COPYRIGHT © 1981,
1984, 1987, 1990, 1993   By WEST PUBLISHING COMPANY
COPYRIGHT ©1996   By WEST PUBLISHING COMPANY
                          610 Opperman Drive
                          P.O. Box 64526
                          St. Paul, MN 55164–0526

Printed in the United States of America

03 02 01 00 99 98 97 96   8 7 6 5 4 3 2 1 0

Library of Congress Cataloging in Publication Data

Schuler, Randall S.
    Human resource management : positioning for the 21st century /
Randall S. Schuler, Susan E. Jackson.—6th ed.
        p.   cm.

    Includes bibliographical references and index.
    ISBN 0–314–06123–1 (alk. paper)
    1. Personnel management.   2. Personnel management—Case studies.
I. Jackson, Susan E.   II. Schuler, Randall S. Managing human
resources.   III. Title.
HF5549.S24895   1996
658.3—dc20
                                                            95–24154
                                                               CIP

◆ DEDICATION

*Dedicated to Students Preparing
to Conquer the Challenges of
the 21st Century.*

Contents

CHAPTER 3 *Establishing Fair Policies and Procedures* 76

CHAPTER 4 *Organizational Changes and Human Resource Planning: Focusing on the Key Issues   110*

CHAPTER 5 *Job Design: Meeting the Needs of the Business and Employees   150*

CHAPTER 6   *Job Analysis: Knowing Who Does What*   174

CHAPTER 7   *Recruitment: Developing a Pool of Candidates*   214

CHAPTER 8   *Selection and Placement: Picking from the Applicant Pool*   256

CHAPTER 9   *Socialization, Training, and Development: Ensuring Workforce Capability*   298

CHAPTER 10   *Performance Appraisal: Measuring Who Is Doing What Well   342*

CHAPTER 13 *Performance-Based Pay: Rewarding Performance Contributions* *464*

CHAPTER 14 *Indirect Compensation: Providing Benefits and Services* *502*

CHAPTER 15 *Occupational Safety and Health: Reducing the Incidence of Deaths, Injuries, and Diseases 536*

CHAPTER 16 *Unionization and Collective Bargaining: Representing the Employees 562*

CHAPTER 17 *Human Resource Information Systems and Assessment: Getting and Using the Facts 600*

CHAPTER 18 *The Human Resource Department: Linking Human Resources with the Business 624*

Preface

Increasingly, chief executive officers (CEOs) of companies, from the very largest multinational firms to the smallest domestic firms, claim that the management of people is vital to their success today and will continue to become more vital as we enter the 21st century. Thus, it is not surprising to hear CEO Bill Gates of Microsoft say, "The most important thing I do is hire bright people." Howard Schultz, CEO of Starbucks, says it this way: "Hire people smarter than you and get out of their way." General Electric's CEO Jack Welch expands on this a bit: "Without the right people in place, strategies can't get implemented." All three are suggesting that managing human resources is not only possible but no longer a choice: to be successful in today's highly competitive marketplace, they must have the best people available everywhere in their organizations.

Expanding this imperative is the reality that the global marketplace is now of concern and a challenge to American business. It is also becoming more and more strategic for American business. Just fifteen years ago, exports accounted for only 15 percent of the U.S. gross domestic product (GDP). Today, exports account for 30 percent. Some U.S. firms, such as General Motors, Ford, Quaker Oats, Coca-Cola, and Dow Chemical, generate substantial earnings in the global marketplace. Of the top ten pharmaceutical companies in the world, a majority are based in America. Of the top twenty-five industrial sectors in the world, the largest firms in half of them are American. In the service sector alone, U.S. firms dominate the top five hundred. This is particularly important given that the worldwide service economy accounts for more than 60 percent of the world's GDP and for most of the newly created jobs in industrial economies. Managing human resources effectively is also a challenge facing businesses worldwide. According to Floris Maljers, CEO of the British-Dutch company Unilever, a top-ten company in *Fortune's* Global 500, "Limited human resources, not unreliable capital, are the biggest constraint when companies globalize." Clearly, then, the global environment can only become more important as we enter the 21st century.

The world around us is changing. No longer can we Americans consider our share of the "good life" a given. If we are to maintain some semblance of that life, we as individuals, as organizations, and as a society will have to fight actively for it in an increasingly competitive global economy. So the new world economy offers challenges and opportunities for everyone!

PURPOSES OF THIS BOOK

Human Resource Management: Positioning for the 21st Century, Sixth Edition, attempts to provide a detailed understanding of just how important human resource management is to firms today as they enter the 21st century. A careful reading of this book will also give a comprehensive understanding of what effective firms in competitive environments are doing to manage their human resources as successfully as possible. Because firms are different from each other in many respects—such as size, location, technology, products or services, and corporate culture—this text uses many different companies as examples, including Wal-Mart, AT&T, Microsoft, Southwest Airlines, General Electric, Eaton, Avon, Saturn, Levi Strauss, Swiss Bank Corporation, Chrysler, Coca-Cola, Dow Chemical, Disney, Lincoln Electric, Aetna, Weyerhaeuser, Federal Express, UPS, PepsiCo, and Aid Association to Lutherans. These firms are effective year after year and are considered to be innovators in the management of their human resources.

To further describe the major issues facing human resource management today, this book returns again and again to several key themes: partnership, ethics, globalization, managing change, diversity, teamwork, and linking human resource management with the business. You will encounter these issues in one form or another throughout your working life, no matter what path your career takes. Even governments in the United States are challenged by these issues as they strive to improve their quality, to deal with the nation's ever-more-diverse workforce, and to help make and keep America competitive.

Line managers are often at the front of the operation, managing people, so much of an organization's success depends on how skillfully they do their jobs. This book considers human resource management issues from the perspectives of the line manager, the employee, and the human resource manager, all working in *partnership*. Managing human resources effectively is the responsibility of everyone in the organization. The 21st century will witness even greater cooperation among HR managers, line managers, and employees as teams strive to make their organizations more capable of success. Thus, this book is written for everyone who is working, or will one day work, in an organization.

The international arena is critical to business and human resource management today. This text explores various aspects of this issue, describing how other countries manage their human resources and discussing the human resource concerns of U.S. firms operating in other nations.

This edition also conveys the importance of managing human resources with an awareness of the needs of the business and of the environment, which includes legal and regulatory agencies, competitors, customers, and suppliers.

ORGANIZATION OF THIS BOOK

Our guiding principle in presenting this exciting material is that of a flow model. That is, we begin by describing the human resource activities that apply to individuals before they come to the organization and then as they move from newly hired job applicant to seasoned veteran. Before seeking job candidates, organizations should understand the environments in which they operate, including their economic, social, and demographic environments as well as their legal environment. They should also understand how their own characteristics influence their human resource needs. With these understandings, organizations can plan for the number and types of employees they need. This process includes comparing present and future needs in light of information about such concerns as labor market demand, competition, and the strategy of the organization. Information about job design and job requirements is necessary to further specify types of knowledge, skills, and abilities. Decisions are made about where and how to seek job applicants. The HR department in partnership with line managers and employees may need to develop tests to screen job applicants and select those most likely to succeed. After selection, employees become socialized and may receive training to ensure they can perform their jobs. Once ready to go, employees need performance standards. Their performance should be evaluated, and any performance deficiencies identified and corrected. A system of direct and indirect pay for the employees must also be established. At the same time, issues of employee safety and health must be addressed. If employees belong to unions, organizations will need to engage in collective bargaining and contract negotiations. Human resource information systems can be useful in conducting all of these activities, which most often are coordinated by a company's Human Resource Department.

The chapters of this text reflect this flow model. The first three chapters explain what managing human resources is about and identify the characteristics of the environment influencing the effective management of human resources. Each of the remaining chapters discusses one of the other human resource activities, beginning with a brief description of its purpose and importance.

✸ FEATURES OF THIS EDITION

Several features are incorporated into this edition:

◉ *"Managing Human Resources for the 21st Century":* These features describe in some detail the human resource activities of companies familiar to most readers. They are used to convey how effective companies are managing their human resources.

◉ *"Positioning for the 21st Century":* The purpose of these features is to suggest what firms should start working on today if they want to be ready for the events of the 21st century. To successfully implement many human resource practices requires time— time to analyze, plan, implement, and evaluate and revise.

◉ *"Using Data for the 21st Century":* In preparing for the 21st century, firms can watch and learn from other firms, or decide on their own what is required. In either case, a data-based approach is called for. The "Using Data" features provide data for use in developing human resource practices that can be implemented by the 21st century.

◉ *Discussion Questions:* The discussion questions at the end of each chapter seek to determine your understanding of the material found in the chapter. They include material in the body of the chapter and in the "Managing," "Positioning," and "Using Data" features. Thus, by the time you finish reading and studying all the chapters, you should know a great deal about human resource management, about what particular companies are doing today to manage their human resources, and about what companies should be preparing to do as they enter the 21st century.

◉ *In-Class Projects:* The in-class projects at the end of the chapters ask you to discuss the human resource activities used by the two companies in the end-of-text integrative cases. For some chapters, these cases provide plenty of evidence. For others, they provide little and you will need to investigate further or make educated guesses based on the material in the chapter and on your own experience.

◉ *Field Projects:* The field projects at the end of each chapter direct you to investigate human resource practices in companies in your neighborhood or locale. They may ask you to contact companies directly or to gather information about companies from the library or from others who know the companies.

◉ *Case Studies:* The case studies at the ends of some chapters offer challenge and variety. It is up to you to analyze what is going on and suggest improvements. In some instances, discussion questions are presented to guide your thinking; in other instances, you are on your own to determine the issues most relevant to the material in the chapter. Except in the two end-of-textbook integrative case studies, the companies in these cases are disguised, although their problems and challenges are not.

NEW FOR THIS EDITION

Every chapter in this edition has been extensively rewritten and reorganized to incorporate the most current ideas, research results, and real examples of human resource practices in action. The text provides more opportunities for you to build your human resource management skills, especially from the point of view of the line manager in partnership with the HR manager and the employees. Thus, an additional case study has been included in some chapters. Some chapters also have role-plays and exercises, and many have field projects. At the end of the book are two integrative case studies, one on Lincoln Electric (a for-profit, manufacturing company) and one on Aid Association for Lutherans (a non-profit, service firm). Each of these case studies has extensive descriptions of how the management of human resources is linked with the needs and objectives of the business. In each chapter, in-class projects ask you to describe in detail the nature of the human resource activities specific to that chapter and how they are related to the objectives of the companies.

To deepen your understanding of companies and their human resource management activities, each chapter opens with a "Managing" feature on a company that is then referred to throughout the chapter and in later chapters. Thus, by the time you have finished the book, you should be familiar with a large number of companies and the approaches they use to manage their human resources in a manner consistent with their needs and objectives.

SUPPLEMENTARY MATERIALS

Supplementary materials for *Human Resource Management: Positioning for the 21st Century,* Sixth Edition, prepared by Randall S. Schuler, include

- An Instructor's Resource Manual, which contains
  —Chapter outlines
  —Lecture enhancements, including experiential and skill-building exercises and end-of-chapter case notes
- A Test Manual which includes multiple-choice, true-false, and short essay questions with answers referenced to pages in the text
- WesTest, a computerized version of the test bank
- Transparency masters
- Acetate transparencies of the key transparency masters
- Videos, including short segments on companies illustrating topics discussed in various chapters, and additional videos in West's Human Resource Management Video Library (these are available to qualified adopters).

Additional materials include *Personal Computer Projects for Human Resource Management,* Second Edition, by Nicholas J. Beutell; and *Cases in Management, Organizational Behavior and Human Resource Management,* Fifth Edition, by Randall S. Schuler and Paul F. Buller. All these materials are available from West Publishing Company.

 ## ACKNOWLEDGMENTS

As with the previous editions, many fine individuals were critical to the completion of the final product. They include Paul Buller at Gonzaga University; Peter Dowling at the

University of Tasmania in Australia; Hugh Scullion at the University of Newcastle in England; Paul Sparrow at Manchester Business School in England; Shimon Dolan at the University of Montreal; Stuart Youngblood at Texas Christian University; Gary Florkowski at the University of Pittsburgh; Bill Todor at the Ohio State University; Nancy Napier at Idaho State University; Vandra Huber at the University of Washington; John Slocum at Southern Methodist University; Lynn Shore at Georgia State University; Mary Ahmed at Grand Forks; Ed Lawler at the Center for Effective Organizations, University of Southern California; Hrach Bedrosian at New York University; Lynda Gratton and Nigel Nicholson at the London Business School; Chris Brewster and Shaun Tyson at the Cranfield Management School; Michael Poole at the Cardiff Business School; Paul Stonham at the European School of Management, Oxford; Jan Krulis-Randa and Bruno Staffelbach at the University of Zurich; Albert Stahli and Cornel Wietlisbach at the GSBA in Zurich; Per Jenster and Jean Marie Hiltrop at IMD; Susan Schneider and Paul Evans at INSEAD; Jason Sedine at ISA/HEC; Stewart Black and David Ricks at Thunderbird; Mark Mendenhall at the University of Tennessee, Chattanooga; Helen De Cieri and Denise Welch of Monash University; Yoram Zeira of Tel-Aviv University; Dan Ondrack, the University of Toronto; Vladimir Pucik, Cornell University; Moshe Banai, Baruch College; Steve Kobrin, Wharton School; Steve Barnett, York University; Carol Somers, Lowell University; Christian Scholz, University of Saarlandes; Pat Joynt, Henley Management College; Reijo Luostarinen, Helsinki School of Economics and Business Administration; Mickey Kavanagh, SUNY, Albany; Wayne Cascio, University of Colorado, Denver; Ricky Griffin, Texas A&M University; Ed van Sluijs, University of Limberg; Joy Turnheim, New York University; and Mark Huselid, Rutgers University.

The following individuals provided many good ideas and suggestions for changes and alterations in their roles of reviewers and evaluators:

Janet C. Barnard
Rochester Institute of Technology

Debra Cohen
George Washington University

Gary W. Florkowski
University of Pittsburgh

Keith Hattrup
New York University

Mark A. Huselid
Rutgers University

Stella Kaplow
Columbia University

Marianne J. Koch
University of Oregon

Kenneth A. Kovach
University of Maryland at College Park

Oliver J. Mulford
Mankato State University

Christina E. Shalley
University of Arizona

Ann C. Wendt
Wright State University

Jon M. Werner
University of South Carolina

Caroline Wiley
University of Tennessee at Chattanooga

Stuart A. Youngblood
Texas Christian University

Several human resource managers, practicing line managers, and publishers also contributed in many important ways to this edition, particularly with examples and insights from their work experiences. They include Mike Mitchell, Judith Springberg, Tom Kroeger, Patricia Ryan, Margaret Magnus, Betty Hartzell, Don Bohl, Bob Kenny, Jack Berry, Steve Marcus, Paul Beddia, Mark Saxer, John Fulkerson, Cal Reynolds, Jon Wendenhof, Joan Kelly, Michael Losey, Jo Mattern, Larry Alexander, Nick Blauweikel, Mike Loomans, Sandy Daemmrich, Jeffery Maynard, Lyle Steele, Rowland Stichweh, Bill

Maki, Rick Sabo, Bruce Cable, Gil Fry, Bill Reffett, Jerry Laubenstein, Richard Hagan, Horace Parker, and Johan Julin.

The following individuals graciously provided case and exercise materials: George Cooley, Bruce Evans, Mitchell W. Fields, Hugh L. French, Jr., Peter Cappelli, Anne Crocker-Hefter, Stuart Youngblood, Ed Lawler, John Slocum, Jeff Lenn, Hrach Bedrosian, Kay Stratton, Bruce Kiene, Martin R. Moser, James W. Thacker, Arthur Sharplin, and Jerry Laubenstein.

The support, encouragement, and assistance of many individuals were vital to the production of this work. They include Lou DeCaro, who worked extensively and carefully in the preparation of the final chapter drafts; and Dave Rogers and George Daly, management department chair and dean, respectively, of the Stern School of Business. A special thanks to Vandra Huber for her contributions in the two previous editions. Also, several people at West Publishing deserve our special thanks for their help and support: Esther Craig, developmental editor, Sharon Adams Poore, acquisition editor, Cliff Kallemeyn and Paul O'Neill, production editors, and Carol Yonish, promotion manager. Without their professional dedication and competence, this book would not have been possible.

Randall S. Schuler and Susan E. Jackson
New York, New York

Human Resources: Competing Effectively in the 21st Century

The people who work here don't think of Southwest as a business. They think of it as a crusade.

HERB KELLEHER, CEO, Southwest Airlines Company
Fortune's Number One Leader in American Business[1]

With yearly sales of about $12 billion, the Weyerhaeuser Company is one of the largest paper and forest products companies in the world. Headquartered in Federal Way, it spreads most of its forty thousand employees throughout North America. Its major competitors include Georgia-Pacific Corporation, International Paper Company, and Westvaco Corporation.

Today, in the mid-1990s, the Weyerhaeuser Company is successful in many respects, yet it continually strives to improve. Its guiding *vision* is "To be the best forest products company in the world." Leading the company toward this vision is John W. Creighton, Jr., ("Jack Creighton") chief executive officer, who describes the company's *key strategies* as

- Making Total Quality the Weyerhaeuser way of doing business
- Relentlessly pursuing full customer satisfaction
- Empowering Weyerhaeuser people
- Leading the industry in forest management and manufacturing excellence
- Producing superior returns for our shareholders

The company's vision and these key strategies are in clear focus today, but before competition intensified to its present level, their importance was not so apparent. Through the 1970s, the firm enjoyed fairly consistent growth and financial success. Then, in the 1980s, things began to change: global and domestic competition roared in at the same time the national economy went into recession and the housing industry entered a major slump. These conditions created overcapacity in the paper industry. Suddenly the company's long-successful strategy of being a large-commodity lumber and paper business was no match against the tactics of new, smaller, and speedier competitors who focused more on the customer.

Faced with a do-or-die crisis situation in the 1980s, top management decided to decentralize operations and concentrate attention on the customer. They created three major divisions, or strategic business units: forest products, paper products, and real estate. The decentralized operating structure was motivating for those running the independent business units. But decentralization created new problems, too. In decentralized firms, it is easy to lose a feeling of identity with the larger company; inefficiencies due to duplication creep into the operation, and potential synergies may not be realized, so resources are underutilized.

The challenge of reducing the disadvantages of decentralization without losing its advantages was tackled by Creighton upon becoming CEO. He and a new senior management team established the company's new vision. Shared by everyone in the company, this vision helps align business objectives across the strategic business units. Supporting this vision and the company's key strategies is a set of common *values*, which are also shared by everyone in the company:

- *Customers:* We listen to our customers and improve our products and services to meet their present and future needs.
- *People:* Our success depends upon people who perform at a high level working together in a safe and healthy environment where diversity, development, and teamwork are valued and recognized.
- *Accountability:* We expect superior performance and are accountable for our actions and results. Our leaders set clear goals and expectations, are supportive, and provide and seek frequent feedback.
- *Citizenship:* We support the communities where we do business, hold ourselves to the highest standards of ethical conduct and environmental responsibility, and communicate openly with Weyerhaeuser people and the public.
- *Financial Responsibility:* We are prudent and effective in the use of the resources entrusted to us.

The vision and these common values facilitate coordination and cooperation between the people spread out across the different divisions.

Restructuring has helped Weyerhaeuser focus on its customers, be innovative, and become more efficient. But according to Creighton and his senior management team, ultimately it is the people—not the organizational structure—that make the company successful. In the preceding list of values, Weyerhaeuser's people have a prominent position. Furthermore, the values list describes how senior management expects people to behave in order to drive the business objectives. Managers' behaviors should support safety and health, diversity, teamwork, high performance, and total quality. Managers should empower employees, talk with customers, team with others in the company, and communicate effectively with everyone. Human resource practices play a central role in changing managers' old behaviors to be consistent with the new organization and the new expectations. Compensation, training and development, and performance management systems all must be aligned to deliver a clear and consistent message that encourages and supports the behaviors that can drive the business objectives.

The past ten years of change have not been easy for Weyerhaeuser. But through the cooperation of everyone in the company and with a new way of managing human resources, considerable success has been achieved. Yet the company is seeking ways to improve and move into an even better position for even more intense competition in the 21st century.[2]

 ## MANAGING HUMAN RESOURCES FOR THE 21st CENTURY

Managing human resources for the 21st century is high on the business agenda. Successful CEOs see human resources as assets that need to be managed more conscientiously, that is, in tune with the business, if their firms are to be competitive. They understand that aligning human resources with the new direction of the business may take several years. Thus, they are working now at moving their human resource assets into line with the business needs of the future.

As companies like Weyerhaeuser approach the subject of managing human resources for the 21st century, they draw upon the skills and knowledge of line managers, human resource (HR) professionals, and all other employees. In these firms, the special expertise of HR professionals in the HR department are used by, and in cooperation with, line managers and other employees.

Managing human resources engages everyone, and it takes time. It involves attending to the concerns of the moment while keeping a longer-term perspective in mind. It also involves continuously improving and changing, activities that take time to put in place and produce results. Consequently, the phrase "managing human resources for the 21st century" includes (a) the people management activities, policies, and practices that firms can use to compete effectively now, and (b) the many changing forces (e.g., technology, business restructuring, legal and social concerns) that organizations need to attend to today in order to ensure they are positioned to compete effectively in the 21st century.

 ## USING HUMAN RESOURCES TO COMPETE IN THE 21st CENTURY

Like Jack Creighton and Herb Kelleher, a growing number of other business leaders understand the importance of human resources for competing in the 21st century:

The best companies now know, without a doubt, where productivity—real and limitless productivity—comes from. It comes from challenged, empowered, excited, rewarded teams of people. It comes from engaging every single mind in the organization, making everyone part of the action, and allowing everyone to have a voice—a role—in the success of the enterprise. Doing so raises productivity not incrementally, but by multiples.

JACK WELCH, CEO, General Electric Company[3]

We're not anywhere near world class at a lot of these things [in the automobile industry]. The only way we can beat the competition is with people. That's the only thing anybody has. Your culture and how you motivate and empower and educate your people is what makes the difference.

ROBERT J. EATON, CEO, Chrysler Corporation[4]

Limited human resources—not unreliable capital—are the biggest constraint when companies globalize.

FLORIS A. MALJERS, CEO, Unilever N.V.[5]

If you take a look at the sources of sustainable, competitive advantage during the last decade, the only one that has endured has been the quality of the people who work for you.

JIM ALEF, EXECUTIVE VICE PRESIDENT AND HEAD OF HUMAN RESOURCES, First Chicago Corporation[6]

Because people are important to short- and long-term competitiveness and survival, business analysts pay attention to whether companies effectively manage their human resources domestically and globally.[7] For example, the *Fortune* ratings of America's most admired corporations, published early each year, considers the *ability to attract, develop, and keep talented people* a primary performance dimension, along with long-term investment value, financial soundness, use of corporate assets, quality of products and services, innovation, quality of management, and community and environmental responsibility.[8] Why do *Fortune* and other business magazines such as *Inc.* and *Money* include among their criteria of successful businesses the ability to manage human resources well?

Competitive Necessity and Organizational Success

According to Massachusetts Institute of Technology economist Lester C. Thurow, one reason business analysts value HR management is that firms will need human talent in order to compete in the 21st century: "Consider what are commonly believed to be the seven key industries of the next few decades—microelectronics, biotechnology, the new materials industries, civilian aviation, telecommunications, robots plus machine tools and computers plus software. All are brainpower industries."[9] If brainpower drives the business, attracting and keeping great talent becomes a necessity. But even for companies in industries other than the seven Thurow refers to, great human resource management increases success. Here being successful means effectively serving the interests of the organization itself, stockholders and investors, customers, employees, society, and suppliers.[10]

Recent studies show that firms that manage their human resources effectively have higher levels of profitability, higher annual sales per employee (productivity), higher market value, and higher earnings-per-share growth—in other words, they meet the needs of the organization, stockholders, and investors. Effective HR management can meet the needs of the employees in several ways: as firms survive, expand, and increase their profitability, they provide more employment security, more job opportunities, and higher wages. Successful human resource management serves the needs of society by elevating the standard of living, strengthening legal regulations and ethical guidelines, and controlling the effect of the firm on the surrounding community—that is, it contributes positively to society, which in turn supports a favorable corporate image in the mind of the public.[11]

The Best Get the Best

Like business analysts, the general public pays attention to whether a company has a good reputation for effectively managing its human resources. Besides reading business magazines such as *Fortune, Inc.,* and *Money,* they refer to lists such as *The One Hundred Best Places to Work, A Great Place to Work,* and *America's Top One Hundred Internships.* Lists like these are especially popular among students graduating from college, who view firms high in the rankings as desirable places in which to land their first full-time job. Dissatisfied workers who are looking for better employment situations read these lists too.

The result, over time, is that the best get the best: a good reputation for attracting, developing, and keeping good talent acts like a magnet drawing the best talent to the firm, which then leverages this advantage. When Lincoln Electric Company in Cleveland, Ohio, announced it was planning to hire two hundred production workers, it received over twenty thousand responses. When BMW Incorporated announced that it had selected Spartanburg, South Carolina as the site for its first U.S. production facility, it received more than twenty-five thousand unsolicited requests for employment. Numbers this large make it more feasible for Lincoln Electric and BMW to hire applicants who are two to three times more productive than their counterparts in other manufacturing firms. The best-gets-the-best cycle helps explain why, according to a recent study, the market value of firms increased after their names appeared on *Working Mother* magazine's list of the one hundred best companies for working mothers.[12]

Gaining Competitive Advantage

Because competition is the name of the game, especially for firms in highly competitive environments, such as Southwest Airlines, General Electric (GE), Lincoln Electric, and Weyerhaeuser, companies seek ways to compete that can last a long time and cannot easily be imitated by competitors. Harvard's Michael Porter refers to this as the desire of firms to gain competitive advantage.[13] Firms seek to gain competitive advantage in many ways: For example, Wal-Mart Stores uses rapid market intelligence so that the right products are always available in the right amounts. McDonald's Corporation enters into agreements with shopping mall developers to secure prime locations in their facilities. Au Bon Pain and Starbuck's negotiate special supplier arrangements to ensure that they receive some of the best coffee beans. Mrs. Field's Incorporated has a great information system that enables the firm to carefully monitor and enhance the service of each store outlet on a daily basis.

Firms also gain competitive advantage through their wise and innovative use of human resources. In fact, according to auto industry expert Maryann N. Keller, the "enduring advantages will come from making better use of people."[14] She nominates Saturn Industries' dealers and Toyota Motor Corporation's Georgetown, Kentucky, plant workers as examples of the kind of competitive advantage that will last: whole groups of carefully picked, highly motivated people determined to make customers happy.[15]

A Future Job Assignment for Managers

Given the importance of effectively managing human resources, it should come as no surprise that more and more companies value those who are particularly skilled in this area. According to the global consulting firm Korn/Ferry International, which conducted a worldwide study of fifteen hundred CEOs, expertise in managing human resources would be the second most important attribute for CEOs going into the 21st century; only strategic planning was ranked more important.[16] In another large international study conducted jointly by Towers Perrin and the IBM Corporation, nearly 60 percent of the line executives who were asked agreed that by the start of the 21st century, a position in human resource management would be viewed as a key experience for line managers.[17] In the past, taking such assignments often was viewed as synonymous with being sidetracked. But now, as companies and their managers realize success by improving how well they manage their human resources, these assignments are seen as critical components of that success.[18]

❖ HUMAN RESOURCE OBJECTIVES: SERVING MULTIPLE STAKEHOLDERS

At Harley-Davidson, we are committed to a corporate Vision that mandates how we run our businesses. Our Vision says: "Harley-Davidson, Inc. is an action-oriented, international company—a leader in its commitment to continuously improve the quality of profitable relationships with stakeholders. . . . Harley-Davidson believes the key to success is to balance stakeholders' interests through the empowerment of all employees to focus on value-added activities.[19]

Stakeholders are the institutions and people who influence and are influenced by how well human resources are managed.[20] They include the organization itself, stockholders and investors, customers, employees, society, and the strategic partners of the business (e.g., suppliers), as illustrated in Exhibit 1.1. When success is defined as effectively serving the interests of these groups, their needs define a firm's fundamental human resource objectives.

The Organization

Productivity—the value of goods and services produced by each employee—is an important "bottom-line" goal of all business organizations. As a nation, our ability to earn more money and enjoy a higher standard of living depends on productivity improvement. After experiencing meager productivity increases of less than 1 percent during the 1980s and into the early 1990s, by the mid-1990s, U.S. companies were registering rather strong productivity growth rates of more than 3 percent. Particularly outstanding increases were seen in the automobile, machinery, chemical, food processing, and computer sectors.[21] For example, in the automobile industry, productivity, measured as thousands of dollars of output per employee, increased more than 30 percent between 1988 and 1994. In several industries today, the productivity of U.S. companies exceeds that of firms in any other nation, including Japan and Germany.[22] This rather dramatic change in the overall rate of productivity growth has come about for several reasons, including improvement in how companies manage their human resources. As we move into the 21st century, productivity improvement through better management of human resources, such as that provided by Ford Motor Company's total quality program (Quality Is Job One) and Chrysler's team-based management system, will continue to be important.[23]

From the mid-1980s to the mid-1990s, large-scale research projects generated substantial evidence linking human resource management practices to bottom-line profitability and productivity gains. To help draw attention to this evidence, in 1993, the U.S. Department of Labor summarized much of it in a report titled *High Performance Work Practices and Firm Performance*.[24] For example, one study of sixty *Fortune* 1000

■ *Exhibit 1.1*
Stakeholders of Human Resource Management

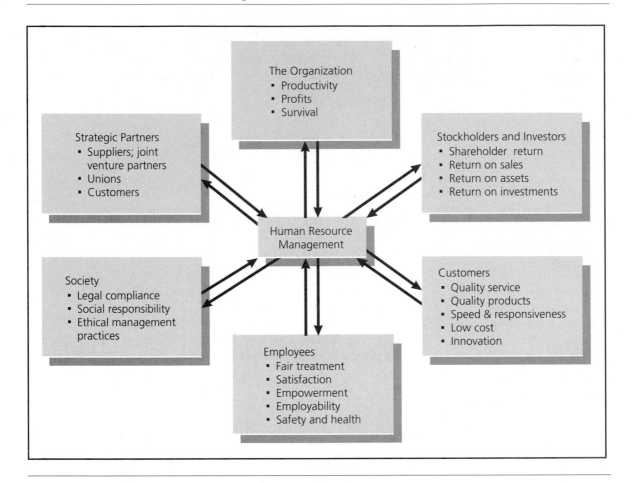

Companies involved asking thousands of employees to describe their job and their organizations. The responses were used to form an index to reflect how much emphasis was placed on human resources. The research results showed a strong association between profitability and emphasizing human resources, as measured by average return on assets over a five-year period.[25] An international study focusing on sixty-two automobile plants, eighteen located in North America, also demonstrated the importance of managing human resources. This study found a strong relationship between productivity and systematically integrating human resources management with a flexible production system (e.g., coordinating recruitment practices, the use of work teams, job rotations, training, and compensation). For similar vehicles produced in plants with similar technology, the use of modern integrative approaches to managing human resources resulted in faster production and higher quality.[26]

But productivity increases do not always translate into profitability increases. Many factors determine profitability. In the automobile business, design and operating efficiency are determinants, as are the costs of components used to make the final product. Together these factors help explain why Chrysler makes more profit per vehicle than Ford and General Motors.[27] Nonetheless, all three of these firms have been and are trying to manage their employees as effectively as possible.

Managing Human Resources for the 21st Century at FedEx

Between 1973 and 1994, FedEx added more than seventy thousand employees to its payroll. In 1990, as the United States' largest express transportation company, headquartered in Memphis, Tennessee, FedEx was the first service company to win the coveted Malcolm Baldrige National Quality Award. Since day one, its basic philosophy of doing business, as stated by founder and Chief Executive Officer Frederick W. Smith, has been People, Service, and Profit. Its motto is 100 Percent Customer Satisfaction.

This highly successful company understands the importance of its people. With a business that relies on individuals delivering packages overnight to customers anywhere, 100 percent customer satisfaction comes only from managing human resources as if they really matter. Highlighting its concern for managing human resources, FedEx formulated a philosophy of managing people based upon these cornerstones:

- no layoffs;
- guaranteed fair treatment;
- survey, feedback, action;
- promotion from within;
- profit sharing; and
- an open-door policy.

The company also has a pay-for-performance and pay-for-knowledge program, which is based on interactive video training and job knowledge testing for its thirty-five thousand customer-contact employees. Before couriers ever deliver a package, they receive at least three weeks of training. Because FedEx is constantly making changes or additions to its products and services, it also must continually update its training programs. According to Larry McMahan, vice president of human resource development, "We can't support a customer-oriented objective without having a strong emphasis on training."

A strong emphasis means, for example, that employees at hundreds of FedEx locations around the United States can readily access a twenty-five-disk training curriculum, which covers topics such as customer etiquette and defensive driving. It means that customer-contact employees take a job knowledge test every six months; the company pays each employee for four hours of study and preparation and for two hours of test taking. The knowledge required to do well on the test is so job related that performance on the test essentially reflects performance on the job. As an incentive for employees to get serious about doing well on the test, the company links their compensation to performance on the test. Employees who excel in applying their knowledge to job performance become eligible for additional proficiency pay.

FedEx dedicates an enormous amount of time, money, and effort to managing its human resources because it knows that doing so gives it an edge over its competitors when it comes to satisfying customers. FedEx manages people knowing that doing so really matters.[28]

Support from Top Management. Top managers in some companies become convinced that improving their human resource management practices is worthy of their attention when dramatic financial and productivity improvement can be directly traced to those practices. Consider the case of Levi Strauss Associates' Blue Ridge, Georgia plant. After gainsharing and quality enhancement programs were introduced in the plant, unit costs decreased 5.5 percent within a year.[29]

In some companies, the value of human resources is unquestioned and practices are continually scrutinized in order to find new ways to improve productivity and profitability. Federal Express Corporation is one such company. Years of relentless attention to how people are managed have helped FedEx maintain a position of leadership in a highly competitive industry. This company has developed a complex and integrated system of human resource practices, all designed to keep employees focused on the needs of customers and the business. Its system was not simply copied intact from another

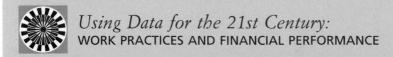

Using Data for the 21st Century:
WORK PRACTICES AND FINANCIAL PERFORMANCE

The most comprehensive study of work practices and financial performance is based on a survey of over seven hundred publicly held firms from all major industries. This study examined the use of HR in the following areas:

personnel selection	performance appraisal	incentive systems
job design	promotion systems	grievance procedures
information sharing	attitude assessment	labor-management participation

Firms using effective HR practices—or what were deemed the "best practices"—in these areas were generally found to have superior financial performance. The 25 percent of firms scoring highest on the index performed substantially higher on two key performance measures: annual shareholder return and gross return on capital.

After accounting for other variables likely to influence financial performance—such as industry characteristics—the human resource index remained significantly related to both performance measures: annual shareholder return and gross return on capital.[30]

Quartile of Human Resource Practice Index

Performance Measure	Bottom 25 Percent	Second 25 Percent	Third 25 Percent	Top 25 Percent
Annual Shareholder Return	6.5%	6.8%	8.2%	9.4%
Gross Return on Capital	3.7%	1.5%	4.1%	11.3%

company, nor did the firm develop it by applying some formula that could guarantee a correct solution. Rather, through a period of many years, FedEx developed its own unique set of practices to fit its specific situation (see "Managing Human Resources for the 21st Century at FedEx"). Over time, it developed a workforce that is uniquely qualified for its needs. By continuously changing and improving various practices within its human resource management system, FedEx strives to stay ahead of competitors who might try to copy its system, thereby maintaining its competitive advantage. This has certainly benefited the stockholders and investors, and other key stakeholders.

Stockholders and Investors

According to the U.S. Department of Labor report *High Performance Work Practices and Firm Performance,* firms with state-of-the-art work practices have substantially higher annual sales, market value, profits, and earnings-per-share growth. The precise numbers are described in "Using Data for the 21st Century: Work Practices and Financial Performance;" in general, they indicate that it pays for a firm to manage its human resources as effectively as possible.

Further support comes from an analysis of the firms that are recognized as having some of the most effective human resource practices. From firms listed in *The One Hundred Best Companies to Work for in America* in 1993, those with the most effective pay and benefits, availability of opportunities, job security, pride taken in work and company, level of openness and fairness, and friendliness and camaraderie were also likely to be strong economic performers according to a variety of indicators.[31]

◉ In terms of total shareholder return (the sum of stock price appreciation and dividends paid), the annual return for the one hundred best firms in 1993 was 19.5 percent over that in the previous eight years, compared with a 12 percent annual return for the three thousand largest companies in America.

◉ The financial performance of firms after they have been chosen as one of the one hundred best is also illuminating. Firms among the one hundred best in 1984 had an annual total return of 15 percent in the eight subsequent years, also above the average 12 percent for the three thousand largest companies.

◉ About two-thirds of the firms in 1993's one hundred best ranked in the top half of their industry in return on sales and in return on assets.[32]

Another study focused on companies that had gone through major changes and transformed their corporate culture from a traditional top-down form to a more participatory, bottom-up culture. Companies that made a change to greater employee involvement and participation reaped rewards such as higher returns on sales and investments in subsequent years.[33]

Customers

As Weyerhaeuser Company and FedEx and others have found, improving customer satisfaction is a primary means through which human resource management practices affect success. Reducing costs and improving product quality are two ways we generally think of improving customer satisfaction. But, as many companies have now learned, customers react to more than just these.[34] Good service is also important. Satisfied customers usually return to purchase more products and services in the future. Because return business can cost less than new business, improving customer retention by as little as 5 percent has been shown to improve profits by 28 percent for auto service, 35 percent for business banking, and 125 percent for credit card service.[35]

Exhibit 1.2 shows the results from a study of two thousand customers who purchased goods and services from five different service companies. When asked to allocate one hundred points to the five characteristics shown in the exhibit, on average, customers gave only eleven points to the tangible product or service (e.g., the food purchased or the report delivered). The remaining points were allocated to characteristics that more directly reflect the interactions with service providers. And, as the second bar graph in Exhibit 1.2 shows, customers often reported that these interactions were less than satisfactory.[36] With nearly 75 percent of current U.S. gross domestic product (GDP) being generated in the service sector, few companies can be satisfied with this situation.

Service companies win or lose during the moments of contact between employees and customers. This point was not lost on one company official:

As I was putting on paper some of my reflections on managing a service company, I realized that it was actually during the instant of contact between customer and staff that the future of the company hung in the balance. I call it the moment of truth. . .

JAN CARLZON, CEO and Chairman (Retired), Scandinavian Airlines System[37]

This moment of truth, it turns out, is often the moment when customers get a glimpse of how a firm manages its human resources. When the internal climate of the organization is positive, with employees generally getting along well and not leaving the company at too rapid a pace, customers report they are more satisfied and intend to return.[38] For example, using a sixty-second customer survey to study 771 stores, Sears, Roebuck and Company learned that the stores where customer service was best also had lower

■ *Exhibit 1.2*
Customer Ratings

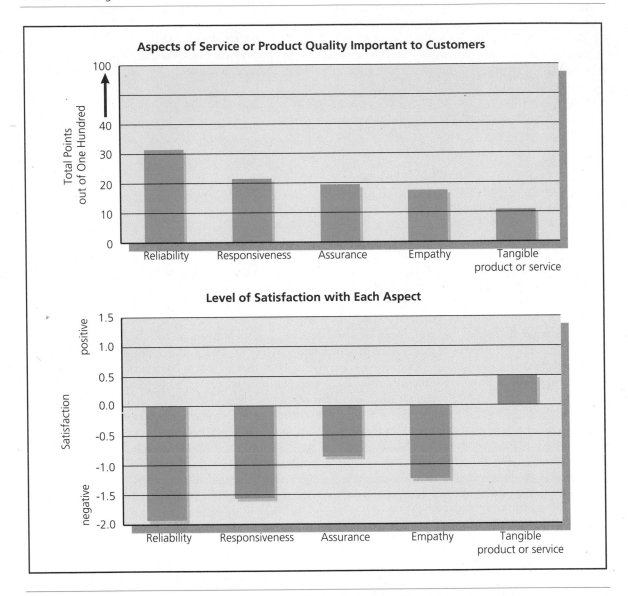

Aspects of Service or Product Quality Important to Customers

Level of Satisfaction with Each Aspect

SOURCE: Based on V. A. Zeithaml, A. Parasuraman, and L. L. Berry, *Delivering Quality Service* (New York: Free Press, 1990).

turnover rates.[39] Herb Kelleher at Southwest Airlines strongly acts on the belief, "If you don't treat your own people well, they won't treat other people well."[40]

Because frontline employees—such as the FedEx delivery people, the attendants at Disney theme parks, the sales clerks at Nordstrom, or the flight attendants at Southwest Airlines—are so important to service delivery, some experts have argued that service companies should be literally turned upside down.[41] Service providers should control important decisions, and everyone else should provide secondary support. Marketing campaigns, operations management systems, and practices for managing human resources should all be coordinated with customers' needs in mind. The objective? To create a *passion* for service by everyone in the company.

Focusing Employees on the Customer. Approaches to managing human resources appear to play a significant role in creating a passion for service, which is ultimately experienced by customers. For example, in financial services, passion for service appears to be strongest when employees are carefully selected for their service orientation, are trained extensively, receive plenty of performance feedback, and get paid fairly.[42]

Regardless of *how* they seek to satisfy customers, most companies recognize customers as primary stakeholders who wield considerable power, which is felt throughout the organization. To meet customers' demands for higher quality, for instance, companies such as Weyerhaeuser, Southwest Airlines, and FedEx are organizing to maintain an environment for quality excellence conducive to full participation and personal and organizational growth for their employees. This is the criterion for human resource utilization used by the committee that evaluates companies considered for the Malcolm Baldrige National Quality Award. How can a company meet this objective? These are some of the HR suggestions in the Baldrige guidelines:

- Promote cooperation such as internal customer-supplier techniques or internal partnerships.
- Promote labor-management cooperation, such as partnerships with unions.
- Use compensation systems based on building shareholder value.
- Create or modify recognition systems.
- Increase or broaden employee responsibilities.
- Create opportunities for employees to learn and use skills that go beyond current job assignments.
- Form partnerships with educational institutions to develop employees or to help ensure the future supply of well-prepared employees.[43]

These guidelines are, admittedly, unique—but they produce positive results:

> A sample of Baldrige National Quality Award finalists was used to examine the change in financial performance of firms after they implemented comprehensive changes in work practices; altogether, 15 companies considered exemplary in their customer-driven approach to quality, strong leadership, continuous improvement, and employee involvement were analyzed. The adoption of those exemplary practices were associated with better employee relations, improved operating procedures, greater customer satisfaction, and enhanced operating results. The average annual increase in market share after implementing new practices was 13.7%. Operating results, such as return on assets and return on sales, improved for all but two of the reporting companies after the adoption of these practices.[44]

National Baldrige Award guidelines for managing human resources in a way consistent with delivering quality services and products were developed because in the 1980s, the need for improved quality was recognized as a national priority. Companies have no similar guidelines to consult as they strive to meet customers' demands for lower prices, speedier service, or more exciting innovations. So, for companies competing for customer approval in these areas, the challenge of developing appropriate approaches to managing human resources is substantial. Potential ideas will emerge as we return to this discussion in later chapters.

Employees

You give us an opportunity to have a say-so and we can do a good job.

CALVIN THOMAS, Assembler, Honda of America, East Liberty, Ohio[45]

Organizations that recognize and respond to the needs of employees and provide opportunities for development and involvement provide a higher quality of working life, thereby increasing their ability to attract and retain the best talent. Many aspects of human resource management contribute to a good quality of working life: training and development to improve employees' skills and knowledge; job designs that allow employees to really use their knowledge and skills; management practices that give employees responsibility for important decisions; selection and promotion systems that ensure fair and equitable treatment; safe and healthy physical and psychological environments; and work organized around teams. Such practices increase employee commitment, satisfaction, and feelings of empowerment.[46]

The feature "Positioning for the 21st Century: Getting Everyone Involved" describes in more detail just how organizations are increasing employee commitment, satisfaction, and empowerment in order to be more effective. Notice how the organizations described by Edward E. Lawler III, using HR practices now sometimes referred to as high-performance work practices, are able to manage in ways that benefit both employees as individuals and the business. An illustration of this is managing to ensure that employees are flexible and adaptable.

Flexible and Adaptable Employees. Firms in highly competitive environments must move quickly and often. Doing so requires a workforce that rapidly adjusts to new technologies, strategies, and competitors' practices. Thus, being responsive to employees' concerns also involves preparing employees for inevitable change. When employees are not prepared for and capable of change, their employability decreases and their economic livelihood is threatened. Human resource management practices play a major role in meeting employees' concerns about their long-term employability.[47] For example, continuous training prepares the workforce for change and develops employees' confidence in their own ability to continuously learn new ways of working. Regular employee assessments, feedback, and career management activities provide the information employees need understand their strengths and weaknesses and to prepare for the future. Ultimately, by developing their employees, employers help ensure that the workforce is employable in good jobs that pay well enough to maintain the high standard of living to which Americans have grown accustomed.[48]

Finally, responsiveness to employees' concerns requires including the employees' perspectives when making business decisions that have major implications for employees. Constant change and adjustment can create stress within organizations, which can have debilitating consequences in the long term.[49] To avoid straining the workforce and the organization unnecessarily, the longer-term needs of the company and of employees should inform decisions about how to respond to immediate pressures.[50] For example, hiring more employees in response to a spurt in orders and sales may seem like the obvious solution to reducing back orders, but a longer-term view recognizes that more hiring now may mean having to lay people off when business slows down again in two or three years. For another example, after a decade of downsizing, managers have learned that reducing the scope of a business does not always solve the problems of high costs and inefficiencies. According to the consulting firm of Arthur D. Little, "Most major corporate downsizings have failed to produce what was expected."[51]

Society

Legal Regulations. To be effective, businesses must be responsive to broader societal concerns and comply with an extensive set of legal regulations regarding human resources.[52] By doing so, firms establish their legitimacy and gain acceptance and support from the community; ultimately, they increase their chances for long-term survival.[53]

Positioning for the 21st Century:
GETTING EVERYONE INVOLVED

"The enormous changes in corporate structures and needs over the past decade have necessitated a refocusing of management approaches," according to Edward E. Lawler III, director of the Center for Effective Organizations at the University of Southern California. Lawler's research from the mid 1980s to the mid 1990s focused on exactly what it means for organizations to adopt new management approaches. Although his research mainly concerned modern manufacturing plants, he now concludes that several principles of management apply in any product or service organization, large or small, wanting to be highly effective. He generally defines *effectiveness* in terms of *high-quality, customer-driven organizations* that survive and flourish by staying ahead of competitors with new and better products and services.

According to Lawler, effective organizations are those that make extensive use of *self-managing teams* and *a relatively limited number of hierarchical levels of management.* These two features facilitate individuals working in teams that are responsible for serving an identifiable customer or producing a whole product. In turn, this enables individuals to feel that they have control over a real business. Thus, in effective organizations, individuals really feel a sense of ownership in what they are doing and a sense of responsibility and accountability for the success of their organizations. For example, the Digital Equipment Corporation plant at Enfield, Connecticut, allows teams to deal directly with suppliers and customers for the electronic boards that the teams make.

Effective organizations do not restrict the use of teams to the production floor only, but extend the team concept to all areas of the organization. This broader use of self-managed teams further flattens the organization by reducing the number of supervisors and managers throughout the operation.

The use of teams is extended so that cross-functional teams work together. Cross-function integration might combine manufacturing, product engineering, and product design. This produces a better product and also a better understanding by all employees of the needs of the business. Employees' understanding is enhanced with information technology that allows workers in the manufacturing area to have direct access to marketing and sales information and even to answer questions from customers as they produce the products and services.

In today's effective organizations, *reward systems* compensate individuals for being in teams, for gaining more skill-based competencies, for learning and continuously improving, and for meeting business and organizational performance goals. Of course, the teams themselves have a significant input in compensation decisions, such as deciding when employees have attained mastery of needed skill-based competencies. Some of these important competencies are related to the use of information and data technology. Effective organizations are networked with computers. They rely extensively on videos for learning; television screens link employees in various parts of the firm.

Along with all the above, effective organizations use the tools and principles of total quality management, such as problem-solving approaches and continuous commitment to process and product improvement. Continuous training is available for all employees on topics ranging from technical job details to business strategy. Thus, throughout the most effective organizations, one finds employees who are committed, involved, and continuously improving both themselves and their organizations.[54]

Codes of conduct for some aspects of business behavior take the form of formal laws, and many of these have implications for managing human resources. In addition, businesses are subject to regulation through several federal agencies, including the Occupational Safety and Health Administration, the Equal Employment Opportunity Commission, the Office of Federal Contract Compliance Programs, and the Immigration and Naturalization Service. They must also attend to the actions of various state and city equal employment commissions and human rights, and civil rights commissions. Finally, multinational corporations (MNCs) must be aware of the employment laws in other countries. Because they affect virtually all human resource management activities, many different laws, regulations, and court decisions are described throughout this book, beginning with an overview in Chapter 3.

Social Responsibility and Ethics. Formal laws and regulations establish relatively clear guidelines for how society expects a company to behave, but effective companies respond to more than simply the formal statements of a community's expectations.[55] The most effective companies understand that the enactment of formal laws and regulations often lags behind public opinion by several years. Indeed, unless a community's most strongly held values are being violated, legal restrictions are unnecessary. Long before legislation is agreed to, communities communicate their expectations and attempt to hold organizations accountable for violations of those expectations. In turn, proactive organizations stay attuned to public opinion and use it as one source of information that may shape their own management practices. For example, WMX Technologies (formerly Waste Management) of Oak Brook, Illinois, is building an ethical culture that demonstrates the firm's commitment to encouraging and supporting behavior consistent with the norms and values of society (see "Managing Human Resources for the 21st Century at WMX Technologies").

In addition to ensuring that their internal functioning is consistent with society's expectations, some companies interpret social responsibility to include active involvement in the external community. Ben and Jerry's Homemade Incorporated, the Vermont ice cream company, is a great example. It prints its "social performance report" right after the president's letter in its annual report. The company's credo, Turning Values into Value, reflects a philosophy that centers on creating a socially responsible firm, which means giving back to the community. When asked to describe what would make him happiest, former President and founder Bennett R. Cohen replied, "I'd like to see Ben & Jerry's act as a force for social change in trying to help deal with some of the root causes of poverty and starvation and disease and illiteracy."[56] The firm's Partnerships—subsidized franchises located in areas of high unemployment, like Harlem, with all profits returned to the community—reflect this vision.[57] Respect and concern for people permeates the company, which pays employees well above the average in Vermont, offers generous benefits, and aggressively strives to make business decisions that are consistent with the concerns of employees.[58]

Ben and Jerry's is not the only company getting involved in the community. Southern California Edison Company has established a $6.5 million training center in downtown Los Angeles. State Farm Mutual Automobile Insurance Company, BankAmerica Corporation, and Sumitomo Bank of California also participate in their communities by offering low-cost redevelopment loans and many socially needed projects and institutions.[59] The Walt Disney Company is one of several making connections with education. For example, Walt Disney World employees also serve as teachers to students who take on-site classes to learn about leisure and entertainment industries. At Epcot Teachers' Center, school teachers learn to use entertainment and communication techniques to improve student learning.[60] Being socially responsive in these and other ways can directly affect specific activities in managing human resources. For example, it may impact the type of employees the company chooses to hire, the criteria used to evaluate their performance, the scheduling and coordinating of activities within work units, reward and recognition systems, and so on.

Managing Human Resources for the 21st Century at WMX Technologies

WMX Technologies Corporation (Oak Brook, IL), the largest U.S. waste services company, with over $6 billion in sales, is taking a leading role in building ethics awareness into the company culture for its 60,000 employees. Under the impetus of Chairman and CEO Dean Buntrock and an Executive Environmental Committee, Waste Management is seeking to gain employee commitment and leadership awareness through a number of management systems.

Overall responsibility for the effort belongs to Jodie Bernstein, vice president of environmental policy and ethical standards, also general counsel for Chemical Waste Management and a former general counsel for the Environmental Protection Agency and the Department of Health, Education and Welfare (now Health and Human Services) in Washington. She believes that explicit and active management of ethical issues is vital to [WMX Technologies] because of the nature of its business, but it's also becoming increasingly important to other businesses as well. "Increasingly, we are seeing a breakdown in government's ability to regulate environmental and other ethical issues, and there is a growing public distrust of government interference in these matters. Moreover, on the individual level, we just can't make the assumptions we used to about our shared value systems. The diverse workforce and our increased globalization mean we have to recognize that people have different ideas about what is and isn't ethical. Rather than leave things up to chance, we're going to spell it out for people."

Rules versus Climate

"In some areas, like compliance with EPA regulations, for example, we tell people exactly what the rules and expectations are. Falsifying information on a regulatory filing, for example, means immediate dismissal. But we think it has to go beyond that. Ethics is more than following the rules. You can't make enough rules to cover all the things that can come up, so it's important that all employees have a general level of ethical awareness, so that they will at least be asking the right questions. And you have to create a climate in which it's possible—easier, even—for employees to do the right thing. Most of the programs we are developing focus on this latter area: increasing awareness of ethical issues and building an ethical climate throughout the company."

ETHICS COMMUNICATION

To do that, the company is adapting many of its existing human resource and communication systems. Under Jodie Bernstein's direction, explicit business conduct guidelines are being written, and she is considering the establishment of a regular ethics column in the employee publication. Ethics goals are also being developed for the performance appraisal system, which already includes factors related to environmental compliance and health and safety. The company is also trying to rejuvenate an existing employee hotline program to encourage more use. Established in 1984, the hotline may be used by employees who wish to call attention to a situation they find disturbing or to ask questions on ethical, environmental, or safety issues.

The bottom line, according to Bernstein, is ethical leadership: "This is the lifeblood of our company. We are an environmental services company. How we handle these issues is critical to our success."[61]

Working with Strategic Business Partners

In the U.S., we tend to think of firms as autonomous organizations, with clear boundaries separating one from another. However, such an image is overly simplistic. A more realistic image portrays firms as nodes in a web of relationships. Other firms in the web might include suppliers, joint venture partners, potential merger partners, and partners in coalitions formed for community service and political action. In some cases, even customers are viewed as strategic business partners, especially when they are other businesses instead of individual consumers. All of these interfirm relationships potentially involve issues of human resource management.

Suppliers. A company's suppliers include the organizations that provide the company with resources needed to conduct business. The resources needed by most companies include capital, material, information, and people. Suppliers of people might include schools, employment agencies, and other firms. It is easy to understand why suppliers of people should be considered important strategic partners for managing human resources. What about other types of suppliers?

Firms that supply raw materials or component parts clearly are strategic partners, especially for companies competing on the basis of quality. To improve quality, improvements in raw materials or component parts can and must always be found. As organizations such as Xerox Corporation, the National Aeronautics and Space Administration (NASA), and Ford have learned, eventually a stage is reached where the quality of the product cannot be improved without improving the quality of the materials coming in. That is, the organization has to work with its suppliers to improve their total quality.[62] The Baldrige Award for quality essentially requires companies to demonstrate that their suppliers also have total quality management (TQM) programs in place. And because much of TQM involves managing human resources, the supplier becomes a key stakeholder for human resource management. AT&T's total quality approach specifically includes a partnership with the firm's suppliers, as shown in Exhibit 1.3. Certainly the Weyerhaeuser Company's total quality management system includes its many suppliers.

■ *Exhibit 1.3*
AT&T's Total Quality Approach

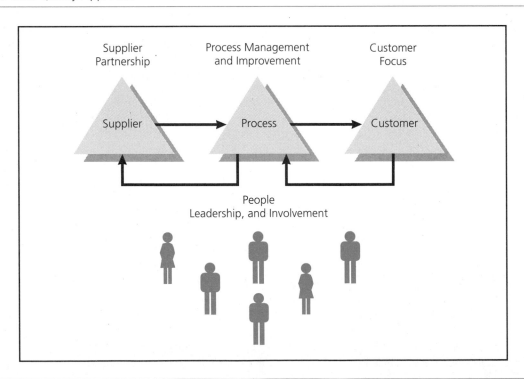

Supplier firms are also of special importance to companies because of their mutual interest in legal compliance. For example, companies that sell to the federal government, called federal contractors, develop affirmative action plans and in turn ask their suppliers to do the same. Compliance with the Americans with Disabilities Act of 1990 requires that companies obligate their suppliers to also adhere to the mandates of the act.

Unions. A special supplier is the union that represents workers and potential workers. Firms such as GE, AT&T, Xerox, and the three U.S. automakers look to the unions for joint discussion on issues such as improving productivity, the quality of working life, and outsourcing. In these firms, the union leadership and members have moved from a traditional adversarial relationship to a collaborative, problem-solving relationship. Thus, although the proportion of union membership shrank from the mid-1980s to the mid-1990s, it still plays a vital role in supplying the ideas and motivated workers necessary for companies seeking to be globally competitive and profitable. (This is not to say, however, that adversarial relationships do not exist today, but that they are diminishing as we enter the 21st century.)

Customers. On occasion, the firm may also treat customers as strategic partners and help them improve their quality. If a dealership (customer) that sells Ford cars improves its service orientation, then it might sell more cars. The more it sells, the more Ford will benefit. So why should Ford not help its dealers with their own TQM programs? Similarly, insurance companies recognize that both they and their corporate customers benefit by managing human resources in ways that ensure the safety and health of employees. Thus, it is in the best interests of both the suppliers of insurance and the buyers of their policies to collaborate in the area of health and safety.

SPECIFIC ACTIVITIES IN MANAGING HUMAN RESOURCES: A HISTORICAL PERSPECTIVE

To serve the stakeholders of human resource management—for example, through organizational productivity, customer satisfaction, responsiveness to employees' concerns, responsiveness to the law and society, and working with suppliers—companies employ many specific human resource management activities. This book groups these activities into chapters, with activities to meet challenges posed by the environment in Chapter 2, activities for managing employees fairly in Chapter 3, and so on.

As with many aspects of the way businesses operate, the way they approach managing people has changed rather dramatically during the 20th century.[63] This book focuses mostly on understanding how companies within the United States are managing human resources as we approach the 21st century. Some of the activities described reflect new developments, whereas others are approaches honed through decades of research and analysis.

A full appreciation of current approaches benefits from some understanding of their historical evolution. Exhibit 1.4 presents a thumbnail sketch of the changing concerns of human resource management within the United States.

At the beginning of the 20th century, Frederick W. Taylor helped shape management practices. Trained as an engineer, Taylor emphasized the importance of developing precise analytical schemes to select, train, evaluate, and reward production workers for the purposes of motivating them, controlling their behaviors, and improving productivity.

◼ *Exhibit 1.4*

Changing Concerns of Human Resource Management

Time Period	Primary Concern	Employers' Perceptions	Techniques of Interest
Before 1900	Production technologies	Employee needs are not important.	Discipline systems
1900–10	Employee welfare	Employees need safe conditions and opportunity.	Safety programs, English language classes, inspirational programs
1910–20	Task efficiency	Employees need high earnings made possible with higher productivity.	Motion and time study
1920–30	Individual differences	Employees' individual differences should be considered.	Psychological testing, employee counseling
1930–40	Unionization	Employees are adversaries.	Employee communication programs, anti-unionization techniques
	Productivity	Group performance affects productivity.	Improving conditions for groups
1940–50	Economic security	Employees need economic protection.	Employee pension plans, health plans, fringe benefits
1950–60	Human relations	Employees need considerate supervision.	Supervisor training (role-playing, sensitivity training)
1960–70	Participation	Employees need involvement in task decisions.	Participative management techniques
	Employment laws	Employees from different groups should all be treated equally.	Affirmative action, equal opportunity
1970–80	Task challenge and quality of working life	Employees need work that is challenging and congruent with abilities.	Job enrichment, integrated task teams
1980–90	Employee displacement	Employees need jobs—lost through economic downturns, international competition, and technological changes.	Outplacement, retraining, total quality; customer focus
1990–2000	Productivity, quality, and adaptability	Employees need to balance work and nonwork and to make contributions.	Linking the needs of the business, training, globalization, ethics, diversity, workplace accommodation

SOURCE: Adapted from S. J. Carroll and R. S. Schuler, "Professional HRM: Changing Functions and Problems," in *Human Resources Management in the 1980s,* ed. S. J. Carroll and R. S. Schuler (Washington, D.C.: Bureau of National Affairs, 1983), 8–10.

During the second quarter of the century, the focus shifted somewhat to acknowledging the importance of the work group's influence on employees. Elton Mayo and his work at the Hawthorne plant (the "Hawthorne studies") focused on improving individual productivity by experimenting with changing the work group's composition and incentive schemes, in addition to its environmental conditions, such as the lighting and physical arrangements. Knowledge of groups and the effect of groups on individuals advanced during the 1930s and into the 1940s. World War II refocused attention on the importance of improving selection procedures for people doing more complex jobs (e.g., for fighter pilots and secret service agents).

During the 1950s and 1960s, practices developed in the military, such as assessment centers, spread into the private sector. From the 1920s on, a bureaucratic view of personnel activities predominated. The use of practices such as formal performance appraisals, selection testing, and centralized employment decisions; the presence of a full-time personnel director; and the presence of rule books and extensive record keeping became increasingly common throughout most sectors of the economy, often with the support of industrial unions.[64]

During the 1970s, the term *human resource management* emerged and began to replace the older term *personnel management*. The new term reflected a broader perspective, which included issues such as safety and health, stress, employee satisfaction, and industrial relations. As the century is drawing to a close, *human resource management* is used to acknowledge the importance of employees as corporate assets. The skills, knowledge, and experiences of employees have economic value to an organization because they enable it to be productive and adaptable.[65] Like other assets, employees have value in the marketplace; but unlike other assets, they have a potential value that can be fully realized only with their cooperation. Furthermore, human resources are now recognized as sources of potential competitive advantage.[66] Competitive advantage is gained by implementing a value-creating strategy that competitors cannot easily copy and sustain.[67] Creating and re-creating such strategies is now recognized as a primary objective for human resources management. Frank Calamita, an executive at Sony Music Entertainment, describes the changing importance of people this way: "The only aspect of the people aspect used to be, 'What is the head count?' Now they say, 'Let's take each one of these strategic issues and look through the lens of human resources.' "[68]

As in Weyerhaeuser, current approaches to managing people within any particular company reflect both the past and the process of letting go of the past in order to prepare for the future. As environmental change quickens, more and more companies are concluding that some of the traditional approaches to managing human resources, which are rooted in the organizations of the past, must be modified. Intense international and domestic competition is forcing major companies to reassess themselves. Reassessment often culminates in fundamental changes in technologies, organizational structures, business strategies, and human resource management philosophies and practices.[69] Thus, the decade of the 1990s has emerged as a period of experimentation in new approaches to managing human resources within the context of new organization and work designs. Organizations are rapidly learning from this experimentation in order to be positioned for the 21st century.

THE CONTEXT FOR MANAGING HUMAN RESOURCES IN THE 21st CENTURY

Chapters 2, 3, and 4 of this text describe several variables that shape current approaches to managing human resources, and that will continue to evolve throughout the 1990s. As these chapters reveal, organizations must attend to many aspects of their environment. As firms position for the 21st century, however, some of these aspects will receive much more attention than ever before. Three particularly important aspects are the complex international context; increasing diversity in external labor markets and in the internal workforce; and new organizational structures that delegate responsibility for work to teams rather than individuals.

The Global Arena

Although it is true that within the United States, companies vary widely in how they manage human resources, the variations that appear around the world are often even more dramatic. As more and more U.S. companies reach out to take advantage of the resources and markets available in other countries, managers are discovering that they cannot ignore the international arena and its many permutations in managing human resources. Indeed, they will benefit from welcoming them:

> As companies' global ambitions grow, many fast-track executives now see foreign tours as necessary for career advancement. Gerber CEO Al Piergallini, who is building markets in Latin America and Central and Eastern Europe, says foreign assignments will be "emphasized" in the future as part of normal career development for his executives. As a result, Gerber's country manager in Poland feels he has an edge over many of his colleagues. "My overseas experience sets me apart from the rest of the MBA bunch," says Jan Lower. "I'm not just one of hundreds of thousands."[70]

Therefore, throughout this book the discussion returns repeatedly to comparisons of how managing human resources differs between several countries, especially the countries in Europe and Asia and the other members of the North American Free Trade Agreement (NAFTA) (i.e., Mexico and Canada). These particular countries include the United States' largest trading partners, the locations of many joint ventures and strategic alliances involving U.S. companies, and the locations of many of the major competitors of U.S. companies. Readers who are particularly interested in cross-cultural and international human resource management should consult the sources referenced throughout the chapters.

Workforce Diversity

Increased awareness of global diversity is accompanied by increased awareness of the diversity present within the domestic workforce—perhaps not coincidentally. Successful organizations recognize diversity as an issue that demands attention.[71] According to Stona J. Fitch, vice president of manufacturing for Procter and Gamble Company, the first companies that achieve a true multicultural environment will gain a competitive advantage. Diversity provides a much richer environment, a variety of viewpoints, greater productivity.[72] And, not unimportant, it makes work much more fun and interesting.

As organizations develop effective domestic multiculturalism, they appear to expand their appreciation of the many other dimensions of diversity that characterize their workforce. For example, organizations develop initiatives to encourage the understanding and appreciation of differences in age, language, background, and physical capabilities. Northern States Power (NSP) Company (Minnesota), a utility firm serving the Minneapolis–St. Paul area, attends to more than twenty types of workforce diversity (see Exhibit 1.5). Throughout this book, diversity initiatives at companies like NSP are described to illustrate how paying attention to this aspect of the environment shapes human resource management practices.

The U.S. workforce has, of course, always been diverse. And diversity within organizations is certainly increasing. But changes in the composition of the workforce alone cannot account for the attention this issue has drawn in the 1990s. The importance of workforce diversity, and the consequences of ignoring it, has been highlighted by other changes, especially increased use of teams.

Workplace Differences Valued at NSP

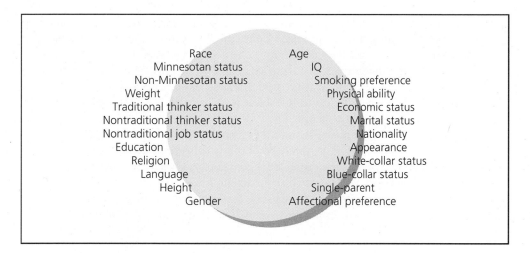

Race	Age
Minnesotan status	IQ
Non-Minnesotan status	Smoking preference
Weight	Physical ability
Traditional thinker status	Economic status
Nontraditional thinker status	Marital status
Nontraditional job status	Nationality
Education	Appearance
Religion	White-collar status
Language	Blue-collar status
Height	Single-parent
Gender	Affectional preference

Teams and Teamwork

Located in Wooster, Ohio, is one of *Fortune* magazine's most admired companies: Rubbermaid Incorporated. Its success depends upon developing new products for customers. With more than five thousand rubber products such as storage boxes, mops, mailboxes, and spatulas, the company continually pumps more than 14 percent of its profits into R&D. However, Richard D. Gates, head of product development, thinks that the firm's success in developing new products is not just due to the amount of money the organization spends.

> Most ideas for products flow from a single source: teams. Twenty teams, each made up of five to seven people (one each from marketing, manufacturing, R&D, finance, and other departments), focus on specific product lines, such as bathroom accessories. So successful has been the team approach to innovation that Dick Gates fears to contemplate a world without it. "If we weren't organized that way," he says, a look of concern spreading over his face, "who would be thinking about ice cube trays? Who would be thinking about johnny mops?"[73]

Many firms now use teams and teamwork.[74] Team-based approaches to work can increase innovation, improve quality, and shorten the time it takes to transform an idea into a product that is available in the marketplace. To create and orchestrate teams, people need to be selected, appraised, compensated, and trained in ways that reflect the unique relationships that develop between employees who work together. Most companies know—or at least believe—that people working in teams should not be managed just the same as people who work more or less independently. Nevertheless, teamwork really is a somewhat new phenomenon in the American workplace, so considerable experimentation in how best to manage teams is still taking place around the country. Some practices now viewed as experimental will undoubtedly become commonplace within the next decade. Therefore, positioning for the 21st century requires understanding how teamwork is changing human resource management in leading companies; accordingly, illustrative examples and suggestions appear throughout the remaining chapters of this book.

✦ A ONE BEST WAY?

Activities related to managing human resources occur in all companies, from the smallest to the largest. At a minimum, every company has jobs, which comprise a set of responsibilities. To get these jobs done, the firm hires people and compensates them in return for the work they do. To hire, the company generally finds that it must recruit a few potential employees and then select among them. Few companies continue to pay a person who cannot or will not perform satisfactorily, so at least some measurement of performance generally occurs—even if it is just to keep track of how many hours were worked. To ensure that people know what they are supposed to do, some instruction and training are usually given, though these may be minimal. Employees' work is carried out in a physical context, which may be plush or dangerous and is increasingly off-site. Their work also occurs in an interpersonal context, which may be informal or governed by an explicit contract. Eventually, of course, employees are dismissed, retire, or simply leave voluntarily. Because no employee stays forever, every company must manage the process of exit. Thus it is reasonable to conclude that practically all firms do some human resource management, at least at the most fundamental or basic level.

Distinguishing Characteristics of Successful Firms

What distinguishes firms that are relatively successful in achieving their HR objectives is their capacity to choose and implement the appropriate human resource activities, policies, and practices. This requires both technical expertise and systematic analysis.

Technical Expertise. Firms can distinguish themselves by being more technically competent than other firms. Technical knowledge about how to manage human resources accumulated through most of the 20th century, and was established from the early 1970s to the mid-1990s. As a result of thousands of research studies, we know a great deal about how to design effective methods of selecting people, how to assess performance, how to design training programs, how to design pay systems, and so on. Like any body of technical knowledge, however, our understanding of how to manage people effectively is based on what has worked in the past. As conditions change, some of our knowledge may become obsolete. In addition, much of the technical knowledge we have was developed by experts working in narrowly defined subareas of human resource management—for example, compensation specialists, training specialists, and so on. Specialists in each area have often been guided by the desire to answer the questions "*In general,* what are some basic principles (e.g., of compensation, training, etc.) that seem to apply?" Technical specialists do not often consider questions such as "How do the training activities within a specific organization affect the way employees will react to a particular type of compensation plan?"

Because of constantly changing conditions and because our technical knowledge has been created by specialists, we should not expect that technical knowledge alone will be a sufficient basis for effective human resource management. Managing people effectively requires using the available technical knowledge in a thoughtful and systematic way.[75]

Systematic Analysis. Effective companies take advantage of the power of human resource policies and practices by using them systematically. A *systematic approach* has four defining characteristics. First, a systematic approach involves considering how all the many specific practices for managing people *together* affect the attitudes and behaviors of employees working in various jobs. Human resource policies and practices that are consistent with each other and coordinated with each other communicate the same message to employees.[76] A performance appraisal system that evaluates employees on the basis of the attainment of long-term goals, coupled with a compensation system that rewards employees on the same basis sends a clear message to employees. On the other hand, a human resource policy that describes employees as the most valuable resource, coupled with constant layoffs and little training sends conflicting messages. Consistency across all human resource policies and practices results in consistency and clarity about what is expected, what is rewarded, and what is important.

Second, a systematic approach involves taking into account the unique characteristics of the company, including the company's history, top management's goals and the strategies they intend to pursue, the corporate culture, the size of the company and the way it is structured, the technologies people use, and so on. As a consequence of this, we find that successful firms, even in the same industry, can have rather different human resource activities. For example, different companies in the same industry can compete for different customers, using different competitive strategies.[77]

The strategy pursued by a company is related to what customer satisfaction means in the context of *that particular company*. For example, companies competing through innovation seek to satisfy customers by creating something totally new and different. In contrast, those competing on quality seek to satisfy customers by offering products or services that predictably meet rigid specifications at a low cost. For example, Nordstrom is a retail department store that competes on the basis of customer service, whereas Sears, which is in the same industry, competes largely on the basis of low cost and brand names. Although both are fine organizations in the same industry, they have substantially different HR practices and philosophies. These differences reflect their different approaches to retailing and the needs that result from these. (See "Managing Human Resources for the 21st Century: Sears versus Nordstrom.")

In firms that manage their employees systematically, managers know why they lead their people the way they do: their entire set of HR practices has been explicitly developed to match the needs of their employees and customers, and the strategies of the business. In this way, they all fit each other and fit the qualities of the company.[78]

Third, a systematic approach involves looking at the constantly changing aspects of the environment. To be effective, human resource practices must be sensitive to changes in the economy in general and the labor market in particular; the actions of competitors and strategic partners; myriad laws and regulations, both current and proposed; and even political action groups.[79] Chapter 2 examines these considerations. Exhibit 1.6 illustrates how the many human resource management activities are interconnected with the many elements of the internal and external contexts of HR.

Because one must consider so many internal and external elements when choosing how to manage a company's human resources, no "one best way" will be effective under all circumstances. Consequently, some trial and error is inevitable. Jerome H. Laubenstein and his team at the Insurance Product Services (IPS) Department at Aid Association for Lutherans (AAL) have certainly experienced this (see the AAL case at the back of this book). This leads us to the fourth defining characteristic of a systematic approach to managing human resources. In a systematic approach, the process of trial and error is driven by information and data, from beginning to end. Information and data are gathered before changes are made, and are used to decide what changes should be made; continued monitoring during the change process facilitates midstream adjustments; and after a change is in place, data are used to evaluate the intended and unintended consequences. In other words, a systematic approach ensures that the

Sears and Nordstrom are legends in the retailing industry. Sears has been the world's largest retailer for generations and has outlasted all its historical competitors. During the 1980s, Nordstrom set service and growth standards for the industry. Although Sears stumbled in this period—as did most department stores—it eventually reorganized with improved performance. These two firms have very different employment practices, yet they are practices that make sense for their operations. Here, the practices are compared for sales positions, a key job in retailing.

SEARS

Sears has been and remains a pioneering firm in the science of employee selection. It relies on sophisticated selection tests that it has refined over time so that they now boast extremely high predictive power. Once hired, employees receive training in company practices. Management also keeps track of employee attitudes and morale through frequent and rigorous employee surveys.

Two practices are especially noteworthy in the management of sales representatives. The first is that sales employees receive intensive training in Sears products, in the company's operating systems, and in sales techniques. The second is that most sales employees work on straight salary. Only the employees in the big-ticket departments like appliances receive commissions, and those are modest. Sears also has had a "no-layoff" policy and hires almost no temporary workers.

Sears is in the retail business, and service is part of what it sells. But it is service of a different kind from Nordstrom's, in part because its product line is dominated much more by housewares than by fashion. Customers buying home appliances or hardware want information about the products and how they are used. Sears also sells financing and warranties, reasonably complicated items that require some background knowledge. As evidenced by its marketing (The Name You Can Trust), Sears trades in part on a reputation for steering the customer in the right direction. Salary pay systems, as opposed to commissions, create no incentives to push products irrespective of customer needs or to cut back on "nonselling time" associated with providing information.

With this strategy, training is important, and turnover therefore is costly—hence, the emphasis on selection as well as job security. Personal relationships with customers also help build this reputation for honest and reliable service. Sears customer satisfaction data show that the stores with the lowest employee turnover and the least temporary help have the highest satisfaction ratings. A restructuring of Sears during 1992 and 1993 smashed its no-layoff policy but left the other principles of employment intact. In fact, the amount of training for sales representatives was increased and the limited commission-based pay was reduced from 3 percent to 1 percent.

NORDSTROM

Nordstrom operates with virtually none of the formal personnel practices advanced by Sears. Indeed, its practices appear downright primitive in comparison. Nordstrom's hiring is decentralized, using no formal selection tests. Managers look for applicants with experience in customer contact (although prior *retailing* experience is often seen as a minus), but the main qualities seem to be pleasant personalities and motivation. The company has only one rule in its personnel handbook: "Use your best judgment at all times." Individual sales clerks virtually run their areas as private stores. Nordstrom maintains a continuous stream of programs to motivate employees and help them pursue the goal of providing intensive service, but it offers only a modest amount of formal training. Its pay system is heavily loaded toward commissions, which makes it possible for sales clerks to earn a sizable income. Nordstrom sales personnel are also ranked within each department according to their monthly sales; the most successful are promoted, and the least successful let go. Virtually all managers are promoted from within.

In Nordstrom's fashion-oriented retail business, customers do not demand detailed knowledge of the products. Rather, they require personal contact—emotional energy, in part—and hustle: running across the store to match an item, remembering an individual customer's tastes, and so on. More impulse purchases are made in fashion than in other segments of retailing, and so the efforts of the sales clerks can especially increase such sales. What Nordstrom gets from its employment system is an intense level of personal motivation and customer contact. The commissions, internal competition, and motivation programs provide the drive, and autonomy and the absence of rules allow that drive to be exercised. Many new hires do not survive—Nordstrom has among the highest turnover in the industry—but because the investment in each employee in relatively small (selection and training costs are low), such turnover is not a real problem for the company.[80]

■ *Exhibit 1.6*
The Contexts of Managing Human Resources

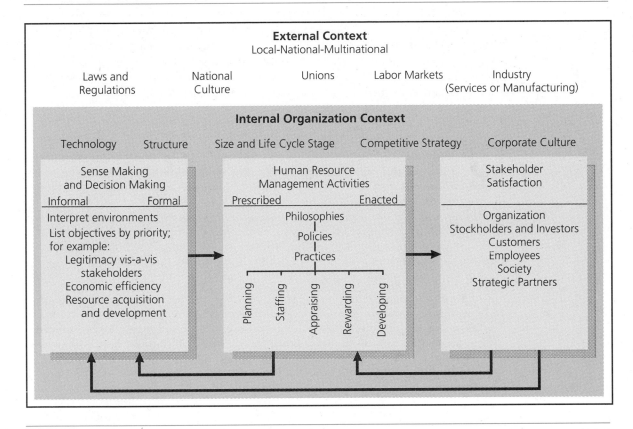

SOURCE: Adapted from S. E. Jackson and R. S. Schuler, "Understanding Human Resource Management in the Context of Organizations and Their Environments," *Annual Review of Psychology* (1995), 254.

organization and its employees learn from their mistakes and successes.[81] Chapter 4 discusses the importance of careful planning for changes that affect the way people are managed; Chapter 17 returns to this important topic to discuss monitoring and assessing the consequences of such changes.

Managing to Compete versus Managing Like Everyone Else

Unfortunately, most companies probably manage without being thoughtful and systematic. Instead of constantly tailoring their people management system to fit their own unique situation, many companies continue to do things the same way year after year. Ask why salespeople in the shoe section are paid on commission and people in toys are not, and you are likely to be told, "That's just the way we've always done it." When companies do change the way they manage people, they may do so for the wrong reason. Why did that small retail food chain just send all its middle managers to off-site wilderness training? "Everybody in the industry's doing it—we can't be the only ones who don't." Why did your insurance company start randomly listening in on calls from customers? "The new telecommunications system we installed last year included it as a no-cost feature, so we decided we should use it."

Why Human Resource Practices Matter

Whether a company chooses its human resource practices carefully or somewhat haphazardly, those practices can be powerful influences on behavior. Used wisely—that is, systematically linked to the needs of the company's customers, employees, and business strategy—they can transform a lackluster company into a star performer. Used unwisely, they can create havoc. Sears, for example, discovered that a new and different compensation system it installed unintentionally encouraged employees to break the law, as the company explained in this newspaper announcement:

An Open Letter to Sears Customers

You may have heard recent allegations that some Sears Auto Centers in California and New Jersey have sold customers parts and services they didn't need. We take such charges very seriously, because they strike at the core of our company—our reputation for trust and integrity.

We are confident that our Auto Center customer satisfaction rate is among the highest in the industry. But after an extensive review, we have concluded that our incentive compensation and goal-setting program inadvertently created an environment in which mistakes have occurred. We are moving quickly and aggressively to eliminate that environment.

To guard against such things happening in the future, we're taking significant action:

- We have eliminated incentive compensation and goal-setting systems for automotive service advisors—the folks who diagnose problems and recommend repairs to you. We have replaced these practices with a new non-commission program designed to achieve even higher levels of customer satisfaction. Rewards will now be based on customer satisfaction. . .

[other actions were also listed in this letter.]

Ed Brennan
Chairman and CEO
Sears, Roebuck and Co.[82]

According to the framework described here, this failure at Sears occurred because the new compensation system did not fit the rest of what the company was doing. Nor did it fit with the other HR practices of Sears. Consequently, the employees were unable to perform as the company had intended. This example helps explain why many companies become reluctant to change the way they manage people, once they have an effective HR system. To change one HR practice and not others is nearly impossible. And to change HR practices without there being a change in the business may even be unwise—except in firms that are not already managing their human resources effectively. The examples of Sears and Nordstrom also illustrate why not all *new* HR practices are picked up by all firms: they just may not fit!

What this says to line managers looking for ways to improve operations is, "Be careful." Being careful means gaining an understanding of what works and under what conditions it works. Because of pressures for constant improvement, managers seek the best ways of doing things. Increasingly, they do so through *benchmarking,* a systematic process of finding out who is most well-known for a practice and then learning what they do. The term *high-performance workplace practices* is used to describe a bundle of the best HR practices. Although benchmarking may identify and label some practices as the best (singly or in bundles), managers need to examine the conditions under which they work. Individual incentive pay may be a "best practice" for Lincoln Electric, but it may not work at AAL. Managers should resist the temptation to jump on the "best practices" bandwagon without learning more about the context in which those practices work. Without this additional knowledge, it may be better to avoid changing.

Even once an informed decision has been made, it takes time to change a set of HR practices. Thus, it takes patience and it takes confidence to know that things will work out. Top management support is needed here to prevent the organization from retreating to its previous practices. This is why human resource management practices can be used to gain and maintain competitive advantage. It is also why firms that want to become more successful in the 21st century must begin to position their HR activities today.

 PARTNERSHIP IN MANAGING HUMAN RESOURCES

Human resources should not be managed just by those in a human resource department. All company managers are responsible for leading people. No department alone can effectively manage a company's human resources. So, regardless of whether a line manager ever holds a formal position in human resource management, she or he will be accountable for the task of managing people. In the long run, every manager's portfolio of knowledge and skills must reflect this reality: "There is a saying at Merck that goes like this, 'human resources are too important to be left to the HR department.' Fully one-third of the performance evaluation of the managers is related to people management."[83]

The Line Manager Has Always Been Responsible

In small businesses, the *owner* must have HR expertise because he or she will be building the company from the ground up. This reality is clearly reflected in the various popular magazines targeted to small-business owners—for example, *Inc., Money, Success,* and *Entrepreneurship.* These publications devote a great deal of space to discussing issues related to managing the people who make up a small company. Eventually, as a company grows, the owner may contract out some of the administrative aspects related to managing people (e.g., payroll), or delegate some of the responsibilities to a specialist, or both. As the company grows even larger, more specialists may be hired—either as permanent staff or on a contract basis to work on special projects, such as designing a new pay system. But, as with other business activities, these specialists will not bear all responsibility for the project. For example, many companies have a marketing department; nevertheless, they employ people outside that department to conduct marketing activities. Similarly, most companies have a few people with special expertise in accounting; nevertheless, employees throughout the company perform accounting activities. The same is true for human resource management activities.

This book treats managing human resources as a responsibility shared by everyone in the company—line employees and professionals in the human resources department and top-level executives and entry-level new hires. Consistent with the stakeholder model in Exhibit 1.1, this partnership can even extend to HR working with managers in supplier firms, with customers, and even with members of community organizations. Yet, for the most part, on a day-to-day basis, the firm's line managers have responsibility for actually managing most people in an organization. Those who recognize the importance of this responsibility work in partnership with HR professionals who have specialized knowledge and skills, as described more extensively in Chapter 18.

Partnership between line managers and HR professionals is the ideal situation, but it is not happening in all companies. In the worldwide survey published by IBM and Towers Perrin, CEOs and human resource managers indicated that more partnering was needed by the year 2000. Exhibit 1.7 details the shifting HR responsibilities of line managers. Although it appears that line managers will be much more involved in the

■ *Exhibit 1.7*
An Emerging Role for Line Management

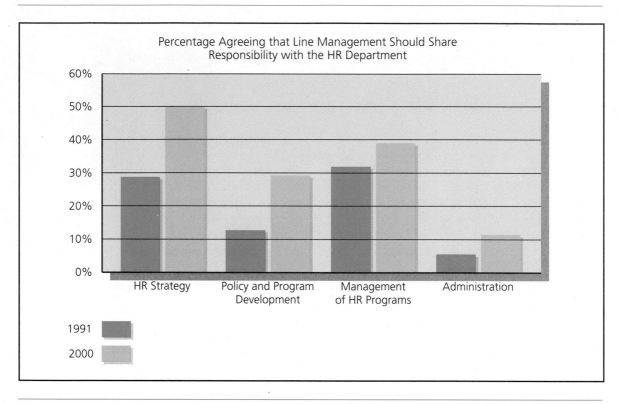

SOURCE: Adapted from "Priorities for Competitive Advantages: A Worldwide Human Resource Study" (IBM and Towers, Perrin, 1992), 26.

crafting of HR strategy, policy and program development, and the management of HR programs, their level of involvement in the administrative details of HR is likely to remain low.

Employees Are Now Sharing the Responsibility

The responsibilities of line managers and HR professionals are especially great, but partnership involves even more sharing of responsibility. Each employee in an organization, regardless of their particular job, also shares some of the responsibility. For example, employees commonly write their own job description. Some even design their own job. Employees may also be asked to provide input for the appraisal of their own performance or the performance of their colleagues and supervisors, or both. Perhaps most significant, employees assess their own needs and values and must manage their own career in accordance with these. Doing so effectively involves understanding many aspects of their employer's human resource management practices. As we move toward the 21st century, we all need to position ourselves for the future. For all of us, learning about how effective organizations are managing human resources is an essential step for getting into position.

This theme of partnership, of working together to manage human resources, is highlighted throughout this book in a feature called "Partnership in Managing Human

Partnership in Managing Human Resources

Line Managers	Human Resource Professionals	Employees
Include HR professionals in the formulation and implementation of business strategy.	Work closely with line managers and employees to develop and implement HR activities.	Work closely with line managers and HR professionals to develop and implement HR activities.
Work closely with HR professionals and employees to develop and implement HR activities.	Work with line managers to link activities to the business.	Accept responsibility for managing their own behavior and career in organizations.
Accept shared responsibility for managing the human resources of the company.	Work with employees to help them voice their concerns to management.	Recognize the need for flexibility and adaptability.
Set policy that is supportive of ethical behavior.	Develop policies and practices to support ethical conduct.	

Resources." Each "Partnership" section illustrates some ways this process of working together can be played out in various areas of human resource management.

 ## SUMMARY

Managing human resources is critical to the success of all companies, large and small, regardless of industry. The more effectively a firm manages its human resources, the more successful the firm is going to be.

Using the stakeholder framework, companies define success by how well they serve their stakeholders. Stakeholders include those who have a claim on the resources, services, and products of the companies. Although stakeholders influence all parts of an organization, they affect some aspects more than others, and some aspects are affected by more stakeholders. The stakeholders who make a significant claim on human resource management, and thus define a firm's general human resource objectives, include (but are not limited to) the organization itself, the stockholders and investors, society, the customers, the employees, and the suppliers. It is, in part, the existence of these powerful stakeholders that makes managing human resources a challenging and important task, because their claims sometimes conflict.

Managing employees requires the coordination of many human resource activities. Every activity, whether it be a value, policy, or practice, sends a message to employees. If all these activities are sending different messages, the employees are likely to respond in rather unpredictable ways. Thus, all HR activities must be coordinated with each other. HR activities must also be coordinated to fit the organization: its history, its strategies, its technology, the values and goals of its top management, its size, and its products and services.

The art of managing human resources is made even more challenging by the complex and changing context in which it takes place. For virtually all organizations, the competitive environment is no longer domestic; it is global. Therefore, a company's approach to managing human resources may need to take into account both the unique culture of the headquarters location as well as all the cultures of many other countries.

Thus, there is no one best way to manage employees. Organizations need to manage their human resources to fit their unique situation. This involves using information and data, which is why a theme in this book is "Using Data for the 21st Century." It is also why another theme of this book is "Partnership for the 21st Century." Organizations need more knowledge than that of just one group of individuals—for example, HR professionals in the HR department. They need a partnership between everyone who is working in the organization. In the following chapters, this partnership theme appears repeatedly. Also appearing repeatedly are the themes of diversity management, teams and teamwork, global realities, and organizational change. Organizational change is emphasized for two reasons: (1) rapid change is everywhere, in technology, in the workforce, in the world, and in the customers; and (2) for virtually all organizations, positioning for maximum competitiveness in the 21st century will require a change in the way they manage their human resources.

LOOKING AHEAD

Because managing human resources is the responsibility of everyone in organizations, we want to provide you with as much relevant information as possible. And because managing human resources is an art as well as a science, we want to provide you with as much opportunity for application as possible. To achieve these goals, this book includes many examples of what companies are doing for today and to position themselves and their human resources for the 21st century. We encourage you to get to know more about these companies by using on-line data retrieval services; reading company reports, business magazines, and newspapers; and even interviewing employees of these companies during the course in order to better understand why firms manage their human resources the way they do.

Cases

This book includes two types of cases: short, end-of-chapter cases, and two longer, summary cases at the back of the book. The two longer cases—one on Lincoln Electric, the other on the Insurance Product Services Department at Aid Association for Lutherans—are referred to throughout the book. They are provided so that you can see examples of how firms are systematically managing all their human resource activities through partnership and consistent with the characteristics of their organizations and the concerns of their stakeholders. Note that although the case of AAL focuses on the IPS Department, it is referred to as the AAL case.

These cases reflect several differences: one is manufacturing, the other service; one is the entire company, the other is a major unit of a company; one is in an urban area, the other in a rural area; and one has global operations, the other is solely domestic. Because these two longer cases cover all the HR activities, you are asked to analyze parts of them in each chapter. They thus complement the shorter, end-of-chapter cases that focus attention only on the specific issues addressed in a particular chapter.

Organization of the Book

Because the environmental context greatly influences the effective management of human resources, the several key context variables illustrated in Exhibit 1.6 are discussed in the next two chapters. After this setting is established, the text discusses how these variables affect human resource management: they require organizational change, they demand human resource planning, and they influence the types of jobs to be performed. These topics in turn set up the discussions in the remaining chapters in this book, which closely mirror the experience of an individual being recruited, hired, appraised, compensated, and developed, all within the context of a safe and healthy work environment, with and without union representation.

 Discussion Questions

1. What has the Weyerhaeuser Company been doing that demonstrates the value of managing human resources?
2. What are the four major reasons why organizations need to manage human resources well today and as they position themselves for the 21st century?
3. Using the stakeholder framework, outline the objectives that HR needs to be concerned with from all its major stakeholders.
4. Describe the relationships between managing human resources and the objectives of the organization.
5. Describe the relationships between managing human resources and the objectives of the stockholders and investors.
6. Describe the relationships between managing human resources and the objectives of the customers.
7. Describe the relationships between managing human resources and the objectives of the employees.
8. Describe the relationships between managing human resources and the objectives of society.
9. Describe the relationships between managing human resources and the objectives of strategic business partners (e.g., suppliers, joint venture partners).
10. Describe the importance of being systematic in managing human resources.
11. What are the implications and conclusions of the feature "Managing Human Resources for the 21st Century at Sears and Nordstrom"?
12. Describe the theme of the feature "Partnership in Managing Human Resources."

 In-Class Projects

1. Read the two cases at the end of this textbook, entitled "Lincoln Electric Company" and "Organizational Change: Planning and Implementing Teams at AAL and IPS." Then, using the stakeholder framework illustrated in Exhibit 1.1, develop a schematic illustration that identifies the stakeholders of each company, shows the relative importance of each stakeholder to each company, and shows the HR objectives relevant to each stakeholder. Be as specific as possible.

   Once your schematic illustration is developed, discuss the implications of the various HR objectives facing these two companies. Are any of them in conflict with each other? Based on your knowledge of the two companies, do they need to be doing things that they seem not to be doing now?
2. Because we will be using Lincoln Electric and AAL cases throughout the remaining chapters, you may wish to discover more information about each of these companies. To begin your analyses, write down what you think are the HR values and policies of Lincoln Electric and IPS/AAL. Using the choices in Exhibit 1.8 (see next page), begin to check off what you think best describes the HR practices in each company. We will be discussing these practices more in the following chapters, so you may wish to come back to this as we go along.

■ *Exhibit 1.8*
Human Resource Management Practice Choices

Planning Practice Choices

Informal ------- Formal
Short-Term ------- Long-Term
Explicit Job Analysis ------- Implicit Job Anaylsis
Job Simplification ------- Job Enrichment
Low Employee Involvement ------- High Employee Involvement

Staffing Practice Choices

Internal Sources ------- External Sources
Narrow Paths ------- Broad Paths
Single Ladder ------- Multiple Ladders
Explicit Criteria ------- Implicit Criteria
Limited Socialization ------- Extensive Socialization
Closed Procedures ------- Open Procedures

Appraising Practice Choices

Behavioral Criteria ------- Results Criteria
Purposes: Development, Remedial, Maintenance
Low Employee Participation ------- High Employee Participation
Short-term Criteria ------- Long-Term Criteria
Individual Criteria ------- Group Criteria

Compensating Practice Choices

Low Base Salaries ------- High Base Salaries
Internal Equity ------- External Equity
Few Perks ------- Many Perks
Standard, Fixed Package ------- Flexible Package
Low Participation ------- High Participation
No Incentives ------- Many Incentives
Short-Term Incentives ------- Long Term Incentives
No Employment Security ------- High Employment Security
Hierarchical ------- Egalitarian

Training and Development Practice Choices

Short Term ------- Long-Term
Narrow Application ------- Broad Application
Productivity Emphasis ------- Quality-of-Work-Life Emphasis
Spontaneous, Unplanned ------- Systematic, Planned
Individual Orientation ------- Group Orientation
Low Participation ------- High Participation

SOURCE: Adapted from R. S. Schuler, "Human Resource Management Practice Choices," in R. S. Schuler, S. A. Youngblood, and V. L. Huber, eds., Readings in *Personnel and Human Resource Management,* 3rd ed., St. Paul, MN: West Publishing, 1988.

3. Describe the following for

a. The Lincoln Electric Company
- The business objectives
- The major factors influencing these business objectives
- The HR objectives
- The major factors influencing these HR objectives

Going forward:

Why are these HR objectives likely to need changing (assuming you agree that they will need to change)? How and why are the business objectives and HR objectives likely to change?

b. The AAL company
- The business objectives
- The major factors influencing these business objectives
- The HR objectives
- The major factors influencing these HR objectives

Going forward:

Why are these HR objectives likely to need changing (assuming you agree that they will need to change)? How and why are the business objectives and HR objectives likely to change?

The Environment: Creating Challenges for Human Resource Management

It is our belief that, with trade barriers coming down, the world is going to be one great big marketplace, and the one who gets there first does the best.

DONALD SHINKEL, Vice President, Wal-Mart Stores[1]

Managing Human Resources for the 21st Century at the General Electric Company

General Electric (GE) Company's dramatic changes during the 1980s and early 1990s reflect a company adjusting to an increasingly competitive environment in innovative ways that mesh its human resource policies with the needs and strategy of the business.[2]

During the 1970s, GE's chief executive, the highly regarded "financial wizard" Reginald H. Jones, built the firm into a strong financial performer. He also led a diversification effort that put the company into about one hundred different businesses, ranging from manufacturers of appliances and lightbulbs, to coal mines and producers of TV sets and computer chips. Company earnings per share rose an average of 4.9 percent yearly. But in the process of building a profitable and diverse conglomerate, Jones also created a massive organization mired in bureaucracy. Reporting requirements were legendary. For example, one manager finally had to stop computers from generating seven daily reports on sales of hundreds of thousands of products; the paper from just one of those reports stood twelve feet high!

In 1981, Jack Welch assumed the post of GE's chief executive officer. In picking Welch as his successor, Jones supported Welch's objective of making the $27-billion GE a "world class competitor," able to thrive in an increasingly global marketplace. As he took the helm of a strong yet somewhat complacent firm, one of Welch's key tasks was to "instill in . . . managers a sense of urgency when there is no emergency," and prepare the company to meet the challenges of the 1980s and 1990s.

Welch saw the world marketplace as a tough and increasingly competitive playing field that eventually would be dominated by a few large firms. To compete in such a field, Welch believed, GE had to operate only in markets in which it could be the first or second player worldwide. This led to major restructuring: GE exited all but about fourteen businesses, reducing its labor force by 25 percent. By the mid-1990s, GE had gone from 420,000 employees to 200,000 employees through layoffs, attrition, and divestiture of businesses.[3]

In addition to the external competitive forces driving change, GE's increasingly diverse workforce has also posed a challenge. Like other American firms, GE is a place where employees with "different career objectives, different family aspirations, [and] different financial goals" are working side by side. Welch wants them to "share directly in GE's vision, the information, the decision-making process, and the rewards." In practical terms, this means Welch and his two hundred highest ranking managers must build a commitment to the changes resulting from restructuring among the other 99.9 percent of the company's two hundred thousand employees.

According to Welch, managing human resources effectively is part of the solution to positioning GE for the 21st century. In planning and staffing business units for the future, for example, Welch seeks managers who are "business leaders," able to "create a vision, articulate the vision, passionately own the vision, and . . . relentlessly drive it to completion." GE's business leaders must be open and willing to change. Identifying and preparing future leaders is so important that Welch regularly reviews files of selected employees from the time they join the firm, and evaluates each person's potential for future positions.

To increase productivity and reward performance, GE is shifting responsibility for decision making down the line. To expose weaknesses and reduce mediocrity, Welch consolidated the layers of line management. For managers, spans of control went from an average of six or seven subordinates to an average of ten to fifteen. Welch's reasoning? "Overstretched" managers perform better on important tasks because they have no time for trivia and no time to interfere with subordinates' tasks. Larger spans of control mean people down the line take on more responsibility and show their ability to perform. Welch also reduced corporate staff and forced remaining staff units to ask how they could help people on the line "be more effective and competitive."

Training and communication are top priorities for the firm. Welch takes his message directly to employees during training sessions at GE's in-house university in Crotonville, New York, which trains five thousand employees annually. To improve communication and further reduce bureaucracy, GE initiated a program called Work-Out in late 1989. The heads of the business units meet regularly with subordinates to identify and eliminate unnecessary activities—meetings, reports, and unproductive work. The process also seeks to identify better ways to evaluate and reward managers.

Finally, Welch is trying to move GE's labor unions toward the new way of thinking and managing. He wants labor, as well as white-collar managers, to gain a sense of "ownership" of the company and its direction.

During the 1980s and early 1990s, GE overhauled its strategy, streamlined business lines to compete for the future, and began to change the way people were being managed. As the company moves toward the 21st century, managing human resources effectively plays an important role in the success of the firm's strategy.[4]

 ## ENVIRONMENTAL FORCES

As the GE example illustrates, changes in the environment often precede changes in organizations.[5] In response to new economic and competitive conditions, for example, large corporations may reassess their portfolio of businesses. Such reassessments often culminate in a decision to shed one or more business units; or to build up a business by pursuing a new strategy; or to expand through acquisitions; or to branch out into the global arena; or to "rightsize," de-layer, reengineer, or otherwise fundamentally change the operations of the company; or to make any combination of these adjustments. The rapidly changing world of business profoundly affects the daily life of employees, their families, and the communities in which they live.

Economic and business conditions are not the only important environmental forces a company must attend to. Societal conditions, such as population levels and educational trends, directly affect the availability of labor and the characteristics of the people who are eventually hired as employees. In addition, the preferences of employees and the legal environment constrain the manner in which companies operate and the way they treat their employees. This chapter describes global economic and business conditions and discusses their implications for how companies are managing human resources. Then, Chapter 3 turns to a discussion of how employees' concerns and legal constraints influence the ways companies manage their human resources.[6]

Which Environmental Forces Are Most Important?

Exhibit 2.1 lists many of the changing environmental conditions affecting business today. Which of these do you think business leaders consider most important as they position their companies for the 21st century? Take a moment to choose and rank these changes. What are the implications of these forces for managing human resources in the 21st century? Doubtless you can think of many, and doubtless all are important for the stakeholders of organizations.

 ## THE GLOBAL ECONOMY

Consumers All Over the Globe

Because of their relative wealth, U.S. consumers have been considered the largest market in the world for several decades. But as we enter the 21st century, various political and economic changes are opening up potentially large consumer markets in other countries. Therefore, the world market is becoming increasingly more important for both small and large U.S. firms. Global population figures help put the U.S. market in perspective. In

■ *Exhibit 2.1*

Environmental Forces Affecting the Management of Human Resources

Many observers have predicted significant changes in the work and business environment for the twenty-first century. Choose and rank the **five** changes you think will have the most effect in the twenty-first century. Use 1 to indicate the highest effect, 2 to indicate the next highest effect, and so forth.

Environmental Changes	Rank
a. Increased national and international competition	_____
b. Increased governmental regulation	_____
c. Globalization of corporate business structure	_____
d. Growth in nontraditional business structures (e.g., business alliances, joint ventures)	_____
e. Globalization of the economy and breakdown of trade barriers	_____
f. Increased energy costs	_____
g. Increased reliance on automation and technology to produce goods and services	_____
h. More sophisticated information and communication technology	_____
i. Changing attitudes of society toward business	_____
j. Heightened concern about pollution and natural resources	_____
k. Heightened focus on total quality and customer satisfaction	_____
l. Changing employee values, goals, and expectations (e.g., less loyalty to current employer)	_____
m. Fewer entrants into the workforce	_____
n. Inadequate skills of entrants into the workforce	_____
o. Cross-border application of employee rights	_____
p. Changing composition of the workforce with respect to gender, age, or ethnicity, or any combination of these	_____
q. Greater concerns about the confidentiality of personal information	_____

SOURCE: Adapted from *Priorities for Competitive Advantage: A Worldwide Human Resource Study* (IBM and Towers Perrin, 1992): 11. Used by permission.

1995, slightly more than 5.5 billion people lived on this planet, 250 million in the United States. By the year 2000, the worldwide population will be around 6 billion, with 275 million living in the United States.[7]

With the average American's income and purchasing power growing at a relatively slower pace today versus thirty years ago, it is easy to see why many companies seek growth opportunities in other markets. The result? In the early 1970s, exports accounted for only 15 percent of U.S. GDP, whereas in the mid-1990s, exports accounted for 30 percent of the GDP. Indeed, several U.S. firms obtain *most* of their earnings in the global marketplace. These include General Motors, Ford, IBM, Quaker Oats Company, Coca-Cola Company, and Dow Chemical Company.[8] But this is just a small piece of the story. For many U.S. industries, foreign sales now account for between one-third and two-thirds of total sales. These industries include

- ⊚ Computers and office equipment (59 percent foreign sales)
- ⊚ Machinery (51 percent foreign sales)
- ⊚ Autos and auto parts (44 percent foreign sales)
- ⊚ Tobacco (41 percent foreign sales)
- ⊚ Chemical products (39 percent foreign sales)
- ⊚ Transportation equipment (34 percent foreign sales)[9]

Labor Markets around the World

Huge markets for products and services are not the only things enticing companies to enter the global arena. Foreign labor markets also attract interest. At 1994 growth rates, the labor force in developing nations alone will expand by about 700 million people by the year 2010, and the U.S. labor force by only 75 million.[10] Furthermore, opportunities for productivity growth are much greater in developing countries.[11] Between 1988 and 1992, for example, U.S. productivity increased by about 3 percent and Mexico's by more than 6 percent.[12] The reasons for these differences in productivity potential are many, but simple demographics tell much of the story. As Exhibit 2.2 shows, the workforce is generally older in developed countries and younger in developing countries. Furthermore, education levels are rising more rapidly in developing countries. For example, in 1970, less than 25 percent of all college students were from developing countries. By 1990, about 50 percent of all college students were from developing countries.[13]

For employers seeking flexible and adaptable workers, the young and newly educated workforces in developing countries are particularly attractive. Thus, it is not surprising that many firms headquartered in developed countries now have a large proportion of their workforce located elsewhere. For example:

- The Ford Motor Company has half its employees outside the United States.
- Philips Industries, N.V., has three-fourths of its employees working outside the Netherlands.
- More than half of Matsushita Electric's employees are outside Japan.
- Just over half of L. M. Ericsson's staff work outside Sweden.[14]

U.S. business leaders expect to continue to rely on foreign sources of labor. When 402 senior executives surveyed by *Business Week* were asked, "Do you think the proportion of your full-time work force that works outside the U.S. will be higher or lower (in one year)?" they responded like this:[15]

Higher	33%
Same	9%
Lower	26%
No overseas workforce	30%
Not sure	2%

Expatriates

The number of U.S. expatriates was estimated to be around 125,000 in 1994. As we enter the 21st century, this number is expected to move upward, perhaps only to 130,000.[16] This rate of growth does not mirror that of global trade because many U.S. multinational companies are staffing their international operations with people from the local country and other countries. Although the number of U.S. expatriates is modest, the positions occupied are extremely important to the companies. In many situations, U.S. multinationals even include an overseas posting as a necessary step in an employee's career.

One can also become an international employee by working for a non-U.S. firm operating in the United States. Increasingly, non-U.S. companies are sending their executives to the United States, so more and more American workers have non-American bosses. For example, some four-hundred thousand Americans work in U.S. subsidiaries of Japanese firms, usually with Japanese bosses.[17]

The International Workplace

Globalization means more than just sending executives abroad to run an essentially monocultural, foreign operation. It also means much more international travel to conduct business; indeed, from the early 1970s to the mid-1990s, the number of

◼ *Exhibit 2.2*

Share of Workforce under Age Thirty-Four in Developed versus Developing Countries (Projections for the Year 2000)

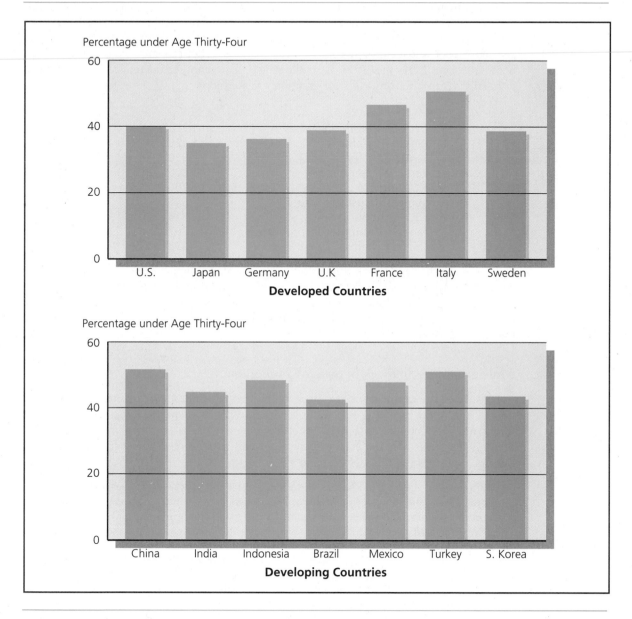

Note: Developed and developing countries are defined by the International Labor Office.
SOURCE: Based on data reported in W. B. Johnston, "Global Workforce 2000: The New World Labor Market." *Harvard Business Review* (March–April 1991): 115–27.

foreigners entering the United States on business rose an astounding 2,800 percent![18] And, increasingly, globalization means developing a truly multinational workforce at a single location. For example, at the Rotterdam headquarters of Unilever, a Dutch-British corporation whose products include Lipton Tea, the staff consists of employees from thirty different nations.[19]

For U.S. companies that require high skill levels in areas such as science and engineering, the issue of whether to adopt an international approach is simply no longer even a question. Declining test scores and lack of interest among U.S. students mean these companies must seek needed talent in other countries.[20] Because of the skills shortage at home and the resulting high wages demanded by skilled Americans, each year some thirty-five thousand U.S. companies request visas, especially for physical therapists, civil engineers, and people in computer-related jobs.[21] Reflective of what is happening here, between 1991 and 1993 the following U.S. computer-related companies were granted visas to hire foreigners for computer-related jobs:

Company	Number of Visas
Data Consultancy Services	1,255
Digital Equipment	1,129
Syntel	930
Borland International	800
HCL America	700
Complete Business Solutions	541
VSLI Technology	316
Tandem Computer Incorporated	267
Oracle Systems Corporation	258[22]

The skills shortage is not unique to the United States. Japan faces a similar problem. According to a report published by Japan's Science and Technology Agency, the percentage of college students interested in engineering has been declining steadily.[23] As is true in the United States, interest has shifted away from the sciences toward management and law.

Multinational Alliances between Companies

Finally, even if a company is not itself multinational, multinational interdependencies may permeate the business. For example, Exhibit 2.3 shows how companies around the world are interconnected through interdependencies based on two major computer operating systems. To understand how complex these global interdependencies can become, consider the following factual example:

Natural gas owned by Indonesia's oil agency, Pertamina, flows out of a well discovered by Royal Dutch Shell into a liquification plant designed by French engineers and built by a Korean construction company. The liquified gas is loaded onto U.S. flag tankers, built in U.S. yards after a Norwegian design. The ships shuttle to Japan and deliver the liquid gas to a Japanese public utility, which uses it to provide electricity that powers an electronics factory making television sets that are shipped aboard a Hong Kong–owned container ship to California for sale to American farmers in Louisiana who grow rice that is sold to Indonesia and shipped there aboard Greek bulk carriers. All of the various facilities, ships, products, and services involved in the complex series of events are financed by U.S., European, and Japanese commercial banks, working in some cases with international and local government agencies. These facilities, ships, products, and services are insured and reinsured by U.S., European, and Japanese insurance companies. Investors in these facilities, ships, products, and services are located throughout the world.[24]

Developing and managing employees in this world of joint ventures and strategic alliances poses challenges for which few companies are prepared.[25] As described in "Managing Human Resources for the 21st Century at Merck and Company," these challenges include merging different cultures, compensation systems, and business strategies—which would be difficult enough if two U.S. companies were involved but is even more complicated when a U.S. company is working with a French company.

◼ *Exhibit 2.3*

Global Competing Networks: IBM and AT&T

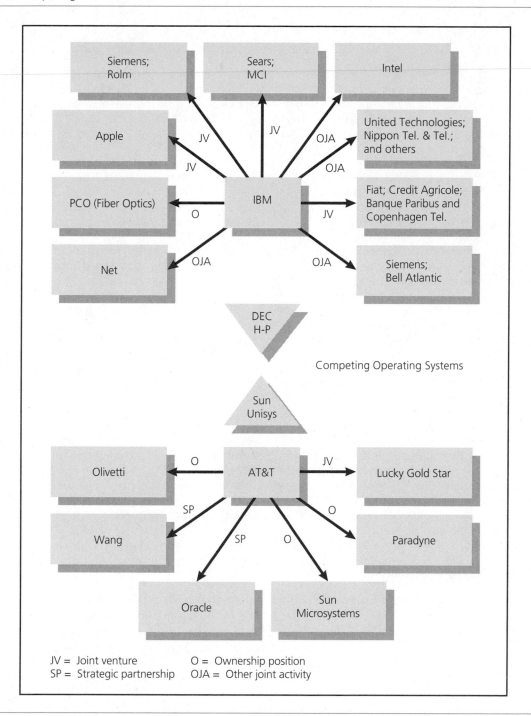

SOURCE: Based on J. B. Quinn, "The Intelligent Enterprise," *The Executive,* (6(4),1992): 48–63. Used with permission of the Academy of Management.

Managing Human Resources for the 21st Century at Merck and Company

Whitehouse Station, New Jersey–based Merck & Company Inc. is the world's largest maker of prescription drugs, with 37,000 employees worldwide and revenues of more than $8.5 billion. Despite having all of these resources on hand, Merck has improved particular elements of its business by using resources of other companies more capable than itself in specific areas. In turn, Merck has offered its resources to those companies for their growth.

It began back in 1990 when Merck teamed up with Wilmington, Delaware–based E. I. DuPont. DuPont had a $700 million pharmaceutical business. Because the chemical producer's area of expertise wasn't the pharmaceutical business, however, it lacked the development capability for these products that Merck has. It did have approximately 300 scientists and a substantial research budget, however. By forming a joint venture, Merck could help develop and bring to market DuPont's experimental compounds.

The partnership was successful. Today, DuPont Merck Pharmaceutical Company—the company created from the joint-venture—is a *Fortune* 500 business worth more than a billion dollars.

The success of that alliance has prompted several others. Johnson & Johnson·Merck Consumer Pharmaceuticals Co. was formed when several of Merck's overseas patents were expiring and Merck wanted to modify the products for over-the-counter sales—something in which Johnson & Johnson has expertise. Two of Merck's other large enterprises have been formed overseas: The Astra-Merck Group is a strategic alliance between Merck and the Swedish

company AB Astra, and Pasteur Merieux, Serums, et Vaccins is an alliance in France. Although each of these businesses was formed for different strategies, all were pursued so that the companies involved could accomplish a desired result more rapidly and at a lower cost than each could do on its own.

From the beginning of each of these joint enterprises, HR has been involved. The function must resolve most of the issues surrounding the melding of two companies; issues such as the blending of two corporate cultures, two different compensation strategies and two different business strategies. "There's a real challenge in the alliances in merging cultures and strategies and I think HR plays a key role in helping the companies resolve the issues," says Eric Marquardt, director of executive compensation for Merck. For example, when Merck teamed up with its French alliance, one of HR's greatest challenges was developing a reward system for employees. Merck promotes ownership of the company and has profit-sharing pay programs. Because these concepts aren't part of the French culture, a system had to be developed to satisfy both parties.

Other challenges that HR undertakes for these alliances deal with staffing. It has been involved in determining who will head the joint ventures—whether the CEOs will come from one of the parent companies or from the outside—and in developing packages to attract these people, as well as employees from the two parent companies, to the new assignments. The service HR offers to the company in these strategic alliances makes it an important element for their success.[26]

The Virtual Corporation. Joint ventures and strategic alliances such as those shown in Exhibit 2.3 may be just the beginning. In the future, the so-called virtual corporation may take hold. What is it? In the minds of a few executives who are focused on the future, it is a temporary network of companies with diverse core competencies who quickly form a collaboration to take advantage of fleeting opportunities. Having exploited these opportunities, the "corporation" may disband as swiftly as it formed. The temporary firm will have no hierarchy, no central office, and no organizational chart.[27]

To get in on the action, companies will need a reputation as a desirable partner. Of course, they will also need a core competency in an area such as technology or marketing. But in addition, they will need people who are both able and motivated to cross organizational boundaries easily and be productive in a "temporary" job, yet remain loyal to the home base.

MANAGING HUMAN RESOURCES IN THE GLOBAL ECONOMY

Faced with unprecedented levels of foreign competition at home and abroad, firms are beginning to recognize how important it is to find and nurture the human resources required to implement global strategies. As we move into the 21st century, more and more companies will see opportunities that can be seized only by adopting a global perspective, and the question of how best to staff and manage such organizations will become more pressing. The situation has been described like this: "Virtually any type of international problem, in the final analysis, is either created by people or must be solved by people. Hence, having the right people in the right place at the right time emerges as the key to a company's international growth. If we are successful in solving that problem ... we can cope with all others."[28] Apparently, many companies underestimate the complexities involved in international operations, and poor management of human resources is responsible for many business failures in the international arena:

> The primary causes of failure in multinational ventures stem from a lack of understanding of the essential differences in managing human resources, at all levels, in foreign environments. Certain management philosophies and techniques have proven successful in the domestic environment: their application in a foreign environment too often leads to frustration, failure and underachievement. These "human" considerations are as important as the financial and marketing criteria upon which so many decisions to undertake multinational ventures depend.[29]

Global Corporate Cultures

Managing human resources in a global economy presents many substantial challenges. Transporting a corporate culture successfully around the world is perhaps the greatest challenge. When a company's operations are flung across great distances and many national cultures, corporate culture glues the pieces together. According to Calvin Reynolds, senior counselor from New York City–based Organization Resources Counselors, "If you don't have a strong set of cultural principles from which to function, when people get overseas, they're so lacking in clarity that no one knows where they're going."[30]

ABB. The Swiss-Swedish firm Asea Brown Boveri (ABB) is one global firm with a strong corporate culture. "We think of ABB as a company without regard to national boundaries. . . . We just operate on a global basis," explains Richard Randazzo, vice president of human resources. The corporate culture—focused on making money, taking action, using a hands-on approach, and traveling to wherever business opportunities arise—is not insensitive to national cultures, however. Indeed, the firm insists that its 213,000 employees working in 1,300 national companies adapt the corporate culture to blend with the local cultural scene. Local activities, in turn, influence the ABB corporate culture because local learning is shared across borders. For example, ABB's approach to equal employment opportunity in Europe will reflect its U.S. experience. This is because European countries have become actively concerned with issues of equal employment opportunity only recently, whereas the United States has many years of experience addressing these concerns.[31]

PCI. Pepsi-Cola International (PCI) is another company with a strong corporate culture that is now being successfully transported across national borders. But this was not always true: "In 1985, there was some confusion about what it took to be individually successful in Pepsi-Cola International. There was no shared value system or vocabulary for describing individual performance. For example, in the socialist countries the concept of individual performance was practically nonexistent, whereas in Germany it carried the same meaning as it does in the United States. The business was beginning to develop and grow at a rapid rate, and the pressures on individual managers were considerable."[32] Since then, PCI, which employs five thousand people and operates in over 150 countries, has worked hard to establish a common understanding of its business objectives and values, which are shown in Exhibit 2.4.

PCI made many changes in the way it managed its managers, some of which are described in "Positioning for the 21st Century: Management Development at Pepsi-Cola International." As the PCI experience reveals, the evolution of multinational enterprises is increasing the importance of effectively managing human resources. It is also increasing the need for firms to recognize and incorporate cultural differences in the ways they manage their human resources.

National Cultural Differences

Some people see ongoing business globalization creating worldwide enterprises that transcend, and perhaps eventually replace, national borders:

> This latest round of reorganizations comes from companies that have streamlined domestic operations and now are looking for efficiencies abroad. The result: dramatic changes in the way these U.S. giants work. Their aim: to break down national barriers inside the companies. IBM, for instance, is organizing its marketing and sales staffs into 14 industry groups, such as banking and retail, rather than by country.
>
> The shakeup at Ford is even more dramatic: It is merging its large and culturally distinct European and North American auto operations and plans to later fold in Latin America and the Asia-Pacific region. Why bother? Chairman Alexander J. Trotman sees Ford as being in "an all-out race" to make more efficient use of its engineering and product development money against rapidly globalizing rivals.[33]

This may be tomorrow's reality, but in today's reality, country-to-country differences remain somewhat intact and most companies assume that flexible corporate cultures are needed. Rather than displacing or ignoring the national culture, a flexible corporate culture adapts to the local cultural conditions.

■ *Exhibit 2.4*

The Most Common Values Making up the Mind-Set at Pepsi-Cola International

Business	To be the world's leading soft drink company
HR Focus	To be a world-class company where business results and career satisfaction are synonymous
Business Objectives	• Committed bottling organization
	• Uncompromising dedication to quality
	• Development of talented people
	• Focus on growth
	• Quality business plans
Shared Values	• Leadership
	• High standards of personal performance
	• Career/skill development
	• Balancing teamwork and individual achievement

SOURCE: Pepsi-Cola International company material provided by J. F. Fulkerson for J. R. Fulkerson and R. S. Schuler, "Managing Worldwide Diversity at Pepsi-Cola International," in S. E. Jackson, ed., *Diversity in the Workplace: Human Resource Initiatives* (New York: Guilford Press, 1992). Used by permission.

Positioning for the 21st Century:
MANAGEMENT DEVELOPMENT AT PEPSI-COLA INTERNATIONAL

Pepsi-Cola International always knew it needed a certain kind of savvy, intelligent manager to succeed in the complex world of international production and marketing. But just to be sure, the international division quantified its values and expectations, says John Fulkerson, personnel director for Pepsi-Cola International (Somers, NY).

"We recently studied 100 successful managers and 100 unsuccessful managers, with the help of the Center for Creative Leadership, and came up with 11 qualities that seem to make a difference in success at Pepsi-Cola International. We looked at very junior to very senior managers over a three-year period.

"We were not surprised by any of the qualities— especially the top three:

- The ability to handle business complexities
- The ability to lead and manage people
- Drive and a results orientation.

"All these qualities support our company's success and results orientation, which lies at the heart of our corporate culture. It sounds hard to maintain a workable corporate culture when doing business across cultures. However, Pepsi International has built a set of values that transcend petty differences and apply to everyone, everywhere.

"What's more important is how you treat people. We operate on the principles of telling people what we expect, showing them how to develop, and helping them reach the goals. Those ideas work in any of the countries where we do business.

"People are more similar than we think; they want the same things. They want to be successful. That even applies in the Communist bloc countries. After all, they invited us in. They just want to be successful, too.

"Our 1,200 international employees help us sell 40 billion 8-ounce servings of Pepsi annually in 145 countries through 16 regional offices. Our people need to be mature and savvy. They must be able to handle complex business and understand global issues.

"We need these kinds of people to do business in the complex international arena, and Pepsi-Cola needs people like this to operate in the result-oriented culture that (former Pepsi chairman) Don Kendall pioneered here. We key on results because, especially in international, you quickly learn there are 100 ways to do anything. . . .

"Our culture centers around clear communication of the expected results, and risk taking with no punishment for making mistakes. Along with this expectation that our mature, savvy people will know what to do is another expectation that they'll know when it's time to ask for help. We emphasize the criticality of communication. We make it known that we expect, for example, a manager in Spain to know when its appropriate to check with New York to see what Australia is doing in a certain circumstance. If you talk to others you lessen the chance of making a mistake.

"Our culture also tells managers that being defensive will get you nowhere and that you are not viewed as being mature if you just complain. Things are very open and above board here, and that is even reflected in a formalized personnel program we call 'Instant Feedback.' It's a system for reinforcing our desire to have constant quick communication.

"Some cultures don't like this, and we are flexible. For example, in the Far East, you can't give feedback in front of peers, you wait until you're alone. In Latin America, on the other hand, people are much more vocal in discussing performance issues. They throw it out on the table and it's a jump ball.

"Though we try to emphasize similarities in our culture, and hope that most of our values cut across cultures, we are not unmindful of varying customs in different cultures and regions. We're willing to modify our practices to get results, because wanting results is at the heart of our culture.[34]

PCI. PCI illustrates this approach. PCI is fundamentally a feedback-driven company. Its culture includes the use of "instant feedback," coaching, accountability-based performance appraisals, and developmental feedback. These activities occur in every country, and the objective is always to improve performance. But feedback sessions look somewhat different depending on the local culture. For example, Americans might give each other feedback in public, but this would never occur in most Asian cultures. In Asian countries, the person receiving feedback may do a lot of head nodding, which means only that the message is being heard. If they disagree with what they are hearing, some Latins will argue strongly during a feedback session. And employees in some countries—for example, India—will insist on being given very specific and detailed feedback.[35]

PCI has a strong corporate culture. Nevertheless, to operate effectively in different countries, PCI managers must understand differences among country cultures. This is also true for most managers in other international companies. In the 21st century, many more managers will need to understand how these cultural differences influence employees' behaviors and the systems organizations use for managing human resources.

What Is Culture? *Culture* has many definitions, but generally it is used to refer to societal forces that shape behavior. Members of a cultural group share a distinct way of life founded on common values, attitudes, ways of viewing the world, and behaviors. Members socially transmit these elements of culture across generations, often with little reflection or even intention. Culture can be so subtle that we are unaware of its effects on us. But when confronted with a different culture, suddenly it is easy to see its effects on *other* people![36]

Culture's Effects on Personal Relationships. Travelers often experience cultural differences as novel, even enjoyable. However, people living and working in a new country for extended periods of time often find such differences unsettling. Adjusting to a new culture challenges one's own frame of reference; sometimes one's sense of self and national identity come into question. Self-doubt combined with culture shock—a psychological disorientation caused by being in a situation where you do not recognize and understand social cues—can lead to negative feelings about the members of other cultural groups. Negative behaviors toward others may soon follow. It is now generally recognized that culturally insensitive attitudes and behaviors stemming from ignorance or from misguided beliefs often cause business failure.[37]

Culture's Effects on Business Practices. Activities such as hiring, promoting, rewarding, and dismissal all reflect aspects of national culture.[38] When expatriates take assignments abroad, ignorance of cultural differences detracts from their ability to be effective. Consider the case of the Australian general manager sent to Indonesia to manage a new mining venture. As often happens, the expatriate was running a unit staffed with local people. The local manager responsible for recruitment could not understand why the expatriate general manager was upset when he hired most of his extended family to fill jobs, rather than recruiting people with the required technical competence. He was simply fulfilling his duty to family—since he was in a position to employ most of his relatives, he was obligated to do so. The Australian, however, interpreted the Indonesian's actions as nepotism, a negative practice according to his own value system.[39]

Dimensions for Comparing National Cultures. The most widely known framework for comparing cultures was developed in the early 1980s by Geert Hofstede, a Dutch researcher who surveyed over 116,000 employees in seventy-two national subsidiaries of a large international firm, thirty-eight occupations, and twenty languages.[40] The four dimensions of culture described by Hofstede and the relative ranking of ten selected countries on these four dimensions are shown in Exhibit 2.5.

■ *Exhibit 2.5*

Culture Dimension Scores for Ten Countries

	PD	ID	MA	UA
United States	40 L	91 H	62 H	46 L
Germany	35 L	67 H	66 H	65 M
Japan	54 M	46 M	95 H	92 H
France	68 H	71 H	43 M	86 H
Netherlands	38 L	80 H	14 L	53 M
Hong Kong	68 H	25 L	57 H	29 L
Indonesia	78 H	14 L	46 M	48 L
West Africa	77 H	20 L	46 M	54 M
Russia	95*H	50*M	40*L	90*H
China	80*H	20*L	50*M	60*M

Notes: Column headings are as follows:

PD = Power distance. The degree of inequality among people that is considered normal: from relatively equal (small power distance) to extremely unequal (having a large power distance).

ID = Individualism. The degree to which people prefer to act as individuals rather than as members of groups. The opposite of individualism can be called collectivism, so collectivism is low individualism.

MA = Masculinity and its opposite pole femininity. The degree to which tough values like assertiveness, performance, success, and competition, which in nearly all societies are associated with the role of men, prevail over tender values like the quality of life, maintaining warm personal relationships, service, care for the weak, and solidarity, which in nearly all societies are more associated with women's roles.

UA = Uncertainty avoidance. The degree to which people prefer structured over unstructured situations. Structured situations are those involving clear rules as to how one should behave.

Results are as follows among fifty three countries and regions:

H = Top Third

M = Middle Third

L = Bottom Third

*Estimated

SOURCE: Adapted from G. Hofstede, "Cultural Constraints on Management Theories," *The Executive* (February 1993): 91. Used by permission of the Academy of Management.

Cultural differences such as those described in Exhibit 2.5 undoubtedly account for some country differences. But country differences in human resource management may also be due to economic and political systems, laws and regulations, and labor market conditions. Furthermore, within a single country, industry and organizational characteristics may account for some differences in managerial practices and employee behaviors.

 ## DIFFERENCES IN HUMAN RESOURCE PRACTICES ACROSS INDUSTRIES

Industry refers to a distinct group of productive or profit-making enterprises. The U.S. and global economies can be carved up into many different industry sectors, commonly classified by Standard Industrial Classification (SIC) numbers. Two of these sectors are manufacturing and service.[41]

The Manufacturing and Service Sectors

During the 19th century, the U.S. economy was based on agriculture, trades, and crafts. Henry Ford's assembly line quickly changed all that, and for most of the 20th century, mass manufacturing industries dominated the U.S. economy. During the industrial era, most of the U.S. workforce moved off the farm and out of small shops into large, formal business organizations. Their work focused on producing, distributing, and selling standardized goods. Formal approaches to managing human resources were developed in this context.

As we approach and move into the 21st century, the U.S. economy is completing yet another transformation, this time from a manufacturing to a service economy. The second half of the 20th century saw the number of blue-collar production jobs cut in half, while white-collar administrative and service jobs tripled.[42] Exhibit 2.6 shows how the U.S. Bureau of Labor Statistics (BLS) classified the jobs Americans held in 1990 and where the BLS expected job growth and decline by the year 2005.

As the transformation of our economy unfolds, it is becoming clear that managing human resources in the service sector demands a new approach. A service company that manages its employees the same way big manufacturing firms do will probably not be successful.

Managing Human Resources in the Manufacturing and Service Sectors

Three characteristics distinguish services from manufacturing, and they all have implications for managing human resources. First, most services involve something intangible. Second, the customer and employee usually collaborate in the production-and-delivery process for services. Third, production and consumption of services are usually simultaneous; that is, as soon as a service is produced, it is already being received and "consumed" by the customer.[43] In theory, these distinctions are sometimes sharply drawn, but in reality, many firms cannot be easily classified as service versus manufacturing because their activities include both components. Furthermore, some types of services are more intangible and simultaneous than others. Exhibit 2.7 illustrates this point: the dinner at a nice restaurant evidently has some tangible product (the food), as well as some intangibles (the ambience, the waitperson's manner, etc.).

For supervisors, the intangible nature of services makes it difficult to monitor employee performance directly, so traditional means of quality control—the inspect-and-reject model—are useless. The imperative for service employees is getting the job done right on-line the first time. This means employees must be fully capable of monitoring their own performance. It also means supervisors must trust employees to monitor themselves.[44]

In services, the customer plays a unique role. Because they are essential to service delivery, sometimes customers are actually thought of as partial employees. This means they are subject to being managed by the company and they can be expected to participate in the process of managing regular employees.[45] For example, employers in the service sector often ask customers for input in the performance appraisals of regular employees.[46]

Differences in the nature of manufacturing and service also have implications for other HR practices, including recruitment, compensation, the employment of temporary workers, the development and maintenance of appropriate organizational climates and cultures, and stress management.[47] For example, more employee training and socialization occur in services than in the manufacturing sector.[48] Also, it appears as if service firms can benefit more by attending carefully to the personal characteristics of employees, such as friendliness and a pleasant smile, instead of focusing *solely* on skills and abilities. However, some evidence suggests that this is also occurring in some manufacturing firms, particularly firms that are pursuing total quality and continuous improvement. In these situations, firms want employees with technical skills *and* a willingness to work cooperatively with others in teams.[49]

◼ *Exhibit 2.6*

Current Jobs and Projected Growth for Selected Categories of Work (in Thousands)

	1990	Growth by 2005		1990	Growth by 2005
Executive, Administrative, and Managerial			**Technical Support**		
			Engineering technicians	755	25–34%
General managers and top executives	3,100	14–24%	Licensed practical nurses	644	35% or more
Accountants and auditors	985	25–34%	Computer programmers	565	35% or more
Financial managers	701	25–34%			
Restaurant and food service managers	557	25–34%	Medical technologists and technicians	258	14–25%
Personnel and labor relations managers	456	25–34%	**Production**		
Marketing, advertising, and PR managers	427	35% or more	Miscellaneous production workers	1,997	5–13%
Engineering and data processing managers	315	25–34%	Supervisors	1,800	5–13%
			Metal-working and plastic-working machine ops	1,473	–4–4%
Health services managers	257	35% or more	Apparel workers	1,037	–5% or more
Marketing and Sales			**Repairs and Installation**		
Retail sales workers	4,754	25–34%	General maintenance mechanics	1,128	14–24%
Manufacturers' and wholesale sales reps	1,944	14–24%	Automotive mechanics	757	14–24%
Service sales reps	588	35% or more	Electronic equipment repairers	444	5–13%
Insurance agents and brokers	439	14–24%	**Unskilled Labor**		
Real estate agents, brokers, and appraisers	413	14–24%	Miscellaneous unskilled workers	2,082	5–13%
Securities and financial services sales reps	191	35% or more	Freight, stock, and material movers	881	5–13%
Administrative Support			Construction trades helpers	549	5–13%
Traffic, shipping, and stock clerks	3,755	5–13%	**Miscellaneous Service**		
Secretaries	3,576	14–24%	Chefs, cooks, and kitchen workers	3,100	25–34%
General office clerks	2,737	14–24%	Janitors and cleaners	3,000	14–24%
Word processors and data entry keyers	1,448	–4–4%	Nursing and psychiatric aides	1,374	35% or more
Information clerks	1,400	35% or more	**Professional**		
			Registered nurses	1,727	35% or more
Transportation and Material Moving			Engineers	1,519	25–34%
Truck drivers	2,700	14–24%	Secondary school teachers	1,280	25–34%
Other transportation workers	698	5–13%	Lawyers and judges	633	25–34%
Construction Trades			Physicians	580	25–34%
Carpenters	1,077	14–24%	Computer systems analysts	463	35% or more
Electricians	548	25–34%			
Highway maintenance workers	151	14–24%			

SOURCE: Adapted from W. Woods, "The Jobs Americans Hold," *Fortune* (July 12, 1993):54–55.

■ *Exhibit 2.7*
Ratings of Goods and Services by MBA Students

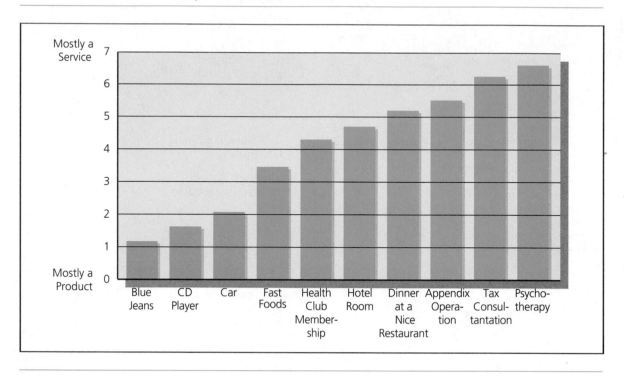

SOURCE: Based on materials in D. Iacobucci, "An Empirical Examination of Some Basic Tenets in Services: Goods-Services Continua," in *Advances in Services Marketing and Management*, (Greenwich, CT: JAI Press), (Vol. 1, 1992): 23–52.

◈ THE CHANGING ORGANIZATIONAL ENVIRONMENT: NEW TECHNOLOGIES

American executives feel a sense of vast impending change in the external environment—and external changes often mean that internal changes will soon follow. As they look at the highly competitive international marketplace, executives see that the 1990s have been tougher than the 1980s, and that the 21st century will be tougher still. They see companies being forced to develop new approaches to managing, and they see the need to make decisions faster. New technologies and new organizational structures help solve some of the challenges created by the change to a more global economy—and these new technologies and structures, in turn, mean new approaches to managing human resources.

Leaner and More Flexible Production Systems

Technology generally refers to the equipment and knowledge used to produce goods and services. Today's organizations are discarding yesterday's technologies and replacing them with new technologies.[50] For example, going is Henry Ford's mass production system; arriving as its replacement is the "lean" production system developed by Eiji Toyoda of Toyota and his production genius, Taiichi Ohno:

Just as the mass-production principles pioneered by Henry Ford and General Motors' Alfred Sloan swept away the age of craft production after World War I, so the ideas of Toyoda and Ohno are today chipping away at the foundations of mass production. We call their system "lean" production because it uses less of everything than a comparable mass-production operation: half the human effort in the factory, half the manufacturing space, half the investment in tools, half the engineering hours to develop a new product. Lean production is built not simply on technical insight but on a precisely defined set of relationships that extends far beyond the factory floor to encompass designers, suppliers and customers.[51]

The new production systems are not just leaner—they are also more flexible. Mass production was used to produce standardized goods at low cost, using special-purpose, product-specific machines and semiskilled labor. But now consumers are demanding more specialized products. Flexible specialization is a modern form of production that shares some of the features of the craft modes of production that were common prior to the industrial revolution.[52]

With this newer technology, jobs are more complex, so both production and managerial employees need more skills and higher levels of skill.[53] These skills are costly—a fact not lost on the organizations using flexible production technologies. To reap the highest returns from the money they spend on compensation, firms using the more modern technologies more often link pay to performance.[54] Until the early 1990s, performance-based pay was almost unheard of for American production workers, owing in part to the nature of assembly lines and in part to union opposition to such plans. But the modern technologies, combined with statistical process control techniques like those used for total quality management, may fit well with some types of performance-based compensation.

Telematics

Factory automation is just one example of how computers can change an organization. More than ever before, companies of all types operate through computers. Consider this: A birthday card that plays *Happy Birthday* contains more computer power than existed on the entire earth in 1950.[55] The year 1950 was about the time many of today's top executives were born. Now some 32 million households have personal computers. Office automation, data communications, voice mail, and information systems all are being implemented together faster than ever to virtually revolutionize the ways we organize and do work. The so-called telematics technologies encompass

- Mainframe computers and associated information systems
- Microcomputers and word processors
- Networking technologies
- Telecommunications technologies
- Reprography and printing
- Peripherals

Filmmaker George Lucas is one of the many people who enthusiastically embrace this revolution: "I see us in the beginnings of the real digital revolution now. This is one of those sociological, historic pivot points that changes the way all society is going to work forever. It's as dramatic a change as the Industrial Revolution was. To a lot of people it's scary because the world is turning upside down, but for those who like the future, it's exciting."[56]

Computers facilitate speed, flexibility, decentralization, and staying in close touch with the customer. For example, for banks and brokerage firms, computers enable customers to do their business from their homes, their offices, and while traveling almost anywhere in the world. Computers can also let customers look inside an organization. The trucking firm Pacific Intermountain Express gives customers access to its computers so that they can check the status of their shipments.[57] These technologies also help organizations enhance quality by ensuring that suppliers deliver better parts and services. Already, retail chains are linked with their suppliers so that they know the timing and the nature of needed shipments. For example, The Limited (an upscale retail store with headquarters in Columbus, Ohio) tracks consumer preferences every day through point-of-sale computers. Orders, with facsimile illustrations, are sent by satellite to suppliers around the U.S. and in Hong Kong, South Korea, Singapore, and Sri Lanka. Within days clothing from distant points begins to collect in Hong Kong. About four times a week a chartered 747 brings it to the company's distribution center in Ohio, where goods are priced and shipped to stores within 48 hours.[58]

New Organizational Structures and Corporate Cultures

Whether in the factory, in the office, in the home, on the road, or in the air, computers change organizational structures and corporate cultures. Because information is instantaneously available, top-level managers can bypass middle managers and get information directly from first-line managers. Thus, telematics technologies redefine authority structures.[59] With these technologies, traditional managers may no longer be needed.

> A few observers believe that computers in the workplace will lead to far more than better information and better products. Shoshana Zuboff, a professor at the Harvard Business School and author of *In the Age of the Smart Machine,* argues that computerization undermines traditional forms of authority and breaks down barriers between job categories and functions. "You have people doing work which is more abstract, more analytical," says Zuboff. "People not considered managerial in the past are managing information." Zuboff concludes that the role of the managers will have to be redefined in the Nineties. Says she: "Since managers are no longer the guardians of the knowledge base, we do not need the command-control type of executive."[60]

In summary, telematics help organizations decentralize decision making, making organizations more flexible and responsible. At the same time, they create many new challenges related to managing human resources.

New Skills

Many of the HR management challenges raised by telematics are related to the new skills needed to work with the new technologies: "Several factors are driving the shift toward new skills for work: greater use of information technologies, the move away from craft and assembly manufacture and toward computer-mediated processes, the larger amount of knowledge work in almost every occupation, new requirements for education and the ability to manage complexity, and the redesign of many jobs to include computer-based work. Frequently, several skills will be folded into one job, often with a new title and greater individual responsibility."[61]

Overall, the skill mix of the economy is moving rapidly upscale, with most new jobs demanding more education and higher levels of language, math, and reasoning skills.[62] Unfortunately, the skills of American students are falling behind those of students in other countries (see, e.g., Exhibit 2.8).

As jobs are redesigned, companies find they cannot take full advantage of available technologies until many workers are trained and retrained. After installing millions of

■ *Exhibit 2.8*
High School Student Performance in Science

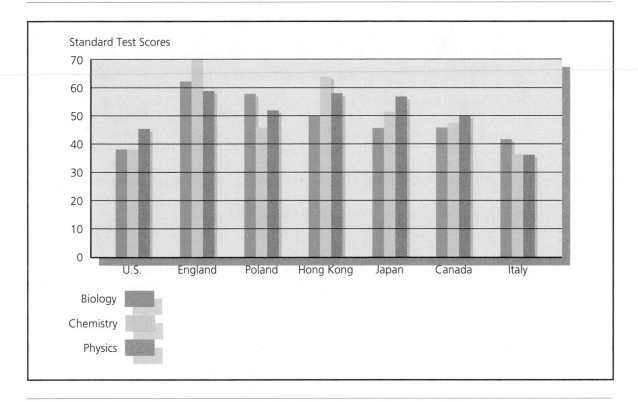

SOURCE: U.S. Department of Education, *Digest of Education Statistics* (Washington, DC, 1989), table 348, p. 391.

dollars worth of computers in its Burlington, Vermont, factories, the IBM Corporation discovered that it had to teach high school algebra to thousands of workers before they could run the computers.[63] David T. Kearns, former chairman and CEO of Xerox and subsequently deputy secretary of education and then chairman and president of New American Schools Development Corporation, believes that the mismatch between the skills needed in the new workplace and the skills available in the U.S. labor market represent a significant national challenge: "[T]he American workforce is running out of qualified people. If current demographic and economic trends continue, American business will have to hire a million new workers a year who can't read, write, or count. Teaching them how, and absorbing the lost productivity while they're learning, will cost the industry $25 billion a year for as long as it takes."[64]

Merry I. White, professor of comparative sociology at Boston University and author of *The Japanese Education Challenge,* sees the skills gap created by new technologies as central to the ability of the United States to compete effectively in the global economy, noting that "[m]uch of the success of Japan stems from the fact that its blue collar workers can interpret advanced mathematics, read complex engineering blueprints, and perform sophisticated tasks on the factory floor far better than blue collar workers in the U.S."[65] Many top executives share this concern, which is one reason why more companies are partnering with educators.[66] In Minneapolis, Minnesota, for example, corporate contributions underwrote much of the planning activity for the successful restructuring of the city's school system. Similar partnerships have been formed throughout the country.[67]

Some estimates suggest that by the year 2000, 75 percent of all employees will need to be retrained in new jobs or taught new skills for their old jobs.[68] Consequently, corporate trainers are looking for faster and more effective methods for delivering new skills and learning.[69] An example of what one business in Ohio is doing to train and educate its workforce is given in the feature "Managing Human Resources for the 21st Century at Will-Burt."

Training is not the only aspect of HR affected by new technologies. A study of 512 manufacturing firms that had adopted advanced manufacturing technology and just-in-time inventory systems found that these technologies were also associated with more selective hiring, better use of performance appraisals as developmental (versus evaluational) tools, and compensation packages that reflected the value of employees in the external labor market.[70] Furthermore, new communication technologies in particular make it possible for organizations to fundamentally change their structures and for employees to experiment with working at home.

ORGANIZATION SIZE

What Does Size Mean?

When companies are discussed, sometimes *size* refers to financial indicators, such as total assets or total sales; and other times it refers to the number of people employed. Unless stated otherwise, this text uses *size* to refer to the number of employees.

Descriptions of size—small, medium, large—can also be confusing. The federal government typically defines small organizations as having fewer than 500 employees, and large organizations as having more than 500 employees. Business leaders and media reporters often use *small* to mean fewer than 100 employees and *medium* to mean 100 to 500 employees. Generally, firms with over 500 employees are considered large by everyone.

The Consequences of Size

The size of an organization has many consequences, especially for managing human resources. For example, many federal laws and regulations concerning employment apply only to firms with fifteen or more employees; whereas state and city legislation may apply to firms of all sizes.

Although exceptions exist, generally, the larger the organization, the more developed its internal labor market and the less its reliance on the external labor market. In contrast, the smaller the organization, the less developed its internal labor market and the greater its reliance on the external labor market. As it relies more on the internal labor market, the organization depends more on itself in deciding how much to pay people and on whether job evaluations, job classifications, and internal equity will be used. As it relies more on the external labor market, the organization depends less on itself and more on what other organizations are doing when deciding issues such as pay rates and external equity.

The size of an organization also affects the duties and responsibilities of line managers. For example, because organizations with fewer than one hundred employees often have no HR department and no HR professionals, their line managers usually have full responsibilities for designing and carrying out all the activities related to recruitment,

Managing Human Resources for the 21st Century at Will-Burt

Dennis Donahue, president of Will-Burt, Inc., a $20 million machine-parts manufacturer in Orrville, Ohio, confesses that when the company started a remedial training program for employees in 1985, it wasn't just for the benefit of the employees. "The company had to save itself," he says. "The reasons weren't altruistic, to be honest with you."

With 2,000 hours of rework a month and a 35 percent product-rejection rate, Will-Burt teetered on the brink of bankruptcy. The company hired professors from nearby University of Akron and set up classrooms in the factory. Classes were mandatory and included basic math courses, as well as reading and other subjects.

Now, eight years later, the company has not only saved itself, it is thriving. According to Donahue, Will-Burt spends less than 1 percent of annual sales on remedial training. But as a result, defective products have fallen from 8 percent of sales to 2 percent. Employee tardiness has dropped, as well—from 70 late employees a day to 2 in seven months. Disability costs also have been cut.

Central to the program was math instruction. "If the worker does the math wrong in making a product, the quality is bad," says Donahue. "They have to have a certain level of math skills, especially with the computers we're using now."

But some employees weren't eager to learn the new math, especially when they felt they were being held up for ridicule. "The employees didn't react very well to the program at first," admits Donahue. "When we started getting publicity for it, they thought management was telling people we had dumb employees.

"Now they understand there is a nationwide problem of employees not being able to do calculations on new machinery. It's being received better. Part of that has to do with everyone in the plant—secretaries, purchasing people, as well as lathe operators—taking the courses."

Will-Burt is now held up as a shining example. The Department of Labor endorsed the program, and the National Association of Manufacturers will include it in a remedial training package it plans to offer its 13,000 members.[71]

interviewing, selection, compensation, training, performance measurement, and so on. Some assistance may be available from an administrative assistant or outside vendors such as Automatic Data Processing (ADP), which handles payrolls—but for the most part, in small firms, the key partnership is between line manager and employee.[72]

As a company grows larger, many dynamics can change its approach to managing human resources.[73] For example, because their activities affect many people, larger companies attract more attention from the media and from government regulators, and this puts more pressure on them to be socially responsive. Also, sufficient economies of scale mean that larger companies are better able to take advantage of more costly HR technologies. In addition, larger firms are more likely to

- Have narrowly defined jobs that use less variety of skills
- Manage for "high involvement" of employees
- Rely less on temporary staff
- Use more sophisticated procedures to recruit and select employees
- Include self-ratings and peer ratings as input for performance appraisals
- Pay employees more
- Put more pay at risk through the use of bonuses and long-term incentives
- Test employees for drugs
- Use due process procedures to handle grievances[74]

In general, then, larger companies are more likely to have more sophisticated systems for managing employees.

This is not to say, however, that all large organizations will evolve the same HR activities. In fact, we must be careful not to assume that all the major differences in HR activities exist mainly between small and large firms. Major differences can also exist between firms that are large and jumbo sized, like the 86,000-employee FedEx and the 286,000-employee United Parcel Service of America (UPS). The feature "Managing Human Resources for the 21st Century at UPS and FedEx" explains that because of its larger size, UPS has a much greater need for coordination mechanisms, which it meets in part with specific human resource activities.

Finding the Right Size

Unfortunately, larger companies often become bureaucratic, and also hierarchical. As organizations grow, management layers tend to proliferate and the ability to react swiftly to changing market demands and increased competition tends to be reduced. Many organizations restructure to change one or both of these features. Indeed, in a recent poll of HR executives at the United States' largest one hundred companies, 42 percent said they are grappling with downsizing, rightsizing, mergers and acquisitions, and change management.[75] Emory Mulling, president of a firm specializing in outplacement, describes the situation this way: "Not only are large corporations downsizing, but selective downsizings by small to midsize firms are occurring as well. Whole departments are cutting out levels of management or combining departments where efforts have been duplicated. . . . I see job eliminations continuing for the next 10 years or so because of global competition and technology. . . .We're in the midst of long-term corporate restructuring, not cyclical reductions."[76] Details of the effect of this activity on managing human resources are presented in Chapter 4.

 ORGANIZATIONAL STRUCTURE AND FORM

An organization's structure and form describe the allocation of tasks and responsibilities among individuals and departments; they designate the nature and means of formal reporting relationships as well as the groupings of individuals within the organization.[77] The structural forms generally recognized for domestic firms include functional departmentalization, product-based divisionalization, geographic divisionalization, matrix organization with dual reporting relationships, and several network arrangements. Different structures arise in response to a variety of internal and external forces, including technological demands, organizational growth, environmental turbulence, size (as illustrated by the UPS and FedEx examples), and business strategy.[78] Each structural form creates unique challenges for managing human resources.

Departmental Structure

Businesses with a single product or service often have a departmental structure. Careers in these types of companies generally focus narrowly on developing single-function, "silo-like" expertise. Departmentalization can easily engender feelings of commitment and loyalty to functional groups (accounting, marketing, R&D), and turn organizational decision making into a competitive sport in which departments battle over turf and resources.[79] Customers are almost always the losers of these battles. According to Richard C. Palermo, a vice president for quality and transition at Xerox, "If a problem

Managing Human Resources for the 21st Century at UPS and FedEx

It is difficult to find two companies with more different people management systems than FedEx and UPS.

FEDEX

FedEx has no union, and its workforce is handled using most of the current practices in human resource management. For example, individual and group performance are assessed, and both influence pay. The company has pay-for-suggestion systems, quality-of-work-life programs, and a variety of other arrangements to "empower" employees and increase their involvement. The most important of these may be its Survey-Feedback-Action program, which begins with subordinates completing climate surveys and performance reviews of management, and ends with each work group developing a detailed action plan to address the problems identified by the surveys and reviews.

Employees at FedEx have had an important role in helping to design the way work is organized and the way technology is used. And their hustle and motivation have helped make FedEx the dominant force in the overnight mail business. These initiatives have been so successful that FedEx was the first service company to win the Malcolm Baldrige award.

One goal at FedEx is that every employee should be empowered to do whatever is necessary to get a job done. The company's decentralized authority and lack of detailed rules would lead to a chaotic pattern of disorganized decisions in the absence of a strong set of common norms and values. FedEx instills those norms and values with an intensive orientation program and communication efforts that include daily information updates broadcast to each of its more than two hundred locations. Empowering individual employees also demands giving them the information and skills to make good decisions. FedEx requires that employees pass, every six months, interactive skills tests that are customized to each location and employee, and the results are tied to a pay-for-skill program.

UPS

UPS has none of the people management practices found at FedEx. Employees have no direct say over work organization matters. Their jobs are designed in excruciating detail by a staff of more than three-thousand industrial engineers according to time-and-motion studies. Drivers, for example, are told how to carry packages (under their left arm) and even how to fold money (faceup). The performance of individual employees is measured and evaluated against company standards for each task, and it is assessed daily. The firm makes no efforts at involving employees other than in collective bargaining over contract terms through the Teamsters' Union, which represents drivers.

The union at UPS does not appear to be the force maintaining this system of work organization. The initiative on work organization issues has been with management, which has shown little interest in moving toward work systems such as the kind at FedEx. Indeed, the view from the top of the company has been that virtually all the company's problems could be addressed by improving the accountability of employees—setting standards for performance and communicating them to workers.

REASONS FOR THE DIFFERENCE

The material rewards for working at UPS are substantial and may, in the minds of employees, more than offset the low level of job enrichment and the tight supervision. The company pays the highest wages and benefits in the industry. It also offers employees gain-sharing and stock ownership plans. UPS remains a privately held company owned by its employees. In contrast to FedEx, it fills virtually all higher job openings (98 percent) from within, offering entry-level drivers excellent long-term prospects for advancement. As a result of these material rewards, UPS employees are also highly motivated and loyal to the company. At UPS, the productivity of drivers, the most important work group in the delivery business, is about three times higher (measured by the number of deliveries and packages) than it is at FedEx.

Why might it make sense for UPS to rely on highly engineered systems that are generally thought to contribute to poor morale and motivation, and then offset the negative effects with strong material rewards, especially when FedEx offers an alternative model with high levels of morale and motivation and lower material rewards? Differences in technology do not explain these differences in HR management. FedEx is known for its pioneering investments in information systems, but when UPS responded with its own wave of computerized operations, its basic organization of work did not change.

Products and Size

The employment systems in these two companies are driven by the firms' business strategies. FedEx is the much smaller company, operating until recently with only one hub, in Memphis, Tennessee, and focusing on the overnight package delivery service as its platform product. UPS, in contrast, operating with multiple hubs, has a much wider range of products. Although its overnight delivery volume is only 60 percent of FedEx's, its total volume is nine times as large—11.5 million deliveries a day versus 1.2 million.

Coordination

The scale and scope of UPS's business demands an extremely high level of coordination that may only be achievable through highly regimented and standardized job design. The procedures must be very similar, if not identical, across operations if the different delivery products are to move smoothly across a common network that links dozens of hubs. Changes in practices and procedures essentially have to be systemwide to be effective. Such coordination is incompatible with the significant levels of autonomy in employee decision making found at FedEx. It is compatible, however, with the systemwide process of collective bargaining allowed at UPS.

In short, the scale and scope of UPS's business demands a level of coordination that does not fit with individual employee involvement and a "high-commitment" approach. UPS substitutes a system of unusually strong material rewards and performance measurement to provide alternative sources of motivation and commitment. At FedEx, having historically one hub meant the firm faced fewer coordination problems, which allowed considerable autonomy and participation in shaping decisions at the work group level, and more of a high-commitment approach.[80]

has been bothering your company and your customers for years and won't yield, that problem is the result of a cross-functional dispute." He calls this Palermo's law. And Palermo's corollary is "People who work in different functions hate each other."[81]

Divisional Structure

Multiproduct or multiservice firms often take a divisionalized form, with each division serving a different customer need (product-based divisions) or a different customer base (geographic divisions). Divisionalized firms tend to be more externally focused than are firms structured around functional departments, and they emphasize bottom-line results over process. To support their results focus, divisionalized firms are more likely to offer stock ownership and bonuses for companywide performance.

In divisionalized companies, each division, sometimes called a strategic business unit (SBU), usually operates autonomously; coordination between divisions may be modest, at best. However, too little coordination among divisions can create problems for the total corporation. To offset this problem, many large companies began to adopt matrix structures during the 1970s and 1980s.

Matrix

In a matrix structure, employees report to more than one boss, with each boss responsible for a different aspect of the organization.[82] For example, a clothes designer artist might report to the vice president of marketing *and* the vice president of outerwear. These vice presidents, in turn, might report to a general manager for manufacturing *and* a general manager for the North American region. In this type of structure, managers must coordinate with each other in assigning work to their subordinates, evaluating employee performance, and so on. The vast majority of medium and large companies in the United States are structured around functional departments, divisions, or some hybrid of these in a matrix form. Increasingly, firms such as GE, Eaton, and Weyerhaeuser are using common corporate visions, missions, values, and principles to help provide some unity and means of coordination.

Mergers and Acquisitions

During the 1980s, U.S. firms restructured through mergers and acquisitions (M&As) at a dizzying pace. M&As subsequently slowed somewhat, but they remained popular as a strategy for improving organization effectiveness. Novell Incorporated, which sells computer networking software, uses M&As aggressively to penetrate markets and diversify its offerings. In 1993, for example, Novell worked on five acquisition deals.[83]

For Novell, a major objective of M&As is to acquire the skills and talents of people employed by another company. According to Ernest J. ("Tim") Harris, Novell's senior vice president of HR, "The reason a company will buy another company many times is not only because of the technology but definitely because of the people that developed that technology and make it successful in the marketplace. You need to ensure that you can continue to operate the company and develop the technology on an ongoing basis, and the best way to do that is by having an integration that's successful enough to maintain continuity and continued employment for the people who are part of that entity."[84]

To ensure that executives think through all the HR issues when merging companies, Novell developed the *Merger Book.* Its two-thousand questions pertaining to HR serve as a road map for all Novell's M&A activities. The *Merger Book* helps the company keep the best talent, by facilitating smooth integration between companies. Information gathering and analysis are the heart of the process.[85]

Teams

As the 21st century approaches and begins, new structural forms are popping up. These new forms strive to replace hierarchy with horizontal flatness, and they avoid bureaucratic sluggishness in favor of speed. They also link people together in cross-organization alliances.[86] In the newer horizontal and weblike structures, work is more likely to be carried out in temporary and permanent teams of employees. Team goals and projects replace individual ones to a great degree.

When organizations restructure around teams, they often adopt a whole new way of thinking and operating. Some companies even come up with completely new ways to depict their organization's structure. For example, when Eastman Chemical Company went from a traditional hierarchical structure to a flatter, more horizontal structure, it chose the image of a familiar food item:

> "Our organizational chart is now called the pizza chart because it looks like a pizza with a lot of pepperoni sitting on it," says Ernest W. Deavenport Jr., who as president is the pepperoni at the center of the pie. "We did it in circular form to show that everyone is equal in the organization. No one dominates the other. The white space inside the circles is more important than the lines."
>
> Each pepperoni typically represents a cross-functional team responsible for managing a business, a geographic area, a function, or a "core competence" in a specific technology or area such as innovation. The white space around them is where the collaborative interaction is supposed to occur.[87]

Structuring around teamwork, in place of individual performance, has major consequences for managing human resources. For example, organizations with team-based designs may need to use new methods of job analysis, assessment, recruitment, and socialization.[88] The most obvious change in all types of HR practices is that team members take responsibilities previously reserved for supervisors. For example, in GE's $3 billion lighting business, which is organized worldwide around one hundred process and program teams, as many as twenty peers and other employees may be involved in appraising a person's performance.[89] Exhibit 2.9 shows typical responsibilities of self-directed teams.

According to Terry Ennis, who helped E. I. duPont deNemours and Company (Du Pont) reorganize its businesses into horizontal forms, changing from hierarchical to horizontal "is the hardest damn thing to do. It's very unsettling and threatening for people. You find line and function managers who have been honored and rewarded for what they've done for decades. . . . [Now] our goal is to get everyone focused on the business as a system in which the functions are seamless."[90] In other words, the new organization expects managers who previously acted pretty autonomously using the "organize, direct, and control" management style, to work in teams that collaborate in all their activities.[91] Teams and the skills to work in them are discussed in detail in Chapter 5.

Reengineering. To design self-managing teams, reengineering processes are often used. *Reengineering*—also called process management—is an inside-out approach to organization design. It starts with obtaining the customer's perspective to identify key performance objectives.[92] These often include shortening up cycle times, lowering costs, and improving quality. Extensive analyses are then done of all tasks required to achieve the objectives. Then teams are usually designed around key processes. The goal is to have everyone in the organization feel ownership for their part of the work. For example, at Hallmark Cards Incorporated, the greeting card maker, a functional structure has been redesigned into a team arrangement with work groups organized around particular greeting card holidays, like Valentine's Day and New Year's Day. A team of writers, artists, lithographers, accountants, and so on now sit together to produce a card design. One-on-one conversations replace many of the old interdepartment mailings, deliveries, and approval signatures.[93]

Structures That Cross Country Borders

The effect of structure is particularly evident in multinational companies and international joint ventures. Many terms can be used to describe global organizational

■ *Exhibit 2.9*
What Self-Managing Teams Manage

Activity	Percentage of Teams Performing the Activity
Setting work schedules	72%
Training	65
Setting performance targets	57
Dealing directly with external customers	58
Conducting performance appraisals	47
Dealing directly with vendors and suppliers	45
Budgeting	36
Hiring	29
Firing	22

SOURCE: Adapted from B. Filipczak, "The Teaming of America," *Training* (October 1993): 58.

structures, including *multinational, transnational,* and *mixed.*[94] Briefly, *multinational structure* refers to an organization that has operations in more than one country and whose major business decisions are made at the headquarters. *Transnational structure* refers to an organization that also has operations in more than one country but whose major business decisions are likely made throughout the world. This structure often results from the growth of companies and the nature of the business. As companies grow, they may set up major operations in different countries. These operations may become so large, or local conditions may require, that they almost operate as independent companies, each responsible for its own major business decisions. If this structure arises as a result of the type of product—for example, groceries—it may also be called a *multidomestic structure.*

Some MNCs become more complex by having more than one major business. This results in a *mixed structure.* For example, CIBA, an MNC with ninety thousand employees, is headquartered in Basel, Switzerland. Its pharmaceutical and agricultural businesses are likewise headquartered in Basel, but its composites business is headquartered in Los Angeles, California, near its major customers, U.S. defense contractors. Thus, major business decisions get made in several locations. Because the products of CIBA's businesses are made worldwide, these businesses are also referred to as global business divisions. Some of these divisions, in turn, have operations in several countries, resulting in multiple businesses operating in one country. CIBA's agricultural and pharmaceutical divisions have operations in the United States. To help coordinate these, a country headquarters division is also located in the United States. Corporate headquarters at Basel has to coordinate the operations of all the global business divisions and country headquarters divisions.

All these global organizational structures represent alternative solutions to the problems of differentiation, integration, uncertainty, and risk management in an international environment.[95] Each structure has unique implications for how people are managed, with the fundamental challenge being how to use HR activities to link globally dispersed units while also adapting to the societal requirements of host societies.[96] Thus, the key phrase that multinational companies use, "Think global, act local," has many HR implications. Similar challenges and implications also accompany MNCs from different countries when they seek to collaborate in an international joint venture.[97]

❖ ORGANIZATIONAL LIFE CYCLE

The concept of organizational life cycle is adapted from the concept of product life cycle developed in marketing. It relates growth in sales revenues to the age of the organization, and states that organizations, like products, go through different stages of development: start-up, growth, maturity, and decline. Changing managerial priorities characterize organizations in these various developmental stages.[98] These changing priorities, in turn, have implications for HR management. For example, they have been used to argue that selection criteria and assessment methods for top-level executives need to be matched to life cycle stages.[99] The role requirements of CEOs in a rapidly growing firm are quite different from those that founding CEOs may have been good at performing when the company was in its start-up phase. Because CEOs find it difficult to switch roles, outsider CEOs are likely to be hired when the firm enters a growth phase. Similarly, the roles of the CEOs and top-level executives change again as the firm moves out of a period of rapid growth and into a stage of maturity or perhaps decline. These changes in the needs of the organization, in turn, influence staffing decisions.[100]

The life cycle concept is useful as a heuristic for thinking about how HR activities might vary across organizations, as well as for planning how an organization may need to change its activities as it evolves. Its use is illustrated in more detail in Chapter 11, where life cycle stages are related to compensation practices.

COMPETITIVE STRATEGY

Competing successfully at home or abroad requires a clearly articulated competitive strategy. Some firms attempt to offer the lowest-priced goods and services. Some emphasize excellence of quality, with cost being a secondary consideration. Some put most of their energy into creating and developing new and unique goods and services that no one else offers.[101] Still others use various combinations of these strategies. For example, they may seek to keep costs low by finding innovative ways to deliver their services in the marketplace. These different ways of competing are significant for managing human resources because they help determine needed employee behaviors. That is, for competitive strategies to be successfully implemented, employees have to behave in certain ways. And for employees to behave in certain ways, human resource practices need to be put in place that help ensure that those behaviors are explained, are possible, and are rewarded.

Quality Improvement, Customer Focus

Delivering quality goods and services is a continual challenge forced on organizations by consumers as well as by domestic and international competition. Customers continue to demand high-quality products and are willing to buy from whoever offers those products. To keep matters interesting, the ante on playing in the international arena of high quality keeps going up: what was acceptable quality yesterday is unacceptable today. Thus, organizations must continue to pursue quality improvement with a vengeance— and success requires managing human resources appropriately.

Does the quality of service you get from a bank have anything to do with the treatment you get from the bank's tellers? Does the quality of your stereo, VCR, CD player, or car have anything to do with the level of motivation, dedication, training, and commitment of the individuals making these products? Quality depends on the people we are dealing with as well as on the people behind the scenes who make the products. Total quality depends upon all parts of the organization working together. Consequently, organizations are bound to give increasing attention to their human resources as they continue to seek to enhance quality. The most complete treatment of quality improvement in this text appears in Chapter 4.

Cost Reduction

We all want quality—but if you see two products or services with equally great quality, which will you buy? Price may not be all you consider, but it is likely at least one concern. In order to offer products or services at lower prices, organizations seek to be as efficient as possible. One way to be more efficient is to lower production costs— especially labor costs. Because much of our economy is based in the service sector, labor costs are substantial in most companies. Thus, from the mid-1980s to the mid-1990s, many large organizations reduced workforces as one approach to lowering costs.

Another way to lower costs is hiring contingent workers and subcontracting work out to other companies. *Contingent workers,* as discussed in Chapters 5 and 7, are individuals who are hired for a limited time, are subject to dismissal on short notice, and typically do not receive as many benefits as regular employees.[102] With subcontracting arrangements, workers are not even employees of the host firm. For example, IBM subcontracted with Pitney Bowes Incorporated to run its mailrooms, stockrooms, and reproduction operations. Many companies outsource their payroll activities to payroll processing firms such as ADP. As these examples illustrate, a desire to lower costs may be a major reason companies develop networked structures.

Innovation

A third way to compete is by offering new products and services. Some observers believe that the United States should concentrate on innovation as a strategy for competing worldwide. If we cannot make the cheapest products or the highest quality products, at least we can develop products no one else has and get them to market faster than anyone else. Other nations can copy and improve U.S. products, but this takes time. The United States has not typically copied and imitated the products of others; it has traditionally valued the creative individual, the entrepreneur, and the pioneer. This aspect of our culture can be used to gain a competitive advantage over others.

Unquestionably, innovation occurs through people. It takes talented people managed very effectively to come up with good new ideas. The challenge in the future is for more firms to create these conditions and stay ahead of competitors worldwide who are trying to catch up.

An innovation strategy requires risk taking and tolerance of inevitable failures. Therefore, HR practices in firms pursuing this strategy should be used to give employees a sense of security and to encourage a long-term orientation.[103]

Speed and Responsiveness

Concern about quality, cost, and innovation reflects the general issue of being responsive to the environment. The world order is changing and will continue to change. Although some trends are somewhat predictable, increasingly, changes are becoming unpredictable and are having a greater effect on managing human resources. Speed and responsiveness, as well as accuracy, have become critical. Decentralized decision making helps companies make decisions faster, and with more knowledge of the customer. But it requires companies to empower their employees—that is, to give their employees the power and ability to make organizational decisions.[104]

The changing market may also require organizations to be able to quickly reduce, expand, or fundamentally change their workforce. A contingent workforce allows a company to reduce output in line with market demand. Longer term, in anticipation of major market changes, companies can train their employees to enable them to serve different customers, use new machinery, or sell new products. With speed and responsiveness growing in importance as we approach and enter the 21st century, many companies are experimenting with new approaches to managing human resources with the goal of increasing workforce flexibility.

TOP MANAGEMENT

Ultimately, top managers are responsible for directing people effectively. They exercise their responsibility through their own actions, or inaction, and through the messages they send to all other employees. If top managers minimize the importance of people to the organization's overall success, so will line managers. In turn, those in the human resource department will perform routine administrative activities and make few attempts to experiment with new ideas. Minimally effective human resource management is the likely result. Conversely, top managers can be the champions of effective human resource management.

Goals, Visions, and Values

The stated goals and the subsequent standards of excellence that an organization establishes give clear cues to employees, telling them what is important and what behaviors are required. Thus, goals help determine the criteria against which workers and their behaviors will be evaluated. The criteria, in turn, determine the kinds of people attracted to the organization, the way they are evaluated, and who is eventually promoted to the top ranks.

At Southwest Airlines, these dynamics are clearly visible—to employees and passengers alike. From the beginning, CEO Herb Kelleher has tried to establish a unique vision. He wants his company to overflow with "an insouciance, an effervescence." Counterbalancing this lighthearted aspect of Kelleher's vision is a tough-minded pursuit of high productivity, which is necessary to successfully pursue Southwest's strategy to keep costs low. In an industry where labor costs account for 30 percent or more of expenses, and a company where 80 percent of employees belong to unions, Kelleher's vision and ability to bring it to life impress most observers, but the company's productivity tells the story best: compared with competitors such as American Airlines, Delta Air Lines, Northwest Airlines, United Air Lines, and USAIR, Southwest serves two to three times as many passengers per employee and employs only 50 percent to 75 percent as many employees per aircraft.[105]

At the Weyerhaeuser Company, one common value is *people*. This value describes the organization's philosophy of what employees mean and how they are to be managed. Specifically, it means

- People are mature, responsible individuals who want to contribute.
- People hold themselves to high standards of integrity and business ethics; they are responsible stewards of the land and environment.
- Our work environment is based on mutual respect, personal satisfaction, and growth opportunities for everyone.
- People recognize that teamwork, cooperation, and a clean, safe, well-maintained workplace are essential to fulfilling our customer commitments.
- Continuing education is an ongoing commitment that involves everyone.

Weyerhaeuser, like Southwest Airlines, takes its value statements very seriously. They are used to shape the wording of the firm's policies and then to guide and evaluate the development of specific HR practices, such as leadership and management development. The details of how the company enacts its philosophy are presented in Chapter 4.

Organizational Culture

Organizational culture represents an organization's value system. It reflects the organization's regard for customers, suppliers, competitors, the environment, and employees. For example, Southwest's Kelleher describes the mood around his company as "a kind of hoo-hah brio." Humor is important in this company. Passengers are treated to little amusements such as the following announcement heard over the intercom: "Good morning ladies and gentleman. Those of you who wish to smoke will please file out to our lounge on the wing, where you can enjoy our feature film."

Human Resource Philosophy. One aspect of organizational (or corporate) culture is a company's HR philosophy. To understand the HR philosophy at Southwest, consider Kelleher's description of how top management selects employees: "What we are looking for, first and foremost, is a sense of humor. . . . Then we look for people who excel to satisfy themselves and who work well in a collegial environment. We don't care that much about education and expertise, because we can train people to do whatever they have to do. We hire attitudes."[106]

In some companies, the HR philosophy is a formal statement describing how people are to be treated and managed. Typically, however, HR philosophy statements are very general, allowing interpretation at more specific levels of action within an organization.

Fair and Ethical Behavior

Top management also shares responsibility for ensuring that employees are treated fairly and that everyone behaves ethically. Here, as in other aspects of the total human resource management system, top managers set the tone through their own actions as well as through the policy statements they endorse. Policies regarding fair treatment and ethical conduct can shape many specific aspects of a company's practices and, therefore, the conduct of all employees. Some observers even argue that corporations are a major force that can strengthen, or may weaken, the basic fabric of society.[107] The topics of fairness and ethics are introduced in some detail in Chapter 3.

INTERNATIONAL COMPARISONS

Three sets of international comparisons may be made for human resource management: worldwide population figures, worldwide educational attainment levels, and human resource management in Mexico.

Worldwide Population and Educational Attainment

Between the mid-1990s and 2020, the industrializing nations are expected to increase their population in an amount equal to the total population of the industrialized nations. As this happens, the average age of the population in the industrializing nations will decrease, and the average age of the population in the industrialized nations will increase. We will also see substantial differences in educational attainment levels (see Exhibit 2.10). These international trends mean an increasing worldwide labor supply with a large component of highly educated individuals. Exhibit 2.11 reveals where labor was distributed around the world in 1994.

From a human resource management point of view, the expected trends in world population and educational attainment can facilitate the globalization of businesses; it may be feasible for companies to open up shops in literally any part of the world. What other possible implications do you see?

Human Resource Management in Mexico

The United States is rapidly developing a strong trade relationship with Mexico, where workers can match the skills of about 70 percent of U.S. laborers. Many Mexican employees work in manufacturing plants, often called maquiladoras, owned by foreign companies, many based in the United States. Most maquiladoras are located along the U.S.–Mexico border, but activity farther south in the major cities is growing.

■ *Exhibit 2.10*

Share of Students by Industrialized Nations

Year	Ages 15–18 (High School)	Ages 19–22 (College)
1970	44% of 160 million	77% of 26 million
1985	30% of 280 million	51% of 58 million
2000	21% of 450 million	40% of 115 million

Note: Industrialized nations include those in North America, western Europe, and the Asia-Pacific region.
SOURCE: Compiled from W. B. Johnston, "Global Workforce 2000: The New World Labor Market," *Harvard Business Review* (March–April 1991): 115–29.

The maquiladoras grew in response to the Border Industrialization Program, established in 1965 to increase Mexico's level of industrialization; to create new jobs; to raise the domestic income level; to facilitate the transfer and absorption of technology and related skills; and to attract much-needed foreign exchange. The program permitted duty-free import of all tools (equipment, raw materials) required for production if the final product was to be exported. During the 1970s and 1980s, the auto industry predominated economic activity along the U.S.–Mexico border. In the early 1990s, activity diversified to include electronics, pharmaceuticals, paper, glass, and many other products. With NAFTA, this activity will likely expand even more, productwise and throughout Mexico.

■ *Exhibit 2.11*

Workforce Size of Several Major Countries in Three Regions of the World

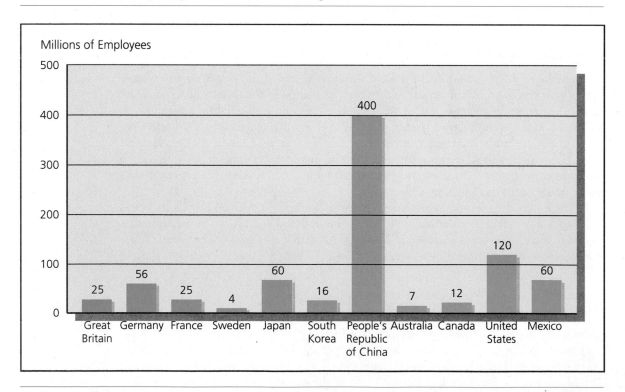

Positioning for the 21st Century:
NAFTA'S EFFECT

HR professionals who think they won't be affected by NAFTA because their companies are remaining in America may have to think again. The fact is, approximately 150,000 low-skill, low-wage jobs are expected to go south over the next few years. In return, approximately 325,000 jobs are expected to be created as U.S. exports to Mexico increase. Politics aside, the hope is that many of these new positions will be created in the more high-tech industries. This shift in market will allow for—even demand—a more skilled labor force. "Basically, we want a high-skill, high-wage economy," says Jerome Rosow, president and founder of the Work in America Institute in Scarsdale, New York. "If we're exporting some work to Mexico that's low-skill and low pay, it's really not the kind of work we should have long-term in our economy."

And who will create this high-skill, high-wage labor force? Yes, part of the responsibility will fall upon HR's shoulders in the form of training. And get as much of a head start as possible, because when change comes, it will come with a bang. "Companies have to rethink their training and their preparation and their upgrading of workers for better jobs," says Rosow. "As technology and the work processes become more sophisticated, and change becomes more rapid, companies can't go out and buy labor in our labor market with all the skills they need. It just doesn't exist."

HR professionals must play a role in giving today's work force the skills they'll need in the future. That includes not only those just entering the workplace, but workers who've been there a while. Indeed, Rosow recommends that HR give special attention to employees who entered the work force several decades ago straight out of high school. He says that these individuals are likely to lack good on-the-job training.

No, HR won't have to do this all alone. Luckily, some help is on the way. When the Reemployment Act of 1994 was completed in March, it promised to lay the groundwork for a new system that will assist workers in getting the training and counseling they need to ascend to higher-wage jobs. The $13 billion Act also includes programs to help dislocated workers (and presumably, there may be some more, post-NAFTA) to receive job training.

The School-to-Work Opportunities Act also focuses on providing better-trained workers. The $300 million Act is intended to assist students not going to college to transition into the workplace, providing support that many baby boomers were denied.

However, this doesn't mean that all our problems are solved. For instance, although Rosow, the former assistant secretary of labor, likes the general objectives of the Acts, he says that the Reemployment Act is too dependent on action by the states. This is risky, he says, "because the states have a very uneven ability and concern with employment issues."

So human resources does have an active role to play: advocate of employee training. Workers need someone to go to bat for them. "They can't pull themselves up by their own bootstraps," says Rosow, "no matter how willing or anxious they are—unless the employer begins training them and upgrading them. [Employers] aren't as loath to invest in technology as they are to invest in training—and that's really the big problem."

Training benefits the employer as much as the employee, particularly if, as predicted, we're seeing the beginnings of a shift to high-skill jobs. And change may be a good thing: Currently, the United States has the highest proportion of poverty of any industrialized city in the world, and the proportion is growing faster than any other. Combined with responsive training, Rosow sees NAFTA as a way to get people back in the middle class: "For the country as a whole, it means more jobs and better jobs."[108]

Historically, low labor costs have been the primary reason foreign firms were drawn to Mexico. The dramatic differences between Mexican and U.S. labor costs are obvious to auto companies such as Ford. For example, in 1994, Ford assemblers in Mexico were paid about $1.55 an hour, whereas those in the United States were paid about $17.38 an hour. The average pay for top-skilled workers at Ford plants was $2.87 an hour in Mexico, compared with $20.21 an hour in the United States. With NAFTA, these wages are expected to rise, as are the benefits workers receive. As manufacturing becomes more automated, however, Mexican workers will need to acquire higher levels of skill in order to operate new technologies and remain attractive to foreign employers.[109]

Will Mexico's educational system respond to the new demands and prepare tomorrow's workforce for the skills it will need in the 21st century? Will employers find that the low labor costs mean they can easily afford to provide the training to Mexican workers? Will Mexican workers become more skilled than U.S. workers as a result? What does the future hold for Mexico? And what effect will NAFTA have on the United States? One description of how NAFTA is likely to influence trade relations and human resources management is presented in "Positioning for the 21st Century: NAFTA's Effect."

⊕ SUMMARY

This chapter began by asking you to predict some significant changes in the economic and business environment for the 21st century (Exhibit 2.1). The results from almost three thousand CEOs and HR leaders worldwide for these same items are described in the feature "Using Data for the 21st Century: Environmental Forces Affecting Human Resources." Those results, and probably yours as well, suggest that the late 1990s and early 2000s will be filled with rapid change, challenge, uncertainty, and intense global competition. They appear to be saying that for organizations in the 21st century to be successful, they need to be:

- Capable of rapid response
- Flexible and adaptable
- Lean and concerned about costs
- Conscious of quality
- Focused on the customer
- Able to use innovation

For these organizational characteristics to result in success, they need to be complemented by employees who are:

- Adaptable
- Committed
- Motivated
- Skilled and reskilled
- Highly energetic
- Comfortable with diversity, complexity, and change
- Good team players
- Ethical

Creating and sustaining a workforce with these characteristics is the job of everyone in an organization, from the CEO to the most junior individual employees. For many companies and many individuals, the future represents a call for change. New policies and practices must be developed to guide and support new types of employee behaviors.

Using Data for the 21st Century:
ENVIRONMENTAL FORCES AFFECTING HUMAN RESOURCES

Priorities for Competitive Advantage: A Worldwide Human Resource Study was released in 1992. For this study, IBM and the consulting firm Towers, Perrin surveyed almost three-thousand chief executive officers and human resource managers of worldwide firms in twenty countries. The firms were selected because they are effective and are in highly competitive environments. Translated into eight languages, the survey was based on the premise that characteristics of the environment significantly affect human resource management. A major objective of the study was to find out which characteristics had the most effect in the early 1990s and were likely to have the most effect in the year 2000. The researchers were also interested in knowing whether the characteristics with the most effect would be different from one country to the next.

The results of the study strongly support the premise that the environment plays a major role in shaping human resource management around the world. The following table shows the environmental characteristics regarded as being most important to human resource management, overall. These forces were more important to some countries than others.

Increased levels of national and international competition refer to more commerce and competition from firms in countries all over the world. Globalization of the economy refers to what a firm must do to compete on a global basis—for example, operate in all countries of the world or in just some. Notice that results are presented with no indication of the present or of the year 2000; regarding the effect of the environment, respondents said, "The future is today."

Geographic Differences for the Six Most Important Environmental Forces

The Most Important Environmental Forces for Human Resources	Relative Importance Across All Countries	Relatively High Ratings in . . .	Somewhat Lower Ratings in . . .
National and international competition		Mexico, Brazil	Japan, United States
Focus on quality and customer satisfaction		Latin America, Australia	Japan, Korea
Changing employee values		Korea, Japan, Germany	Latin America, Italy
Globalization of the economy		Latin America, Italy	Japan, United States
Fewer entrants into the workforce		Japan	Latin America, Korea, Australia
Changing workforce demographics		Japan, United States	Latin America, Korea, Australia

SOURCE: Based on *Priorities for Competitive Advantage: A Worldwide Human Resource Study* (IBM and Towers Perrin, 1992): 13.

Discussion Questions

1. What did GE do to respond to the changing environment from the mid-1980s to the mid-1990s?
2. What is the effect of domestic and international competition on managing human resources?
3. What labor market changes are likely to have the most significant effect on human resource management? Describe the nature of the effect.
4. What effects are economic and organizational trends having on human resource management?
5. Will U.S. employers provide more basic education to U.S. workers in the future, or will they choose instead to develop the skills of workers in countries where the costs of labor are lower?

6. How do PCI's management development practices reflect cultural differences?
7. How do size and life cycle stage influence how a company manages its human resources?
8. Compare and contrast the differences in how FedEx and UPS manage their human resources.

9. Describe how top management affects the way a company handles its human resources.
10. Compare and contrast the environmental forces in the United States and Mexico, and their effect on managing human resources.

 ## In-Class Projects

1. Using the Lincoln Electric case at the end of the text, describe how the following environmental forces affect and relate to the company's HR practices and policies:
   a. The global economy
   b. The firm's current technology
   c. The size of the firm (primarily by number of employees, but also by sales)
   d. The firm's form of organization, particularly its use of teams versus individuals
   e. The firm's competitive strategy
   f. Top management's philosophies, visions, and values

2. Using the AAL case at the end of the text, describe how the following environmental forces affect and relate to its HR practices and policies:
   a. The global economy
   b. The firm's current technology
   c. The size of Jerry Laubenstein's IPS group (primarily by number of employees, but also by sales)
   d. The firm's form of organization, particularly its use of teams versus individuals
   e. The firm's competitive strategy
   f. Top management's philosophies, visions, and values

 ## Field Projects

1. Pick an organization with which you are familiar; it may range anywhere from very small to very large. Identify and describe the characteristics of its environment, and explain how these characteristics affect the management of human resources.
2. Interview four people, two from each of two different organizations. Ask them to describe their organization's culture, particularly as it relates to managing people. Tell the class about any differences and explain them.
3. Analyze the labor force in your area. Report on the number employed, the type of work people have, employee pay levels, the number unemployed, and so

forth. Answer these questions: How are the characteristics of the local labor force viewed by companies in the area? Are these characteristics an attraction for companies? Is the labor force more attractive for some types of companies and less attractive for other types of companies? Explain.
4. Choose several companies in your area. For each company, ask several people what they know about the company in terms of the way it manages its human resources. What type of culture do people associate with the company? How do the public's images about a company's culture affect the company's ability to attract and retain the best talent?

Case Study:

THE SHERWIN-WILLIAMS COMPANY: POWER OF THE ENVIRONMENT

 Spread throughout the United States and North America, the Cleveland, Ohio–based Sherwin-Williams Company has claimed for years that it sells enough paint to cover the earth. Perhaps you have seen its logo of the earth being covered with a can of red paint. Well, this is just part of the eighteen-thousand-person, $3 billion company. Its largest business unit is the Stores Group, which operates about two-thousand paint stores across the United States. These stores sell to do-it-yourself retail customers, as well as professional painters and industrial customers. They are the exclusive channel of distribution for Sherwin-Williams–brand products. The Coatings Group is responsible for product development and manufacturing and also sells other brands of paint products to major retail customers such as hardware stores, home centers, and mass merchandisers. The Automotive Division is a major player in the automotive aftermarket; it provides a variety of specialty coatings to original equipment manufacturers.

Sherwin-Williams felt the effect of the external environment back in 1977, the first year in its 111-year existence that it lost money. Shortly after that, the reigning CEO, Walter Spencer, resigned. For the first time in its history, the company went outside to recruit a new CEO. John G. Breen quickly took the company into a significant cultural and organizational change. Beginning in 1979 and through the 1980s, the culture altered dramatically from paternalistic to performance based. The management style became aggressive and demanding. A centralized structure was replaced with a decentralized, autonomous one. These changes occurred while the organization went through two major strategies. The first strategy was a turnaround; the business had to be saved. The key business issue during this period, from 1979 into the early 1980s, was survival and was characterized by the slogan "Cash Is King." Management emphasis was on expense control, working capital management, financial controls and systems, and divestiture of nonprofitable businesses. The planning horizon was one day at a time. Once the financial stability of the organization had been secured, the second strategy was set in place. This strategy emphasized growth. From the mid-1980s forward, the growth strategy was evidenced by the business goals of profitable growth, sales development and market share, product quality, acquisitions

in the core business, and longer-term planning. During this period, the saying that captured the spirit became "Paint Is King."

These business changes in turn greatly affected the human resource function. Driven by the new corporate culture and structure, new HR policies and practices were rolled out. Here are some typical examples of how HR practices changed from the time of the turnaround to the time of new growth:

- HR planning went from short-term survival concerns to longer-term development concerns.
- Staffing went from heavy outplacement to ongoing hiring at all levels.
- Performance appraisal criteria shifted from an emphasis on short-term, bottom-line results to a focus on longer-term issues such as leadership development and feedback.
- Compensation for top management went from high risk, high reward to above average pay for high performance.

The only constants during these times of perpetual change were the beliefs and values of the company. These included a fundamental belief that managers are paid for improvement and that smart people plus hard work equals success. Other cornerstones of the Sherwin-Williams culture included these beliefs:

- winning is better than losing;
- truth is what you can put a number on;
- problems are to be faced, not avoided;
- personal integrity above all is essential.

During these times, the HR department had to deal with its own structure. The key to the effectiveness of the HR strategy at Sherwin-Williams was an effective partnership between the HR professionals and operating managers. Human resource responsibilities continued to be pushed out into the divisions and to the line managers while the corporate HR staff became smaller and shifted to a group of highly specialized professionals providing technical expertise to the division staffs in such areas as employment law, compensation, benefits, labor relations, management development and HR planning, and consulting.

These changes, made in response to developments in the environment (competition at the business level and a new business strategy, culture, and structure at the HR level) were successful. Yet, neither Sherwin-Williams nor any other firm is able to assume that the environment will ever again be relatively constant and predictable. To this day, the HR staff at Sherwin-Williams continues to make changes and adjustments in the HR operations because of changes in the environment and the line managers continue to act in true partnership by actually taking responsibility for many HR activities.

Discussion Questions

1. In addition to the change in leadership and business strategy, what other forces in the environment were probably influencing the HR activities at Sherwin-Williams during the 1980s and early 1990s?
2. In what ways can companies like Sherwin-Williams monitor their environment to anticipate what if any changes may be needed in their HR activities?
3. If Sherwin-Williams expands globally, what new HR issues is it likely to encounter?

Establishing Fair Policies and Procedures

There's no magic. What will make all the difference in business will be how well you train your work force, how well you motivate—and how well you empower.

ROBERT EATON, CEO, Chrysler Corporation[1]

The Coors Brewing Company, headquartered in Golden, Colorado, is famous for its beer and for its procedures for managing employees fairly. Headed by the family heir, Peter H. Coors, Coors Brewing Company realized in 1978 that it had to develop better relations with employees. A bitter confrontation between the union that had represented the employees for nearly fifty years and the management preceded a failed strike against the company. Employees voted to decertify the union, but this left them unprotected from what they saw as the potential abuses of management.

Employees were afraid that management would take control from them and give them no recourse in such matters as discipline. According to Richard Kellogg, who was involved in the grievance process at that time and later became Coors's HR director, representatives for the workers told William K. Coors, who was head of the company: "Our employees are frightened because they've had this union here that was taking care of our needs and making sure that discipline was meted out fairly. Now we don't have that and we've got to either find a way to provide it or ultimately the employees will bring in another union."

The company acted swiftly. Borrowing from a Coors subsidiary, Coors Container Company, the HR department set up a peer review system designed to give employees a chance to air their complaints and have their coworkers take part in evaluating whether those complaints were legitimate. HR believed that such a system would benefit employees and management alike. Others in senior management, including the Coors family members, were not so positive. They feared that every disciplinary action would be considered unfair and so would be reviewed by the peer system, and, in turn, would be reversed. Despite their concerns, they agreed to put the system in place. The system includes hearings over all forms of discipline including first warnings, final warnings, suspensions without pay, and terminations. Regardless of the issue, the process is this:

An employee who's unsatisfied with the application of a company policy—but not the policy itself—may file an appeal with his or her employee-relations representative within seven working days. The employee-relations representative then sets up an appeal board by randomly selecting two members of management and three employees from the same job category as the appellant.

A hearing is held, orchestrated by the employee-relations representative. At the hearing, the supervisor describes the circumstances surrounding the discipline. The employee then explains why the supervisor's action was unfair. Board members may ask questions of both parties during the proceedings and also may request testimony from witnesses.

When the board members are satisfied that they have all the information that they need, they privately discuss the case. They decide by majority vote on one of three outcomes: to uphold the action; to reduce the severity; or to overturn the action completely. The board's decision is final.[2]

Management's fears appear to have been unfounded: in the system's first ten years, an average of only 9 percent of management's decisions were overturned by the review boards. In 1993, appeal boards reversed only three of sixty-two decisions appealed and modified only nine. Management also recognizes the added value of the review board: Coors has never lost a wrongful termination case in court. According to Ed Cruth, employee relations manager for the company: "If we can't substantiate or uphold a termination internally with an appeal board, we can almost guarantee it wouldn't be upheld in front of a jury. And if it is upheld internally, then we feel comfortable that it's going to be upheld in front of a jury."

Although its system has been very successful for the company and its seven thousand employees, Coors is quick to point out that it may not work as well for other firms. Any process of this type needs to be structured to fit with an organization's specific culture and needs. Cruth concludes: "Whatever system a company sets up has to be perceived by the employees as being fair. Management must be willing to allow employees to participate in decision making, and if they are not willing to do that, then it won't work."[3]

MANAGING EMPLOYEES FAIRLY

Managing employees fairly is fundamentally about balancing the rights and responsibilities of management and employees. Establishing policies and procedures by which employees can appeal actions of management—as Coors did—is one way to ensure that balance is maintained, particularly in environments where employees lack union representation and coverage. Other topics that may be addressed by management policies and procedures include all forms of harassment, terminations, and privacy. These topics reflect our society's values and its legal framework.

Managers, HR professionals, and employees all play important roles in ensuring that human resources are managed fairly. Working together, they can establish workplace policies, procedures, and practices to help ensure that significant employment decisions are made with fairness and due process, respect for the rights and responsibilities of employees and employers, justice, and as much information as possible. This is the meaning of the phrase "managing employees fairly."

SOCIETAL CONCERNS ABOUT FAIRNESS

Chapter 2 described the many economic and business forces that help to shape the approaches companies use to manage their human resources. Much of our discussion in Chapter 2 reflected the importance to American companies of profit making. In a pure capitalistic economic system, managers on behalf of shareholders would seek to maximize profits free of noneconomic external constraints—that is, without constraints other than those imposed by consumers and competitors. In the real world, effective U.S. businesses address the concerns of many stakeholders; businesses and consumers do not make decisions based solely on economic *self*-interests, they also acknowledge the interests of the broader society.

In this chapter, we begin to consider how societal concerns influence the ways companies manage human resources. At the societal level, a fundamental concern is that employees be treated *fairly*. People believe that fairness is a desirable social condition—we want to be treated fairly, and we want others to view us as being fair.[4] Companies that rank high as the best places to work generally emphasize fairness as part of their corporate culture because fairness creates the feeling of trust that is needed to "hold a good workplace together."[5]

The concept of fairness has many connotations, so ensuring fair treatment can be a major challenge for employers. Furthermore, society's view of what constitutes fair treatment of employees is in constant flux, so companies must continually readjust. Many practices that were considered fair at the beginning of the 20th century had become illegal by the middle of the 20th century. Similarly, practices considered fair today may no longer be legal in five or ten years. Of course, for companies operating internationally, being responsive to multiple societal concerns becomes particularly complex.

What does it mean to be treated fairly? Do we automatically feel that we have been treated unfairly when things do not turn out in our favor? What do people do when they have been treated unfairly? We address these and related questions in this chapter. The chapter begins by explaining how employees evaluate whether they have been treated fairly and how this affects their behavior at work. Next, we describe workplace policies, procedures, and practices that employers use to ensure fair treatment of employees. As you will see, some approaches to workplace fairness mirror the procedures used in the U.S. courts. In the United States, the legal system helps define and interpret for society

Partnership in Managing Employees Fairly

Line Managers	Human Resource Professionals	Employees
Set policy for the treatment of employees in workplace issues.	Ensure that line managers set policy in accordance with legal considerations.	Accept responsibility to respect the rights of other employees.
Accept responsibility for one's behavior in dealing with employees.	Develop policies, procedures, and practices that support and are consistent with fair and ethical behavior by everyone in the organization.	Work with HR professionals in establishing policies, procedures, and practices for dealing fairly with workplace issues.
Show concern for due process and fair treatment.	Help keep employer and employee rights and responsibilities in balance.	Accept responsibility for behaving fairly and ethically toward one's employing organization.
Be proactive in attempts to understand employees' views about fairness.		

the meaning of fair treatment within employment settings. Thus, this chapter concludes with an overview of the legal rights and responsibilities of employers and employees.

 ## THE LABOR FORCE AND LEGAL INSTITUTIONS AS KEY STAKEHOLDERS

The concerns of our broader society are communicated through, and supported by, the actions of two primary stakeholders: the labor force and legal institutions.

The Labor Force

Members of the labor force communicate their concerns in both direct and indirect ways. As free agents, they communicate their concerns to employers directly. For example, when deciding which company to work for, a potential employee evaluates whether a company pays a fair wage, whether it offers desirable benefits, whether the corporate culture is appealing, and so on. When making these evaluations, perceptions of what is "fair," "desirable," and "appealing" reflect the potential employee's concerns. The free agency of job applicants, combined with the diversity of the U.S. labor force, means that companies must consider a broad array of labor force concerns in order to attract and hire the best talent.

Once hired, employees continue to express their concerns and they also evaluate whether their employer is addressing those concerns. Indirectly, or informally, employees may voice their concerns in daily conversations at work. Many companies also offer formal channels of expression, such as employee surveys and employee grievance systems.

Finally, union members voice their concerns directly when they collectively bargain with employers over working conditions and compensation.

Legal Institutions

Legal institutions provide indirect channels for the labor force to use in communicating their concerns to employers. Through elected government representatives, members of the labor force initiate and ultimately create federal and state laws. Through their tax payments, employees pay for the operations of a vast array of government agencies and courts, which are responsible for interpreting and enforcing the laws. Thus, employment laws should be thought of not only as legal constraints; they are also sources of information about the issues that potential employees are likely thinking about as they decide whether to join or leave an organization.

 ## WHAT FAIRNESS MEANS TO EMPLOYEES

Consider the following two situations and imagine that you are the employees involved. How do you feel? And what will you do?

A Missed Promotion—Michelle Chang graduated with her MBA five years ago. Since then, she has worked for a large financial services company as an industry analyst. Her performance reviews have always been positive. She and her peers assumed she was on the company's informal fast track. But recently, she has begun to wonder. After the manager of her unit left last month for a better opportunity at another firm, Michelle applied for the job. She did not get the promotion. To her surprise, the person chosen to be the new boss for her unit was Jim Johnson, a twenty-year veteran of the firm who was transferred in from Chicago. After three weeks at his new job, it is obvious that Jim's previous experiences have not provided him with the knowledge he needs. Michelle feels that the company's decision to give Jim the job is a signal that her future may not be as bright as everyone thought. Perhaps it is time to look into possibilities at other companies.

An Unexpected Layoff—Bill Markham works in the same firm as Michelle and Jim. He has been with the organization about seven years, coming there after working for twelve years at a large computer company and for eight years as an independent consultant. As manager of the Information Services Department, he has been responsible for managing all the company's computer specialists. Last week, the firm unexpectedly disclosed plans for a major reorganization of Information Services. To "improve efficiency," the company has decided to decentralize several staff activities. In the new structure, the activities of the Information Services Department will be carried out by generalists who will work within each of the firm's several divisions. Of course, everyone knew that the words *improve efficiency* are code, meaning the size of the Information Services staff will be reduced. But Bill was not worried when he heard the announcement; he expected to be assigned to the largest division and had already begun discussing the idea of a major move with his family. He was shocked when he learned that he was going to be let go. He appreciated the firm's offer to pay for outplacement counseling, but he wondered whether he should accept its decision as final. As a fifty-something white male, he imagined that finding a new job would be pretty tough. Maybe he should put up a fight.

How much trust in their employer do Michelle and Bill feel. Has each person been treated fairly? What other information might you want before concluding whether this company is treating employees fairly?

From the mid-1970s to the mid-1990s, social and organizational scientists conducted numerous studies designed to improve our understanding of concepts such as fairness and justice. This research has shown that people's perceptions of fairness reflect at least two features of the situations they find themselves in: the actual *outcomes* and the *procedures* used in arriving at these outcomes. These two features are referred to as distributive justice and procedural justice, respectively.[6]

Distributive Justice

Not surprisingly, people prefer favorable outcomes for themselves. In the cases of Michelle and Bill, a promotion is better than no promotion and a transfer is better than being let go. In another case, nonsmokers will view a new policy banning smoking at work as more fair than will smokers.[7]

Nevertheless, we do not necessarily feel that we have been treated unfairly when we do not get the best possible outcome. Instead, perceptions of fairness hinge on how our own outcomes compare with the outcomes of other people, taking into account our own situation and the situations of others. In evaluating the fairness of her situation, for example, Michelle compares her outcome with Jim's. If Michelle felt that the outcomes she and Jim experienced reflected their relative qualifications, then Michelle probably would accept the situation as fair even though she did not get promoted. Furthermore, Michelle and Jim's coworkers use similar heuristics in evaluating their employer. When Michelle's coworkers see that she has been unfairly treated, they not only feel bad about what happened to Michelle, they may also conclude that their employer generally treats employees unfairly.

Fair Pay. Consider how you evaluate whether people are paid fairly on two counts: the level of pay people receive and changes in pay over time (e.g., due to raises). Generally, people see pay as fair when they believe that the distribution of pay across a group corresponds to the relative value of the work being done by each person. Similarly, when the relative sizes of raises correspond to the relative performance levels of people in the unit, people are likely to feel fairly treated. As these examples illustrate, in the workplace, distributive fairness is perceived under conditions of *equity,* or merit-based decision making.[8]

In the early 1990s, issues of equity were salient in the ongoing public discussion about CEO compensation, when critics began asking some tough questions: Is it fair that the average CEO earned twenty to thirty times as much as the average engineer, teacher and factory worker? Is it fair that CEO pay has been growing at a pace that is twice the rate of growth in pay for these other workers?[9] What arguments would convince you that this distribution of outcomes is fair?

Typical American employees generally consider equity when evaluating fairness at work; employees from other countries and cultures may see things quite differently. American culture is individualistic, whereas many other cultures are more collectivistic. In collectivistic cultures, concern for social cohesion is greater than in the United States. Going along with a perspective that focuses more on groups, people from collectivistic cultures value *equality* of treatment and treatment based on *need,* and they allocate rewards accordingly.[10] Thus, from a collectivistic perspective, Michelle might be viewed as having been treated fairly. Michelle was treated the same as her coworkers (equally), and perhaps Jim needed the job more than did Michelle. What implications might these differences across countries have for managing human resources in a global organization?

Procedural Justice

Perceptions of justice depend on more than the relative distribution of outcomes: beliefs about the entire process used to determine outcomes also come into play. The term *procedural justice* refers to perceptions about fairness in the process. For example, Michelle and Bill might wonder *how* their company made its decisions in their situations.

Research suggests that in American culture, a procedure is considered fair if:

- The information used to make the decision is appropriate and accurate.
- The basis for making the decision is clearly explained.
- All legitimately interested parties are given the opportunity to have input into the decision process.
- Attention is paid to ensuring that the less powerful parties are protected from abuse by the more powerful parties.
- All interested parties have equal and open access to the system.
- The system is relatively stable and consistent over time.
- The system is flexible enough to be responsive to changing conditions and unique circumstances.[11]

With these criteria in mind, how would you design a procedure for detecting harassment and disciplining those involved? For deciding who to fire or lay off? How would you design drug-testing procedures? Before addressing such issues, it is useful to consider how employees react when they feel they have been treated unfairly, and to consider possible legal constraints.

REACTIONS TO FAIR AND UNFAIR TREATMENT

When employees feel they have been treated unfairly, they can react in many different ways. Consider again the situation of Michelle. If you were Michelle, you would probably consider actions that fall into one of the following categories:

a. Exit the organization and put the incident behind you;
b. Stay and simply accept the situation as something you must tolerate;
c. Stay but engage in negative behaviors that help you restore your sense of fairness (e.g., shorten your hours a bit; stop attending unnecessary meetings and functions);
d. Voice your concern to people inside the organization (e.g., discuss the situation with your colleagues; talk about it with a mentor; talk to someone in the employee relations office);
e. Voice your concern to external authorities (e.g., explore possible legal action; talk to the press).[12]

Quit? For high performers like Michelle, choice a, quitting, may be the best alternative. From the organization's perspective, however, having Michelle leave and perhaps join the competition may be the least desirable alternative. From society's perspective, turnover caused by feelings of injustice is undesirable because it tends to reduce productivity.[13]

Stay and Accept the Situation? Alternative b would be better for Michelle's employer, but it is probably not very common because few people easily shrug off injustices suffered at the hands of their employers. Instead, their outlook sours. Employees who stay in situations that they believe are unfair lose confidence in the competence of management and feel they cannot trust management.[14] Employees who feel unfairly treated also report feeling dissatisfied and uncommitted to both their employers and the goals their employers set for them.[15]

Seek Revenge? Feelings of injustice affect behavior, not just attitudes, even for employees who decide not to quit because of unfair treatment. Therefore, reactions that fall into categories c and e are possible. Employees attempt to maintain a sense of balance in their relationship with employers. If a legal issue is involved, employees may seek legal solutions. Often, however, feelings of unfairness arise in response to perfectly legal management behavior. This was illustrated quite dramatically in a company that temporarily cut employees' pay.

The company was a large manufacturer of aerospace and automotive parts. Owing to the loss of two contracts, temporary pay cuts were required at two of the company's three plants. Everyone at the two plants took a 15 percent pay cut for ten weeks, including management. The situation created a natural opportunity for the company and a researcher to learn more about how best to implement pay cuts, so a small experiment was conducted. In one plant, the company tried to convey how much it regretted the pay cuts, explained that the pay cuts would eliminate the need for layoffs, and assured employees that no favoritism would occur. At a full meeting with the employees, top management spent an hour answering employees' questions. At the second plant involved, the pay cut was announced at a brief fifteen-minute meeting with no apology and very little explanation. The third plant was used as a control group. Employees' reactions were assessed in terms of theft rates, turnover, and responses to a survey. At both the plants taking pay cuts, theft rates went up during the weeks the cuts were in effect and then went back down again when full pay was restored, particularly at the plant where the inadequate explanation was given (see Exhibit 3.1). Turnover in this

◼ *Exhibit 3.1*
Pay Cuts and Employee Theft

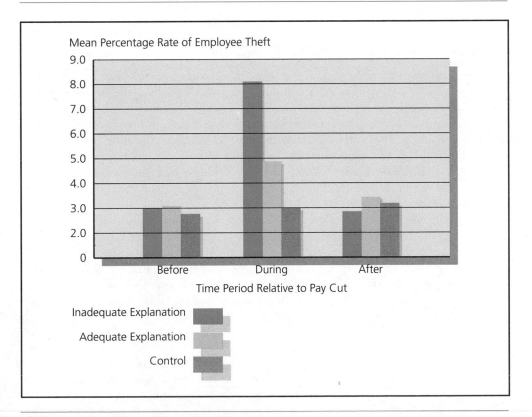

SOURCE: J. Greenberg, "Employee Theft as a Reaction to Underpayment Inequity: The Hidden Cost of Pay Cuts," *Journal of Applied Psychology* 75 (1990): 565.

plant also soared, from 5 percent to 23 percent. Survey results confirmed that employees at this plant did not understand how their pay cut was determined and felt they were treated unfairly.[16] As this company found out, people are sensitive to changes that disturb their sense of equity, and will seek ways to rebalance the scales if they are tipped.[17]

Talk to Others in the Organization? The way companies *manage* situations can greatly influence how employees react.[18] One aspect of managing situations effectively involves using formal organizational systems to deal with conflicts and disputes. By fully explaining *how* decisions are made and by offering employees opportunities to *voice* their concerns and have their questions answered (choice d), employers can minimize negative employee reactions. In well-managed companies, employees' feelings of dissatisfaction are intentionally surfaced and used to stimulate positive changes that actually benefit both employees and employers.[19]

MANAGING TO ENSURE FAIR TREATMENT

Managers use a variety of procedures, policies, and practices to ensure fairness. As you read about these, keep in mind that good systems are not enough. The interpersonal relationships between members of the organization also influence the management of fairness. Inevitably, employees sometimes feel that a decision or procedure is unfair. Sensitive supervisors and managers who acknowledge these situations and express their concern can minimize the disruptive effects of the situations. As simple as it seems, apologies reduce anger.[20]

Grievance Procedures

Formal grievance procedures are one way to encourage employees to voice their concerns and seek constructive resolutions. In unionized settings, the presence of such procedures had already become nearly universal by 1950.[21] Almost all public and private unionized employees are covered by contracts that specify formal written grievance procedures, and most of these culminate in final and binding arbitration by a third-party arbitrator.[22] Historically, the picture has been quite different for nonunion employees. In 1950, formal procedures were almost never available to these employees. By the late 1980s, only about half of America's largest corporations had some type of formal complaint resolution system.[23]

The growing popularity of formal complaint resolution is consistent with managers' belief that employees have a right to fair treatment.[24] Such systems seem to be more common in younger organizations and in those that have adopted other HR policies that favor employees,[25] perhaps because they help establish a positive corporate culture in which conflicts are resolved through compromises that acknowledge the legitimate interests of both disputing parties.[26] When they work well, grievance systems may also help lower the legal costs associated with resolving disputes in the courts.

Fair treatment at Coors. Fairness systems like the one at Coors are particularly helpful in environments where employees lack the representation and negotiating power of a union.[27] Coors's appeal process gives employees a voice in how they are treated. This voice combined with peer review ensures a better balance of power. Over time, employees learn to trust and use the procedures.[28] Clearly, the inclusion of an appeal process is one good approach to managing situations that can potentially raise employees' concerns about fairness.[29]

Proactive Policies and Practices

Is the absence of a formal system for processing employees' complaints necessarily bad business? It may seem so at first, but some companies may choose not to support such systems for good reasons. Grievance systems are reactive. They focus the attention and energy of disputants on the past, and formalize a process for *naming* an injured party, *blaming* someone or something for the injury, and *claiming* a remedy.[30]

Given limited resources, some organizations choose to develop and promote proactive policies and practices designed to prevent the need for formal grievance procedures.[31] Proactive approaches to ensuring fair treatment might include, for example, formal performance appraisals, frequent informal feedback, progressive discipline policies, annual surveys to monitor employees' attitudes and perceptions, benefits packages designed to meet the diverse needs of employees, employee involvement in managerial decision making, management training in how to treat employees fairly, and frequent use of communication channels.

LEGAL REGULATION TO ENSURE FAIR TREATMENT

American society is perhaps the most litigious in the world. In 1992 alone, 21 million lawsuits were filed, 50 percent more than in 1984. No wonder we have so many lawyers—more than twice as many per capita as England, three times as many as Japan, and six times as many as Switzerland.[32] Legal activity regarding employment issues is a significant portion of this general picture.[33] In 1993, eighty-eight thousand charges of employment discrimination were filed with the federal agencies that handle most such lawsuits! Over ninety thousand lawsuits were expected in 1994.[34] Exhibit 3.2 shows in more detail the bases for these lawsuits.[35]

The legal environment communicates society's concerns through state and federal laws, regulations, and court decisions. Failure to comply with societal expectations as defined by this environment may result in monetary fines, imprisonment, and court orders that constrain future activities. In general, the legal system is designed to encourage socially responsible behavior.[36]

To understand how the legal environment affects the way companies manage human resources, it is helpful to understand the U.S. legal system in general. What types of laws and regulations exist? How do disputes move through the system? What types of remedies can the system offer? It is also helpful to understand the many specific laws and regulations that are promulgated and enforced by this system.

U.S. companies must act in accordance with several different types of laws, including constitutional laws, statutory laws, administrative regulations, executive orders, and common laws.

Constitutional Laws

In countries that have one, the constitution is the fundamental law of the land. The U.S. Constitution is the oldest written constitution still in force in the world. It defines the structure and limits of the federal government and allocates power among the federal government and the states. All fifty states also have written constitutions. State and federal laws must be consistent with the U.S. Constitution.

■ *Exhibit 3.2*

Bases of Alleged Discrimination in Equal Employment Opportunity Commission Charges

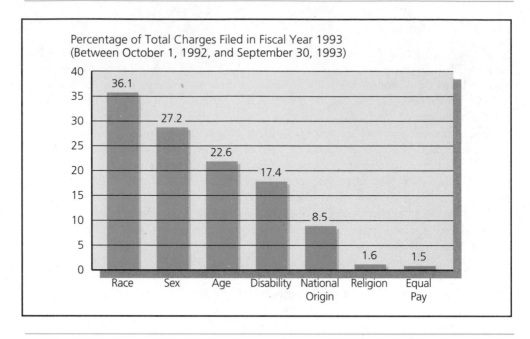

Percentage of Total Charges Filed in Fiscal Year 1993
(Between October 1, 1992, and September 30, 1993)

SOURCE: "Record Number of EEOC Charges Filed in Fiscal Year 1993," *Fair Employment Practices Guidlines* (January 27, 1994): 9.

In the area of employment, one section of the U.S. Constitution that is particularly important is the Fourteenth Amendment, which guarantees due process and equal protection. This amendment also prohibits state actions that are inconsistent with federal law. Because of its equal protection clause, the Fourteenth Amendment often plays a role in cases involving reverse discrimination.

Statutory Laws

The U.S. Constitution gives Congress all power to make laws on behalf of the federal government. Paralleling the federal instrument, state constitutions give lawmaking power to state-level governmental bodies. The resulting federal and state laws are called *statutes.*

One especially important federal employment law has been Title VII of the Civil Rights Act. As originally enacted in 1964, Title VII prohibited discrimination by employers, employment agencies, and unions on the basis of race, color, religion, sex, or national origin. A 1978 amendment prohibited discrimination against pregnant women. In 1991, a new version of the Civil Rights Act went into effect. The new law reinforces the intent of the Civil Rights Acts of 1964 but states more specifically how cases brought under the act should proceed.[37] The Civil Rights Act and other key federal statutes are described in more detail in Exhibit 3.3.

State laws must be consistent with federal law, but this does not imply that they are the same. Two important differences between state and federal laws are common. First, state laws often cover companies that are not covered by federal laws. For example, federal employment laws such as Title VII often apply only to businesses with fifteen or more employees, but similar state laws often apply to even smaller businesses. Second,

■ *Exhibit 3.3*
Major Federal Statutes

Statute	Parties Affected	Purpose
Fourth Amendment	All citizens	Provides freedom from illegal search and seizure
Fifth Amendment	All citizens	Provides that no person shall be deprived of life, liberty, or property without due process of law
Fourteenth Amendment	All citizens	Prohibits abridgment of federally conferred privileges by actions of the state
National Labor Relations Act of 1935 (Wagner Act)	Nonmanagerial employees in private industry not covered by the Railway Labor Act (RLA)	Provides right to organize; provides for collective bargaining; requires employers to bargain; requires unions to represent all members equally
Fair Labor Standards Act of 1938 and subsequent amendments (FLSA)	Most interstate employers; certain types of employees are exempt from overtime provisions—executive, administrative, and professional employees and outside salespeople	Establishes a minimum wage; controls hours through premium pay for overtime; controls working hours for children
Equal Pay Act of 1963 (amendment to the FLSA)	Same as for FLSA except no employees are exempt	Prohibits unequal pay for males and females doing essentially equal work, with equal skill, effort, and responsibility, under similar conditions
Civil Rights Act of 1964 and Title VII, as amended by EEOA of 1972 (CRA of 1964)	Employers with fifteen or more employees, employment agencies, and labor unions	Prevents discrimination on the basis of race, color, religion, sex, or national origin; establishes the Equal Employment Opportunity Commission (EEOC)
Executive Order 11246 of 1965 as amended by Executive Order 11375 of 1966	Federal contractors and subcontractors with contracts over $50,000 and fifty or more employees	Prevents discrimination on the basis of race, color, religion, sex, or national origin; establishes the Office of Federal Contract Compliance (OFCC)
Executive Order 11478 of 1969	Federal agencies	Prevents discrimination on the basis of race, color, religion, sex, or national origin
Freedom of Information Act of 1966	Federal agencies only	Allows individuals to review employers' records on them and bring civil damages
Equal Employment Opportunity Act of 1972 (EEOA)	Adds employees of state and local government and educational institutions; reduced number of employees required to fifteen	Amends Title VII; increases enforcement powers of EEOC

state laws are often predecessors to federal law and in this sense tell us what to expect in the future at the federal level. For example, Massachusetts passed the first minimum wage legislation in 1912, which was a predecessor of the federal Fair Labor Standards Act of 1938 (FLSA). New York had adopted a fair employment law in 1945 and about half the states had similar laws by the time the Civil Rights Act of 1964 was passed at the federal level. Florida, Maine, and the District of Columbia had each adopted family leave legislation before the federal Family and Medical Leave Act of 1993 was enacted.

■ *Exhibit 3.3*
Major Federal Statutes (continued)

Statute	Parties Affected	Purpose
Age Discrimination in Employment Act of 1967 as revised in 1978 and 1986	Employers with more than twenty-five employees	Prevents discrimination against persons age forty and over, and states compulsory retirement for some workers
Occupational Safety and Health Act of 1970 (OSHA)	Most interstate employers	Ensures as far as possible that every working man and woman in the nation will have safe and healthful working conditions and that our human resources will be preserved
Employee Retirement Income Security Act of 1974 (ERISA)	Most interstate employers with pension plans (no employer is required to have such a plan)	Protects employees covered by a pension plan from losses in benefits due to mismanagement, plant closings and bankruptcies, and job changes
Privacy Act of 1974 (Public Law 93-579)	Federal agencies only	Allows individuals to review employers' records on them and bring civil damages
Pregnancy Discrimination Act of 1978	Same as for CRA of 1964	States that pregnancy is a disability and, furthermore, must receive the same benefits as any other disability; allows individuals to review employers' records on them and bring civil damages
Guidelines on Sexual Harassment, 1980	Same as for EEOA of 1972	Defines standards for what constitutes harassment
Drug-Free Workplace Act of 1988	Federal contractors with contracts exceeding $25,000	Requires employers to maintain drug-free workplaces
Americans with Disabilities Act of 1990	Virtually all employers (employers with fifteen or more employees by 1994)	Protects against discrimination against individuals with disabilities
Civil Rights Act of 1991 (CRA of 1991—amends CRA of 1964)	Same as for CRA of 1964, plus U.S. citizens working abroad for an American employer or for a foreign corporation controlled by an American employer	Protects groups against discrimination (as does the 1964 act), but makes provision for jury trials and punitive compensation
Glass Ceiling Act of 1991	Same as for CRA of 1991	Empowers the Glass Ceiling Commission to focus greater attention on eliminating artificial barriers for the advancement of women and members of minorities
Family and Medical Leave Act of 1993	Employers with fifty or more employees	Allows workers to take up to twelve weeks' unpaid leave for pregnancy or illness of close family member

Administrative Regulations

At both the federal and state levels, the legislative and executive branches of government can delegate authority for rule making and enforcement to an administrative agency. For example, the federal Equal Employment Opportunity Act of 1972 gave power to enforce Title VII of the Civil Rights Act to the Equal Employment Opportunity Commission

(EEOC). The EEOC also administers the Equal Pay Act and the Age Discrimination in Employment Act of 1967.

In carrying out their duties, agencies such as these make rules—often called standards, guidelines, or decisions; conduct investigations; make judgments about guilt; and impose sanctions. In practice, this means these federal agencies have the responsibility and authority to prosecute companies they believe are in violation of the law. Furthermore, they generally require companies to monitor their own behavior and file reports, either at preset time intervals or following particular types of events. For example, the Occupational Safety and Health Administration (OSHA) conducts safety and health inspections, investigates accidents and alleged hazardous conditions, issues citations for violations, levies fines, collects mandatory reports prepared by employers, and compiles statistics on work injuries and illnesses. Agencies can also acquire information directly through inspections and audits.

Executive Orders

U.S. presidents shape the legal environment by approving and vetoing bills passed by Congress and by influencing how vigorously administrative agencies carry out their duties and responsibilities. In addition, the President can create law by issuing executive orders that specify rules and conditions for government business. Organizations that do work for the federal government are referred to as government contractors. In the area of employment, the actions of government contractors are most affected by Executive Order 11246, issued in 1965 by President Lyndon B. Johnson. Like Title VII, Executive Order 11246 prohibits discrimination on the basis of race, color, religion, or national origin. It applies to federal agencies and to federal contractors and subcontractors. In 1966, Executive Order 11375 was issued to prohibit discrimination based on sex by these employers.

Whereas Executive Orders 11246 and 11375 parallel federal law that applies to all employers, Executive Order 11478, issued in 1969, has no parallel in federal statutory law. Executive Order 11478 requires that employment policies of the federal government be based on merit.

Common Laws

Common laws are rules made by judges as they resolve disputes between parties. The U.S. system of common law is rooted in English common law, which was established after the Normans conquered England in 1066. To help unify the country, William the Conqueror established the King's Court. Its purpose was to develop a common set of rules and apply them uniformly throughout the kingdom. Decisions were based on the opinions of judges. Important decisions were recorded and subsequently referred back to as *precedent* (examples) for making future decisions. When new types of disputes arose, judges created new law to resolve them. This system is still in effect today in England.

Unlike English judges, U.S. judges do not make laws, they only interpret and apply them. But their interpretations continue in the tradition of setting precedent to decide new cases. The use of precedent to decide cases, referred to as the doctrine of *stare decisis,* helps employers anticipate how the courts might rule should they find themselves involved in a similar case.

Consider the 1971 decision of the U.S. Supreme Court in *Griggs v. Duke Power Company.* Griggs was an African American male who applied for a job at the Duke Power Company but was not accepted because he lacked a high school diploma. The lawsuit charged that Duke Power Company had engaged in racial discrimination. By requiring a high school diploma, the firm deemed that fewer African American applicants would be qualified for available jobs. Furthermore, given the work performed in these jobs, mandating a high school diploma seemed questionable.

In its decision in favor of Griggs, the Supreme Court argued that Title VII prohibited not only overt racial discrimination but also practices that are fair in form, but discriminatory in operation. This meant that *direct* evidence of intentional discrimination would not be necessary to pursue cases under Title VII. Cases of discrimination could also be brought using statistics showing a disproportionate rate of rejection for members of groups protected by Title VII. Disproportionately high rejection rates would be considered evidence of illegal discrimination if the practice leading to these rates (e.g., requiring a high school diploma) cannot be shown to be related to job performance.

In writing their decision, the justices of the Supreme Court made it clear that they wished employers to accept responsibility for ensuring that they could prove usefulness of the criteria they used in making employment decisions. But over time, the Supreme Court slowly changed, and gradually its decisions began to suggest a different point of view. In particular, the 1989 decision in *Wards Cove Packing Company v. Atonio* appeared to suggest that (*a*) plaintiffs would have more responsibility for proving that a particular practice resulted in discrimination, and (*b*) employers accused of illegal discrimination would have less responsibility for proving that an apparently discriminatory employment practice was justified by business necessity.

This apparent shifting in the Supreme Court's interpretations of the Civil Rights Act of 1964 generated considerable debate among some segments of our society, including legal scholars, social scientists, and employers. This debate culminated in the passage of the Civil Rights Act of 1991. In establishing this new law, Congress sought to clarify and reassert its view of what constitutes fair employment practices; this and other new laws make clear that the intent of Congress was consistent with earlier court decisions and was misconstrued in later decisions, such as *Wards Cove.* The feature "Positioning for the 21st Century: The Burden of Proof Grows Heavier" explains how this shift affects HR management.

As the preceding discussion of the Civil Rights Act illustrates, court rulings indicate how laws have been interpreted when applied to specific employment disputes. When interpreting the implications of court decisions, keep in mind that rulings made by the Supreme Court carry the most weight because the decisions of all other federal and state courts are subject to review by the Supreme Court. Exhibit 3.4 lists several Supreme Court rulings of particular importance for managing human resources within employment settings. As you read through this exhibit, remember also that even a ruling by the Supreme Court can be overruled should Congress decide that it is not consistent with society's view of socially responsible behavior.

REMEDIES TO DISPUTES IN CIVIL LITIGATION

Although we read about some cases in the newspapers, most civil suits never actually reach the stage of a formal trial. Instead, they are resolved privately. For cases that are resolved in court, two common remedies are monetary damages and settlement agreements.

Monetary Damages

If a legal right has been violated and has resulted in injury, the defendant may be required to pay monetary damages to the plaintiff. Compensatory monetary damages are

Positioning for the 21st Century:
THE BURDEN OF PROOF GROWS HEAVIER

The 1991 Civil Rights Act has redefined discrimination and exposed employers to greater financial liability. The law now in effect reversed several Supreme Court rulings and shifted the burden of proof for cases of intentional discrimination from the employee to the employer. In addition, workers who successfully prove they were discriminated against now can receive compensatory and punitive damages that previously were not allowed. Under the original civil rights legislation, employees could only receive reinstatement, back pay and attorneys' fees.

The total amount of compensatory and punitive damages allowed by the law is determined by the number of employees at the company and cannot exceed the following limits:

- $50,000 for companies with 15 to 100 employees;
- $100,000 for employers with 101 to 200 employees;
- $200,000 for companies with 201 to 500 employees;
- $300,000 for employers with over 501 employees.

These damages would be added on top of attorneys' fees, which can range anywhere between $40,000 and $150,000, according to professionals in the employment law field. Companies also may be responsible for paying the fees of expert witnesses called by the plaintiffs, which often range between $10,000 and $15,000.

Legal experts agree that damages will be awarded more easily now because an employee can have his or her case heard before a jury. Previously, discrimination cases were tried before judges, many of whom were considered more sympathetic to employers. Juries, on the other hand, historically have decided against businesses and awarded plaintiffs huge sums of money for damages.

"The Civil Rights Act, on top of the Americans with Disabilities Act (ADA), is the final kick in the pants for managers," said attorney Fred Sullivan of the Springfield, Mass., firm Sullivan & Hays. "Managers have to think differently."

The underlying question employers need to consider regarding any potentially liable action is, "How can this be perceived differently than the way we perceive it," Sullivan added.

"The Civil Rights Act and the ADA place more limitations on recruiting as well as discharging employees," said Howard Flaxman, an attorney with the Philadelphia firm Blank, Rome, Comisky & McCauley. "The stakes are very high right now."

THE BURDEN IS SHIFTED

The stakes are higher because any employer brought before a court on a "disparate impact" discrimination case today must prove that the challenged employment practice was a result of a business necessity. In the past, companies only had to submit evidence of a business justification, and the employee was responsible for persuading the court against the employer's evidence.

The act also shifts the burden of proof to employers in dual motive cases, that is, cases in which both lawful and unlawful factors were involved. Before, a company that used an illegal factor, such as race or gender, to make an employment decision could prevail if it proved that the same decision would be made even if that factor were not considered. Now an employer must show that only lawful factors were used to make the employment decision. The employee only has to prove that his or her protected status, such as race, gender, or disability, was a "motivating factor" in the decision regardless of other factors involved.[38]

AN EMPLOYER'S DEFENSE

Companies now must review all of their personnel policies to protect themselves against any litigation that could result from the new law.

"With juries, the issue is more of fairness, not discrimination. That's the issue even though it's not supposed to be," Flaxman said. "Juries are punishing employers who appear to be almost cavalier in their attitude."

"You want to show to the jury that efforts went beyond what was normally expected," Sullivan added. "Go beyond the final warning; issue a second warning."

Major Supreme Court Rulings That Help Define the Rights and Responsibilities of Employers and Employees

Diaz v. Pan American World Airways (1971)
The primary function of an airline is to transport passengers safely from one point to another. Therefore, not hiring males for flight attendants is discriminatory. *Business necessity* is established.

Griggs v. Duke Power Company (1971)
Tests that have adverse effects on the hiring of members of minority groups cannot be used unless the employer demonstrates they are job related. Also, for plaintiffs to win a case involving discrimination, it is not necessary to establish intent to discriminate.

Marshall v. Whirlpool (1980)
Employees have the right to refuse job assignments that constitute a clear and present danger to life or limb. However, employers are not required to pay if, as a result, employees are sent home because of no work.

Arizona Governing Committee v. Norris (1983)
Pension payouts by employers should be equal for women and men, and past unequal treatment of women must be cured by retroactive funding of pensions. This decision is in essence the second half of the issue. The first half was rendered in the Supreme Court decision *Los Angeles Department of Water and Power v. Manhart,* which stated that requiring larger contributions by females than males into pension programs is discriminatory.

National Labor Relations Board v. Transportation Management (1983)
Employees are protected by the National Labor Relations Act when helping organize employees. If an employee claims to be fired for trying to organize a union but the employer claims that the dismissal was for poor performance, the employer has the burden of proof. In cases where such "mixed" motives for employer action may exist, the employer must prove the case.

Scott v. Sears Roebuck (1985)
Employers are responsible for the acts of coworkers only if they knew or should have known of the acts and took no action.

Horn v. Duke Homes (1985)
Employers have strict liability for sexual harassment by supervisors. Full back pay was required for plaintiff who had been terminated.

Glasgow v. Georgia Pacific Corporation (1985)
A sexual harassment argument may be made on the basis of creating a hostile work environment. A company may be found to have made a sexually harassing environment a condition of employment if the harassment went on for a long time with the organization doing nothing.

Meritor Savings Bank v. Vinson (1986)
Sexual harassment is a form of sex discrimination prohibited by Title VII of the Civil Rights Act and employers may be liable for condoning a hostile work environment.

Chalk v. U.S. District Court for the Central District of California (1987)
Although viewed as being disabled by virtue of being infected with AIDS, a teacher was otherwise able to perform his job within the meaning of the Rehabilitation Act of 1973 and, therefore, should be allowed to teach.

O'Connor v. Ortega (1987)
Workplace privacy is, for the first time, a recognized right.

Hopkins v. Price Waterhouse (1989)
A female accountant who successfully claimed that sexual stereotyping prevented her promotion should receive the award of a partnership.

Dimaranan v. Pomona Valley Hospital (1991)
Employers can restrict the use of foreign languages only when there is a compelling business-related necessity to do so.

EEOC v. Arabian American Oil Company (1991)
Title VII of the Civil Rights Act of 1964 has no application to U.S. organizations employing U.S. citizens to work abroad. However, the Age Discrimination in Employment Act and the Civil Rights Act of 1991 do have application.

Harris v. Forklift Systems (1993)
The Supreme Court affirmed the "reasonable woman" standard by sending the case back to the appeals court stating that Harris did not have to prove that she was psychologocially damaged for her boss' behavior to claim sexual harassment.

Arrington v. Wilks (1995) and Martin v. Wilks (1995)
The Supreme Court upheld the lower courts' rulings that, because of its success in redressing the imbalance of minority representation in the city of Birimingham's firefighters, the existing affirmative action program was no longer necessary.

intended to help victims retrieve what they have lost, for example, back pay and attorneys' fees. Punitive damages are intended specifically to punish wrongdoers and deter future wrongdoing. A 1993 case illustrates how these remedies work:

> Firing employees and making examples out of them can prove costly for employers if such actions are not based on clear facts. This point is illustrated starkly in a Texas case, where damages in excess of $15 million were awarded a former Procter & Gamble employee who was fired after being accused of stealing a $35 telephone.
>
> The employee had worked for P&G for 41 years and, according the his attorney, had an unblemished record. He had purchased the phone with his own money and was not reimbursed because he had lost the receipt. Later, a security guard stopped the employee as he was leaving work and discovered the phone in his belongings. After an internal investigation, P&G fired the employee and announced through internal notices that he had committed a theft. The employee sued for libel, saying P&G used him as an example to prevent other thefts.
>
> Procter & Gamble committed actual malice in falsely accusing the employee of stealing the phone, the jury in the case decided. The jury awarded the employee $14 million in punitive damages and more than $1 million for actual damages to the employee's character and damages to his mental and physical well-being (*Hagler v. Procter & Gamble Manufacturing Co.,* 1993).[39]

Settlement Agreements

Court proceedings can be lengthy and costly. When the objective is correcting employer wrongdoing, court procedures often are not the most expedient. The U.S. Justice Department and administrative agencies can speed the process of ensuring that employers engage in responsible behavior by negotiating a settlement. When lawsuits are resolved by a settlement agreement, the defendant (employer) usually does not admit to wrongdoing. Nevertheless, it may agree to pay money to the plaintiff or plaintiffs. And it may agree to conduct itself according to the court's specific directives. The first settlement agreement regarding unfair employment practices was negotiated with AT&T and its twenty-four operating companies. In 1973, the firm agreed to (*a*) pay $15 million to thirteen-thousand women and two-thousand men of color who had been denied pay and promotion opportunities, and (*b*) develop goals for employing women and people of color in all jobs in all of its seven-hundred establishments. In 1992, State Farm Insurance agreed to pay a total of $192 million to women and people of color who had been denied jobs because of the company's discriminatory recruitment, selection, and training practices.[40]

In another settlement, the courts recognized that the circle of victims in organizations that engage in unfair employment practices can be surprisingly large. In 1993, Shoney's Incorporated's restaurant chain agreed to pay $105 million to victims of the company's blatant racial discrimination. Most of the plaintiffs were African American employees, but some settlement money also was awarded to white managers and supervisors who were dismissed because they refused to follow orders to terminate African-American employees.[41]

 ## ALTERNATIVE DISPUTE RESOLUTION

A growing number of businesses are using *alternative dispute resolution (ADR)* to resolve charges of employment discrimination or wrongful termination. Working out a dispute before it reaches litigation can promote goodwill between management and employees and reduce the adverse publicity often associated with legal disputes.[42] It can also reduce legal costs to both employers and society.

Mediation and arbitration are the two most common forms of alternative dispute resolution. Internal review procedures, such as those used at Coors, can also be thought of as alternative dispute resolution systems.

Mediation

Mediation is the most popular form of ADR, partly because its format is more flexible than that of other proceedings. All concerned parties come before a third-party neutral (the mediator), who may be appointed by a judge or selected by the parties or their attorneys. Parties to a civil dispute may be ordered into mediation by the court, or they may volunteer to submit to the process in an effort to settle the dispute without litigation.

Arbitration

Arbitration is also a popular method of alternative dispute resolution. It can be included in the employment contract or it may be court ordered. Here are some key ways that arbitration differs from mediation:

- Arbitration is more formal and often more expensive. Attorneys must actually present their cases in a formal manner.
- The third-party neutral might be an expert in the industry involved. The third-party neutral may be a single arbitrator or a panel of three. Arbitrators are selected by national organizations, by a judge, or by the parties themselves.
- Arbitrators have some powers, in that they may make an award after hearing both sides of the case.
- Arbitration often is specified long before any actual dispute arises. Arbitration clauses are frequently written into employment contracts or collective bargaining agreements.
- Arbitration may be binding or nonbinding. Employment or labor contracts that call for arbitration in the event of a dispute should specify whether the arbitration will be binding. If the award is nonbinding, the process could lead to a trial. If it is binding, the arbitrator's decision is final, subject to a very limited right of appeal.

 ## MANAGERS' RESPONSIBILITIES FOR ENSURING FAIRNESS IN THE WORKPLACE

The task of managing to ensure fairness in the workplace is complex. To succeed, managers must behave in ways that are consistent with societal expectations regarding employee and employer rights and responsibilities. Failure to do so jeopardizes the success of their companies.

During the 20th century, society's expectations gradually shifted, hinting at trends for the future. Whereas once the doctrine of employment-at-will seemed to give employers the right to treat employees in almost any way they wished, a more balanced approach to employment relations began to evolve. Early in the century, the rights of most concern to employees were basic conditions of work. Both the rhetoric of union organizers and early workplace legislation reflected these concerns. In comparison, from the mid-1970s to the mid-1990s, much attention focused on the right to equal opportunities in employment: women's opportunities should equal men's, and members of minority groups should have the same opportunities as members of the majority. As we enter the 21st century, concerns about equal opportunity remain salient. Nevertheless, several shifts in perspective are apparent.

Fairness for All Groups

One shift has been to begin recognizing that unfair discrimination can take many forms. Eliminating discrimination on the basis of race and gender has been the focus of most attention in the recent past. As we move into the 21st century, however, it is increasingly evident that members of many other demographic groups sometimes are victims of unfair discrimination. Gradually, legal protections have been extended to prohibit more and more types of discrimination.[43] Nevertheless, for members of some groups, no legal protection is currently available, and it is probably safe to predict that regardless of how broadly the reach of legal protection eventually extends, some groups of employees will always remain vulnerable to legal unfair treatment. In other words, legal compliance will likely never guarantee total workplace fairness. Ensuring workplace fairness requires attending to the fabric of the organization's culture.

Fairness in All Aspects of Employment Relations

A second shift in perspective has been the recognition that concerns about fairness and equal opportunity are relevant to many aspects of managing people. For many years, the term *equal opportunity* had been interpreted to mean equal hiring opportunities for entry-level jobs. In other words, attention focused most often on assessing whether unfair discrimination was occurring when hiring new organizational members, especially for jobs that had very large numbers of applicants, that is, entry-level jobs. As we move into the 21st century, this type of fairness is recognized as only a small piece of a much larger pie. Concerns about fairness permeate all aspects of managing human resources and are as relevant to people at the top of the organization as to people at lower levels.

Fairness and Ethics

It is easy to emphasize the responsibility of employers to treat employees fairly. Fairness is a two-sided coin, however, and the other side is the responsibility of employees to treat their employers fairly. This side of the coin is often referred to as ethics. The feature "Managing Human Resources for the 21st Century at J. P. Morgan" illustrates the point that fairness and ethics depend upon mutual respect and concern.

In many firms, the responsibilities of employees are spelled out in policy statements on conflicts of interest:

> Conflict-of-interest policies are often implemented by employers to ensure ethical business conduct and high standards of integrity. Generally, such policies specify that the best interests of the company must be employees' foremost concern in all business dealings.
>
> Typical conflict-of-interest policies prohibit employees from serving, in any capacity, a competitor of a company with which the employer does business. Such policies also may require employees to:
>
> - Disqualify themselves from involvement in transactions that could lead to personal financial gain or other benefits for the employees;
> - Refuse gifts or entertainment offered by anyone who has a business relationship with the employer; and
> - Refrain from using company information for personal gain or divulging proprietary information to anyone who would use it in a manner detrimental to the employer.[44]

By developing and using these policies, the employers essentially define unethical and ethical behavior. Thus, what is fair is defined not so much by the larger society, but by the specific organization. However, organizational and societal definitions may overlap. For

Managing Human Resources for the 21st Century at J. P. Morgan

A guiding philosophy of J. P. Morgan and Company Incorporated's approach to managing human resources is that the contract between the firm and its employees should be based on mutual commitment. From the firm's perspective, a fair situation requires that employees and the firm live up to each other's expectations. These expectations are spelled out in a company document entitled *Mutual Commitment: Guiding Principles of the Relationship between Morgan and You.* The excerpt below addresses the area of ethics:

Ethics: We insist on the highest standards of personal and professional conduct so that we will be deserving of our clients' and colleagues' trust.

The firm expects you to:
Act with personal and professional integrity.
Understand and comply fully with the letter and spirit of laws and regulations, as well as the firm's rules and policies.
Safeguard the firm's reputation.
Preserve the confidentiality of information about our clients, colleagues, and the firm.
You can expect the firm to:
Engage in business activities that are consistent with its reputation for integrity.
Articulate its standards and rules clearly.
Provide you with support in making legal and ethical decisions.
Refuse to tolerate illegal, unethical, or unprofessional conduct.

example, the company may say that departing employees cannot take company secrets. It would justify such a policy in the courts on the basis that taking company secrets and documents is stealing. Regardless, managers must know the policies of the firm they are joining. Then they must decide if they can live up to the policies based on whether they agree that the expectations are fair.

Managers will always need to be alert to employees' concerns about fairness. Yet, at particular times in history and in particular organizations or industries, specific fairness issues are particularly salient and in need of attention. Today, three such concerns are harassment, employment-at-will, and privacy.

HARASSMENT IN THE WORKPLACE

Harassment creates an offensive and hostile work environment that prohibits effective performance; leads to expensive financial settlements and negative publicity that tarnishes the organization's image; and, ultimately, interferes with the ability of the organization to attract and retain the best talent. Indeed, whole industries can be hurt when the public learns about unfavorable workplace climates. For example, when *Business Week* carried a story about the "flurry of employment-discrimination charges" that had been brought against the brokerage firm Kidder, Peabody and Company Incorporated, it pointed out that of all sexual harassment suits filed with the EEOC, the proportion coming from the financial services industry was rising dramatically.[45]

What Is Harassment?

In 1980, the EEOC issued guidelines stating that sexual harassment is a form of sex discrimination. This view was consistent with several earlier court decisions (*Tomkins v. Public Service Electric and Gas Company*, 1977; *William v. Saxbe*, 1976; *Barnes v. Costle*,

1977; *Heelen v. Johns-Manville Corporation,* 1978). According to the guidelines, verbal and physical conduct of a sexual nature is harassment when the following conditions are present:

- Submission to such conduct is either explicitly or implicitly made a term or condition of an individual's employment.
- Submission to, or rejection of, such conduct by an individual is used as the basis for employment decisions affecting that individual.
- Such conduct has the purpose or effect of substantially interfering with an individual's work performance or creating an intimidating, hostile, or offensive working environment.

In 1993, the EEOC issued regulations that broadened the types of harassment considered illegal.[46] Under the new regulations, employers have a duty to maintain a working environment free of harassment based on race, color, religion, gender, national origin, age, or disability. Furthermore, conduct is harassment if it creates a hostile, intimidating, or offensive work environment; unreasonably interferes with the individual's work; or adversely affects the individual's employment opportunities. Harassing conduct includes such things as racist epithets, raunchy jokes, and ethnic slurs, and usually, though not always, it has to be systematic.

The 1993 regulations clarify that the standard for evaluating harassment is whether a "reasonable person" in the same or similar circumstances would find the conduct intimidating, hostile, or abusive. The perspective of the victim—her or his race, gender, age, place of origin, and so forth—has an important place in the evaluation. This is an expansion of the "reasonable-woman" standard articulated in *Ellison v. Brady* (1991). There the court said that "unsolicited love letters and unwanted attention . . . might appear inoffensive to the average man, but might be so offensive to the average woman as to create a hostile working environment." The "average woman" in this case became the "reasonable woman," and this standard was reaffirmed later in *Harris v. Forklift Systems* (1993).[47]

Finally, the 1993 EEOC guidelines clearly state that employers are liable for the acts of those who work for them if they knew or should have known about the conduct and took no immediate, appropriate corrective action. Employers who fail to draw up explicit, detailed antiharassment policies and grievance procedures may put themselves at particular risk.

Preventing Harassment

Strategies to *prevent* harassment begin with a clear policy statement describing the management philosophy. At Northern States Power, a letter from CEO James J. Howard to employees reads, in part: "All of us have the right to be treated fairly, with dignity and respect. Any violation of this right simply will not be tolerated. We will continue to enforce a 'Zero Tolerance' approach to all forms of discrimination and harassment. Inappropriate behavior will result in the strict use of our Positive Discipline program with the possibility of termination. . . . Join me in making this a company that respects men and women of all ages, races, backgrounds, affectional orientations and physical abilities."[48]

To support such policy statements, effective strategies include the following:[49]

- Raise affirmatively the issue of harassment. Acknowledge that it may be present in the organization, and make all employees aware of the company's position on harassment.

- Build in checkpoints designed to detect harassment. For example, review all discharges to ensure that the employee was clearly performing poorly and had been given adequate opportunity to improve.
- Set up reporting procedures for harassed employees to use. Employers are responsible for taking immediate and appropriate corrective action when harassment occurs. To do so, they must first be aware of its happening. In designing reporting procedures, protections are needed to assure harassed employees that they will not experience retaliation for reporting the situation.
- Establish procedures for corroborating a harassment charge, and give the person accused of harassment opportunity to respond immediately after charges are made. Due process must be provided the alleged perpetrator as well as the alleged victim.
- Specify a set of steps in a framework of progressive discipline for perpetrators of harassment. These could be the same steps used by the organization in treating any violation of organizational policies.

Implementing these strategies does not guarantee elimination of harassment, but it does help communicate the company's expectations and provides a fair means for enforcing appropriate behavior. Training programs further support efforts to prevent harassment. Awareness-training programs can help employees understand the pain and indignity of harassment. If they are comprehensive and used aggressively, such programs can be highly effective. According to one study, the estimated cost for training ranges from $5,000 for a small company to $200,000 for a large one. These bargain rates compare favorably against the costs of losing key employees, incurring negative publicity, and handling expensive lawsuits. According to one attorney who specializes in defending companies against sexual harassment lawsuits, employers spend an average of $200,000 on each complaint that is investigated in-house and found not to be valid. For claims that are valid and end up in court, you can add the cost of the average court verdict for sexual harassment, which is $225,000. Given that 90 percent of the *Fortune* 500 Companies have dealt with sexual harassment complaints, and 25 percent have been sued repeatedly, it is easy to see why one labor lawyer compares the total cost of harassment to the cost of asbestos—in the $1 billion range.[50] And, like asbestos's, harassment's true cost can never be adequately expressed in dollar terms.

EMPLOYMENT-AT-WILL

As the industrial era was beginning, near the end of the 19th century, employers managed their businesses under the assumption that they had the right to terminate employees for any reason. This right is known as the *employment-at-will* rule. It is a common-law rule with historical roots in medieval England. In the United States, one Tennessee court explained it as follows: "All may dismiss their employee(s) at will, be they many or few, for good cause, for no cause, or even for cause morally wrong without being thereby guilty of legal wrong" (*Payne v. Western and A.R.R Company,* 1884).

Limits to the Employment-at-Will Doctrine

The courts still recognize the force of at-will employment, but during the 20th century, numerous regulations and court decisions acknowledged that employers should not have absolute autonomy to end a person's employment. Giving employers too much self-government would be harmful to employees and essentially nullify all employee rights. Thus, the Civil Rights Act, the Age Discrimination in Employment Act, and the

Managing Human Resources for the 21st Century at GE

A former employee of the General Electric Company was awarded $13.4 million by a federal judge [December 4, 1992,] for bringing forward evidence that the company defrauded the United States in a scandal involving the sale of military jet engines to Israel.

The award was the largest to date under the federal whistle-blower statute.

The award was made to Chester L. Walsh, a former General Electric manager in Israel, for informing the Justice Department of a scheme in which GE conspired with an Israeli Air Force general to submit bills for fictitious parts and testing equipment. The bills were accepted and paid by the Pentagon.

General Electric, based in Fairfield, Connecticut, pleaded guilty to four federal criminal fraud charges and agreed to pay $9.5 million in fines and $59.5 million to settle a related civil case. The Israeli general, Rami Dotan, was convicted of bribery and fraud charges in Israel and is serving a 13-year prison sentence.

Under the *Federal False Claims Act,* whistle-blowers may receive 15–25 percent of any settle-ment or any financial recovery won by the government.

In his ruling, United States District Judge Carl B. Rubin in Cincinnati said the case against General Electric "would have been difficult, if not impossible, to sustain" without documents that Mr. Walsh smuggled from Israel. The judge awarded Mr. Walsh 22.5 percent of the Government's settlement, or 90 percent of the maximum award he could have received under the law.

Such a large award is a rebuff to the Justice Department and General Electric, which had argued that Mr. Walsh did not deserve such a large award because he did not bring his accusations directly to the company as corporate policy requires and that he delayed acting for several years. . . .

Judge Rubin said in the ruling that whether Mr. Walsh should have shared his information earlier was not at issue, and he cited Mr. Walsh's argument that he feared retribution from the company and possible physical danger from General [Dotan].[51]

Americans with Disabilities Act each curtail employers' use of the employment-at-will doctrine by stating that certain personal characteristics (race, sex, age, etc.) cannot be used as justification for employment decisions of any kind, including termination. In addition, the National Labor Relations Act prohibits discharge for union-organizing activities or for asserting rights under a union contract, even if the employee in question had a record of poor performance (*National Labor Relations Board v. Transportation Management,* 1983).[52] When employees are represented by a union, the union contract replaces the termination-at-will doctrine and specifies the conditions under which an employee may be fired.

Individual employees are not the only beneficiaries of changing views about employment-at-will; society also has a stake in this issue. For example, it is clearly to the benefit of society in general to have employees who are willing to expose the unethical and illegal behaviors of their employers. To encourage employees to "blow the whistle," we must offer them some protection, as illustrated in the feature "Managing Human Resources for the 21st Century at GE."

In 1994, fair employment practices prohibited employers from terminating employees for doing the following:

⦿ Whistle-blowing (for example, opposing and publicizing employer policies or practices that violate laws such as the antitrust, consumer protection, or environmental protection laws)

◉ Being garnished for any one indebtedness
◉ Complaining or testifying about violations of equal pay, wage, or hour laws
◉ Complaining or testifying about safety hazards or refusing an assignment because of the belief that it is dangerous
◉ Engaging in union activities, provided there is no violence or unlawful behavior
◉ Engaging in concerted activity to protest wages, working conditions, or safety hazards
◉ Filing a workers' compensation claim
◉ Filing unfair labor practice charges with the National Labor Relations Board (NLRB) or a state agency
◉ Filing discrimination charges with the Equal Employment Opportunity Commission or a state or municipal fair employment agency
◉ Reporting Occupational Safety and Health Administration violations
◉ Cooperating in the investigation of a charge against the company[53]

Permissible Termination

In union settings, employers often agree to contracts that include clauses stating that employees will be terminated only for good cause. Although this doctrine is not an explicitly stated condition of employment for most nonunion workers, these workers may implicitly expect it to apply to them. Few employees expect their jobs to be guaranteed for life regardless of their own behavior. Nevertheless, employers and employees do not always agree on what constitutes "good cause" for termination, and many disputes on this issue have been resolved in the courts. The decisions of the courts suggest that termination is fair and legal when it occurs for the following reasons:

◉ Incompetence in performance that does not respond to training or to accommodation
◉ Gross or repeated insubordination
◉ Civil rights violations such as engaging in harassment
◉ Too many unexcused absences
◉ Illegal behavior such as theft
◉ Repeated lateness
◉ Drug activity on the job
◉ Verbal abuse
◉ Physical violence
◉ Falsification of records
◉ Drunkenness on the job[54]

At the federal level and for most states, the law does not require employers to have good cause for terminating employees. But changes are in the wind. For example, the state of Montana *does* have a good-cause requirement. Violations of the standard are punishable by damages awards of up to four years' wages or salary, plus attorneys' fees. The Montana statute also encourages employers to develop and use grievance procedures to resolve disputes internally. Following Montana's lead, the Uniform Law Commissioners developed the Model Employment Termination Act for other states to adopt, so continued changes can be expected at the state level. As we move into the 21st century, it seems likely that fewer and fewer employees will accept the 1884 view of what constitutes fair termination, and more and more employees will expect employers to adopt procedurally fair practices.

Similarly, the courts are expressing new views about acceptable reasons and procedures for terminating employees. Decisions of the past ten years emphasize the value of procedural justice. That is, termination of employment should be the last step in a series of documented steps designed to ensure that an employee understood that performance problems existed and had opportunity to improve. Furthermore, all evidence and material relevant to each step should be documented and filed. Even though an employer may have the right to discharge an employee, the employer may be required to show evidence indicating that none of the protections against wrongful termination was violated.

❖ EMPLOYEE PRIVACY

Simply stated, the right to privacy is the right to keep information about ourselves to ourselves. Nowhere in the Bill of Rights are private-sector employees directly guaranteed a right to privacy. Perhaps this is why Henry Ford faced no resistance from the government when he sent social workers to the homes of employees to investigate their personal habits and family finances. He and other early industrialists were free to monitor whether employees went to church and to check up on the dating habits of their young female employees. Such invasions of privacy went hand in hand with the doctrine of employment-at-will.

Although the U.S. Constitution does not guarantee us the right to privacy, in 1965, the U.S. Supreme Court concluded that various guarantees stated in the Constitution (e.g., the Fourth Amendment's protection against illegal search and seizure) have the effect of creating zones of privacy.[55] Since then, new state and federal legislation has begun to address employee privacy rights more explicitly. The best example of this at the federal level is the Family Education Rights and Privacy Act of 1974, also known as the Buckley Amendment. It allows students to inspect their educational records and prevents educational institutions from supplying information without students' consent. Employee rights to control private information were also a consideration in the passage of the Employment Polygraph Protection Act of 1988, which gives individuals the right to refuse to take a polygraph test as a condition of employment for most jobs.

Other privacy legislation is of a much weaker form. Rather than giving individuals control over who gets what information, most statutes simply give individuals a right to access and verify the information others already have.

The Privacy Act of 1974 was the first major statute to address issues of privacy directly. This act, which applies only to federal agencies, gives individuals the right to verify information collected about them and used in selection and employment decisions. It allows individuals to determine which records pertaining to them are collected, used, and maintained; to review and amend such records; to prevent unspecified use of such records; and to bring civil suit for damages against those intentionally violating the rights specified in the act. The Privacy Act is consistent with the Freedom of Information Act of 1974, which allows individuals to see all the material a federal agency uses in its decision-making processes.

In contrast to federal employees and citizens affected by the decisions of federal agencies, public-sector employees are relatively unprotected against employers, who have the ability to access and use information, often without the knowledge or consent of employees or job applicants. Two laws establish exceptions to this generalization: The Fair Credit and Reporting Act of 1970 permits job applicants to know the nature and content of credit files, which can easily be obtained by potential employers and used as they wish. And the Employee Exposure and Medical Records Regulation of 1980 gives employees the right to access their on-the-job medical records and records that document their exposure to toxic substances.

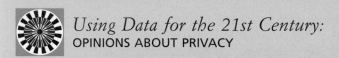

Using Data for the 21st Century:
OPINIONS ABOUT PRIVACY

In 1993, Louis Harris and Associates, a firm that specializes in opinion polls, surveyed a national cross section of one-thousand private-sector employers.

Activity	Percentage who Say Employers Should NOT Be Able to Do It
Verify education levels attained	81%
Forbid employees to engage in dangerous sports and hobbies	90%
Forbid alcohol consumption off the job	93%
Forbid tobacco consumption off the job	88%
Require overweight employees to lose weight	80%
Require genetic testing	88%
Require AIDS testing	73%
Test job applicants for drugs	30%

SOURCE: Adapted from "Employer Intrusions Shunned," *Bulletin to Management* (September 1, 1994): 280.

Concerns about privacy also are addressed by state-level legislation. Several state laws—for example, in California, Connecticut, Maine, Michigan, Oregon, and Pennsylvania—give employees access to their human resource files and define what information employees are and are not entitled to see, as well as where, when, and under what circumstances employees may view their files.[56]

Issues of privacy will continue to be debated into the 21st century. Questions to be answered include: How much access should employers have to medical records? Is there any nonmedical information that employers should not have the right to obtain, and are all methods of monitoring employees acceptable? Should employers have the right to use information about employees' behavior off the job when making employment decisions? The feature "Using Data for the 21st Century: Opinions about Privacy" shows how U.S. workers and HR executives feel about some such questions.

Access to Medical Information

Health insurance costs grew so dramatically from the mid-1980s to the mid-1990s that many employers now feel pressure to do whatever is necessary to reduce them. One way to lower these costs is to employ people who make little use of health care services, because insurance for such employees is less expensive. Like insurance companies, employers can predict how much health care a person is likely to need if they have information about variables that put people into high-health-risk categories: Does she smoke? Is he overweight? Does she abuse alcohol? other drugs? Does he exercise regularly? like to bungee jump or drive too fast?

A study of four thousand employees by DuPont documented the following additional annual costs associated with several personal behaviors and conditions:[57]

Average smoking habit	$960
Excessive weight	$401
Alcohol abuse	$369
Elevated cholesterol	$370
High blood pressure	$343

Data like these support General Mills' policy of lowering workers' insurance premiums if they lead healthy lives, as measured by behaviors such as not smoking, drinking little to no alcohol, controlling blood pressure and cholesterol, and wearing seat belts. They also support Turner Broadcasting System's policy of not hiring people who smoke, and help explain why drug testing has quickly gone from a rare to a routine practice: whereas in 1987, only about 1 out of 5 employers conducted drug testing, by the mid-1990s, about 9 out of 10 do so.[58]

It appears that employers can penalize or even terminate employees because of some types of conditions associated with high health care costs. But other employee conditions are clearly protected. The Americans with Disabilities Act (ADA) protects anyone with a history of drug use who has successfully completed or is currently engaged in rehabilitation—with some exceptions, especially when public safety may be at risk. The ADA also states that a medical exam may be given only after a conditional job offer has been made. Then, the offer may be rescinded only if the exam reveals a condition that would prevent the applicant from performing the job, and cannot be accommodated. Under the ADA, medical records are supposed to be kept separate from other human resource records and treated as confidential.[59]

The ADA protects primarily people with disabilities. It does not address directly the question of how employers might use information about genetic makeup. Advances in our understanding of the link between genetics and disease susceptibility raise new concerns about medical privacy. Should a twenty-five year-old applicant for a sales job be required to undergo genetic screening for diseases that she may experience when she reaches middle age? Is it fair to penalize workers with high cholesterol, given that genes as well as diet affect cholesterol levels?

Access to Nonmedical Information

Employers who seek medical information usually do so for good reasons. They may be concerned about how to keep health insurance costs as low as possible, which benefits the company's bottom line and may ultimately mean that healthy employees see a bigger paycheck. Or they may be concerned about protecting employees and customers from contagious diseases or unsafe behavior by employees carrying out their duties.[60] Medical information seems to be directly relevant to such concerns.

What about other concerns? For example, research has shown linkages between watching violent TV and movies and engaging in violent behavior.[61] With violence in the workplace becoming a major issue in our society, should employers be allowed, perhaps even expected, to attempt to screen out employees whose viewing behaviors suggest they are likely to be violent?[62] Or suppose an employer wants to ensure that employees do not engage in illegal behaviors of various sorts, such as industrial espionage, drug dealing, or insider trading: Does this give the employer the right to listen in on employees' telephone calls? Do employers have the right to access and use all computer files on employees' office PCs? May employers monitor all employee E-mail communications, regardless of whom they are sent to?[63]

Do employers have the right to obtain all possible information about on-the-job behavior? Are all methods of monitoring on-the-job behavior acceptable? How would you feel if you discovered that your employer, as part of an effort to detect the illegal behavior of another employee, made a videotape of you while you were in the bathroom or lockerroom, installed a monitoring device to learn what magazines you were reading during your lunch break, and hired undercover agents to pose as employees as a way to keep tabs on workers? This is what the Campbell Soup Company did—before terminating sixty-two employees.[64]

> Nearly all 62 of the workers ... were let go primarily on the strength of accusations by undercover agents who posed as shift workers during a four-month investigation. The agents produced no videotapes of wrongdoing, no audiotapes, no traces of cocaine or marijuana residue—in short, none of the corroborating evidence typically required for conviction in a court. ... [The experience of one employee, Mr. Guelde] is fairly typical of how the operation worked. ...
>
> On the night of Dec. 4, 1992, a supervisor escorted him to a conference room, where he listened for 90 minutes as an undercover agent asked about two occasions when he said Mr. Guelde was observed in a men's room ingesting cocaine through his nose. A company representative entered the room toward the end of questioning.
>
> Stunned, Mr. Guelde responded by saying he had not used illegal drugs since trying marijuana in high school. He also demanded a drug test immediately, but was denied one. ...
>
> Each of the 61 other workers was summoned to the same kind of interview, lasting as long as six hours, and each was asked to sign a statement that included a confession. Mr. Guelde refused to include a confession. Other workers admitted wrong-doing but said later they acquiesced only out of exhaustion, frustration, fear or with the understanding that their jobs would be spared for 'telling the truth,' as Mr. Iorio [the union lawyer] said. ...
>
> In the year since their dismissals, only a quarter of the workers have found meaningful jobs, Mr. Iorio ... said. Mr. Guelde is one of the better-off ones, making $8.95 an hour in a scrap-metal plant. Several days after his arbitration hearing ended in November, he praised Campbell for its attempt to sweep out problems.
>
> 'What they're doing is good,' he said. 'There's no place for drugs in the workplace. I just think they went about it all wrong. They should have brought in the police; then no one could fight it. The police would have needed more evidence.'
>
> 'But meanwhile,' he added, 'they have wrecked my whole life because of it.'[65]

 ## INTERNATIONAL CONSIDERATIONS

Termination Liabilities

In many countries, termination of employment is viewed as a harsh action that is potentially harmful to employees. Consequently, in fairness to employees, employers are held responsible for minimizing its negative consequences. Most countries have some traditional or legally required practices that come into play in the event of a plant closing or a substantial reduction of the workforce.[66] In general, these practices create more extensive and costlier employer obligations than do layoffs in the United States and Canada. One such obligation is the payment of cash indemnities that are in addition to individual termination payments required by law, collective bargaining agreements, or individual contracts.

Furthermore, in many countries, a company that wishes to close down or curtail operations also must develop a "social plan" or its equivalent, typically in concert with unions and other interested stakeholders. The plan may cover continuation of pay, benefit plan coverage, retraining allowances, relocation expenses, and supplementation of statutory unemployment compensation. Frequently, a company planning a partial or total plant closing must present its case to a government agency. In the Netherlands, for example, authorities may deny permission for a substantial workforce reduction unless management is able to demonstrate that the cutback is absolutely necessary for economic reasons and that the company has an approved social plan.

Employee-Employer Expectations in Mexico

When operating abroad, as when operating at home, complying with legal regulations is one step toward managing fairly. To be truly effective, however, managers need to realize that perceptions of fairness reflect cultural assumptions and values—not just legal realities. Managers who are insensitive to the broader social fabric will find it difficult to anticipate employees' reactions to how they are treated. Unenlightened managers run the risk of triggering negative employee reactions. To illustrate this, consider the culture of Mexico.

Mexico's social structure is similar to its family structure, and its institutions—whether government, business, or church—resemble an authoritarian, paternalistic family. A plant manager, like the president of Mexico, fills a fatherly role, rather than a mere organizational function.

Mexican law and history reflect the Mexican view that the employer has a moral and paternal responsibility for all its employees, even when the workers have a union. Mexican employees are not just working for a paycheck: they tend to expect to be treated as the "extended family" of the boss; they expect to receive a wide range of services, including food baskets and medical attention for themselves and their families, apart from social security. Medical benefits are not considered "an extra" or discretionary; they simply fulfill the employer's role and responsibilities.

Corresponding to these expectations, employees have a reciprocal obligation to be loyal, to work hard, and to be willing to do whatever is requested of them. American managers who accept the Mexican sense that a job is more than a paycheck and who try to fulfill the expectations of their employees can reap the benefits of these reciprocal expectations.

 ## SUMMARY

Workplace fairness is a complex issue that touches all employees and all employers. When managing human resources, the question "What is fair?" may be difficult to answer. Historically, the power to determine workplace conditions rested largely in employers' hands. Gradually, society recognized that this was unfair and a shift in the power balance was needed. Numerous laws now sanction some employer actions because they are clearly unfair to employees. Some practices that employers once considered fair are now illegal.

A first step toward ensuring workplace fairness, therefore, is legal compliance. With the many laws and regulations governing relationships between employers and employees, you might wonder whether managers can really be expected to know all the rules. As the owners of Tiffany English Pub (a.k.a. TGI Friday's Incorporated) found out, ignorance is no excuse for violation of the law. The restaurant had a policy that tips were the property of the restaurant. This policy, the owners reasoned, meant they could hire servers at rates below the minimum wage and use the tips to bring the pay level up to the minimum wage. The servers sued, and the restaurant owners were found to be in violation of the Fair Labor Standards Act. The court found the restaurant liable for over $34,000 in damages plus $17,000 in attorneys' fees, but then refused to allow damages.

The restaurant argued that it should not be responsible for paying damages, based on a provision of the FLSA that allows the court to deny damages if an employer proves it had a reasonable basis for believing it was not in violation. The owners stated at the trial that this was their first experience as employers, having previously been farmers. The lower court was sympathetic to this argument, stating that "the restaurant . . . simply did not know and did not understand exactly what it was to do with respect to these records on these waiters." But eventually the U.S. Court of Appeals heard the case. It did not accept the employers' excuse, and concluded: "Even inexperienced businessmen cannot claim good faith when they blindly operate a business without making any investigation as to their responsibilities under the labor laws. Apathetic ignorance is never the basis of a reasonable belief" (*Barcellona v. Tiffany English Pub,* 1979).

Legal compliance is expected of employers. By following the laws, employers should at least be able to protect themselves from losing lawsuits alleging unfair employment practices. However, workplace fairness is more than an issue of legal compliance. Even legal employer actions may be considered unfair by employees. For example, drug-testing practices are becoming routine. They are accepted as legal by the courts. Does this mean employees agree that drug testing is fair? Not necessarily. Employees tend to evaluate whether drug testing is fair on a case-by-case basis. They weigh issues of invasion of privacy, threats to safety and health, the specific procedures used to conduct the drug tests, and the penalties associated with failing a drug test.[67] Even the American Medical Association prefers to see employers use other means for detecting drug use, such as simple eye-hand coordination tests.[68]

Managing human resources fairly requires an understanding of how employees evaluate fairness. Managing in ways that meet the principles of distributive and procedural justice is one approach to creating fair employment conditions. In addition, because perceptions of fairness constantly change, employees' attitudes about fairness should be determined and taken into account when establishing policies. Finally, managers need to understand that the same policy and the same outcome can be perceived as relatively fair or unfair depending on the attitudes they display and the amount of respect they show for the concerns of employees.

 Discussion Questions

1. Why does the peer review system at Coors Brewing Company work so well?

2. Why should companies be concerned about managing employees fairly?

3. What is the employment-at-will doctrine? Why were courts in the late 1880s more willing to uphold the doctrine than are courts today?

4. How would you distinguish a just from an unjust dismissal? Is this distinction easier to make for low-level jobs than for high-level or managerial jobs? Explain.

5. The industrial, occupational, and demographic composition of the labor force shifted from the mid-1970s to the mid-1990s. How might these specific shifts coincide with the heightened interest in employee rights in the 1990s?

6. Develop counterarguments for the following arguments in support of the employment-at-will doctrine:

a. If the employee can quit for any reason, the employer can fire for any reason.

b. Because of business cycles, employers must have the flexibility to expand and contract their workforce.

c. Discharged employees are always free to find other employment.

d. Employers have economic incentives not to discharge employees unjustly; therefore, their power to terminate should not be restricted by laws.

7. What workplace policies and procedures would you recommend for firms to be fair in their efforts to downsize and lay off employees?

8. What kinds of behaviors might constitute sexual harassment? How can an organization prevent those types of behaviors from occurring?

9. Due process has been interpreted as the duty to inform an employee of a charge, solicit employee

input, and provide the employee with feedback in regard to the employment decision. How can a grievance procedure ensure this type of due process for an employee accused of sexual harassment? How

can the grievance procedure protect the victim of the alleged harassment?

10. What are the major issues involved in the privacy rights of employees?

 ## In-Class Projects

LINCOLN ELECTRIC

1. What is the evidence that Lincoln Electric manages employees fairly? Do you consider any aspects of Lincoln's practices unfair? If so, what are they and why are they unfair?

2. In what ways would you expect Lincoln's treatment of its employees to change if it opened a plant in Mexico? Why?

3. Describe what Lincoln's management appears to expect from employees. What does Lincoln agree to give employees in return? How do the expectations and responsibilities of Lincoln's management relate to notions of distributive and procedural fairness?

AAL

1. What is the evidence that AAL manages employees fairly? Do you consider any aspects of AAL's practices unfair? If so, what are they and why are they unfair?

2. In what ways would you expect AAL's treatment of its employees to change if it opened a plant in Mexico? Why?

3. Describe what AAL's management appears to expect from employees. What does AAL agree to give employees in return? How do the expectations and responsibilities of AAL's management relate to notions of distributive and procedural fairness?

 ## Applied Projects

1. Assess employers' responses to the AIDS epidemic. This issue has become extremely controversial because some employers have fired workers who reveal they have the disease and others have instituted AIDS-screening procedures during employee selection. Key questions include: What are the rights of AIDS victims? What are the rights of non-AIDS-infected coworkers? What are employers' rights and responsibilities?

2. Find and interview an individual who has experienced sexual harassment on the job. Report to the class on the content of the interview, including such things as where the harassment took place, who was involved, how long the situation lasted, what the harasser or harassers did, how the victim felt, what

the perspective of the harasser was, and how the problem was resolved or what the victim is trying to do to resolve it.

3. Consult BNA's *Fair Employment Practices* manual, *Labor Relations Reporter,* or *Labor Arbitration Reports* to find recent cases that involve a charge of unjust dismissal. Address the following questions: What type of job was involved? What are the characteristics of the discharged employee (age, sex, prior history with the company)? Did the company have a grievance procedure? On what basis did the employee contest the discharge? What did the judge or arbitrator rule? Why? State whether you agree with the outcome of the cases, and explain your position.

Case Study:
WHAT'S WRONG WITH WHAT'S RIGHT?

 Stuart Campbell, age thirty-five, moved slowly down the front steps of the courthouse and squinted as the last rays of sunlight pierced downtown Cleveland. It had been a long day, spent in court recalling the details of his past employment with Nako Electronics, a major marketer of audiotapes in the United States. Nako Electronics had and still has a considerable stake in Stuart. The arbitrator's decision and an award of $500,000.00 plus interest of $82,083.50 was a bitter pill for Nako to swallow for having terminated him.

Stuart hesitated for a moment at the bottom of the courthouse steps and came back to the present; he had agreed to meet his attorney, Jim Baldwin, at the Steak and Brew for a couple of drinks and to unwind from the courtroom tension. His spirits began to pick up as he maneuvered through the city traffic, but he could not help thinking how within a year, a good job had gone bad.

Five years ago, Stuart was riding high as the Midwest representative for Nako, covering Ohio, West Virginia, and Pennsylvania. A hard driver, he boosted the sluggish sales of Nako audiotapes from less than $300,000 to $2 million in about fourteen months. In fact, a year ago, business was going so well for Stuart that he began driving a Mercedes-Benz 450 SEL.

That's when Mike Hammond, vice president of marketing at Nako Electronics, took notice of Stuart. On one of his visits to Stuart's territory, Mike commented that he really liked Stuart's car. Mike remarked that he was making a trip to California soon. "I distinctly remember Mike saying he would like to have a Buick," Stuart testified. "He didn't want anything as fancy as I had, because a new Buick would be adequate and, after all, he wanted me to bear the expense!"

Not only did Stuart refuse to go along with Mike's car scheme, but he also refused to invest in a phonograph cartridge business begun by Mike, which Stuart believed was a phony. In fact, Mike approached all the sales representatives of Nako Electronics to invest in the cartridge company at $1,250 a share, whereas Mike and two other associates paid $1 a share for 80 percent of the stock.

In the year following Stuart's successful boost of sales of Nako audiotapes and Hammond's thwarted attempts at commercial shakedown, Nako increased Stuart's sales quota by more than 75 percent. It also sabotaged a substantial proportion of his sales by refusing to give his large customers promotional assistance. Finally, Nako fired Stuart without explanation, and the income from his sales dropped to zero.

Mike was not in court that day to defend himself; he had died unexpectedly six months before of a heart attack. Instead, during the trial, Nako Electronics had to defend a number of allegations made against Mike. Stuart's attorney made sure that two of Stuart's former fellow sales representatives testified that they were mysteriously fired after refusing Mike's demands to invest in his side company. Nako argued that it did not need a reason to fire Stuart, and, besides, Stuart was not meeting his new, increased sales quota. Moreover, the company argued, the deceased Mike could not very well defend himself against the charges of Stuart and others.

Stuart had rehashed these details many times with his attorney both during the private arbitrator hearing and during numerous rehearsals for the trial. As he arrived at the Steak and Brew, he hoped he could put these memories behind him. After a few drinks, Jim summarized the day's proceedings and expressed cautious optimism for the final outcome. "But you know, Stuart," mused Jim, "if you would have kicked in the ten or fifteen K that Hammond demanded, you would have outlived that old goat, and you'd have a business worth over $4 million in sales today, and we wouldn't be having this drink!" ◉

Case Questions

1. Why did the arbitrator award Stuart so much money?
2. Was the arbitrator's decision a just and fair one?
3. Did Nako have to give Stuart a reason for firing him?
4. If Stuart's firing was due to his failure to invest in Mike's side company, could Nako defend the firing in court?
5. Could Stuart have done anything, legally, to avoid being fired?
6. How do you think Stuart's former coworkers at Nako reacted to what happened to Stuart?

SOURCE: Stuart A. Youngblood, Texas Christian University.

Organizational Changes and Human Resource Planning: Focusing on the Key Issues

People always ask, "Is the change over? Can we stop now?" You've got to tell them, "No, it's just begun." They must come to understand that it is never ending. Leaders must create an atmosphere where people understand that change is a continuing process, not an event.

JACK WELCH, CEO, General Electric Company[1]

Managing Human Resources for the 21st Century at AT&T's Global Business Communications Systems

In the mid-1980s, people wondered whether AT&T could survive the rigors of competition. By the mid-1990s, influential people were asking whether AT&T might be the influential winner in a global contest of communications and computing as it pursued its strategy to be the world's networking leader. AT&T in 1994, with three hundred thousand employees, fifty thousand of them overseas, had the right pieces to put together the success puzzle. It had the network in place to keep up with customers' insatiable demand for information. It had the research, development, manufacturing, sales, and service to meet customers' needs.

During those ten years, AT&T transformed from a stodgy monopolistic institution into a nimble competitor. Organized into more than twenty business units was the twenty-six-thousand-employee Global Business Communications Systems (GBCS) unit. Like that of AT&T's other business units, GBCS's transformation into a nimble competitor was greatly facilitated by the actions of the HR department. Two key contributions were linking HR to the strategic needs of the business, and repositioning the HR department.

GBCS was formed in 1992 through a merger of two AT&T business units, Business Communications Systems (BCS), which sold telecommunications systems and services to large clients, and General Business Systems (GBS), which served smaller customers. Jerre Stead was hired by AT&T chairman Robert E. Allen to run GBCS. Stead was seen as a business leader with proven experience outside of AT&T who was capable of bringing a new strategy and management philosophy to AT&T.

The first order of business for the newly formed unit was developing a set of strategic business principles. These principles would reflect management's overall direction for successfully achieving its business objectives, and they would guide all day-to-day actions, from handling a customer's inquiry to manufacturing a system. Five business principles emerged:

- Make people a key priority.
- Use the total quality management approach to run the business.
- Profitably grow by being the leader in customer-led applications of technology.

- Rapidly and profitably globalize the business.
- Be the best value supplier.

These principles serve as a guiding force in linking employees with the needs of the business.

Management also identified seven values to guide decisions and behavior:

- Respect for individuals
- Dedication to helping customers
- Highest standards of integrity
- Innovation
- Teamwork
- Accountability
- Excellence

These values support the GBCS vision and mission. The vision states the organization's purpose: "To be your partner of choice: dedicated to quality, committed to your success."

The mission describes a broad plan of action: "To be the worldwide leader in providing the highest quality business communications products, services, and solutions."

LINKING HUMAN RESOURCES TO THE STRATEGIC BUSINESS NEEDS OF GBCS

When President Jerre Stead selected Fred Lane, an experienced AT&T line manager, to head the HR organization in the fall of 1991, he asked Lane to "reexamine every aspect of our people dimension." Stead emphasized the need to "engage the workforce" and to create an environment that "supports our people as our only sustainable, competitive advantage."

Lane and his staff tackled the task of developing a strategic plan and management system for human resources that would meet these objectives. The result was the HR Strategy and Planning Model. This blueprint provides an overall perspective for viewing relationships and linkages that exist within the business even as the business continues its transformation process.

A critical step in developing the strategic plan was crafting an HR mission statement: "To create an environment where the achievement of business goals is realized through an acceptance of individual accountability by each associate and by his or her commitment to performance excellence."

REPOSITIONING THE HUMAN RESOURCE ORGANIZATION

Implementing the HR strategic plan called for new roles, new competencies, new relationships, additional resources, and new ways of operating—for both GBCS associates and HR. Prior to its reorganization, the HR group within GBCS provided salary administration, HR information systems, staffing support, and other related administrative services. HR had to transform itself *from* its role as provider of basic personnel services *to* a strategic function that would be seen as adding value to the entire organization.

With support from Jerre Stead, GBCS repositioned human resources as a key member on the senior management team with responsibility for providing leadership on strategic HR issues. Since this repositioning and the merger of the two business units, both revenues and return on investment have been increasing and customer satisfaction goals are being attained.[2]

The feature "Managing Human Resources for the 21st Century at AT&T's Global Business Communications Systems" highlights several things: (1) managing people effectively is vital to the success of businesses in today's highly competitive environments; (2) as businesses change their strategies, objectives, missions, and values, a systematic plan should guide the way they manage human resources; (3) in turn, HR departments should change their HR activities to link with the strategies, objectives, mission, and values of the business; and (4) as HR departments link to their businesses, they will reposition themselves, develop new competencies, and develop new ways of organizing in order to better serve their customers. In other words, as we move into the 21st century, major environmental and hence organizational changes will require the systematic and well-planned integration of HR activities.

 ## MANAGING ORGANIZATIONAL CHANGES AND HUMAN RESOURCE PLANNING

Through the 21st century, organizations will need to respond to many events associated with changes in the environmental forces that affect them. Because many of these changes involve people and will affect people, they have major implications for managing human resources and they raise significant issues for the stakeholders of human resources. To address these implications effectively, organizations need to understand the changes themselves *and* understand the process of change. As Jack Welch suggests in the quote introducing this chapter, managers must accept and get their employees to accept the idea that change is both necessary and a continuous process. The environmental forces necessitating organizational change are certainly likely to vary over time and across different businesses, but the process of change will be constant.

This chapter looks at three examples of organizational changes that have major implications for managing human resources and that are likely to remain into the 21st century: (a) the continued move to a total quality, customer-focused strategy, as in the example of GBCS at AT&T; (b) organizational restructurings and the consequent downsizing and layoffs; and (c) comprehensive initiatives to respond to the concerns of an increasingly diverse workforce. This chapter also describes the process of change and the role of HR professionals in that process. (Chapter 18 presents greater detail about how HR departments can be repositioned to be effective in this change process.) Because addressing these three organizational changes requires that future human resource requirements be anticipated and fulfilled, the chapter then discusses systematic HR planning tools and techniques. The relationships between these changes and activities are shown in Exhibit 4.1.

Managing organizational changes takes time in part because realigning human resource capabilities with new organizational conditions takes time. Furthermore, the process of change itself takes time: because organizations are complex systems with multiple interdependencies, bringing about change involves collaboration and partnerships between line managers, HR professionals, and all employees. Possible activities of these three groups are shown in the feature "Partnership in Managing Organizational Changes and Human Resource Planning." Ideally, this collaboration occurs during all phases of change, beginning with an understanding of the nature of the organizational changes and continuing through HR planning, implementation, reassessment, and readjustment. The phrase "organizational changes and HR planning" refers to the activities and processes related to aligning, redesigning, and repositioning an organization's human resources.

TOTAL QUALITY MANAGEMENT (TQM) STRATEGIES

In essence, *total quality management strategies* are systematic and coordinated companywide efforts to continuously improve the quality of a firm's products and services. Increasingly, these are focused on the customer. In total quality, the key to customer-focused strategies is the question "What is quality?" Its answer: "Quality means delivering loyalty-producing products and services along all dimensions of quality with a single effort."[3]

For manufacturing products, the dimensions of quality include:

- *Performance:* A product's primary tangible operating characteristic. Examples are a car's ability to accelerate and a television set's picture clarity.
- *Features:* Supplements to a product's basic functioning characteristics, such as one-touch power windows on a car.

■ *Exhibit 4.1*
The Relationship between Changes and Human Resource Management

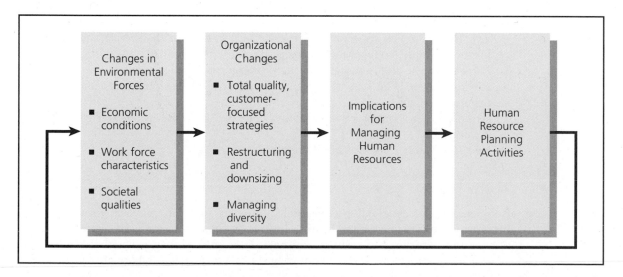

Partnership in Managing Organizational Changes and Human Resource Planning

Line Managers	Human Resource Professionals	Employees
Be aware of the implications of managing human resources in organizational changes like restructuring and diversity.	Identify the HR implications of business plans.	Participate in training programs to improve total quality.
Work with employees to become comfortable with change.	Train employees in total quality procedures and techniques.	Enhance skills and abilities for flexibility and change.
	Help establish policies and procedures for downsizing and diversity.	Respond to empowerment programs and actively participate in team activities.
Choose the best type of structure and decide which employees need to be outplaced.	Facilitate change.	Learn to work with diversity in organizations.
	Identify a supply of human resources to help match the needs of line managers.	
Describe one's business plans and HR needs	Develop HR programs to match supply and demand for employees.	

⊚ *Reliability:* A probability of not malfunctioning in a specified time period.
⊚ *Conformance:* The degree to which a product's design and operating characteristics meet established standards.
⊚ *Durability:* A measure of product life.
⊚ *Serviceability:* The speed and ease of repairing a product.
⊚ *Aesthetics:* How a product looks, feels, tastes, and smells.
⊚ *Perceived Quality:* Quality as defined and judged by the customer.[4]

For services, the dimensions of quality include:

⊚ *The Tangibles:* The appearance of the physical setting for the service, including the location, people, communication materials, and equipment.
⊚ *Reliability:* The ability to perform the promised service dependably and accurately.
⊚ *Responsiveness:* The extent to which an employee helps customers and provides prompt service.
⊚ *Assurance:* An employee's knowledge, courtesy, and ability to convey trust and confidence.
⊚ *Empathy:* Caring, individualized attention.[5]

The Importance of Total Quality Management

Competition, domestic and international, is growing more intense each year. The need for organizations to change and continually improve quality has never been greater. Many organizations in the 21st century will have little choice: they will either continually change and improve quality, or go out of business—or they may be bought up by others or forced to merge in order to survive.

The beneficial outcomes of pursuing total quality management strategies are greater than mere survival, as shown in Exhibit 4.2. The desirability of these and related outcomes provide strong incentives for undergoing the necessary changes and dealing with the implications for managing human resources.[6]

The Elements of Total Quality Management Programs

The Ford Motor Company, which has become a leader in quality improvement programs, pursues total quality by following the principles of W. Edwards Deming. These fourteen principles guide Ford's approach:

- Create consistency and continuity of purpose.
- Refuse to allow a commonly accepted level of delay for mistakes, defective material, or defective work.
- Eliminate the need for and dependence upon mass inspection.
- Reduce the number of suppliers. Buy on statistical evidence, not price.
- Search continually for problems in the system and seek ways to improve it.
- Institute modern methods of training, using statistics.
- Focus supervision on helping people to do a better job. Provide the tools and techniques for people to have pride of work.
- Eliminate fear. Encourage two-way communication.
- Break down barriers between departments. Encourage problem solving through teamwork.
- Eliminate the use of numerical goals, slogans, and posters for the workforce.
- Use statistical methods for continuing the improvement of quality and productivity, and eliminate all standards prescribing numerical quotas.
- Remove barriers to pride of work.

◼ *Exhibit 4.2*
The Deming Chain Reaction

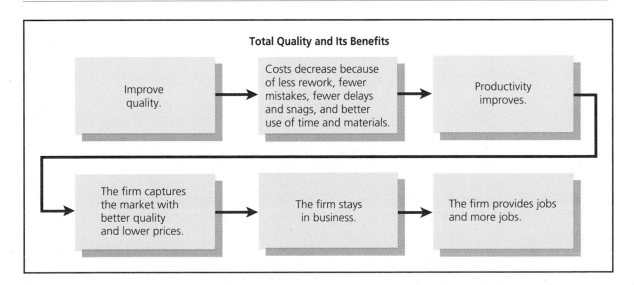

Total Quality and Its Benefits

Improve quality. → Costs decrease because of less rework, fewer mistakes, fewer delays and snags, and better use of time and materials. → Productivity improves. → The firm captures the market with better quality and lower prices. → The firm stays in business. → The firm provides jobs and more jobs.

SOURCE: Adapted from W. E. Deming, *Out of Crisis* (Cambridge: MIT Press, 1986).

⊚ Institute a vigorous program of education and training to keep people abreast of new developments in methods, materials, and technologies.

⊚ Clearly define management's permanent commitment to quality and productivity.[7]

Thus, pursuing total quality change requires dedication, commitment, and employee involvement.

The Role of People in Total Quality Management

For most organizations, the human resource component is one of several that a company must manage effectively in improving quality. This is clear when you look at the criteria used to evaluate companies competing for the Baldrige Award—companies such as Federal Express, AT&T, Xerox, Cadillac Motor Car Division, Texas Instruments Incorporated, and Motorola. Exhibit 4.3 shows the seven components used in scoring the companies applying for the Baldrige Award in 1995.[8]

Not all companies pursuing total quality management apply for the Baldrige Award. Some seek certification that is more widely recognized worldwide: ISO 9000. ISO 9000 certification is based on a series of five quality system standards developed by the International Organization for Standardization in Geneva, Switzerland. These standards, which have been adopted by many companies within the European Union, apply more to managing the technical components of an organization. Most of the areas addressed in the 150 ISO 9000 criteria are covered in category 5.0 of the Baldrige criteria, Process Management.[9] The ISO 9000 criteria do not include specifications for HR, as do the Baldrige criteria. Nevertheless, as firms strive to meet the technical standards, they will undoubtedly also begin to change their human resource practices, because people are ultimately the initiators and implementors of change.

New Ideas for Quality. At Corning, the total quality approach is about people, according to James R. Houghton, the chief executive officer. Corning's employees often provide good ideas for product improvement. To carry through on their ideas, they form short-lived "corrective action teams" to solve specific problems: "Employees . . . give their supervisors written 'method improvement requests,' which differ from ideas tossed into the traditional suggestion box in that they get a prompt formal review so the employees aren't left wondering about their fate. In the company's Erwin Ceramics plant, a maintenance employee suggested substituting one flexible tin mold for an array of fixed molds that shape the wet ceramic product baked into catalytic converters for auto exhausts."[10]

Empowerment. For other firms pursuing total quality, customer-focused strategies such as the feedback systems at Corning, Ford, Southwest Airlines, General Electric, Weyerhaeuser, and Eaton are also in place; teamwork is permitted and facilitated; decision making, autonomy, and responsibility are a part of everyone's job description; and job classifications are flexible. Giving workers more decision-making ability, autonomy, and responsibility is referred to as *empowerment.* Empowering workers appears to be critical to getting employees more committed and involved.[11] In fact, employers that mesh total quality programs with empowerment efforts are twice as likely to report significant improvements in their products and services, according to a survey of 126 companies by the Wyatt Company and the Manufacturers Alliance for Productivity and Innovation. At these companies, "[e]mpowerment measures included increased use of functional or cross-functional work teams, decentralization of decision-making, and redesign of jobs, functions, and work groups."[12]

■ *Exhibit 4.3*
Scoring the Baldrige Award

1995 Examination Categories/Items	Point Values	
1.0 Leadership		90
1.1 Senior Executive Leadership	45	
1.2 Leadership System and Organization	25	
1.3 Public Responsibility and Corporate Citizenship	20	
2.0 Information and Analysis		75
2.1 Management of Information and Data	20	
2.2 Competitive Comparisons and Benchmarking	15	
2.3 Analysis and Use of Company-Level Data	40	
3.0 Strategic Planning		55
3.1 Strategy Development	35	
3.2 Strategy Deployment	20	
4.0 Human Resource Development and Management		140
4.1 Human Resource Planning and Evaluation	20	
4.2 High Performance Work Systems	45	
4.3 Employee Education, Training, and Development	50	
4.4 Employee Well-Being and Satisfaction	25	
5.0 Process Management		140
5.1 Design and Introduction of Products and Services	40	
5.2 Process Management: Product and Service Production and Delivery	40	
5.3 Process Management: Support Services	30	
5.4 Management of Supplier Performance	30	
6.0 Business Results		250
6.1 Product and Service Quality Results	75	
6.2 Company Operational and Financial Results	130	
6.3 Supplier Performance Results	45	
7.0 Customer Focus and Satisfaction		250
7.1 Customer and Market Knowledge	30	
7.2 Customer Relationship Management	30	
7.3 Customer Satisfaction Determination	30	
7.4 Customer Satisfaction Results	100	
7.5 Customer Satisfaction Comparison	60	
Total Points		1000

Quality Circles and Other Problem-Solving Groups

The development, implementation, and utilization of quality circles have helped involve all organizational members in total quality strategies.[13] A *quality circle* is a voluntary group of workers who have a shared area of responsibility.[14] They meet together periodically to discuss, analyze, and propose solutions to quality problems. They are taught group communication processes, quality concepts, and measurement and problem analysis techniques, and are encouraged to draw on the resources of the company's management and technical personnel to help them solve problems. In fact, they sometimes take the responsibility for solving quality problems, and for generating and evaluating their own feedback.

A quality circle is usually a normal work crew, with from five to ten members. The leader works as a group facilitator and not as a boss. If the department requires more than one circle, then a second leader is trained and a second circle is formed. The circle calls on technical experts to help solve problems. Circle meetings are usually held on company time and on company premises. When companies have unions, the union members and leaders are encouraged to take an active role in the circle, to attend leader training, and to become fully aware of circle principles.

In companies such as Intel, Selectron, Southwest Airlines, Motorola, AT&T, and Xerox, employee groups may be named problem-solving groups, leaderless teams, or continuous improvement teams.[15] Regardless of their name, the discussions, training, and problem solving of these groups are critical to TQM.

The introduction of quality circles and problem-solving teams may seem like a small intervention for creating change, but as many companies have learned, it can affect the design of jobs, selection criteria, training programs, performance evaluation methods, pay systems, reporting relationships, and so on.

The Eaton Corporation's Total Quality Strategy

The feature "Managing Human Resources for the 21st Century at the Eaton Corporation" describes one company's efforts to transform a traditional structure into one driven by TQM. The Eaton example illustrates several points about total quality initiatives. First, it illustrates the role and importance of people and the human resource department in a major organizational change. Second, it shows the linkage between the needs of the business and human resource management. Third, it illustrates the partnership between human resource professionals, line managers, and employees in the development and implementation of the plan for continuous quality improvement. Fourth, it illustrates the usefulness of surveys, data, and feedback in the process of organizational change.

Communication

Communication is fundamental to all types of organizational change efforts, and efforts to improve quality are no exception.[16] Communication is built into human resource practices such as performance management and compensation.[18] It is also facilitated by organizationwide programs that encourage and legitimate horizontal communication, that is, information flowing from individual to individual, team to team, and division to division. At Weyerhaeuser, the role of communication is spelled out in the firm's statement of values:

> People require open, timely, two-way communication to contribute to the company's success. This means that
>
> - Business direction is clear and broadly communicated across the organization.
> - People have the information they need to perform their jobs.
> - People's ideas and suggestions are valued and mechanisms exist to evaluate and act on them in a timely manner.
> - Communication is continuous, honest, and two-way, and employees continuously measure its effectiveness.
> - Employees share ideas across the organization in support of continuous improvement and implement the most reliable methods.

Like Weyerhaeuser, the Global Business Communications Systems unit of AT&T uses several specific HR practices to get people to communicate in all directions. Exhibit 4.4 describes these. Note that each practice has built-in feedback mechanisms. These

Managing Human Resources for the 21st Century at the Eaton Corporation

Eaton Corporation in Cleveland, Ohio, is a *Fortune* 500 Company and a worldwide manufacturer of thousands of products in six industries, including truck components, engine components, automotive and appliance controls, commercial and military controls, industrial controls and power distribution components, hydraulics and general products, and semiconductor equipment. Fully 80 percent of its products are number one or number two in their respective markets. During the early 1990s, the average productivity of its fifty thousand employees improved more than 4 percent annually, resulting in products that earned the firm more than $5.5 billion in sales.

Owing to the highly competitive nature of its businesses, success and ultimately survival depend upon delivering high-value products to the customer. Delivering high value means giving world-class quality at competitive prices. To do this, most companies like Eaton pursue total quality management strategies—and quickly recognize that success in total quality management depends upon success in managing human resources.

At Eaton Corporation, success in managing human resources is not left to chance. It begins at the top and works its way down through the organization. Eaton believes in the value of empowerment at all levels, so the divisions of the company are fairly decentralized. Nevertheless, all the divisions subscribe to total quality management, with latitude given for tailored approaches to attaining it. Within this framework, Nickolas L. Blauwiekel, division manager of human resources for the Automotive and Appliance Controls Operations (AACO) Division in Carol Stream, Illinois, and a group of key managers used the corporate-developed Eaton Philosophy Audit Process to support their unit's quality improvement activities.

Blauwiekel started the Eaton Philosophy Audit Process program in 1992 to help support the division's Quality 1st+ Program. The Quality 1st+ Program is designed to help AACO meet and exceed its goal as expressed in its mission statement, which is "To provide total customer satisfaction while creating growth and value through total quality of performance in all facets of our business." The Quality 1st+ Program encompasses activities devoted to business systems improvement, cycle time reduction and process improvement, and improving the way people are managed. The Eaton Philosophy Audit Process falls within this last category. The seven values that make up the Eaton philosophy, "Excellence through People," are

- Focus on the positive behavior of employees
- Encourage employee involvement in decisions
- Communicate with employees in a timely and candid way, with emphasis on face-to-face communications
- Compensate employees competitively under systems which reward excellence
- Provide training for organization/individual success
- Maintain effective performance appraisal systems
- Emphasize promotion-from-within throughout the Company
- Select managers and supervisors who demonstrate an appropriate blend of human relation skills and technical competence

Essentially, each of the divisions' 15 plants is audited every two to three years. During a typical audit, an audit team, headed by Blauwiekel, visits the plant for a day and a half. The team members conduct structured interviews with various groups of employees at all levels of the organization, 50 to 100 percent of the plant's employees. Before leaving, the audit team gives an initial summary of its findings to the plant manager. After a few weeks, the plant manager receives a written formal report and is asked to share the results with all plant employees. Within two months, the plant manager is asked to send back to Blauwiekel's office an "action plan" to assess the level of implementation of the Eaton Philosophy. The action plan serves as a benchmark when the next audit team visits the plant.[17]

---

make communication a *process* rather than a one-time, one-way event.[19] At Xerox, one employee described a consequence of better communication this way: "Now, I can go to my boss and say, 'Boss, you and I need to talk about meeting our customer's requirements by that Thursday deadline. Thanks to Leadership through Quality, the boss must respond appropriately and begin to work with me on the problem.' "[20]

GBCS Communication Programs

Practice	Description	Feedback Mechanism
Ask the President	Program that allows associates to write, phone, or mail questions or concerns to the president of GBCS.	Receipt is acknowledged within twenty-four hours. Written response from Pat Russo is sent within forty-eight hours.
AnswerLine	Program that allows associates to call a toll-free number with questions, issues, or requests for business-related information.	Call is acknowledged within seventy-two hours. Written or telephone response is sent to associate from subject expert.
Chats	Small, face-to-face group meetings with the business unit president and GBCS associates.	Associates receive immediate feedback at meeting on issues raised or question asked. Associates provide feedback to Pat Russo by survey following the meeting.
Bureaucracy Busters	Program that allows all associates to submit ideas to recommend changes to existing policies or processes that will reduce or eliminate bureaucracy.	Receipt is acknowledged within forty-eight hours. Associate may receive a written acceptance decision, share-of-stock award, or recognition.
All Associates Broadcasts	*Video:* Quarterly video broadcasts to all associates. Associates can view live at sixty-plus sites, dial a toll-free number and listen to the broadcast, or view a tape after the broadcast.	Associates may call in during broadcast and ask questions. Questions are answered live if time allows. All questions and answers are published electronically after the broadcast. Associates may provide feedback by survey after the broadcast.
	Audio: As-needed audio broadcasts on specific subjects. Associates dial a toll-free number and listen to the broadcast live or can listen to a recording for several days after the initial broadcast.	Live questions and answers occur during call. Associates may provide feedback by survey after broadcast. Trends show an increase in Ask the President calls after each All Associates Broadcast.
Performance Excellence Partnership (PEP)	Performance and developmental initiative that ensures that all associates have measurable objectives linked to GBCS business objectives.	Coach-associate review is conducted and objectives are revised three times (minimum) a year. Objectives and accomplishments are discussed in total at annual salary review. Associates provide upward feedback to coach twice a year.
Progress Sharing Plan (PSP)	Compensation plan for all GBCS associates that links pay to business results.	Monthly results are published in *Goalposts.* Quarterly results are published in *Bigger Bucks Bulletin.*
Recognition programs	Various programs that allow coaches or associates or both to nominate each other for performance recognition.	Peer-coach recognition takes place; awards are made.
Associate Opinion Survey (AOS)	Semiannual survey to all associates that assesses their feelings about the work climate. The Associate Excellence Index (AEI) is GBCS's key measure of associate value.	Business unit results are shared through various communication vehicles. Group results are shared down to the lowest level possible while still maintaining the anonymity and integrity of data.

SOURCE: Adapted from M. J. Plevel, F. Lane, S. Nellis and R. S. Schuler, "AT&T Global Business Communication Systems," *Organizational Dynamics* (Winter 1994): 70.

MANAGING DOWNSIZING AND LAYOFFS

In their quest for efficiency, survival, global competitiveness, and profitability, many firms are also going through another form of organizational change: they are restructuring their operations. Almost without exception, this means lost jobs and layoffs.[21] Here are some *conservative* estimates of the number of jobs lost in major firms from the early 1990s to the mid-1990s:

Company	Staff Cutbacks
IBM	85,000
AT&T	83,500
General Motors	74,000
U.S. Postal Service	55,000
Sears	50,000
Boeing	30,000
NYNEX	22,000
Hughes Aircraft	21,000
Martin Marietta	15,000
DuPont	14,800
Eastman Kodak	14,000
Philip Morris	14,000
Procter and Gamble	13,000[22]

Given numbers like these, it is easy to understand why people are feeling insecure. For example, whereas in the early 1980s, about 75 percent to 80 percent of employees described their job security as good or very good, by the early 1990s, only 50 percent or 55 percent did so.[23] These feelings of insecurity are likely to continue into the 21st century, particularly in larger organizations. Fortunately, many firms recognize that restructuring, downsizing, and layoffs significantly affect the lives of employees. Many firms are also developing policies and procedures designed to help those who lose their jobs assess their own strengths and weaknesses and prepare for a possible career change.

The Survivors' Side of Downsizing and Layoffs

The employees who remain in the company—the survivors—are also affected by layoffs.[24] Facing the threat of job loss and seeing others lose *their* jobs can be a traumatic and bitter experience.[25] It appears, however, that the *process* by which jobs are eliminated can make a difference. In summarizing the effect of job loss resulting from an acquisition, one study concluded that loss of attachment, lack of information, and a perception of "apparent managerial capriciousness" as the basis for decisions about who will be terminated, cause anxiety and an obsession with personal survival.[26] The negative cycle of reactions may not be inevitable. If survivors feel that the process used to decide who to let go was fair, their productivity and the quality of their job performance may not suffer as much. The same study found that "it was apparently not the terminations *per se* that created . . . bitterness but the manner in which the terminations were handled. Those who remained . . . expressed feelings of disgust and anger that their friends and colleagues were fired . . . [and] felt guilty that they were not the ones who were let go because they believed their coworkers performed at least as well or better than they did."[27] Thus, in developing human resource policies, procedures, and practices for effective downsizing and layoffs, even the needs of survivors require attention.

A process model that recognizes all employees and their desire for fairness in downsizing and layoffs is shown in Exhibit 4.5.

■ *Exhibit 4.5*
Process Model for Developing and Implementing Downsizing Plans

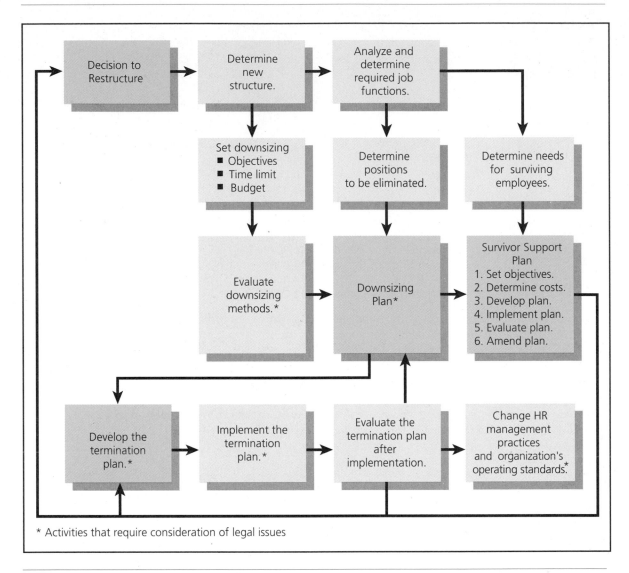

* Activities that require consideration of legal issues

Managerial Responsibilities during Downsizing

As with any major organizational change, the steps of diagnosing the current situation and developing a careful plan to implement change are essential. But even the best plan is little guarantee that chaos will not break out. The process of carrying out change is not just about strategies and plans; it is also about relationships between the people in a company and it is about personal character. Perhaps the greatest challenge to managers is maintaining employee morale while the actions of the company seem to say, "You are not valuable." A manager who had the challenge of maintaining the morale and performance of employees until the closing of more than six General Motors auto plants offers the following tips for how to be effective in such situations:

■ *Exhibit 4.5 (Continued)*

Components of the Downsizing Plan
• Methods employee terminations (volutary-involuntary, termination-retirement, redeployment)
• Phases of the plan and time schedule
• The termination plan
• The survivor support plan (before, during, and after downsizing)
• The communication plan (what information will be given to whom and when)
Components of the Termination Plan
• Management-supervisor training re termination interviews
• The severance package determined key variables: age, years of service, employability and so forth
• Type and extent of employee assistance given: outplacement services, retraining, referrals, extended benefits
• Notice of termination: lead time allowed, work or pay
• Method of termination interview and by whom, method of exit
• The communication program: what information will be given to whom, when, by whom, and how
Components of Survivor Support Plan
• Management-supervisor training—re addressing survivor concerns and morale problems
• The communication program: what information will be given to whom, when, by whom, and how
• Stress counseling
• Information sessions: objectives, roles, performance requirements, career opportunities
• Employee development program: retraining for increasing survivor skills, and career planning independent of the organization
Other HR and Organizational Components
• restructuring and supporting compensation packages
• Employee development program: career paths, redefining security, career planning, development of required knowledge, skills, and abilities
• Changes in operating standards and procedures

SOURCE: Adapted from N. Labib and S. H. Applebaum, "Strategic Downsizing: The Human Resource Perspective," *Human Resource Planning* (Fall 1993): 243.

Communicate. *Give notice as far in advance as possible—certainly before workers read it in the paper. Be thorough and repetitious, because they may not be able to absorb everything the first time.*

Be visible. *Take personal responsibility for guiding people through the change. Don't just have an "open door" policy; wander around outside your office.*

Be honest. *False hope isn't helpful for anyone. Be blunt about the plant closing, even if you don't know the exact date.*

Be positive. *Reward top performers and implement worker ideas for improvements. Also, encourage plant tours by schoolchildren and customers. They imply that workers are worth showing off.*

Demand more. *Remind workers that improving skills will help the plant today and make them more marketable later.*

Keep the plant looking good. *Clean it, paint it. Don't let the equipment deteriorate. Morale is iffy enough already.*

CRAIG B. PARR, Manager General Motors' Pontiac-West Assembly Plant[28]

Positioning for the 21st Century:
LAYING OFF EMPLOYEES IN A DIGNIFIED WAY

Now that downsizings and reorganizations have become a necessary part of business for most U.S. companies, there are many workers who wouldn't be surprised if they received a layoff notice at some time in their careers. This doesn't mean, however, that employees relish the idea of being laid off. What they want most is to be treated with dignity during the process. Here are 10 basic principles that HR professionals can use to help managers lay off or eliminate employees in a respectful way. These principles include:

1) Conduct the meeting in private. A terminated employee has the right to a private severance meeting conducted by the employee's supervisor, not someone from the HR department. Because termination is a personal issue, employees want to hear the news from their supervisors, not from someone they don't know.

2) Keep the meeting short and to the point. The meeting should last no more than 10 to 15 minutes. Employees want to know the facts. They don't want nuances and indirect language. As soon as the employee is seated, explain why you called him or her in: "Fred, I'm sorry, but your position has been eliminated." Repeat the statement if necessary, and ask if he or she understands it.

3) Offer support and compassion, but don't give hope of reversing the decision. For example, tell the employee that this decision has been reviewed at the highest levels, and there's no possibility for appeal. Tell him or her that efforts have already been made, without success, to find him or her another assignment.

4) Explain why the company made the decision. Tell the employee why he or she is being laid off: a change in the company's strategic direction, or whatever is the reason for the decision. Don't argue about issues that should have been resolved long ago. Be firm in telling the employee that the decision is made, and it's final.

5) Don't make discriminatory statements. Be aware of the many U.S. laws on discrimination and wrongful termination. The HR department should be involved in giving managers advice on what they can and can't say to employees.

6) Control your emotions. Don't try to keep the employee from leaving the room (you could be accused of false imprisonment); don't touch (you could be prosecuted for assault and battery); don't yell (you could be accused of intentional infliction of emotional abuse).

7) Give the severance package in writing. When doing this, explain that the company wishes to make the employee's transition as painless as possible. Express confidence in the employee and his or her prospects. Remind the person that this termination was a business decision, and that you'll do all you can to help him or her.

8) Encourage the employee to take positive, rather than destructive, actions. Tell the person to follow the advice of the outplacement consultant who will help him or her move in a positive career direction.

9) Plan a graceful exit. Walk the employee to the door or bring the outplacement consultant to him or her.

10) Inform other employees, customers, and suppliers of the decision. Don't criticize the employee. Make the statement simple and non-blaming, such as, "Joe left the company to pursue other interests."

There should be no winners and losers in a termination. All parties should come out as whole as possible with a promise for a better future.[29]

Additional recommendations are provided in "Positioning for the 21st Century: Laying Off Employees in a Dignified Way," which illustrates the partnership between HR professionals and line managers.

Legal Considerations in Downsizing and Layoffs

Closing Notification. The stress imposed by a loss of employment can be severe. Indeed, the suicide rate among displaced workers is almost thirty times the national average. Clearly, society has a legitimate interest in minimizing the harm to workers, their families, and their communities. Several states now recognize the importance of plant or office closings and relocations and are considering legislation to control them. Maine and Wisconsin require prenotification and penalize employers who move plants or offices without it. At the federal level, the Worker Adjustment and Retraining Notification Act took effect in 1989. It mandates that employers give employees sixty days' notice of layoffs of fifty or more employees where the number constitutes one-third of the workforce. It also requires employers to give prenotification of layoffs of five hundred or more workers, regardless of the total number of workers at the company. The act covers all businesses that employ one hundred or more employees, excluding part-timers.[30]

Where a union represents the workers, the right of employers to move production facilities is greatly affected by the National Labor Relations Act (NLRA), section 8(a). It has been clearly established that employers must bargain over the effects of a plant closing and relocation in most situations. Companies must negotiate with the union before they make a decision to move if the nature of the employer's operation at the new location does not change in any basic way (*NLRB v. Dubuque Packing Company,* 1991).

Layoff Notification. Under the Worker Adjustment and Retraining Notification Act, layoffs that are temporary in nature or downsizings that are permanent but do not involve a complete shutdown do not require advance notification. HR needs to ensure that the entire process is not in violation of the Age Discrimination in Employment Act, which covers workers aged forty and above. This is true whether organizations downsize by layoffs or early retirements, with or without incentives. It appears that downsizing programs that are directed at easing out older workers specifically are in violation of ADEA. However, in attempts to survive and reduce expenses, employers are able to reduce their overall head count including workers over age forty (*Schibursky v. IBM Corporation,* 1993).

Alternatives to Layoffs

Regardless of the cause, the loss of a job can be traumatic for employees. To assuage the difficulty of this transition, organizations are pursuing several different strategies.[31]

Job Sharing. Rather than terminating those with less seniority or poor performance, some companies have initiated job-sharing programs. Job sharing involves reducing an individual employee's workweek and pay. This helps the company cut labor costs and may actually lead to higher overall productivity because each employee is working more concentrated hours. One apparent cost-related disadvantage is that expenses per employee may increase because benefits costs are usually a function of the number of employees, not the number of hours worked or amount of pay. On the other hand, cost savings are realized by reduced severance pay, unemployment insurance, outplacement and employee assistance expenses, and so on. Although few studies have investigated the payoffs of this alternative, Motorola found that implementing job sharing, rather than layoffs, saved an average of $1,868 per employee, or almost $1 million overall, in one plant.[32]

Early Retirement. Age-based mandatory retirement is illegal for most employees because it is considered a form of unfair discrimination under the ADEA. This means employers cannot rely on attrition due to retirement as a planned form of downsizing. Instead, early retirement programs often attempt to create voluntary attrition.[33] The key to a successful early retirement program is understanding the needs of targeted employees and providing incentives that meet those needs. Incentives may include pension payments before and after age sixty-two, when Social Security payments start, and company-paid health and life insurance. Alternatively, a company may maintain its current retirement program but lower the qualifying age in order to increase the pool of potential retirees.

 MANAGING DIVERSITY

The publication in 1987 of the U.S. Department of Labor monograph *Workforce 2000* created a widespread awareness of the need for business to develop competence in managing a workforce filled with diversity of many types.[34] One chart from *Workforce 2000* dramatically shows that the *entry-level* workforce in the year 2000 will be much more diverse than the 1985 workforce in general (see Exhibit 4.6). After reading and digesting *Workforce 2000,* many managers realized, "Successful organizations will react to diversity as the important business issue it is by implementing proactive, strategic human resource planning."[35] Today, this view is very widely shared.

The Importance of Managing Diversity

Surveys of business leaders confirm the perception that interest in managing diversity successfully is widespread. For example, in one study of 645 firms, 74 percent of the respondents were concerned about increased diversity, and of these, about one-third felt that diversity affected their corporate strategy. Why are companies so concerned? The two primary reasons cited were a belief that supervisors did not know how to motivate their diverse work groups, and uncertainty about how to handle the challenge of communicating with employees whose cultural backgrounds result in differing assumptions, values, and even language skills.[36]

As the term *managing diversity* implies, the organizational interventions that fall within the realm of this label focus on ensuring that the variety of talents and perspectives that already exist within an organization are well utilized.

Organizations that attack the diversity issue with full force do so because they believe that taking action is a strategic imperative. For most organizations, simply knowing the facts about workforce diversity—which are now parading as headlines in our daily newspapers—does not stimulate major changes in management practices. The facts are most significant when they are considered in the context of the changing business

■ *Exhibit 4.6*
New Entrants into the Labor Force

Category	Labor Force 1985	Net New Workers 1985–2000
Native white men	47%	15%
Native white women	36%	42%
Native non-white men	5%	7%
Native non-white women	5%	13%
Immigrant men	4%	13%
Immigrant women	3%	9%
Total workers	115,461,000	25,000,000

SOURCE: Adapted from U.S. Department of Labor, *Workforce 2000* (Washington, DC 1987): xxi.

environment: increased emphasis on the highly interpersonal task of providing quality service, globalization of markets and businesses, and the increasing use of work teams are all making diversity management a high priority. These changes are bringing more and more people from diverse backgrounds into contact with each another, and, at the same time, mean that businesses are becoming more reliant on person-to-person contact as a way to get things done. Add to these trends the changing demographics of both consumers and the workforce, and the stage is set for diversity to emerge as a strategic business issue.

Dimensions of Diversity

Many companies, such as Northern States Power, understand and value many dimensions of diversity, including gender, ethnicity, culture, age, functional areas of expertise, religion, lifestyle, and so on. By considering just three aspects of diversity, you may begin to understand the bigger picture.

Gender Diversity. In the late 1950s, when many of the CEOs of the 1990s were entering the labor force as young professionals, they were almost exclusively men. Back then, men were receiving 95 percent of the MBA degrees awarded and 90 percent of the BBA degrees. As these men are finishing their careers, forty years later, the picture is dramatically different. In 1990, women received approximately 31 percent of the MBA degrees awarded, as well as 39 percent of the law degrees, 13 percent of the engineering degrees, and half of all undergraduate degrees.[37]

Today, females are better educated than ever before, and more are choosing to be in the active labor force. Furthermore, gender-based segregation within organizations is gradually decreasing, although in 1990, women held fewer than 0.5 percent of the top jobs in major corporations.[38]

Maximizing the productivity of women is essential to achieving competitiveness. This often requires attacking the artificial barrier of a male-dominated corporate culture. As the CEO of Avon Products has noted: "Cultural discrepancies can come out in little ways. We used to have a lot of white male traditions at Avon. We bought season tickets to sporting events, and we called the annual management outing President's Golf Day. Our first two women officers complained. . . . We realized these activities were no longer appropriate. They were too male-oriented and unwittingly made others feel like outsiders."[39]

According to one survey, 60 percent of women executives in large firms feel that their organization's male-dominated corporate culture is an obstacle to the success—that is, productivity—of women.[40] These women may be underestimating the problem. In a poll of 241 *Fortune* 1000 CEOs, nearly 80 percent of the respondents said women face barriers that keep them from reaching the top. And of those who admitted that barriers exist, 81 percent identified stereotypes and preconceptions as problems women face.[41]

Cultural Diversity. After gender diversity, cultural (including ethnic) diversity is the second most frequently noted change in the workforce. Cultures have consequences that are easily experienced but more difficult to describe. For many people, the concept of culture conjures up images of the exotic customs, religions, foods, clothing, and lifestyles that make foreign travel—as well as trips into the ethnic enclaves in our local cities—both stimulating and enjoyable. These aspects of a foreign culture can be experienced without ever engaging in conversation with someone from that culture.

The deeper consequences of culture—such as values and ways of interpreting the world—cannot be handled merely by changing menus and policies. And it is these deeper consequences that organizations are struggling with today. When people with different habits and world views come together in the workplace, misunderstandings and conflicts inevitably occur as a result of dissimilar expectations and norms. Employees who behave according to the cultural adage that "the squeaky wheel gets the grease" may be viewed as offensive and undesirable teammates by employees who were taught that "the nail that sticks out gets hammered down." Employees behaving according to the latter adage may be viewed as ineffective by those following the former.

Several circumstances seem to account for employers' current recognition that cultural diversity requires active management. First, although the proportion of African Americans in the United States has remained stable, their employment patterns have changed considerably during the affirmative action era, with substantial integration occurring for clerical, technical, and skilled crafts jobs.[42] Also, although often overlooked, educational levels of African Americans have risen during this time, providing another stimulant for workplace integration. Second, although the number of immigrants entering this country each year is relatively small, over the years, the number of employees with strong ties to another national culture grows owing to the continuing effect of nationality on second- and third-generation citizens.[43] Third, the variety of the immigrant population has itself increased, as Asians and Latins from dozens of countries join European immigrants. Fourth, insightful business leaders recognize that they can use their multicultural domestic workforce as an educational resource and training ground for learning some of the tough lessons associated with conducting business internationally.

Age Diversity. In developed countries such as the United States, the median population age has been increasing. Along with this comes the bulging ranks of "older" employees trying to climb the corporate ladder, which creates havoc for traditional, hierarchical organizations. Such organizations are structured to accommodate large cohorts of entry-level employees and smaller cohorts of employees at more advanced career stages. These organizations tend to segregate employees by age. Organizational elders supervise the cohorts who will soon replace them, who in turn supervise their own replacements.

But these old hierarchies are a dying breed. As layers of hierarchy are removed, previously segregated generations of employees find themselves working together and even rotating jobs among themselves. Often, the result of all these forces is an unfamiliar reversal of roles. As one restaurant manager put it, giving orders to older workers "is sort of like telling your grandma to clean the table." If younger generations find this uncomfortable, so do older generations. As one working retiree explained: "For 30 years I was a supervisor, and then one night I step out of one role and into another. . . . When you're being supervised by someone younger, you see a lot of things that aren't going to work, but you have to bite your tongue."[44]

The combination of changes in the age distribution of employees and new, flatter organizational structures means that three generations of workers can find themselves working side by side. Even if employees from these generations were all born and raised in the United States, they will differ in their values and attitudes about work, their physical and mental functioning, and the everyday concerns that reflect their stages in the life cycle. Of course, within each generation, gender and cultural variety also abound, yielding a workforce that reflects the complete palette of human potential.[45]

Diversity Managers

Businesses are taking the diversity issue very seriously—so seriously, in fact, that many large corporations have followed Digital Equipment Corporation's early lead, which was to create a new job with the title *manager of valuing differences*. For example, Honeywell Incorporated has a director of workforce diversity, and Avon Products has a director of multicultural planning and design.[46] What do the people with such titles do? Fundamentally, their jobs are about creating change in organizations. Long term, their goals include changing corporate cultures. Short term, their goals include changing the behaviors of individuals and ensuring that all employees fulfill their potential.

To achieve these goals, managers of diversity engage their organizations in many types of activities designed to create change. For example, Hewlett-Packard Company conducts training sessions for managers to teach them about different cultures and ethnic groups and about their own gender biases and training needs.[47] Procter and Gamble has implemented "valuing diversity" programs throughout the company. A mentor program designed to retain black and female managers was developed at one plant, and one-day workshops on diversity were given to all new employees.[48] Equitable Life Assurance encourages minority group members to form support groups that periodically meet with the CEO to discuss problems in the company pertaining to them. At Avon, women have made significant inroads into management, however, more remains to be done. To help improve the progress of women and minority group members, the company uses councils that represent various groups, each having a senior manager present at meetings. These councils inform and advise top management.[49]

Breaking the Glass Ceiling. The *glass ceiling* is a barrier that although hard to see, nevertheless prevents women and people of color from gaining access to promotions. Until recently, the dominant approach has been to focus on helping nonmajority individuals develop a "winning style" to succeed in a "white man's" world. This has worked to some extent, but it is not enough. The more long-term approach to helping break the glass ceiling, and the one that might determine whether businesses will survive in the future, is to ensure that the workplace has no artificial barriers to performance in day-to-day activities or to advancement. That way, everyone can offer their individual talents to a company, rather than suppress them to conform to deep-rooted prejudices.

Until companies change their culture to become truly merit based, a short-term practical approach is for women and people of color to be aware of the kinds of behavior management prefers and to respond to those preferences. Some believe that "[t]o be successful in upper management, women must constantly monitor their behavior, making sure they are neither too masculine nor too feminine."[50] Some women in upper management have achieved success by altering their behavior to what is desirable to the male management hierarchy already in place. Nevertheless, simply expecting everyone to change themselves to "fit" into the existing culture of upper management is not the long-term solution. The long-term objective is to increase an organization's effectiveness by improving management practices. Changing organizational norms, policies, and structures that inhibit full utilization of the workforce is the goal.[51]

Because organizations have so little experience in changing their culture to fit a more diverse workforce, it is too soon to say what approaches to change are the most effective. Nevertheless, we can examine some of the many strategies companies are experimenting with.[52]

Several activities focus on increasing awareness of discriminatory attitudes and practices. For example, managers can be trained to work and manage in a diverse workforce, and everyone can be educated about how our reliance on stereotypes is often counterproductive. Managers and supervisors can work with their employees to identify ways in which traditional performance-ranking and performance-rating systems can be improved so that they do not perpetuate disadvantage. Task forces can be formed to plan new programs and make recommendations for change based on problems discovered in the workplace. These task forces could also review and monitor such programs on a continuing basis.

Other programs can be implemented that will benefit a diverse workforce by helping everyone reach their potential. For example, career planning can be used to ensure that everyone has the opportunity to gain experience, knowledge, and exposure as well as to provide career guidance. Mentorship programs can be encouraged as a means of giving everyone access to advice from the upper ranks. Companies can address the need to balance work and family by offering more generous adoption- and pregnancy-related leaves of absence and flexible hours (some even provide on-site child care, flexible projects, and opportunities to work at home).[53]

Companies that have taken action to remove the glass ceiling are already seeing results. For example, Merck reports that about 25 percent of its middle managers were women in 1990, versus approximately 10 percent in 1980,[54] and the Prudential Insurance Company of America had 50 percent women managers in 1990 versus 30 percent in 1980.[55]

These are just a few of the interventions that can chip away at the glass ceiling in organizations. In the best companies, such activities fit within a larger strategic plan focused on improving organizational effectiveness. Guidelines for developing such plans are provided later in this chapter.

Basic Principles

Many options and choices must be made when introducing initiatives for working through diversity, but a few basic principles seem to apply for all circumstances.[56]

Develop a Comprehensive Understanding of the Many Types of Diversity in the Organization and Decide Which to Address. The first task is to develop awareness of the many possible types of diversity that exist in organizations. The next task is to learn the facts about the relevant aspects of diversity.

What do the numbers indicate about the backgrounds of people in the organization and the way diversity is distributed throughout the organization? Do people with diverse backgrounds work closely together, or are they segregated into homogenous subgroups based on occupation, hierarchical level, or geographic location? Facts such as these may be readily available in the database of the organization's human resource information system, but if not, then some basic research may be needed.

Are some subgroups of employees more likely to report dissatisfaction with their coworkers or the type of supervision they receive? Are turnover patterns different among different groups of employees? Do promotion rates differ among subgroups? Is everyone equally satisfied with the career opportunities they see? Answers to questions such as these may be easy to obtain in organizations that routinely survey employees to assess attitudes. In organizations without such ready information, systematic research may be needed.

The next task is to rank the dimensions of diversity that the organization needs to address. This task should go hand in hand with a discussion of the objectives for any new initiatives and should subsequently be used throughout all phases of planning, implementing, evaluating, and revising diversity initiatives.

Stay Close to the Customers. To be effective, new initiatives must be bought by all the relevant constituencies. In this sense, the constituencies are appropriately thought of as customers. The customer metaphor emphasizes the importance of designing and delivering initiatives that all affected parties see as valuable, are aware of, and evaluate positively. To achieve this objective, close contact with customers is essential. This includes contact with both primary customers, who are targeted as the direct users of a product or service, and secondary customers. For example, if flexible work schedules are the "product," primary customers are the employees whose work schedules are made more flexible; secondary customers include the managers and supervisors of these employees, and, in some cases, the coworkers.

During the design phase, customers can provide valuable information about their needs, as they conceptualize them; the conditions under which they would "buy" the product or service; constraints that might interfere with their ability to use particular product or service; alternatives that they view as competition for the proposed product or service; and, ultimately, suggestions for how to modify the proposed product or service prototype to make it most appealing. Without this input, well-intentioned change agents are likely to develop initiatives that are never bought by the customers of interest.

Anticipate Possible Problems and Be Prepared to Deal with Them. Any new initiative can run into unanticipated problems, and diversity interventions are no exception. Even the most thorough planning process will not completely prevent problems. Because of the sensitive nature of some types of diversity initiatives, it is particularly important to be prepared for the consequences. For example, if employees are suddenly convinced that the organization really wants to know about incidents of racism, sexism, or any other kind of "ism," several such complaints may suddenly surface. These may implicate an employee who had never been identified as creating problems in the past. In such a circumstance, procedures should be in place for investigating the complaints and resolving the situation fairly.

For another example, employees who attend a training program may feel that the program itself perpetuates destructive stereotyping. Awareness training programs and special skills programs such as assertiveness training can easily backfire if they seem to highlight differences that employees have worked hard to obliterate because the differences are devalued by the organization's culture. A fine line must be walked in programs that attempt both to acknowledge some of the differences that characterize members of different demographic groups *on average,* and to reduce the tendency we all have to rely on stereotypes. Even the most experienced trainer may offend a few participants, so it is desirable to have a mechanism for handling employees' complaints.

Finally, when organizations announce that they value differences and support diversity, they should be prepared to have employees point out contradictions between words and actions. For example, all printed materials will come under scrutiny, from annual reports to announcements for company-sponsored social events. The company's advertising materials will also be examined from a new perspective. Other organizational elements that may suddenly be criticized more openly include the types of clubs frequented by top-level executives; the types of community events and programs supported, or not supported, by company donations; and the types of awards and gift certificates offered to employees as incentives or bonuses. An organization that intends to be serious about supporting diversity should be prepared, even eager, to make adjustments in many spheres of activity, including those not directly linked to a specific human resource initiative.

Institutionalize New Learning. Initiatives for creating organizational changes are likely to involve many different people working on many different specific projects in many different places over a long period of time. Throughout this process, a tremendous number of qualitative and quantitative data will be generated. A lot of these data will be gathered systematically during the planning and evaluation phases of a new initiative.

Typically, standard operating procedures ensure that such systematically collected data are summarized and recorded in the form of a report.

Recording what has been learned is the first step toward institutionalizing what has been learned. The second step involves disseminating the learning throughout the organization. Dissemination of learning can be achieved in numerous ways. Redesigning formal policies and practices is perhaps the most fundamental method but is also the most difficult and complex. Training programs are another popular vehicle, but these often reach only a few employees. Therefore, other methods should be constantly sought with the objective of creating a continuous stream of learning that immerses all employees. Such methods could include scheduled times for sharing log notes during staff meetings, hot lines that people may call when they have questions or when they wish to add new information to an available resource, special features in company newsletters (e.g., a monthly listing of "new lessons" submitted by employees), information anecdotes incorporated into speeches given by high-level executives, memorable quotes posted on bulletin boards, short essays published in company-sponsored literary forums, and so on.

TOP MANAGEMENT LEADERSHIP AND THE PROCESS OF CHANGE

It is now widely recognized that for change to occur in organizations, leaders must get others to change *and* they themselves must also change.[57] Changes such as those toward focusing on the customer, managing for total quality, using diversity to advantage, empowering employees, and operating with fewer levels of management all start at the very top and cascade down. Robert B. Haas, the CEO of Levi Strauss, describes his firm's attempt to create an organization that reflects these qualities: "What we're trying to do around here is syndicate leadership throughout the organization. . . . In a command and control organization, people protect knowledge because it's their claim to distinction. But we share as much information as we possibly can throughout the company. Business literacy is a big issue in developing leadership. You cannot ask people to exercise broader judgment if their world is bounded by very narrow vision."[58]

New Leadership Behaviors

CEOs and all other managers must change before other employees will. Managers have to move from the command-and-control style to empowering, visioning, cooperating, and supporting. They must also change the way they behave with respect to suppliers and customers outside the organization, the environment, social and ethical issues of business and society, and the strategy and direction of the organization. These changes in leadership are seen as vital to many organizations today, and they are not likely to occur unless systematic strategies are in place to help managers make them. Companies like Eaton Corporation, General Electric, Levi Strauss, Federal Express, and Weyerhaeuser are systematically linking specific on-the-job experiences and training and development programs to the new behavioral competencies required in the new organizational forms. Some companies are even establishing leadership institutes.

Leadership Institutes. In the late 1980s, Weyerhaeuser's Forest Products Company (FPC) established its own leadership institute to help its managers change their behaviors. Within FPC, Chief Executive Charles W. Bingham, his executive team, and the director of strategic education, Horace Parker, concluded that a major strategic repositioning called for upgrading the firm's human capabilities through executive development:

How the organization was sold on the worth of an executive development program is an important lesson. The trump card used in closing the deal was to involve the executives at various levels of the organization in the planning stages. During those stages, they came to see, as did the executive team, that an intensive development program such as the Leadership Institute was not an expensive frill but a prerequisite for survival. The Leadership Institute, top management was convinced, would be a powerful catalyst that could accelerate the normal process of change—of everything from a corporate culture to how a salesperson deals with customers.[59]

Working with others in human resource management and with the top management team, FPC created a leadership institute where managers could come to discuss the new strategy and its implications for them. In addition, the institute offered training to help managers acquire needed skills, knowledge, and leadership styles. A success, this institute grew into a total quality company program. By 1994, the entire Weyerhaeuser Company used the institute to help managers learn new leadership behaviors. The new leadership behaviors identified as critical for total quality management flow directly from what leadership means to the company:

We are committed to leadership behavior that empowers people to fully contribute to company goals. This means that

- Leadership behavior and standards are well defined and understood throughout the organization and are linked with company values.
- The criteria for selecting leaders include demonstrated commitment to company values and leadership skills.
- Leaders set clear goals and expectations and inspire others to meet them.
- Development is provided for existing and current leaders.
- Leaders seek and use feedback to improve their leadership skills.
- A key measure of leadership success is the development of others.

Management Development on-the-Job. When systematically developed and coordinated by the HR department, education and job experiences can go a long way toward helping managers change themselves and, in the process, change their organizations.

As described in Chapter 1, the Weyerhaeuser Company has gone from a centralized structure to a decentralized structure and now to a decentralized structure coordinated through shared vision, values, and leadership philosophy. At the same time, it has moved from a maker of undifferentiated commodity products to one of customer-focused, total quality products. Continuous management development helps ensure that all these changes last and continue to filter down in the company. Frequent meetings between top managers are one type of activity facilitating on-the-job development. Working as a team develops, shares, and coordinates efforts to help each individual manager learn more about the company as a whole. A deeper understanding of the business puts each manager in a better position to lead in ways that are consistent with the several separate businesses, yet coordinated to reflect the functions of these businesses as part of one larger company. In addition, the Weyerhaeuser Company, like the Eaton Corporation, uses surveys to measure whether managers exhibit leadership behaviors that are consistent with the company's strategy, values, and vision.

Survey Development and Feedback. As Nick Blauwiekel at the Eaton Corporation has indicated, constant and continuous change and improvement need measurement systems. Eaton uses surveys to systematically gather information about total quality management in its plants, and feeds the results back to the plant managers and all the plant employees. This is all a part of the Eaton Philosophy Audit Process. Although the data are collected by interview teams rather than written surveys, the team asks specific

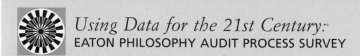

Using Data for the 21st Century: EATON PHILOSOPHY AUDIT PROCESS SURVEY

Of the Eaton Philosophy values discussed today, please evaluate how successful your organization has been in implementing each value. Audit teams are asked to gain a consensus on the evaluation of the trend for each value in the success of implementation, for example, our facility has improved substantially since the last audit visit. Base your evaluation on the question, "Has the facility improved on implementing this value since the last audit team visit?"

The values the facility is trying to implement include:

- Focuses on the positive behavior of employees
- Encourages employee involvement in decisions
- Communicates with employees in a timely and candid way, with emphasis on face-to-face communications
- Compensates employees competitively, under systems which reward excellence
- Provides training for organization/individual success
- Maintains effective performance appraisal systems
- Emphasizes promotion-from-within throughout the Company
- Selects managers and supervisors who demonstrate an appropriate blend of human relation skills and technical competence

questions and records this information very systematically. Examples of the questions asked (that reflect the common eight values listed earlier in "Managing Human Resources for the 21st Century at the Eaton Corporation") are shown in "Using Data for the 21st Century: Eaton Philosophy Audit Process Survey." Here, the HR department plays a critical role in determining what information is needed, how to get it, and who to feed it back to. And again, the line managers are working in partnership with the HR department and the employees to make this all happen.

Weyerhaeuser also uses data to support its change efforts. Believing that people are central to instituting total quality management and making other changes in the organization, CEO Jack Creighton and his top senior management team have developed and use a leadership behaviors survey. The survey contains items that reflect all the values of the company (listed in Chapter 1). Each executive gives the survey to her or his subordinates and asks them to evaluate the boss (anonymously, of course). The surveys are sent to an outside firm that scores them and sends the executive the results. The executives subsequently identify action plans for self-improvement. Through their own improvement, these executives also serve as role models for other managers in the company. As this leadership survey process cascades down the organization, more and more managers exhibit behaviors that are consistent with the needs of total quality management. The success of the process is built upon involvement, data collection, feedback, and development plans for improvement.

 THE ROLE OF THE HUMAN RESOURCE DEPARTMENT IN ORGANIZATIONAL CHANGE

From hiring and firing to training and performance management, every HR activity influences human resources and, thus, the success or failure of most efforts for organizational change and competition.[60] Keeping HR systems aligned with business strategies such as total quality management will be a major HR challenge going into the 21st century. AT&T and the Eaton Corporation provide specific illustrations of how the HR department can facilitate strategic business goals. In general, the HR department can:

⊚ Help formulate the firm's strategic business principles and strategies
⊚ Identify an HR mission or culture consistent with the business needs
⊚ Identify the key strategic HR imperatives that result from the business principles and strategies
⊚ Develop and implement HR initiatives and activities consistent with the HR culture

At AT&T, Fred Lane first helped develop the GBCS's key business principles and strategies, as well as the organization's seven values. Then Lane and his HR group developed their own mission statement. At the same time, using input from other managers, they identified the key strategic HR imperatives. Subsequent to this, they developed some very specific HR activities that link HR with the business. The details of these business principles, strategic HR imperatives, HR mission, and HR initiatives are shown in Exhibit 4.7.

Partnership between Human Resources and Line Managers

Line managers play a critical role in developing strategic HR imperatives. They contribute by providing answers to questions such as:

1. What are the specific HR implications of your business strategy and plan? (Implications will vary, of course, by the time horizon of the business plan.)
2. What types of skills not presently available will be needed?
3. What action steps are you taking to ensure that these skills will be available?
4. What types of skills presently available will no longer be needed?
5. What action steps are you taking to ensure a minimum of redundant skills: retraining? transfer? promotion? termination?
6. What employee behaviors do you need in order to make the implementation of your business strategy and plan a success?
7. What specific objectives do you have for each of questions 1 to 6?
8. Who is responsible for meeting these objectives?
9. What measures of success vis-à-vis the objectives are you using?
10. What contingency plans for revision and updating are available?
11. What do you need from the HR department to help you be successful?

❖ HUMAN RESOURCE PLANNING

In general, today the term *human resource planning* refers to the efforts of firms to identify the human resource implications of organizational changes and of key business issues, in order to align their human resources with needs resulting from those changes and issues.[61] Earlier, in times of environmental stability, human resource planning focused on matching human resource demand with human resource supply. At that time, forecasting human resource needs and planning the steps necessary to meet those needs was largely a numbers game. This process typically consisted of developing and implementing plans and programs to ensure that the right number and type of people were available at the right time and place to serve relatively predictable business needs. For example, if business was growing at 10 percent, top management would continue to add to the workforce by 10 percent: it worked before, it would work again.

GBCS' Human Resource Strategy and Planning Model

GBCS Business Principles	GBCS Human Resource Strategic Imperatives	Human Resource Mission	Focus Areas	Human Resource Plan Initiatives
Make *people* a key priority.	→ I. Associates actively take ownership for the business success at all levels, individually and as teams by improving associate value.			Learning forums such as Change Management and You GBCS Strategy Forum PEP Workshop Quality Curriculum
Use the *total quality management* approach to run our business.	→ II. GBCS HR contributes to increased shareholder value by achieving process improvements that increase productivity and customer satisfaction.		Cultural change →	Communication Platform Ask the President AnswerLine All Associates Broadcasts Bureaucracy Busters Associate dialogues
Rapidly and profitably globalize the business.	→ III. Ensuring GBCS HR readiness to expand its business initiatives into global markets which requires a business partner that is sensitive to the unique needs of various cultures and people.			Diversity Platform Pluralistic Leadership: Managing in a global society Celebration of Diversity National Diversity Council
Profitably grow by being the leader in customer-led applications of technology.	→ IV. HR strategic plans and processes support and are integrated with GBCS' strategic and business planning processes so that the HR Management System attracts, develops, rewards and retains associates who accept accountability for business success.	→ To create an environment where the achievement of business goals is realized through an acceptance of individual accountability by each Associate and by his/her commitment to performance excellence.	Rewards and recognition →	Progress Sharing Plan (PSP) Special Long Term Plan (SLTP) Recognition Platform Partner of Choice Trailblazers President's Council Achiever's Club Local recognition programs Touch Award
Be the *best value supplier.*	→ V. GBCS HR provides a level of service to internal and external customers that establishes the HR organization as their value added business partner. VI. The HR Leader and team are competent to provide leadership and support to GBCS by championing HR initiatives that contribute to GBCS's success.		Ownership →	Performance Excellence Partnership (PEP) Associate surveys ASI (Associate Satisfaction Index) AOS (Associate Opinion Survey) Organizational effectiveness Work teams Process teams

SOURCE: M. J. Plevel et al., "AT&T Global Business Communications Systems: Linking HR with Business Strategy," *Organizational Dynamics* (Winter 1994): 64.

From Numbers to Issues

Today, because the environment is changing organizations so dramatically, human resource planning has become more of a dynamic, volatile issues game.[62] The question is, "What are the issues of most importance to the business?" Increasingly, the key business issues flow from dynamic organizational changes, but they can also result from situations associated with greater predictability. Then the questions are: What are the HR implications? How can we orchestrate the way people are managed, in order to address the issues successfully? Yes, human resource planning still involves numbers, but as illustrated by AT&T and Eaton, it often involves much more: (1) crafting mission and value statements consistent with the business; (2) ensuring that employees understand and buy into the process of change; (3) systematically aligning the appropriate HR activities based upon an explicit understanding of the business; and (4) creating a dynamic human resource planning process that mirrors the business planning process and that identifies key changes and implications for managing human resources.

The human resource planning process must consider both the long-term and short-term HR implications of organizational changes. In fact, firms might typically go out five years in their planning and then work back to the present. Exhibit 4.8 shows the integration between business and human resource planning across several time horizons. This process can be used in dealing with the three major organizational changes already discussed in this chapter, or any other changes or key business issues specific to a particular company. Using human resource planning helps ensure that the human resource implications of organizational changes and key business issues are dealt with systematically and thoroughly.

FIVE PHASES OF THE HUMAN RESOURCE PLANNING PROCESS

Regardless of the time horizon or the issues, the HR planning process has five phases.[63]

Phase 1: Identify the Key Business Issues

The first phase of human resource planning involves gathering data to learn about and understand all aspects of the organization's environment. This helps the organization anticipate and plan for issues arising from both stable and dynamic conditions. For example, planning for increased global competition based on cost could involve assessing current labor productivity and probable future productivity. If a company is going to expand its revenue by 10 percent over each of the next five years, it *may* need more employees. Or perhaps improved technologies will mean a need for fewer employees. HR planners and line managers together would need to figure out just what the staffing implications are. To do this, they might use their HRIS (human resource information system) to measure performance levels in specific divisions, offices, occupational groups, or positions.

The organizational structure might also be examined. Is the distribution of positions at the top, middle, and lower levels of the organization appropriate for the organization of tomorrow? Which specific activities or functional areas can be expected to experience particularly severe growth or contraction? Where will the work and workers be located in the future: in the United States or abroad? in a central location, in regional offices, or in employees' homes?

■ *Exhibit 4.8*

Dynamic Linkages between Components of a Fully Integrated System of Business and Human Resource Planning

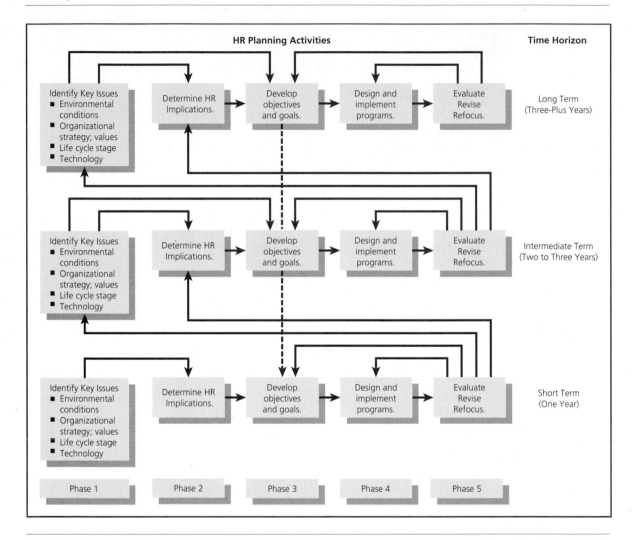

SOURCE: Adapted from S. E. Jackson and R. S. Schuler, "Human Resource Planning: Challenges for Industrial/Organizational Psychologists," *American Psychologist* (February 1990): 225.

Phase 2: Determine the Human Resource Implications

The objectives of the second phase are (a) to develop a clear understanding of how the information generated during phase 1 affects the future *demands* of the organization, and (b) to develop an accurate picture of the current *supply* available internally.

Forecasting Human Resource Demands. A variety of forecasting methods—some simple, some complex—can be used to determine an organization's demand for human resources. The type of forecast used depends on the time frame and the type of organization, the organization's size and dispersion, and the accuracy and certainty of available information. The time frame used in forecasting the organization's demand for human resources frequently parallels that used in forecasting the potential supply of human resources and the needs of the business. Comparing the demand and supply forecasts then determines the firm's short-, intermediate-, and long-term needs.

Forecasting involves approximations—not absolutes or certainties. The forecast quality depends on the accuracy of information and the predictability of events. The shorter the time horizon, the more predictable the events and the more accurate the information. For example, organizations are generally able to predict how many graduates they need for the coming year, but they are less able to predict how many they will need for the next five years.

A study indicates that 60 percent of major firms conduct some form of human resource forecast. More than half of these firms prepare forecasts for both the short term (one year) and the long term (five years). The emphasis is generally on predicting human resource demand rather than supply, perhaps because firms believe they have more control over demand than supply. In fact, more than half of the firms predict *only* demand, and only one-third formally forecast both supply and demand.[64]

Two classes of techniques that HR planners and line managers can use to determine their company's projected demand for human resources are *judgmental forecasts* and *conventional statistical projections*.

Judgmental forecasting employs experts and includes the most common method of predicting human resource demand, *managerial estimates.*[65] These estimates, based upon experience and familiarity with the employee productivity rates, can be made by top managers. Alternatively, the review process can begin at lower levels of management, with the results sent to higher levels for refinement. Useful information can include data on current and projected productivity levels, market demand, and sales, as well as current staffing levels and mobility information.

Another way to make judgments about human resource demand is the *Delphi technique.* At a Delphi meeting, experts take turns at presenting their forecasts and assumptions to the others, who then make revisions in their own forecasts. This combination process continues until a viable composite forecast emerges. The composite may represent specific projections or a range of projections, depending on the experts' positions.

A related method is the *nominal group technique.* Several people sit at a conference table and independently list their ideas on a sheet of paper.[66] The ideas presented are recorded on larger sheets of paper so that everyone can see all the ideas and refer to them in later parts of the session.

The Delphi and nominal group techniques are similar in process, but the Delphi technique is more frequently used to generate predictions, and the nominal group technique is more frequently used to identify current organizational problems and solutions to those problems.

Although all these judgmental forecasts rely on less data than those based on statistical methods such as linear and multiple linear regressions, they tend to dominate in practice.[67]

Forecasting Human Resource Supplies. Forecasted supply can be derived from both internal and external sources of information. Internal sources of supply are generally the focus at this stage of planning. External sources are considered in later phases, as part of the process of designing the practices needed to prepare for the future.

As with forecasting demand, two basic techniques help forecast internal labor supply: judgmental and statistical. Once made, the supply forecast can be compared with the human resource demand forecast to help determine, among other things, action programming for identifying human resource talent and balancing supply and demand forecasts. More often, however, the forecasting of labor supply is short-range, with the focus often on budgeting and controlling costs.

Forecasts for periods of five or more years, if made, usually address the company's need to plan for managerial replacements.[68] Two judgmental techniques used by organizations to make supply forecasts are replacement planning and succession planning. *Replacement planning* involves developing replacement charts to show the names of the current and potential occupants of positions. Potential promotions can be estimated by the performance levels of employees currently in jobs, and their development needs. Incumbents are listed directly under the job title. Individuals likely to fill potential vacancies are listed directly under the incumbent.

Succession planning is similar to replacement planning except that it is usually longer term and more developmental. Companies are practicing succession planning now more than ever, as they recognize that great leadership is needed to be effective in today's business environment. These same companies realize that what makes a good manager today may not be what makes a good manager in the future.

> *Renewed attention is focused on Human Resources and the strategic role it plays in securing our future success. Emphasis will grow on conducting meaningful interactive performance reviews linked to career development, training and education, and, very importantly, succession planning.*
>
> LINCOLN KROCHMAL, MD, President and CEO, Unilever Research, U.S.[69]

Consequently, companies such as AT&T, Unilever, and Allstate Insurance Company are trying to identify what will make a good manager in the years ahead and to design developmental activities to make sure the right people will be available with the right skills at the right time.[70]

Phase 3: Develop Human Resource Objectives and Goals

After phase 2 is completed, a great deal of descriptive information about current and future conditions is available. The next phase involves interpreting this information and using it to establish priorities and set objectives and goals.

With a short time horizon, which is often the time frame adopted for downsizing efforts, objectives are often easy to state in quantifiable terms. Examples of short-term human resource objectives include increasing the number of people who are attracted to the organization and apply for jobs (the applicant pool); attracting a different mix of applicants (with different skills, in different locations, etc.); improving the qualifications of new hires; increasing the length of time that desirable employees stay with the organization; decreasing the length of time that undesirable employees stay with the organization; and helping current and newly hired employees quickly develop the skills needed by the organization. Such objectives can generally be achieved in a straightforward way by applying state-of-the-art human resource management techniques and working with line managers to ensure agreement with and understanding of the program objectives.

The issues of total quality management and diversity management usually involve adopting intermediate- and long-term time frames for setting objectives. Differences in the types of objectives established for the shorter and longer term reflect differences in the types of changes that are feasible with two to five additional years of time. Thus, whereas short-term objectives include attracting, assessing, and assigning employees to jobs, intermediate-term objectives are more likely to include readjusting employees' skills, attitudes, and behaviors to fit major changes in the needs of the business, as well as adjusting human resource practices to fit changes in the needs of employees.

Longer-term objectives might include creating a major change in the corporate culture or positioning the firm to compete in totally new businesses.

Phase 4: Design and Implement Human Resource Policies, Programs, and Practices

Whereas the focus of phase 3 was establishing *what* to accomplish, phase 4 addresses *how* to accomplish it. What specific HR policies, programs, and practices will help the organization achieve its stated objectives? A great variety of activities can be designed during this phase. These include diversity programs to make organizations more attractive to a broader array of applicants; programs to improve socialization efforts so that good employees want to remain with the organization; programs to downsize or rightsize the organization, such as early retirement incentives and generous severance packages to complement the normal attrition process; and programs to empower employees and increase participation in order to ensure success in a change to total quality management. GBCS at AT&T established a communication platform (program), a diversity platform, and a performance excellence partnership during this phase (see Exhibit 4.7).

Phase 5: Evaluate, Revise, and Refocus

When a company offers a product to the external marketplace, it is almost certain to evaluate the success of that product using some type of objective indicator. Likewise, the success of products and services offered in the company's internal marketplace should be monitored closely. In this phase, the objectives set during phase 3 again come into play, for these define the criteria to be used in evaluating whether a program or initiative is successful or is in need of revision. For example, if personal self-development is the only objective one hopes to achieve from holding diversity awareness workshops, then asking employees whether the workshop experience was valuable may be the only data that should be collected. However, when large investments are made for the purposes of reducing turnover, attracting new or different employees to the firm, or improving team functioning, or all three, then data relevant to these objectives should be examined. As addressed more in Chapter 17, an HRIS facilitates evaluation by allowing for more thorough, rapid, and frequent collection of data.[71] The Eaton Corporation's audit process survey to measure how well a plant is doing in terms of the Eaton philosophy illustrates how evaluation data can be used both to monitor progress and to inform future actions. Where less-than-ideal conditions are found, the plant manager meets with the employees to develop a plan of action for improvement. In this case, the evaluation phase can also be thought of as the analysis phase for the next round of planning.

Evaluation of human resource plans and programs is an important process not only for determining the effectiveness of human resource planning but also for demonstrating the significance of both human resource activities and the human resource department in the organization as a whole. Without this phase, the improvement process can slow down significantly.

 SUMMARY

Change is everywhere, and as the 21st century approaches and unfolds, it becomes more pervasive and intense. Consequently, the organizations that are learning to deal with major change associated with the key business issues of today are positioning themselves quite nicely for the future. Some of the key issues companies are working on today include pursuing total quality management, managing downsizing and layoffs, and managing diversity. Each of these issues involves organizations and their people in major organizational change efforts. Successful organizational change, in turn, requires effective human resource planning. When major business issues are involved, the cycle of anticipating change, planning and carrying out change, and evaluating and readjusting becomes continuous. Change becomes the constant in managing human resources effectively.

Total quality management affects all aspects of an organization. For human resource management, one significant implication is the need to identify the appropriate HR policies and practices for total quality. Although no one set of HR policies and practices is the best, some are much more appropriate than others. The challenge is for each firm to select those that are most compatible with the rest of the organization, for example, top management's values, the technology of the organization, the nature of jobs, and the philosophy of the organization. The features on AT&Ts Global Business Communications Systems unit and on the Eaton Corporation illustrated just how complex this process can be, yet also just how significant the outcomes of effectively aligning the HR activities with total quality management are.

Downsizing and layoffs may result when companies manage for efficiency. Organizations are likely to continue in their efforts to become more competitive and efficient because of the worldwide onslaught of intense competition. As they do so, they are likely to find that some approaches are more effective than others. Effective approaches help companies to become more competitive while also attempting to minimize the negative side effects by respecting the rights of individuals to fairness and due process. Here, again, we see the importance of considering the needs of the employee as a key stakeholder in programs to manage human resources.

Managing diversity is another people-related business issue that is likely to remain a challenge well into the 21st century. Just as the workforce is becoming more diverse, so the need for organizations to maximize the skills and abilities of all employees is becoming even more critical if organizations are to be globally competitive. This means that major organizationwide changes must be put in place to ensure that all employees are given a fair chance for training and advancement and that ideas as well as people move throughout the organization. And just as diversity is an expansive phenomenon, so are the human resource activities that can be put in place to support organizationwide initiatives to manage diversity effectively.

Common to all these major issues are the necessary involvement of top management, the necessary involvement of the HR department, and the necessary use of human resource planning. Without the leadership and support, and even change, of top management, these three major issues are not likely to be effectively managed. At Weyerhaeuser, Jack Creighton and his top management staff realized that before they could expect the rest of the company to embrace total quality management, first they had to change. So change they did, and then the rest of the organization followed. The HR department helped the organization determine the content of the needed changes (e.g., what skills the employees needed), and the process of change (e.g., who should change first and how fast the changes should be made). Like any effort that affects the entire company, the changes required a great deal of business and human resource planning.

Human resource planning is critical for organizations engaged in organizationwide change efforts. This is because these programs involve many resources and require the change-modification-alignment of many HR policies and practices. Selecting, designing, and implementing the appropriate policies and practices requires a great deal of information, wise judgment, and managerial skills. A quick review of downsizing indicates just how much planning is required to do an effective job when laying off large numbers of employees while at the same time making conditions favorable for those who stay.

Proceeding through the tried-and-true steps and phases of human resource planning can help ensure that most of the bases are covered and that everything and everyone are in nearly the right place at nearly the right time.

 ## Discussion Questions

1. Describe how AT&T's Global Business Communications Systems unit went about linking its HR activities with the business.
2. What value do you think GBCS's vision and mission have in linking HR activities with the business?
3. Total quality management is a major organizational program; what implications does it have for managing human resources?
4. What lessons are offered by the feature "Managing Human Resources for the 21st Century at the Eaton Corporation"?
5. What aspects of downsizing and layoffs make some of these efforts more effective than others?
6. What are the legal considerations in downsizing and layoffs?
7. Describe the meaning of *managing diversity*.
8. What must the top management in most organizations do in order to manage total quality, downsizing and layoffs, and diversity successfully?
9. Describe the role of the HR department and its partnership with line managers and employees in making major organizational changes.
10. Describe how HR planning is different today than in earlier days when conditions were more stable and predictable.
11. Describe the phases of human resource planning.

 ## In-Class Projects

Lincoln Electric

1. Describe the objectives of the organizational change and planning activities at Lincoln.
2. Describe the degree to which these objectives are serving the business and HR objectives of Lincoln.
3. Describe Lincoln's organizational change and planning activities.
4. Describe the degree to which these activities are serving the organization's objectives.
5. How can the organizational change and planning activities be improved?

AAL

1. Describe the objectives of the organizational change and planning activities at AAL.
2. Describe the degree to which these objectives are serving the business and HR objectives of AAL.
3. Describe AAL's organizational change and planning activities.
4. Describe the degree to which these activities are serving the organization's objectives.
5. How can the organizational change and planning activities be improved?

Lincoln Electric and AAL

What characteristics of top management leadership do Donald F. Hastings and Jerry Laubenstein demonstrate?

Note: While there have not been many organizational changes at Lincoln Electric, there have been many at IPS/AAL. Much of your analysis here, therefore, might be more extensive and easier because of the detail provided in the end-of-text summary case on IPS/AAL.

 ## Field Project

Choose a company, either through a personal visit or by reading about it, and identify major organizational changes it is experiencing. Describe their implications for managing the organization's human resources. Then describe how these implications will affect the firm's HR activities.

Case Study:
PEOPLES TRUST COMPANY

The Peoples Trust Company first opened its doors to the public on June 1, 1875, with a total salaried staff of eight members: a treasurer; a secretary; and six assistants, three of whom held the positions of day guard, night guard, and messenger. Located in a large midwestern city, the original company occupied the basement floor of a new five-story office building with an electric-bell system, steam heat, and steam-driven elevator.

During its early years, the trust company concentrated its activities on providing vault services to its customers for the safekeeping of tangible items and securities. Management was able to develop the reputation of being a highly conservative trust company that concentrated on a relatively small and select market of wealthy individuals from the local area. In the years following, the vault service was retained as an accommodation to its customers, but the company's emphasis slowly shifted from vault service to a wider range of banking and trust services.

Until the early 1900s, banking services overshadowed trust services in terms of asset volume. Following the turn of the century, trust assets began to grow at an increasing rate. Over the years, the company was able to achieve an impressive record of sound and steady growth. According to a story often told in banking circles, "Peoples Trust was so conservative that they prospered even during the Depression!"

In 1973, with the appointment of a new president, a new era began for Peoples Trust Company. Between 1973 and 1982, trust assets under supervision rose by $145 million, and savings deposits increased by more than $20 million.

Accompanying this growth was the company's desire to fashion a new image for itself. In 1989, Robert Toller assumed the presidency of Peoples Trust. In 1982, he remarked, "[I]t should be said that the old concept of a trust involving merely the regular payment of income and preservation of capital is largely obsolete." Accordingly, the Investment Division of the company had been expanded and strengthened. Similar changes had been effected in the Trust and Estate Administrative Group and other customer service units. Among these were the improvement of accounting methods and procedures, the installation of electronic data processing systems, and the complete renovation of the company's current eight-floor building and facilities. Most recently, the company has extended its services into the field of management consulting. This had been acknowledged as a "pioneer" step for a banking institution. The president recently characterized the company as "an organization in the fiduciary business."

At the time these data were gathered, the company had a total of 602 employees. Of this number, 109 were in what is considered the "officer-group" positions of the company—that is, positions in which they were legally empowered to represent the company in a transaction. The company's relations with its employees over the years have been satisfactory, and Peoples Trust is generally recognized by city residents and those in suburban areas as a good place to work. The company hires most of its employees from the local area.

Before 1990, Peoples Trust provided satisfactory advancement opportunities for its employees, and it was possible for a young high school graduate who showed promise on the job to work up gradually to officer status. Graduates of banking institutions were also sought for employment with the company. Ordinarily, individuals were considered eligible for promotion to the jobs above them after they had thoroughly mastered the details of their present positions.

Before 1990, the total staff of the company was small enough so that there was no need to prepare official organization charts or job descriptions. Virtually all the employees knew each other on a first-name basis, and they were generally familiar with each other's area of job responsibility. New employees were rapidly able to learn "whom you had to go to for what."

In 1990, the company management called in an outside consultant to appraise its organizational structure and operations and to confer on the rapid expansion and diversification of banking services that the company had planned. The presence of the consultants and the subsequent preparation of organization charts and job descriptions reportedly "shook up a lot of people"—many feared loss of their jobs or, at least, substantial changes in the nature of work and assignments. However, there was little overt reaction among the officer-level employees in terms of turnover and other indexes of unrest.

Over the years, it had been the policy of the company to pay wages that were at least average or a little above the average paid by comparable banking organizations in the area. This, combined with favorable employee relations and the stable and prestigious nature of the work, resulted in a low turnover of personnel. The bulk of employee turnover occurred among the younger employees who filled clerical positions throughout the company's various departments.

Since 1990, the personnel picture at Peoples Trust has been shifting. Several changes have taken place in the top management of the company. By adding several new customer services, the company has altered the very nature of its business. This has resulted in a trend toward the "professionalization" of many of the officer-level positions in that these positions now require individuals with higher levels of education and broader abilities. The effect of these changes on current employees has been a matter of concern to several executives in the company, particularly to John Moore, manager of the Organization Planning and HR Department. Moore describes his picture of the situation as follows:

INTERVIEW WITH JOHN MOORE, VICE PRESIDENT, ORGANIZATION PLANNING AND HUMAN RESOURCES

Our problem here is one of a changing image and along with it the changing of people. As a trust company, we had no other ties with an individual's financial needs . . . we could only talk in terms of death. We wanted to be able to talk in terms of life, so we got active in the investment-advisory business.

The old wealth around here is pretty well locked up, so we wanted to provide services to new and growing organizations and to individuals who are accumulating wealth. Our problem is one of reorientation. We used to provide one service for one customer. We now want to enter new ventures, offer new services, attract new customers. The problem has become one of how to make the change . . . do we have the talent and the people to make the change?

We have a "band" of people [see Exhibits 1 and 2] in our organization . . . in the thirty-five–to–fifty age-group, who came in under the old hiring practices and ground rules. Given the new directions in which our company is moving and the changing job requirements, it's clear that, considering their current qualifications and capabilities, these individuals have nowhere to go. Some have been able to accept this; and this acceptance includes watching others move past them. Others have difficulty accepting it . . . a few have left . . . and we haven't discouraged anyone from leaving. For those who can't accept it, there is the problem of integrating their career strategy with ours. We've articulated our objectives clearly; now individuals need clarification of their own strategies.

As I see it, change caught up with these individuals. They had on-the-job training in their own areas, but that doesn't help them much to cope with the new demands. New functional areas are being melded on top of old

ones. For example, marketing is new; so is electronic data processing. They both require qualities that our existing employee staff didn't have.

To date, we have not approached any of these people in an individual way to discuss their problems with them. Our objectives are to further develop these people, but we'll first have to get the support of the department managers who supervise them.

We want to find ways to further develop people of the kind represented by this group through a variety of approaches. I am thinking here not only of formal job training in management development, but also of management techniques that would help individuals identify new kinds of qualifications or possible new standards of performance they must take into consideration in planning their own personal growth.

We also have to find ways to provide more opportunities for minorities and women in the organization, particularly at the officer level. Peoples Trust is a federal contractor, and we would like to be seen as an affirmative action employer and an organization where everyone has an equal chance for employment and promotion.

We have to change the conditioning of old times throughout the company. A recently hired MBA is now an officer. Years ago, that couldn't have happened so rapidly. And not everyone here is in agreement that the appointment I just mentioned *should* have happened the way it did. We have to develop support in our company for the new recruiting image.

There are two things which really concern me most about this whole problem:

1. We have a problem in underutilization of resources.
2. There is a problem which is presented to the growth and development of the company in having some of the individuals I have been discussing settled into key spots.

The company really bears the responsibility for the current situation as I described it. In addition, what this all means to me is that our HR function may change considerably over the coming year.

Other company executives expressed their views of the problems outlined by Moore as follows:

INTERVIEW WITH FRED BELLOWS, HUMAN RESOURCE PLANNING

Historically, we have been conservatively managed . . . you might say "ultraconservatively." But now we want to change that image. Several years ago, there was a revolution in top management. In 1989, Mr. Toller took over and brought in young people, many not from the banking field but from other types of business and consulting organizations. Our employment philosophy may be stated as follows: "We want above-average

■ *Exhibit 1*
Key Personnel Needing Development

Name	Age	Education	Date of Hire	Positions Held
Linda Horn	37	Two years at a technical institute of business administration	1985	Messenger Clearance clerk Accounting clerk Unit head (working supervisor) Section head (supervisor)
Richard Gaul*	30	Two-year junior college program in business administration	1987	Business machines operator Section head (supervisor) Operations officer
Fred James	35	BA degree from a local university, American Institute of Banking	1986	Loan clerk Teller Accounting unit head (working supervisor) Section head (supervisor)
Fran Wilson*	35	One year at a local university	1991	Methods analyst Operations unit head (working supervisor) Systems programmer Property accounting Department head
Martin Pfieffer*	32	Prep school	1987	Messenger Accounting clerk Section head (supervisor) Department head
James Klinger	38	BA degree from a local university	1982	Messenger Accounting clerk Records clerk Unit head (working supervisor) Administrative specialist
Karen Kissler*	35	BA degree from a local university co-op program	1984	Messenger Real property specialist Assistant estate officer
Charles Ferris	42	Two-year junior college program in business administration, American Institute of Banking	1972	Messenger Deposit accounting section head (supervisor) Unit head (working supervisor)
William Jagger	54	High school	1959	Messenger Trust liaison clerk Accounting clerk Bookkeeping section head
Thomas Geoghigan*	42	Two-year junior college program in business administration	1979	Messenger Securities accountant Property custodian Office manager Assistant operations officer

SOURCE: John Moore drew from his files a list of ten individuals who he felt were representative of the group whose lack of appropriate experience or qualifications created a roadblock to their future development and advancement with the company. These individuals are described in this exhibit.
*Officer

people . . . for above-average pay . . . and we want to give them a chance to learn and grow and move with the organization." This applies mainly to those in whom we see management-level potential.

They are told in their employment interview that if they don't see opportunity with us, then they should leave. This is in contrast to the old philosophy that this is a secure place to work, that you can stay here by keeping

■ *Exhibit 2*
Peoples Trust Company Organization Chart

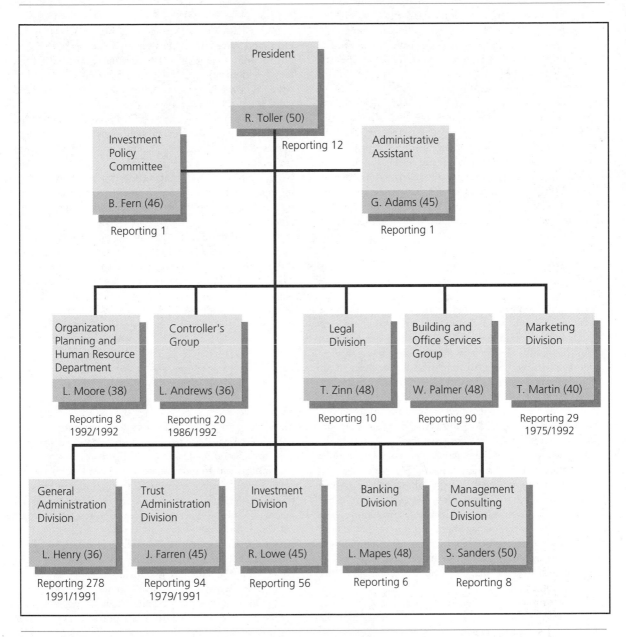

SOURCE: Numbers in parentheses indicate managers' ages. These are included for planning purposes only. Numbers below positions indicate numbers of subordinates.

*Year in which manager joined the company and year in which he or she assumed current position. For example, Larry Andrews joined Peoples Trust Company in 1986 and became controller in 1992.

your nose clean, and that you can sit and wait for potluck to become a trust officer.

Many people are caught in this changing philosophy. A case in the Trust Administration Division is a good example. There we have an employee in a grade ten job who has been with the bank eight years. We just hired a new person out of college who we put in that same grade, ten. Now they're both at the same level, but they're entirely different people in terms of education, social background, etcetera.

Now, the head of our Trust Division bucks this sort of thing. She argues that we don't need all "stars" in the company. Yet, the president wants young, dynamic individuals who can develop and be developed. So I'm trying to get the Trust Division to define, What does the job really require?

We have a number of people with two years of accounting training who have been with the company anywhere from six to nine years. Under our old system, they'd be okay, but under the new system, they're not. They're not realistic about their future. Our problem is that we're being honest, but few are getting the message.

We bring in a new individual . . . ask others to train that person . . . and then promote that person over their heads. We have people whose jobs we could get done for a lot less money. When, if ever, do we tell them to go elsewhere?

INTERVIEW WITH LARRY ANDREWS, CONTROLLER

There is no question but that there has been a complete revolution around here. In the past, we were in business to serve the community, to handle small accounts, to help the small investor who needed investment service. Our motto was "Help anyone who needs help." Our employees were geared to this kind of work orientation and felt at home with it. They could easily identify themselves with this sort of approach to doing business. Most people were quite comfortable; their personal goals coincided with the company goal.

But we found that we couldn't make any money conducting this kind of business. So, we've had to extend our services to attract people who have money and can afford our service. Now the company goal has changed. For example, the Trust Department is now concerned with the management of property in general. The "dead man's bank" has become the "live people's service organization." So we've had to create a kind of snob appeal that too many of our people can't identify with or don't believe in.

Many problems have emerged from these changes. Before, individuals' knowledge of the details of their jobs was their greatest asset. They worked to develop that knowledge and protected it. Now—and I'm speaking of supervisory jobs—the important factor is to have some familiarity with the work but to be able to work with people; to get others to do the detail. Too many of our people still don't understand this. . . .

The route to the top is no longer clear. Over a five-year period, this organization has changed. There have been reorganizations, new functions created, and some realignment of existing functions. Many who felt they had a clear line to something higher in the organization now find that that "something" isn't there anymore.

We've had lots of hiring-in at higher levels. Many old-timers have been bypassed. In some cases, the new, outside hirees came into jobs that never existed before, or were hired into a job that had previously existed but which is now a cut above what it was before. What used to be a top job is now a second or third spot.

What we need now are people who are "professional managers"—by that, I mean a supervisor versus a technical specialist. Years ago, supervision could be concentrated in a few key individuals . . . but in the past five years, we've grown 20 percent to 30 percent and have a management hierarchy. A person used to be able to grow up as a technical specialist and develop managerial skills secondarily.

To a small extent, it's a matter of personality too. We have a new president, and what is acceptable to him differs from what was acceptable to his predecessor. There's a new mix of personal favoritism that goes along with the new vogue. Technical specialists are "low need" as far as the company is concerned. I estimate we now have about thirty people in this category in officer-level jobs.

INTERVIEW WITH TOM MARTIN, MARKETING DIVISION HEAD

There have been many changes over the past six years. Mr. Toller took a look at the entire organization . . . and then hired a consultant to do an organizational study. It was sort of an outside stamp of approval.

His hope was to move some of the dead wood . . . the senior people who were past their peak and didn't represent what the company wanted anymore in its managerial and officer staff. Few of these individuals have the capacity to change, and for others, it may already be too late to change. Many had leveled off in their development long before these changes came about, and the changes just made it more apparent. Early retirement has been given to some of those over sixty. Others remained as titular head of their departments, but in essence report to a younger person who is really running the department.

Banking used to be a soft industry . . . you were hired and never fired. If you were a poor performer, you were given a lousy job that you could stay at. No one was ever called in and told to shape up. The pay was so poor it attracted people who wanted to work in a sheltered area, and they were satisfied to try and build a career in that area. So it was a job with low pay, high prestige, and some opportunity.

Our biggest problem is to convince people that they are not technicians anymore, that they are to *supervise* their subordinates and work to develop them. Apparently, for many older individuals, and younger ones, too, this is an impossible assignment. They can do the jobs themselves, but having anyone else do it in any other way runs against their grain.

If our rate of growth over the next ten years is as fast as the previous ten years, I'm afraid we can only absorb about 50 percent of our most promising people.

INTERVIEW WITH JANE FARREN, TRUST ADMINISTRATION DIVISION HEAD

We have several people for whom there is very little opportunity anymore. We just don't see any potential in these people. There are about fifteen of them who are in their forties and are really not capable of making any independent decisions. We're trying to get them to see other opportunities ... both inside and outside the company. For example, our Real Estate group was big in the 1970s and 1980s. We're trying to make it important again, and there may be some opportunities in that area.

To give you an idea of the problem we're faced with: One individual is really a personality problem. He's an attorney, but he can't get along with others. He wants people to come to him; he focuses on detail too much; and he has great difficulty in telling others what to do and how to do it. He has to do the job all by himself.

Another individual: We gave him a section to supervise, but he really hasn't measured up. But, he was the president's pet. I suppose we'll let him continue on ... he's fifty-seven ... and then retire him early.

INTERVIEW WITH L. HENRY, GENERAL ADMINISTRATION DIVISION

The company has been undergoing basic change. In the past, if people demonstrated technical competence, they were promoted, and that was fine while the company was a small, stable group and everyone knew what the other was thinking. But then, many in the senior group began to retire. With this "changing of the guard" and the growth of the company, many of us have lost communication with our counterparts. Many of us are new in this field, new to this company, and, of course, new to each other. But we recognize this, so half the communication problem is solved. In a sense, we're not constrained by "how it was done before."

My people have reacted to all this change by sitting back and waiting, seeing which way things are going to go, then I guess deciding whether they are going to join you or not. Most of my people are relatively recent employees—as a matter of fact, of the 278 people in my division, only 11 have been with the company more than ten years. Conversion to more advanced computer systems will really create a lot of changes in my area. ◉

SOURCE: This case was prepared and updated by Hrach Bedrosian, New York University, 1995.

Job Design: Meeting the Needs of the Business and Employees

We see the pilots as team leaders. We need to communicate effectively with each of the other work groups, even though the others work quite differently and some do their jobs on the ground. Soft skills are every bit as important to a pilot as the knowledge of how the hydraulic system works. If you don't have the capacity to get the input, insight and perspective of your co-workers, you're operating at a disadvantage.

PETE WOLFE, Captain, Southwest Airlines Company[1]

Managing Human Resources for the 21st Century at Lincoln Electric

In 1994, the production workers at Lincoln Electric in Cleveland, Ohio, received bonuses averaging between $18,000 and $22,000. Their total pay, including wages, profit sharing, and bonuses averaged almost $50,000. According to Paul J. Beddia, vice president of HR for Lincoln, the company's productivity rate was two to three times that of any other manufacturing operation that uses steel as its raw material and that employs more than one thousand people (Lincoln has about three thousand employees in the United States and more than twenty-five hundred outside the United States). Lincoln is widely cited as a firm with a highly motivated workforce, despite a lack of benefits. Lincoln has no paid holidays. It has no sick days that are paid by the firm. Workers must accept job reassignment and overtime as mandatory. They are awarded no seniority or special parking spaces or special cafeterias. Workers also take care of their own retirement needs. Yet, the postprobationary turnover is less than 3 percent a year and the company receives nearly one thousand unsolicited job applicants or resumes a month.

How does Lincoln do it? Although the firm's piecework system is credited with its high level of employee motivation, job design and job analysis are fundamental to making it all happen. What is seen today reflects the history of Lincoln. Its famous piecework system was established in 1914, the heyday of Frederick W. Taylor and scientific management. The jobs are—and have been—narrowly and clearly defined for individual work. The jobs and the procedures to perform them efficiently have been systematically and scientifically measured. The workers know what to expect, and they are trained to do a broad variety of jobs. With this combination, Lincoln is able to assign employees to a variety of jobs at a moment's notice without any loss of quality. The nature of the jobs allows specific and clear job descriptions to be made so that everyone knows what each job is about. Any changes to improve the jobs can be made through suggestions that are carefully studied by industrial engineers.

Thus, at a time when many organizations are implementing job enrichment and team-based job designs, Lincoln Electric remains an example that the scientific approach to job design can still work under some conditions for some individuals.[2]

The feature "Managing Human Resources for the 21st Century at Lincoln Electric" shows that the scientific management approach to job design can work very effectively. Although job enrichment programs are becoming popular, the more narrowly defined jobs from the days of scientific management may still be used. The scientific management approach to job design facilitates the writing of clear and understandable job descriptions. These, in turn, make it easier for everyone to learn how to do a job and for each person to learn several jobs. Thus, employees rotate from job to job, based on the customers' demands for products and services.

But there may be a time when the jobs themselves need to be changed. New technologies may alter the way work gets done. Or jobs may need to provide more motivational value to employees in anticipation of a workforce that is more productive, satisfied, involved, and committed. Or jobs may need to accommodate to the physical capabilities of individuals. More and more, jobs redesign occurs as part of a total organizational reengineering effort.

Companies can also change the time and location in which a job is performed. Such changes may be made for the same reasons that companies change the nature of a job: in response to new technology, to improve employee outcomes, to accommodate to physical capabilities, or to meet the needs of a reengineered company.

Job design is of tremendous importance to individuals, organizations, and society. For individuals, job designs shape the fabric of everyday life. In doing so, they shape society as a whole. For organizations, job designs are an integral piece of the structural foundation. In determining how work is done, they influence almost every aspect of managing human resources, including recruitment, selection, appraisal, compensation, training and development, safety and health, and union-management relations.

JOB DESIGN

Job design is the process by which the characteristics and qualities of jobs are determined and created. How should that hamburger be flipped, when, and by whom? Should the nurses at the hospital work rotating shifts, or is it better to always have the same staff on the graveyard shift? After the layoffs, will everyone just be expected to work harder, or is there a smarter way to design the work? Job design is the issue such questions raise. This chapter begins by identifying the purposes and importance of job design, then discusses alternative approaches to job design, and finally addresses legal considerations. In reading this material, keep in mind that the jobs that exist in most organizations have already been designed, either intentionally or by accident, so the issue of interest is really job *re*design. In this text, the term *job design* refers to creating new jobs as well as modifying existing jobs.

PURPOSES AND IMPORTANCE OF JOB DESIGN

Since the times of Frederick W. Taylor and scientific management, jobs such as those at Lincoln Electric have been designed for technical efficiency (finding the one best way to produce a product) and productivity (obtaining maximum use of human and physical

 Partnership in Job Design

Line Managers	Human Resource Professionals	Employees
Identify job design needs.	Identify job design needs.	Assist in job design.
Assist in job design and redesign.	Assist in job design and redesign.	Provide feedback about reactions to job design.
Empower employees and facilitate teamwork.	Help line managers and employees adjust to empowerment and teamwork.	Adopt a positive attitude and be willing to change.
Propose accommodations to employees.	Monitor and evaluate job design alternatives.	Accept responsibility for continually learning new ways to work.
Accommodate to employees.	Develop workplace accommodations.	Assist peers throughout the change process.
Work with HR professionals to align HR systems with job designs.	Work with line managers to align HR systems with job designs.	Request job accommodations, if needed.

resources).[3] Today, job design is taking on renewed importance as organizations look for ways to attract and accommodate to a workforce that is diverse in terms of age, gender, lifestyle, and capability. New organizational strategies are also stimulating discussions about how best to design. For example, companies such as Xerox and GE empower workers on their jobs and organize work in teams to facilitate high-quality and low-cost strategies. In pursuing its customer-focused strategy, TIE/Communications, a supplier of telecommunications equipment, realized that its technical specialists needed to take on some totally different job duties so that they could function as "ambassadors to the customers." In their new jobs, technicians would interact with the customers, find out the problems their customer's faced, and recommend solutions.[4] Even the San Diego Zoo has redesigned its jobs. In the old days, a keeper did the keeping and a gardener did the gardening: jobs were narrow and clearly defined. In the late 1980s, the zoo restructured to develop "bioclimatic zones," into which visitors enter and enjoy a naturalistic combination of plants and animals. In this new environment, the old narrow jobs do not make sense. Now, workers perform in teams and share tasks.[5]

APPROACHES TO JOB DESIGN

Regardless of the objectives to be met by job design, several different approaches may be used. Some approaches fit some purposes better than others, and, ultimately, all the approaches can be blended to fit an organization's unique needs. Each approach is grounded in its own discipline. These approaches, and their associated disciplines, are as follows:

- Mechanistic approach, based in mechanical engineering (also called scientific management)
- Human factors approach, based in biology and physiology
- Motivational approach, based in organizational psychology[6]

Mechanistic Approach

Using the mechanistic approach, which is also referred to as scientific management, job designers (typically, industrial engineers) take special pains to design jobs so that tasks can be performed as efficiently as possible. These tasks lend themselves well to time-and-motion studies and to incentive pay systems, each for the purpose of obtaining high productivity. Usually, the jobs of interest involve mostly physical activity rather than mental activity. For the sake of efficiency, work is often portioned into small, simple, standardized tasks that can easily be performed with little training. Each job involves essentially one task, which is performed over and over by one person. Consequently, each person and each job are highly specialized, as are the tools and procedures associated with the job. Traditional assembly line jobs and modern fast-food jobs are mechanistically designed.

Frederick W. Taylor, the father of this approach, believed such jobs would improve productivity because the performance of the workers was less dependent on employee initiative: "Under the old type of management, success depends almost entirely upon getting the 'initiative' of the workmen, and it is indeed a rare case in which this initiative is really attained. Under scientific management the 'initiative' of the workmen (that is, their hard work, their goodwill and their ingenuity) is obtained with absolute uniformity and to a greater extent than is possible under the old system."[7] In Taylor's new system, management's job also changed; specifically, the managers' responsibility became to determine scientifically precisely how to divide work into tasks; to select and train people to do the tasks; to ensure that the work is done in accordance with the "many rules, laws and formulae which replace the judgment of the individual;" and to "take over all the work for which they are better fitted." Taylor's philosophy was to clearly separate back work from brain work. The intent was not to demean in any way the work of laborers, nor was it to work people beyond their limits. Rather, the philosophy stressed the idea that the systematic collection and analysis of data was the best way to learn how to get work done as efficiently as possible. Employees could not be expected to collect such data and analyze it while also doing the work.

Some aspects of the mechanistic approach continue to be used today, although often in a modified form that reflects a newer philosophy about the involvement of workers in the design process. Successful use of this approach can be found at the Disney theme parks, where ride operators perform perfectly scripted roles repeatedly and predictably throughout their days and nights. Consistent with a view that high-quality service is reliable service—that is, the same regardless of time, place, or customer—Disney employees learn to anticipate every eventuality. To avoid seeming too mechanical in their performances, they even rehearse the ad-lib's. Such a mechanistic approach may seem counterintuitive for service-based companies, but it makes sense if the success of the business depends on high volume and low costs. These business imperatives are also common in fast-food restaurants and convenience stores.

UPS. Through meticulous application of the mechanistic approach to job design, the United Parcel Service has grown highly successful despite stiff competition. In the business where "a package is a package," UPS succeeds by its scientific work standard method. This method has been the key to gains in efficiency and productivity since the privately held company was founded in 1907.

In the 1920s, UPS engineers cut away the sides of UPS trucks to study how the drivers performed. The engineers then made changes in equipment and procedures to enhance workers' efficiency. In the 1990s, studies continued to be used to monitor the behaviors of workers. More than one thousand industrial engineers used a time study to set standards for a variety of closely supervised tasks. In return, the UPS drivers, all of whom are Teamsters, earn wages of approximately $17 an hour plus benefits. Because of the company's success in these endeavors, it was able to offer employees good job security.

Human Factors Approach

Human factors to be taken into account in designing jobs include the physical dimensions of the human body, the mechanical principles that govern physical movements, and physiology.[8]

Knowing the physical dimensions of the human body—such as the average width of the palm, the distance between hip and neck or between knee and ankle—aids in the design of equipment used on the job, including tools, machines, furniture, and vehicles. The objective of the human factors approach is to design equipment that fits the full range of physical features found in the population of people likely to be using the equipment. The human factors approach is often referred to as *ergonomics.*

Knowing the biomechanical principles that govern physical movement and muscle functioning helps in the design of equipment that minimizes the amount of stress and fatigue experienced as a result of doing work. For example, with an understanding of the biomechanics of the wrist, arm, and shoulder, office equipment can be designed to minimize the development of the painful carpal tunnel syndrome, which is characterized by numbness, tingling, soreness, and weakness in the hand and wrist.[9]

Finally, an understanding of the physiology of circulation, respiration, and metabolism allows work tasks to be designed to maximize the efficient use of energy. For example, with an understanding of how the body uses nutrients and oxygen when exerting moderate to heavy effort, work can be designed to maximize beneficial aerobic metabolism and minimize fatigue-inducing anaerobic metabolism.

Human Factors for an Aging Workforce. The human factors approach to job design has proved useful in automobile factories, where the physical capabilities of the workforces have changed. Union members protected from layoffs by their seniority are still at the same jobs, but they are now considerably older. At Chrysler's Jeep plant in Detroit, the average age is fifty-two, about six years above the industry average. Physically, this workforce simply does not perform at the level of a younger workforce, such as Japan's, where the average autoworker is age thirty-four. According to industrial relations expert Harley Shaiken: "The traditional way of improving productivity has been to speed up the line, but you can't do that with older workers. . . . you have skill and experience, which can be positive factors if you know how to harness them, [but] you can't rely on 52-year olds working at the limit to dig you out of a hole."[10]

To thrive, the auto industry has had to redesign its plants, installing ergonomic equipment to ease the strain. For example, overhead conveyor belts tilt auto bodies at angles that make assembly work less physically demanding, and the air guns used to drive screws are designed to reduce the stresses that cause carpal tunnel syndrome. Gyms have been installed, and workers have taken "back classes" to learn how to lift without injuring themselves.

Motivational Approach

If the mechanistic approach to job design focuses on tasks and the human factors approach focuses on the body, what is left for the focus of the motivational approach? The mind and heart. Of course, this is the terrain of psychologists.

The motivational approach begins with the assumption that jobs can be designed to stimulate employee motivation and to increase job satisfaction. This assumption is not incompatible with the human factors approach, but it does conflict with the mechanistic approach. Two types of motivational approach are commonly used: the individual contemporary approach and the team contemporary approach.

Individual Contemporary Approach. As shown in Exhibit 5.1, for employees who value meaningfulness, responsibility, and knowing the results, job enrichment to provide five core job characteristics leads to positive personal and work outcomes.[11]

Several different strategies can be used to design jobs with the motivating core characteristics. For example, with *job rotation,* each job remains the same but the employee moves from one job to another over a period of time. This increases task variety and, depending on the jobs involved, may also increase skill variety and boost job identity.

When job rotation is used, each job is usually narrowly defined. In contrast, *job enlargement* expands the tasks in a job. Thus, job enlargement is the opposite of scientific management. The objective of job enlargement is increasing skill variety. Task identity may also improve because employees in enlarged jobs often complete a "whole and identifiable piece of work." Job enlargement is usually achieved through *horizontal loading,* that is, adding more duties with the same types of task characteristics. This approach may increase skill variety, but it is also likely to foster resentment because the employee is expected to do more of the same. Therefore, some employees may benefit

■ *Exhibit 5.1*
The Core Job Characteristics Model

Core Job Characteristics	Critical Psychological States	Outcomes
Skill variety Job identity Job significance	Meaningfulness of the work	Less absenteeism Less turnover High satisfaction High motivation High-quality work performance
Job autonomy	Responsibility for outcomes of the work	
Feedback from job	Knowing the actual results of the work activities	

SOURCE: Adapted from J. R. Hackman and G. R. Oldham, *Work Redesign* (Reading, MA: Addison-Wesley, 1980): 77, Fig. 4.2. Reprinted with permission.

more from *job enrichment,* which uses *vertical loading* of responsibility, thereby closing the gap between who does the planning, organizing, and controlling of work and who actually does the work.[12]

Consider the following simple changes made to improve the jobs of 526 tellers working in thirty-eight banks in the Southwest:[13]

Before Job Redesign	After Job Redesign
Tellers cashed checks, and accepted deposits and payments; tellers referred travelers and commercial customers to special clerks; bookkeepers posted checks, deposits, and so forth.	Tellers handled all these tasks, increasing skill variety and job identity; tellers were given autonomy to handle large, significant transactions for local accounts.
Feedback on errors was available at the end of the day or the next day.	Feedback about errors was available almost immediately.
No feedback was available about work volume.	Feedback about volume was continuously displayed on a computer monitor.
Tellers had no signature line to sign off on.	Tellers signed their names for each transaction, in recognition of their responsibility for the work.

The tellers found their new jobs to be more motivating, and, importantly, their job performance improved significantly.

Of course, this is only one example, so you might still wonder, "Does designing jobs according to the model shown in Exhibit 5.1 really work?" Dozens of studies involving thousands of employees in many types of jobs indicate that the answer to this question is yes. Both performance and job satisfaction go up after jobs are redesigned to provide more skill variety, task identity, significance, autonomy, and feedback.[14] These beneficial outcomes are especially likely to be seen among employees with high *growth needs.* Such people enjoy challenges, like to be creative and innovative, and are comfortable being in positions where they have high levels of responsibility.[15]

Today, providing job autonomy appears to be a particularly effective way to obtain high worker commitment and total quality, because many employees value responsibility, which flows from having job autonomy. Companies that offer employees autonomy realize that the implications of changing the work reach far beyond simply the design of the job. Many other aspects of managing human resources must be aligned to fit these new jobs. In particular, companies where jobs are designed to give high levels of autonomy usually have these characteristics:

- They invest a lot of time and effort in hiring, to make sure new recruits can handle workplace freedom.
- Their organizational hierarchy is flat.
- They set loose guidelines, so workers know their decision-making parameters.
- Accountability is paramount. Results matter as much as and sometimes more than process.
- High-quality performance is always expected.
- Openness and strong communication are encouraged.
- Employee satisfaction is a core value.[16]

Thus, for companies wanting to redesign jobs and empower their employees, making the change is not as simple as it might at first seem. Nevertheless, many large companies like AAL, FedEx, and the Eaton Corporation have been moving in this direction. Small companies like the following are by nature already there:

ACTION INSTRUMENT, San Diego, California, Instrument Manufacturer
Two hundred employees, $25 million in sales

Urges employees to solve problems that they discover. Sets loose boundaries to define scope of autonomy.

ALPHATRONIX, Research Triangle Park, North Carolina, Maker of Optical Storage Systems
Seventy employees, $11.8 million in sales

Puts recruits through up to five interviews, then assigns them their own projects. Has employees set their own goals and timetables for project completion.

JOB BOSS SOFTWARE, Minneapolis, Minnesota, Developer of Factory Software
Forty employees, $2.3 million in sales

Encourages employees to take ownership of their jobs. Hires rigorously, trains well, and then grants employees wide latitude. Has managers act more as facilitators than as bosses.[17]

Team Contemporary Approach. Whereas the individual contemporary and scientific approaches design jobs for individuals, the team contemporary approach designs jobs for groups of individuals. These team designs generally show a concern for the social needs of individuals as well as the constraints of the technology. Teams of workers often rotate jobs and may follow the product they are working on to the last step in the process. If the product is large—for example, an automobile—teams may be designed around sections of the final car; each group then passes its section to the next team.

In the team contemporary design, each worker learns to handle several duties, many requiring different skills. When faced with decisions, teams generally try to involve all members. Thus, teams can satisfy preferences for achievement and task accomplishment and some preferences for social interaction. When team members work well together, team decisions and behaviors result in greater output.

Today, teamwork has become so critical for organizations that many are elevating it to a core value.[18] As a core value at Weyerhaeuser, it is stated and defined as follows:

Teamwork: Business results are improved by using teams to combine the talents and ideas of people. That means:

- People work together and empower each other to be successful.
- People have the skills and information that enable them to participate as effective team members and decision makers.
- Diverse work teams, cross-functional and multicultural, are formed where opportunities exist to enhance business results across organizations.

Managing Human Resources for the 21st Century at Kodak

When the 1980s came to a close, the picture of the future was fuzzy for the black-and-white film division of Rochester, New York–based Eastman Kodak Company. The division, which produces seven thousand products from 250 product lines, was regarded by employees as the worst place in the company to work. It suffered from budget overruns, huge inventories, waste, poor deliveries, and late delivery of products. It was actually losing money for the company. In August 1989, "Mother" Kodak gave the division eighteen months to turn around its financial performance or stop making product.

It met the challenge. Led by a fifteen-member team made up of managers from the division (on which the HR manager played a significant role), the fifteen hundred employees of the black-and-white division reengineered their workplace from a traditional manufacturing process organized by functions to a team-driven process organized by work flow. The flow system flattened out the organization, breaking down the boundaries between functions and eliminating the every-function-for-itself mentality. It created a seamless process for the manufacture of film and paper from raw materials at one end to finished goods at the other.

Today, the black-and-white division—nicknamed Team Zebra—is one of Kodak's leading business units in product quality, customer satisfaction, and overall operating efficiency. Working in teams, employees increased on-time delivery rates to 95 percent. They cut inventories in half within the first two

years after the reorganization, saving a total of $50 million. They reduced waste by 75 percent, generating $40 million in cost reductions within the first two years, without cutting down on the number of products produced. In fact, they increased productivity by 15 to 20 percent each year.

The results of the department's turnaround are significant. Just as significant, however, is how the department accomplished the turnaround. Changing to an empowered, team-based enterprise required transforming an entire culture and mindset. Stephen J. Frangos, manager of Kodak's black-and-white division at the time of the reorganization, credits an active HR strategy as key.

That strategy encompassed relying on the company's inner human resources rather than investing in new equipment and technical programs, or cutting costs and dropping product lines. It required encouraging risk taking, using positive reinforcement to unleash creativity, and creating an empowered environment. It also required refining practices that increased the organization's capabilities in the areas of the selection of people, rewards and recognition, appraisals, work structures, capability building, and communications.

Martha Britt, human resource manager for the black-and-white division at the time of the reorganization, says, "We had to put together a strategy that would build the capability, the understanding, and the desire of the fifteen hundred partners to play a key role in turning the business around."[20]

- We continuously measure employee involvement and develop action plans to improve.
- Where work interdependencies exist, work teams are utilized.[19]

Although teamwork may be unusual for some employees, it appears that most employees are able to adapt to it. It may take time to install teams and attain high levels of teamwork, but the benefits can be substantial, as illustrated in the feature "Managing Human Resources for the 21st Century at Kodak."

Taking Time to Learn Teamwork. Because working in teams is new to many employees and organizations, making the change to teams takes time. Effective teamwork and organizational success do not happen overnight. Typically, teams start out making only a few decisions. After time, training, and familiarity, they begin to make many more decisions. Essentially, the team members pass through stages of greater empowerment (decision making). In each new stage, they make more decisions, until they can eventually be called *self-managed teams*.

Tasks about which self-managed teams can make decisions include these:

- Perform routine equipment maintenance.
- Ensure workplace cleanliness.
- Stop production for quality problems.
- Assign daily tasks.
- Make team-member assignments.
- Identify training needs.
- Select team members.
- Develop work methods and procedures.
- Ensure workplace safety.
- Monitor and report on unit performance.
- Set team production goals.
- Provide training.
- Coordinate work with suppliers and vendors.
- Discipline employees.
- Prepare unit budgets.
- Conduct performance appraisals.[21]

Being Successful. Getting to the point where a team is self-managed and is capable of making decisions and performing related activities requires change and commitment in several organizational areas. According to one large study, several barriers may inhibit the success of working teams. The study was conducted by Wilson Learning Corporation of Eden Prairie, Minnesota, which offers team development training. To improve its understanding of clients' needs, Wilson conducted two hundred fifteen-minute interviews with team facilitators and administrators, plus twenty-five hour-long interviews. It also used survey responses from twenty-five thousand people working in forty-five hundred teams. Wilson concluded that the biggest barriers to effective teams had little to do with the team process itself, but it had a lot to do with organizational barriers. For example, most teams operated in companies that continued to use individual-based compensation and performance appraisal systems. Teams also felt hampered by their inability to access crucial information from their own companies, which were concerned about leakage of proprietary information.[22] The feature story about Kodak's Team Zebra illustrates the importance of making system-level changes when redesigning jobs around teamwork.

Individual team members also create barriers to effective team designs. It is not enough to change the job design; people need to change, too. Perhaps most important, employees need to develop new skills. The areas in which employees often need individual training, according to Michael Leimbach, director of research for Wilson Learning Corporation, include the following:

- *Advocating.* Team members must learn how to "sell" their point of view to others.
- *Inquiring.* Employees should know how to listen to other team members, as well as to "interview" other employees for needed information.
- *Tension Management.* Instead of avoiding conflict, workers should learn how to create constructive conflict and manage the resulting tension.
- *Sharing Responsibility.* To become a "team player," employees should learn to align personal objectives with the team's objectives, and understand their roles in creating shared outcomes.
- *Leadership.* Employees should understand their roles in leading the team to success.
- *Valuing Diversity.* A team's success results largely from members' differences in expertise, expectations, personalities, and work styles. Therefore, team members should learn to value their differences, instead of striving for sameness.
- *Self-Awareness.* Employees must be willing and able to accept constructive criticism from others, and must learn to be self-critical.[23]

Besides these changes in the administrative system and in individual team members, total support must be available from all line managers and union representatives. Ultimately, the success of a team depends on effective partnership.[24]

Which Design to Use?

Exhibit 5.2 lists some of the advantages and disadvantages of each approach to job design. Clearly, no single approach is the best approach. In fact, often, a combination of approaches is needed. Which approach a company chooses necessarily depends in part on cost considerations and the available technology. It can also depend on the task. For example, one study of forty-five projects at a dozen large companies revealed that teams are especially effective for developing and launching new products, but product modification is better done by individuals.[25] And as it did at UPS and FedEx, the selection of a design approach may even depend on the sheer size of the company.

Job design choices depend as well on the rest of what is happening in the company. In particular, they may depend on the history of the company. For example, UPS and Lincoln Electric have long histories of using the mechanistic and human factors approaches to job design.

Of course, the effectiveness of each approach also depends on the nature of the workforce, particularly the physical and psychological needs of workers. At Kodak, FedEx, and AAL, the employees respond positively to their jobs. Working under rather

■ *Exhibit 5.2*

Comparison of Job Design Approaches

Approach	Advantages	Disadvantages
Mechanistic	Ensures predictability Provides clarity	May be boring May result in absenteeism, sabotage, and turnover
Human factors	Accommodates jobs to people Breaks down physical barriers Makes more jobs accessible to more people	May be costly for some jobs Is impractical if structural characteristics of the organization make job change impossible
Motivational Individual contemporary	Satisfies needs for responsibility, growth, and knowledge of results Provides growth opportunity Reduces boredom Increases performance Improves morale	May not work for people who prefer routine May require higher pay May be difficult to implement for jobs that are hard to enrich Requires some changes in the total HR system
Team contemporary	Provides social interaction Provides variety May improve service provided to customers Reduces absenteeism problem	May not work for people who prefer to work alone Requires training in interpersonal skills Requires a long time to make a major change May require major changes in the structure of the organization and in the HR system

different job conditions, the employees at Lincoln Electric and UPS also respond positively.

Whether a particular approach is effective may also depend on what top management believes is necessary for the success of the business. For example, based on all the information it had, Kodak Team Zebra's management thought changing to teamwork was critical to the survival of the business.

At AAL, Jerry Laubenstein and his team thought teams would be critical to serving the needs of their field agents and the ultimate customer, the policyholder. But this was only one piece of the puzzle. Job changes within the Insurance Product Services Department were preceded by a change in the vision, mission, business structure, and desired outcomes. These changes, in effect, became the data that Laubenstein and his IPS employees used to redesign their jobs around teams. These changes are summarized in the feature "Using Data for the 21st Century: Context for Job Design at IPS."

Management's views of its responsibility to society as a whole may also play a role in choosing how to design work. For example, since 1985, the Chicago Marriott has teamed up with the International Association of Machinists Center for Administering Rehabilitation and Employment Services (IAM CARES) to provide training and jobs for people with severe disabilities. "The benefit for us is that we hire a percentage of these kids and therefore give back to the community," explains Bryon Petersen, director of HR at the Chicago Marriott. For people with learning disabilities or who have low intelligence, jobs designed according to Taylor's mechanistic approach may be ideal. But Petersen is also quick to point out that partnership is key to this program's success—in this case, Marriott's partnership with the IAM CARES staff is essential because the IAM CARES staff will jump in to resolve problems. IAM CARES agrees that partnership is essential; it needs support from Marriott's CEO, HR, and direct supervisors.[26]

ALTERNATIVE WORK ARRANGEMENTS FOR EMPLOYEE ACCOMMODATION

The growing number of single-parent families, the high costs of commuting, the desire for larger blocks of personal time, and the desire of older workers to reduce their hours, all create conflict for today's workers. Alternative work arrangements can reduce the stresses caused by such conflict between job demands, family needs, leisure values, and educational needs. Thus, organizations increase their attractiveness to a more diverse pool of applicants if they are willing to accommodate work schedules to individuals.

Offering flexibility in time schedules, job sharing, and telecommuting arrangements are also ways to comply with the ADA. For these and a variety of other reasons, many firms are restructuring jobs:

In a survey conducted by New York City–based William M. Mercer, Inc., three-fourths of the nearly 3,400 responding mid- to large-size companies report that they have restructured jobs in one or more ways. Here are the most common alterations:

- ⊚ About 80% of the companies reporting changes in job structure support their full-time work force with regular, part-time employees. Most provide benefit coverage to these workers, and 72% allow them to participate in a savings or 401(k) plan.
- ⊚ Almost half (1,000) of the 2,550 employers that reported having restructured jobs offer job-sharing arrangements, in which two part-time employees fill what would otherwise be one full-time job.
- ⊚ More than half (63%) of those that restructured jobs allow employees to choose flexible work schedules, such as a workweek of four 10-hour days rather than the traditional five

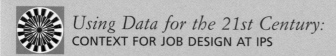

Using Data for the 21st Century:
CONTEXT FOR JOB DESIGN AT IPS

Several types of data drove AAL's IPS reorganization and redesign efforts. First came the industry data, which convinced CEO Richard L. Gunderson that AAL needed to cut costs by over $50 million over a five-year period. Next came the company's data. With a mandate for change, a team of twelve managers was assembled to systematically collect data internally. After receiving training in how to conduct structured interviews, the team interviewed two-hundred employees selected to represent the broad array of perspectives within the organization. The data they collected helped define the current situation at AAL and established the need for change. Then, within the IPS unit, data collection and use continued. The IPS management team held a retreat to share views (soft data) and craft a vision to guide its efforts. These were the results:

IPS MISSION

To enable the agent, the primary customer, to do an even better job of serving the policyholder, the ultimate customer.

IPS VISION AND STRUCTURE

Regionalization plus "one-team" processing.

DESIRED OUTCOMES

1. A *customer-driven* organization. Customers are field staff and members. Being customer driven includes:

   • Listening to the customer for wants or needs
   • Being responsive and proactive to customer wants or needs

   • Acknowledging that the customer's problem is the provider's problem
   • Seeing the provider as a problem solver rather than an order taker
   • Informing and educating the customer
   • Using customer-informed measures of how well customer needs are being met

2. A strong *team* relationship with the field staff and internal support units. The need for *networking* is heavily stressed.
3. A *flat* organization with fewer levels of supervision and fewer staff.
4. *One-stop* processing as fully as possible to avoid the delays and lack of ownership associated with an assembly line approach.
5. A quality management team that will model participative management, more involvement of employees in deciding how work is to be accomplished, and more decision-making authority for employees in carrying out their day-to-day assignments.

A systematic use of data gave the change effort direction early on. Then, following the changes, data were again collected systematically, in order to monitor and evaluate. One source of data was monthly employee feedback sessions held with department heads. Another was a survey conducted periodically to assess attitudes. The survey proved especially helpful for identifying problems that needed to be addressed during the job redesign implementation. Finally, AAL kept an eye on the bottom line, and it was able to document that all its efforts eventually paid off, as evidenced by a 29 percent increase in productivity.[27]

8-hour days. However, half of these organizations offer flexible work schedules only to selected individuals.

◉ Only one-fifth (20%) of the organizations are implementing telecommuting programs. Those that do, however, generally benefit from the arrangements, describing them as "fairly successful" (61%) or "very successful" (36%).[28]

Although these alternative accommodations are popular, a substantial number of workers are still on some form of standard schedule.

Standard Work Schedules

In the 1860s, the average workweek was seventy-two hours—twelve hours a day, six days a week. It was fifty-eight hours in 1900, and is approximately forty hours today. Standard work schedules include day, evening, and night sessions as well as overtime, part-time, and shift work. Since the end of World War I, shift work systems have become more prevalent in industrialized countries. Currently, about 20 percent of all industrial workers in Europe and the United States are on shift work schedules.[29] The percentage of employees on part-time schedules has also increased steadily.[30]

All these standard work schedules have advantages and disadvantages. Initially, employees may select a given schedule, but after that, the days of the week (five) and the hours of the day (eight) are generally fixed. Because employee preferences and interests change over time, what was once an appropriate work schedule may at some point no longer be so. If alternative arrangements are not provided, the employee may leave the organization. Furthermore, as they lose employees, organizations may have a difficult time attracting similar types of people with similar preferences. As a result, it pays to give employees a choice between a nonstandard and a standard schedule, as well as a choice of hours, days, total number of hours a week, and even total number of hours a year.

Flextime Schedules

Flextime, a nonstandard work schedule, is popular with organizations because it can decrease absenteeism; increase employee morale; induce better labor-management relations; and encourage a high level of employee participation in decision making, control over the job, and discretion. Simply stated, flextime gives employees daily choice in the timing of work and nonwork activities.[31] Consideration is given to *band width,* or the maximum length of the workday. This band, often ranging between ten and sixteen hours, is divided into core time and flexible time. *Core time* is when the employee *has* to work; *flexible time* is when the employee *chooses* to work. Exhibit 5.3 shows how a twelve-hour band width can be divided into blocks of flexible and core times.

Among the advantages of flextime is its ability to increase overall employee productivity. It also allows organizations to accommodate employee preferences, some of which may be legally protected, such as reasonable religious obligations. On the other hand, flextime forces the supervisor to do more planning; sometimes makes communication difficult between employees, especially those with different schedules; and complicates the task of keeping records of employees' hours. Furthermore, most flextime schedules still require employees to work five days a week.

Compressed Workweeks

An option for employees who want to work fewer than five days a week is *compressed workweeks.* By extending the workday beyond the standard eight hours, employees generally need to work only three to four days to equal a standard forty-hour week. At two General Tire and Rubber plants, some employees work only two twelve-hour shifts each weekend and yet are considered full-time employees because weekend hours are weighted as "time-and-a-half." Compressed workweeks are a regular part of certain occupations, such as nursing.

Compressed workweeks permit an organization to make better use of its equipment while decreasing turnover and absenteeism. Legal and scheduling problems may

■ *Exhibit 5.3*
Flextime Scheduling

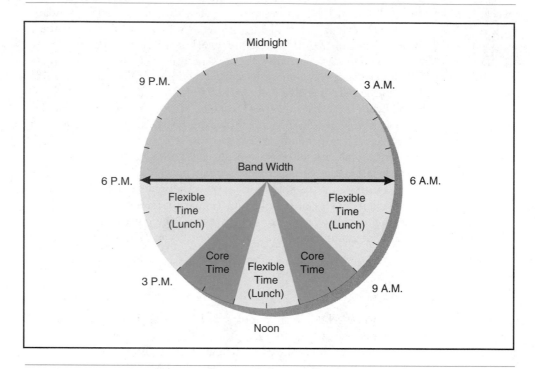

SOURCE: Adapted from A. Cohen and H. Gadon, *Alternative Work Schedules: Integrating Individual and Organizational Needs* (Reading, MA: Addison-Wesley, 1978), 35. © 1978. Reprinted with permission.

accompany such arrangements, but legal exceptions can be made, and scheduling can become a joint negotiation process between supervisors and employees.

Permanent Part-Time Schedules, Job Sharing, and Contingent Schedules

Traditionally, part-time work has meant work that lasted only for a short time, such as temporary clerking in retail stores during holiday periods. Now some organizations have designated *permanent part-time positions.* A permanent part-time work schedule may be a shortened daily schedule (e.g., from 1:00 P.M. to 5:00 P.M.) or an odd-hour shift (e.g., from 5:00 P.M. to 9:00 P.M.). Organizations may also use permanent part-time schedules to fill in the remainder of a day composed of two ten-hour shifts (representing a compressed workweek).[32]

Job sharing is a particular type of part-time work. In job sharing, two people divide the responsibility for a regular full-time job. Both may work half the job, or one may work more hours than the other. Traditional part-time workers generally receive little or no indirect compensation, but workers on permanent part-time and job-sharing schedules often do. The benefits of these workers are not equal to those of full-time workers but are prorated according to the amount of time worked.

Both permanent part-time work and job sharing provide the organization and individual with opportunities that might not otherwise be available. They offer staffing flexibility that can expand or contract to meet actual demands, using the skills of employees who are at least as productive as, if not more productive than, regular full-time employees. Individuals benefit from being able to enjoy permanent work with less than a full-time commitment to the company.

For staffing flexibility, companies may also use *contingent workers,* those working under temporary arrangements. Contingent workers, in contrast to permanent part-time workers, have a more temporary relationship with the company and therefore may be less loyal.

Electronic and Industrial Cottages

Work-at-home arrangements can be made for people with a full-time commitment to the company and for those wanting only part-time employment.[33] Increasingly, individuals who work at home can easily be plugged into the office through their computers. In essence, the employee's home then becomes an *electronic cottage.* Individuals can also take home work that involves assembly, such as small toys. After a batch is done, the worker takes it to the regular plant and turns it in for more parts. In this case, the home becomes an *industrial cottage.*[34]

The use of industrial and electronic cottages is increasing. These arrangements offer workers another choice as well as more freedom. One drawback is the difficulty of protecting the health and safety of employees at home. Another is the difficulty of ensuring that employees are paid a fair wage for their work. Also, state and federal laws may restrict home work: for example, a federal law prohibits commercial knitting at home. The restrictions must be dealt with carefully if the use of these cottages is to remain a viable option.

Telecommuting

An extension of the industrial and electric cottages is telecommuting. It allows interaction with the office while working at home or while traveling. You see many people with portable, cellular telephones on the street or in their cars, conducting business. This is a form of telecommuting. Cellular or mobile phones, fax machines, and PCs are making it possible for people to do work almost anytime and anywhere. Although it may be difficult for a company to monitor the performance of people who telecommute, this is becoming another way companies can accommodate to and attract employees.[35]

LEGAL CONSIDERATIONS IN JOB DESIGN

Today, companies are concerned not only about creating jobs from the beginning, as with small firms just starting, but also with creating new job designs from existing jobs. A job redesign effort at AT&T was an early example of how job redesign can be used to accommodate the physical differences between men and women. In the mid-1970s, AT&T entered into an agreement with the Equal Employment Opportunity Commission to increase the representation of women in telephone line repair jobs, which had been male dominated. To achieve this objective, AT&T had to accommodate to the physical differences in size between men and women by changing the job design for telephone pole climbers. The telephone line repair workers had to climb up the poles by placing their feet on horizontal bars on either side of the poles. With the old job design, most women were unable to climb the poles simply because the bars were too far apart. AT&T resolved this situation by reducing the distance between the bars. Although this change had to be made on several thousand poles, the accommodation was regarded as "reasonable."[36]

Positioning for the 21st Century:
AMERICANS WITH DISABILITIES ACT OF 1990

"I have a doctor's note that says I can return to my job, but I have to avoid contact with latex," medical technician Dan Coleman explained.

"I'm truly sorry, but we can't accept this," HR director Pat Kubricki responded. "All medical technicians have to wear rubber gloves in compliance with safety rules, so there's no way you can come back to work and avoid contact with latex."

Was this employer's action justified?

Facts: A worker whose duties included emergency medical work had been employed more than ten years without any problems on the job. Due to increasing concerns over blood-borne pathogens such as AIDS, new health guidelines required the employee to wear latex gloves on the job whenever he might have contact with bodily fluids. The employee eventually developed an allergy to both the gloves and a powder in the gloves that made them easier to get on and off.

In time, the employee became so highly sensitized that he had an allergic reaction to powder residue on the steering wheel of a vehicle that previously had been operated by another employee wearing the latex gloves. After he suffered a series of allergic reactions requiring emergency medical care, a doctor told the employee that for him to be completely risk free, everyone in his workplace would have to stop using the latex gloves.

The employee eventually missed so much work that he used up all his sick leave. When he attempted to return to work, he brought a doctor's note explaining that he must "avoid all contact with latex and latex products." The employer refused to allow his return, saying it would be impossible for the employee to avoid such contact.

The employee objected to the decision, asserting that it amounted to termination. He charged that the employer was obligated to make reasonable accommodations to facilitate his return to work.

Decision: The employer must reinstate the worker and accommodate his disability.

Discussion: The employee's medical records show that he is fully able to perform his job duties as long as he avoids contact with latex gloves and the powder in the gloves, the arbiter notes. Therefore, the arbiter finds, the "entire department would have to be supplied with vinyl or powderfree, hypoallergenic latex gloves" in order for the employee to return to his job.

Supplying different gloves is an "entirely reasonable accommodation" to protect the job of a ten-year employee, the arbiter says. The cost of the accommodation would be "minimal," at about $150 extra a year, he points out. Moreover, medical journals suggest that the prevalence of latex allergies is increasing, and it is likely that other employees would eventually develop allergies to latex as well. Finding the accommodation an appropriate solution to the problem, the arbiter orders the employer to reinstate the employee with back pay and supply new gloves to all employees.[37]

Reasonable accommodation is now a common term because of the Americans with Disabilities Act of 1990. For organizations with fifteen or more employees, the ADA "prohibits bias against qualified individuals with disabilities in all aspects of employment and requires employers to make reasonable accommodations for such individuals so long as the accommodations do not pose an undue hardship to the employer's business."[38] Exactly what this reasonable accommodation means in practice varies with the nature of the company. AT&T had to change the spacing of horizontal bars. Subsequently, bars were replaced by spiked shoes. Because it believed it had found an unusually effective employee, UPS considered it reasonable to spend $11,000 for equipment that enabled a blind man to work as a computer programming instructor.[39] Another employer was told that it was reasonable to supply different gloves to all its medical personnel when one worker developed an allergy to latex and the powder in latex gloves (see the feature "Positioning for the 21st Century: Americans with Disabilities Act of 1990").

[D]etermining what is "reasonable" is a fact-specific issue that will vary with the employer and individual in question. Under various circumstances, appropriate accommodations might include such things as making existing facilities readily accessible, job restructuring, modifying work schedules, acquiring or modifying equipment or devices, or providing readers or interpreters.

At the same time, an accommodation is not required if it would impose on the employer's business an "undue hardship"—i.e., a significant difficulty or expense. Factors that must be considered to ascertain whether an accommodation would impose an undue hardship include:

- The nature and cost of the accommodation;
- The size, type, and financial resources of the specific facility where the accommodation would have to be made;
- The size, type, and financial resources of the covered employer; and
- The covered employer's type of operation, including the composition, structure, and functions of its work force, and the geographic separateness and administrative or fiscal relationship between the specific facility and the covered employer.

Thus, legal considerations in job design influence the nature of job activities and the context in which the job takes place, making more jobs available to more people. The result can be a situation in which the individual, the company, and society all win.

When recreating existing jobs, such as many firms are doing when they move to total quality management, firms may wish to involve employees in the process. They may even create a self-managed team to allow employees to make many decisions. As the team begins to make its decisions, the company, the line management, and the HR professionals need to be aware of the National Labor Relations Act.

Under the National Labor Relations Act, where a union represents the employees, the employer must consider that almost all issues, including the establishment of programs to change job designs, may need to be negotiated with the union. In many cases, employers and unions work together cooperatively.[40] When this is done, the NLRA requires employers to provide information to the union, when requested, for purposes related to the job design program.

When the employees are not represented by a union, employers may implement job design programs unilaterally—with some limitations. For example, employers may not be able to create and dominate employee teams for the sake of modifying job and working conditions. According to the National Labor Relations Board in the cases of *Electromation* (1992; 1994) and *DuPont* (1993), this may constitute illegal behavior because it undermines the role of union activity.

INTERNATIONAL COMPARISONS: GERMANY

In electronics products, automobiles, and appliances, Germany appears to be well ahead of other countries in modifying or reducing the conventional assembly line and its simple, repetitive jobs. This enlightened position in alternative job design utilization is a product of the work humanization movement in Germany, initially funded by the German government in 1974 and maintained by the cooperative relationship between labor and management. Many companies also furnish their own funds for work design innovation projects.

Although each company's project may result in different types of job design, common emphasis is placed on enlarging assembly jobs by adding more complex tasks. One goal is to ensure that the job cycle is more than one and one-half minutes, the point below which employees have been found to become dissatisfied with a job. As a consequence of experiments in various companies, three major ways are being used to modify the traditional assembly line and its jobs. In *group assembly,* workers rotate jobs as they follow the product from the first to the last step in the assembly process. This is the notion of the "work island," where workers have the opportunity to socialize and are tied together by a group incentive pay plan. With *individual workstations,* work is done by the individual in a cycle time of ten to fifteen minutes. During this time, the worker assembles a major subcomponent of the total product—for example, an electric motor for a washing machine. Finally, *assembly lines* are being modified to make work easier and lighter. Where the assembly line cannot easily be replaced, as in automotive production, it has been altered so that the worker stands on a platform moving at the same speed as the car.

 ## SUMMARY

The worker-job relationship can be effectively managed with knowledge of job design. Increasingly, job design is seen as a way to accommodate a diverse workforce that ranges from individuals who prefer repetitive tasks to individuals with disabilities. Alternative work arrangements such as telecommuting are also used to meet the needs of this diverse workforce. Many forms of job design and alternative work arrangements enable organizations to more effectively match individual needs with job demands and conditions.

To determine exactly who needs or prefers which type of job design and accommodation, human resource managers and line managers need to talk with individuals and diagnose the job situation. The best solution may be a combination of job designs and work arrangements.

 ## *Discussion Questions*

1. Why does Lincoln Electric have so much of its operation based on piecework?
2. What other HR practices support the piecework system at Lincoln Electric?
3. Describe the alternative approaches to job design.
4. Describe how core job characteristics influence the psychological states of employees (see Exhibit 5.1).
5. What topics should employees be trained in to become self-managed teams?
6. Describe the job changes made in Kodak's Team Zebra operation.
7. What issues influence the choice of a job design approach?
8. Describe how data were used to guide and evaluate job design changes within the IPS Department of AAL.
9. How can alternative work arrangements be used to accommodate jobs to employees?
10. How might telecommuters affect companies' attempts to use teamwork?

 ## *In-Class Projects*

1. Describe the following for the Lincoln Electric Company:
   a. The objectives of its job design activities
   b. The degree to which these objectives are serving its business and HR objectives
   c. Its job design activities
   d. The degree to which these activities are serving its objectives

Going forward:

How can the job design activities be improved?

2. Describe the following for AAL:
   a. The objectives of its job design activities
   b. The degree to which these objectives are serving its business and HR objectives
   c. Its job design activities
   d. The degree to which these activities are serving its objectives

Going forward:

How can the job design activities be improved?

 Field Project

Interview an overnight delivery person—you might have to interview them as they are walking!—and ask them to describe the nature or characteristics of their job: number of skills used, degree of freedom, and so forth. Report to the class your findings in terms of the job characteristics model.

 Exercise: Data Entry Operations

JOB OBJECTIVE

To enter information from printed or written sources into computer data files.

CURRENT SITUATION

This unit contains fifteen employees reporting to one supervisor. They handle a wide variety of data entry work, which is supplied by various departments and groups. Some jobs are small; others involve entering up to one hundred thousand bits of information. Some work comes with a due date; the remainder has been prescheduled on a routine basis.

The work is supplied to the data entry employees by an assignment clerk. She attempts to see that each employee gets exactly one-fifteenth of the work. The assignment clerk looks at each project before she assigns it to a data entry employee, and makes sure it is legible. If it is not, she gives it to the supervisor, who returns it to the originating department.

Usually, the data entry unit is able to enter about sixty-five thousand data points per employee per day. Because of the exactness required for this work and the cost of doing it, the completed data files are sent to verifiers to review, to help keep errors to a minimum. However, some errors are not discovered until after the finished job is returned to the client. Turnover is high, and many due dates are not met.

ASSIGNMENT

Listed below are some activities that might improve work performance. Read through the list and decide which things you would or would not do, and put an X on the appropriate line next to each item. Then decide which action you would take first, and number it 1. Continue to rank all the activities you would do.

Possible changes:	Would	Would Not	Rank Order
1. Make sure the forms from which the data entry employees get their information are arranged in the best way.	_____	_____	_____
2. Let some data entry employees decide whether or not their work should be verified.	_____	_____	_____
3. Tell the data entry employees to do first the work that has specific due dates.	_____	_____	_____
4. Train the assignment clerk so that she can help with data entry when the workload is heavy.	_____	_____	_____
5. Split the group so that fewer data entry employees report to a supervisor.	_____	_____	_____

6. Have the data entry employees inspect the material they receive for legibility.

_____   _____   _____

7. When errors are discovered, feed back the details to the data entry employee who made them.

_____   _____   _____

8. Have the data entry employees verify their own work.

_____   _____   _____

9. Assign responsibility for entering all of a particular job to an individual.

_____   _____   _____

10. Arrange for departmental client contacts for certain employees.

_____   _____   _____

11. Let some data entry employees schedule their own day.

_____   _____   _____

12. Make sure that jobs for a particular group or account always go to the same employee.

_____   _____   _____

Case Study:

JOB REDESIGN AT AID ASSOCIATION FOR LUTHERANS (AAL)

 Jerome (Jerry) H. Laubenstein, vice president of the insurance product services (IPS) department at AAL, is wondering what is the best way to improve work conditions and the performance of his five hundred employees. Currently his employees are broken down into three major groups: clerks (the majority), technicians, and managers.

AAL is a nonprofit fraternal society (mutual benefit association) with 1.5 million members (customers) throughout the United States. AAL has over $6 billion in assets, putting it in the top 2 percent of life insurers. In the early 1980s AAL grew dramatically, nearly doubling in size to approximately two thousand employees. Unfortunately productivity did not increase at the same rate. It was this later point that drew the attention of Richard L. Gunderson, the new president and CEO in 1985. Knowing that AAL, though nonprofit, still must compete with other insurers, Gunderson established the goals of cutting costs by $50 million over five years and of reducing the number of jobs by 250. At the same time, he remained committed to the society's policy of no layoffs or terminations. Thus, workforce reductions would occur only through attrition.

Laubenstein was even more aware of what was going on than Gunderson; after all, it was his department. He also had in his hands the results of a survey that had been done by his five newly appointed regional managers and by two hundred employees who had volunteered to help improve the department. They had an interest in improving things, too. In the past few years, as the department grew management layers were added and the clerks and technicians were left with less discretion. In addition to this, they worked on jobs that were narrowly defined and unconnected to other employees' jobs. The work of each employee was passed on to others randomly and very inefficiently. It took an average of twenty days for the company to get back to the policyholder. This was also due in part to the climate that had been created over the past few years, described by some "waiting for marching orders."

Laubenstein was determined to do something that would be useful to the employees and to AAL. Based upon the survey, his fundamental premises were that the number of separate job classes that existed in the department would be reduced from the current 167 and

that the concept of self-directed teams would be put in place. Thus, the functional structure was not sacred, and neither were the jobs of the managers.

Discussion Questions

When Jerry said that the number of jobs will be reduced from 167, he means to say that there are now 167 unique job descriptions. He would like to reduce this number in order to reduce the degree of job specialization. This would help in the coordination of the tasks to be done in serving the client (the field agent) and the ultimate customer, the buyer of the policies.

1. How can Jerry use the concept of self-directed teams here? That is, how can he use the tearm contemporary task design approach? Are his employees able/willing to adapt to this approach?
2. In your task design, how are you able to reduce the number of unique job descriptions? How many unique jobs do you have?
3. Based on the concepts of empowerment and participation, *how* should Jerry go about making the changes you have just described you would make?

Optional
Role-Play: Jerry Laubenstein

Suppose you are Jerry Laubenstein, vice president of the insurance department at AAL. Based upon the situation at AAL, you have decided to go ahead and make several changes in the departmental structure and jobs. With information from two hundred employee volunteers and your five regional managers, you have decided to base many of your changes upon the concept of self-directed teams. This means that all your employees, most of whom have not been to college, will work in specific teams and learn many tasks (will become multiskilled). Thus far, most have worked alone—like the typical officeworkers of many companies—and have used only a few skills, which they learned ten years ago. They have established their routines in life and family situations, as have most people. Most are not planning to go anyplace in life other than where they are now.

You are about to talk with one of the employees, Marie Saxer, about the changes you want made. This employee represents the three hundred workers who were not part of the survey group. She supports the current situation and believes that a change is not necessary. You depend on her cooperation and cannot afford to lose her, or any of the other workers.

Your challenge is to explain to Marie the changes you want. You want her to cooperate and explain your changes to the other workers in a way that they can understand and accept.

Role-Play: Marie Saxer

You are Marie Saxer, one of the three hundred employees who were not involved in the survey of how to improve the situation at AAL. As a consequence, you know nothing about what is going on. This is typical for AAL: the managers have rarely spoken with the workers in the past, except to tell them what to do and when to do it. Because you are a gifted speaker and full of energy, the other workers elected you to be their representative and find out what is going on. Presently, you and the others who were not in the survey group are not interested in changing. You have gotten used to things the way they are. You know what to do, and you have established relationships with the workers around you. You have good social relationships with many of the workers during the weekends.

You are now to see Jerry Laubenstein, the new vice president of the insurance department. He wants to convince you to cooperate with him and go along with the changes he has decided on after considering the suggestions of two hundred volunteer workers and the five regional managers. You are not impressed with Jerry because he does not associate with the employees and does not seem to care about the workers. You are comfortable with your life now and are looking forward to retirement in twenty more years. You and your coworkers are not interested in changing, and you know that Jerry really needs to keep you around because good workers are impossible to find. ◉

Case Study:
REDESIGN OR RELOCATE?

During the past five years, productivity and worker satisfaction at the Jackson Toy Company have been declining. Productivity is now so low that Dr. Helen Jackson, the company's founder and president, is considering closing the plant and moving south, although she wants to retain the company.

When Jackson, a mechanical engineer, started the company in 1980, she installed an assembly line so that workers could become specialized at their jobs and, hence, very productive. The employees were quite productive during the first ten years of operation. Then, several younger, newly hired employees began complaining about the repetitive, boring nature of the work. About that time, Jackson began to notice a decline in productivity. Her response was to assume that pay was too low. Whereas many of the original employees were essentially "second-income earners," the newly hired employees were younger and were moonlighting in order to earn more money, and they were coming to work too tired to work efficiently. Consequently, she increased everyone's salary by 20 percent. Since she had seventy-five employees, this represented a substantial increase in payroll expense. Nevertheless, she was concerned about productivity as well as the "plight" of the workers.

About two months after the salary increase, Jackson noted that the level of productivity had not increased. In fact, it had actually declined slightly. Disappointed, but resolved to do something, Jackson called the local university. Professor Erin Brief, a specialist in job redesign, suggested that Jackson either completely redesign the jobs for the employees or implement a job rotation program. Although it would be more costly to completely redesign the jobs, Professor Brief recommended that alternative. Jackson wondered if it would be more trouble than it was worth.

Discussion Questions

1. On what basis would Brief recommend job redesign?
2. What would you recommend to Jackson? Why?
3. Was increasing salaries by 20 percent a valid way for Jackson to test her assumption about the cause of the productivity problems? What would you have done?

Job Analysis: Knowing Who Does What

With the job families, we're trying to get rid of all the extraneous details and allow managers and their employees to do what is needed to serve their customers extremely well.

MARY FITZER, Director of Base Salary Development, Aetna Life and Casualty Company[1]

The forty-thousand-person Hartford, Connecticut–based Aetna Life and Casualty Company is a leading provider of insurance and financial services. Its lines of business include health care, casualty coverage for commercial and personal property, life insurance, and assets management. After years of great success, Aetna's profits started to decline in 1987. This happened partly because the company had a product line that was too large and too diversified and because some of its businesses were unprofitable. Also, overhead expenses exceeded the industry average in many cases. Consequently, Aetna's services could not be offered at prices that were competitive with those of specialty insurers such as GEICO Corporation and Progressive Corporation.

Beginning in 1992, CEO Ronald E. Compton, a forty-year veteran of Aetna, began a concerted effort to get the company back on the road to profitability. At the shareholders' meeting in 1993, he promised to position Aetna in the top half of the Dow Jones Insurance Industry Index by 1997. Like other large insurers in the industry, such as ITT Corporation, Hartford Fire Insurance Company, and Cigna Corporation, Aetna started eliminating unprofitable lines of businesses. These included its individual health and reinsurance operations. At the beginning of 1994, Compton announced plans to stop selling guaranteed investment contracts (GICs) and single-premium annuities to pension plans. At the same time, he announced that 10 percent of the workforce would be laid off. Perhaps as important, Compton announced that "this is not the end of changes."

In addition to eliminating people and lines of business, Aetna is becoming more efficient and effective at what it does. It has been reengineering many areas of the business, and through the use of new technology, it hopes to increase its return on equity to 12 percent, which is the industry average.

The corporate human resource department has been a partner in Aetna's reengineering efforts. Specifically, it has been working to ensure that the new work environment is consistent with Aetna's vision and core values. The Aetna vision is stated as follows: "Aetna's employees have worked together to create one of the world's leading providers of insurance, financial and health care services. We strive to offer unmatched customer service and to achieve superior financial performance. To attain greatness, we have become a multi-niche company that is quick, flexible and right in a challenging environment. Our employees demonstrate the highest levels of integrity and competency. In all we do, our policy is to go beyond the expected."[2] Aetna's three core values are invest in people, build trust, and inspire excellence.

The first core value—"Invest in people"—influences how work is structured throughout the company. Specifically, Aetna's commitment is to be sure that "all employees have the opportunity to reach their potential."[3] This implies that careers progress along logical paths within the company. Job analysis is the human resource management tool at the heart of efforts to map out these paths.

Using job analysis, the human resource department has helped the company reduce more than seven thousand individual jobs to two hundred job families. In effect, they have redesigned jobs to give more latitude to the employees and to managers, particularly in terms of rewarding people for results achieved. The old job classification system specifically delineated tasks employees were supposed to do. This discouraged employees from taking on additional responsibilities. With the new job families, employees can perform many tasks *and* be rewarded for doing so, without having to go through a promotion procedure and without having to revise the job description. Broader job families are particularly useful in organizations like Aetna, that have reduced the layers of management and, in the process, reduced the opportunities for advancement through promotion.

Job families give employees and line managers more, but not unlimited, flexibility. This is where job analysis comes in. Aetna used job analysis to define the boundaries and content of its job families. Like kinship families, job families describe groupings of related members. But in this case, the members are tasks, related through their common reliance on particular skills and abilities. Identification of these groupings of related tasks is consistent with the core value "Invest in people" because it shifts the focus to a consideration of each person's current and potential capabilities.

As the feature "Managing Human Resources for the 21st Century at Aetna" suggests, job analysis provides a basis for establishing the relationship between HR systems and the needs of a business. At Aetna, the new job families help reduce bureaucracy. Consistent with a partnership philosophy for managing human resources, job families help managers and employees decide which new tasks can be added to a person's job and how to compensate that person without their having to wait for authorizations from a centralized HR unit. Consequently, both managers and employees get more involved in human resource management decisions.

Creating job families is just one of the many uses for job analysis results. Others include developing measures of job performance, designing training programs, developing criteria to use when selecting people to fill a job, and developing a compensation structure that is internally equitable. This chapter describes the legal considerations involved in job analysis, the sources and methods organizations use to conduct job analysis, and specific job analysis techniques employed in organizations today. Subsequent chapters illustrate how job analysis results are used to integrate several aspects of the total HR system.

❖ JOB ANALYSIS

Job analysis is the process of describing and recording information about job behaviors and activities.[4] Typically, the information described and recorded includes the purposes of a job, the major duties or activities required of the jobholder, and the conditions under which the job is performed. On the basis of the job analysis results, *job descriptions* can be written and *worker specifications* can be developed to detail both what the jobholder is expected to do and the knowledge, skills, and abilities (KSAs) and other characteristics needed to perform the job. This relationship between job analysis, job descriptions, and worker specifications is illustrated in Exhibit 6.1

The term *job* refers to one or more positions (which are held by individuals) that are functionally interchangeable in the organization. The term *job families* refers to a group of jobs that can be treated as similar for a given administrative purpose, such as compensation. Usually, jobs in the same family involve similar but not identical types of tasks and require similar skills and abilities. Thus, job families are closely related to what many people think of as occupational categories.

❖ PURPOSES AND IMPORTANCE OF JOB ANALYSIS

Much of what happens to individuals at work depends on the jobs they currently hold or the ones they aspire to or both. For example, recruitment procedures, selection methods, performance measurement, training programs, and compensation are all designed around the demands of jobs. For these human resource management practices to be effective, the jobs must be clearly understood by both the organization and the jobholders. Job analysis provides this understanding.

Job analysis also serves several specific purposes:

- Provides job applicants with realistic job information regarding duties, working conditions, and requirements
- Identifies relationships between supervisors and subordinates
- Aids in defining each employee's duties and related tasks
- Provides the information base necessary to make employment decisions consistent with the Civil Rights Acts of 1964 and 1991

■ *Exhibit 6.1*
Relationships and Aspects of Job Analysis

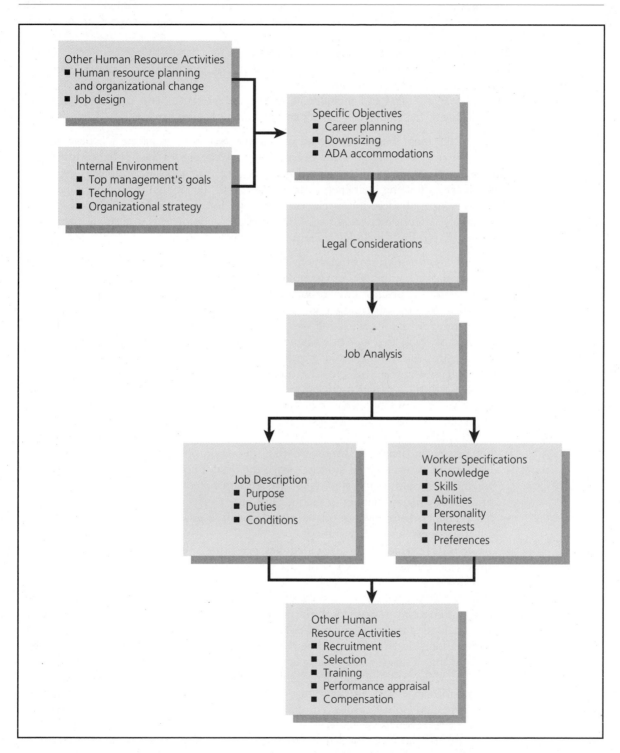

- Can help organizations comply with the Americans with Disabilities Act of 1990
- Prescribes the importance of and time requirements for a worker's effort
- Serves as a basis for training, career planning, and career development
- Is used in determining the relative worth of jobs, and thereby serves to maintain external and internal pay equity
- Can serve as a tool that facilitates job redesign and change
- Can facilitate organizational change by identifying redundancies during mergers, acquisitions, and downsizing
- Guides supervisors and incumbents in writing references and preparing résumés, respectively, for employees leaving and seeking new employment[5]

Often, the most immediate use of job analysis results is preparing job descriptions (see Exhibit 6.2). In many ways, job descriptions serve as part of the written contract that governs the employment relationship. Employees use their job descriptions as guides to their behavior, directing their energies to the aspects of the job that seem most important. Supervisors use job descriptions in evaluating performance and providing feedback. Consequently, a job description needs to represent a complete and accurate picture of job duties. Typically, it includes seven items of information:

- *Job title* defines a group of positions that are interchangeable (identical) with regard to their significant duties. For example, a company with fifty accounting assistants has fifty accounting positions but probably has fewer than five discernible job titles. Job titles can be deceptive if they are not appropriately linked to job duties, creating problems for the organization. For example, if jobs in different departments erroneously carry the same title when in fact they involve different duties, people may be inappropriately transferred to a job they cannot perform, or people with truly different jobs may all be sent to a training program that does not serve everyone's needs, or distinct jobs that appear to be redundant may be mistakenly eliminated in efforts to improve efficiency. Thus, in determining whether jobs are similar, it is important to focus on the degree of overlap in job duties rather than on any similarity in job titles.[6]
- *Department* or division indicates where in the organization the job is located.
- *Date* the job was analyzed indicates when the description was prepared and perhaps whether it should be updated. A job description based on a job analysis conducted prior to any major changes in the job is of little use.
- *Job summary* is an abstract of the job; it can be used for job posting, recruitment advertisements, and salary surveys.
- *Supervision received and given* identifies reporting relationships. If supervision is given, the duties associated with that supervision should be detailed under work performed.
- *Work performed* identifies the duties and underlying tasks that make up a job. A task is something that workers perform or an action they take to produce a product or service. Duties are a collection of tasks that recur and are not trivial. For maximum informational use, duties should be ranked in terms of the time spent on them as well as their importance; a duty may take little time to complete but be critical to job success. Weighted duty statements rank work for incumbents, are useful in establishing performance standards, and may help in determining whether job accommodations for individuals protected under the Americans with Disabilities Act are reasonable. A concise weighted listing of job duties is also used to determine whether jobs are exempt from overtime provisions of the Fair Labor Standards Act and whether two jobs with different titles are similar in skill, effort, responsibility, and working conditions, as provided by the Equal Pay Act.[7]

Functional Title: Corporate Loan Assistant   Department: Corporate Banking
Date: June 1996   Location: Head Office

Note: Statements included in this description are intended to reflect in general the duties and responsibilities of this classification and are not to be interpreted as being all inclusive.

Relationships

Reports to: Corporate Account Office A or AA; or Sr. Corporate Account Officer B or BB
Subordinate staff: None
Other internal contacts: Various levels of management within the Corporate Banking Department
External contacts: Major bank customers

Summary Statement

Assist in the administration of commercial accounts, to ensure maintenance of profitable Bank relationships.

Domains

A. Credit Analysis (Weekly)
   Under the direction of a supervising loan officer: Analyze a customer company's history, industry position, present condition, accounting procedures, and debt requirements. Review credit reports, summarizing analysis and recommending course of action for potential borrowers; review and summarize performance of existing borrowers. Prepare and follow-up on credit reports and Loan Agreement Compliance sheets.
B. Operations (Weekly)
   Help customers with banking problems and needs. Give out customer credit information to valid inquirers. Analyze account profitability and compliance with balance arrangements; distribute to customer. Direct Loan Note Department in receiving and disbursing funds and in booking loans. Correct internal errors.
C. Loan Documentation (Weekly)
   Develop required loan documentation. Help customer complete loan documents. Review loan documents immediately after a loan closing for completeness and accuracy.
D. Report/Information System (Weekly)
   Prepare credit reports, describing and analyzing customer relationship and loan commitments; prepare for input into Information System. Monitor credit reports for accuracy.
E. Customer/Internal Relations (Weekly)
   Build rapport with customers by becoming familiar with their products, facilities, and industry. Communicate with customers and other banks to obtain loan-related information and answer questions. Prepare reports on customer and prospect contacts and follow-up. Write memos on events affecting customers and prospects.
F. Assistance to Officers (Monthly)
   Assist assigned officers by preparing credit support information, summarizing customer relationship, and accompanying on calls or making independent calls. Monitor accounts and review and maintain credit files. Coordinate paper flow to banks participating in loans. Respond to customer questions or requests in absence of assigned officer.
G. Assistance to Division (Monthly)
   Represent bank at industry activities. Follow industry/area developments. Help Division Manager plan division approach and prospect for new business. Interview loan assistant applicants. Provide divisional back-up in absence of assigned officer.
H. Knowledges and Skills (Any item with an asterisk will be taught on the job)
   Oral communications skills, including listening and questioning. Intermediate accounting skills. Writing skills. Researching/reading skills to understand legal financial documents. Organizational/analytical skills. Social skills to represent the Bank and strengthen its image. Sales skills. Knowledge of Bank credit policy and services.* Skill to use Bank computer terminal.* Knowledge of bank-related legal terminology. Independent work skills. Work efficiently under pressure. Interfacing skills. Knowledge of basic corporate finance.
I. Physical Characteristics
   See to read fine print and numbers. Hear speaker twenty feet away. Speak to address a group of five. Mobility to tour customer facilities (may include climbing stairs). Use of hands and fingers to write, operate a calculator.
J. Other Characteristics
   Driver's license. Willing to: work overtime and weekends occasionally; travel out of state every three months/locally weekly; attend activities after work hours; wear clean, neat businesslike attire.

SOURCE: Used by permission of Biddle & Associates, 2100 Northrop Avenue, Sacramento, California, 1995.

Partnership in Job Analysis

Line Managers	HR Professionals	Employees
Work with HR managers to determine whether jobs need to be analyzed or reanalyzed.	Communicate with line managers and employees about the importance of job analysis.	Understand the purposes and importance of job analysis.
Help decide who should conduct the job analysis and for what purposes.	Work with line managers to determine whether jobs need to be analyzed or reanalyzed and for what purposes.	Help line managers recognize when major changes in a job indicate the need for job analysis or reanalysis.
Help identify incumbents to participate in job analysis.	Serve as a job analysis expert, or help select an external vendor to conduct job analysis.	Provide accurate information for the job analysis process.
Provide technical documents to the job analyst.	Ensure that line managers and employees are aware of legal considerations.	Adapt to the changing nature of the job and be willing to show flexibility in performing new job tasks.
Participate in job analysis through interviews and questionnaires.	Prepare job descriptions with line managers and employees.	
Facilitate job incumbents' participation in job analysis.		

⦿ *Job context* deals with the environment that surrounds the job. For example, a job may be conducted outdoors (construction worker), in close quarters (film editor), in remote areas (forest ranger), in high temperatures (chef), or in low temperatures (meat cutter). It may involve extensive standing (sales clerk), sitting (data entry clerk), or exposure to fumes (fiberglass fabricator), noise (drill press operator), electrical shocks (electrician), diseases (laboratory technician), or stress (pension fund manager). Information on these job components provides an understanding of the setting in which work is conducted.[8]

What are the sources of this wealth of information, and what methods are used to collect it? Should any legal considerations be kept in mind when conducting job analysis? These are the key questions to be addressed when an organization conducts a job analysis.

Regardless of which techniques are used, job analysis is the backbone of nearly all the human resource activities described in the chapters ahead. Therefore, partnership among line managers, HR managers, and all employees is essential (see the feature "Partnership in Job Analysis").

✦ LEGAL CONSIDERATIONS IN JOB ANALYSIS

Because they serve as the basis for so many fundamental employment decisions, a company's job analysis procedures will almost certainly be scrutinized by legal and professional experts if the company is sued over its employment practices. Consequently, a large body of legal opinion and regulatory guidelines has evolved. By using these to inform their job analysis practices, companies can accomplish two compatible goals: legal compliance and the development of a sound base of information upon which to build an effective system of human resource management.

The Uniform Guidelines

The legal issues in conducting job analysis have been articulated in the federal government's 1978 Uniform Guidelines on Employee Selection Procedures (Uniform Guidelines) and several court decisions. The primary purpose of the Uniform Guidelines is to help employers select employees using job-related and fair procedures. The courts have established that the only way to be sure that selection procedures—as well as many other employment procedures—are job related and fair is to conduct a job analysis.[9] Section 14.C.2 of the Uniform Guidelines states that "there shall be a job analysis which includes an analysis of the important work behaviors required for successful performance." Any job analysis should focus on work behaviors and the tasks associated with them.[10]

Where job analysis has not been performed, the validity of selection decisions has been successfully challenged (*Kirkland v. New York Department of Correctional Services* [1974]; *Albemarle Paper Company v. Moody* [1975]). Numerous court decisions have also been handed down regarding job analysis and promotion and performance appraisal. For example, in *Brito v. Zia Company* (1973), the court stated that the performance appraisal system of an organization is a selection procedure and therefore must be validated—that is, it must be anchored in job analysis. And in *Rowe v. General Motors* (1972), the court ruled that to prevent discriminatory practices in promotion decisions, a company should have written objective standards for promotion. In *United States v. City of Chicago* (1978), the court stated that standards for promotion not only should be objective but should describe the job to which the person is being considered for promotion. These objective standards can be determined through job analysis.[11]

Americans with Disabilities Act

The Americans with Disabilities Act prohibits bias against qualified individuals with disabilities who can perform the "essential functions" of a job with or without reasonable accommodations. Employers should conduct job analysis to identify essential functions and formulate job descriptions to facilitate compliance with this law. Written job descriptions may provide evidence, although not conclusive, of a job's essential functions and serve as a baseline for performance reviews. Therefore, written job descriptions must be accurate and must correspond to the current requirements of the job.

An accurate job description results from a thorough, well-designed job analysis that

- Specifies minimum educational requirements and training
- Describes what is done
- Does not include unneeded requirements
- Estimates the time spent on each duty
- Determines the minimum required experiential qualifications
- Describes mental functions
- Outlines physical functions
- Describes the current manner of doing the job
- Specifies the required output level
- Lists the environmental forces in the workplace

- Describes the equipment used
- Builds flexibility into the description
- Specifies how the job is supervised[12]

 SOURCES OF INFORMATION USED IN JOB ANALYSIS

Information about a job can be obtained from the current incumbents; supervisors; or trained job analysts, such as members of the HR staff or outside consultants. Because each person sees the job from a different perspective, the results of a job analysis may differ, depending on the information source.[13]

Job Incumbents

Job incumbents have direct knowledge of their jobs. Often referred to as subject matter experts (SMEs), incumbents usually provide data through participation in an interview or by responding to a questionnaire.

One concern in job analysis is selecting which particular job incumbents to include. For example, if your publishing firm employs thirty copy editors, do you need to obtain information from them all? Many companies feel that it would be inefficient to survey everyone, so they select only a sample. These companies have to be sure a *representative* sample of incumbents participates: men and women, members of different ethnic groups and nationalities, younger people as well as older ones, people who work in different divisions or regions, and so on.[14]

Line managers and incumbents usually agree about whether an incumbent performs specific tasks and duties. However, incumbents tend to see their jobs as requiring greater skill and knowledge than do line managers or outside job analysts. One reason for this difference is that job-specific information is more salient to incumbents who perform the work than to outsiders. The difference may also be due to a self-enhancement bias. Because job analysis is related to many human resource outcomes—for example, performance appraisal, compensation—incumbents, and, to a lesser extent, their supervisors, may exaggerate job duties in order to maximize organizational rewards and self-esteem.[15]

Although incumbent ratings may be slightly enhanced, there are still good reasons to include them in the job analysis process. First, they are the source of the most current and accurate information about the job. Second, their inclusion allows line managers and incumbents to gain a shared perspective about job expectations. Third, their inclusion can increase perceptions of procedural fairness and reduce resistance to changes that might be introduced on the basis of job analysis results.

Supervisors

Like incumbents, supervisors have direct information about the duties associated with a job. Therefore, they are also considered SMEs. Yet, because they are not currently performing the job, supervisors may find it more difficult to explain all the tasks involved in it. This is especially true of tasks the supervisors cannot observe directly, such as mental tasks or tasks performed out in the field. On the other hand, supervisors who have seen more than one job incumbent perform a job bring a broader perspective to the job analysis process. Whereas an incumbent provides information about what she or he in particular does, supervisors can provide information about the tasks *typically* associated with the job. Supervisors also may be in a better position to describe what tasks *should* be included in the job, and what tasks *could* be included if the job is to be redesigned.[16]

Trained Job Analysts

Some methods of job analysis require input from trained job analysts. Supervisors or incumbents could be taught to serve as job analysts, but usually outside consultants or members of the company's HR department perform this role.

The advantage of enlisting the help of trained job analysts is that they can observe many different incumbents working under different supervisors in different locations, and so forth. Thus, they should be able to provide more consistency in the data collection process. Trained job analysts also can read through organizational records and technical documentation and provide information culled from these indirect sources. Furthermore, trained experts are more likely to appreciate fully the legal issues associated with conducting job analysis. Nevertheless, like every other source of information, trained job analysts are imperfect. One drawback to using their skills is that, like supervisors, they cannot observe all aspects of a job. Also, they may rely too much on their own stereotypes about what a job involves, based on the job title, rather than attending to all the available information. Finally, especially in the case of outside consultants, their services may be expensive.

Selecting Information Sources

Because incumbents, supervisors, and trained job analysts each have associated advantages and disadvantages, a good strategy is to include some of each of these sources. In addition, although this is seldom done, anyone who interacts with an incumbent during the job performance—peers, support staff, subordinates, customers—may be considered a source of job analysis information. Including sources such as these is especially valuable if the results of the job analysis will be used to develop criteria for assessing job performance.

METHODS OF COLLECTING JOB ANALYSIS INFORMATION

Just as many sources provide information about jobs, many methods are used to obtain that information. Four common methods are observations, interviews, questionnaires, and diaries.

Observations

As Frederick Taylor understood quite well, observing workers as they perform their jobs provides rich information about the tasks involved. Observation may include videotaping, audiotaping, and even electronic monitoring. Physical measurements of activities performed, such as measuring objects that must be moved, and descriptions of how equipment is operated often require some observation of the job as it is being performed.

Interviews

Some jobs include tasks that are difficult to observe. A better way to understand such jobs may be to conduct interviews with the various people touched by them. For example, to really understand the job of a software designer who develops customized graphics programs for commercial printers, you might interview job incumbents, their supervisors, members of their product design teams, staff members who write the computer codes to implement their design, and the customers who ultimately define their objectives.

Questionnaires

Questionnaires are often used when information is being collected from many job incumbents, because they are more economical than interviews or observations. This is especially true when a job has a large number of incumbents. Questionnaires may be developed for specific circumstances, or standardized questionnaires may be purchased from external vendors. Standardized questionnaires are more economical, and often an added benefit is that the vendor can provide useful information from a larger database. On the other hand, customized questionnaires usually yield information that is much more specific to the particular jobs involved. This feature is especially useful for writing meaningful job descriptions and for developing performance measures. Questionnaires may be administered in a paper-and-pencil form or, as is increasingly the case, by computer.

Diaries

One drawback of observations, interviews, and questionnaires is that the information they yield is likely to be dependent on the time it happens to be collected. Whatever is most salient at the time of the interview is most likely to find its way into the job analysis results, for example. Diaries offer one solution to this problem. If job incumbents and supervisors keep a diary over a period of several weeks, the job analysis results are less likely to be biased by the timing of the analysis. For jobs that vary at different times of the year, diaries may be especially valuable.

SPECIFIC JOB ANALYSIS TECHNIQUES

The most common and widely used techniques for conducting job analysis include methods analysis, functional job analysis, standardized job analysis questionnaires, customized task inventories, integrated approaches to job analysis, and managerial job analysis. Many organizations use another technique, called the Hay Plan, but almost always in conjunction with the development of a compensation system.[17]

Methods Analysis

Methods analysis focuses on analyzing *job elements,* the smallest identifiable components of a job. This method would be used to assess minute movements in order to identify inefficient actions of workers or actions that cause undue strain. For example, based on methods analysis, UPS drivers are told how to carry packages (under the left arm) and even how to fold money (face-up); little is left to the workers' discretion. The resulting efficiencies can be very beneficial for the employees and the company.

Although many organizations have shifted away from methods analysis, it is still used in a number of companies that, like UPS and Lincoln Electric, rely heavily on human labor to carry out repetitive and routine tasks accurately and efficiently. Paradoxically, the use of new technologies, collectively referred to as *programmable automation,* also increases the need for methods analysis. Examples of programmable automation technologies include computer-aided design (CAD), computer-aided manufacturing (CAM), computer-aided engineering (CAE), flexible manufacturing systems (FMS), group technology, robotics, and computer-integrated manufacturing (CIM).

The new manufacturing technologies may require a quantum jump in a manufacturing organization's precision and integration. To prevent process contamination, for example, it is no longer possible to rely on people who have a "feel" for their machines, or just to note on a blueprint that operators should "remove iron filings from the part." Automated machine tools can produce parts to more exacting specifications than can the most skilled human machinist, but to do so, they need explicit, unambiguous instructions: Where is the blower that removes the filings, and what is the orientation of the part during operation of the blower?[18] These instructions are given in the form of computer programs. Therefore, the new hardware requires new skills on the part of managers—an integrative imagination, a passion for detail. It also makes it increasingly important to study and document work processes. Several specific tools and techniques are available for conducting the necessary methods analysis.

Flow Process Charts. Flow process charts are used to examine the overall sequence of an operation by focusing on either the movement of an operator or the flow of materials. For example, they have been used in hospitals to track patient movements, in grocery stores to analyze the checkout process, in small-batch manufacturing facilities to track the progress of material from machine to machine, in banks to examine the sequence associated with document processing, and in general to track supervisor-incumbent interactions during a performance appraisal interview. These charts can become particularly useful in efforts to redesign or reengineer the work a person, group, or company performs.

Worker-Machine Charts. Worker-machine charts are useful for envisioning the segments of a work cycle in which the equipment and the operator are busy or idle. The analyst can easily see when the operator and the machine are working jointly or independently. One use of this type of chart is to determine how many machines or how much equipment an operator can manage.

A *team process chart* is an extension of the worker-machine chart. Rather than focusing on the operations of a single operator and a machine, it simultaneously plots the worker-machine interfaces for a team of workers. Such charts are particularly useful for identifying equipment utilization and for pinpointing bottlenecks in interdependent tasks.

Time-and-Motion Studies. Time-and-motion study originated in industrial engineering and the work of Frederick Taylor and Frank Gilbreth. Lincoln Electric and UPS are perhaps the most widely quoted examples of firms using time-and-motion study today. With this technique, in essence, work measurement determines standard times for all units of work activity in a given task or job. Combining these times gives a standard time for the entire job. Exhibit 6.3 summarizes the formulas associated with this type of analysis.

In time-and-motion formulas, observed time is simply an average based on several observations. Normal time is the observed time adjusted for worker performance; this is found by determining a performance rating for observed performance. The performance rating is an estimation of the difference between the normal rate at which a worker could be expected to perform and the observed rate. The adjustment is necessary because workers may deliberately slow down or speed up the processes when observed. For instance, a performance rating of 1.20 indicates that an observed pace is much faster than

■ *Exhibit 6.3*
Time-and-Motion Computations

Variable	Formula	Note
Observed Time	$OT = t_i/n$	
Normal Time	$NT = OT*PR$	
Standard Time	$ST = NT(1 + A)$	Allowance as a percentage of NT
	or	
	$ST = NT/(1 - A)$	Allowance as a percentage of total time
Where		

A	=	Allowance Percentage
n	=	Number of Observations
NT	=	Normal Time
OT	=	Observed or Average Time
PR	=	Performance Rating
ST	=	Standard Time
t_i	=	Time Observed for the ith Observation

normal. By comparison, a performance rating of 0.80 indicates that observed performance is slower than normal (which may be the case if the job is being studied to set rates of pay). Standard time is the normal time adjusted for normal work interruptions. These interruptions may include personal delays (getting a drink of water, going to the washroom) and variable allowances specific to the job (mental or physical effort, lighting, atmospheric conditions, monotony, and detail).

Standard times can be used as a basis for wage incentive plans (incentives are generally given for work performance that takes less than the standard time), cost determinations, cost estimates for new products, and the balancing of production lines and work crews.[19] Establishing standard times is a challenge of some consequence because the time it takes to do a job can be influenced as much by the individual doing the job as by the nature of the job itself. Consequently, determining standard times often requires measuring the "actual effort" the individual is exerting and the "real effort" required. This process often involves trying to outguess someone else.

Work Sampling. Work sampling is a technique for determining standard times as well as another form of methods analysis. It is the process of taking instantaneous samples of the work activities of individuals or groups of individuals.[20] The activities observed are timed and then classified into predetermined categories. The result is a description of the activities by classification and by the percentage of time each takes.

Work sampling can be done in several ways. The job analyst can observe the incumbent at predetermined times; a camera can be set to take photographs at predetermined times; or, at a given signal, all incumbents can record their activity at that moment.

Work sampling was used in a study to examine the differences between successful managers and effective managers. Successful managers were defined as those who moved up formal hierarchies quickly, whereas effective managers were defined as those who achieved high levels of quality and quantity of work performance and satisfaction. Managers in general were found to spend their time in the following activities: traditional management (32 percent), routine communication (29 percent), human resource management (20 percent), and networking (19 percent). Effective managers spent less time on networking activities and more on human resource management activities, compared with successful managers.[21] If this study had been conducted in a company you owned, how would you have used the results to improve your company's performance?

Functional Job Analysis

The U.S. Training and Employment Service developed functional job analysis (FJA) to improve job placement and counseling for workers registering at local state employment offices. As in methods analysis techniques, trained observers conduct FJA. However, with FJA, the observers use a complex rating system to describe the activities of jobs, rather than measuring activities directly. The trained analysts describe jobs in terms of the extent to which they involve three types of activities: working with *data*, dealing with *people*, and handling *things*. For each of these aspects, the analysts provide a rating of the level of functioning required by the job (see Exhibit 6.4).

FJA is both a conceptual system for defining the dimensions of worker activity and a method of measuring worker activity levels. Its basic premises are as follows:

- A fundamental distinction must be made between what gets done and what workers do to get it done. Bus drivers do not carry passengers; they drive vehicles and collect fares.
- All jobs require workers to relate to data, people, and things to some degree.
- In relation to things, workers draw on physical resources; in relation to data, on mental resources; and in relation to people, on interpersonal resources.
- Although workers' behavior or the tasks they perform can apparently be described in an infinite number of ways, only a few definitive functions are involved. Thus, in interacting with manufacturing machines, workers feed, tend, operate, and set up; in interacting with vehicles or related machines, they drive or control them. Although these functions vary in difficulty and content, each draws on a relatively narrow and specific range of worker characteristics and qualifications for effective performance.
- The functions appropriate to dealing with data, people, or things are hierarchical and ordinal, proceeding from the complex to the simple. Thus, to indicate that a particular function—say, compiling data—reflects the job requirements is to say that it also includes lower-function requirements, such as comparing, and excludes higher-function requirements, such as analyzing.[22]

■ *Exhibit 6.4*
Functional Job Analysis Ratings

Data	People	Things
0 = Synthesizing	0 = Mentoring	0 = Setting Up
1 = Coordinating	1 = Negotiating	1 = Precision Working
2 = Analyzing	2 = Instructing	2 = Operating, Controlling
3 = Compiling	3 = Supervising	3 = Driving, Operating
4 = Computing	4 = Diverting	4 = Manipulating
5 = Copying	5 = Persuading	5 = Tending
6 = Comparing	6 = Speaking, Signaling	6 = Feeding, Offbearing
	7 = Serving	7 = Handling
	8 = Taking Instructions, Helping	

SOURCE: Adapted from U.S. Department of Labor, Employment Service, Training and Development Administration, *Handbook for Analyzing Jobs* (Washington, DC, 1972): 73.

■ *Exhibit 6.5*
Sample *DOT* Entry

166.267-018 JOB ANALYST (profess. & kin.) alternate titles: personnel analyst

Collects, analyzes, and prepares occupational information to facilitate personnel, administration, and management functions of organization: Consults with management to determine type, scope, and purpose of study. Studies current organizational occupational data and compiles distribution reports, organization and flow charts, and other background information required for study. Observes jobs and interviews workers and supervisory personnel to determine job and worker requirements. Analyzes occupational data, such as physical, mental, and training requirements of jobs and workers and develops written summaries, such as job descriptions, job specifications, and lines of career movement. Utilizes developed occupational data to evaluate or improve methods and techniques for recruiting, selecting, promoting, evaluating, and training workers, and administration of related personnel programs. May specialize in classifying positions according to regulated guidelines to meet job classification requirements of civil service system and be known as Position Classifier.

SOURCE: U.S. Department of Labor, *Dictionary of Occupational Titles,* 4th ed. (Washington, DC, 1991).

Dictionary of Occupational Titles. The U.S. Department of Labor has used FJA as a basis for describing thousands of jobs. These results are made available to the public in the *Dictionary of Occupational Titles (DOT)*. An example of a *DOT* entry appears in Exhibit 6.5.

The identification codes in the *DOT* provide a significant amount of information. For a job analyst, this code is 166.267-018. The first three digits (166) are the occupational code, which in this case means Professional, Technical, and Managerial Occupations. The next three digits (267) represent the degree to which a jobholder typically has responsibility for and judgment over data (2 - Analyzing), people (6 - Speaking, Signaling) and things (7 - Handling). The final three digits (018) indicate the alphabetic order of titles within the occupational group having the same degree of responsibility and judgment.

In addition to describing jobs, the *DOT* classifies them into nine job families:

- Professional, technical, and managerial
- Clerical and sales
- Service
- Agricultural, fishery, forestry, and related occupations
- Processing
- Machine trades
- Bench work
- Structural work
- Miscellaneous

This system is likely to change in the near future. The Department of Labor's Bureau of Labor Statistics has been charged with revising the Standard Occupational Classifications (SOCs) for the 21st century in recognition of the growth that has occurred in the number and diversity of service sector jobs since the current system was developed.[23]

Today, a number of private and public organizations use many aspects of FJA. A line manager in a small business, for example, who has to prepare job descriptions and specifications, might start with the *DOT* to determine general job analysis information and to find a job description that can be adapted to the specific conditions in the company. The *DOT* can also help companies as they expand and create jobs they have never had before, in part because it provides a job description that can be used for recruitment of new talent.

In the future, employers can expect even more help from the Department of Labor. As described in the feature "Using Data for the 21st Century: Skill Standards, Assessment, and Certification," the government's SCANS project is working with employers as well as educators to develop standards for defining and assessing the skills needed to perform the jobs described in the *DOT.* This shift in emphasis, from job tasks to skill requirements, is clearly consistent with the types of organizational changes occurring as companies like Aetna strive to become flatter and more flexible in their ability to use human resources effectively.

Standardized Job Analysis Questionnaires

Like the functional job analysis approach, standardized job analysis questionnaires rely on ratings of job behaviors. However, these questionnaires generally do not need to be completed by a highly trained job analyst. Instead, they rely primarily on incumbents' and supervisors' responses, or perhaps the ratings of a human resource manager.

The items on standardized questionnaires are intentionally written to be generally applicable to a wide variety of jobs. For example, consider the job of salesperson in an ice cream parlor. Relevant items from a standardized questionnaire might read "Works in an enclosed area that is cold" and "Chooses among items that differ in terms of color."

The value of using such general statements is that it allows you to analyze all types of jobs using the same items. For example, you could use the same questionnaire to analyze the jobs performed by the production workers who make ice cream, packers who prepare it for shipping, drivers who deliver it to locations around town, and salespeople who eventually serve it to customers.

Two of the most widely used standardized job analysis questionnaires are the *Position Analysis Questionnaire (PAQ)* and the *Job Element Inventory (JEI).*

Position Analysis Questionnaire. The *PAQ* is often described as a worker-oriented method of job analysis. The term *worker-oriented* was coined to describe the idea that the items on the *PAQ* can be applied to the activities and behaviors of all workers, regardless of the specific jobs they perform.[24] The *PAQ* items tend to be abstract, but they are not quite as abstract as the FJA's three dimensions of data, people, and things.

The creator of the *PAQ,* Ernest J. McCormick, started with two assumptions: (a) relatively few work behaviors exist across all jobs, and (b) all jobs can be described in terms of how much they involve each of these behaviors.[25] Based on these assumptions, he developed a structured questionnaire containing 194 statements that describe worker behaviors. These statements are organized into six divisions:

- ◉ *Information Input:* Where and how does the worker get the information used in performing the job? Examples are written materials and near-visual differentiation.
- ◉ *Mental Processes (Information-Processing Activities):* What reasoning, decision-making, planning, and information-processing activities are involved in performing the job? Examples are problem solving, and coding and decoding. A sample item is shown in Exhibit 6.6.
- ◉ *Work Output:* What physical activities does the worker perform, and what tools or devices are used? Examples are, respectively, assembling and disassembling, and keyboard devices.

Several large-scale educational reform initiatives that have advanced through Congress and in many states have major implications for businesses. These initiatives emerged from a rethinking of national priorities. For nearly half a century, the federal government's support of research was shaped by the cold war. Then, with a new world order came less reliance on a military-industrial complex. Broad national objectives placed greater emphasis on industrial performance and productivity, and increased preoccupation with international comparisons in education and business. A number of new legislative and federal initiatives addressed skills and competencies.

SCANS AND A NATIONAL JOB ANALYSIS

The Secretary's Commission on Achieving Necessary Skills (SCANS) was the first of several ambitious national policy initiatives that focused more closely on the work setting than on the schools. The commission's charge was to examine demands of the workplace to determine whether the current workforce was capable of meeting those demands. Four objectives were identified:

- Define the skills needed for employment.
- Propose acceptable levels in these skills.
- Suggest effective ways to assess proficiency.
- Develop a strategy to disseminate the findings to the nation's schools, businesses, and homes.[26]

The most enduring aspect of the SCANS work is the definitions of foundation skills and competencies, which were widely disseminated and adopted by many businesses, states, and local communities. SCANS helped stimulate a national dialogue between leaders in business, education, local communities, training, and labor, concerning workplace skills and human capital, as well as providing a framework for further work on skills. In 1994, a national job analysis study was underway to empirically identify competencies, subcompetencies, and illustrative behaviors common across most jobs, in order to increase mobility and enhance developers' portable credentials.[27] The core competencies have evolved from the SCANS project, but additional competencies may emerge through a study of national occupations. These ongoing efforts will also attempt to identify and define characteristics of high-performance workplaces.

VOLUNTARY INDUSTRY-BASED SKILL STANDARDS AND CERTIFICATION

In 1992, the National Advisory Commission on Work-Based Learning held hearings on the issues of voluntary skill standards and certification. This program encourages and facilitates the development of consortiums of industry, labor, educational institutions, trainers, and community groups to (a) identify cross-occupational standards required for broad clusters of occupations (primarily occupations that do not require a college education) within an industry, but across organizations; (b) develop valid assessments to determine the attainment of the skill standards; and (c) develop mechanisms for portable credentialing that would generalize across occupations within a cluster and across organizations within an industry.

Over sixteen grants have already been provided primarily to industry trade associations that are responsible for developing consortiums that in turn develop broad skill standards for clusters of representative occupations.

After nearly two years of legislative activity, another effort at national educational reform, the Goals 2000: Educate America Act, was signed into law in the spring of 1994.[28] This law has several purposes. Title I establishes seven national educational goals and objectives. Several are directly relevant to the workplace. For example, goal 3 requires every school to ensure that students are prepared for responsible citizenship, further learning, and productive employment in our nation's modern economy. Another goal states that by the year 2000, every adult citizen will be literate and will possess the knowledge and skills necessary to compete in a global economy. All these citizens will have the opportunity to acquire knowledge and skills to adapt to new technologies, work methods, and markets through education, vocational or technical training at the workplace, or other programs.

Title VII establishes the National Skill Standards Board. Skill standards are defined as the level of knowledge and competence required to successfully perform work-related functions within an occupational cluster. The purpose of the National Skill Standards Board is to stimulate the development of a voluntary national system of skill standards, assessments, and certifications that will be used:

- By the nation, as a cornerstone of the national strategy to enhance workforce skills
- By the nation, to ensure development of a high-skills, high-quality, and high-performance workforce
- By industries, to inform trainers and prospective employees of necessary skills
- By employers, to assist in evaluating prospective employees and in training incumbents
- By labor, to enhance employment security through portable credentialing
- By students and entry-level workers, to determine the skills and competencies required for high-wage jobs
- By trainers and educators, to determine the appropriate training services required
- By the government, to evaluate public funding of skills training
- To facilitate opportunities for members of minorities and for women
- To facilitate linkages between all components of the workforce investment strategy and school-to-work transition and job training

THE SOC AND THE DOT

At the heart of these initiatives is the need to develop a common definition, language, and taxonomy of skills. Two efforts underway within the Department of Labor (DOL) are relevant to this central issue. First, the DOL's Bureau of Labor Statistics is charged with revising the Standard Occupational Classification (SOC) system used to classify and describe occupations. It is examining a variety of national occupational classification systems used by the military, census bureau, DOL, and Office of Personnel Management, as well as systems in place internationally. The desire is to create an integrated skill-based system that can be universally adopted.[29]

The second initiative is the revision of the widely used *Dictionary of Occupational Titles (DOT)*. In May 1993, the Advisory Panel for the Dictionary of Occupational Titles (APDOT) issued a report recommending the use of a content model for the revised *DOT*. The content model is "intended to provide a coherent and integrated system that identifies the most important types of information about jobs and workers. . . . it embodies a view of occupational analysis that reflects the characteristics both of occupations (through the use of 'job-oriented' descriptors) and people (through the use of 'worker-oriented' descriptors) as well as the broader

labor market." The model is organized into four sections:

- Worker attributes (e.g., aptitudes and abilities, basic skills, cross-functional skills, occupation-specific skills, personal qualities, education, experience)
- Work context, work, and job (e.g., organizational structure and climate, physical work conditions, design characteristics)
- Work content and outcomes (e.g., general and specific tasks and work steps, services provided, products produced)
- Labor market context (e.g., labor market trends for specific occupations, locations of jobs)

In addition, APDOT recommended

- Changes in the data collection process, moving from analysts' observations to structured interviews
- Use of automated technology for the collection of data, and the construction of a database that can be easily and often revised
- Coverage of all occupations, but at a level of detail dictated by the empirical needs and intended uses (although the implication is that greater emphasis and detail may be placed on occupations in high-growth and high-skill areas)
- A systematic program of research on the *DOT* and "staffing-up" of the technical staff at the DOL responsible for this effort

CLOSING THOUGHTS

Several trends emerged across these initiatives. First, the desire to move from very specific task statements to more general behavioral descriptors that cross occupations and even work settings is common to all efforts. The traditional mechanistic approach for analyzing each individual job classification is viewed as preventing the type of occupational migration that is increasingly required for open systems. Second, the desire for a common nomenclature to describe skills as well as jobs is found throughout all initiatives. The fragmented and highly specialized occupational classification systems developed throughout federal agencies and the private sector are barriers to the cross-walk of occupational information needed in research and applications. Third, states and local communities are viewed as key stakeholders in such efforts, as are business and labor. Finally, the skill assessments must conform to existing civil rights laws—placing a heavier burden on employment assessments.[30]

■ *Exhibit 6.6*
Sample *PAQ* Item for Mental Processes

INFORMATION PROCESSING ACTIVITIES

In this section are various human operations involving the
"processing" of information or data. Rate each of the
following items in terms of how *important* the activity
is to the completion of the job.

Code Importance to This Job (I)
N Does not apply
1 Very minor
2 Low
3 Average
4 High
5 Extreme

39 _____ Combining information (combining, synthesizing, or intergrating information or data from two or
more sources to establish new facts. hypotheses, theories, or a more complete body of *related*
information, for example, an economist using information from various sources to predict
future economic conditions, a pilot flying aircraft, a judge trying a case, etc.)

40 _____ Analyzing information or data (for the purpose of identifying *underlying* principles or facts by
breaking down information into component parts, for example, interpreting financial reports,
diagnosing mechanical disorders or medical symptoms, etc.)

41 _____ Compiling (gathering, grouping, classifying, or in some other way arranging information or data
in some meaningful order or form, for example, preparing reports of various kinds, filing
correspondence on the basis of content, selecting particular data to be gathered, etc.)

42 _____ Coding/decoding (coding information or converting coded information back to its original form,
for example, "reading" Morse code, translating foreign languages, or using other coding systems
such as shorthand, mathematical symbols, computer languages, drafting symbols, replacement
part numbers, etc.)

43 _____ Transcribing (copying or posting data or information for later use, for example, copying meter
readings in a record book, entering transactions in a ledger, etc.)

44 _____ Other information processing activities (specify) _____

SOURCE: E. J. McCormick, P. R. Jeanneret, and R. C. Mecham, *Position Analysis Questionnaire* (Occupational Research Center. Department of
Psychological Sciences, Purdue University. West Lafayette, IN). © 1969 by Purdue Research Foundation. Used by permission.

- *Relationships with Other People:* What relationships with other people are required
  in performing the job? Examples are instructing and contacts with the public or
  customers.
- *Job Context:* In what physical or social contexts is the work performed? Examples are
  high-temperature and interpersonal conflict situations.
- *Other Job Characteristics:* What other activities, conditions, or characteristics are
  relevant to the job?[31]

Each element is rated on scales such as extent of use, importance to the job, and amount
of time spent performing.

The *PAQ* has been used to analyze hundreds of jobs held by thousands of people. The results from many of these job analyses have been centrally stored in a database to allow comparisons between similar jobs in different organizations. Using the very large data set generated with the *PAQ*, research has been conducted to determine whether a small number of dimensions of work behaviors can be used to describe all jobs. The results of this research suggest that work involves five basic dimensions:

- Having communication, decision-making, or social responsibilities (e.g., working with people, supervising and planning activities)
- Performing skilled activities (e.g., using technical devices or tools, doing manual precision work)
- Being physically active, and related environmental conditions (e.g., performing activities that require full use of the body, and the setting in which this occurs—such as loading pallets in a factory)
- Operating vehicles and equipment (e.g., working with machines that require the use of sensory and perceptual processes)
- Processing information (e.g., working with data of all types, which may or may not involve using machines such as computers)[32]

The *PAQ* database also contains information about the relationships between *PAQ* responses, job aptitudes, and pay rates for the labor market. Thus, the *PAQ* is a potential selection and job evaluation tool, as well as a job analysis tool.

Note that the methods used to link *PAQ* scores to needed employee qualifications were subjective. They involved asking knowledgeable people to indicate what qualifications they believed would be needed to perform a job with particular characteristics. Because many experts' opinions are represented, using *PAQ* data to set qualification levels is less subjective than using a supervisor's opinion. However, no direct evidence suggests that obtaining a given test score means an applicant is more or less likely to perform well.

Care is also needed in using the *PAQ* to set compensation rates, because the *PAQ* data reflect only the external labor market; they do not take into account the unique value a job may have within a particular organization. If care is not taken, jobs highly valued by an organization but less valued in the external labor market could be paid at too low a rate, communicating the wrong message to employees.

Another concern with the *PAQ* is that it must be bought from a consulting firm; consequently, direct costs appear high.

Finally, a postcollege reading comprehension level is required to respond to the items on the *PAQ*. Thus, the *PAQ* is not well suited to job analysis situations in which less-educated job incumbents or supervisors serve as raters.[33]

Job Element Inventory. Closely modeled after the *PAQ*, the 153-item *JEI* has a readability index estimated to be at the tenth-grade level and is explicitly designed for completion by incumbents. For example, the *PAQ* item "Dirty Environment (situations in which workers and/or their clothing easily becomes dirty, greasy—environments often associated with garages, foundries, coal mines, highway construction, furnace cleaning)" is "Work where you easily become dirty" on the *JEI*. The dimensional structure of the *JEI* is similar to that of the *PAQ*. The advantage of the *JEI* lies in the cost savings associated with having incumbents rather than trained analysts complete the instrument.[34]

Customized Task and Work Behavior Inventories

A customized inventory is a listing of tasks or work behaviors, called items, for the jobs or group of jobs being analyzed, with a provision for various types of ratings to be made for each item listed. Usually, tasks or work behaviors are rated in terms of importance, frequency, and difficulty.[35] These inventories are customized in that they are developed from the ground up for each new customer, such as a company or a unit within a company or a manager. In a *task* inventory, the items are very specific. It is therefore not unusual to have two hundred to three hundred items on a task inventory. In comparison, a *work behavior* item refers to a larger chunk of work, which usually involves doing several specific tasks. As a consequence, customized inventories based on work behavior items are shorter and more user-friendly. The trade-off is that the results are somewhat less specific.

When responding to a task or work behavior inventory, the job incumbent, supervisor, or job analyst checks the appropriate scale responses for each item listed. If the job of HR analyst were analyzed using a customized work behavior inventory, a part of the inventory might look like Exhibit 6.7. Because the inventory method is based on a structured questionnaire, it is easy and quick to score and analyze. The results can be readily processed by computer and used for recruitment, selection, and compensation.

The development of customized task or work behavior inventories requires large samples of employees and complex statistical analysis, so the use of these instruments is usually limited to organizations that employ many people in the same occupation (police, firefighters, data entry clerks). For example, the use of these inventories is fairly widespread in city and state governments, the military, and large companies that have many incumbents performing the same job. In fact, much of the early development work carried out to generate this method of job analysis was conducted by the U.S. Air Force and AT&T.[36]

How are the statements for task and work behavior inventories developed? Often, several steps are involved. For example, the procedures used by Psychological Services, Inc., a consulting company that provides job analysis services to businesses, include observation and group interviews. The critical incident technique may also be used.

Observation and Interviews. At Psychological Services, the observation phase consists of on-site visits in which the job analysts observe the job being performed by incumbents and review samples of the materials, forms, and equipment used in the job. Brief, informal interviews may be conducted during this phase, if needed, to clarify observations and identify the purpose of employee activities. This step is intended to familiarize job analysts with various aspects of the job.

Following the observation phase, subject matter experts—usually experienced job incumbents and their supervisors—are invited to a group interview meeting. These experts generate a list of work behaviors performed on the job and a list of KSAs necessary for adequate performance of those work behaviors. The work behaviors are described using a standardized format. Work behaviors are stated as verbs and objects of verbs (e.g., "Check reports"), followed by a *how* statement specifying what procedures, materials, or tools are used ("by careful proofreading"), and a *why* statement specifying the expected result, output, or product ("to ensure that there are no errors"). Twelve to eighteen work behaviors are typically identified for each job.[37] These work behaviors are then used as the items in a job analysis questionnaire like the one excerpted in Exhibit 6.7.

Ratings from the questionnaire are arithmetically combined to arrive at a description of the job. Work behaviors included in the job description are screened based on their combined ratings. Each work behavior must meet several minimum rating criteria in order to be a "qualifying" work behavior. For instance, work behaviors must be performed by over half of all job incumbents to be considered qualifying behaviors.

Job Analysis Questionnaire for Human Resource Analyst I

Work Behaviors	A. Is the work behavior performed in the position? 1 = Yes 0 = No	B. For each work behavior, indicate the percentage of time spent performing it. The percentages should be whole numbers (i.e.,0, 1, 5, 10, 15, etc.) and must total exactly 100.	C. How important is it that this work behavior be performed acceptably? 4 = Critical 3 = Very Important 2 = Moderately Important 1 = Slightly Important 0 = Of No Importance	D. Is it necessary that employees new to the position be able to perform this work behavior? 1 = Yes 0 = No
1. *Counsels employees* on various matters (career opportunities, policies and procedures, insurance and retirement options, personal problems relating to employment, etc.) by listening, asking relevant questions, and noting alternative courses of action in order to improve employee management relations.	1 0	_____ %	4 3 2 1 0	1 0
2. *Disseminates information* (job vacancies and requirements, insurance and retirement programs, merit system rules, regulations, and procedures, etc.) to applicants, employees, and the public verbally or through written materials or by both methods in order to provide direction for recruiting efforts and personnel practices as well as to inform individuals of opportunities for which they are eligible and benefits to which they are entitled.	1 0	_____ %	4 3 2 1 0	1 0
3. *Prepares reports* (e.g., records management reports, HUD reports, manpower reports) by collecting, organizing, and summarizing statistical data, historical documents, or verbal records, or all three, in order to assist in the development and interpretation of policies, procedures, rules, and regulations as well as to provide information to the public or administration or both.	1 0	_____ %	4 3 2 1 0	1 0
4. *Interviews applicants or employees* in a structured or unstructured manner to investigate applicant or employee complaints, grievances, or adverse action appeal cases and to identify qualified applicants for specific job vacancies.	1 0	_____ %	4 3 2 1 0	1 0
5. *Conducts job analyses* by reviewing written records (e.g., job descriptions, class specifications), observing and interviewing job experts, and administering questionnaires in order to obtain information for examination development.	1 0	_____ %	4 3 2 1 0	1 0

SOURCE: Based on the customized work behavior inventory used by Psychological Services, Inc., Glendale, CA. Used with permission.

■ *Exhibit 6.8*
Job Analysis Results for Human Resource Analyst I

			Work Behavior		
					Percentage
			Mean	Median	Rating
Item		Percentage	Percentage	Importance	Necessary
Number	Work Behavior	Who Perform	of Time Spent	Rating*	at Entry
1	Counsels employees.	100	5	2.0	0
2	Disseminates information.	100	33	3.0	0
3	Prepares reports.	100	11	3.0	0
4	Interviews applicants.	100	14	2.0	0
5	Conducts job analyses.	0	0	0.0	0

Note: Ratings for importance and necessity at entry are based on the responses of the SME who perform the task.
*Scale for median importance rating:
3 = Critical
2 = Very Important
1 = Moderately Important
0 = Of Slight or No Importance

Exhibit 6.8 shows partial results of work behavior ratings for the job of HR analyst. Statement 5 in this exhibit, which was generated in the first step of the job analysis, will now be eliminated because it does not meet the minimum rating criterion.

Critical Incident Technique. The critical incident technique (CIT) involves having people who are knowledgeable about a job describe the critical job incidents that represent effective or ineffective performance.[38] Those describing the incidents are also asked to describe what led up to the incidents, what the consequences of the behavior were, and whether the behavior was under the incumbent's control. Here is a critical incident report written by a librarian, as an example of effective job performance:

> A person who was apparently somewhat disturbed came into the library and started yelling obscenities. When I heard the commotion, I came out of my office and tried to calm him down. I was really afraid he might hurt someone or cause some damage to our collection. I spoke with him for about ten minutes and finally convinced him to step outside. As soon as he did so, I had a staff member call the police and I went outside to try to keep him from leaving the area until the police arrived. Luckily, nothing more happened once we went outside. Later that day, however, a reporter from the local TV news came by and wanted the full story. I told her the basic flow of events but tried not to say anything that would reflect poorly on the library or compromise the rights of our intruder. We were all happy to see that the story was not carried on the ten o'clock news that evening.

After the critical incident reports are gathered (often, several dozen are obtained from incumbents in the job), the job analyst writes task statements. For example, the librarian's critical incident report was used to create task statements like these:

◉ Handles serious disturbances created by users of the library.
◉ Represents the library to members of the news media (e.g., reporters).

The major disadvantages of customized task inventories are the time required to gather the critical information used to develop the task statements, and the complex data analysis required after task ratings have been obtained. For example, one job analysis conducted for an organization with 120 positions (i.e., 120 employees) involved 106,000 task ratings; another job analysis for an organization with 3,600 positions involved 1.8 million ratings.[39] Desktop computers can handle the analysis of data sets like these, and they can be used to collect the data.[40] Some researchers have even experimented with using artificial intelligence systems to generate task statements.[41]

With the help of technology, the primary obstacles to this job analysis technique are being effectively addressed, so in the near future, even small organizations will be able to use customized task inventories. Then they too will benefit from the advantages of the rich base of information that can be generated. For example, by reading a job description developed using this method, it is easy to picture what the job involves. Rather than generating abstract descriptions that could apply to any job, this method creates specific descriptions that clearly outline the tasks required. This advantage also makes it easier to develop training programs for people who will do the job.[42]

Managerial Job Analysis

The job analysis methods described so far in this chapter are generally used for nonmanagerial jobs. A number of special concerns arise in analyzing managerial jobs. One is that managers adjust job duties to fit their styles rather than adjusting their styles to fit the job. Also, it is difficult to identify what a manager does over time because activities vary from hour to hour and day to day. As immediate situations or exceptions arise, the content of a manager's job changes. Despite these complications, several methods have been developed to analyze managerial jobs.

Management Position Description Questionnaire. The *Management Position Description Questionnaire (MPDQ)* is a standardized questionnaire containing 197 items related to managers' concerns, responsibilities, demands, restrictions, and miscellaneous characteristics.[43] These items have been condensed into the following thirteen essential components of managerial jobs:

- Product, market, and financial planning
- Coordination of other organizational units and personnel
- Internal business control
- Product and service responsibility
- Public and customer relations
- Advanced consulting
- Autonomy of action
- Approval of financial commitments
- Staff service
- Supervision
- Complexity and stress
- Advanced financial responsibility
- Broad HR responsibility

The *MPDQ* is designed for analyzing all managerial positions, so responses are expected to vary by managerial level in any organization and also across different organizations. The *MPDQ* is appropriate for creating job families and placing new managerial jobs into the right job family; developing selection procedures and performance appraisal forms; determining the training needs of employees moving into managerial jobs; compensating managerial jobs; and developing selection procedures and performance appraisal forms.

Behavioral Job Descriptions. Building on the work of the *MPDQ* are behavioral job descriptions (BJDs). BJDs use three categories of behaviors to distinguish how managerial jobs at the same level in the organization may differ. BJDs recognize that managerial jobs differ by function (e.g., marketing, manufacturing, human resources) and by organizational level (e.g., executive vice president, middle manager, supervisor). The main focus of BJDs is to differentiate jobs by behaviors regarding the

- effect of the managers' activities,
- type of interpersonal contacts, and
- managers' approaches to accomplishing work.

Exhibit 6.9 shows how two similar product manager jobs in two different departments of the same company could vary on these three behaviors. Combined results based on the *MPDQ* and on BJDs can illustrate differences in responsibilities, concerns, demands, restrictions, and behaviors by levels within the organization and within those levels. Such information may suggest that rather different recruitment and selection strategies are needed for various positions that may at first glance seem similar.

Supervisor Task Description Questionnaire. Whereas the *MPDQ* and BJDs can be used to describe, compare, classify, and evaluate management jobs at all levels, the *Supervisor Task Description Questionnaire (STDQ)* is limited to the work of first-line supervisors. The questionnaire describes one hundred work activities of first-line supervisors in areas such as

- Working with subordinates
- Planning subordinates' work
- Planning and scheduling work
- Maintaining efficient production and quality
- Maintaining safe and clean work areas
- Maintaining equipment and machinery
- Compiling records and reports

A study of more than 250 first-line supervisors in forty plants showed that these job responsibilities were universal, regardless of technology or product type.[44]

Integrating Job Analysis with Identification of Worker Specifications

Recall that worker specifications refer to the skills, knowledge, abilities, and other characteristics (e.g., personality) that someone needs to perform a job effectively. Information about worker specifications is essential if job analysis results are going to be used to develop procedures for selecting people to perform jobs. This information can also be very helpful for developing recruitment strategies and for designing training programs.

Recall the example from earlier in this chapter involving a customized work behavior inventory for the job of HR Analyst (refer back to Exhibits 6.7 and 6.8). The consulting company that provided the human resource analyst example in Exhibits 6.7 and 6.8, as well as other similar consulting companies, used an integrated approach to job analysis. Thus, in addition to the information generated by the customized work behavior inventory, it also provided information about the KSAs relevant to the job. The procedures used to obtain KSAs are as follows:

During the group interviews used to identify work behaviors, the subject matter experts (usually incumbents and supervisors) are also asked to identify all the KSAs they think may be necessary to perform each work behavior. To ensure that everyone

■ *Exhibit 6.9*
Profiles of Two Product Manager Jobs

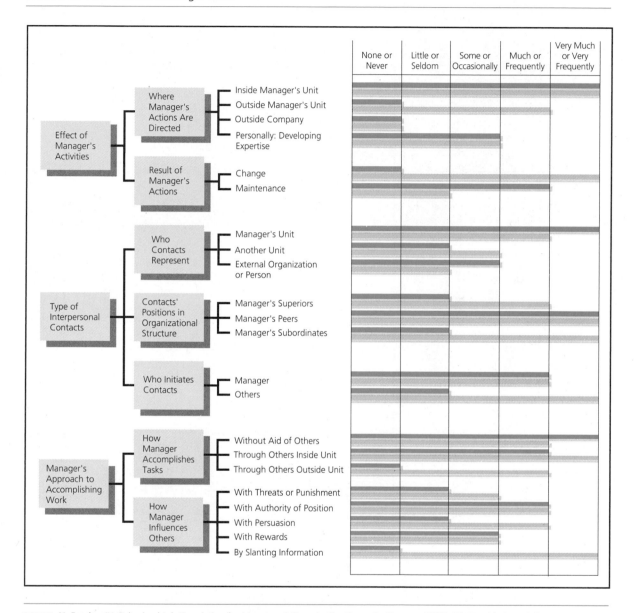

SOURCE: N. Fondas, "A Behavioral Job Description for Managers," *Organization Dynamics* (Summer 1992): 50. Used by permission.

understands the meaning of potentially important KSAs, the central content of each KSA is explicitly stated and examples are often provided.

Based on the results of the group interview meeting, a KSA rating questionnaire is created. The questionnaire is distributed to subject matter experts, preferably experts other than those who participated in the group interview meeting. The questionnaire asks respondents to evaluate the KSAs along a number of dimensions: importance, whether a new incumbent needs the KSA upon entry to the job, and the extent to which the KSA distinguishes a superior incumbent from an adequate one. Respondents are also

■ *Exhibit 6.10*
Job Analysis for Human Resource Analyst I

KSA Ratings

KSA Definitions	E. Is the KSA used in the position? 1 = Yes 0 = No	F. How important is this KSA to acceptable job performance? 4 = Critical 3 = Very Important 2 = Moderately Important 1 = Slightly Important 0 = Of No Importance	G. Is it necessary that employees new to the position possess this KSA? 1 = Yes 0 = No	H. To what extent does this KSA distinguish between superior and adequate new employees? 3 = To a great extent 2 = Considerably 1 = Moderately 0 = Not at all
A. *Knowledge of HR Procedures* refers to the knowledge of the working rules and regulations. Included are policies on overtime, absences, vacations, holidays, sick leave, court leave, selection, promotion, reassignment, disciplinary actions, terminations, grievance procedures, performance appraisals, and so forth, as outlined in relevant manuals.	1 0	4 3 2 1 0	1 0	3 2 1 0
B. *Knowledge of organizational structure* refers to the knowledge of whom to contact when various situations arise. Included is the knowledge of interrelationships between organizational units. Also included is the knowledge of lines of authority and responsibility within organizational units.	1 0	4 3 2 1 0	1 0	3 2 1 0
C. *Knowledge of laws and ethics* refers to the knowledge of legal and ethical standards to be maintained in HR work. Included are ethical considerations governing general professional practice (e.g., confidentiality of records) as well as state and federal regulations governing fair employment practices (e.g., EEO legislation and the *Uniform Guidelines on Employee Selection Procedures*.	1 0	4 3 2 1 0	1 0	3 2 1 0
D. *Computer skill* refers to skill in the use of a computer terminal. Included is a basic knowledge of the keyboard and of computer terminology.	1 0	4 3 2 1 0	1 0	3 2 1 0

SOURCE: The KSA Rating Inventory shown is based on the Integrated Job Analysis method used by Psychological Services, Inc., Glendale, CA. Used with permission.

◼ *Exhibit 6.11*

Job Analysis Results for Human Resource Analyst I

KSA Ratings

Item Letter	KSA Description	Percentage Who Use	Median Importance Rating*	Percentage Rating Necessary at Entry	Median Rating Distinguishing Superior Employees**
A	Knowledge of HR procedures	100	2.5	0	3.0
B	Knowledge of organizational structure	100	2.0	0	1.0
C	Knowledge of laws and ethics	100	2.0	50	2.5
D	Computer skill	100	1.0	0	0.5

Note: All ratings are based on the responses of the SMEs who use the KSA.
*Scale for importance rating:
   3 = Critical
   2 = Very Important
   1 = Moderately Important
   0 = Of Slight or No Importance
**Scale for extent to which KSA distinguishes superior from average employees:
   3 = To a great extent
   2 = Considerably
   1 = Moderately
   0 = Slightly or not at all

asked to allocate one hundred points to the KSAs on the basis of each KSA's relative overall importance to the job, the relative amount of each KSA required to perform the job, and the relative frequency with which each KSA is used. Exhibit 6.10 represents a portion of a KSA rating questionnaire. The KSAs shown were among those identified as important for the job of HR analyst. Thus, the questionnaires in Exhibits 6.7 and 6.10 would be used together. Exhibit 6.11 shows partial results obtained from the analysis of the KSA ratings.

The final step of an integrated job analysis procedure often involves asking experts to indicate the linkage between KSAs and work behaviors. An example of a questionnaire used to collect this information is shown in Exhibit 6.12. When combined with the information obtained from the work behavior and KSA sections of the questionnaire, this linkage information helps provide answers to questions such as: Which KSAs are essential for a job applicant to have upon entering the job? Which abilities are so peripheral to the job that they should definitely not be used to screen out potential new hires?

Developing Job Families and Career Paths

The initial results of job analyses are typically many separate and unique job descriptions and employee specifications—as many as there are unique jobs. Often, however, these unique jobs are not greatly different from each other. That is, employees who perform one job may be able to perform several others. And increasingly, this flexibility is what employers need. This is why organizations group jobs into families. Jobs are placed in the same family to the extent that they require similar worker specifications or have similar tasks or are of similar value to the organization.[45]

■ *Exhibit 6.12*
Work Behavior–KSA Linkup Ratings

Instructions to Job Incumbents

Refer to both your list of work behaviors and your list of KSAs to answer the following question, which involves linking work behaviors to KSAs.

To what extent is each KSA required in order to perform each work behavior?

2 = Necessary (the work behavior cannot be performed without the KSA)

1 = Helpful (the work behavior is performed more easily with the KSA)

0 = Not Used (the KSA is not used in performing the work behavior, although it *may* be needed in performing other work behaviors.

Answer this question for each KSA that you use and for each work behavior that you perform. If you do not perform a work behavior or use a KSA, do not complete any linkup ratings for the work behavior or KSA. Record a rating in every box where a work behavior you perform and KSA you use intersect.

Complete all the ratings for KSA A before rating KSA B, and so on.

KSA

Work Behavior	A	B	C	D	E	F	G	H	I	J	K	L
1												
2												
3												
4												
5												
6												
7												
8												
9												
10												
11												
12												

SOURCE: Based on the work behavior–KSA linkup ratings questionnaire used by Psychological Services, Inc., Glendale, CA. Used with permission.

Adding to worker flexibility is the growing use of *broadbanding,* or the clustering of jobs (even job families) into wide tiers for the purposes of managing employee career growth and administering pay. Broadbanding has become an attractive alternative to traditional job and pay structures.[46]

A growing number of companies favor broadbanding because it fits their flatter organizational structures by collapsing multiple salary grades with narrowly defined pay ranges into fewer salary grades with more pay potential. Broadbanding also clusters more job descriptions into broader job family categories. Job descriptions are still used, but they encompass a broad class of jobs rather than specific jobs. Of course, at some organizations, such as AT&T and Microsoft, technological changes occur so rapidly that traditional job analysis is all but impossible. And increasingly, job requirements are hard to specify because the company does "whatever the customer wants." In these situations, job analysis becomes much more dynamic and fluid. Here, the HR professionals, line managers, and employees all need to value flexibility and adaptability. These changes in the nature of "jobs" have major implications for virtually all other HR activities as organizations enter the fast-paced world of the 21st century.

As organizations restructure, the practice of creating job families and broad job bands based on the skills needed may become more popular. The Exploration Division of British Petroleum Company (BPX) has used this approach to completely restructure its career paths, as described in the feature "Positioning for the 21st Century: Skill-Based Career Paths at BPX."

When BPX recognized the value of having a more flexible organization, they used job analysis to restructure the way they organized work and, consequently, the way people within the organization behave. In their new structure, BPX has job families that group together jobs of similar content and then they use skill-based information about the jobs in each family to link together jobs in different families. Thus job content and worker specifications (skills) form the warp and woof of the organization's total job fabric.

The End of the Job?

Today's environment requires organizations that are adaptable and individuals who are flexible. At the same time, organizations also need highly repetitive and reliable behavior in order to produce and deliver high-quality goods and services, and individuals typically need to know what is expected and need some degree of certainty and predictability.

Most job analysis methods used today were developed in a time when everything was a bit more stable and predictable. People could be hired to do a particular job. This arrangement was convenient for management and workers, *except* when management wanted the workers to change or to do something "not in their job descriptions."

As organizations restructure using principles such as broadbanding and skill-based career paths, jobs are disappearing. And "what is disappearing is not just a certain number of jobs—or jobs in certain industries or jobs in some part of the country or even jobs in America as a whole. What is disappearing is the very thing itself: the job. That much sought after, much maligned social entity, a job, is vanishing like a species that has outlived its evolutionary time."[47] We can see this happening today in organizations such as BPX; BMW in Spartanburg, South Carolina; Nissan Motor Manufacturing in Syrma, Tennessee; and Honda in Marysville, Ohio. These firms are hiring applicants to work for the company rather than to do a specific job. The organization has specific jobs that can be described, but each employee must be able to meet the requirements of several jobs. With good job descriptions in place, workers know what is expected and the company gains flexibility in being able to have workers move around as needed. This model is also used at Lincoln Electric, which is why its workforce is very productive.

As organizations struggle to adapt to high-speed changes in technology—in the labor pool, and in worldwide markets—it becomes clear that the old command-and-control forms of management no longer work.

Innovations must stream forth continuously. Decisions must be made at the drop of a fax. To maintain productivity and flexibility, managers must depend on the increasingly complex skills of the people they manage.

One organization that has been struggling with this challenge is the Exploration Division of British Petroleum (BPX), the third-largest oil company in the world, having locations dotting the globe. Like many other organizations that have grown and scored major business successes, BPX also had accumulated layers of bureaucracy. Career paths had become a *time-in-grade* system, and career success had come to be equated with management titles. Individual contributors, such as engineers and other technology experts, had to switch over to management if they wanted to advance to the top levels of the company.

This needed to change if BPX was to realize its vision of success. Senior management wanted to shift to a more dynamic system that would challenge employees constantly to gain and apply the new skills needed by the business. The framework the company devised for creating this strategic shift was a set of *skills matrices*.

Each skills matrix describes steps in the career ladder—from the lowest level to the highest—along the vertical axis, and describes the skills and competencies that were required for each step across the horizontal axis.

Because BPX needed talented individual contributors to support its technology mission as much as it needed managers to support its business mission, it created skills matrices for two types of employees: (1) people who want to go into management and (2) people whose talents and expertise lie elsewhere (individual contributors). The management matrix is common across all the job families, but the individual contributor path is unique to each job family.

This dual-track system was designed by multidisciplinary teams of BPX staff members from various locations around the globe. On the teams were representatives of all the types of employees who would be affected by the shift: managers, individual contributors, human resource people, and senior executives.

Together they developed the descriptors for skills and levels of performance that applied to their particular job families—*not* descriptions of specific jobs. These multinational teams developed a common set of paths on a global basis: drilling managers in Aberdeen, South Dakota, for example, would have the same career path as drilling managers in Alaska.

To bridge the gap between existing skills and what the business needed, the teams created *development matrices*. These were not *pre*scriptions but *de*scriptions. They were designed to stimulate each individual's thinking about how his or her skills might be developed through a variety of approaches—not just formal training but also coaching, on-the-job experimentation, self-study, and so on. The matrices, which are distributed throughout the company, are so detailed that employees can see precisely what types of roles are available in BPX and what levels of performance are required at each level.

Recognizing that both business cycles and people's interests change with increasing frequency, BPX decided to make the system flexible. Employees are not locked into either the management track or the individual contributor track; they can move from one to the other and back again. However, no one moves up or laterally until she or he has demonstrated sufficient competency in the current role.

This flexibility also allows BPX to rotate a person temporarily from an individual role into a management role, or vice versa, to deepen his or her understanding of the interdependence of technology and business decisions. The company expects this to stimulate new ideas, open up thinking, and free the flow of information.

In addition to opening up new avenues for increasing productivity, the matrices provide support for other human resource initiatives. For example, BPX has launched an *upward feedback* program, in which employees rate their bosses' people management skills.

Descriptions in the skills matrices also provide stimuli for discussions the supervisors have with their work groups and later with their own managers. The matrices also are linked to a new *personal development planning* system that individuals use for professional growth and self-marketing within the company.

What are the benefits to BPX from replacing job descriptions with a matrix reflecting skills and behaviors?[48]

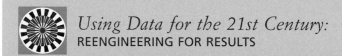

Using Data for the 21st Century:
REENGINEERING FOR RESULTS

REDESIGN AT IBM

IBM Credit Corporation, a subsidiary of IBM that finances the company's computers and services, significantly improved its performance through reengineering, Michael Hammer and James Champy say. The company used to handle its credit process through a lengthy, multistep process that began with a telephone call from a sales representative. When the call was received, information would be written down by one employee, the customer's credit would be checked by another, and the corporation's standard contract might be modified by a third. A fourth person would determine the appropriate interest rate, and a fifth person would create a contract to be delivered to the sales rep. The process took from six days to two weeks.

In examining this routine, IBM executives found that it took only ninety minutes of actual work to process an application, and the remaining time was taken up by moving forms from one department to the next. As part of its reengineering effort, IBM replaced four of the specialist positions with one generalist position to handle the entire process from start to finish. The executives challenged the assumption that each credit application was unique and difficult to process, finding instead that most applications could be handled by one person with access to the appropriate data.[49]

Reengineering

The need for flexibility and adaptability is also associated with reengineering efforts. According to the leading experts in the field, Michael Hammer and James Champy, "*Reengineering* involves 'radical redesign' of existing structures and procedures, not just 'fiddling' with what is already in place. Thus, reengineering is not for organizations looking for small, incremental improvements ... but for organizations requiring 'dramatic' increases in their performance."[50]

A frequent consequence of reengineering is the need to alter the jobs—not only their content but also their shape. As a result, employees are typically confronted with the need to adapt to new conditions. Because reengineering efforts can result in substantial reconfigurations, they must be done right, beginning with systematically collected data. The feature "Using Data for the 21st Century: Reengineering for Results" describes how IBM and Ford used data to move ahead with reengineering. It also describes some immediate results: the creation of generalists from specialists at IBM, and the reduction of the workforce from 500 to 125 in the accounts payable department at Ford.

Another example of reengineering is the extensive effort to redesign operations to focus on customers at AAL's IPS Department. One consequence of this change effort was the elimination of traditional individual job descriptions. Now IPS uses team job descriptions with individual personal assignments.

INTERNATIONAL COMPARISONS

MODAPTS

In more than forty countries, including Korea, Japan, Germany, England, Australia, and the former Soviet Union, a type of time-and-motion study called MODAPTS is utilized to assess the elements that make up manufacturing, government, banking, and dental jobs. Little known in the United States, MODAPTS is fundamentally simple. It is based on the assumption that the time taken for any body movement can be expressed in terms of a multiple of the time taken for a simple finger move. The time for a finger move is called a MOD and is set at 129 milliseconds. The code of a MODAPTS move consists of a mnemonic character (e.g., G = Grasp) and a number, which is the MOD value of that movement. Thus, a hand move becomes M2 (129 milliseconds × 2).

The MODAPTS system answers four questions:

- What is a reasonable time for a nondisabled-for-the-task person to carry out a defined task?
- What is a reasonable output for a nondisabled person in a given time period?
- What are the relative efficiencies of two or more ways of performing the task?
- When a particular person takes longer than the average nondisabled person to perform a specific task, what is the degree of deficiency?

An advantage of MODAPTS is that a series of twenty-one "workability" tests have been developed to assess the functional capabilities of workers against the performance standard of a "nondisabled" individual. The results of the test can be used to place people on tasks that maximize their strengths, to train workers in areas of identified deficiencies, to redesign jobs to minimize worker deficiencies, and to determine if a performance loss is due to injury or disability. Testing materials cost less than $50, and individuals with or without disabilities such as cerebral palsy can be tested.[51]

Japan

Japanese organizations select individuals on the basis of their fit with the company rather than on the basis of how they can do a particular job. In essence, individuals are organizational applicants rather than job applicants. In a culture where lifetime employment and continuous training are more common than in the United States, and where less attention is paid to the issue of unfair discrimination, *job* analysis takes on much less significance.

The Japanese system of lifetime employment, *shushin koyo,* comes close to a guarantee that once employees join a company, they will stay with it until retirement age. The employees will not decide halfway through their careers to move to another company, nor will the employer decide to dismiss the employees before retirement, except under extreme circumstances. (This guarantee has generally applied to men only; women have usually left their jobs once they were married or pregnant.)

With lifetime employment, recruitment, selection, and human resource planning are recognized as vital activities, especially in a dynamic global environment in which products and competitors are constantly changing. Training and development programs must be accurately planned so that employees will be prepared for new tasks and new environments. Thus, human resource plans must be more closely linked to the plans of the business. And because these plans change, workers need to be flexible. Practices of selecting people for the company and not the job help provide this flexibility.

Although neither required by law nor formalized by a written contract, lifetime employment is encouraged by and endorsed by the Ministry of Labor and Nikkeiren (the Japan Federation of Employers' Associations) and is practiced by major employers. It does not appear to be practiced within smaller companies, such as vendors and small parts suppliers, although major corporations are known to provide extra benefits to valued employees within vendor companies as a means of encouraging lasting relationships with those vendors. Although lifetime employment has been a cornerstone in Japanese employment practices, increasing levels of international competition, shrinking profit margins, and slowing economic growth are making the practice less feasible.[52]

SUMMARY

The creation and maintenance of effective organizations today require that the worker-job relationship be understood and managed. Job analysis provides information about what jobs are and how individuals should perform them. Job analysis information can be collected from a variety of sources using several different methods. It provides information for job descriptions and serves as input to the development of worker specifications. With modifications that consider the worker-organization interface as well as the worker-job interface, the process of job analysis serves as a basis for linking together all human resource activities and also linking these activities to the needs of the business.

The choice of a job analysis method should be a result of the intended purpose, as defined by the type of human resource issue to be served by the analysis, as well as practical concerns.

Regardless of the approach, it is important to bear in mind that job analysis serves as the backbone for nearly all the human resource activities described in the chapters ahead. The value of job analysis will become even more apparent in the following two chapters on recruiting and selecting.

 Discussion Questions

1. How is the use of job families being linked to the business at Aetna Life and Casualty?
2. How do job descriptions differ from job specifications?
3. What are the advantages and disadvantages of time-and-motion study? (Refer also to Chapter 5.)
4. Despite the deemphasis on Taylor's scientific management in organizations, why should today's organizations have a firm understanding of the elemental motions that constitute many jobs?
5. What are the important legal considerations in job analysis?

6. Can job analysis make human resource functions—such as recruitment, performance appraisal, and compensation—less legally vulnerable? Explain.
7. Do most jobs change over time? If so, what might cause them to change? What implications does this have for job analysis?
8. How does the use of job families give companies more flexibility with their employees?
9. How can job descriptions give clarity to workers and yet also flexibility to the organization?
10. How does BPX benefit from replacing job descriptions with a matrix reflecting skills and behaviors?

 In-Class Projects

1. Describe the following for the Lincoln Electric Company:
   a. The objectives of Lincoln's job analysis
   b. The degree to which these objectives are serving the business and HR objectives of Lincoln
   c. Lincoln's job analysis activities
   d. The degree to which these activities are serving Lincoln's objectives

   Going forward:

   How can the job analysis activities at Lincoln be improved?

2. Describe the following for AAL:
   a. The objectives of AAL's job analysis
   b. The degree to which these objectives are serving the business and HR objectives of AAL
   c. AAL's job analysis activities
   d. The degree to which these activities are serving AAL's objectives

   Going forward:

   How can the job analysis activities at AAL be improved?

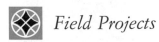

Field Projects

1. Obtain one or more job descriptions from local organizations (e.g., businesses, hospitals, or service organizations) and analyze them in terms of completeness as described in this chapter. To what extent do they provide information regarding performance standards, worker activities, equipment used, job context, job characteristics and worker specifications, or personality requirements? Find out what job analysis methods were used by the organization to collect the information in the descriptions, who provided the information, and how long ago the information was collected. Suggest specific improvements.

2. This exercise will give you experience in conducting a job analysis as well as in writing a job description. To complete this project:

   a. Select a job you are interested in knowing more about or might like to perform during some stage of your career. Pick a professional job (e.g., manager, financial analyst, chemical engineer, museum curator, dietician), not a skilled or semiskilled job.

   b. Select a method to conduct your job analysis.

   c. Select a person or persons to interview, observe, and so forth. Identify that person and give her or his telephone number.

   d. Conduct your job analysis.

   e. Type up a complete job description for the position. Rank the job duties in order of their importance. Indicate the amount of time spent on each task. Also indicate the criticality of error if this task is performed incorrectly.

   f. On a separate typed sheet, explain the method of job analysis you used, why you chose it, and its strengths and weaknesses.

   g. Respond to this question: "From the perspective of (1) an employee and (2) a manager, why is it important to have an accurate, up-to-date job description for the position being analyzed?"

Case Study:
JOB DESCRIPTIONS AT HITEK

 Jennifer Hill was excited about joining HITEK Information Services after receiving her MBA. Her job involved examining compensation practices, and her first assignment was to review HITEK's job descriptions. She was to document her work and make recommended changes, which would include reducing more than six hundred job descriptions to a manageable number.

BACKGROUND

To its stockholders and the rest of the outside world, HITEK is a highly profitable, highly aggressive company in the computer business. It provides software and hardware to businesses and individuals as well as numerous government organizations. From its inception in the late 1970s, it has maintained its position on the leading edge by remaining flexible and adaptable to the turbulent environment in which it operates. It is a people-intensive organization that relies enormously on its human resources; therefore, it is in HITEK's best interests to establish policies and procedures that nurture productivity and enhance the satisfaction of its employees.

Because the computer industry is growing at an incredible pace, opportunities for placement are abundant, and the competition for high-quality human resources is tremendous. HITEK has grown about 30

■ *Exhibit 1*
HITEK's Organizational Chart

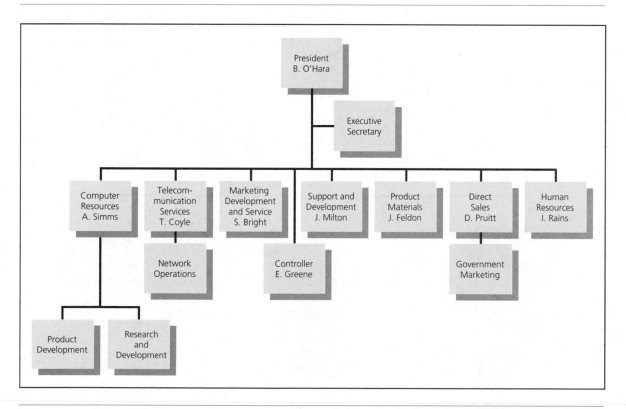

percent in the last three years, and its management knows that as easily as it attracts new employees, it can lose them. However, its turnover rate (14 percent) is about average for its industry.

HITEK remains relatively small, at one thousand employees, and it prides itself on its "small team company culture." This culture is maintained partly by the use of a computer mail system that can put any employee in touch with anyone at HITEK, and by the utilization of open office spaces. The relatively flat, lean organizational structure (see Exhibit 1) and the easy accessibility of all corporate levels also promotes an open-door policy. All in all, employees enjoy working for HITEK, and management is in touch with the organization's "pulse."

With the notable exception of the human resource department, organizational units impose few rules at HITEK. Work in a department is often shared by all levels of employees, and positions are redefined to match the specific skills, abilities, and interests of the incumbent. "Overqualified" and "overachieving" individuals

are often hired but are then promoted rapidly. Nothing is written down, and if newcomers want to know why something is done a certain way, they must ask the person or persons who created the procedure. Extensive horizontal linkage connects departments, perpetuating the blurring of distinctions between departments.

THE HUMAN RESOURCE DEPARTMENT

The human resource department stands in stark contrast to the rest of HITEK. About thirty people are employed in the department, including the support staff members, or about one human resource employee for every thirty-three HITEK employees. The vice president for human resources, Isabel Rains, rules the department with an "iron fist." Employees are careful to mold their ideas to match Isabel's perspective. When newcomers suggest changes, they are told that "this is the way things have always been done" because "it's our culture." Most of the human resource functions are bound by written rules and standard operating procedures; and, because de-

■ *Exhibit 2*
The Structure of the Human Resource Department at HITEK

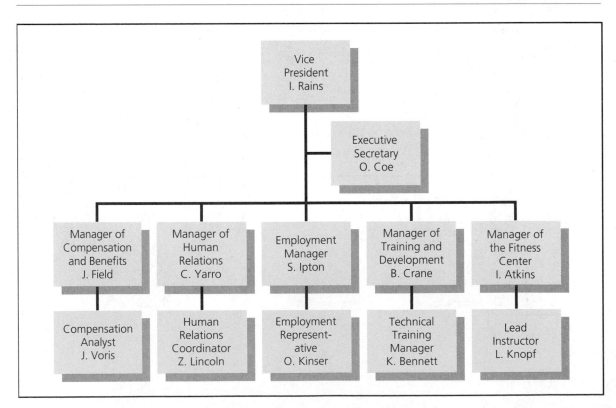

partment employees know their job descriptions well, there is little overlap in duties.

With the exception of one recruiter, all the incumbents whose positions are represented in Exhibit 2 are women. Only half of them have degrees in industrial relations or human resource management, and only one-fourth have related experience with another company. Most of them have been promoted from clerical positions. In fact, some employees view the vice presidency as a "gift" given to Isabel, a former executive secretary, the day after she received her bachelor's degree at a local college. In other departments, it is widely believed that professional degrees and related experience lead to expertise.

One incident that conveyed the department's image to Jennifer Hill occurred during her second week on the job. While preparing a job description with Dave Pruitt, Jennifer explained that she would submit the job description to Janet Voris for final approval. Dave became confused and asked, "But Janet is only a clerical person; why would she be involved?"

JENNIFER HILL'S DUTIES

At HITEK, the pool of job descriptions had grown almost daily as newcomers were hired, but many of the old job descriptions were not discarded, even when obsolete. Other job descriptions needed updating. Jennifer spent some time thinking about how to proceed. She considered the uses of the job descriptions and what steps she would need to take to accomplish all that was expected of her. Support from within the department was scarce because other employees were busy gathering materials for the annual review of HITEK's hiring, promotion, and development practices conducted by the Equal Employment Opportunity Commission.

After six harried months on the job and much frustration, Jennifer had revised all the descriptions that were still needed (examples of "old" and "new" job descriptions appear in Exhibits 3 and 4). She was also beginning to develop some strong opinions about how the human resource department functioned at HITEK and what needed to be done to improve its effectiveness and its image. She decided to arrange a confidential lunch with Billy O'Hara. ◉

Discussion Questions

1. What are the goals of HITEK? of the human resource department? Why does the conflict between these different goals create problems for HITEK?
2. Why is it important for HITEK to maintain a professional, competent human resource function?
3. Jobs change frequently at HITEK. Should the human resource department simply discontinue the practice of job analysis and stop writing job descriptions?
4. What steps should Jennifer Hill take in performing the tasks assigned to her? How do your answers to the earlier questions affect your answer to this one?
5. Is the "new" job description (Exhibit 4) better than the "old" one (Exhibit 3)? Why or why not?
6. What should Jennifer suggest to the president concerning the image and operation of the human resource department?

SOURCE: Written by M. P. Miceli, Ohio State University, and Karen Wijta, Macy's.

■ *Exhibit 3*
An "Old" Job Description

Associate Programmer

Basic Objective	Perform coding, testing, and documentation of programs, under the supervision of a project leader.
Specific Tasks	Perform coding, debugging, and testing of a program when given general program specifications.
	Develop documentation of the program.
	Help implement the system and train its users.
	Report to the manager of management information services as requested.
Job Qualifications	Minimum: (a) BA or BS degree in relevant field or equivalent experience or knowledge; (b) programming knowledge in FORTRAN; (c) good working knowledge of business and financial applications.
	Desirable: (a) computer programming experience in a time-sharing environment; (b) some training or education in C and object-oriented programming language.

Exhibit 4
A "New" Job Description

Associate Programmer

General Statement of Duties	Performs coding, debugging, testing, and documentation of software under the supervision of a technical superior. Uses some independent judgment.
Supervision Received	Works under close supervision of a technical superior or manager.
Supervision Exercised	Performs no supervisory duties.
Examples of Duties	(Any one position may not include all the duties listed, nor do listed examples include all duties that may be found in positions of this class.)
	Confers with analysts, supervisors, or representatives of the departments, or all three, to clarify software intent and programming requirements.
	Performs coding, debugging, and testing of software when given program specifications for a particular task or problem.
	Writes documentation for the program.
	Seeks advice and assistance from supervisor when problems outside of realm of understanding arise. Communicates any program specification deficiencies back to supervisor.
	Reports ideas concerning design and development back to supervisor.
	Helps implement the system and train end users.
	Provides some support and assistance to users.
	Develops product knowledge and personal expertise and proficiency in system usage.
	Assumes progressively complex and independent duties as experience permits.
	Performs all duties in accordance with corporate and departmental standards.
Minimum Qualifications	Education: BA or BS degree in relevant field or equivalent experience or knowledge in computer science, math, or other closely related field.
	Experience: No prior computer programming work experience necessary.
	Knowledge, Skills, and Abilities: Ability to exercise initiative and sound judgment. Knowledge of a structured language. Working knowledge in operating systems. Ability to maintain open working relationships with supervisor. Logic and problem-solving skills. System flowchart development skills.
Desirable Qualifications	Exposure to FORTRAN, C, and object-oriented programming languages; some training in general accounting practices and controls; effective written and oral communication skills.

Recruitment: Developing a Pool of Candidates

In business, there is only one true long-term competitive advantage and key to stakeholder satisfaction: People. Our ongoing challenge at Harley-Davidson is to ensure that we have the most talented employees in our industries addressing the many issues of our markets and keeping us ahead of our competitors.[1]

Managing Human Resources for the 21st Century at Microsoft

Microsoft Corporation is one of the biggest success stories in America today. Chairman and CEO William H. Gates has grown the company from its birth in 1975 to a healthy young adulthood in which it employed more than fifteen thousand people, with an average age of 31.2 years, in 1995. Microsoft, based in Redmond, Washington, is continually ranked among the most admired companies and often singled out as the most innovative company in the United States. It is not at all unusual for the firm to introduce as many as fifty new products in one year, including many international versions. The success of Microsoft has made millionaires of many current and past employees, including Gates, who reportedly has about 78 million shares of Microsoft stock.

According to many observers and Microsoft vice president Jeff Raikes, the firm is "high horse-power, high energy." Gates is described by most as "brilliant and totally focused on the company." He expects the same in others and serves as a role model for most. As CEO, he not only stays abreast of what is happening within Microsoft but is continually seeking opportunities to work closely with other manufacturers. For example, Microsoft and Xerox are jointly developing a new generation of printers and fax machines. Microsoft also works closely with its customers. According to Dorothy Cooney, Aetna's direc-

tor of information technology and a customer of Microsoft, "Our joint commitment with Microsoft is important to us; it's a big part of how we're making quantum leaps in effectively using technology to improve customer service and reduce expenses, while bringing increased order to our technology environment, which all brings bottom-line benefits to our customers, users, and shareholders."

To achieve all this success and involvement in an industry in which total product lines become obsolete within five years, Microsoft needs great people, and it needs a lot of them. Acting on the premise that a company succeeds only because of its people, Gates gets involved in the recruitment at Microsoft. Indeed, ask Gates what was the most important thing he did last year and he answers, "I hired a lot of smart people." Not surprisingly, this means that Microsoft does a lot of recruiting and hiring.

"Today, with revenues approaching $5 billion, Microsoft is hiring almost one hundred people per week. . . . finding and hiring the best people is the number one priority of Microsoft. They recruit at 137 campuses four times per year, review 120,000 resumes per year, interview 7,400 [recruits] and eventually hire 2,000 of them. And they succeed while having a reputation for paying below-market wages."[2]

At Microsoft, getting the right people into the organization is so important that the chairman gets personally involved in the firm's recruiting and selection. Of course, this also means that other top managers do the same. Together, the top managers devote so much time and attention to recruiting and selection because they believe it is vital to the long-term survival and success of the business.

RECRUITMENT

Recruitment involves searching for and obtaining qualified job candidates in such numbers that the organization can select the most appropriate person to fill its job needs. In addition, it should be concerned with satisfying the needs of the job candidates.[3] Consequently, recruitment not only attracts individuals to the organization but also increases the chance of retaining the individuals once they are hired. Thus, *recruitment* is the set of activities used to obtain a pool of qualified job applicants.

The key activities that are part of recruitment include (1) determining the organization's long- and short-range needs by job title and level in the organization; (2) staying

Partnership in Recruitment

Line Managers	Human Resource Professionals	Employees
Identify present and future job openings.	Use information from line managers to prepare recruitment activities.	Participate in recruitment efforts such as referring the company to others.
Prepare descriptions of job duties and skills needed to fill jobs.	Develop sources and methods of recruiting to ensure a sufficient number of qualified applicants.	Work with HR professionals and line managers in the organization's efforts to effectively manage workforce diversity.
Prepare for interviews with job applicants.	Ensure that equal employment considerations are met and workforce diversity is effectively managed.	Become part of a succession plan or talent pool for further training and development.
Work with HR professionals on equal employment and workforce diversity.	Develop and maintain succession plans and replacement charts.	
Help identify potential talent for future promotion and staffing.		

informed of labor market conditions; (3) developing effective recruiting materials; (4) developing a systematic and integrated program of recruitment in conjunction with other human resource activities and with the cooperation of the line managers and employees (see the feature "Partnership in Recruitment"); (5) obtaining a pool of qualified job applicants; (6) recording the number and quality of job applicants produced by the various sources and methods of recruiting; and (7) following up on applicants, those hired and not hired, in order to evaluate the effectiveness of the recruitment effort. All these activities must be accomplished within a legal context.[4]

The result of these recruitment activities is the identification of a pool of potentially qualified applicants from which to select and place job applicants. These relationships are shown in Exhibit 7.1.

PURPOSES AND IMPORTANCE OF RECRUITMENT

The general purpose of recruitment is to provide an organization with a pool of potentially qualified candidates. The specific purposes of recruitment are as follows:

- To link with and be consistent with the strategy, the vision, and the values of the company (An example of how these characteristics influence recruitment is described in the feature "Managing Human Resources for the 21st Century at Chubb and AIG." Note that Chubb tries to recruit undergraduates and graduates who look like its customers; AIG, in contrast, hires employees away from other firms.)
- To determine the organization's present and future recruitment needs in conjunction with major organizational changes, human resource planning, job design, and job analysis

■ *Exhibit 7.1*
Relationships and Aspects of Recruitment

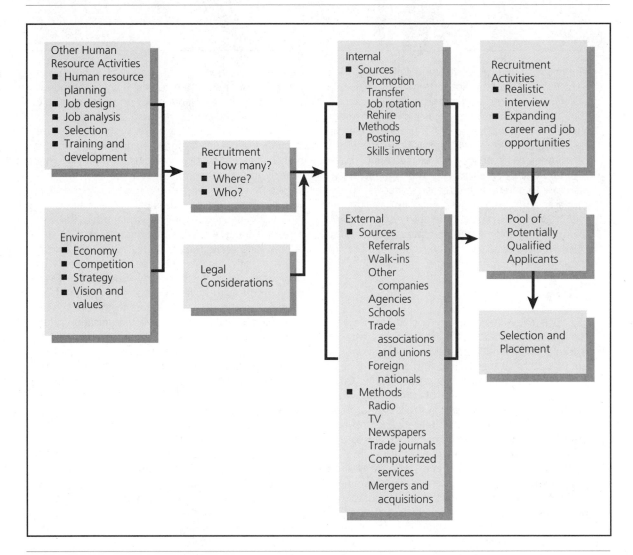

- To increase the pool of qualified job applicants as efficiently as possible
- To support organizational initiatives in managing workforce diversity
- To help increase the success rate of the selection process by reducing the number of obviously underqualified or overqualified job applicants
- To help reduce the probability that job applicants, once recruited and selected, will leave the organization after only a short period of time
- To coordinate recruitment efforts with selection and training programs (as also illustrated in the feature on Chubb and AIG)
- To evaluate the effectiveness of various techniques and locations of recruiting for all types of job applicants
- To meet the organization's responsibility for affirmative action programs and other legal and social considerations regarding workforce composition[5]

Managing Human Resources for the 21st Century at Chubb and AIG

The property and casualty business of the insurance industry is based, perhaps more directly than other businesses, on knowledge and skills. For example, the ability to identify and assess risk in unique situations is its central issue. Thus, employees and the practices used to manage them are at the heart of competencies needed to be successful in this business. These practices vary widely, apparently in response to different competitive strategies. The two property and casualty firms that are very different with respect to people management are Chubb Corporation and American International Group (AIG). Yet both are among the most profitable firms in the entire insurance industry.

CHUBB

Chubb is often described by competitors as being the best at what it does. Chubb does not create new markets or expand the ones it is in through low prices; instead, it tries to find the very best risks that will provide high returns on its premiums. Chubb often goes after customers of other firms who it believes are good risks, identifies "gaps" or problems in their coverage, and offers them superior insurance protection. The core competency that makes these efforts possible is superior underwriting skills.

Chubb also looks for customers who are willing to pay a premium for superior service that is manifested by intensive customer contact. It has a reputation for being the insurer of choice for the very wealthy.

In short, Chubb earns above-market profits by targeting customers who will pay some premium for superior products and service and by identifying particularly good risks that are not spotted by competitors and that will earn the company high profits.

Human Resource Practices

Chubb makes a substantial investment in its employees, and that investment begins with recruiting. Historically, it has gone to the most prestigious undergraduate schools and hired graduates who, regardless of major, have good interpersonal and communication skills upon which insurance-specific skills could be built. It has been argued that the

recruiters have searched for applicants who look like Chubb's customers, often coming from backgrounds that create contacts and make them comfortable with potential customers in the monied class.

New hires complete several months of intensive training and testing before beginning work in the branch into which they were hired. Then, for the next six to twelve months, they work in an apprenticelike system in the field with established underwriters who provide a great deal of supervision.

The company goes to great lengths, through career planning, to ensure that the new workers stay around long enough so that this substantial investment in skills can be recouped. First, it keeps its underwriters from the boredom of desk jobs, which often produces turnover elsewhere, by making them agents. Sending the underwriters to the field to do the selling is key. It eliminates communication problems that otherwise exist between sales and underwriting functions, by eliminating the intermediary role of agents. The underwriter gets better information for assessing risks and also provides customers with better service, including better information about their risks. The superior abilities of the employees make it possible to combine the sales role with the underwriting job.

Second, Chubb fills vacancies internally, moving people frequently and retraining them for new jobs. The pace of work eventually results in some people voluntarily leaving the organization, but they rarely go to other insurance companies and more typically become independent agents, helping to expand the network for Chubb's business. This turnover has the added benefit of expanding what would otherwise be very limited career opportunities for those remaining.

AIG

American International Group achieves its high level of profitability in a different way than Chubb, but it also relies on its human resources. AIG is a market maker. It identifies new areas of business, creates new products, and benefits from "first-mover" advantages in getting to those markets. It was the first insurer allowed into Communist China and later moved into Russia. AIG thrives in markets where it has little competition, often insuring high-risk operations that competitors avoid. Once companies that compete on price enter its markets, AIG may move on to another market.

Human Resource Practices

AIG's competencies are in marketing—identifying new business areas—and in changing quickly. It pursues the latter with a set of policies that are virtually the opposite of Chubb's. It operates in a highly decentralized manner by creating literally hundreds of subsidiary companies, each targeted to a specific market. It creates new companies to attack new markets and staffs them by hiring experts with industry skills from other firms. It has been known to hire away entire operations from competitors, typically for much higher pay. AIG has little interest in developing commonalities across its companies, given that its "core competency" is variation, and therefore has no need to manage its companies

tightly from the center. The executives in each company are managed through a series of financial targets—with generous rewards for meeting them—and are otherwise given considerable autonomy in running the businesses.

When a market dries up or tough competition arrives, a company in that market may close down and the employees will be let go to return to the industry's labor market. These quick market changes would make it difficult for AIG to recoup the investment it would need to develop necessary market-specific skills itself, so it relies on the outside labor market instead.

The advantages of speed in attacking markets effectively make other ways of competing difficult. For example, hiring experienced employees away from competitors without offering any real job security means that AIG needs to pay top dollar to get them. Furthermore, the need to quickly change the competencies of employees as AIG enters and exits markets means that AIG cannot rely on the development of internal employees to satisfy its needs.[6]

Managing Workforce Diversity

Increasingly, organizations are recognizing the value in having a workforce that is as diverse as the customers and communities they serve. Thus, recruiting for diversity has become a strategic issue. For example, the Weyerhaeuser Company has diversity as a key value because it is fundamental to the success of the business:

Weyerhaeuser recruits and retains the best available talent. To do that, we must create an atmosphere where a diverse workforce feels welcome and valued. This means that

- Our criteria and measures for success are focused on the customer and recognize the power of diverse styles and perspectives.
- Our commitment to diversity is reflected in all our processes to select, develop, promote, and reward people. Weyerhaeuser considers people's varied backgrounds to be assets to the company and a long-term source of competitive advantage.
- The Weyerhaeuser workplace measurably reflects the diversity of our communities and our customers.
- Education and coaching are provided to encourage the workforce to embrace our diversity strategy.
- Women and people of color participate in decision making at all levels of the company, from the board of directors to the individual contributor.
- Leaders communicate and model their commitment to diversity.
- Discrimination based on non-job-related issues is not tolerated and is appropriately dealt with.

Many other firms have embraced diversity in the same way for years. Levi Strauss, for example, is recognized as among the most culturally and ethnically diverse companies in the United States, with 56 percent of its twenty-three thousand employees being other than American-born caucasians. Fifteen percent of top management were people of color, and 30 percent were women. Levi Strauss views this diversity as a way to ensure that the company is in touch with the many perspectives of its customers.[7]

Specific Initiatives. In managing diversity, human resource managers are reassessing and sometimes modifying several key activities. Recruiting activities and outreach programs are often among the first to be scrutinized. At US West, through the partnership efforts of Jack A. MacAllister and Darlene Siedschlaw, diversity efforts have included all employees through a philosophy of pluralism, as described in "Managing Human Resources for the 21st Century at US West." Notice that the search firms hired by US West to obtain job candidates are dropped if they fail to supply a pluralistic mix of job candidates.

SOURCES AND METHODS FOR OBTAINING JOB APPLICANTS

Fundamentally, the objectives of recruitment always include the identification of a pool of qualified applicants. From this pool, a portion is selected as being the *most* qualified, and they are invited to join the company. In the best-case scenario, the applicants of most interest to the company accept the company's offer and then become productive employees. Furthermore, the applicants who are not selected have a positive experience and develop a favorable image of the company and its products and services. They may become applicants again in the future, and they may encourage their friends to view the company as an employer of choice. In other words, the recruitment process not only generates a pool of applicants, it also is an exercise in marketing.

When designing a recruitment program, the first step is establishing the objectives. What are the characteristics of the ideal recruit? Do we need people who want to stay with the company for a long time, or are we looking for a short-term commitment? Do we want people with well-developed skills, or are we looking for people who are capable and eager to learn? Are we prepared to pay top dollar, or should we look for people who will be attracted to our company despite the modest compensation we offer? Are we interested in finding people who are different from our current employees, to bring in new perspectives, or is it important to maintain our status quo?

Once the objectives of recruitment efforts have been clarified, the next two questions to address are *where* and *how* to recruit people.

Internal Sources

Internal sources include present employees who become candidates for promotions, transfers, and job rotations, as well as former employees who are available for rehires and recalls.

Promotions. The case for promotion from within rests on sound arguments. Internal employees may be better qualified. Even jobs that do not seem unique require familiarity with the people, procedures, policies, and special characteristics of the organization in which they are performed. Employees are likely to feel more secure and to identify their long-term interests with an organization that provides them the first choice of job opportunities. Availability of promotions within an organization can also motivate employees to perform. At Chubb, internal promotions motivate employees and give them reason to stay with the firm. After having invested a lot of training dollars in each person, the firm is not anxious to lose him or her.

Managing Human Resources for the 21st Century at US West

It was fifteen years ago that current chairman Jack MacAllister introduced what he called "sensitivity training" to employees at Northwestern Bell (which later became a subsidiary of US West), saying it was a positive investment of shareholders' money because racism and sexism directly affected the bottom line.

Today, as companies prepare to manage the changing workforce of the future, there's evidence that MacAllister's foresight has already paid off.

For example, in 1992, women held 21 percent of the jobs in US West's top 1 percent salary level of $68,000 or more; since the introduction of the Accelerated Development Program for Women of Color three years before, the ratio of directors to employees who were women of color had decreased from 1:289 to 1:98; and the company's employee base closely mirrored that of the general population.

At US West, pluralism (the company's concept to denote valuing human diversity) is achieved largely through a commitment from the top. "Pluralism isn't an option at US West," says Darlene Siedschlaw, the company's director of EEO and affirmative action. "If you're going to change the texture of the corporation, you have to change everybody."

At the officer level, compensation is tied to whether or not that person has participated in Leading a Diverse Workforce, the company's three-day diversity training program, and has been supportive of his or her employees doing the same.

Compensation is also tied to the profiles of the employees, from a pluralistic standpoint, who are being promoted and hired within that top-ranking executive's organization.

The same standards are applied externally as well. According to Siedschlaw, the company has gone so far as to stop doing business with search firms that do not supply US West with a pluralistic mix of job candidates.

For employees, US West offers eight well-established resource groups that provide a forum in which to discuss their concerns. Each year, representatives from each group, which range from Friends, a group for employees with disabilities, to Voice of Many Feathers, an American Indian employee resource group, have the opportunity to meet with approximately forty of the company's top executives to make their concerns known.

Despite the strides Englewood, Colorado–based US West has made to manage its changing workforce, the company does not pretend to have all the answers, as demonstrated by Siedschlaw. When employees from other companies call to find out more about the company's pluralism program, she tells them: "We don't have a pluralism program because a program has a start and a finish. What we have is a philosophy called pluralism and what we're trying to do is change the texture of this corporation, and that's ongoing."[8]

To assist with maintaining an internal promotion policy, organizations use succession planning and replacement planning charts. *Replacement planning* charts list the current and potential occupants of positions in the firm. Potential promotions and developmental needs are indicated by the performance levels of employees. Incumbents are listed directly under the job title. Individuals likely to fill potential vacancies are listed next. An example of a replacement chart is shown in Exhibit 7.2.

Succession planning is similar to replacement planning except that it is usually longer term and more developmental. With rapidly changing environments, organizations are planning successions more than ever. Realizing that what makes a good manager today may not tomorrow, many companies use HR planning activities to identify what *will* make a good manager in the future. Then, developmental activities, such as job rotations

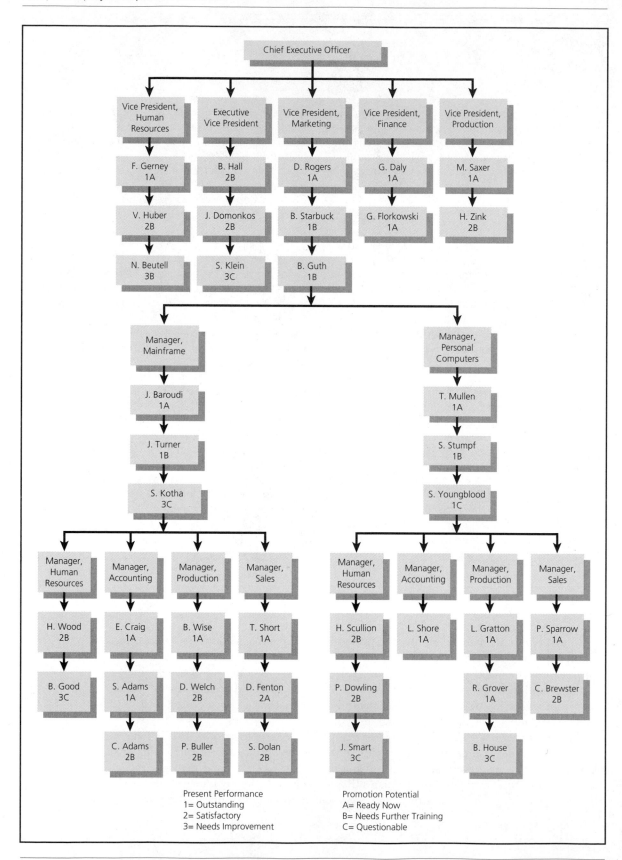

Present Performance
1= Outstanding
2= Satisfactory
3= Needs Improvement

Promotion Potential
A= Ready Now
B= Needs Further Training
C= Questionable

and key task assignments, can be offered as a way to ensure that the right people are available with the right skills at the right time.

According to Frank Berardi of the corporate human resource department at Allstate Insurance: "While there is some concern for numbers, it is primarily the concern for skills that [line managers] are worried about and they want HR to help them develop management education programs and new succession programs. So this is a business issue that is HR in nature."[9]

In part owing to unpredictable events such as key individuals leaving the company, and the desire to give more people a chance for promotion, firms are starting to develop internal *talent pools* from which people can be recruited for new job openings throughout the company. If the company in Exhibit 7.2 used a talent pool, the employees would not be stacked in small divisional and functional jobs; instead, all these individuals would be in one big job or management grouping, differentiated only in terms of the job *levels* into which each person was ready to be moved.

Whether a company uses replacement charts or the talent pool concept, internal recruitment can be much less expensive in terms of time and money. By comparison, outside recruits often earn higher salaries, plus the costs of relocating a new recruit and her or his family may range from $50,000 to $500,000. The result, especially if the new recruit fails to contribute as expected, may be dissatisfaction among the current employees. In addition, the incentive value of promotions diminishes.[10]

Counterbalancing these advantages are several disadvantages associated with a promotion-from-within policy. One is the possibility of not finding the best-qualified person. Even if the best person is found, he or she may not take the promotion for personal reasons, such as a desire to stay in familiar surroundings. Other disadvantages include infighting between candidates vying for a position, and inbreeding. Inbreeding exists when someone who is familiar with the organization has come to accept its ways of doing things. Such people are less likely to come up with creative and innovative ideas for improvement.

Given these advantages and disadvantages, it is not surprising that most companies do some internal promoting and also some external recruiting. Often, the type of employee sought determines whether the organization looks inside or outside. For example, many organizations such as AIG tend to hire highly trained professionals and high-level managers from the outside.

Transfers. Transfers occur when current employees are moved laterally to different *types* of jobs. Transfers often are used to develop employees with a broad view of the organization—a view that may be necessary for future promotions.

Job Rotations. Whereas transfers are likely to be considered somewhat permanent, job rotations are usually temporary. Like transfers, job rotations can be used to expose employees to various aspects of organizational life. For example, they are often used in management training programs. Job rotation has also been used to relieve job burnout for employees in high-stress occupations. For example, the Utah Department of Social Services has a program in which human service workers swap jobs with workers in other divisions or with employees in federal agencies for up to one year. At the end of the contracted period of service, employees have the opportunity to return to their original positions or remain in their new positions. Such programs give employees different perspectives as well as the opportunity to try out new positions without fear of failure. Management, in turn, gets a chance to preview the employees before making a long-term commitment.

Rehires and Recalls. Each week, thousands of employees are temporarily laid off from work and more are recalled to former jobs. Recalls may even occur at top-level positions in some companies. For example, when American Express found it had been weakened by a steady drain of its marketing talent, it turned to its retired former head of the Travel-Related Services unit for help.[11] Rehiring former or laid-off employees is a relatively inexpensive and effective method of internal recruiting. The organization already has information about the performance, attendance, and safety records of these employees. Because they are already familiar with job responsibilities, rehires may be better performers than recruits from other sources. In addition, they tend to stay on the job longer and have better attendance records.

In deciding whether to use rehiring as a recruitment strategy, organizations need to weigh the costs against the benefits. Rehiring and recalling are particularly beneficial to organizations that have seasonal fluctuations in the demand for workers, such as department stores, canneries, construction companies, ski resorts. For example, canneries in eastern Washington State recall large numbers of employees—some who have been on the payroll for more than twenty years—each summer and fall during the apple harvest. Mail-order companies like L. L. Bean continually bring back a large share of their laid-off workforces between September and December, the busiest months of the years, to help reduce employment costs.

The downside of this recruitment approach is that employee commitment may be low. By the time of the recall, a qualified recruit may have found alternative employment—possibly with a major competitor. Finally, because of turnover, an organization's contribution to unemployment compensation programs is likely to increase. However, many firms like L. L. Bean develop long-term relationships with their seasonal workers, so they are as committed to quality service as the regular employees.[12]

Internal Methods

Internal applicants for job vacancies can be located by posting a notice on the bulletin board, word of mouth, examining company personnel records, perusing promotion lists based on performance, obtaining ratings from assessment activities, checking seniority lists, and looking at lists generated by the skills inventory in an organization's HRIS.

Job Postings. Job postings prominently display current job openings to all employees in an organization. They serve the following purposes:

- Provide opportunity for employee growth and development
- Provide equal opportunity for advancement to all employees
- Create a greater openness in the organization by making opportunities known to all employees
- Increase staff awareness of salary grades, job descriptions, general promotion and transfer procedures, and what constitutes effective job performance
- Communicate organizational goals and objectives and allow each individual the opportunity to help find a personal fit in the organizational job structure

Although job postings are usually found on bulletin boards, they also appear in company newsletters and are announced at staff meetings. Increasingly, job posting is becoming high-tech. At Microsoft, individuals can e-mail the recruiting department and obtain a listing and description of jobs currently open. Although specific salary information is sometimes included, job grade and pay range are more typical. Job postings offer several benefits: improved morale, a way to see more opportunity for job variety, better matching of employee skills and needs, and the ability to fill positions at a low cost.[13]

These benefits are not always realized. Potential problems that arise with job posting include the following:

- Conflicts are sometimes created if an "heir apparent" in the department is passed over in favor of a candidate from another department or division.
- Conversely, the system may lose credibility if it appears that the successful candidate within the department had been identified in advance and the managers were merely going through the motions in considering "outsiders."
- The morale of unsuccessful candidates may suffer if feedback is not handled carefully.
- If two or three equally qualified internal candidates apply, it may be more difficult to choose among them, and the political aftermath may be greater.

Skills Inventories. Most organizations have skill-related information buried in human resource files. When it is needed, much time and effort may be required to get at it. A formal skills inventory aggregates this information through the use of a human resource information system.

Any data that can be quantified can be coded and included in a skills inventory. Common information includes name, employee number, job classification, prior jobs, prior experience, and salary levels. The results of formal assessments, such as those conducted in assessment centers or using work sample tests, are usually included. Skills inventories also should include the employee's job interests, geographic preferences, and career goals. Using this type of information, a company can ensure that potential job assignments meet individual as well as organizational goals.

Skills inventories are only as good as the data they contain. Because people's skills and interests change over time, maintaining a good database can be time-consuming and somewhat costly. Still, skills inventories help ensure fairness because they make it easier to identify and consider all internal candidates with the necessary qualifications for a position.[14]

External Sources

Recruiting internally may not produce enough qualified applicants, especially in a rapidly growing organization or one with a large demand for high-talent professional, skilled, and managerial employees. Therefore, organizations often must recruit from external sources.

Recruiting from the outside has a number of advantages, including bringing in people with new ideas. If internal candidates would require training in order to be qualified, it may be cheaper and easier to hire an already trained professional or skilled employee. External sources can also supply temporary employees who give the organization more flexibility to expand or contract the workforce.

In general, organizations need to use both internal and external sources of recruitment. A summary of the advantages and disadvantages of these sources appears in Exhibit 7.3. To see how the type of job being filled relates to methods and sources of recruitment, consult Exhibit 7.4.

Employee Referral Programs. Employee referral programs are, in effect, word-of-mouth advertisements through which current employees refer applicants from outside the organization. Because of the involvement of current employees, this recruiting method blends internal with external recruitment and is a low–cost-per-hire means of

■ *Exhibit 7.3*
Advantages and Disadvantages of Recruitment Sources

INTERNAL SOURCES

Advantages	Disadvantages
Better morale of promotee	Inbreeding
Better assessment of abilities	Possible morale problems of those not promoted
Lower cost for some jobs	Political infighting for promotions
Increased motivation for good performance	Need for strong management development program and
Need to hire only at entry level	training programs
Faster filling of openings	Prevention of new ideas

EXTERNAL SOURCES

Advantages	Disadvantages
"New blood," new perspectives	Possibility of selecting someone who does not "fit"
Lower cost than training a professional	Possibility of causing morale problems for internal
No group of political allies in organization already	candidates not selected
Possibility of bringing competitors' secrets, new insights	Longer "adjustment" or orientation time
Help in meeting equal employment needs	Possibility of bringing in an attitude of "This is the way we
	used to do it at XYZ Company"

SOURCE: Adapted from R. L. Mathis and J. H. Jackson, *Personnel: Contemporary Perspectives and Applications,* 7th ed. (St. Paul: West Publishing Co., 1994): 210. © 1994. Reproduced by permission. All rights reserved.

recruiting.[15] Informal referral programs consist of informing current employees about job openings and encouraging them to have qualified friends and associates apply for positions. Formal referral programs reward employees for referring skilled applicants to organizations. Employees may be awarded as little as $15, or as much as $2,000 for referring someone with a critical skill such as robotics engineering or specialized nursing care. The financial incentives may be linked to a recruit's completion of an application, acceptance of employment, or completion of work for a specified time period.

Compared with other external recruiting methods, for most occupations, employee referrals result in the highest one-year survival rates. One explanation for this success is that employees provide a balanced view of organizational life. Another explanation is that employees tend to recruit applicants who are similar to them in skills, interests, and abilities. Since employees are already both qualified and adjusted to the organizational culture, this matching process increases the likelihood that applicants also will fit into the environment.

At first thought, referring individuals who are similar in type—age, gender, race or ethnicity, and religion—may also be expected to be beneficial. However, such referrals—particularly if they are *required* for employment—may be detrimental or even illegal with regard to equal employment opportunity obligations.[16]

Walk-in Applicants. Some individuals become applicants by simply walking into an organization's employment office. As illustrated in Exhibit 7.4, walk-ins are especially prevalent for clerical and service jobs; managerial, professional, and sales applicants are seldom walk-ins.[17]

Like employee referrals, walk-ins are relatively casual and inexpensive. Unlike referral applicants, walk-in applicants may know less about the specific jobs available and may come without the implicit recommendation of a current employee. This may be a disadvantage, since current employees would be reluctant to refer or recommend

■ *Exhibit 7.4*
Recruiting Sources and Methods by Occupation

	Percent of Companies					
	Any Job Category*	Office/ Clerical	Production/ Service	Professional/ Technical	Commissioned Sales	Managers/ Supervisors
(Number of companies)	(245)	(245)	(221)	(237)	(96)	(243)
Internal Sources						
Promotion from within	99%	94%	86%	89%	75%	95%
Advertising						
Newspapers	97	84	77	94	84	85
Journals/magazines	64	6	7	54	33	50
Direct mail	17	4	3	16	6	8
Radio/television	9	3	6	3	3	2
Outside Referral Sources						
Colleges/universities	86	24	15	81	38	45
Technical/vocational institutes	78	48	51	47	5	8
High schools/trade schools	68	60	54	16	5	2
Professional societies	55	4	1	51	19	37
Community agencies	39	33	32	20	16	9
Unions	10	1	11	1	—	1
Employee referrals	91	87	83	78	76	64
Walk-in applicants	91	86	87	64	52	46
Employment Services						
State employment services	73	66	68	38	30	23
Private employment agencies	72	28	11	58	44	60
Search firms	67	1	**	36	26	63
U.S. Employment Service	22	19	20	11	7	7
Employee leasing firms	20	16	10	6	2	**
Computerized resume service	4	**	—	4	—	2
Video interviewing service	2	**	**	1	—	1
Special Events						
Career conferences/job fairs	53	20	17	44	19	19
Open house	22	10	8	17	8	7
Other	9	5	5	7	6	7

*Percentages for each job category are based on the number of organizations that provided data for that category, as shown by the number in parentheses.

SOURCE: Bureau of National Affairs, *Personnel Policies Forum,* survey no. 146, Recruiting and Selection Procedures (Washington, DC, 1988; updated 1993): pp. 4–5. Reprinted by permission.

unsatisfactory applicants. Nevertheless, walk-in applicants who are hired generally have turnover rates similar to those of referral applicants.[18]

This method tends to be a passive source of applicants. Furthermore, walk-in applicants are likely to come from the immediately surrounding area. Consequently, walk-in recruitment may generate an inadequate pool of candidates. This problem can be reduced by using open-houses to attract walk-in applicants from a larger geographic area.

Employment Agencies. Public and private employment agencies are a good source of temporary employees—and an excellent source of permanent ones. American public employment agencies operate under the umbrella of the U.S. Training and Employment

Service; it sets national policies and oversees the operations of *state employment agencies,* which have branch offices in many cities. State employment agencies provide a wide range of services, most of which are supported by employer contributions to state unemployment funds. The agencies offer counseling, testing, and placement services to everyone and provide special services to military veterans, members of some minority groups, colleges, and technical and professional people.

The Social Security Act provides that, in general, workers who have been laid off from a job must register with the state employment agency in order to be eligible for unemployment benefits. These agencies have rosters of potential applicants. Nationwide, they are networked to form job banks. These job banks have one drawback: the Training and Employment Service and its state agencies do not actually recruit people but only passively assist those who come to them. In addition, those who do come in are often untrained or only marginally qualified for most jobs.

Private employment agencies—sometimes called headhunter or search firms—serve professional, managerial, and unskilled job applicants. Agencies dealing with unskilled applicants often provide job candidates that employers would have a difficult time finding otherwise. Many employers looking for unskilled workers do not have the resources to do their own recruiting or have only temporary or seasonal demands for these workers.

Private agencies play a major role in recruiting professional and managerial candidates.[19] Between the mid-1980s and the mid-1990s, the executive recruiting industry grew phenomenally. Some estimates suggest that the search firm industry in 1994 generated more than $200 million annually in billings.

The fees charged by these agencies may be as high as one-third of the first year's total salary and bonus package for a job to be filled. Thus, this can be an expensive recruitment method for the employer. The costs may be much greater than the fees charged. In the prescreening process, for example, the search firm may err in rejecting a candidate who would do well, which poses additional cost to the organization.[20] To minimize such costs, close monitoring of the search firm's activities is necessary. Also, search firms often prescreen applicants who are already working with other organizations. They may call people they believe fit the company's needs, and discuss a job, but then never identify those people as having been considered for the job. Because of this, the process is apt to be secretive and counter to the openness that is desirable in an organization's employment process.

Yet another drawback is that a search firm generally cannot approach executives it has recently placed, and it may have agreements with its clients that limit its ability to approach the clients' employees. This limits the pool of applicants considered by a search firm, which is why IBM took the unusual action of hiring *two* search firms when it needed to find a successor to John F. Akers, its former CEO.[21]

In spite of these drawbacks, headhunter firms are doing well, especially when it comes to helping talented people who work in troubled companies find new positions.[22] They are also helping companies that cut too deeply during layoffs and now need people to fill the gaps. Says one executive recruiter, "We've become their management development arm. . . . instead of spending over $1 million to develop someone inside, companies would rather pay a $150,000 fee in order to recruit outside."[23]

Other Companies. Companies such as General Electric and Procter and Gamble are noted for their management development programs and their systematic way of developing people through job assignments. These practices can produce great managers, but they also provide a talented pool of potential candidates for other companies to raid:

So many companies have been rejuvenated by the arrival of a new chief executive drawn from the management of the General Electric Company that many investors feel as if they have hit a jackpot when their companies announce such recruiting coups.

Companies that hire GE executives usually get managers who have experience running businesses that would be among the nation's largest companies if they were independent. Most have also been through GE's widely admired management training courses and have absorbed GE's global perspective.[24]

Employees in companies known for their outstanding managers have always been contacted by private employment agencies; increasingly, they are being contacted directly by the company that wants them.

Management development programs are expensive, and some firms do not have them because they think it is foolish to train managers just to be hired by others. This view may be shortsighted for two reasons. First, the developing firm still gets its "pick of the litter," and second, having a good reputation for development serves as a powerful recruitment tool for lower-level jobs.

Temporary Help Agencies. Complementing the private agencies that provide applicants for full-time positions are more than forty-five hundred temporary help agencies, which can provide applicants for assignments lasting from a day to one or two years. These temporary workers are a part of the 40 million to 50 million American workers labeled the *contingent workforce*.[25] As more and more companies find it preferable to hire temporary workers, temporary help agencies have experienced a real boom. Their business is further fueled by the growing number of skilled and semiskilled individuals who prefer to work less than a forty-hour week or on a schedule of their own choosing. Temporary employment also provides a way to preview different jobs and work in a variety of organizations. For employees, temporary work is a good way to learn about possible new careers. Good temporary employees, or temps, often receive permanent job offers as well. Furthermore, temps may receive higher pay than members of the organization's permanent staff, although they also generally forgo any benefits.

Organizations are using temporary help agencies more than ever because some hard-to-get skills are available nowhere else. This is especially true for small companies that are not highly visible or cannot spend time recruiting. In addition, many organizations need people for only a short time. Getting them without an extensive search—while staying flexible enough to reduce the workforce without costly layoffs and potential unemployment compensation payments—is an obvious advantage.[26]

Trade Associations and Unions. Unions for the building trades and maritime industry assume responsibility for supplying employers with skilled labor. This practice takes many labor decisions, such as job assignment, out of company hands. However, the Taft-Hartley Act restricts hiring halls to a limited number of industries.

Trade and professional associations are also important sources for recruiting. Their newsletters often provide notices of employment opportunities, and their annual conferences provide a forum where employers and potential job applicants can meet. Communities and schools have adopted this idea and now bring together large numbers of employers and job seekers at *job fairs*. Of course, with only a limited time for interviews, such fairs serve only as an initial step in the recruitment process. Nevertheless, they are an effective means for introducing employers and applicants.

Schools. Schools can be categorized into three types: high schools, vocational and technical schools, and colleges and universities. All are important sources of recruits for most organizations, although their importance varies depending on the type of applicant sought. For example, if an organization is recruiting managerial, technical, or professional applicants, then colleges and universities are the most important source. These institutions become less important when an organization is seeking production, service, office, and clerical employees (see Exhibit 7.4).

Recruiting at colleges and universities is often an expensive process, even if the recruiting visit eventually produces job offers and acceptances. Approximately 30 percent of the applicants hired from college leave the organization within the first five years of their employment. The rate of turnover is even higher for graduate management students. Some people attribute typically high rates of turnover to the lack of job challenge provided by many organizations. Organizations claim, however, that people just out of college have unrealistic expectations. Partly because of the expense and partly because of the availability of midlevel managers in transition, organizations are now reexamining the necessity of hiring college graduates for some jobs.

Nevertheless, college placement services are helpful when recruiting in particular fields—such as engineering and microelectronics—and when seeking highly talented and qualified women and members of minority groups. In addition, because some colleges and universities provide placement services to alumni, campus recruiting can be an effective means to developing a pool of experienced applicants.

Foreign Nationals. In some professions—such as chemical engineering, software engineering, and others that involve high-tech skills—labor shortages cause employers to recruit foreign nationals, often from overseas or through college placement offices. Foreign nationals may be employed in operations in the United States or abroad. When they work abroad, they serve as *host-country nationals* (persons working in their own country, not the country of the parent company) or *third-country nationals* (persons working in a country that is neither their own nor that of the parent company). One novel practice, where U.S. firms contract out work to Russian scientists, represents a global solution to a domestic skill shortage, and it is also an economical way to get highly skilled workers:

> Scientists in Russia are signing Western contracts as fast as they can to supplement dwindling incomes. A Russian computer scientist, Boris A. Babayan, is setting up a laboratory in Moscow for Sun Microsystems, Inc., based in Mountain View, Calif., that will employ his team of about 50 software and hardware designers. Mr. Babayan created the supercomputers used by the Soviets to design nuclear arms. Sun Microsystems will pay each of his team's members a few hundred dollars a year—ample pay by Moscow standards.[27]

Under the Immigration Reform and Control Act of 1986 and the Immigration Act of 1990, it is unlawful for employers to hire foreigners who are not authorized to work in the United States. Since foreign nationals are critical to their operations, U.S. companies have made increased efforts to ensure that these employees either are or become legal.

External Methods

Advertising—on radio and television, in the local paper, in national newspapers such as the *Wall Street Journal,* and on electronic bulletin boards—is one of a broad variety of methods used to recruit from external sources.

Radio and Television Advertisements. Of the approximately $3 billion spent annually on recruitment advertising, most is spent on printed ads. Only a tiny percentage is spent on radio and television. Some companies are reluctant to use these media because they fear the ads will be too expensive or the company will look desperate and damage its conservative image. In reality, of course, there is nothing inherently desperate about using radio and television. Rather, the implied level of desperation depends on what is said and how it is delivered. Recognizing this, organizations are increasing their recruitment expenditures for radio and television advertisements, with favorable results.[28]

Newspaper and Trade Journal Advertisements. Traditionally, newspapers have been the most common vehicle of external recruiting. They reach large numbers of potential applicants at a relatively low cost per hire. Newspaper ads announce openings of all types, from unskilled to top-level managerial positions. They range from matter-of-fact to creative. According to Arte Nathan, HR manager, Mirage Resorts Incorporated gets great results with well-placed newspaper ads:

> Five months before [a new] building opens, we open our employment offices and put image advertising [related to our casino-hotels' themes] in the newspaper. The initial ad for the Mirage said, "We're looking for 5,000 people who wouldn't mind working in a tropical rain forest with live sharks and a volcano that erupts every 30 minutes." Treasure Island's ad said: "We're looking for roughians [*sic*], scalawags and other people who don't mind a good fight while they're working." We received 57,000 applications for the 6,500 Mirage positions and close to 70,000 for Treasure Island's 5,000. Our intention in HR was to get a giant applicant pool and then screen for several traits: personality, stability and some type of experience.[29]

Trade journals enable organizations to aim at a much more specific group of potential applicants. Unfortunately, long lead times are required, so the ads can become dated. This problem is quickly disappearing as we approach and enter the 21st century, however, because more and more trade associations have electronic bulletin boards, which supplement the printed ads.

Whatever the medium, preparing ads requires considerable skill. Many organizations hire advertising firms to do this. An advertising agency must be chosen with the same care used to select a private recruiting agency.[30]

Computerized Service Listings. A newer and much less common external recruitment method is the computerized recruiting service. This service works as a place to both list job openings and locate job applicants. Job/Net is one such service:

> Personnel officers using a Job/Net terminal "can find people in fifteen minutes that it would take eight hours to find going through paper resumes," says Janice Kempf, a vice-president and cofounder. M/A Com, a microwave and telecommunications company in Burlington, Massachusetts, recently hired a $30,000 quality-control engineer through Job/Net. "If we paid an agency fee, it would have been $6,500 to $7,000," says Richard L. Bove, the staffing and development manager. He adds that the service lets him see more resumes of qualified people and lets him choose people who don't require expensive relocation.[31]

A number of on-line employment services and bulletin boards provide relatively inexpensive and valuable information. These include the following:

E-Span. Lists professional and managerial positions. Accessible through America Online, Compuserve, Genie.

Help Wanted—USA. Lists professional jobs. Accessible through America Online, the Internet.

Online Career Center. Lists professional jobs. On the Internet.

Federal Job Opportunity Board. Lists Federal Government openings. On the Internet. Also, Fedworld.

Career Connections. Engineering, manufacturing, marketing and computer jobs. Also has service for recent college graduates. On the Internet.[32]

Positioning for the 21st Century:
TIPS FOR HIRING TECHIES

How does your company recruit technical workers? Still hanging that tacky Job Openings sign by the plant gate? Or maybe you're running cryptic classifieds. Are you happy with the results? . . .

As technicians assume larger responsibilities in the new economy, employers will have to take the same care in hiring them as they would candidates for positions in management. Indeed, some are already adopting many of the same recruitment strategies. More technical workers are coming to their fields from colleges and specialized trade schools, making on-campus recruiting a fruitful way to find younger technicians with the latest skills. When Union Pacific wanted to hire candidates for its newly created data integrity analysis positions who had the capability of growing into management slots, for example, it dispatched its recruiters to colleges located near its National Customer Services Center in St. Louis. Moreover, many technical academies, like the DeVry Institute of Technology, stay in close contact with their alumni, offering employers a way to find experienced techies.

Some innovative employers and private employment agencies are reaching the technicians they need where they live, which for an ever-increasing number of them is in cyberspace. The Internet now carries some 800 listings of job openings daily—many of them for technical workers. Twenty companies in the Boston area—including Wellfleet Communications, Medtronic, and Addison-Wesley—are testing a new Internet recruitment service called Argus Virtual Classifieds. Developed by a company called Computer-Based Communications in suburban Lexington, Argus allows Internet job seekers to log on to some 150 listings weekly, which provide far more detail about the nature of the work, required qualifications, and compensation than a conventional newspaper classified ad can.[33]

One old tried-and-true hiring technique—word-of-mouth references—works especially well for finding the technicians your company needs. Technical workers form what Stanford University ethnographer Stephen R. Barley calls "communities of practice." Membership in these informal craft networks consists of technicians who are employed by vendors of technical equipment and the end users. In addition to the technical information they share with one another, they swap tips on which companies are hiring. So if you're looking for a good technician, why not ask one who already works for you?

Another use of computer technology is for the recruitment of high-tech applicants in cyberspace. The feature "Positioning for the 21st Century: Tips for Hiring Techies" highlights the efforts required by firms such as Wellfleet Communications in order to attract "high-demand" professionals.

Acquisitions and Mergers. In contrast with other external methods, acquisitions and mergers can facilitate the immediate implementation of an organization's strategic plan. When an organization acquires a company with skilled employees, this ready pool may enable the organization to pursue a business plan—such as entering a new product line—that would otherwise be unfeasible. However, the need to displace employees and to integrate a large number of them rather quickly into a new organization means that the human resource planning and selection process becomes more critical than ever.[34]

Open Houses. An excellent way to introduce individuals to the organization and also attract individuals who might not otherwise apply is to hold an open house—to open the doors so that people can come in and take a look at the company and learn about jobs that might be available. Such events can give the individual a realistic organizational preview and the firm a chance to look at potential applicants in a fairly informal setting.

When an open house is held during a weekend, the firm might also attract applicants who are working during the weekdays.

Contract Recruiting. In response to employment cycles and the need for cost containment, some firms hire a *contract recruiter.* Contract recruiters are consultants who accept temporary assignments, typically for three to six months; become an integral part of the HR staff; and address recruitment problems. Although employment activity accounts for a majority of their assignments, contract recruiters are increasingly involved in a variety of human resource issues, ranging from compensation and benefits to employee relations, equal access, and equal opportunity.

Contractors are available immediately, without the expense of employee benefits. Unlike regular employees, they are easily replaced without the trauma of a termination. For example, GTE Corporation in Needham, Massachusetts, won a major contract, assuring the government that twelve hundred professionals would be onboard within sixteen months. At the peak of recruiting, twelve contractors worked full-time as an instant employment staff, establishing a recruiting and selection system. The number diminished to two at the end of the sixteen months. Before leaving, the consultants recruited, hired, and trained their own replacements.

When Fidelity Investments opened up a new consumer division in Salt Lake City, Utah, rather than rely on a corporate staff to recruit applicants, the firm trained human resource graduate students in Fidelity's selection procedures. En masse, these contract recruiters enabled Fidelity's new office to become operational within two months.[35]

Contingent Workforce Recruiting. Another way to give individuals and companies a preview of each other is to recruit individuals from the contingent workforce. This method is likely to grow significantly in the years ahead:

> Like the tolling of an iron bell, a gloomy statistic has begun to resonate with many Americans: by some calculations, more than one out of four of us is now a member of the contingent work force, people hired by companies to cope with unexpected or temporary challenges—part-timers, freelancers, subcontractors, and independent professionals. As the name suggests, such workers typically lead far riskier and more uncertain lives than permanent employees; they're also usually paid less and almost never receive benefits. In large U.S. companies, their numbers have been growing lately in the scramble to get leaner and more efficient by shedding full-time workers for contingent ones. Indeed, a few analysts of trends predict that by the year 2000 fully half of all working Americans—some 60 million people—will have joined the ranks of these freelance providers of skills and services.[36]

The contingent workforce helps some companies meet the demands of flexibility and change. AT&T's version of the contingent workforce is "in-house employee pools." AT&T employees who join these pools can be assigned to a wide variety of jobs on any given day or week.

The notion of a contingent workforce is often considered a negative employment trend for employees. However, one large study of nearly seven thousand workers suggests that a pool of employees who are not promotable is beneficial to core employees. In effect, the contingent workforce creates a "hidden escalator" that allows core employees to advance.[37] The availability of temporary workers also facilitates implementation of temporary leave policies, which benefit core workers. Some temporary help agencies believe that the Family and Medical Leave Act of 1993 in particular will drive more companies to make greater use of the services of professional and managerial temps.[38]

Multiple Sources and Methods

Because of a growing skill shortage, some organizations need new recruiting solutions, so they experiment with sources and methods not used before.[39] This includes advertising in movie theaters and through cable television, using video teleconferencing for recruitment interviews, and trying to entice retired senior citizens back to work. Days Inns of America, a national motel chain, is doing exactly this. According to Richard A. Smith, executive vice president for Days Inns:

> Days Inn started actively recruiting older employees in the mid-1980s when, because of a shrinking labor market, we had to look for alternative labor sources to fill jobs. We couldn't find all the individuals needed to fill 65 to 85 positions a week at our largest reservation center, which at that time was in Atlanta, Georgia. Fast-food restaurants were gobbling up the labor market. The senior market seemed the most likely for us.
>
> Days Inn started with an exhibit at a local job fair for seniors. With assistance from older employees already on the payroll, the company organized its own job fair, which was held on a Saturday and was well publicized. It attracted about 100 older applicants and 75 to 85 were hired, many of whom still work for the company. Once the company had about 85 older employees, it relied on these employees rather than on additional job fairs to pass the word that the company wanted to hire additional seniors.
>
> People who are 55 years old or older are hired for both part-time and full-time positions at the reservations center at starting wages of $4 to $6 an hour. As is true with other Days Inn employees, they are not required to pass a physical examination. In addition, because the reservation system is a 7-day-a-week, 24-hour-a-day operation, new hires can virtually choose their own schedules.[40]

As companies face increased skill shortages, they are becoming more skillful at recruiting. But they are also doing this in an environment where downsizing is occurring. Consequently, many organizations are concerned with work flow management.

Work Flow Management

Throughout the early 1990s, companies in the United States and then in Japan and Europe were downsizing—at both managerial and nonmanagerial levels. While these organizations were concerned about outplacement of employees, they were hiring at the same time.

> *Even in tough times, we have to bring some level of entry-level talent into the organization to keep the business revitalized.*
>
> ANDY ESPARZA, Director of Recruitment and College Relations AT&T Global Information Solutions (formerly NCR)[41]

During this period, many smaller companies were hiring only; downsizing occurred mainly in the largest companies in America. Nonetheless, in most firms, employees were coming and going.

The process of recruitment seeks to ensure that the best are attracted to the firm and the best stay. Because of rapid changes in technology, the need for balancing is even more important. Companies cannot afford to be without the latest technological skills, so they must continually look at their recruitment methods and sources to make sure needed skills are coming in and perhaps unneeded skills are being outplaced or retrained. In this respect, HR planning and recruitment work hand in hand. Together, these activities need to address the needs of the business, attend to (and use!) new technologies, and adjust to the ever changing nature of the workforce. Recruitment is a dynamic activity today, concerned about the inflow as much as the outflow of a company's human resources.

❖ JOB SEARCH AND RECRUITMENT FROM THE APPLICANT'S PERSPECTIVE

For organizations to effectively attract potentially qualified candidates, they need to understand the behaviors and preferences of the diverse workforce. How do candidates differ in their job search activities? Are some sources better for some types of job applicants? Knowing how candidates are attracted means understanding where they get their information regarding job availability and what they react to the most. For example, one study involving several large companies found that students are attracted to companies that provide more information in their ads. When ads tell about the company, the job, and the job benefits, students are more likely to follow up and apply for the job.[42] Another study found that applicants who obtained information from both formal and informal sources had more knowledge about the job than those who relied on only one source.[43] And informal sources may provide more accurate information.[44]

What Sources Attract

Informal sources—referrals from friends and relatives, direct applications—top the list of sources used by recruits across all jobs. In addition, these sources result in the highest one-year job survival rates. Individuals who get help from friends and relatives also tend to accept lower wages, perhaps because they give in to pressure to accept job offers.

More formal sources, such as classified advertisements and private employment agencies, have lower survival rates but are used more often by managerial and clerical employees. Salaries secured through private employment agencies may be higher than those obtained through other methods. This is because the recruiter's fee is contingent on the salary level accepted, so the recruiter as well as the applicant will likely be pushing for a higher salary.[45]

In addition to understanding the appeal of these different sources, companies also seek to understand what knowledge is likely to have the most effect on a candidate's decision to consider them. The feature, "Using Data for the 21st Century: Do Recruiters and Recruiting Practices Really Make a Difference?" indicates that job seekers' perception of job fit is affected by job and company characteristics; thus, these must be managed effectively in the recruitment process. The behaviors of the recruiters also make a big difference. Effective recruiters show sincere interest in applicants, and, in return, applicants show more interest in the job.[46] A national study of recruitment for engineering graduates revealed that students not only responded to the interpersonal skills of recruiters but also preferred recruiters who were similar to them in terms of gender and education. Contrary to conventional wisdom, recruits did not respond more favorably to line managers or engineers than to human resource personnel.[47] Given that recruiters sell the organization to employees, perhaps they should be trained just as if they were selling the firm's products. Instead, whereas salespeople generally receive several weeks of training, recruiters seldom receive more than a few hours.

Evaluating Job Offers

Just as organizations have ideal requirements for job applicants, recruits have preferences for jobs. Several variables, including occupational choice and organizational choice, influence applicants' evaluations of job options.

Occupational Choice. Choosing an occupation involves a narrowing process, which begins in childhood and continues through adulthood. Whereas almost any occupation is

Using Data for the 21st Century:
DO RECRUITERS AND RECRUITING PRACTICES REALLY MAKE A DIFFERENCE?

Imagine that you own a toy company. With the baby boomlet in full swing, orders are growing at a fast pace. To keep up, you need to expand your manufacturing facility and hire a couple of good managers. When you offer the best applicants a job, what will determine whether they say yes? Does it make a difference whom you choose to do the job of recruiting, or can you just give this task to whoever is most easily spared? Does the recruitment process itself really make much difference?

To develop a better understanding of how job applicants view recruiting practices, one team of researchers decided to conduct intensive, open-ended interviews with a few job hunters. The researchers asked placement directors from four colleges of a large university to identify job seekers who were as different from each other as possible in terms of sex, race, grade point average, and so on. Forty-one job seekers were identified and then interviewed early in the campus recruiting season and again near the end, eight to ten weeks later. The interviews were recorded, transcribed, and then content analyzed.

The results showed that job seekers' early perceptions of how well they fit a job were affected most by job and company characteristics, then by contacts with recruiters, and then by contacts with other people in the company besides recruiters. Important job and company characteristics included status of the functional area the job was in, company reputation and management ethics as presented in the media, attitudes toward the product, and HR practices—such as whether the company was hiring new managers and at the same time laying some

people off. By the end of the recruiting season, most people reported that the recruiters made a big difference in how they felt about a job. By this time, the average job seeker in the study had completed eighteen interviews, made more than six site visits, and received three offers.

In many instances, recruiters made jobs that initially appeared unattractive seem attractive. Positive impressions were created by the status of recruiters and whether recruiters made applications feel "specially" treated. On the other hand, almost all job seekers reported that some recruiters or recruiting practices or both created poor impressions and made some jobs seem less attractive. Timing was especially important here, with slow or late decisions being a major reason for negative impressions. Recruiters were viewed as more important by job seekers who had more job offers to choose from. Also, women (compared with men) viewed recruiters as more important. Many women (50 percent) reported some "offensive" interactions with recruiters, including remarks made about their personal appearance, negative comments about "minority" groups other than women (e.g., older workers), and mail addressed to "Mr." even after the initial interview. Another interesting finding was that the best applicants were more likely than weaker applicants to interpret recruiting practices as indications of what the employing *organization* was like rather than assuming the practices were just a poor reflection on the particular recruiter involved.

Clearly, this study suggests that every employer should select recruiters carefully and put its best foot forward when it begins the hiring process.[48]

a potential choice in childhood, people have usually focused on one or two by young adulthood. These choices are influenced by economic issues, including the realities of the labor market; psychological issues, such as individual needs, interests, and abilities; and sociological issues, including exposure to the occupation through parents and relatives. The process draws to a close when an organization offers a position that most clearly meets the applicant's needs.[49]

Organizational Choice. Most individuals make an occupational choice and then choose an organization within that occupation. Several variables affect organizational choice.

Although it has often been assumed that job seekers generate as many options as possible and simultaneously evaluate them, job search activities are usually not this intense. In fact, job seekers typically have only a hazy notion of their options.[50] The objective of most job seekers is to find a minimally acceptable, rather than optimal, job. As a result, job opportunities are usually evaluated *sequentially*. If a job meets minimum qualifications, it is accepted; if it does not, the sequential search process continues.

The exception is job search activities after college. In high-demand fields—for instance, software writing and mechanical and electrical engineering—new graduates often have more than one offer to consider *simultaneously*. Traditionally, organizations provide these individuals with job information and give them time to consider various job options. Increasingly, however, organizations are adopting strategies that bring high-potential students to the company's attention earlier in the process to ensure acceptance of its job offers.[51]

Organizational choices are also affected by location, by whether the applicant believes the organization's values match her or his own, and by specific job attributes.[52] An important job attribute is an individual's *noncompensatory reservation wage:* the minimum pay necessary to make a job offer acceptable. Prior compensation levels, the length of unemployment, and the availability of accurate salary information all affect an individual's reservation wage. Evidence suggests also that males have higher reservation wages than females. One reason is that females have been found to undervalue their work abilities. Another may be that males are exposed to more job opportunities.[53]

Once a reservation wage is met, job seekers adopt a *compensatory approach* in which trade-offs are made between different job attributes, including higher levels of compensation and the type of compensation plan.[54] In one large study, more than fifty thousand male and female applicants to the Minnesota Gas Company were asked to rank the importance of ten job attributes. Both sexes tended to rank the importance of company and coworkers higher for themselves than for others, and higher than benefits, hours, and pay. Job applicants agreed that pay was important to others but were less willing to admit that it was important to them. For females, the type of work was ranked most important, whereas job security was ranked higher by males.[55]

INCREASING THE POOL OF POTENTIALLY QUALIFIED APPLICANTS

To gain a competitive edge, organizations must understand and meet the needs of job seekers. To increase the likelihood that high-potential employees will be successfully recruited, hired, and retained, organizations can adopt a variety of strategies. Providing alternative work schedules and other forms of job accommodation can certainly be helpful, as can management development programs. Effective methods and processes of conveying job and organizational information are also very helpful. As they work to expand the applicant pool, recruiters and HR professionals need to reject unselected applicants with tact and carefully follow truth-in-hiring guidelines.

Conveying Job and Organizational Information

The traditional approach to recruitment involves matching the job applicant's skills, knowledge, and abilities with the demands of the job. A more recent approach also matches the job applicant's personality, interests, and preferences with the job and with organizational characteristics. The activities at Chubb, described earlier in this chapter, reflect this approach. For effective human resource management, getting the job applicants to stay is as important as recruiting job applicants who can do the job. Both objectives are facilitated by devoting attention to the job interview, having a job-matching program, developing appropriate policies regarding job offer acceptances, and carefully timing recruitment procedures.

Job Interview. The interview is a vital aspect of the recruitment process. A good interview provides the applicant with a realistic preview of what the job will be like. It can entice an applicant to join an organization, just as a bad interview can turn him or her away. The quality of the interview is just one aspect of the recruitment process. Other things being equal, the chances of a person's accepting a job offer increase when interviewers show interest and concern for the applicant.

The content of the recruitment interview also matters. Some recruiters assume that it is in the company's best interest to tell job applicants only about the positive aspects of a job and the company. However, studies by the life insurance industry show that providing both positive and negative information, in what is called a realistic preview, actually increases the number of eventual recruits. In addition, those who receive both types of job information tend to be more committed and less likely to quit once they accept the job.[56] The type of interview that conveys positive and negative information is referred to as a *realistic job preview.*

> A realistic job preview can be given as part of the recruitment process before an individual has accepted a job, or as part of the orientation or socialization process that takes place after job acceptance. Such previews can take many forms, including written descriptions of the job, film or video tape presentations, and samples of the actual work. Although they may differ in form or mode of presentation, all realistic job previews are alike in presenting all relevant aspects of a job as accurately as possible. Since new or potential employees usually have inflated ideas or expectations about what a job involves, a realistic preview usually *reduces* these overly optimistic expectations. In effect, even though it presents a complete and accurate picture, a realistic preview primarily serves to acquaint new or prospective employees with the previously unknown negative aspects of a particular job.[57]

If job applicants pass an initial screening, they should be given the opportunity to interview with a potential supervisor and even with coworkers. The interview with the potential supervisor is crucial, because this is the person who often makes the final decision.

Job Matching. Job matching is a systematic effort to identify people's knowledge, skills, and abilities, and their personalities, interests, and preferences, and then match them to the job openings. Increasing pressure on organizations to effectively recruit, select, and place new and current employees may make an automated job matching system worthwhile. For example, Citibank's job matching system for nonprofessional employees evolved from an automated system designed to monitor requisition and internal placement processes. The system is used to identify suitable positions for staff members who wish to transfer or who are seeking another job because of technological displacement or reorganization. The system also ensures that suitable internal candidates will not be overlooked before recruiting begins outside the organization. Thus, the system appears not only to help recruit people and ensure that they stay, but also to provide a firm basis for job-related recruitment and selection procedures.

Policies Regarding Job Offer Acceptance. Employers can influence job applicants' selection decisions through the amount of time they allow individuals to ponder an offer. Given unlimited time, most job seekers will delay decision making until they have heard from all the organizations in the job search net. Although potentially advantageous to the job seeker, the lack of a deadline places the organization at a distinct disadvantage. Unless the number of openings exceeds the number of applicants, the organization cannot extend an offer to a second-choice candidate until a decision is made by the preferred candidate. Thus, most organizations have recall policies, and job seekers may find themselves having to accept or reject a minimally acceptable offer before receiving a preferred offer. The short- and long-term effects of time deadlines need further investigation before definitive conclusions can be drawn about their effectiveness.

Timing of Recruitment Procedures. In markets where recruiting occurs in well-defined cycles, as in college recruiting, organizations can enhance their chances of obtaining high-potential candidates through early entry into the process. For example, high-technology companies begin the recruitment process by involving high-potential college juniors in summer internships or cooperative education programs. Progressive organizations also bypass traditional second-semester campus interviews and invite high-potential candidates directly to corporate headquarters early in the senior year. Most major accounting firms have job offers out and accepted by the end of the calendar year. Such strategies are designed to induce commitment from top graduates before they are exposed to competing firms. Organizations that rely on traditional second-semester senior year interviews and long selection processes may find themselves in a less competitive position.[58]

Rejecting with Tact

When a new Toyota plant opened in Georgetown, Kentucky, the applicant pool reached forty thousand for twenty-seven hundred assembly line openings. Thousands more applied for the three-hundred office jobs.[59] Like other "high-demand" organizations, Toyota faced a new challenge to recruiting: rejection with tact.

Consider what happens when one hundred applicants apply for one position with a bank. Only one applicant will be accepted, leaving ninety-nine potential employees or customers. If these rejected candidates feel angry at the bank, they may never again purchase services from the organization. If the application procedures are viewed as unfair, too lengthy, or too impersonal, the rejected candidates may also share their dissatisfaction with friends and associates.

Several characteristics of rejection letters make a difference. Statements that are friendly (e.g., "Thank you for applying; good luck in the future"), include a personalized address and a correct salutation (*Ms., Mrs., Miss,* or *Mr.*), and summarize the applicant's job qualifications leave positive impressions. Including statements about the size and excellence of the application pool and about the person who was offered the job (e.g., "the person hired had ten years' experience and was certified in arbitrage") reduce disappointment and increase perceptions of fairness. However, employers are becoming a bit cautious about disclosing too much. If the rejected candidate disagrees with the reasoning, litigation could ensue.

Including a statement that the applicant's résumé will be kept on file increases the likelihood that the applicant will continue to use the organization's services or buy its products. But promises made in rejection letters can serve as binding contractual obligations. Thus, a promise should be made only if the organization intends to keep it.

The timeliness with which rejection letters are mailed also is important to applicants. Not only should a recruitment and selection timetable be specified to applicants, but also the organization should meet its self-imposed deadlines.[60]

Following Truth-in-Hiring Guidelines: Ethics in Recruitment

Is it ethical for firms to promise something to a job candidate in order to make the firm attractive and then not deliver on the promise? Accepting a job offer can have far-reaching implications for a person's life—it can affect where the person lives, how much stress the person experiences commuting to work, where the person's children attend school, where a partner works, income levels, and so on. Viewed in this light, persuading a person to take a job becomes a big responsibility. Clearly, the only ethical approach is to engage in an honest exchange of information with job applicants.

If a firm's representatives do make false promises to job candidates, the firm can face costly lawsuits, as in *Stewart v. Jackson and Nash* (1992). Such truth-in-hiring lawsuits have yielded damage awards as high as $10 million. Thus, truth-in-hiring appears to be a legal as well as ethical issue that is of importance to both the individual and the organization.[61] The HR department can assist by ensuring that line managers and others involved in recruiting interviews are trained and are aware of their legal and ethical responsibilities so that they do not make exorbitant promises just to attract a favorite job applicant.

 ## LEGAL CONSIDERATIONS IN RECRUITMENT

Legal considerations play a critical role in the recruitment and hiring processes of most companies in the United States. For example: "Federal Express Corporation is firmly committed to afford equal employment opportunity to all individuals regardless of age, gender, race, color, religion, national origin, citizenship, physical handicap, or status as a Vietnam era or special disabled veteran. We are strongly bound to this commitment because adherence to equal employment opportunity principles is the only acceptable way of life. We adhere to those principles not just because they're the law, but because it's the right thing to do."[62]

Although much of the legal framework facing human resource management is directed at employment decisions concerning hiring, firing, health and safety, and compensation, legal considerations begin with the organization's search for job applicants, whether inside or outside the organization. The equal employment laws most directly relevant to recruitment are those describing affirmative action programs (AAPs).

Affirmative Action Programs

Affirmative action programs are intended to ensure proportional and fair representation of *qualified* employees on the basis of race, color, ethnic origin, sex, and disability.[63] Many firms have AAPs (see Exhibit 7.5). These programs generally arise from three different conditions: federal contracts, past discrimination, and voluntary action.[64]

Federal Contracts If a company has a federal contract greater than $50,000 and has fifty or more employees, it is referred to as a federal contractor and is required to file, with the Office of Federal Contract Compliance, (OFCC), a written plan outlining steps to be taken for correcting underutilization in places where it has been identified.

Affirmative action programs are designed to facilitate an organization's commitment to provide and achieve proportional representation or parity, or to correct underutilization, in its workforce with the relevant labor market of protected group members. Title VII of the Civil Rights Act of 1964 includes in this group women, African Americans, Hispanics, Native Americans, Asian Americans, and Pacific Islander Americans. The

■ *Exhibit 7.5*
Corporate Affirmitive Action Programs

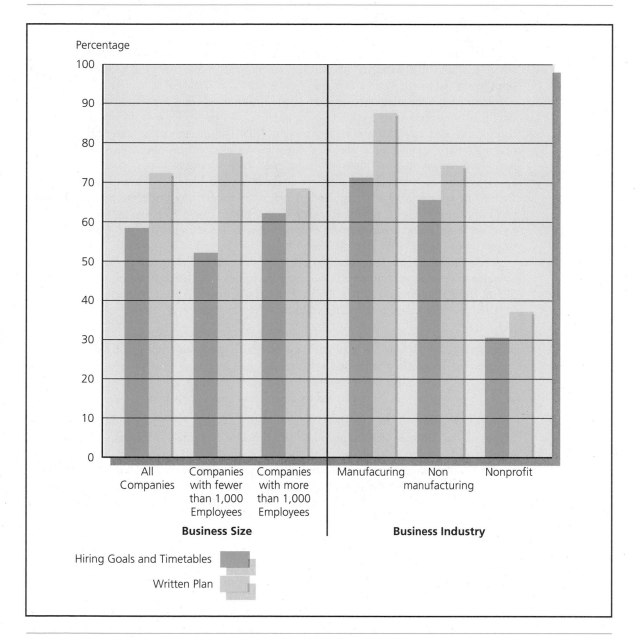

Note: Some written affirmative action plans are only statements and do not include goals and timetables.
SOURCE: Bureau of National Affairs. Used by permission.

components of affirmative action programs for federal contractors are specified by the Department of Labor in the OFCC. These AAPs are enforced by the OFCC and the Equal Employment Opportunity Commission through Executive Order 11246.

The specified components of AAPs for federal contractors include utilization and availability analyses, goals, and timetables. A *utilization analysis* determines the number of members of minorities and women employed in different jobs within an organization. An *availability analysis* measures how many members of minorities and women are available to work in the relevant labor market of an organization. If an organization is employing fewer members of minorities and women than are available, a state of *underutilization* exists.

The *relevant labor market* is generally defined as the geographic area from which come a substantial majority of job applicants and employees. Published sources of population data such as the *Standard Metropolitan Statistical Analysis* may provide initial guidance in determining this defined area. Within a relevant labor market, availability data can be gathered from sources such as the *U.S. Census,* local and state chambers of commerce, and city and state governments. Because organizations may fill some job openings with applicants in the local area and others with applicants from across the nation, organizations may have several relevant labor markets.

After the utilization and availability analyses are completed, goals and timetables are written to specify how an organization plans to correct any underutilization. Because goals and timetables become the organization's commitment to equal employment, they must be realistic and attainable. An example of a utilization plan for one job group in an organization is shown in Exhibit 7.6.[65]

Federal contractors are also required to take affirmative action to employ and advance in employment qualified disabled individuals at all levels of employment (section 503 of the Rehabilitation Act of 1973). The Rehabilitation Act, as amended in 1980 and in 1990 by the Americans with Disabilities Act, names three categories of protected persons:

⦿ Any individual who has a physical or mental impairment that greatly limits one or more of life's major functions
⦿ Any individual who has a history of such an impairment
⦿ Any individual who is perceived as having such an impairment

The impairments in the first category are usually evident conditions such as amputations, Down's syndrome, paralysis, hearing or visual problems, and so forth. Impairments in the second category cannot be readily discerned. Nevertheless, some employers shy away from applicants whose medical histories include cancer, heart disease, diabetes, and similar health problems, perhaps out of fear that a recurrence or other effects of the disease will result in increased insurance costs, a higher rate of absenteeism, and decreased efficiency. In one case, an employer refused to hire a worker who had leukemia because he was prone to infection from even minor injuries, but a Wisconsin circuit court found that the man was qualified to perform his job so the company could not refuse employment.

Notice that an employer's misconceptions can bring an individual who is not actually disabled under the coverage of the act or a similar state law. That is what happened when an employee was terminated because his employer thought he had epilepsy. The Washington Court of Appeals awarded the worker two years' back pay and ordered him reinstated. Also included are individuals who have suffered from alcoholism and drug abuse and individuals who are well but test positive for the AIDS virus.[66]

The Americans with Disabilities Act of 1990 permits medical exams only after the job offer has been made. The offer can be made conditional upon the results of the exam, but the employer must make reasonable accommodation. Before the job offer is made, the employer can describe the essential functions to the individual, but the employer cannot inquire about any disabilities the applicant might have.

■ *Exhibit 7.6*
Utilization, Goals, and Timetables

Job Group: ABC
As of: 2/14/96
Availability source: Eight-factor analysis

	Male	Female	White	Black	Hispanic	Asian	Native American	Minority	Total
Current Utilization									
Employees (#)	193	7	186	4	3	6	1	14	200
Employees (%)	96.5	3.5	93.0	2.0	1.5	3.0	0.5	7.0	
Availability (%)	88.0	12.0	66.0	15.0	14.0	4.0	1.0	34.0	100.0
Underutilized?	No	Yes	No	Yes	Yes	Yes	Yes	Yes	
Based on expansion of 36									
Goals									
Long-range goal (%)	—	15.0	—	15.5	14.5	4.0	1.0	35.0	100.0
Long-range goal (#)	—	35	—	37	34	9	2	82	236
Annual placement (%)	—	22.5	—	21.0	19.7	7.2	1.8	49.7	
Timetables									
If 12 openings (5.1% turnover)—Employment opportunities 1st year = 48									
Years to goal (#)	—	14	—	15	15	1	3	15	
Hired 1st year	—	11	—	10	9	3	<1	24	
Hired 2nd year on	—	3	—	3	2		<1	6	
If 24 openings (10.2% turnover)—Employment opportunities 1st year = 60									
Years to goal (#)	—	7	—	11	10	1	2	9	
Hired 1st year	—	14	—	13	12	4	1	30	
Hired 2nd year on	—	5	—	5	5		<1	12	
If 47 openings (19.9% turnover)—Employment opportunities 1st year = 83									
Years to goal (#)	—	4	—	5	5	1	1	4	
Hired 1st year	—	19	—	17	16	6	2	41	
Hired 2nd year on	—	11	—	10	9			23	
Projected openings 18 (7.6% turnover)—Employment opportunities 1st year = 54									
Years to goal (#)	—	10	—	14	14	1	2	11	
Hired 1st year	—	12	—	11	11	4	<1	27	
Hired 2nd year on	—	4	—	4	4		<1	9	
Utilization Analysis									
Employees (#)	193	7	186	4	3	6	1		200
Employees (%)	96.5	3.5	93.0	2.0	1.5	3.0	0.5		
Availability (%)	88.0	12.0	66.0	15.0	14.0	4.0	1.0		100.0
Should have (#)	176	24	132	30	28	8	2		
Underutilized?	No	Yes	No	Yes	Yes	Yes	Yes		
Calculation type	—	Z	—	Z	Z	Z	P		
Statistical value	—	3.59	—	5.05	4.99	0.54	0.73		
Z or probability	—	0.00	—	0.00	0.00	0.59	0.36		
Significant?	No	Yes	No	Yes	Yes	No	No		
Additional needed	—	8	—	16	15	—	—		

The rules further provide that employers with fifty or more employees who hold federal contracts totaling more than $50,000 must prepare written affirmative action programs for disabled workers in each of their establishments—for example, in each plant or field office. This condition must be met within 120 days after the contractor receives the federal contract. Those who hold contracts or subcontracts of less than

$2,500 are not covered by this act. Those with federal contracts that range from $2,500 to $50,000 are required to include an affirmative action clause in their contracts, but they do not need a written affirmative action plan.

To aid its efforts to attain its specified goals and timetables, an organization must make sure its employment policies, practices, and procedures facilitate goal attainment. This generally requires an assessment to determine whether underutilization exists. If it does, the organization's policies, practices, and procedures need to be modified.

Past Discrimination. A federal court may require an AAP if it finds evidence of past discrimination in a suit brought against the organization through the Equal Employment Opportunity Commission. An AAP under these conditions is generally part of a *consent decree,* a statement indicating the specific affirmative action steps the organization will take.

In April 1992, State Farm reached a settlement with women who had filed for damages in a past-discrimination suit. Worth $157 million, it was the largest settlement ever brought under the Civil Rights Act of 1964.[67]

> State Farm Insurance Co. agreed to set aside for women half of its new sales agent jobs in California over the next 10 years, and to pay damages and back pay to women who were refused sales jobs during a 13-year period, according to a consent decree settling a long-running sex bias case against the company.
>
> Female employees filed a class action suit in 1979, claiming that State Farm in California had discriminated against women in recruitment, hiring, job assignments, training, and termination decisions. A federal district court found the company had discriminated and was liable for damages to all women who unsuccessfully applied for or were deterred from applying for trainee agent jobs since 1974. The settlement covers 1,113 sales jobs that became vacant and were filled by men between 1974 and 1987, and is expected to result in back pay awards totaling between $100 and $300 million.
>
> The agreement provides that State Farm will use its best efforts to give women 50 percent of the trainee agent appointments each year for the next decade. The company is required to nominate one woman in each of its three California regions to serve as a recruitment administrator to train agency managers to recruit and retain qualified women. In addition, procedures were specified for the company to follow in publicizing openings for sales agent jobs. (*Kraszewski v. State Farm,* 1988).

Although goals set by consent decrees, or as part of the federal contractor's AAP, only specify percentages to be used as targets, these are often misconstrued as *quotas.* Setting strict quotas would generally be a violation of the Fourteenth Amendment, as well as being inconsistent with Title VII's protection against all employment discrimination. The courts have generally held in favor of goals as the only way to reverse previous practices of discrimination (*Detroit Police Officers' Association v. Coleman Young,* 1979; *Maehren v. City of Seattle,* 1979; *City of St. Louis v. United States,* 1980).

Nevertheless, the issue of reverse discrimination is being heard. For example, the Supreme Court ruled that federal courts could not ignore a seniority-based layoff policy and modify a consent decree to prevent the layoff of Black workers (*Firefighter Local Union 1784 v. Stotts,* 1984). In related cases, the Supreme Court has ruled that there are limits to the use of rigid racial and ethnic criteria to accomplish remedial objectives (*Fullilove v. Klutznick,* 1980; *Richmond v. Croson,* 1989; *Coalition of Black Maryland State Troopers v. Evans,* 1993). Remedies that go far beyond correcting past injustices and harm current employees may not be upheld (*Ensley Branch, NAACP v. Siebels,* 1994; *Black Fire Fighters Association of Dallas v. City of Dallas,* 1994). Reverse discrimination as it relates to recruitment is an issue for organizations establishing voluntary AAPs.

Voluntary Action. Organizations such as Weyerhaeuser and Levi Strauss may voluntarily establish goals for hiring and promoting women, members of minority groups, and individuals with disabilities. The exact content of such AAPs depends on the organization and the extent to which various groups are underrepresented.

Organizations that establish their own voluntary affirmative action programs may benefit from using EEOC guidelines that support such programs. The key considerations in a legal voluntary AAP are that it be remedial in its purpose, limited in its duration, restricted in the effects of its reverse discrimination (i.e., not an absolute ban on members of the majority group), and flexible in its implementation. When an organization's voluntary AAP has these characteristics, the risk of losing a reverse discrimination suit may be minimized, although it is not eliminated (*Martin v. Wilks,* 1989).

Regardless of the impetus for a company's affirmative action efforts, their presence often stimulates people to think more systematically about their recruitment efforts. Unfortunately, the disciplined approach associated with AAPs—that is, defining the relevant labor market and tracking how recruitment efforts affect both who is offered a position and who accepts job offers—usually is used only for lower-level positions. One consequence is the apparent existence of glass ceilings, which the Department of Labor defines as "artificial barriers based on attitudinal or organizational bias that prevent qualified individuals from advancing upward in their organizations."[68] Based on its intensive study of nine large corporations, the Department of Labor concluded that recruitment methods contributed to the problem of glass ceilings. Specifically, it identified these problems:[69]

- *Reliance on Networking—Word-of-Mouth:* In some companies, mid- and upper-level positions were filled by senior executives through word-of-mouth referrals. In some of these instances, corporate executives had learned of individuals, interviewed them casually (at luncheons or dinners), and made them an offer, outside the formal recruitment process. The net result of these activities was a diminished opportunity for the career advancement of women and members of minorities.
- *Reliance on Networking—Employee Referrals:* In some companies, elaborate employee referral systems are in place. Employees are paid for referring individuals who are subsequently hired. In one company reviewed by the Department of Labor, the review team could not establish if this system was discriminatory, but no members of minorities or women were hired into mid-levels and upper levels of the company through this process. Moreover, no members of minorities or women were in midlevel or upper-level positions doing this referring.
- *Corporate Use of Executive Search and Referral Firms:* All companies reviewed by the Department of Labor used search and referral firms during the period under review. One company appeared to fill almost every upper-level management position through search firms. Most of the companies failed to make executive recruitment firms aware of their equal employment and affirmative action obligations under the law. Specifically, when these companies asked a search agency for a candidate pool, many of them did not make any effort to ensure that the search firm reached out to identify qualified minorities and women. In addition, when the search firm sent forward a slate with no members of minorities or women, the contractors did not demonstrate any good-faith effort to broaden the pool of candidates.
- *Job Postings:* In some companies, vacancies were posted up to a certain level, above which employees were not made aware of advancement opportunities. Their only hope was reliance on networking. In addition, although the personnel director and EEO director are generally directly involved in the staffing of lower-level positions, in

some companies, above a certain level, those individuals do not appear to have a very substantive role in the hiring process.

- *Interview Process:* In addition to the type of recruitment used, the recruitment process itself can, at times, be a barrier for women. A Wellesley College Center for Research on Women study found that holding interviews for prospective sales representatives in hotel rooms is intimidating especially for women, and reduces the possibility of finding qualified women applicants. As an alternative strategy for hiring sales representatives, managers, and professionals, some corporations have developed comprehensive and sophisticated recruitment programs for attracting promising candidates to the corporations.[70]

To remedy these problems, which are now more widely recognized than they were when the Department of Labor's Glass Ceiling Commission first began its investigation, several actions can be taken. For example, one company developed a management intern program aimed at recruiting recent minority and female college graduates, as well as sponsoring scholarships for members of minorities and women in disciplines related to the company's business. Others planned to remedy problems related to the glass ceiling and affirmative action with better use of search firms and other forms of recruitment, record keeping, and internal monitoring. Creating awareness training for its top executives was the first step of one company, which also conducted an internal cultural audit to identify obstacles or barriers that hinder individuals from meeting their career goals. Important to the success of all such interventions is maintaining merit as the actual and perceived basis for employment decisions.[71]

INTERNATIONAL COMPARISONS

Japan

In Japan, the recruitment of graduates traditionally takes place once a year only, although this has changed somewhat since an economic slowdown in the early 1990s caused many firms to evaluate their HR practices.[72] In a company's direct recruitment, college professors play a dominant role. Company Y may ask Professor X to recommend so many students with special qualifications in certain fields. The selection process depends on the students' future occupational class. Students who major in the social sciences, law, or the humanities will enter administrative jobs, such as planning, human resources, sales, or purchasing. Students majoring in technical disciplines will enter technical jobs. The selection procedures differ for these occupational classes.

Aspiring administrators are asked to apply directly to employers for jobs. Following the formal application, the candidates are asked to appear for a set of interviews with company employees, managers, and executives. The basic criteria for hiring—besides an employee's potential or ability—are a "balanced" personality and moderate views. The evaluation of job candidates is often supplemented by background checks assigned to private investigators who interview the candidates' neighbors and acquaintances, check local police records, and examine family histories. Those who pass the last round of interviews are invited to sit for the company entrance examination. Officially, this exam should determine who is best qualified for the job, but in many corporations, over 90 percent of candidates are preselected on the basis of earlier interviews. The exam usually asks essay questions on such topics as family background, career and life objectives, or the applicant's strengths and weaknesses. A number of firms are actually using the exam as an assessment tool to determine the career interests of new employees.

Firms rely on intermediaries—that is, college professors—for selection decisions, especially when evaluating technical candidates, for a number of reasons. First, it is difficult to evaluate a student's technical potential on the basis of a short interview only, when most interviewers have little up-to-date technical background. If a company waited for a written examination, it would not preselect and would risk losing the best candidates to the competition. Professor recommendations circumvent both problems. Second, because of the competition for graduates, recruiters cultivate good relations with college professors, who then recommend individual firms to students. In this way, the firms expect to get their "fair share" of talent and simultaneously prevent a self-defeating bidding war that not only would raise the starting salaries for selected jobs but, more critical, would disrupt the carefully balanced compensation structures of internal labor markets. And last, college grades are not considered a valuable selection tool. What matters are the educational credentials of the school from which the student is graduating. Given the intense and rigorous competition to enter first-tier schools, the companies rely on the university entrance examination as an indicator of the employee's "latest ability."

During the 1970s, many elements of Japanese management practice demanded modification. Economic growth rates were declining and automation was broadly implemented. At this point, Japanese companies began hiring significantly fewer workers in entry-level positions. This resulted in the average age of employees increasing as they moved up the seniority ladder. In turn, pressure was added on average wage costs. The most powerful and negative effect of this era was the low morale caused by few opportunities for real advancement.

The Japanese responded to these problems quickly, instead of ignoring them. They increased their flexibility in employment with temporary transfers of surplus employees to other companies that are part of the "extended organization." This form of organization, called *keiretsu,* is a vertical linkage of companies that are mutual suppliers and customers.[73]

Mexico

A key HR concern for a company operating in Mexico is staffing. Recruiting for low-wage workers is relatively uncomplicated, because these workers constitute the majority of the labor pool. For example, at operations in cities on the U.S.-Mexico border, the maquiladora region, approximately 90 percent of employees are low-wage workers.

It is not as easy to staff high-level positions. To begin with, U.S. companies question whether to hire locally or employ an expatriate. One thing they need to consider is that under current Mexican labor law, no more than 10 percent of a foreign company's employees may be non-Mexican.

But even if they decide to hire expatriates, many companies have difficulty getting these American employees to relocate. Expatriates worry about pollution and its effects on their health, says Kevin Duffy, director of employee relations for Nabisco International, a division of New York City–based RJR Nabisco. Duffy says that this and other situations in Mexico contribute to an image problem.

"The infrastructure in general, from roads to schools to sewers to housing, is a problem." Does this mean that expatriates should be excluded from considerations? "If you have critical areas of expertise that you need that do not seem to be available in the market, then it may require an expat, but it should be relatively short-term, say two to three years, while developing the local talent."[74]

Schaumburg, Illinois–based Motorola, which has had operations in Mexico for more than twenty years, has hired expatriates, but views their employment more as a strategic choice than an act of desperation. Rebecca Lotsoff, manager of international compensation, says, "[But] that's probably not something you'll do long-term, because expats are very expensive."[75]

So U.S. companies may decide to use local talent. But focusing on the Mexican market for high-level talent can be challenging. Because of generally low educational levels in Mexico and a past lack of management development, a good manager may be hard to find:

> *What makes it difficult is not that there are no good Mexican executives. In fact, I think the Mexican executives are excellent. The problem is, there are so many companies opening doors and growing their businesses, there's just not enough to go around.*

FERMIN DIEZ, Principal and General Manager, Mexico City Office, Towers Perrin[76]

Recruitment in Mexico relies heavily on networking, especially for professionals, supervisors, and even managers. Of course, there is nothing wrong with networking itself, as long as it is simply a way of guiding good people to good jobs. The potential problem with networking anywhere is that it may begin to reflect the attitude "It's not what you know, it's who you know." Nabisco, which has maintained a presence in Mexico for some time but initiated new operations in 1992, has run into this problem more than once:

> *The problem is that even with executive recruiters, you may get a social referral as opposed to a person who's been referred on his or her technical merits.*

KEVIN DUFFY, Director of Employee Relations, Nabisco International[77]

The solution to this situation is to recruit more actively, more diligently, and more creatively:

> *Really find out what [the former jobholder's] responsibilities were and what their talents are because job titles can be inflated in Mexico; they don't necessarily reflect the job abilities.*

REBECCA LOTSOFF, Manager of International Compensation, Motorola[78]

Locals and U.S. expatriates are not the only sources for recruiting managers. Fermin Diez of Towers Perrin suggests investigating other Latin American countries:

> The cost may be less than for other expats, because they already have the language and cultural background and so require little training. Also, many Latin American executives view a move to Mexico as a career stepping stone, and so may be willing to take a more modest compensation. Recruitment can also be successful closer to home. Nabisco hunts down entry-level professionals at such U.S. colleges as University of Texas and Texas A&M, which have high populations of well-educated Mexicans with every desire to return to their home.[79]

Europe

Recruiting involves many activities and Europe includes many countries.[80] In Germany, especially the former West Germany, clerical and professional jobs are largely filled by apprentices. To attract new candidates and retain current employees, companies offer flexible hours, but they tend to neglect training and reskilling. The most difficult individuals to recruit in Germany are engineers and qualified manual workers.

The Scandinavian countries—Denmark, Finland, Norway, and Sweden—have fewer recruitment problems than any other countries in Europe. The one job category that presents an exception to this rule is the health profession, for which it is most difficult to recruit. Most clerical, manual, and managerial jobs are filled by wide use of external and internal advertising. In Scandinavian countries, staffing requirements are planned further in advance than in other European countries, often two years into the future.

In France, Ireland, the United Kingdom, and the Netherlands, vacant positions of all sorts—clerical, professional and technical, managerial—are filled with the help of recruitment agencies. These countries recruit foreigners more widely when prospective employees in the home labor market are not available.

Spain, Portugal, and Turkey experience difficulty when trying to recruit technicians and information technology professionals. Organizations in these countries have introduced a great number of working practices to facilitate the recruitment of those with scarce skills, including relaxed qualifications, training for new employees and retraining for current employees, increased pay benefits, and organizational relocation. Staffing requirements are rarely planned more than one year in advance. This lack of forecasting might partly account for the recruitment difficulties faced by the organizations in these countries.

SUMMARY

After human resource needs have been established and job requirements have been identified through job analysis, a recruiting program produces a pool of job applicants obtained from internal or external sources.

Effective recruitment addresses not only the needs of the organization but also those of the individual and of society. Individuals' needs figure prominently in two aspects of recruiting: attracting candidates and retaining desirable employees. Society's needs are most explicitly defined by various federal and state regulations in the name of equal employment opportunity.

Keeping legal considerations firmly in mind, the organization must recruit sufficient numbers of potentially qualified applicants so that the individuals selected are adequately matched to jobs. This matching will help ensure that the individuals will perform effectively and not leave the organization. An organization can attract and retain these job applicants by numerous methods and through various sources. Although some methods and sources are more effective than others, the ones chosen often reflect the type of applicant sought.

Discussion Questions

1. Is recruiting more important to a firm like Microsoft than to one like General Motors? Explain.
2. What are the purposes of recruitment? How do these purposes affect other organizational activities?
3. Compare and contrast the recruiting methods and philosophies of Chubb Insurance and AIG. Explain the reasons for similarities and differences.
4. How does human resource planning contribute to effective recruitment? What are the roles of the line manager and human resource manager in each of these activities?
5. Why do some organizations use mostly external searches, whereas others use mostly internal searches?
6. Recruitment involves finding not only the right number but also the right kind of applicants. Are some recruitment sources "richer" than others—that is, do they yield more information about the applicants? Explain.

7. How has the legal environment affected recruitment? Have its effects been positive or negative for organizations? Explain (refer back to Chapter 3).
8. How do recruitment activities affect the diversity of a company's workforce?
9. How can organizations increase their attractiveness to potential job applicants?

10. How can organizations increase the chances that applicants will stay once hired?
11. How is recruiting conducted by firms in Japan?
12. What alternatives do U.S. firms have for staffing operations in Mexico?

 ## In-Class Projects

1. Describe the following for Lincoln Electric:
   a. The recruitment objectives
   b. The degree to which these objectives are serving the business and HR objectives of Lincoln
   c. The recruitment activities
   d. The degree to which these activities are serving the objectives of Lincoln

Going forward:

How can Lincoln's recruitment activities be improved? How could the effectiveness of these improvements be evaluated? Be specific.

2. Describe the following for AAL:
   a. The recruitment objectives
   b. The degree to which these objectives are serving the business and HR objectives of AAL
   c. The recruitment activities
   d. The degree to which these activities are serving the objectives of AAL

Going forward:

How can AAL's recruitment activities be improved? How could the effectiveness of these improvements be evaluated? Be specific.

 ## Field Projects

1. Outline information that should be contained in a realistic job preview by a firm seeking to attract the best MBA students. State if and how this depends upon the type of industry and part of the country, and whether or not it involves an overseas assignment.
2. Given that work organizations will be competing for a diverse pool of labor in the near future, it will be critical for organizations to manage diversity effectively. Assume you are in charge of recruiting clerical employees from a labor pool with a large percentage of single parents. What programs might the organiza-

tion develop and implement to attract qualified single parents? Outline the content of these programs and the rationale for them. Keep in mind the relevant legal constraints that influence managing human resources.
3. By the time we reach the 21st century, recruitment will probably be more high-tech than it is today. Interview several people who work in high-tech environments and ask them to imagine what recruiting will be like in five years. Describe how new technology is likely to change the recruitment process.

Case Study:
THE NEW RECRUIT

 Stan Fryer, project leader at General Instruments (GI), knew that today would be one of those proverbial Mondays that managers so often fear. Stan's boss and group manager, Harry Hoskinsson, had left town on business the previous Friday and would not return until the following week. General Instruments, a defense contractor in Palo Alto, California, employs nearly one thousand engineers and designs and manufactures a number of electronic systems for nuclear submarines. Recruiting qualified engineers has been difficult because of the competitive market in Palo Alto and the fairly substantial cost-of-living increase for anyone relocating to the area.

Stan's immediate problem concerned June Harrison, a single, twenty-three-year-old systems engineer who was hired three weeks ago upon graduation from San Diego State. Much to Stan's surprise, June had submitted a letter of resignation, stating personal reasons as the cause of her departure. Stan also had a memo from June's supervisor, Lou Snider, describing the events leading up to June's resignation.

As Stan reconstructed these events, it seemed that June was expecting overtime payment in this week's paycheck because of extra hours she had put in over the previous three weeks. However, Lou had neglected to file the proper payroll paperwork so that June could receive her overtime in the current pay period. This did not surprise Stan, given Lou's prior history of not getting the job done in other supervisory positions at GI. Apparently, Harry had spoken to Lou about filing excessive overtime for his section, so Lou had decided to spread out some of the overtime charges over several pay periods.

Lou had not realized that June had finally secured an apartment in Palo Alto (she had been renting a room in a nearby hotel) and had committed herself to make a three-month payment and deposit with her paycheck and the additional overtime payment she was expecting. When June realized what was going to happen, she called Harry to set up a meeting to discuss how she could cover her housing expenses. June remembered that, when she was being recruited, Harry emphatically told her to contact him if she ever needed anything or

had any problems settling into her new job at GI. Harry was in a bit of a rush to make a staff meeting, so he agreed to see June early the following day. When June reported to Harry's office the next morning, she was understandably upset when Harry's secretary told her that Harry had left town on a business trip. With that, she returned to her office and drafted her resignation letter.

As Stan contemplated how to resolve his "Monday morning" problem, he recalled the speech Harry had given him two years ago when he joined GI. Harry had made clear his distaste for young engineers who tended to live beyond their means and to count on bonuses and overtime as if they were regular and assured components of their paycheck. Nonetheless, Stan decided, despite Harry's speech, GI must try to arrange for a loan covering June's housing expenses and, more important, to persuade her to reconsider her hasty decision.

No sooner had Stan decided on a course of action than June appeared in his doorway. She had done some thinking over the weekend, after talking with another GI project engineer, a temporary employee hired only for the duration of his project. It seemed that temporary employees earned about 20 percent more than comparable permanent employees at GI, although they received considerably fewer benefits (such as retirement and health insurance). June made a proposal to Stan: She would retract her resignation letter if GI would permit her, in effect, to quit and be rehired as a temporary project engineer. Otherwise, she planned to leave GI and accept a standing offer she had received from an engineering firm in her home city of San Diego. As Stan listened, he wondered how Harry would have handled this situation. To Stan, June's proposal sounded like blackmail. ◉

Discussion Questions
1. Should June have resigned over the overtime issue?
2. Should GI accept June's proposal of hiring her as a temporary employee?
3. How could the recruiting process for June have been done better?
4. Was the socialization process for June lacking something? If so, what?

Case Study:
NORTHEAST DATA RESOURCES

George Wellington closed the door behind him and slumped into his desk chair with an air of resignation. He had just returned from a meeting of the Executive Committee of Northeast Data Resources (NDR), where personnel layoffs had been decided upon. As director of human resources at NDR, he realized that he would be responsible for both developing the process by which the layoffs would take place and assisting the managers responsible for the actual implementation. These would not be pleasant tasks, particularly in light of the human resource program he had begun to implement over the past four years.

Wellington pulled out a pad of paper from the top desk drawer and began to scribble notes. He had found that in times of pressure, it was best to get some perspective on the situation before taking action. The drastic character of this situation required a review of the growth of Northeast Data Resources from its inception in 1979 to the present. It was the first crisis the young company had been forced to face.

BACKGROUND OF THE COMPANY

In 1979, four young engineers formed a partnership to create the basis of NDR. Three of them had worked for a large national data processing company. They had recognized the high potential in the computer industry, particularly for a product that filled a vital need in this growing field. The fourth engineer, working in a research program with a large university, was asked to join them because of his expertise in the computer field.

Jack Logan was the prime mover of the new company. He had been working for nearly five years on a project within the data processing company to develop ways to protect its computer systems from being copied by competitors. The primary objective in this project was to ensure that a customer would have to purchase the entire system rather than use a number of different systems. Jack saw the opportunity to sell a service that would do just the opposite—link various competing systems into an integrated unit.

He and Charlie Bonner developed a black box that could connect at least two types of computer systems already on the market. They worked in Jack's basement for two years to perfect this instrument. Another six months of testing revealed that it was very effective. Two other engineers, George Miller and Al Grant, had begun to work with them in order to expand the box to tie together three other systems with which they had experience.

The four men decided to strike out on their own and found that their innovation and daring paid off. The first two years of their new enterprise were both exhilarating and demanding. NDR subcontracted the production of the black box to a small manufacturing company, and the partners divided responsibilities between marketing and continuing research. Jack and Charlie carried the marketing and organizational functions, and George and Al worked to streamline the instrument itself.

Early success in securing contracts with some key customers and fears about loss of the exclusive information about the unpatented invention led to a decision to go into full production. An old plant was leased and renovated, and workers were hired to begin the process of building the black box for distribution. Within two years, the company had grown from four partners to nearly one hundred people. By 1989, NDR had expanded to about seven hundred people and had become the focus of attention for a number of investors. The invention, now dubbed Omega I, had become a product competitors emulated but with little success.

Jack assumed the responsibilities of chairman and president, with Charlie as executive vice president in charge of operations. George and Al stayed in the lab, with more interest in research and development, being willing to act more in an advisory capacity on managerial decisions.

Jack saw the need to consolidate and expand the overall operations of the company. Production and distribution now overflowed into three buildings separated by nearly ten miles. He negotiated a contract with the economic development committee of Newbury, a New England town about forty miles away, to help construct a new building to house headquarters and the plant. The town agreed to help NDR through reduced taxes; water and sewage hookups at a minimal charge; arrangements with local banks to secure a loan for construction of the plant; and development of a federal grant to train new workers at the plant. In exchange, NDR agreed to move its entire operation to Newbury within the next two years. It helped Newbury in its search for new industry while assuring NDR of a secure base of operations for the future.

The Newbury headquarters was close enough to the old facilities that NDR lost few of its present staff because of the change. But the growth in business demanded an increase in workforce. Engineers with sophisticated skills in computer science were hired to expand the system capability. Often, international engineers were the only ones available, and the importation of English, Australian, and a few European professionals gave an international flair to the small company. New factory workers from Newbury and surrounding towns were hired so that the production shifts could be expanded from one to two. The training grants secured by the town helped to equip new workers, and the integration with more experienced workers moved smoothly. Empty managerial slots required hiring mostly from the outside. A new vice president of manufacturing came from a large industrial company in the Midwest. The new vice president of finance had a solid résumé that included most recently financial experience with a large conglomerate but before that two stints with growing companies much like NDR. The staffing of the growing company proceeded professionally.

FUTURE OF THE COMPANY

The phenomenal growth of NDR in old industrial New England rivaled that of the computer companies developing in California's Silicon Valley. NDR's workforce had evolved to 1,350 by 1992. Sales increased from $75,000 for two small initial contracts in 1979 to nearly $20 million by 1992. The opening stock price of $7 a share moved to between $8 and $9 and hovered there in 1991. But a feature article in a national stock advisory report about NDR led to an upward move in the summer of 1992 to $15. Even without paying a dividend in its thirteen years of existence, it had become an attractive investment.

Jack had taken time during the summer of 1992 to begin the process of strategic planning. Convinced that he and his executive committee could and should do this alone, he decided not to engage outside consultants to develop a costly set of plans. His projection was that the computer industry would grow nearly ten times in size over the next decade. Conservatively, the company could expect to hold its share of the market, which meant a doubling of sales in five years, to $40 million, and an increase of up to $70 million by 2004. Expansion was the key to maintaining its market share and holding its own against the handful of competitors that had begun to appear by 1992.

In shaping the strategy, Jack began to map out a new marketing plan that would guarantee NDR's position in the national market instead of the eastern United States market alone. He saw new customer possibilities, in the fields of insurance, financial institutions, and state and local governments. He negotiated an option to buy the factory of a watch company moving south. Its building was about thirty-five miles away in the heart of another old industrial New England town with a pool of skilled workers available to be retrained. He began to develop some ideas about how many new staff would be needed and the kind of capital necessary to finance this expansion.

GEORGE WELLINGTON'S CAREER AT NDR

George Wellington stopped his writing and reviewed the rapid growth of NDR up to this point. He remembered vividly his first few months at the company. He had moved to a nearby town to retire in the serenity of New England. His career had begun immediately after he completed his MBA from a leading eastern university where he had concentrated on management and human resources. He had begun work in the HR area with a major corporation in New York. Six years in the field had led him next into marketing and then into strategic planning with another company. The last seven years of his full-time career had been with a prestigious consulting firm in New York where he had focused on a variety of problems for a host of clients. His decision to retire had been prompted by a dislike for traveling and a desire to settle down where his children had located.

In retirement, George continued to do part-time consulting work. He still found the travel excessive, but he had recognized a need to be fully active in business to be happy. His search for a nontraveling part-time job was successful when Jack Logan met him at a chamber of commerce luncheon in Newbury and hired him as a consultant to help with the transition from the old to the new facilities. He remembered the challenges associated with coordinating the efforts of not only NDR personnel but outside contractors and town officials as well.

The flawless nature of the transition into the new plant made the president recognize that he needed George full-time. George agreed to stay only another six months as a special assistant to Jack. He carried out a variety of projects for Jack and quickly became an integral part of the management team at NDR.

The president called in George one day and showed him an organization chart he was reworking. "George, I know that your six months are nearly up, but I need you around here on a permanent basis. I just don't know where to put you on this chart. How about becoming director of human resources for NDR? That is the only important position which we haven't filled here in the past few months, and it would allow me to have you close at hand for help on those big decisions."

George asked for some time to think through his decision, and within a week agreed to a full-time position. Although Jack sometimes acted as if he believed HR was a somewhat unnecessary staff function, George would have a chance to help him understand the importance of human resources to this company. George began immediately to develop a plan for human resources at NDR.

His plan for that function at NDR had three major elements: a five-part program of activities to bring NDR up-to-speed to face future competitive challenges, a plan to staff his unit, and a plan for where to locate his office.

1. **The Program**
   • *Gathering employee information:* He had his staff develop a file on each employee, with a record of hiring date, previous experience and employers, salary, job title, and so forth. This was stored in a computer so that he could have rapid recall for evaluation.

- *Performance appraisal system:* He developed a new appraisal system that incorporated a three-page form to be completed twice a year by immediate supervisors. The annual review was tied to salary and bonus decisions. He experimented with it in two engineering sections over a two-year period and then was able to get Jack to mandate it for all of NDR beginning in 1991. The results from the 1991–92 year were compiled and filed for future use.
- *Personnel policy manual:* In 1991, a new personnel policy manual was developed that detailed the policies and procedures as well as benefits for all personnel at NDR. It met with some initial negative reaction by those who had enjoyed a variety of benefits from the early days of the company. But the imprint of Jack on the manual quelled the complaints and ensured uniformity in the policies.
- *Equal Employment Opportunity and affirmative action program:* The highly technical character of the NDR business and its presence in a small New England town made both EEO and AA difficult to pursue. A visit to George by an EEO field investigator regarding the case of a former worker led George to move quickly to formulate this program. The data were gathered on minority hiring and promotion and then a plan was designed for increasing the percentage of members of minorities in all categories and the number of women in management in particular. Jack resisted the immediate implementation of the program with the argument that the federal government would soft-pedal civil rights in employment so that business-people did not need to worry. George accepted this decision with reluctance but got an agreement to update the plan periodically as well as pursue informally a goal of more integration of the workforce.
- *Management development program:* The rapid growth of NDR created many new managerial positions. Hiring from the outside became one method by which to increase the number of managers, but George believed that the key to the company's future lay in developing them from within. He negotiated a contract with a professor of management at a local university to design and teach a course in management for selected employees. George and the professor team-taught a six-week course for twenty midlevel managers in 1990. Its success led to an offering three times a year to both managers and potential managers.

2. The Staff

George became director of HR in the spring of 1989. He selected four professionals and two secretaries to work with him. Two professionals came from outside NDR and two from within. All four had experience in human resource management but needed more training. One was encouraged to enter an MBA program on a part-time basis with a concentration in human resource management. The other three were sent to local and national seminars to upgrade skills and understanding in the various areas of HR management. But at the heart of their training was George, drawing on his vast experience and encouraging his younger colleagues to learn through experimentation and discussion.

3. The Office Location

The final design of the NDR headquarters had not been decided when George became a consultant to the project, so he had taken primary responsibility for the design of the corporate office area. Later, as director of HR, he negotiated some changes in the office assignments so that his office was located at one of the major entrances and exits of the building. It was a primary thoroughfare for engineers and managerial personnel arriving in the morning and leaving at night. It was also a stop along the way to the new cafeteria that had just opened.

George had chosen this location for a reason. He felt that human resource departments must have high visibility and availability. Being in the middle of a key thoroughfare allowed people to recognize the central function of his unit in the operation of NDR. It encouraged questions about policies and procedures. It also gave the HR management staff the chance to get to know all the managers and professionals within a short period of time. This provided instant recognition and a capacity to deal with problems on a much more personal basis. George himself was always at his desk working before most of the staff arrived, and usually left after 6:00 P.M. This gave him considerable visibility with managers, who often worked late.

George's images of the first few years were succeeded by thoughts about the past two months with his staff. He had begun to engage them in the planning process by asking them to think about NDR for the next five years. He had sketched out the growth projections of Jack and then provided some parameters within which to think about staffing. Each member of his professional staff was to develop a short presentation on four consequences for HR management:

1. Effect on the size of our workforce
2. Effect on the mix of skills needed in the workforce
3. Effect on the recruitment efforts from outside NDR and the development efforts within
4. Effect on the working conditions within the company itself, both physically and organizationally

The first meeting four weeks ago had produced some very good reports. With one exception, the four had done a lot of homework and some imaginative thinking about the future with regard to how the HR management plan would fit into the NDR overall strategic plan. George had collated and refined the projections and redistributed them to the professional staff, asking for further thought and more specific targets for the next five years. He asked for input for his own report to the president, which he had hoped would be ready by December 1992.

THE PRESENT DILEMMA

The work had now come to an abrupt halt, although George had not alerted the staff to the discussion taking place within the executive committee until the day before. Jack's projections about the future had been overly optimistic.

Two weeks ago, Jack had asked George to meet him at 8:00 P.M. He laid out a report on the results from the first quarter of this fiscal year and then a chart that traced the sales of the last nine quarters. The last two quarters showed a significant decline. Jack said, "The decline is now a trend and not simply a blip on the screen as I had thought." The loss of five key contracts totaling nearly $3 million over the past six months plus the entry of a new competitor in the southeastern market had been responsible for the dramatic sales drop. At the same time, profits had suffered as well because of the increased expenses from a decision to increase the size of the engineering and financial service departments. The president admitted that his projections had been too optimistic and that something had to be done immediately. The cash flow problem had emerged as the most important pressure in this situation. The budget had to be pared while efforts to increase revenue were intensified.

George studied the figures carefully and agreed reluctantly to both the conclusions and the recommendations reached by Jack. The two men took some time to sort through the various options available, but it always came back to drastic cuts in personnel. George urged Jack to call a meeting of the executive committee in the morning and provide the data to them with encouragement to diagnose the problem and solutions to it. He argued that any solution must be a product of consensus of the committee.

The meeting caught everybody by surprise, as they had accepted the president's projections of growth despite a temporary decline in sales. Two weeks of intensive debate among the executives had led to the meeting that morning, which defined the exact personnel cuts to be made. It was agreed that twenty-five engineers, fifty production workers and supervisors, and twenty-five others from various departments would be laid off within the next two weeks. In addition, fifteen new marketing and sales personnel would be added as soon as possible to carry out a new marketing thrust aimed at a different market segment.

There had been heated discussion about the exact number to be laid off and hired, with considerable friction between the vice presidents of production, engineering, and marketing. The blame for the crisis was shouldered by Jack, who asked that the executives

recognize that they had to work together to resolve this problem if the future of NDR was to be assured. George, as the director of personnel, was given the task of coordinating the identification of the people to be laid off, although the actual decisions would rest with the three vice presidents. There were no criteria for the decisions, although all agreed that loyal and trusted employees who had been with NDR for a number of years should be released only as a last resort.

THE DIRECTOR'S RESPONSIBILITY

The acrimonious debate of the morning still echoed in George's ears that afternoon. He tore the pages on which he had been writing off the pad and began a new one as he started to determine how the layoffs should be handled. His mood was a far cry from the exuberance with which he had begun the process of developing a five-year human resource plan just two months ago. Cutbacks in personnel demanded the same precision and careful thought in planning and action as hiring and promotion. There was less excitement about retrenching than about growing, because it affected the livelihood of many familiar people.

George jotted down the important questions in three different areas as he mapped out his thinking on this problem:

1. **The Layoffs**
   - Criteria to be used?
   - Data available on employees?
   - Effect of EEO and AA on decisions?
   - Severance pay and benefits?
   - Procedure for layoffs?
2. **The New Hires**
   - Skills needed in marketing and sales?
   - Available resources for positions?
   - Salary and benefit package?
   - Procedure for hiring?
3. **The HR Management plan**
   - Immediate effect on five-year HR management plan?
   - What if only temporary reversal of growth trend? (Commitments to rehire or not?)
   - Effect on employee morale now and in future?

George recognized that he had a lot of work to do. He struggled to regain his sense of professionalism as he began to detail the options available for each of the questions. His days as a consultant and manager had given him little experience in the arena of layoffs. But Jack had given him the responsibility, and he knew that the future of NDR would depend heavily on how it handled this crisis. ◉

SOURCE: D. Jeffrey Lenn, George Washington University. This case is meant to be not an example of effective or ineffective human resource management but an example for teaching and discussion purposes.

Selection and Placement: Picking from the Applicant Pool

Hire people smarter than you and get out of their way.
HOWARD SCHULTZ, Chief Executive, Starbuck's Corporation[1]

Managing Human Resources for the 21st Century at Coca-Cola and Pepsi

Few products appear to be more similar than soft drinks, yet the "cola wars" between Coca-Cola and Pepsi show how even organizations with highly similar products can be differentiated by their business strategies.

COKE'S DOMINANCE

Coke is the most recognized trademark in the world. First marketed some seventy years before Pepsi, Coke is, literally, part of American history and culture. In World War I, for example, Coca-Cola bottling plants went to Europe along with the U.S. armed forces. With such enormous recognition in the market, Coke's business strategy centers on maintaining its position and building on its carefully groomed image. Compared with other companies its size, Coca-Cola owns and operates few ventures—especially now that its brief fling with Columbia Pictures is over—and has relatively few bottling franchises with which to deal. Indeed, the largest franchisee, which controls 45 percent of the U.S. market, is owned by Coca-Cola itself.[2]

Given its dominance, the Coke trademark is something akin to a proprietary technology, and Coca-Cola's business strategy turns on subtle marketing decisions that build on the trademark's reputation. This is not to suggest that running Coke's business strategy is easy. Rather, the decisions are highly constrained within a framework of past practices and reputation. (One reason New Coke was a debacle, it can be argued, was that it broke away from the framework represented by Coke's tradition.)

Managing Coca-Cola therefore requires a deep firm-specific understanding and feel for the trademark that cannot be acquired outside the company or even quickly inside it. What Coke does, then, is both teach that culture and hang onto it. Coke typically hires college graduates—often liberal arts majors and rarely MBAs—with little or no corporate experience and provides them with intensive training. Jobs at Coke are very secure, virtually lifetime positions for adequate performers, and a system of promotion from within and seniority-based salary increases provides the carrot that keeps employees coming back day after day. The organizational culture is often described as familylike with a high degree of employee loyalty. Decision making is very centralized; the people management system ensures that only career Coke managers who have been thoroughly socialized into worrying about the company as a whole get to make decisions affecting the company. The company allows little autonomy and has a low tolerance for individual self-aggrandizement: no one wants an unsupervised, low-level decision backfiring on the trademark. To reinforce the centralized model, performance is evaluated at the company or division level.

PEPSI's CHALLENGE

Pepsi is not Coke. Pepsi has prospered by seeking out the market niches where Coke is not dominant and then differentiating itself from Coke. From its early position as a price leader ("Twice As Much for a Nickel") to contemporary efforts at finding a "New Generation" of consumers, Pepsi cleans up behind the Coke trademark.

One way Pepsi has found new markets is to become highly diversified. Its fast-food operations—Taco Bell, Pizza Hut, Kentucky Fried Chicken Corporation—provide proprietary outlets for Pepsi soft drinks. Pepsi markets more aggressively to institutional buyers like hotels and restaurants than does Coke, which is focused on individual consumers. Pepsi also has many more bottling franchises that operate with some autonomy.[3]

Given its marketing strategy, Pepsi faces a much more diversified and complicated set of management challenges.[4] It needs more innovative ideas to identify market niches, and it needs the ability to move fast. Its people management system makes this possible. Pepsi hires employees with experience and advanced degrees, high-performing people who bring ideas with them. In particular, Pepsi brings in advanced technical skills. Within the company, Pepsi fosters individual competition and a fast-track approach for those who are successful in that competition. The company operates in a much more decentralized fashion, with each division given considerable autonomy, and performance is evaluated at the operating and individual levels. Restructuring in the early 1990s moved the firm toward further decentralization and introduced a stock option program, designed to push entrepreneurial action down to individual employees.

Pepsi employees have relatively little job security, and the company does not have a strong promotion-from-within policy. One Pepsi insider commented, "Whenever anybody is either over 40 or has been in the same Pepsi job for more than four or five years, they tend to be thought of as a little stodgy."[5] In part because of higher turnover, Pepsi employees have significantly less loyalty to the company than do their counterparts at Coke. Indeed, the main issue that unites them, some say, is their desire to "beat Coke."

What Pepsi gets from this system is a continuous flow of new ideas (e.g., from experienced new hires), the ability to change quickly (e.g., by hiring and firing), and the means for attacking many different markets in different ways (e.g., decentralized decision making with individual autonomy).[6]

 ## SELECTION AND PLACEMENT

Selection is the process of obtaining and using information about job applicants in order to determine who should be hired for long- or short-term positions. *Placement* is concerned with matching individuals to jobs, based on the demands of the job and the knowledge, skills, abilities, preferences, interests, and personality of the individual. Effective selection and placement, as described in the feature "Managing Human Resources for the 21st Century at Coca-Cola and Pepsi," involve finding the match between the organizations' needs for qualified individuals and the individuals' needs for jobs in which they are interested.

Selection and placement decisions seek to put the right person in the right job. Whether a person is "right" may depend on the match between the person's KSAs and the *job*'s demands, as well as the match between the person's personality, interests, and preferences and the opportunities and culture associated with the *total organization*.[7] The job involved may be newly created or the result of retirement, transfer, voluntary termination (turnover), demotion, or discharge. The right person may be found outside or inside the organization. The final selection and placement decision may be to hire a new job applicant or to transfer one from within the organization. Or the decision may be not to hire a particular applicant or set of applicants, but rather to go out and do more recruiting. Or the decision may be to "put on hold" some applicants who are qualified but for whom no jobs are currently open. Or, although generally not thought of as such, the final selection and placement decision may be to demote or terminate an employee. This is the special case of "selecting out."[8] As far as equal employment laws are concerned, all decisions about hiring, transfer, promotion, demotion, layoff, termination, and admittance to training programs are regarded as selection decisions.

 ## PURPOSES AND IMPORTANCE OF SELECTION AND PLACEMENT

Selection and placement procedures provide the essence of an organization—its human resources. When done well, these procedures ensure that a company has employees who perform well, resulting in high productivity.

Consider the time, effort, and money invested by some organizations to select their workforce:

- Toyota (USA) screens fifty thousand applications for three thousand factory jobs in the initial staffing of its plant in Georgetown, Kentucky. Each employee hired invests at least eighteen hours in a selection process that includes an exam on general knowledge, a test of attitudes toward work, an interpersonal skills assessment center, a manufacturing exercise designed to provide a realistic job preview of assembly work, an extensive personal interview, and a physical exam.

⊙ AFG Industries builds two new float glass plants. The plants use practices—such as work teams, extensive training, and skill-based pay—that create a high level of employee involvement. The hiring process for factory workers includes screening of formal résumés (not job applications), personality testing, preemployment training that simulates some plant jobs, interviews with panels of managers or employees or both, and a medical exam.

⊙ Sun Microsystems was the fastest-growing U.S. company in 1990–95, with annual growth averaging more than 100 percent. Filling open jobs is critical to Sun's effectiveness, phenomenal growth, and profitability. Yet the firm's hiring process is extremely time-consuming and labor intensive. Potential hires at all levels are brought into the organization from four to seven times for interviews with up to twenty people. The process is full of ambiguity, lacks formal rules, and demands that all applicants solve problems to get themselves hired.[9]

The value of using several sophisticated selection practices by employers was demonstrated in a study of 201 companies from several industries, listed in *Dun's Business Rankings.* Companies reported their use of practices such as conducting validation studies, using structured interviews, and administering cognitive tests. The researchers showed that companies that used these practices had higher levels of annual profit, profit growth, and overall performance. The relationship between use of these practices and bottom-line performance was especially strong in the service and financial sectors, as defined by SIC codes.[10]

Some of the specific purposes served by selection and placement procedures are as follows:

⊙ Enable organizations to implement their particular business strategies, as suggested in the examples of Coca-Cola and Pepsi.[11]

⊙ Ensure that financial investments in employees pays off. For example, hiring an employee with a starting salary of $25,000 and annual cost-of-living adjustments (COLAs) of only 1.5 percent and no benefits involves an investment of $128,000 in that employee over five years and $578,092 over twenty years.

⊙ Evaluate, hire, and place applicants in jobs that match their interests.

⊙ Treat applicants fairly and thereby minimize the negative consequences associated with discrimination.

⊙ Minimize multimillion-dollar verdicts and settlements in litigation brought by victims of criminal, violent, or negligent acts perpetrated by employees who should not have been hired or kept in their jobs.

⊙ Help fulfill hiring goals and timetables specified in affirmative action programs.

To serve these purposes effectively, selection and placement must be congruent with the internal and external environment, integrated with other human resource activities (see Exhibit 8.1), and done in a manner consistent with legal regulations. In combination, these elements often determine whether the company is most likely to look for job candidates internally or externally. For jobs above the entry level, promotion from within is a standard practice in most organizations.[12] Nevertheless, many job vacancies above the entry level are filled by outside sources especially when someone with considerable skill is needed. External hiring also occurs when organizations are caught by surprise and have no internal individual ready to take the job. This may occur because of a sudden change in business strategy or a desire to take advantage of unpredictable business

■ *Exhibit 8.1*
Relationships and Aspects of Selection and Placement

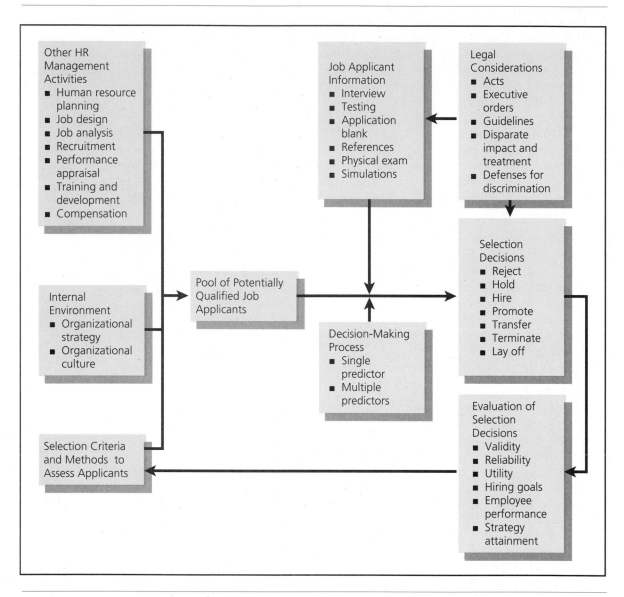

opportunities. For example, when the job to be filled is that of general manager for a division or business unit, the evidence from a few studies suggests that matching the experience profiles of applicants to the defined strategy leads to better performance. So, if the strategy of a company shifts, the company may need to look externally in order to find a person with the right profile for the new job.[13]

Organizations are increasingly realizing what Reginald H. Jones, former chairman and CEO of the General Electric Company, has noted: "[B]usinesses with different missions require quite different people running them."[14] As a result, particular characteristics, skills, abilities, values, and perspectives of executives need to match particular types of business strategy.[15] For example, a study by Hay Associates reports that when a

Partnership in Selection and Placement

Line Managers	Human Resource Professionals	Employees
Identify staffing needs through articulating business strategies.	Develop and choose selection tests that are reliable and valid.	Maybe interview candidates who work in the group.
Help HR professionals identify appropriate criteria for evaluating the performance of new hires and new placements.	Coordinate the administrative aspects of the selection process.	Maybe help select new group members.
Help HR professionals develop selection tools.	Arrange interviews between the applicant and line managers.	Maybe apply for internal transfers, promotions, and so forth.
Coordinate the selection process with the applicant and HR professionals.	Conduct data analyses to establish validity and to determine how to combine results from multiple tests.	Maybe identify appropriate criteria for evaluating performance.
Maybe administer and score some selection tests.	Provide education and training to all employees involved in the selection process.	
Understand and comply with relevant legal regulations.	Monitor selection outcomes to ensure equal opportunity for all.	
Provide information to other organizations that are conducting reference checks.	Keep complete and accurate records for possible use in defending the organization against lawsuits.	
Facilitate the organization's accommodation to the Americans with Disabilities Act.		

business is pursuing a growth strategy, it needs top managers who are likely to abandon the status quo and adapt their strategies and goals to the marketplace. Because insiders are slow to recognize the onset of decline and tend to persevere in strategies that are no longer effective, top managers need to be recruited from the outside. Outsiders are not always helpful, however. When a business is pursuing a mature strategy, what is needed is a stable group of insiders who know the intricacies of the business.

For selection processes to achieve strategic objectives, line managers must be involved in the process and work with HR professionals (see the feature "Partnership in Selection and Placement"). In fact, they may even need to take the lead.[16]

Partnership in Selection and Placement

Line managers help identify the need for staffing through the organization's human resource planning activity, assist with job analysis and strategy identification, evaluate job applicants, and eventually evaluate employee performance. All these activities engage line managers regardless of whether hiring is from external or internal applicant pools. When internal promotions and transfers are contemplated, however, line managers' involvement often escalates.

Role of Managers in Promotion and Transfer. Promotions can occur within a department, a division, or an entire organization. They also can occur between nonmanagerial positions (e.g., from Typist I to Typist II), between managerial positions, and between a nonmanagerial and a managerial (or supervisory) position.

Although a promotion generally is a vertical move in the organization, it may be a move to another job at the same level but with more pay or status. A transfer generally is a move at the same level and pay. This type of move is becoming more common in companies because downsizing and restructuring have reduced the promotion opportunities. Both broadbanding and the use of talent pools facilitate the transfer process.

In some organizations and under some circumstances, immediate supervisors have limited control in deciding who to promote or transfer out of their unit, but they usually have considerable say in who will move into the unit. They search for qualified candidates and help choose the best candidate. This process is probably carried out in close consultation with one or more higher-level supervisors who ultimately have to approve the choice. In many companies, immediate supervisors have almost total control over selection decisions, especially promotion and transfer decisions. When a new job is being created, they may be able to determine exactly who will be promoted by writing the job description to fit only one person. This is not necessarily a fair practice, but it is common.

Managers can also try to control the final decision by stacking the deck to confirm their favorite candidate. To make the selection process appear legitimate, a manager may select several candidates, in addition to the favorite, for others to evaluate. The catch is that the other candidates are far less qualified than the favorite. The whole selection process becomes superficial, allowing only one "real" choice.

A line manager can also become involved as a sponsor or mentor—often a manager at a higher level in the organization "adopts" and looks out for an employee—ensuring that an individual's strengths are noted by others. Here is where HR professionals face the challenge of trying to ensure that the promotion process is open yet at the same time recognizing the preferences of managers and supervisors who will eventually become the boss of the newly hired or newly placed candidate. Formal programs for identifying potential candidates for promotion and up-to-date human resource information systems help speed the process of identifying potential candidates. They can also ensure fairness in the process by giving everyone a chance regardless of where they are currently working or for whom they are working. In the final analysis, however, if managers have control over selection and placement decisions, they should accept responsibility for making these decisions wisely. As the feature "Positioning for the 21st Century: Workers Are a Small Firm's Most Valuable Asset" indicates, the ability to make good decisions in this area requires time and demands an understanding of the process.

Role of the Human Resource Department. In larger organizations, the human resource department is usually responsible for gathering detailed information about applicants and arranging interviews between job applicants and line managers. Organizations and applicants both can benefit by having these activities centralized in the HR department because

- Applicants go to only one place to apply for all jobs in the company, which is convenient.
- The company can consider each applicant for a variety of jobs, which is efficient.
- Outside sources of applicants can clear employment issues through one central location.
- Operating managers can concentrate on their operating responsibilities, which is especially helpful during peak hiring periods.

Positioning for the 21st Century:
WORKERS ARE A SMALL FIRM'S MOST VALUABLE ASSET

For many small businesses, payroll is easily the single largest expense. Yet business owners often are more knowledgeable about products, plants, equipment, and other assets than about their most expensive asset—people.

The reason for this is obvious: people cannot be neatly measured the way raw materials can.

However, an increasingly competitive marketplace is causing many businesses to pay closer attention to this one resource that truly sets them apart from their competition.

The challenge of business today is not simply to find the most qualified worker, but to find a good match between workers and jobs.

The logical approach is to make a concerted effort to get to know employees and candidates—not only their job skills and general intelligence, but their drives, needs, interests, and behavioral makeup as well—and then use that information to make a good placement.

Managers must do a number of things both in the hiring process and on the job to understand the people who do the work and manage them accordingly:

- Job candidates should undergo multiple interviews, answering the same questions from different people. This provides an opportunity to compare notes on a given candidate's responses. It also provides a chance for several people to get to know the candidate and to decide how that personality would fit into the department.
- On the job, managers should make it their mission to learn more about what motivates employees. They can begin by making themselves more available to employees—at workstations, in the lunchroom, on breaks, and during weekly meetings. Keeping the door open to questions and comments tells employees that their contributions are important and gives managers insight into what is happening on the front lines.
- In the planning process, employees should be kept involved and shown that management has an interest in their development on the job. Managers need to define jobs clearly, so that employees know what is expected of them.

Managers also should discuss individual career plans so that people know where they fit into the company's long-term plans and what goals they must achieve.

Performance appraisals need to be done in an open, constructive fashion. And efforts to build work teams need to be openly explained and developed with employees.

Organizing and bringing objectivity to the process by which executives learn and manage their workers is another issue altogether.

Many business owners and managers rely on a predictive index—a process that teaches managers how to identify each employee's potential and match the employee with suitable jobs. They can also use the process to manage employees in their everyday duties.

Consider the experience of Peter Flood, president of Hudson, a company that makes coatings, sealants, and paint additives. The company was about to hire a supervisor who had a top-notch résumé and interviewed beautifully. The job was managing a new division.

Flood decided to try the predictive index approach before making the offer. The process indicated the candidate was not particularly suited for a supervisory position, and tended toward an adversarial management style. A further check into the candidate's work history revealed that this was a problem in previous management positions.

If Flood had relied solely on the résumé and interview to make that hiring decision, the company would have spent several months and thousands of dollars integrating the wrong person into a crucial position.

The outcome would have practically guaranteed dissatisfaction for both the company and the supervisor. And the effects most assuredly would have put an untold strain on other relationships in the company, including those with customers.

The critical step is going beyond the standard business approaches of evaluating employees to learn more about what they are suited to do and how they can be motivated to perform to their greatest potential.

Economist Ronald Hoffman said, "There is only one free lunch in economics—an increase in efficiency."

When American business truly learns how to understand and manage its employees as individuals, then it will have not only a "free lunch" but a veritable banquet.[17]

⦿ Hiring is done by specialists trained in staffing techniques, so the selection decisions are often better, resulting in better employee performance.

⦿ Costs may be kept low by avoiding duplication of effort.

⦿ People who know about the many legal regulations relevant to selection handle a major part of the hiring process, which improves both legal compliance and fairness to job applicants.

Multibusiness companies such as Pepsi may have several human resource departments, each serving the unique needs of its own business. This type of partial decentralization helps ensure that selection and placement are consistent with the strategy, history, and culture of each business unit.

A decentralized HR structure does have potential disadvantages, however, especially if each division or unit operates independently, selecting only from among its own employees and not from the whole workforce. Decentralization may also mean that each unit relies on its own performance appraisal systems, so even if candidates from other divisions become internal applicants, they may be difficult to evaluate. This reality is magnified in global firms: regions of the world may become virtually unrelated to each other and the human resources of one region completely off-limits to the others.

Fundamentally, the role of a company's HR department or departments is helping ensure that the best candidates available are placed into open positions. To carry out this role, HR must make sure the organization has the information it needs to identify who is the best candidate. It also must make sure the selection decision is based only on relevant information and that the most qualified person does not lose out because of prejudice and stereotyping that are irrelevant to job qualifications. As the feature "Using Data for the 21st Century: Age Bias in Hiring Is Prevalent" shows, unfair discrimination persists especially among less successful companies. This responsibility requires careful attention to the legal environment.

Finally, HR's role includes helping the organization persuade applicants to accept job offers. To fulfill this responsibility requires sensitivity to the perspectives of job applicants.

The Role of Applicants. Applicants almost always care deeply about the outcomes of selection decisions and can have strong reactions to their experiences. Consider the following stories:

⦿ A married graduate student with a 3.9+ grade point average reported that the first three questions in one company's psychological assessment procedure involved inquiries about her personal relationships with her husband and children. Although the company asked her what she thought of the procedure before she left, she lied because she was afraid that telling the truth would eliminate her from further consideration. Because of dual-career constraints, she continued to pursue an offer, but noted that if she got one, her first on-the-job priority would be to try to get the assessor fired.

⦿ A male MBA told how he had originally planned to refuse to submit to psychological testing, but was persuaded by his girlfriend that it would be a more effective form of protest to pursue the offer and then pointedly turn it down.

⦿ The first interview question asked of a female MA student was, "We're a pretty macho organization. . . . Does that bother you?" Unfortunately, it did, and she simply wrote the company out of her future interviewing plans. (When . . . this incident [was later relayed] to an audience of corporate recruiters, a male recruiting director raised his hand and asked, "What's wrong with that?")[18]

Applicants' reactions to selection processes clearly affect their decisions about whether to pursue job opportunities in a company. Equally important, these early experiences serve as an organization's first steps in a socialization process that will

Using Data for the 21st Century:
AGE BIAS IN HIRING IS PREVALENT

A recent study of age bias in hiring provides two key messages for employers. First, employers that discriminate on the basis of age in hiring, whether deliberately or inadvertently, are vulnerable to the use of testers employed by the EEOC and state fair-employment agencies—a practice generally approved by the courts. Second, organizations that do not discriminate on the basis of age in hiring generally appear to be more successful than those that do.

The study, which was sponsored by the American Association of Retired Persons (AARP) and was conducted by the Fair Employment Council of Greater Washington (FEC), found that when younger applicants and older applicants apply for the same type of positions with the same credentials, older workers encounter discriminatory reactions more than 25 percent of the time. Interestingly enough, the results also indicate that disparities in treatment were less prevalent among more successful firms.

THE METHODOLOGY

In the study, the FEC employed the relatively new technique of employment testing to measure the extent of age discrimination in hiring. Testing operates in the manner of a controlled experiment: Two applications are submitted simultaneously that represent job seekers who are identical in job-relevant qualifications but who differ in one demographic dimension—in the present case, age.

Operating under carefully developed research guidelines, the FEC mated pairs of résumés—one for a fifty-seven-year-old and the other for a thirty-two-year-old—to a random sample of 775 large firms and employment agencies nationwide. The résumés indicated that the applicants were identically qualified in job-relevant characteristics, such as education and work experience. The responses to the résumés were then monitored and compared.

Typically, candidates for employment are unaware how other candidates are treated. Therefore, applicants denied the opportunity to enter the interviewing and hiring process do not know whether other applicants with similar credentials have been treated in the same fashion. The use of this testing technique gave the FEC a unique insight into employers' initial reaction to an applicant's age.

THE RATE OF DISCRIMINATION

Of the 775 tests that were conducted, 79 received some positive response indicating that a position was available and the firm was interested in one of the applicants. Among these 79 cases, the thirty-two-year-old applicant was favored 43 percent of the time and the fifty-seven-year-old applicant was favored 16.5 percent of the time, for a net difference of 26.5 percent. Therefore, in slightly more than one test in four, the older worker was treated less favorably despite having qualifications identical to those of his or her younger counterpart.[19]

continue for several months after an applicant is eventually hired.[20] Therefore, it is essential to consider how applicants view the recruitment and selection activities of the company.

The Perspective of the Applicant

At the heart of applicants' concerns appears to be the desire to be treated fairly. Perceptions of fairness in selection processes undoubtedly are created by many variables, including the content of the measures used to select people, the administration of the process, and the outcomes of the process.[21]

Content of Selection Measures. Research on applicants' reactions to selection procedures show unequivocally that applicants prefer a process that involves them in activities that have obvious relevance to the job opening. To applicants, work samples and simulations usually seem more relevant than cognitive paper-and-pencil tests and handwriting analysis, for example, and perhaps for this reason applicants consider them to be more fair.[22] Applicants may react negatively to poorly conducted interviews. Offensive or discriminatory questions obviously send negative messages, but so do questions that appear to be superficial or irrelevant.[23]

Administration of the Selection Process. Applicants also attend to the process: Did the company tell them what it was evaluating and why? Did it provide feedback about how they scored? Did it appear to respect their desire for confidentiality? Did the company representatives behave professionally and appear to take the task seriously? Was the company respectful of their time and need for information about their chances for a positive outcome? Did it seem to treat all candidates equally, or did it treat some more equally than others? Did the process appear to recognize the potential for applicants to misrepresent themselves, and take steps to ensure that honesty was not penalized? Effective selection includes managing these and many other aspects of the process.[24]

Outcomes of the Selection Process. Whereas the content and administrative features of a selection process are experienced primarily by applicants, the outcomes are visible to a broader array of people. These include the acquaintances and coworkers of applicants who tell stories about the process, the new coworkers of successful applicants, the managers inside an organization who participated in the process, and people who served as references for applicants. Based on who is selected and who is rejected, all these constituencies form opinions about whether a company uses fair procedures and makes wise choices about who to hire or promote. Even the news media offer comments about executive selection decisions. They also publish reports concerning the demographic characteristics of successful applicants at specific companies. Consider, for example, the results of a study conducted by the *Wall Street Journal,* which compared the percentages of women hired into managerial jobs for companies in several different industries. These results clearly suggest that within any given industry, some companies appear to be more "fair" in terms of selecting women to fill managerial jobs.[25]

OVERVIEW OF THE SELECTION PROCESS

Regardless of the specific purpose for selection—for example, entry hire, promotion, or transfer—the process generally involves the following basic steps:

1. Assess the job demands and organizational needs to establish the criteria of interest.
2. Infer the type of person needed to establish which predictors are likely to be useful.
3. Design a method or process that allows both the organization and the applicant to gather job-related information.
4. Synthesize the information collected and make selection decisions.

Of course, the process does not end when the organization makes its decision. The candidate must ultimately make a final decision about whether to accept the new position and under what conditions. As the person enters the new position, accommodation, socialization, and training activities may all be involved. And, as time passes, both the organization and the new job incumbent will reevaluate their decisions.

Assess the Job Demands and Organizational Needs

An understanding of the specific tasks required by a job and the organizational context surrounding the job develops from job analysis as well as, more generally, human resource planning. Ideally, a systematic job analysis would be conducted for all jobs in an organization. In reality, job analysis is more likely to be conducted for lower-level and midlevel jobs and for jobs that encompass many positions.

For positions near the top of the organization, "job analysis" may or may not be systematic and very likely will be subjective rather than quantitative. At the level of CEO, for example, it may consist of a discussion among members of the board of directors.[26] Understanding the organization's culture and strategy, and perhaps future changes in technology or the nature of the business, may help HR managers fill positions from CEO all the way down to entry-level worker.

The objective of all this analysis is to establish the relevant *criteria,* which often describe the critical elements of job performance. For example, in a corporate loan assistant's job, accurately documenting decisions is probably more critical than keeping the office desks clean and organized. At Coca-Cola, the criteria of interest include loyalty and the ability and willingness to learn through the company's intensive training program. What criteria are most important at Pepsi?

Infer the Type of Person Needed

Organizations make selection decisions on the basis of information about one or more *predictors.* Generally, these predictors fall within three broad categories:

- Knowledge, skills, and abilities (KSAs)
- Personality, interests, and preferences
- Other characteristics essential to job performance

Predictor information serves as the basis for making projections and inferences about how well applicants, if placed in a particular job, will perform.

The most often assessed predictors are knowledge, skills, and abilities relevant to the job. But some firms care more about a person's attitudes and basic values. If used appropriately in combination with information about the culture and strategy of the firm, attitudes and values may be good predictors of future satisfaction in the job,[27] as well as of motivation and perhaps performance.

Core values also come into play when hiring managers and executives, according to a poll of U.S. CEOs.[28] When jobs are ambiguous and supervision is minimal, knowing that the job incumbent has the appropriate values can be reassuring. Presumably, the person's character can be relied on to function like a trustworthy compass, pointing him or her in the right direction.

Employers can also gather information about other characteristics. For example, they can ask about information relevant to the terms and conditions of employment, including willingness to obtain licenses required by law; to travel or to work split shifts, weekends, or under adverse conditions such as in confined facilities and with high noise levels; to adhere to uniform requirements or business-related grooming codes; to supply tools required on the job but not provided by the employer; and to complete required training. Although these characteristics offer no indication of how well candidates will perform, applicants unwilling to comply with job requirements can be disqualified from further consideration.

Choose Job-Related Predictors. A great deal of information often *can* be gathered and used to evaluate candidates; whether that information *should* be gathered and used depends on the likelihood that it will lead to a better selection decision. The information gathered about applicants needs to be clearly relevant to the job. The objective is to use information that predicts the subsequent outcomes of concern—that is, the criteria—and avoid using information that will not predict these outcomes. It is especially important to avoid using information that may unfairly discriminate against members of certain subgroups, such as women, disabled people, African Americans, and older people.

In technical and legal literature, the term *validity* describes the usefulness of a predictor for correctly inferring the future job behavior of applicants. For example, unstructured interviews generally have low validity, whereas structured interviews that include questions tailored to the job and situation of interest generally have high validity.[29] In general, high validity means that the decision maker can be confident that low predictor scores will translate into low scores on the specified criteria and high predictor scores will translate into high scores on the criteria.

For most predictors, validity depends on what you want to predict. For example, a personality test that assesses gregariousness may be valid for predicting performance as a fund-raiser for the city ballet company, but it is probably useless for predicting performance as a highway landscape designer. How can you be sure that a given measure is valid for the situation of interest? Three basic strategies are used to ascertain whether inferences based on predictor scores will be valid:

- Content validation
- Criterion-related validation
- Validity generalization

All these strategies require a job analysis to determine job tasks and working conditions as the first step. Ideally, an organizational analysis will also have been conducted. Then, the three strategies diverge. (For more detailed information on these strategies, consult Appendix A.)

Content validation is the most commonly used strategy. Based on job analysis information, it involves building a rational argument to link job content to predictors. In the simplest case, an expert job analyst determines which predictors appear to map onto the content of the job. For example, if the job analysis reveals that 70 percent of the job involves data entry, the job analyst might conclude that an appropriate selection tool is a work simulation test. If a board of directors concludes that 50 percent of the job of the new CEO will be identifying partners for new joint ventures, the job analyst, in this case a member of the board, might conclude that past experience in establishing joint ventures is a reasonable predictor to use for the selection decision.

This basic content validation strategy can be substantially improved. A more rigorous approach is to involve a wider range of people in judging whether a predictor is likely to be job related. Integrated job analysis procedures serve this purpose. As described in Chapter 6, these procedures ask job incumbents and supervisors to rate the extent to which specific skills and abilities are needed to perform the job. Although such judgments are necessarily subjective, one's confidence is increased when several subject matter experts agree that a particular skill is needed.[30]

Criterion-related validation uses more definitive data to establish a relationship between predictor scores and criteria. It involves assessing people on the predictor and also assessing their actual performance in the job. For example, if a ballet company wanted to decide whether gregarious people are better fund-raisers, it could ask all its current fund-raisers to take a personality test. Then it could correlate the fund-raisers' scores on gregariousness with their performance. If gregariousness and fund-raising performance were correlated, criterion-related validity would be established.

Validity generalization is relatively new and still somewhat controversial. Nevertheless, it has been gaining favor since the mid-1980s and may continue to gain popularity as we approach and enter the 21st century. Briefly, the validity generalization strategy rests on the assumption that the results of criterion-related validity studies conducted in other companies can be generalized to the situation in your company. For example, suppose ten other organizations have already shown that gregariousness tends to correlate with fund-raising success. Even if the correlation was not strong in all those organizations, and even if the type of fund-raising was quite different, you might nevertheless conclude that gregariousness is likely to be a valid predictor of fund-raising success for your ballet company.

Each of these strategies has associated advantages and disadvantages. For example, the criterion-related validation strategy has the advantage of documenting empirically that a predictor is correlated with performance in a particular job in a particular organization. However, the strategy can be costly and is not applicable for jobs that have only a few incumbents (e.g., CEO). Content validation strategies are more feasible, but they also depend more on subjective judgment. Validity generalization may be cost-effective, but you will not know whether results from other organizations will hold in your organization until after you make a selection decision. Furthermore, whereas the legal credibility of the other strategies is well-established, validity generalization has not been sufficiently tested in the courts.

Design a Method for Selection to Assess Fit

Decide How to Measure Predictors. For each predictor of interest—each skill, ability, personality aspect, physical ability, and so forth—multiple means can be used to assess each applicant. For example, information can be obtained using application forms, résumés, and reference checks. Most organizations use interviews of some type at one or more steps in the process. Who should conduct these interviews? At what stage in the process? What exactly should be assessed through the interview? If paper-and-pencil tests are to be given, which characteristics will these be used to assess: personality? cognitive ability? both? For internal candidates, past performance will undoubtedly be of some interest; how should this be assessed? Using sales volume figures? ratings and evaluations from supervisors and peers? How far back in the records should you go? These and many similar questions arise during the process of designing a selection method and process. Exhibit 8.2 illustrates how a company might use several different methods to capture all the information it wishes to use in selecting a corporate loan assistant.

Because each bit of information contributes to the final decision, the quality of information used determines the quality of the final outcome. One aspect of information quality that is especially important is *reliability*. The reliability of a measure (e.g., an interview, a mathematical reasoning test, or a work simulation) is the degree to which the measure yields dependable, consistent results. Unreliable measures produce different results depending on the circumstances. Different circumstances could include having different people administer and score the measure (e.g., having several different interviewers screen applicants), or administering the measure while different events are occurring (e.g., giving a mathematical reasoning test in August versus during the week immediately after everyone files their tax statements).

Reliable measurement tools yield equivalent results time after time regardless of incidental circumstances; this is referred to as *test-retest reliability*. Reliable tools also yield equivalent results regardless of who uses them; this is referred to as *inter-rater reliability*. Unreliability translates into greater measurement error. Greater measurement error, in turn, translates into decision errors concerning who to hire, promote, transfer, and so on.

Decide When to Measure Each Predictor. Often, selection decisions progress through several steps, with each progression to a new step based on some information

■ *Exhibit 8.2*

Selection Matrix: Possible Selection Methods for Several Knowledges and Skills

For Job: Corporate Loan Assistant (Internal Hires)
Date: 2 / 25 / 96

Code	Qualifications (Knowledge and skills)	Used to Rank?	SAF	WKT	ST	PCD	SOI	DAI	BI/REF	PAF
MQ	1. Communication	Yes	X				X	X	X	X
MQ	2. Math		X		X					
MQ	3. Writing		X							X
MQ	4. Reading		X		X					X
MQ	5. Researching		X							
MQ	6. Organizing	Yes	X							X
MQ	7. Listening	Yes	X				X			X
MQ	8. Social skills		X				X			X
MQ	9. Sales	Yes								X
MQ	10. Interpreting	Yes					X			
MQ	11. Bank policy									
MQ	12. Bank services	Yes	X	X				X		X
MQ	13. Computer									

MQ = Is a minimum qualification
MT = May be acquired through training or on the job (desirable); preference may be given to those who possess this knowledge or skill
MA = Can be accommodated within reason
WT = Will be acquired through training or on the job; not evaluated in the selection process
Will applicants be ranked by how much of this knowledge or skill they possess?
SAF = Supplemental Application Form
WKT = Written Knowledge Test
ST = Skills Test
PCD = Physical Capability Demonstration
SOI = Structured Oral Interview
DAI = Departmental Appointment Interview
BI/REF = Background Investigation/Reference Check
PAF = Performance Appraisal Form

SOURCE: Adapted from a form supplied by Biddle & Associates, 2100 Northrop Ave., Sacramento, CA. Used with permission.

about how the candidate scores in terms of one or more predictors. Exhibit 8.3 illustrates a typical progression. Clearly, each piece of information used throughout this process has the potential to determine the final outcome. Perhaps less clearly, information used early in the process is, in effect, weighted the most heavily—applicants who fail to do well early in the process fail by default on all the later steps. For example, suppose an applicant for a systems analyst position in a life insurance company scores poorly on a mathematical reasoning ability test given to all applicants who pass the initial interview. This person may never be given the opportunity to show her skills by completing a work simulation.

■ *Exhibit 8.3*
Possible Steps in the Selection Process

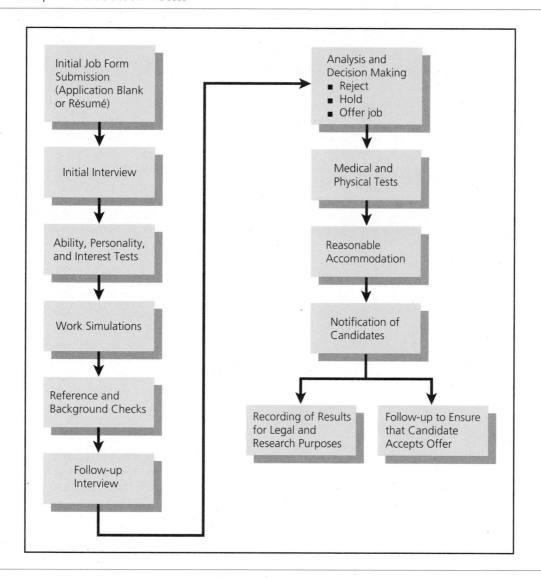

Consider Economic Utility. In general, the economic value of using a specific predictor is a function of the cost of acquiring the information and the value of performance gains that can be expected as a result of using that information. Information gleaned from résumés and brief screening interviews costs relatively little to acquire compared with information from multiple interviews, background investigations, and medical exams. Nevertheless, expensive information may be worth acquiring if it enables the organization to make better decisions *and* if substantial consequences are attached to making better decisions. More expensive procedures may be justified when, for example,

- Tenure in the job is expected to be relatively long.
- Incremental increases in performance reap large rewards for the organization.
- Many applicants are available to choose among.

Expensive procedures may not be justified if, for example,

- Progressively higher tax bites are associated with increased profits.
- Labor costs are variable and rise with productivity gains.
- Labor markets are tight, which makes it less likely that the best candidates, once identified, can be enticed to take the position[31]

For details about how to conduct an economic utility analysis, consult Appendix A.

Evaluate Legal and Social Acceptability. Finally, the acceptability of the selection methods and process must be designed with legal regulations and social norms clearly in mind.[32] Legal acceptability does not ensure social acceptance. Although the courts may agree that an employer's procedures are legally defensible, members of the public, including potential employees and customers, may not accept them. As employers enter the 21st century, their ability to compete effectively in the labor market may depend on their willingness to move beyond the minimum standards for fairness defined by legal regulations and strive to meet the more complex standards for fairness held by potential employees and interested members of the general public.

Synthesize Information and Choose Appropriate Candidates

Upon reaching this final step, a large amount of information of many types—some of it easily quantified and some of it very "soft"—may be available for a large number of applicants. To complicate things further, some applicants might be considered simultaneously for more than one job opening. Combining and synthesizing all available information to yield a yes-or-no decision for each possible applicant-job match may be a fairly complex task. Alternative approaches to combining and synthesizing information may lead to very different final decisions, so this step takes on great significance for both applicants and the organization. When more than one selection device is used, information can be combined in three ways.

Multiple-Hurdles Approach. In the multiple-hurdles approach, an applicant must exceed fixed levels of proficiency on all the predictors in order to be accepted. A score lower than the cutoff score on one predictor cannot be compensated for by a higher-than-necessary score on another predictor. Underlying this approach is the assumption that some skills or competencies are so critical that inadequacy guarantees the person will be unsuccessful on the job.

Compensatory Approach. Since most jobs do not have absolute requirements, a compensatory approach is commonly used. This approach assumes that good performance on one predictor can compensate for poor performance on another—for instance, a high score on an interview can compensate for a low score on a written examination. With a compensatory approach, no selection decisions are made until the completion of the entire process. Then, a composite index that considers performance on all predictors is developed.

Combined Approach. Many organizations use a combined approach. First, one or more specific requirements—for instance, pass the state bar or the CPA examination—must be met. Then, once these hurdles are jumped, scores on the remaining predictors are combined into an overall measure of job suitability. Consider college recruiting. Many organizations interview only college students with GPAs that exceed a specific level (first hurdle). To be offered a site visit, the candidate must pass a campus interview (second

■ *Exhibit 8.4*

Knowledge, Skills, and Abilities Required for Teamwork

I. Communication skills
   A. Understand verbal and nonverbal communications
   B. Listen without evaluation
   C. Give to others feedback that can be used
   D. Encourage others to contribute
   E. Facilitate communication across teams
II. Problem-solving skills
   A. Identify problems with others
   B. Gather data to diagnose
   C. Propose and analyze alternative solutions
   D. Implement solutions
   E. Evaluate results
III. Group member skills
   A. Understand group stages of development
   B. Manage group dynamics
   C. Understand social, task, and individual roles
   D. Have knowledge of team project planning, goal setting, execution, evaluation, and learning
   E. Manage group conflict
   F. Understand interaction styles of group members
   G. Recognize the variety of types of teams used in organizations
IV. Performance management skills
   A. Understand need for team mission and objectives
   B. Monitor and measure group performance
   C. Understand self-management and team management concepts
   D. Have ability to learn from past experiences

SOURCE: Based on M. J. Stevens and M. A. Campion, "The Knowledge, Skill and Ability Requirements for Teamwork: Implications for Human Resource Management," *Journal of Management* 20 (1994): 505–30; B. Dumaine, "The Trouble with Teams," *Fortune* (September 5, 1994): 86–92; N. R. F. Maier, "Assets and Liabilities in Group Problem Solving: The Need for an Integrative Function," *Psychological Review* (April 1967): 239–49; R. Klimoski and R. G. Jones, "Staffing for Effective Group Decision Making: Key Issues in Matching People and Teams," *Team Effectiveness and Decision Making in Organizations*, R. A. Guzzo and E. Salas, eds., (San Francisco: Jossey-Bass, 1995).

hurdle). At corporate headquarters, the applicant must take aptitude tests, participate in an assessment center, and be interviewed. A composite index that takes into consideration scores in all three areas is then used to make the final selection (compensatory approach).

Example: Selecting for Teamwork. Companies that are trying to enhance their competitiveness by improving quality seem to agree that the employees at the front line—for example, the production workers—are key to improving and delivering quality. Thus, they devote considerable time and effort to selecting production workers. In high-quality manufacturing environments, work is now organized around teams, so selecting people who can be effective as team players is essential. Exhibit 8.4 lists several types of knowledge, skills, and abilities that are likely to be needed in team-based organizations. To assess such characteristics, some organizations have developed and use very sophisticated approaches, including those listed for production team workers in Exhibit 8.5.[33] In this exhibit, each box represents one step in a series of multiple hurdles. A compensatory approach is used to combine the information within each step and decide whether to involve the applicant in the next step. Sophisticated hiring procedures are also recommended for other workers, as described in the feature "Positioning for the 21st Century: Workers Are a Small Firm's Most Valuable Asset," shown earlier in this Chapter.

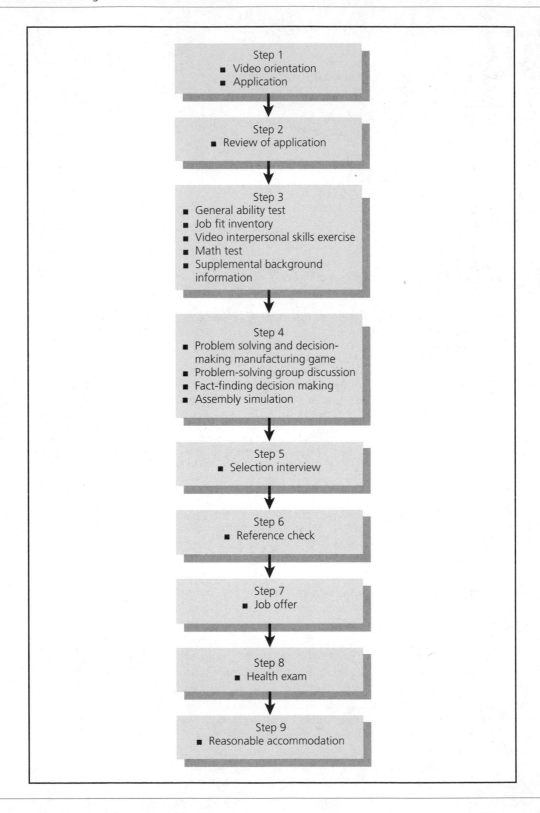

Step 1
- Video orientation
- Application

Step 2
- Review of application

Step 3
- General ability test
- Job fit inventory
- Video interpersonal skills exercise
- Math test
- Supplemental background information

Step 4
- Problem solving and decision-making manufacturing game
- Problem-solving group discussion
- Fact-finding decision making
- Assembly simulation

Step 5
- Selection interview

Step 6
- Reference check

Step 7
- Job offer

Step 8
- Health exam

Step 9
- Reasonable accommodation

✷ TECHNIQUES FOR OBTAINING JOB APPLICANT INFORMATION

A variety of selection techniques are available for obtaining applicant information. These techniques vary in terms of what they measure, what they cost, the number of firms using them, and their usefulness for predicting various outcomes.[34]

Application Blank and Background Information

Application Blank. Premised on the assumption that past behavior is a good predictor of future performance, the application blank is a form seeking information about the applicant's background and present status. Usually this information is used as an initial or preemployment screen to show whether the candidate meets the minimum job requirements. The form often asks for details of educational achievements and work experience. Validity evidence indicates that educational requirements are predictive of job tenure. Both educational and experience requirements may be useful in selecting individuals for high-level, complex jobs, not jobs that require a short learning period.

Although not prohibited per se, many traditional questions are now considered "red flags" of discrimination and should be avoided, including some about the following topics:

- *Demographic Information:* Questions related to race should be avoided because essentially no conditions legally allow one to make an employment decision on the basis of race. An exception to this may arise if a firm needs to fulfill a legally mandated affirmative action plan. Age, gender, religion, and national origin may be considered if they are related to a bona fide occupational qualification, but this can be difficult to prove, so questions regarding them may be avoided. Proof of age and citizenship can be required after hiring.
- *Commitments:* Questions about marital status, dependents, spouse's job, and child care arrangements need to be asked of both men and women and given equivalent weight for both if they are asked at all. It is acceptable to ask if applicants have any social, family, or economic responsibilities that would prevent them from performing job duties.
- *Arrests and Convictions:* Inquiries about arrest records are not permissible under any conditions, but employers may ask about convictions.
- *Disabilities:* Disabilities may be considered after the job offer is made. The guidelines contained in the Americans with Disabilities Act must be followed closely.
- *Physical Requirements:* Height and weight may be queried for a few jobs. Care should be taken to ensure that physical requirements are valid, because they tend to discriminate against some ethnic groups (Hispanics, Asians) and against women.
- *Affiliations:* Catchall questions about organization affiliations (e.g., country clubs, fraternal orders, lodges) must be avoided. However, it is acceptable to ask about professional memberships that relate to specific jobs.

The accuracy of applicant-generated information is also a concern. Verified Credentials reports that almost 30 percent of the résumés it checks contain false information. Distortions vary from a wrong starting date for a prior job to inflated college grades to actual lies involving degrees, types of jobs, and former employers. The most common distortions relate to length of employment and previous salary.[35]

Biographical Information Blank and Biodata Tests. In addition to the application blank, or even as a substitute for it, employers may administer a *biographical information* *blank (BIB).*[36] A BIB generally requests more information from the applicant than does an application blank. For example, in addition to name, present address, references, skills, and type of education, the BIB may request a degree of preference for such things as working split shifts, being transferred, working on weekends, or working alone. Exactly which items are asked should be based on the nature of the job. If the job does require split-shift work, a BIB item that indicates any preference for split shifts may be a good predictor of turnover.[37]

Biodata tests are a variation on this theme of obtaining information about past and current activities. They ask autobiographical questions on such subjects as extracurricular activities (e.g., "Over the past five years, how much have you enjoyed outdoor recreation?"), family experiences as a child, and recent and current work activities (e.g., "How long were you employed in your most recent job?"). Responses to these questions are empirically keyed based on research that usually involves hundreds of respondents.[38] Biodata information alone can be quite effective as a predictor of performance and it can also be effective when used with an interview.[39]

Reference and Background Verification. Because some job applicants falsify their past and current qualifications, employers are stepping up efforts to check references thoroughly (see the feature "Positioning for the 21st Century: Investigating Applicant Fraud"). Instead of relying on unstructured reference letters, which are always positive, some organizations are using outside investigators to verify credentials, others are personally contacting prior employers to get reference information firsthand, and still others have structured the reference process to acquire only job-specific information (goals, accomplishments, degree of supervision).[40]

Another reason for the increased rigor in reference checking is negligent-hiring lawsuits. Consider the following case:

A woman raped by a cable television installer . . . sued the installer's employers—a cable television franchise and its independent contractor. She claimed that they gave the installer a master key to her apartment, which he used to enter her dwelling on the night of the attack. Because his employers gave him a master key to the apartments, the woman argued that they owed their customers a special duty to ensure that he was not a violent criminal. But they had failed to check his criminal record. The employers settled out of court for $250,000.[41]

Unfortunately, it is getting more difficult to get information, because of the potential for defamation-of-character suits. Previous employers are becoming "street-smart," limiting the type of information they give out about former employees. However, reference checks of an applicant's prior employment record are not an infringement on privacy if the information provided relates specifically to work behavior and to the reasons for leaving a previous job.

Written Tests

The most common types of written tests measure ability, personality, interests and preferences.

Aptitude and Ability Tests. Aptitude and ability tests measure the potential of an individual to perform, given the opportunity. Used in the United States and Europe since the turn of the 20th century, these devices are useful and valid. The number of distinct aptitudes and abilities of potential relevance to job performance is debatable, but generally aptitudes and abilities fall into three broad groupings: cognitive (e.g., verbal, quantitative), psychomotor (perceptual speed and accuracy), and physical (e.g., manual

Positioning for the 21st Century:
INVESTIGATING APPLICANT FRAUD

Q-1—What are the items most likely to be falsified on a résumé or employment application?

A-1—Education, work experience, and references. Some people claim to have degrees that they don't have, and some make claims of work experience that are fraudulent. These are just some of the reasons that more and more human resource departments are asking their company's security professionals to help screen job applications and make sure that the candidates are what they say they are.

Q-2—How do applicants falsify their education credentials on a résumé or application?

A-2—What dishonest applicants exaggerate most often is the amount of their schooling. For example, applicants may indicate that they have a bachelor's or master's degree when, in fact, they don't.

Often, an investigation will reveal that the applicant was enrolled in the degree program at the college or university listed; however, the applicant never actually completed the requirements for the degree. Or applicants will claim to have graduated from an accredited technical institute, but upon investigation, the "institute" turns out to be a bus driver's school.

Q-3—What about work experience?

A-3—The "creative" applicant often counterfeits the length of time of a previous job, the responsibilities held, or the compensation received. On rare occasions, an applicant may list employment that never took place at all, perhaps with a fictitious employer.

Applicants with unsatisfactory employment records attempt to disguise the facts. Sometimes, people will say that they worked from January to December when they actually worked only from January to June, and were terminated from a job.

Deceitful applicants also tend to inflate their former salaries in an attempt to make themselves look better than they are.

Q-4—What problems have you found in checking references?

A-4—Unscrupulous applicants may also list fake references to round off their other deceptions. They will list actual people who have never heard of them or fictitious people, hoping that the names and titles will give credence to their claims and that you will not bother to contact the references.

Q-5—How much information on the application or résumé should you check?

A-5—You should devise a checklist to clarify what education and experience are essential for any position that needs to be filled. By defining what is essential and what is nonessential, you will not have to verify more information than is required.

Although it is important to confirm applicants' credentials, you may not need to check everything unless you suspect that some information may be false. If a degree is not required for the position, you may not need to contact the school, provided everything else on the application appears satisfactory.

State and federal laws may limit what information is available to you or impose rules on how you should go about obtaining certain information. For instance, credit checks conducted for employment purposes must conform to the guidelines established by the federal Fair Credit Reporting Act and any applicable state laws.[42]

---

dexterity, physical strength and ability).[43] Numerous studies document the usefulness of such tests for a wide variety of jobs.[44]

Exhibit 8.6 shows sample items for measuring seven types of cognitive abilities. Standard Oil Company has developed a cognitive ability test of management reasoning and judgment, and other firms have developed programmer aptitude tests.[45]

■ *Exhibit 8.6*

Samples of Cognitive Ability and Psychomotor Tests

Verbal Comprehension involves understanding the meanings of words and their relationships to each other. It is measured by such test items as:

Which one of the following words means most nearly the same as *dilapidated:*
(1) new   (2) injured   (3) unresponsive   (4) run-down   (5) lethargic

Word Fluency involves the ability to name or make words, such as making smaller words from the letters in a large one or playing anagrams. For example:

Using the letters in the word *measurement,* write as many three-letter words as you can in the next two minutes.

_____   _____   _____   _____   _____

_____   _____   _____   _____   _____

Number Aptitude involves speed and accuracy in making simple arithmetic calculations. It is measured by such test items as:

Carry out the following calculations:

```
  429        7,983        721 × 52 = _____        4,920 ÷ 6 =_____
+762       −6,479
```

Inductive Reasoning focuses on the ability to discover a rule or principle and apply it to the solution of a problem. The following is an example:

What number should come next in the sequence of five numbers?
1   3   6   10   15
(1) 22   (2) 21   (3) 25   (4) 18

Memory relates to having the ability to recall pairs of words or lists of numbers. It is measured by such test items as:

You have thirty seconds to memorize the following pairs. When the examiner says stop, turn the page and write the appropriate symbols after each of the letters appearing there.
A @   C #   E Δ   G ?
B >   D *   F +   H $

Perceptual Speed is concerned with the ability to perceive visual details quickly and accurately. Usually these tests are timed and include such items as:

Make a check mark in front of each pair below in which the numbers are identical. Work as fast as you can.
1. 755321 753321
2. 966441 966641
3. 334579 334579

Motor Skill—Aiming involves the ability to respond accurately and rapidly to stimuli. For example:

Place three dots in as many circles as you can in 30 seconds.
○ ○ ○   ○   ○   ○○   ○   ○

SOURCE: Modified from M. D. Dunnette, *Personnel Selection and Placement* (Monterey, CA: Brooks/Cole Publishing, 1966), 47–49.

Many jobs involve not only a wide range of cognitive abilities but also psychomotor and physical skills. For example, a bank teller needs the motor skills to operate a computer or a ten-key calculator and the finger dexterity to manipulate currency.

Psychomotor abilities are varied, with each being highly specific and showing little relationship to other psychomotor abilities or to cognitive or physical abilities. For instance, control precision involves finely controlled muscular adjustments (e.g., moving a lever to a precise setting), whereas finger dexterity entails skillful manipulation of small objects (e.g., assembling nuts and bolts).

Ability tests are useful for selecting applicants in many occupations. However, only some categories of ability tests may be predictive of job performance in a specific position. For instance, sensory tests, which measure the acuity of a person's senses, such as vision and hearing, may be appropriate for such jobs as wine taster, coffee bean selector, quality control inspector, and piano tuner. Clerical tests focus primarily on perceptual speed; specific tests such as the Minnesota Clerical Tests measure these skills in a job-relevant context.

Personality Tests. *Personality* refers to the unique blend of characteristics that define an individual and determine her or his pattern of interactions with the environment. A variety of approaches for psychological assessment can be used to measure personality, but paper-and-pencil tests are probably the most common.[46] Although most people believe that personality plays an important role in job success or failure, U.S. employers have shied away from measuring it for a variety of reasons. After many years of research, it appeared as if personality seldom predicted performance. But this early conclusion may have been inaccurate.[47]

Recent advances in the academic community's understanding of the nature of personality suggest that employers may have abandoned personality measures too early. The most significant advance has been the realization that most aspects of personality can be captured using only a few basic dimensions. Often referred to as the Big Five, these are

- Extraversion (sociable, talkative, assertive)
- Agreeableness (good-natured, cooperative, trusting)
- Conscientiousness (responsible, dependable, persistent, achievement oriented)
- Emotional stability or instability (tense, insecure, nervous)
- Openness to experience (imaginative, artistically sensitive, intellectual)[48]

Although not all these aspects of personality are likely to be relevant to performance in all types of jobs, some meaningful links seem to exist.[49] The most important dimension for predicting job performance across a variety of jobs and a variety of occupational groups is conscientiousness. In general, conscientious people perform better, and this seems to be even more true for managerial jobs characterized by high levels of autonomy.[50] Not surprisingly, extraversion is somewhat predictive of performance in jobs that involve social interaction, such as sales and management, but these linkages are actually not very strong.

One other personality characteristic is attracting a lot of attention among employers—namely, personal integrity, also referred to as honesty. Employee theft is often cited as a primary reason for small-business failures, with some estimates suggesting it is the cause of up to 30 percent of all failures and bankruptcies.[51] In retailing, inventory shrinkage (unexplained losses in cash, tools, merchandise, and supplies) is a major problem, requiring companies to invest large amounts in security systems. In a survey of nine thousand employees by the Justice Department, one-third admitted stealing from their employers. And, unfortunately, white-collar crime involving millions of dollars regularly makes the news.

Problems of this scope and magnitude help explain why employers administer approximately 5 million integrity tests annually.[52] Undoubtedly, not all these tests are equally valid. But they appear to be more effective than the polygraph tests previously used by employers (which were found to be highly unreliable and are now, under the Employee Polygraph Protection Act of 1988, effectively banned for use in employment screening). Substantial evidence now indicates that psychological measures of personal integrity can successfully be used to predict dishonest and disruptive work behaviors—for instance, theft and disciplinary problems.[53] From the applicants' perspective, it appears that paper-and-pencil integrity tests are favored over more invasive procedures, such as lie detectors and background checks.[54]

Sometimes simply giving a test can help solve a company's problems. A convenience food-store chain recently gave an honesty test to a few hundred employees and told them how to correct the test themselves. The employees' exposure to the test and the process of self-correction, according to Mr. Keller, prompted an immediate two-thirds reduction in inventory theft.[55] Thus, although less predictive of job success than cognitive ability tests, carefully developed personality assessments can be inexpensive additions to the selection process for a few jobs.

Important legal issues can arise in the use of some personality tests. Invasion of privacy and possible discrimination may be especially problematic if tests are not carefully chosen. As the feature "Managing Human Resources for the 21st Century at Target Stores" describes, an invasion of privacy can be costly to the employer.

Interest and Preference Inventories. Interest inventories assess applicants' preferences for different types of work and work situations.[56] Such inventories are useful in matching people to jobs they will enjoy.

Representative items from an interest inventory include the following:

For each set, write an *M* next to the activity you most like and an *L* next to the activity you least like.
1. _____ Go to a concert.
   _____ Play tennis.
   _____ Read a book.
2. _____ Work in the garden.
   _____ Go hiking.
   _____ Paint a picture.

As these items illustrate, interests and preferences are reflected in the behaviors people engage in voluntarily. Interest and preference inventories are most often used to assist people during their early struggles with deciding which types of occupations or careers suit them. For example, high school and college counselors often advise students based on results from the *Strong Vocational Interest Blank*. With massive downsizing, outplacement counselors serving unemployed adults also use such inventories to help people develop midlife career strategies and evaluate potential changes in occupation. In all these settings, the assumption is that people will be both more satisfied and more likely to perform satisfactorily in jobs that match their interests. Some evidence supports this idea, and also shows a tendency for satisfied jobholders to remain in their jobs longer.[57] Thus, it may be wise for employers to use interest inventories as part of their placement activities.

Work Simulations

Work simulations, often referred to as work sample tests, require applicants to complete verbal or physical activities under structured "testing" conditions. Rather than measure

Managing Human Resources for the 21st Century at Target Stores

Target Stores has agreed to pay approximately $2 million to settle a class-action privacy suit filed by a group of applicants for security jobs. As part of the company's job-screening process, applicants were required to answer questions about religion, sexual orientation, and other personal issues in a psychological test. The California State Court of Appeal earlier had ruled in the case that employers may not screen out job applicants by using non-job-related psychological tests. Target had argued that the test was needed to weed out emotionally unfit applicants. The state supreme court agreed to review the case, but Target settled before the case was heard by the court.

Employers already had become more cautious of psychological testing even before this case, owing to the Americans with Disabilities Act, which requires that a legitimate, business-related reason must exist to require employees to take medical exams. (A psychological test likely will be considered a medical exam under the law.) Although the law allows more breathing room for testing applicants, it still requires that such test results be used only to evaluate a person's ability to perform the essential functions of the job. If not, the employer is forced to consider reasonable accommodation for the position.[58]

what an individual knows, they assess the individual's ability to do. Work sample tests are somewhat artificial because the selection process itself tends to promote anxiety and tension.[59]

Because they replicate the actual work, these tests are not easy to fake. They also tend to be more valid than almost all other types of selection devices and the least likely to create problems due to unfair discrimination. Unfortunately, they are usually expensive to develop so they are only cost-effective when large numbers of applicants are to be examined. They are also expensive to administer, though, so the total price is lower if they are placed at the end of a selection process, when the number of applicants tested is smaller.

Assessment Centers

Assessment centers evaluate how well applicants or current employees might perform in a managerial or higher-level position.[60] As described in "Managing Human Resources for the 21st Century at Hamilton Standard," these centers can be particularly effective at selecting team-oriented candidates. More than twenty thousand companies used this method in 1994, and its use grows each year because of its validity in predicting whether job applicants will be successful or unsuccessful.[61]

Assessment centers usually involve six to twelve people, although they may involve more. Customarily, they are conducted off the premises for one to three days. The performance of the attendees is usually rated by managers who are trained assessors. Typically, the purpose of the program is to help determine the potential promotability of applicants to a first-line supervisor's job.

At a typical assessment center, candidates are evaluated using a wide range of techniques. One activity, the *in-basket exercise,* creates a realistic situation designed to elicit typical on-the-job behaviors. Situations and problems encountered on the job are written on individual sheets of paper and set in an in-basket. The applicant is then asked to arrange the papers by priority. Occasionally, the applicant may need to write an action

Managing Human Resources for the 21st Century at Hamilton Standard

Organizations that place a high value on selecting the right people and developing them to be high performers often use assessment centers. By using these centers, employers can observe candidates in exercises or work simulations instead of only in an interview situation. Although assessment centers produce positive results, most do not evaluate a candidate's ability to perform effectively on a team.

The assessment center at a division of Windsor Locks, Connecticut–based Hamilton Standard is an exception. Hamilton Standard Commercial Aircraft Electronics Division of United Technologies (HSCAE) manufactures environmental and jet-engine control systems for commercial aerospace applications. When Hamilton Standard was awarded a contract on the Boeing 777 in 1991, the company moved HSCAE to Colorado Springs, Colorado.

Once in Colorado Springs, an HSCAE leadership team designed a flat organization based on self-directed teams to produce the relatively low volumes of high-quality products that were necessary at the plant. To allow the teams to follow the product through all areas of production, HSCAE decided to hire and train a multifunctional workforce, certified in a variety of technical, business, and people skills. HSCAE created an assessment center to find these new team members.

Because of the company's progressive job requirements and work environment, it had two critical considerations:

1. Current team members needed to be involved in the selection process.

2. The program needed to assess individuals' abilities to work in teams, learn such generic work skills as hand-eye coordination, follow written instructions, and learn technical skills.

To meet these requirements, the company implemented a multistep selection program. This process begins with an information session for candidates who submit résumés to the company. Brought in groups of about 150 people for an interactive two-hour session, candidates learn about the organization's product and HSCAE's employee expectations. At the end of the session, candidates are invited to complete applications.

Preparing current team members to participate on selection teams is a crucial second step. Individuals throughout the Colorado Springs facility go through extensive training to become certified in résumé and application review, telephone interviewing, technical interviewing, and consensus-exercise evaluation.

The assessment center process evaluates sixty-five to seventy candidates on a single Saturday. During the week prior to the Saturday session, candidates participate in two three-hour assessments. The first is a battery of tests that measure the candidates' generic work skills. Then, candidates complete the *College Placement Exam,* conducted by the local community college. This is used to validate high school training. Although these assessments help HSCAE identify strengths and weaknesses, candidates are not selected or rejected based on their results.

When the candidates come in on Saturday, forty-five to sixty trained HSCAE employees conduct technical and general interviews and evaluate the Team Consensus Exercise, in which candidates participate during the three-hour evaluation.

In the technical interview, all candidates are presented with a flowchart of the manufacturing process, which is used to identify areas in which they could add value.

Next, the general interview evaluates a candidate's understanding of such business issues as the material flow process, configuration management, computer, finance, and human resource skills.

In the Team Consensus Exercise, candidates work in teams of six to build a model airplane. Six trained evaluators assess the candidates in these areas of team performance: participation, support of the process, interpersonal skills, quality of thought, mode of behavior, and flexibility. At this time, evaluators discuss each candidate and all hiring decisions are made by group consensus.

After almost two years, the assessment center has achieved outstanding results. Through the center, HSCAE has been able to recruit and retain a talented, cross-functional workforce whose certified skills cover more than fifty-two areas. Further, the teams have improved customer-acceptance rates while lowering costs, making HSCAE a highly competitive supplier of aerospace electronics.[62]

response on a piece of paper. The problems or situations described to the applicant involve different groups of people—peers, subordinates, and people outside the organization. The applicant is usually given a time limit and is often interrupted by phone calls meant to create more tension and pressure.

Other tests used in managerial selection are business games and the leaderless group discussion. *Business games* are living cases. That is, they ask individuals to make decisions and live with them, much as does the in-basket exercise.

In the *leaderless group discussion (LGD),* a group of individuals is asked to discuss a topic for a given period of time. At IBM's assessment center, participants must make a five-minute oral presentation about the qualifications of a candidate for promotion. During the subsequent group discussion, they must defend their nomination of the candidate with five or more other participants. Participants are rated on their selling ability, oral communication skill, self-confidence, energy level, interpersonal competency, aggressiveness, and tolerance for stress. LGD ratings are useful predictors of managerial performance in a wide range of business areas. In addition, prior experience in LGD does not affect current LGD performance.

Because in-baskets exercises, business games, and LGDs tend to be useful in managerial selection, they are often used together in an assessment center.[63] As candidates go through these exercises, their performance is observed by a specifically trained team of observers or assessors drawn from the local management group. After the candidates have finished the program, these assessors meet to discuss the candidates and prepare performance evaluations based on their combined judgments of the candidates in such areas as organizing and planning, analyzing, making decisions, controlling oral communications, conducting interpersonal relations, influencing, and exhibiting flexibility. The composite performance on the exercises and tests is often used to determine an assessment center attendee's future promotability. It may also be used to develop the organization's human resource planning and training needs, as well as to make current selection and placement decisions. This rating is generally given to the attendee, who in turn can use it for his or her own personal career planning purposes.

Assessment centers have been used effectively in manufacturing companies, the government, military services, utility companies, oil companies, the foreign services, and educational institutions. They appear to work because they reflect the actual job environment and measure performance on multiple job dimensions, and because two or more trained raters with a common frame of reference evaluate each participant's behavior. These centers are often criticized as costing too much—$50 to over $2,000 for each applicant. However, annual productivity gains realized by selecting managers through assessment centers average well above administrative costs.[64]

Selection and Placement Interview

Job offers go to the applicants who *appear* most qualified, because it is often impossible to determine from available data who really *is* most qualified. Although appearances can be deceiving, the job interview and the perceptions gained from it still constitute the tool most heavily used to determine who gets a job offer.[65] As shown in Exhibit 8.3, interviews occur at both the beginning and during the selection process. Their usefulness depends on several variables.

Degree of Structure. An unstructured interview involves little preparation. The interviewer merely prepares a list of possible topics to cover and, depending on how the conversation proceeds, asks or does not ask them. Although this provides for flexibility, the resulting digressions, discontinuity, and lack of focus may be frustrating to the

Positioning for the 21st Century:
YOU AND YOUR COMPUTER

Employers can improve employee selection by making computers an integral part of the interviewing process, suggests Brooks Mitchell, president of Aspen Tree Software and author of a new book on the use of computers in employee selection.

Typically, "front-line" hiring is performed by junior managers who do not possess much interviewing experience and spend only five to ten minutes on each job candidate, Mitchell observes. Calling employee selection the most important personnel task carried out by human resource managers in conjunction with line management, Mitchell says it cannot properly be done in such a short amount of time. Accordingly, he asserts, the hiring process currently used by most employers needs to be closely scrutinized and given more priority.

Although human interaction will always be needed in an interview, a computer can perform the parts of the interview process that most managers do not want to do, such as questioning an applicant on previous employment, according to Mitchell. These types of questions can be asked in a multiple-choice format on a computer, and the software can be programmed to tailor upcoming questions to prior answers. For example, if an applicant answers on the computer that he turned down a prior job offer with a $20,000 salary because the pay was too low, the computer might be prompted to tell the applicant that the current job opening pays $18,000 a year, to ensure continued interest, he explains.

Overall, a structured computer interview ensures that the important questions are not forgotten, while eliminating personal bias and the hesitancy of many managers to ask sensitive questions, Mitchell says. It also delivers substantial time savings, since a computer can ask more questions in a given period of time than can a human, he notes.[66]

interviewer and interviewee. More important, unstructured interviews result in inconsistencies in the information collected about the candidates.

In a structured interview, all the applicants are asked the same questions in the same order. Usually, the interviewer also has a prepared guide that suggests which types of answers are considered good or poor. Although structuring the interview restricts the topics that can be covered, it ensures that the same information is collected on all candidates. As a result, managers are less likely to make snap and possibly erroneous judgments.[67]

Computerized interviews help both line managers and HR professionals make better judgments in the interview process, as described in the feature "Positioning for the 21st Century: You and Your Computer." Another alternative that minimizes snap judgments is the semistructured interview. Questions are prepared in advance, the same questions are asked of all candidates, and responses are recorded. However, follow-up questions are allowed to probe specific areas in depth. This approach provides enough flexibility to develop insights, along with the structure needed to acquire comparative information.

Systematic Scoring. Job interviews also vary in the degree to which results are scored. At one extreme, an interviewer merely listens to responses; forms an impression; and makes an accept, reject, or hold decision. Alternatively, raters are given specific criteria and a scoring key to evaluate responses to each question. This approach helps ensure that applicants are evaluated against the same criteria. Systematic scoring also tends to minimize "halo bias," in which an interviewer judges an applicant's entire potential on the basis of a single characteristic, such as how well the applicant dresses or talks.

Number of Interviewers. Typically, applicants are interviewed by one person at a time. Unfortunately, managers sometimes overlap in their coverage of some job-related questions and miss others entirely. An applicant may have not four interviews but one interview four times. This is a time-consuming process in which the interviewer's and applicant's impressions may vary, depending on what was discussed. These problems can be overcome by using a *panel interview,* in which several individuals simultaneously interview one applicant. Because all decision makers hear the same responses, panel interviews produce more consistent results. They may also be less susceptible to the biases and prejudice of the interviewers, especially if panel members come from diverse backgrounds.[68] On the other hand, panel interviews are expensive because many people are involved. However, if applicants are to be interviewed by more than one manager and nonmanager anyway, panel interviewing may be more efficient and reliable than, and as cost-effective as, individual interviews.

A variation of the panel interview is the *team interview.* Glenna Sue Davis, HR and quality control manager at A. E. Staley Manufacturing Company's potato starch facility, says: "I feel it's important to get a perspective from the people who will be working directly with the new hire. . . . Team interviewing also provides me with a more in-depth sense of what traits are needed to successfully fill a position."[69] Davis tries to get at least four or five people involved and ensures a mix of male and female interviewers. The team approach provides another benefit in that decisions are shared and are more likely to be supported by the staff.[70]

Training. Left on their own, interviewers tend to form their own impressions based on whatever criteria are most important or salient to them. For example, an applicant might be rejected by one interviewer for being "too aggressive" but accepted by another for being "assertive." Consequently, interviewers must be trained to interpret information consistently. At A. E. Staley, Davis stresses that she and her staff "do a couple of training sessions on our wants, needs, and priorities. Then we put together the questions we'll be asking—of course, every applicant will be asked the same questions."[71]

Frame-of-reference training (which is also used to reduce inconsistencies in performance ratings) involves teaching interviewers (or raters) a common nomenclature for defining the importance of each component of behavior that is to be observed in the interview (or rating).[72] This can be accomplished by having potential interviewers develop questions and a scoring key. Alternatively, an interviewer's ratings for "practice" interview questions can be compared with normative ratings given by other interviewers. Such training brings individual perceptions into closer congruence with those of the rest of the organization.

Medical and Physical Tests

Although not all organizations require medical exams or physical tests, these are being given in increasing numbers. One consequence is a concern about genetic screening.

General Health Examinations. Because of their high cost, health examinations have often been among the final steps in the selection process. But under the Americans with Disabilities Act of 1990, these exams may be given only after a job offer has been made.[73] Before the offer is made, employers should only describe the job's functions and ask if the applicant is capable of performing the job. Employers cannot inquire at this stage about any disabilities. Postoffer physical and medical exams that tend to screen out people with disabilities must be job related. Attempts at accommodation should be made and documented.

Guidelines for assessing physical abilities have been developed that detail the sensory, perceptual, cognitive, psychomotor, and physical requirements of many jobs—for example, police officer, firefighter, electrical powerplant worker, telephone line worker, steel mill laborer, paramedic, maintenance worker, and numerous mechanical jobs. When applied carefully, these physical requirements—not physical examinations per se—are extremely useful in predicting job performance, worker's compensation claims, and absenteeism. Although non-job-related exams can be given if they are given to everyone, any elimination of members of protected groups will need to be defended as job related. And even then accommodation efforts must be made.

To accommodate workers with disabilities, organizations should also explore whether equipment can be "reasonably" adapted to facilitate their work. Guidelines on inexpensive adaptations for most types of machinery are available from the federal government.[74] This concern is also particularly relevant for employees since the passage of the ADA. In fact, the act is giving employers an opportunity to review their entire set of policies regarding job applicants and employees with disabilities.

Genetic Screening. Each year, hundreds of thousands of job-related illnesses and deaths occur. Many of these are attributable to chemical hazards. Genetic screening identifies individuals who are hypersensitive to harmful pollutants in the workplace. Once identified, these individuals can be screened out of chemically dangerous jobs and placed in positions in which environmental toxins do not present specific hazards.[75] Genetic screening is not covered by the ADA.

Although cost-effective genetic tests have not yet been developed, 1 percent of major firms already use genetic screening, and 15 percent are considering genetic tests in the future. As scientific research on genetic screening continues, the debate over the ethics of basing employment decisions on immutable traits is likely to grow.[76] It also seems probable that organizations will be pressured to develop engineering controls that minimize or eliminate workplace pollutants. These controls would be the preferred alternative to genetic screening, a selection criterion over which an individual has no control.[77]

Drug and Alcohol Testing. Drug and alcohol abuse are said to cost U.S. industry more than $100 billion annually.[78] Consequently, firms are likely to continue drug testing. Federal contractors have no choice. According to the Drug-Free Workplace Act of 1988, firms that do business with the federal government must have written drug use policies. Regardless of what methods are used for drug testing, a key issue in adopting a drug policy is establishing a disciplinary procedure: "If a drug policy does not state specifically that disciplinary actions will be taken when an employee tests positive for drug use, there's no reason to test. Drug testing doesn't make sense if you're not willing to take disciplinary action based on a confirmed positive test result. A policy calling for discipline in such a circumstance doesn't have to require termination. Rehabilitation can be required as an alternative."[79]

The Americans with Disabilities Act protects applicants and employees who are in recovery programs, but not current drug and alcohol users. Testing for illegal drugs is not considered a medical exam under the ADA and is, therefore, permissible.

AIDS Testing. Persons with AIDS and HIV are protected by the Rehabilitation Act of 1973 (*Chalk v. United States District Court for the Central District of California,* 1987) and the Americans with Disabilities Act. Because AIDS and HIV are a major challenge in today's workplace, organizations are establishing guidelines concerning them. Companies such as IBM, Levi Strauss, DuPont, AT&T, and Johnson and Johnson have endorsed these guidelines:

◉ People with AIDs or who are infected with HIV, the AIDS-causing virus, are entitled to the same rights and opportunities as people with other serious illnesses.
◉ Employment policies should be based on the scientific evidence that people with AIDS or HIV do not pose a risk of transmitting the virus through ordinary workplace contact.
◉ Employers should provide workers with sensitive and up-to-date education about AIDS and about risk reduction in their personal lives.
◉ Employers have the duty to protect the confidentiality of employees' medical information.
◉ Employers should not require HIV screening as part of general preemployment or workplace physical examinations.[80]

 ## LEGAL CONSIDERATIONS

Numerous acts, executive orders, guidelines, professional standards, and agencies affect selection practices in most organizations.[81] Their effect is not direct in the sense of mandating procedures to be used. Rather, it is indirect: legal constraints operate by defining what constitutes illegal discrimination and specifying how employers can successfully defend themselves if they are charged with illegal discrimination.[82] The effects of numerous acts and executive orders are described in Chapters 3 and 7. Here we describe the effects of federal guidelines and professional standards.

Federal Guidelines and Professional Standards

Guidelines describe the procedures that organizations should use to comply with acts and orders. In particular, they explain how to develop and use selection tools, such as tests, and how organizations can assess whether their procedures may be considered discriminatory.

Federal Guidelines. The first set of federal guidelines was issued in 1970 by the EEOC, which intended to provide a workable set of ideal standards for employees, unions, and employment agencies. Those guidelines defined tests as being "all formal, scored, qualified or standardized techniques of assessing job suitability, including . . . background requirements, educational or work history requirements, interviews, biographical information blanks, interview rating scales and scored application blanks."

Following the issuance of the guidelines, the courts began using them as a sort of checklist of *minimum* standards for test validation, rather than as a flexible set of *ideal* standards, as intended. Concern over this trend prompted the Equal Employment Opportunity Coordinating Council to develop a set of uniform guidelines, to be used by all federal agencies, that were based on sound psychological principles and were technically feasible. As a result, the Federal Executive Agency (FEA) Guidelines were published in 1976, followed by the Uniform Guidelines on Employee Selection Procedures in 1978. The Uniform Guidelines were issued in a fourteen-thousand-word catalog of do's and don'ts and questions and answers for hiring and promotion. It contains interpretation and guidance not found in earlier EEOC guidelines and is generally considered the most complete and useful legal document relevant to selection and placement.

The EEOC also has published other guidelines. On November 10, 1980, it issued Guidelines on Discrimination because of Sex. These guidelines are premised on the assumption that sexual harassment is a condition of employment if women are exposed to it more frequently than men. Six weeks later, the EEOC issued its Guidelines on Discrimination because of National Origin. These guidelines extended earlier versions of this protection by defining national origin as a *place* rather than a *country*. It also revised the "speak-English-only rules." This means employers can require that English be spoken if they can show a compelling business-related necessity. On September 29, 1981, the EEOC issued guidelines on age discrimination, in essence, identifying what the Age Discrimination in Employment Act meant to do and what it should mean to employers and employees.

Under the Guidelines on Discrimination because of Religion, an employer is obliged to accommodate the religious preferences of current and prospective employees unless the employer demonstrates undue hardship. It appears, however, that if an employer shows "reasonable attempts to accommodate," the courts may be satisfied that no religious discrimination has occurred (*State Division of Human Rights v. Rochester Housing Authority*, 1980; *Philbrook v. Ansonia Board of Education*, 1986).

Regarding interpretive guidelines for compliance with the Americans with Disabilities Act, the best currently available document is the *Technical Assistance Manual on Employment Provisions*, published by the EEOC in 1992. This document provides valuable guidance in such areas as explaining how to identify essential job functions, acceptable interviewing strategies, and the appropriate timing and use of medical examinations.[83]

Professional Standards. Selection processes are also monitored by the American Psychological Association (APA), which includes among its members many experts in testing and individual assessment. In 1966 and again in 1974, the APA released its *Standards for Education and Psychological Tests*. These were updated in 1985 and were again revised in 1994.[84] In 1975 and again in 1987, the Society for Industrial-Organizational Psychology (SIOP) published its *Principles for the Validation and Use of Personnel Selection Procedures*. Drawing from relevant research, these help clarify issues regarding test fairness and discrimination. They were also under review in 1995.[85]

 PROVING ILLEGAL DISCRIMINATION

Although federal laws explicitly prohibit discrimination, nowhere in the law is discrimination defined. Usually, the court system decides whether or not illegal discrimination has occurred. Broadly speaking, however, the law prohibits differential treatment of employees on the basis of membership in particular groups defined by race, color, religion, national origin, sex, age, physical and mental handicap, and status as a disabled or Vietnam-era veteran. Discrimination on all other bases or qualifications is untouched by federal law, except when it is disguised as legal discrimination.[86]

Prima Facie Cases

In a typical discrimination lawsuit, a person alleges discrimination due to unlawful employment practices. The person may first go to the Equal Employment Opportunity Commission office. The EEOC may seek out the facts of the case from both sides, attempting a resolution. Failing a resolution, the person may continue the case and file a suit. In the first phase of the suit, the person filing it (the plaintiff) must establish a prima facie case of discrimination. This is done by showing disparate treatment or disparate impact.

Disparate Treatment. Illegal discrimination against an individual is referred to as *disparate treatment.* A prima facie case of disparate treatment exists when an individual can demonstrate the following:

- The individual belongs to a protected group.
- The individual applied for a job for which the employer was seeking applicants.
- Despite being qualified, the individual was rejected.
- After the individual's rejection, the employer kept looking for people with the applicant's qualifications.

These conditions, which suggest intentional discrimination, were set forth in *McDonnell Douglas Corporation v. Green* (1973).

For individual applicants, demonstrating a case of disparate treatment can be difficult. One reason is that discrimination can be subtle, so the applicant may never really realize that a decision was made on the basis of personal characteristics. Also, most of the decision processes are not visible to applicants. Rejected applicants, especially external ones, seldom know how other applicants performed or even who was eventually hired. In part for these reasons, the law also provides other means for establishing a case of illegal discrimination—specifically, the logic of disparate impact.

Disparate Impact. Unfair discrimination against an entire protected group is called *disparate impact.* The Supreme Court specified the basic criteria for establishing a prima facie case of disparate impact in *Griggs v. Duke Power.* Cases of disparate impact can be brought on the basis of three types of statistical evidence.

One type of evidence is *comparative statistics* showing the rates at which members of protected versus nonprotected groups have been hired, fired, promoted, transferred, or demoted. The Uniform Guidelines state that disparate impact, also called adverse impact, is demonstrated when the selection rate "for any racial, ethnic, or sex subgroup is less than four-fifths or 80 percent of the highest selection rate for any group." This so-called bottom-line criterion, which focuses on the consequences of a selection decision rather than on its intent, applies to *each part* of the selection process as well as to the process as a *whole* (*Connecticut v. Teal,* 1982). For enforcement purposes, employees file EEO-1 report forms, which the EEOC has authority to audit.[87]

Disparate impact can also be based on *demographic statistics* of the labor market. That is, an employer's selection procedures can be shown discriminatory in a prima facie sense if the employer's workforce fails to reflect parity with the race or sex composition of the relevant labor market. Organizations may determine their relevant labor market in several ways. One is by identifying where 85 percent of current employees reside. Another is by identifying where job applicants reside. A third approach—preferred by the EEOC—is by identifying where potentially qualified applicants reside, even if the organization's current recruitment efforts do not reach this market. Prima facie cases of this type can be successfully defended by employers if they can show that statistical parity exists, that is, that the proportions of protected group members in their organization's workforce mirror the proportions in the relevant labor market.

The third basis for establishing a case of disparate impact is *concentration statistics.* The argument here is that a prima facie case of illegal discrimination exists to the extent that protected group members are located in one particular area or job category in the organization. For example, equal numbers of male and female employees may be hired into entry-level jobs in the organization, but the females may be placed predominately in secretarial jobs. This type of practice creates "glass walls" between job categories and job families. Furthermore, because the route to the top of an organization often begins in jobs dominated by men, these glass walls contribute to the problem of "glass ceilings."

Bases for Defending Discriminatory Practices

Once a prima facie case of disparate treatment or disparate impact has been established, the employer is given the opportunity to defend itself.[88] An organization accused of illegal discrimination may be able to successfully defend its employment practices by showing that the demonstrated discrimination is legally justified. Discriminatory employment practices can be acceptable if they are used on the basis of

- Job relatedness
- Business necessity
- Bona fide occupational qualifications
- Bona fide seniority systems
- Voluntary affirmative action programs

Job Relatedness. In discrimination cases, the employer bears the burden of showing that a selection decision is based on job-related information. To demonstrate *job relatedness,* the company must show that the information used (e.g., interviews, ability tests, education requirements) to make decisions about who to hire or how to place a new hire is related to an employee's being successful on the job (*Watson v. Fort Worth Bank and Trust,* 1988). Employers can use either logical argument or statistical evidence to demonstrate job relatedness. To be effective, either type of defense requires evidence that the important components of the job were determined through job analysis. For example, a typing test is arguably an appropriate selection device for an administrative assistant if a job analysis shows that people in this job spend 60 percent of their time on data entry; it may not be an appropriate selection device if people in the job actually spend less than 5 percent of their time typing.

Business Necessity. Showing the job relatedness of a selection procedure is not always possible. The law recognizes this, and allows companies to defend their selection procedures by showing *business necessity*—that is, they must show that the selection decision was based on a factor (e.g., pregnancy) directly related to the safe and efficient operation of the business. In cases where the logic for arguing business necessity is strong, demonstrating that a specific selection procedure is job related may not be necessary (see *Spurlock v. United Airlines,* 1972). However, the courts and the language of the Civil Rights Act of 1991 define this exception in very narrow terms. For example, the courts have stated that "the test is whether the alleged purpose is so essential to the safe and efficient operation of the business as to override any racial impact" (*Robinson v. P. Lorillard Company,* 1971) and "necessity connotes an irresistible command" (*United States v. Bethlehem Steel Company,* 1971).

Bona Fide Occupational Qualifications. The defense of *bona fide occupational qualifications (BFOQ)* is permitted for decisions based on sex, religion, and national origin only—not race or color.[89] To use this defense, the employer must show that the discriminatory practice is "reasonably necessary to the normal operation of that particular business or enterprise." For example, women can be barred from contact positions in an all-male, maximum security prison (*Dothard v. Rawlinson,* 1977).

Bona Fide Seniority Systems. As long as a company has established and maintained a seniority system without the intent to discriminate illegally, it is considered bona fide (*International Brotherhood of Teamsters v. United States,* 1977; *United States v. Trucking Management,* 1981; *American Tobacco v. Patterson,* 1982). Thus, promotion and job assignment decisions can be made on the basis of seniority.[90] In a major decision, the U.S. Supreme Court ruled that seniority can also be used in the determination of layoffs, even if doing so reverses effects of affirmative action hiring (*Firefighters Local Union 1784 v. Stotts,* 1984).

Voluntary Affirmative Action Programs. For voluntary affirmative action programs to be a defense against illegal discrimination, they must be remedial in purpose, limited in duration, restricted in effect, flexible in implementation, and minimal in harm to innocent parties (*Wygant v. Jackson Board of Education,* 1986; *International Association of Firefighters Local 93 v. City of Cleveland,* 1986; *Black Fire Fighters Association of Dallas v. City of Dallas,* 1994; *Ensley Branch, NAACP v. Seibels,* 1994).

 INTERNATIONAL CONCERNS

Selecting Employees for U.S. Companies Operating Abroad

The number of American expatriate employees is relatively small, but their importance to companies operating in the international markets is relatively large. Without effective expatriate managers and nonmanagers, U.S. companies are essentially unable to operate successfully abroad. Nevertheless, the ineffectiveness of expatriate employees—also called parent-country nationals (PCNs)—is alarmingly commonplace. Consequently, American-based multinational companies not only need to obtain candidates for expatriate positions but also must ensure that those employees are effective on the job.

Expatriate managers perform their daily activities in the context of the parent company's headquarters, the host country's government, the parent company's government, and a local culture that is often quite different from their home culture. In addition, expatriate managers typically operate in a culture with a different language—a major obstacle for many of them.[91] Thus, for expatriate managers to be successful, they need the skills not only to perform the specific type of job but also to perform the general duties required by six major categories of relations: (1) internal relations with their coworkers, (2) relations with their families, (3) relations with the host government, (4) relations with their home government, (5) external relations with the local culture, and (6) relations with the company's headquarters. Pepsi-Cola International selects its expatriates on the basis of how likely they are to perform well in eleven areas (see Exhibit 8.7). Using these success characteristics for selection, as well as for structuring a related management development program, can go a long way toward increasing the likelihood of expatriate managerial success.[92]

Typically, expatriate employees fill only a few positions in U.S. companies operating abroad. Most of the employees are host-country nationals (HCNs), who are usually selected using host-country practices.[93]

A growing but still relatively small number of positions are filled by third-country nationals (TCNs), individuals from neither the host country nor the parent country. They are often selected by the parent firm using practices similar to those used in selecting expatriates.[94] The pros and cons of selecting these three types of individuals are listed in Exhibit 8.8.

■ *Exhibit 8.7*

PCI Success Characteristics for Performance Measurement and Management

1. *Ability to Handle Business Complexity:* Figuring out what needs to be done and charting a course of action
2. *Results Orientation and Drive:* Focusing on an outcome and driving for completion
3. *Ability to Lead and Manage People:* Directing the work of and motivating others
4. *Executional Excellence:* Putting ideas into action
5. *Organizational Savvy:* Knowing how the organization works and how to maximize it
6. *Composure under Pressure:* Staying focused in the international pressure cooker and still getting things done
7. *Executive Maturity:* Always acting with maturity and good judgment
8. *Technical Knowledge:* Understanding and applying technical knowledge
9. *Positive People Skills:* Knowing how to get along with people from all cultures
10. *Effective Communication:* Knowing how to communicate cross-culturally
11. *Impact and Influence:* Being able to get things done when faced with obstacles

SOURCE: Adapted from J. R. Fulkerson and R. S. Schuler, "Managing Worldwide Diversity at Pepsi-Cola International," in *Diversity in the Workplace: Human Resources Initiatives,* ed. S. E. Jackson. (New York: Guilford Press, 1992): 258.

Human Resource Practices

The practice of using one's own human resource practices abroad is referred to as *ethnocentrism.* Allowing operations in different countries to develop and use their own human resource practices is called *polycentrism.* Developing practices that can be applied in all countries, with modest adjustments to local conditions, is called *geocentrism.*

As firms go global, they may go through a period of trial and error, seeing what works and what does not. Firms that have been successful because of their human resource practices may be inclined to insist that those practices be used elsewhere and may adapt only after getting feedback from the locals.

Legal Considerations

In the Civil Rights Act of 1991, Congress affirmed its policy that American civil rights laws—specifically Title VII of the 1964 Civil Rights Act and the Americans with Disabilities Act—apply to the employment practices of American multinationals relative to U.S. citizens employed in their foreign operations. Essentially, the act reversed the decision of the U.S. Supreme Court in *EEOC v. Arabian American Oil Company* (1991), which had concluded that Congress had *not* intended to apply Title VII to the foreign operations of American multinational firms. Furthermore, the Age Discrimination Employment Act of 1967 was amended in 1984 to protect American workers over the age of forty against discrimination by U.S. companies abroad.

The U.S. District Court in Washington, D.C., has ruled that U.S. law can even replace the laws of other nations:

> A long-standing German labor policy of mandatory retirement at age 65 does not shield an employer from the *Age Discrimination in Employment Act*'s protections for American workers in Germany, a federal district court rules.
>
> The case involves a non-profit U.S. corporation well known for two of its broadcast services—Radio Free Europe and Radio Liberty—that employs more than 300 U.S. citizens at its Munich facility. The mandatory retirement policy, contained in the employer's union contract, is found in most collective bargaining agreements in Germany. Two employees discharged because of their age filed a bias suit under ADEA. The employer conceded that the employees had been discharged because of age but argued that ADEA's "foreign laws" exemption—allowing actions taken in order to avoid violating the laws of a foreign country—applied. The "nearly ubiquitous contract terms" are considered to have "legal force" in Germany, the employer contended.

■ *Exhibit 8.8*

Selecting Managers: Pros and Cons of PCNs, HCNs, and TCNs

PARENT-COUNTRY NATIONALS

Advantages

- Organizational control and coordination is maintained and facilitated.
- Promising managers are given international experience.
- PCNs are the best people for the job.
- The subsidiary will likely comply with the company objectives, policies, and so forth.

Disadvantages

- The promotional opportunities of HCNs are limited.
- Adaptation to the host country may take a long time.
- PCNs may impose an inappropriate headquarter style.
- Compensation for PCNs and HCNs may differ.

HOST-COUNTRY NATIONALS

Advantages

- Language and other barriers are eliminated.
- Hiring costs are reduced, and no work permit is required.
- Continuity of management improves, since HCNs stay longer in positions.
- Government policy may dictate the hiring of HCNs.
- Morale among HCNs may improve as they see the career potentials.

Disadvantages

- Control and coordination of headquarters may be impeded.
- HCNs have limited career opportunities outside the subsidiary.
- Hiring HCNs limits opportunities for PCNs to gain overseas experience.
- Hiring HCNs could encourage a federation of national rather than global units.

THIRD-COUNTRY NATIONALS

Advantages

- Salary and benefit requirements may be lower than for PCNs.
- TCNs may be better informed than PCNs about the host-country environment.

Disadvantages

- Transfers must consider possible national animosities
- The host government may resent the hiring of TCNs.
- TCNs may not want to return to their own countries after assignment.

SOURCE: Adapted from P. Dowling, R. S. Schuler and D. Welch, *International Dimensions of Human Resource Management,* 2nd ed. (Belmont, CA: Wadsworth, 1994): 57.

Policies and practices, even when embodied in contracts, are not "laws," the court says, distinguishing a country's established "policy" from a foreign law. The former cannot deny Americans working abroad ADEA's protections against age discrimination, the court explains, ruling that "where a foreign labor union policy collides" with a law of the United States, the U.S. law "cannot be expected to bow down" (*Mahoney v. RFE/RL,* 1991).[95]

Some say that this is a rather ethnocentric policy. It is furthered by the practice of applying U.S. laws to foreign firms operating in the United States—which in 1994 employed about 5 million American workers:

> As many as one-third of Japanese firms with operations in the U.S. have been confronted with lawsuits for discrimination in their employment practices relative to their American employees in the U.S. Part of the problem may be a lack of knowledge about U.S. employment laws. But more to the point (and one which must concern all multinational firms) is the conflict between the national culture and employment practices of the parent firm and the employment laws in the overseas locations. As is true with the multinational enterprises (MNEs) from some other countries as well, Japanese firms tend to use only parent-country (i.e, Japanese) executives to run their American subsidiaries, providing few of the perquisites and no opportunities for promotion to the top management slots for their American managers . . .
>
> The preceding discussion notwithstanding, Japanese firms in the U.S. may well be protected in their staffing practices, at least at their top tiers of management. The Seventh Circuit Court of Appeals has ruled that Japanese subsidiaries operating in the U.S. may legally prefer Japanese citizens over U.S. citizens and *Civil Rights Act* prohibitions against discrimination on the basis of national origin do not apply. According to the ruling in *Fortino v. Quasar Co.,* Title VII of the *1964 Civil Rights Act* is preempted by a treaty between Japan and the U.S. which permits companies of either country to prefer their own citizens for executive positions in subsidiaries based in the other country.[96]

 SUMMARY

Organizations want to ensure that they hire job applicants with the abilities to meet job demands. Increasingly, they also want to ensure that job applicants will also stay with the organization. Thus, organizations may want to match the job applicant's needs and the rewards offered by the job qualities and organizational context.

To match individual knowledge, skills, and abilities to job demands and to match individual personalities, interests, and preferences to job and organizational characteristics, organizations need to gather information about job applicants. The three most common methods—interviewing, testing, and application blanks—must operate within legal regulations. These legal regulations are intended to ensure that information is collected, retained, and used in recognition of the individual's rights to equal opportunity in employment and to privacy, and of the organization's right to select individuals who will be productive on the job.

The types of information and the methods used to obtain information for selection vary according to characteristics of the job and of the organization. For example, assessment centers are apt to be used for managerial jobs, and physical ability tests for manufacturing and public health and safety jobs. How many different predictors are used may depend in part on the type of job as well as on labor market conditions and the costs associated with the selection tests in comparison with their benefits.

Increasingly, U.S. organizations are operating in other countries. Because the globalization of many U.S. companies is just beginning, gaining information about managing expatriates and learning how other countries manage their employees are likely to be of interest for some time.

Discussion Questions

1. Describe the selection practices at Coca-Cola, Pepsi, and Pepsi-Cola International and explain the similarities and differences.
2. A frequent diagnosis of an observed performance problem in an organization is, "This person was a selection mistake." What are the short- and long-term consequences of so-called selection mistakes? If possible, relate this question to your own experiences with organizations.
3. Successful selection and placement decisions are dependent on other human resource activities. Identify these activities, and explain their relationships to selection and placement.
4. Given all the weaknesses identified with unstructured interviews, why are interviews a popular selection device? How could you improve the typical job interview to overcome some of its potential weaknesses?
5. Describe the partnership in selection and placement.
6. Describe the most important legal considerations that all managers should be aware of when they participate in selecting people to fill jobs in their units.
7. Why are the best people often not the ones hired for the job?
8. What characteristics should companies consider when selecting expatriate managers?
9. What are the considerations in selecting from among PCNs, HCNs, and TCNs?

 In-Class Projects

1. Describe the following for Lincoln Electric:
   a. The objectives of the staffing activities—recruitment and selection
   b. The extent to which these staffing activities are serving the business and HR objectives of Lincoln
   c. The criteria being used to select applicants
   d. The extent to which these criteria are serving the business and HR objectives of Lincoln
   e. The specific methods and procedures being used to select applicants
   f. The extent to which these methods and procedures are serving the business and HR objectives of Lincoln

Going forward:

How can the staffing activities at Lincoln Electric be improved?

2. Describe the following for AAL:
   a. The objectives of the staffing activities—recruitment and selection
   b. The extent to which these staffing activities are serving the business and HR objectives of AAL
   c. The criteria being used to select applicants
   d. The extent to which these criteria are serving the business and HR objectives of AAL
   e. The methods and procedures being used to select applicants
   f. The extent to which these methods and procedures are serving the business and HR objectives of AAL

Going forward:

How can the staffing activities at AAL be improved?

 Field Projects

1. Prepare a job description for a job you are interested in performing. Detail a selection process for the position. Your report should describe the following:
   a. Selection procedures to be used. If you will use a cognitive ability test, identify which one. If you will use a situational interview, describe the questions that will be asked. If you will use a personality test, identify the specific test.
   b. Provide a rationale for the choice of each selection device.
   c. Outline the order in which the selection devices will be administered and explain the rationale for the ordering.
   d. Specify how information will be combined: using a compensatory, multiple hurdles, or combination

Case Study:
AZTEC: STAFFING WITH THE RIGHT PEOPLE

 John Blair, the human resource manager at Aztec Industries, a medium-sized electronics company, was just told by company president Martha Klein that Aztec has received a very large contract from Sony Corporation of America. Both know that success in filling this order is likely to mean a great deal of business in the future. John's concern is with finding and hiring two hundred new, qualified employees to work on the Sony contract, which needs to be filled within twenty-four months.

In the past, Aztec's growth rate required adding only twenty-five new employees a year. With Dallas, Texas, nearby, John never found it difficult to find enough people to fill job openings, although inevitably some new employees quit or failed to perform adequately. Never had the company needed to hire so many people so quickly, and never had the company been so concerned about meeting the high standards of a major customer. In addition, most of the new jobs had to be filled with semiskilled and skilled employees. Previously, most new hires were unskilled workers who filled jobs that simply involved a six-step assembly process. Consequently, when John needed job applicants, he just advertised in the *Dallas Tribune* and selected workers on a "first-come, first-served" basis.

John realizes that he must abandon his previous selection policy. He knows it will be necessary to find out the skills of the job applicants and place them in the jobs they are qualified to perform. But performing the job is not John's only concern. He realizes that other behaviors such as absenteeism, cooperation, loyalty, concern for quality, flexibility, and willingness to retrain will affect the successful fulfillment of the Sony contract. He sees this as possibly the time to systematically develop an entire set of human resource practices and get line managers more involved in the process. First things first, however: he needs to hire two hundred new, qualified applicants. ◉

Discussion Question
What are all the activities Blair must do to be successful here?

approach. Detail how the selection devices will be scored.
   e. Finally, specify the costs associated with your selection process.
2. One source of illegal discrimination and waste of human resources comes from worker specifications—minimum ability, experience, or education standards, or all three—that are higher than necessary for adequate job performance. To prevent such problems, organizations must establish appropriate specifications and evaluate applicants fairly on how well they meet these specifications. Talk with a human resource manager of a company and ask how she or he arrives at the specifications for various jobs. Report to the class about what you learn. You may wish to invite the manager to class to describe the procedures used by the company to establish worker specifications and selection criteria.

Socialization, Training, and Development: Ensuring Workforce Capability

The development of our best people is the personal responsibility of management.
ROBERTO C. GOIZUETA, CEO, Coca-Cola Company[1]

What do people have to do with the success of the world's largest retailer? Everything!

The late Sam Walton, founder of Wal-Mart, believed that the essence of being successful in retailing is giving customers what they want. Yes, they want a great selection at the lowest possible prices. But they also want friendly and knowledgeable service that is easily and readily available. In today's highly competitive environment with major national retailers such as Safeway Incorporated, Home Depot, Kmart Corporation, Sears, Roebuck and Company, and J. C. Penney Company, and with regional and local stores such as Meijers Incorporated, most customers can easily get great selection at low prices. What they cannot get as easily is good service.

Walton knew that people were important to his success. His golden rules of retail competition reflect this philosophy: share your profits; motivate your associates (employees)—with money, ownership, high goals, competition, and career development; communicate everything to your associates; appreciate everything your associates do for the company; celebrate your successes; and listen to everyone. Besides these rules focused on people were a few others: commit to and be passionate about the business, control costs, exceed customers' expectations, and ignore conventional wisdom (Walton was always told that a town of fifty thousand could not support a discount store for very long; that's about the size of the typical town supporting Wal-Mart stores today!).

Just how much has paying attention to people and managing human resources paid off for Walton and Wal-Mart? The first Wal-Mart store opened in Bentonville, Arkansas, in 1962, when Walton was forty-four years old. About fifteen years later, the market value of Wal-Mart stock was $135 million. In 1994, it was over $60 billion. The number of employees has gone from fewer than 50 to more than 525,000—only General Motors has more employees in the United States. Wal-Mart's profits and revenues have seen double-digit growth every year. The number of stores has gone from one to around two thousand.

From his humble beginnings, Walton created a great deal of wealth for himself and his family, and also for many others. Typical of the people who have worked for the company for more than twenty years is "[o]ne Arkansas worker, Joyce McMurray, [who] said [in 1994] that since she joined the company as a high school graduate in 1969, her profit-sharing account had grown to $492,230, including an increase of $175,000 in the last year." McMurray's good fortune is due to one of Walton's golden rules of retailing: share the profits with your associates.

How does Wal-Mart do it? It starts with the philosophy that it is easier to take care of the associates you have than to replace them and train others. With this premise, the company automatically makes a commitment to do a great job selecting (and, therefore, recruiting) and motivating associates. Having a very generous profit-sharing plan that is tied directly to performance outcomes motivates associates and attracts many others who like to make a "good living."

In addition, the company trains and retrains associates, thoroughly and frequently, to provide knowledgeable and friendly service. But what exactly makes the associates friendly? Here is where culture and communication come in. Walton believed in visiting the stores and talking to the associates and customers. Today, although he is not here, his legacy remains strong in part because his management team was thoroughly socialized into his way of doing things. Typical is Andrew H. Wilson, one of fifteen regional vice presidents, who is constantly traveling to the stores and telling the associates the same thing Walton told them: "My job isn't important. You're the people who make it happen." The associates at Wal-Mart believe him. They have heard the same thing for years, and they have seen the managers at Wal-Mart "walk the talk." Related to this humble profile assumed by the managers is the role they play to support the importance and value of the associates: the managers constantly ask the associates, "Is there anything we can do for you?"

Wal-Mart also emphasizes a team spirit: "It takes a team, and we're the team." It's also important to have fun: team rallies and singing by the associates and managers are not uncommon.

Profit sharing and a down-to-earth management style seem to have created and to sustain a company in which the associates truly care about the customer, which contributes directly to the success of the firm. And because many of the qualities of Wal-Mart and its managers are hard for competitors to duplicate, the firm's approach to managing human resources is hard to beat.[2]

The feature "Managing Human Resources for the 21st Century at Wal-Mart" highlights the importance of socialization, training, and development: without these, the company would be far less successful than it is today. The feature also emphasizes that it takes several human resource practices systematically linked together to manage human resources effectively. Leadership, rewards, and teamwork are all necessary, too.

 ## SOCIALIZATION, TRAINING, AND DEVELOPMENT

Employee socialization, training, and development are an organization's *intentional* efforts to improve current and future performance by increasing capabilities.[3] Specifically, *socialization* refers to teaching the corporate culture and philosophies about how to do business, *training* refers to improving skills needed today or very soon, and *development* refers to improving skills over the long term. In practice, of course, these apparently clear distinctions become blurred, since the three types of activities are components of an (ideally) integrated system. This system is referred to simply as a training system, even though it encompasses all three components.

The need for socialization, training, and development may arise for many reasons. Upon entry into a new job or a new organization, all employees initially need to "learn the ropes"—that is, through socialization, they need to learn how things are done in the new environment, including things they cannot find written in any policy-and-procedures manual.[4] In addition, new hires may have insufficient skills; technological changes may result in a need for new job skills; job redesign may require employees to learn more skills; employees who are transferred or promoted may require new skills and knowledge; a new product may require technologies not before used by employees; or changes in company strategy may mean that senior management needs to adopt new leadership behavior and acquire new business knowledge. In some of these cases, the need for socialization, training, and development can be immediate; in others, future needs can be anticipated and planned.[5] Exhibit 9.1 provides a detailed picture of the specific types of training typically offered by large U.S. companies.

 ## PURPOSES AND IMPORTANCE OF SOCIALIZATION, TRAINING, AND DEVELOPMENT

Commitment and Performance

When done well, socialization creates intensely loyal employees. Companies that have perfected the socialization process include IBM, Wal-Mart, Procter and Gamble, and Morgan Guaranty Trust Company of New York.

Often, the socialization process begins before the employee is hired. At Procter and Gamble (P&G), for example, an elite cadre of line managers trained in interviewing skills probes applicants for entry-level positions in brand management, for qualities such as the "ability to turn out high volumes of excellent work." Through the interviewers' questions, applicants begin to learn about the organization's culture. Only after successfully completing at least two interviews and a test of general knowledge are applicants flown to P&G headquarters in Cincinnati, Ohio, where they endure a day-long series of interviews. These interviews are two-way communications that continue the socialization process at the same time that selection decisions are being made.

If applicants pass the extensive screening process, they then confront a series of rigorous job experiences calculated to induce humility and openness to new ways of

■ *Exhibit 9.1*
Specific Types of Training

Type of Training	Total	Percentage of Organizations with One Hundred or More Employees That Provide This Training		
		By In-House Staff	By Outside Consultants or Suppliers	By Both In-House Staff and Outside Consultants or Suppliers
New-employee orientation	85	75	1	9
Leadership	75	17	14	44
Performance appraisals	74	50	4	19
Interpersonal skills	70	18	10	41
Train-the-trainer	70	18	21	30
Team building	69	19	10	40
Listening skills	69	24	11	33
Personal computer applications	68	21	8	38
Hiring and selection process	67	33	10	23
Time management	67	20	16	31
Problem solving	65	21	9	35
Decision making	64	20	11	33
New-equipment operation	63	31	4	29
Conducting meetings	63	26	9	28
Word processing	63	23	11	28
Delegation skills	63	19	14	30
Sexual harassment	62	28	9	25
Managing change	62	17	13	32
Safety	62	25	3	34
Product knowledge	61	42	3	17
Quality improvement	60	17	6	37
Public speaking and presentation	59	16	15	29
Stress management	59	16	14	29
Goal setting	59	22	7	29
Data processing and MIS	58	14	18	26
Computer programming	57	10	24	22
Diversity	56	18	12	26
Motivation	55	16	8	32
Writing skills	54	14	13	26
Negotiating skills	53	13	15	24
Planning	50	17	6	28
Strategic planning	48	15	9	24
Marketing	45	9	13	23
Creativity	44	14	10	20
Finance	44	10	15	19
Substance abuse	43	11	14	19
Smoking cessation	41	12	17	12
Ethics	39	16	10	13
Outplacement and retirement planning	38	16	11	11
Purchasing	35	14	9	13
Reading skills	31	8	14	10
Reengineering	28	6	7	15
Foreign language	23	3	13	7
Other (topics not listed)	3	0.7	0.8	1

Note: The figures in this table are based on 1,119 responses.
SOURCE: Adapted from "1994 Industry Report," *Training* (October 1994): 49. Used by permission.

Partnership in Socialization, Training, and Development

Line Managers	Human Resource Professionals	Employees
Provide top management commitment and support.	Coordinate with line managers in assessing socialization, training, and development needs.	Identify personal socialization, training, and development needs with HR professionals and line managers.
Cooperate with HR professionals and employees in identifying socialization, training, and development needs.	Develop programs to fit the needs of the business and the needs of employees.	Actively participate in socialization, training, and development programs.
Take responsibility for guiding the socialization of all direct reports.	Maybe participate in program delivery.	Accept some responsibility for seeking out and using resources outside the organization to meet personal needs for socialization, training, and development.
Help employees develop plans for their own training and development.	Inform all employees of available programs.	
Maybe serve as a mentor to employees.	Evaluate programs against stated objectives and revise when appropriate.	Maybe help deliver formal programs.
Maybe participate in the delivery of on-site and off-site training programs.		Provide socialization and perhaps training to peers on the job.

doing things. Typically, this phase of socialization involves long hours of work in a pressure cooker environment. Throughout this phase, new employees learn transcendent company values and organizational folklore, including the importance of product quality and stories about the dedication and commitment of employees long since retired. This intense socialization results in increased commitment to the success of the company, willingness to work long hours, and decreased absenteeism and turnover.[6]

After this initial socialization come training and development. A major purpose of training is to remove deficiencies, whether current or anticipated, that cause employees to perform at less than the desired level. Training for immediate performance improvement is particularly important to organizations with stagnant or declining rates of productivity. It is also important to organizations that are rapidly incorporating new technologies and consequently increasing the likelihood of employee obsolescence.

With their longer-term focus, development activities prepare employees for future career moves, even if these have not yet been identified. Development activities also ensure that employees are qualified for the positions to which they aspire.

As in the Weyerhaeuser Company (see Chapters 1 and 4), training and development are vital to organizations adapting to the new, more competitive business environment. Like socialization, training and development can strengthen the level of commitment of employees to the organization and magnify their perceptions that the organization is a good place to work. Stronger commitment can result in less turnover and absenteeism, thus increasing an organization's productivity.[7] More and more, experts are recognizing that training and development can benefit society by enabling individuals to be productive and contributing members of organizations. These are among the reasons why U.S. corporations spend an estimated $50 billion annually on formal employee training programs that use an estimated 1.5 billion hours of time for the 47 million–plus employees who participate.[8]

Top Management Support. In some companies, managers view socialization, training, and development as too costly and too long-term to justify.[9] In other companies, annual training budgets register in the millions. For example, at Motorola, training represents 4 percent of total payroll and about 1 percent of annual sales. Motorola gives all employees at least forty hours of training a year, and hopes to quadruple this number by the year 2000.[10] A commitment to training investment by leaders such as Sam Walton, Robert Galvin of Motorola, and D. Wayne Calloway of PepsiCo is critical to the success of an organization's efforts.[11] The rewards for top management support are impressive: "Motorola calculates that every $1 it spends on training delivers $30 in productivity gains within three years. Since 1987 the company has cut costs by $3.3 billion—not by the normal expedient of firing workers, but by training them to simplify processes and reduce waste. Sales per employee . . . doubled [from 1987 to 1992], and profits . . . increased 47%."[12]

Without top management support and commitment, the major focus of an organization is likely to be on other activities. This is particularly true when the organization has short-term goals and desires immediate results; this situation allows too little time to wait for the benefits of training and development. Top managers at Motorola and PepsiCo began to emphasize training and development at the same time they recognized that they had to develop their people and businesses in order to be effective.

Although a few exceptional companies recognize the value of training investments, most U.S. companies invest much less than their competitors in other regions of the world. For example, a recent study of seventy auto assembly plants from twenty-four companies in seventeen countries showed that newly hired production workers in U.S.-owned plants received an average of only about 40 hours of training during their first six months on the job, compared with an average of about 300 hours for similar workers in plants owned by citizens of Japan and about 260 hours for similar workers in plants headquartered in the newly industrialized countries of Korea, Mexico, Taiwan, and Brazil.[13]

Role of Employees

The effectiveness of an organization's training system requires the support and cooperation of all employees in the system—top management's support alone is not sufficient. For example, self-managed teams often take responsibility for training their own members.[14] Similarly, as organizations begin to embrace a philosophy of continuous learning and improvement, more active participation in the design and delivery of the organization's training system by all stakeholders is seen as both desirable and necessary.[15]

Although most employees are not actively involved in designing and delivering training systems, most organizations depend heavily on employees' seeking opportunities to use the available system to their advantage. For example, many companies sponsor informal events designed to provide employees opportunities to meet other people in the company, develop informal networks and support groups, and even establish mentoring relationships. By participating in such activities, employees facilitate their own socialization into the organization, and potentially reap longer-term benefits such as greater income, job satisfaction, and a better sense of personal identity.[16] More formal activities may also be offered to employees on a voluntary basis. For example, career-planning workshops, tuition reimbursement for job-related course work, and support for attending professional conferences are often available. Research indicates that these opportunities are more likely to be used by employees who acknowledge their own needs for improvement and have developed a specific career plan.[17]

Linking with the Needs of Customers

Organizations can use their socialization, training, and development activities to link with the needs of customers. For example:

> [D]esigning, manufacturing and operating increasingly complex high-technology systems demands advanced knowledge and hands-on expertise. That's why Siemens USA—one of the world's leading manufacturers of high-technology equipment—conducts a variety of training programs for many of its 27,000 employees, as well as for its customers, all across America.
>
> Siemens USA courses are designed to meet the special needs of customers and their markets. For example, on-the-job training for customers ensures that all the capabilities of the company's technologically advanced systems are fully utilized, and all their benefits are fully realized. Similarly, the special classes for Siemens USA engineering, manufacturing, service and administrative personnel are designed to sharpen skills, enhance professional knowledge, and improve service expertise and effectiveness.
>
> Constant, specialized training is one of the ways Siemens is fulfilling their commitment to keep customers and employees ahead of the competition in a fiercely changing, tough and complex high-technology marketplace.[18]

Similarly, in the low-margin, highly competitive world of department store sales,

> Seattle-based Nordstrom has turned exacting standards of customer service into a billion-dollar annual business. . . .
>
> A major ingredient in Nordstrom's success is the quality of the salesclerks. They are paid about 20% better than those of competitors, and they are selected, trained and encouraged to do almost anything within reason to satisfy customers. In Seattle, a store salesclerk personally ironed a customer's newly bought shirt so that it would look fresher for an upcoming meeting. Thomas Skidmore, vice president of a Los Angeles–area real estate brokerage, tells of bringing back a squeaky pair of year-old shoes to a local Nordstrom outlet, hoping merely for repairs. Instead, he got a new pair of shoes free.[19]

The growing importance of a business philosophy focused on the customer means training activities are on the rise in many companies across America today. As these companies are discovering, effective training is a relatively complex and challenging activity, owing in part to the multitude of relationships training and development have with other human resource activities, as shown in Exhibit 9.2.

 ## DETERMINING SOCIALIZATION, TRAINING, AND DEVELOPMENT NEEDS

Employees sometimes receive training for reasons other than need. For example, in some organizations, attendance at an executive training program serves as a reward for past performance. In other organizations, participation in training programs is a ritual that signals to newly promoted employees as well as to members of their former work groups that a change in status has occurred (e.g., a rank-and-file employee is now a manager). Most often, however, training is offered on the basis of need—to rectify skill deficiencies,

■ *Exhibit 9.2*

Relationships and Consequences of Socialization, Training, and Development

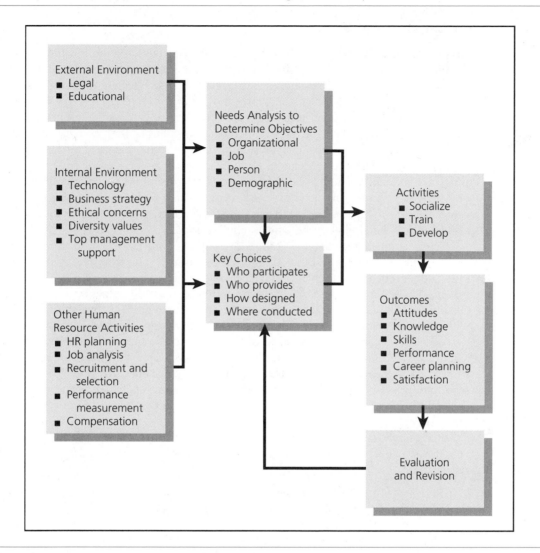

to provide employees with job-specific skills, or to prepare employees for future roles they may be given.[20]

Socialization is needed by almost any new employee and by current employees moving into new jobs or to new units within the company. Therefore, formal assessments of an individual's need for socialization are seldom undertaken. *In*formal assessments may occur, however, based on employees' individual circumstances. Whether accurate or not, for example, companies or managers may assume that applicants recruited from sources that have yielded good performers in the past need little socialization. They may also assume that internal placements require less socialization than new hires.

Although fewer than one-third of all U.S. companies conduct formal needs assessment, it is a vital part of a training system.[21] Without determining the need for training, an organization cannot guarantee that the right training will be provided for the right trainees.

The needs assessment process is detailed in Exhibit 9.3. It shares many similarities with the general model of human resource planning activities described in Chapter 4.

Organizational Needs Analysis

According to many training experts, attaining the objectives of the business should be the ultimate concern of any training and development effort.[22] Therefore, conducting an organizational needs analysis should be the first step in effective needs assessment. It begins with an examination of the short- and long-term objectives of the organization and the trends that are likely to affect these objectives. It can include a human resource analysis, analyses of efficiency indexes, and an assessment of the organizational climate.

The organizational needs analysis should translate the organization's objectives into an accurate estimate of the demand for human resources (as described in Chapter 4). Efficiency indexes, including cost of labor, quantity of output (productivity), quality of output, waste, and equipment use and repairs, can provide useful information. The organization can determine standards for these indexes and then analyze them to evaluate the general effectiveness of training programs.

Organizational analysis also can address the organization's performance in the "softer" domains that constitute the corporate culture. For example, it may reveal a misalignment between the current value system in the organization and the values espoused by top management. Many companies today espouse values such as focusing on customers, following ethical business practices, and supporting diversity, yet behavior within these companies often fails to reflect those values.[23] In such cases, training for everyone in the company—regardless of their specific job, may be called for.[24] Thus, for example, a recent survey by Louis Harris and Associates for the Conference Board showed that 79 percent of major U.S. corporations either currently offer (63 percent) or plan to offer (16 percent) diversity training for their managers, whereas 65 percent either are conducting (39 percent) or plan to conduct (26 percent) such training for all other employees.[25]

Increasingly, ethics training is a part of a firm's effort to build an ethical culture. In a recent survey of more than one thousand members of the American Management Association,

> [s]eventy-three percent of managers surveyed said they probably would resign if their boss insisted that they carry out some action they strongly believed was unethical.
>
> Most of the [survey] participants agreed that corporate codes of ethics and ethics workshops were helpful to understand issues and help guide them through their daily decision making. However, more than three-quarters of these managers noted that their companies did not offer such workshops. Almost half said that their firms did not have a written code of ethics.[26]

According to Karen Alphin, its employee communications director, Chemical Bank's Decision-Making and Corporate Values program addresses issues that are of interest not only to bankers but also to ethical individuals. Convinced of the need for "a conversation about ethics," Polaroid Corporation set up a major internal conference that brought philosophers, ethicists, and business professors to the company for lectures and discussions of ethical concepts.[27] As the need for ethical behavior increases, more organizations may reconsider their training programs and offer courses in ethics.[28]

Different Strategies, Different Needs. Even if they are in the same industry, two companies with different business strategies may adopt very different training systems, as illustrated in the feature "Managing Human Resources for the 21st Century at Boston Consulting Group and at McKinsey and Company."

■ *Exhibit 9.3*
Training Program Model

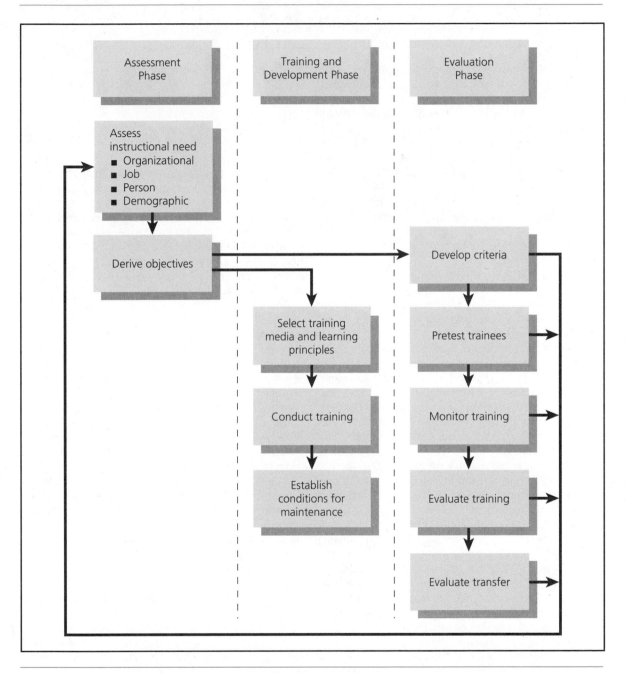

Note: Many other models for instructional systems are used in the military, in business, and in education. Some of the components of this model were suggested by these other systems.
SOURCE: Adapted from I. I. Goldstein, *Training: Program Development and Evaluation* (Monterey, CA: Brooks/Cole, 1986): 8.

Managing Human Resources for the 21st Century at Boston Consulting Group and at McKinsey and Company

Boston Consulting Group (BCG) and McKinsey and Company are among the world's leading strategic consulting firms. Both have worldwide operations, and their reputations for thoughtful leadership and quality service to management are comparable. Both hire from the best undergraduate and MBA programs, competing for the top students. Both have rigorous selection procedures and exceptional compensation.

Yet the characteristics of the people the two firms hire and the way these employees are managed differ in line with the ways the companies approach their markets.

BOSTON CONSULTING GROUP

BCG tends to attract candidates with very broad perspectives on business. Some previously started their own companies, and others leave BCG to found new companies. BCG also maintains something of a revolving door with academia, hiring business school professors as consultants and sometimes losing consultants to faculty positions in business schools. Once hired, consultants jump right into work, although they are closely supervised, and the formal training they receive is likely to be from outside courses.

BCG has an entrepreneurial environment, expecting each project team to come up with its own innovative approach. Each office is even thought to have a slightly different culture. BCG pays less than many of its competitors but offers more individualized incentive pay, reinforcing the entrepreneurial culture.

Although BCG has some "products," such as time-based competition and capabilities-based strategies, these approaches are not the source of its competency. Indeed, some of them, like the Growth-Share matrix, are well publicized and basically given away. The value added comes from a customized application to the client's situation. Many of BCG's projects start not with these products but rather with a blank-slate approach. What clients buy, therefore, are original solutions and approaches to their problems. And these approaches begin with consultants whose varied backgrounds and entrepreneurial spirit help produce a unique product.

MCKINSEY AND COMPANY

McKinsey historically hired all its new employees from on-campus recruiting and rarely hired from other employers. It tends to prefer candidates with backgrounds in technical areas, such as engineering and computer science, who have depth in some functional area of business. Its new entrants vary little in terms of management experience and come in with few consulting ideas. If McKinsey consultants leave, they are more likely to take senior line management positions in corporations than to move into entrepreneurial positions.

McKinsey provides new consultants with extensive training on the company's method of project execution and management, even though this is highly tailored to each client's situation. McKinsey's size—it employs three thousand consultants, compared with eight hundred at BCG—may create scale economies in training new entrants that make it easier for the firm to provide programs itself. The firm expects the career path to the highest position, senior partner, to take approximately twelve years—versus six to eight years at BCG—which gives the consultants a long time to learn how to fit in.

In terms of its consulting product, the company is known for the "McKinsey way." McKinsey strives to provide its clients with consistent services; its clients know what to expect from the project teams. The firm's products and techniques are regarded as proprietary and are not publicized. Its core competency, therefore, is in the consistent products and techniques that constitute the McKinsey way. To have consultants deliver that product in the same way across companies and countries, McKinsey takes bright people with strong skills and adapts them to the product. This standardization is especially notable given the far-reaching nature of McKinsey's empire. Half its senior partners are abroad, and twenty-seven of the thirty-three offices it has opened since 1980 were outside the United States in 1994.[29]

Increasingly, companies are recognizing that by establishing a new strategy and a new set of objectives they create an immediate need for a major training and development initiative. Here, the organizational analysis begins by identifying the demands of the new strategy on human resources. Only after this is done can implications for training and development be identified. As companies such as Weyerhaeuser, GE, Eaton, Ameritech Corporation, Motorola, and AT&T have discovered, significant training and development needs often arise from strategy-driven changes in the nature of managerial jobs.

Job-Needs Analysis

As described in Chapter 6, the specific content of present or anticipated jobs is examined through job analysis. For existing jobs, information on the tasks to be performed (contained in job descriptions), the skills necessary to perform those tasks (drawn from job qualifications), and the minimum acceptable standards (gleaned from performance appraisals) are gathered. This information can then be used to ensure that training programs are job specific and useful.

The process of collecting information for use in developing training programs is often referred to as job-needs analysis. In this situation, the analysis method used should include questions specifically designed to assess the knowledge, skills, and abilities needed to perform the job. Therefore, an integrated job analysis approach is appropriate.

For jobs that have yet to be created, expert information and predictions can be made relevant to their anticipated content and complexity. For example, in 1985, it was predicted that the

> next generation of manufacturing managers will need to know computer-aided design and computer-aided manufacturing (CAD/CAM), computer-integrated manufacturing (CIM), group technologies, flexible manufacturing, "just-in-time" inventory control, manufacturing resource planning (MRP), robotics, and a whole litany of other techniques and technologies in manufacturing.
>
> They're going to have to understand systems thinking, as more and more of the major corporations move toward the globalization . . .
>
> They'll have to develop different perspectives on managing a work force as the concepts of lifestyle employment, worker participation, and job enrichment extend further and further through the American enterprise system.
>
> Perhaps most importantly, they are going to have to have a well-developed understanding of corporate strategies, not only to find those organizations and subunits of organizations in which they will be most comfortable and successful, but also to be able to take an important role in determining and directing those strategies.[30]

This prediction has come true. Companies that began to prepare for this situation in 1985, by developing their future managerial talent, have a reasonable chance at surviving in today's hypercompetitive manufacturing environment.

Increasingly, jobs require a great deal of teamwork and cooperation. This is significantly affecting the skills and thus training required for employees in many companies. Exhibit 9.4 profiles the skills and characteristics needed of employees in a team-oriented, total-quality, modern manufacturing plant.

Person-Needs Analysis

After information about the job has been collected, the analysis shifts to the person. A person-needs analysis identifies gaps between a person's current capabilities and those identified as necessary or desirable. Person-needs analysis can be either broad or narrow in scope. The broader approach compares actual performance with the minimum

■ *Exhibit 9.4*
Team Member Skills and Characteristics

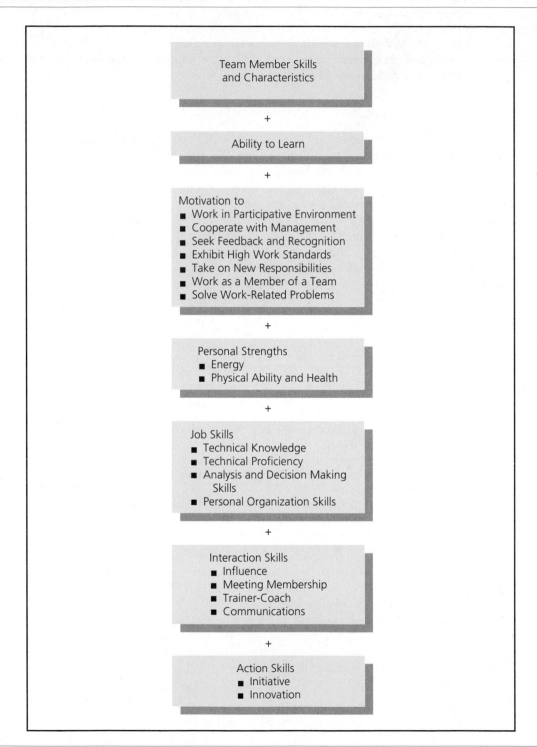

SOURCE: Used with the permission of Douglas Bray, Chairman, Development Dimensions International

acceptable standards of performance. The narrower approach compares an evaluation of employee proficiency on each required skill dimension with the proficiency level required for each skill. The first method is based on the actual, current job performance of an employee; therefore, it can be used to determine training needs for the current job. The second method, on the other hand, can be used to identify development needs for future jobs.[31]

Whether the focus is on performance of the job as a whole or on particular skill dimensions, several different approaches can be used to identify the training needs of individuals.[32]

Output Measures. Performance data (e.g., productivity, accidents, customer complaints), as well as performance appraisal ratings, can provide evidence of performance deficiencies. Person-needs analysis can also consist of work sample and job knowledge tests that measure performance capability and knowledge.[33] Major advantages of such measures are that (a) they can be selected according to their strategic importance; (b) they often are easily quantified; and (c) when they show improvements, the value of training investments is readily apparent. For example, a study of Michigan manufacturing firms that received state training grants showed that increasing training from fifteen to thirty hours reduced scrap by 7 percent.[34] A major disadvantage is that such indicators reflect the past and may not be useful for anticipating future needs.

Self-Assessed Training Needs. The self-assessment of training needs is growing in popularity. At Motorola, for example, "[e]ach year [top managers] require the employee and his or her supervisor to identify what the business needs are for the department and the business, as well as the skill needs and deficiencies of the individual."[35] A recent study of training practices in major U.S. firms showed that between 50 and 80 percent of all corporations allow managers to nominate themselves to attend short-term or company-sponsored training or education programs. Self-assessment can be as informal as posting a list of company-sponsored courses and asking who wants to attend, or as formal as conducting surveys regarding training needs.[36]

Exhibit 9.5 shows sample questions from a managerial self-assessment survey. Surveys are convenient tools for self-assessment. More time-consuming methods may be needed in some circumstances. For example, when WMX Corporation conducted a needs analysis on the topic of ethics, it used interviews to ask managers to identify the issues that were most troubling to them. The themes identified by managers were then used to create teaching cases for a four-hour management training module that was one of the company's many activities intended to build an ethical corporate culture.[37]

Self-assessment is premised on the assumption that employees, more than anyone else, are aware of their skill weaknesses and performance deficiencies. Therefore, they are in the best position to identify their own training needs. One drawback of self-assessment is that individuals may not be aware of their weaknesses, especially if the organization does a poor job of providing honest feedback during performance appraisals. Also, employees may be fearful of revealing their weaknesses and so may not accurately report their training needs. In both cases, reliance on self-assessment may result in individuals' not receiving education that is necessary for them to remain current in their fields. On the other hand, employees who are forced to attend programs that they believe they do not need or that do not meet their personal training needs are likely to become dissatisfied with training and to lack the motivation to learn and transfer skills.

One way to improve upon the idea of self-assessment is to weave it into a larger set of activities that all clearly address the employees' long-term career concerns. This

◼ *Exhibit 9.5*

Sample Questions from a Self-Administered Training Needs Survey

Please indicate in the blanks the extent to which *you* have a training need in each specific area. Use the scale below.
   To what extent do you need training in the following areas?

To no extent 1	2	3	4	To a very large extent 5

Basic Management Skills (Organizing, Planning, Delegating, Problem Solving)

_____ 1. Setting goals and objectives
_____ 2. Developing realistic time schedules to meet work requirements
_____ 3. Identifying and weighing alternative solutions
_____ 4. Organizing work activities

Interpersonal Skills

_____ 1. Resolving interpersonal conflicts
_____ 2. Creating a development plan for employees
_____ 3. Identifying and understanding individual employee needs
_____ 4. Conducting performance appraisal reviews
_____ 5. Conducting a discipline interview

Administrative Skills

_____ 1. Maintaining equipment, tools, and safety controls
_____ 2. Understanding local agreements and shop rules
_____ 3. Preparing work flowcharts
_____ 4. Developing department budgets

Quality Control

_____ 1. Analyzing and interpreting statistical data
_____ 2. Constructing and analyzing charts, tables, and graphs
_____ 3. Using statistical software on the computer

SOURCE: Modified from J. K. Ford and R. A. Noe, "Self-Assessed Training Needs: The Effects of Attitudes toward Training, Managerial Level and Function," *Personnel Psychology* 40 (1987): 39–53.

approach is illustrated in the feature "Managing Human Resources for the 21st Century at Granite Rock."

Attitude Surveys. Attitude surveys completed by a supervisor's subordinates or by customers or by both also can provide information on training needs. For example, when one supervisor receives low scores regarding her or his fairness in treating subordinates, compared with other supervisors in the organization, the supervisor may need training in that area.[38] Similarly, if the customers of a particular unit seem to be particularly dissatisfied compared with other customers, training may be needed in that unit. Thus, customer surveys can serve a dual role: providing information to management about service and pinpointing employee deficiencies.

Surveys can also be completed by higher-level managers to identify the development needs of the cadre below them. Such surveys can be used to identify which skills are important for managerial effectiveness. Differences in opinions can serve as a basis of discussion about what is really necessary for managerial success in today's environment. Generally, the results of attitude surveys can contribute significantly to the design of a training program.

Managing Human Resources for the 21st Century at Granite Rock

Granite Rock is a small family-owned business, employing fewer than four hundred people. It is headquartered in a small town in the central coast region of California. Its HR staff is small, too—three people. But they think big. And nothing about the success of the multimillion-dollar company is small. Everything it does, it does in a big way.

It has to. Not so many years ago, the Watsonville-based construction materials supplier was competing with companies similar in size and resources. That all changed when, around 1987, many of those companies sold out to well-endowed multinational corporations. Granite Rock executives realized that for their company to come out ahead of the competition, it had to offer superior customer service and quality products.

So that is what it does. Granite Rock's concrete products consistently exceed the industry performance specifications by one hundred times. The reliability of several of its key processes has reached the six-sigma level (3.4 errors per 1 million chances to err, a goal most high-tech companies hoped to reach by 1995). And it delivers more than 90 percent of its product on time, topping the on-time delivery average of a prominent national company that Granite Rock benchmarked.

The strategy works. Granite Rock has been gaining market share every year since 1987; its market share in 1994 was double what it was back then. And by continuously responding to customers' needs (it surveys its customers annually, asking them to rate Granite Rock against its competitors), it aimed to build a 10 percent lead over its nearest competitor for each indicator of customer satisfaction by 1995.

The company's success at serving its customers can be credited in large part to its Total Quality Program, which earned it the coveted Malcolm Baldrige National Quality Award in 1992. The cornerstone of the TQM program is a commitment to employee development and training.

Development begins with the Individual Professional Development Plan (IPDP), a system that allows employees to set developmental goals in conjunction with the firm's needs. Together with his or her supervisor, each employee sets goals each year for skill development and job accomplishments. Management, in roundtable sessions, reviews the goals and determines the educational and training needs required for meeting them.

The company backs this goal setting with ample opportunity for training. Granite Rock University, its training program, offers all employees seminars, courses, and lectures on at least fifty different subjects. The types of offerings fall into five categories: quality-process skills; maintenance skills; sales and service skills; product or technical skills; and health, wellness, and personal growth. Granite Rock covers the cost of off-site training, be it through college courses or at professional conferences.

Granite Rock employees average thirty-seven hours of training each year, at an average cost of $1,697 for each employee. This is three times more than the mining industry average and thirteen times more than the construction industry average. As a result, revenue earned per Granite Rock employee has risen to approximately 30 percent above the national industry average. Not bad for a small company.[39]

Demographic-Needs Analysis

Organizations should conduct demographic studies to determine the training needs of specific populations of workers.[40] For example, Frito-Lay conducted a special assessment to determine whether women and members of minority groups in its sales force would benefit from special training. According to Dave Knibbe, Frito-Lay management development director, the needs assessment was critical to evaluating different ways in which the organization could facilitate more rapid career advancement for these employees.

More generally, research indicates that different groups have different training needs. For example, first-line supervisors need more technical training (e.g., in record keeping and writing), midlevel managers rate HR courses as most important for meeting their needs, and upper-level managers rate conceptual courses (e.g., in goal setting and planning skills) as critical to their development.[41] In one study, male managers were found to need training in listening, verbal skills, nonverbal communication, empathy, and sensitivity; women managers, on the other hand, needed training in assertiveness, confidence building, public speaking, and dealing with male peers and subordinates.[42]

Demographic-needs analysis can also be used to assess whether all employees are given equal access to growth experiences and developmental challenges, which are known to be useful on-the-job methods for promoting skill development.[43] For example, one large study of managers compared the developmental experiences of men and women. In general, men were more likely to have been assigned to jobs that presented difficult task-related challenges (e.g., operation start-ups and "fix-it" assignments), whereas women were more likely to have been assigned to jobs that presented challenges caused by obstacles to performance (e.g., a difficult boss or a lack of support from top management).[44] Presumably, successful performance in the face of task-related challenges is the more valuable currency in work organizations. Therefore, if a company finds demographic differences such as these, it might conclude that an intervention is needed to assure men and women equal access to valuable developmental challenges—and equal exposure to debilitating obstacles.

SETTING UP A TRAINING SYSTEM

Successful implementation of training and development programs depends on selecting the right programs for the right people under the right conditions.[45]

Who Participates?

The answer to the question "Who will participate?" depends in part on the results of the person-needs analysis. It also depends on how many employees are to be trained simultaneously. If only one or two employees are to be trained, then on-the-job approaches such as coaching are generally cost-effective. If large numbers of individuals need to be trained in a short period of time, then programmed instruction may be the most viable option.

When larger groups are to be trained, questions arise concerning how to sequence participation across groups and how to compose the groups. When everyone has been targeted as needing training, as is often the case with major corporate change efforts, top managers often participate first, and other employee groups are scheduled in hierarchical sequence. But as Medtronic learned when it introduced diversity training throughout the company, this common approach may not be the best: "[W]hen we trained [the] first corporate group, the managers told us they wished they had gone through with employees at other levels, so now we do that. We mix different levels of managers and supervisors in the same group, since that is a part of diversity as well."[46]

As the Medtronic example suggests, decisions about who participates in a group training session may influence how much learning occurs during the session. Furthermore, when employees who work side by side attend training sessions together, they may find it easier to transfer their learning back to the work site because coworkers can provide feedback and friendly coaching.

Who Provides?

Socialization, training, and development activities may be provided by any of several people, including

- The supervisor
- A coworker, such as a lead worker or a buddy
- An internal or external subject matter expert
- The employee

Which of these people is selected to teach often depends on where the program is held and what skill or skills are taught. For example, literary and technical skills are usually taught by the immediate job supervisor or a coworker, although technical skills may also be taught by internal or external subject matter experts. A basic organizational orientation is usually handled by a member of the HR staff. Interpersonal, conceptual, and integrative skills for management are often taught by training specialists, university professors, or consultants.

A concern with relying on supervisors and coworkers as trainers is that although they may perform adequately, they may not be able to instruct others. They may also teach others their own shortcuts rather than correct procedures. On the other hand, immediate supervisors or coworkers may be more knowledgeable than anyone else about work procedures. If coworkers or managers are to be trainers, they should receive instruction on how to train and should be given sufficient time on the job to work with trainees.[47]

Subject matter experts may not be familiar with procedures in a specific organizational culture. As a result, they may be respected for their expertise but mistrusted because they are not members of the work group. Still, if no one in the immediate work environment possesses the knowledge needed, or if large numbers of individuals need to be trained, the only option may be to hire experts.

Self-paced instruction is also an option. Trainees benefit from this method by learning at a speed that maximizes retention. However, if they are not given incentives to complete the instruction in a specified period of time, they may place it on the back burner.

DEVELOPING PROGRAM CONTENT

A training program must have content congruent with its learning objectives. Three types of learning objectives that the organization may be concerned about are cognitive knowledge, skill-based outcomes, and affective outcomes.[48]

Cognitive Knowledge

Cognitive knowledge includes the information people have available to themselves (what they know), the way they organize this information, and their strategies for using this information. Of these, what people know is by far the type of cognitive knowledge that most organizations try to address through training systems.

Company Policies and Practices. Orientation programs are frequently used for building cognitive knowledge. These programs brief new employees on benefit programs and options, advise them of rules and regulations, and explain the policies and practices of the organization:

A first-rate orientation system for new-hires can reduce turnover rates, decrease employee learning time, and improve quality and productivity throughout the organization, according to Edmund McGarrell, Jr., supervisor of special projects at Corning Glass Works. Addressing the American Management Association's 56th Annual Human Resource Conference, which was held in New Orleans, McGarrell stresses that the company's orientation process is designed to provide new-hires with "red carpet treatment" that will turn them into highly skilled, involved, and committed employees.[49]

Typically, orientation programs inform new employees about equal employment opportunity practices, safety regulations, work times, coffee breaks, the structure and history of the organization, and perhaps the products or services of the organization. Usually, they do not tell employees about the politics of the organization—for example, that the organization may soon be going out of business, that it may be merging with another company, or even that an extensive layoff may soon occur.

Basic Knowledge and the Three Rs. Increasingly, organizations are concerned about cognitive knowledge of a more basic nature: the three Rs (reading, writing, and arithmetic). Training programs designed to correct basic skill deficiencies in grammar, mathematics, safety, reading, listening, and writing have been projected to continue to grow to the year 2000.[50] The feature "Managing Human Resources for the 21st Century at Will-Burt," in Chapter 2, illustrates just how important basic skill training can be to companies.[51] In particular, as the movement toward total quality management grows, the importance of basic math and statistical knowledge grows. Statistical tools are fundamental to W. Edwards Deming's approach to quality, which is improvement by the numbers. To improve quality, one must know the causes of poor quality. *Statistical process control (SPC)* techniques provide employees a means for determining these causes. SPC is the practice of using the tools of statistics to help control the quality of operating processes.

Also basic to total quality is knowledge about how to diagnose and solve problems. A fishbone diagram (see Exhibit 9.6) provides a cognitive strategy and a way of structuring information that facilitates effective use of available information. Thus, basic knowledge about fishbone diagrams can help employees analyze the procedures, people, policies, and plant characteristics that are helping or hindering a company's efforts to improve its quality.

The Big Picture. Employees striving for or currently in managerial positions may need knowledge about the organizational structure, the organization's products and services, the organization's business strategies, and changing conditions in the environment. Much of this type of knowledge is learned through standard job assignments as well as through temporary developmental learning experiences, such as serving on a task force or taking an overseas assignment. Adapting to complex and changing environments is often a responsibility for top and middle managers, and conceptual training helps such employees make new associations. Cognitive knowledge is at the heart of today's emphasis on creativity and entrepreneurship, and on making major changes in an organization's strategy, objectives, vision, and values at firms such as Microsoft, GE, Weyerhaeuser, and Eaton.

Skill-Based Outcomes

Skill-based outcomes include the development of technical and motor skills.[52] Whereas cognitive knowledge is, essentially, inside the head, skills are evident in behaviors. Whereas cognitive learning often involves studying and attending to information, skill-based learning generally involves practicing desired behaviors.

■ *Exhibit 9.6*
Fishbone Diagram for Total Quality Management

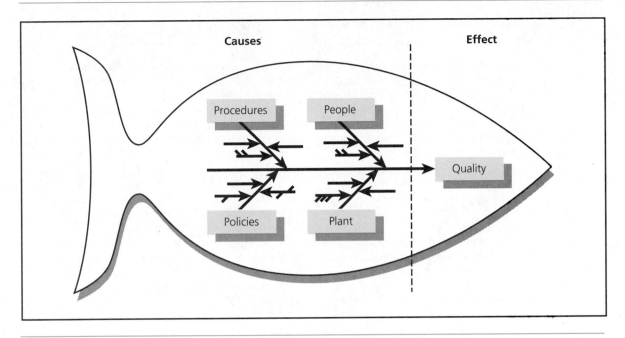

Owing to rapid changes in technology and the implementation of automated office, industrial, and managerial systems, technological updating and skill building have become a major thrust in training.[53] Skills in communication, conducting performance appraisals, team building, leadership, and negotiation are also increasingly in demand. In fact, training for these types of skills tops the list of training needs for lower- level and midlevel managers. The development of interpersonal skills is also important for employees who interface with the public, such as sales associates.[54] The feature "Managing Human Resources for the 21st Century at Microsoft: Experiential Board Games" describes how Microsoft uses business games to train its sales staff in planning and team building.

Affective Outcomes

When the desired result of socialization training or developmental experiences is a change in motivation, attitudes, or values, or all three, the learning objectives of interest are affective outcomes.

At the Walt Disney Company, all newly hired "cast members" participate in an orientation and training program at Disney University. New hires first receive an overview of the company and learn about its traditions, history, achievements, and philosophy. In addition, they learn about the key Disney "product"—happiness—and their roles in helping to provide it. Next, each cast member learns about the benefits— health, social, recreational—of being part of the Disney "family;" gains more direct information about his or her role in the production; and has a tour of the complex. Tailored to reflect the needs of each type of cast member and group, the initial orientation and subsequent training have a theme of bringing new hires into the family

Managing Human Resources for the 21st Century at Microsoft: Experiential Board Games

"We started with experiential board games for sales training six years ago this January at our regional sales meetings," said Susan Sullivan-Sibert, senior sales training consultant at Microsoft Corporation. Today, all company sales people at all levels and locations throughout the United States have experienced a game called The Gold of the Desert Kings, and many have played other special-purpose games that relate to company and training objectives.

CHOOSING GAMES

"When we first got started, our objective at the time was for our sales force to become more focused on planning, and a secondary objective was team building," Sullivan-Sibert said.

"There are a lot of companies that make these games, and each one, like Eagle's Flight, where we get our games, has a number of products for different purposes. We looked all around.

"You can choose products that match your needs and goals as closely as possible, but you can't customize the games. The customization to your company's specific needs comes in the debrief—the hour-long discussion of what happened in the game—when the facilitator can point to specific occurrences during play that relate directly to corporate goals."

WHAT HAPPENS

In The Gold of the Desert Kings, the game Microsoft has used most often, a group comes into a room that has tables scattered all around. Three to six people are in each group—one group to a table. Already on each table is a large desert road map and a packet of information that is not to be opened until the participants are instructed to open it. Also on the table is desert headgear—hats and scarves.

"The instructor or facilitator comes into the room—not as an instructor, but playing a role, the role of the person who is going to lead everyone through the desert," the trainer said. "There's a script, welcoming the participants and explaining that there is a big mission ahead of them. They must go to a mountain mine for gold."

Instructions are issued quickly with no repetition and no allowance for questions. Employees are told that the first team back home gets the most money for their gold, that they have twenty-five three-minute days to accomplish the mission, and that they have a prescribed quantity of resources for the journey. Water and food must be consumed daily. Weather can be a big problem.

"We tell them it is a competition, and with salespeople, competing is not something we have to urge them to do. We also tell them that 30 percent of the teams usually die in the desert because they have run out of food," Sullivan-Sibert explained.

"There's more, but that's the idea."

The training consultant said she plays music during the game. Not soothing music. "It's meant to be distracting—just like in the world.

"When I facilitate, I watch the behavior so I will be prepared for the debrief. It's interesting to see the choices the players make. Salespeople are not known for taking the safe route."

Sullivan-Sibert said most players race up to the mountain and back, going for the greater amount to be given for the gold, but the first team back may not have done it all right.

"Sometimes I ask teams in the debrief, 'What could you have accomplished if you had stayed out longer, instead of rushing back to get the most for your gold?' Then it starts to click with the players, because Microsoft doesn't reward for the first one in. We reward for doing the best possible job with a given project, always trying to stop and ask ourselves, 'What is the maximum I can do here?' We're in business for the long haul, and that's what The Gold of the Desert Kings teaches. And it shows the price you pay for not planning."

OTHER GAMES FOR OTHER GOALS

Two years ago, Sullivan-Sibert said, Microsoft trainers introduced another game to salespeople. Since they had already been through The Gold of the Desert Kings, they thought they had it down, but they got a surprise.

"This game, called Promises, Promises, had a whole different focus. It stressed working together but not in work teams. Rather, it demonstrated how to work with outside resources, the value of relying on people reporting to different areas."

The game taught another key Microsoft theme—that there is plenty of business, plenty of everything to go around, that wiping out the competition is harmful to the marketplace.

"We don't repeat games," Sullivan-Sibert said. "We do follow up with other more traditional development methods to reinforce the same lessons learned in the games. As everyone knows, you can't run one program and expect to instantly get great team building, or great leadership. The games are just a piece of the pie that will help get people moving in the right direction. And they do have a lasting effect. We can see it from the language people pick up from the games and continue to use."[55]

and developing a team sense, as well as a focus on courtesy to guests, safety, and putting on a good show (entertainment).[56]

The objectives of building team spirit and socializing employees into the corporate culture are not the only affective outcomes of a training system. In fact, training activities often are designed in part to develop employees' feelings of mastery and self-confidence. For example, mentoring programs not only provide information, they also provide the feedback and supportive encouragement that give employees confidence in their ability to take on new tasks and make decisions that might otherwise seem too risky. Self-confidence enhances task performance.[57] This is a point not lost on athletes, their coaches, or sportscasters—nor, apparently, is it lost on the many companies now providing wilderness training. Although the evidence is sparse, testimonials and some research indicate that participating in outdoor group adventures boosts self-confidence.[58]

CHOOSING A PROGRAM LOCATION

Three types of locations for training activities are on the job, on-site but not on the job, and off-site. Decisions about location may be constrained by the type of learning that is to occur—cognitive, skill based, or affective—as well as by cost and time considerations. Exhibit 9.7 summarizes the advantages and disadvantages of several learning formats according to their location.

On the Job

On-the-job training (OJT) occurs when employees learn their jobs under direct supervision. Trainees learn by observing experienced employees and by working with the actual materials, personnel, or machinery, or all three, that constitute the job. An experienced employee trainer is expected to provide a favorable role model and to take time from regular job responsibilities to provide job-related instruction and guidance.

One advantage of OJT is that transfer of training is high. That is, because trainees learn job skills in the environment in which they will actually work, they readily apply these skills on the job. Assuming the trainer works in the same area, the trainee receives immediate feedback about performance. However, on-site training is appropriate only when a small number of individuals need to be trained and when the consequence of error is low. Also, the quality of the training hinges on the skill of the manager or lead employee conducting it.[59]

■ *Exhibit 9.7*

Advantages and Disadvantages of Training Programs by Location

Type of Program	Advantages	Disadvantages
On the Job		
Job instruction training	Facilitates transfer of learning	Interferes with performance
	Does not require separate facilities	Damages equipment
Apprenticeship training	Does not interfere with real job performance	Takes a long time
	Provides extensive training	Is expensive
		May not be related to job
Internships and assistantships	Facilitate transfer of learning	Are not really full jobs
	Give exposure to real job	Provide vicarious learning
Job rotation	Gives exposure to many jobs	Involves no sense of full responsibility
	Allows real learning	Provides too short a stay in a job
Supervisory assistance and mentoring	Is informal	Means effectiveness rests with the supervisor
	Is integrated into job	
	Is inexpensive	May not be done by all supervisors
On-Site But Not on the Job		
Programmed instruction	Provides for individualized learning and feedback	Is time-consuming to develop
	Provides for fast learning	Is cost-effective only for large groups
Videotapes	Convey consistent information to employees in diverse locations	Are costly to develop
	Are more portable than film	Do not provide for individual feedback
Videodisks	Store more information than tapes	Are extremely costly to develop
	Allow for fast-forward	Offer limited courseware
	Are portable	
Interactive video training	Draws on more senses	Is costly to develop and implement
	Provides for self-paced learning and feedback	Requires diverse staff to develop
Telecommunication training	Provides for latest insights and knowledge	Is costly and difficult to set up
	Speeds up communications	Is not feasible for small firms
	Is standardized	
Off the Job		
Formal courses	Are inexpensive for many	Require verbal skills
	Do not interfere with job	Inhibit transfer of learning
Simulation	Helps transfer of learning	Cannot always duplicate real situations exactly
	Creates lifelike situations	
Assessment centers	Help transfer of learning	Are expensive to develop
	Provide a realistic job preview	Take time to administer
Role playing	Is good for interpersonal skills	Cannot create real situations exactly; is still playing
	Gives insights into others	
Sensitivity training	Is good for self-awareness	May not transfer to job
	Gives insights into others	May not relate to job
Wilderness trips	Build teams	Are costly to administer
	Build self-esteem	Are physically challenging

Job Instruction Training. The disadvantages of on-the-job training can be minimized by making the training program as systematic and complete as possible. *Job instruction training (JIT)* was developed to provide a guide for giving on-the-job skill training to white-collar and blue-collar employees as well as technicians.[60] Because JIT is a technique rather than a program, it can be adapted to training efforts for all employees in off-the-job as well as on-the-job programs.

JIT consists of four steps: (1) careful selection and preparation of the trainer and the trainee for the learning experience to follow; (2) a full explanation and demonstration by the trainer of the job to be done; (3) a trial on-the-job performance by the trainee; and (4) a thorough feedback session to discuss the trainee's performance and the job requirements.[61]

Apprenticeship Training, Internships, and Assistantships. Another method for minimizing the disadvantages of on-the-job training is combining it with off-the-job training. Apprenticeship training, internships, and assistantships are based on this combination.

Apprenticeship training is mandatory for admission to many skilled trades, such as plumbing, electronics, and carpentry. These programs are formally defined by the U.S. Department of Labor's Bureau of Apprenticeship and Training and involve a written agreement "providing for not less than 4,000 hours of reasonably continuous employment . . . and supplemented by a recommended minimum of 144 hours per year of related classroom instruction." The Equal Employment Opportunity Commission allows the United States' forty-eight thousand skilled trade (apprenticeship) training programs to exclude individuals aged forty to seventy, because these programs are part of the educational system aimed at youth.[62] To be most effective, the on- and off-the-job components of an apprenticeship program must be well integrated and appropriately planned and must recognize individual differences.

Somewhat less formalized and extensive are the internship and assistantship programs. *Internships* are often part of an agreement between schools and colleges, and local organizations. As with apprenticeship training, individuals in these programs earn while they learn, but at a lower rate than that paid to full-time employees or master crafts workers. Internships are a source not only of training but also of realistic exposure to job and organizational conditions. *Assistantships* involve full-time employment and expose an individual to a wide range of jobs. However, because the individual only assists other workers, the learning experience is often vicarious. This disadvantage is eliminated by programs of job or position rotation and multiple management.[63]

Job Rotation. *Job rotation programs* are used to expose employees to and train them in a variety of jobs and decision-making situations. The extent of training and long-run benefits it provides may be limited, because employees are not in a single job long enough to learn very much and may not be motivated to work hard since they know they will move on in the near future.

Supervisory Assistance and Mentoring. Often the most informal program of training and development is supervisory assistance or mentoring.[64] *Supervisory assistance* is a regular part of the supervisor's job. It includes day-to-day coaching, counseling, and monitoring of workers on how to do the job and how to get along in the organization. The effectiveness of these techniques depends in part on whether the supervisor creates feelings of mutual confidence, provides opportunities for growth, and effectively delegates tasks.

Mentoring, in which an established employee guides the development of a less-experienced worker, or protégé, can increase employees' skills, achievement, and understanding of the organization. At AT&T Global Information Systems, for example, protégés are usually chosen from among high-potential employees in middle or entry-level management. Each executive is encouraged to select two people to mentor, and must decide how to develop the relationships. Usually, executives counsel their protégés on how to advance and network in the company, and they sometimes offer personal advice.[65]

On-Site but Not on the Job

Training at the work site but not on the job is appropriate for required after-hours programs and for programs in which contact needs to be maintained with work units but OJT would be too distracting or harmful. It is also appropriate for voluntary after-hours programs and for programs that update employees' skills while allowing them to attend to their regular duties.

For example, when a major Northeast grocery store chain switched to computerized scanners, it faced the problem of training thousands of checkers spread out across three states. The cost of training them off-site was prohibitive. Yet management also was fearful about training employees on the job, lest their ineptitude offend customers. To solve the problem, the grocery chain developed a mobile training van that included a vestibule model of the latest scanning equipment. Checkers were trained on-site but off the job in the mobile unit. Once the basic skill of scanning was mastered, employees returned to the store, and the trainer remained on-site as a resource person. According to one store manager, the program was effective because employees could be trained rapidly and efficiently, yet no customers were lost owing to checker errors or slowness.

Company Schools and Executive Education Programs. A growing trend in the United States is the development of *company schools and executive education programs* tailored to the needs of the company. Company schools focus on the education of employees and sometimes customers. McDonald's Hamburger University, begun in 1961, is among the oldest corporate universities. Started in a basement, the center now trains more than twenty-five hundred students annually in the fine details of restaurant and franchise operations. General Electric, an advocate of training and development for years, has an up-to-date facility in Croton-on-Hudson, New York, that it uses for divisional and group training. Corporate schools have also been developed by such diverse firms as AT&T, Ford, Arthur Andersen, Motorola, United Airlines, Chase Manhattan Corporation, Kodak, and Digital Equipment.

Motorola dedicated its $10 million Galvin Center for Continuing Education in 1986. The facility contains 88,000 square feet of classrooms, individual instruction centers, an auditorium, lounges, dining facilities, and a fitness center. In affiliation with the National Technological Union, a consortium that teaches by satellite, Motorola offers courses leading to three master's degrees. It has also opened Motorola University, where it teaches total quality management to its own employees. In addition, it teaches TQM to faculty from business and engineering schools.[66]

Like a growing number of corporations, Motorola is committed to company-based education. In fact, recent research suggests that 65 percent of all major firms offer some form of executive education. Today, many corporate colleges offer degrees, and hundreds of corporations offer courses leading to degrees.

In providing company schools and executive education, corporations, large and small, can help their employees obtain state-of-the-art knowledge, both technical and managerial. In the process, employees develop an ability to adapt continuously to changing conditions. This can then make it easier for organizations to institute major changes such as a movement to total quality management.[67]

Programmed Instruction. *Programmed instruction (PI)* is an old on-site training method. Here, the instructional material is broken down into frames and programmed for the computer. Each frame represents a small component of the entire subject to be learned, and each frame must be learned successfully before the next one can be tackled.

An advantage of PI is that large numbers of employees can be trained simultaneously, with each learner free to explore the material at her or his own pace. In addition, PI includes immediate and individualized feedback. The downside is that development costs are high, especially for computerized PI. Although the development of several authoring systems has eased the burden of developing PI modules, instruction still must be carefully planned. It is estimated that one hour of programmed instruction requires fifty hours of development work. Consequently, this approach is effective only if canned programs (e.g., word processing and database tutorials) are used or if large numbers of employees are to be trained so that development costs for an original program can be justified.

Videotapes. At its most basic level, video training includes taped instruction that can be stopped and started at any point. *Videotapes* can be used on-site or off-site and have generally replaced films for organizational training. Because they are less expensive than traditional training films, their use has increased rapidly in recent years.

An advantage of videotape is that instruction can be standardized. For example, Pizza Hut faced the challenge of training ten thousand employees in various locales on such matters as competing with Domino's Pizza in the home delivery market, new products (e.g., pan pizza), safe driving, and customer service. Professionally prepared video presentations were mailed out to its individual locations, and the training was then provided on-site to each shift of workers. Cost savings for this program versus traditional off-site or on-site training were substantial.

Videodisks. Organizations with large budgets for training are replacing videotapes with videodisks. A *videodisk* relies on a laser beam instead of a needle to pick up images and project them on a television screen. Although more expensive to produce than simple videotape programs, videodisks provide higher-quality images, quicker starts and stops, and greater durability. Because disks are much smaller than tapes, they are also easier to transport and utilize.

The newness of videodisk technology and the lack of standardized courseware make these systems cost-ineffective for small companies. Still, corporations such as Kodak are relying on videodisks for training in business, computer logic, mechanics, and new technology. For example, Kodak uses videodisks to keep its scientists and engineers updated on technological advances.

Interactive Video Training. *Interactive video training (IVT)* combines the best features of PI with the best attributes of videotape or videodisk instruction. Interactive video programs, typically formatted on a CD-ROM, present a short video and narrative presentation (on tape or disk) and then require the trainee to respond to it. Usually, the video program is attached to a personal computer, and the learner responds to video cues by using the keyboard or by touching the screen. This sequence—packaged program, learner response, and more programmed instruction—provides for individualized learning.

Interactive video has been used by a variety of organizations. Kodak developed an IVT system to train office personnel in the use of a new word processing system. The Kodak system relied on two computer screens. On one screen, through a videodisk, a model demonstrated how to use the software package; on the adjacent screen, written instructions, as well as the trainee's word processing output, were displayed. Support staff could complete their training on-site. If a trainee forgot portions of the program, they could repeat those segments by merely walking over to the on-site training center and calling up the modules of concern.

Interactive video training has been used to train four hundred thousand General Motors workers in occupational health and safety procedures, and to train Dow Chemical employees in how to deal with petrochemical hazards. Electrical workers have learned how to solve complex wiring problems by tracing patterns on touch-sensitive screens.

On the downside, the development and equipment costs associated with IVT are high. Hardware alone can cost between $6,000 and $12,000, and a master videodisk between $2,000 and $5,000. For sophisticated programs, more than five hundred hours may be spent developing one hour of training, with costs running as high as $150,000. Also, a sizable and diverse staff is needed to make IVT work. Instruction designers, scriptwriters, programmers, video producers, and subject matter experts are all needed. Still, IVT offers fast, effective training, and, as its popularity increases, its development and hardware costs should drop, making it more affordable to small organizations.

Telecommunication Training. In 1987, the Public Broadcasting System (PBS) entered the field of satellite training with the establishment of the National Narrowcast System (NNS). Produced in cooperation with the American Society for Training and Development (ASTD), the network offers more than five hours of daily programming by microwave to subscribing businesses, public agencies, and colleges and universities. Contractors are free to tape programs for six months to one year, and the system has nine training tracks targeted for specific groups (e.g., sales, supervision, computer literacy, and effective communications).

The major advantage of *telecommunication training* is its potential for speeding up communications within large corporations. A cost study conducted by Kodak estimates that a new product training program beamed by satellite to three cities costs $20,000. However, Kodak also estimates that it would cost five to six times that amount to send engineers and managers on the road to do the same training. More important, six weeks of training time is saved, which is invaluable in a competitive industry.[68]

Off the Job

When the consequence of error is high, it is usually more appropriate to conduct training off the job. For example, most airline passengers would readily agree that it is preferable to train pilots in flight simulators rather than have them apprentice in the cockpit of a plane. Similarly, it is usually useful to have a bus driver practice on an obstacle course before taking to the roads with a load of schoolchildren.

Off-the-job training is also appropriate when complex skills need to be mastered or when employees need to focus on specific interpersonal skills that might not be apparent in the normal work environment. For example, it is difficult to build a cohesive management work team when members of the team are constantly interrupted by telephone calls and subordinate inquiries. Team building is more likely to occur during a retreat, when team members have time to focus on establishing relationships.

However, the costs of off-the-job training are high. Transfer of knowledge to the workplace is also a concern. Research has shown that the more dissimilar the training environment is to the actual work environment, the less likely trainees will be to apply what they learn to their jobs. For example, the transfer-of-knowledge problem is minimal for vestibule training, in which trainees work with machines that are comparable to the ones in their actual work environment. However, it may be difficult to apply teamwork skills learned during a wilderness survival program to a management job in a large service organization.

Formal Courses. *Formal courses* can be directed either by the trainee—using programmed instruction, computer-assisted instruction, reading, and correspondence courses—or by others, as in formal classroom courses and lectures. Although many training programs use the lecture method because it efficiently and simultaneously conveys large amounts of information to large groups of people, it does have several drawbacks:

- It perpetuates the authority structure of traditional organizations and hinders performance because the learning process is not self-controlled.
- Except in the areas of cognitive knowledge and conceptual principles, the transfer of learning to the actual skills and abilities required to do the job is probably limited.
- The high verbal and symbolic requirements of the lecture method may be threatening to people with low verbal or symbolic aptitude.
- The lecture method does not permit individualized training based on individual differences in ability, interests, and personality.

Because of these drawbacks, the lecture method is often complemented by other training methods.

Simulation. *Simulation,* which presents situations that are similar to actual job conditions, is used for both managers and nonmanagers.[69] A common simulation technique for nonmanagers is the *vestibule method,* which simulates the environment of the individual's actual job. Because the environment is not real, it is generally less hectic and more safe than the actual environment; as a consequence, trainees may have trouble adjusting from the training environment to the actual environment. However, the arguments for using a simulated environment are compelling: it reduces the possibility of customer dissatisfaction that can result from on-the-job training, it can reduce the frustration of the trainee, and it may save the organization a great deal of money because fewer training accidents occur. Not all organizations, even in the same industry, accept these arguments. Some banks, for example, train their tellers on the job, whereas others train them in a simulated bank environment.

Assessment Centers. An increasingly popular simulation technique for managers is *assessment centers.* Assessment centers are also especially useful for identifying potential training needs. Whether used for training or selection, they appear to be a valid way to make employment decisions.[70] In fact, certain aspects of the assessment center, such as management games and in-basket exercises, are excellent for training and need not be confined to these programs.

Regardless of where they are used, *management games or business games,* like the experiential board games used at Microsoft, can be used to develop a variety of skills, such as teamwork in a group setting. In contrast, *in-basket exercises* are more solitary. The trainee sits at a desk and works through a pile of papers found in the in-basket of a typical manager, setting priorities, recommending solutions to problems, and taking any necessary action in response to the contents.[71]

Although in-basket exercises tend to be enjoyable and challenging, the extent to which they improve a manager's ability depends in part on what takes place afterward. An analysis of what happened and what should have happened in business games and in-basket exercises, when done by upper-level managers in the organization, should help trainees learn how to perform like managers. The opportunity for improvement may be drastically reduced if the trainees are left to decide what to transfer from the games or exercises to the job.

Role-Playing and Sensitivity Training. Whereas simulation exercises may be useful for developing conceptual and problem-solving skills, two other types of training are used for developing human relation or process skills. Role-playing and sensitivity training develop managers' interpersonal insights—awareness of self and of others—for changing attitudes and for practicing human relation skills, such as leading or interviewing.

Role-playing generally focuses on understanding and managing relationships rather than facts. The essence of role-playing is to create a realistic situation, as in the case discussion method, and then have the trainees assume the parts of specific personalities in the situation. The usefulness of role-playing depends heavily on the extent to which the trainees get into the parts they are playing. If you have done any role-playing, you know how difficult this can be and how much easier it is to simply read the part. However, when the trainee does get into the role, the result is a greater sensitivity to the feelings and insights that are presented by the role.

In *sensitivity training,* individuals in an unstructured group exchange thoughts and feelings on the "here and now" rather than the "there and then." Although being in a sensitivity group often gives individuals insight into how and why they and others feel and act the way they do, critics claim that these results may not be beneficial because they are not directly transferable to the job.[72]

Wilderness Trips. To increase employees' feelings about the here and now and raise their self-esteem, organizations sometimes use programs that involve physical feats of strength, endurance, and cooperation. These can be implemented on *wilderness trips* to the woods or mountains or even water:

> Everyone goes overboard during strategic planning meetings of the Meridian Group. But that doesn't bother Harvey Kinzelberg, 43, chairman of the $250-million-a-year Illinois computer-leasing firm, the nation's third largest. On the contrary, he requires it. Twice a year Kinzelberg charters a boat in the Caribbean, puts his top executives aboard, and leads them in a five-day brainstorming session cum scuba-diving expedition.... As often as three times a day, the company's managers pause from strategizing, strap on air tanks and face masks, and go for a plunge in the briny.
>
> Kinzelberg claims the downward bound excursions focus his executives' attention on business by eliminating the ... distractions of the office. More important, he says, they foster team spirit...."In the potentially life-threatening environment underwater," he explains, "you realize that you depend on everyone else in the company not just for your livelihood in business but for your life as well."
>
> Excursions in the deep also provide the benefits of a different perspective, says Kinzelberg.... After spearing and killing a large barracuda, as he did on a recent dive, Kinzelberg finds that the sharks he faces in business seem like small fries.[73]

Whereas many firms such as General Electric, General Foods, Knight-Ridder, General Motors, and CIBA use some variation of outdoor experiences in their management training with success, many others, such as Microsoft, question the degree of transfer to the job that these experiences offer. Firms using outdoor experiences recognize this concern and thus articulate the link between the skills developed in the experiences and the skills and competencies needed by the managers on the job. They also are sensitive to employee differences in order to ensure that these experiences can be accommodated to an increasingly diverse workforce.

 MAXIMIZING LEARNING

Even when the technique is appropriate, learning may not take place if the experience is not structured appropriately. Exhibit 9.8 details learning principles that increase the success of training.[74]

■ *Exhibit 9.8*
Learning Principles to Increase the Effectiveness of Training

Setting the Stage for Learning

1. Provide clear task instructions.
2. Model appropriate behavior.

Increasing Learning during Training

1. Provide for active participation.
2. Increase self-efficacy.
3. Match training techniques to trainees' self-efficacy.
4. Provide opportunities for enactive mastery.
5. Ensure specific, timely, diagnostic, and practical feedback.
6. Provide opportunities for trainees to practice new behaviors.

Maintaining Performance after Training

1. Develop learning points to assist knowledge retention.
2. Set specific goals.
3. Identify appropriate reinforcers.
4. Train significant others in how to reinforce behavior.
5. Teach trainees self-management skills.

Following up on Training

1. Evaluate effectiveness.
2. Make revisions as needed.

Setting the Stage for Learning

Before launching a training program, a trainer or manager needs to consider how information will be presented. In addition, he or she must consider the beliefs of trainees regarding task-specific competencies.

Clear Instructions. If task instructions are unclear or imprecise, learning is hampered. Employees must know what is expected in order to perform as desired. Clear instructions establish appropriate behavioral expectations. Training expectations should be stated in specific terms. The conditions under which performance is or is not expected should be identified, along with the behavior to be demonstrated.

To set the stage for desired performance, it is also useful to specify up front what the reward will be for performing as desired. Trainees are more likely to be motivated if they know that successful performance can lead to positive reinforcement (e.g., promotion, pay raise, or recognition) or can block the administration of negative reinforcement (e.g., supervisory criticism or firing).[75]

Behavioral Models. Even when instructions are clear, the desired behavior still may not occur if the trainee does not know how to perform it. This problem can be overcome through *behavioral modeling,* which is a visual demonstration of desired behavior. The model can be a supervisor, coworker, or subject matter expert, and the demonstration can be live or videotaped. The important thing is to show employees what needs to be done before asking them to do it.[76]

Care is needed in choosing an appropriate behavioral model. If the model makes the task look too simple, trainees may quit the first time they encounter a difficulty. Thus, models should show not only how to achieve desired outcomes but also how to overcome performance obstacles.

Increasing Learning during Training

Although employees should be responsible for their own learning, organizations can do much to facilitate this.

Active Participation. Individuals perform better if they are actively involved in the learning process. Organizational help in this area can range from encouraging active participation in classroom discussions to establishing a set of programs to assist managers in a major strategic change. Participation may be direct (e.g., hands-on training) or indirect (e.g., role-plays and simulations). The important point is to hook the individual on learning. Through active participation, individuals stay more alert and are more likely to feel confident.[77]

Self-Efficacy. Even with modeling, learning may not occur if people have feelings of low self-efficacy. *Self-efficacy* is a trainee's beliefs about a task-specific ability. If individuals dwell on their personal deficiencies relative to the task, potential difficulties may seem more formidable than they really are. On the other hand, people who have a strong sense of self-efficacy are likely to be motivated to overcome obstacles.

The choice of an appropriate training method is critical to self-efficacy. In a recent study, a group of trainees was taught how to use computer spreadsheets. People low in self-efficacy performed better when one-on-one tutorials were conducted; individuals with high self-efficacy (who believed they could easily learn how to use spreadsheets) performed better when appropriate behavior was merely modeled. Consequently, before choosing training techniques, the level of self-efficacy for each trainee should be determined.[78]

Enactive Mastery. Self-efficacy increases when experiences fail to validate fears and when skills acquired allow for mastery of once-threatening situations. This process is called *enactive mastery*. To facilitate task mastery, trainers should arrange the subject matter so that trainees experience success. Whereas this may be easy when tasks are simple, it can be quite difficult when tasks are complex.

Solutions include segmenting the task, shaping behavior, and setting proximal goals. Task segmentation involves breaking a complex task into smaller or simpler components. For some jobs (e.g., laboratory technician), the components (e.g., drawing blood, culturing a specimen, and running a blood chemistry machine) can be taught individually and in any order. For other jobs (e.g., engineer, chauffeur, and interviewer), segments must be taught sequentially because task B builds on task A and task C builds on task B.[79]

Shaping includes rewarding closer and closer approximations to desired behavior. For example, when managers are learning how to conduct a selection interview, they can be reinforced for making eye contact and for developing situational questions.

The setting of *proximal goals,* or intermediary goals, also increases mastery perceptions. Consider a software developer with an overall objective of developing a new word processing package. Proximal goals might include meeting a project specifications deadline, developing algorithms for fonts by a set deadline, developing an algorithm for formatting paragraphs, and so on. These proximal goals all lead to the attainment of the distal, or overall, objective.[80]

Feedback. For individuals to master new concepts and acquire new skills, they must receive accurate diagnostic feedback about their performance. When feedback is not received or is inaccurate, the wrong behaviors may be practiced. Feedback can be provided by a supervisor, coworkers, customers, computers, or the individual performing the task. It must be specific, timely, based on behavior and not personality, and practical. If a performance discrepancy exists, the feedback should also be diagnostic and should include instructions or modeling of how to perform better.[81] The Weyerhaeuser Company and Eaton Corporation use surveys to make sure managers get a lot of feedback on how well they are doing as managers.

Practice. The goal of skill training is to ensure that desired behavior occurs not just one time but consistently. This is most likely to occur when trainees are able to practice and internalize standards of performance. Even mental practice appears to help improve performance.[82] Practicing the wrong behaviors is detrimental; therefore, practice must follow specific feedback.

For some jobs, tasks must be overlearned. *Overlearning* includes internalizing responses so that the trainee does not have to think consciously about behavior before responding. For example, if a plane is losing altitude rapidly, a pilot must know immediately how to respond. The pilot has no time to think about what should be done. The emergency routine must be second nature and internalized.

Maintaining Performance after Training

Following employees' exposure to socialization, training, and development experiences, the environment needs to support the transfer of new behaviors to the job, and their maintenance over time.

Learning Points. First, new skills and information are more likely to be retained when learning points are developed. *Learning points* summarize key behaviors—particularly those that are not obvious—and serve as cognitive cues back on the job. Although learning points can be written by trainers, trainee-generated learning points—even if they are of lower quality—enhance recall and lead to better skill acquisition and retention.[83]

Specific Goals. Without goals, people have little basis for judging how they are doing.[84] Specific goals for subsequent performance should be challenging but not so difficult as to be perceived impossible. They also should not be set too early in the learning process, as explained in the feature "Using Data for the 21st Century: Are Goals for Learning a Help or Hindrance?"

Reinforcers. Learning new behaviors is difficult and threatening. To ensure that trainees continue to demonstrate the skill they have learned, behavior must be reinforced. Reinforcement can be positive (e.g., praise and financial rewards) or negative (e.g., "If you perform as desired, I will quit screaming at you"), but it must be contingent on performance.[85]

Significant Others. Trainers must also teach significant others to look for and reinforce desired changes. If a person labeled a troubled employee continues to be viewed as such, the person has no incentive to display new behavior. If, however, a supervisor or coworker responds positively to a positive change in behavior, the frequency with which the new behavior will be displayed is likely to increase.

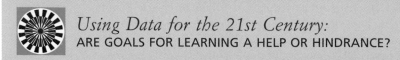

With rapid changes in technologies and the gap between the skills needed by employers and those available in the workforce growing wider, organizations will be spending more resources than ever before on training. To maximize their ability to compete, employers will be looking for the best training methods available. What are the ideal training conditions for teaching adults new skills? Do individual differences in basic ability levels influence the learning process? Specific and difficult goals are known to encourage good performance on tasks that people are familiar with, and they are used frequently as part of management by objectives. Can goals be used effectively to speed the learning process as well?

These questions were addressed in experiments involving 1,010 U.S. Air Force trainees. The task for these trainees was to learn air traffic control. Using a simulator, they practiced landing DC10s, prop planes, 747s, and 727s. To do the task well, trainees had to learn to manage four runways, twelve different holding patterns, and a queue stack of planes requesting permission to land. As they were learning, wind speeds, wind directions, and ground conditions (e.g., icy, wet, dry) changed randomly. Performance scores reflected how many planes landed safely, how many rule violations occurred, and how many planes ran out of fuel and crashed.

To study how goals influenced learning, goals were set at different stages of their learning. In the first experiment, trainees with no goals were compared with those given a specific and difficult goal very early in their training, when they were simply trying to understand the task and the rules. The early goals had no positive effect on performance and they appeared to interfere with learning. In the second experiment, goals were set later in the learning sequence, after trainees understood the task but while they were still honing their skills. These later goals proved to be effective: trainees with difficult goals landed more planes safely. These results suggested that goals influence the learning of complex tasks differently depending on when they are set. If they are set too early, they can interfere with performance because they detract attention from the task at hand. Instead of focusing on the task, people spend too much time monitoring their behavior. For complex tasks, it appears to be better to set performance goals later in the learning process, after trainees have mastered some of the basic skills but while they are practicing to achieve higher levels of performance. At this stage, additional performance improvement depends mostly on skill practice rather than on cognitive activity. This means that the monitoring behaviors that people engage in when they are trying to achieve a difficult goal do not interfere with performance at this stage of learning.

Finally, a third study found that the beneficial effects of goals were greater for low-ability trainees than for high-ability trainees. This suggests that to deliver effective training programs, trainers need to take into account the basic abilities of trainees and the trainees' learning stage, especially if they set goals for trainees. If trainers ignore these variables, they may inadvertently create conditions that actually interfere with the learning process.[86]

Self-Reinforcement. Because it is not always possible for significant others to reinforce an individual worker, a long-term objective should be to teach employees how to set their own goals and administer their own reinforcement. When people create self-incentives for their efforts, they are capable of making self-satisfaction contingent on their own performance. The challenge here is to ensure that personal goals are congruent with organizational goals, which leads to self-management.[87]

Longer-term Follow-up. All too often, even when training has been successful, participants who want to change their behavior get back to work and then slowly slip back into their old patterns. This results in a significant loss of effectiveness of the training program. One approach to help prevent this from happening is an action plan. At Eaton Corporation, Nick Blauwiekel feeds back the results of the Eaton Audit Survey to the plant managers and asks each manager to develop an action plan to remove any deficiencies.

Another approach is a contract. Each participant writes an informal agreement near the end of a training program, stating which aspects of the program he or she believes will have the most beneficial effect back on the job and then agreeing to apply those aspects. Each participant is also asked to choose another participant from the program, to whom a copy of the contract is given and who agrees to check up on the participant's progress every few weeks.

 ## EVALUATING THE EFFECTIVENESS OF SOCIALIZATION, TRAINING, AND DEVELOPMENT

As is true for all human resource management practices used by a company, the value of socialization, training, and development activities can be enhanced through continual evaluation and revision. Because evaluating and revising HR activities is so important, this text devotes an entire chapter (Chapter 17) to a discussion of how to assess effectiveness. Here we simply note that for socialization, training and development most experts agree that evaluation should include at least these four components:

1. *Reactions of participants:* Short questionnaires (often referred to as "smile sheets") are a popular way to measure employees' reactions to their experiences. Was the instruction clear and helpful? Did the participants like the program? Do they see how it is relevant to their work? Do they believe they learned something from the experience? These are the most commonly-used measures of training effectiveness.

2. *Learning:* To assess learning, simple tests can be given to determine whether participants acquired the knowledge and skills of interest. *Can* participants perform tasks they couldn't perform before (e.g., conduct an appraisal interview, negotiate a contract)? Do participants have information they didn't have before? *Can* they talk meaningfully about new issues (e.g., workforce diversity, ethics, global strategies)?

3. *Behavior or Performance Change:* Effective training does more than give participants new capabilities. It also results in actual changes in behavior. *Do* participants behave differently than they did before? *Do* they perform their job better than they did before?

4. *Results:* Ultimately, the objective of socialization, training and development is to produce results. Has productivity improved? Have complaints and grievances declined? Are customers more satisfied with the service they receive? Has the bench strength of the management talent pool increased?

By obtaining information to answer questions like these, a company can assess the effectiveness of its current practices. Equally important, such data provides useful guidance for improving future approaches to socialization, training and development.

 ## LEGAL CONSIDERATIONS IN TRAINING AND DEVELOPMENT

Legally, an applicant cannot be eliminated from the selection pool just because she or he lacks a skill that can be learned in eight hours. Thus, it is important to determine what skills are needed to perform a job, what skills an applicant possesses, training programs that can remove any deficiencies, and the time necessary to complete these programs.

Discriminatory Training Practices

For current employees, bans on discrimination extend to on-the-job training and one-day introductions to new jobs or equipment, as well as to affirmative action and formal apprenticeship and training programs. However, admission to formal training programs can be limited to those under a certain age, as long as those passed over are not women or members of minorities who have previously been denied training opportunities. Specific discriminatory training practices can often be determined by the responses to the following questions:

- Are members of minorities and women given the same training opportunities as white males? Be careful! Advertising and recruiting practices come into play here.
- Are requirements for entry into a training program (i.e., tests, education, or experience) job related, or are they arbitrary?
- Are nearly all machine functions or other specialized duties that require training performed by white or male workers?
- Does one class of trainees tend to get more challenging assignments or other special training opportunities?
- Do supervisors know what constitutes training? It could be almost any learning experience, from OTJ instruction in how to fit a drill bit to a two-week seminar on complex sales procedures.
- Who evaluates the results of instruction or training—only white males?
- Are all trainees given equal facilities for instruction? Are they segregated in any way?
- Do a disproportionate number of females or members of minorities fail to pass training courses? If so, why? Do they have lower qualifications upon entering the program? Do they receive inferior instruction? Do they receive less support from their supervisors when attendance in the course conflicts with job duties?

Defenses against Charges of Discrimination

To defend against charges of discrimination, companies can show that the training programs were conceived and administered without bias. This will be exceedingly difficult to do unless companies have the foresight to document their training practices. Thus, they should follow these guidelines:

- Register affirmative action training and apprenticeship programs with the Department of Labor. This must be done in writing. Include the goals, timetables, and criteria for selection and evaluation of trainees. Such a record will help prove job relatedness and lack of intent to discriminate. It can also help prove that an organization's program was not used as a pretext to discriminate.
- Keep a record of all employees who wish to enroll in the training program. Detail how each trainee was selected. Keep, for at least two years or as long as training continues, application forms, tests, questionnaires, records of preliminary interviews, and anything else that bears on an employee's selection or rejection.
- Document all management decisions and actions that relate to the administration of training policies.
- Monitor each trainee's progress. Provide progress evaluations, and make sure counseling is available.
- Continue to evaluate the results even after completion of the training.

Role of the Supervisor

Supervisors, managers, and executives, as well as their employees can be sued for violations of fair and equal employment laws.

What can employers do? The best protection against liability for personnel-related actions is better training for managers and supervisors as to the consequences of their actions. Many employers promote people to supervisory levels based on their expertise and their performance as individual contributors to the company, not on their managerial abilities. Employers need to train these employees in the "science of people management," in [the words of Lucille E. Brown, a partner at the law firm Schatz and Schatz, Ribicoff and Kotkin]. "This is absolutely necessary both for the employer and for the supervisor's self-development." Employers should encourage and train supervisors and managers to

- Document personnel issues such as performance and conduct, at the time the performance or conduct becomes a problem.
- Assess objectively employee performance and conduct.
- Review carefully communications concerning or directed to employees.[88]

GOVERNMENT SUPPORT

Support from federal and state governments can defray some training costs and provide already trained employees; for instance, the state of South Carolina supplied substantial financial support to encourage BMW to locate its first U.S. plant in Spartanburg. It can also enable employees to obtain training and jobs. Currently, support from the federal government is funneled through block grants to states and through the Office of Federal Contract Compliance Programs under provisions in the Job Training Partnership Act of 1982. Under that act, grants are provided to states, which in turn train economically disadvantaged youths and adults as well as workers whose jobs have been eliminated.[89]

INTERNATIONAL CONCERNS

Managing for Globalization

A few things seem certain, and one is that "globalization" will continue to be an inescapable buzzword. Businesses will operate in an ever more interconnected world. With continuing advances in computers and communications, world financial markets will meld. Manufacturing prowess will appear almost suddenly in new Taiwans and South Koreas.

A shrinking world will mean an expanding clock. Managers will have to shape organizations that can respond quickly to developments abroad. As speed and agility become paramount virtues, we will see even more decentralization, with responsibility closer to the operating level.[90]

Organizations are having to develop a world or global structure and perspective. Human resource policies need to mirror the necessary organizational characteristics. According to Gillette's CEO, Alfred M. Zeien, developing senior managers on an international scale takes a great deal of time (see "Managing Human Resources for the 21st Century at Gillette").

Pepsi-Cola International

At PepsiCo and Pepsi-Cola International, the idea that everyone can lead even small components of the business is critical. Employees are encouraged to find ways to improve continuously.[91]

To build the kind of global organization needed in the year 2000 and beyond, PCI embraces the selection and development of leaders from many different cultures. Discussions among the senior staff of PCI led to the conclusion that a leadership

Managing Human Resources for the 21st Century at Gillette

Rome was not built in a day. Neither was Gillette's international management team. According to Gillette chairman and CEO Alfred M. Zeien, it takes at least twenty-five years to build an international management corps that possesses the skills, experience, and abilities to take a global organization from one level of success to the next.

Gillette, through its senior management team, has learned that developing managers through international assignments helps the business grow. The firm's International Trainee Program is one of the company's key strategies for building its worldwide management corps. Its other key international staffing strategy is hiring and developing foreign nationals to staff its operations globally. Many of these managers have become part of Gillette's growing expatriate corps.

Interestingly, fewer than 15 percent of the company's expatriates are natives of the United States; at least 85 percent come from one of the other twenty-seven countries in which it has operations.

For the most part, Gillette hires foreign nationals to staff management positions in countries other than the United States. Often, however, the organization first identifies these individuals while they are studying at U.S. universities for their MBAs. The new hires typically work at Gillette's Boston headquarters for a year, then return to their home countries, much like trainees in the International Trainee Program.

After these managers work in their home countries for about four years, Gillette typically moves them on to other countries and other assignments. As Gillette managers build their international experience, they also teach and develop other potential managers within the organization.

Often these managers with international experience are prime candidates for positions that open up when the company enters new markets or into joint ventures. Such was the case with its new joint venture in the fall of 1992 with a company in China.

Because Gillette first began planning the joint venture in China more than three years before implementing it, it began identifying individual managers then who would be right for assignments in that new business.

As Gillette expatriate Bob McCusker puts it, "Gillette has a lot of resources that we can apply to our new ventures." McCusker says he finds it gratifying when individuals who work in a new Gillette venture in one area go on to help develop new ventures in other areas.

Gillette's policy of giving its managers international experience attracts individuals seeking international careers. Gillette managers constantly are on the lookout for individuals who show interest and promise in moving through the Gillette organization worldwide. "One of my responsibilities is to look for people who are promotable internationally," says Jorgen Wedel, president of Braun USA and a native of Denmark. "We need people who have a more global understanding of the business, and we need managers who can manage that business. I think it's one of the key responsibilities of management today."

Dieu Eng Seng agrees. Seng is the area vice president of Oral-B, Asia Pacific. A native of Singapore, Seng's past service with Gillette has included assignments in Australia, Singapore, China, Hong Kong, Malaysia, and the United States. "One of my key objectives is to identify, recruit, and develop competent managers. I'm confident that from these good people will generate a flow of business growth and profits into the future."

International management teams clearly are not built in a day. They are not even built in a year. In Gillette's case, careful planning and constant attention to international development can, however, yield employees that support and grow a business successfully from one decade to the next.[92]

program should be designed for all senior executives. The result was the Executive Leadership Program.

In developing this program, an outside consultant and the management development staff of PCI compiled a list of thirty-three leadership practices that reflect the actions leaders and managers are expected to take in running their businesses. Now, at least every eighteen months, the top one hundred officers of PCI have their performance reviewed anonymously by their subordinates against these leadership practices. The results of this review are fed back to senior staff during the Executive Leadership Program. Some of the questions asked to review these practices are: To what extent does the executive regularly share business results and plans? To what extent does the executive articulate a vision for the business? To what extent does the executive value cultural diversity? A sample of the topics included in the Executive Leadership Program appears in Exhibit 9.9.

The Executive Leadership Program is targeted at improving personal leadership behaviors as well as solving practical leadership questions such as those that arise in starting a new bottling plant or dealing with the career development concerns of a specific work unit. During the program, each senior executive receives confidential counseling about specific behaviors that need to change for that executive to manage her or his work group more effectively. In addition, each executive is expected to share her or his survey results with the work group that provided the data, and ask how the executive can help make the work group more effective.

In general terms, the leadership program is seen as culturally neutral. Although cultural differences are discussed, the focus is on how best to demonstrate a practice regardless of the country of application. Once again, however, typical survey results are likely to vary. For example, an executive in Eastern Europe, where the concept of competition is just taking hold, is less likely than an executive in Japan to hear about goals, targets, and the need to beat the competition. Thus, although cultural differences do exist, the practice of doing the survey is common.

When this program was initially installed, participants had some significant misgivings about the confidentiality of the data. An outside consultant was called in to ensure confidentiality. The program has now passed the confidentiality hurdle, and many participants are eager to attend and find out how they can improve their personal performance. In general, the program provides an intense forum for the discussion of

■ *Exhibit 9.9*

Sample Topics for Pepsi-Cola International Executive Leadership Program

	Leadership			Management	
Module	Establishing a vision for the business	Aligning people to accomplish the vision	Motivating and inspiring people	Performance management	Skill transfer
Practice Examples	Communicating an exciting vision of the future for our business	Communicating priorities in clear and simple terms	Communicating high personal standards	Establishing clear, specific performance goals and standards	Communicating the importance of developing strong and functional skills
	Integrating PCI's cultural priorities into a vision for our business	Encouraging an open discussion of business problems and issues	Valuing individual and cultural diversity	Demonstrating a commitment to long-term career development	Helping subordinates learn new skills

SOURCE: Adapted from J. Fulkerson and R. S. Schuler, "Managing Worldwide Diversity at Pepsi-Cola International," in *Working through Diversity: Human Resources Initiatives,* ed. S. E. Jackson (New York: Guilford Publications, 1992): 260.

leadership and management issues; these discussions, in turn, provide data about needed human resources practices and interventions.

A different program, called Excellence in Management, is used for midlevel managers. Questionnaires (translated at local discretion) and feedback are again used, as in the executive program. The midlevel program focuses primarily on basic managerial skills such as delegating, managing conflict, and being more effective in an organization that is mature, decentralized, and international. The midlevel program is designed more around strategy execution issues.

The two leadership programs at PCI focus on improving personal effectiveness and exploring ways to improve executive and managerial effectiveness in an international, culturally diverse organization. The attendees for these programs commonly represent a half dozen different nationalities, which provides a unique opportunity to practice problem sharing and problem solving with a diverse group of colleagues.

Expatriate Training

The training and development of U.S. expatriates present special problems. Management development of expatriates should take up where selection leaves off. Although only a few companies provide expatriate training, it is critical. The basic aspects of this training include the following:

- Development of expatriates before, during, and after foreign assignments
- Orientation and training of expatriate families before, during, and after foreign assignments
- Development of the headquarters staff responsible for the planning, organization, and control of overseas operations[93]

This range of training is aimed at bringing about attitudinal and behavioral changes in the expatriates, expatriates' families, and the staff (in the United States and abroad) responsible for the multinational operations.

One form of expatriate training is *cross-cultural training*. Although expatriates are important, their numbers in any one firm are limited. Thus, many firms offering cross-cultural training use outside vendors:

> Cross-cultural programs usually take the form of a three-to-five-day immersion course in the assigned country's values, customs and traditions. Although a few companies . . . teach these courses themselves, more often than not (and especially in the U.S.) firms use outside consultants for such instruction. Most consultants have a basic training module for each country, which they tailor to a client company's particular requirements. [The consulting firm] Moran, Stahl & Boyer . . . for example, begins with a basic program, which becomes more specific depending on client needs. Its three-day predeparture program covers everyday life in the country in question, area studies, doing business in the country, the role of women in the foreign culture, as well as culture shock and the stress executives and their families are likely to experience. Sessions make use of nationals of the country and are designed to prepare executives and their families for situations they will actually encounter.[94]

> Cross-cultural training is perhaps the main growth area in the training field, and more and more companies include it as a part of predeparture programs. The primary beneficiaries of this new emphasis on cross-cultural training are departing executives themselves. But companies stress that spouses and children may benefit as much [as] or even more than executives from this type of instruction, since it is they who are "out" in the local community daily and need to be sensitive to and knowledgeable about the culture. In contrast, most of an executive's time is spent in the somewhat insulated office environment. Therefore, more and more companies have begun offering the training to families as well as executives.[95]

By having an extensive development effort, multinational companies can help increase the effectiveness of their expatriate managers. Such a program can also encourage more domestic managers to apply for expatriate positions. To make expatriate positions really attractive, however, multinational companies must also offer commensurate salaries.[96] This makes it expensive for companies to have expatriate managers. For example, in 1994, it would cost a company almost $200,000 a year to maintain an expatriate manager in Japan, whereas a similar midlevel manager would earn about $60,000 in the United States.

 SUMMARY

Rapidly changing technology, illiteracy, foreign competition, and changes in organizational strategy are putting pressure on organizations to socialize, train and develop employees. This requires careful attention to needs assessment, program development and implementation, and evaluation. Four types of needs analysis—organizational, job, person, and demographic—are designed to diagnose systematically the short- and long-term human resource needs of an organization. When actual performance and desired performance differ, training is needed.

Following effective needs analysis, socialization, training and development activities must be designed and implemented. Setting up these activities involves deciding who will be trained, who will train, where the training will occur, and what methods will be used. Cost considerations, as well as the types of skills to be acquired (basic, interpersonal, or conceptual) and the location of the training (on the job, on-site, or off the job), affect the selection of appropriate methods.

Regardless of the method chosen, the content of the training should be designed to maximize learning. Principles to consider include clear instructions, proper role models, active participation, feedback, and practice. These should be viewed in relationship to the trainees' self-efficacy or competency beliefs. It is also important to examine the work environment to ensure that new behaviors will be reinforced rather than punished.

The last major phase of socialization, training and development is evaluation. Not only should reactions to training be assessed, but also the degree of learning, the change in job behavior, and organizational outcomes should be examined against objectives.

Globalization creates many new challenges, and developing managers who will be effective everywhere in the world is among the greatest of these. The examples of Pepsi-Cola International and Gillette illustrate how the most competitive firms are effectively developing their managers now in order to prepare for the 21st century.

 Discussion Questions

1. How is training at Wal-Mart related to the organization's other HR practices?
2. How do the HR practices and the business strategy of Wal-Mart compare with those of Sears and Nordstrom (see Chapter 1)?
3. Describe and explain the three major phases involved in setting up any training system.
4. Reflect for a moment on your own work experience. What benefits did your former (or present) employer receive by socializing and training you? Why did your employer not just hire someone who could perform the job without training?
5. What legal considerations influence training and development decisions? How can training and development programs avoid potential legal problems? (See Chapter 3 for a legal refresher.)
6. Explain how and why the training activities at Boston Consulting Group and at McKinsey Company differ.

7. What design principles can enhance the learning that takes place in training and development programs?
8. As a manager, what indicators would you need in order to decide whether a low-performing subordinate was a selection mistake or merely in need of training? If possible, illustrate this dilemma with an example from your own organizational experience.
9. Discuss the strategic role of socialization, training and development activities.
10. What training material is needed to prepare expatriates?

 In-Class Projects

1. Describe the following for Lincoln Electric:
   a. The socialization, training and development objectives
   b. The degree to which these objectives are serving the business objectives of Lincoln
   c. The socialization, training and development programs and activities
   d. The degree to which each of these serves the business objectives of Lincoln
   Going forward:

   How can the socialization, training and development programs and activities at Lincoln be improved?

2. Describe the following for AAL:
   a. The socialization, training and development objectives
   b. The degree to which these objectives are serving the business objectives of AAL
   c. The socialization, training and development programs and activities
   d. The degree to which each of these serves the business objectives of AAL
   Going forward:

   How can the socialization, training and development programs and activities at AAL be improved?

 Field Project

Identify two firms in the same industry. Then compare and contrast their socialization, training and development practices as was done in the feature "Managing Human Resources for the 21st Century at Boston Consulting Group and at McKinsey and Company" (page 308).

Case Study:
THE BUZZY COMPANY DOWNTURN: SETTING UP A DEVELOPMENT AGENDA

THE CHALLENGE

During his regular weekly staff meeting, Lou Topman, president of the Buzzy Company, expressed his serious concern over the report he had just received. "I have indications that there is not enough *enthusiasm* prevalent throughout the Buzzy plant," he stated emphatically. "We are not going to tolerate such an attitude," Lou continued. "Buzzy people are always enthusiastic, and you, the staff members, are going to help me straighten this out!"

Most of the staff members realized that a recent business slowdown had necessitated a sizable reduction in workforce, causing many key people to question their own job security. To avoid the stigma of being laid off, many employees were actively seeking and accepting positions in other companies. Those who remained were becoming conscious of protecting their job status. Established informal communication networks were being broken as a result of people leaving. Many staff members wondered when they could expect Buzzy's employee and financial recovery.

Lou told his staff that this trend had to be reversed. Somehow, they would have to bring about a management renewal to ensure the successful achievement of the company's newly established objectives. The president charged each member of his staff to consider carefully methods for overcoming the present dilemma.

THE BUSINESS SITUATION

Financially, the Buzzy Company had operated profitably over the years, with about 80 percent of the business based on defense. However, in 1979, changes in the defense market coupled with an altered economic environment began to reverse the trend. By 1982, consumer sales were up to 70 percent of the company's total. Since 1988, an unexpected decrease in sales had caused considerable alarm throughout the organization. In an effort to remain profitable in the face of declining sales, the company management found it necessary to make corresponding and significant reductions in the workforce. In addition, wages became essentially frozen.

As viewed from top management levels, the business prospects for the future, by contrast, looked encouraging. In anticipation of improved business prospects, Lou had redirected Buzzy's business objectives toward the opportunities that would most likely yield the highest return on investment.

THE PROBLEM

Lou and his immediate advisers recognized that the achievement of their newly established business objectives would require the support of an effective management organization to execute their carefully formulated plans. Unfortunately, Lou did not see the uncertainty that shrouded the general workforce as a major obstacle to the achievement of company goals. This problem was the surprisingly sticky subject that generated considerable discussion at the next few weekly staff meetings. Many staff members thought personal motivation was eating away at the vital organs of the organization. It finally became obvious to everyone that unless the current trends were reversed, the company would be faced with replacing key individuals.

Because of the mounting concern expressed frequently by the members of his staff, Lou appointed a special task force to investigate the problem, to evaluate various alternative solutions, and to make appropriate recommendations. The task force consisted of the director of industrial relations, Dave Peoples; the executive assistant to the president, Kate Ryan; the director of research and development, Alan Dees; the vice president of finance, Sharise Marcus; and the director of business planning, Fred Guth. The makeup of the group was intended to represent a broad spectrum of company interests and talents.

Following its appointment, the task force held a series of meetings to accomplish its assigned task. It was decided that interviews with selected employees should be conducted to gather data relating to the problem. A reputable consultant firm was retained to assist in the investigation.

It was agreed that the survey data obtained from interviews throughout the company revealed at best an incomplete picture of the real problems facing the company. This was attributed to a reluctance to speak freely about real concerns given the current setting of uncertainty. As a consequence, the task force decided that qualified interviewers from outside the company were needed to obtain the data necessary for an intelligent definition of the problem.

Accordingly, Burke and Associates was retained to conduct confidential interviews, analyze the data, and identify pertinent problem areas. The results of this activity, as summarized by Burke and Associates, revealed that "the central problem was communication throughout the organization—upward, downward, and laterally." This opinion was confirmed by the earlier reluctance of people to discuss their concern freely with company interviewers.

In addition, Burke and Associates interviews with many in management positions indicated a widespread desire to improve their management skills. For example, many managers wanted to learn how to make better use of time in the execution of their assigned job.

Based on the findings of the consultants and its own independent investigations, the task force concluded that a management development program, specifically designed to address the identified problems and needs of the Buzzy organization, could contribute greatly toward the achievement of company objectives. The group then considered alternative methods of implementing such a program.

ALTERNATIVE SOLUTIONS

Three alternative approaches to implementing the recommended management development program were considered by the task force.

Plan A: Use Existing In-House Talent

The adoption of Plan A would involve the identification of individuals presently within the company who possess the unique talents required to implement such a program. The task force members agreed that the qualifications of the selected individuals would have to include

- An advanced degree with at least a minor in education or psychology or both
- Previous related experience in the field of management development
- A keen appreciation of the unique problems and their relation to the company

Once selected, the individuals would become thoroughly familiar with the problems, investigate appropriate management training objectives directed toward the specific needs, and administer the resulting management development program.

Plan B: Hire a Professional Management Training Director

If Plan B were recommended by the task force and adopted by the company, a lengthy sequence of activities and events would occur, beginning with the preparation of a fairly comprehensive description of the job to be performed, in terms of not only the immediate problems at hand but also the longer-range requirements associated with continuing management development training. Having established such a job description, the company would then advertise for prospective applicants. The qualifications and salary requirements would be carefully screened, and the best-qualified director would be selected. The new management training director would then begin an extensive orientation period, during which

he or she would become familiar with the company, its people, and their interrelated problems. Based on his or her perception of the situation and understanding of the assignment, the training director could select an appropriate management development program and administer it.

Plan C: Engage a Professional Consulting Firm

Plan C would involve identifying qualified professional consulting or management development firms. Having selected a firm whose capabilities best matched the specific needs of Buzzy, the company would then contract for services including the following:

- Confidential interviews with a representative sample of management and supervisory personnel
- An analysis of the results of these interviews to verify the previously identified problems
- Identification of other problem areas revealed by the interviews
- Proposal of a management development program
- If acceptable to the company, execution of the program

EVALUATION OF ALTERNATIVE SOLUTIONS

Having defined its alternative solutions, the task force then evaluated these in terms of their advantages and disadvantages, their respective probabilities of successfully achieving the specific objectives, and their required investment of resources versus expected returns.

As seen by the task force, Plan A offered the unique advantage that the qualified individual selected from within the company might already be well aware of the problems facing the company. Also, it was felt that such an insider would probably be more personally concerned than an outsider, because of her or his established involvement with the company.

Several disadvantages to Plan A were also recognized. It was generally conceded that the task force was not likely to find an individual employed by the company with the required qualifications. Even if it did, making this person available for this assignment would probably require hiring another individual to fill the resulting vacant slot. Also, the reluctance on the part of potential trainees to respond openly during interviews would still exist to some degree and thereby diminish the effectiveness of the interviews.

In general, the members of the task force believed that Plan A had a low probability of successfully achieving the required objectives. Also, although the investment needed to implement the plan was thought to be the lowest, the expected results were similarly valued low.

Plan B would afford the company an opportunity to more closely match the capabilities of the selected individual to the requirements of the job, thereby improving the probability of successfully achieving the objectives. Also, this approach would have less effect on existing operations than if an existing employee were transferred out of a critical position into the new slot.

On the minus side, Plan B would require a considerable amount of time just getting to the point where the program could begin. Preparing the job description, advertising, screening applicants, selecting and hiring, orientation—all these activities would have to precede the actual planning and execution of the program.

In considering the level of investment required for Plan B, the task force concluded that it probably would cost slightly more than Plan A and would likely yield a better result.

The advantages of Plan C were seen to include the following:

- The resulting management development program would be specifically tailored to the needs of Buzzy by qualified, experienced professionals trained to recognize the critical problems and needs of the company.
- The time required to prepare and plan the selected management development program would be considerably shorter than that for Plans A and B.
- The probability of successfully achieving the company's objectives would be high based on the proven performance of the particular consulting firm selected.
- The routine company operations would incur minimal disruption, since most of the effort would be performed by people outside them.

The only disadvantage seen by the task force was the somewhat higher ongoing cost of conducting the program, compared with what it would cost to use one of the so-called in-house plans.

THE BEST SOLUTION

The task force selected Plan C, stating the following reasons orally to Lou at the next staff meeting:

- Shortest time to implement the program
- Highest probability of successfully achieving program objectives
- Least effect on routine company operations
- Most reasonable investment based on expected return

After considering several possible consulting firms for the plan C assignment, the task force selected Burke and Associates based on its earlier involvement and its acknowledged reputation as a leader in its field.

IMPLEMENTATION

The task force then wrote its report to Lou. The substance of its assignment was summarized briefly, followed by the problem definition, alternative solutions considered, evaluation of the alternatives, and conclusions and recommendations for subsequent action.

Lou accepted the conclusions and recommendations of the task force, thanked its members for their participation in this special assignment, and relieved them of any further responsibilities. He then directed Dave to proceed with the approach recommended by the task force.

Shortly thereafter, in response to a request from Dave, Burke and Associates submitted its proposal for instituting a management development program at Buzzy. The program, to be coordinated and administered by the Human Resource Department, was designed for individuals responsible for developing strategies for human effectiveness within their organization. The program addressed five major areas of interest and concern:

1. *Communication Laboratory:* A one-day session aimed at solidifying the work group into a team. The method includes both structural and nonstructural techniques. Communication barriers are examined and approaches to alleviating the problems are developed.
2. *Managing Management Time:* A one-day seminar that examines the content of a manager's day as opposed to the efficiency with which he or she carries out activities. Special considerations include the art of delegation, the rightful assumption of responsibility, and the use of leverage in time management.
3. *Motivation and Job Enrichment:* A one-day seminar exploring a basic philosophy of management relating to people. Consideration is given to needs that on the surface appear to be motivational but are not. The actual motivation needs are explored with an eye to immediate practical application. The application of motivation concepts to the task of job enrichment is featured.
4. *Managerial Performance Standards:* A one-day seminar in which managers learn the technique of writing managerial performance standards. They study the methods of determining with their supervisor how they will be quantifiably measured before the performance review takes place. Specific emphasis is placed on effective performance review, and controlling performance standards is discussed.
5. *Development Sessions:* A series of development sessions conducted every fourth Friday, covering such items as problem analysis, decision making, conference skills, managerial skills, technical skills as related to budgeting and finance, organizational structure, and the like. These seminars are given by individuals having expertise in these categories.

After reading this proposal, Dave smiled to himself and began to prepare the necessary internal papers to begin the program. ◉

SOURCE: B. Evans and H. L. French, Jr. This case is adapted from *Case Problems in Personnel and Human Resource Management,* ed. R. S. Schuler and S. A. Youngblood (St. Paul, MN: West Publishing Co., 1986).

Performance Appraisal: Measuring Who Is Doing What Well

The company views each employee's performance strategically as a means to help Chaparral gain competitive advantage. To accomplish this, the company links careful selection and training programs with performance expectations. In addition, Chaparral's basic philosophy of pushing decision making to the lowest level in the company has resulted in employees taking responsibility for self-management.

GORDON E. FORWARD, President, Chaparral Steel Company[1]

The term *mystery shopper* may conjure up the image of a detective meticulously tasting a firm's product or peering through a magnifying glass to look for the secret ingredient—but Au Bon Pain Company's mystery shoppers are nothing like this caricature. Instead, they are normal people who are paid $10 a visit to be part of the Boston-based restaurant chain's team-based performance appraisal program. According to Ron M. Shaich, Au Bon Pain's co–chief executive, the program is designed to ensure that the company meets its corporate mandate of attaining excellence in product, environment, and service. "If you've got customers, you ought to be looking at what you do through a customer's eyes," he contends.

With 1,250 full-time and 3,000 part-time people on its payroll, evaluating performance was not an easy task for the $135 million–plus 225-store firm—that is, until it implemented its mystery shopper program. Now, anonymous non-company-affiliated customers, recruited through newspaper advertising, buy meals and fill out behavior-based appraisals on the restaurants, their food, and their service. Before actually evaluating performance, all shoppers receive a three-hour training session on the company's customer service philosophy, and are given samples of the food as it should be prepared so that they can effectively evaluate how it was prepared.

The mystery shoppers visit each store three times over four weeks, during breakfast, lunch, and dinner. They spend at least twenty minutes—thirty is average—during their visits. More visits are made if a district manager is concerned about the service or cleanliness of a particular unit. Other hospitality firms shop more or less frequently than does Au Bon Pain; the important thing, Shaich contends, "is that the appraisal be systematic and statistically significant."

Figuring out what to target in the area of food, environment, and service was not simple. The num-

ber of questions on the evaluation form has been whittled down from a high of two hundred to the current sixty. Some questions, such as, "Does the rail in front of the counter have smudge marks on it?" have been pulled in favor of instructions more critical to measuring quality and service, such as, "Note a small piece of trash (straw, napkins, etc.) or an area of crumbs or other minor spills on the floor. Check Yes if cleaned within 10 minutes."

Performance appraisal also involves areas that the mystery customers cannot evaluate. District managers check up on such things as whether cooked chicken is being kept warm at 140 degrees Fahrenheit, and in-house managers monitor the performance of bakers, prep people, and cleanup crews.

PEGS FORMULA

Au Bon Pain's appraisal system is entitled PEGS—Product, Environment, and Great Service—and focuses on the twelve specific criteria Au Bon Pain feels are most important to attaining its corporate mission. Questions assess everything from food availability to length of waiting time to whether the server restated the order when it was handed to the customer. PEGS scores are tallied (e.g., ten of twelve criteria met) and transformed into a percentile ranking (e.g., 83.3 percent).

According to Joy Pomeroy, the company's first store manager and current head of Retail Quality Control, the program has significantly improved customer service because employees now know what is expected of them and receive feedback on how well they met expectations. Overall site performance scores have risen from an average of 72 percent to an average of 82 percent. Approximately twenty people from stores receive rave reviews each week, about the same number as when the program was launched.[2]

Au Bon Pain's mystery shopper program shows how the performance appraisal process can help an organization implement its business objectives. In addition, it typifies the way strategic plans can be linked to performance appraisal for individual employees as well as for business units. Au Bon Pain's performance appraisal process is strategic because it helps the company meet its customer service and food quality objectives. The process incorporates many of the components of a system that is capable of eliciting peak performance among employees at all levels. Performance expectations are communicated to employees in advance. The goals are difficult but attainable. Individual and strategic business unit goals are intertwined. Raters are trained and have an opportunity to observe performance. Feedback is immediate, precise, and behaviorally based. In addition, valued rewards are linked to performance outcomes.

PERFORMANCE APPRAISAL

Employees may learn about how well they are performing through informal means, such as by favorable comments from coworkers, but *performance appraisal* refers to a formal, structured system for measuring, evaluating, and influencing an employee's job-related attributes, behaviors, and outcomes, including absenteeism. Its focus is on discovering how productive the employee is and whether he or she can perform as or more effectively in the future, so that the employee, the organization, and society all benefit.[3] The terms performance appraisal and performance evaluation can be used interchangeably.

This chapter describes performance appraisal more completely, delineates system objectives, and reviews components of an effective performance appraisal system. It also examines the determinants of performance appraisal,[4] and discusses some ethical issues associated with electronic monitoring. Chapter 11 describes in more detail how to ensure that the entire performance management system works to maximize performance.

PURPOSES AND IMPORTANCE OF PERFORMANCE APPRAISAL

A recent study identified twenty different purposes of performance information, which can be grouped into four categories: (1) evaluations that emphasize between-person comparisons, (2) development that emphasizes changes within a person over time, (3) systems maintenance, and (4) documentation of human resource decisions (see Exhibit 10.1).[5] Increasingly, a fifth category is being added: alignment of appraisal with the needs of the business. This is illustrated in the feature "Managing Human Resources for the 21st Century at Au Bon Pain."

Aligning Performance Appraisal with the Business

How effectively the performance appraisal system achieves the twenty purposes shown in Exhibit 10.1 depends on how successfully the organization aligns and integrates performance appraisal with strategic business objectives. Performance appraisals are integrated with strategic objectives for a variety of reasons. First, strategic performance appraisal, as it is called when linked to the business, aligns the goals of the individual with those of the organization; that is, it embodies the description of actions employees must exhibit and results they must achieve to make a strategy come alive.[6] Second, such a process provides a means for measuring the contribution of each work unit and each employee. Third, performance evaluation contributes to the administrative actions and decisions that enhance and facilitate strategy, such as assessing current skill levels of employees and planning how to prepare the workforce for the future.

Performance information can be particularly useful during strategic transformation, which often requires new or different skill mixes. For example, when Kodak made a strategic shift, it recognized it would need engineers familiar with photo processing and electronics to carry out new corporate objectives and move the firm into new markets.

■ *Exhibit 10.1*

Top Twenty Uses of Performance Appraisal Information

Use	Rating*	Rank
Between-Person Evaluation		
Salary administration	5.6	2
Recognition of individual performance	5.0	5
Identification of poor performance	5.0	5
Promotion decisions	4.8	8
Retention and termination decisions	4.8	8
Layoffs	3.5	13
Within-Person Development		
Performance feedback	5.7	1
Identification of individual strengths and weaknesses	5.4	3
Determination of transfers and assignments	3.7	12
Identification of individual training needs	3.4	14
Systems Maintenance		
Development of individual corporate goals	4.9	7
Evaluation of goal attainment by individuals, teams, and strategic business units	4.7	10
Human resource planning	2.7	15
Determination of organizational training needs	2.7	15
Reinforcement of authority structure	2.6	17
Identification of organizational development needs	2.6	17
Human resource system auditing	2.0	20
Documentation		
Documentation of HR management decisions	5.2	4
Meeting of HR management legal requirements	4.6	11
Criteria for validation research	2.3	19

*Ratings were based on a seven-point scale measuring the effect of appraisal on different organizational decisions and action, where 1 = No Effect, 4 = Moderate Effect, and 7 = Primary Determinant.

SOURCE: Based on J. N. Cleveland, K. R. Murphy, and R. E. Williams, "Multiple Uses of Performance Appraisal: Prevalence and Correlates," *Journal of Applied Psychology* 74 (February 1989): 130–35.

Kodak's strategic alternatives ranged from developing the skills of existing employees to acquiring engineers from the outside. On first thought, hiring engineers from the outside was appealing; a more careful analysis showed it would be more effective to train existing employees—namely, the chemists who would otherwise no longer be needed with the implementation of the new strategy—to handle engineering responsibilities. In choosing this alternative, Kodak recognized that its chemists already had a strong scientific background. More important, they had a detailed knowledge of the photo processing industry and a well-grounded commitment to Kodak. Kodak set up corporate-sponsored technical training. An arrangement was made with a nearby university for the chemists to earn their engineering degrees. For Kodak, this strategic decision was easier to make because its appraisal process made available information regarding the competencies of current employees.

The fourth and final reason for linking appraisal with the needs of the business is its potential to identify the need for *new* strategies and programs. At Pepsi-Cola International, the overall business goal is to accelerate corporate growth ahead of global market growth. To achieve this objective, the company conducts upward, or reverse, evaluations regularly. Performance information recently pointed to a deficiency in corporate training. To address this deficiency, the multinational firm established an umbrella organization to deliver training programs around the world. Performance data also were the catalyst for the development of Pepsi-Cola International's Designate Program. This program brings non–U.S. citizens to the United States for a minimum of eighteen months of training in the domestic Pepsi system. The program was developed to provide in-depth experiential training that would build a skill base among expatriate employees, because appraisals indicated skill deficiencies. Having a knowledgeable workforce was viewed as a necessary first step in attaining Pepsi-Cola International's overall growth objective and its under-lying business goal of developing talented people to drive the growth in Pepsi brands.[7]

Roadblocks in Aligning Performance Appraisal with the Business

Organizations are not always successful in using performance appraisals strategically with the business. One reason is that line managers do not fully understand performance appraisal basics. Most managers spend far more time acquiring technical competencies (e.g., in the areas of accounting, marketing, and operations management) for entry into an organization than they do learning to manage human resources. Yet, skillfully managing performance appraisals can help line managers achieve their corporate mandate to get things done through other people.

   Another roadblock to the effective use of performance appraisals is that managers fail to see the payoff for conducting them. A recent study shows that most organizations offer no obvious organizational incentives for managers to do a good job of appraising employee performance. In fact, usually, managers so dislike the associated excessive paperwork and unpleasant confrontations with employees that they try to avoid the process entirely. This, of course, is shortsighted.

   A third reason performance appraisals fall short of achieving strategic objectives is the ambiguity around who owns responsibility for managing human resources. Does performance management fall in the domain of human resource departments or line departments?[8] But debates about who is responsible miss the point. Line managers, HR professionals, and employees all need to work in partnership to ensure that appraisals are effective and fair to everyone concerned (see the feature "Partnership in Performance Appraisal"). Without doubt, when appraisal is aligned with the business, everyone's knowledge can be very useful. And without doubt, everyone should be knowledgeable about how the appraisal process fits within a system of performance management practices.[9]

LEGAL CONSIDERATIONS IN PERFORMANCE APPRAISAL

As shown in Exhibit 10.1, performance information partly determines pay, promotions, terminations, transfers, and other types of key decisions that affect both the well-being of employees and the productivity of a company. Thus, society has a vested interest in seeing to it that high-quality information is used for these important decisions. Numerous pieces of legislation and court decisions provide guidance in how to collect and use performance information that serves the legitimate concerns of business while protecting the rights of employees. Particularly relevant are the Civil Rights Acts of 1964 and 1991, the Americans with Disabilities Act of 1990, and the Age Discrimination in Employment Act of 1967.

   When companies make employment decisions on the basis of performance apprais-als, they are in effect using the appraisals as selection criteria. Thus, the appraisals must be based on identifiable job-related criteria (*Stringfellow v. Monsanto Corporation*, 1970; *United States v. City of Chicago,* 1978). For example, the U.S. circuit court in *Brito v. Zia*

Partnership in Performance Appraisal

Line Managers	Human Resource Professionals	Employees
Work with HR professionals and employees to develop business-relevant criteria for appraisals.	Work with line managers and employees to develop the criteria for appraisals.	Work with line managers and HR professionals to develop criteria for appraisals.
Develop an understanding of how common appraisal errors can be avoided.	Coordinate the administrative aspects of the appraisal process.	Maybe appraise the work of other employees.
Fill out appraisal forms carefully and conscientiously.	Train everyone who provides appraisal information (e.g., peers, subordinates, and supervisors) how to avoid errors in appraisal.	Maybe appraise personal performance.
Give constructive and honest feedback to employees.	Train line managers to give feedback.	Maybe appraise the boss.
Seek and accept constructive feedback about personal performance.	Support line managers in efforts to keep the performance management system going.	Seek and accept constructive and honest feedback.
Use performance information for decision making.		Strive to improve personal performance.

Company (1973) found that Zia Company was in violation of Title VII when a disproportionate number of employees of a protected group were laid off because of low performance scores. The critical point was that the performance scores were based on the supervisor's best judgments and opinions, not on important components of doing the job. The best way to determine whether appraisal criteria are job related is to do a job analysis (*Albemarle Paper Company v. Moody*, 1975). Then, using a content validity argument, the employer can show that the performance appraisal system is designed to ensure that performance scores reflect the important components of the job.[10]

Once the appropriate performance criteria are established, standards for defining the degree of desirability or acceptability of employee performance on each job criterion are established. To ensure that all aspects of job performance are assessed, several criteria may be required. In such cases, a performance standard must be established for each criterion. Establishing standards is necessary for legal considerations, and it is also consistent with management principles for ensuring adequate job performance.[11] For example, it would be unreasonable to expect an employee to put in the extra effort and overtime that may be needed to reach a standard for performance if the employee is unaware of what the standard is. From the employee's perspective, using performance standards that were never communicated to the employee would be viewed as unfair, as well. Consistent with these arguments, the courts have established that employers are responsible for communicating performance expectations to incumbents in advance of the evaluating period. In *Donaldson v. Pillsbury Company* (1977), an employee who was dismissed was granted relief because she had never been shown her job description, which would have specified performance criteria.[12]

In most companies, the performance appraisal process includes the use of paper-and-pencil appraisal forms. The content of these forms should reflect the critical job components. For example, if output quantity is a critical performance criterion, appraisal forms that ask supervisors to indicate general impressions—such as how "personable" or "valuable" the employee is—may lead to an inappropriately negative appraisal. Then, if the appraisal result is used to justify a negative employment decision, the affected employee may have sufficient evidence to establish a prima facie case of illegal discrimination.

Appraisal forms on which the raters checkmark attributes such as leadership, attitude toward people, or loyalty are often referred to as *subjective forms*. In contrast, appraisal forms where the evaluation involves specifically defined behaviors or outcomes—such as level of output, level of specific goal attainment, or number of days absent—are often called *objective forms*. Although the law does not prohibit the use of subjective forms (*Roger v. International Paper Company*, 1975), the courts generally frown upon it (*Albemarle Paper Company v. Moody*, 1975); *Oshiver v. Court of Common Pleas*, 1979; *Baxter v. Savannah Sugar Refining Corporation*, 1974; *Rowe v. General Motors*, 1972) because it may not produce fair or accurate evaluations. Consequently, the courts have ruled that when disparate impact is found, all performance appraisal procedures—objective or subjective—must be shown to be job related (*Watson v. Fort Worth Bank and Trust*, 1988).

A condensed set of recommended actions for developing and implementing a legally defensible appraisal system is detailed in Exhibit 10.2. All these recommendations are also consistent with the development of an effective performance management system that is linked strategically to business objectives.

 ## ACTIVITIES AND PROCESSES FOR A PERFORMANCE MANAGEMENT SYSTEM

The entire set of activities that support the development and use of performance appraisals is often referred to as the performance management system. The general steps

■ *Exhibit 10.2*
Prescriptions for Legally Defensible Appraisal Systems

1. Job analysis to identify important duties and tasks should precede development of a performance appraisal system.
2. The performance appraisal system should be standardized and formal.
3. Specific performance standards should be communicated to employees in advance of the appraisal period.
4. Objective and uncontaminated data should be used whenever possible.
5. Ratings on traits such as dependability, drive, or attitude should be avoided or operationalized in behavioral terms.
6. Employees should be evaluated on specific work dimensions rather than on a single global or overall measure.
7. If work behaviors rather than outcomes are to be evaluated, evaluators should have ample opportunity to observe ratee performance.
8. To increase the reliability of ratings, more than one independent evaluator should perform appraisals whenever possible.
9. Behavioral documentation should be prepared for extreme ratings.
10. Employees should be given an opportunity to review their appraisals.
11. A formal system of appeal should be available for appraisal disagreements.
12. Raters should be trained to prevent discrimination and to evaluate performance consistently.
13. Appraisals should be frequent, offered at least annually.

SOURCE: Adapted from H. J. Bernardin and W. F. Cascio, "Performance Appraisal and the Law," in *Readings in Personnel and Human Resource Management*, 3d ed., ed. R. S. Schuler, S. A. Youngblood, and V. L. Huber (St. Paul: West Publishing Co., 1988): 239.

in developing a performance management system are detailed in Exhibit 10.3. Exhibit 10.4 shows the components that make up AT&T's Global Business Communications Systems' approach to performance management, which it refers to as Performance Excellence Partnership (PEP). How well the system works depends in part on how well everyone works together when deciding what to evaluate, when to conduct appraisals, and who should evaluate performance.

What to Evaluate

Once the important job duties and tasks are delineated, performance criteria can be developed. *Criteria* are dimensions against which the performance of an incumbent, a team, or a work unit is evaluated. Together, they are the performance expectations individuals and teams strive for in order to achieve the organization's strategy. If jobs have been designed well, with attention paid to how job demands relate to strategic business needs, then conducting a job analysis should ensure that performance appraisals reflect strategic concerns. The job analysis should also capture the more general role expectations held for members of the organization. These expectations often have more to do with organizational citizenship behavior than with job performance per se, but they may be no less important to measure and attempt to improve.[13] Examples of these behaviors include:

■ *Exhibit 10.3*
Steps in Developing a Performance Management System

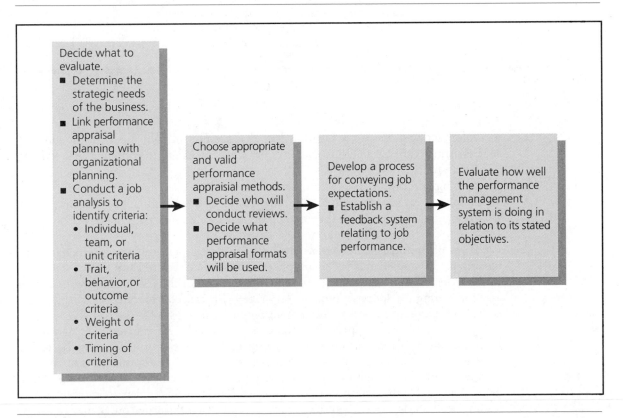

■ *Exhibit 10.4*
GBCS's Performance Excellence Partnership

Component	Purpose	Human Resource Critical Focus Area*
Objective setting	Focuses on objectives and drives performance. Must be realistic and linked to the business goals. Must be specific, measurable, achievable, relevant, and timely (SMART). Is monitored a minimum of three times a year.	O
Performance feedback	Is an ongoing process that provides valid, constructive developmental feedback related to objective attainment. Must be SMART and given a minimum of three times a year.	O
Annual performance review	Focuses on achievement of objectives, how they were achieved, criticality to the business, and degree of difficulty. January 1993, GBCS converted to a merit review process based on AT&T service anniversary date, for management associates. This reinforces objective setting as an ongoing process for the total team.	O
Upward feedback	Provides associates the opportunity to give anonymous feedback to coaches regarding specific dimensions of leadership and behavior related to values.	O
Development	Consists of planning and implementing actions designed to enhance individual and team performance. Examples include training, education, task force assignments and so forth.	O
Reward and recognition	Are key elements of PEP's success. Take many forms, such as noncash awards, unique work assignments, and so forth. GBCS's recognition and compensation systems are specifically designed to recognize or pay associates for behaviors and results that are part of PEP and contribute to GBCS's success.	R

*R = Rewards and Recognition, O = Ownership.
SOURCE: Adapted from M. J. Plevel et al., "AT&T Global Business Communications Systems: Linking HR with Business Strategy," *Organizational Dynamics* (winter 1994): 66.

◉ Volunteering to carry out task activities that are not formally a part of the job
◉ Persisting with extra enthusiasm or effort when necessary to complete task activities successfully
◉ Helping and cooperating with others
◉ Following organizational rules and procedures even when doing so is inconvenient
◉ Endorsing, supporting, and defending organizational objectives[14]

Types of Performance Criteria. Three basic types of performance criteria have been identified. *Trait-based criteria* focus on the personal characteristics of an employee. Loyalty, dependability, communication ability, and leadership skill exemplify traits often assessed during the appraisal process. This type of criteria concentrates on what a person is, not what a person does or does not accomplish on the job.

Whereas trait-based appraisal instruments can easily be constructed, they may not be valid indicators of job performance. What is assessed as performance must be related directly to the job. Unfortunately, the link between traits and performance is often weak, or at least difficult to establish clearly because traits are difficult to define. To one person, being dependable may mean showing up to work on time every day; to another person, it may mean staying late when the boss requests it; to a third person, it may mean not using sick days even when you are really sick. Because of these concerns, trait-based performance measures are not generally defendable in the courts. This may seem to be at odds with the potential value placed on building a corporate culture around having the right kinds of people as defined by personal qualities that extend beyond job skills. Does the position of the courts mean that difficult-to-measure personal qualities should not be evaluated as part of the performance appraisal process? No; they can be included if the company can make a shift from a *trait* focus to a *behavioral* focus.

Behavior-based criteria focus on how work is performed. Such criteria are particularly important for jobs that involve interpersonal contact, such as those at Au Bon Pain. For example, whether cashiers are friendly and pleasant with Au Bon Pain's customers is critical to the image of the store in the minds of customers. Therefore, the company has generated a list of specific behaviors that employees should engage in, and these behaviors get measured by mystery shoppers.

As organizations struggle to create a culture in which diversity is valued and respected, behavioral criteria are proving useful for monitoring whether managers are investing sufficient energy in their own development. Imagine how difficult it would be to evaluate whether a manager achieved a traitlike criterion such as "Values the diversity of subordinates." A performance criterion like this provides little guidance to the manager about what actually to *do,* and would be equally difficult for the manager's superior to evaluate meaningfully (although subordinates may be quite willing to express their opinions!). For the purpose of performance management, more effective criteria would be specific behaviors. For example, one company uses the following items to assess management accountability for diversity:

- Does your business plan include a diversity strategy?
- Are you a member of a diversity focus group or steering committee?
- Have you attended a diversity workshop or seminar during the past twelve months?
- What percentage of employees in your organization have individual development plans?
- Has your organization formed a diversity focus group?
- Has anyone in your organization filed complaints of discrimination or harassment during the past twelve months? If yes, what is their current status?

Behavioral criteria, when combined with performance feedback, are particularly useful for employee development. With behaviors clearly identified, an employee is more likely to exhibit the acts that lead to peak performance. Behavioral criteria are less appropriate for jobs in which effective performance can be achieved using many different behaviors. Still, even in these jobs, the identification of the most appropriate behaviors serves as a useful guideline for most employees' actions. Because they relate specifically to what employees do on the job, behavioral criteria tend to be legally defensible.

With the increased emphasis on productivity and international competitiveness, *outcome-based criteria* are enjoying rising popularity. These criteria focus on what was accomplished or produced rather than on how it was accomplished or produced. Outcome-based criteria may be appropriate if the company does not care how results are achieved, but they are not appropriate for every job. They are often criticized for missing critical but evasive aspects of the job—such as quality, which may be difficult to quantify. For example, the number of cases handled annually by a lawyer can easily be counted, but the result will not indicate the quality of legal counsel given or the resolution of the cases. For another example, it is far easier to assess the number of word processing errors an administrative assistant makes than it is to assess his skill in screening office calls and visitors.

Furthermore, a results-at-all-costs mentality may plague outcome-based appraisals. For example, a collection agency used the outcome-based criteria "Collects large sums of money" as its sole measure of performance. Although large sums of money were collected, the agency ended up being sued because its agents used threats and punitive measures to amass collections.

Linkage to Organizational Goals. Regardless of which type of criteria get measured during the appraisal process, the performance management system becomes strategic to the extent that these criteria are clearly linked to organizational goals. This linkage almost always involves an inferential leap. Consider the job of assistant vice president in a bank. Behavioral criteria for this job may include "Phones arbitrageurs and traders within ten minutes of order receipt." Outcome-based criteria may include "Generates $5 million in sales each month." For both criteria, the strategic linkage assumes that an aggregation of these individual performances relates to total profitability of the bank for a specific quarter. Line managers must evaluate whether such assumptions are reasonable. If they are not, managers should ensure that better criteria are developed.

Single or Multiple Criteria. Coordinating market activities may be the only duty for a particular job. More often, however, jobs are composed of many different duties and related tasks. For the assistant vice president job of a market research firm, the primary duty of coordinating market activities may be accompanied by other duties such as staying abreast of current events and closing out daily market activities. If job analysis identifies all these duties as important, all should be measured by the performance appraisal instrument.

If the form used to appraise employee performance lacks the job behaviors and results that are important and relevant to the job, the form is said to be *deficient*. If the form appraises anything either unimportant or irrelevant to the job, it is *contaminated*. Unfortunately, many performance appraisal forms used in organizations today are deficient and contaminated.

One theory of performance suggests that a limited set of performance domains can be used to capture all aspects of nearly any job. This theory defines performance in terms of what people do, not what they produce. The eight domains thought to capture all aspects of performance are:

- Job-specific task performance
- Non-job-specific task performance (which includes tasks performed by everyone in a large group of jobs or a job family)
- Written and oral communications
- Effort (demonstrated consistently, frequently, and even under adverse conditions)
- Personal discipline (e.g., not engaging in substance abuse, following rules)
- Facilitation of peer and team performance (e.g., providing support and training, serving as a good role model)
- Supervision and leadership (positively influencing subordinates' performance)
- Management and administration (e.g., articulating goals for the enterprise, monitoring goal accomplishment, allocating resources).[15]

Not all jobs will include all these activities. Nevertheless, this general taxonomy may serve as a useful checklist when thinking through the types of criteria that might be relevant to a particular job.

Weighting of Criteria. For jobs involving more than one duty, another question must be asked: "How should these separate aspects of performance be combined into a composite score that facilitates comparisons of incumbents?" One way is to weight all the criteria equally. The simplest approach is to use weights generated through job analysis. Statistical procedures such as multiple regression also can be used to determine appropriate weights for each job dimension. With these procedures, greater weights get assigned to dimensions that are most strongly associated with overall performance evaluations.

When to Evaluate

The timing of performance measurement should also reflect strategic considerations. Two aspects of timing are cycle length and appraisal dates.

Most organizations require formal performance review sessions at six-month to one-year intervals. This type of *regular cycle* makes some sense, since it fits with the natural rhythm of the organization. However, some experts argue that the evaluation period should correspond to the natural *time span of the job,* that is, the length of time it takes to recognize the performance level of someone who is doing the job. In the case of some simple, lower-level jobs, the time span may be as short as a few minutes; in the case of a senior-level management job, the appropriate time period may be as long as several years. In an advertising agency, account executives receive evaluation feedback after each presentation. In a research firm searching for a genetic marker, the time period would be much longer.[16]

Assessing performance on a cycle that roughly approximates the characteristics of the job can be advantageous. If performance is assessed before it can be reasonably measured, misassessment is likely. If the time period is too long, motivation and performance may suffer significantly. This is particularly detrimental in the case of a poor performer, who will likely not know how to improve performance until it is too late.

The evaluation period may also depend on the purpose of the appraisal. For communication and evaluation purposes, the focus should be on current employee performance during a single performance period. For promotion and training decisions, an examination of performance across multiple appraisal periods may be of use. If performance is steadily increasing or is consistently high, a promotion may be justified. If performance remains consistently low, training may be necessary.

Many organizations conduct performance appraisals according to when employees join the organization. This approach, referred to as the *anniversary model,* spreads out the workload for doing appraisal, making the appraisal task less overwhelming. However, the anniversary model typically does not tie individual or team performance to the overall performance of the organization, and thus compromises the strategic benefits of the appraisal process. Furthermore, research suggests that ratings given to employees early in the year are higher or more lenient than ratings given later. This is particularly likely if raters or appraisers must use a "curve" so that they can allocate only specific numbers of high and low ratings. A third drawback is that the organization does not know how the supervisor is appraising performance and therefore cannot determine how well the total organization is performing until the year is over and all evaluations have been completed.

Another common approach is called the *focal-point system.* In this system, all employees are appraised at approximately the same time, usually the end of the fiscal or calendar year. The major advantage of this system is that supervisors can look at all individuals, report to them, and get a sense of how their performances compare during the same time period. Similarly, top management can compare the performances of different strategic business units to assess how well they are meeting corporate objectives. Such comparative information is particularly important if performance information is used for compensation decisions. Because the link to compensation is central to Lincoln

Electric, its line managers spend up to two weeks doing appraisal. The HR department spends several weeks before this making sure the line managers have all the necessary data, for instance, on absenteeism and productivity.

One major disadvantage of focal-point reviews is that they produce a tremendous workload at one time. This burden can be reduced in two ways: first, by having clear criteria against which to evaluate performance, and second, by ensuring that subordinates share with their supervisors the responsibility for defining performance criteria and documenting accomplishments relative to performance standards.

Another major disadvantage of focal-point reviews is that they can create artificial productivity cycles that reflect merely the timing of appraisals. For example, if a law firm measures performance each year at the end of November for deciding bonus payouts, an employee's billable hours may begin to peak in the immediately preceding weeks and then drop below normal as everyone takes time to recover from the frenzy.

Who to Have Conduct the Evaluation

Sources of performance data include supervisors, employees themselves, peers or team members, subordinates, customers, and computer monitoring. The relevance of each source needs to be considered before the rating method is chosen.

Critical in determining who should conduct an appraisal are the amount and type of work contact the evaluator has with the person being evaluated. The quantity and quality of *task acquaintance* may vary with organizational level as well as with proximity of the worker and the rater.[17] Team members, customers, and subordinates see different facets of an individual's task behavior than do supervisors. For example, a customer is more likely to observe the behavior of a sale's representative—for instance, greeting the customer or closing the sale—than is a first-level supervisor. Similarly, customers are among the best observers for Au Bon Pain's employees, which is why that company has the mystery shopper element in its appraisal. The important point is that no one—not even the employee—has complete information. A worker may know what he or she has done but not be aware of the results of that behavior in terms of customers' reactions or the bottom line. On the other hand, a supervisor has access to more information about results and comparative sales performance than do employees or customers. Thus, involving multiple raters in the evaluation process generally is the best approach.

When evaluations from supervisors, subordinates, peers, and employees themselves are all used, they are often referred to as 360-degree appraisals. Such appraisals are especially useful for providing developmental feedback.

Appraisal by Superiors. The term *superior* in this context refers to the immediate boss of the subordinate being evaluated. Many companies assume that the superior knows the subordinate's job and performance better than anyone else and so give all the responsibility for appraisal to this person. However, appraisal by superiors has drawbacks. First, because superiors usually have power to reward and punish, subordinates may feel threatened. Second, the evaluation is often a one-way process that makes the subordinate feel defensive. Third, the superior may not have the necessary interpersonal skills to give good feedback. Thus, little coaching takes place; employees tend not really to hear the negative feedback they are given; and justification of actions prevails.

Because of the potential legal liabilities and the desire to have the best appraisal data possible, organizations often invite other people to share in the appraisal process. This increases the reliability and perceived fairness of the appraisal process. In addition, it creates greater openness in the performance appraisal system and enhances the quality of the superior-subordinate relationship. These benefits are not without cost, however.

Evaluations obtained from other sources often bypass natural lines of authority (organizational hierarchy) or reverse the usual authority structure (upward evaluations) and may be prohibited by contractual agreements (e.g., union-management contracts).[18]

Self-Appraisal. The use of self-appraisal, particularly through subordinate participation in setting goals, was made popular as a component of management by objectives, often referred to as MBO. Subordinates who participate in the evaluation process may become more involved and committed to the goals. Subordinate participation may also help clarify employees' roles and reduce role conflict.[19]

Companies such as Chaparral use self-appraisals because they are effective tools for programs focusing on self-development, personal growth, and goal commitment. However, self-appraisals are subject to systematic biases and distortions. Self-ratings often are more lenient than those obtained from supervisors, although they correspond more closely to supervisory ratings when extensive performance feedback is given, and when incumbents know that their ratings will be checked against objective criteria.[20]

A variant on self-appraisal is self-initiated appraisal. Roger Flax, president of Motivational Systems, a New Jersey management and sales training company, says: "There's a lot of assuming that in small companies employees are motivated so there's not a lot of formal appraisal. One answer may be the employee initiated appraisal in which employees are told they can ask for a review from their manager. The on-demand appraisal doesn't replace a conventional semi-annual review, but it promotes an attitude of self-management among workers and often makes critiques more honest."[21] Flax suggests that employees ask for as many reviews as they feel they need. Listed below are seven questions he believes employees should ask themselves and their managers in their self-initiated appraisals:

- On a scale of 1 to 10, how does my performance rate?
- What are the strongest elements of my work?
- What are the weakest elements?
- Why didn't I get a 10 (the highest rating)?
- Where can I go in my job or career in the next eighteen months to four years?
- What skills, training, or education do I need to get to that point?
- What specifically can we agree on that I can do, beginning tomorrow?

Although self-appraisals are being used by more and more companies in the United States, firms must exercise caution in interpreting their results. The feature "Using Data for the 21st Century: Cultural Differences" suggests that self-appraisal may be influenced by cultural differences.

Peer or Team-Member Appraisal. The use of team-member appraisals is likely to increase into the 21st century in light of corporate America's focus on employee participation, teamwork, and empowerment. One reason is that appraisals by peers have been shown to be useful predictors of future performance.[22] Another reason is that performance appraisals conducted on an individual basis do not contribute to the team-building efforts that are an important element in today's participative management style.

Team-member involvement in the appraisal process can take many different forms. Jamestown Advanced Products Incorporated, a small metal fabrication firm, had to deal with the issue of employee tardiness. According to the team members' assessment of the problem, one person's late arrival disrupted everyone else's schedule, reduced team performance, and consequently lowered financial bonuses. Traditionally, a tardy employee lost some wages but could still receive a quarterly performance bonus. Team

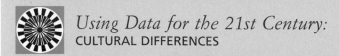

Using Data for the 21st Century:
CULTURAL DIFFERENCES

Are self-evaluations of performance always lenient? Do workers in collective cultures, which discourage boasting about individual accomplishments, evaluate performance the same way as American workers do? Or is the leniency bias merely a product of Western culture's emphasis on individuality? As the world economy becomes globalized and more multinational firms find themselves operating in many different countries, these questions become more important. Also, a growing portion of the U.S. labor force includes people with non-Western cultural backgrounds. How will this diversity affect the performance evaluations used by companies to make important decisions?

In Western cultures, subordinates tend to evaluate themselves more favorably than do their supervisors. This effect occurs across different types of employees (clerical, managerial, blue-collar), for different types of rating scales, and for appraisal done for different purposes. Leniency in self-ratings is consistent with the notion that people view themselves in a positive light. The tendency to have a positive self-image and to project a positive self-image to others is common in Western culture, which stresses individual achievement, self-sufficiency, and self-respect. In contrast, collectivistic cultures encourage interpersonal harmony, interdependence, solidarity, and group cohesiveness. They do not draw attention to individual achievements in the interest of interpersonal harmony.

Are workers in collectivistic cultures more modest than their American counterparts when it comes to rating their own job performance? To find out, an international team of researchers examined the performance ratings of over nine-hundred pairs of supervisors and their subordinates. The ratings of people working in the Republic of China (Taiwan) were compared with those of American supervisors. In conducting this cross-cultural research, English-language versions of the rating scales were translated into Chinese and then translated back into English to be sure that a good translation had been achieved.

When Chinese workers evaluated their own job performance and their own desire to work, they gave themselves lower ratings than did their supervisors. Their ratings were also lower than the ones American workers gave to themselves. Consistent with the belief of collectivistic cultures that wisdom comes with age, younger workers rated themselves lower than did their supervisors, and the self-ratings of younger workers were lower than those of older workers.

The researchers concluded that the use of self-ratings by multinational firms may create bias against Chinese employees and against other employees from collectivistic cultures. Such employees may rate themselves lower than equally performing Anglo-Americans. Also, Chinese employees may be reluctant to engage in impression management behaviors and self-promotion (e.g., making sure their supervisor knows about their accomplishments). As a result, their supervisors may give them lower ratings than they deserve. If the ratings are used for evaluation purposes, the result may be unintended discrimination and unfair treatment, as well as lower morale and ineffective use of the best talent.[23]

members thought this was not fair. The work team was encouraged to set performance standards for its members and to identify consequences for low performance. After the team batted around the issue of how much lateness or absenteeism it could tolerate and how punitive it should be, it reached agreement: employees could be tardy—defined as one minute late—or absent without notice no more than five times a quarter. Beyond that, they would lose their entire bonus.

In addition to defining performance expectations, Jamestown team members commonly serve as evaluators; the coworker who is at an individual's side all day has an excellent opportunity to observe that individual's behavior. Common performance dimensions on which team members have evaluation expertise include

- Attendance and timeliness (e.g., "Attends scheduled group meetings")
- Interpersonal skills (e.g., "Is willing to give and take on issues," "Is not unreasonably stubborn")
- Group supportiveness (e.g., "Offers ideas or suggestions for the group to use on the project," "Supports group decisions")
- Planning and coordination (e.g., "Contributes input to help other team members perform their assignments")[24]

Firms such as Jamestown have learned that team members may also provide useful information for evaluating how well the team as a whole is functioning. Exhibit 10.5 is a measure containing statements that can be used to assess overall team cohesiveness, drive (motivation), and productivity. Using this measure, different groups can be compared with each other or the same group can be compared at different points in time. Line managers and HR professionals can use both member appraisal and overall appraisal to help employees analyze their teams and improve team effectiveness.

Upward, or Reverse, Appraisal. Organizations such as Johnson and Johnson and Sears have been surveying employees for their opinions of management for years, but in general, this type of appraisal, called *upward appraisal* or *reverse appraisal,* is still catching on. Major firms that are out in the front of this movement include Amoco Corporation,

---

■ *Exhibit 10.5*

Representative Appraisal Statements to Measure Team Cohesiveness, Drive, and Perceived Productivity

---

Please describe the extent of your agreement with the following statements:

Cohesiveness
1. The people in my work group pitch in to help each other.
2. The people in my work group do not get along with each other.
3. The people in my work group take an interest in each other.
4. The members of my work group share a lot of team spirit.
5. The members of my work group regard each other as friends.
6. The members of my group are very cooperative with each other.
7. My group's members know that they can depend on each other.
8. My group's members stand up for each other.
9. The members of my group work together as a team.

Drive
10. My group tackles a job with enthusiasm.
11. The group I work with has quit trying. (R)
12. My group is full of vim and vigor.
13. The work of my group seems to drag. (R)
14. My group works hard on any job it undertakes.
15. My group shows a lot of pep and enthusiasm.

Productivity
16. My group turns out more work than most groups in the company.
17. My group turns out as much work as our supervisor expects.
18. My group has an excellent production record.
19. My group gets a job done on time.
20. My work group has an excellent production record.

Note: Items are scored on a 1–7 scale, with 1 being Strongly Disagree and 7 being Strongly Agree. Items marked with "(R)" should be reverse scored.

SOURCE: Based on R. M. Stogdill, *Group Productivity, Drive and Cohesiveness* (Columbus, OH: Bureau of Business Research, 1965): 65–75.

Chrysler, Cigna, and DuPont. These firms use subordinates' ratings of how their bosses manage in order to improve operations, make their organizations less hierarchical, and develop better managers.[25] For example: "Employee requests prompted Amoco to adopt an upward appraisal system. The system includes a voluntary employee questionnaire that solicits feedback on a supervisor's participative leadership, creativity, and performance management. The questionnaire—titled the "Leadership Development Process"—has been computerized to allow employees to answer anonymously from their own terminals. Feedback results are incorporated into Amoco's week-long, mandatory training sessions for middle-level managers."[26]

Although subordinates often do not have access to information about all dimensions of supervisory performance, they do have frequent access to information about supervisor-subordinate interactions. When asked, for example, subordinates usually complain that they do not get enough feedback.

One drawback to upward feedback is that subordinates may not always evaluate performance objectively or honestly, especially if their ratings are not anonymous.[27] To protect anonymity, evaluations need to be made by at least three or four subordinates and turned in to someone other than the supervisor being evaluated.

Customer Appraisal. As the feature on Au Bon Pain illustrated, appraisals by customers are appropriate in a variety of contexts. For example, a medical clinic in Billings, Montana, routinely has patients rate desk attendants and nursing personnel on behaviors such as courtesy, promptness, and quality of care. Domino's Pizza hires mystery customers who order pizzas and then evaluate the performance of the telephone operator and delivery person. Doyle Ripley, owner of a carpeting firm in Utah, uses a customer checklist to monitor the on-site performance of carpet installers (see Exhibit 10.6). According to Ripley: "When you've got installers out on jobs everywhere, it's impossible to check their work. The advantage of our appraisal instrument is that it educates customers regarding what to look for in a quality installation job. Simultaneously, it provides us with inexpensive performance feedback. From the installer's perspective, the system works well because any problems can be resolved immediately without being recalled back to the job." To encourage customers to return the surveys, Ripley holds a monthly drawing for free carpet shampooing. Installers with the highest ratings are recognized monetarily and praised verbally.

Computer Monitoring. Owing to new technology, it is becoming increasingly easy to gather performance data by computer.[28]

Based on a survey of 301 U.S. employers, the study estimates that 20 million Americans may be subject to electronic monitoring other than telephone monitoring.

Employers typically monitor employees to check work flow, investigate theft, review job performance, prevent harassment, prevent personal use of software, and investigate industrial espionage, according to a study released by the International Labor Organization. U.S. workers are most susceptible to being monitored, the study adds, because there currently are no laws in the United States to restrict employers from using such practices. In contrast, Austria, Belgium, Germany, the Netherlands, and Sweden restrict the use of technical devices to monitor employee behavior and performance. In these countries, the study notes, employees must agree to monitoring or at least be consulted before electronic surveillance commences.[29]

Although computer monitoring may be fast and seemingly objective, many employees have become concerned enough to raise several legal and ethical questions, including, Do we have a right to privacy? and Is it ethical to monitor employee whereabouts constantly? In addition to an increase in stress, musculoskeletal problems, and headaches, electronic surveillance can result in paced work, apathy, reduced peer social

■ *Exhibit 10.6*
Sample Customer Evaluation Form for a Carpet Installer

Name _____ Date _____

Address _____

Your business and satisfaction are important to us. To help ensure quality installation and service, we would appreciate your help in completing this postage-paid evaluation form and returning it to our store. Each statement is intended to describe and point out things to look for in a quality installation. This completed evaluation form will qualify you for our monthly drawing, good for two free rooms of carpet cleaning, which can be used within one year from the date of this drawing.

Please circle *Y* if the installer met the statement or *N* if the installer did not meet the statement.
1. Y N The installer consulted with the customer on the location of all seams and placed them in the most desired areas.
2. Y N All seams were located in closets or low-traffic areas other than doorways.
3. Y N The seams are not visible.
4. Y N The seams feel secure.
5. Y N The installer avoided property damage (e.g., scratches or mars on baseboards, walls, or doors) while installing carpet.
6. Y N The installer stretched the carpet tightly enough to avoid all wrinkles, waves, and bubbles.
7. Y N The installer trimmed and tucked all carpet edges flush with walls or metal stripping or both.
8. Y N The installer cleaned up the entire area, leaving no scraps.
9. Y N The installer went over the job with the customer and ensured satisfaction.

Additional Comments (use the back of this form if necessary): _____

_____

_____

_____

For office use only

SCORE _____
(Y = 3, N = 0)

SOURCE: Modified from a project report submitted by D. Ripley et al. (University of Utah, 1987).

support, fear of job loss, and lack of control over tasks, the study concludes.[30] More discussion and advice on electronic monitoring is in the feature "Positioning for the 21st Century: Electronic Employee Monitoring."

❖ PERFORMANCE APPRAISAL FORMATS

The development of a rating format follows systematic job analysis, the identification of criteria and appropriate raters, and decisions about the timing of appraisals. Although direct measures for performance appraisal are available for some jobs, by far the most widely used formats are judgmental. The simplest classifications are the norm-referenced, absolute standards, and output-based formats, each of which may be supplemented by essays.[31]

Norm-Referenced Appraisals

For many types of human resource decisions, the fundamental questions often are, Who is the best performer in the group? Who should be retained, given that we have to cut

Positioning for the 21st Century:
ELECTRONIC EMPLOYEE MONITORING

Electronic monitoring comes in several forms. Computers can measure the output of machine operators, the number of calls made by a telemarketer, or the number of keystrokes or entries made by computer operators. Customer service telephone conversations can be recorded or monitored live.

Monitoring the performance of employees is the subject of growing controversy. Backers of privacy rights point not only to privacy concerns but also to studies indicating that electronic monitoring in the workplace increases stress.

CONSIDER PRIVACY RIGHTS

Although the U.S. Constitution does not convey any guarantee of privacy to private-sector employees, courts in some states have held that their state constitutions do provide certain privacy protections for those employees. But whether such protections apply in workplace settings where an employer has a legitimate right to monitor performance is thus far unclear.

As a practical matter, privacy attorney Bradd Siegel advises employers to *always* notify employees of any intent to monitor employee conversations. Once an employer has done so, an employee can no longer expect telephone conversations that take place in the workplace to be safeguarded by the employee's right to privacy, Siegel says. An employee who has been given such notice no longer has a "reasonable expectation of privacy."

"You have to exercise good judgment when monitoring employee conversations," says Siegel. "Giving your employees notice that you'll be monitoring their telephone conversation doesn't give you carte blanche." On the other hand, if an employer listens in for fifteen minutes on a personal conversation because it has reason to believe that trade secrets or other proprietary information is being divulged, such lengthy telephone monitoring will likely be considered legitimate.

EXPLAIN THE REASONS

Siegel advises employers to explain the reasons for a telephone monitoring program as clearly as possible so that employees understand why their telephone conversations are being monitored. "That doesn't guarantee that everyone will be happy about it, but it reduces the number of employees who will be disgruntled and unhappy," he says.

"Another thing to keep in mind," says Siegel, "is that an employer who excessively measures employee performance via electronic means runs the risk of creating stress that can increase the employer's workers' compensation costs." Siegel's point: One needs to keep a proper balance between the desire to measure employee performance and the desire to maintain high levels of employee productivity.

CAUTION FOR EMPLOYERS

If electronic monitoring is used for performance evaluations, employers must monitor all employees in the same job category. If you monitor some employees and not others, you run the risk of discrimination charges—especially if the employees being monitored fall into protected groups.[32]

our workforce? Who should be assigned a specific task? For these types of decisions, one of several norm-referenced performance formats are appropriate.

Straight Ranking. In straight ranking, the superior lists the incumbents in order, from best to worst, usually on the basis of overall performance. Incumbents can also be ranked with regard to their performance of specific duties. Rankings such as these are appropriate only in small organizations. As the number of incumbents increases, it becomes difficult to discern differences in their performance—particularly for average incumbents. Alternative ranking can help.

Alternative Ranking. The first step in alternative ranking is to put the best subordinate at the head of the list and the worst subordinate at the bottom. The superior then selects the best and worst from the remaining subordinates, placing the best second on the list, the worst next to last. The superior continues to choose the best and worst until all subordinates are ranked. The middle position on the list is the last to be filled.

Paired Comparison. The paired comparison approach involves comparing each incumbent with every other incumbent, two at a time, on a single standard to determine who is "better." A rank order of the individuals can be obtained by counting the number of times each individual is selected as the better of a pair. An advantage of this approach over traditional ratings is that it overcomes the problem of an "evaluation set." That is, it forces the rater to compare the performance of each incumbent to the performances of all other incumbents.

Several potential problems exist with paired comparison, however. If the number of incumbents is large, the total number of comparisons may be unmanageable: $n[(n-1)/2]$ = The Total Number of Comparisons, where n is the number of individuals; thus, for twenty-five incumbents, three hundred comparisons must be made if only overall performance is evaluated. Intransitivity in judgment is another problem. It occurs if incumbent A is rated better than B, and B is rated better than C, but C is rated better than A.

Forced Distribution Method. A problem with straight ranking, alternative ranking, and paired comparison is that each person is assigned a unique rank. This suggests that no two subordinates perform exactly alike. Although this may be true, many supervisors believe that some incumbents perform so similarly that individual differences cannot be discerned. Forced distribution was designed to overcome this complaint. The term forced distribution is used to describe the appraisal format where a superior is forced to distribute subordinates across several categories of performance. A common forced distribution scale may be divided into five categories, with a fixed percentage of all subordinates in the group falling within each category. A typical forced distribution looks like this:

	Lowest	Next Lowest	Middle	Next Highest	Highest
	10%	20%	40%	20%	10%
Number of Employees	5	10	20	10	5

This method creates problems for supervisors who believe that the pattern of performances from people being evaluated does not conform to the fixed percentages.

Comments on Norm-Referenced Methods. Regardless of the approach, norm-referenced methods usually are based on the assumption that performance is best captured or measured by one criterion—overall performance. Because this single criterion is a global measure and is not anchored in any objective index, such as units sold, the results can be influenced by subjectivity. As a consequence, the rankings lack behavioral specificity and may be subject to legal challenge.[33] Peer comparisons were used in *Watkins v. Scott Paper Company* (1976), *Albemarle Paper Company v. Moody* (1975), and *Brito v. Zia Company* (1973). The courts ruled against the companies in all three decisions, saying the comparisons were not based on objective performance criteria, or that the companies failed to establish that they were.

Another critical problem facing the rater is that no information regarding the absolute level of performance is available. Because these methods yield ordinal rather than interval data, managers do not know whether the best performer in a group is actually outstanding, average, or poor, or whether two individuals with adjacent ranks are quite similar or quite different. Finally, these formats do not provide useful information for the job incumbent to act on.

Absolute Standards Formats

With norm-referenced methods of evaluation, the rater is forced to evaluate the individual, team, or strategic unit in relation to similar others. In contrast, formats that use absolute standards allow evaluators to assess performance in relation to specified criteria. Consequently, they can give two people or two units identical ratings.

Graphic Rating Scales. Graphic rating scales are the most widely used form of performance evaluation. Introduced in the 1920s, they were touted as useful because direct output measures were not needed and the rater was free to make as fine a judgment as desired. The scales as originally developed and as used today consist of performance descriptions and unbroken lines with various numbers positioned along the lines and sometimes with descriptive adjectives below.

As shown in Exhibit 10.7, graphic rating scales vary considerably in terms of the clarity with which the performance dimension is delineated, the number of rating categories, and the specificity of the anchors (short definitions) associated with the rating categories. In this exhibit, scales A to C require the rater to define the dimension. This obviously leads to different interpretations by different raters. Although scales D and E do a better job of defining work quality, they still provide latitude for disagreement. Scale F is problematic in a different way: although it provides the most extensive definition of work quality, the rater must consider more than one aspect of performance quality. In addition, scale F provides anchors for only three general groups of scale values, although twenty-five discrete scale values can be used.

The primary advantage of the graphic rating scale format is its simplicity. The major disadvantage is its lack of clarity and definition, which makes legal defensibility questionable. Even when raters are trained, they still might not define a specific trait similarly.[34]

Behaviorally Anchored Rating Scales. Dissatisfaction with graphic rating scales led to the development of absolute standards formats that use more specific behavioral criteria. The most systematic of these approaches relies on critical incidents (see Chapter 6) to replace ambiguous graphic scale anchors, creating behaviorally anchored rating scales (BARS).[35] These scales were developed to provide results that subordinates could use to improve performance and that would allow superiors to be more comfortable in giving feedback.

The process for developing a BARS generally corresponds to the first steps in the critical incidents method of job analysis—that is, collecting incidents describing competent, average, and incompetent behavior for each job category. These incidents are then grouped into broad overall categories or dimensions of performance—for example, administrative tasks and interpersonal tasks. Each dimension serves as a criterion for evaluating performance. Another group of individuals lists the critical incidents pertinent to each category. Exhibit 10.8 shows an example of one such criterion or category—transacting loans—and the critical incidents pertinent to it. This exhibit also shows the next step: assigning a numerical value (weight) to each incident in relation to its contribution to the criterion. A higher weighted incident means higher performance. This format was developed on the basis of the corporate loan assistant's job described in Exhibit 6.2.

■ *Exhibit 10.7*

Sample Graphic Rating Scales for Work Quantity

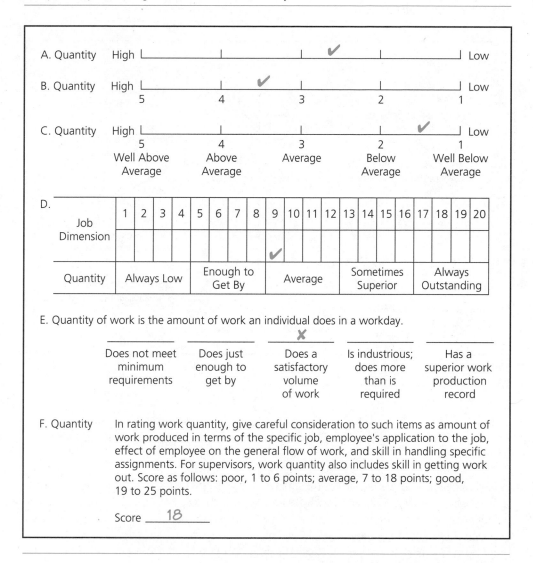

Armed with a set of criteria with behaviorally anchored and weighted choices, superiors can rate their subordinates with a form that is relatively unambiguous in meaning, understandable, justifiable, and easy to use. Yet the form has its limitations. Because most BARS forms use a limited number of performance criteria—for example, seven—many of the critical incidents generated in the job analysis stage may not be used. Thus, the raters may not find appropriate categories to describe the behaviors, or critical incidents, of their subordinates.[36] Similarly, relevant incidents may be worded such that the rater cannot match an observed behavior with the dimension and anchors on the form.

Another concern with BARS is that an incumbent can simultaneously display behavior associated with high and low performance. For example, a corporate loan assistant could prepare follow-up documentation in a timely manner and also receive

■ *Exhibit 10.8*

Sample Behaviorally Anchored Rating Scale for One Dimension of the Work Performance of a Corporate Loan Assistant

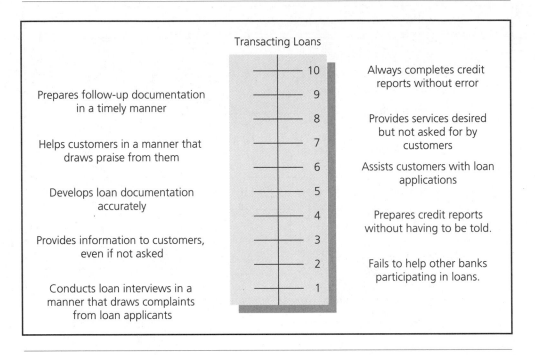

complaints from loan applicants about rudeness and inappropriate questioning. In a situation such as this, it is difficult for the rater to determine whether the rating should be high or low.

Mixed Standard Scales. Mixed standard scales (MSSs) were developed to eliminate some of the problems associated with BARS. As with BARS, critical incidents underscore the development of these scales. The format consists of sets of three statements that describe high, medium, and low levels of performance for a specific performance dimension. These items have been scaled using a process similar to that employed in the development of BARS. Behavioral examples for the dimensions are arranged randomly on the rating sheet. Unlike BARS, in which scale values are known, MSSs have no values attached to the behavioral incidents. Instead, the rater makes one of the three responses (such as +, 0, and −) to each example. Exhibit 10.9 shows an example of a mixed standard scale developed to evaluate the performance of grocery store checkers.

Once gathered, the ratings in Exhibit 10.9 will be transcribed by the human resource department, usually by computer, into numerical ratings, with more points given for + than for 0 and for 0 than for −. For example, a checker who receives a + rating for all three store maintenance items might receive a rating of 9 (three points for each +) on that dimension; a checker who receives two 0s and a + might receive a rating of 7 (two points for each 0 and three points for the one +) on the same dimension.

A drawback of mixed standard scales is that because scale values are not known, developmental information is lost. An advantage of the MSS format is that the rater is not dealing with numbers. Consequently, some of the most common errors associated with

■ *Exhibit 10.9*

Representative Mixed Standard Scale Items for Grocery Store Checkers

---

Name _____ **Rater** _____
Store _____ **Date** _____

Mark each of the numbered statements in one of three ways:
+ indicates the checker performs better than this statement.
0 indicates the checker performs exactly like this statement.
− indicates the checker performs worse than this statement.

_____ 1. Arrives late to work for one shift a week (T)
_____ 2. Averages twenty three items a minute when checking (C)
_____ 3. When business is slow, hangs around the check stand talking to other checkers (M)
_____ 4. Arrives late to work once a month (T)
_____ 5. When business is slow, cleans the stand, helps with light stocking, or performs other tasks (M)
_____ 6. Averages eighteen items a minute when checking (C)
_____ 7. Arrives late for work two shifts a week (T)
_____ 8. Averages thirty six items a minute when checking (C)
_____ 9. When business is slow, cleans check stand (M)

Note: (T) = Tardiness, (C) = Checking, (M) = Maintenance.

rating are overcome (rating errors are discussed later in this chapter). In addition, an analysis of rater response patterns can identify raters whose use of the scales is haphazard. Finally, once developed, MSSs are relatively easy to use.[37]

Behavioral Observation Scales. A more recent development in behavioral scales is called the behavioral observation scale (BOS). Like BARS and MSSs, these scales are derived from critical incidents of job behavior. BOSs differ, however, in that job experts are asked not what level of performance incumbents illustrate, but how frequently they engage in the behaviors. Scores are obtained for each behavior by assigning a numerical value to the frequency judgment. For example, a score of two may be assigned if a behavior is almost always observed. These scores can be summed to get an overall rating. Exhibit 10.10 includes examples of BOSs. The examples of ineffective performance are reverse scored so that all the statements can be presented in the same way.

The advantages of BOS include the following: (1) It is based on a systematic job analysis. (2) Its items and behavioral anchors are clearly stated. (3) In contrast with some other methods, it allows employees to participate in the development of the dimensions—through the identification of critical incidents in the job analysis—which facilitates understanding and acceptance. (4) It is useful for performance feedback and improvement because specific goals can be tied to numerical scores (ratings) on the relevant behavioral anchor (critical incident) for the relevant performance criterion or dimension. (5) It appears to satisfy the Uniform Guidelines in terms of validity (job relatedness) and reliability.

The limitations of BOS are connected with some of its advantages, especially the time and cost for its development as compared with that of graphic rating formats. Although

■ *Exhibit 10.10*

Sample Behavioral Observation Scale Items for a Maintenance Mechanic

---

In completing this form, circle
0– if you have no knowledge of the employee's behavior
1– if the employee has engaged in the behavior 0 to 64 percent of the time
2– if the employee has engaged in the behavior 65 to 74 percent of the time
3– if the employee has engaged in the behavior 75 to 84 percent of the time
4– if the employee has engaged in the behavior 85 to 94 percent of the time
5– if the employee has engaged in the behavior 95 to 100 percent of the time

Customer Relations   **Behavior Frequency**

1. Swears in front of customers (e.g., operators and vendors) (R) 0 1 2 3 4 5
2. Blames customer for malfunction (R) 0 1 2 3 4 5
3. Refers to customers by name or asks for his or her name when first introduced ... 0 1 2 3 4 5
4. Asks operator to demonstrate what she or he was doing at the time of the malfunction ... 0 1 2 3 4 5

Teamwork

1. Exhibits rude behavior that coworkers complain about (R) 0 1 2 3 4 5
2. Verbally shares technical knowledge with other technicians 0 1 2 3 4 5
3. As needed, consults fellow workers for their ideas on ways to solve specific problems ... 0 1 2 3 4 5
4. Given an incomplete assignment, leaves a clear, written tie-in for the next day shift to use ... 0 1 2 3 4 5
5. Works her or his share of overtime 0 1 2 3 4 5

Planning

1. Estimates repair time accurately 0 1 2 3 4 5
2. Completes assigned jobs on time 0 1 2 3 4 5
3. Is able to set job priorities on a daily or weekly basis 0 1 2 3 4 5
4. Even when the job is not yet complete, cleans up area at the end of the shift ... 0 1 2 3 4 5
5. Identifies problems or potential problems that may affect repair success or completion time ... 0 1 2 3 4 5

Planned Maintenance Repairs

1. Executes planned maintenance repair, requiring no follow-up 0 1 2 3 4 5
2. Adjusts equipment according to predetermined tolerance levels; commits no errors ... 0 1 2 3 4 5
3. Replaces components when necessary rather than when convenient or easy ... 0 1 2 3 4 5
4. Takes more time than allotted to complete a planned maintenance repair (R) ... 0 1 2 3 4 5

Note: "R" deontes item is reverse scored.

SOURCE: Adapted from V. L. Huber, *Validation Study for Electronics Maintenance Technical Positions* (Washington, DC: Human Resource Development Institute, AFL-CIO, 1991); prepared under Grant No. 99-9-0264-98-090-02 from the Employment and Training Administration, U.S. Department of Labor.

the behavioral orientation of BOSs appears, on the surface, to be an advantage, evidence suggests that raters do not respond to these scales in terms of behaviors, but rather use their overall, subjective evaluations to guide their ratings. Evidence also suggests that most raters do not have sufficient time or ability to accurately assess the frequency with which behaviors are observed. The accuracy demanded for effective BOS ratings may best be achieved through computer monitoring.[38]

Comments on Absolute Standards Formats. The use of absolute standards formats is expected to increase for two reasons. First, the service sector of the economy is growing rapidly. For this sector, *how* the work is performed is critical to job success and is often viewed as the way to gain a competitive edge; having clear behavioral standards for employees is integral to success in both respects. Second, employee development is increasing in importance. Behavioral formats, unlike graphic or norm-referenced formats, provide useful information for modifying the behavior of employees.

On the other hand, absolute standards formats can be difficult and time-consuming to develop. The exception is graphic rating formats, which are simple to develop but not generally legally defensible. From a cost-benefit perspective, the development of behavioral formats should be restricted to jobs that have many incumbents or for which the job processes are critical to job success. Even then, relying exclusively on behavioral formats may mean that the real essence of many jobs, especially managerial and highly routine jobs, is not captured. For these types of jobs, actual outputs produced—regardless of the behaviors used to obtain them—may be the most useful. When these conditions exist, output-based formats may be best.

Output-Based Formats

Output-based formats focus on job products as the primary criteria. Like the norm-referenced and absolute standards approaches, this one presumes that job analysis was used to identify critical job duties and tasks. Once duties are identified, the level of proficiency that an employee must attain is determined. Four variants of output-based appraisal formats are used: management by objectives, the performance standards approach, the direct index approach, and accomplishment records. Regardless of the format, effective output criteria should include the components listed in Exhibit 10.11.

Management by Objectives. Management by objectives is widely used in both private- and public-sector settings.[39] MBO begins with the establishment of goals or objectives for the upcoming performance period. Then, the superior and subordinate delineate an appropriate strategy for goal attainment. Experienced and high-performing

■ *Exhibit 10.11*
Components of Effective Output-Based Performance Criteria

- ◉ *Specific Parameters:* Identify how well the behavior must be performed or how high the output must be to be considered acceptable. Specificity reduces variability in performance and in ratings.
- ◉ *Deadlines:* Identify the deadline for completion of the task or attainment of the output level.
- ◉ *Conditions:* Point out any qualifications associated with attaining the standard—for example, whether the production schedule is adhered to—because many circumstances beyond the control of the incumbent may hamper goal attainment.
- ◉ *Priorities:* Ensure that incumbents understand which standards are most important. Supervisors and incumbents can weight them, or weights can be derived from the job description.
- ◉ *Consequences:* Specify the consequences of attaining or not attaining the specified level of performance.
- ◉ *Congruent Goals:* For employees performing similar jobs, assign comparable goals.

managers can develop their strategies on their own; the freedom to perform the job in the way they think best is reinforcing in and of itself. For less experienced or low-performing incumbents, the supervisor may need to intervene. Clearly delineating how a goal is to be attained reduces ambiguity and makes goal attainment more likely. Strategy development includes outlining the steps necessary to attain each objective, as well as any constraints that may block attainment of the objective. Finally, it is necessary to specify the responsibilities of the incumbent and of the supervisor.

At the conclusion of the performance period, actual performance is evaluated relative to the agreed-on objectives. Here, it is useful to develop an appropriate scoring algorithm. Because people do not synthesize multidimensional data well, each objective should be scored separately. Scoring algorithms can be either simple (indicating whether the objective was or was not met) or complex (signaling how far above or below the objective actual performance was). After evaluation, the superior and subordinate jointly explore the reasons goals were not attained or were exceeded. This step helps determine training needs and development potential.

The final step is to decide on new goals and possible new strategies for goals not previously attained. At this point, subordinate and superior involvement in goal setting may change. Subordinates who successfully reached the established goals may be allowed to participate more in the goal-setting process the next time.[40]

Management must be clearly committed to the process if the MBO system is to be effective. When management is committed and goals cascade from the top down, supervisory complaints are reduced by more than 20 percent and employee satisfaction increases. In addition, productivity gains average 56 percent; without management commitment and a shared vision, productivity gains average a meager 6 percent. Management must recognize, though, that MBO systems do not lead to immediate increases in productivity. On average, it takes about two years after implementation for MBO systems to work effectively.[41]

Remember that the objectives are only guidelines that facilitate two-way communication. They can and should be changed if the job changes or the situation changes. In some organizations, superiors and subordinates work together to establish goals; in others, superiors establish goals for work groups or individuals; in still others, goals are derived from time-and-motion studies (see Chapter 6). Goals can refer to desired outcomes to be achieved, means for achieving those outcomes, or both. They may be related to the routine activities that constitute day-to-day duties or to the identification and solution of problems that hamper individual and organizational effectiveness; they may also be innovative or have special purposes.[42]

Performance Standards Approach. Although similar to MBO, the performance standards approach uses more direct measures, with emphasis placed on the verifiability of performance. Standards are generally more numerous and more detailed than objectives. Exhibit 10.12 shows some performance standards for a graphic artist. Notice that the standards include indicators of expected performance as well as exceptional performance.[43]

Direct Index Approach. The direct index approach differs from the other output-based approaches primarily in how performance is measured. It measures performance by objective, impersonal criteria, such as productivity, absenteeism, and turnover. For example, a manager's performance may be evaluated by the number of the manager's employees who quit or by the employees' absenteeism rate. For nonmanagers, measures of productivity may be more appropriate. These can be broken into measures of quality and measures of quantity. Quality measures include scrap rates, number of customer

■ *Exhibit 10.12*
Verifiable Performance Standards for a Graphic Artist

Accomplishment	Performance Measures and Standards

Product logos	1. All agreed-on deadlines are met.
	2. Vendor costs are within the agreed-on budget.
	3. Designer's hours are within plus or minus 10 percent of the agreed-on budget.
	4. Supervisor is satisfied that the logo
	   a. Reproduces well in various sizes and in three dimensions
	   b. Can be used in one color, line art, and halftone versions
	   c. Conveys the function of the product
	   d. Has a strong identity and reads well
	   e. Uses type in a unique manner
	   f. Has high-quality art
	5. Client is satisfied that the
	   a. Image conveyed to the public is the image the client wants to convey
	   b. Message is clear
	   c. Logo is easily recognizable
	   d. Typeface matches the personality of the product or program
	6. Designer exceeded expectations. This occurs when one or more of the following conditions are met: the logo design wins an award; customers say they are excited about using the logo; the logo is used for ten years; the logo graphic gets public recognition without the accompanying text.

SOURCE: Adapted from J. Zigon, "Making Performance Appraisal Work for Teams," *Training* (June 1994): 62. Used by permission.

complaints, and number of defective units or parts produced. Quantity measures include units of output per hour, number of new customer orders, and sales volume. Exhibit 10.13 provides some examples of direct indexes for several jobs.

Accomplishment Records. A relatively new type of output-based appraisal is the accomplishment record. It is suitable for professionals who claim, "My record speaks for itself," or who maintain that they cannot write standards for their jobs because every day is different. With this approach, professionals describe their achievements relative to appropriate job dimensions, on an accomplishment record form. Their supervisors verify the accuracy of the accomplishments. Then, a team of outside experts evaluates the accomplishments to determine their overall value. Although time-consuming and potentially costly because outside evaluators are involved, this approach has predicted job success for lawyers. It also has face validity because professionals believe it is appropriate and valid. Exhibit 10.14 shows an accomplishment rating for using knowledge.[44]

Comments on Output-Based Formats. With the increased emphasis on performance enhancement, the use of output-based appraisal continues to increase. The major advantage of these formats—when used correctly—is that they provide clear, unambiguous direction to employees regarding desired job outcomes. When exceptional performance also is specified (see Exhibit 10.12), these scales can motivate the average as well as exceptional employee. Research indicates that when the criteria used in output-based rating formats is specific, extraneous variables such as the ratee's prior evaluation, the order of evaluation, salary, and even personal characteristics like gender are less likely to bias judgments. When standards fail to specify an exact level of performance or a time period, these variables do bias performance ratings.

The disadvantages of output-based formats are that they require time, money, and cooperation to develop. Furthermore, they may not capture the essence of job perfor-

■ *Exhibit 10.13*
Examples of Direct Indexes of Performance

Job	Direct Indexes
Salesperson	Dollar volume of sales over a fixed period
	Number of new customers
	Number of delinquent accounts collected
	Net sales per month in territory
	Penetration of the market
Manager	Number of employee grievances
	Cost reductions
	Unit turnover
	Absenteeism
	Unit safety record
	Timeliness in completing appraisals
	Employee satisfaction with supervisor
	Division productivity
	Diversity of new hires
Police officer	Number of arrests for felony offenses
	Number of shots fired in the line of duty
	Number of complaints
	Clearance rates
	Average response time
Scientist	Number of patents
	Number of grants
	Number of technical articles written or cowritten
	Number of solo-authored manuscripts
Computer scientist	Number of coding sign-offs
	Response time for requests
	Number of lines of code written
	Number of bytes of compiled code
Administrative assistant	Number of letters prepared
	Word processing speed
	Number of errors in filing
	Number of jobs returned for reprocessing
	Number of calls screened

mance, so important job behaviors may be ignored in the evaluation process. Also, the production of desired products or output may induce unintended competition among employees. This problem can be overcome if the output-based appraisal system is carefully designed, building on job analysis and utilizing training for raters. Under these conditions, output-based formats are highly useful decision tools. Results can be used to make between-employee comparisons and to develop employees, as well as to document organizational actions.

Creating a New Performance Appraisal Format

In selecting an appraisal format, organizations increasingly seek to identify some of their unique concerns and characteristics. They are saying, "We must do everything possible to make sure the appraisal format fits with what we are trying to do, with what we stand for and what we say is important to this company." Thus, most organizations now select some new type of rating format that fits where top management needs and wants to take the business. The feature "Managing Human Resources for the 21st Century at the

Exhibit 10.14
Accomplishment Record for Using Knowledge

Using Knowledge
Interpreting and synthesizing information to form legal strategies, approaches, and lines of argument; developing new configurations of knowledge, innovative approaches, solutions, and strategies; selecting the proper legal theory; using appropriate lines of argument, weighing alternatives, and drawing sound conclusions.

Time period: 1996

General Statement of what you accomplished:
I developed three new legal theories that could be used to justify jurisdiction in areas previously thought to be foreclosed as a result of a Supreme Court decision on equal employment.

Description of exactly what you did:
I located and analyzed every judicial opinion discussing the "fair employment" jurisdiction, and demonstrated that sound legal arguments could be developed to support the firm's action.

Awards or formal recognition:
The CEO sent me a note thanking me for my efforts.

The information was verified by: Lou DeCaro, Director

Rating: 4.5*

---

*On a 6.0 scale
SOURCE: Adapted from L. Hugh, "Development of the Accomplishment Record Method of Selecting and Promoting Professionals," *Journal of Applied Psychology* 69 (1984): 135–46.

Chrysler Corporation" shows that the format selected is often less important than the process used in selecting and adapting it to the organization.[45] That is why many managers now talk about the performance management system and about getting employee involvement and understanding.

✦ APPRAISALS FOR PREDICTING FUTURE PERFORMANCE

Occasionally, it is useful to appraise how employees would perform on a future job—generally, one to which they would be promoted. The assessment center method, which is used to determine the managerial potential of employees, evaluates individuals as they take part in a large number of activities conducted in a relatively isolated environment. In a typical assessment center, an employee may spend two or three days going through a series of activities, including management games, leaderless group discussions, peer evaluations, and in-basket exercises. Advantages of the assessment center include its validity and its ability to "open up" the process by which an organization identifies future managers, giving more employees a chance to have their potential tested and recognized.

Occasionally, employees find themselves placed in jobs or parts of the organization that are less visible to top management. This, combined with having a supervisor who fails to make fair evaluations of present performance, may bury some employees in the organization. An assessment center program that employees can volunteer to attend helps reduce this potential for early burial.

Potential limitations of the assessment center method are its creation of "crown princes and princesses," its focus on competition rather than cooperation, and its cost. However, the creation of a special class of employees is less likely under a program where those who attend the centers can either be nominated by their supervisors or volunteer themselves. The nature of the activities in the center, including the degree of cooperation

Managing Human Resources for the 21st Century at the Chrysler Corporation

In the early 1980s, the Chrysler Corporation was about at the end of its rope. Through the coordinated efforts of Lee A. Iacocca, his management team, and the employees and the United Automobile Workers (UAW) union, and a little help from the federal government, Chrysler staged a rather dramatic turnaround. In 1994, with global sales of $35 billion, making it the world's eleventh largest manufacturing organization, it is again able to call itself one of the Big Three U.S. automakers. As with any successful turnaround, Chrysler's depended on many things going right. It required the dedication of the workforce to survival and improvement, and it seemed to help a great deal if all the employees felt they were part of the team. In late 1988, Chrysler began a reverse appraisal process. To implement the process, it formed a steering committee representing top management and UAW leadership. This was done to ensure that both management and non-management were involved from the beginning; the program was not to be seen as one imposed by management.

Because it was a new program, Chrysler decided to initially develop and test it in two units within the Vehicle Engineering Division. In this way, the process could be worked out, perfected, and then used in other areas. To help ensure that the change process was as objective as possible—and run as effectively as possible—Debra Dubow, a management development specialist in another Chrysler division, was brought in to manage it. The process included developing a new appraisal instrument. This involved gathering data to determine what criteria should be used to appraise the bosses; later on, everyone would be trained in how to use the new appraisals. "Dubow first pulled together a cross section of employees from the two pilot groups, ranging from vice presidents and union management to first-line supervisors and mechanics. Through this sample of approximately 50 persons, she was able to gather valuable input from different levels of managers and employees, as well as recognize and head off resistance to the new project that might be encountered along the way."[46] The result of Dubow's discussions with her initial sample was that Chrysler would develop its own performance appraisal form, not buy an existing one from another organization. The categories of criteria that Dubow and her team decided to consider using initially were those already being used to evaluate employees in the traditional boss-subordinate process. The final appraisal form they developed, after many rounds of discussions and revisions, included many of those categories. However, the team had to write the definitions of each category to fit the appraisal of the boss. Examples of these definitions include

- *Teamwork:* "My supervisor promotes cooperation and teamwork within our work group"
- *Communication:* "My supervisor learns current business information and communicates it to our work group"
- *Quality:* "My supervisor demonstrates meaningful commitment to our quality efforts"
- *Leadership:* "My supervisor demonstrates consistency through both words and actions"
- *Planning:* "My supervisor provides reasonable schedules so that my commitments can be met"
- *Development of the work force:* "My supervisor delegates responsibilities and gives me the authority to carry out my job."[47]

It was determined that each category would be evaluated on a 1–5 (Almost Never–to–Almost Always) scale.

By the summer of 1989, two pilot groups from top management volunteered to be the first to have their employees appraise their performance. The data were gathered on the appraisal forms, and the results were read by computer scan. The data were converted by computer to provide managers with individual reports. The managers then met with their employees to discuss the results and develop an action plan for improvement. This entire process was intended to focus on behaviors that managers can change. Once the top management went through this first round, the process cascaded down, reflecting the philosophy "Do as I do," rather than "Do as I say." At each level, the action plans for improvement became the measure of accountability: the next time around, the managers would be asked to discuss how well they had done on their plans with their employees.

Because of the magnitude of this change, the implementation is still going on. It had, however, already gone through more than six thousand employees in the division. And other divisions were volunteering to implement the program.

In appraising the overall success of the program, Dubow is candid, admitting that the changes are more anecdotal than cultural. In certain areas, workers report better feelings of communication, and managers report better awareness of how they're impacting their groups. Individually, they're more cognizant of interpersonal and career growth areas and are becoming better at coaching employees.

Dubow admits Chrysler's reverse-appraisal program is too new to have had a major organizational impact. Therefore, it's too difficult to tie it to product results. Says Dubow, "The second round of the process should be more telling."[48]

or competitiveness, can be regulated to match the needs of the organization and its environment. The relatively high cost of the assessment center approach suggests that to justify its use, the organization must clearly identify its benefits, such as the value derived from a better, more diverse, and bigger pool of potential managers.

Once performance potential is identified, organizations can use the results to help fill in replacement charts or talent pools. Using the same information, organizations can also establish career-planning and training programs to eliminate any gaps between current and needed skills.[49]

THE RATING PROCESS

Despite the prevalence of potentially effective performance appraisals, organizations and employees are still somewhat uneasy about using them. This uneasiness centers on the vulnerability of these measures to intentional as well as unintentional bias, both of which threaten the accuracy of the final results. Unintentional cognitive errors often occur simply because human beings are imperfect information processors. In addition, the social setting and specific organizational circumstances may come into play.

The quality of performance judgments depends, in part, on the information processing capabilities or strategies of the decision maker.[50] As shown in Exhibit 10.15, the performance rater first attends to and recognizes relevant information, which is then aggregated and stored in the rater's short-term memory. Because of long appraisal periods, information is condensed further for storage in long-term memory. When a performance judgment needs to be made, information relevant to the category to be rated is retrieved from memory. Recalled information about behaviors and outputs is then compared against the rater's standards. An evaluation is made based on aggregated data retrieved from memory and any additional information used by the rater either intentionally or unintentionally. Finally, before the evaluation is recorded officially, it may be revised depending on possible reactions of the incumbent or higher-level managers, the goals the rater hopes to achieve through the appraisal process, and even organizational norms.[51] Unfortunately, the fallibility of managers combines with this process to create numerous types of errors.[52]

Rating Errors

When criteria are not clearly specified and no incentives are associated with rating accuracy, a variety of errors occur during the rating process. These errors can affect all stages of the process, as shown in Exhibit 10.15, but their effects are most clearly seen at the final stage, after ratings have actually been recorded.

■ *Exhibit 10.15*
The Performance Appraiser's Rating Process

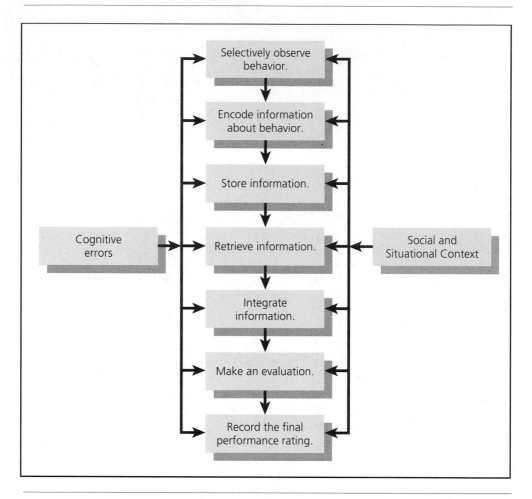

Halo and Horn. Halo and horn errors occur with a tendency to think of a person in general as more or less good or bad, which is reflected in judgments of specific performances as either good or bad. For example, performance on a single dimension may be so outstanding or so critical that it overshadows performance on other tasks. Or a personal characteristic, such as sex, race, or age, may be associated with a stereotype of how the person performs. In either case, the rater does not make meaningful distinctions when evaluating specific dimensions of performance. When negative performance on one dimension supersedes any positive performance, the error is sometimes referred to as a horn error. When the error is to provide favorable ratings on all dimensions, it is called a halo error.[53]

Leniency. Another common and often intentional rating error is called leniency. Leniency occurs when, to avoid conflict, a manager rates all employees in a particular work group higher than they should be rated objectively. This is particularly likely when high ratings are not sanctioned by the organization, when rewards are not part of a fixed and limited pot, and when dimensional ratings are not required.

Strictness. At the opposite extreme from leniency is the error of strictness, in which ratees are given unfavorable ratings regardless of performance level. Inexperienced raters who are unfamiliar with environmental constraints on performance, raters with low self-esteem, and raters who have themselves received a low rating are most likely to rate strictly. Rater training that includes a reversal of supervisor-incumbent roles and confidence building can reduce this error.

Central Tendency. Rather than use extremes in ratings, some raters tend to evaluate all ratees as average, even when performance actually varies. This bias is referred to as the error of central tendency. Raters with large spans of control and little opportunity to observe behavior are likely to rate most incumbents in the middle of the scale rather than too high or too low. This is a "play-it-safe" strategy. Central tendency may also be the by-product of the rating method. The forced distribution format requires that most employees be rated average.

Primacy and Recency of Events. The typical appraisal period, six months to a year, is far too long for any rater adequately to retain in memory all performance-relevant information. As a cognitive shortcut, raters may use initial information to categorize a ratee as either a good or a bad performer. Subsequently, information that supports the initial judgment is amassed, and unconfirming information is ignored. This error is referred to as the *primacy bias.*

Conversely, a rater may ignore employee performance throughout the appraisal period, until the appraisal interview draws near. When the rater then searches for cues about performance, recent behaviors or outputs are most salient, so recent events receive more weight than they should. This *recency-of-events error* can have serious consequences for a ratee who performs well for six months or a year but then makes a serious or costly error in the last week or two before he or she is evaluated.

Contrast Effects. If criteria are not clear or if ranking systems are used, contrast effects will occur. When compared with weak employees, an average employee will appear outstanding; when evaluated against outstanding employees, an average employee will be perceived as a low performer. Again, the solution is to have specific performance criteria established prior to the evaluation period; then, any employee with adequate performance receives an acceptable rating.

Escalation of Commitment. The costly error called escalation of commitment results when managers are unable to cut their losses. Consider this situation: A new midlevel manager has joined the department you manage. You expected excellent performance, but early reports suggest that she is not doing well. Should you fire her? After all, you cannot afford to carry a low performer. On the other hand, you have invested in her training, and she may just be learning the ropes. Research indicates that if you made the initial hiring decision, you are likely to escalate your commitment and invest in her a bit longer. You may even provide her with additional training so that she can succeed. On the other hand, if you did not make the initial decision, your investment is lower and you are more likely to recommend immediate termination. According to decision experts, when faced with negative feedback about a prior decision, the decision maker feels the need to reaffirm the wisdom of having invested time and money. Further commitment of resources somehow justifies the initial decision.[54] This bias, which may have some beneficial consequences, can be managed by setting in advance limits on involvement and commitment.

Anchoring and Adjustment. Prior performance information often anchors judgments about current performance, making ratings that depart from the prior ratings less likely. The tendency to use prior information inappropriately to make current judgments is referred to as the anchoring and adjustment bias. This bias can be controlled by limiting access to prior rating information and by having clear, concise performance standards and performance output data available to use in judging current performance.

Self-Fulfilling Prophecy. The anchoring and adjustment bias may partially account for the phenomenon of self-fulfilling prophecies: candidates evaluated positively tend to perform better in the future than do those initially evaluated low. Such judgments have been shown to affect supervisor-incumbent interactions. High performers receive more positive feedback and believe more in their ability than do low performers. Consequently, they perform better or receive higher evaluations or both.[55]

Strategies for Increasing Rater Accuracy

Even the best performance management system may not be effective when so many extraneous variables impinge on the performance appraisal process. Therefore, employers are wise to implement strategies that minimize appraisal errors.

Design an Effective Appraisal System. Initially, the appraisal process should include the following features:

- Each performance dimension addresses a single job activity, rather than a group of activities.
- Each performance dimension is rated separately, and the scores are then summed to determine the overall rating.
- The raters can observe the behaviors of ratees on a regular basis while the job is being accomplished.
- Terms like *average* are not used on rating scales because different raters have various reactions to them.
- Raters do not have to evaluate large groups of employees, especially all at the same time.
- Raters are trained to avoid such errors as halo and horn, leniency, strictness, central tendency, and primacy and recency of events.
- Raters are trained to share a common frame of reference.[56]

In sum, performance ratings tend to be more accurate when the rating criteria, the record of performance accomplishments, and the rating scales are precise. Research also suggests that when all three of these elements are in place, evaluators are not only more accurate in their ratings but also more confident about their ratings.

Provide Memory Aids. Behavior diaries and critical incident files are useful memory aids.[57] The emphasis here is on recording behaviors or outcomes—good or bad—that relate to an employee's or work group's performance. These are then reviewed at the time the performance appraisal is conducted. This process helps ensure that the rater uses all available and relevant information; it is particularly helpful when the assessment period is six months to a year long. Consulting a behavioral diary or a critical incident file before rating reduces recency and primacy errors, yielding more accurate measures of performance. One enterprising firm has even created an electronic diary-keeping software package, just for this purpose. Using an expert system, the program is designed to help managers keep track of key incidents and then use this information systematically and analytically in making appraisals. Using menus and performance dimensions likely to be relevant to a broad array of jobs, the program guides the managers through a BARS-like evaluation, complete with examples of specific behaviors relevant to each dimension, and then produces a narrative description of the employee's performance.[58]

Provide Rater Training. Rating accuracy can also be improved through training that focuses on improving the observation skills of raters. Frame-of-reference training is one useful approach. A comprehensive frame-of-reference training program might include the following steps:

1. The raters are given a job description and instructed to identify appropriate criteria for evaluating the job.
2. When agreement is reached, the raters view a tape of an employee performing the job.
3. Independently, the raters evaluate the videotaped performance, using the organization's appraisal system.
4. The raters' evaluations are compared with each other and with those of job experts.
5. With a trainer as a facilitator, the raters present the rationales for their ratings and challenge the rationales of other raters.
6. The trainer helps the raters reach a consensus regarding the value of specific job behaviors and overall performance.
7. A new videotape is shown, followed by independent ratings.
8. The process continues until consensus is achieved.[59]

Organizations that cannot afford to develop videotapes or that use MBO performance standards can accomplish similar results using written performance profiles instead of videotapes of behavior.

Increase Self-Efficacy. Raters also should be trained to be critical. This is best accomplished by increasing their self-efficacy, or beliefs that they *can* rate accurately and *can* handle the consequences associated with giving negative feedback. Self-efficacy can be increased through observing someone else's success in handling the appraisal process, practicing the behaviors, and receiving coaching and feedback on how to do it better.

Reward Accurate and Timely Appraisals. Another potential cause of rating inaccuracy—particularly leniency—is a lack of rater motivation. Without rewards, raters may find it easier to give high ratings than to give accurate ratings.[60] If this is the case, a straightforward strategy for increasing rater motivation is to base salary increases, promotions, and assignments to key positions partly on the performance as a rater. Ratings done in a timely manner and a fair manner (as measured by employee attitude surveys) should be rewarded. Human resource audits can be performed, in which a random sample of supervisory ratings is examined for thoroughness, completeness, and timeliness.

Diffuse Responsibility. Often, the ratee believes that the rater is solely responsible for a poor evaluation and any subsequent loss of rewards; the rater may also believe this. Research suggests that this negative effect can be minimized by relying on the judgments of multiple raters. The diffusion of responsibility frees each rater to evaluate more accurately. Furthermore, an incumbent is less likely to shrug off negative information when multiple raters are involved.[61] One recent study showed that multiple raters acting as a group may be especially effective in producing accurate ratings, because discussion among members of the group helps overcome the various errors and biases of individuals.[62]

 ## THE DISAPPEARANCE OF PERFORMANCE APPRAISAL?

Typically, in companies focusing on total quality, the basis for appraisal begins to reflect team-oriented criteria rather than solely individual-oriented criteria. Longer-term criteria are added to supplement the more traditional shorter-term criteria. Peer reviews and customer evaluations are added to supplement traditional supervisory appraisals.

Usually, these changes do not take place with one big bang; they occur gradually, giving people time to adjust to the new ways. Just as important, organizations need to experiment with what they are doing. New ways of doing things generally have to be adapted to specific conditions facing a given company. In the instance of performance appraisal, companies may reach a point in the change process when they ask, "Do we even need performance appraisal?"

Firms have used performance appraisal systems for a long time. They will probably not abandon them wholesale, but some are at least starting to ask, "Why do we do appraisal?" As firms address this question, they may see that they do it more to *control* than to develop or improve employee performance—and they do it because they assume they need to. If employee goals are different from organizational goals, then—the assumption goes—firms have to monitor and control what employees do. In some cases, firms are finding that the assumption is wrong: employees can have goals that coincide with the organization's. W. Edwards Deming, a father in the field of quality management and statistical process control, acted on the assumption that employees will do their best when management treats them accordingly. In fact, he argued that, in terms of performance problems, *management*—not employees—is largely responsible for performance problems.

Such questioning could eventually result in dramatic changes in how organizations measure performance. This has already happened in a few firms. Nevertheless, most companies will continue to use some form of individual performance appraisal, even those pursuing total quality management, in part because such appraisal provides the basis for making decisions about how to pay people, who to promote, where to transfer people, and so forth.

SUMMARY

Human variability is a fact of life, especially organizational life. Much of human resource management involves attending to this variability. This chapter and the next discuss how organizations manage performance variability and use that variability as the basis for making employment decisions.

The strategic use of performance appraisals seeks to be sure that measures of performance reflect business objectives. This approach is gaining in popularity as firms begin to understand how performance appraisals can be used to enhance organizational effectiveness. Employees tend to do what is expected and what they believe is valued by "the system," as generally defined by the performance appraisal system. So, when firms such as Grand Union develop performance appraisal criteria that communicate the company's concern about teamwork and customer satisfaction, they are more likely to get teamwork and customer satisfaction from their employees. Thus, for firms wanting to produce total quality or total customer satisfaction or both, such as L. L. Bean, Au Bon Pain, Chaparral, and Chrysler, these criteria should appear in the performance appraisals of all employees.[63]

The activity of performance appraisal is part of a performance management system that evolves over time. Such systems are premised on the beliefs that the performances of individuals vary over time and that individuals can exert some influence over their performance. Thus, an effective performance management system generally serves two purposes: (1) an evaluative purpose of letting people know where they stand and (2) a developmental purpose of providing specific information and direction to individuals, so that they can improve their performance. Performance appraisal is, therefore, linked to other human resource activities such as compensation, promotion, planning, development and training, and validation of selection systems for legal compliance.

Special emphasis is placed on the need for job analysis as a means of developing job-related performance criteria. In general, the more subjective the performance appraisal approach, the more vulnerable the performance appraisal system to legal challenge. Although various approaches to performance appraisal exist, they can be classified into three broad categories: norm referenced, absolute standards, and output based. The choice of the best approach is a function of several criteria: the purpose of the performance appraisal system (evaluation or development or both), the costs of developing and implementing the system, the degree to which rater errors are minimized, and user acceptance of the system.

Despite the most well laid plans for a performance management system, human resource professionals are often frustrated by the failure of line managers to conduct performance appraisals consistently. A number of obstacles contribute to resistance from managers: they may not have opportunities to observe subordinates' performance; they may not have clearly specified performance standards to use when making judgments; as human judges, they realize they are prone to errors and may be concerned about how these errors get translated into consequences for their subordinates' lives; and they may view performance appraisal as a conflict-producing activity and therefore avoid it. For these reasons and others, it is important to examine not only why and how performance appraisal data are gathered but also, as the next chapter explores, how they are used.

 Discussion Questions

1. Explain the role of performance appraisal in the success of Au Bon Pain.
2. How can performance appraisal forms be developed to minimize supervisory errors?
3. Why does employee performance vary even after employees have successfully passed rigorous organizational selection and placement procedures? How can a performance management system address this performance variability?
4. Assume, in turn, the identity of each of the following persons: a subordinate, a superior, and a human resource professional. Answer this question for each person: "What purpose can a performance appraisal serve for me?" Are the purposes served by a perfor-

mance appraisal for these three people congruent or conflicting? Explain.
5. Why is job analysis essential for the development of a performance appraisal?
6. What are the three major approaches to performance appraisal? Give an example of each approach.
7. How does the performance appraisal approach called BARS function? BOS? mixed standard? What advantages are offered by each of these approaches? What disadvantages?
8. Performance appraisal approaches often differ based on whether behavior or the results of behavior (outcomes) are evaluated. Give examples from organizations with which you are familiar, in which one

approach might be preferred over the other. Explain why.

9. Teachers often complain that students should not be asked to evaluate teacher performance. Argue the position that students should be asked. What poten-tial rater errors are students likely to commit? How can these be minimized? Are these errors similar to the types teachers might commit when evaluating student performance? Explain.

 In-Class Projects

1. Describe the following for Lincoln Electric:
   a. The objectives of its performance appraisals
   b. The extent to which these objectives are serving the business and HR objectives of Lincoln
   c. The performance appraisal criteria
   d. The extent to which these criteria are serving the business and HR objectives of Lincoln

Going forward:

How can the performance appraisal activities at Lincoln be improved?

2. Describe the following for AAL:
   a. The objectives of its performance appraisals
   b. The extent to which these objectives are serving the business and HR objectives of AAL
   c. The performance appraisal criteria
   d. The extent to which these criteria are serving the business and HR objectives of AAL

Going forward:

How can the performance appraisal activities at AAL be improved?

 Field Projects

1. Assume you want to convince top management that your firm's performance appraisals should be strategically linked to the overall business plan. What arguments do you use to convince top management to use performance information strategically? What arguments do you use to build a case for strategic linkages?

2. Assume you are the vice president of operations for a one-thousand-person firm that makes and markets specialized computer circuit boards. You have been asked to develop an appropriate performance appraisal system for the firm's five-hundred-plus software and hardware engineering professionals. What type or types of appraisals do you recommend, and why? What arguments can you make to convince the CEO and the board of directors to adopt your new appraisal system?

3. Assume that your company, an international consulting firm, puts you in charge of developing output-based performance appraisals. Develop a flowchart, including time lines, detailing the steps that will be taken and the decisions that will be needed to develop the new measures.

4. Assume that a fast-food chain has invited you in to make suggestions to improve its quality of customer service. Top management believes that improving service will mean that prices and margins can be increased. Although these managers understand that such things as the type of food and the physical appearance of the restaurants may need to change to improve the quality of service, they want you to tell them about the human resource implications. What are your suggestions, and what are the HR implications?

Case Study:

PERFORMANCE APPRAISAL AT ESSEX

Percy Sharp sat at his desk, looking over the performance appraisal form he had just completed on Bob Maxwell, one of his insurance underwriters. Bob was on his way to Percy's office for their annual review session. Percy dreaded these appraisal meetings, even when he did not have to confront employees with negative feedback.

A couple of years before, Essex Insurance Ltd., which had experienced very rapid growth, decided to implement formal appraisals. All supervisors had been presented with the new appraisal form, which included five different subcategories in addition to an overall rating. Supervisors were asked to rate employees on each dimension using a scale from 1 (unacceptable) to 5 (exceptional). They were also advised to maintain a file on each employee into which they could drop notes on specific incidents of good or poor performance during the year to use as "documentation" when completing the appraisal form. They were told they could only give an overall rating of "1" or "5" if they had "substantial" documentation to back it up. Percy had never given one of these extreme ratings because he wasn't diligent about recording specific incidents in employee files; he believed it was just too time-consuming to write up all of the documentation necessary to justify such a rating. There were a couple of employees in his department who deserved a "5" rating, in Percy's opinion, but so far no one had complained about the appraisals they received from Percy.

Bob was one of Percy's "exceptional" workers. Percy had three or four specific examples of exceptional performance in Bob's file but, looking over the form, he could not clearly identify the category in which they belonged. "Oh well," Percy said to himself, "I'll just give him 3s and 4s. I don't have to justify those, and Bob has never complained before." One of the categories was "Analyzing Work Materials." Percy had never understood what that meant or whether it was relevant for the job of insurance underwriter. He had checked "3" (satisfactory) for Bob, as he did on all the evaluations he did. He understood the meaning of the other categories—Quality of Work, Quantity of Work, Improving Work Methods and Relationships with Co-workers—although he was confused as to what a "3" or a "4" indicated about each category.

Bob knocked on Percy's door and came in. Percy looked up and smiled. "Hi, Bob. Sit down. Let's get through this thing so we can get back to work, OK? ◉

Case Questions:

1. Does Percy feel very comfortable giving Bob his performance appraisal?
2. What problems do you see with the appraisal system Percy is using?
3. What are Bob's likely reactions to being told by Percy that he scored 3s and 4s even though he is one of Percy's exceptional workers?
4. What suggestions do you have for improving performance appraisals at Essex?
5. What might be the benefits of an improved system for Bob, for Percy, and for the company?

Using Appraisals to Maximize Performance

To embed our values, we give our people 360-degree evaluations, with input from superiors, peers, and subordinates. These are the roughest evaluations you can get, because people hear things about themselves they've never heard before. But they get the input they need, and then the chance to improve. If they don't improve, they have to go.

JACK WELCH, CEO, General Electric Company[1]

It is 8:00 A.M. in Park City, Utah, a ski resort community thirty miles southwest of Salt Lake City. Debra J. Fields, founder and CEO of Mrs. Fields Incorporated, has just arrived at her office. Sipping herbal tea and nibbling on a Mrs. Fields muffin, she turns on her desktop computer, presses a few keys, and calls up the cookie emporium's Retail Operations Intelligence (ROI) system. The state-of-the-art software networks all retail outlets to the company's headquarters and allows corporate officials to communicate with all store managers and vice versa. Simply stated, it allows store managers, district managers, and regional directors across the United States to have daily contact with Fields and the rest of the company's top administrative staff.

Clicking through a couple of menus, Fields finds what she is looking for—yesterday's sales figures for all 650 cookie emporium outlets, including those in Hong Kong, Tokyo, Singapore, and Sydney. Since the ROI system tracks sales continuously through cash registers, a summary report of the preceding day's performance test results appears on the screen within seconds. By pressing a few more keys on the computer, Fields can tell which stores did the best and which did the worst, or which stores met their sales projections and which did not. Armed with this information, Fields begins her favorite task of the morning—calling store managers to congratulate them on their performance. According to Paul Quinn, vice president of management information systems: "People can't believe that she knows so quickly how they did the day before. It makes them feel as if she's watching and that she cares."

The twenty modules or applications of the ROI system also allow Fields's management philosophy and skills to filter throughout the company to help sell cookies. When the company was started in Palo Alto, California, Fields set hourly sales quotas for herself and baked up the day's inventory based on daily experience. It was her policy (and still is) not to sell a product that was more than two hours old. Through the ROI's production planning module, store managers know how many units of a particular cookie they can expect to sell to meet projections from hour to hour, how much dough must be prepared, and when to bake to maximize sales and minimize loss. The system also charts hourly progress

versus projections and makes suggestions on how to keep selling cookies.

Information obtained through the ROI system also can be used to motivate managers and staff. For example, Janet Oskinski, manager of a Mrs. Fields store in Costa Mesa, California, provides her employees with individualized, daily bonus reports to let them know how close they are to reaching their goals. The computer even flashes reinforcing messages such as "Congratulations, you're doing great" as employees reach performance milestones.

The system also is a decision aide and can help diagnose performance ailments and develop high-potential employees. This is done by strategically integrating all human resource functions through the ROI. For example, after a store manager conducts an initial screening interview, a half-hour computer interview is administered to each applicant and then computer analyzed. By automating and standardizing the selection process on computer, the company can select the employees who are most likely to be successful.

Once hired, employees participate in the ROI skill assessment. This module tests employees to make sure they are qualified to do their jobs. Immediate grading with on-line tutorials for questions incorrectly answered is provided. If any performance deficiencies are found, additional computer-aided training is provided. The computer also provides refresher courses for existing employees. For example, when an employee was not performing as effectively on the job as he could have been, store manager Oskinski directed him to work on the computer located in the back of the store for a few hours. "When he returned, his performance improved," Oskinski explains, adding that you can tell employees they need to sell more, but if they do not know how to do it they will not perform as expected. "Computer training assures that trainees know the ingredients of a successful sale as well as other aspects of the cookie business," says Osinski.

According to Randy Fields, president of Mrs. Fields's parent company (and Debra Fields's husband), the ROI system was designed to keep the corporation administratively lean and flat. Nanette Mathieu, director of operations, was promoted from store manager to her current position in just four years. Much of the knowledge she now possesses was acquired through the ROI system. The system also freed her to do what she does best—manage people. "If you're supposed to be the expert and the manager who's going to build sales, the last thing you should be doing is sitting at your desk working numbers," says Mathieu. "You should be developing your team."

Since implementing the new system in 1985, sales at Mrs. Fields have continued to increase. Also, employee turnover is substantially lower than for other companies in the fast-food industry at all levels.[2]

 ## USING PERFORMANCE APPRAISALS TO MAXIMIZE PERFORMANCE

As the feature "Managing Human Resources for the 21st Century at Mrs. Fields" shows, companies are finding out that their best chance for attaining peak performance at the individual, team, and organization levels lies with establishing a strategically aligned performance management system *and* giving employees feedback as quickly as possible on how well they are doing. Although performance management systems are as individual as the goals and objectives of organizations, to be successful, they must mesh with key aspects of the organizations' overall approaches to managing human resources.

Performance measurement, which necessarily reflects the past, is not an end to be achieved. Rather, it is a means for moving into a more productive future. For performance appraisals to achieve their potential, it is not sufficient to just *do* them; employees must *act* on them. Usually, supervisors have responsibility for communicating the results of appraisals to their subordinates and helping their subordinates improve in the future. Conversely, subordinates usually have responsibility for seeking honest feedback and using it to improve their performance. Human resource professionals can facilitate the effective use of appraisal by training supervisors in the art of feedback and by providing skill- and knowledge-building resources to employees.

These principles may seem straightforward, yet few organizations can claim to have perfected their performance management systems. Numerous hindrances to performance maximization are inherent in organizational life. This chapter describes several of these and offers recommendations for how to deal with them. It begins by describing sources of conflict in performance management and strategies to resolve conflict. Next, it discusses the components of appraisal processes that evoke peak performance, paying special attention to the appraisal interview and the appraisal context. Then, it explains how to diagnose performance problems and how to improve performance. It concludes by examining performance appraisal in different countries.

 ## OBSTACLES TO PERFORMANCE APPRAISAL

Performance appraisal touches on an emotionally charged activity: the assessment of a person's contribution to an organization. The signals a person receives about this assessment affect self-esteem and subsequent performance. When everything is going well, appraisal is easy. Everyone wants to give and get feedback that says "You do not need to change." But today's competitive environment does not usually accept the status quo. Instead, it mandates improvement. Improvements often come slowly, in part because of conflicts inherent in the appraisal process. These conflicts interfere with honest data gathering, data sharing, and data use. The result? Performance appraisals are often given low marks from employees, employers, and experts. Often, these low marks reflect larger systemic problems. They also reflect a normal preference for positive social interactions.

Lack of Strategic Integration

Performance appraisal processes often lead to conflict because their goals are not aligned with the organization's overall objectives. One explanation for this is that traditionally, human resources have not been given the same priority as other resources during strategic planning. As a consequence, the performance management system evolves in isolation from strategic initiatives rather than in anticipation of them. Another explanation is that building such linkages takes time as well as other resources. Therefore, even when a company recognizes problems of strategic misalignment, it may not be willing to commit these resources unless it anticipates a sure and immediate payoff.[3]

The experiences of Metropolitan Property and Casualty Insurance Company of Warwick, Rhode Island, illustrate the scope of investment that may be needed to achieve strategic alignment. The company decided to evaluate its performance appraisal system as part of a larger corporation change effort. To begin, it established employee focus groups to review and evaluate the existing system. The focus groups' discussions revealed that dissatisfaction was far greater than expected. Rather than supporting the strategies of the organization, stakeholders viewed the appraisal process as demotivating. Employees particularly abhorred appraisals as something done *to* them by the manager, rather than *with* them. They saw appraisals as backward, focusing on the past rather than providing direction for the future. The timing of appraisals, which was every six to twelve months, was viewed as nonsensical and inappropriate. These revelations prompted Metropolitan Property and Casualty to conduct an environmental scan to find out how exemplary firms were using appraisals far more effectively.

Armed with both internal and external information, an employee-management team created a new performance management system. Called Focus on Achievement, the new program was built on the organization's mission: "We will provide an environment in which individuals effectively utilize their skills and creativity and receive recognition for their contributions." Exhibit 11.1 summarizes the differences between Metropolitan's old system and its new strategically aligned system. At the heart of the new system is a shift in emphasis, from evaluation of the past to development for the future.

Viewing performance management as an ongoing process, Metropolitan launched its Focus on Achievement program by reviewing its organizational goals and strategies with all employees. This is now done at the beginning of each year. Within this context, each employee develops a personalized achievement plan; this is a statement of individual vision: What do I value in the company? What do I want to become and achieve on the job during the next year? In addition, job responsibilities are reviewed to identify activities that can be eliminated to enhance effectiveness. Employees also develop personal action plans in which they specify primary customers, identify stretch goals, and identify indicators that serve as criteria for assessing effectiveness. The employees review their proposed plans with their supervisors at this point, and then, during the year, checkpoint meetings may be called by the employee or manager. At year-end, employees receive recognition for their *achievements.* An employee who established an ambitious plan but did not fully achieve it may receive greater recognition than one who exceeded a simpler plan.[4]

Power and Politics

By definition, a performance appraisal system has legitimate power to influence job incumbents. Higher-ranking employees typically evaluate lower-ranking and less power-

■ *Exhibit 11.1*

Components of Metropolitan Property and Casualty's Performance Management System

Component	Old versus New Methods	
	Performance Appraisal	Focus on Achievement
Goal	Evaluation	Achievement
Manager	Program controller	Partner
Employee	Passive person	Initiator
View	Rearview mirror	Prospective
Outcome	Performance rating	Improved performance
Timing	Once a year	Ongoing
Links	None	Corporate goals
Rewards	Based on rating	Based on contribution
Theme	Control	Sharing
Criteria	Determined by manager	Suggested by and mutually determined with employee
Customer	No input	Input
Development plan	Sometimes included	Essential element
Individual vision	Not discussed	Basis for the plan
Atmosphere	Often confrontational	Supportive

SOURCE: Adapted from "A New Focus on Achievement," *Personnel Journal* (February 1991): 73–75.

ful employees. In addition, appraisal results lead to formal organizational consequences such as monetary rewards, promotion, and dismissal, as well as to informal consequences such as public criticism and special privileges. Such consequences generally are recognized as affecting ratees, but appraisal results also have consequences for the organization and for raters. If appraisals are contaminated by a rater's concern about the consequences for himself or herself, distorted and inaccurate information is used as a basis for future action. Dynamics such as these lessen the strategic value of appraisal information and actions based on that information. Exhibit 11.2 provides examples of the motives that might produce distorted rating behaviors. The behaviors are categorized as defensive or assertive and tactical or strategic. Tactical behavior seeks to secure a short-term political goal and is episodic. In comparison, strategic behavior involves a longer time frame and is used to develop characteristics that will yield long-term results.[5]

According to a recent study, the main reason managers distort ratings is to avoid conflict with subordinates. They may also believe that high ratings will be reciprocated during upward appraisals. Politically motivated managers may rate their subordinates higher than deserved in order to appear successful themselves, to enlist subordinate cooperation for future work, to enhance their popularity, or to compare favorably with other supervisors. Conversely, managers may give out strict ratings in order to create an image as a taskmaster, to signal a change in leadership, or to motivate employees to work even harder.[6]

Low ratings often have some negative consequence (e.g., firing or demotion) for employees—consequences for which the manager may not want to be held personally responsible. As a career military officer put it: The political environment in the Armed Forces has been such that an officer MUST have ALL superior ratings or he or she won't move up. ANY glitch in your ratings and you're out or plateaued. Therefore, we all play the game: My commanding officer gives me high ratings and I do the same for my men and women. While the military is trying to change all this, it's going to take a cultural revolution before any significant progress will be made.

■ *Exhibit 11.2*

Examples of the Motives Behind Distortions in Performance Appraisal Ratings

	Tactical Motive	Strategic Motive
Defensive Motive	*Deflated Ratings* ■ To attribute poor unit performance to individual subordinate problems ■ To provide an excuse for anticipated poor unit performance ■ To keep valuable employees who would otherwise be promoted or transferred ■ To control greater proportions of discretionary funds by restricting merit awards *Inflated Ratings* ■ To avoid complaints about poor supervision or a poor performance appraisal process ■ To avoid personal confrontations with subordinates over lower-than-expected ratings	*Deflated Ratings* ■ To attribute poor unit performance over several periods to a subordinate's lack of ability ■ To pave the way to increase future unit evaluations and to claim greater personal responsibility for future effectiveness *Inflated Ratings* ■ To attend to other supervisory responsibilities by avoiding potential subordinate grievances concerning appraisal
Assertive Motive	*Deflated Ratings* ■ To comply with superiors' demands for high work standards ■ To comply with informal demands of superiors for a normal distribution of ratings ■ To increase the perceived coercive power of the supervisor, that is, the perception that slacking off results in punishment or fewer rewards *Inflated Ratings* ■ To enhance the image of work unit effectiveness as a form of self-enhancement ■ To motivate employees to reciprocate with higher performance ■ To promote troublesome individuals out of the work unit ■ To inflate subordinate ratings of leadership or supervisory competence	*Deflated Ratings* ■ To increase perceptions of superiors' esteem and competence by maintaining high standards *Inflated Ratings* ■ To increase or maintain subordinate liking ■ To claim credit for aggregated unit excellence under conditions of ambiguous criteria ■ To increase the perceived reward power of the supervisor, that is, the idea that hard work is financially rewarded ■ To increase prestige with ratees by making them eligible for more merit increases

Stakeholder Goals

Goal conflict between the various constituents who have a stake in the appraisal process may hinder attempts to maximize performance. From organizational and individual goals come two sets of conflicts. One is between the organization's evaluative and developmental goals. When pursuing an evaluative goal, a superior makes judgments that affect the subordinate's career and immediate rewards. Communicating these judgments can create an adversarial, low-trust relationship between superior and subordinate. This, in turn, precludes the superior from performing as a problem solver and coach, which is essential to serving developmental goals.

The second set of conflicts arises from the various goals of the employees who are being evaluated. On the one hand, these individuals want valid feedback that gives them information about how to improve and where they stand in the organization. On the other hand, they want to verify their self-image and obtain valued rewards. Supervisors must strive to be both open and protective, to help employees meet both sets of goals.[7]

Perceptual Focus

Another hindrance to using performance appraisals effectively is the differing perspectives that the players bring to the process. For the subordinate (the actor), the perceptual focus is outward. Most salient are environmental forces (the supervisor, availability of supplies, coworkers) that interfere with the subordinate's ability to perform. For the supervisor (observer), the perceptual focus is on the subordinate and her or his motivation and ability. These differences can lead to conflict, especially when it comes to identifying the causes of poor performance. Low-performance situations accentuate a natural tendency that we all share, which is to account for performance in a self-serving manner. To protect their egos, employees attribute their own poor performance to external circumstances—a difficult task, unclear instructions, lack of necessary equipment, and other situations that often implicate the supervisor. Supervisors also wish to protect their egos, which may mean denying responsibility for the subordinate's poor performance and instead attributing causes to the employee's own deficiencies.

Similar self-serving perceptual biases may also dampen the expected effects of positive appraisals. When we perform well, the natural tendency is to take full credit for our performance. We use positive evidence to reinforce our high opinion of ourselves, discounting the role external forces may have played. The self-interested perspective of observers, however, leads them to view our success as due to such things as chance or luck and the support we received from others.[8] Add to this our general feeling that we are better-than-average performers, and the scene is set for a potentially dysfunctional cycle: Employees believe they perform well and deserve credit for having done so; their supervisors often evaluate their performance less favorably, and these evaluations are perceived as unfair. When supervisors do recognize good performance, employees may perceive the recognition as merely what they deserved, leaving supervisors to wonder why their subordinates are not more grateful.

Of course, not all subordinates or all employees are equally susceptible to these perceptual biases, but few are completely immune, either. So all experience some of the negative consequences. Also, all can improve by understanding these dynamics.

Consequences of Inherent Conflicts

Among the several consequences of the conflicts inherent in performance appraisal are ambivalence, avoidance, defensiveness, and resistance. The organization demands that superiors act as judge and jury in telling subordinates where they stand, and subordinates expect it; nevertheless, supervisors may feel uncertain about their judgments and anxious about how subordinates will react to negative feedback. This latter feeling is intensified when superiors have not been trained in giving feedback. Subordinates are equally ambivalent because they want honest feedback, yet they also want to receive rewards and maintain their self-image. In addition, if they are open with their superiors in identifying undeveloped potential, they risk the chance that the superiors may use this to evaluate them unfavorably.

DESIGNING APPRAISAL PROCESSES TO ATTAIN MAXIMUM PERFORMANCE

Can the appraisal system and feedback sessions be designed to minimize appraisal conflicts, attain perceptual congruence, and maximize performance among individual workers and work teams?[9] Yes, it can, with the help of some useful strategies.

Use Appropriate Performance Data

The first step in reducing conflict and perceptual differences is to use performance data that focus on specific behaviors or goals. Performance data that focus on personal attributes or characteristics are likely to prompt defensiveness because they are difficult for the superior to justify and because they affect the subordinate's self-image. Marilyn Moats Kennedy, managing partner of Career Strategies, a management consulting company in Wilmette, Illinois, says:

> It's important to critique the behavior of an employee, not the employee himself.
> If you bark, "You have a bad attitude," to your receptionist, for example, you'll likely find yourself facing a very defensive employee. You'll probably get better results if you say, "When someone steps up to your desk, I'd like them to get the distinct impression that you're delighted to see them."[10]

The delivery of performance information needs to be well-timed, also. Performance expectations need to be communicated at the beginning of the appraisal period and then reinforced with feedback. In general, immediate feedback is most useful. Delays may be necessary, however, if the subordinate is not yet ready to receive the performance information. Feedback also should involve the amount of information the receiver can use rather than what the evaluator would like to give. Overloading a person with information reduces the possibility that he or she will use it effectively. An evaluator who gives more data than can be used is most likely satisfying a personal need (e.g., pride in not holding anything back) rather than helping the other person.[11]

360-Degree Feedback, Upward Evaluations, and Professional Coaching. Increasingly, major companies are concluding that appropriate feedback is 360-degree feedback, or feedback from multiple sources reflecting multiple perspectives, especially for managerial employees, and especially from employees upwards to their bosses. Use of these upward evaluations appears to be a critical component of 360-degree feedback in the best companies. In 1993, *Fortune* magazine surveyed the companies ranked number one in their industries according to *Fortune*'s annual *Most Admired* list. Of these thirty-seven companies, representing thirty-seven industries, twenty reported using upward evaluations, and most of these used the results for determining pay and promotion. Using this approach to appraisal, UPS realized that it needed to give its managers more training in how to develop the skills of their employees.

For high-level executives, 360-degree feedback may prompt the company to invest in individualized, professional coaching. According to one account, the typical candidates for such coaching are one of two types:

The first is usually a white man in his late 40s who has soared because he's an outstanding engineer or has mystical intuition about coming reversals in exchange rates. He has recently been promoted to a position where he has authority over people not like himself, folks in marketing perhaps or communications. "The only management style he knows is how to shout orders and take names," observes Alicia Whitaker, director of global career planning for Colgate. "He makes people feel like idiots for coming to him with a question or suggestion." He finishes people's sentences for them, refuses to listen, and castigates not only his own subordinates but also those of peers, so that people in other departments refuse to work with his people.

The second category is typically a woman, not necessarily white, about a decade younger than the male archetype. Her brilliance and dedication to the job have catapulted her through the lower ranks. Now, however, she must work with equally talented peers, and she hasn't mastered the complex game of competition and cooperation played at her new managerial level. She sees male chauvinism everywhere; some is real, some imagined. She isolates herself and her section from the rest of the company.[12]

The general purpose of such coaching and feedback is improving the organization's ability to achieve its strategic objectives.

The feature "Positioning for the 21st Century: Performance Management in the Round" suggests that firms should give strong consideration to using 360-degree feedback.

Ensure Fairness

To minimize the emotionally charged atmosphere that surrounds the performance appraisal process, managers also need to take steps to ensure that the process is perceived as fair and equitable. Appraisal programs are viewed as fair to the extent that they provide for:

- *Consistency:* Performance standards are applied consistently to all incumbents. Allowances are not made frequently for workers with special problems, nor are high performers expected to carry more than their own weight.
- *Familiarity:* The use of diaries to record worker outputs, frequent observation of performance, and management by "wandering around" increase a supervisor's job knowledge and consequently create the impression that the supervisor and the appraisal are fair.
- *Solicitation of Input:* Information regarding performance standards, as well as strategies to attain them, needs to be solicited prior to evaluation. More important, this information should be used constructively.
- *Opportunity to Challenge or Rebut the Evaluation:* Consistent with the problem-solving interview (discussed later in this chapter), employees need to be able to challenge or rebut evaluations. Due process procedures (discussed in Chapter 3) are useful here.

Furthermore, outcomes of the appraisal process must be distributed fairly. For example, in a merit-based system, ratings need to reflect the levels of performance attained, and recommendations for salary increases and promotions need to reflect these ratings.[13]

Empower Employees

Part of the difficulty in managing the appraisal process is collecting and maintaining information on all employees. As a manager's span of control increases in size, the task grows to unmanageable levels. Shifting the responsibility for performance record keeping

Positioning for the 21st Century:
PERFORMANCE MANAGEMENT IN THE ROUND

Employers can better manage the performance of their workers if they replace traditional employee evaluations with 360-degree feedback systems, asserts Mark R. Edwards, president of the consulting firm TEAMS Incorporated of Tempe, Arizona.

A DIAGNOSTIC TOOL

In contrast to the traditional approach, where a single supervisor rates employee performance, multiple-source systems allow evaluations to be conducted by a group of colleagues and internal customers who form a circle around the employee. According to Edwards, employees are much more likely to respond constructively to a group's suggestions on how to improve their performance. As a result, the evaluation process becomes more of a diagnostic tool for employee development and less of an instrument to judge and discipline employees.

Ten years of research at some of the largest employers in the country, including DuPont, Dow Chemical, and Disney, provides compelling evidence that multiple-source evaluation systems are much more fair than single-source approaches, Edwards adds. The 360-degree system has even been upheld as more reliable than single-source evaluations in several wrongful discharge lawsuits, he notes. The evaluation process produces more valid results because it involves a group of people who interact with the employee in many different ways. For the same reason, the process has proved to be less susceptible to gender and ethnicity biases than are single-source evaluations.

DESIGNING AN EVALUATION SYSTEM

As organizations become flatter and move toward team-based management structures, multiple-source evaluation systems can play an integral role in facilitating participation and enhancing productivity, Edwards notes. The essential elements of an effective 360-degree feedback system, he says, include the following:

1. *Establish feedback criteria:* The first step in developing a multiple-source assessment system is selecting evaluation criteria and developing a behavior profile, so that employees can be assessed relative to a model and not coworkers. The process of defining evaluation criteria should be participative. For the system to work effectively, stakeholders in the organization must be given the opportunity to get involved up front in the process.

2. *Select evaluation teams:* Do not limit evaluation teams to the employees' closest colleagues. To get the most out of multiple-source assessments, the group should reflect the employees' internal customers. Teams should consist of five to eight members, including the employee being evaluated. Employees then have the opportunity to compare their self-evaluations with the group's assessments.

3. *Conduct the evaluations:* Evaluation forms can be distributed in hard copy or electronically. Using an electronic mail system is one very efficient method for carrying out the process. It is important, however, to establish procedures for ensuring the anonymity of evaluators and the confidentiality of their responses.

4. *Create summary reports:* After the evaluation forms are collected, summary data should be tabulated and put into a format that is easily understood by employees.

5. *Analyze results:* Along with the raw results of the evaluations, provide employees an analysis of the data that will help clarify and focus areas of strength and weakness in their performance.

6. *Intervene to improve behavior:* The final step is to use evaluation results to improve employee performance. Instead of focusing only on problems, seek to identify structural constraints to improvement, and attempt to change those constraints. For example, does the employee have the necessary training and tools to perform the job, and are internal procedures clearly communicated?[14]

to the job incumbent helps resolve this problem, while increasing perceptions of fairness. To carry out this responsibility, incumbents first need training in writing performance standards and in collecting and documenting performance information. Incumbents must feel free to renegotiate performance standards that have become obsolete or unattainable owing to constraints. Thus, open two-way communication is needed, as in a climate of trust.

Delegating performance management responsibility offers several advantages. First, subordinates are no longer passive participants, reacting to supervisor directives. Second, because subordinates are identifying performance hurdles and bringing them to the attention of managers, defensiveness is reduced. Third, supervisors are free to manage and coach rather than patrol and police. Finally, subordinates feel ownership for the process.

At Southwest Texas Methodist Hospital, employees are empowered to call a "powwow" any time a problem needs to be resolved. Powwows are brief, impromptu problem-solving meetings designed to improve patient care, increase productivity, and involve employees in the decision process. As operationalized, a powwow must focus only on patient care or job-related issues and can be called by simply announcing it. The employees who are involved complete all work that cannot wait and then join the powwow. The person calling the powwow acts as a leader—stating the problem, leading the discussion, and ensuring that the powwow is brief (less than five minutes). The leader must inform a supervisor about the problem and the solution. Powwows also can be a policy-making forum and may result in changes in written policies and procedures.[15]

Establish Interlocking Goals

To resolve the problem of goal conflict between stakeholders, new goals can be established that integrate the needs of all parties. For example, retailers have historically had different performance management systems for buyers and sellers. Buyers usually are evaluated on gross margins, managers on sales and management (the use of people skills, service, etc.).

At Neiman Marcus Group, the two systems were merged to give the buyer and the department manager a stake in both ends of retailing. According to Craig Innes, senior vice president of human resources at Neiman Marcus:

> Buyers and managers receive a monthly Base Profit Contribution Report. The buyer's report lists all the gross margin components, including handling and merchandise preparation. The buyer can use this information to negotiate with the manager. The manager's report lists all the expenses involved in selling such as draw versus commission pay. This information allows the manager to determine that sales productivity is covering the cost of selling. Our profit contribution reporting system works because it merges the goals of buyers and sellers and forces them to look at the business more wholistically.[16]

Conflicting goals between stakeholders become especially salient in organizations using cross-functional teams to complete short-term or long-term projects. For such teams, diverse members typically are drawn from different parts of the organization. In some cases, team members may even come from other organizations. For example, at Bell Labs, engineers typically work in a research lab and also serve as members of project teams that include customers for the products they design.[17]

Members of successful cross-functional teams must break through the walls that traditionally separate departments, divisions, and even whole organizations, and learn to operate as a cohesive unit. A major part of their challenge is managing the team's performance. The company will hold the team accountable for a final product, but the team usually must manage the activities that eventually lead to that product. Much of this management task involves creating interlocking goals for the individual members. Individuals in the team need to understand their own responsibilities and goals, and also how the set of interlocking goals within the team relate to the team's ability to deliver its end product on time.

Conduct Problem-Solving Performance Appraisal Interviews

Performance management is an ongoing process, punctuated by formal appraisals. The performance appraisal interview often is the centerpiece of the formal appraisal. During the interview, supervisors and subordinates meet to exchange information, including evaluations of performance and ideas for how to improve. Setting goals for the future may also be on the agenda. Used well, the interview can be an effective tool for minimizing or resolving conflicts.

Advance Preparation. To signal to employees that performance matters, the interview needs to be scheduled in advance. In setting up the interview, the manager and employee should reach agreement regarding its purpose and content. For example, will the subordinate have an opportunity to evaluate the performance of the supervisor, or will the evaluation be one way? Will the interview be restricted to evaluating past performance or to mapping out a strategy for future performance, or will it be open to both tasks? By discussing these issues before the actual interview, both participants have time to prepare. If subordinates are empowered, advance notice will give them sufficient time to update their performance records and do a self-review.

Interview Content. Initiating and carrying out an effective interview session requires both coaching and counseling skills. Supervisors need to listen to and reflect back what subordinates say with regard to performance, its causes, and its outcomes. Too often, the interview process breaks down and supervisors end up telling employees how well or poorly they are doing and selling them on the merits of setting specific goals for improvement. This may seem efficient for the supervisors, but subordinates feel frustrated trying to convince their superiors to listen to justifications for their performance levels. As a result, they discount feedback and become entrenched in past behavior.

A more effective approach is to use the appraisal interview as a problem-solving session. This approach centers on sharing perceptions and identifying solutions to problems. Active and open dialogue is established between superior and subordinate. Goals for improvement are established mutually by supervisor and subordinate. This type of interview is difficult for most supervisors, so prior training in problem solving and in giving and receiving feedback should be provided.

Appropriate Follow-Up. Follow-up is essential to ensure that the behavioral contract negotiated during the interview is fulfilled. Because changing behavior is hard work, supervisors as well as subordinates tend to put behavioral agreements on the back burner. Consequently, supervisors should verify that subordinates know what is expected, have strategies to perform as desired, and realize the consequences of good or poor behavior. They should also monitor behavior, provide feedback, and immediately reinforce new behaviors that match desired objectives. In the absence of feedback and reinforcement, new behaviors will probably not become habit. Reinforcement can be as simple as a pat on the back or a compliment ("That was nice work, George"), or as tangible as a note placed in the employee's file.[18] For some behaviors, constant monitoring may be needed. Consider this example:

> I'm inclined to yell. I know I shouldn't. So I got a gadget, a mechanical daisy with sunglasses and guitar that sits in a glass and oscillates with the volume of my voice. It tells me when I'm yelling. Also, I instructed my secretary to hold up a stop sign when I'm screaming at someone. Like a recovering alcoholic, I take it one day at a time. Patience, patience. Tolerance, tolerance.
>
> A FORTY-NINE-YEAR-OLD BANKER[19]

Designing performance management systems with all the characteristics needed to maximize performance will not guarantee perfect performance—in some cases, for example, individuals may lack the ability to perform—but it should improve performance. Also, satisfaction with the system may go up.[20,21]

 ## DIAGNOSING PERFORMANCE

The interview provides a mechanism by which performance information can be exchanged, but it is only one component of an effective performance management system. For the system to work well, and for performance to be maximized, the information on which the interview is based must be accurate and the cause of any deficiency must be pinpointed.

Identifying Performance Gaps

Goals and absolute behavioral standards can be used to identify performance deficiencies by determining how well an employee does in relation to them. If an employee had a performance goal of reducing the scrap rate by 10 percent but reduced it by only 5 percent, a performance gap exists. This method is valid if the goals and standards are not contradictory and if they can be quantified, and if the subordinate's performance can be measured in the same terms.[22]

Some organizations identify gaps by comparing the performance levels of individuals, units, or departments. For example, organizations with several divisions might measure the overall performance of each division by comparing it with the overall performance of every other division, with divisions ranked at the bottom identified as having performance gaps. This is not an effective strategy for diagnosing performance gaps. Even units at the bottom of the ranking may have met their established goals, and, conversely, those at the top may not have met their goals.

Finally, gaps can be spotted by completing a checklist of symptoms, like the one in Exhibit 11.3. Although such a checklist does not identify the causes of the performance discrepancies, more than one "yes" indicates that the line manager should probe deeper.

Regardless of the method used to discover if a performance deficiency exists, once one is detected, managers should examine the causes underlying it.

Identifying Causes of Performance Deficiencies

To uncover the reasons for performance deficiencies, a number of questions can be asked, based on a model of the determinants of employee behavior in organizations.[23] This model enables HR professionals and line managers to diagnose performance deficiencies and correct them in a systematic way. In general, the model says employees perform well if the following performance facilitators are present:

◼ *Exhibit 11.3*
Sample Checklist for Identifying Performance Problems

Read each question and relate it to your knowledge of the incumbent. If you are thinking "yes" in response to a question, place a check mark next to that item. If not, leave it blank.

Do Peers Complain That

_____ 1. She is not treating them fairly?
_____ 2. He is not carrying his own weight?
_____ 3. She is rude?
_____ 4. He is argumentative and confrontational?
_____ 5. She is all talk and no action?

Do Customers

_____ 1. Always ask for someone else to help them?
_____ 2. Complain about her attitude?
_____ 3. Complain that he has made promises to them that he has never fulfilled?
_____ 4. Say she is bad-mouthing you, the organization, or the organization's products?
_____ 5. Complain that he is too pushy?

Do You

_____ 1. Find it difficult to get your own work done because you spend so much time with him or his problems and mistakes?
_____ 2. Worry about what she will say to customers and clients?
_____ 3. Check his work often because you are afraid of mistakes?
_____ 4. Do work yourself that you should have delegated to her?
_____ 5. Assign work to others because they can do it faster or better than he can?
_____ 6. Hear about her mistakes from your boss or others?
_____ 7. Sometimes find out that he has lied to you or stretched the truth?
_____ 8. Seldom think of her when you are deciding who should get an important assignment?

Does the Incumbent

_____ 1. Infrequently complete assignments on time?
_____ 2. Often show up to work late or not at all?
_____ 3. Always have an excuse for poor performance?
_____ 4. Wait to be assigned additional work rather than asking for more work when an assignment is completed?
_____ 5. Rarely complete assignments in the way you want?
_____ 6. Ignore suggestions for improvement?

- ◉ Ability
- ◉ Interest in doing the job
- ◉ Opportunity to grow and advance
- ◉ Clearly defined goals
- ◉ Certainty about what is expected
- ◉ Feedback on how well they are doing
- ◉ Rewards for performing well
- ◉ Punishments for performing poorly
- ◉ Power to get resources to do the job[24]

Exhibit 11.4 shows most of these determinants and specific questions to ask in pinpointing the causes of performance deficiencies. Negative responses indicate that an item is probably a cause. Based on a series of such responses, the likely causes of a performance deficiency can be established. Then, action plans for improvement can be developed.

■ *Exhibit 11.4*
Sample Checklist for Diagnosing the Causes of Performance Deficiencies

Check the determinants of performance or behavior that apply to the situation you are analyzing.

	Yes	No
I. Knowledge, Skills, and Abilities		
A. Does the incumbent have the skill to perform as expected?	_____	_____
B. Has the incumbent performed as expected before?	_____	_____
C. Does the incumbent believe he or she has the ability to perform as desired?	_____	_____
D. Does the incumbent have the interest to perform as desired?	_____	_____
II. Goals for the Incumbent		
A. Were the goals communicated to the incumbent before the performance period?	_____	_____
B. Are the goals specific?	_____	_____
C. Are the goals difficult but attainable?	_____	_____
III. Certainty for the Incumbent		
A. Has desired performance been clearly specified?	_____	_____
B. Have rewards or consequences for good or bad performance been specified?	_____	_____
C. Is the incumbent clear about her or his level of authority?	_____	_____
IV. Feedback to the Incumbent		
A. Does the incumbent know when he or she has performed correctly or incorrectly?	_____	
B. Is the feedback diagnostic so that the incumbent can perform better in the future?	_____	_____
C. Is there a delay between performance and the receipt of the feedback?	_____	_____
D. Can performance feedback be easily interpreted?	_____	_____
V. Consequences to the Incumbent		
A. Is performing as expected punishing?	_____	_____
B. Is not performing more rewarding?	_____	_____
C. Does performing as desired matter?	_____	_____
D. Are there positive consequences for performing as desired?	_____	_____
VI. Power for the Incumbent		
A. Can the incumbent mobilize the resources to get the job done?	_____	_____
B. Does the incumbent have the tools and equipment to perform as desired?	_____	_____

SOURCE: Based on R. F. Mager and P. Pipe, *Analyzing Performance Problems, or "You Really Oughta Wanna"* (Belmont, CA: Fearon Pitman, 1970).

The process people use to explain their own and others' behavior is called *attribution*. Understanding attribution helps one predict what causes and responses line managers are likely to attach to the performance deficiencies they see in their subordinates. These explanations for behavior serve as the basis for deciding how to change behavior. If the explanations are wrong, plans for changing behavior will probably be ineffective.

Line managers attribute subordinates' deficiencies to either internal causes (the subordinates) or external causes (the subordinates' environment). Internal attributions include explanations such as low effort (motivation) or low ability; external attributions include task interference, bad luck, lack of organizational rewards, and poor supervision. Managers are more likely to make internal attributions to the extent that the incumbent (1) performs poorly on other tasks, (2) performs poorly when other incumbents perform well on the same task, and (3) has performed poorly on the same task in the past. Furthermore, managers are likely to focus on motivation over ability if an incumbent has performed the task adequately in the past but is not doing so now.[25]

Whether the manager makes internal or external attributions influences the strategy for performance improvement selected by the manager.[26] If internal attributions are made, the manager is more likely to select strategies aimed at changing the subordinate, such as retraining or reprimands. If external attributions are made, the manager is more likely to select strategies that modify the environment, such as changing the job design or bringing in more rewards and punishments.

STRATEGIES FOR IMPROVING PERFORMANCE

When performance deficiencies are found, line managers and HR professionals can do many things to improve employees' performance. They can use the following suggestions for acting on the causes of deficiencies identified in Exhibit 11.4, except for ability. If lack of ability is the cause, then training is needed (see Chapter 9).

Positive Reinforcement

A *positive reinforcement (PR)* system can be designed based on the principles of reinforcement theory.[27] Positive reinforcement involves the use of positive rewards to increase the occurrence of the desired performance. It is based on two fundamental principles: (1) people perform in ways that they find most rewarding to them; and (2) by providing the proper rewards, it is possible to improve performance. A PR program focuses on the job behavior that leads to desired results, rather than on the results directly. It uses rewards rather than punishment or the threat of punishment to influence that behavior, and attempts to link specific behaviors to specific rewards. This model operates according to the law of effect, which states that behavior that leads to a positive result tends to be repeated, whereas behavior that leads to a neutral or negative result tends not to be repeated. Thus, an effort is made to link behavior to its consequences.[28] A positive reinforcement program is installed by four basic steps, as shown in Exhibit 11.5.[29]

   Conduct a Performance Audit. Performance audits examine how well jobs are being performed. Without them, many managers believe that their operations are going better than they actually are. For instance, Emery Air Freight Corporation conducted a performance audit on the way it was shipping packages. The cost of freight is considerably reduced if all the small packages going to a particular city are put in large

■ *Exhibit 11.5*
Steps in a Positive Reinforcement Program

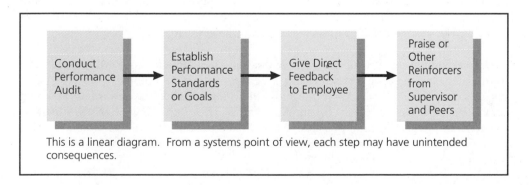

This is a linear diagram. From a systems point of view, each step may have unintended consequences.

containers. The managers involved in this part of the operation estimated that large containers were used in shipping about 90 percent of the time. The audit showed that the actual frequency was only 45 percent of the time.[30] If possible, workers should be involved in performance audits, since they know more about the job than anyone else.

Establish Performance Standards and Goals. Standards are the minimum levels of performance accepted; goals are targeted levels of performance. Both should be set after a performance audit and should be tied directly to the job. Goals and standards should be measurable and attainable. Goals should be challenging but not impossible to reach; perfection is never possible. Goals and standards are best formed on the basis of observation and common sense, and they should be as precise as possible. "Better identification with the organization" and "increased job satisfaction" are too general to be goals or standards.

Where possible, the workers should help establish their own goals. At Emery Air Freight, the employees in the Chicago customer service department set and reached a standard higher than the one management would have set for giving customer answers within a specified time period.[31] However, time does not always allow for giving employees all the information they need to establish a reasonable goal.

Give Feedback to Employees about Their Performance. The third step in a positive reinforcement program is to give workers the basic data they need in order to keep track of their own work. The standards of performance for many jobs are not clearly stated; even when they are, they are seldom available to the worker. A woman in an insurance company described her routine as follows: "I glance through the form to see if it is completely filled out. Then I separate the blue copies from the yellow copies and put them in different piles." When asked what purpose the form served, how it was used, and where the different copies went, she reported that she did not know. She had no idea if the information on the form was accurate, and she did not know the consequences if the form was incompletely or incorrectly filled out. All she knew was that each line of the form had to have something on it or the document had to be returned to another department.

Performance standards are ineffective without constant measurement and feedback. The feedback should be neutral rather than evaluative or judgmental and, if possible, should come directly to the worker rather than to the supervisor. Prompt, direct feedback provides the knowledge the worker needs in order to learn. Feedback allows the worker to know whether performance is improving, remaining the same, or getting worse. When the managers and employees at Emery Air Freight understood that only 45 percent of all small packages going to one location were being shipped in containers, and feedback and positive reinforcement were given, the workers soon hit the standard of 95 percent. The change resulted in savings of about $65,000 a year.[32]

Offer Employees Praise or Other Rewards Tied Directly to Performance. The fourth step in a positive reinforcement program—offering employees praise or other rewards tied to performance—is the most important one. If the reward is praise, it should be expressed in specific, quantitative terms. "Keep up the good work, Chris," is too general. A better form of praise is: "Mary, I liked the imagination you used in getting the product packed. You are running fairly consistently at 97 percent of standard. After watching you, I can understand why."

One common reward is money. Although money is very effective as a motivator, many organizations cannot afford to use it that way often. Other rewards can be just as effective, though. They include praise and recognition tied to the specific job behavior, the opportunity to choose activities, the opportunity to personally measure work improvement, and the opportunity to influence coworkers and management.

Rewards for specific performance should be given as soon as possible after the behavior has taken place. Reinforcement should be frequent and predictable at the beginning of a change, and can become less frequent and less predictable after the desired performance level is reached.

Several different types of reward schedules have been developed, among them continuous reinforcement and partial reinforcement. Under continuous reinforcement, the employee is rewarded every time the correct performance occurs. When this schedule is used, performance improves rapidly, but it can regress just as rapidly when the reinforcement is removed. In addition, managers find it difficult or impossible to reward performance continuously. Therefore, in most cases, managers should use partial reinforcement, rewarding correct behavior only part of the time. They may choose from a number of partial reinforcement schedules, perhaps the most effective being the variable ratio schedule. Under this schedule, reinforcement is given after an average number of desired responses but not precisely at that average point; the time of dispensation varies so that it cannot be predicted exactly.[33] In most organizations, pay occurs on a fixed interval schedule, such as once a week or once a month; pay increases and promotions occur on a variable interval schedule; and praise, recognition, and similar rewards occur on a partial reinforcement schedule.

Whatever schedule is used, managers should provide positive reinforcement as employees come close to the standard, shifting perhaps from a continuous to a partial reinforcement schedule as they get very close to the standard. At the beginning, managers might have to look carefully for even small changes in behavior in order to give positive reinforcement; otherwise, behavior might not improve.

The six basic rules for using reinforcement are

1. *Do not reward everyone the same way.* Using a defined objective or standard, give more rewards to the better performers.
2. *Recognize that failure to respond also has reinforcing consequences.* Managers influence subordinates by what they do not do as well as by what they do; a lack of reward thus can also influence behavior. Managers frequently find the job of differentiating between workers unpleasant but necessary. One way to differentiate is to reward some and withhold rewards from others.
3. *Tell people what they must do to be rewarded.* If employees have standards against which to measure the job, they can arrange their own feedback system to let them make self-judgments about their work. They can then adjust their work patterns accordingly.
4. *Tell people what they are doing wrong.* Few people like to fail; most want to get positive rewards. A manager who withholds rewards from subordinates should give them a clear idea of why the rewards are not forthcoming. The employees can then adjust their behavior accordingly rather than waste time trying to discover what behavior will be rewarded.
5. *Do not punish anyone in front of others.* Constructive criticism is useful in eliminating undesired behavior; so is punishment, when necessary. However, criticizing or punishing anyone in front of others lowers that person's self-respect and self-esteem. Furthermore, other members of the work group may sympathize with the punished employee and resent the supervisor.
6. *Be fair.* Make the consequences equal to the behavior. Do not cheat an employee out of just rewards; if someone is a good worker, say so. Some managers find it difficult to praise; others find it difficult to counsel an employee about what is being done

wrong. A person who is overrewarded may feel guilty, and one who is underrewarded may become angry.[34]

Positive Discipline Programs

Some organizations improve performance through the use of positive discipline or nonpunitive discipline.[35] The essential aspects of positive discipline programs are illustrated in the following example:

> When disciplinary discussions have failed to produce the desired changes, management places the individual on a one-day, "decision making leave." The company pays the employee for the day to demonstrate the organization's desire to see him or her remain a member of the organization and to eliminate the resentment and hostility that punitive actions usually produce. But tenure with the organization is conditional on the individual's decision to solve the immediate problem and make a "total performance commitment" to good performance on the job. The employee is instructed to return on the day following the leave with a decision either to change and stay or to quit and find more satisfying work elsewhere.[36]

This program puts the responsibility for the employee's behavior into the hands of the employee. It tells the employee, however, that the company cares and will keep the employee as long as she or he makes a commitment to do well. If the employee makes the commitment, the company has a good employee. If the employee decides to leave, she or he has no real cause to blame the company. This type of program appears to work.[37]

Employee Assistance Programs

As the feature "Using Data for the 21st Century: Today's EAPs Make the Grade" indicates, employee assistance programs (EAPs) help employees with chronic personal problems that hinder their job performance and attendance.

Successful employee assistance programs have the following attributes:

- Top management backing
- Union or employee support
- Confidentiality
- Easy access
- Trained supervisors
- A trained union steward, if in a union setting
- Insurance
- Availability of numerous services for assistance and referral
- Skilled professional leadership
- Systems for monitoring, assessing, and revising

Even though EAPs are designed to provide valuable assistance to employees, many employees in need fail to use them unless faced with the alternative of being fired. When so confronted, however, their success rate if they do attend an EAP is high. Successful results can translate into substantial gains in employee performance and reductions in absenteeism that far outweigh the costs of an EAP.[38]

Self-Management

Self-management is a relatively new approach to resolving performance discrepancies. It teaches people to exercise control over their own behavior. Self-management begins when people assess their own problems and set specific (but individual), hard goals in relation to those problems. Next, they discuss ways in which the environment facilitates

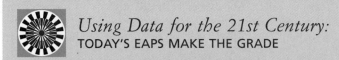

Using Data for the 21st Century:
TODAY'S EAPS MAKE THE GRADE

No matter how you try to measure them, employee assistance programs (EAPs) made the grade in the early 1990s: not only did more companies have successful programs, but those programs were addressing more types of problems and saving companies more money than ever.

Overall, American organizations invest as much as $798 million annually in EAPs. But for every dollar employers invest, recovery of loss is estimated at $5. That's $3.9 billion recovered from loss annually, according to statistics compiled by the Employee Assistance Professionals Association (EAPA), based in Arlington, Virginia. Recovery from loss is money that otherwise would have been spent on absenteeism, sick benefits, and work-related accidents.

In fact, a survey of fifty companies published in *American Management Magazine* showed that EAPs were responsible for substantial cost reductions, including declines of 33 percent in the use of sickness benefits, 65 percent in work-related accidents, 30 percent in workers' compensation claims, and 74 percent in time spent on supervisor reprimands. Individual worker absenteeism traceable to alcohol abuse dropped 66 percent.

TAILORED SOLUTIONS

EAPs were originally created to battle alcoholism but have since expanded to address family, financial, and legal problems.

Thus, demographics—and geography—play a large role in determining the type of EAP a company adopts. No two are the same. Carpenter Technology Corporation in Reading, Pennsylvania, for example, happens to be located about one hundred miles from Atlantic City, New Jersey. "Our proximity allows for a whole lot of gambling in the casinos. And Eastern Pennsylvania's got a wealth of horse tracks where a lot of our employees spend a lot of money and time," says Gregory DeLapp, EAP administrator for the company's thirty-six hundred employees. "On the financial end, you've got everything from problems related to plastic financing to the other extreme, which is owing money to all the wrong people, for gambling debts." The company's EAP helps employees stop seeking short-term solutions such as cash advances or loans and achieve a long-term solution through counseling or referral.

NUMBER ONE PROBLEM: MARITAL

Marital and family relationship problems tend to be the most common problems employees bring to their EAPs, even though substance abuse continues to have more of an effect on job performance and costs more to treat. In fact, marital and family problems account for 40 to 50 percent of the referrals EAPs receive, says Keith McClellan, president of the Employee Assistance Society of North America (EASNA), based in Oak Park, Illinois.

But even though EAPs have evolved over the years, they have not strayed too far from their roots. "We had a good salesman recently who was referred by his boss because he went to a company function that served alcohol, and he began to drink too much," recalls Susan Swan-Granger, executive director of Employee Assistance of Central Virginia. "He also began to talk too much, and he put his foot in his mouth a couple of times to his boss and to his vice president. And the next day, he didn't even remember it. They could have terminated him for insubordination, but they didn't. Instead they insisted that he refer himself to the EAP."

And that, perhaps, best demonstrates the continuing ideals of EAPs; they rehabilitate rather than punish—for that, they earn an A.[39]

or hinders goal attainment. The challenge is to develop strategies that eliminate blocks to performance success. Put another way, self-management teaches people to observe their own behavior, compare their outputs to their goals, and administer their own reinforcement to sustain goal commitment and performance.[40]

Although self-management is effective for a variety of performance problems, its implementation can be tricky—particularly for the manager. Managers often perceive a threat of loss of power and ultimately importance as they realize that their subordinates are to become to a large extent their own managers. They also soon recognize that their repertoire of skills is at least in part obsolete. According to Jim Kouzes, president of Tom Peters Group, self-management entails coaching on the part of the manager: "If you want people to do what's right, teach them what's right and then show them by your own behavior."[41]

Telecommuting. As we approach and enter the 21st century, telecommuting and other forms of employment-at-a-distance are gaining ground; consequently, the role of self-management in the total performance management system will also grow. In places like Arizona and California, telecommuting got started as a way to reduce air pollution caused by commuters, but the practice has spread rapidly for a variety of reasons, including employees' needs for flexibility. According to one estimate, by 1992, 6.6 million Americans were telecommuters.

To the surprise of many managers, several studies show that telecommuting improves productivity. The success of telecommuting arrangements shows that employees clearly are capable of self-management. On the other hand, managers of telecommuters often realize that they lack the skills needed to effectively manage self-managing employees. According to Carol Nolan, telecommuting manager for Pacific Bell in Los Angeles, part of the problem is managers' views of their own roles: " 'We've done a good job of convincing managers they must see their employees to make sure they're doing the work,' says Nolan. She points to the success of the book *In Search of Excellence,* which promoted management by walking around the office [p. 43]."

The trick, it seems, is to replace direct supervision with management by results. This skill requires some learning and developing a degree of trust in employees. As a person in charge of about two dozen telecommuters at Apple Computer put it, "It's been a significant step forward in my maturation as a manager to become more focused on objectives rather than on how the work gets done."[42]

Punishment

Even though most employees want to conduct themselves in a manner that is acceptable to the organization and their fellow employees, problems of absenteeism, poor work performance, and rule violation do arise. When informal discussions or coaching fails to neutralize these dysfunctional behaviors, formal disciplinary action is needed. The following discussion complements the one in Chapter 3.

The objective of punishment is to decrease the frequency of an undesirable behavior. Punishments can include material consequences, such as a cut in pay, a disciplinary layoff without pay, a demotion, or, ultimately, termination. More common punishments are interpersonal and include oral reprimands and nonverbal cues, such as frowns, and aggressive body language.

Punishment is frequently used by organizations because it can achieve relatively immediate results. In addition, it is reinforcing to supervisors in that they feel they have taken action. It is an effective management tool for the following reasons:

◉ Discipline alerts the marginal employee that his or her low performance is unacceptable and that a change in behavior is warranted.
◉ Discipline has vicarious reinforcing power. When one person is punished, it signals other employees regarding expected performance and behavioral conduct.
◉ If the discipline is viewed as appropriate by other employees, it may increase their motivation, morale, and performance.

Punishment can also have undesirable side effects, however. For example, an employee reprimanded for low performance may become defensive and angry toward the supervisor and the organization. As many news reports attest, this anger may result in sabotage (destroying equipment, passing trade secrets) or retaliation (shooting the supervisor). Punishment also frequently leads only to a short-term suppression of the undesirable behavior, rather than its elimination. Another concern is that control of the undesirable behavior becomes contingent on the presence of the punishing agent. When the manager is not present, the behavior is likely to be displayed. Finally, the employee may not perceive the punishment as unpleasant. For example, an organization with a progressive disciplinary procedure may send an employee home without pay for being late one too many times. If this occurs at the beginning of the fishing season, the employee may relish the excuse not to go to work.

The negative effects of punishment can be reduced by incorporating several principles, including the following:

- Provide ample and clear warning. Many organizations have clearly defined disciplinary steps. For example: the first offense might elicit an oral warning; the second offense, a written warning; the third offense, a disciplinary layoff; the fourth offense, discharge.
- Administer the discipline as quickly as possible. If a long time elapses between the ineffective behavior and the discipline, the employee may not know what the discipline is for.
- Administer the same discipline for the same behavior for everyone every time. Discipline has to be administered fairly and consistently.
- Administer the discipline impersonally. Discipline should be based on a specific behavior not a specific person.

Because the immediate supervisor or manager plays the integral role in administering discipline, the human resource department should educate managers and supervisors about the organization's disciplinary policies, and train them to administer the policies.[43]

When Nothing Else Works

Helping employees—especially problem ones—to improve their work performance is a tough job. It is easy to get frustrated and to wonder if we are just spinning our wheels. Even when we want our efforts to work, they sometimes do not. Still, when we conclude that "nothing works," we are really saying that it is no longer worth our time and energy to help the employee improve. This conclusion should not be made in haste, because the organization has already invested a great deal of time and money in the selection and training of its employees. Nevertheless, some situations may require drastic steps, including when:

- Performance actually gets worse.
- The problem behavior changes a little—but not enough.
- The problem behavior does not change.
- Drastic changes in behavior occur immediately, but improvements do not last.

If, after repeated warnings and counseling, performance does not improve, then four last recourses are available.

Transferring. Sometimes, the employee and the job are just not well matched. If the employee has useful skills and abilities, it may be beneficial to transfer her or him. Transferring is appropriate if the employee's performance deficiency would have little or no effect on the new position. The concern is that a job must be available for which the problem employee is qualified.

Restructuring. Some jobs are particularly unpleasant or onerous, causing employees to behave as if they too are unpleasant and onerous. For these positions, the solution may be redesigning the job, rather than replacing the employee. It may also make sense to redesign a position to take advantage of an employee's special strengths. For example, if an employee has extraordinary technical expertise, job redesign might add duties that utilize this expertise.

Firing. Firing is generally warranted for dishonesty, habitual absenteeism, substance abuse, and insubordination, including flat refusals to do certain things requested and consistently low productivity that cannot be corrected through training. Unfortunately, firing, even for legitimate reasons, is unpleasant. In addition to the administrative hassles, documentation, and paperwork involved, supervisors often feel guilty. The thought of sitting down with an employee and delivering the bad news makes most supervisors anxious. As a result, they put off firing and justify the delay by saying that they will not be able to find a "better" replacement. Still, when one considers the consequences of errors, drunkenness, or being under the influence of drugs on the job, firing may be cost-effective. Ensuring that the process is seen as fair will go a long way toward getting even this unfavorable decision accepted.

Neutralizing. Neutralizing a problem employee involves restructuring that employee's job in such a way that his or her areas of needed improvement have as little effect as possible. It means assigning noncritical tasks in which the employee can be productive. Because group morale may suffer when an ineffective employee is given special treatment, neutralizing should be avoided whenever possible. However, temporary neutralizing may be practical and even benevolent for a valued employee who is close to retiring or suffering unusual personal distress due to illness or family problems.[44]

Arbitration

Arbitration has long been used in unionized environments, and its popularity is spreading. The National Conference of Commissioners on Uniform State Laws has suggested a new employment statute that would let most fired employees take their case to a neutral arbitrator. Some companies have initiated their own in-house arbitration where a panel party composed of one's peers hears an appeal.

Arbitration is viewed as an effective alternative to costly legal suits that often evolve following the last step in the disciplinary process—termination. Some say, however, that by turning to arbitration, an employee may actually give up the protection legally afforded in some cases, such as that offered under the Age Discrimination in Employment Act. The experience of the Marriott Hotel Corporation suggests, however, that by entering into arbitration, an employee is almost as likely as the employer to win. In addition, both the employer and employee learn the results of in-house arbitration in weeks rather than in years as might happen in a case passing through the judicial system.[45]

INTERNATIONAL CONCERNS

Pepsi-Cola International

Communication in an international environment is difficult under the best of circumstances. It presents ample opportunities for misunderstanding in terms of language and, as any diplomat knows, in terms of intent. At Pepsi-Cola International, the overlay of 150 potentially different cultures makes it likely that some level of misunderstanding on almost any topic will occur on a regular basis. The problem of understanding what performance is expected from an individual cannot be left solely to a statement of values.[46]

In the early 1980s, it was clear to almost every manager in Pepsi-Cola International that expectations for individual performance standards varied from country to country, and all too often they were dependent on the manager's good intentions. For example, in Eastern Europe, it was acceptable for a manager to meet the quota and essentially take the rest of the day off, but in Germany, continuous improvement in output and efficiency was expected. Thus, a simple, yet direct, and culturally flexible tool was needed to develop more consistency in managing performance. The answer turned out to be something that most sophisticated human resource executives would have called too simple and not sufficiently structured to work globally: instant feedback.

Instant Feedback. Instant feedback is at the top of a chain of feedback systems designed to improve and maintain high levels of personal performance (see Exhibit 11.6).

Pepsi-Cola International is fundamentally a feedback-driven organization. Feedback is part of every tool used to measure and improve performance. Stated simply, the principle of instant feedback says that if you have a problem or an idea about any aspect of the business or about an individual's performance, then the organization demands that you raise the issue appropriately and discuss it maturely.

The original vehicle that delivered this message was a twenty-minute videotape. The tape used dramatizations and explanations to explain how instant feedback is now a part of the everyday vocabulary of Pepsi-Cola International. It is heard when someone with an issue or problem says to another individual, "Let me give you some instant feedback." With busy travel schedules and frequent phone contact and constant time pressure, instant feedback has become a shorthand for getting to the point and communicating clearly.

But perhaps the most fascinating aspect of instant feedback is that it has worked in every culture, with some modifications. Americans use it because it suits the fast-paced way they do business. Canadians may say that Americans are too direct, and some Europeans may say that Americans are too demanding and critical. In most Asian cultures, feedback may be tough and direct but should never be given in public. Also in some Asian cultures, a lot of head nodding occurs during instant feedback, which Americans might assume indicates agreement but really only signifies that the message has been heard. Some Latins will argue very strongly if they do not agree with the feedback, and some people from India and other countries will insist on a great deal of specificity.

◼ *Exhibit 11.6*
Chain of Feedback Mechanisms at PCI

What	Frequency
Instant feedback	Daily
Coaching (performance management)	Event
Accountability-based performance appraisals	Yearly
Development feedback	Yearly
Human resource plan	Yearly

SOURCE: J. R. Fulkerson and R. S. Schuler, "Managing Worldwide Diversity at Pepsi-Cola International," in *Working through Diversity: Human Resources Initiatives,* ed. S. E. Jackson (New York: Guilford Publications, 1992).

In any cultural context, the performance message of instant feedback gets delivered and a healthy debate may ensue. The focus of instant feedback is always how to improve business performance and is not directed against cultural styles. Some would argue that this method is nothing more than effective communication, but that is only partially correct. It is communication directed at solving performance problems. Although total cultural neutrality is not possible, instant feedback says that it does not really matter how you do it as long as you do it.

Four other individual performance management mechanisms Pepsi-Cola International employs are also listed in Exhibit 11.6. The intent of each tool is to improve individual performance vis-à-vis business objectives. For example, Pepsi-Cola International has a workshop on performance management that is designed to help managers and employees understand how and why performance management is a competitive advantage and why it can help ensure individual success. This workshop, delivered by local staff, takes the concept of instant feedback as a starting point and links the feedback tools together. The intent is to ensure that performance management occurs in a manner that is as culturally neutral as possible. The performance management workshop may be delivered in the local language, and attendees are encouraged to find ways to apply the principles in concert with local customs and culture.

International Comparisons

United States. To understand what is distinctive about the U.S. culture, forty international managers—all non–U.S. nationals who were familiar with the U.S. business culture—were interviewed and asked to identify cultural aspects that underlie the U.S. system of management. Thirty-six felt that a strong commitment to the philosophy of meritocracy is a distinctively American societal value. *Meritocracy* emphasizes fairness, evaluating people on their work-related contributions. The managers also noted the short-term orientation in America as emphasized by annual appraisals based solely on current performance.

In other cultures, meritocracy is not so firmly established as a guiding principle. In its place is more concern for status, family ties, and loyalty to the supervisor or organization. Recent performance is not always the most important criterion. Behavior over time, and the potential for the future are emphasized much more.[47]

Evidence also suggests that U.S. managers believe in a "master-of-destiny" viewpoint, where, if a person works hard and has the ability and motivation to perform, he or she will be able to advance in the company. A more fatalistic view predominates in many other countries. That is, persons are born into a certain class, and, no matter what they do, they are not able to improve their standing. In such a culture, a performance management system may not be needed.[48]

Americans also have very specific ideas about performance appraisal criteria. For example, management guru Peter Drucker writes: "An employer has no business with a man's personality. Employment is a specific contract calling for specific performance and for nothing else."[49] Other societies base performance judgments much more on the "whole man or woman" than on actual job performance.

Pacific Rim Countries. Although actual practices vary by country, most Pacific Rim companies use informal and formal appraisal processes to develop and reward employee performance. However, they appear to rely less on sophisticated formalistic systems than do U.S. companies. That is, most dialogue on performance occurs informally either one-on-one or in groups, rather than in a formal review session.

Korea. In Korea, performance appraisal systems are in place in almost all large and most small companies. Since promotions are based primarily on seniority, performance appraisal is conducted primarily for counseling and development. The scope of performance appraisal does vary across enterprises, with some enterprises approaching the process formally, almost ritualistically, and other enterprises approaching it very informally.

One reason appraisal practices vary in scope is that many Koreans believe that the cooperative nature of work makes it impossible to differentiate performance levels between employees with any degree of accuracy. As a result, variables such as seniority, loyalty, proper attitude, and initiative are at least as important as actual job performance.

Practices at Sunkyong are representative of the more formalized approach to appraisal in Korea. The appraisal process begins with an extensive self-assessment inventory that is completed by the employee. Results are discussed with the employee's immediate supervisor and later with the supervisor's supervisor. Extensive peer assessments are also used. In other companies, the appraisal review consists of nothing more than informal individual counseling sessions.[50]

People's Republic of China. Since the 1978 Cultural Revolution, management practices in the People's Republic of China (PRC) have undergone significant changes. Most notable is a shift from a Stalinist system of industrial management (with centralization, detailed plans, and standard operating procedures) to a new motivational system that emphasizes responsibility and performance. Since 1984, the imperative has been to calculate profit before action, rather than vice versa.

At the enterprise level, these changes were accompanied by a move from participatory management in the Yan'an tradition (with pluralistic decision making and tight control) to a new structure of collective leadership. According to the PRC Decision Document of 1984, "Modern enterprises must have a minute division of labor, a high degree of continuity in production, strict technological requirements and a high degree of cooperation." This document also prescribes that enterprises must specify in explicit terms the requirements for each work post and the duties of each worker and staff.

As a result of these reforms, performance in Chinese enterprises has received increasing emphasis. In the past, profits reverted directly to the state. Since the Cultural Revolution, a portion of profits can be held out and distributed to employees. Even by Western standards, performance bonuses—even for low-level workers—are high, averaging as much as one-third of a worker's annual salary. Still, the allocation of these rewards is based upon organizational rather than individual performance.

Regarding a shift in values, a recent study found that objective performance was the most important determinant of performance ratings of both U.S. and Chinese decision makers. However, unlike Americans, Chinese were significantly influenced by employee loyalty and dependability when making performance judgments. Apparently, traditional Chinese cultural values of defining performance in broad terms still linger.[51]

Performance evaluation in China also includes one unique facet: self-criticism. The format of meetings held to provide self-criticism, called Hsiao-tsu sessions, is advocated by the central committee of the national government. The official objective is to create more cohesive groups through identifying insensitive and other dysfunctional behaviors. As operationalized, they appear to serve as upward appraisal sessions in which lower-ranking employees can make perceived or real mistreatments known to management.[52]

Japan. On first thought, performance appraisal would seem to be an unnecessary control mechanism for the Japanese enterprise, which emphasizes job rotation; slow promotion; and group, rather than individual, loyalty. As William Ouchi, a cross-cultural management expert, notes, Japanese employees are controlled in a subtle, indirect manner that contrasts greatly with the explicit, formal control system used in the United States.[53]

Still, an increasing number of Japanese firms are using formal appraisals to evaluate the contribution of employees and to develop them into better employees. However, the concept of performance has a different meaning in Japan than in Western countries. For example, merit ratings are based on educational attainment and job ability characteristics such as communication skills, cooperativeness, and sense of responsibility, rather than on work results. The Japanese concept of performance includes not only the achievement of results but also the expenditure of a good-faith effort.[54]

 ## SUMMARY

Ineffective employee performance plagues all organizations at least some of the time. For a performance management system to be effective, it must facilitate the gathering of performance appraisal data and enable the manager to use this information. Organizations that have developed effective performance management systems reap the rewards of productivity, quality work life, and legal compliance.

Because of the dual purposes of evaluation and development, conflicts in the appraisal system are inevitable. These conflicts, if unaddressed, will cripple the effectiveness of any performance management system. From a design perspective, an effective performance management system can avoid inherent conflicts by (1) focusing on behavior rather than on subjective traits; (2) using multiple sources of appraisal information to improve reliability and validity and thus ensure that the process is fair; (3) delegating appraisal responsibility to employees; (4) establishing goals that integrate the needs of all parties; and (5) conducting effective problem-solving appraisal interviews.

Although many motivation theories explain human performance in organizations, a single diagnostic framework has been provided to help appraisers get at the root cause of a performance problem. Using this framework to understand performance gaps provides a basis for choosing different strategies to improve performance. From a developmental perspective, strategies that involve participation and job clarification encourage self-directed improvement. Ultimately, problem employees may require outside assistance through counseling or EAPs. Control of behavior can also be achieved by linking rewards to behavior or using group or organizational norms. It may be necessary in some cases to neutralize the negative behavior or in extreme cases to fire the employee, but these strategies should be used only when all else fails.

 ## *Discussion Questions*

1. How does Mrs. Fields make its feedback system impersonal yet helpful?
2. What are the sources of conflict inherent in performance appraisal? How can they be managed?
3. What must organizations consider in designing processes to ensure peak performance?
4. With what causes are performance deficiencies associated? What are the respective strategies used to correct those performance deficiencies?

5. What are the advantages and disadvantages of having a 360-degree feedback system?
6. Assume you are supervising employees who fall into one of three categories: (1) effective performers who have lots of potential for advancement; (2) effective performers who lack motivation or ability, or both, for potential advancement; and (3) ineffective performers. It is performance appraisal time, and you must plan interviews with subordinates from each of

these three categories. How will your interviews differ? How will they be similar?

7. What are the advantages of self-management for the organization? for the individual?

8. Discuss the ramifications of neutralizing employees' performance.

9. Describe the feedback system used by PCI worldwide. How can it vary across cultures?

10. Describe some differences in performance appraisal feedback in different countries of the world.

 ## In-Class Projects

1. Answer the following questions for Lincoln Electric:
   a. What level of conflict is inherent in its performance appraisal system?
   b. What are the most likely sources of performance appraisal deficiencies?
   c. What strategies are used to improve employee performance?
   d. How could you improve the organization's feedback and improvement programs?

2. Answer the following questions for AAL:
   a. What level of conflict is inherent in its performance appraisal system?
   b. What are the most likely sources of performance appraisal deficiencies?
   c. What strategies are used to improve employee performance?
   d. How could you improve the organization's feedback and improvement programs?

 ## Field Projects

1. Margarita Rodriguez was seen smoking a cigarette in her car about forty minutes before her scheduled time to leave work. Carl Otto, a coworker, was seen at the same time sitting in his car. Margarita tried to explain to her supervisor why she was in her car at the time, but she was never heard; she was simply fired. "It isn't fair to fire me when Carl received a day's suspension for the same offense," shrieked Margarita. "Carl has a much better work record than you," retorted the supervisor. "He's never had an attendance problem. You were suspended for another attendance infraction two months earlier and knew that the next incident would result in discharge. Therefore, you're fired."

   Was this discharge fair, or should Margarita be reinstated?

2. Omar DiPalma is a forty-year-old vice president of marketing for a large corporation. He recently promoted a promising young regional sales manager, Linda Thomas, to assistant vice president of sales for the western states. Although Linda is viewed as showing real promise in the organization, Omar feels she is focusing too much on meeting monthly quotas when she should be looking at the big picture. He wants to get her on the right wavelength but is not sure what he should do. Outline a specific plan of action for him.

3. Your company has decided to go international and open offices in several foreign countries. You plan to employ host-country nationals for all but the top few positions. Before implementing a performance management system, what questions will you want to ask? What will be the key components of your system?

Case Study:

ASSESSING THE PERFORMANCE OF COURIERS AT AAP

 The Atlantic Association of Pathologists (AAP) was founded in 1992 as a for-profit regional pathology laboratory. Since its inception, AAP has secured contracts with five of six hospitals in the Atlanta area and has expanded its scope throughout the southeastern United States. By centralizing laboratory operations, using the latest in computerized assessment, and achieving quick turnaround, AAP has gained economies of scale. As a result, AAP has grown to four times its original size and now has 321 employees.

One of AAP's major needs is to transport specimens from draw sites to the central operation. To meet this need, AAP employs couriers who pick up and drive specimens and other items between AAP and its clients. The courier position is an entry-level position requiring little education or training. It does require the ability to meet rigid deadlines and a safe driving record.

Since incorporation, the demand for couriers has increased six times, and couriers now number thirty. Unfortunately, turnover has been equally high. It is not uncommon for a courier not to show up for a shift. AAP has also fired ten couriers for poor performance in the past three years. Because pickups have to occur on schedule, AAP has had to rely on overtime, with some couriers working more than sixty hours a week. The inconsistency in service has resulted in AAP's losing one of its hospital contracts. Additional complaints about slow service, rudeness, and lack of knowledge on the part of couriers have filtered in from the private physicians and veterinarians served.

Because AAP's competitive advantage lies in its ability to provide quick, efficient off-site laboratory services, Kyra Burns, human resource manager, has targeted courier services as one of her first priorities. Since being hired two months ago, she has rewritten and standardized the courier's job descriptions (see Exhibit 1). Next she plans to tackle AAP's performance appraisal system. However, corporate officers are resisting her plans. The following comment is typical of management's view: "It's a low-skill 'dime-a-dozen' position. All the couriers do is drive, and if they don't work out, the company can simply replace them."

Kyra has found out that courier overtime cost AAP $100,000 this past year, or about 25 percent of total payroll for couriers. The selection of new couriers took more than 250 hours and cost more than $50,000. The problem of improving courier performance is exasperating because 70 percent of the couriers' time is spent driving to and from AAP—out of the supervisors' sight. Therefore, it is difficult to get a clear picture of what is actually going on at client sites. Another potential problem is that the couriers have more than one supervisor. Besides their immediate supervisor, they also report to the administrative technologist of the courier department and to a medical doctor who coordinates medical services.

At the heart of the performance problem is AAP's current performance appraisal system, including the current appraisal form (see Exhibit 2). Some of the supervisors complain that feedback is not specific to the employees' job. They also point out that many of the levels on the behavioral checklist are not mutually exclusive, so they are forced to check two behavioral characteristics within one area. For example, when evaluating responsibility, raters sometimes are forced to check both characteristics 1 and 2.

The system also poses problems with rater bias. For the twenty couriers who were rated during the last performance appraisal period, the average score was 3.8, which is significantly above the expected average score of 3.0. No couriers received a score lower than 2.0. Although high scores may have been justified in some cases, they were given even to employees the managers wanted to fire. This made it difficult to justify terminating individuals for performance deficiencies. However, couriers as a group received lower individual scores than did all other employees as a group, who averaged 4.1. Couriers who received a high rating on one dimension tended to receive high ratings on all others.

To make matters worse, the human resource budget is limited, with little money available for revising the performance appraisal system or for training raters.

Armed with this gloomy knowledge, Kyra sat at her desk, pondering where she should go from here. ◉

SOURCE: Modified from a project report by K. Steadman, R. Sutton, and V. Madsen (University of Utah).

Discussion Questions

1. What rating biases are associated with the current appraisal format?
2. Will changing the appraisal format alleviate the problems with courier performance? Why or why not?
3. Assuming that the current appraisal system needs to be changed, what type of rating format would you recommend?
4. Who should evaluate the performance of couriers?
5. What can be done to increase the commitment of AAP managers to performance appraisal?
6. Discuss the relationships between selection, appraisal, and training, and their implications for improving the performance of couriers.

■ *Exhibit 1*
Position Description

___

Title: Courier

Position Summary

Under the direction of lead courier-dispatcher, administrative technologist, and medical supervisor, provides timely and efficient transport of specimens, slides, mail supplies, and company personnel to and from AAP and its affiliated clients. Acts as a liaison in a public relations capacity by providing clients with needed information and handling customer complaints.

Supervision Received

Lead courier-dispatcher. When asked, takes direction from medical supervisor and administrative technologist.

Supervision Given

None

Duties

1. Drives to and from AAP and its clients.
2. Locates the appropriate pickup or receiving areas, or both.
3. Picks up, sorts, and properly packages items for transport.
4. Delivers items to the appropriate receiving area.
5. Adjusts time schedule and driving routes to accommodate pickups.
6. Creates a favorable public relations environment.
7. Properly handles and delivers interdepartmental mail.
8. Maintains equipment such as coolers, radios, and automobiles in working condition. Reports problems within one hour.
9. Keeps an accurate daily log of activities such as dispatch time, arrival time, breaks, and lunch.
10. Handles cash for COD pickups and makes change for petty cash.

Skills and Abilities

Ability to (1) closely follow a prescribed time schedule; (2) drive safely and effectively in heavy traffic and in poor road conditions; (3) determine and follow the quickest route between designated contact points; (4) make independent decisions about scheduling; (5) handle client relations when presented with conflicting client demands; (6) read, write, and speak English; and (7) lift and carry packages and boxes weighing up to fifty pounds.

Requirements

Twenty-one years old or older
Good driving record as shown by a current motor vehicle record
Class C driver's license
Good visual acuity
Willingness to handle or be exposed to blood, urine, feces, tissue, and other samples from humans and animals
Willingness to work overtime as required

___

Employee Performance Appraisal Form

Employee Name _____ Date _____

Department ____Couriers_____ Position ____Lead Couriers_____

Observations: List comments, strengths, areas for improvement.

Behavior Ratings: Check the one characteristic that best applies.

Quality of Work (refers to accuracy and margin of error):
- _____ 1. Makes errors frequently and repeatedly
- _____ 2. Often makes errors
- _____ 3. Is accurate; makes occasional errors
- _____ 4. Is accurate; rarely makes errors
- _____ 5. Is exacting and precise

Quantity of Work (refers to amount of production or results):
- _____ 1. Usually does not complete workload as assigned
- _____ 2. Often accomplishes part of a task; others must help
- _____ 3. Handles workload as assigned
- _____ 4. Turns out more work than requested
- _____ 5. Handles an unusually large volume of work

Timeliness (refers to completion of task, within time allowed):
- _____ 1. Does not complete duties on time
- _____ 2. Is often late in completing tasks
- _____ 3. Completes tasks on time
- _____ 4. Usually completes tasks in advance of deadlines
- _____ 5. Always completes all tasks in advance of time frames

Attendance and Punctuality (refers to adhering to work schedule as assigned):
- _____ 1. Takes longer or more frequent breaks than most; is usually tardy or absent
- _____ 2. Takes longer or more frequent breaks than most; is often tardy or absent (comment)
- _____ 3. Usually ensures that breaks do not cause inconvenience; normally is not tardy or absent
- _____ 4. Makes a point of being on the job and on time
- _____ 5. Is extremely conscientious about attendance and punctuality

Responsibility (refers to completing assignments and projects):
- _____ 1. Usually does not assume responsibility for completing assignments
- _____ 2. Is at times reluctant to accept delegated responsibility
- _____ 3. Accepts and discharges delegated duties willingly.
- _____ 4. Accepts additional responsibility
- _____ 5. Is a self-starter who seeks out more effective ways to achieve results or seeks additional responsibilities

Cooperation with Others (refers to working and communicating with supervisors and coworkers):
- _____ 1. Has difficulty working with others; is usually unwilling to perform assignments, and rarely assists others
- _____ 2. Sometimes has difficulty working with others and often complains when given assignments
- _____ 3. Usually is agreeable and obliging; generally helps out when requested
- _____ 4. Works well with others; welcomes assignments, and is quick to offer assistance
- _____ 5. Is an outstanding teamworker; always assists others and continually encourages cooperation by setting an excellent example

Performance Summary (include strong areas and areas for future emphasis in improving performance or developing additional job skills):

Employee Comments or Concerns:

Signatures:
Human Resource Director _____ Date _____

Employee _____ Date _____

Supervisor _____ Date _____

Monetary Compensation: Developing Methods of Payment

To the extent that auto insurance is a commodity, our biggest differentiator is our people. We want the best people at every level of the company, and we pay at the top of the market.

PETER B. LEWIS, Chairman, Progressive Corporation[1]

Managing Human Resources for the 21st Century at Northern Telecom

When a telecommunication system malfunctions, the pressure to restore service is intense. Every second without a dial tone can cost the customer sales and the company customer relations. Recognizing the competitive advantage to be gained from fast, reliable service, Northern Telecom Limited set increased customer service as its number one objective. To determine the best way to launch this strategic initiative, Telecom examined its customer service ratings in thirteen key areas. Overall, customer service rated a respectable 72 on a scale of 0 to 100, but both management and employees knew that it could be improved to enhance Telecom's reputation as a high-quality supplier.

Telecom zeroed in on two opportunity areas: (1) shortening the time required to install new equipment and (2) diagnosing, troubleshooting, and repairing service outages on the initial call. Success in both areas was seen as a function of having a versatile, flexible, and knowledgeable workforce in the field of cable service. Since increased spending on skills training is only wise if employees stay with the company and apply their knowledge, Telecom established a second objective of building a highly skilled and committed workforce.

Telecom also needed to resolve a concern with pay inequity. Traditionally, company divisions used different salary structures, pay grades, and career ladders. Because technicians and engineers from different divisions often found themselves on the same job, pay equity was continually being questioned.

After researching different approaches to attain these objectives, Telecom's planning team settled on skill-based pay to drive its strategic initiative. This solution allowed Telecom to meet its last objective—pay fairness—while avoiding the difficult task of adjusting one division's pay to agree with another's; previous attempts to combine pay plans had failed in the company.

The resulting program was named Fast Forward. *Fast* refers to Telecom's focus on time-based solutions, and *Forward* describes the direction to be advanced by the company and employees when skills are developed. The theme of reciprocity—the company will do well if employees do well, and vice versa—was used to better link business objectives to employee rewards.

Here is how the program was designed: First, a development team identified skill requirements for the major job families to be included in the plan. The skill sets for technicians were built from existing procedure manuals for installing equipment. By comparison, the skill hierarchy for technical support engineers had to be developed from scratch. Seven key dimensions of work were identified for these engineers: hardware, software, customer database, documentation, network interface, written communication, and interpersonal interaction. For each dimension, managers ranked the skills from most to least difficult. Then they bundled the skills into four separate blocks, one for each level or title in the technical support engineer job family. Because Telecom's jobs are dynamic, job bundles are now routinely reviewed to keep the inventory current.

The fundamental difference between Telecom's Fast Forward pay plan and its predecessor is that employees now progress through a job ladder at their own pace, based on their ability to learn new skills. Under the old, job-based system, an employee could not advance unless the company had an opening at the next higher level and the employee had sufficient seniority. Under Fast Forward, technicians gradually progress from level to level on average every six months. Career ladders can be branched by moving from associate status to technical support status.

The second development step involved determining rates of pay for Fast Forward skill bundles. This was no easy task, since pay data to fit a whole job family rather than individual jobs had to be extracted from traditional pay surveys. Determining the minimum rate of pay for a job bundle was relatively easy, since the salary range could be matched to the entry-hire rate for the labor market. After various alternatives were considered, the maximum was established on the basis of the average rate of pay for tasks at the senior job level. Applying these guidelines to the technical family produced a salary range with a 270 percent spread (job-based pay ranges typically have a 30 to 60 percent spread). Fast Forward's broad pay range was broken into segments called target pay zones, which correspond to the skill blocks (e.g., associate, field technician, field test technician).

With skill-based pay, salary increases typically are given only for skill accomplishment. Because quality of service is important to Telecom, the Fast Forward program was modified to include merit pay. Employees are reviewed annually on their individual anniversary dates for increases based on performance rather than skill flexibility. Merit increases advance salary up to an employee's skill target high, but not beyond.

The final component of Telecom's skill-based pay plan is a skill assessment-certification program, a process for evaluating employee skill levels to determine skill grade advancement. The assessment process developed for technicians is relatively straightforward compared with the one developed for technical support engineers. The former involves a simple hierarchy of skills; the latter includes abstract problem-solving and interpersonal abilities.

When an employee believes he or she has mastered a specific skill level, a preassessment discussion with the supervisor is held. Next, skill accomplishments are documented for review by the assessment committee. A Qualified rating is given to employees

who can perform a skill unaided; a Perform rating is assigned to those who need some direction; and a Trained designation is used to note that employees have received instruction. To earn a certificate, participants must not only learn the designated skills but also demonstrate their proficiencies on the job. An extensive training system supports Telecom's skill-based pay program.

What has been the outcome of Fast Forward? Since it was implemented, Telecom's overall customer satisfaction rating has surpassed 75, with installation ratings improving from 70 to 74. Turnover among the highly mobile technician workforce has been reduced from 16 percent to 7 percent. Complaints about salary differences have all but disappeared now that all employees are paid on the same system.[2]

Northern Telecom's Fast Forward pay system reflects three recent trends in compensation management. First, faced with major challenges to their survival, more companies than ever view compensation as a strategy to drive their business. That is, they recognize that compensation not only can attract, motivate, and retain employees but also enhances organizational competitiveness, survival, and profitability. Second, an increasing number of firms are replacing traditional job-based pay systems, in which employees are paid for the particular jobs they are performing, with skill-based pay systems, in which employees are paid for the range, depth, and types of skills they demonstrate. Third, whereas the use of skill-based pay traditionally has been restricted to high-involvement, continuous-process manufacturing plants, many firms now see that skill-based and other new pay plans are flexible enough to be used in a wide variety of industries, including service firms that employ white-collar professionals.

Other issues in total compensation include the following: How are wages really determined? How do we know when people are paid fairly? How do we decide the wage rate for a given individual? Chapters 12 to 14 address these and many other issues in compensating employees.

MONETARY COMPENSATION

A total reward system includes both monetary and nonmonetary compensation. *Monetary compensation* involves the assessment of employee contributions in order to distribute fairly and equitably both direct compensation and indirect compensation (benefits) (see Exhibit 12.1).

Nonmonetary rewards, which include career and social rewards, are often highly valued by employees:

For nine years Steve O'Donnell was David Letterman's head writer. Asked if he personally dreamed up anything that could be considered a pillar of the show, he thinks a moment. "Well . . . I came up with the top ten lists." Did he ever get any special compensation tied to that

■ *Exhibit 12.1*
Components of a Total Reward System

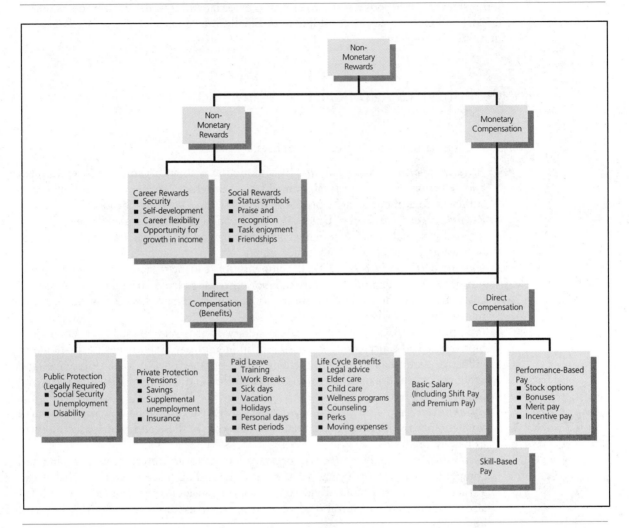

particular contribution? "No. It never occurred to me. I did get a couple of thousand dollars to edit the two top ten books that came out, but I did that because I thought it was important to get them to the public the right way. I'm probably the biggest simp about money of anybody over 12 years old. A pat on the back, making Dave happy, the thrill of hearing the audience laugh—that's what matters most."[3]

Nonmonetary rewards are clearly important for organizations to attend to. For instance, job security has become important in the mid-1990s era of substantial and continuous layoffs by large employers.[4] Recognizing this, some employers offer job security in exchange for no increase in monetary rewards.[5] Readjustments in nonmonetary rewards such as status symbols, praise, and recognition often accompany efforts to change a corporate culture. Furthermore, opportunities for career growth and development may help a firm attract and retain valuable talent. Nevertheless, Chapters 12 to 14 focus on the role of monetary compensation in managing human resources.

This chapter begins with a discussion of compensation's purposes and importance, and then describes the strategic decisions that must be made in designing a compensation system. Next, it looks at the roles of the external and internal environments and of internal and external equity considerations. Finally, it examines contemporary issues and international concerns.

PURPOSES AND IMPORTANCE OF MONETARY COMPENSATION

Compensation serves several major purposes:

- *Attracting potential job applicants:* In conjunction with an organization's recruitment and selection efforts, the total compensation program can help ensure that pay is sufficient to attract the right people at the right time for the right jobs.[6]
- *Retaining good employees:* Unless the total compensation program is perceived as internally equitable and externally competitive, good employees (those the organization wants to retain) are likely to leave.[7]
- *Gaining a competitive edge:* Total compensation can be a significant cost of doing business. Depending on the industry, labor costs range from 10 to 80 percent of total costs. To gain a competitive advantage, an organization may choose to automate or to relocate to areas where labor is cheaper.
- *Increasing productivity:* Whereas nonmonetary awards may influence an employee's motivation and satisfaction, the design of monetary pay systems has been shown to influence performance and productivity.[8] Still, because of individual differences and preferences, an organization must determine the correct blend of monetary and nonmonetary rewards.
- *Administering pay within legal regulations:* Several legal regulations are relevant to total compensation. An organization must be aware of these and avoid violating them in its pay programs.
- *Facilitating strategic objectives:* An organization may want to create a rewarding and competitive culture, or it may want to be an appealing place to work so that it can attract the best applicants. Total compensation can attain these objectives and can also further other organizational objectives, such as rapid growth, survival, and innovation.[9]
- *Reinforcing and defining structure:* The compensation system can help define an organization's structure, its status hierarchy, and the degree to which its people in technical positions can influence those in line positions.

These objectives are interrelated. When employees are motivated, an organization is more likely to achieve its strategic objectives. When pay is based on the value of the job or the relevant job-based skills, the organization is more likely to attract, motivate, and retain its employees. Nonmonetary rewards become more important in attaining these objectives as monetary rewards decrease.[10]

No other human resource activity has more relationships with other human resource activities and with the internal and external environments than does monetary compensation, as Exhibit 12.2 illustrates. Perhaps more than ever, compensation is viewed as key to effectively managing human resources consistent with the needs of the business and the needs of employees. The appropriate blending of direct and indirect compensation makes it possible for companies to address both sets of needs simultaneously.

■ *Exhibit 12.2*
Relationships and Consequences of Monetary Compensation

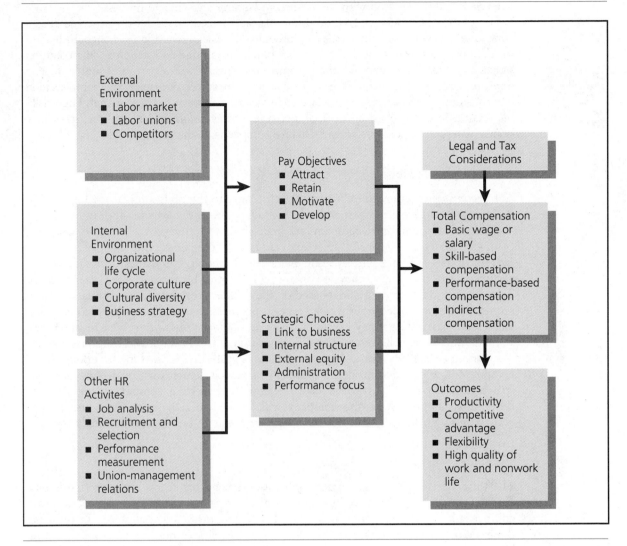

STRATEGIC DECISIONS IN DESIGNING A COMPENSATION SYSTEM

Increasingly, firms are developing compensation systems that support the needs and characteristics of the business and that are sensitive to anticipated social and legal pressures. To do this, businesses must make a series of critical decisions regarding the distribution of monetary compensation among their basic elements.

The Business Strategy

The first decision in compensation design is whether to view the system as an integral aspect of business strategy or to think of it as a support system. As the feature "Managing

Human Resources for the 21st Century at Northern Telecom" shows, the implementation of a compensation system can signal a shift in and actually drive the business strategy when it is fully integrated with the business planning and change process.

Employers like General Electric, Motorola, and Allied Signal have discovered that a compensation system can encourage employees to embrace organizational change. Instead of handing out automatic annual pay increases based on job title and seniority—the common practice in the old economy—these companies reward teamwork, measurable quality improvements, and the acquisition of new skills.[11] In other companies, the compensation system is designed to accommodate or complement the strategy, but not drive it. High-risk–high-return incentive plans at financial investment firms accommodate the strategy; a new bonus plan that supports a strategic initiative complements the strategy.[12]

Internal Pay Structure

The second decision in compensation design relates to the philosophy to be followed in designing the internal pay structure. By decoding the variables that appear to explain why different people in a company get paid as they do, employees discern what the company values and rewards. In many traditional companies, the value of one's job reflects one's level in a bureaucratic hierarchy. In other companies, jobs are valued according to how central they are to the core of the business activity. At Northern Telecom, pay differences are now based on the skill level of employees—a relatively new approach. The premise underlying a strategic perspective is that considerable discretion exists to design different pay hierarchies even in organizations with similar technologies. For example, Bonneville International Corporation, a Utah broadcast group, has a single pay structure for all nonexempt employees in all divisions. One of Bonneville's competitors takes a decentralized approach to pay, and each division has its own pay structure and rates.[13] Regardless of the specific approach a company takes, the pay differentials found within the company will be evaluated by employees and judged according to whether the internal pay structure seems to be fair and internally logical.

External Equity

The third decision in designing a compensation system has to do with external equity. From a strategic perspective, external equity refers to the positioning of a firm's compensation relative to the positioning of its competitors' compensation. In the past, the issue of external equity was typically framed as a simple question: "Should we lead, lag, or match the pay rates of labor market competitors?" When almost everyone's pay was predominately a basic salary with few benefits, this simple view made sense. In today's highly competitive environment, however, external equity has become more complex because companies are now creatively mixing several forms of pay. Base salary is no longer the only piece that really matters. For example, to support a high-volume strategy, sales representatives at one company may receive a low base salary ($20,000) with a high bonus potential ($40,000). At another company, a high base salary ($50,000) coupled with merit pay may support a customer service objective. When choosing which company to work for, employees will consider not only the level of typical pay but also their comfort with the risk-return trade-off. The former pay plan shifts most of the risk to the employee, and the latter leaves a greater portion of risk with the company.

Compensation Administration Policies

The policies used to administer compensation represent the fourth decision point in the design of a compensation system. Choices here include the amount of information to be disclosed to employees, the involvement of employees in the development of the plan, and the nature of a dispute resolution process. Each decision may affect how well integrated the total system is and how well it serves business needs. For example, should the company state broad policies to employees or communicate the details of the pay structure? Some firms may involve employees directly in the development of the pay plan, including the evaluation of their jobs; other firms may have outside consultants or even an automated expert system evaluate jobs, and then simply inform employees of the final outcome—that is, how much they will be paid.

Performance Focus

The fifth decision to make in designing a compensation system is whether to focus on performance. General Dynamics Corporation's top 25 executives receive a large bonus each time the firm's stock price rises $10 a share and stays there for ten days. Although executives have to wait a while for the money, this plan has drawn widespread criticism among union leaders and Wall Street analysts because it seems to encourage management to focus on short-term gains at the expense of long-term profitability. In general, the proportion of pay placed at risk, the degree of pay differentiation among peak and competent employees, and the relative emphasis on individual versus team versus corporate performance all have strategic implications.[14] (These will be described in more detail in Chapter 13.)

Linkage to Other Business Needs and Practices

Total compensation is linked to the needs and characteristics of a business when top management believes that compensation affects the company's overall performance. A tight linkage is most likely when monetary compensation is managed through a true partnership (see the feature "Partnership in Monetary Compensation"). If designed and implemented well, compensation policies and practices encourage desired employee behaviors, which in turn support the business objectives. Although business objectives shape the many decisions a company makes about how to design pay, they cannot be treated in isolation. Other forces from the external and internal environments also come into play.

ROLE OF THE EXTERNAL ENVIRONMENT

Three forces in the external environment that directly shape compensation design decisions are the labor market, legislation, and unions.

Labor Market

The labor market influences the design of compensation in two ways. First, the degree of competition for labor partly determines the lower boundary or floor for pay level. If a company's pay level is too low, qualified labor will not be willing to work for the company. Thus, shortages in the labor market (internal or external) provide those who are qualified to fill available jobs with opportunities to negotiate better terms of employment. Demand drives labor prices up to a point, but high prices in turn attract more entrants to the market. At the same time, they push employers to seek alternatives, such as foreign labor supplies, where prices may be lower, or technology that reduces the need for labor.

Partnership in Monetary Compensation

Line Managers	Human Resource Professionals	Employees
With HR, ensure the alignment of the pay system with the business.	With line managers, ensure the alignment of the pay system with the business.	Take responsibility for understanding the pay system.
With HR professionals, determine how to value jobs and people.	Design the process for job evaluation to involve line managers and job incumbents.	Maybe participate in job evaluation.
Work with HR to communicate the pay system.	Analyze the external market.	Indicate preferences for indirect pay.
Make and communicate pay decisions.	Develop processes to measure performances or skills, or both.	Maybe assess the levels of performance or skill, or both, of self and others.
	Assess employees' preferences.	
	Work closely with line managers to finalize pay.	
	Work with line managers to communicate the pay system.	

Sometimes, the alternatives involve changing the conditions of work in order to make employment in the organization more attractive to the available labor force. For example, firms such as American Express Travel Related Services Company Incorporated (TRS) have designed and implemented major new pay initiatives to ensure their ability to attract and retain qualified employees. The feature "Using Data for the 21st Century: Responding to Changing Workforce Concerns at American Express Travel Related Services" provides a vivid example of how the labor market can shape a company's compensation strategy.

Legal Considerations

A sociological analysis of all congressional bills introduced from 1951 to 1990 revealed that different visions of work and family have been dominant at different periods, reflecting the changing concerns of the labor market.[15] The three visions are separate spheres, equal opportunity, and work-family accommodation. As Exhibit 12.3 illustrates, legislative support for these different types of bills has changed substantially along with the entrance of more women into the workforce and changing societal norms. During the middle of the 20th century, barriers between work and family were considered normal and even desirable. As we enter the 21st century, legislators are encouraging employers to remove such barriers and actively support employees' simultaneous involvement in the spheres of work and family.

The bills introduced in Congress often reflect employees' concerns, but only a few receive sufficient support to be passed into law. Like other aspects of managing human

Using Data for the 21st Century:
RESPONDING TO CHANGING WORKFORCE CONCERNS AT AMERICAN EXPRESS TRAVEL RELATED SERVICES

The first formal recognition that workforce diversity might be an important issue for Travel Related Services (TRS), and for American Express in general, occurred within corporate human resources, serving American Express as a whole. This was consistent with the primary mission of the corporate staff, which is to scan the environment for important trends and to conduct strategic planning. The event that brought diversity to the attention of corporate human resources was the release of *Workforce 2000* by the Hudson Institute in 1987. Detailing the changing nature of the U.S. economy and labor market, the report projected a clear picture of the workforce in the year 2000.

In response to *Workforce 2000,* the senior vice president of human resources for corporate American Express amassed a think tank to address what was then called the Workforce Challenge. The group was formed to study and discuss the implications of *Workforce 2000,* and to determine the relevance of changing demographics for American Express. Given the fast-paced and growing nature of American Express's business, which required a large number of new employees each year, the think tank members were particularly concerned about the company's ability to attract and retain qualified employees in the face of a shrinking and increasingly diverse labor pool. Therefore, they decided to focus on the issues of attraction and retention of employees. They selected several key customer service jobs and collected the following data for each: number of persons within that position, average tenure, average training time, average time until competent, and rate of turnover.

In June 1988, the think tank released a report with these figures to American Express's senior management. The report highlighted very clearly the high cost of turnover for American Express. It also emphasized that attracting and retaining qualified customer service personnel were critical for American Express, and would become much more critical as the workforce began to grow at a slower rate and as it became more diverse.

Senior management reacted quickly to the think tank's report. At the next senior management meeting (a two-day event held every eighteen months), in October, the entire first day was devoted to the Workforce Challenge. The day began with an impassioned speech by the president of American Express, in which he posed the Workforce Challenge as "the most difficult—and most important—challenge facing American Express." He argued that the company needed to attack the changing labor market "with the same dedication we do any other market." As he saw it, "[T]he company's very survival [was] at stake."

Following the president's speech, the senior managers of each subsidiary were given the task of addressing the Workforce Challenge within their own subsidiaries. Within TRS, the largest of the subsidiaries, the task was handed to the human resource staff at the headquarters in New York.

Given the think tank's conclusions, the senior management of human resources at TRS felt that its biggest challenge would be attracting and retaining employees in the face of a shrinking labor pool and increasing diversity with respect to values, expectations, lifestyles, and family responsibilities. After careful consideration, senior management decided that the first thing to do was to collect data from its own workforce. The managers hoped that by better understanding the needs and concerns of current workers, they could determine the requirements for attracting and retaining workers of similar caliber in the future. They also decided to focus on needs and concerns with respect to balancing work and family. This had been a growing concern within TRS human resources, and the think tank's report highlighted the urgency of addressing it.

The senior managers were surprised to learn that they were perceived as unresponsive to employees' needs. Their survey suggested that employees wanted to be treated as whole and unique individuals with legitimate interests and needs outside the workplace. For this to occur, a significant departure from the existing culture at TRS would be required. Traditionally, TRS had striven to maintain an exchange-based relationship with employees—where all employees were treated equally, and where family and personal issues were kept separate from work issues.

Several employee focus groups were asked to identify specific policies and benefits that employees felt were needed. Participants were asked the following: "If you were offered an identical job, for the same pay and in the same city, what would it take, in terms of specific benefits and policies, to make you accept the offer?" Based on the employees' responses, fourteen possible benefits and policies were identified. To decide which of these to adopt, TRS analyzed all of them in light of the benefits and policies of the sixteen firms considered to be TRS's major competitors in the labor market nationwide, and projected costs. Based on these analyses, four initiatives were ultimately selected for implementation, with the rollout beginning in 1990 under the HR strategy titled Becoming the Best Place to Work. The four initiatives and the key advantages associated with each are shown in the following exhibit:[16]

• *KidsCheque and FamilyCheque:* Child care subsidy for all full-time employees; subsidy for employees' dependents who are physically or mentally incapable of caring for themselves

• *Workplace Flexibility:* Flexible alternatives in scheduling, including flextime, job sharing, and part-time work; flexible return from family and sick leave, with continuing coverage of regular benefits

• *Sabbaticals:* Paid sabbaticals for community service for up to twelve months, depending on years of service, with same job guaranteed for up to three months and comparable job guaranteed after three months; unpaid sabbaticals for personal pursuits for up to three months for employees with ten-plus years of service, with same job guaranteed

• *Improved Part-Time Benefits:* Benefits comparable to those of full-time employees after six months of employment

TRS's 1990 Human Resource Initiatives

1990 Initiatives	Key Advantages					
	Attraction Retention	Marketplace Differentiation	Increased Productivity	To Meet Marketplace Competition	Community Relations	Personal Development
KidsCheque and FamilyCheque	X	X	X			
Sabbaticals	X	X	X		X	X
Workplace Flexibility	X	X	X	X		
Improved Part-Time Benefits	X			X		

■ *Exhibit 12.3*
Congressional Support for Bills Adopting Different Visions of Work and Family

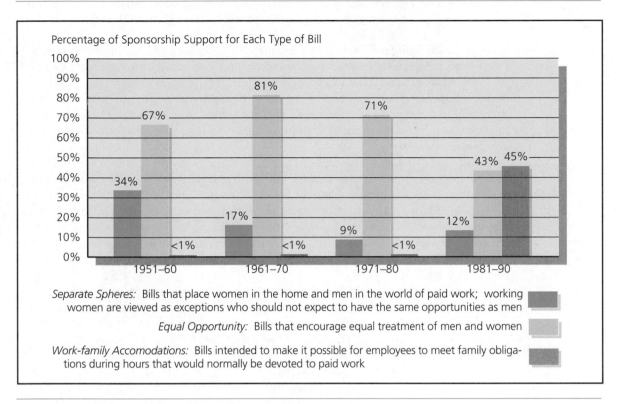

Percentage of Sponsorship Support for Each Type of Bill

Separate Spheres: Bills that place women in the home and men in the world of paid work; working women are viewed as exceptions who should not expect to have the same opportunities as men

Equal Opportunity: Bills that encourage equal treatment of men and women

Work-family Accomodations: Bills intended to make it possible for employees to meet family obligations during hours that would normally be devoted to paid work

SOURCE: Based on data presented in P. Burstein, R. M. Bricher, and R. L. Einwohner, "Policy Alternatives and Political Change: Work, Family, and Gender on the Congressional Agenda," *American Sociological Review* 60 (1995): 67–83.

resources, the compensation activities are shaped by a plethora of laws and regulations, covering topics such as taxation, nondiscrimination, fair wages, a minimum wage, the protection of children, hardship pay for employees who work unusually long hours, and income security through pension and welfare benefits (the last are described in Chapter 13).

In 1994, a standard workweek was considered to consist of five eight-hour days, but this was not always the case. In 1840, six thirteen-hour days was considered normal. During the next one hundred years, state by state, legislation redefined the norm. In 1913, when Henry Ford introduced the eight-hour day at a $5-a-day minimum wage, most of his competitors still expected sixty hours of work a week from employees. Significant national legislation governing hours and wages was passed in the 1930s,[17] and additional legislation followed in the 1960s.

Davis-Bacon and Walsh-Healey Acts. The first federal law to protect the amount of pay employees receive for their work was the Davis-Bacon Act of 1931. This act required organizations holding federal construction contracts to pay laborers and mechanics the prevailing wages of the majority of the employees in the locality where the work was performed. The Walsh-Healey Public Contracts Act of 1936 extended the Davis-Bacon Act to include all organizations holding federal construction contracts exceeding $10,000 and specified that pay levels conform to the industry minimum rather than the area minimum. The Walsh-Healey Act also established overtime pay at one and one-half times the hourly rate. These wage provisions did not include administrative, professional, office, custodial, or maintenance employees, or beginners, or disabled persons.

Fair Labor Standards Act. Partly because the coverage of Davis-Bacon and Walsh-Healey was limited to employees on construction projects, the Fair Labor Standards Act of 1938, or Wage and Hour Law, was enacted. This set minimum wages, maximum hours, child labor standards, and overtime pay provisions for all workers except domestic and government employees. The Supreme Court extended the coverage to include state and local government employees in 1985 (*Garcia v. San Antonio Metropolitan Transit Authority*).

Under the Fair Labor Standards Act, the minimum wage began at $0.25 an hour and had reached $4.25 as of April 1, 1991 (although several states had set their minimum wage rates above this national rate). Still, subminimum wages are permitted for learners in semiskilled occupations, apprentices in skilled occupations, messengers in firms engaged primarily in delivering letters and messages, handicapped persons working in sheltered workshops, students in certain establishments, and employees who receive more than $30.00 a month in tips (up to 40 percent of the minimum requirement may be covered by tips).[18]

To prevent abuses regarding children, the act prohibits minors under the age of eighteen from working in hazardous occupations. For nonhazardous positions, the minimum age ranges from fourteen to sixteen, depending on the type of work to be performed and whether the employer is the child's parent.[19]

The act also establishes who is to be paid overtime for work and who is not. Most employees covered must be paid time and a half for all work exceeding forty hours a week. These are called *nonexempt employees.* Several groups of individuals are exempt from both the overtime provision and the minimum wage provision. *Exempt employees* include workers in firms not involved in interstate commerce, workers in seasonal industries, certain highly paid commission workers, workers in motion picture theaters, and others. Executives, administrators, and professionals are also exempt from overtime pay and minimum wage laws in most organizations. However, trainee managers and assistant managers are considered nonexempt and should thus be paid overtime.

To be exempt, professionals must spend 80 percent of their work hours in the following tasks:

◉ Doing work requiring knowledge acquired through specialized, prolonged training
◉ Exercising discretion or judgment
◉ Doing work that is primarily intellectual and nonroutine[20]

The criteria for exempt status as an executive or administrator include spending at least 80 percent of work time in the following tasks:

◉ Undertaking management duties
◉ Directing the work of two or more employees
◉ Controlling or greatly influencing hiring, firing, and promotion decisions
◉ Exercising discretion

In both cases, a comprehensive job analysis is necessary to determine whether a job is exempt.

The feature "Using Data for the 21st Century: Record Fines at Food Lion" shows that the Fair Labor Standards Act was alive and well in the mid-1990s.

Using Data for the 21st Century:
RECORD FINES AT FOOD LION

A record settlement of Fair Labor Standards Act (FLSA) charges requires Food Lion Incorporated to pay more than $16 million in back pay and civil penalties.

The settlement between the Salisbury, North Carolina, supermarket chain and the Department of Labor (DOL) calls for Food Lion to pay $13.2 million for back wages to current and former Food Lion employees, $2 million for civil penalties arising from overtime and minimum wage violations, and $1 million for civil penalties for child labor violations. According to DOL, these amounts individually are the highest ever paid by a private employer in each category.

The charges stem from a complaint filed by the United Food and Commercial Workers (UFCW) on behalf of some 330 current and former Food Lion employees. The union alleged that the company's "effective scheduling" policy had resulted in employees' working thousands of hours of overtime for which they were not paid. Under the policy, Food Lion would allocate a set number of hours for employees to complete assigned tasks. According to UFCW, the time allocated was often inadequate, and employees would have to work overtime, without compensation, to complete the tasks.

Food Lion consistently denied the allegations, citing an internal policy that prohibits employees from working off the clock. However, the Labor Department proceeded with an investigation of the overtime allegations, and uncovered some thirteen hundred violations of the FLSA's child labor provisions. Subsequently, DOL threatened to take Food Lion to court if it would not agree to settle the charges.

In addition to paying $16.2 million, Food Lion agrees to post copies of the settlement agreement at all of its more than one thousand stores, train its management staff on compliance with FLSA regulations, and file quarterly reports with the Labor Department on compliance with FLSA regulations and the implementation of a compliance plan. Among other things, the compliance plan calls for the company to conduct periodic audits of its FLSA compliance, to designate a labor standards intermediary to oversee and coordinate companywide compliance, and to provide an internal dispute resolution procedure for employees to complain about alleged FLSA violations in the future. In agreeing to the settlement, Food Lion does not admit to committing any FLSA violations.[21]

Equal Pay Act. A fourth provision of the Fair Labor Standards Act was added as an amendment in 1963. Called the Equal Pay Act, this extension prohibits an employer from discriminating "between employees on the basis of sex by paying wages to employees . . . at a rate less than the rate at which he pays wages to employees of the opposite sex . . . for equal work on jobs the performance of which requires equal skill, effort and responsibility, and which are performed under similar working conditions."

To establish a prima facie case of wage discrimination, the plaintiff needs to show that a disparity in pay exists for males and females performing substantially equal, not necessarily identical, jobs. The amount of skill, effort, and responsibility and the working conditions required by each job must be assessed through careful job analysis. Job contents rather than the window dressing of job titles should be examined. If jobs are found to be substantially equal, wages for the lower-paid job must be raised to match those for the higher-paid position. Freezing or lowering the pay of the higher-paid job is unacceptable.

Four exceptions can be used to legally defend unequal pay for equal work: the existence and use of a seniority system, a merit system, a system that measures earnings or quality of production, or a system based on any additional characteristic other than gender. If the employer can show the existence of one or more of these exceptions, a pay differential may be found to be justified.

Civil Rights Acts. Title VII of the Civil Rights Act of 1964, and the Civil Rights Act of 1991 provide broader legal coverage for pay discrimination than does the Equal Pay Act. These acts can enter into equal-pay-for-equal-work cases, as well as cases where the jobs are comparable but not identical.

Comparable Worth. An important concept in compensation is comparable worth. The heart of the *comparable worth* theory is the contention that, although the "true worth" of nonidentical jobs may be similar, some jobs (often held by women) are paid a lower rate than others (often held by men). Resulting differences in pay that are disproportionate to the differences in the "true worth" of jobs amount to wage discrimination. Consequently, according to comparable worth advocates, legal protection should be provided to ensure pay equity.

Several state and local governments and unions have passed comparable worth or pay equity legislation, and many businesses have also taken action on pay equity issues. The feature "Positioning for the 21st Century: Pay Equity" describes these issues and how they can be addressed.

Internationally, comparable worth is an idea that has been around for some time:

> "The International Labor Organization (ILO), the Geneva-based agency of the United Nations the U.S. joined in 1934, adopted an international convention on comparable worth almost 35 years ago. And what the ILO's experience shows is that while comparable worth may have helped reduce the gap between male and female wages in some countries that have tried it, it hasn't eliminated that gap. But neither has it led to the major economic or bureaucratic headaches that its critics prophesy."[22]

Since its adoption, more than one hundred governments—but not that of the United States—have ratified the ILO's convention. These include most of the nations of Western Europe, Canada, Australia, New Zealand, Japan, and more than seventy developing countries.[23]

Wage Deduction Laws. Three federal laws influence how much employers may deduct from employee paychecks. The Copeland Act of 1934 authorized the secretary of labor to regulate wage deductions for contractors and subcontractors doing work financed in whole or in part by a federal contract. Essentially, the Copeland Act was aimed at illegal deductions. Protection against a more severe threat from an employer with federal contracts was provided in the Anti-Kickback Law of 1948. The Federal Wage Garnishment Law of 1980 also protects employees against deductions from pay for indebtedness. It provides that only 25 percent of one's disposable weekly earnings or thirty times the minimum wage, whichever is less, can be deducted for debt repayment.

Labor Unions

The presence of a union in a private-sector firm is estimated to increase wages by 10 to 15 percent and benefits by about 20 to 30 percent. Also, the wage differential between unionized and nonunionized firms appears to be greatest during recessionary periods and smallest during inflationary periods. Whether the increased compensation costs in unionized firms translate into higher output is widely debated. Some researchers contend that, by improving employee satisfaction, lowering turnover, and decreasing absenteeism,

Positioning for the 21st Century:
PAY EQUITY

Pay equity is a policy that provides businesses the competitive edge to meet the challenges of the 21st century, declares the National Committee on Pay Equity. A consistent, fair pay policy whereby all workers are paid equally for work of equal value produces a more productive and better-motivated workforce, which, in turn, promotes recruitment and retention of good workers.

"Smart employers recognize that future profits depend on current investment in their most vital resource: their people," says the coalition of labor, women's, and civil rights groups in its report, *Pay Equity Makes Good Business Sense.*

Women and men of color are concentrated in lower-paying jobs. In addition, when women and men of color occupy traditionally white-male-dominated positions—even after accounting for legitimate reasons for pay differences such as differing skills, work experience, and seniority—women and men of color are still paid less, contends the pay equity committee's publication.

Discriminatory wage practices account for between one-quarter and one-half of this disparity in wages, says the report.

WHAT IS PAY EQUITY?

Pay equity, also known in the United States, Canada, and Europe as equal pay for work of equal value, is broader than equal pay for equal work. Pay equity is a means of eliminating race, ethnicity, and gender as wage determinants within job categories and between job categories, the report says.

Many businesses pay women and men of color less than white males. This result is often unintentional and due in part to personnel systems and wage structures that retain historical biases and inconsistencies that are, in fact, discriminatory, explains the report.

A pay equity policy examines existing pay policies that underpay women and men of color and activates steps to correct the discrimination.

HOW TO ACHIEVE PAY EQUITY

A comprehensive audit is the first step in implementing a pay equity policy, explains the committee's report. The audit should examine the following areas for inequities and needed changes:

- Job evaluation
- Market pricing
- Pay administration
- Recruitment

In the area of pay administration, the audit should scrutinize each individual component of a business's system, including salary range design, salary grades, pay differentials, and the determination of hiring rates. Additional items to be examined for inequities include promotion rates, merit increases, incentive programs, and performance and seniority elements in the pay system.

PAY EQUITY IS NOT COSTLY

Following the lead of public employers, many private-sector businesses are already incorporating pay equity analyses in their annual budget proposals. "The cost of pay equity adjustments," reports the committee, usually has been "between 2 and 5 percent of payroll."

In no cases have the wages of any workers been lowered in order to achieve pay equity, reports the committee, because the objective of pay equity is to remedy wage inequities for underpaid workers, not to penalize another group of employees.[24]

---

unions have a positive effect on net productivity. Others contend that the gains in productivity are not equivalent to the increased compensation costs.[25]

Unions also have pushed for wage escalation clauses, which increase wages automatically during the life of a contract. One way unions have accomplished this is to tie wage increases to changes in the consumer price index. However, whereas cost-of-living adjustments were popular in the 1960s and 1970s, the number of workers covered by COLAs declined during the 1980s and early 1990s, when the consumer price index decelerated and concerns about job security increased in priority during contract negotiations.

Another way unions have affected compensation practices has been through the establishment of two-tiered wage systems. In such a system, the contract specifies that employees hired after a specific date will receive wages that are as much as 50 to 80 percent lower than those of their higher-seniority peers working on the same or similar jobs. Two-tiered pay systems increased in use during the 1980s because unions viewed them as less painful than wage freezes and salary cuts for existing employees.[26] American Airlines, United Air Lines, Greyhound, McDonnell Douglas Corporation, and Ingersoll-Rand Company have had two-tiered wage systems to help reduce total fixed costs.[27]

In addition to determining how much employees are paid, unions have shaped the way total pay is allocated among wages, performance-based pay, and benefits. For example, the International Association of Machinists opted to set aside $0.10 an hour for skill retraining rather than take a $0.05-an-hour increase in direct pay. According to Seattle Local president Tom Baker, union members are concerned more with long-term job security than with short-term gains in salary. With the establishment of the $12 million annually funded Career Mobility program, union members are being retrained for higher-level jobs that also pay better.

A different, but equally useful, strategy was employed at Crown Zellerbach Corporation. To reduce fixed labor costs without reducing the total wages of unionized workers, the International Woodworkers of America and management opted for an incentive pay plan. Under this system, workers earn about $3 more an hour than before, when they earned straight wages. In exchange for shifting greater risk to the workers, the company gave the union more say in work-related decisions. Thus, workers gained additional involvement and higher salaries, and the company won reductions in fixed labor costs.[28]

Finally, the nature of union-management relationships within a firm have important implications for pay system design and administration. Some unions take an active part in job evaluation to protect their interests in rational wage structures. Others preserve customary relationships, seeking job security and resisting changes in job content and wage rates. Skill-based pay programs such as the one instituted at Northern Telecom (see pages 415–416) are more likely to work if the union is willing to trade job and financial security for the work assignment flexibility that skill-based pay demands.

ROLE OF THE INTERNAL ENVIRONMENT

In addition to the many aspects of the external environment that influence monetary compensation, are many aspects of the internal environment. The following four are aspects of the organization introduced in several earlier chapters, particularly Chapter 2, and elaborated upon in this section.

Organizational Life Cycle

The choice of a specific compensation mix is constrained by an organization's life cycle. As suggested in Exhibit 12.4, firms grow rapidly during some stages and slowly during others. During the start-up phase, they emphasize product and market development. Attracting key contributors and facilitating innovation are the focus issues for managing human resources. Still, risk is high, sales growth is slow, and earnings are low, so the

■ *Exhibit 12.4*

Potential Pay Mixes for Different Stages of Organizational Life

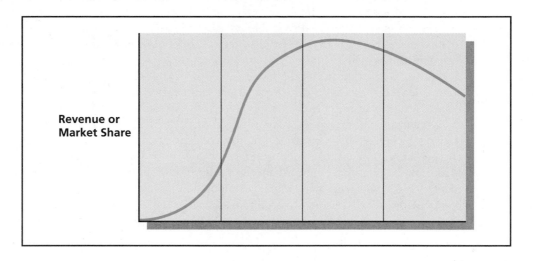

| | Life Cycle Stage | | | |
	Start-Up	Growth	Maturity	Decline
Organization Characteristics				
HR management focus	Innovation, attracting key contributors	Recruiting, training	Retention, consistency	Cutting back, management
Risk profile	High	Moderate	Low	Moderate to high
Compensation Strategy				
Short-term incentives	Stock bonus	Cash bonus	Profit sharing, cash bonus	Unlikely
Long-term incentives	Stock options (broad participation)	Stock options (limited participation)	Stock purchase	Unlikely
Base salary	Below market level	At market level	At or above market level	At or below market level
Benefits	Below market level	Below market level	At or above market level	At or below market level

SOURCE: Adapted from D. B. Balkin and L. R. Gomez-Mejia, "Compensation Systems in High Technology Companies," in *New Perspectives on Compensation,* ed. Balkin and Gomez-Mejia (Englewood Cliffs, NJ: Prentice-Hall, 1987), 269–77.

company offers base salary and benefits below the market. Counterbalancing these are broad-based short- and long-term incentives, designed to stimulate innovation and its associated rewards.

During the growth stage, sales grow rapidly, with moderate increases in earnings. To keep up with increased demand for products and services, the organization must grow rapidly. The human resource focus is on rapid recruitment and training to develop the human capital. Bonuses may be offered for innovation and sales growth, and stock options may be offered to encourage employees to think about the long-term growth of the company.

During the maturity stage, growth is slower and more orderly because the market is saturated with the product. High entry costs and exit barriers keep the number of competitors low, so organizations can focus on profitability. During this stage, performance, consistency, and retention of peak performers are the issues that arise in managing human resources. Profit sharing, cash bonuses, and stock awards tied to short- or long-term growth may be offered to retain key contributors, along with competitive base pay and benefits.

During the decline stage, the human resource focus shifts to cutting back as market shares decline. Base salary and benefits are competitive at best, and may drop below market levels as management attempts to reduce expenditures.[29]

Organizational life cycles have received wide attention as a heuristic device for designing compensation systems, but the concept has critics. More than one set of compensation policies may be appropriate for any given stage in the cycle. Furthermore, organizations often have more than one product, each at a different stage of development. This complexity may make it impossible to cleanly classify a firm and its compensation mix according to a particular stage of development.[30]

Organizational Culture

Organizations differ in the values, norms, and expectations that make up their cultures. Compensation systems reflect organizational values. For example, in hierarchical organizations, clan-type cultures emerge. Loyalty is exchanged for the organization's long-term commitment to the individual. Reward allocations are based on supervisors' qualitative and subjective evaluations of employees. In this culture, members share a sense of pride in the "fraternal network."

By comparison, market cultures link rewards objectively and explicitly to performance. Contractual obligations specified in advance define the relationship between the individual and the organization. Market cultures are not based on loyalty, cooperation, or a sense of belonging, and members feel less constrained by norms, values, or allegiance to accepted ways of doing things. Market cultures encourage personal initiative, feelings of ownership, and a sense of responsibility.

These are only two examples of how corporate cultures influence compensation systems. As stated in Chapter 2, organizational cultures can be described in many ways, and their effects on human resource management can be quite complex.[31]

Cultural Diversity

The cultural diversity of today's workforce and the growing problems of international operations are beginning to influence the design of compensation systems. David Jamieson, president of the Jamieson Consulting Group, and Julie O'Mara, president of O'Mara and Associates, summarize the issues associated with compensation in the 1990s: "The value of money, response to public recognition, the desire for professional and peer respect, and the need for challenging assignments all vary according to lifestyle and culture. The importance of these rewards to individuals affects their motivation, productivity and satisfaction. A greater variety of rewards is clearly called for in an era of cultural diversity."[32] Cultural diversity among U.S. employees can be substantial. Often, however, companies fail to recognize the importance of cultural values until they broaden their activities beyond U.S. borders.

As companies become transnational, they begin to adopt a global perspective that recognizes alternatives to the traditional U.S. model. Such firms face the difficult task of administering rewards in multiple cultures, each emphasizing different values and reward priorities.

Consider compensation practices in the People's Republic of China. Here, a person of good character is expected to be less occupied with the self than with the group and to be more concerned with citizenship behaviors (altruism, attendance, and conscientiousness) that benefit the group than with individual outcomes. To reinforce this culture, all workers, regardless of rank or occupation, receive an identical basic wage (e.g., forty yuan a month). Workers also get subsidies for rent, transportation, food, sanitation, retirement, education, and general welfare. Only minimal differentials are given for differences in job responsibility and seniority. Performance-based pay, which accounts for as much as one-third of total pay, is related to the activities of the organization, not of the individual worker. This compensation mix contrasts sharply with pay practices in less collectivistic, Western countries.[33]

What are the implications for a company striving for a consistent corporate culture in operations flung around the globe? How can workers with different cultural heritages be brought together to work in multicultural teams if the home-country compensation systems do not all encourage the same approach to work behavior? These are the types of questions raised by the global workplace.

Organizational Strategy

A recent study by the American Compensation Association indicates that two-thirds of all firms implementing changes in their pay system do so because of fundamental changes in the way they view and define their markets. That is, the selection of the right compensation mix is highly dependent on what a company needs from its employees to match its strategy initiative, be that strategy for entrepreneurial development, for dynamic growth, to extract profit, for liquidation or divestiture, or for turnaround.[34]

General Dynamics has pursued a turnaround strategy. Faced with a shrinking market, the company eliminated more than ten thousand jobs through layoffs and attrition, drastically cut spending on plants and equipment, and sold several nonmilitary subsidiaries. In support of this strategy, top executives were offered short- as well as long-term incentives linked to stock prices. Employee involvement at the top was high. At lower levels, wages were frozen and jobs eliminated. Participation in compensation activities was held to a minimum, perks were limited, and a standard, fixed severance package with no incentives was offered.

Tandem Computers, in comparison, has pursued an entrepreneurial strategy. To encourage employees to innovate, to take more risks, and to assume responsibility, compensation practices are flexible, contain many perks and long-term incentives (stock options or stock appreciation rights), and encourage high employee participation. Tandem's compensation philosophy is to reward people fairly but not necessarily equally. Although stock options are awarded equally to all employees, cash bonuses are awarded only to top performers. A "night on the town" is given to people who make a special contribution. To further recognize employee contributions, peak performers (selected by their supervisors and peers) annually attend a special retreat at a resort. The retreat creates a place for top performers to relax, network, become acquainted, and brainstorm on key issues facing the business.[35]

Supporting Total Quality Management. Do you regard a smile and a "Thank you for shopping" from the cashier of the local store as examples of quality customer-oriented service? Many people do and, in fact, are willing to pay more for the goods in stores, such as Nordstrom, that have salespeople who engage in such behaviors. Whereas selection practices, socialization, and training can all help ensure that employees will be able and willing to engage in courteous, friendly behaviors, compensation systems provide the supporting structure that motivates employees to display these behaviors even under the most trying circumstances:

> Organizations that institute quality programs should structure their compensation practices to reward quality, concludes a report by the Hay Associates. Compensation practices alone cannot make quality initiatives succeed, the report says, but they can help motivate employees to take responsibility, find innovation, and reduce costs.
>
> The shift to quality often requires fundamental organizational change, the report warns. Additionally, most organizations try several approaches to quality before they find the system that works best for them. Whatever the new quality process entails, however, the following elements must be present to ensure its success:
>
> ◉ Management must be committed to the quality movement and not looking for a "quick fix;"
> ◉ Management must define quality outcomes and have measurement systems to gauge progress toward those outcomes;
> ◉ Management must empower the workforce and shift the focus from individual effort to teamwork; and
> ◉ Management must link pay to quality improvement goals.[36]

According to one recent study of more than one hundred business units across 41 corporations, egalitarian pay systems also seem to facilitate a quality strategy. Egalitarian systems are characterized by relatively less pay differential between lower-level and upper-echelon employees. As pay differentials increase, employees are less likely to feel fairly treated. At the same time, their attention to quality apparently declines. Thus, in this study, customers' ratings of product quality were lower for business units with less egalitarian pay structures.[37]

Because employees' perceptions of internal equity are so important for organizations, sophisticated techniques have been developed to facilitate the design of internally equitable pay structures.

INTERNAL EQUITY: DETERMINING THE RELATIVE WORTH OF JOBS

Job evaluation involves the systematic, rational assessment of jobs to determine their relative internal worth.[38] Internal job worth reflects a job's importance or its contribution to the overall attainment of organizational objectives. By design, job evaluation focuses internally; it does not take into account market forces or individual performance—these are managed through other techniques that ensure external equity and employee equity, respectively.

Job evaluation is closely related to job analysis, but they are not identical. As described in Chapter 6, the objective of job analysis is to determine the content of jobs: what tasks are performed, what responsibilities employees have, and, perhaps, what skills and abilities are used. Obtaining this information is an essential prior step to job evaluation. Job evaluation then asks, "What is the relative value of jobs with various contents and responsibilities involving the use of various skills and abilities?"

As with any administrative procedure, job evaluation invites give and take. Consensus building is often required among stakeholders (incumbents, managers, HR representatives, union officials) to work out conflicts that inevitably arise about the "relative" worth of jobs to an organization. The use of group judgments throughout the job evaluation process helps ensure that these conflicts are addressed, producing a pay structure that is more congruent with organizational values than one based solely on external market valuations of worth.[39]

Choosing among job evaluation processes depends on several variables:

- *Legal and Social Background:* The choice of job evaluation methods may be limited by collective bargaining arrangements or by what is legally acceptable.
- *Organizational Size and Structure:* In small firms, simple systems such as ranking may be appropriate. In multiplant enterprises, more complex methods may be needed.
- *Management Style:* Management style can vary from autocratic to democratic. It will primarily affect the scope of worker participation in the design and application of a job evaluation scheme.
- *Labor-Management Relations:* No job evaluation scheme can succeed unless the workers accept it. Indeed, the results of many job evaluation programs have been totally rejected because of union opposition. To prevent this, organizations may choose a plan that provides for worker participation.
- *Cost in Time and Money:* Job evaluation, like other HR activities, costs time and money. An up-front cost is incurred in developing a tailor-made plan. Canned programs may also be costly in terms of dollars and user acceptance. Usually, job evaluation takes between six and twelve months for firms with more than five hundred employees.[40]

As this list suggests, establishing a job evaluation system involves several major decisions. The three major decisions concern whether to use a single plan or multiple plans, what job evaluation method to follow or whether to use a skill-based pay plan, and how to set up a process to drive the plan.

Single Plan versus Multiple Plans

Traditionally, organizations have used different job evaluation plans for different job families (e.g., clerical, skilled craft, and professional). This approach assumes that the work content of jobs in different families is too diverse to be captured by one plan. For example, manufacturing jobs may vary in terms of working conditions and physical effort, whereas professional jobs usually vary in terms of technical skills and knowledge. Proponents of multiple plans contend that these differences require the use of unique evaluation systems tailored to the job.

However, persuasive arguments have been made against using multiple job evaluation systems within a single organization. From a strategic perspective, the use of multiple systems is incongruent with the objective of using internal pay differentials to communicate a coherent message to employees regarding what is valued by the organization. For example, if the strategy is to focus on customers, it may be logical to use potential for affecting customers as a variable to determine the relative worth of all jobs within the company. Also, the use of a single system for valuing all jobs has been proposed as a partial solution to the problem of sex-based inequities.

Proponents of pay equity assert that only if jobs are evaluated using the same criteria can the relative value of all jobs be fairly determined. When separate plans are used, it is much easier to discriminate against specific classes of jobs (e.g., clerical versus skilled) because direct comparisons of segregated jobs can be avoided.

Developing a firm-specific job evaluation system with universal variables selected in accordance with the company's strategy and culture is clearly more difficult than adopting off-the-shelf job evaluation systems developed for specific occupational groups.

Nevertheless, companies such as Control Data and Hewlett-Packard have concluded that the extra effort of developing a tailored system pays off. Thus, these companies use a set of core variables to provide some common basis for evaluating all jobs, and they supplement this with another set of variables unique to particular occupational groups.

Traditional Job Evaluation Methods

Traditional job evaluation methods focus on the job as the unit of interest. Some methods evaluate the whole job, whereas others evaluate components of jobs using compensable factors. Job evaluation approaches also vary with regard to the type of output produced. For example, the factor comparison method evaluates jobs directly in dollar worth, whereas the point rating system requires the conversion of points to dollars.

Ranking Method. The least specific job evaluation method is ranking. One approach to ranking relies on the market value of each job. Alternatively, jobs can be ranked on the basis of such variables as difficulty, criticality to organizational success, and skill required.

The ranking method is convenient when only a few jobs need to be evaluated and when one person is familiar with them all. As the number of jobs increases and the likelihood of one individual's knowing all the jobs declines, detailed job analysis information becomes more important, and ranking is often done by committee. Especially when a large number of jobs are to be ranked, key or benchmark jobs are used for comparison.

One difficulty in the ranking method is that all jobs must be different from each other. Making fine distinctions between similar jobs is often difficult, so disagreements often arise.

Job Classification Method. The job classification method is similar to the ranking method, except that classes or grades are established and the job descriptions are then grouped under them. Pay grade classification standards specify in general terms the kinds and levels of responsibilities assigned to jobs in each grade, the difficulty of the work performed, and the qualifications required of incumbents. According to compensation experts George Milkovich and Jerry Newman: "Classes can be conceived as a series of carefully labeled shelves on a bookshelf. The labels are the class descriptions which serve as the standard against which the job descriptions are compared. Each class is described in such a way that it captures sufficient work detail and yet is general enough to cause little difficulty in slotting jobs."[41]

No matter how lengthy and comprehensive the pay grade narratives, the placement of a specific position into a pay grade can be tricky. Two steps can be taken to make this process easier: (1) make the job descriptions accurate and complete and (2) include benchmark jobs in each class. *Benchmark jobs* are jobs that are common across a number of different employers. Because the job content is relatively stable, external wage rates for these jobs are used for setting internal pay. Benchmark jobs can serve as reference points or judgment anchors against which the content of other jobs can be compared.

A particular advantage of the job classification method is that it can be applied to a large number and a wide variety of jobs. As the number and variety of jobs in an organization increase, however, the classification of jobs tends to become more subjective. This is particularly true when an organization has a large number of plant or office locations and thus jobs with the same title may actually differ in content. Because it is difficult to attend to the true content of each job in such cases, the job title becomes the guide to job classification.[42]

Factor Comparison Method. Approximately 10 percent of employers evaluate jobs using the factor comparison method. This approach uses *compensable factors,* or job attributes, to evaluate the relative worth of jobs inside the organization. Although organizations differ in their choices, compensable factors should be work related and acceptable to all stakeholders. Factor comparison differs from other job evaluation processes because it systematically links external market rates of pay with internal, work-related compensable factors.

To begin the process, the compensable factors are defined. Then, benchmark jobs are chosen, and a compensation committee allocates wage rates for each benchmark job to each compensable factor, as shown in Exhibit 12.5. After all benchmark jobs are slotted across compensable factors, the rate of pay is determined for nonbenchmark jobs. To do this, nonbenchmark jobs are compared against each benchmark job to determine whether they are of greater or lesser value. The total wage for a nonbenchmark job is the sum of the slotted wages across all compensable factors.

Although the factor comparison method is a quick way to set wage rates, it has the potential to perpetuate traditional pay differentials between jobs because the wage rates for other jobs are determined against externally anchored pay rates. Another concern is that the relationship between jobs may change as external rates of pay shift for benchmark jobs. In spite of these limitations, the factor comparison method is a definite improvement over ranking and classification.

Point Rating Method. The most widely used method of job evaluation is the point rating (or point factor) method. This consists of assigning point values for previously determined compensable factors and then adding them to arrive at the overall worth of

■ *Exhibit 12.5*
Factor Comparison Ratings for Benchmark Positions in a Small-Batch Manufacturing Facility

Pay per Hour	Skill	Effort	Responsibility	Working Conditions
$5.25	Parts inspector			
5.00				
4.75				
4.50	Crane operator			Common laborer
4.25		Common laborer	Crane operator	
4.00			Drill or press operator	
3.75		Crane operator		
3.50		Parts inspector	Parts inspector	
3.25		Riveter		
3.00	Drill or press operator	Drill or press operator		Guard
2.75		Guard		Crane operator
2.50				
2.25	Riveter			Riveter
2.00				Drill or press operator
1.75			Guard	
1.50				Parts inspector
1.25	Guard		Riveter	
1.00	Common laborer		Common laborer	
0.75				
0.50				
0.25				

438

■ *Exhibit 12.6*
Sample Point Evaluation System

Compensable Factor	First Degree	Second Degree	Third Degree	Fourth Degree	Fifth Degree
1. Job knowledge	50	100	150	200	NA
2. Problem solving	50	100	150	205	260
3. Impact	60	120	180	240	NA
4. Working conditions	10	30	50	NA	NA
5. Supervision needed	25	50	75	100	NA
6. Supervision given	30	60	90	120	150

Note: NA = Not Applicable, which means that this degree level is not used for the relevant compensable factor

a job. Compensable factors may be adapted from existing point evaluation plans or may be custom designed to reflect the unique values of an organization. Regardless of how they originate, factors should be *weighted* relative to their importance. For example, a research-and-development firm may assign more points to education and experience factors than would a manufacturing facility. Conversely, the manufacturing facility may assign more points to a working conditions factor than would an accounting firm. The point evaluation system presented in Exhibit 12.6 has six compensable factors. The total maximum number of points in this system is 1,000, and the total minimum number of points is 225. Notice that the maximum points assigned to the factors can easily be translated into weights expressed in percentages. To obtain the factor weights, simply divide the maximum points for each factor by the total points possible (1,000). This yields the following weights for factors 1 to 6, respectively: 20 percent, 26 percent, 24 percent, 5 percent, 10 percent, and 15 percent.

Once factors are chosen and weighted, the next step is to construct scales reflecting the different degrees within each factor. Exhibit 12.7 shows descriptions for five degrees of the problem-solving factor in Exhibit 12.6. Notice that each degree is anchored by a description of the typical tasks and behaviors associated with that degree.

■ *Exhibit 12.7*
Example of a Compensable Factor and Related Degree Statements

Problem Solving

This factor examines the types of problems dealt with in your job. Indicate the one level that is most representative of most of your job responsibilities.

Degree 1: Actions are performed in a set order according to written or verbal instruction. Problems are referred to supervisor.

Degree 2: Routine problems are solved and various choices are made regarding the order in which the work is performed, within standard practices. Information may be obtained from various sources.

Degree 3: Various problems are solved that require general knowledge of company policies and procedures applicable within area of responsibility. Decisions are made based on a choice from established alternatives. Actions are expected to be within standards and established procedures.

Degree 4: Analytical judgment, initiative, or innovation is required in dealing with complex problems or situations. Evaluation is not easy because there is little precedent or information may be incomplete.

Degree 5: Complex tasks involving new or constantly changing problems or situations are planned, delegated, coordinated, or implemented, or any combination of these. Tasks involve the organization of new technologies or policies for programs or projects. Actions are limited only by company policies and budgets.

■ *Exhibit 12.8*
Hay Compensable Factors

Mental Activity (Problem Solving)	Know-How	Accountability
The amount of original, self-starting thought required by the job for analysis, evaluation, creation, reasoning, and arriving at conclusions. Mental activity has two dimensions:	The sum total of all knowledge and skills, however acquired, needed for satisfactory job performance (evaluates the job, not the person). Know-how has three dimensions:	The measured effect of the job on company goals. Accountability has three dimensions:

Mental Activity (Problem Solving)

The amount of original, self-starting thought required by the job for analysis, evaluation, creation, reasoning, and arriving at conclusions. Mental activity has two dimensions:

- The degree of freedom with which the thinking process is used to achieve job objectives without the guidance of standards, precedents, or direction from others
- The type of mental activity involved; the complexity, abstractness, or originality of thought required

Mental activity is expressed as a percentage of know-how for the obvious reason that people think with what they know. The percentage judged to be correct for a job is applied to the know-how point value; the result is the point value given to mental activity.

Know-How

The sum total of all knowledge and skills, however acquired, needed for satisfactory job performance (evaluates the job, not the person). Know-how has three dimensions:

- The amount of practical, specialized, or technical knowledge required
- The breadth of management, or the ability to make many activities and functions work well together; the job of company president, for example, has greater breadth than that of department supervisor
- A requirement for skill in motivating people

A chart can be used to assign a number to the level of know-how needed in a job. This number—or point value—indicates the relative importance of know-how in the job being evaluated.

Accountability

The measured effect of the job on company goals. Accountability has three dimensions:

- Freedom to act, or the relative presence of personal or procedural control and guidance; determined by answering the question "How much freedom has the job holder to act independently?"—for example, a plant manager has more freedom than a supervisor under his or her control
- Dollar magnitude, a measure of the sales, budget, dollar value of purchases, value added, or any other significant annual dollar figure related to the job
- Effect of the job on dollar magnitude; a determination of whether the job has a primary effect on end results or has instead a sharing, contributory, or remote effect

Accountability is given a point value independent of the other two factors.

Note: The total evaluation of any job is arrived at by adding the points (not shown here) for mental activity, know-how, and accountability.

After factors and underlying degrees are delineated, a job's worth can be assessed. Typically, a compensation committee is chosen to assess job worth. The committee includes a cross section of stakeholders (e.g., managers, union officials, hourly workers, and workers from various job families) who are trained in the use of the job evaluation process. They independently evaluate each job—that is, they determine the degree level for each factor for each job. Committee members usually discuss their evaluations, and debate continues until consensus is reached on the value of each job. At the end of the process, each job has a total point value that reflects its relative worth.

Like other job evaluation plans, the point factor method incorporates the potential subjectivity of the job analyst. Thus, it has the potential for wage discrimination. Bias or subjectivity can enter (1) in the selection of the compensable factors, (2) in the assignment of relative weights (degrees) to factors, and (3) in the assignment of degrees to the jobs being evaluated. At stake here are equal pay and job comparability. To make sure its point factor evaluation system is free from potential bias and is implemented as objectively as possible, an organization may solicit the input of job incumbents, supervisors, and job evaluation experts, as well as that of human resource professionals.[43]

Hay Guide Chart-Profile Method. One widely used job evaluation system combines features of the point evaluation and factor comparison methods of job evaluation. The

Hay Guide Chart-Profile has been particularly popular for evaluating executive, managerial, and professional positions, but is also widely used for many others including technical, clerical, and manufacturing positions.

Operationally, the Hay system relies on three primary compensable factors: problem solving, know-how, and accountability (see Exhibit 12.8). Point values are determined for each job, using the three factors and their subfactors. In addition, jobs are compared to each another on the basis of each factor. The former approach parallels traditional point evaluation processes, and the latter parallels factor comparison methods.

According to Hay Associates, which developed this method, a major advantage of this system has been its wide acceptance and usage. Because organizations worldwide use the system, Hay can provide clients with comparative pay data by industry or locale. Another advantage of the system is that it has been legally challenged and found acceptable by the courts.

Still, the Hay Guide Chart-Profile Method, like any canned, or standardized, system, may not reflect a particular organization's true values. Thus, each organization needs to consider whether the Hay system's problem-solving, know-how, and accountability factors are truly congruent with the organization's values. For example, under the Hay system, the job of an airline pilot usually receives between 289 and 333 points, the point range typically associated with the job of a first-line supervisor. However, pilots with major airlines often make six-figure salaries, whereas no first-line supervisors make comparable salaries. A better way to evaluate airline jobs is to design a job evaluation specifically for them. This can be done by selecting compensable factors that are appropriate for an airline and weighting the factors in a way that is appropriate to the specific application.[44]

In recognition of the idea that different companies are likely to value different aspects of a job, Hay Associates has been developing a new system called Dynamic Pay. Perhaps this new Hay method will eventually replace the old Hay Guide Chart-Profile Method.

Skill-Based Pay

A growing number of organizations, academics, and consultants assert that the conventional job evaluation processes are easily abused and ill-suited to the needs of today's organizations. Critics contend that conventional job-based pay approaches:

- Support rigid hierarchical organizations that suppress employee motivation and creativity
- Assume that people are commodities that can be made to "fit" defined roles
- Are inappropriate in today's flatter organizations where small, flexible teams of multiskilled people make better economic sense than a large number of single-skilled individuals
- Are inappropriate in the service sector, where future success lies in the knowledge workers possess rather than in the jobs they are assigned[45]

Because of these concerns, companies such as Northern Telecom, General Foods, Aid Associations for Lutherans, General Motors, Honeywell, Mead Corporation, Procter and Gamble, and Anheuser-Busch Companies are implementing skill-based pay, alternatively called pay-for-knowledge or multiskilled pay, to gain a competitive advantage.

Skill-based pay rewards employees for the range, depth, and types of skills they are capable of using. This is a very different philosophy from the conventional job-based approaches. It moves the compensation of workers toward the approaches used to evaluate many types of professionals.[46] Research-and-development firms have used a related approach, called maturity curves, since the 1950s to evaluate the contribution of engineers and scientists. With this method, a series of curves is developed to provide differing levels of worth to individuals. The underlying principle is that professionals with more experience and knowledge are more valuable to the organization. Similar approaches are used to pay elementary and secondary school teachers and apprentices in skilled crafts, who receive pay increments based on educational levels and seniority.

Skill-based pay is premised on the same assumption, namely, that a person who can do more different tasks or who knows more is of greater value and should be paid according to capabilities, not according to job assignment. The important distinction between skill-based pay and the maturity curve approach is that with maturity curves, pay increases occur automatically at particular time intervals. With skill-based pay, pay goes up only after the worker demonstrates an ability to perform specific competencies. In one version of skill-based pay, pay goes up as new tasks or knowledge areas are mastered. This is a multiskill system. For a machine operator, the relevant skills might include an assembly task, a material handling and inventory task, and maintenance tasks. Alternatively, pay may be pegged to the employee's *level* of skill or knowledge within a job domain. For example, supervisors might demonstrate increasing skills and knowledge in job domains such as budget planning and analysis, employee performance management, and marketing.

Skill-based pay systems differ in a variety of ways from conventional job-based pay, some of which are summarized in Exhibit 12.9. Another difference between skill-based pay and job-based pay concerns seniority. Traditionally, seniority, or time in grade, played

■ *Exhibit 12.9*

Comparison of Skill-Based and Conventional Job-Based Pay Systems

Component	Skill-Based System	Job-Based System
1. Determination of worth	Tied to evaluation of skill blocks	Tied to evaluation of total job
2. Pricing	Difficult because the overall pay system is tied to the market	Easier because wages are tied to benchmark jobs in the labor market
3. Pay ranges	Extremely broad; one pay range for entire cluster of skills	Variable, depending on type of job and pay grade width
4. Evaluation of performance	Competency tests	Job performance measures
5. Salary increases	Tied to skill acquisition as measured by competency testing	Tied to seniority, performance appraisal ratings, or actual output
6. Role of training	Essential to attain job flexibility and pay increases for all employees	Necessitated by need rather than desire
7. Pay growth opportunities	Greater opportunities; anyone who passes competency test advances	Fewer opportunities; no advancement unless there is a job opening
8. Effect of job change	Pay remains constant unless skill proficiency increases	Pay changes immediately to level associated with new job
9. Pay administration	Difficult because many aspects of pay plan (training, certification) demand attention	Contingent upon the complexity of job evaluation and pay allocation plan

SOURCE: Adapted from G. E. Ledford, "Three Case Studies on Skill-Based Pay: An Overview," *Compensation and Benefits Review* (April 1990): 11–23; H. Tosi and L. Tosi, "What Managers Need to Know about Knowledge-Based Pay," *Organizational Dynamics* (Winter 1986).

a large role in job-based pay systems; more time in the job was assumed to correspond to greater value. With skill-based pay, value is more closely aligned with skill than with seniority.

As described in the Northern Telecom feature (see pages 415–416), the design of a skill-based pay plan involves developing a set of skill blocks, defining progression paths through the skill blocks, and formulating rules that govern the speed of movement through the skill blocks and their associated pay levels. Issues such as training and certification are more complex and much more important in skill-based pay than in job-based pay. Finally, internal equity—the fairness of pay levels within the organization—is more important in skill-based pay than in job-based pay. This is because the pay for each step in the progression is set in relation to the pay for all other steps, not in relation to the external market rate for each pay grade.

Although skill-based pay is relatively new, preliminary research has identified a number of consequences of this system. First, skill-based pay creates an environment that facilitates worker rotation. This may reduce absenteeism and may ease job assignment pressures for management. Because workers are motivated to learn higher-level skills, they will likely be paid more than the job evaluation rate of the specific jobs to which they are assigned. However, overall labor costs may be lower owing to enhanced workforce flexibility and productivity.[47]

Skill-based pay systems represent a truly different approach to designing a compensation system. The approach may not fit all situations. In fact, a large study comparing *Fortune* 1000 companies to companies using skill-based pay found substantial differences in many other aspects of their cultures and their total systems for managing human resources (see Exhibit 12.10).

Overall Assessment

As Helen Murlis and David Fitt, directors of Hay Management Consultants, noted: "[j]ob evaluation is not a wholly scientific process since it relies on evaluators making judgments about jobs based on facts presented to them. Once this reality is accepted, the true value of formal job evaluation can be seen for what it is: a means of improving objectivity and attaining perceptions of internal equity."[48] The acid test of any scheme's validity is whether it produces results that are acceptable to both jobholders and managers, and are perceived as fair and reasonable. Formal job and skill evaluation schemes are capable of meeting these objectives when they promote genuine participation by all employees—including job incumbents and their managers, as well as union representatives, where appropriate. Participation also smooths the process of communicating and justifying results to employees.

EXTERNAL EQUITY: BUILDING A COMPETITIVE WAGE STRUCTURE

Whatever method is used to determine internal equity, the next step is to develop a wage structure that takes into account the realities of the external labor market. For the pay structure to be usable, pay rates must be somewhat comparable to those in the external market. Achieving both internal equity and external equity is the ultimate objective. Both types of equity are important if an organization is to be successful in attracting, retaining, and motivating employees.[49] Achieving external equity involves (1) conducting a wage survey of the external market, (2) setting the wage policy, and (3) developing a wage structure including ranges, flat rates, or incentives.

Power-Sharing Practices

Survey Feedback — 58 / 27
Participation Groups — 43 / 10
Self-Managing Teams — 34 / 0
Job Enrichment — 30 / 3
Quality Circles — 11 / 5
Mini-Enterprises — 4 / 1

Information-Sharing Practices

Unit's Results — 91 / 54
Business Plans and Goals — 80 / 47
New Technologies — 64 / 25
Competitor's Results — 49 / 21

Formal Training

Job-Specific Skills — 81 / 35
Cross Training — 65 / 11
Quality Control — 55 / 9
Team Building Skills — 52 / 8

Alternative Rewards

Non-Monetary Awards — 50 / 40
All-Salaried Systems — 49 / 23
Cafeteria Benefits — 43 / 34
Employee Stock Ownership Plans — 33 / 46
Profit Sharing — 24 / 33

Skill Based Pay Sites
Fortune 1000 Companies

SOURCE: Adapted from G. E. Ledford, Jr., "Skill-Based Pay: Results of a Large Scale Study" (Los Angeles: University of Southern California, 1992)

Conducting a Wage Survey

To make use of data from a wage survey, an organization first needs to select appropriate benchmark jobs. These jobs should have relatively stable content. They should also represent the entire job structure under study and, if at all possible, all functions.

Next, the organization must define the relevant labor market for each benchmark job.[50] Three variables are commonly used to determine the relevant market: the occupation or skill required, the geographic location (the distance from which applicants would be willing to relocate or commute), and the other employers competing for labor. The relevant geographic labor market for a vice president of sales for Microsoft Corporation may be the entire United States; by comparison, the relevant labor market for an accounts receivable clerk may be Greater Seattle.

Once the labor market is defined for each benchmark job, survey data must be collected. In some cases, the company may conduct its own wage and salary survey; however, it may be less costly to purchase a survey from a consulting firm or to use labor market data from the public domain. Regardless of how survey data are obtained, the process is filled with subjective judgments and the results are likely to depend in part on idiosyncratic issues taken into account by the people conducting the analysis.[51] Thus, as is true for other steps in the process of designing the pay system, involving multiple people with multiple perspectives is a good strategy.

After the appropriate market wage and salary information is collected, it is plotted against the company's job evaluation points to determine a policy line for pay in the external market (see Exhibit 12.11). Why does an organization need to calculate the policy line? Because market data are not available for all jobs. The market policy line makes it possible to estimate what the market pays for jobs that are similar to those in the company but are not among the benchmark jobs included in the market survey.

Deciding on a Pay Policy

Once a policy line for external pay has been calculated, an organization has sufficient data to set its own pay policy line. If the company wants simply to match the market, it may set its policy line equal to the line for the external market. The choice of a pay policy is influenced by the pay rates of major competitors, the firm's profits or losses, surpluses or shortages of qualified workers, the stage of the firm's development, the role of performance-based pay (described in Chapter 13), the strength of union demands, the organizational culture, and so forth.[52]

An evaluation of all these influences will help the company decide whether to lead, match, or lag the market. The rationale behind a lead policy is to maximize the company's ability to attract and retain quality employees and to minimize employee dissatisfaction with pay. A lead policy signals employees that they are valued by the firm. A concern is whether the additional pay attracts and retains the best or merely the most applicants. It is also uncertain how much a firm needs to lead others to gain a distinct competitive advantage. Finally, the pay rates of other firms tend to escalate and eventually match the leader's rates.

By far the most common policy is to match the competition. Although this approach does not give an employer a competitive advantage, it does ensure that the firm is not at a disadvantage. One way to maximize the effectiveness of a match policy is to implement annual pay adjustments prior to major recruiting periods. By doing so, the organization essentially leads the market for the first half of the year and lags the market during the last half of the year.

The option to lag the market may hinder a firm's ability to attract potential employees unless other variables—such as job security, benefits, locale, and job content—compen-

■ *Exhibit 12.11*
Pay Rates Based on Market Survey Results for Benchmark Jobs

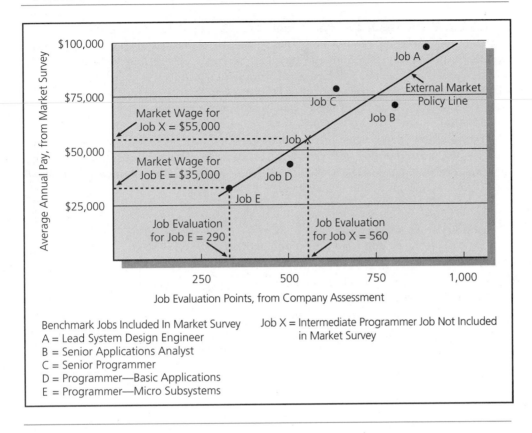

Benchmark Jobs Included In Market Survey
A = Lead System Design Engineer
B = Senior Applications Analyst
C = Senior Programmer
D = Programmer—Basic Applications
E = Programmer—Micro Subsystems

Job X = Intermediate Programmer Job Not Included
in Market Survey

sate for the low base pay.[53] In this case, however, companies may be able to take advantage of the possibility that employees will not notice small variations from the market policy.

Little evidence suggests that one of these strategies is more effective than another for attracting applicants. The most important consideration is whether the pay policy is congruent with the organization's overarching HR strategy. For example, KSL Television in Salt Lake City, Utah, has a corporate objective of being a broadcast leader in the Intermountain West. In support of this objective, executives of the television station set their pay policy line at 5 percent above the market. According to Jean Bishop, vice president of human resources: "The cost of replacing and training a highly skilled engineer, a technical operator, or producer is substantial. We wanted to be proactive in our efforts to attract and retain these people. On the other hand, we didn't want to position our pay line higher than anticipated productivity increases would support. Therefore, leading the market by 5 percent was considered appropriate. It is high enough to signal our employees and competitors that we are a leader but not so high that our revenues can't support it." By comparison, Luther Child Center, a not-for-profit agency in Everett, Washington, has set a goal of matching its competitors in pay and in benefits. "We were losing some of our best therapists to our competitors. When we conducted a market survey, we found that our compensation package was not competitive. While we'd like to be a pay leader, our funds are restricted, so we've settled on matching rates of pay," HR director Janet Allen explains.

Developing a Pay Grade Structure

Once the firm's pay policy line has been set, a pay grade structure can be developed.

Job-Based Pay Grade Structure. Exhibit 12.12 shows a pay grade structure for a conventional job-based pay system. The boxes are associated with a spread of job evaluation points (the job grade) and a range of pay.[54] Several different jobs may be within one box. These jobs will have similar evaluation points, if not content. The boxes may be the same size or may vary in height, but generally they ascend from left to right. This reflects the association of higher pay levels (shown on the vertical axis) with more valued jobs.

In establishing pay ranges, the corporate pay line generally serves as the midpoint. Maximums and minimums are generally set at a percentage above and below that amount. The difference between the two is the pay range. Some common ranges above and below the pay grade midpoint include

Nonexempt	
Laborers and tradespeople	Up to 25%
Clerical, technical, and paraprofessional workers	15–50%
Exempt	
First-level managers, and professionals	30–50%
Middle and senior managers	40–100%

For the firm depicted in Exhibit 12.12, six equal-interval pay grades were established, each with a width of one hundred points. Each grade has a pay range of $500. For pay

■ *Exhibit 12.12*
Pay Grade Structure for a Conventional Job-Based Pay System

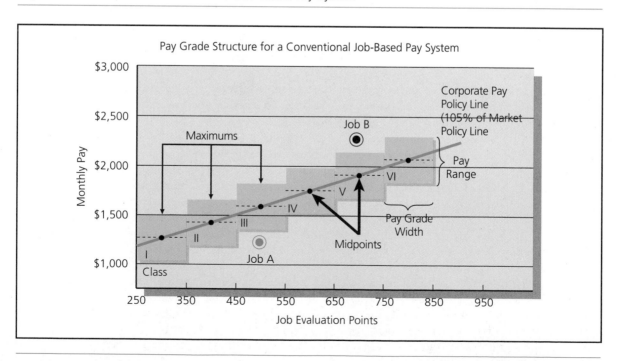

grade II, the range goes from $1,125 (minimum) to $1,625 (maximum) a month; the midpoint is $1,375 a month.

Occasionally, jobs fall outside the established pay structure. When a job falls *below* the established minimum (see job A in Exhibit 12.12), it is *blue circled,* and usually a wage adjustment (sweetener) is made to bring the job within the established pay range. When a job is overpaid (see job B in Exhibit 12.12), it may be *red circled*—that is, as long as the current incumbent remains in the job, the pay rate remains unchanged; when the incumbent leaves the job, the rate will be adjusted downward to put the job back in the established range.

Compa-Ratio. To determine how management is actually paying employees relative to the pay line midpoint, managers often rely on an index called a compa-ratio:

Compa-Ratio = Average Rate of Pay for Employees within a Pay Grade ÷ Range Midpoint

A compa-ratio of less than 1.00 means that on average, employees in the pay grade are being paid below the midpoint. Translated, this means that on average, employees are being paid below the intended policy. A valid reason for this may be that employees as a group were hired relatively recently or are poor performers or were promoted so rapidly that they have not reached the upper half of the pay range.

A compa-ratio greater than 1.00 means that, on average, the organization is paying more than the stated policy. This might occur when employees as a group "top out" because they stay in the same job a long time without getting promoted to jobs in higher grades.

Pay Grades for Skill-Based Pay. The establishment of external equity is more complex with skill-based pay systems than with job-based pay systems. For instance, Northern Telecom could not directly compare any particular pay levels in its skill-based pay plan with pay levels of other firms using job-based pay. Although organizations using skill-based pay rely on the market to set pay levels, they use market data to set minimum, maximum, and average pay levels for the entire job family, not to peg each particular skill step in the pay system to jobs found in the outside markets. Exhibit 12.13 depicts the salary guidelines for Northern Telecom's field technician job family. Notice that it contains five competency levels with an overall pay range of 270 percent. Target high rates suggest maximum rates of pay for employees at a specific competency level.

As with job-based pay, organizations employing skill-based pay differ in their pay policies relative to the external market. According to Peter LeBlanc, director of compensation, Northern Telecom matched the market by setting the minimum of the salary range at the labor market entry rate. The maximum was established on the basis of the average rate of pay for the senior job in the firm's traditional benchmark ladder.

HR officials at a Honeywell ammunition plant in Joliet, Illinois, adopted a different policy. Traditionally, the ammunition industry has been a low-wage industry. However, average wages in the area of the Honeywell plant were relatively high, owing partly to the number of unionized industrial plants in the region. According to HR manager William Tyler, "This meant that paying wages that were competitive in the local labor market risked making the organization uncompetitive in its business market." Skill-based pay was viewed as a way out of this pricing nightmare. Entry wages were pegged at a rate that was low for the area but competitive within the industry. Pay rates rose sharply as employees reached higher skill levels—that is, each new skill was worth an additional $0.90 an hour. With a total of five levels, this produced a pay range of $4.50. According to Tyler, level 3 was pegged at slightly above the area average, and level 4 was priced at well above the area average. Company officials believed that by the time employees

■ *Exhibit 12.13*

Skill-Based Pay Guidelines for Northern Telecom's Field Technician Job Family

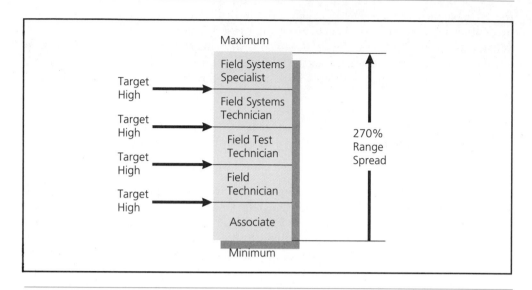

reached level 4, they would be so productive that the facility could afford to pay them the higher rate.[55]

◈ CONTEMPORARY ISSUES IN DESIGNING PAY SYSTEMS

Among the several contemporary issues that affect the design of monetary compensation systems, four are of particular importance: (1) How can differences in the order in which jobs are ranked on internal (job evaluation) and external (wage survey) variables be reconciled if they do not agree? (2) To what extent should employees be able to participate in determining job value? (3) What are the advantages and disadvantages of pay secrecy? (4) What is needed for employees to be satisfied with their pay?

Reconciling Internal and External Equity Imbalances

As discussed in the feature "Using Data for the 21st Century: What Matters Most?" external and internal data as well as a firm's compensation strategy differentially affect job worth decisions. Sometimes differences between market rates and job evaluation results can be resolved by reviewing the basic decisions associated with evaluating and pricing particular jobs. Sometimes survey data can be ignored or benchmark jobs can be changed or jobs can simply be reevaluated. In cases where the disparities persist, judgment is required to resolve them. In reconciling discrepancies, several problems can arise, including market differentials, pay compression, and comparable worth.

Pay Differentials. One way the discrepancy between internal and external pay equity can be resolved is to establish temporary market differentials. Consider the dilemma confronting KSL Television. To resolve problems of pay inequity, the broadcast firm conducted a job evaluation study and then collected market data for key positions. The

Using Data for the 21st Century:
WHAT MATTERS MOST?

Researchers have long recognized the existence of large differentials in pay for the same job, even in a single local labor market. Although the magnitude of interfirm differentials for the same job title—as much as 300 percent—makes it unlikely that the difference in pay is due to job content alone, the causes of these differentials have not been well understood. This is a serious omission in our knowledge of compensation, because job pay decisions are critical strategic concerns affecting whether firms will lead, lag, or match the market; whether pay structures will be steep or flat; whether particular jobs will receive unique compensation treatment; and whether internal or external considerations will drive job rates.

To better understand the sources of pay differentials, researchers Carolyn Weber and Sara Rynes examined how compensation managers from a wide variety of industries determine pay rates for jobs. They used a policy-capturing approach, in which 411 trained compensation analysts were provided simulated information about current job pay, market survey rates, and job evaluation results. The analysts were instructed to assign new pay rates in dollars per month to nine jobs on the basis of the following pieces of information: job title and description, current pay rate, median market survey rate, and job valuation points. The primary objective of the study was to determine how compensation managers make job pay decisions when alternative sources of information about job worth suggest different outcomes. To make the simulation realistic, conflicting information was built into it through the market survey and job evaluation data. Both bits of information varied in terms of whether they indicated the job to be priced was over- or undervalued. The compensation experts were told to evaluate the nine jobs "according to the same priorities that would be used in their own organization." Information was also collected on whether the firms that employed the compensation analysts tried to meet, lead, or follow the market and whether they were unionized.

Consistent with expectations, both job evaluation (internal equity) and market survey information (external equity) figured prominently in compensation managers' job pay decisions. However, compensation managers relied *more* on market information than on job evaluation information. According to the researchers, most employers do not openly communicate the details of their job evaluation ratings, thus employees are more likely to know about market rates than job evaluation rates. Hence, they are more sensitive to deviations from market practices than to deviations from job evaluation results. Still, the preeminence of market rates in setting job pay is problematic for those who advocate the use of job evaluation to attain internal pay equity.

An organization's pay strategy also played a prominent role in the setting of wages in two ways. Managers from market-leading firms and internally oriented firms assigned significantly *higher* pay levels to jobs than those from market-meeting and externally oriented firms. Put another way, internally oriented respondents were distinguished more by their reluctance to act on market data than by any tendency to place greater emphasis on job evaluation.

Evidence also suggested that pay policies vary by industry. Public utilities and services were less likely to report external orientations than were diversified and multiple-classification organizations. The researchers also found that unionized organizations were more likely to be pay leaders, and expanding organizations were more likely to be followers or meeters. Public-sector compensation managers were more likely to be market followers. Still, these organizational variables affected assigned pay levels *less* than did pay strategies themselves.

Weber and Rynes concluded that most compensation is administered in such a way that decisions about job pay (internal and external equity) precede and hence severely constrain decisions about individual pay (employee equity). Although some experts have suggested that the whole notion of paying for jobs is fast becoming obsolete, the persistence of basic techniques for setting job pay, in the face of vast changes in labor and product market conditions, suggests that job pay decisions are likely to remain important determinants of individual earnings for some time to come.[56]

job evaluation positioned the job of a broadcast engineer technician (624 of 1,200 points) in pay grade VI. The pay range for this grade was set at $20,000 to $26,000, well below the average rate of pay of $28,900 in the external market. This discrepancy persisted even following a check of the job evaluation and wage survey data. Because engineers with broadcast experience are difficult to find, KSL executives considered reassigning the job to a higher pay grade (they had done this in the past). Although this would provide a "quick fix," the long-term consequences—particularly if other employees found out about the reclassification—could be disastrous, threatening the validity of the entire compensation system. To preserve the integrity of the system while meeting market demands, KSL left engineering jobs in appropriate grades but paid a market differential. As long as the external market rate of pay was higher than the station's policy line, engineers would receive a $2,900 market differential; when the labor market imbalance corrected itself, the differential would be eliminated.

Pay Compression. Pay compression results when wages for jobs filled from outside the organization are increasing faster than wages for jobs filled from within the organization. As a result, pay differentials among jobs become very small, and the traditional pay structure becomes compressed. Consider the dilemma faced by fast-food restaurants that traditionally pay wages at or near the minimum wage. When Congress increased the minimum wage to $4.25 in 1991, these firms had to decide whether to shift the entire wage structure upward in order to maintain differentials or to allow pay differences to narrow. Compression is also an issue for professional organizations—such as engineering and law firms and colleges and universities—where new graduates command salaries equal to or above those of professionals with more experience.

The problem of compression has no one correct solution. Ultimately, a company considers the costs and consequences of eliminating compression problems (e.g., by raising the pay of more senior job incumbents to keep pace with the changing market) versus letting compression drive employee behavior (e.g., through psychological withdrawal or active job hunting among employees with compressed pay), and chooses a course of action that seems reasonable.

Participation Policies

Job evaluation judgments, like other human resource decisions, can be made by a variety of constituents including compensation professionals, managers, and job incumbents. Traditionally, compensation professionals and managers had the most involvement in the design of compensation systems. Recently, however, employee involvement in job evaluation has been emphasized. For example, 64 percent of all labor agreements require incumbent involvement. As many as half of all companies involve their employees in designing and implementing their compensation plans.[57] Employee participation in job evaluation also is a key feature of what is called new pay.[58] New pay gives employees ownership over their work outcomes. For example, the Polaroid Corporation, having established its policy of openness, involves employees in making salary decisions. Employees are also involved in job evaluation to get a broad understanding of the process by which job value is established.

Job Evaluation Committee. One common way to increase involvement is to establish a job evaluation committee composed of management, nonmanagement, and union representatives. Individuals on such a committee should be knowledgeable about a wide range of jobs. It may also be useful to co-opt antagonists. Involving representatives from all areas improves communication and increases the likelihood that the organization's values will be reflected in the job evaluation system. Of course, this also increases the potential for conflict. For example, managers may try to distort job evaluation ratings of a favorite or superstar employee so that the pay for that employee can exceed the maximum permitted for a job of that value. Conversely, compensation professionals will want to preserve pay equity at all costs. Although it takes time, working through such conflicts is worthwhile because managers and employees are less likely to accept the results of a job evaluation study when they are not consulted.

Self-Participation. A newer method of employee participation allows employees to set their own wage rates. One way of doing this is to let employees vote on who should get a raise. At Romac Industries, a pipe fitting plant, an employee requests a pay raise by completing a form that includes information about her or his current pay level, previous raise, requested raise, and reasons for thinking a raise is deserved. The employee then "goes on board." His or her name, hourly wage, and photograph are posted for six consecutive working days. The employees then vote, and the majority rules. Although top-level managers cannot vote, they can veto a raise. But this has not yet happened because management has learned that employees can responsibly set their own wages if they trust management and have a sufficient understanding of the "cost of doing business."[59]

Pay Secrecy

According to organizational etiquette, asking others their salaries is generally considered gauche. In a study at DuPont, all employees were asked if the company should disclose more payroll information so that everyone would know everyone else's pay. Only 18 percent voted for an open pay system. Managers also favor pay secrecy, because it makes their lives easier. Without knowledge of pay differentials, employees are less likely to confront supervisors about inequitable pay. Consequently, managers do not have to defend or justify their actions.[60]

Despite these common perceptions, open communication about pay practices may be desirable for several reasons. First, some research indicates that employees tend to overestimate the pay of those with lower-level jobs and to underestimate the pay of those with higher-level jobs. Because pay differentials are designed to motivate employees to seek promotion, this misperception may be detrimental to employee motivation. After all, why should an employee in training gain experience and accept greater responsibility for meager increases?

A second reason for an open pay policy is that considerable resources have been devoted to developing a fair and equitable system. For managers and employees to gain an accurate view of the system, they must be informed.

A third and potentially more important reason is that pay is a powerful motivator only when its linkage to performance is explicitly stated and known to employees. For an employee to perform well, he or she must know what performance is desired, what the reward for performing well will be, and what the consequences of performing poorly will be.

Finally, a fourth reason for openness is that having a policy forbidding employee discussions of pay is illegal: "The National Labor Relations Board has reaffirmed that an employer rule [made by the Automatic Screw Products Company] forbidding employees to discuss their salaries constitutes interference, restraint, and coercion of protected employee rights under the National Labor Relations Act. The Board thus concludes that an employer promulgating or enforcing such a rule violates the National Labor Relations Act."[61]

Many employers specify that the range for an incumbent's job and other jobs in a typical career path should be communicated. Some organizations also detail the typical increases associated with low, average, and top performance. A concern in communicating these increases is that the organization may not be able to maintain the same pay schedule in the future. If increases are lower in subsequent years, some employees may be dissatisfied. Furthermore, if policies are not carefully worded to permit employer flexibility, changes in policies may be viewed as a breach of a legal contract. Nevertheless, if it is made clear that the size of the bonus pool is contingent on the profitability of the organization, these problems can be avoided.

Satisfaction with Pay

If organizations want to minimize absenteeism and turnover through compensation, they must make sure employees are satisfied with their pay. Armed with an understanding of the determinants of pay satisfaction, organizations can develop practices that are likely to result in such satisfaction. Three major determinants are pay fairness, pay level, and pay administration practices.[62]

Pay Fairness. Pay fairness refers to what people believe they deserve to be paid in relation to what others deserve to be paid. People tend to determine what they and others deserve to be paid by comparing what they give to the organization with what they get out of the organization. If they regard the exchange as fair or equitable, they are likely to be satisfied. If they see it as unfair, they are likely to be dissatisfied.[63]

Fairness can be increased by providing a "voice" and due process to employees. Thus, organizations must establish formal appeal procedures as discussed in Chapter 3. These procedures vary in degree of formality and in how independent they are from traditional lines of authority. Union contracts often prescribe a formal system in which complaints are first filed with the immediate supervisor. If a satisfactory resolution is not attained, the appeal moves forward to a higher level of management.

Pay Level. People compare their pay levels with what they believe they should receive. They are then satisfied if the "should" level of pay equals the actual level of pay, or dissatisfied if the actual level is less than the "should" level.

Increasingly, pay level satisfaction is being related to differences in pay levels for employees at different levels in the organization.[64] These disparities in wages have been growing in recent years. Observes David Sirota, chairman of the corporate polling firm Sirota and Associates: "CEOs say 'We're a team. We're all in this together, rah, rah, rah.' But employees look at the differences between their pay and the CEO's. They see top management's perks—oak dining rooms and heated garages, vs. cafeterias for the hourly guys and parking spaces half a mile from the plant. And they wonder: 'Is this togetherness?' "[65] As the disparity between pay levels for top management and pay levels for everyone else widens, the wonder grows.[66]

Pay Administration Practices. What does our understanding of pay issues suggest for pay administration practices? First, if employers wish to attract new employees and keep them satisfied with their pay, the wages and salaries offered should approximate the wages and salaries paid to other employees in comparable organizations—in other words, external equity must exist.

Second, the pricing of jobs can enhance pay satisfaction when it is perceived as embodying a philosophy of equal pay for jobs of comparable worth. The determination of equal pay for equally valued work can be aided by sound job evaluations.

Third, pay-for-performance systems must be accompanied by a method for accurately measuring the performance of employees and must be open enough so that employees can clearly see the performance-pay relationship. This is discussed further in Chapter 13.

Fourth, compensation rates and pay structures should be continually reviewed and updated if necessary. Over time, the content of jobs may change, thus distorting the relationships between the jobs' true worth and their job-evaluated worth.

Finally, trust and consistency must be maintained. Employees must perceive that the organization is looking out for their interests as well as its own. Without trust and consistency, pay satisfaction will sink, and pay will become a target for complaints regardless of the real issues.[67]

 ## INTERNATIONAL CONCERNS

As the environment for many business firms in the United States becomes more global, international compensation becomes a more significant element of total compensation.[68]

Objectives of International Compensation

When developing international compensation policies, a multinational corporation seeks to satisfy several objectives. First, the policy should be consistent and fair in its treatment of all categories of international employees. The interests of the MNC are best served when all international employees are relatively satisfied with their compensation package and perceive that they are treated equitably. Second, the policy should help attract and retain personnel in the areas where the MNC has the greatest needs and opportunities. Third, the policy should facilitate the transfer of international employees in the most cost-effective manner for the MNC. Fourth, the policy should be consistent with the overall strategy and structure of the MNC. Finally, the policy should ensure that compensation motivates employees. Some professional international HR managers would say that motivation is the major objective of their compensation programs.[69]

Compensation in Multinational Corporations

In general, the first issue facing MNCs when designing international compensation policies is whether to establish an overall policy for all employees or to distinguish between parent-country nationals and third-country nationals. This differentiation may diminish in the future, but in the mid-1990s, it was very common for MNCs to distinguish between these two groups.

MNCs even tend to differentiate among types of PCNs (expatriates). Separate types of policies may be established based on the length of assignment (temporary transfer, permanent transfer, or continual relocation) or on the type of employee. Cash remuneration, special allowances, benefits, and pensions are determined in part by such classification. Short-term PCNs, for example, whose two- or three-year tours of duty abroad are interspersed with long periods at home, may be treated differently than career PCNs, who spend most of their time working in various locations abroad. Both these groups are different from TCNs, who often move from country to country in the employ of one MNC, or several MNCs, headquartered in a country other than their own: for example, a Swiss banker may be in charge of a German branch of a British bank. In effect, TCNs are the real global employees, the ones who can weave together the far-flung parts of an MNC. As the global MNC increases in importance, TCNs will likely become more valuable and thus will be able to command levels of compensation equivalent to those of PCNs.

For PCNs, the most widely used policy emphasizes "keeping the expatriate whole"—that is, maintaining a salary level relative to that of the PCN's colleagues plus compensating for the costs of international service.[70] The basis of this policy implies that foreign assignees should not suffer a material loss owing to their transfer. This policy can be accomplished through the balance sheet approach, which is designed to equalize the purchasing power of employees at comparable position levels living overseas and in the home country, and to provide incentives to offset qualitative differences between assignment locations.[71]

Expatriate Expenses. Five major categories of outlays cover all the types of expenses incurred by PCNs and their families:

- *Goods and Services:* Home-country outlays for items such as food, personal care, clothing, household furnishings, recreation, transportation, and medical care
- *Housing:* The major costs associated with the employees' principal residences
- *Income Taxes:* Payments to federal and local governments for personal income taxes
- *Reserve:* Contributions to savings, payments for benefits, pension contributions, investments, education expenses, Social Security taxes, and so forth
- *Shipment and Storage:* The major costs associated with shipping and storing personal and household effects

Thus, MNCs seek to develop international packages that are competitive in all the following aspects of compensation:

- Base salary
  Wages—home rate and home currency, as well as local rate and local currency
  Salary adjustments or promotions—home or local standard
  Bonuses—home or local currency, home or local standard
  Stock options
  Inducement payment or hardship premium—percentage of salary or lump-sum payment, home or local currency
  Currency protection—discretion or split basis
  Global salary and performance structure

- Taxation
  Tax protection
  Tax equalization
  Other services

- Benefits
  Home-country program
  Local program
  Social Security program
  Car

- Allowances
  Cost-of-living allowances
  Housing standards
  Education expenses
  Relocation expenses
  Perquisites
  Home leave
  Shipping and storage costs

Not all these aspects of international compensation come into play for every expatriate; nevertheless, expatriates are still rather expensive. Costs to post an expatriate can be anywhere from three to seven times the expatriate's home base salary. Thus, global firms face high compensation bills if they need to staff with expatriates.

To understand some of the issues MNCs face, consider the base salary decision. The term base salary acquires a somewhat different meaning when employees go abroad. At home, base salary denotes the amount of cash compensation that serves as a benchmark for other compensation elements (e.g., bonuses and benefits). For PCNs, base salary is the primary component of a package of *allowances,* many of which are directly related to base salary (e.g., foreign service premium, cost-of-living allowances, housing allowances, and tax protection) as well as the basis for in-service benefits and pension contributions.

When applied to TCNs, base salary may mean the prevailing rate paid for a specific skill in the employee's home country. Typically, companies use local compensation levels as guidelines when developing HCN compensation policies. Conditions that force compensation policies to differ from those in the United States include inflation and differences in the cost of living, housing, security, schooling, and taxation. For example, it is far less costly to recruit a construction engineer from Spain or Taiwan to work in the Middle East than to recruit someone from the United Kingdom or the United States to work in the Middle East.

> More than half of American companies now tie base salaries to the home countries of the third-country national they employ, rather than to U.S. or host-country salary structures, according to a survey of 117 international companies by Organization Resources Counselors Inc. The number of companies doing this has risen from 38% to more than 52% in just two years, and the trend includes those with small as well as large PCN populations. The primary objective is cost saving, since base pay levels of most other countries are currently below those of the U.S.[72]

The base salary of a PCN is usually paid either in the home currency at the home rate or in the local currency at the local rate paid for the same job. Similarly, salary adjustments and promotional practices may be fashioned according to either home-country or local standards. In some select cases, global salary and performance structures have been implemented.

Cultural Imperatives

To succeed in an ever changing international environment, MNCs must look beyond next year's goals and develop clear but flexible long-term compensation strategies: "An effective managerial reward system should be linked to long-term corporate strategy and should anticipate changes in employees' valence for different organizational rewards. On the one hand, multi-national settings make the complex task of developing such a system even more difficult; on the other hand, the fact that the corporation operates in many different environments permits the establishment of unique reward programs, unavailable in more conventional environments."[73]

In addition, MNCs need to match their compensation policies with their staffing policies and general human resource management philosophies. If, for example, an MNC has an ethnocentric staffing policy—that is, it staffs positions with expatriates chosen by headquarters—its compensation policy should be one of keeping the PCN whole. If, however, the staffing policy follows a geocentric approach—that is, the MNC staffs positions with the best people, regardless of nationality—the MNC will need to consider establishing for key managers a system of international base pay in a major reserve currency such as the U.S. dollar or the deutsche mark. This system will allow the MNC to deal with considerable variations in base salaries for managers, such as the following: "In Switzerland, a department head working for a medium-sized company earns $60,000. The same executive in Germany earns only $49,000. But in the U.S., the equivalent job pays only $45,000, according to a survey by Business International Corporation. However, the gap increases as U.S. executives climb the corporate ladder. At the highest levels, CEOs in the U.S. average $727,000 while those in Switzerland average only $214,000 and in Germany only $171,000."[74]

In addition to pay practices that vary from country to country, MNCs must deal with salary management systems that differ radically from West to East. European and North American MNCs usually base compensation on the type of work individual employees or classes of employees perform and the skill required for each defined job position. In Hong Kong and Singapore, individual performance and skill can dramatically affect compensation. Japanese companies tend to pay employees according to their age and seniority as well as group or company performance, offering little or no pay differential for individual performance or exceptional skills. Latin American firms often continue to pay aging, nonproductive workers as much as they do young, vigorous ones because they cannot force them to retire without making additional payments on top of termination indemnities. Clearly, a company cannot ignore the compensation practices of the countries in which it operates. Ignorance of local custom invites disaster; knowledge of the laws, practices, and employer obligations in each country should form the basis for all international compensation decisions.

Compensation Practices in Other Countries

Japan. The Japanese are fond of saying the Imperial House has three sacred treasures. The first of these is lifetime employment. The second, which stems from lifetime employment, is the traditional seniority system that determines not only wages but also the timing of promotions. Under this system, an employee rarely works under someone with less time in service, assuming both have similar educational backgrounds. This system has its roots in the traditional *oyabun-kobun* (parent-child) relationship, which attaches great respect to the older or senior member of the family (or company). The third treasure of the Imperial House is the enterprise (or company) union.

Initially, individual companies pay almost the same starting salary for every new employee hired upon graduation from either high school or college. After that, an employee's annual earnings increase according to the merit rating system. In addition, earnings will increase annually by seniority, even if an employee's job responsibilities remain unchanged, until the age of mandatory retirement, which in the mid-1990s was commonly sixty years of age.

A distinguishing feature of the Japanese wage system is the provision for a semiannual bonus or wage allowance, separate from the annual incremental rate. Usually paid without exception, even in times of recession, the bonus amount is closely related to both the general economy and the profitability of the company. Generally, the equivalent of five to six months' salary is paid in bonuses at midsummer and at the end of the year.

In addition to basic salary, Japanese workers customarily receive housing or a housing allowance, daily living support (including transportation, meals, and workers' uniforms), cultural and recreational benefits, and medical and health care.[75]

Europe. The development of the European Union has brought greater use of the European currency unit (ECU) within business. This common currency, already being used by some European firms, will facilitate the mobility of workers across nations. Having a similar effect is the movement toward *Europay,* which is the practice of developing a common pay policy regardless of the organization's national origin and extent of location throughout Europe. This practice, primarily targeted for top management, recognizes the need to treat European operations as truly one market and their employees as truly all European.

Further comparisons among wage levels within Europe and throughout the world are shown in Exhibit 12.14. As indicated, European nations, almost without exception, have the highest pay per hour for production workers in manufacturing.

Mexico. Although inexpensive low-skill labor in Mexico (see Exhibit 12.15) has been a recurring theme, in truth, this labor is more expensive than many have been led to believe, because the numbers are not necessarily indicative of real pay. Under Mexican labor law, employees' pay is figured to include compensation for holidays and weekends, so the concept of per-hour pay does not translate. As a result, straight comparisons between hourly pay in the United States and in Mexico can understate Mexican wages by 40 percent.

■ *Exhibit 12.14*

Employee Compensation Costs: Selected Countries versus the United States, 1993

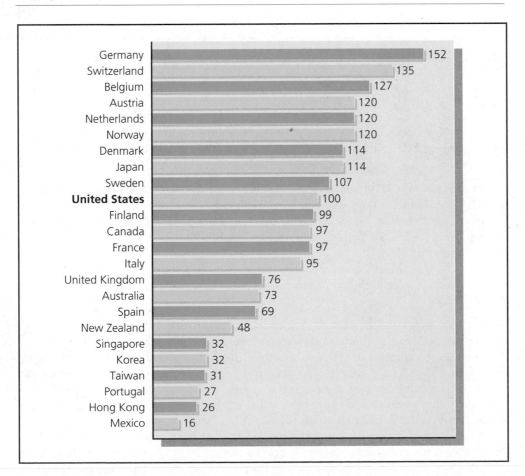

Country	Value
Germany	152
Switzerland	135
Belgium	127
Austria	120
Netherlands	120
Norway	120
Denmark	114
Japan	114
Sweden	107
United States	100
Finland	99
Canada	97
France	97
Italy	95
United Kingdom	76
Australia	73
Spain	69
New Zealand	48
Singapore	32
Korea	32
Taiwan	31
Portugal	27
Hong Kong	26
Mexico	16

SOURCE: "Labor Costs in Manufacturing by Nation," *Bulletin to Management* (August 4, 1994): 245. Used by permission.

■ *Exhibit 12.15*
Mexican-U.S. Pay Comparison

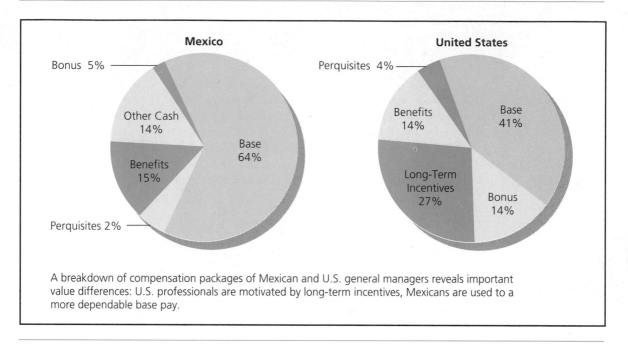

A breakdown of compensation packages of Mexican and U.S. general managers reveals important value differences: U.S. professionals are motivated by long-term incentives, Mexicans are used to a more dependable base pay.

SOURCE: Hewitt Associates, as presented in G. Flynn, "HR in Mexico: What You Should Know," *Personnel Journal* (August 1994): 36. Used by permission.

Cash allowances also play a major role in compensation in Mexico. Employees receive them as part of their total compensation package in addition to base pay. Some are required by law, many are customary. Those required by law are:

◉ *A Christmas Bonus:* Fifteen days' pay is given to all employees with one year or more of service. Most employers provide a month's pay.
◉ *A Vacation Premium:* An additional 25 percent of pay is the required minimum. Most employers provide 80 percent, although on the border it is common to see only the minimum provided.
◉ *Profit Sharing:* Most companies (new operations are sometimes exempted) must distribute 10 percent of their pretax profits each year among all employees, excluding the CEO.

Given these requirements, Hewitt Associates calculates that for production workers, average pay per hour is about $6 in Mexico, compared with $16 in the United States. However, as companies snatch up available cheap labor and call for even more, lower-skilled workers are beginning to have more leverage in pay demands. "One of the long-term expectations that people have about NAFTA is that the salary levels, particularly for lower-echelon employees, will rise," according to Fermin Diez, a general manager of Towers, Perrin in Mexico City.

Compensation for executives in Mexico has also been underestimated. A 1994 Hewitt report states that executives in Mexico may earn 10 to 25 percent more than their U.S. counterparts. This difference is due to supply and demand—and the limited supply of Mexican executives is expected to be able to demand more as companies continue to flood into Mexico. This is particularly true for executives with skills specific to industries becoming more prevalent in Mexico: telecommunications, computer hardware and software, consumer products, and banking.

In addition to base pay and cash allowances, Mexican executives are accustomed to perks to designate status differences. Says Rebecca Lotsoff, manager of international compensation at Motorola: "One thing that is very much rewarded is prestige. A Mexican compensation package for an executive includes such things as a club membership and a big fat title." Alejandro Palma, intercultural business specialist for the Redwood City, California–based Clarke Consulting Group, says that desire for status perks is particularly prevalent at middle-management levels. This, he says, is because in Mexico's hierarchical culture, midlevel managers have a very limited decision-making role. "They are very interested in personal status and the semblance of authority, because in reality, they don't have that authority," Palma says.[76] Other differences between the compensation of U.S. and Mexican general managers are shown in Exhibit 12.15.

 ## SUMMARY

Organizations are being forced to develop strategic compensation practices in light of a cost-conscious, competitive business environment that demands high quality and a continuous flow of new products. Compensation programs must be consistent with the organization's culture and the needs of its business. In addition, compensation practices must adhere to the Fair Labor Standards Act and Equal Pay Act. Concern over comparable worth is causing organizations to consider the manner in which rates of pay are determined for male- and female-dominated positions.

Job evaluation is a systematic, rational assessment of the value of jobs that is designed to establish internal equity in jobs. Ranking and job classification methods focus on evaluating the whole job. These methods are premised on intuitive judgments about job worth. Preferable methods include point evaluation and factor comparison, both of which evaluate jobs using compensable factors.

In conducting a job evaluation study, a decision needs to be made regarding whether to custom design or buy a system. Although it may be more expedient to buy a standardized system, such a system may not reflect organizational needs and values. Another decision is whether to use one or several evaluation plans. To ensure systemwide equity, a single job evaluation plan is usually preferred over multiple plans. Still another decision is who should evaluate the worth of jobs. The greater the involvement of incumbents, the more likely they are to accept the results of the job evaluation study. Alternatively, an organization can choose a pay-for-knowledge or skill-based pay system in which pay increases with job skill or flexibility.

Once their worth is determined, jobs must be priced. Job evaluation procedures are more relevant to establishing relative job value than to setting actual wage rates. To help establish actual wage rates, organizations often use market survey data, especially for jobs that have identical or nearly identical counterparts in the marketplace. This procedure should be done with caution: it involves subjectivity and, therefore, is open to potential wage discrimination charges. Organizations should be careful in using market rates that perpetuate wage differentials that are obviously discriminatory. Fair evaluations should be conducted to help reduce that likelihood.

In establishing wages, organizations can also rely on employees themselves. In the few companies that have tried this approach, employees have set their own wages responsibly without management's altering the procedures or changing decisions. The method is most successful in organizations where employees and management have mutual trust and where employees are provided with information to help them understand the business objectives and financial status of the company.

Establishing wages and determining which job evaluation method to use are only two components of compensation. Other components include selecting the best performance-based pay plan and obtaining benefit from indirect compensation. Chapters 13 and 14 discuss these components.

 ## Discussion Questions

1. Describe Northern Telecom's efforts to link total compensation with the needs of the business.
2. What purposes can total compensation serve? Can the purposes vary across different organizations? Explain.
3. What forms of pay and rewards make up total compensation?
4. What are four basic wage issues that any job evaluation system must address?
5. Describe the basic mechanics of the traditional job evaluation methods.

6. Describe the similarities and differences of skill-based pay and traditional job-based pay systems.
7. How do firms establish the actual pay levels for each job?
8. Are the CEOs of U.S. firms overpaid relative to those of firms in other countries? What issues should be considered in setting pay rates for CEOs?
9. What are the components of the typical expatriate's compensation package?
10. How do the base salaries of expatriates differ from the base salaries of employees in the United States?

 ## In-Class Projects

1. Describe the following for Lincoln Electric:
   a. Lincoln's total compensation plan objectives
   b. The degree to which these objectives are serving the business and HR objectives of Lincoln
   c. Lincoln's total compensation plans and activities
   d. The degree to which these plans and activities are serving Lincoln's objectives

Going forward:

How can the compensation activities at Lincoln Electric be improved?

2. Describe the following for AAL:
   a. AAL's total compensation plan objectives
   b. The degree to which these objectives are serving the business and HR objectives of AAL
   c. AAL's total compensation plans and activities
   d. The degree to which these plans and activities are serving AAL's objectives

Going forward:

How can the compensation activities at AAL be improved?

 ## Field Projects

1. The head of engineering comes to you, the compensation analyst, and asks to pay a "hotshot" more than the current pay range allows. The manager contends that the company will lose this person if it does not pay her what she is worth. You know that good engineers are difficult to find, but your company has a firm policy about pay ranges. What do you tell the head of engineering?
2. You are the head of administrative services for a nonprofit charity fund, which has just completed a pay audit. Much to your surprise, the audit reveals that the current rates of pay for accounting clerks,

accountants, and grounds keepers exceed significantly those dictated by the external market. One strategy for remedying this discrepancy is to freeze the wages of employees in these jobs. However, fund administrators are afraid of the reaction if they find out that employees are being paid above-average wages. What will you do about this dilemma, and why?
3. You are a member of the management team for a major accounting firm that employs two hundred accountants. Traditionally, these accountants have been salaried but have been awarded overtime or

time off for excess work during tax season. You have heard about skill-based pay and are thinking that it may be appropriate for your firm. Discuss the pros and cons of implementing skill-based pay in an accounting firm. Would you make the switch?

 Exercise: Motivation and Pay Raise Allocation

STEP 1: PREPARATION FOR GROUP MEETING

Individually, read the instructions to the *Employee Profile Sheet* shown in the exhibit, and decide on a pay increase for each of the eight employees. Write your decisions in both dollars and percentages. Be prepared to explain your decisions in class.

STEP 2: GROUP MEETING

In a group, share the recommendations you made in step 1 and explain your reasons. After all group members have reported, analyze and try to explain differences among everyone's recommendations. Then develop a set of recommendations that the group can agree on. Appoint a spokesperson to present the group's recommendations to the class.

The group may also decide to totally re-vamp the current pay system, e.g., make it more incentive-based. Describe what changes you recommend here. A spokesperson should be appointed to present the group's recommendations to the class.

■ *Exhibit 12.16*
Employee Profile Sheet

You must make salary increase recommendations for eight individuals whom you supervise. They have just completed their first year with the company and are now to be considered for their first annual raise. Keep in mind that you may be setting precedents that will shape future expectations and that you must stay within your salary budget. Otherwise, there are no formal company policies to restrict you as you decide how to allocate raises. Write the raise you would give each person in the space to the left of each name. You have a total of $50,000 in your budget for pay raises.

$ _____ % _____ **Arnold J. Adams.** Adams is not, as far as you can tell, a good performer. You have discussed your opinion with others and they agree completely. However, you know that Adams has one of the toughest work groups to manage. Adams' subordinates have low skill levels and the work is dirty and hard. If you lose Adams, you are not sure that you could find an adequate replacement. Current salary: $60,000.

$ _____ % _____ **Bruce K. Berger.** Berger is single and seems to lead the life of a carefree swinger. In general, you feel that Berger's job performance is not up to par, and some of Berger's "goofs" are well known to other employees. Current salary: $63,750.

$ _____ % _____ **Carol C. Carter.** You consider Carter to be one of your best subordinates. However, it is quite apparent that other people don't agree. Carter has married into wealth and, as far as you know, doesn't need any more money. Current salary: $67,000.

$ _____ % _____ **Daniel Davis.** You happen to know from your personal relationship that Davis badly needs more money because of certain personal problems. Davis also happens to be one of your best managers. For some reason, your enthusiasm is not shared by your other subordinates, and you have heard them make joking remarks about Davis' performance. Current salary: $64,000.

$ _____ % _____ **Ellen J. Ellis.** Your opinion is that Ellis just isn't cutting the mustard. Surprisingly enough, however, when you check with others to see how they feel you find that Ellis is very highly regarded. You also know that Ellis badly needs a raise. Ellis was recently divorced and is finding it extremely difficult to support a young family of four as a single parent. Current salary: $60,750.

$ _____ % _____ **Fred M. Foster.** Foster has turned out to be a very pleasant surprise, has done an excellent job, and is seen by peers as one of the best people in your group of managers. This surprises you because Foster is generally frivolous and doesn't seem to care very much about money or promotions. Current salary: $62,700.

$ _____ % _____ **Gloria K. Gomez.** Gomez has been very successful so far. You are particularly impressed by this because Gomez has one of the hardest jobs in your company. Gomez needs money more than many of your other subordinates and is respected for good performance. Current salary: $65,250.

$ _____ % _____ **Harriet A. Hunt.** You know Hunt personally. This employee seems to squander money continually. Hunt has a fairly easy job assignment, and your own view is that Hunt doesn't do it especially well. You are thus surprised to find that several of the other new managers think that Hunt is the best of the new group. Current salary: $61,500.

SOURCE: Adapted from material copyrighted by Edward E. Lawler III.

Case Study:

ELITE SOFTWARE INCORPORATED

 Elite Software Incorporated (ESI) develops, produces, and markets business applications programs for personal computers. Most of its customers are small businesses that use the programs for record keeping in their financial, manufacturing, marketing, and human resource functions. ESI's main product, MiniCalc, was one of the first and most successful business applications programs on the market, and it was responsible for most of ESI's growth from 40 employees at the end of 1989, to 135 in 1992, to 310 employees by the end of 1994. Recently, the demand for the MiniCalc has slowly declined as new products that have more powerful features have been introduced to the market. ESI had anticipated the decline of MiniCalc and the responses of its competitors and is now developing a new, more powerful business applications program, the MaxiCalc, which is designed to replace its predecessor. Unfortunately, unforeseen problems have delayed MaxiCalc's market introduction. Turnover of programmers has resulted in work disruptions, and this has contributed to the delay. MaxiCalc is now six months behind its scheduled introduction to the market. Frank Laver, vice president of HR, is aware that the survival of the company depends on MaxiCalc's being brought to market without any further delay. He is also concerned that ESI be able to come out with more new products over the next several years.

In response to the problem of programmer turnover and Frank's troubleshooting, a meeting of the ESI Compensation Committee was organized. Those present were Ken Mitchell, CEO and president; Frank; Sam Rose, vice president of finance; and Carolyn Jones, manager of compensation. The purpose of the meeting was to develop an incentive pay plan that would moti-

vate and reinforce employees to design and develop new products at ESI. The pay incentive should also contribute to retaining employees in order to ensure far fewer disruptions due to turnover of programmers and other employees.

The committee explored the pros and cons of many possible incentive pay plans. It was able to narrow its choice down to three possible plans:

- *A Profit-Sharing Plan:* Under this scheme, all ESI employees would share a portion of the company's profits. Profits would be reported quarterly, and employees would receive a share of them.
- *A Cash Bonus:* The cash bonus would be given to employees in work groups on a one-time basis contingent upon the successful achievement of certain work group targets and goals.
- *An increased Merit Pay Budget:* The size of the merit pay budget would be increased so that each employee's pay raise would be perceived as more meaningful. ◉

Discussion Questions

1. What type of competitive strategy is ESI trying to pursue?
2. Which incentive plan should be selected by the Compensation Committee? Present the details of your decision and your rationale.
3. What behaviors are really needed from the employees if ESI is to be successful in pursuing its competitive strategy?
4. Should ESI consider other compensation alternatives besides these three? Explain.
5. What HR management practices should definitely be avoided?

Performance-Based Pay: Rewarding Performance Contributions

Our famous incentive pay plan is just part of the story! To explain why our workers are as motivated as they are requires an understanding of our basic philosophy, which is centered around the importance of people. The people we work with and the customers we serve deserve the very best we can offer at all times. Our main employee focus is to encourage growth by involvement, participation and teamwork. Thus, we strive to create an environment where employees can achieve company goals and personal goals simultaneously.

PAUL J. BEDDIA, Vice President of Human Resources, Lincoln Electric Company[1]

Managing Human Resources for the 21st Century at Lincoln Electric: Quality Focus in an Incentive Pay Plan

In 1987, when Donald Hastings became president of Lincoln Electric Company, total quality management became a major program. The desire was to build quality into the process rather than testing it at the end of the production line—primarily for electric motors and arc welders. Lincoln's efforts under Hastings have paid off: 25 percent fewer inspectors are needed, now that the employees assume the responsibility for quality, yet quality ratings and employee productivity are up.

With quality playing such an important part in Lincoln's strategy, it has been included in the firm's famous incentive plan. In one component of this plan, the merit rating system, workers' quality is specifically evaluated and compensated. Workers receive merit ratings or report cards twice a year, and these determine the amount of bonus each worker receives at the end of the year. The four criteria in the merit rating are output, quality, dependability, and personal characteristics. The other components of Lincoln's incentive pay plan are a base wage, piecework payments, profit sharing, job security, and an employee stock ownership plan.

Do these components work? Lincoln's productivity level is two to three times that of comparable organizations. Average employee compensation is over $50,000. And Lincoln is dominant in the markets it serves.[2]

The feature "Managing Human Resources for the 21st Century at Lincoln Electric: Quality Focus in an Incentive Pay Plan," with the feature "Managing Human Resources for the 21st Century at Lincoln Electric" in Chapter 5, and the end-of-book case, illustrates how performance-based pay enhances worker productivity and company success. These features together also reveal the complexity of Lincoln's total compensation system, which includes several performance-based incentives as well as a no-layoff policy that was adopted in 1959. Without job security and the workers' trust in top-level managers, the entire incentive system might be far less effective.

Several human resource practices support the performance-based pay component of Lincoln's HR system, and it is this larger system that accounts for effective employee behavior. Nevertheless, performance-based pay is a very powerful cornerstone in the system. This chapter examines performance-based pay exclusively, focusing first on its purposes and importance for attaining organizational objectives. Next, this chapter describes several methods for linking pay to performance, including those that emphasize individual performance and those that reward the performance of the larger group as a whole. In addition, it examines compensation for special groups, such as sales personnel and executives. Finally, it focuses on legal and international issues associated with performance-based pay.

PERFORMANCE-BASED PAY

External and internal equity, as discussed in Chapter 12, focus on the value of jobs in the labor market and to the organization, respectively. Together, they establish the base pay for specific jobs in an organization. In contrast, performance-based pay centers on the value of the performance contribution of an individual, a team, or an organization unit. Payment is then determined by the amount of that performance contribution.[3]

Performance-based pay can take many forms. The most widespread form, and the most familiar, is merit ratings used to determine salary increases.[4] *Merit pay* has three key features: it emphasizes individual performance; the performance it rewards is usually subjectively measured; and it provides permanent increases—once a merit raise is given, the resulting base pay will be higher regardless of future performance. In contrast, most other methods of paying for performance are episodic in nature. That is, pay is given for one occurrence of performance (the occurrence might last a day, a week, a quarter, or the duration of a project) and does not permanently affect future base pay rates. In these systems, the opportunity to earn additional pay for the next episode of performance invites employees to exert effort in the future. Consistent with this distinction, the term *incentive-based pay* refers to all methods of paying for performance that do not involve changes in base pay.[5]

According to recent surveys of U.S. companies of all sizes, the use of performance-based pay is on the increase. Most U.S. companies have used merit pay to reward performance for decades, but dissatisfaction with merit raises as the sole incentive for improving performance seems to be leading to greater use of incentive-based pay, such as bonuses and profit sharing. Currently, approximately one-third of U.S. companies offer incentive pay to nonmanagement employees, often in addition to merit-based salary increases.[6] According to Steven Gross, a vice president of Hay Management Consultants: "This is the hottest area in compensation today. Just about every major company is examining its pay strategy."[7]

Exhibit 13.1 details some questions to ask when considering whether to implement performance-based pay.[8] A systematic approach to performance-based pay requires a thorough assessment of these questions.

PURPOSES AND IMPORTANCE OF PERFORMANCE-BASED PAY

Performance-based pay and the pay differentials it can provide serve a multitude of purposes in today's firms.

Attaining Strategic Goals

Organizations wanting to use pay strategically often feel they must link pay directly to performance in order to reinforce strategic initiatives.[9] For example:

> In early 1989, the Fibers Department of E.I. DuPont de Nemours and Co. initiated a major shift from straight hourly or salary-based pay to one in which employees' compensation rests on their unit's overall performance. As an effort to view employees as "stakeholders" of the

---

 Exhibit 13.1

Ten Questions to Answer before Implementing a Performance-Based Pay System

---

1. Is pay valued by employees?
2. What objective or objectives will the performance-based pay system have?
3. Are the values of the organization conducive to a performance-based pay system?
4. What steps will be taken to ensure that employees and management are committed to the system?
5. Can performance be accurately measured?
6. How frequently will performance be measured or evaluated?
7. What level of aggregation (individual, group, or organization) will be used to distribute rewards?
8. How will pay be tied to performance (e.g., through a merit increase, bonus, commission, or incentive)?
9. Does the organization have sufficient financial resources to make performance-based pay meaningful?
10. What steps will be taken to control and monitor the system?

---

firm's future and to build a sense of teamwork, the compensation plan bases pay on the department's profits and losses. One employee described it as a shift from being paid for "coming to work" to being paid for how well a business unit succeeds.

The plan pays employees based on how well their department meets its performance goals. Thus, employees in the fibers department could receive one to twelve percent above their base pay, depending upon the department's performance; this also means fibers department employees could receive up to 6 percent more in pay than their counterparts in other departments.[10]

DuPont's plan, which covered twenty thousand employees, was devised by a thirteen-member task force, which spent two years on it. But DuPont, like other companies, soon realized that implementing its plan was unexpectedly difficult, when a business downturn meant employees fell short of their profit goal. Rather than withhold the 6 percent pay-for-performance bonus it had designed, DuPont pulled the plug on the plan to avoid demoralizing a workforce that had been toiling harder than ever owing to recent downsizings that had reduced its size by nearly 25 percent.[11]

One way to avoid such missteps, according to Monsanto Company's director of compensation, is by designing incentive pay systems built around the performance of smaller work units rather than plantwide achievements. The objective is to define carefully the strategic objectives of the smaller groups and to ensure that the system ties pay to outcomes that workers feel they can really control.

Another way to avoid such missteps is to consider carefully whether strategic objectives will actually be served by performance-based pay. In some cases, there may be good reasons to link pay increases to something other than performance. Perhaps paying people for gaining seniority would be a better strategic choice. For example, Orrefors, a Swedish manufacturing firm, has positioned itself in the marketplace as a high-end producer of unique handmade glass products. To attract and retain the highly talented craftspeople it needs, Orrefors implemented a pay system that links salary increases with tenure and, presumably, skill level. The company argues that glassmaking demands a long apprenticeship period—often a decade of learning. Young people frequently are willing to remain in a job only so long without a financial incentive. Thus, those who are willing to learn the craft of glassmaking and who remain with the company for the apprenticeship period will receive increasingly higher wages.[12]

Another form of seniority-based pay, the maturity curve, is popular in high-technology and research-and-development firms as noted in Chapter 12. This approach plots a graph using the years of applicable experience accumulated by an employee since receiving a bachelor's degree as the x-axis, and the rate of pay in dollars as the y-axis. With a maturity curve approach, a series of curves can be developed to provide differing levels of worth (performance ratings) for individuals with the same years of experience.[13] This helps reduce the perception that employees are practically entitled to increases.

Performance-based pay, depending on the amount, sends a clear message that there are no entitlements; the strong will prosper, and the weak will not. Organizational cultures that promote risk taking—rather than stability and growth through tried-and-true methods—encourage the use of performance-based pay systems.

Reinforcing Organizational Norms

Pay for performance also can be used to communicate and reinforce organizational norms. For example, Airborne Freight Corporation of Seattle, Washington, revised its incentive packages to link pay directly to the corporate goals of growth, profitability, service, cost control, and productivity. According to Richard Goodwin, vice president of human resources for the overnight delivery and international freight-forwarding company: "We tend to attract young, aggressive managers at Airborne and we encourage internal competition to the point of publicly ranking peers on sales volume and revenue performance. Our incentive system supports these norms.[14]

Some companies have also begun using the notion of paying for performance to establish norms regarding the valuing of workforce diversity. For example, at Corning Incorporated, a leader in creating a corporate culture that embraces diversity, executives receive an extra 10 percent if they meet their goals for diversity management.[15]

Motivating Performance

Money is a powerful motivator because it is valued directly as a reward and because it facilitates the purchase of items that are valued. According to one recent study, pay-for-performance systems reliably increase productivity between 1 and 35 percent when they are introduced.[16] Consider the effect of a small performance reward at Creole Foods of Opelousas, Louisiana. When Alex Chachere took over as president, he found a lethargic workforce content to ship fewer than 3,500 cases per month, far below the company's potential—so he devised a bonus plan. Every month that shipments topped 7,000 cases, workers would divide up an additional 25¢ per case. If the cost of sales stayed under 50 percent, they would get another 10¢. Chachere expected them to reach these targets in a year or so. The first month, they shipped about 8,000 cases. The following year, the company's twenty-eight employees averaged 30,000 cases per month, and Chachere paid $77,000 in bonuses. "That's a lot of money," he admits, "but the day we discontinue the bonuses is the day I quit."[17]

Recognizing Differential Contributions

The difference in performance between peak-performing employees and low-performing employees averages three to one and can be as much as twenty to one.[18] Another objective of performance-based pay is to recognize this differential. Good pay and larger increases help retain employees, and good performers are the ones managers most want to keep. In addition, an employee who is rewarded for good performance will be more likely to continue performing well than one who is not appropriately rewarded.[19]

DESIGNING EFFECTIVE PERFORMANCE-BASED PAY SYSTEMS

Even though most employees are told their raises are based on merit, only one-third *believe* that is so.[20] The problem is that many plans are not designed systematically.

Although performance-based pay systems can substantially improve productivity, poor design and implementation can suppress their potential effectiveness. To be effective, performance-based pay systems must successfully deal with three major issues: specifying and measuring performance, specifying the reward, and gaining employee acceptance.[21]

Specifying and Measuring Performance

All the concerns of performance appraisal must be addressed for any system that links pay to performance to be effective. If the performance measurement system focuses on one component of performance and incentives are given for a different component, employees will be confused and managers will wonder why the incentives do not work.

One conflict to watch for is that of speed and efficiency versus quality and customer satisfaction. Companies often say both sets of objectives are important, and they may really mean it. But if speed and efficiency are easier than quality and customer satisfaction to measure accurately, the incentives may weight them more heavily, leading employees to give them priority when situations force a trade-off.

Another conflict to watch for is that of competition versus cooperation among employees. Even when work is organized around individuals and not teams, cooperation among employees can be beneficial. Incentive systems that pit employees against each other in order to win rewards, instead of encouraging each employee to compete against an objective performance goal, are likely to cut off information sharing and other forms of coworker support.

The problem of competition versus cooperation also arises when incentives are linked to a division's performance but not to the performance of the total company. This is why AT&T has performance-based pay that is driven by the performance of the small work team, of the division, *and* of the company. AT&T wants managers to cooperate with other managers in their own divisions, but not to compete with managers in other divisions. For example, cooperation between the long-distance division and the credit card unit was necessary for the firm to offer a 10 percent discount on calls made with AT&T's universal cards. Explains compensation director Bruce Hollister, "If managers are focused exclusively on their divisions' profits instead of the whole company, it is far tougher to get them to cooperate."[22] Not surprisingly, when incentives are tied to one's own job performance, concern about organizational citizenship fades.[23]

As more and more companies consider paying for skill acquisition, they may face a third conflict, namely that between focusing on performance in the current job and preparing for future jobs. Motorola discovered this conflict when it introduced pay for developing reading and math skills. Team members resented it when their colleagues disappeared to school for weeks, at full pay, leaving the teams weaker. Compensation director Maggie Coil says the workers complained about the mixed message they were getting and the conflict between self-development and teamwork: "They came to us and said, 'Would you guys get a grip? Make up your minds what you really want from us.' "[24]

Specifying the Reward

Rewards for performance can be of many types, ranging from a feeling of personal satisfaction, to public recognition and small tokens, all the way to substantial monetary payments and stock ownership.

Recognition versus Money. The term pay for performance does *not* include intangible rewards or tokens offered as a form of recognition. Nevertheless, rewards such as these can be effective, and companies may include them as part of a total reward system based on performance. For example, AT&T's Global Business Communications Systems unit has a multipronged recognition system as part of its total reward package, as shown in Exhibit 13.2.

Although the term incentive pay is generally not used to refer to rewards that consist mostly of social recognition, in practice, no clear lines separate such rewards from those that are primarily monetary. Regardless of the specific form of the reward, for it to be effective it must be valued by employees. Because the value of a reward is only partly a function of its monetary worth, judging "how much is enough" is mostly a matter of speculation or trial and error. According to one noted expert, a noticeable and meaningful merit increase is probably between 6 and 7 percent—and consequently, many

■ *Exhibit 13.2*
GBCS's Recognition System

Program	Purpose	Eligible Employees*	Nomination Process	Selection Process
Achievers Club	Motivates and recognizes associates, who meet the established performance criteria	All associates	Nomination is based on attainment of performance criteria.	Selection is based on attainment of performance criteria.
Bureaucracy Busters	Encourages associates to recommend changes to existing processes and policies, that will reduce and eliminate bureaucracy	All GBCS associates	A *Proposal for Accelerated Action* is submitted to the program's coordinator; all associates may nominate.	Selection is made by the appropriate functional organization.
Partner of Choice	Recognizes individuals or teams, or both, that demonstrate a dedication to quality and exhibiting the organization's values; recognizes associates outside GBCS if they are part of a GBCS team	All GBCS associates	Nominations are submitted to the program's coordinator; all associates may nominate.	The selection team consists of six associates of all levels, from various organizations throughout the country.
President's Council	Recognizes associates for outstanding contributions; provides an opportunity for members to interact with the Quality Council on initiatives affecting the value equation	All GBCS associates	Coaches nominate.	Selection is made by the GBCS Quality Council.
Touch Award	Honors associates for outstanding social or community contributions	All GBCS associates	A nomination is submitted to the program's coordinator; all associates may nominate.	Selection is made by the GBCS President's Council.

*All associates, regardless of category or type, are eligible for recognition programs implemented within the business unit.
SOURCE: Adapted from M. Plevel et al., "AT&T Global Business Communication Systems: Linking HR with Business Strategy," *Organizational Dynamics* (Winter 1994): 68. Used by permission.

employees never notice the incentive pay they receive.[25] Perhaps the best advice is to intentionally use both recognition and monetary incentives. This is what Au Bon Pain does.

Recall that Au Bon Pain asks mystery customers to evaluate the performance of its restaurants and their employees. To establish a direct relationship between performance and rewards, managers whose employees score 100 percent in all twelve of the categories that are evaluated receive an on-the-spot bonus of twenty Club Excellence Dollars—dubbed CDs. These dollars can be traded for items in a company catalog. Most items are in the $10–$70 range and include such things as Au Bon Pain sunglasses and portable cassette players. In addition, winner's names are posted on the store's bulletin board next to a list of the criteria for the program, and all winners receive personal letters of congratulations from company officials. Thus, it is not clear whether Au Bon Pain's employees are motivated more by the monetary worth of these rewards or by the social recognition that goes with them.

Size of Reward. Companies clearly make different choices in the sizes of the incentives they offer.[26] Although the average for nonexecutives is about 7 percent, at Lincoln Electric, the incentive is 100 percent. Even within the same company, employees in different jobs usually have different percentages of their pay placed "at risk," with the general pattern being proportionately more incentive-based pay as they move up in the hierarchy.

Form of Payment. Besides simply cash, a company may choose to give employees large prizes (e.g., all-expenses-paid vacations), direct stock awards, or stock options, or any combination of these. These different forms of payment can be used to achieve different types of strategic objectives. For example, Domino's Pizza combines performance-based rewards with a form of off-the-job training in disguise. The company spends $1 million holding its Distribution Olympics. Top-performing employees from across the United States are identified, flown to the national headquarters, and paid to spend three days playing job-related games at this unique event. According to a Domino's spokesperson, the games encourage employees to hone their job skills and produce a better product. They also enhance Domino's fundamental belief that the contribution of every employee matters. Winners of the games garner substantial cash prizes.[27]

Gaining Employee Acceptance

Although few employees are likely to object to playing Domino's games, employee opposition can be a major obstacle to the successful implementation of more consequential performance-based pay, especially incentive plans. Employees may worry, for example, that incentives will result in work speedups or will put some percentage of the workforce out of a job. Another legitimate concern may be that performance targets will be too difficult or out of the employees' control. These anxieties may be especially likely if employees do not understand the system.[28]

When group performance serves as a criterion for incentive pay, individualistic U.S. employees may resent having to depend on others for their rewards. And if trust in management is low, employees may not believe the figures when management tells them how the financial performance of their business unit translates into the size of the pool available for bonuses. This was the problem confronted by Evart Products Company, an auto parts supplier. In the third year of a new gain-sharing plan, bonuses suddenly fell from over $1,000 for each employee to nothing. "Some of the employees we interviewed believed that the calculations had been unfairly manipulated by management so that there was no way to earn the bonuses," reported a researcher who studied the situation.[29]

An incentive plan appears to work best when:

- The plan is clearly communicated.
- The plan is understood, and bonuses are easy to calculate.
- The employees have a hand in establishing and administering the plan.
- The employees believe they are being treated fairly.
- The employees have an avenue of appeal if they believe they are being treated unfairly.

- The employees believe they can trust the company and therefore believe they have job security.
- The bonuses are awarded as soon as possible after the desired performance.

Assuming that these issues are successfully addressed, a viable performance-based pay system can be developed.

STRATEGIC DECISIONS IN DESIGNING A PERFORMANCE-BASED PAY SYSTEM

Several specific strategic decisions are associated with designing a performance-based pay system that will support the behaviors needed by a company. These include deciding the method used for linking pay to performance, the level of aggregation used when distributing rewards, and the timing of the reward.

Methods for Linking Pay to Performance

As shown in Exhibit 13.3, three methods for linking pay to performance are available. These options differ in the level of guaranteed base pay, the relationship of base pay to the market, the amount of performance pay, the method used to allocate performance pay, the permanency of performance-based pay, and the portion of total pay that is at risk.

■ *Exhibit 13.3*
Total Compensation under Traditional, Incentive and Earnings-at-Risk Pay Plans

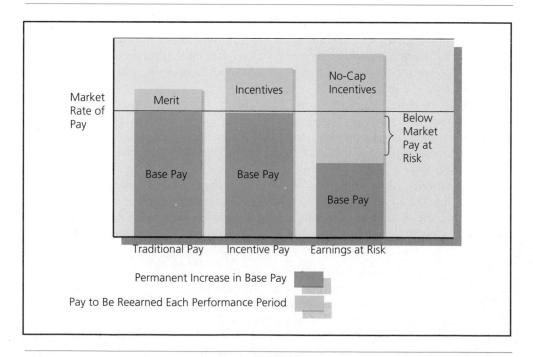

Traditional Pay Plans. With traditional pay plans, base pay (the entitlement to be received regardless of performance) is set at the market rate. A small pool of money is set aside to reward performance. Under such plans, performance usually is not directly assessed. Instead, firms use indicators of performance (e.g., standards and behavioral descriptors) as measured through the performance appraisal processes. Because performance measures are likely to be viewed as being less accurate, the size of a merit pay adjustment typically is smaller than that awarded under the incentive and earnings-at-risk plans.

A recent survey indicated that 72 percent of blue-collar workers and 56 percent of white-collar workers prefer straight wages over *any* type of incentive play plan.[30] With traditional pay plans, even if subsequent performance remains the same or declines, merit increases awarded in a preceding year are not revoked. Therefore, traditional pay entails little risk for the employee. From the organization's perspective, however, traditional pay plans are costly and risky. They permanently increase wage costs without guaranteeing permanent increases in performance.

Incentive Pay Plans. Like traditional pay systems, incentive plans peg base pay at the market rate. Additional compensation is available through bonuses or other forms of payment for peak performance. Under some plans, compensation of a specified amount is tied to specific goals established and communicated to participants before the start of the performance period. The emphasis is on specific actions performed in pursuit of the goals. In other plans, the size of payment is based on an after-the-fact assessment of the outcomes, with no precise agreement made in advance concerning how payments will be allocated: top management assesses the company's performance and allocates a portion of profits to employees in the form of a bonus. Because employees do not know in advance what performance and what level of that performance will be rewarded, this type of system is less likely to be effective in achieving specific strategic objectives.

Although typically a cap is placed on incentive pay, the earning potential is usually much greater with an incentive plan than with a traditional plan. The risk is that the incentive pay supplement must be reearned each performance period. For example, between 1983 and 1993, Boeing Company employees received annual bonuses that were approximately 30 percent of their gross pay, instead of wage increases. For a full-time worker making $12 an hour, these bonuses averaged about $7,740 a year. If the annual bonuses had instead been wage increases, each employee would have received a total of about $25,940 more during the same period.[31]

Still, incentive pay systems provide an "upside earnings opportunity" with minimal risk to the employee. In the worst-case scenario, the employee earns what the market pays for the job, and there is always the potential to earn more if goals are exceeded.[32]

Earnings-at-Risk Pay Plans. Traditional and incentive pay systems provide rewards for individual or group performance as a supplement to historically guaranteed base pay amounts that equal the market rate. By comparison, earnings-at-risk (EAR) plans involve reductions in base pay to below-market levels. In essence, employees must earn their way back to the level that would have been guaranteed under a traditional or incentive pay plan. But they also have the potential for unlimited earnings.

According to Cathe Johnson, manager of compensation planning for Motorola's semiconductor business sector: "When base pay for the job lags the market, there is no longer a safety net. Additional earnings are possible if goals are exceeded, but income will be lost if goals are not met. The worst case scenario is that if the employee does not reach his or her performance goals, the standard of living will be lowered."[33] As

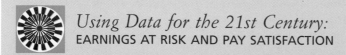

Using Data for the 21st Century:
EARNINGS AT RISK AND PAY SATISFACTION

Earnings-at-risk (EAR) systems have gained popularity in many industries including retail banking because of their potential to reduce fixed costs and ensure long-term employment stability. As operationalized in banks, EARs cut base pay levels to below market levels and reward employees for selling products (e.g., new accounts, loan packages, and even insurance) rather than merely servicing customer accounts. While these systems result in a wider range of possibilities for total take-home pay, since they place no upper limit on earnings, they do add elements of risk and uncertainty that may be foreign to a retail banking culture. In contrast to real estate sales, and garment manufacturing, the conservative retail banking industry has traditionally placed a relatively high value on commitment and longevity rather than productivity. Thus, the implementation of an EAR plan may meet with employee resistance and dissatisfaction.

Because little research has been devoted to examining the effects of EAR pay programs, Seattle-based researchers Karen Brown and Vandra Huber examined pay satisfaction before and after the introduction of an EAR plan in a retail bank. The two researchers wanted to understand whether an EAR system differentially would affect pay process as well as pay outcome satisfaction. In addition, they wanted to determine the antecedents to pay satisfaction before and after implementing an EAR system.

The research was conducted in a large publicly held bank in a western region of the United States where the economy is very stable. The bank was in extremely good financial health at the time of the study and was not associated with the savings and loan industry, which had experienced downturns. All branch employees were surveyed at two points in time, just prior to the implementation of a reduced-base EAR pay plan, and several months after the plan had gone into effect and just before the beginning of a new fiscal year.

The first survey was mailed to bank employees along with a letter from bank officials encouraging employees to complete them. A total of 101 employees responded to both surveys. At the time that the first survey was distributed, a traditional "upside earnings" variable pay plan was in place. Employees received a base salary set at the market rate. In addition, they were eligible for quarterly bonuses based on branch performance determined by the net present value of each bank product. Six months after the EAR pay system was implemented, the second survey was distributed. Six months was chosen because it provided enough time for employees to sufficiently experience the pay system but not so much time that turnover, known to be high in retail banking, would result in a substantial degradation of the employee population base.

A statistical process called multivariate analysis of variance was used to examine the changes in pay process and pay outcome satisfaction before (time 1) and after (time 2) the implementation of the EAR system. This analysis showed that implementing an EAR pay plan significantly affected both aspects of pay satisfaction. Employees were moderately satisfied with pay *outcomes* (how much they earned) before the EAR system was implemented (Average = 4.43) but were significantly less satisfied once it was in place (Average = 3.05). The change in pay administration *procedures* also led to a significant decline in pay process satisfaction (Time 1 Average = 3.77; Time 2 Average = 2.88). Under the old system, employees were significantly more satisfied with their pay outcomes than with the pay process. Under the new system, employees were equally dissatisfied with pay outcomes and pay process. Apparently, the view of the new incentive system was so negative that it washed out differences in process and outcome ratings found under the old system.

To determine if the changes in pay satisfaction would occur even when total pay did not decrease, a second set of analyses was conducted. Here, only respondents for whom pay had either stayed the same or increased were included. Again, both pay process satisfaction and pay outcome satisfaction declined. Apparently, changing a pay system even when one benefits from the change leads to dissatisfaction. Because satisfaction decreased for wage gainers as well as for wage losers, the opportunity for receiving higher pay appears to have been overshadowed by the reduction in the steady portion of their paychecks upon which the employees had come to rely.

The study found that process and outcome satisfaction were tied to an individual's reward-for-effort beliefs. When employees perceived that they were not getting sufficient rewards for their job efforts, dissatisfaction with the way pay was administered as well as with the level of pay received increased. A second important variable is pay system understanding. An employee's understanding of how pay is tied to performance is more important than the actual mechanics of the plan. Under the old system, understanding was related to both pay process and outcome satisfaction. When the new system was implemented, understanding affected satisfaction with the pay process. The researchers concluded that if the EAR system had been explained better or differently, pay satisfaction may not have declined to the extent that it did.

Tenure was also found to be a significant predictor. Employees with greater tenure were more dissatisfied with the new pay system than were employees with less tenure. The authors noted that as the workforce continues to age, it may be more and more difficult for service organizations to convince their employees that riskier pay plans are in everyone's best interests.

In sum, the implementation of an EAR system must be handled with great care, and strong consideration must be given to its fit with the organization and its employees.

Based on the high dissatisfaction associated with the EAR pay system, the bank returned to the variable pay system that had been in place at the time of the first survey. Base pay was raised to match the market rate, and variable pay was administered in the form of bonuses.[34]

explained in the feature "Using Data for the 21st Century: Earnings at Risk and Pay Satisfaction," such plans may not be acceptable to employees who are used to more traditional reward structures that ensure earnings stability.[35] For some employees, such as salespeople who work on straight commission, placing their earnings at risk is just considered normal. And increasingly, top-level executives are being asked to accept compensation packages that put greater portions of their earnings at risk.

Level of Aggregation for Reward Distribution

Performance can be measured at the individual, work team, department, plant, strategic business unit, or organization level. One variable influencing the aggregation decision is the ease with which performance can be objectively measured. If individual performance can only be evaluated by subjective supervisory ratings, then it may be appropriate to move to a higher level of aggregation—for example, team or strategic business unit. Moving to a higher level tends to yield more objective measures of performance, such as labor costs, profits, and cost savings. The trade-off is that the tie to individual performance is less direct; the gain is that the tie to achieving the company's business objectives is more clear.

Technological constraints may dictate the appropriate level of aggregation. Team or business unit incentives are more appropriate than individual incentives when work flows are interdependent (as in small-batch manufacturing or the development of an advertising campaign) or when the work flows are machine paced (as on an assembly line). Systems in which work outputs are conditional on the receipt of information or materials from someone else also are good candidates for team-level or business unit-level incentive plans.[36]

A third variable affecting the choice of aggregation level relates to the type of behavior an organization needs in order to attain its strategic initiatives. Airborne Freight wants its salespeople to be entrepreneurs. Therefore, it utilizes individual incentive plans that are associated with greater competition, increased performance pressure, and greater risk taking.[37] Team incentive plans, on the other hand, reinforce behaviors that promote collective rather than individual success. In addition, they offer reinforcement to ensure that all team members help to attain objectives. Although the perceived connection between pay and individual performance is weaker, this may be offset by an increase in cooperation. Team and organization incentive plans also are less costly administratively and less difficult to administer than individual pay systems.

Timing of Reward

Generally speaking, the more quickly rewards follow desirable behavior, the more potent the rewards are in evoking subsequent desirable behavior. Delayed rewards may (1) decrease desired behavior (because the employee does not see an immediate consequence), (2) increase dissatisfaction and frustration among high performers, and (3) increase undesired behavior that occurs during the interval between performance and the receipt of the reward.

Unfortunately, in most companies, incentive pay is received from several weeks to a year after the performance being rewarded. Several practical circumstances could cause the delay. Task cycles may not be conveniently equal to calendar cycles, or performance information may not be readily available. Also, the delay may be part of a cost-containment strategy: the longer the company delays paying the incentive, the longer it can use the money for its own purposes.

One way to minimize the problems associated with delayed rewards entails developing performance contracts. Upon completion of agreed-upon work at an agreed-upon date, the performance pay is distributed. If the time frame is too short to be managed, then feedback or supervisory recognition can be provided intermittently until the formal reward can be delivered.[38]

However, it can be advantageous to delay the distribution of performance pay. For example, the Utah firm Exhibit Systems builds one-of-a-kind industrial displays. Traditionally, the company paid its salespeople at the time a contract was signed. The immediacy of the reward created problems. According to Dennis Peterson, a partner in the firm: "Once the sales person received his commission, he moved on to the next sale. We received complaints from our designers that the sales reps were not cooperating. Production workers also complained that the reps were slow in providing specifications for displays." The company also was running a large number of accounts receivable.

To alleviate these problems, the commission plan was redesigned. Sales representatives now receive one-half of their commission when the industrial display has been built and the customer has signed off on it. The remainder of the commission is paid when the account is paid in full. Now, Peterson notes, salespeople work closely with designers and construction teams to ensure that the product is built to customer specifications. In addition, the plan encourages sales personnel to play an active role in collecting accounts receivable.

MERIT-BASED PAY PLANS

Traditional performance-based pay has been the cornerstone of public and private compensation systems for many years. It is best exemplified by merit pay plans.

Although cost-of-living increases are on the decline, more than 80 percent of all organizations still use some form of merit pay.[39] Merit pay plans differ along several dimensions. First, some plans include other variables besides performance—such as cost of living, job or organizational seniority, or comparability in pay grade—in the pay adjustment formula. Second, plans differ in the way the merit increase is calculated: some award an absolute amount, others award a percentage of base salary, still others rely on merit grids (discussed later in this chapter). Third, merit increases may be distributed more often than once a year or delayed in times of budget crisis.[40]

The concept of merit pay has been implemented in a variety of ways, but all merit pay plans share two characteristics. First, some portion of employees' pay is based on their rated performance in a previous time period. Second, the merit increase awarded in one evaluation period carries over into the base salary for future evaluation periods.

Performance Assessment

Fundamental to an effective merit pay system is a credible and comprehensive performance appraisal system. Without a reliable assessment of performance, it is impossible to relate pay to performance in a way that is motivating.

Performance appraisal processes are often subjective. The criteria may be contaminated or deficient. Supervisors all too frequently evaluate incumbents according to preconceived biases. Regardless of the appraisal form—whether it is based, for instance, on behavior, output, or traits—rating errors such as leniency and halo are rampant.[41] Therefore, supervisors and employees often disagree on evaluation results. When pay hinges on evaluation results, confrontation and mistrust often escalate.[42]

A related concern is that appraisals in general—and merit pay systems specifically—emphasize individual rather than group goals. This may promote a "what's-in-it-for-*me*" attitude that does little to boost productivity—particularly in the team-oriented 1990s.

Merit Increase Size

Under merit pay plans, pay raises are recommended by the department heads for the employees being supervised. This is usually carried out within the constraints of a merit pool budget. Since the total of all increases cannot exceed the budget percentage for the department, small merit pay pools are problematic. As Charles Peck, a compensation expert with the Conference Board, based in New York, notes:

> Merit increases tend to be expensive and, contrary to their intent, not strongly related to performance. Usually everybody gets something. This so dilutes the salary increase budget that the top performer's increase is not large enough to be significant (especially after it is prorated over the number of pay periods in the year and subjected to withholding). On the other hand, the poor performer is getting more than he or she should have, which is nothing. If the concept of pay for performance is rigorously applied, there must be zero pay for zero performance.[43]

In 1982, the median increase granted to merit recipients was 8.8 percent. The difference between the median raise and the highest raise was 5.5 percent; the difference between the median raise and the lowest raise was 3.9 percent. In later years, merit budgets declined steadily, and from 1990 to 1994, they averaged 5 percent. In the early 1990s, the typical merit pay difference between satisfactory and excellent performance at the $40,000 level averaged $17 a week after taxes.[44] The result of all this is that the employees who are most dissatisfied are the ones the company least wants dissatisfied—the top performers.

Merit Increase Guidelines

Three types of merit increase guidelines are commonly used to tie pay to performance. The simplest specifies pay increase percentages for different levels of performance. For example, a performance-rating schedule can be paired with a merit increase schedule as follows:

Pay Increase Level					
	1	2	3	4	5
Performance Rating	Unacceptable	Below average	Competent	Above average	Superior
Merit Increase	0%	2%	4%	6%	8%

To give supervisors some latitude, ranges may be used for the merit increases—for example, 0–1 percent for unacceptable performance, 2–3 percent for below average performance, and so on. Another option is to vary the timing of increases—for example, every eight months for high performers versus every fifteen months for low performers.

A more complex system involves the development of a merit pay grid. As shown in Exhibit 13.4, this approach considers the individual's position in the salary range, as well as performance. At any performance rating higher than Below Average, an employee whose current base pay is lower will receive a larger percentage increase in pay than an employee whose current base salary is higher. Although the percentage of merit increase is greater in the lower quartiles, the absolute size of the merit increase is often larger in the higher quartiles, provided the merit budget is large enough and the grid is designed correctly.

Since employees tend to confuse market adjustments and performance pay, they may perceive the merit pay grid approach as unfair because equally performing employees do not get equal percentage increases in pay. Although employee education may help to minimize this problem, a more practical approach is to decouple performance and market pay adjustments and award each type of increase separately.

Overall Assessment

According to Edward E. Lawler III, an expert on reward system design, merit increases do not work well because they are plugged into antiquated pay systems. In the early 1900s, many jobs were in manufacturing and agriculture and involved the production of relatively simple, high-volume products. This is not the case today. If we've learned anything in 40 years of researching reward systems, it's that merit pay is a terrible way to increase productivity—particularly for the service, information-processing, and high technology-based industries of the 1990s and the approaching 21st century.[45] Still, most U.S. workers are paid under merit systems. This situation will likely have changed substantially by the 21st century because of the productivity gains associated with incentive pay plans.

■ *Exhibit 13.4*
Sample Merit Pay Grid

	Merit Increase Based on Current Position in the Salary Range			
Performance Rating	First Quartile	Second Quartile	Third Quartile	Fourth Quartile
1. Unacceptable	0%	0%	0%	0%
2. Below Average	2%	0%	0%	0%
3. Competent	8%	6%	4%	2%
4. Above Average	10%	8%	6%	4%
5. Superior	12%	10%	8%	6%

✵ INCENTIVE PAY PLANS

Top executives have long received bonuses and incentives based on company financial results. Recent surveys indicate that approximately 90 percent of executives receive bonuses that account for about 50 percent of their total pay. Now, incentives, as well as earnings-at-risk pay plans, are being used more frequently to reward rank-and-file employees, too. One report shows that more incentive pay plans had been adopted in the early 1990s than in all the 1970s or 1980s and that more incentive plans were on the way.[46]

Interest in incentive pay has stepped up for several reasons. First, production improvements are necessary if the United States intends to retain a leadership role in an increasingly global market. Second, America has shifted to a service economy. In service companies, compensation can account for up to 80 percent of the operating budget; consequently, incentive pay is spreading into banks, hospitals, and other labor-intensive service providers.

A third reason for increased interest in incentive pay is the discrepancy between the level of compensation paid to top executives and the levels paid to other workers. Incentive plans are one way to allow all workers to share in company prosperity. Finally, there is a growing awareness that traditional pay plans often do a poor job of linking pay to performance. If organizations are to achieve their strategic initiatives, then pay needs to be linked to performance in such a way that it aligns the goals of the employee and of the organization.

Although endless variations on the theme exist, seven performance-based pay approaches predominate (see Exhibit 13.5). Note that these plans can be implemented as either incentive pay or earnings-at-risk plans; in particular, stock rewards tend to put earnings at risk.

Lump-Sum Bonus

With increased emphasis on cost-effective human resource practices, firms are questioning the traditional practice of granting annual salary or merit increases. Consider an employee who performs outstandingly one year and is given a 15 percent merit pay increase. The next year, for whatever reason, the employee does not perform as well, or even adequately, yet the original salary increase is a permanent cost for the organization. Besides being economically unsound, merit increases administered in this way may demotivate other employees because an employee who has performed well previously may have a higher base pay rate than an employee who is currently performing well, and may thus receive a larger dollar increase.

To rectify this situation, many firms are replacing merit increases with semiannual or quarterly performance bonuses. These bonuses often are distributed in one lump sum.[47]

Bonuses hold several advantages over salary increases. First, they increase the meaning of pay. A lump-sum payment of $5,000 is more striking than a before-tax increase of $100 a week. A wise employee can leverage the value of the bonus further by investing it carefully; he or she may be less likely to do this when an increase is spread throughout the year. Second, bonuses maximize the relationship between pay and performance. Unlike permanent salary increases, they must be earned continually by above average performance year in and year.

A major constraint with this, as well as any, performance-based pay system is measurement. If subjective appraisal criteria are used, the fairness of the system may be undermined and the motivational potential of the bonus may be lost.

■ *Exhibit 13.5*

Definitions and Characteristics of Performance-Based Pay Programs

Plan Type	How It Works	Advantages	Disadvantages
Lump-sum bonus (5 percent of total pay)	Payment in lieu of merit increase; not added to base salary	Allows company to control fixed-wage costs and benefits; is a more visible reward than a merit increase	May be based on subjective appraisal; may be resented by employees because not everyone gets something
Instant incentive (3 percent of total pay)	Special payment to an individual for a noteworthy achievement (e.g., devising a cost-saving plan)	Allows employee to benefit from cost-saving ideas; is easy to administer	Emphasizes quantity, not quality; may provide individual rewards that are too small to encourage employee participation
Individual incentive (10–20 percent of total pay)	Payment based on measured individual performance, such as in a piecework system	Produces high rate of productivity; links labor costs to performance; is easy to explain and administer	Promotes competition; has standards that are difficult to calculate; is inappropriate for interdependent tasks
Team incentive (10 percent of total pay)	Uniform award to all members of a group based on achievement of predetermined goals	Improves productivity; promotes teamwork, utilizes reinforcing power of coworkers, and creates goal interdependence	Promotes competition between groups; may cause workers to resent low performers
Profit sharing (6 percent of total pay)	Uniform payment to all employees based on corporate profits; payments made in cash or deferred into a retirement fund	Is guaranteed to be affordable; unites company and employees' financial interests; provides retirement income in some cases; raises productivity	May lead workers to ignore long-term performance; forces company to open its books; may be seen as a gift
Gain sharing (3 percent of total pay)	Plan to measure productivity of a unit or organization and to share the value of productivity gains	Allows employees to learn more about business; links labor costs to firm performance; improves performance	Requires measurable standards; is difficult to administer; is not workable if trust is low; may pay bonuses even when unprofitable
Restricted stock and stock options (15 percent of total pay)	Grant of stock subject to restrictions or stock option grant to an employee ordinarily not eligible for such an award	Increases loyalty; provides retirement income; enables employees to share in firm's success	May focus on short-term earnings, not long-term profitability; is difficult to explain; loses motivational power in economic downturns

Occasionally, traditional merit pay and bonus plans are combined. For example, reasoning that excellence is the standard, not the exception, a broadcast firm set its pay policy line at 5 percent above that of the external market. Pay grade minimums were also established so that entry-level trainees with no experience could be paid less. Merit increases were awarded until an employee's base salary reached the pay grade midpoint. Then, annual salary increases were replaced with an annual performance bonus for all excellent or above average employees. Depending on the employee's base salary, these bonuses ranged from $1,000 to $5,000.

Lincoln Electric's bonus system makes headline news because the bonuses can be quite large. But at Lincoln, bonuses are just one piece of a complex incentive-based pay system (see Exhibit 13.6). The bonus calculation, which is what makes Lincoln's production workers wealthy, is described in the feature "Managing Human Resources for the 21st Century at Lincoln Electric: Calculating Employee Bonuses."

■ *Exhibit 13.6*
Components of Lincoln Electric's Incentive Plan

Lincoln's incentive plan combines job security with a lucrative compensation progam. Below is a summary of the plan's elements.

Features	Description	Criteria
Job security	A thirty-hour workweek is guaranteed.	Employees are eligible after three years of service. • Pay rates are not guaranteed. • Job transfers may be necessary. • Overtime is required during peak demand. • Guaranteed hours may be terminated by the company with a six-month notice.
Base wage	Standard job evaluation procedures are used to set the base wage. However, job evaluation and market requirements determine the actual dollar value of jobs.	Job evaluation compensable factors include skill, responsibility, mental aptitude, physical application, and working conditions.
Piecework	For every job that can be standardized, normal time-study procedures are employed to establish piece rates.	Piece rates are based on the following calculation for consistency and to eliminate constant revisions: 1934 wage rates times cost of living, which fluctuates with the index (Bureau of Labor Statistics). This product is then compared with the average skilled hourly rate of the area to determine the adjustments to the piece rate.
Advisory board	Employees elect representatives to an advisory board. All employees, except department heads and members of the engineering and time-study departments, are eligible.	The advisory board analyzes suggestions that lead to organizational progress. Savings from implemented suggestions have ranged from $2,400 to over $200,000.
Merit ratings	Twice a year, managers appraise employee performance through a merit-rating program.	This program uses four report cards. Each card rates work performance on one of the following: output; quality; dependability; and personal characteristics, such as the ability to come up with ideas; and cooperation.
Profit sharing	All business profits are split three ways: among the company, the shareholders, and the employees.	The company receives seed money; the shareholders receive a dividend; and the employees receive a year-end, profit-sharing bonus.
Year-end bonus	The annual cash bonus closely approximates the employees' annual earnings.	An employee's bonus is a function of his or her total annual earnings, biannual merit ratings, and company profits.
Employee stock ownership plan	Each employee has the opportunity to purchase a limited number of shares of company stock a year.	Employees are eligible after one year of service. On retirement or termination of employment, the company has the option to repurchase the stock.

SOURCE: Adapted from C. Wiley, "Incentive Plan Pushes Production," *Personnel Journal* (August 1993): 90. Used by permission.

Managing Human Resources for the 21st Century at Lincoln Electric: Calculating Employee Bonuses

Under the Lincoln Electric Incentive Plan, employees at Cleveland-based Lincoln Electric Company receive bonuses based on their productivity. The bonuses are determined by a simple bonus-factor formula.

First, the board of directors sets the amount of the year's bonus pool, based on a recommendation by the chair. The chair looks at such factors as how much money the company has made, how much seed money is needed, and how much money is needed for taxes and dividends. The average bonus pool during a recent ten-year period was 10.6 percent of sales revenue.

The company then divides this bonus pool amount by the total wages paid. This quotient is the bonus factor. A bonus factor of 1.00 means that the bonus pool is the same as the total companywide wages. This past year, the bonus pool was approximately 75 percent of wages paid.

Once the bonus factor has been determined, the company calculates bonuses by multiplying the bonus factor by individual earnings and merit ratings. Here is an example: A production worker earned $35,000. His merit rating is 100 percent, or 1.00. The bonus factor is 0.75. The formula for determining his bonus is as follows:

$$
\begin{array}{ll}
\$35,000 & \text{(earnings)} \\
\underline{\times 1.00} & \text{(merit rating)} \\
\$35,000 &
\end{array}
$$

$$
\begin{array}{ll}
\$35,000 & \\
\underline{\times 1.75} & \text{(bonus factor)} \\
\$26,250 & \text{(bonus)}
\end{array}
$$

According to Paul Beddia, vice president of HR at Lincoln, employees must pay for their own hospitalization insurance, which costs approximately $3,000. The company deducts this money from employees' year-end bonuses. Thus, this production worker receives a bonus of $23,250 (before taxes), bringing his annual pay to $58,250.[48]

Instant Incentive

Unlike other performance-based pay systems, instant bonuses are not based on formulas, special performance criteria, or goals. Sometimes called lightning-strike bonuses, these performance awards are designed to recognize the exceptional contributions of employees. Utilized by 95 percent of all firms, they recognize length of service (88 percent), special achievement (64 percent), and innovative ideas (42 percent). Often, they consist of certificates, plaques, cash, savings bonds, or flower arrangements.

Longevity. To recognize longevity, most companies give pins or other jewelry—for instance, a $30 pin for five years and a $300 watch for twenty years. Longevity awards are also used in the health services as a strategy to retain professionals in critical demand areas. For example, hospitals may offer $1,000 cash bonuses to nurses who join the staff and work for a full year. Typically, the cash awards cost less than recruiting, selecting, and training new hires.

Achievement. Bonuses for achievement usually target performance in areas of particular strategic value, such as safety, customer service, productivity, quality, or attendance. Recipients typically are nominated by peers or supervisors to receive awards including gifts, savings bonds, dinner certificates, and cash incentives ranging from $150 to more than $1,000.

When designed well, the activities associated with these bonuses effectively focus attention on core values and business objectives. Data I/O Corporation, an electronics manufacturing company in Redmond, Washington, makes extensive use of achievement bonuses. For example, all members of a computer-aided electronics software development team—such as engineers, technical writers, shippers, and quality assurance personnel—garnered $60 dinner certificates when the product was released. Two high achievers in the groups also earned weekend trips for two to San Francisco, including $1,500 in airline and motel expenses. On other occasions, recognition plaques, mugs, T-shirts, and pen sets have been distributed. Monthly, an employee is recognized for her or his contribution to Data I/O. Recognition brings a parking place by the front door, an engraved plaque, and verbal acknowledgment in a company meeting. These recognition bonuses are slightly different from the ones provided at AT&T's Global Business Communication System (see Exhibit 13.2).

Innovation. To encourage more innovative ideas, many companies have suggestion systems that involve some form of instant incentive. According to the National Association of Suggestion Systems, its nine hundred members received nearly 1 million suggestions from their employees, resulting in savings of over $2 billion in 1990. Crowley Maritime Corporation's Ship Us an Idea is typical of most suggestion plans. The shipping company receives an average of twenty suggestions a month from its one thousand employees. Employees earn between $50 and $150 for most ideas and may earn up to 10 percent of the cost savings for significant ideas. A presidential award of $1,000 is given annually for the best idea. According to Moon Hui Kim, program developer, the benefits far outweigh the $6,000–$10,000 annual program administration costs.[49]

Individual Incentive

Individual incentives are among the oldest and most popular form of incentive pay. In this type of plan, individual standards of performance are established and communicated in advance, and rewards are based on individual output. Individual incentives are used by a significant minority (35 percent) of all companies in all industry groups except utilities. Utility firms have been slower to implement such plans owing to their history of regulation, which limits workforce autonomy.

A variety of individual incentive plans exist. These plans differ in terms of the method of rate determination. When the work cycle is short, units of production generally serve as the method of rate determination. For long-cycle jobs, the standard is typically based on the time required to complete a unit. Individual incentive systems also vary with regard to the constancy with which pay is a function of production level. One option is to pay a consistent amount at all production levels, for instance, $0.25 a carton for all cartons shipped. Alternatively, pay may vary as a function of production level. For example, employees may be paid $0.25 a carton for up to one thousand units a day, and $0.37 a carton beyond this threshold.

Individual incentive plans also share a common job analysis foundation. As discussed in Chapter 6, time-and-motion studies are often employed to determine how wages are tied to output. The challenge is to identify a "normal" rate of production.[50]

Piecework Plan. Piecework, like Lincoln Electric's, is the most common type of individual incentive pay. In this plan, employees are paid a certain rate for each unit of output. Under a *straight piecework plan,* employees are guaranteed a standard pay rate for each unit. The standard pay rate is based on the standard output and the base wage rate. For example, if the base pay of a job is $40 a day and the employee can produce at a normal rate twenty units a day, the standard rate may be established at $2 a unit. The normal rate is more than what time-and-motion studies indicate but is supposed to represent 100 percent efficiency. The final rate may also reflect the bargaining power of the employees, the economic conditions of the organization and industry, and the amount the competition is paying.

In a *differential piece rate plan,* more than one rate of pay is set for the same job. This plan can be operationalized in different ways. The Taylor Differential Plan consists of a higher rate of pay for work completed in a set period of time. For work that takes longer to complete, the rate of pay is lower. Merrill Lynch and Company, a large stock brokerage firm, instituted a commission plan similar to the Taylor plan. Sales personnel having higher sales volume receive higher rates of commission than do sales personnel with lower volume.[51]

Standard Hour Plan. The standard hour plan is the second most common type of individual incentive plan. This approach is based on setting a standard time for each unit of production. Tasks are broken down by the amount of time it takes to complete them, which can be determined by historical records, time-and-motion studies, or both. The normal time to perform each task becomes a standard.

If you go into an automobile repair shop, you will probably see a chart indicating the labor rates associated with various types of repair. These reflect the use of standard hour plans. Each rate includes the rate paid to the mechanic who does the work plus the premium charged by the owner of the shop. The rate is fixed regardless of how long it actually takes to do the repair. Thus, the mechanic and the shop owner both have incentives to ensure that the work is completed in a shorter amount of time than that used to set the standard rate. Consider a standard time of two hours and a rate of $16 an hour, of which the mechanic is paid $12 an hour. In this system, the mechanic receives $24 for each unit of work completed, regardless of the actual time spent. If the mechanic completes six units in an eight-hour day, he receives 6 × $24, or $144. This is substantially more than $96, which would be the "expected" rate of pay for eight hours, based on four units.

Executive Incentive Plan. Individual incentives are also commonly used to award top-level managers. According to a recent survey, in fact, only 48 of the CEOs of America's 350 largest companies received no individual incentives.[52] Executive incentive plans use a formula to relate incentives to the attainment of corporate or strategic business unit goals, with the various goals weighted. In addition to cash, incentive pay includes such things as restricted stock grants (free shares given to the CEO for staying with the company), performance shares or performance units (free shares or cash for achieving multiyear goals), and stock option grants.

Debate over the effectiveness of executive incentives has raged for many years. For one thing, the pay of U.S. executives seems excessive relative to the pay of rank-and-file employees and of CEOs in other countries. In 1995, the ratio of the pay of CEOs to the pay of rank-and-file employees was 40 to 1 in the United States, compared with 17 to 1 in Germany and only 10 to 1 in Japan.

These are the types of figures that make news, but "the relentless focus on how much CEOs are paid diverts public attention away from the real problem—how CEOs are paid," according to compensation experts Michael Jensen and Kevin J. Murphy. After studying the pay of CEOs in fourteen hundred companies over an eight-year period, the researchers contend that the "incentive" compensation of top executives is virtually independent of corporate performance and is no more variable than that of hourly workers. Unfortunately, current incentive pay for CEOs too often is treated as an entitlement program rather than as a way to motivate outstanding performance.

To rectify the problem, the researchers recommend building greater performance variability into executive pay, restructuring incentive pay so that salaries, bonuses, and stock options provide big rewards for superior performance and big penalties for poor performance. This can be accomplished by ensuring that CEOs own substantial amounts of company stock and face the real prospect of being fired as a result of poor performance.[53] In other words, the suggested solution is to put more earnings at risk.

Team Incentive

Team incentives fall somewhere between individual plans and whole-organization plans such as gain sharing and profit sharing. Performance goals are tailored specifically to what the work team needs to accomplish. Strategically, they link the goals of individuals to those of the work group (typically ten people or fewer), which, in turn, are usually linked to financial goals.[54] According to Judy Huret, a principal with Towers, Perrin in San Francisco, team incentives improve employees' "line of sight" regarding what they need to do as a group to enhance profits. For example:

> An insurance company was encountering friction between two different departments—data processing and claims. The claims people said the data processing staff never met its deadlines. The data processing people said the claims people kept changing their minds and made unreasonable demands. When the company instituted a team-incentive plan, senior management facilitated a discussion between the two departments and informed them that their incentive award would be linked to how well they worked together to meet customer needs.
>
> The claims group then clearly outlined the specifications and timetable necessary to meet customer service needs and discussed them with data processing. Data processing developed a detailed project plan and shared it with claims. Now that both groups understand the ultimate objective, they can work together to achieve a common goal. The amount of their incentive award will depend on how quickly and how well the team goal is met.[55]

Assuming that the prerequisites listed in Exhibit 13.7 are met, team-based incentives offer four major advantages compared with individual incentive systems. First, the mere presence of team members who have some control over rewards evokes more vigorous and persistent behavior than is evidenced when individuals work alone. Second, the likelihood that conflicting contingencies (peer pressure) will evoke counterproductive control over behavior is reduced. Third, the strength of the rewards is increased, since they are now paired with group-administered rewards, such as praise and camaraderie. Research also suggests that the performance of a group is higher than that attained by individual group members—although not as high as that of the best person in the group. Fourth, the performance of another group member (usually the high performer) can serve as a model, encouraging other team members to imitate successful behavior.[56]

But just as it takes more than piecework to ensure high productivity at Lincoln Electric, it usually takes more than just a team-based incentive plan at most companies.

■ *Exhibit 13.7*
Prerequisites for the Effective Administration of Group Incentives

1. Everyone who is on the team, including indirect contributors and support staff members, is eligible.
2. Team performance is measurable.
3. Performance standards are communicated to team members before the performance period.
4. The incentive system is easy to understand.
5. Team members receive regular feedback on their progress toward performance targets. Graphs, charts, and statistical analyses provide useful ongoing feedback.
6. Team members believe they can affect performance outcomes.
7. The organizational culture is congruent with team problem solving and participation.

For example, at AAL, a team-based incentive plan is integrated with an individual incentive program, market survey data, and a skill-based pay plan. These interrelated components are described in the feature "Managing Human Resources for the 21st Century at AAL: A Varied Approach to Compensating Teams."

Types of Teams. As more and more companies restructure work around teams, new team structures are likely to proliferate. Different team structures may require different forms of pay. For example, three types of teams are commonly found in today's organizations:

Parallel Teams: Teams operate in a structure that functions in parallel to the regular organization chart. Often staffed by volunteers who serve the team on a temporary assignment, the typical tasks of such teams include creating reports and making suggestions for improvements in the company. The team's work is usually a small portion of each member's full responsibility.

Project Teams: Project teams may operate in a parallel structure or they may be integrated as part of the formal organization structure. Such teams often have a somewhat stable core of members with diverse areas of specialized expertise. They often are self-managing and have a broad mandate to develop innovative products or services. The team's work may be a part- or full-time responsibility for each member.

Work Teams: Work teams are fully integrated into the organization structure. They have clear, narrow mandates usually centered around producing products or providing services. Membership in these teams is usually stable and the team's work is each member's full-time responsibility.[57]

The very different natures of these team types mean that no single approach to rewarding the performance of team members would fit all three. Exhibit 13.8 shows how two leading experts recommend structuring the performance-based pay for these three types of teams.

Although team-based incentives are promising, they involve administrative responsibilities that are as great as those associated with individual incentive plans. Job analysis is still necessary to identify how to structure the teams and to ensure that workloads are equivalent among teams. Also, team incentives may produce unintended side effects, including competition between groups, that may or may not compliment goal attainment. Another concern is *social loafing,* where group performance declines because team members, consciously or subconsciously, lower their inputs, believing that others in the group will pick up the slack.[58] This is less likely to happen in plans that provide for broad-based employee participation and involvement, such as the Scanlon Plan, described later in this chapter.

Profit Sharing

Introduced first in the Gallatin glasswork factory in New Geneva, Pennsylvania, in 1794, *profit-sharing plans* in American business now number approximately 430,000. As defined by the Council of Profit Sharing Industries, these plans include any procedure under which an employer pays or makes available to regular employees, special current or deferred sums based on the profits of the business, in addition to their regular pay.[59] A recent study indicates that some 25 percent of small firms offer profit sharing, and these companies seem to gain more in productivity as a consequence, compared with larger firms.[60]

Profit-sharing plans fall into three categories. *Current distribution plans* provide a percentage of profits to be distributed quarterly or annually to employees. *Deferred plans* place earnings in an escrow fund for distribution upon retirement, termination, death, or

Managing Human Resources for the 21st Century at AAL: A Varied Approach to Compensating Teams

Aid Association for Lutherans (AAL), a fraternal-benefits society, leaves nothing to chance when it comes to compensating members of its insurance service teams. The company, which is based in Appleton, Wisconsin, has devised a four-legged compensation stool, which allows it to:

- Recognize individual achievements
- Reward team productivity
- Compensate employees for the acquisition of new skills
- Remain competitive with its salary structure

AAL has fifteen service teams, organized geographically, that perform all the services necessary for the company's insurance products. For example, a team, comprising twenty-five employees, can underwrite a policy, pay a claim, change beneficiaries, and modify coverage levels. Furthermore, team members can provide these services for any product, be it life, health, or disability insurance.

Before developing the team structure in 1987, the company organized these services functionally, according to the type of product. Service requests traveled from unit to unit, increasing the amount of time needed to help a customer and boosting the chance for errors.

"By moving to teams, we were challenging employees to see the whole job, rather than just the piece they performed individually," explains Jerry Laubenstein, vice president of insurance services. "But we also wanted them to learn additional jobs that could help the team as a whole, and we wanted the team to find ways to boost its overall performance."

To promote all these changes, AAL revamped its compensation structure completely to include four main elements:

1. *A Skill-Based Pay Program:* The company has implemented a skill-based pay system that compensates individuals for each additional skill they acquire in an effort to help the team. As one of the first organizations to implement skill-based pay for white-collar workers, AAL developed a dictionary that describes all the services per-

formed by team members and lists their associated dollar values. Employees are paid a base wage for the primary service they perform, and they can receive incremental pay increases for each service added to their repertoire of skills.

2. *A Team Incentive Program:* AAL has implemented a team incentive program through which the entire team is awarded an annual bonus based on three elements

   - Productivity
   - Customer satisfaction
   - Quality of work

   This team incentive can be worth as much as 10 percent of an employee's annual compensation.

3. *The Use of Market Data:* The company now relies heavily on market data to ensure that employees are paid competitive wages.

4. *An Individual Incentive Program:* AAL has added an incentive component that recognizes outstanding achievement by individual employees. This lump-sum incentive is paid once a year only to employees who are already paid at market value. This incentive is worth as much as 6 percent of an individual's compensation.

AAL's compensation structure did not change all at once, Laubenstein says, and several problems occurred along the way. "We went to teams in 1987 and didn't put any incentives in place until 1989. Then we moved entirely to team incentives, where we didn't recognize individuals at all. This caused a lot of problems with employees who were used to being recognized individually. Finally, in 1991, we modified the program to recognize both individual and team achievements."

Is the program working? "We're on a journey, and we haven't reached the destination yet," Laubenstein cautions. "But in the five years that we've been in teams, we've increased our productivity by 40%. Surveys reveal that more than 90% of our customers are satisfied with the level of service they're receiving. I'd say things are coming along well."[61]

■ *Exhibit 13.8*
Pay Systems for Different Types of Teams

	Type of Team		
Feature	Parallel	Project	Work
Base pay	Job based	Skill based	Skill based
Pay for performance			
Individual	Merit pay for job performance	Possible if team assessed	Unusual but possible if team assessed
Team	Recognition or cash for suggestions	Possible at end of project	Possible if team independent
Unit	Possible gain sharing	Profit sharing or gain sharing	Profit sharing or gain sharing
Participation	Design of sharing plan	Assessment of individuals	All aspects of design and administration
Communication	Open about rewards for improvement	Open about skill plan and rewards for performance	Highly open

SOURCE: E. E. Lawler III and S. G. Cohen, "Designing Pay Systems for Teams," *ACA Journal* (Autumn 1992): 17. Used by permission.

disability. These are the fastest-growing type of plan owing to tax advantages. About 20 percent of firms with profit-sharing programs have *combined plans*. These distribute a portion of profits immediately to employees, setting the remaining amount aside in a designated account.

Profit-sharing plans are designed to pay out incentives when the organization is most able to afford them. Often, these plans do not have clear strategic objectives. Furthermore, employee involvement is not necessarily an important component of them. Both these characteristics rob many profit-sharing plans of their potential motivational value. The motivational potential of deferred plans is questionable also because employees may not see the relationship between their performance and the profitability of the firm. Results such as those at Lincoln Electric, Nucor Corporation, Chrysler, Wal-Mart, and Hallmark, however, suggest that profit sharing can be very motivational when it is accompanied by employee participation and feelings of involvement.[62]

Gain Sharing

Gain-sharing plans are premised on the assumption that it is possible to reduce costs by eliminating wasted materials and labor, developing new or better products or services, or working smarter. Typically, gain-sharing plans involve all employees in a work unit or firm.[63]

The median gain-sharing payout is 3 percent, substantially less than the average 5 percent merit increase. Still, gain-sharing plans represent a fast-growing type of performance-based pay, with more than 15 percent of all firms using them in 1995 and another 15 percent of all firms anticipating using them in the next few years.[64]

Three generations of gain-sharing plans have evolved.

First-Generation Plans. Two plans—Scanlon and Rucker—were developed in the Depression Era. Both focus on cost savings relative to historical standards. The Scanlon and Rucker Plans are built around the following four principles:

- ◉ A management philosophy emphasizing employee participation
- ◉ A formula to share the benefits of productivity-generated savings among employees and the employer

◉ Employee committees to evaluate ideas

◉ A formal system for gathering and implementing employee suggestions on ways to increase productivity or reduce costs[65]

Even though the Scanlon and Rucker Plans share a common philosophy, they differ in one important aspect: the Scanlon Plan focuses only on labor cost savings. Suppose that the historical costs of labor for your firm are $1 million a year. If actual labor costs are less than anticipated costs ($800,000), a portion ($50,000) of the money saved is placed in a set-aside fund in case labor costs soar in subsequent quarters. The remaining savings ($150,000) are split among the company and the employees.[66] In contrast, the Rucker Plan ties incentives to a wide variety of savings. A ratio is calculated that expresses the value of production required for each dollar of total wages.

Both plans are appropriate in small, mature firms employing fewer than five hundred workers. Since standards are based on past performance, simple and accurate measures of performance are needed. Because of the heavy involvement of all employees, the culture must be open, trusting, and participative.[67]

Second-Generation Plans. Beginning in the 1960s, a second generation of gain-sharing plans began to emerge. These differ from first-generation plans in several respects. First, they focus on labor *hours* saved, rather than labor *costs* saved. Detailed time-and-motion studies are conducted to develop engineered standards of physical production. Because of the depth of analysis required, employees typically are not involved in the development of the plan. This may reduce perceptions of fairness.

Unlike first-generation plans, second-generation plans include nonproduction workers in the measurement of the organization's productivity and in the distribution of variable pay, realized from cost savings. ImproShare, developed by industrial engineer Mitchell Fein, is typical of second-generation plans. It has been adopted in a wide array of firms, including service-sector firms such as hospitals and financial institutions.

Exhibit 13.9 compares the details of the calculations of the Scanlon, Rucker, and ImproShare plans.

Third-Generation Plans. According to Marc Wallace, who studied new pay practices in forty-six firms, a third generation of gain-sharing plans is emerging that "is so different from first and second generation models that the term gain-sharing may no longer be appropriate."[68] Third-generation plans encompass a much broader range of organizational goals.[69] They have definite terms, which support the current business plan.

An example of this is in use at one U.S. company:

Employees of a Cleveland steel manufacturer called L-S Electro-Galvanizing Co. see their participation rewarded through a gain-sharing plan negotiated with the United Steelworkers.

■ *Exhibit 13.9*
Calculations for Selected Gain-Sharing Plans

Scanlon Plan Base Ratio
[(Sales Dollars − Returned Goods) ± Inventory] / [(Cost of Work and Nonwork Time Paid + Pension + Insurance)]

Rucker Plan Base Ratio
(Cost of All Wages and Benefits) / (Sales Dollar Value of Product − Goods Returned − Supplies, Services, and Material)

ImproShare Plan Base Formula
[(Standard Value Hours Earned, Current Period) × (Total Actual Hours Worked, Based Period / Total Standard Value Hours Earned, Based Period)] / [(Total Hours Worked, Current period)]

L-SE, as the company is known, is a joint venture between the American steel company LTV Corp. and Japan's Sumitomo, explains Ken Pohl, senior director of participative work systems with the company. The two firms joined forces after American automakers made known their intention to use rust-resistant, electro-galvanized steel in their cars, technology available only in Japan at that time, he says.

L-SE began as a nontraditional workplace with high levels of participation, Pohl says. An important motivator at the company, he adds, is a gain-sharing plan that allows employees to share in the company's success. The plan is administered by a labor-management committee and applies to all team members equally, he explains.

The plan is structured so that payouts are capped at 25 percent of an employee's wages and overtime, says Chris Vance, an official with USW Local 9126. A reasonable set of objectives is defined twice annually and amended if necessary.

Gain-sharing payouts are based largely on production levels, according to Pohl, who notes that the formula has been adjusted upward as productivity has improved. So far, the plan's average payout has been 18 percent and there have been several maximum payouts, he says.[70]

As with Lincoln Electric's plan, this method of compensation works because of other aspects of the total system used for managing human resources in the company.

Characteristics of Successful Incentive Pay Plans

Successful incentive pay plans share several characteristics. First, they are based on a clear vision of the organization's strategy and culture—that is, they tie individual, team, or organization rewards to business priorities.

Second, they provide sufficient time for implementation—one to two years—and they keep score, indicating expected results through clearly measurable goals and evaluating accomplishments against those goals. The plans are continually audited and controlled to ensure that they stay on course.

Third, they provide a wide margin in which employees can exercise discretion and add value to the firm. This is accomplished by having fewer management levels and fewer job titles. Broader, simpler definitions of employee work responsibilities are the rule, rather than the exception. Programs are flexible, focusing more on the needs of the business rather than adherence to a performance formula.

Finally, successful plans provide a sunset (i.e., an expiration date) so that rewards are not viewed as entitlements, and employees celebrate when they are successful.

Exhibit 13.10 lists questions to evaluate the effectiveness of incentive pay plans. A firm should expect to spend more than $40,000 on a task force to complete the initial

■ *Exhibit 13.10*
How to Tell a Live Plan from a Dead One

Does the plan capture attention?   Are employees talking more about their work and the incentive program? Are they celebrating early successes under the plan?

Do employees understand the plan?   Could you walk up to a participant, ask how the plan works, and get a technically correct answer? Do employees know what they need to accomplish in order to earn payments?

Does the plan communicate about the business?   Has the plan contributed to knowledge about the business? Do employees have a better understanding of how their individual and collective efforts impact the bottom line?

Does the plan pay out when it should?   Are payouts occurring for actual results against goals and being withheld when they are not met? Or is the plan becoming another entitlement by paying out under all circumstances?

Is the business unit performing better?   Can we point to the operation of the reward plan and conclude that we are actually performing better as a result? Are profits up? Have we gained market share?

SOURCE: M. J. Wallace, *Rewards and Renewal: America's Search for Competitive Advantage through Alternative Pay Strategies* (Scottsdale, AZ: American Compensation Association, 1990): 15.

study, including the development of communication materials, and to administer and implement the program. Gain-sharing plans also involve significant additional cost to administer the database and generate the reports upon which payouts depend. According to Wallace, firms typically underestimate the time and money it takes to develop stable, accurate standards for tracking performance and calculating awards.[71]

 ## PAY THAT PUTS EARNINGS AT RISK

Merit-based and incentive-based pay systems apply to a large percentage of the workforce. However, they are generally not often used for sales personnel and high-level executives, who frequently have their earnings placed at risk.

Some companies have pushed the notion of at-risk pay throughout the organization. For example:

> [F]actory workers at Nucor's five steel mills earn meager base wages ($5.80 to $9.02) per hour, less than half the typical union [rate]. Yet bonuses based on the number of tons of acceptable quality steel produced, bump total pay to more than $32,000, about $2,000 more than [that of] unionized counterparts. Workers who are late lose their bonus for the day; workers who are more than 30 minutes late lose their bonus for the week.
>
> Department managers at Nucor earn yearly bonuses based on return on plant assets and plant managers receive bonuses based on return on equity. At year end the company distributes 10 percent of pretax earnings to employees. As a result of this, Nucor turned out more than twice as much steel per employee than larger steel companies.[72]

Arguably, Lincoln Electric's pay plan also puts employees' earnings at risk, as does any incentive plan that does not guarantee income that is near the market average. In other words, earnings at risk is a matter of degree. Employees take the most extreme risks with commissions and stock payments.

Commissions

Because a large part of a salesperson's job is unsupervised, performance-based compensation programs are useful in directing sales activities. More than half of all sales plans use a combination of salary and individual or group incentives.[73] Only 20 percent of all sales personnel are paid by straight incentives, however.

As companies rethink their strategic objectives, they often evaluate their current pay system for salespeople, who represent the company to their valued customers. IBM's recent restructuring provides a vivid example. IBM has approximately thirty thousand employees who sell its products and services around the world. According to one general manager: "In the old days, we'd give a branch manager a revenue quota, and that would be it. We'd see him at year end and he'd tell us how he did."

IBM's new strategy is to focus much more on customer satisfaction and profits. To implement this strategy, CEO Louis Gerstner wants to be sure salespeople think about the implications for IBM of the deals they cut with customers. To achieve the appropriate focus within the sales force, he dramatically restructured its commission system. In 1993, only 6 percent of commission pay was tied to profits; in 1994, 60 percent was tied to profits (not overall revenue)—and the other 40 percent was tied to customer satisfaction, in order to reduce the temptation to simply push fast-turnover, high-profit products. The firm supports the new pay system by giving salespeople access to information that was before closely guarded: the margins for the products they sell. This example clearly illustrates the powerful role sales commissions are believed to exert over behavior.[74]

Exhibit 13.11 shows the types of components most commonly found in pay plans for salespeople. Note that approximately 30 percent of all sales personnel are paid a straight salary. This may be appropriate when the major function of the salesperson is providing customer service or "prospecting new accounts under low-success conditions." Straight salary plans are also appropriate in jobs demanding high technical expertise but little ability to close sales. Consider the job of a product engineer for a software publishing house. Duties of this job might include developing and executing sales and product training programs, participating in trade shows, promoting new products, and meeting with distributors to encourage them to push product lines. In such jobs, a high salary to attract technically competent individuals is more critical than incentives to close the sale.

The advantages of a straight salary program are several. From the salesperson's viewpoint, it takes the ambiguity out of the salary process. It is also simpler to administer. If nonsales functions (e.g., paperwork and customer support) are important, salaried sales personnel are more willing to perform them. The drawback is that straight salaries reduce the connection between performance and pay. Commissions make this link directly.

Straight Commission. Usually, the term *commission* refers to pay based on a percentage of the sales price of the product. The percentage received by the salesperson depends on the product being sold, industry practices, the organization's economic conditions, and special pricing during sales promotions.

■ *Exhibit 13.11*
Basis for Incentive Pay for Field Sales Personnel

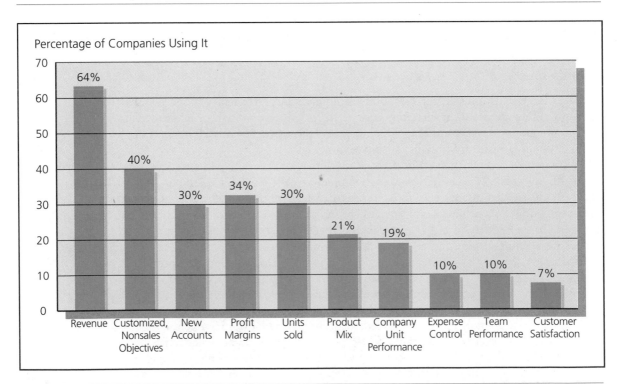

SOURCE: Based on a survey conducted by Hewitt Associates, as represented in G. Fuchsberg, "Selling Isn't Everything," *Wall Street Journal* (April 13, 1994): p. R8.

In establishing a sales commission program, the following questions need answering:

- What are the strategic objectives to be achieved?
- What criteria will be used to measure performance?
- Are territories equivalent in sales potential?
- Will commission rates vary by product or vary depending on sales level?
- Will earnings have a cap?
- What will be the timing of commission payments (e.g., monthly or quarterly)?

Once these questions are answered, a program can be set up.

Under commission-only plans, responsibility for generating an income rests directly on the salesperson. The more sales, the greater the earnings; no sales means no income. When these are accepted by employees as legitimate pay plans, their effect on behavior is enormous. Seattle-based Nordstrom, with more than sixty-five stores, $3 billion in annual sales, and a growth rate of twenty percent, pays its salespeople entirely on commission. Through this method, the salespeople earn about twice what they would at a rival's store.[75] Unfortunately, such incentives can be so powerful that they elicit unintended behaviors, as when Sears Auto Centers in California were nailed for making unnecessary repairs on customers' cars (described in Chapter 1).[76]

Combined Plans. Because of concerns about the negative effects of straight commission plans, more than half of all sales compensation plans combine base salary and commissions. In setting up a combined plan, the critical question is, "What percentage of total compensation should be salary and what percentage should be commission?" The answer depends on the availability of sales criteria (e.g., sales volume, units sold, product mix, retention of accounts, and number of new accounts) and the number of nonsales duties in the job. Commonly, these plans are based on an 80-to-20 salary-to-commission mix. However, organizations wishing to push sales over customer service functions may utilize different ratios—60-to-40 or even 50-to-50.

The commission portion of the sales compensation can be established in two ways. The simplest is to combine the commission with a draw. The salesperson receives the draw, or specific salary, each payday. Quarterly or monthly, the total commission due the salesperson is calculated. The amount taken as a draw is deducted, with the salesperson receiving the remainder. Alternatively, bonuses can be given when sales reach a specific level.[77]

Stock Payments

Among the top 350 U.S. firms, the median CEO pay, including base and incentives, was $1.17 million in 1993, an increase of 8.1 percent over the median pay in the preceding year. At the extreme, Walt Disney's Michael D. Eisner received total direct compensation of $203 million, mostly by exercising stock options. More typical of the top-paid CEOs was Alan C. Greenberg of Bear Stearns Companies, who received $15.9 million, of which $15.7 million was a bonus. By comparison, David D. Glass, CEO of Wal-Mart, the nation's hottest retailer, got a miniscule $250,000 stock options grant besides cash pay of $630,000.[78]

Although bonuses are the most prevalent nonsalary compensation device used by companies to reward their executives, according to a Conference Board survey of 580 large U.S. firms,[79] stock options run a close second in popularity.

Stock Options and Stock Option Plans. A stock option is an opportunity for a manager to buy the organization's stock at a later date but at a price established when the option is granted. Approximately 75 percent of energy, manufacturing, and insurance firms provide such plans.[80]

With stock option plans, stockholders vote to create a pool of shares—usually about 5 percent of the total number outstanding—out of newly issued shares. Over a period of years, employees are given the right to buy stock in the future at today's price. Most options last ten years, with executives typically allowed to exercise half their options after two years and the entire grant after three.

In theory, options are supposed to motivate an employee to make a company's stock more valuable. The backbone of executive compensation programs, the awarding of stock options, is premised on the assumption that the plans encourage executives to "think like owners." After all, they profit only if the stock price goes up. However, critics contend that companies without stock option plans do as well as companies with them. According to management consultant James H. Carbone: "Options don't really make managers walk in the owner's moccasins. Only after executives exercise options do they truly become owners. Until then, they have no capital at risk. If the stock sags, they can expect a new grant the next year at a lower price."[81]

Despite such critics, many companies are encouraging their CEOs in particular to forgo salary increases and cash bonuses and take instead stock options as their rewards. Robert Levine, CEO of Cabletron Systems Incorporated, a high-tech maker and installer of computer cable systems, shares this philosophy. The idea is that it is more palatable for CEOs to show more modest cash gains when those lower in the company ranks seem to be pushing harder for less. J. E. ("Ted") Newall, president and CEO of Canada's Nova Corporation of Alberta, a natural gas pipeline company, has taken this philosophy to the extreme. In 1994, he decided to accept *no* salary or bonus for two years, drawing only stock for compensation. Clearly, this arrangement put him at significant risk. As he says, "That's what corporate governance is all about."[82] His salary in 1994 was a mere $52,000—less than that of many of his employees. But his income from stock bonuses during the preceding few years was said to be worth over $1 billion.[83]

In the future, performance-based pay will be even more prevalent for executives because under current tax law, pay in excess of $1 million must be offered through a formal, written performance-based plan in order for the company to claim deductibility.

In high-growth companies, stock options flourish. The primary reason is that stock options are the only major form of compensation that never shows up as a cost on a company's profit and loss statement. Instead, the money paid for option shares and the tax break the company may get (based on the spread between the strike price and the exercise price) show up only on the balance sheet. As a result, employees can earn millions from options at no apparent cost to the company.[84]

Several other advantages make stock options particularly well suited to high-growth companies. Stock options avoid both earnings charges and the need for immediate cash outlays. When the options are exercised, the company does not have to lay out any money but does receive back the value of the initial stock purchase price. This money can then be used to meet business objectives. Also, the company receives a tax deduction for the amount of income realized by the executive—producing additional cash through tax savings. In comparison, companies that give cash incentives must charge against earnings for financial reporting purposes.[85]

Since the Economic Recovery Tax Act of 1981, most companies with stock option plans have used *incentive stock options (ISOs)*. When an ISO is exercised, an executive pays only 20 percent capital gains on the first $100,000 of appreciated value. Although this is far less than the previous 50 percent tax rate, these programs still require a large cash investment. Consequently, some companies are experimenting with *stock apprecia-*

tion rights (SARs), which allow executives to realize capital gains of stock options without purchasing stocks.[86]

Restricted Stock Grants. An alternative approach entails the award of stock at no or very low cost. In most cases, employees are required to work a set period of time—usually three to five years—before they are vested in the plan.

Restricted stock is a potent program for attracting and retaining executives. Microsoft Corporation uses stock grants to attract and retain peak performers. The software leader's policy of "getting it right" demands that the firm have top-notch, creative programmers. Finding and retaining such talent is difficult given the tight national market and Microsoft's stringent hiring requirements. Once the firm finds its programmers, it relies on incentive pay to motivate and retain them. Rather than pay high salaries (Bill Gates's base salary is less than half that of the average CEO) or dispense perks (no company cars are provided), Microsoft evaluates programmers yearly and places them on one of six levels. As a programmer reaches the top two levels—the equivalent of becoming a partner in a law firm—a big celebration is held and the employee receives significant stock awards. Does the program pay off? Employees think so—particularly the dozens who are now millionaires.[87]

Phantom Stocks. A third option involves the award of phantom stocks. Here, participants receive a cash payment equal to the full value of stock in the future, not just its appreciation. An advantage of phantom stock programs is that even private companies can establish them.

Phantom stocks are also useful to retain key performers in a merger. Consider the dilemma faced by Fine Organics Corporation, an $8.2 million chemical manufacturer in Lodi, New Jersey. Fine Organics was buying two small companies and wanted to retain key personnel in the acquired companies without diluting the ownership control by broadening the base of regular shareholders. Company officials considered setting up a second tier of stock options without voting rights, but, because Fine Organics had been incorporated as an S corporation, Internal Revenue Service regulations prohibited the introduction of a second-tier plan. CEO William J. Reidy says: "We were trolling about for some kind of compromise solution and heard about phantom stock. The basic scheme was simple. Instead of real stock, we'd give peak performers a document that, at the time it was issued, had a value of zero. As the book value of combined equity, namely Fine Organics and the acquired company, increases, the amount of the increased value is added to the original zero value. At an agreed-upon point, the employee can cash in the phantom stock for the gain in value."[88]

In implementing these plans, it is important to keep the financial terms simple. If the company is publicly traded, the value can be tied to the book value of the stock. If not, it can be based on the board of directors' assessed value. In selling the plan to employees, Reidy advises presenting it as a win-win proposition. One benefit, for example, is that no tax bill is associated with the receipt of phantom shares. Phantom stock, unlike regular stock grants, is considered a form of deferred compensation by the IRS.[89]

✳ LEGAL CONSIDERATIONS

Legal and tax considerations play a major role in executive compensation. They also arise for lower- and midlevel employees, although in a less prominent role. By definition, pay "discrimination" based on performance—not job title, rank, or status—is an inevitable and appropriate outcome of a properly administered performance-based pay system. Performance-based compensation is intended to create behaviors that lead to the accomplishment of organizational goals. Rewards that are administered contingently—that is, according to performance—cause increases in subsequent employee performance and expressions of satisfaction among high performers.[90] They encourage low performers to perform at a higher rate or to exit the organization. The legal issue, then, is not whether to discriminate in pay but how to do so fairly.

Under Title VII of the Civil Rights Act of 1964, the Civil Rights Act of 1991, and the Equal Pay Act of 1963, a supervisor may be charged with unlawful discrimination by an employee in a protected group who believes that a pay raise, bonus, or other incentive was denied on a basis not related to performance. Performance-based pay can be given for reasons other than performance and still be legal, however. Assuming they apply equally to all employees, defensible nonperformance bases include the following:

- Position in salary range
- Time since last increase
- Size of last increase
- Pay relationships within the company or department
- Pay levels of jobs in other companies
- Salaries of newly hired employees
- Budgetary limits

What is critical for both merit and incentive pay is that the same rules be used to give raises fairly and consistently among all employees. Data such as those in Exhibits 13.12 and 13.13 cause many people to believe that unfair pay discrimination persists in many organizations today. Although some of the pay differentials in these exhibits can be explained by years in the labor market, study after study has shown that human capital variables such as education, experience, and performance do not account for them.

INTERNATIONAL CONCERNS

If a multinational corporation utilizes any type of incentive bonus system, a policy is usually established.[91] Bonuses may be according to either parent- or host-country policies. Actual payments can be made in either local or foreign currency and may often be a combination of the two or the choice of the recipient. For example, most U.S. financial services companies have an overall policy of paying PCNs according to the U.S. salary structure, including its bonus programs and salary increase practices. Most often, this compensation is paid partly in U.S. dollars and partly in the local currency. The local-currency portion is generally pegged to pay ordinary living expenses, and bonuses are typically paid in U.S. dollars. Salary practices for TCNs tend to vary more widely and may be paid according to the home structure, a U.S. structure, or the host-country structure. U.S. MNCs need to keep in mind that potential incentives such as stock options may lose their value for TCNs and HCNSs because they are tax advantaged only in the United States.

Questions that MNCs generally address when planning for their incentive bonuses include these:

- What techniques can be used to provide management incentives abroad?
- Incentive bonuses help many companies achieve their objectives at home, but can they be used as effectively in subsidiary operations?
- How can companies design appropriate incentive bonuses for managers in an area suffering from rapid inflation?[92]

■ *Exhibit 13.12*

Earnings by Educational Level and Sex

Median Weekly Earnings of Full-Time Wage and Salary Workers, 1992 Annual Averages in Dollars

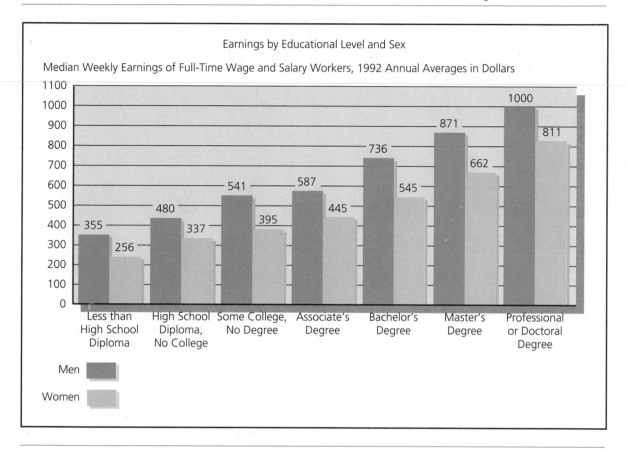

SOURCE: A Bureau of National Affairs graphic based on data from the Bureau of Labor Statistics, in "Is Discrimination the Source of Differential Earnings?" *Bulletin to Management* (August 19, 1993): 262. Used by permission.

American MNCs frequently link stock opportunities to executive performance. Recent tax changes in a number of Western countries make stock ownership more feasible than in the past.[93]

Parent-country nationals often receive a salary premium as an inducement to accept a foreign assignment or to compensate for any hardship suffered owing to the transfer. Under such circumstances, the definition of hardship, eligibility for the premium, and amount and timing of payment must be addressed. For cases in which hardship is determined, MNCs often refer to the U.S. Department of State's Hardship Post Differentials Guidelines to determine an appropriate level of payment. As others have noted, however, international comparisons of the cost of living pose many problems.[94] TCNs do not receive these payments as often as PCNs. Foreign service inducements, if used, are most commonly made in the form of a percentage of salary, usually 5 to 40 percent of base pay. Such payments vary depending on the assignment, actual hardship, tax consequences, and length of assignment. In addition, differentials may be considered: for example, if a host country's workweek is longer than that of the parent country, a differential payment may be made in lieu of overtime, which is not normally paid PCNs or TCNs.

■ *Exhibit 13.13*

Earnings by Educational Level and Race

Median Weekly Earnings of Full-Time Wage and Salary Workers, 1992 Annual Averages in Dollars

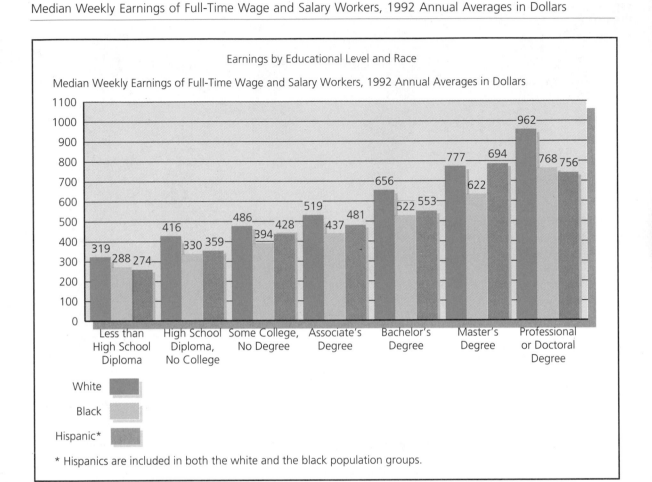

Earnings by Educational Level and Race

Median Weekly Earnings of Full-Time Wage and Salary Workers, 1992 Annual Averages in Dollars

White
Black
Hispanic*

* Hispanics are included in both the white and the black population groups.

SOURCE: A Bureau of National Affairs graphic, in "Is Discrimination the Source of Differential Earnings?" *Bulletin to Management* (August 19, 1993): 262. Used by permission.

Currency protection also affects compensation. Several alternatives for this protection exist. Employers may use discretion for individual PCNs or follow a standard split basis for all PCNs. A split basis may be applied case by case, depending on the particular country assignment. For local-currency payments, a policy concerning exchange rate adjustments is necessary to ensure that all employees are treated fairly.

Incentive Pay in Mexico

Although popular in the United States, performance-based pay may ruffle a few feathers in Mexico, especially among line employees. Why? Workers receiving more pay could be viewed as having connections to the higher echelons. Variable pay creates distance. "It's much more important for a Mexican person to have a congenial working environment than it is to make more money," says Alejandro Palma, intercultural business specialist for Clarke Consulting Group. "There have been cases where very good workers, ones who have performed well and received [pay] recognition for that, have left the company because they felt ostracized by their co-workers."

Arturo Fisher, a consultant for Hewitt Associates who specializes in Latin America, knows of variable pay plans that have worked, but he too expresses concern at their use. "[Mexicans] are more oriented to guaranteed situations, guaranteed pay. So, pay at risk is OK, but you have to communicate it a little bit more."

Instead, Palma suggests other reward strategies, such as making the outstanding worker a team leader. This plays into the desire for respect without isolating the worker, he says: "Employees-of-the-month programs, where it's on a rotating basis, not permanent like salary compensation, seem to be OK, because everyone has a chance." Other incentives include family days or other activities including workers' relatives.[95]

 # SUMMARY

Performance-based pay systems continue to attract the attention of many human resource managers, and line managers continue to ask whether pay can be used to motivate their employees. The success of many incentive plans indicates that pay can motivate job performance, although many problems can arise because of the myriad issues associated with the implementation of performance-based pay systems.

Despite the potential motivational value of performance-based pay systems, most organizations continue to choose essentially nonperformance-based plans. Some organizations believe that performance-based pay systems are not possible because of the lack of appropriate conditions or because of the cost. However, if organizations can measure performance, and if everyone thinks the system is fair and tied to the objectives of the organization, paying for performance should increase profitability.

Which performance-based pay plan to use must be determined by several variables, such as the level at which job performance can accurately be measured (individual, department, or organization), the extent of cooperation needed between departments, and the level of trust between management and nonmanagement. A specific organization's decision to use performance-based pay may be limited by issues such as management's desire to have performance-based pay, management's commitment to take the time to design and implement one or several systems, the extent to which employees influence the output, the extent to which a good performance appraisal system exists, the existence of a union, and the degree of trust in the organization. Whether the organization is public or private influences the decision, too. Generally, only private organizations utilize incentive systems. Both private and public organizations, however, can and do use merit pay systems. A final major consideration is the extent to which employees will understand and accept the plan.

 ## *Discussion Questions*

1. Describe in detail all the parts of compensation linked to performance at Lincoln Electric. How much credit for Lincoln's success do you give to the incentive system?

2. What are the major purposes of performance-based pay systems?

3. What obstacles are there in performance-based pay?

4. If possible, describe a performance-based pay system that you have directly experienced. Did the system work? If not, why not?

5. Under what conditions would you expect a performance-based pay system to have the greatest likelihood of success?

6. Debate the following assertion: If selection and placement decisions are made effectively, individual performance should not vary by a great deal; therefore, a performance-based pay system is not needed.

7. Design an incentive system you would want to have for yourself. Then, design an incentive system for your employees. Specify all conditions and assumptions as needed.

8. Describe the several types of incentive pay plans.

9. What is an earnings-at-risk plan?

10. What are the issues in setting up a performance-based program in an international compensation program?

 ## In-Class Projects

1. Describe the following for Lincoln Electric:
   a. Lincoln's incentive plan objectives
   b. The degree to which these objectives are serving the business and HR objectives of Lincoln
   c. Lincoln's incentive plans and activities
   d. The degree to which these plans and activities are serving the objectives of Lincoln

Going forward:

How can Lincoln's incentive compensation activities be improved?

2. Describe the following for AAL:
   a. AAL's incentive plan objectives
   b. The degree to which these objectives are serving the business and HR objectives of AAL
   c. AAL's incentive plans and activities
   d. The degree to which these plans and activities are serving the objectives of AAL

Going forward:

How can AAL's incentive compensation activities be improved?

 ## Field Project

Interview two or three employees of a company in your area. Ask whether they are paid on the basis of their performance. If so, ask how performance is measured and what percentage of total pay is based on performance. If they are not so paid, find out if the employees would like to be paid for performance, and if so, under what type of plan—merit or incentive based. Identify the reasons employees use in preferring one type of plan over another.

Case Study:

LINCOLN ELECTRIC COMPANY

 Use the Lincoln Electric Company case at the end of the book for this chapter's case. Use the questions for this chapter's in-class project as a basis for your analysis.

Indirect Compensation: Providing Benefits and Services

There was a time when increased health care costs could be made up through increases in the prices of our products. This is now impossible.

EDGAR S. WOOLARD, JR., CHAIRMAN, DuPont[1]

Managing Human Resources for the 21st Century at Rockwell International

The bad news comes in a telephone call to Daniel P. Heslin, the employee benefits director of the Rockwell International Corporation. Doctors attending to an employee report that she has leukemia. They want to do a bone marrow transplant. The cost: more than $100,000. Will Rockwell pay?

Experts at various medical centers tell Rockwell it is customary not to perform such a transplant on people older than forty because the chances for success are slim. The patient is fifty, and she is very weak. Rockwell's insurance administrator, the Metropolitan Life Insurance Company, recommends denying payment—but the final decision belongs to Rockwell. Like a growing number of large firms, Rockwell is self-insured. Metropolitan Life administers its plan; but Rockwell must decide how to distribute its health care investment.

Like his counterparts at companies across the United States, Heslin has become accustomed to such difficult issues. In an attempt to aggressively control medical costs that are rising about 20 percent a year, American benefits managers have been forced to adopt the role of a pinstriped referee in a game where the field keeps expanding and the calls get tougher.

"As a society, we want the best and it's hard to say no—particularly to someone who is dying," Heslin says. Indeed, in the case of the worker with leukemia, Metropolitan eventually withdrew its opposition and Rockwell agreed to pay for the treatment. The rationale was that the company would refuse payment only if the procedures were clearly excluded by the plan or were clearly not medically necessary. The bone marrow transplant was performed. The patient died six weeks later.

Heslin's job is a daunting one in several other ways. Each of Rockwell's businesses has its own benefits arrangement, and Rockwell has a lot of businesses, with a total of about 350,000 employees, retirees, and dependents in almost every state and twenty foreign countries. The vastness of the program is complicated by Rockwell's effort to slow the growth of medical costs. By 1990, Rockwell was spending about $0.5 billion a year on health benefits. That's a substantial amount of money, yet Rockwell's health care costs are lower than those of most companies.

To contain costs, Rockwell's strategy is to pay medical expenses related to injuries or illness and not to pay medical expenses for procedures deemed nonessential, cosmetic, experimental, or covered under the less comprehensive provisions of Rockwell's vision or dental plans. Rockwell pays for heart, pancreas, and bone marrow transplants and for expensive tests like magnetic resonance imaging (MRI) and computerized axial tomography (CAT) scans. However, it will not pay for other things such as in vitro fertilization, sex change operations, and some treatments for temporomandibular joint syndrome (a jaw disorder), and it has eliminated payment for radial keratotomy, an operation on the cornea to correct nearsightedness.

Rockwell's strategy makes sense in theory, but it does pose some ethical dilemmas. For example, an employee of impeccable health habits who is having trouble conceiving a child must pay his or her own way for fertility treatments, whereas an employee whose illness is related to potentially modifiable habits like smoking, heavy drinking, or bad diet still has expenses covered by the company.

The final decision on what Rockwell will cover rests with Robert H. Murphy, senior vice president for organization and human resources—the boss of Heslin's boss—who reports to Rockwell's chairman. Like many executives in charge of benefits, Heslin and his colleagues do not have a medical background. For expertise, they rely on the insurance company, the company medical department, and consultants. Heslin received his bachelor's degree in business administration and worked in human resources at three different companies before joining Rockwell in 1975 as a regional benefits manager.

Heslin also is in charge of life insurance, vacation and leave time, and pensions and saving plans. "But these days, easily 55 percent of my time goes to health care," he says, "up from about 20 to 25 percent six years ago." Much of the additional time is devoted to developing strategies to control medical costs. For example, outside consultants review each mental health and substance abuse case to determine how long a hospital stay is warranted. "The idea is to prevent [the need for] the miraculous cure that always comes after 28 days, just as the hospital insurance runs out," Heslin says. "We are not looking to roll back the benefits but to channel them into more effective care."

The importance of aggressively handling long-term catastrophic cases was driven home by a study conducted by a Dallas consulting firm that helps Rockwell analyze its costs. It found that 5 percent of employees accounted for half the health care dollars spent. Excluding the catastrophic cases, health care costs would have risen only 11 percent rather than nearly 20 percent.

Rockwell also is trying to save money by being more flexible. Consider the potentially high cost of a head injury case that causes paralysis. Rather than paying for long-term hospitalization, Rockwell will pay for the purchase of wheelchair ramps and a specially equipped van so that the employee can move home as soon as possible.

Another strategy for handling soaring costs involves larger employee contributions to health care.

Rockwell employees now contribute about $500 annually for their health coverage, cover a $250 deductible, and bear 30 percent of health care costs up to $2,500. (Deductibles in most firms are $100, and cost sharing is usually set at 10–20 percent.) Such out-of-pocket costs are hard to accept for employees who think a faceless insurance company is paying the bill. To correct this misperception, Rockwell has launched a major communication campaign designed to teach workers that the insurance company is merely the claims administrator, the company pays the bills.[2]

In addition to its high value, indirect compensation is generally exempt from employee-paid income taxes. As the cost of indirect benefits grows in proportion to the total cost of compensation, organizations are becoming more concerned about the number and type of benefits they provide, the management of benefits, and cost containment. As a result, benefits management has moved from the rear ranks into the firing line of strategic management. Furthermore, indirect compensation, particularly health care and workers' compensation, is of interest to all levels of government.

This chapter discusses indirect compensation—also called employee benefits and services—and the role it plays in fulfilling organizational objectives. First, it outlines the objectives and organizational and environmental influences affecting the strategic management of benefits. Then, it looks at legal considerations. Next, it reviews public and private protection programs, such as workers' compensation and pension plans. It also focuses on health care benefits, paid leave, and life cycle benefits such as child and elder care. It concludes with a discussion of administration issues, including cost-benefit analyses, and some international comparisons.

INDIRECT COMPENSATION

The benefits and services that organizations provide include:

- ◉ Public protection programs
- ◉ Private protection programs
- ◉ Health care benefits
- ◉ Paid leave
- ◉ Life cycle benefits

Several of these categories are mandated by federal and state governments and therefore must be administered within the boundaries of laws and regulations. Many others are provided voluntarily by companies and vary with the company.

Although the specific elements of plans vary, employee benefits and services are generally defined as in-kind payments to employees for their membership or participation in the organization. These payments provide protection against health and accident-related problems and ensure income at retirement. Legally required payments include

Social Security, unemployment compensation, and workers' compensation; private protection programs include health care, life insurance, and disability insurance. Retirement income is provided through pensions and savings plans. Benefits programs also include pay for time not at work—for instance, vacations, holidays, sick days and absences, breaks, and washup and cleanup. A growing category of benefits enables employees to enjoy a better lifestyle or to meet social or personal obligations while minimizing employment-related costs. Discounts, educational assistance, and child and elder care fall into this category.

Exhibit 14.1 illustrates the cost of benefits as a share of the total labor costs associated with the "average" U.S. employee.

⊛ PURPOSES AND IMPORTANCE OF INDIRECT COMPENSATION

Companies provide benefits and services primarily to attract and retain valued employees. Until recently, employers were relatively generous; now, the tide is shifting, for several reasons. First, benefits and services are a major, increasingly costly part of total compensation. In 1929, total benefits payments averaged 5 percent of total pay. By 1995, they had risen to an average of almost 40 percent of wages and salaries, or roughly $7 a payroll hour, or $14,000 a year for each employee. Although these numbers vary across industries and by type of worker, the cost of benefits to organizations is, in general, enormous.[3] While wages and salaries increased forty times from the mid-1940s to the mid-1990s, benefits increased five hundred times.[4]

■ *Exhibit 14.1*
Average Annual Employee Benefits and Earnings

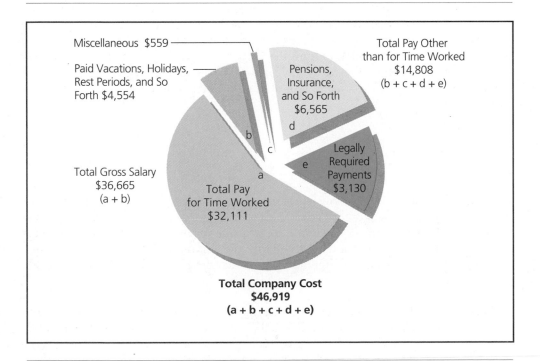

SOURCE: Based on U.S. Chamber of Commerce data for the Bureau of National Affairs (January 5, 1995).

Why do organizations pump so much money into benefits programs? Because they believe that benefits help:

- Attract good employees
- Increase employee morale
- Reduce turnover
- Increase job satisfaction
- Motivate employees
- Enhance the organization's image among employees and in the business community

Unfortunately, ample research demonstrates that these objectives are not always attained, owing largely to inadequate communication. Many, perhaps most, employees do not really know which benefits they receive or how much those benefits are worth. Realizing this, firms such as Rockwell have begun aggressively marketing their benefits packages to tell employees what the company provides to them.[5] Clearly, if employees do not know they receive a benefit, they will not stay with the company in order to retain that benefit.

Indirect compensation also may fail to help a company achieve its objectives if employees regard it as a condition of employment to which they are entitled. Rather than appreciating their employer's concern, employees may view benefits as a social responsibility the employer is obligated to provide.[6]

Even when indirect compensation is regarded as an inducement to work in a particular company, its importance relative to other job factors—for example, opportunity for advancement, salary, geographic location, responsibilities, and prestige—may be low. Furthermore, some of the potential value of a company's benefits package is often lost because each employee values only some of the benefits offered, and may even resent the company's decision to spend money on benefits used only by other employees. Allowing employees to choose their indirect compensation packages is one solution to this problem. As some firms reduce or even eliminate benefits and ask workers to share or even assume their costs, many employees are beginning to realize how expensive benefits can be. Also, they are being forced to decide which benefits are of most personal value,[7] and are thus beginning to learn the range of benefits they can and do receive.

The specific benefits offered by any particular company are determined by many forces in the external environment, as well as a few internal forces.

External Influences

The skyrocketing growth in the types and costs of employee benefits can be traced to several environmental trends.

Wage Controls. Under normal business conditions, employers compete for labor primarily through the wages they offer. During times of major crisis, such as World War II and the Korean War, the government curtailed such activity in order to prevent runaway inflation. Throughout the 20th century, the imposition of wage controls in times of war forced organizations to offer more and greater benefits in place of wage increases, to attract new employees.

Health Care Costs. Health care costs have been increasing at an alarming rate. In 1940, U.S. health care expenses were $4 billion, about 4 percent of the GDP. In 1995, they were more than $1 trillion, or 16 percent of the GDP. For employers, the average health benefits cost for each employee was almost $4,000 in 1995. Regardless of their causes, these increases have had a major effect on indirect compensation.[8]

Union Bargaining. From 1935 into the 1970s, unions were able to gain steady increases in wages and benefits for their members. Practically all benefits are now mandatory bargaining items, which means that employers must bargain in good faith on union proposals to add them.

Federal Tax Policies. Employers prefer not to cover benefits expenses that, for tax purposes, cannot be counted as business costs. Employees, on the other hand, want to receive benefits without the burden of increased taxation. Thus, employers' benefits packages regularly change as the tax codes change.

Inflation. Employee benefits managers, more so than compensation managers, must anticipate the effects of inflation on medical service, education, and pension benefits. For example, double-digit inflation in the 1980s eroded the purchasing power of some retirees' benefits and resulted in adjustments in the retirees' levels of benefits.

Competition. In their recruitment ads and literature, most companies label their benefits packages as competitive. Owing to increased competition, being competitive without spending more often means developing innovative packages to attract and retain employees. Wellness programs, health screenings, and employee assistance programs are examples of relatively new benefits options. Other responses to competitive pressures include flexible benefits plans and cash options offered in place of prepaid benefits packages.[9]

Social Legislation. A variety of laws significantly affect the administration and offering of indirect compensation, including the Family and Medical Leave Act of 1993, the Americans with Disabilities Act of 1990, and the Employee Retirement Income Security Act of 1974 (ERISA). These are described more fully later in this chapter.

Expansion of Social Security. In 1935, the Social Security Act covered 60 percent of all workers. Subsequently, the scope of benefits and the percentage of eligible workers increased substantially. Today 95 percent of all workers were covered and received disability and health benefits in addition to retirement pay.

Internal Influences

The scope of employee benefits has also been affected by organizations and their stakeholders. Initiatives such as major medical insurance, long-term disability plans, and child and elder care allowances reflect a general concern for employees. All were implemented by organizations in response to employee needs. Provisions such as educational assistance benefits, employee assistance programs, and wellness programs have been inspired by pressures to improve productivity and worker skills. More recently, benefits such as subsidies for buying American-made cars and matching funds for charitable giving have been prompted by private businesses' desire to support their country or to be socially responsible.

In a poll conducted by the Employee Benefit Research Institute (EBRI) and the Gallup organization, 84 percent of the Americans surveyed said they consider employee benefits such as pensions, health and life insurance, vacations, and sick leave very important or important in deciding whether to accept or reject a job. Although only 15 percent had ever changed jobs or quit a job based on benefits provided, if given a choice between two identical jobs, only one of which offered benefits, respondents said they would require a salary amount of $10,000 more to accept the job without benefits.

Employee Wants. Traditionally, employers have adopted a "father-knows-best" attitude toward benefits; the company has assumed it knows what is the most appropriate coverage for its employees. As we enter the 21st century, this attitude is being replaced with one of high employee involvement and choice, consistent with employee empowerment.[10] "Choice accounts" that provide various benefits options and allow employees, rather than the company, to allocate benefits dollars are increasingly popular.[11] Exhibit 14.2 shows how employees evaluate the relative importance of several types of benefits.

Human Resource Philosophy. An organization's fundamental beliefs about its employees and the employer-employee relationship set the stage for benefits management. The benefits manager must understand the underlying basis of the philosophy and the extent to which management supports human resources generally and benefits specifically. Some firms adopt an egalitarian approach to benefits and services by insisting that the same set of benefits be provided to all employees. Other firms adopt a more competitive approach, varying benefits with organization level. For example, some firms still have executive lunches and executive parking areas. Many U.S. automakers give larger purchase entitlements with higher ranks—for example, a Ford Escort for low-level managers, a Thunderbird for top executives; two weeks' severance pay for low-level workers, substantial golden parachutes for top officials. Such benefits policies communicate the organization's culture and values to employees.

■ *Exhibit 14.2*
Benefits Employees Consider Most Important

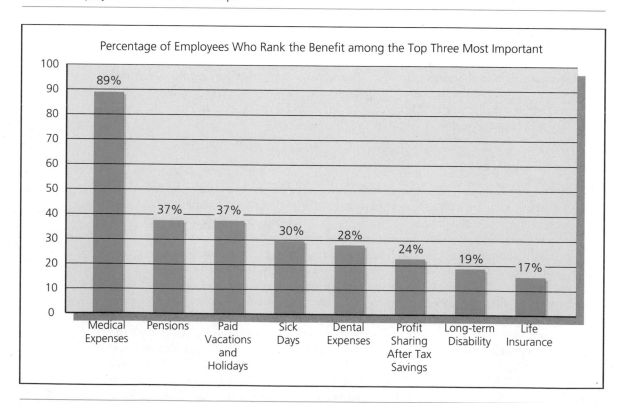

SOURCE: Based on responses from five hundred thousand employees surveyed by Hewitt Associates, as reported in *Employee Benefits in 1995* (Hewitt Associates, Lincolnshire, IL, 1994).

Business Objectives. As described in Chapter 4, comprehensive planning involves assessing external threats and internal forces, setting and ranking goals, establishing timetables, and integrating benefits planning with human resource planning specifically and with the organizational planning process generally. In a study of nonunion firms, benefits emerged as one of the key policy areas that reflects top management's belief in individual worth and equity and as a key area in which to achieve organizational objectives.[12] Exhibit 14.3 provides some examples of business objectives and possible responses from the benefits area.

 ## LEGAL CONSIDERATIONS

Indirect compensation grew rapidly during the Depression, which produced the first major legislation involving benefits. The Social Security Act, passed in 1935, provided old-age, disability, survivors', and health benefits and established the basis for federal and state unemployment programs. The Wagner Act, or National Labor Relations Act of 1935 (NLRA), helped ensure the growth of benefits by strengthening the union movement in the United States. Both the Social Security Act and the Wagner Act continue to play significant roles in the administration of benefits. Since the 1960s, Congress has passed several acts that make this legal environment more complex, including the Equal Pay Act of 1963, the Americans with Disabilities Act of 1990, and the Age Discrimination in Employment Act of 1967 (which were discussed in previous chapters).

Pregnancy Discrimination Act of 1978

The Families and Work Institute, a research group based in New York, found that approximately 4 percent of pregnant employees, or about eighty thousand women a year,

■ *Exhibit 14.3*
Business Objectives and Potential Benefits Responses

Business Objective	Benefits Response
1. To unify the company acquired from the merger, from independent subsidiary to integrated division status, by year-end.	Perform an analysis of an immediate versus a gradual transfer of subsidiary employees into the corporate benefits plan.
2. To develop a working environment that is founded on integrity, open communication, and individual growth.	Develop an employee career-counseling system that provides employees with an opportunity to assess skills and develop competencies. Establish a tuition reimbursement program.
3. To establish the division as a recognized leader in support of its community.	Establish a corporate-giving matching fund.
4. To complete the downsizing of the milling unit by the end of the third quarter.	Develop various termination subsidies such as severance pay, outplacement assistance, and early retirement benefits.
5. To cut accident rates 10 percent by year-end.	Establish an employee assistance program by year-end. Set up a free literacy training program to ensure that all employees can read job safety signs.

are fired for becoming pregnant. A similar figure was generated by a 1985 study conducted by the Census Bureau.[13] Although employees of small businesses and the federal government may legally be treated in this manner, employees in large companies are protected by the Pregnancy Discrimination Act of 1978, which states that pregnancy is a disability and qualifies a person to receive the same benefits as afforded for any other disability. Applying this statute, a state appeals court in Michigan ruled that a labor contract between General Motors and the United Auto Workers was illegal. The contract provided sickness and accident benefits of up to fifty-two weeks but limited childbearing disability to six weeks.[14]

Although the Pregnancy Discrimination Act does not explicitly address this issue, it is now interpreted as also requiring companies to offer the same pregnancy benefits program to wives of male employees and to husbands of female employees. The U.S. Supreme Court ruled in *Newport News Shipbuilding and Dry Dock Company v. EEOC* (1983) that employers who provide to spouses of employees health care insurance that includes complete coverage for all disabilities except pregnancy are violating Title VII of the Civil Rights Act of 1964. In essence, employers must provide equal benefits coverage for all spouses.

Family and Medical Leave Act of 1993

The Family and Medical Leave Act of 1993 requires employers with fifty or more workers to grant an employee up to twelve weeks' unpaid leave annually "for the birth or adoption of a child, to care for a spouse or an immediate family member with a serious health condition, or when unable to work because of a serious health condition. Employers covered by the law are required to maintain any preexisting health coverage during the leave period."[15] The employee taking leave must be allowed to return to the same job or a job of equivalent status and pay—with the exception of some highly paid executives. To be eligible, employees must have worked at a company for at least twelve months and have put in at least 1,250 hours in the year before the leave.[16]

This act is entirely consistent with what some companies have been doing for some time in their efforts to accommodate to an increasingly diverse workforce and make themselves more "family friendly." However, family-friendly policies are more prevalent within a few industries and less prevalent elsewhere. In particular, the chemical, pharmaceutical, commercial banking, and life insurance industries seem to lead the way.[17]

ERISA and Private Employers' Pensions

Building on the foundation of the Revenue Act of 1942, the Employee Retirement Income Security Act of 1974 was designed to protect the interests of workers covered by private retirement plans, especially plans that promise the workers a certain monthly dollar amount upon retirement. It does not require an employer to offer a pension fund. When companies choose to offer pension funds, employees are eligible for private pension fund participation after one year of service or at age twenty-five.[18]

ERISA also established provisions regarding *vesting,* which refers to the time when the employer's contribution belongs to the employee. Three basic options are available:

- Full vesting after ten years of service
- Twenty-five percent vesting after five years of service, with 5 percent additional vesting for years 6 to 10 and then 10 percent additional vesting for years 10 to 15
- Fifty percent vesting after five years of service and when age plus years of service equals 45, with 10 percent additional vesting for each subsequent year of service.

In the past, some companies set up pension funds but then, when necessary, drew upon those funds to pay for operating expenses. Such activity put employees' pensions at great risk. To protect employees against such risk, ERISA prohibits the use of unfunded pension programs that rely on the goodwill of the employer to pay retirement benefits out of current operating funds when needed. Money paid into a pension fund must be earmarked for retirees whether paid in part by the employee or paid solely by the employer (as in noncontributory programs).[19]

Under ERISA, employers are not required to accommodate new or transferred employees who wish to deposit funds into their retirement plans. On a voluntary basis, employers can allow employees to transfer money to individual retirement accounts. When this occurs, the pension funds are said to be *portable*. Increasingly, employers are making it possible for employees to transfer their retirement funds to another firm.

Because ERISA covered only single-employer firms, the Multi-Employer Pension Plan Amendment Act of 1980 was passed to broaden the definition of defined benefit plans to include multiemployer plans. If employers withdraw from multiemployer plans, they, rather than the employees, face liability for doing so and must reimburse employees for money lost.[20]

Economic Recovery Tax Act of 1981

A major provision of the Economic Recovery Tax Act of 1981 is that employees can make tax deductible contributions of up to $2,000 to an employer-sponsored pension, profit-sharing, or savings account, or to an individual retirement account. The act also makes it possible for employers to provide company stock to employees and pay for it with tax credits or to establish a payroll-based plan that facilitates employee stock ownership. Both approaches are referred to as *employee stock ownership plans (ESOPs)*.

Because these plans are attractive to organizations, over 10 million employees have gained direct ownership of stock in their own companies. By the year 2000, 25 percent or more of all U.S. workers will own part or all of their companies.[21]

> The appeal of ownership programs goes far beyond the tax breaks available to ESOPs. At a time when competitive pressures are forcing companies to keep a lid on labor costs, many are using stock plans as a substitute for cash compensation. Stock is being used to fund bonuses, pension and savings plans, and even retiree medical benefits.
>
> Such programs are not without risk, particularly if corporate sponsors go belly-up in future years. But they can help make companies more competitive, enhance productivity, and bolster morale when wage hikes need to be deferred. Because workers are concerned with job security, they represent a source of patient capital that is likely to value long-term performance over short-term profits.
>
> The most intriguing aspect of this trend is the possibility that workers who own a significant share of their companies will want a voice in corporate governance, as has already happened in the case of several companies contemplating mergers. Employers who prepare for this development by setting up mechanisms for dialogue can lay the groundwork for productive cooperation between labor and management in future decision-making. Those who don't may find worker ownership a mixed blessing.[22]

Tax Reform Act of 1986 and Revenue Reconciliation Act of 1993

The Tax Reform Act of 1986 and the Revenue Reconciliation Act of 1993 essentially cap the tax-exempt deferred contribution employees can make to a qualified pension plan that receives favorable tax treatment, such as a 401(k) plan or defined benefit plans. These acts put into force provisions to reduce the disparity of benefits provided high- and low-income employees, to ensure that all employees are treated in a roughly equal manner. Referred to as *nondiscrimination tests,* these provisions essentially limit the absolute amount of money that employees and employers can contribute to their qualified pension plans. The percentage of salary an employer can contribute is based on a maximum employee salary of $150,000. In 1995, employees could set aside, tax deferred, roughly 6 percent of their salaries, to a maximum of approximately $9,000. Prior to 1993, the maximum had been $30,000. Because this cap imposed for highly paid employees a reduction in benefits—both from the employees and from their employers in the form of matching amounts—some firms have set up supplemental executive retirement plans, which do not receive favorable tax treatment.[23] Furthermore, under these acts, for the top five executives in a company, annual pay above $1 million is not tax deductible unless it is performance related.

❖ PUBLIC PROTECTION PROGRAMS

Protection programs are designed to assist employees and their families if and when the employees' income (direct compensation) is terminated, and to alleviate the burden of health care expenses. Protection programs required by the federal and state governments are referred to as public programs, and those voluntarily offered by organizations are called private programs (see Exhibit 14.4).

Social Security System

Public protection programs are the outgrowth of the Social Security Act of 1935. This act initially set up systems for retirement benefits, disability, and unemployment insurance.

■ *Exhibit 14.4*
Protection Programs

Issue	Public Programs	Private Programs
Retirement	Social Security old-age benefits	Defined benefit pensions Defined contribution pensions Money purchase and thrift plans [401(k)s and ESOPs]
Death	Social Security survivors' benefits Workers' compensation	Group term life insurance (including accidental death and travel insurance) Payouts from profit-sharing, pension, or thrift plans, or any combination of these Dependent survivors' benefits
Disability	Workers' compensation Social Security disability benefits State disability benefits	Short-term accident and sickness insurance Long-term disability insurance
Unemployment	Unemployment benefits	Supplemental unemployment benefits or severance pay, or both
Medical and dental expenses	Workers' compensation	Hospital and surgical insurance Other medical insurance Dental insurance

Health insurance, particularly Medicare, was added in 1966 to provide hospital insurance to almost everyone age sixty-five and older.

Funding of the Social Security system is provided by equal contributions from the employer and employee under terms of the Federal Insurance Contributions Act (FICA). Initially, employee and employer each paid 1 percent of the employee's income up to $3,000. In 1995, each paid 6.2 percent of the first $60,600 of the employee's income (for retirement and disability) and 1.45 percent of the total income (for hospital insurance through Medicare).

The average annual Social Security benefit is about $8,300 for a single person and about $15,000 for a married couple, with adjustments routinely made for increases in the consumer price index. The maximum benefits from Social Security in 1995 were around $900 a month for a person who retired in 1988. Retired people age sixty-five to sixty-nine can also earn about $11,000 annually without sacrificing benefits; beneficiaries under age sixty-five can earn about $8,000.[24]

Unemployment Compensation Benefits

To control costs, the Social Security Act dictates that unemployment compensation programs be jointly administered through the federal and state governments. Because income levels vary from state to state, unemployment compensation also varies by state, although the federal rate is the same for all states (in 1995, $133 a month). Consequently, the total tax liability varies greatly across the United States. For example, this liability in Rhode Island is $633 a month and in South Dakota $91 a month. All profit-making organizations pay a tax on the first $7,000 to $10,000 of wages paid to each employee. The contribution rate for employers varies according to the number of unemployed people drawing from the fund. Consequently, employers make larger contributions during periods of higher unemployment. The level of benefits to employees ranges from 50 percent to 70 percent of base salary up to a maximum weekly amount that varies by state. With the passage of the Tax Reform Act of 1986, unemployment compensation became fully taxable, making actual benefit levels much lower.[25]

Workers' Compensation and Disability

As described in the feature "Managing Human Resources for the 21st Century at Steelcase," workers' compensation costs are a major concern to companies. Of the more than 6 million job-related injuries reported annually in the private sector, about half are serious enough for the injured worker to lose work time or experience restricted work activity, or both. In addition, hundreds of thousands of new occupational illness cases are reported each year. Almost 60 percent of these illnesses—most of which are back related—are associated with repetitive motions such as vibration, repeated pressure, and carpal tunnel syndrome. Most require medical care and result in lost work time.[26]

When injuries or illnesses occur as a result of on-the-job events, workers may be eligible for workers' compensation benefits. Administered at the state level and fully financed by employers, these benefits cover costs and lost income due to temporary and permanent disability, disfigurement, medical care, and medical rehabilitation. Survivors' benefits are provided following fatal injuries.

Proactive workers' compensation administrators such as Libby Child at Steelcase are applying a variety of health care cost-containment strategies to workers' compensation, such as:

⊙ Developing networks of preferred provider organizations
⊙ Specifying fees for treating workers' compensation claimants

Managing Human Resources for the 21st Century at Steelcase

Workers' compensation costs are rising dramatically. Payouts in the United States climbed from $22 billion in 1980 to $62 billion in 1990. In California, costs rose so high that firms started leaving the state, taking valuable jobs with them. The state legislature responded by redefining the employee conditions covered by state laws.

Although rules governing compensation insurance differ from state to state, moving a company's operations is not necessarily the best solution to the problem. At least, that was Steelcase Incorporated's conclusion. Steelcase is a high-quality office furniture manufacturer headquartered in Grand Rapids, Michigan. With more than twenty thousand employees in a highly competitive business, it got serious about workers' compensation costs in the 1980s. Under the direction of Libby Child, manager of workers' compensation and medical services, and the leadership of Dan Wiljanen, director of HR, and Jerry K. Myers, president and CEO, Steelcase developed and implemented a "return-to-work" program in 1986 that reduced the average cost of a claim by 50 percent and saved the company more than $24 million in six years.

Steelcase's overall program for reining in workers' compensation costs has two major pieces: (1) A medical review board systematically examines the injured person and the injury situation to make the correct diagnosis of the claim. The intent here is to uncover all the facts and build an atmosphere of trust and understanding between worker and company. (2) A return-to-work component enables workers to get back to work as soon as possible. Once an injury has been diagnosed, the biggest manageable expense is the time in getting the worker back to work. By setting up therapy centers and accommodating working conditions, for most injuries, Steelcase reduced time away from work by 50 percent in six years. Its average cost per claim went from $1,552 in 1983 to $1,213 in 1992 (in California, the average cost per claim went from $6,000 in 1980 to $20,000 in 1992).[27]

- Limiting payments to medically necessary or reasonable procedures
- Requiring precertification of hospital admissions
- Establishing concurrent review of inpatient hospital stays
- Routinely auditing hospital and health care bills[28]

Employers also are jumping on the cost-containment bandwagon. For example, Sprague Electric Company in Concord, New Hampshire, assembles a team consisting of the worker's supervisor, a rehabilitation counselor, and the firm's personnel and human resource manager. Using physician input and videotaped demonstrations of the employee's job, the team identifies job components the worker can still perform, as well as appropriate accommodations that need to be made.[29]

 PRIVATE PROTECTION PROGRAMS

Private protection programs are offered by organizations but are not required by law. They include retirement income plans, capital accumulation plans, savings and thrift plans, and supplemental unemployment benefits and guaranteed pay. Some firms also offer work options for retirees, including temporary full-time and permanent part-time employment.

The various retirement income plans can be classified in terms of whether they are qualified or nonqualified. A *qualified plan* covers a broad, nondiscriminatory class of employees, meets Internal Revenue Code requirements, and consequently is qualified to receive favorable tax treatment. For example, the employer's contributions to the plan are tax deductible for the current year and employees pay no taxes until retirement. *Nonqualified plans* do not adhere to the strict tax regulations, cover only select groups of employees, and consequently do not receive favorable tax treatment.[30]

Pension Plans

The largest category of private protection plans is pensions. Four out of five employees in medium and large firms are covered by some type of private pension or capital accumulation plan and rely on these plans to provide future security. A less well known fact is that the twenty largest pension funds, thirteen of them for public employees, hold one-tenth of the equity capital of America's publicly owned companies. All told, institutional investors—primarily pension funds—control close to 40 percent of the common stock of the country's largest businesses. Pension funds also hold 40 percent or more of the medium- and long-term debt of the country's bigger companies. Thus, employees, through their pension funds, have become America's largest retirement bankers, lenders, and business owners.[31]

Defined Benefit Plans. With a defined benefit pension plan, the actual benefits received on retirement vary by the employee's age and length of service. For example, an employee may receive $50 a month for each year of company service. Some employers and unions prefer defined plans because they produce predictable, secure, and continuing income. Another advantage of such plans is that they are carefully regulated by the Employee Retirement Income Security Act. In addition to reporting rules, disclosure guidelines, fiduciary standards, plan participation rules, and vesting standards, defined benefit plans must adhere to specific funding-level requirements and be insured against termination due to economic hardship, misfunding, or corporate buyouts.

The Pension Benefit Guaranty Corporation (PBGC) administers the required insurance program and guarantees the payment of basic retirement benefits to participants if a plan is terminated. The PBGC also can terminate seriously underfunded pension funds. In July 1991, it moved to do exactly that with Pan Am's pension fund. The airline had missed three required funding contributions over the past year. According to James Lockhart, executive director for PBGC, the PBGC had to act immediately to keep the pension insurance safety net strong for workers and retirees and stem the rising costs for companies with well-funded pension plans.

In the case of Pan Am, PBGC covered the contributions of 34,000 workers, including 11,000 retirees enrolled in Pan Am's Cooperative Retirement Income Plan and 750 participants in the Defined Benefit Plan for Flight Engineers. According to Lockhart, PBGC lost more than $600 million owing to the mismanagement of this plan alone. Losses like this explain why PBGC's long-term deficit topped more than $2 billion in 1995 and why retirement programs are threatening to be the next "savings and loan crisis" as we head into the 21st century.[32]

Defined Contribution Plans. Eighty percent of new plans are defined contribution plans. With this type of plan, each employee has a separate account to which employee and employer contributions are added. If only the employer contributes it is a *noncontributory plan.* When both contribute it is a *contributory plan.* Typically, the employee must activate the plan by agreeing to contribute a set amount of money; the employer then matches the percentage contribution to a specific level. Defined contribution plans are more prevalent in competitive, participative, organizations.

The two most common types of defined contribution plans are money purchase and tax-deferred profit-sharing plans. With *money purchase plans,* the employer makes fixed, regular contributions for participants, usually a percentage of total pay. Employees may also make voluntary contributions. The maximum amount for any employee is equal to 25 percent of earned income, up to a maximum of $30,000 for all defined contribution plans combined. Monies are held in trust funds, and the employee is given several investment options that differ in terms of the degree of risk and growth potential. At retirement, accumulated funds are used to provide annuities. In some cases, lump-sum distributions may be made.

Tax-deferred profit-sharing plans allow employees to share in company profits using a predetermined formula. Monies contributed to these plans are set aside until retirement, when the employees can cash in their profits. From the employer's perspective, tax-deferred profit-sharing plans are useful because they may deduct up to 15 percent of a participants' compensation (up to an income level of $200,000) for contributions. In addition, they pass on the investment risk to employees.[33]

Supplemental Plans

In addition to Social Security and standard pension plans, large firms often offer a supplemental defined contribution plan or a supplemental savings plan. Currently, 30 percent of all employees participate in supplemental plans. Such plans function as the third leg of the retirement income stool; they also provide additional retirement income or serve as a source for accumulating funds to meet short-term needs and goals. These plans take one of two forms: savings plans that work as defined contribution plans, called 401(k) plans, and employee stock ownership plans.[34]

Individual Retirement Accounts

Under current law, an employee who is not an active participant in an employer-sponsored pension plan during any part of a year may contribute up to $2,000 unconditionally to an individual retirement account (IRA), with an additional $250 allowed for a spousal account. The latter provision applies only if a joint tax return is filed. Employees involved in employer-sponsored pension plans also may participate, providing their income does not surpass limits set by the IRS.

HEALTH CARE BENEFITS

Coverage for medical expenses—including hospital charges, physician charges, and other medical services—is the core of a group health plan. Companies also may provide wellness programs, employee assistance programs, and short- and long-term disability insurance. Health benefits—particularly medical insurance—cost far less than what employees would pay on their own. Most employees underestimate the cost of health benefits to the organization and view coverage as an entitlement rather than a valuable gift. In a recent study, more than 80 percent of all workers said their employers are obligated to provide health care for them, but almost half of all employees did not know how much their health insurance cost their employer.

In reality, health care costs more than $1 trillion, and that figure is rising much faster than inflation. Health care consumed about 14 percent of the U.S. gross domestic product in the mid-1990s; by the year 2000, the figure will likely be 20 percent, almost regardless of federal intervention in health care. Companies that buy health insurance for their employees spend, on average, more than thirteen cents of every dollar they make to pay for this coverage. This is 35 to 40 percent more than in other industrialized countries, which already puts the United States at a competitive disadvantage. The burden is no lighter when employees buy their own health insurance, and it will become far worse if the current rate of increase continues—as there is every reason to think will happen.[35]

Employer-funded health care costs, like workers' compensation costs, double every five years. In 1995, health insurance cost employers an average of $300 for each employee every month. To fund rising health care costs, businesses are passing the cost on to consumers. For example, Detroit automakers estimate that $500 to $700 is added to the retail price of each automobile to pay for employee health care costs.[36]

Medical Care Approaches

Employers usually finance and provide medical expense benefits to employees and employees' dependents through insurance companies. However, a variety of other approaches are gaining in popularity as businesses attempt to thwart rising costs.

Insurance Companies. Insurance carriers offer a broad range of health care services from which employers can select coverage. Premiums are set and adjusted depending on usage rates and increases in health care costs. The insurance company administers the plan, handling all the paperwork, approvals, and problems. Proponents of this approach argue that insurers protect the plan sponsor against wide fluctuations in claim exposure and costs and offer opportunities for participation in larger risk pools. Insurance companies also have administrative expertise related to certification reviews, claim audits, coordination of benefits, and other cost-containment services.

On the downside, the insurance company, not the employer, makes decisions regarding covered benefits. Its decisions may go against the corporation's ethics and sense of social responsibility. Companies that subscribe to a specific insurance plan do not have the luxury of ignoring the insurer's advice and doing what they feel is ethical, as Rockwell did in the feature on pages 503–04. The insurance company makes all the tough calls.

Provider Organizations. Blue Cross and Blue Shield are nonprofit organizations that operate within defined geographic areas. Blue Cross plans cover hospital expenses, and Blue Shield plans cover charges by physicians and other medical providers. Typically, these associations negotiate arrangements with their member providers to reimburse the providers at a discounted rate when a subscriber incurs a charge. As originally established, the rate represented full payment for the service and no additional charge was levied. However, as a result of skyrocketing costs in health care, employees may now be asked to pay deductibles ($50 to $250 a year for each person) or a share of the cost of service (10 to 20 percent), or both.

Health Maintenance Organizations. A survey of almost two thousand firms in the mid-1990s found that 63 percent offered health care through *health maintenance organizations (HMOs)*. Health care costs with HMOs have risen only 15.7 percent a year, compared with increases above 20 percent for traditional health care plans. About one-third of all eligible employees or about 35 million people, participate in HMO plans.[37]

The growth in HMOs was stimulated by the passage of the Health Maintenance Organization Act of 1973. This act requires that companies with at least twenty-five employees living in an HMO service area must offer membership in that organization as an alternative to regular group health coverage, provided the HMO meets federal qualification requirements. HMO amendments of 1988 relaxed many of the federal rules governing HMOs and specifically repealed the dual-choice mandate, effective October 1995. This shift in legislative direction is designed to make the HMO field more competitive and, as a result, employers more receptive to using HMOs.

One successful HMO is operated by Deere and Company, the Moline, Illinois–based farm machinery manufacturer. Realizing twenty years ago that its own health care costs were skyrocketing, Deere brought its health care operations in-house and thereby established its own HMO, called the Heritage National Healthplan. Deere has been so successful that it has attracted more than three hundred other company clients, such as Monsanto, Sundstrand Corporation, and Chrysler.[38]

Preferred Provider Networks. *Preferred provider organizations (PPOs)* are a relatively new option in health care delivery. Introduced in the 1980s, these plans covered 55 to 60 million participants in 1990. With these programs, employers contract directly—or indirectly through an insurance company—with health care providers (physicians, dentists, laboratories, hospitals, and so forth) to deliver discounted services to program participants. Because the rates and requirements for these plans are relatively unregulated, employers have a great deal of flexibility in structuring an arrangement.

Unlike HMO participants, employees in a PPO are not required to use the plan's providers exclusively. However, they are usually offered incentives, such as a lower deductible or lower cost-sharing percentage, to use a PPO provider. For example, the employer may cover all the costs of health care provided by a PPO but only 80 percent of the costs of health care provided by physicians outside the PPO network. A concern with PPOs is the potential for antitrust legislation, since these plans ask providers to agree on standard charges for health care services.[39]

Self-Funded Plans. Like Rockwell, a growing number of companies are opting for self-insured or self-funded plans as a way to control medical plan costs and gain relief from state insurance regulations. By eliminating or reducing insurance protection, the employer saves on carrier retention charges (the amount of money not utilized to pay claims), such as state premium taxes, administrative costs, risk and contingency expenses, and reserve requirements. Typically, the employer creates a voluntary employee beneficiary association and establishes a trust whose investment income is tax exempt as long as it is used to provide benefits to employees and their dependents.

Cost-Containment Strategies. To further control costs, firms employ a variety of other strategies such as the following:

- *Hospital utilization programs.* Employers set up a system to review the necessity and appropriateness of hospitalization, prior to admission or during a stay, or both.
- *Coordination of benefits.* Employers coordinate their benefits with those of other providers to prevent duplicate payment for the same health care service.
- *Data analysis.* Employers analyze the available information to determine the most viable cost management approach. Simulations and experience-based utilization assumptions are used to develop models.
- *Managed care.* Many employers are active participants in case management. Interventions include requirements for second opinions and peer reviews.

- *Cost sharing with employees.* By raising deductibles and contribution levels, employers hold the line on overall expenses.[40]
- *Incentives to take care.* By offering incentives, some firms hope to change employees' behaviors so that employees are healthier. This may have substantial merit, but it may also have substantial risks.[41] In the worst case, companies may be in violation of the Americans with Disabilities Act if individuals with specific disabilities are treated differently than other employees without those disabilities. This strategy also may create ethical dilemmas. Although employees may consider it fair to give premium rebates for healthy lifestyles, most would not tolerate raises in premiums for genetically linked conditions.

Wellness Programs

Frustrated with efforts to manage health care costs for employees who already are sick, a growing number of employers are taking proactive steps to prevent health care problems. Moving beyond employee exercise classes and stress management classes, a handful of firms implement well-designed wellness programs to produce significant savings on the bottom line.[42]

For example, the Coors Brewing Company spent ten years fine-tuning its wellness program. For every $1.00 spent on wellness, Coors sees a return of $6.15, including $1.9 million annually in decreased medical costs, reduced sick leave, and increased productivity. According to William Coors, past chairman and CEO, the secret to Coors's success is really no secret: "Wellness is an integral part of the corporate culture." Coors's commitment to wellness includes a health risk assessment, nutritional counseling, stress management, and programs for smoking cessation, weight loss, and orthopedic rehabilitation.

Overweight Coors employees learn about the long-term risks associated with their condition through a health hazard survey. They are educated about the effect of excess weight on the cardiovascular, endocrine, and musculoskeletal systems. Then they receive an individual plan that may include individual counseling, group classes, and medical programs. The company even gives employees a financial incentive if they participate in the program and achieve and maintain their weight loss goal during a twelve-month period. To further encourage involvement, classes are held on-site.

Coors has been sensitive to the ADA requirements (a) that entry into a wellness program cannot be a condition for passing a medical exam and (b) that facilities must be accessible to all:

- At Coors Co. persons with disabilities have complete access to all of the company's facilities and its wellness center, says corporate communications manager Joe Fuentes. Part of the wellness program includes a medical questionnaire that determines employees' "health age" in relation to their "chronological age," Fuentes says. The program is totally voluntary for employees, he adds.
- The questionnaire asks employees whether they smoke, wear a seat belt, have high blood pressure, and exercise, and also includes questions about the employees' medical history, Fuentes says. All Coors employees are covered by their health insurance at 85 percent, he notes. Employees who pass the questionnaire are then covered at 90 percent. If employees fail the test, they can have a plan of action recommended by the community outreach person who runs the program, he explains.
- Test results are confidential and made available only to the community outreach person who administers the survey, Fuentes notes. In addition, employees can choose not to follow up on the test results. Thus far, he says, there have been no legal conflicts with ADA.[43]

Employee Assistance Programs

Whereas wellness programs attempt to prevent health care problems, *employee assistance programs* are specifically designed to assist employees with chronic personal problems that hinder their job performance and attendance. EAPs often serve employees with alcohol or drug dependencies, or both, or those with severe domestic problems. EAPs also help employees cope with mental disorders, financial problems, stress, eating disorders, smoking cessation, dependent care, bereavement, and AIDS. Because the job may be partly responsible for these problems, some employers are taking the lead in establishing EAPs for affected workers.[44] Thus, EAPs serve as a form of indirect compensation that benefits the individual and the firm.

PAID LEAVE

Paid leave is not as complex to administer as benefits from protection programs, but it is more costly, accounting for more than 10 percent of the total payroll. If absenteeism policies are not designed correctly, costs may escalate even further. The two major categories of paid leave are time not worked while off the job and time not worked while on the job.

Off the Job

The most common paid-off-the-job times are vacations, holidays, sick leaves, and personal days. The challenge in administering these benefits is to contain costs while seeking better ways to tailor the benefits to fit employees' needs and preferences.

Vacations and Holidays. Vacations give employees time to recuperate from the physical and mental demands of work. Vacation time is also viewed as an appropriate reward for service and commitment to the organization. Recently, a small number of firms have granted sabbaticals to employees (similar to those in academia), which, after a stated period of service, can be used for self-improvement, community work, or teaching. Tandem Computers, for example, grants six-week sabbaticals plus normal vacation time at full pay. Tandem found that in the short term, such programs have a negative effect on productivity, but in the long term, they enhance productivity.

In setting up vacation programs, several issues need to be addressed: (1) Will vacation pay be based on scheduled hours or on hours actually worked? (2) Under what circumstances can an employee be paid in lieu of a vacation? (3) Can vacations be deferred, or will they be lost if not taken? (4) What pay rate applies if an employee works during a vacation? The trend is toward vacation banking, with employees able to roll over a specified period of unused vacation days into a savings investment plan.[45]

Employees in the United States average about ten paid holidays a year. According to the Bureau of National Affairs in Washington, D.C., employers spend an average of $3,500 for vacations and holidays for the average employee.

Paid Absences. On any given day, 1 million American workers who are otherwise employed will not attend work; they will be absent. In the United States, the absenteeism rate ranges from 2 percent to 3 percent of total payroll, but some organizations report absenteeism in excess of 20 percent. An estimated 400 million person-days are lost each year as a result of employee absenteeism. This is almost ten times the number of person-days lost to strikes over a ten-year period.[46]

In comparison with other countries, the United States is midrange. Japan and Switzerland have lower absenteeism rates; Italy, France, and Sweden report substantially higher rates. The problem in Italy became so severe at one point that the police began arresting some habitual absentees, charging them with fraud.[47]

What makes absenteeism so problematic is the cost of employee replacement. It has been estimated that for every 1 percent change in the national absenteeism rates, the gross domestic product goes down by $20 billion. Absenteeism at General Motors has been estimated to cost $1 billion annually.[48]

Employees fail to show up for work for many reasons—health problems, family problems, bad weather, transportation difficulties, and so forth. Nevertheless, absences are greatly influenced by an organization's formal policies. As the number of paid days off increases, the number of days of actual absence increases proportionally. As pay rates rise, absenteeism also increases, with employees potentially "buying" time off. Consequently, because of lax policies, many organizations unwittingly not only tolerate or accept absenteeism but actually reward it. Their policies make it easier to be absent than to come to work.[49]

Negative strategies to control absenteeism include disciplinary procedures against employees who are absent once a week, once every two weeks, without a physician's excuse, before or after a holiday, after payday, without calling in, or for personal business. This discipline ranges from oral warnings for first offenses, to discharge. Unfortunately, these policies appear to be generally ineffective in controlling absenteeism among habitual offenders.

Programs that reward attendance—with, for instance, cash prizes, bonuses, or conversion of a proportion of unused absence days to vacation days—appear more promising. To prevent unscheduled absenteeism, many organizations grant personal days. The logic here is that employees must notify officials in advance that they will be absent. Self-management programs for habitual offenders also offer some hope for controlling excessive absenteeism.

On the Job

Time not worked on the job includes rest periods, lunch periods, washup times, and clothes-changing and getting-ready times. Together, these are the fifth most expensive indirect compensation benefit.

Another benefit that is growing in popularity is paid time for physical fitness. This is clearly pay for time not worked, but organizations often offer it because of its on-the-job benefit: healthy workers.

LIFE CYCLE BENEFITS

In response to a growing number of single-parent families, two-earner families, aging parents in need of care, and nontraditional families, employers are expanding their benefits packages to address new priorities.[50] Some of these benefits are offered by only a handful of firms. However, employers realize that a failure to address these needs in the near future will restrict their ability to compete. Thus, many employers plan to add these benefits by the 21st century. Life cycle benefits include child care, elder care, and other benefits.

Child Care Services

Recognizing that child care is a shared responsibility, more and more employers are providing some type of child care assistance to their employees. In fact, a survey of more than ten thousand firms employing ten or more workers showed that 63 percent of those firms offered some type of assistance benefits, scheduling help, or services related to child care. Thus, to be competitive in the labor market, firms at least need to survey their employees to find out their preferences and may need to offer a variety of options to meet employee needs.[51] Exhibit 14.5 shows a list of options for employers who want to develop an image of being family friendly. As described in the feature "Managing Human Resources for the 21st Century at Lotus Development," employees can share in the costs of family-friendly benefits through dependent care reimbursement accounts.[52]

Dependent Care Reimbursement Accounts. Dependent care reimbursement accounts have become the most prevalent type of child care benefit in the 1990s. These accounts allow employees to pay for qualified expenses with pretax dollars subject to a use-it-or-lose-it rule. They benefit employees greatly, yet involve minimal administrative costs for the sponsoring organization. The maximum amount an employee can channel into one of these accounts is $5,000 a year. For an employee to participate in a reimbursement account, the child must be under the age of thirteen. The expense must be necessary to permit an employee to work, to permit both husband and wife to work, or to permit a spouse to attend school full-time.[53]

For employees, these accounts offer potential tax advantages. Consider a single parent with a four-year-old daughter. He anticipates child care expenses of $5,000 in the next year. His projected salary for the next year is $35,000. This employee will have $445 more in disposable income using a dependent care reimbursement account:[54]

	Without Account	With Account
Gross salary	$35,000	$35,000
Preelected payroll deduction	−0	−5,000
Adjusted gross salary	35,000	30,000
Estimated taxes (federal income tax and Social Security)	−3,115	−2,670
Net salary	31,885	27,330
Payment from account	+0	+5,000
Available income	31,885	32,330
Payment to child care center	−5,000	−5,000
Disposable income	$26,885	$27,330

■ *Exhibit 14.5*
Family-Friendly Benefits

Summer day camp for dependent	Relocation plannings
Scholarships for dependents	Assistance plans
Summer employment for dependents	Child care referrals
Emergency care for adults	On-site child care
Subsidized tutoring for dependents	Family care leave
Sick-child care	Elder care referrals
On-site child care	Spouse relocation
Elder care	School matching
Flexible scheduling	Adoption benefits

SOURCE: Adapted from B. P. Noble, "Family-Friendly Firms," *New York Times* (May 2, 1993): F25.

Managing Human Resources for the 21st Century at Lotus Development

When Mitch Kapor founded his computer software firm in 1982, he called it Lotus, using a word that represents the state of perfect enlightenment in the Hindu philosophy. It was more than just a name. Kapor's vision was for his company's culture to embody all that the name symbolized.

Today, that corporate culture infiltrates all aspects of the business. It is this culture, more than current trends or legislative babble, that dictates HR policy at the company. And many of those policies enrich the quality of life of Lotus Development Corporation's employees and their communities.

Here is a glimpse of what it is like at the Cambridge, Massachusetts–based company. For starters, the employees are well compensated. The average wage at Lotus is $52,000 a year. In addition, Lotus gives stock options to more than one thousand employees. Its goal is for workers to retire with a pension that amounts to 85–90 percent of their final salaries.

All employees get twelve paid holidays each year, including their birthdays, and five days of paid personal leave. They also receive three weeks of paid vacation after one year of service. After six years with the company, they are eligible for a four-week sabbatical for any purpose.

Benefits include medical, dental, vision, and hearing insurance coverage, and bereavement leave.

In September 1991, Lotus became the first major employer to offer benefits to employees' gay and lesbian spousal equivalents. That is just one example of Lotus's family friendliness. There are many others. Since 1987, long before the federal Family and Medical Leave Act was enacted, the company has allowed both fathers and mothers to take one-month paid parental leaves. It encourages parents to adopt by reimbursing them $2,500. It offers job-sharing opportunities. Twice a month, Lotus brings in lunchtime speakers who frequently address topics focused on the family, such as fatherhood and infertility-adoption. And, at company headquarters, a children's center that opened in 1990 provides child care for up to seventy children a day. Employees are allowed to visit their children frequently, and join in on special events planned by the center.

It is clear that Lotus takes responsibility for the welfare of its workers. In 1992, Lotus moved its manufacturing plant from Cambridge to North Reading. The company made the effort to retain all 650 employees—including approximately 150 mentally handicapped people who work on the final assembly line—by paying the full cost of a rail transit ticket between Cambridge and Reading. A company-run shuttle bus picks up workers throughout the day at the station and brings them to the plant twelve minutes away.[55]

Resource and Referral Programs. Twenty-nine percent of firms offer child care information and referral assistance. These company-sponsored programs counsel employees about day care options and refer them to prescreened local providers. Prescreening helps to ensure that the centers in the network meet minimum care standards and are financially responsible.

The program offered by the Eastman Kodak Company is typical. The leading manufacturer of photographic products and health care products contracted with Work/Family Directions, a national organization that specialized in child care resources and issues, to maintain its Child Care Resource and Referral Program. To provide Kodak employees with detailed information and referrals, Work/Family Directors established contracts with community-based child care agencies throughout the United States. Kodak has also provided start-up costs to develop child care programs in areas of short supply. During this program's first eighteen months, Kodak's funding resulted in the addition of 650 family day care homes in communities where Kodak employees live.[56]

Using Data for the 21st Century:
ALLSTATE INSURANCE COMPANY

Research is an integral part of the decision-making process at Allstate, according to Catherine Higgs, who heads Allstate's human resource research department. With a staff of six professionals, Higgs works closely with managers in the business units and corporate headquarters. The HR research group is one part of the Allstate Research and Planning Center, which reports directly to the chief information officer, with dotted-line relationships to other appropriate functional areas.

Market research, direct market research, financial research, claim research, actuarial research, underwriting research, economic and demographic research, and systems support are areas other than HR that the Allstate Research and Planning Center tackles. Although much of the information is proprietary—such as how to help salespeople be more effective—Allstate shares quite a bit of its research on social issues, such as work-family issues and workforce diversity.

With a twenty-six-year history to draw on, Allstate's research group has a great deal of expertise and data available, including surveys on benefits, work and family, and so on.

1987 BENEFITS SURVEY

In 1987, Allstate conducted a thirty-five-question benefits survey, in which five questions targeted the work and family area. "Then, elder care was not a major problem for employees, probably because they were younger. However, many employees were at a stage where they had responsibility for primary child care," says Higgs.

1988 WORK AND FAMILY SURVEY

In 1988, Allstate conducted a telephone survey of a national sample of employees to learn the extent to which work-family issues were interfering with employees' work hours, how supportive managers were of these conflicts, and how these issues affected absenteeism.

"We found that employees preferred a child care site near their home, not work. That way, if both parents were working, either parent could pick up the child," Higgs says.

Results of this survey resulted in several decisions for Allstate:

- The company decided to provide a child care information and referral service rather than brick-and-mortar child care sites for employees.
- The company instituted a change in policy, allowing up to five days of an illness allowance for use in family situations.
- The company started a leave-of-absence policy, allowing family leaves of up to six months with the same job guaranteed, and of up to two years with a similar job guaranteed and subject to management approval.

1989 SURVEY OF SATISFACTION ON CHILD CARE INFORMATION AND REFERRAL SERVICE

In 1989, Allstate found that employees were satisfied with its Child Care Information and Referral Service; however, care for a sick child remained a difficult issue to deal with. The survey included people planning to have children within the next year or two. Allstate found they had very different perceptions of their needs than did employees who already had children.

1990 SURVEY OF FIVE SITES

In 1990, a major survey of fifteen thousand people in New York, New York, Dallas, Texas, Chicago, Illinois, Los Angeles, California, and Charlotte, North Carolina, found that dependent care cannot be defined as a monolithic problem—that its quality, quantity, and availability varied tremendously by city.

1994 BENEFITS SURVEY

In 1994, Allstate planned to update its survey of comprehensive benefits programs, and also to examine its work and family programs.[57]

On-Site Care Facilities. By 1995, more than two thousand employer-sponsored on-site or near-site care centers were in operation. In San Francisco, office and hotel complexes with more than fifty thousand square feet must either provide an on-site facility or pay into a city child care fund. Although the operation of such centers can be costly, a growing number of employers now accept it as a social and business necessity.

Consider the comments of Dick Parker, director of administrative services for Merck and Company, at groundbreaking ceremonies for its $8 million child care center: "You don't provide child care just because you want to be a good guy. You do it for business reasons. Merck decided to build the center for three reasons: retention, recruitment, and productivity. Child care will become more and more of a recruitment issue in the future. If employees are worried about their child care services[,] that will affect their productivity and retention."[58]

Campbell Soup Company's child care center is located across the street from its corporate headquarters and cares for 110 children. Contending that on-site care cuts absenteeism, reduces distractions for employees, and helps with hiring, the company picks up 40 percent of the weekly expense for each child.[59] The Hacienda Child Development Center in Pleasanton, California, serves multiple employers, including Hewlett-Packard, Computerland Corporation, and Prudential Insurance Company. Operating costs are funded from parent fees and business fees.

Elder Care Services

Twenty-eight percent of employees over the age of thirty spend an average of ten hours a week giving care to an older relative. For a significant faction, this commitment equals a second job. Some 12 percent of workers who care for aging parents are forced to quit their jobs to do so. With aging of the baby boomers, more and more employers are considering ways to help workers who are caring for elderly relatives. Assistance ranges from information and referral programs to specialized care insurance. The Family and Medical Leave Act of 1993 supports employee time off for both child care and elder care.

Information and Referral Programs. In 1990, only 11 percent of employers offered information and referral programs for elder care; by the 21st century, the number could exceed 50 percent. Like dependent care referral programs, company-operated elder care referral programs are designed to help the caregiver identify appropriate community resources.

The program offered by First Interstate Bank of California is representative of today's referral programs. In 1992, an employee survey revealed that about 8 percent of bank employees provided care for one or more elderly or disabled relatives, and 25 percent expected to do so by 1993. Furthermore, 30 percent of supervisors said their subordinates' caring for elderly family members had a negative effect on operations, owing to increased anxiety and health problems, requests for time off, and leaves of absence.

To address this concern, First Interstate investigated setting up its own elder care program. According to Julia Gettinger, manager of work and family programs at the bank: "If a company the size of ours were to do an independent elder care resource and referral program, it could cost up to $100,000 a year. The bank's commitment was substantial, but it wasn't $100,000." To help meet the need for elder care assistance *and* stay within the budget, First Interstate entered into a public-private partnership with the County Division on Aging. The agency is a member of a nationwide resource and referral system for elder care. Linked into the system, First Interstate employees call a toll-free number and talk to a counselor about what resources they need and in what city they need those resources. The counselor calls back with a list of resources including at-home care for the elderly, day care centers, and support groups for the caregiver.[60]

Long-Term Care Insurance. One new and fast-growing option for elder care is long-term care insurance. Although fewer than 15 percent of firms offered this benefit in the mid-1990s, nearly 70 percent expect to offer it by the beginning of the 21st century. This type of insurance covers medical, social, custodial, and personal services for people who suffer from chronic physical or mental illnesses or disabling injury or disease over an extended period of time. Typically, coverage is offered to employees on an employee-pay-all basis. Premium rates are age based, and some plans set a maximum age (typically seventy-nine) for participation. Benefit maximums are related to care site (e.g., nursing home versus day care center) and include lifetime limits.[61]

Other Life Cycle Benefits

With demographic and value shifts, a wider array of lifestyle choices is now available. As a consequence, a rising percentage of workers—such as unmarried couples, divorced people, and single parents—do not fit into conventional benefits packages. Recognizing that people are assets to the organization and that the world of work can never be fully separated from the rest of life, companies on the cutting edge are redesigning their benefits packages to address the needs of all employees.[62]

Adoption Benefits. In 1989, the Communications Workers of America (CWA) negotiated a benefits plan with AT&T that provides a $2,000 allowance for each adoption. That agreement is expected to serve as a model for other unions to follow as part of their bargaining strategy into the 21st century. An adoption benefits plan is a company-sponsored program that assists employees with or reimburses them for the costs associated with the adoption of a child. The most frequently covered benefits include adoption agency fees, attorneys' fees, and court costs. Some plans also include paid or unpaid leave, and a handful cover pregnancy care expenses for the birth mother.

Benefits for Spousal Equivalents. Some companies are now extending "spousal" benefits to same-sex partners and to unmarried opposite-sex partners.[63] For example, the Lotus Development Corporation modified its insurance and benefits policy to offer gay and lesbian partners the same benefits accorded heterosexual spouses. According to Russell J. Campanello, vice president for human resources, "This is fair and equal." To be eligible, unmarried partners of the same sex must live together and share financial obligations. If they break up, the employee must wait one year before registering a new partner. In addition to health care, the plan includes life insurance, relocation expenses, bereavement leave, and a death benefit.[64]

Educational Expense Allowances. Faced with skill obsolescence, downsizing, and retraining demands, most medium and large firms provide some form of educational expense assistance. Most plans cover registration fees, and some assist with graduation, laboratory, entrance examination, professional certification, and activity fees. Typically, these programs require a relationship between the course and some phase of company operations. For example, National Healthcorp, which is headquartered in Murfreesboro, Tennessee, offers tuition assistance to any aide who wishes to become a nurse. The company will pay for up to two years of school in exchange for the aide's promise to stay on staff that long after graduation.

Relocation and Housing Assistance. As housing costs continue to soar, more employers are considering housing assistance as an employee benefit. Seventy-five percent of surveyed New Jersey employers with five hundred or more employees attributed hiring and retention problems to the high cost of housing; 71 percent of surveyed California manufacturers said high housing costs were limiting their business expansion abilities.[65]

Relocation assistance traditionally has consisted of financial help for travel expenses and the cost of moving possessions. If needed, the company might also pay for furniture storage for a limited time as well as for temporary housing. A growing number of firms also offer a variety of allowances and services for transferred employees and high-demand new hires. These benefits include cost allowances for selling a house, expenses for finding a new residence, assistance in finding employment for a spouse, and temporary living expenses.[66]

 ADMINISTRATIVE ISSUES

Although organizations tend to view indirect compensation as a reward, recipients do not always see it that way. This conflict causes organizations to become concerned with how they administer their packages of indirect compensation benefits.

Determining the Benefits Package

The benefits package should be selected on the basis of what is good for the employee as well as for the employer. Knowing employee preferences can often help organizations determine what benefits should be offered. For example, employees in one company indicated a strong preference for dental insurance over life insurance, even though dental insurance was only one-fourth the cost to the company. As workers get older or their incomes increase, the desire for higher pension benefits steadily increases. Employees with children prefer greater hospitalization benefits than do those without.[67]

Allstate Insurance Company takes seriously the need for research into employees' preferences. Starting in 1987, it has continually sought employee input and participation in the design and administration of its plans, as described in the feature "Using Data for the 21st Century: Allstate Insurance Company."

Even if employers know what employees prefer, they may not be able to offer it. According to Jordan Shields, owner of a consulting firm specializing in benefits, a company's size may constrain the benefits it can provide:

> Companies that have fewer than 10 employees may have difficulty finding an insurance carrier, even for basic medical. Dental and vision care insurance options aren't very good. Disability plans for these small companies will be either very restrictive or very expensive.
>
> "If there are between 10 and 24 employees," says Shields, "vision, dental, and disability options are OK. Medical options are a bit easier to find than for the smallest firms, but it still isn't a breeze. At that size, there's no flexibility to offer more than one medical plan." Only after a company has at least 25 employees can it begin to offer a choice of medical plans. . . .
>
> Companies having more than 50 employees, and certainly those with more than 100, have more options and can even participate in partial self-insurance programs. "If you self-insure, then you, as the employer," says Shields, "you're acting partially as the insurance company, which means that if your employees stay fairly healthy and don't file a lot of claims, you won't pay as much in premiums."
>
> As companies grow, they encounter fewer limitations. A firm that has 300–400 employees can choose from among many options and carriers and can establish a large plan that can be

modified easily. However, a firm that grows from 10 to 150 employees within a year or two—which isn't at all unusual for [some] companies—will have major changes to make. Unfortunately, like many other functions at young, fast-growing firms, benefits management tends to lag behind the more urgent line functions.[68]

Providing Benefits Flexibility

When employees can design their own benefits packages, both they and the company come out ahead. At least that is the experience at companies such as Quaker Oats, Ex-Cello, TRW Incorporated, Educational Testing Service (ETS), and Morgan Stanley Group Incorporated.[69] ETS provides a core package of benefits to all employees, covering basic needs such as personal medical care, dental care, disability, vacation, and retirement. In addition, each individual can choose, cafeteria style, from optional benefits or can increase those in the core package. Employees are allowed to change their packages once a year. At Morgan Stanley, about two-thirds of all eligible employees elect their own benefits package over the standard no-choice plan. The options themselves were developed by the employees, working in small discussion groups. Because providing benefits flexibility is so effective, most companies now offer at least some variable benefits.[70]

A recent benefits survey showed that workers want to choose how to pay for their benefits and would modify their benefits if given the opportunity. Among the most preferred benefits are preventive medical care, wellness programs, vision care, and deferred compensation plans. One-third of all employees would prefer expanded medical and dental benefits over other types of benefits.[71]

Communicating the Benefits Package

Considering that most benefits program objectives are not attained, assessment of communication effectiveness would probably produce unfavorable results. This may be partly due to the communication techniques used. Almost all companies use impersonal, passive booklets and brochures to convey benefits information; only a few use more personal, active media, such as slide presentations and regular employee meetings. An especially good technique communicates the total compensation components every day. Increasingly, firms are offering voice response benefits systems. Employees in firms such as Cummins Engine Company in Columbus, Indiana, telephone in to learn about and manage their benefits.[72]

Through communicating the benefits package and providing benefits flexibility, the positive image of indirect compensation can be increased. Hewitt Associates found that 75 percent of all employees who understand its compensation program perceive it as fair, whereas only about 33 percent of all employees who do not understand the system think it is fair. Providing clear information about how to file claims and where to get services tends to bring more employees into the positive-perception camp.[73]

Managing and Reducing Benefits Costs

The trend is clear: more and more organizations are managing and reducing benefits costs. Managing costs means having second opinions and fewer choices in health care coverage. It means making sure that a disability is really a disability and that workers get back to work as soon as possible. It means being proactive and seeking ways to prevent sickness and injury.[74]

Does managing and reducing benefits costs mean eliminating benefits? Certainly, firms are asking workers to share the expenses of their own health care and even retirement. This is a very big issue in the automobile industry. It is consistent with employee empowerment and self-management. Workers are capable of understanding business and cost conditions. By having benefits information, they may be able to help reduce costs without eliminating benefits. For coverage that each individual needs, employers are likely to find ways to not only reduce costs but also maintain employee commitment to the organization. Experiences at Steelcase, Johnson and Johnson, Levi Strauss, Lotus, and Deere all indicate that win-win situations, with extensive employee involvement and understanding, are possible.

Employers in the United States are not the only ones dealing with benefits costs. The issue is also of growing importance in Europe, although employers there face a somewhat different situation. In Europe, most of the health care and pensions are provided by federal governments. Today, however, these governments are seeking ways to balance their budgets, and one way is to get out of the health care- and pension-providing roles. If they do this, employees and governments are likely to look to employers for relief at a time when many of those employers are already paying some of the highest wages in the world (see Exhibit 12.14). Thus, the pressure on European employers to manage and reduce benefits costs is likely to be even greater than it is on U.S. employers.

 ## INTERNATIONAL CONCERNS

Although the precise numbers change frequently, the comparisons in Exhibit 14.6 give a sense of the relative differences in wages, benefits, and working conditions in the United States, Canada, and Mexico.

Mexico

The Mexican Federal Labor Law governs all benefits matters in Mexico. The state labor boards oversee the enforcement of the law.[75] These boards have representatives from the government, labor, and management. The law states that full-time employees should get certain fringe benefits, including six days' paid vacation yearly, a minimum wage (about $15 a day), a 25 percent vacation pay premium, seven paid federal holidays, a profit-sharing plan, social security, and an employer-paid payroll tax that funds employee day care centers.[76]

The employer has twenty-eight days to evaluate the employees' work ethics. After that period, the worker is granted job security and termination becomes difficult. This is especially true in terms of financial liability. For example, an employer that decides to fire a worker who has been with the company for six months could be charged for an additional six weeks, plus vacation pay and bonuses accordingly. It is therefore worthwhile to screen employees before hiring.

An employee is considered tenured after one year of employment. A tenured worker may be dismissed only for causes specifically set out in the Mexican Federal Labor Law—for example, falsifying employment documents, or committing dishonest or violent acts during working hours. For a dismissal to be valid, a written notice of the firing and complete documentation of the offenses must be given.

Upon leaving a firm, employees may receive benefits from three sources:

◉ Social security is mandatory and covers old-age, survivors', and disability pensions, and medical and maternity benefits.
◉ Retirement savings systems require employees to pay into a retirement fund 2 percent of base pay.
◉ Severance pay is a major part of company retirement plans. There are two types: *antiguedad* and *cesantia*. *Antiguedad* is paid upon an employees' voluntary resignation

■ *Exhibit 14.6*

Private-Sector Wages, Benefits, and Working Conditions in NAFTA Nations

	United States	Canada	Mexico
Minimum wage (US dollars)	$4.25 per hour	$3.51 per hour	$0.46 per hour (average)
Maximum workweek	40 hours (8×5)	Varies with province	48 hours (8×6)
Pensions	Optional	Required contribution	Optional
Social security (old age)	Required contribution	Required contribution	Required contribution
Social security (disability)	Required contribution	No provision	Required contribution
Health care benefits	Optional	Required contribution	Required contribution
Unemployment insurance	Required contribution	Required contribution	No provision
Workers' compensation insurance	Required	Yes, varies with province	No provision
Pay equity and comparable worth	No provision	Yes, in Ontario	No provision
Plant-closing notification	60 days	Yes, varies with province	Yes
Severance pay	Optional	Varies with province	90 days' pay
Housing assistance	Optional	Optional	5% base salary
Profit sharing	Optional	Optional	10% net profits
Christmas bonus	Optional	Optional	15 days' pay
Holiday leave	Optional	3+ paid holidays	7 paid holidays
Vacation leave	Optional	10 paid days	6+ paid days
Sick leave	Optional	Paid by government after 3 weeks	Paid by government
Maternity leave	Optional	17 weeks + 24 weeks	12 weeks
Gender discrimination	Prohibited	Prohibited	Prohibited
Race or color discrimination	Prohibited	Prohibited	Prohibited
Religious discrimination	Prohibited	Prohibited	Prohibited
National origin discrimination	Prohibited	Prohibited	No provision
Age discrimination	Prohibited	Prohibited	No provision
Disability discrimination	Prohibited	Prohibited	No provision
Marital status discrimination	No provision	Prohibited	No provision

Note: In all NAFTA countries, states and provinces also have jurisdiction over labor law and may set additional standards.
SOURCE: Adapted from Institute for International Human Resources, Society for Human Resource Management (briefing paper on the North American Free Trade Agreement, January 1993).

after fifteen years of service, an employee's death, or an employee's disability. Compensation is twelve days' pay for each year of service, with a maximum of two times the minimum wage. *Cesantia* is severance paid upon termination without just cause. Just cause is limited to gross misconduct—poor performance is not considered just cause. Severance is not necessary upon retirement. This sets up a problem, because employees are often significantly better off being dismissed than voluntarily retiring. To remedy this, some companies establish informal voluntary retirement programs, with pension plans to allow retiring employees to receive severance pay.[77]

Individual operations can give their own benefits to entice workers, above and beyond the legal requirements. Some of these benefits include transportation, showers at the plant, wages double the minimum wage, subsidized or in some cases free lunches, on-site education, athletic activities, and cosmetics for women workers.

Certain border plants are short of good workers because of the infrastructure of nearby cities. Most northern towns have grown fast, and housing shortages and transportation difficulties cause problems. These conditions have not really affected industry as a whole, but people tend to change jobs in order to work closer to home. The solution for some maquiladoras is to locate in a central area so that most employees are within walking distance.

Most maquiladoras pay the Mexican legal minimum wage, which varies about 10 percent throughout the country. Owing to the pay, turnover may range from 30 percent to 100 percent a year in major cities. The effects of this turnover are higher production costs, poor quality, and higher wages in the local industry. Some maquiladoras have to pay their employees above minimum wage to keep their good workers. Some firms prevent high turnover by making employees feel that they can move up in the company, and offer an increase in salary after a certain amount of service time given to the company.[78]

Canada

In Canada, the sharpest contrasts with the United States concerning compensation are found in indirect compensation, particularly pensions and health care. Yet, even these differences appear relatively minimal. For example, Canada has the Canada Pension Plan (CPP), and the Quebec Pension Plan in the province of Quebec, both of which are similar to the U.S. Social Security system. CPP is a mandatory plan for all employees except federal workers. Like the U.S. Social Security system, CPP pays retirement benefits, disability pensions, benefits for children of disabled contributors, orphans' benefits, and pension benefits to survivors' spouses. Canada also has private pension plans, although fewer than 40 percent of all employees are covered by these plans. The administration of these plans is governed by the Pension Benefits Act, which is less extensive in its regulation of private pension plans than is the U.S. Employee Retirement Income Security Act.[79]

 ## SUMMARY

From the mid-1940s to the mid-1990s, indirect compensation grew substantially more than did direct compensation. This increase occurred despite the lack of evidence that indirect compensation helps to attain the purposes of total compensation. Money, job challenge, and opportunities for advancement appear to serve the purposes of compensation as much as, if not more than, pension benefits, disability provisions, and services, especially for employees aspiring to managerial careers.

This is not to say that employees do not desire indirect benefits. Organizations are offering them at such a rapid rate in part because employees want them. Unfortunately, the specific indirect benefits offered by an organization are not always valued by all employees, and all employees may not even know what benefits are offered. As a result, some organizations now solicit employee opinions about their preferences for compensation programs. Organizations are also becoming more concerned with the communication of their benefits programs. Current evidence suggests that employees' lack of awareness of the contents and value of their benefits programs may partially explain why these programs are not always perceived favorably.

These benefits do not come without costs. To ensure that an organization is getting the most from its indirect compensation, thorough assessments must be made of what the organization is doing, what other organizations are doing, and what employees prefer to see the organization doing. To improve the motivational value of indirect compensation, organizations should try to provide what employees want. As with direct compensation, employees apparently will continue to want more benefits like the ones they now have, as well as some they presently do not have. For example, employees want greater private retirement benefits, more health and insurance coverage, and more time off. Demands for dental coverage, vision care, and legal services will probably increase. Greater educational and career development opportunities are also likely to be demanded by employees.

As more U.S. firms move into international markets, the need to understand international compensation increases in importance. Although practices in countries such as Canada are quite similar to those in the United States, practices in Mexico are not. Mexican employees rely more on seniority than do U.S. and Canadian employees, and have many benefits set by the government.

 ## Discussion Questions

1. What is Rockwell doing to manage its health care costs?
2. As a manager, how can you use indirect compensation to improve productivity?
3. Describe the various components of indirect compensation.
4. Distinguish between public and private protection programs, and give examples of each.
5. How are unemployment benefits derived? What is the status of unemployment compensation?
6. How would you rationalize to your employer the costs of providing a physical fitness facility? How would you assess and compare benefits and costs?
7. Should more companies follow the example of Coors and establish a wellness program? Why or why not?
8. Should more companies follow the example of Lotus and provide ample family-friendly benefits? Why or why not?
9. Compare and contrast indirect compensation in the NAFTA countries.

 ## In-Class Projects

1. Describe the following for Lincoln Electric:
   a. Lincoln's indirect compensation plan objectives
   b. The degree to which these objectives are serving the business and HR objectives of Lincoln
   c. Lincoln's indirect compensation plans and activities
   d. The degree to which these plans and activities are serving Lincoln's objectives

Going forward:

How can Lincoln's indirect compensation activities be improved?

2. Describe the following for AAL:
   a. AAL's indirect compensation plan objectives
   b. The degree to which these objectives are serving the business and HR objectives of AAL
   c. AAL's indirect compensation plans and activities
   d. The degree to which these plans and activities are serving AAL's objectives

Going forward:

How can AAL's indirect compensation activities be improved?

Note: For these projects, use your "best guesses," because the cases do not cover indirect compensation extensively. Your responses here might reflect what effective companies in general do with respect to indirect compensation.

 ## Field Projects

1. Interview a human resource manager in a local company and ask about the organization's benefits program: How has it changed in the past several years? What methods are used to communicate the program to employees? How does the company measure the effectiveness of the benefits? How does it know what the employees want? What is the future of benefits in the company?

2. Go to a local company or a college or university to learn about its pension plan. Discuss with the benefits manager the characteristics of the plan; the benefits the plan provides—to whom, when, and how; the level of vesting in the plan; whether the plan is contributory or noncontributory; how the plan's benefits are communicated; and how ERISA has affected the plan.

Sally Yuen, director of HR for Dough Pineapple's (DP's) Maui, Hawaii, cannery, returns to her office deep in thought. She has just spent the last hour and a half in a lengthy and somewhat heated discussion with cannery manager Danny Sackos. Shrugging her shoulders, Sally wonders if Danny is right. Maybe the company's employee problem is her fault—well, the fault of her department, that is. According to Danny, if she had done a better job selecting employees in the first place, DP would not be in its current mess. "You hired quitters," he argued, pointing to the high turnover among temporary and permanent full-time employees.

DP maintains a regular workforce of 200 employees. Depending on the harvest, as many as 150 temporary employees are also employed. Temporary workers are paid a higher base salary than regular employees—$6.25 an hour. However, they are not eligible for any benefits, including vacation leave, day care, and sick leave. If they are sick, they have to take time off without pay. They also cannot participate in DP's highly successful profit-sharing program and matching pension fund.

Full-time, regular cannery workers are paid $5.00 an hour, $10,400 a year. Although DP's hourly rate is below the industry average of $6.00, employees more than recoup the difference in performance bonuses. To date, DP is the only cannery on the islands to have a state-of-the-art incentive pay program. In fact, it is the only cannery that shares organizational profits with employees at all.

Last year, employees received approximately $2,000 each in bonuses. This amount was lower than usual owing to a hurricane that destroyed almost all of one harvest. Since the program was implemented in 1986, annual bonuses have averaged $8,000 for each employee. And this year, they are expected to be back on target: Sally anticipates that they will be in the range of $10,000 for each employee. Employees have the option of taking the money in one lump sum, in quarterly installments, or in even distributions throughout the next year. According to company policy, employee bonuses will be announced at the next semiannual employee's meeting, which is to be held in six weeks.

Sally also is proud of DP's benefits. Employee benefits as a percentage of payroll average 30 percent in the industry; DP's average 45 percent. All full-time employees with one year's seniority (tenured employees) are eligible to participate in DP's extensive benefits program, which includes such innovations as an on-site day care center (Sally's brainchild, which took her two years to get approved) and an employee assistance program, including free legal assistance. The company also matches, dollar for dollar, employee contributions to a retirement fund and offers two college scholarships annually to employees' children. Sally is particularly proud of DP's fitness center, which can be used by all tenured employees and their families. Swimming lessons are provided free of charge to family members of employees.

Vacation days also are above the industry average. Employees with one to two years of seniority earn one-half day of paid vacation a month; with three to five years' seniority, three-fourths day a month; and with more than five years' service, one day a month. Personal days accrue at the same rate for tenured employees. To prevent abuse, employees calling in absent before or after a holiday or after a payday are charged with an absence of one and one-half days. Employees with less than one year's service and temporary employees are not reimbursed for absences. The failure of any employee to call in to report an absence at least four hours before his or her shift starts is grounds for disciplinary procedures.

By having a core of permanent, tenured employees, DP is assured of having enough workers to meet average production demands. By paying temporary employees base salaries slightly above the labor market average, DP has traditionally had its pick of new employees. The system has been cost-effective because the salaries of temporary employees were only 18 percent over the base pay for cannery employees and well under the hourly rate, with benefits, for permanent tenured employees (estimated at $7.98).

With all this going for DP, Sally wonders where things went wrong. She starts looking for causes by asking her assistant, Mark George, to interview some employees about their view of the situation. He also prepares a report on causes of turnover at DP (see Exhibit 1). According to Mark, the following comments are representative of the feelings of full-time permanent employees:

- "Sure, it's a great place to work, but I'm tired of those young kids walking in off the street and making more than I do."
- "I know, I know, we're eligible to get bonuses, but they just can't make up for a weekly salary—at least not when you have three kids to support."
- "I worry that things are going to be the same as last year. I hung in there, and look what I got, a lousy $2,500. The bottom line is that I still made less than temporary employees and those at the other canneries. I don't like it one bit."

These comments are typical of permanent untenured workers (full-time employees with less than one year of seniority):

- "I got really steamed last month when they docked my pay for being sick. I mean, I was really sick. I was down flat in bed with the flu. Why should I work hard here if I can't even get a lousy day off when I'm sick?"
- "I've worked here seven months already, and I'm pulling my own weight around here. Know what I mean? Well, it doesn't seem right that I should be paid less than those part-timers."

Among temporary workers, characteristic comments are

- "Yeah, we make a good rate of pay, but that's not everything. My wife had to have a C-section last month. Without insurance, it cost me a bundle."
- "I work just as hard as everyone else, so why shouldn't I have the same benefits? I'm getting up there in years. It'd be nice to have a little bit set aside."

In reading these comments, Sally begins to think she cannot win. Maybe the most current employee attitude survey will help (see Exhibit 2); at least, it is worth a try. All she knows is that if she does not come up with a strategy for reducing turnover soon, DP will not have enough trained workers to meet its canning quotas, and the employee bonuses will be lost forever.

Discussion Questions

1. What does the employee attitude survey reveal that is helpful in understanding the turnover problem at DP?
2. What should be Sally's bottom-line response to resolve the current crisis? Are more benefits and services the answer?
3. Describe the relationships between employee status (years in the company) and satisfaction with items 1–7 (Exhibit 2).

■ Exhibit 1
Reasons for Turnover among Employees

	Higher Pay	Better Benefits	Supervision	Moving	Better Job	Job Security	Fired
Permanent Employees							
<1 year	40	22	1	2	3	1	2
1-2 years	10	0	3	3	2	4	1
>2 years	1	0	5	4	4	2	0
Temporary Employees							
<6 months	10	45	4	3	10	17	3
6-12 months	12	23	1	0	2	32	2
>1 year	5	15	2	3	15	19	0

Note: An employee could list more than one reason for quitting.

■ Exhibit 2
Results of the Employee Attitude Survey

	Permanent			Temporary
	<1 year	1-2 years	>2 years	
Satisfaction with:				
1. Pay level	2.1	2.3	2.4	3.4
2. Pay system	1.5	2.4	3.2	3.3
3. Benefits	1.0	3.2	4.1	1.1
4. Supervision	3.4	4.1	3.7	3.3
5. Job	2.4	2.7	3.1	2.3
6. Co-workers	3.3	4.0	4.7	2.3
7. Work environment	3.4	4.1	3.6	2.7

Key: 1 = very dissatisfied, 5 = very satisfied.

Occupational Safety and Health: Reducing the Incidence of Deaths, Injuries, and Diseases

In my opinion, the area that requires the greatest attention is this issue of health and safety.

BENNETT R. COHEN, Chairman of the Board and CEO
Ben and Jerry's Homemade Incorporated[1]

Health and safety get a great deal of attention, yet injuries remain stubbornly high. Any manufacturing company runs the risk, if not certainty, of injury to workers, and Ben and Jerry's of Vermont is primarily a manufacturing company. The type of manufacturing done at the company's three plants offers ample opportunity to hurt a back or to drop a heavy object on a foot or toe. Ben and Jerry's managers have instituted fairly rigorous training methods to prevent these kinds of accidents. But in some areas of the operation, particularly in the Springfield plant, jobs involve motions that are repeated all day long, day in and day out, which can lead to other types of injuries. This is especially true with regard to the manufacture of novelty lines such as Peace Pops and Brownie Bars.

Repetitive motion injuries were first recognized more than two hundred years ago. In modern parlance, these are called cumulative trauma disorders. They result from motions that, although innocent in themselves, are chronically repeated, usually in an awkward or forceful manner, resulting in musculoskeletal disease, pain, or injury. You do not have to work in a factory to get them. Office workers are at risk, and so too are tennis players and runners. But at Ben and Jerry's, work on the manufacturing line is the primary cause.

Injuries of this sort are the most common workplace injuries, and during the working years, between ages eighteen and sixty-four, they are the most common reason for lost work time. Ben and Jerry's has experienced a very high number of workers' compensation claims for these injuries. In 1991, the company paid out 116 percent of workers' compensation premiums on claims, compared with Vermont's average of 17 percent. In 1992, the company's payout percentage soared to 150 percent. In Ben and Jerry's Waterbury plant, injuries rose from 38 to 43 from 1991 to 1992; on the other hand, lost days due to accidents fell significantly from 274 to 148. In Springfield, where the novelty items are made, injuries more than doubled, from 14 to 32, in the same one-year period; lost days due to injuries or accidents rose similarly, from 628 in 1991 to 1,564 in 1992. The figures for the two plants together show that from 1991 to 1992, injuries increased over 44 percent and lost days due to accidents or injuries increased over 88 percent—far greater increases than recorded for sales and production. If each injury had occurred to a separate worker, over 15 percent of the workforce would have experienced some type of injury between 1991 and 1992 (in fact, some workers experienced more than one injury in the year, meaning a smaller percentage of the workforce was actually affected).

One reason Ben and Jerry's may have higher numbers than other companies is, ironically, because people want to be employed there—so much so that workers repeatedly do not report injuries in the early stages for fear of loss of employment. Employees do not fear termination from their job, but some have reported the concern that if they left the company because of disabilities, they might never again get a job that paid as well. Where people have been reluctant to report medical problems, injuries worsened, resulting in longer lost time and greater medical bills.

Another reason for the higher accident figures more recently is that Ben and Jerry's is emphasizing and encouraging early reporting of injuries so as to prevent more serious, chronic injuries later on. Employees who do suffer injuries are the beneficiaries of a generous short-term disability insurance program.

The company also discovered, to its chagrin, that posting consecutive workdays where no one was injured resulted not in greater incentives toward safety, but in an atmosphere where injuries were covered up so as not to break the record. The company has discontinued such emphasis and is now embarking on education, training, and meetings to encourage early reporting of potential injuries. Furthermore, the company has hired a number of consultants who specialize in ergonomics to visit all the plants' operations and revise tools, posture, seating, and activities so as to prevent repetitive motion injuries.[2]

The feature "Managing Human Resources for the 21st Century at Ben and Jerry's Homemade" illustrates some crucial issues about occupational safety and health. One is the increased emphasis firms are putting on safety programs. Another is the benefits associated with workplace safety: a safe work environment keeps employees healthy and productive, and it reduces the workers' compensation costs that firms pay to the state in which they do business. A third issue is the importance of making line managers reponsible for safety through policies, goals, performance appraisal, and compensation. A final issue is the central role of the HR managers. Although not directly involved in the organization's operations themselves, they can still do much to make conditions safer and healthier. (See "Partnership in Safety and Health.)

This chapter introduces these and other issues of occupational safety and health. It first discusses the purposes and importance of occupational safety and health, and then briefly examines the role of the federal government in establishing and enforcing safety standards. Next, it describes the two categories of workplace hazards: (1) the accidents and diseases that produce physiological and physical conditions and (2) the stress and low quality of working life that result when psychological conditions are not optimal. Then, it looks at strategies to improve employee safety and health, including such measures as improved record keeping, job redesign and ergonomics, and educational programs.[3]

OCCUPATIONAL SAFETY AND HEALTH

Occupational safety and health refers to the physiological-physical and psychological conditions of a workforce that result from the work environment provided by the organization. If an organization takes effective safety and health measures, fewer of its employees will have short- or long-term ill effects as a result of being employed at that organization.

Physiological-physical conditions include occupational diseases and accidents such as actual loss of life or limb, repetitive motion injuries, back pain, carpal tunnel syndrome, cardiovascular diseases, various forms of cancer such as lung cancer and leukemia, emphysema, and arthritis. Other conditions that are known to result from an unhealthy work environment include white lung disease, brown lung disease, black lung disease, sterility, central nervous system damage, and chronic bronchitis.

Psychological conditions result from organizational stress and a low quality of working life. These encompass dissatisfaction, apathy, withdrawal, projection, tunnel vision, forgetfulness, inner confusion about roles and duties, mistrust of others, vacillation in decision making, inattentiveness, irritability, procrastination, and a tendency to become distraught over trifles.

PURPOSES AND IMPORTANCE OF OCCUPATIONAL SAFETY AND HEALTH

Some observers feel that U.S. companies do not pay enough attention to safety and health issues:

> We've reached an accommodation with blue-collar death. Forget that a U.S. worker is five times more likely to die than a Swede. . . . Forget that a U.S. worker is three times more likely to die than a Japanese.

Partnership in Safety and Health

Line Managers	Human Resource	Employees
Make safety and health a major objective of the firm.	Work with other professionals such as medical doctors and industrial engineers to develop new programs.	Participate in the development and administration of safety and health programs.
Support the HR professionals' efforts to train all employees in safety and health.	Create HR programs that train employees for safe and healthy behaviors and reward them for their success.	Perform in accordance with established safety and health guidelines.
Allow for employees to have more participation in decision making	Design and deliver stress management programs	Accurately report work-related illnesses and injuries

The sad reality is that blue-collar blood pours too easily. [Occupational Safety and Health Administration] fines amount to mere traffic tickets for those who run our companies. The small fines are simply buried in the cost of production. Blood can be cash accounted, given a number, and factored with other costs.... This has tremendous implications for the union-management relationship, not to mention costs from poor worker morale, lower productivity, and mounting litigation.[4]

Blue-collar workers are not the only ones to suffer from workplace hazards. White-collar workers, including managers, also do so: " 'Stress is the most pervasive and potent toxin in the workplace,' says Leon J. Warshaw, executive director of the New York Business Group on Health, a coalition of businesses concerned about health care. In California, mental stress claims are the most rapidly increasing type of workers' compensation cases, having risen 700 percent in the [1980s]. And a poll [in 1990] found that 25 percent of the employees surveyed at New Jersey businesses suffered from stress-induced ailments."[5] Although the traditional ill effects on the white-collar workforce have been psychological, concern is now growing over physical conditions relating to the unforeseen effects of the computer terminal (e.g., eyestrain, miscarriages, and cumulative trauma disorder) and closed office buildings, where chemical components from sources such as carpeting and structural materials build up and are circulated through the ventilation system.

The Benefits of a Safe and Healthy Work Environment

If organizations can reduce the rates and severity of their occupational accidents, diseases, and stress-related illnesses, and improve the quality of work life for their employees, they can only become more effective. Such an improvement can result in (1) more productivity owing to fewer lost workdays, (2) increased efficiency and quality from a more committed workforce, (3) reduced medical and insurance costs, (4) lower workers' compensation rates and direct payments because of fewer claims being filed, (5) greater flexibility and adaptability in the workforce as a result of increased participation and an increased sense of ownership, and (6) better selection ratios because of the enhanced image of the organization. Companies can thus increase their profits substantially.[6]

Construction is one industry trying to improve its safety and health record:

> The new push for safety, the experts say, is being led by large companies forced by the recession to try to save money and become more competitive by taking advantage of revised insurance industry policies that reward good safety records.
>
> "When companies understand that safety saves them money and increases productivity, they become believers," says Mr. Steven Thies, corporate safety manager for Henkels & McCoy, a 5,000-worker utility construction company based in Blue Bell, Pennsylvania.[7]

The Costs of an Unsafe and Unhealthy Work Environment

The number of workdays lost to injuries increased dramatically from the mid-1980s to the mid-1990s. Statistically, for every 100 full-time workers, the number of days lost to injury went from fewer than 60 in 1983 to almost 100 in 1994.[8] "Back injuries are the most prevalent of all workplace injuries. Every year an estimated 10 million employees in the United States encounter back pain that impairs their job performance. Approximately 1 million employees file workers' compensation claims for back injuries. Billions of dollars are spent each year to treat back pain—$5 billion in workers' compensation payments alone."[9]

Estimates of workplace deaths range from twenty-eight hundred (Bureau of Labor Statistics) to around ten thousand yearly (National Safety Council). In either case, the numbers are significant. Nevertheless,

> Business contends that its health and safety record is much better than generally perceived and has improved over the years. Workplace-related deaths dropped from 18 per 100,000 employees in 1970 to 9 per 100,000 in 1990, according to government records.
>
> When the fact that homicide is the leading cause of workplace deaths, and nearly one-third of all occupational fatalities are the result of car and truck crashes is accounted for, the safety record gets even better.[10]

Of course, these rates differ depending on job type, and sometimes even on the state. For example, the accident rate for 100,000 workers in the United States is 7, but for workers in Alaska's fishing industry, it is nearly 700;[11] in 1992 alone, forty-four Alaskan fishing boats made one-way trips. Another dangerous industry is construction, which places "workers in a constantly changing raw environment where one misstep or forgetful moment can snuff out a life or crush a limb. Pressures to finish a job quickly often push foremen and workers to take risks, industry experts say, amid a macho culture of muscle, sweat, and swagger that tends to belittle safety measures and confuse caution with timidity."[12] Construction, mining, and agriculture are typically the three most dangerous industries nationwide, with yearly deaths for every 100,000 employees being around 32, 43, and 40, respectively.

The costs of workplace deaths and injuries are estimated to be more than $50 billion. Similar costs are estimated for the more than 100,000 workers who annually succumb to occupational diseases. Enormous costs are also associated with psychological conditions. For example, alcoholism, often the result of attempts to cope with job pressures, costs organizations and society over $65 billion annually. Of this, $20 billion is attributed to lost productivity and the remainder to the direct costs of insurance, hospitalization, and other medical items.[13] Perhaps more difficult to quantify, but just as symptomatic of stress and a poor quality of working life, are workers' feelings of lack of meaning and involvement in their work and loss of importance as individuals.

✷ LEGAL CONSIDERATIONS

The legal framework for occupational safety and health can be divided into four major categories: the Occupational Safety and Health Administration, workers' compensation programs, the common-law doctrine of torts, and local initiatives.

Occupational Safety and Health Administration

The federal government's primary response to the issue of safety and health in the workplace has been the Occupational Safety and Health Act of 1970, which created the Occupational Safety and Health Administration and which calls for safety and health inspections of organizations regardless of size, reporting by employers, and investigations of accidents and allegations of hazards. OSHA is responsible for establishing and enforcing occupational safety and health standards and for inspecting and issuing citations to organizations that violate these standards. Two other organizations support the role of OSHA: the National Institute for Occupational Safety and Health (NIOSH) and the Occupational Safety and Health Review Commission (OSHRC). The commission reviews appeals made by organizations that received citations from OSHA inspectors for alleged safety and health violations.[14]

Regardless of whether organizations are inspected, they are required to keep safety and health records so that OSHA can compile accurate statistics on work injuries and illnesses. These records should cover all disabling, serious, or significant injuries and illnesses, whether or not they involve loss of time from work. Excluded are minor injuries that require only first aid and do not involve medical treatment, loss of consciousness, restriction of work or motion, or transfer to another job. Falsification of records or failure to keep adequate records can result in substantial fines. However, the record-keeping requirement was recently qualified:

> An employer may withhold injury and illness records from federal safety investigators if it has a legitimate need to keep the records private, and the Occupational Safety and Health Administration has failed to obtain a warrant granting it access to such documents, the Occupational Safety and Health Review Commission (OSHRC) rules. Rejecting the principle that OSHA compliance officers have unlimited rights to make warrantless examinations of an employer's records, the commission holds that the employer had a reasonable expectation of privacy in safeguarding the information in its injury records. Such documents, OSHRC points out, may contain proprietary information on operations and manufacturing processes that employers may want to keep confidential (*Kings Island Division of Taft Broadcasting Co.,* 1987).[15]

The Access to Employee Exposure and Medical Records Regulation of 1980 requires organizers to show or give employees, their designated representatives, and OSHA the employees' on-the-job medical records. This regulation also requires employers to provide access to records of measurements of employee exposure to toxic substances.

Communication Is Key. The employee's right to know was also strengthened by the Hazard Communication Standard, which went into effect in 1986.[16] Under this standard, employers are required to provide workers with information and training on hazardous chemicals in their work area, at the time of their initial assignment and whenever a new hazard is introduced. According to OSHA, effective communication is the real key and should include information for employees on the following:

⊙ The standard's requirements, and workplace operations that use hazardous chemicals
⊙ Proper procedures for determining the presence of chemicals and detecting hazardous releases

- Protective measures and equipment that should be used
- The location of written hazard communication programs[17]

Workers' Compensation Programs

Whereas OSHA was established to provide protection against accidents and diseases for workers on the job, workers' compensation was established to provide financial aid for those unable to work because of accidents and diseases.[18] For many years, workers' compensation awards were granted only to workers unable to work because of physical injury or damage. Since 1955, however, court decisions have either caused or enticed numerous states to allow workers' compensation payment in job-related cases of anxiety, depression, and mental disorders.[19]

In 1955, the Texas Supreme Court charted this new direction in workers' compensation claims by stating that an employee who became terrified, highly anxious, and unable to work because of a job-related accident had a compensable claim even though he had no physical injury (*Bailey v. American General Insurance Company,* 1955). In another court ruling, *James v. State Accident Insurance Fund* (1980), an Oregon court ruled in favor of a worker's claim for compensation for inability to work due to job stress resulting from conflicting work assignments.[20]

Common-Law Doctrine of Torts

Much of the legal discussion on human resource management is based on statutory law, that is, the body of laws passed by legislatures at the federal and state levels. For example, the Civil Rights Act of 1991, the Americans with Disabilities Act of 1990, and the Occupational Safety and Health Act of 1970 are statutory laws. But the common-law doctrine of torts also plays a role. This body of law consists of court decisions regarding wrongful acts such as personal injuries that were committed by an employee on another employee or even customer and resulted in a lawsuit against the employer.

Employees and customers can obtain damage awards if they demonstrate that the employers engaged in reckless or intentional infliction designed to degrade or humiliate. Few such cases have been successful, in part because workers' compensation programs were designed to remove workplace accidents and injuries from litigation.[21] The cases that have been successfully brought against employers are notable because of the costs involved. For example:

> After a customer in a car rental office argued with the rental agent, the employee struck him with a blow to the head, knocking him to the floor. As the customer lay on the floor, the employee repeatedly kicked him and pummeled him with "judo chops." In the customer's civil action for negligent retention, the evidence showed that the employee had a history of blowing up at and threatening customers. Moreover, the rental company had not disciplined the employee either before or after the incident. A jury awarded the customer $350,000 in compensatory damages and $400,000 in punitive damages (*Greenfield v. Spectrum Inv. Group,* 1985).[22]

Local Initiatives

State, municipal, and city governments may pass their own safety and health laws and regulations that go beyond the coverage of OSHA. Consequently, employers need to be aware of local regulations. Sometimes, these local initiatives offer a glimpse as to what other area governments or even the federal government might do in the future.

Americans with Disabilities Act

Employee layoffs and discharges (terminations) constitute 50 percent of all claims filed under the ADA, and 15 percent of these are for back pain. Victims are entitled to sue for up to $300,000, and many employers are tempted to settle before going to trial in hopes of reaching smaller settlements.[23] Thus, the ADA gives organizations another reason to seek ways to remove hazardous conditions from the work environment.

HAZARDS IN OCCUPATIONAL SAFETY AND HEALTH

As Exhibit 15.1 shows, both physical and sociopsychological aspects of the workplace environment affect occupational safety and health. Traditionally, hazards in the physical environment have received greater attention. Increasingly, however, both OSHA and companies themselves admit that sociopsychological conditions greatly affect health and safety, and they are doing something about it. For example, "at Hoffman-LaRoche, Inc., the Nutley, New Jersey-based subsidiary of the Swiss pharmaceutical concern, employees receive after-hours instruction in a variety of stress management methods. They include meditation, breathing exercises, and a technique called 'dot stopping.' A form of biofeedback, the technique teaches employees to control their stress by recalling a wonderful moment and focusing on the feelings and sensations they had then."[24] Today, efforts to improve occupational safety and health are not complete without a strategy for reducing psychological work-related stress.

Occupational Accidents

Certain organizations, and certain departments within organizations, tend to have higher occupational accident rates than others. Several characteristics can explain this difference.

Organizational Qualities. Accident rates vary substantially by industry. For example, firms in the construction and manufacturing industries have higher incidence rates than do firms in services, finance, insurance, and real estate. But some high-risk firms are taking steps to beat the odds. According to Donald Brush, vice president and general manager at the Barden Corporation, Danbury, Connecticut:

■ *Exhibit 15.1*
Model of Occupational Safety and Health in Organizations

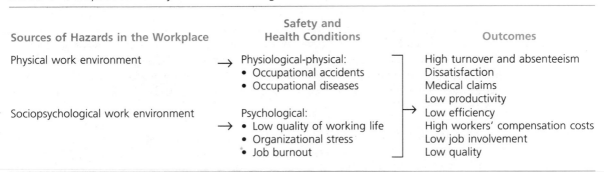

Sources of Hazards in the Workplace	Safety and Health Conditions	Outcomes
Physical work environment	Physiological-physical: • Occupational accidents • Occupational diseases	High turnover and absenteeism Dissatisfaction Medical claims Low productivity
Sociopsychological work environment	Psychological: • Low quality of working life • Organizational stress • Job burnout	Low efficiency High workers' compensation costs Low job involvement Low quality

Over the years, Barden employees assumed that, because we are [a] metal working shop, people were just going to get hurt. Several years ago, we created a Safety and Health Committee that meets monthly to consider our safety and health performance and to effect improvements. More recently, we created a Safety Development Committee whose members included a line superintendent as chairman, the safety engineer, the plant chemist, the occupational health nurse, and the training coordinator—a nice mix of line, staff, and human resource representation. This committee reports to the Safety and Health Committee. Its objective is to develop programs that strengthen safety awareness and performance. While it is too early to prepare a report card, early indications are that results will be favorably impressive. At about the same time, it became clear that the safety engineer was not producing the same results we wanted. After weighing the facts, we created something new and promising. We eliminated the safety engineering position as such and transferred its accountabilities to the Medical Department. The occupational health nurse had previously shown considerable knowledge about safety matters, and her aggressive investigation of accidents and near-misses prompted us to create a new position encompassing both the safety and the medical functions. The occupational health nurse has thus been promoted to a new position entitled Manager of Employee Health and Safety. We believe that this position is unique for a small company, and we are optimistic about results.[25]

Small and large organizations (those with fewer than a hundred employees and those with more than a thousand) have lower incidence rates than medium-sized organizations. This may be because supervisors in small organizations are better able to detect safety hazards and prevent accidents than those in medium-sized ones. And larger organizations have more resources to hire staff specialists who can devote all their efforts to safety and accident prevention.

In general, however, the working conditions (e.g., outdoors versus indoors), and the tools and technology available to do the job (e.g., heavy machinery versus personal computers) most affect occupational accidents. Next in line are the workers themselves.

The Unsafe Employee. Some experts point to the employee as the pivotal cause of accidents. Accidents depend on the behavior of the person, the degree of hazard in the work environment, and pure chance. The degree to which a person contributes to an accident can be an indication of the individual's proneness to accidents. No stable set of personal characteristics *always* contributes to accidents. Nevertheless, certain psychological and physical characteristics seem to make some people *more susceptible* to accidents. For example, employees who are emotionally "high" have fewer accidents than those who are emotionally "low," and employees who have fewer accidents are more optimistic, trusting, and concerned for others than those who have more accidents. Employees under greater stress are likely to have more accidents than those under less stress. Older workers are likely to be hurt less than younger workers. People who are quicker at recognizing visual patterns than at making muscular manipulations are less likely to have accidents than those who are just the opposite.

Many psychological conditions probably related to accident-proneness—for instance, hostility and emotional immaturity—may be temporary states. Thus, they are difficult to detect until at least one accident has occurred. Because these characteristics are not related to accidents in all work environments and because they are not always present in employees, selecting and screening job applicants on the basis of accident-proneness is difficult.

The Violent Employee. Workplace violence is growing rapidly, and employers are being held responsible. Homicide is the biggest cause of death in the workplace today.[26] Although it may be difficult to identify the violent employee before the fact, employers

Positioning for the 21st Century:
THE VIOLENT EMPLOYEE—WARNING SIGNS

If any of the following warning signs are present, employers should consult resource specialists to determine whether monitoring is sufficient or whether immediate action is warranted. Possible resources include a company physician, an employee assistance provider, law enforcement officials, an attorney, or a violence-assessment specialist.

- *Verbal Threats:* Individuals often talk about what they may do. An employee might say, "Bad things are going to happen to so-and-so," or "That propane tank in the back could blow up easily."
- *Physical Actions:* Troubled employees may try to intimidate others, gain access to places they

do not belong, or flash a concealed weapon in the workplace to test reactions.
- *Frustration:* Most cases of workplace violence do not involve a panicked individual who perceives the world as falling apart. A more likely scenario involves an employee who has a frustrated sense of entitlement to a promotion, for example.
- *Obsession:* An employee may hold a grudge against a coworker or supervisor, which, in some cases can stem from a romantic interest.[27]

are urged to be on the lookout for some common signs. These are described in the feature "Positioning for the 21st Century: The Violent Employee—Warning Signs."

Occupational Diseases

Potential sources of work-related diseases are as distressingly varied as the symptoms of those diseases. Several federal agencies have systematically studied the workplace environment, and they have identified the following disease-causing hazards: arsenic, asbestos, benzene, bichloromethylether, coal dust, coke-oven emissions, cotton dust, lead, radiation, and vinyl chloride. Workers likely to be exposed to those hazards include chemical and oil refinery workers, miners, textile workers, steelworkers, lead smelters, medical technicians, painters, shoemakers, and plastics industry workers. Continued research will no doubt uncover additional hazards that firms will want to diagnose and remedy for the future well-being of their workforces.[28]

Categories of Occupational Diseases. In the long term, environmental hazards in the workplace have been linked to thyroid, liver, lung, brain, and kidney cancer; white, brown, and black lung disease; leukemia; bronchitis; emphysema; lymphoma; aplastic anemia; central nervous system damage; and reproductive disorders (e.g., sterility, genetic damage, miscarriages, and birth defects). Chronic bronchitis and emphysema are among the fastest-growing diseases in the United States, doubling every five years since World War II; they account for the second highest number of disabilities under Social Security.[29] Cancer tends to receive the most attention, however, since it is a leading cause of death in the United States (second after heart disease). Many of the known causes of cancer are physical and chemical agents in the environment. And because these agents are theoretically more controllable than human behavior, OSHA's emphasis is on eliminating them from the workplace.

OSHA is also concerned with the following categories of occupational diseases and illnesses: occupation-related skin diseases and disorders, dust diseases of the lungs, respiratory conditions due to toxic agents, poisoning (the systematic effect of toxic materials), disorders due to physical agents, disorders associated with repeated trauma, and all other occupational illnesses.[30] OSHA, therefore, requires employers to keep records on all these diseases.

Occupational Groups at Risk. Miners, construction and transportation workers, and blue-collar and low-level supervisory personnel in manufacturing industries experience the majority of both occupational diseases and occupational injuries. The least safe occupations are mining, agriculture, and construction. In addition, large numbers of petrochemical and oil refinery workers, dye workers, dye users, textile workers, plastics industry workers, painters, and industrial chemical workers are also particularly susceptible to some of the most dangerous health hazards. Skin diseases are the most common of all reported occupational diseases, with leather workers being the group most affected.

Nevertheless, occupational diseases are not exclusive to blue-collar workers and manufacturing industries. The "cushy office job" has evolved into a veritable nightmare of physical and psychological ills for white-collar workers in the expanding service industries. Among the common ailments are varicose veins, bad backs, deteriorating eyesight, migraine headaches, hypertension, coronary heart disorders, and respiratory and digestive problems. The causes of these include the following:

- Too much noise
- Interior air pollutants such as cigarette smoke and chemical fumes—for example, from the copy machine
- Uncomfortable chairs
- Poor office design
- Office technology such as video display terminals[31]

In addition, dentists are routinely exposed to radiation, mercury, and anesthetics, and cosmetologists suffer from high rates of cancer and respiratory and cardiac diseases connected with their frequent use of chemicals.

A Low Quality of Working Life

For many workers, a low quality of working life is associated with workplace conditions that fail to satisfy important preferences and interests such as a sense of responsibility, desire for empowerment and job involvement, challenge, meaningfulness, self-control, recognition, achievement, fairness or justice, security, and certainty.[32] Organizational structures that contribute to a low quality of working life include

- Jobs with low levels of task significance, variety, identity, autonomy, and feedback (see Chapter 5)
- Minimal involvement of employees in decision making and a great deal of one-way communication with employees
- Pay systems not based on performance, or based on performance that is not objectively measured or under employee control
- Supervisors, job descriptions, and organizational policies that fail to convey to the employee what is expected and what is rewarded
- Human resource policies and practices that are discriminatory and of low validity
- Temporary employment conditions, where employees are dismissed at will (employee rights do not exist)
- Corporate cultures that are not supportive of employee empowerment and job involvement

Although these conditions tend to create feelings of poor work life quality, low quality of working life for one individual may not do so for another individual, because of differences in preferences, interests, and perceptions of uncertainty in the environment.

Organizational Stress

Prevalent forms of organizational stress include "the four Ss," organizational change, work pacing, the physical environment, stress-prone employees, and job burnout.

The Four Ss. Common stressors for many employees include the supervisor, salary, security, and safety.[33] Petty work rules and relentless pressure for more production are major stressors that employees associate with *supervisors*. Both deny worker needs to control the work situation and to be recognized and accepted.

Salary is a stressor when it is perceived as being distributed unfairly. Many blue-collar workers feel they are underpaid relative to their white-collar counterparts. Teachers may think they are underpaid relative to people with similar education who work in private industry.

Employees experience stress when they are not sure whether they will have their jobs next month, next week, or even tomorrow. For many employees, lack of job *security* is even more stressful than lack of safety—at least, with an unsafe job, they know the risks, whereas with an unsecure job, they are in a continued state of uncertainty.[34]

Nevertheless, fear of workplace accidents and their resulting injuries or deaths can also be stressful for many workers. When pressure for production is increased, the fear regarding workplace *safety* can rise to the point where production decreases rather than increases. This result, in turn, may lead to a vicious cycle that is counterproductive for the workers and the organization.

Organizational Change. Changes made by organizations usually involve something important and are accompanied by uncertainty. Many changes are made without official warning. Although rumors often circulate that a change is coming, the exact nature of the change is left to speculation. People become concerned about whether the change will affect them, perhaps by displacing them or by causing them to be transferred. The result is that many employees suffer stress symptoms.[35]

Work Pacing. *Work pacing* may be controlled by machines or people. *Machine pacing* gives control over the speed of the operation and of the work output to something other than the individual. *Employee pacing* gives that control to the individual. The effects of machine pacing are severe, because the individual is unable to satisfy a crucial need for control of the situation. It has been reported that workers on machine-paced jobs feel exhausted at the end of their shifts and are unable to relax soon after work because of increased adrenaline secretion on the job. In a study of twenty-three white- and blue-collar occupations, assembly workers reported the highest level of severe stress symptoms.[36]

Physical Environment. Although office automation is a way to improve productivity, it has stress-related drawbacks. One aspect of office automation with a specific stress-related characteristic is the video display terminal (VDT); Sweden and Norway have taken the most measures to deal with these devices. Other aspects of the work environment associated with stress are crowding, lack of privacy, and lack of control—for example, the inability to move a desk or chairs or even to hang pictures in a work area in an effort to personalize it.[37]

Stress-Prone Employees. Yes, people differ in the ways they respond to organizational stressors. A classic difference is referred to as Type A versus Type B behavior. Type A people like to do things their way and are willing to exert a lot of effort to ensure that even trivial tasks are performed in the manner they prefer. They often fail to distinguish between important and unimportant situations. They are upset, for instance, when they have to wait fifteen minutes to be seated in a restaurant, since this is not in compliance with their idea of responsive service. In short, Type A people spend much of their time directing energy toward noncompliances in the environment. Still, Type A people are "movers and shakers." They enjoy acting on their environment and modifying the behavior of other people. They are primarily rewarded by compliance and punished by noncompliance.

Type B people are generally much more tolerant. They are not easily frustrated or easily angered, nor do they expend a lot of energy in response to noncompliance. Type B people may be excellent supervisors to work for—that is, until you need them to push upward in the organization on your behalf. They probably will permit their subordinates a lot of freedom but also might not provide the types of upward support necessary for effective leadership.[38]

Job Burnout

What is job burnout? Job burnout is a particular type of stress that seems to be experienced by people who work in jobs in human services, such as health care, education, police work, ministry, and so on. This type of reaction to one's work includes attitudinal and emotional reactions that a person goes through as a result of job-related experiences. Often the first sign of burnout is a feeling of being *emotionally exhausted* from one's work. When asked to describe how she feels, an emotionally exhausted employee might say she feels drained or used-up, that she is at the end of her rope and is physically fatigued. Waking up in the morning may be accompanied by a feeling of dread at the thought of having to put in another day on the job. For someone who was once enthusiastic about her job and idealistic about what she could accomplish, feelings of emotional exhaustion may come somewhat unexpectedly, though to an outsider looking at the situation, emotional exhaustion would be seen as a natural response to an extended period of intense interaction with people and their problems.

Extreme emotional exhaustion can be very debilitating both on and off the job, so people who are experiencing it must find some way to cope. One common coping reaction is to put psychological distance between one's self and one's clients and to decrease one's personal involvement with them. In moderation, this reaction may be an effective method for creating "detached concern," but when engaged in to excess, the employee may begin to dehumanize or depersonalize the clients. People who have reached the extreme end of the *depersonalization* continuum report feeling they have become calloused by their jobs and that they have grown cynical about their clients.

In addition to emotional exhaustion and depersonalization, a third aspect of burnout is a feeling of *low personal accomplishment.* Many human service professionals begin their careers with great expectations that they will be able to improve the human condition through their work. After a year or two on the job, they begin to realize they are not living up to these expectations. There are many systemic reasons for the gap that exists between the novice's goals and the veteran's accomplishments, including unrealistically high expectations due to a lack of exposure to the job during training, constraints placed on the worker through the rules and regulations of an immutable bureaucracy, inadequate resources for performing one's job, clients who are frequently uncooperative and occasionally rebellious, and a lack of feedback about one's successes. These and other characteristics of human service organizations almost guarantee that employees will be frustrated in their attempts to reach their goals, yet the workers may not recognize the role of the system in producing this frustration. Instead the worker may feel personally responsible and begin to think of himself or herself as a failure. When combined with emotional exhaustion, feelings of low personal accomplishment may reduce motivation to a point where performance is in fact impaired, leading to further experienced failure.

The Consequence of Burnout.   Burned out staff members may *perform more poorly* on the job compared to their counterparts who are still "fired up." Consider as an example the job of an intake interviewer in a legal aid office. For the organization, the intake interview serves as a screening device through which all potential clients must pass. During the interview, specific information about the nature and details of a case must be assessed and an evaluation of the "appropriateness" of the case for the office must be made. Since as many as 40 intake interviews may be conducted per day, it is important that the interviewer work as efficiently as possible. Here the major index of efficiency is the number of forms accurately filled out for further processing. To the extent time is spent talking about problems not relevant for these forms, efficiency decreases.

Now consider the client's perspective. Upon arriving for an interview, the client is likely to be fuming inside as she rehearses in her mind the injustices done her and the retaliations she hopes for. She does not think in terms of the precise statutes encompassing her problem nor of the essential details that make her case worthy of attention. Rather, she is concerned with the problems now being faced by her family. Her primary concern is that her emotional and physical life return to normal—the law seems to offer a solution. For her, the intake interview may be the first chance to explain the problems she is facing. From her perspective, good job performance is displayed by an interviewer who lends a sympathetic ear.

How will the interviewer handle this situation? Typically, the person doing the interview will be a relatively recent graduate of law school with little or no clinical experience to rely on. Socialization has emphasized the supremacy of objectivity. But clearly, adoption of an objective, analytic attitude combined with the pressure to efficiently fill out forms does not add up to the sympathetic ear the client is looking for. The objective interviewer appears unconcerned and the client becomes frustrated. The emotionally involved client becomes an obstacle to detached efficiency, frustrating the interviewer. Whether or not open hostility erupts, both participants are aware of the antagonistic relationship they have formed.

Another unfortunate consequence of burnout is a deterioration of one's *relationships with coworkers*. A study of mental health workers found that people who were experiencing calloused feelings toward their clients also complained more about their clients to their co-workers, thereby generating a negative atmosphere within the work unit. These burned out mental health workers were also absent from work more often and took more frequent work breaks.

Just as burnout leads to behaviors that have a negative impact on the quality of one's work life, it leads to behaviors that cause a deterioration of the quality of one's *home life*. In a study of police families, burnout was assessed in 142 married, male police officers. Their wives were then asked to describe how these officers behaved at home. Emotionally exhausted officers were described as coming home tense, anxious, upset and angry, and as complaining about the problems they faced at work. These officers were also more withdrawn while at home, preferring to be left alone rather than share time with the family. The wives' reports also revealed that officers who had developed negative attitudes toward the people they dealt with also had fewer close friends.

Finally, burnout may eventually lead to *health-related problems.* In the study of police families described above, burnout victims were more likely to suffer from insomnia, use medications of various kinds, and use alcohol as a way of coping.[39]

STRATEGIES FOR IMPROVEMENT

Once the cause of a work hazard is identified, strategies can be developed for eliminating or reducing it (see Exhibit 15.2). To determine whether a strategy is effective, organizations can compare the incidence, severity, and frequency of illnesses and accidents before and after the intervention. OSHA has approved methods for establishing these rates.

Monitoring Safety and Health Rates

OSHA requires organizations to maintain records of the incidence of injuries and illnesses. Some organizations also record the severity and frequency of each.[40]

Incidence Rate. The most explicit index of industrial safety is the incidence rate, which reflects the number of injuries and illnesses in a year. It is calculated by the following formula:

Incidence Rate = (Number of Injuries and Illnesses × 200,000) ÷ (Number of Employee Hours Worked)

The base for 100 full-time workers is 200,000 (40 hours a week times 50 weeks). Suppose an organization had 10 recorded injuries and illnesses and 500 employees. To calculate

■ *Exhibit 15.2*
Sources and Strategies for Improving Occupational Safety and Health

SOURCE	STRATEGEY
Physical Work Environment	
Occupational accidents	Record the accident
	Redesign the work environment
	Set goals and objectives
	Establish safety committees
	Provide training and financial incentives
Occupational diseases	Record the disease
	Measure the work environment
	Communicate information
	Set goals and objectives
Sociopsychological Work Environment	
Stress and Burnout	Establish organizational stress programs
	Increase employees' participation in decision making
	Establish individual stress programs
	Ensure adequate staffing
	Provide adequate leave and vacation benefits
	Encourage employees to adopt healthy lifestyles

the number of employee hours worked, multiply the number of employees by 40 hours and by 50 weeks: $500 \times 40 \times 50 = 1,000,000$. The incidence rate thus is 2 for every 100 workers a year: $(10 \times 200,000) \div (1,000,000) = 2$.

Frequency Rate. The frequency rate reflects the number of injuries and illnesses for every million hours worked, rather than in a year as with the incidence rate. It is calculated thus:

Frequency Rate = (Number of Injuries and Illnesses $\times$ 1,000,000 hours) $\div$ (Number of Employee Hours Worked)

Severity Rate. The severity rate reflects the hours actually lost owing to injury or illness. It recognizes that not all injuries and illnesses are equal. Four categories of injuries and illnesses have been established: deaths, permanent total disabilities, permanent partial disabilities, and temporary total disabilities. An organization with the same number of injuries and illnesses as another but with more deaths would have a higher severity rate. The severity rate is calculated by this formula:

Severity Rate = (Total Hours Charged $\times$ 1,000,000 Hours) $\div$ (Number of Employee Hours Worked)

Controlling Accidents

Designing the work environment to make accidents unlikely is perhaps the best way to prevent accidents and increase safety. Among the safety features that can be designed into the physical environment are guards on machines, handrails in stairways, safety goggles and helmets, warning lights, self-correcting mechanisms, and automatic shutoffs. The extent to which these features will actually reduce accidents depends on employee acceptance and use. For example, eye injuries will be reduced by the availability of safety goggles only if employees wear the goggles correctly.[41] This is more likely when employees accept the responsibility for safety, as is the trend in some firms:

> At Du Pont employees understand that they bear the major responsibility for their own safety. This is even more important today, as Du Pont completes a decade of restructuring for future growth and globalization. The company has reduced its organizational levels—which means less supervision and a more participatory approach to management. With fewer supervisors and managers, there is a greater need for self-management and teamwork. Therefore, the onus is on the individual to assume more responsibility and work in a team to accomplish common objectives—including excellent safety performance.[42]

Ergonomics. Another way to improve safety is to make the job itself more comfortable and less fatiguing, through ergonomics. Ergonomics considers changes in the job environment in conjunction with the physical and physiological capabilities and limitations of the employees.[43] (See Chapter 5 for a discussion of ergonomics.)

In an effort to reduce the number of back injuries, the Ford Motor Company and Eaton Corporation are redesigning workstations and tasks that may be causing musculoskeletal problems for workers. For instance, lifting devices are being introduced on the assembly line to reduce back strain, and walking and working surfaces are being studied to see if floor mats can reduce body fatigue. Videotapes that feature Ford employees performing their jobs both before and after ergonomic redesign are used in training.[44]

In an effort to reduce back injuries, Federal Express has instituted a three-pronged prevention program stressing education, exercise, and the use of back belts, for thousands of package handlers:

The first component of the program raises overall awareness about back injuries through safety training, tips in employee newsletters, and weekly group meetings to discuss safe lifting techniques. The second component prepares workers physically through a pre-shift stretching routine designed to limber muscles. This 10-minute exercise is mandatory for all workers whose jobs involve lifting. The third component—the use of flexible back supports by all package handlers at the company—not only helps physically, but also serves as a constant reminder for employees to lift safely.[45]

Safety Committees. Another strategy for accident prevention is the use of safety committees. The HR department can serve as the coordinator of a committee composed of several employee representatives. Where unions exist, the committee should have union representation as well. Often, organizations have several safety committees at the department level, for implementation and administration, and one larger committee at the organization level, for policy formulation.

Behavior Modification. Reinforcing behaviors that reduce the likelihood of accidents can be highly successful. Reinforcers can range from nonmonetary rewards (such as positive feedback) to activity rewards (such as time off) to material rewards (such as company-purchased doughnuts during a coffee break) to financial rewards (such as bonuses for attaining desired levels of safety).

The behavioral approach relies on measuring performance before and after the intervention, specifying and communicating the desired performance to employees, monitoring performance at unannounced intervals several times a week, and reinforcing desired behavior several times a week with performance feedback.

In two food processing plants, behavior was monitored for twenty-five weeks—before, during, and after a safety training program. Slides were used to illustrate safe and unsafe behaviors. Employees were also given data on the percentage of safe behaviors in their departments. A goal of 90 percent safe behaviors was established. Supervisors were trained to give positive reinforcement when they observed safe behavior. Following the intervention, the incidence of safe behavior increased substantially—from an average of 70 percent to more than 95 percent in the wrapping department and from 78 percent to more than 95 percent in the makeup department. One year after the program, the frequency rate of lost-time injuries was fewer than 10, a substantial decline from the preceding year's rate of 53.8.[46]

Reducing the Incidence of Diseases

Occupational diseases are far more costly and harmful overall to organizations and employees than are occupational accidents. Because the causal relationship between the physical environment and occupational diseases is often subtle, developing strategies to reduce their incidence is generally difficult.

Record Keeping. At a minimum, OSHA requires that organizations measure the chemicals in the work environment and keep records on these measurements. The records must also include precise information about ailments and exposures. Such information must be kept for as long as the incubation period of the specific disease—even as long as forty years. If the organization is sold, the new owner must assume responsibility for storing the old records and continuing to gather the required data. If the company goes out of business, the administrative director of OSHA must be told where the records are.[47] Guidelines for record keeping are given in Exhibit 15.3.

■ *Exhibit 15.3*
OSHA Guidelines for Recording Cases

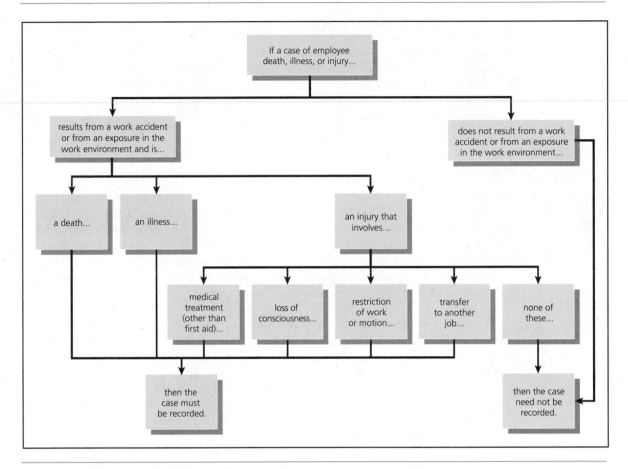

Monitoring Exposure. The obvious approach to controlling occupational illnesses is to rid the workplace of chemical agents or toxins; an alternative approach is to monitor and limit exposure to hazardous substances. For example, the nuclear industry recruits hundreds of "jumpers," who fix the aging innards of the United States' nuclear generating stations. The atmosphere of these components is so radioactive that jumpers can stay in only about ten minutes before they "burn out." Their exposure has to be closely monitored to ensure that it does not exceed five thousand millirems (the equivalent of roughly 250 chest X rays) annually.

Unfortunately, jumpers get rewarded for absorbing the maximum rather than a safe limit of radiation on any given job. Rather than twelve hours of pay for their ten minutes of work, they get a bonus of several hundred dollars each time they burn out. Even with monitoring, it is estimated that three to eight of every ten thousand jumpers eventually will die as a result of radiation exposure.[48]

Some organizations now monitor genetic changes due to exposure to carcinogens—for example, benzene, arsenic, ether, and vinyl chloride. Samples of blood are obtained from employees at fixed intervals to determine whether the employees' chromosomes have been damaged. If damage has occurred, the affected employee is placed in a different job and, where feasible, conditions are modified.

Genetic Screening. Genetic screening is the most extreme, and consequently the most controversial, approach to controlling occupational disease. As noted in Chapter 8, the genetic makeup of individuals may predispose them more or less to specific occupational diseases. By using genetic testing to screen out individuals who are susceptible to certain ailments, organizations lower their vulnerability to workers' compensation claims and problems. Opponents of genetic screening contend that it measures predisposition to disease, not the actual presence of disease, and therefore violates an individual's rights.[49]

Controlling Stress and Burnout

Increasingly, organizations are offering training programs designed to help employees deal with work-related stress. For example, J. P. Morgan offers stress management programs as part of a larger supervisory and management development curriculum. Available to supervisors, professional staff, and officers, these courses are designed to introduce supervisory and management material, information skills, and role definition. The emphasis is on providing concrete information to reduce the ambiguity associated with fast-paced, changing work roles.[50]

Increasing Participation in Decision Making. The importance of being able to control, or at least predict future outcomes is well-recognized. Having opportunities to be self-determining, combined with the freedom and the ability to influence events in one's surroundings, can be intrinsically motivating and highly rewarding. When opportunities for control are absent and people feel trapped in an environment that is neither controllable nor predictable, both psychological and physical health are likely to suffer.

In most organizations, employees are controlled by organizational rules, policies, and procedures. Often these rules and procedures are creations from an earlier era of the organization and are no longer as effective as they once were. Nevertheless, their enforcement continues until new rules are developed. Most often, the new rules are created by people in the highest levels of the organization and then imposed upon people at the lower levels. Sometimes the new rules are an improvement over the old rules, other times they are not. Regardless of whether they are an improvement, the new rules or procedures are likely to be experienced as another event in the organization over which the employees had no control.

Increasing employees' participation in the decision making process and thus *increasing the amount of control* they have can be an effective way to prevent some forms of stress burnout from occuring. For example, a study of hospital nurses found that feelings of emotional exhaustion were linked to feelings of lack of control. Nurses often feel unable to exercise control, either over the behavior of the physicians with whom they are closely interdependent, or over the decisions of the administrators who determine the hours and conditions of their work. Emotional exhaustion was higher for nurses who were less able to influence policies and decisions and for those who had more bureaucratic hassles. Emotional exhaustion was also higher for nurses who had fewer opportunities to be creative in carrying out their work.

Besides giving workers a feeling of control, participation in decision making gives them the power they need to remove obstacles to effective performance, thereby reducing frustration and strain. One effective use of influence would be to persuade others to change their conflicting role expectations for one's own behavior. Through the repeated interchanges required by participative decision making, members of the organization can also gain a better understanding of the demands and constraints faced by others. When the conflicts workers face become clear, perhaps for the first time, negotiation is likely to begin over which expectations should be changed in order to reduce inherent conflicts. Another important consequence of the increased communication that occurs when an organization uses participative decision making is people become less isolated from their coworkers and supervisors. Through their discussions, employees learn about the formal and informal expectations held by others. They also learn about the formal and informal policies and procedures of the organization. This information can help reduce feelings of role ambiguity. It also makes it easier for the person to perform his or her job effectively.

Finally, participation in decision making helps prevent stress and burnout by encouraging the development of a *social support network* among coworkers. Social support networks help people cope effectively with the stresses they experience on the job.

Other potential remedies for workplace stress are described in the feature "Positioning for the 21st Century: Solutions to Workplace Stress." The selection of the most appropriate activity should be based on a thorough analysis of existing safety and health hazards. It should also depend on an assessment of past activities in the organization and of strategies used by other organizations.

Individual Stress Management Strategies. Time management can be an effective individual strategy to deal with organizational stress. It is based in large part on an initial identification of an individual's personal goals. Other strategies that should be part of individual stress management include following a good diet, getting regular exercise, monitoring physical health, and building social support groups. Many large organizations such as Xerox and Coors encourage employees to enroll in regular exercise programs, where their fitness and health are carefully monitored.

Developing Occupational Health Policies

As scientific knowledge accumulates and liabilities rise, more and more organizations are developing policy statements regarding occupational hazards. These statements grow out of a concern that organizations should be proactive in dealing with health and safety problems. For example, Dow Chemical's policy states, "No employee, male or female, will knowingly be exposed to hazardous levels of materials known to cause cancer or genetic mutations in humans."[51]

An example of the growing complexity of the problems associated with workplace hazards is the debate over whether women of childbearing age should be allowed to hold jobs in settings that could endanger fetuses. Johnson Controls Incorporated of Milwaukee, Wisconsin, which makes lead automobile batteries for such customers as Sears and the Goodyear Tire and Rubber Company, responded to this issue by restricting women's access to jobs in its Bennington, Vermont plant. Johnson's management claimed that the factory's air contained traces of lead and lead oxide. Although presumably not high enough to harm adults, the toxin levels were dangerous for children and fetuses. Thus, women were allowed to work in the plant, but only if they were unable to bear children (either because of surgery to prevent pregnancies or because they were too old to have children). According to the company, "The issue was protecting the health of unborn children."

Women's advocates and union leaders argued that the firm was guilty of sex discrimination. Specifically, they claimed that lead levels were too high for men as well; that the firm was deciding for women rather than allowing women to decide for

Positioning for the 21st Century:
SOLUTIONS TO WORKPLACE STRESS

After surveying 1,299 employees, Northwestern National Life Insurance Company researchers suggested the following steps to reduce tension and stress in the workplace:

- *Allow employees to talk freely with each other.* Employees thrive in an atmosphere where they can consult with colleagues about work issues. Moreover, in organizations where employees talk freely with each other, productivity and problem solving are usually enhanced.
- *Reduce personal conflicts on the job.* Employers can reduce stress by training managers and employees on how to resolve conflicts through open communication, negotiation, and respect. Managers can minimize conflicts by treating employees fairly and by clearly defining job expectations.
- *Give employees adequate control over how they do their work.* Employees take greater pride in their work, are more productive, and are better able to deal with stress if they have some control over how they perform their work. Managers who let employees make decisions create an atmosphere that reduces stress and increases job satisfaction.
- *Ensure adequate staffing and expense budgets.* Staff reductions and budget cuts usually increase stress in the long run. Overburdened employees frequently suffer high stress levels, which cause lower productivity, illness, turnover, and accidents.

- *Talk openly with employees.* Open communication between management and employees reduces job stress and helps employees cope with the challenges of the workplace.
- *Support employees' efforts.* When employers show their support of employees' contributions to the organization, stress levels are significantly lower. Managers can show support by regularly asking employees how their work is going, listening to them, and addressing issues that are raised.
- *Provide competitive personal leave and vacation benefits.* Workers who have time to relax and recharge after working hard are less likely to develop stress-related illnesses.
- *Maintain current levels of employee benefits.* Workers' stress levels increase when their benefits are reduced. Employers should determine whether the savings from reduced benefits are worth the risk of employee burnout.
- *Reduce the amount of red tape for employees.* When employees must deal with too much bureaucracy, they become discouraged and demoralized. Employers should ensure that employees' time is not wasted on unnecessary procedures.
- *Recognize and reward employees for their accomplishments and contributions.* A pat on the back, public praise, or a bonus or raise can result in significant increases in employee morale and productivity.[52]

themselves whether to take the risk; that such rules invade women's privacy; and, finally, that the restrictions denied women access to high-paying jobs (a typical factory job in Bennington paid $6.35 an hour, versus $15.00 an hour in the Milwaukee plant).[53]

The situation was made more complex by the reluctance of many workers to leave their jobs to avoid occupational exposure unless they were guaranteed that their income would not suffer. Some workers went so far as to have themselves sterilized to protect their jobs. When the Supreme Court heard this case, it ruled in favor of the workers, thus striking down the company's fetal protection policy (*United Auto Workers v. Johnson Controls, 1991*).

The policies of AT&T and Digital Equipment illustrate alternative strategies. These provide for income protection for pregnant production workers who might be exposed to the toxic gases and liquids used to etch microscopic circuits onto silicon wafers. Other companies are obtaining voluntary consent agreements from employees who choose to stay on hazardous jobs. Although these statements can absolve employers from punitive damages in civil court, they do not alleviate liability under workers' compensation laws and civil disability suits.

Establishing Wellness Programs

Corporations are increasingly focusing on keeping employees healthy rather than helping them get well.[54] They are investing in wellness programs at record rates, and such programs appear to be paying off. A four-year study of fifteen thousand Control Data employees showed that employees who participated in only limited exercise spent 114 percent more on health insurance claims than did coworkers who exercised more. Smokers and obese workers also had higher medical claims. Control Data, which has had its Stay Well program in place since the early 1980s, now markets its program to other organizations such as Philip Morris and the National Basketball Association.[55]

 ## ETHICS IN SHAPING BEHAVIOR

Employers have known for a long time that a small percentage of their workforce is responsible for the majority of their health insurance claims. Originally, they tried to encourage their employees to be healthy by offering to subsidize health club memberships and building exercise facilities and jogging trails, but the results were disappointing. Now, many companies are implementing incentive-based health care programs.

Although no one can deny that health care costs in the United States are spiraling, some question just how far companies should be allowed to go in "encouraging" their employees to shape up. How much should employers be allowed to know about what their employees do in their spare time? Could company policies and practices become so financially attractive that employees would do things they would not otherwise have done?

The potential for creating situations involving ethical or unethical behavior needs to be watched closely. It is too early to tell just how this situation will unfold. Doubtless, employers and employees are concerned about costs and health; perhaps, creative solutions will save the day.[56]

 ## SUMMARY

Employees' health is likely to become increasingly important into the 21st century. Employers are becoming more aware of the cost of ill health and the benefits of having a healthy workforce. The federal government, through OSHA, is also making it more necessary for employers to be concerned with employee health. The government's current concern is primarily with occupational accidents and diseases, both aspects of the physical environment. However, organizations can choose to become involved in programs dealing with the sociopsychological environment as well. If organizations choose not to become involved with improving the sociopsychological environment, the government may prescribe mandatory regulations. Thus, it pays for organizations to be concerned with both aspects of the work environment. Effective programs for both environments can significantly improve both employee health and the effectiveness of the organization.

When the adoption of improvement programs is being considered, employee involvement is not only a good idea but also likely to be desired by employees. Many things can be done to improve both the physical and sociopsychological work environments. Each is different and has its own unique components. Although some improvement strategies may work well for one component, they may not work for other components. A careful diagnosis is required before programs are selected and implemented.

Assuming that a careful diagnosis indicates the need for a stress management program, the challenge is selecting one from the many available. Programs such as time management or physical exercise could be set up so that employees can help themselves cope, or the organization could alter the conditions that are associated with stress. The latter approach requires a diagnosis of what is happening, where, and to whom before a decision is made on how to proceed. Because so many possible sources of stress exist, and because not all people react the same way to them, implementing individual stress management strategies may be more efficient. However, if many people are suffering similar stress symptoms in a specific part of the organization, an organizational strategy is more appropriate.

For many aspects of safety and health, either pertinent information does not exist (as is the case, e.g., with knowledge of causes and effect) or organizations are unwilling to gather or provide it. From a legal as well as a humane viewpoint, it is in the best interests of organizations to seek and provide more information so that more effective strategies for improving safety and health can be developed and implemented. Failure to do so may result in costly legal settlements against organizations or further governmental regulation of workplace safety and health.

 Discussion Questions

1. In what ways are safety and health important issues at Ben and Jerry's?
2. How can strategies to improve the physical work environment and the sociopsychological work environment be assessed?
3. The United States prides itself on freedom, democracy, and free labor markets. Thus, employees should be made responsible for health and safety. In other words, employers who offer riskier employment should simply pay workers more for bearing the risk (a wage premium), and the workers can in turn buy more insurance coverage to cover this risk. Discuss the advantages and disadvantages of this approach.
4. Who is responsible for workplace safety and health? the employer? the employee? the federal government? judges and juries? Explain.

5. How are physical hazards distinct from sociopsychological hazards? What implications do these differences have for programs to deal with these two categories of hazards?
6. Is there such a thing as an unsafe worker? Assuming that accident-prone workers exist, how can effective human resource activities address this problem?
7. Is accident-proneness a reliable trait? If not, does that mean organizations cannot control it? Explain.
8. What incentives does OSHA provide the employer for promoting workplace safety? Explain.
9. How might a company's strategy to prevent occupational accidents differ from a program to prevent occupational disease? In what ways might the programs be similar?
10. Should all employers institute wellness programs for their employees?

 In-Class Projects

1. Answer the following for Lincoln Electric:
   a. How important are safety and health issues at Lincoln Electric? Explain.
   b. What are the most likely types of safety and health issues at Lincoln Electric?
   c. What safety and health programs should be in place at Lincoln Electric? Who should be responsible for them?

2. Answer the following for AAL:
   a. How important are safety and health issues at AAL? Explain.
   b. What are the most likely types of safety and health issues at AAL?
   c. What safety and health programs should be in place at AAL? Who should be responsible for them?

Note: For both of these projects, use your "best guesses" based on what concerns you think effective firms are likely to have.

 Field Project

Visit several local companies and talk to them about safety and health. Specifically, ask them to describe their accident rates over the past few years and what they have been doing to reduce them. Then discuss the same with them about worker illnesses and diseases. Determine the reasons for the changes, e.g., compliance with Americans with Disabilities Act, reduce workers' compensation rates and claims, reduce health insurance costs, etc. Discuss their plans and strategies for the future.

Case Study:

A WEB OF DANGER

Appliance Park is located in Henderson, a small city in western Kentucky next to the Ohio River. It is aptly named for the company, Appliance House, that created several hundred steady manufacturing jobs for its community. Appliance House manufactures washing machines, dryers, and dishwashers at its Appliance Park location. As the major employer in Henderson, it provides jobs for between six hundred and eleven hundred hourly workers, depending on the state of the economy and the housing market. Although new housing starts have slowed considerably in the past two years owing to unusually high interest rates, employment at Appliance Park has stabilized and is expected to rise as production picks up and housing starts increase.

Two weeks ago, a tragedy at Appliance Park was felt throughout the community. On May 2, 1992, Joe Kitner fell to his death at the east plant, where washing machines are assembled. Joe, twenty-four years old, was a local football star in high school and had worked at Appliance Park full-time since his graduation from Henderson Central High School. An investigation of the accident was conducted by representatives of the corporate safety staff and by Teamster local officials who represented the nonexempt workers at Appliance Park.

Although not widely reported, a curious set of circumstances contributed to Joe's death. The assembly line at the washing machine division occupies two stories within a large prefab building on the east side of the park. A rope net or mesh is suspended about thirty feet above the ground-level floor, to catch accessories and parts that drop from an upper conveyor system where some of the assembly of the washing machines is conducted. Periodically, when model changeovers are scheduled on the line, a crew is assigned to switch the setup of the various machines throughout the assembly line. One of Joe's jobs on that crew was to climb out on the net and retrieve the parts that had dropped from the previous production run. The net, although tightly strung, had a hole on one side where a bracket that had fallen previously cut part of the mesh. Even though it was the changeover crew's responsibility to inspect and repair the net, they often overlooked minor rips because of the production time lost in making repairs.

An autopsy revealed that Joe died of a brain hemorrhage suffered when he fell from the net to the concrete floor below. The autopsy also revealed that Joe had a small but malignant brain tumor located near the part of

the brain that controls the central nervous system. Whether the tumor was far enough along to affect his judgment or motor abilities was not stated by the medical examiner, but the autopsy also indicated that Joe had consumed alcohol a few hours before his death, probably at lunch. However, his blood alcohol level was not high enough to have been ruled intoxication using the state driving-while-intoxicated (DWI) standard.

The changeover crew experienced some difficulty replacing Joe. Because the plant was unionized, his job was open to bid, but no one asked for it. Under these circumstances, the company appointed the assembler with the least seniority, to do Joe's job. It selected Luther Duncan.

Although the changeover job comprises several duties, Luther knew that inevitably he would be asked to climb out on the net. He had been on the job for only eight days when his foreman ordered the assembly line shut down for a model changeover for the next production run. At first, Luther decided not to think about what he eventually would have to do, but when his time came to scale the utility ladder to the rope net, Luther balked. No amount of encouragement, cajoling, or threatening would change Luther's mind; he simply was not going up that ladder with Joe's death fresh in his mind.

Stan Fryer, the Teamster steward, pulled Luther aside and pleaded with him to obey his foreman's order to complete the job. Stan even promised to file a grievance concerning the rip on the one side of the net, which still had not been repaired. Luther adamantly refused to proceed. Despite Stan's intervention, Luther's foreman suspended him for the remainder of the day and told him to report, along with Stan, immediately the next morning to the plant superintendent's office. Upon reporting to the superintendent's office, Luther was told he had been dismissed for insubordination. ◉

SOURCE: S. A. Youngblood, Professor of Strategic Human Resource Management, Texas Christian University.

Discussion Questions

1. Was Luther justified in refusing to work?
2. Was the company responsible for the death of Joe?
3. Should Joe also have refused to perform his job, knowing that the net had a tear on one side?
4. Is the changeover job a dangerous job that just has to exist, or should it be eliminated?

Unionization and Collective Bargaining: Representing the Employees

In some cases, [the union] was absolutely right. The protests refocused everyone to the sense of urgency to get the quality problems fixed.

RICHARD G. ("SKIP") LEFAUVE, President
Saturn[1]

Managing Human Resources for the 21st Century at Saturn

In autumn 1991, when Chairman Robert Stempel of General Motors visited the GM Saturn plant in Spring Hill, Tennessee, the workers, wearing black-and-orange armbands, launched a work slowdown. Another strike to get higher wages? No, a protest against the higher production quotas GM was trying to impose on the plant. Although high quality and high quantity can go hand in hand when everything is working right, they cannot be expected to in the early stages of operation. Still in the early stages of their new operation at the Saturn plant, the workers were more concerned about quality—about the car and the customer's satisfaction with it—than they were with quantity of output. They believed that quality was more critical than quantity for the long-term success of the company.

Quality takes commitment, dedication, and training—and the United Automobile Workers (UAW) has never been known for being concerned about either it or quantity. Why were the union workers at the Saturn plant behaving contrary to the traditional stereotype of the union member in the auto industry? Because management was behaving contrary to its stereotype. Management was giving workers more say in the production of the automobile, treating workers as co-owners and as members of teams. Any employee who did not want to fit into this new labor-management relationship could collect a generous severance package—$15,000 to $50,000, depending on length of service.

Reflecting on their original agreement, Stempel and the GM management heard the concerns of the workers at the plant and gave them the benefit of any doubt. These managers knew that Saturn was the test case for whether GM could build cars to compete directly with the top-selling Japanese cars, many of which are also made in the United States, some by UAW members and some by nonmembers.[2]

The events described in the feature "Managing Human Resources for the 21st Century at Saturn" highlight several aspects of unionization and collective bargaining. One is that members of the United Automobile Workers union may indeed be more concerned about quality than any other union members. Another is that the degree of cooperation between the UAW and GM has been high at the Saturn plant, as well as at GM's Buick City plants in Flint, Michigan, NUMMI joint venture in Fremont, California, and plants in the Cadillac Division, winner of the prestigious Malcolm Baldrige Award for quality in 1990.[3]

Another aspect of these events at Saturn is that union-management cooperation can result in benefits to both workers and the company, such as improved quality, lower absenteeism, increased satisfaction, more employment security and training, and increased profitability. It also results in a partnership as described in the feature "Partnership in Unionization." A final aspect is that union-management relationships are dynamic and changing all the time to reflect the changing conditions of the world. For example, new pressures by early 1993 had caused severe strains on Saturn's cooperative spirit. Those pressures included:

- Recent hires who were often less committed to Saturn's employee-participation ideals
- Burnout from fifty-hour-and-up workweeks
- Growing distrust of the union's close ties with Saturn's management
- Anger at lack of elections for key union posts on the shop floor
- A scaling back of training for new workers[4]

As these conditions continue to change into the 21st century, the union-management relationships at Saturn will likely also change. The same is to be expected all around the

Partnership in Unionization

Line Managers	Human Resource Professionals	Employees	Unions
Know and appreciate the historical context of union-management relations.	Train line managers in the legal considerations protecting the unionization rights of employees.	Present views about working conditions to HR professionals and line managers.	Seek to represent employees' views to the company.
Understand why employees are likely to join a union.	Develop HR policies and programs that make for good working conditions.	Desire to have a voice in and influence on workplace conditions, wages, and working hours.	Offer to improve wages and working conditions for members.
Support the efforts of HR professionals in making policies and programs for good working conditions.	Continually survey employees' attitudes so that management knows employees' views and opinions.		Offer to work with management to improve company profitability and ensure company survival.
Manage employees with respect and equality.			
Know what can and cannot be said to employees regarding unionization, during an organizing campaign.			

United States. Changes are likely to occur both in unionization efforts and in the bargaining relationships between existing unions and managements. For example, the UAW is extending its efforts to unionize nonteaching employees in universities. Changes are also occurring within unions as they consider offering alternative forms of membership such as an associate status.[5]

To put into perspective these aspects of union-management relationships, this chapter describes the process of forming a union (unionization) and the characteristics of administering an agreement reached between the union and management (collective bargaining).

UNIONIZATION AND COLLECTIVE BARGAINING

Unionization is the effort by employees and outside agencies (unions or associations) to act as a single unit when dealing with management over issues relating to their work. When recognized by the National Labor Relations Board, a union has the legal authority to negotiate with the employer on behalf of employees—to improve wages, hours, and conditions of employment—and to administer the ensuing agreement.[6]

The core of union-management relations is *collective bargaining*. Collective bargaining generally includes two types of interaction. The first is the negotiation of work conditions that, when written up as the collective agreement (the contract), becomes the basis for employee-employer relationships on the job. The second includes activities related to interpreting and enforcing the collective agreement (contract administration) and resolving any conflicts arising from it.[7]

 ## PURPOSES AND IMPORTANCE OF UNIONIZATION

For employers, the existence of a union—or even the possibility of one—can significantly influence their ability to manage their vital human resources. For employees, unions can help them get what they want—for example, high wages and job security—from their employers. For management, unionization may result in less flexibility in hiring new workers, making job assignments, and introducing new work methods such as automation; a loss of control; inefficient work practices; and an inflexible job structure.

Unions obtain rights for their members that employees without unions do not legally have. This, of course, forces unionized companies to consider their employees' reactions to many more decisions. Nevertheless, in some cases, employers who are nonunion and want to remain that way give more consideration and benefits to their employees. Consequently, it may or may not be more expensive for a company to operate with unionized rather than nonunionized employees.

Unions assist employers through wage concessions or cooperation in joint workplace efforts, such as teamwork programs or Scanlon Plans, allowing employers to survive particularly difficult times and, in fact, remain profitable and competitive. This has been particularly true in the automobile, steel, and airline industries. Unions can also help identify workplace hazards and improve the quality of work life for employees. These ideas and the components of unionization are illustrated in Exhibit 16.1.

 ## LEGAL CONSIDERATIONS

Historical Context

The federal government entered the labor scene in an attempt to stabilize a violent and disruptive labor situation existing in the United States in the 1920s and the 1930s. Court actions and efforts by employers before then had generally suppressed the rights of workers to act collectively to protect their interests.[8] The courts instead protected the "fundamental values of society" by declaring that workers' attempts to band together to increase wages—that is, to form unions—were conspiracies condemned by law (*Commonwealth v. Pullis, Philadelphia Cordwainers, Pennsylvania*, 1806). Thus, the *conspiracy doctrine* was created and given substantial weight in the 1800s. Later, this outright condemnation was modified to include the necessity of applying a "means" test before condemning a union as an illegal conspiracy (*Commonwealth v. Hunt*, 1842). Nevertheless, the courts also used the means test to hamper efforts at unionization.

By the 1880s, the conspiracy doctrine was reinforced by civil instead of criminal law, particularly civil *injunctions*. Injunctions maintain the status quo until disputed legal issues can be resolved. Thus, if workers attempt to join together and strike to attain higher wages, the courts can grant an injunction forcing them to return to work until the legality of the strike is decided. The injunction can be granted quickly, to provide an equitable remedy, without a jury trial and other time-consuming legal proceedings. The effect of injunctions on unionization was particularly evident when the U.S. Supreme Court ruled that they could be used to enforce *yellow-dog contracts*, that is, contracts signed by employees agreeing not to join a union (*Hitchman Coal and Coke v. Mitchell*, 1917).

■ *Exhibit 16.1*
Components of Unionization

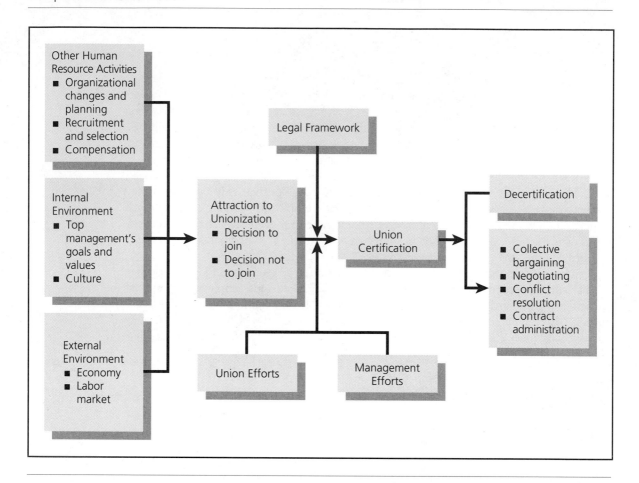

Further protection for the fundamental values of society was provided by the Sherman Antitrust Act, which was passed by Congress in 1890 to limit the ability of organizations (e.g., unions) to engage in acts (e.g., union mergers) that lessened competition. This act, as applied to unions, was upheld by the U.S. Supreme Court in *Loewe v. Lawlor* (1908) (the Danbury Hatters case). The application of the Sherman Antitrust Act to unions was reinforced by the Clayton Antitrust Act of 1914 and subsequent court decisions (*Duplex Printing Company v. Deering*, 1921; *United Mine Workers of America v. Coronado Coal Company*, 1922).

Railway Labor Act

Although the supposed protection of society from unionization was largely maintained throughout the 1920s, early legislation in the railway industry—because of the industry's effect on the public welfare—suggested that it was not sacrosanct. In fact, union activities derived support from the Arbitration Act of 1888; the Erdman Act of 1898, which outlawed yellow-dog contracts in the railway industry; and *Adair v. United States*

(1921), which upheld the unconstitutionality of yellow-dog contracts. These events culminated in the Railway Labor Act of 1926, which brought about the demise of the fundamental-values-of-society doctrine for all industries. This act was passed by Congress in 1926 to prevent labor unrest in the railway industry from having serious economic consequences.[9]

The act specified that employers and employees would maintain an agreement over pay, rules, working conditions, dispute settlement, representation, and grievance settlement. A board of mediation—later called the National Mediation Board—was created to help settle disputes by encouraging, as necessary, negotiation, then arbitration, and finally emergency intervention by the president. A second board—the National Railway Adjustment Board—was created in 1934 to deal with grievances. This board has exclusive jurisdiction over questions relating to grievances or the interpretation of agreements concerning pay, rules, or working conditions; it makes decisions and awards binding on both parties.

National Labor Relations Act

The success of the Railway Labor Act led Congress to enact a comprehensive labor code, called the National Labor Relations Act. Passed in 1935, this act was to restore equality in collective bargaining. Employer refusal to recognize unions, it was claimed, had resulted in poor working conditions, depression of wages, and a general depression of business.

The act affirmed employees' rights to form, join, or assist labor organizations to bargain collectively, and to choose their own bargaining representative through majority rule. As stated in Section 8 of the act, the following were regarded as unfair labor practices on the part of the employers:

- Interference with the efforts of employees to organize
- Domination of the labor organization by the employer
- Discrimination in the hiring or tenure of employees in order to discourage union affiliation
- Discrimination for filing charges or giving testimony under the act
- Refusal to bargain collectively with a representative of the employees

Court interpretation of these unfair labor practices has made it clear that bribing, spying, blacklisting union sympathizers, moving a business to avoid union activities, and other such employer actions are illegal.

The National Labor Relations Board was established to administer this act. Its major function is to decide all unfair labor practice suits.

Labor-Management Relations Act

Employer groups criticized the Wagner Act, as the National Labor Relations Act was also called, on several grounds. They argued that in addition to being biased in favor of unions, it limited employers' constitutional right of free speech, did not consider unfair labor practices on the part of unions, and caused employers serious damage when jurisdictional disputes arose. Congress responded to these criticisms in 1947 by enacting the Labor-Management Relations Act, often called the Taft-Hartley Act. This act revised and expanded the Wagner Act in order to establish a balance between union and management power and to protect the public interest. It introduced the following changes:

- ◉ Employees were allowed to refrain from union activity as well as to engage in it.
- ◉ The *closed shop* (where employees had to join the union if one existed) was outlawed, and employees were required to agree in writing before union dues could be deducted from their paychecks.
- ◉ Employers were assured of their right to free speech, and they were given the right to file charges against unfair labor practices, such as coercing workers to join the unions, causing employers to discriminate against those who do not join, refusing to bargain in good faith, requiring excessive or discriminatory fees, and engaging in featherbedding (excessive staffing levels) activities.
- ◉ Certification elections (voting for union representation) were forbidden to be held more frequently than once a year.
- ◉ Employees were given the right to initiate decertification elections.

These provisions indicated the philosophy behind the act—as Senator Robert A. Taft put it: Simply to reduce the special privileges granted labor leaders.

Labor-Management Reporting and Disclosure Act

Although the Taft-Hartley Act included some regulation of internal union activities, abuse of power and the corruption of some union officials led to the passage of a "bill of rights" for union members in 1959. The Labor-Management Reporting and Disclosure Act, or Landrum-Griffin Act, provided detailed regulation of internal union affairs. Its provisions include the following:

- ◉ Equality of rights for union members in nominating and voting in elections
- ◉ Controls on increases in dues
- ◉ Controls on the suspension and firing of union members
- ◉ Elections every three years for local offices and every five years for national or international offices
- ◉ Restriction of the use of trusteeships to take control of a member group's autonomy for political reasons
- ◉ Definition of the type of person who can hold union office
- ◉ Filing of yearly reports with the secretary of labor

This act was intended to protect employees from corrupt or discriminatory practices of labor unions. By providing standards for union conduct, it eliminated much of the unions' flagrant abuse of power and protected the democratic rights of employees to some degree.

State and Local Employee Regulations

Employee relations regulations at the state and local levels are varied. Some states have no legislation governing their employees, some have legislation covering municipal employees as well. One widespread regulation is that collective bargaining is permitted in most states, and it covers wages, hours, and other terms and conditions of employment. However, it is these other terms and conditions that have caused the most difficulty in interpretation. Managerial prerogatives are usually quite strong, especially for firefighters, police officers, and teachers. The requirement to bargain over certain issues in the private sector is not so stringent as in public organizations at the state or local level. In addition, some twenty states have passed *right-to-work laws,* which prohibit union membership as a condition of employment.

Although the rights and privileges of public-sector labor organizations are not so extensive as those of private-sector organizations, the greatest growth in unionization in recent years has come in the public sector.[10] Indeed, union representation today is substantially higher in the public sector than in the private sector, approximately 35 percent versus 11 percent.

ATTRACTION OF UNIONIZATION

Unions were originally formed in response to the exploitation and abuse of employees by management. To understand the union movement today, we need to examine why employees decide to join unions and why they decide not to.

Decision to Join a Union

Three separate conditions strongly influence an employee's decision to join a union: dissatisfaction, lack of power, and union instrumentality.[11]

Dissatisfaction. When an individual takes a job, certain conditions of employment (wages, hours, and type of work) are specified in the employment contract. A *psychological contract* also exists between employer and employee, consisting of the employee's unspecified expectation about reasonable working conditions, requirements of the work itself, the level of effort that should be expended on the job, and the nature of the authority the employer should have in directing the employee's work.[12] These expectations are related to the employee's desire to satisfy certain personal preferences in the workplace. The degree to which the organization fulfills these preferences determines the employee's level of satisfaction.

Dissatisfaction with the implicit terms and conditions of the employment will lead employees to attempt to improve the work situation, often through unionization. A major study found a very strong relationship between the level of satisfaction and the proportion of workers voting for a union. Almost all workers who were satisfied voted against the union.[13] Thus, if management wants to make unionization less attractive to employees, it must make work conditions more satisfying.

Lack of Power. Unionization is seldom the first recourse of employees who are dissatisfied with some aspect of their jobs. The first attempt to improve the work situation is usually made by an individual acting alone. Someone who has enough power or influence can effect the necessary changes without collaborating with others. The amount of power the jobholder has in the organization is determined by *exclusivity,* or how difficult it is to replace the person, and *essentiality,* or how important or critical the job is to the overall success of the organization. An exclusive employee with an essential task may be able to force the employer to make a change. If, however, the employee can easily be replaced and the employee's task is not critical, other means, including collective action, must be considered in order to influence the organization.[14]

Union Instrumentality. When employees are dissatisfied with aspects of a work environment—such as pay, promotion opportunity, treatment by supervisor, the job itself, and work rules—they may perceive a union as being able to help improve the situation. If they believe that the union may be able to help, they then weigh the value of the benefits to be obtained through unionization against unionization's costs, such as a lengthy organizing campaign and bad feelings between supervisors, managers, and other employees who do not want a union. Finally, the employees weigh the costs and benefits against the likelihood of a union's being able to obtain the benefits—in other words, they determine union instrumentality.[15] The more that employees believe a union can obtain positive work aspects, the more *instrumental* employees perceive the union to be in removing the causes of dissatisfaction. When the benefits exceed the costs and union instrumentality is high, employees are more likely to be willing to support a union.[16] However, as described in the feature "Using Data for the 21st Century: Where Did You Get That Attitude?" research suggests that employees' willingness to support a union is also affected by general attitudes about unions formed early in life.

❖ THE STATE OF UNIONIZATION

Today, the adversarial nature of the union-management relationship has been replaced to a certain extent by a more cooperative one, as suggested in the feature "Managing Human Resources for the 21st Century at Saturn." This change toward relying on collective bargaining has been dictated in part by current trends in union membership, including the shifting distribution of the membership.

Decline in Membership

Union membership in the United States has declined steadily from its high of 35.5 percent of the workforce in 1945. In the mid-1950s, 35 percent of the workforce was unionized. In 1970, the percentage of unionized workers in the labor force was about 25. In 1995, approximately 15 percent of all workers—11 percent in the private sector and 35 percent in the public sector—were represented by unions, down from 23 percent in 1980 and 16 percent in 1992.[17] These percentage declines resulted in part from an increase in service-sector employment and white-collar jobs—both of which historically have had a low proportion of union members. Other contributing circumstances are a decline in employment in industries that are highly unionized, high levels of unemployment, increased decertification of unions, union leadership, union responsiveness to membership, and management initiatives.[18]

To gain more organizational ability, power, and financial strength, several unions have merged. Although mergers may not automatically increase membership, they can mean more efficiency in union-organizing efforts and an end to costly jurisdictional disputes between unions. Increased organizational strength from mergers may also enable unions to cover industries and occupations previously underrepresented in union membership, such as health care and nursing.

Distribution of Membership

Historically, membership has been concentrated in a small number of large unions. In 1976, 16 unions represented 60 percent of union membership, and 85 unions represented just 2.4 percent. Similarly, the National Education Association accounted for 62 percent of all teaching association members. Many employee associations are small because they are state organizations; therefore, their membership potential is limited.

Unions today are exhibiting a substantial and increasing amount of diversification of membership. The most pronounced diversification has occurred in manufacturing. For

Using Data for the 21st Century:
WHERE DID YOU GET THAT ATTITUDE?

The survival of unions depends, in part, on their ability to attract new members and convince employees to vote in favor of union certification. Consequently, numerous studies have examined why people choose to engage in pro-union behavior. The results consistently show that general positive attitudes about unions predict pro-union behaviors. Furthermore, people's general attitudes about unions are quite stable over long periods of time. Such results have led some researchers to conclude that attitudes about unions are formed early in life during a person's "impressionable years," prior to any specific personal experiences with a particular union or a particular employment situation.

A Canadian research team interested in understanding how family socialization experiences influence attitudes toward unions conducted a study of high school and university students. The study focused on two sources of union attitudes: (a) fundamental work-related philosophies and beliefs, and (b) parents' union involvement and attitudes. Work-related philosophies were assessed by students' responses to questions that assessed Marxist work beliefs and humanist work beliefs. For example, Marxist work beliefs would be held by students who agree with statements such as "The work of the laboring class is exploited by the rich for their own benefit." Humanistic work beliefs would be held by students who agree with statements such as "Work can be organized to allow for human fulfillment." The union involvement of each parent was determined by asking students about how often the parent attended meetings and other union-related activities as well as whether the parent was a union member, had ever gone out on strike, or was a union officer.

Students in this study reported that approximately 30 percent of their mothers and 30 percent of their fathers had been union members at some time. When asked whether they would be willing to join a union someday, about 40 percent of the students said yes. Were students' attitudes a result of family socialization processes? Could students' attitudes be predicted from the attitudes and union involvement of their parents? To answer these questions, the researchers developed a statistical model to reflect the linkages between the union activities and attitudes of parents, on the one hand, and the work-related philosophies and union attitudes of their children, on the other hand. The analysis revealed several connections. Perhaps most important was a path that linked parents' participation in unions to their children's Marxist work beliefs, which in turn predicted the children's general attitudes toward unions and their willingness to join a union someday. The children's attitudes toward unions were also strongly related to parents' attitudes and weakly related to the children's own humanist work beliefs.

The results of this study clearly indicate that employees' attitudes about unions are determined partly by family socialization. This result, in combination with the results of other studies that show that attitudes toward unions are quite stable, suggests that union representatives and employers may have less power to change employees' attitudes than is often assumed. Furthermore, it suggests that as union participation declines in successive generations, the attitudes of the following generations are also likely to become less and less pro-union. Given the current pattern of declining union involvement in the United States, can unions survive in the long run? Should they begin communicating with potential future members while these people are still children? How should union officials react to the results of this study?[19]

example, of the 29 unions that represent workers in chemicals and allied products, 26 have less than 20 percent of their membership in a single industry.[20]

Structure of Unionization in the United States

The basic unit of labor unions in the United States is the national (or international) union, a body that organizes, charters, and controls member locals. National unions develop the general policies and procedures by which locals operate, and help locals in areas such as collective bargaining. National unions provide clout for locals because they control a large number of employees and can influence large organizations through national strikes or slowdown activities.[21]

The major umbrella organization for national unions is the American Federation of Labor and Congress of Industrial Organizations (AFL-CIO). It represents about 85 percent of the total union membership.

Every two years, the AFL-CIO holds a convention to develop policy and amend its constitution. Each national union is represented in proportion to its membership. Between conventions, an executive council (the governing body) and a general board direct the organization's affairs; a president is in charge of day-to-day operations.

The executive council's activities include evaluating legislation that affects labor and watching for corruption within the AFL-CIO. Standing committees are appointed to deal with executive, legislative, political, educational, organizing, and other activities. The department of organization and field services, for instance, focuses its attention on organizing activities. Three structures organize the local unions: many of the craft unions are represented by the trade department and the industrial department, and the remaining locals are organized directly as part of the national unions, being affiliated with AFL-CIO headquarters but retaining independence in dealing with their own matters.

About 60 national unions, representing 4.5 million workers, operate independently of the AFL-CIO. Although this separation is not considered desirable by the AFL-CIO, its effect has been diminished substantially since the Teamsters reaffiliated with the AFL-CIO in 1987. About 14 million workers are members in the AFL-CIO.

At the heart of the labor movement are the seventy thousand or so local unions, varying in size up to forty thousand members. The locals represent the workers at the workplace, where much of the day-to-day contact with management and the human resource department takes place. Most locals elect a president, a secretary-treasurer, and perhaps one or two other officers from the membership. In the larger locals, a *business representative* is hired as a full-time employee to handle grievances and contract negotiation. Locals also have a *steward,* an employee elected by her or his work unit to act as the union representative at the workplace and to respond to company actions against employees that may violate the labor agreement. The steward protects the rights of the worker by filing grievances when the employer has acted improperly.

Operations of Unions

The activities of union locals revolve around collective bargaining and grievance handling. In addition, locals hold general meetings, publish newsletters, and otherwise keep their members informed. Typically, however, the membership is apathetic about union involvement. Unless a serious problem exists, attendance at meetings is usually low, and the election of officers often draws votes from less than one-fourth of the membership.[22]

At headquarters, the AFL-CIO staff and committees work on a wide range of issues, including civil rights, job security, community service, economic policy, union-management cooperation, education, ethical practices, housing, international affairs, legislation, public relations, health care, research, safety, Social Security, and veterans' affairs. A publications department produces various literature for the membership and outsiders. National union headquarters also provides specialized services to regional and local bodies. People trained in organizing, strikes, legal matters, public relations, and negotiations are available to individual unions.

National unions and the AFL-CIO are also active in the political arena. Labor maintains a strong lobbying force in Washington, D.C., and is involved in political action committees at the state and local levels. Recently some large national unions have become active in international politics. For example, the United Auto Workers held discussions with Japanese car manufacturers concerning the level of imports into the United States and the construction of Japanese assembly plants here. They have lobbied in Washington, D.C., to restrict car imports in an attempt to bolster U.S. automakers and to increase jobs. They have also lobbied against NAFTA and for health care reform. Thus, to help their membership, unions are expanding their activities on all levels and, in some cases, working with other organizations to attain mutual goals. Unions are also trying to do a more effective job in their organizing campaigns.

✸ THE ORGANIZING CAMPAIGN

One major function of the National Labor Relations Board is to conduct the process in which a union is chosen to represent employees. This is accomplished through a certification election to determine if the majority of employees want the union. The process by which a single union is selected to represent all employees in a particular unit is crucial to the American system of collective bargaining. If a majority of those voting opt for union representation, all employees are bound by that choice and the employer is obligated to recognize and bargain with the chosen union.[23]

Because unions may acquire significant power, employers may be anxious to keep them out. Adding to this potential union-management conflict is the possibility of competition and conflict between unions if more than one union is attempting to win certification by the same group of employees.

The certification process has several stages, as outlined in Exhibit 16.2.[24]

■ *Exhibit 16.2*
Certification Process

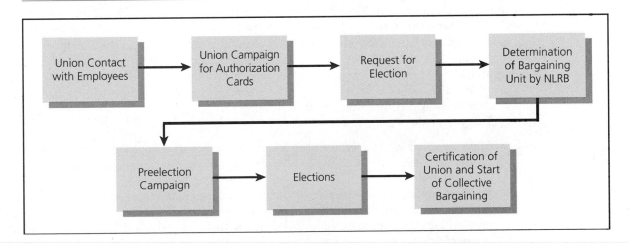

SOURCE: William D. Todor, Professor of Human Resource Management, The Ohio State University.

Campaign to Solicit Employee Support and Request for Election

In the campaign to solicit employee support, unions generally attempt to contact the employees, obtain a sufficient number of authorization cards, and request an election from the NLRB.[25]

Establishing Contact between the Union and Employees. Contact between the union and employees can be initiated by either party. National unions usually contact employees in industries or occupations in which they have an interest or are traditionally involved. The United Auto Workers, for example, has contacted nonunion employees in the new automobile plants that have been built in the South by German and Japanese auto companies.

In other cases, employees may approach the union, and the union is usually happy to oblige. Employees may have strong reasons for desiring this affiliation—low pay, poor working conditions, and other issues relating to dissatisfaction. Because workers generally tend to be apathetic toward unions, however, their concern must become quite serious before they will take action.

At the point that contact occurs between the union and employees, the company must be careful and must avoid committing unfair labor practices. Accordingly, employers should not:

- *Misrepresent the facts:* Any information management provides about a union or its officers must be factual and truthful.
- *Threaten employees:* It is unlawful to threaten employees with losses of their jobs or transfers to less desirable positions, income reductions, or losses or reductions of benefits and privileges. The use of intimidating language to dissuade employees from joining or supporting a union also is forbidden. In addition, supervisors may not blacklist, lay off, discipline, or discharge any employee because of union activity.
- *Promise benefits or rewards:* Supervisors may not promise a pay raise, additional overtime or time off, promotions, or other favorable considerations in exchange for an employee's agreement to refrain from joining a union or signing a union card, to vote against union representation, or to otherwise oppose union activity.

Nor can the union promise benefits or rewards. It would be illegal for the local to bribe workers by offering to waive normal initiation fees for those who signed a card declaring their interest in having union representation prior to the election, or to predict adverse consequences such as the loss of a job for failure to join the union before it was certified (*NLRB v. Savair Manufacturing Company*, 1983). However, free membership can be used as an organizing incentive so long as it extends to everyone who becomes a member up to the time that the first collective agreement is executed. Similarly, it is permissible to reimburse people for lost wages and out-of-pocket expenses incurred while participating in a campaign rally or being at an NLRB hearing. Attendance door prizes also are acceptable, provided their value is not excessive.

Employers also should not:

- *Make unscheduled changes in wages, hours, benefits, or working conditions:* Any such changes are unlawful unless the employer can prove they were initiated before union activity began.
- *Conduct surveillance activities:* Management is forbidden to spy on employees' union activities or to request antiunion workers to do so, or to make any statements that give workers the impression they are being watched. Supervisors also may not attend union meetings or question employees about a union's internal affairs. They also may not ask employees for their opinions of a union or its officers.

◉ *Interrogate workers:* Managers may not require employees to tell them who has signed a union card, voted for union representation, attended a union meeting, or instigated an organization drive.

◉ *Prohibit solicitation:* Employees have the right to solicit members on company property during their nonworking hours, provided this activity does not interfere with work being performed, and to distribute union literature in nonwork areas during their free time.[26]

Employers can:

◉ Discuss the history of unions and make factual statements about strikes, violence, or the loss of jobs at plants that have unionized
◉ Discuss their own experiences with unions
◉ Advise workers about the costs of joining and belonging to unions
◉ Remind employees of the company benefits and wages they receive without having to pay union dues
◉ Explain that union representation will not protect workers against discharge for cause
◉ Point out that the company prefers to deal directly with employees, and not through a third party, in settling complaints about wages, hours, and other employment conditions
◉ Tell workers that, in negotiating with the union, the company is not obligated to sign a contract or accept all the union's demands, especially those that are not in its economic interests
◉ Advise employees that unions often resort to work stoppages to press their demands and that such tactics can cost workers money
◉ Inform employees of the company's legal right to hire replacements for workers who go out on strike for economic reasons[27]

Obtaining Authorization Cards and Requesting the Election. Once contact has been made, the union begins the campaign to collect sufficient *authorization cards,* or signatures of employees interested in having union representation. In the private sector, if the union obtains cards from 30 percent of an organization's employees, it can petition the National Labor Relations Board for an election; procedures in the public sector are similar. If the NLRB determines that sufficient interest exists, it will schedule an election. If the union gets more than 50 percent of the employees to sign authorization cards, it may petition the employer as the bargaining representative. Usually, the employer refuses, whereupon the union petitions the NLRB for an election.

The employer usually resists the union's card-signing campaign. For instance, companies often prohibit solicitation on the premises. Nevertheless, union organizers may earn the right to enter the property and even the building if (1) no other reasonable alternatives for contact exist or (2) the employer regularly permits representatives from other organizations to meet with the workforce on the premises.

Employers are legally constrained from interfering with an employee's freedom of choice. Union representatives have argued that employers ignore this law because the consequences are minimal—and because by interfering, employers can effectively discourage unionism.

During the union campaign and election process, the human resource manager must caution the line managers against engaging in unfair labor practices. These practices, when identified, generally cause the election to be set aside. Outrageous and pervasive violations by the employer can result in certification of the union as the bargaining representative, even if the union has lost the election, if the local can prove that a majority of the employees supported the union prior to the violations. Authorization cards are a common means of establishing this, depending on which type of card was signed. Single-purpose cards indicate that the person is authorizing the union to be his or her representative for collective bargaining outright. Dual-purpose cards express backing for an election and for bargaining. Single-purpose authorization cards have been accepted as evidence of majority status for bargaining orders; dual-purpose cards have not.

Determination of the Bargaining Unit

When the union has gathered sufficient signatures to petition for an election, the NLRB will identify the bargaining unit, the group of employees that will be represented by the union. This process can determine the quality of labor-management relations in the future: At the heart of labor-management relations is the bargaining unit. It is all important that the bargaining unit be truly appropriate and not contain a mix of antagonistic interests or submerge the legitimate interests of a small group of employees in the interest of a larger group.[28]

To ensure the fullest freedom of collective bargaining, legal constraints and guidelines exist for the unit. Professional and nonprofessional groups cannot be included in the same unit, and a craft unit cannot be placed in a larger unit unless both units agree to it. Physical location, skill levels, degree of ownership, collective bargaining history, and extent of organization of employees are also considered.

From the union's perspective, the most desirable bargaining unit is one whose members are pro-union and will help win certification. The unit also must have sufficient influence in the organization to give the union some power once it wins representation. Employers generally want a bargaining unit that is least beneficial to the union; this will help maximize the likelihood of failure in the election and minimize the power of the unit.[29]

Preelection Campaign

After the bargaining unit has been determined, both union and employer embark on a preelection campaign. Unions claim to provide a strong voice for employees, emphasizing improvement in wages and working conditions and the establishment of a grievance process to ensure fairness. Employers emphasize the costs of unionization—dues, strikes, and loss of jobs. Severe violations of the legal constraints on behavior, such as the use of threats or coercion, are prevented by the NLRB, which watches the preelection activity carefully.

The effect of preelection campaigns is not clear. A study of 31 elections showed very little change in attitude and voting propensity after the campaigns. People who will vote for or against a union before an election campaign generally vote the same way after.

Election

Generally, elections are part of the process of determining if unions will win the right to represent workers. Elections can also determine if unions will retain the right to represent employees.

Certification Elections. The NLRB conducts the certification election. If a majority votes for union representation, the union will be certified. If the union does not get a majority, another election will not be held for at least a year. Generally, about one-third to one-half of all certification elections certify the union, with less union success in larger companies. Once a union has been certified, the employer is required to bargain with that union.[30]

Decertification Elections. The NLRB also conducts decertification elections, which can remove a union from representation. If 30 percent or more of the employees in an organization request such an election, it will be held. Decertification elections most frequently occur in the first year of a union's representation, when the union is negotiating its first contract. During this period, union strength has not yet been established, and employees are readily discouraged about union behavior.

 THE COLLECTIVE BARGAINING PROCESS

Collective bargaining is a complex process in which union and management negotiators maneuver to win the most advantageous contract. How the issues involved are settled depends on the following:

- The quality of the union-management relationship
- The processes of bargaining used by labor and management
- Management's strategies in collective bargaining
- Union's strategies in collective bargaining

Union-Management Relationships

The labor relations system is composed of three subunits—employees, management, and the union—with the government influencing interaction between the three. Employees may be managers or union members, and some union members are part of the union management system (local union leaders). Each of the three interrelationships in the model is regulated by specific federal statutes: that of union and management is regulated by the National Labor Relations Act; management and employees by the National Labor Relations Act, Title VII of the Civil Rights Act of 1964, the Civil Rights Act of 1991, and the Americans with Disabilities Act of 1990; and union and employees by the Labor-Management Reporting and Disclosure Act, Title VII of the Civil Rights Act of 1964, and the Civil Rights Act of 1991.[31]

Each group in the labor relations model typically has different goals. Workers are interested in improved working conditions, wages, and opportunities. Unions are interested in these as well as their own survival, growth, and acquisition of power, which depend on their ability to maintain the support of the employees by providing for their needs. Management has overall organizational goals (e.g., increasing profits, market share, and growth rates) and also seeks to preserve managerial prerogatives to direct the workforce and to attain the personal goals of the managers (e.g., promotion or achievement). Government is interested in a stable and healthy economy, protection of individual rights, and safety and fairness in the workplace.

Adversarial Relationship. The goals of workers, unions, management, and governments were often seen as incompatible. Thus, an adversarial relationship emerged, with labor and management attempting to get a bigger cut of the pie, while government oversaw its own interests. In an adversarial relationship between union and management, the union's role is to gain concessions from management during collective bargaining and to preserve those concessions through the grievance procedure. The union is an outsider and critic.[32]

Partnership in Collective Bargaining

Line Managers	Human Resource Professionals	Employees	Unions
Work with HR professionals in developing an effective relationship with union representatives.	Work with line managers in dealing effectively with union representatives.	Bargain in good faith through union representatives with line managers and HR professionals.	Bargain with line managers and HR professionals.
Work with HR professionals and union representatives in resolving grievances.	Develop mechanisms for effective grievance resolution.	Fulfill rights and responsibilities in the union contract.	Seek improvements in conditions and wages.
Engage in cooperative relations with the union and employees.	Move along such issues as total quality management and quality-of-work-life programs.		Be willing to adapt to local conditions and changes in technology and economic conditions.
Know and work with the union-management contract.			

Historically, unions have adopted an adversarial role in their interactions with management. Their focus has been on wages, hours, and working conditions as they attempted to get "more and better" from management. This approach works well in economic boom times but encounters difficulties when the economy is not healthy. High unemployment and the threat of continued job losses have induced unions to expand their role, especially since many of their traditional goals—have already been achieved. Consequently, some unions have begun to enter into new, collaborative efforts with employers, which result in a cooperative relationship.

Cooperative Relationship. In a cooperative relationship, the union's role is that of a partner, not a critic, and the union is jointly responsible with management for reaching a cooperative solution the results of which are shown in the feature "Partnership in Collective Bargaining." Thus, a cooperative relationship requires that union and management solve problems, share information, and integrate outcomes.[33]

Cooperative systems have not been a major component of labor relations in the United States, although they have been built into labor relations in other countries—Sweden and Germany, for example. Increasingly, however, U.S. management and labor are working together cooperatively. Management recognizes that most of the programs they undertake to improve their organization need the acceptance of the union to be successful. Active involvement of the union is a good way to gain this acceptance.[34]

As discussed in Chapter 4, teamwork is a critical component of firms' efforts to improve quality. Unions such as the UAW and the CWA, and firms such as Ford and AT&T are recognizing how important quality is to survival.[35] Consequently, they are unions or their locals, or firms or specific plants are in favor of these "workplace reforms."[36]

In all fairness, it should be noted how difficult the transition from an adversarial to a cooperative relationship is for most unions as well as firms. The recent decision General Motors made to continue its Arlington, Texas plant and close its Willow Run, Michigan plant also illustrated that unions also may have their hands full dealing with locals that experiment more than the parent organization wants them to. For example, Stephen Yokich, a UAW vice president, assailed the union local at Arlington for its willingness to adjust its work schedule.[37]

Processes of Bargaining

Five types of bargaining are used in contract negotiations: distributive, integrative, concessionary, continuous, and intraorganizational.

Distributive Bargaining. Distributive bargaining takes place when the parties are in conflict over the issue, and the outcome represents a gain for one party and a loss for the other. Each party tries to negotiate for the best possible outcome. The process is outlined in Exhibit 16.3.

On any particular issue, union and management negotiators each have three identifiable positions. The union has an *initial demand point,* which is generally more than it expects to get; a *target point,* which is its realistic assessment of what it may be able to get; and a *resistance point,* or the lowest acceptable level for the issue. Management has three similar points: an *initial offer point,* which is usually lower than the expected settlement; a *target point,* at which it would like to reach agreement; and a *resistance point,* or its upper acceptable limit. If, as shown in Exhibit 16.3, management's resistance point is greater than the union's, a *positive settlement range* exists, where working cooperatively to ensure that teamwork programs succeed. Of course, not all negotiation can take place. The exact agreement within this range depends on the bargaining behavior of the negotiators. If, however, management's resistance point is

■ *Exhibit 16.3*
Distributive Bargaining Process

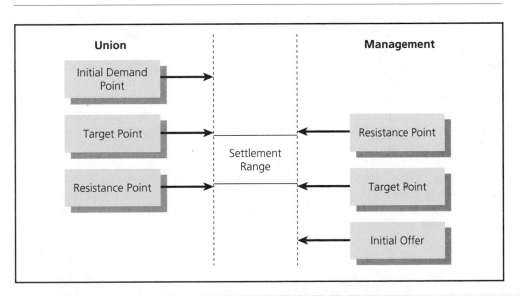

SOURCE: Adapted from R. Walton and R. B. McKersie, *A Behavioral Theory of Labor Negotiations* (New York: McGraw-Hill Book Co., 1965): 43.

below the union's, In such a *negative settlement range,* or bargaining impasse, exists, and there is no common ground for negotiation.[38]

For example, on the issue of wages, the union may have a resistance point of $8.40 an hour, a target of $8.60, and an initial demand point of $8.75. Management may offer $8.20 but have a target of $8.45 and a resistance point of $8.55. The positive settlement range is between $8.40 and $8.55, and this is where the settlement will likely be. However, only the initial wage demand and offer are made public at the beginning of negotiations.

The ritual of the distributive bargaining process is well established, and deviations are often met with suspicion:

> A labor lawyer tells the story of a young executive who had just taken over the helm of a company. Imbued with idealism, he wanted to end the bickering he had seen take place during past negotiations with labor. To do this, he was ready to give workers as much as his company could afford. Consequently he asked some members of his staff to study his firm's own wage structure and decide how it compared with other companies, as well as a host of other related matters. He approached the collective bargaining table with a halo of goodness surrounding him. Asking for the floor, he proceeded to describe what he had done with a big smile on his face and made the offer.
>
> Throughout his entire presentation, the union officials stared at him in amazement. He had offered more than they had expected to secure. But no matter, as soon as he finished, they proceeded to lambaste him, denouncing him for trying to destroy collective bargaining and for attempting to buy off labor. They announced that they would not stand for any such unethical maneuvering, and immediately asked for 5 cents more than the idealistic executive had offered.[39]

Integrative Bargaining. When more than one issue needs to be resolved, integrative agreements may be pursued. Integrative bargaining focuses on creative solutions that reconcile (integrate) the parties' interests and yield high joint benefit. It can occur only when negotiators have an "expanding-pie" perception—that is, when the two parties (union and management) have two or more issues and are willing to develop creative ways to satisfy both parties.[40]

Concessionary Bargaining. Distributive and integrative bargaining are the primary approaches to bargaining; concessionary bargaining often occurs within these two frameworks. Concessionary bargaining may be prompted by severe economic conditions faced by employers. Seeking to survive and prosper, employers seek givebacks or concessions from the unions, promising job security in return. In the early 1990s, this type of bargaining was prevalent, especially in the smokestack industries, such as automobiles, steel, and rubber, and to some extent in the transportation industry. In these groups of enterprises, concessions sought by management from the unions included wage freezes, wage reductions, work rule changes or elimination, fringe-benefit reductions, COLA delays or elimination, and more hours of work for the same pay. Two-tier wage systems were tried in some industries, but problems of inequity and lower worker morale offset much of the savings from lower labor costs.[41] In addition, available evidence suggests that these agreements erode union solidarity, leadership credibility, and control, as well as union power and effectiveness.

Continuous Bargaining. As affirmative action, safety and health requirements, and other governmental regulations continue to complicate the situation for both unions and employers, and as the rate of change in the environment continues to increase, some labor and management negotiators are turning to continuous bargaining. In this process, joint committees meet on a regular basis to explore issues and solve problems of common interest. These committees have appeared in the retail food, over-the-road trucking, nuclear power, and men's garment industries.[42]

Several characteristics of continuous bargaining have been identified:

- ◉ Frequent meetings during the life of the contract
- ◉ Focus on external events and problem areas rather than on internal problems
- ◉ Use of the skills of outside experts in decision making
- ◉ Use of a problem-solving (integrative) approach[43]

The intention of continuous bargaining is to develop a union-management structure that is capable of adapting positively and productively to sudden changes in the environment. This approach is different from, but an extension of, the emergency negotiations that unions have insisted on when inflation or other circumstances have substantially changed the acceptability of the existing agreement. Continuous bargaining is a permanent arrangement intended to help avoid the crises that often occur under traditional collective bargaining systems.

Intraorganizational Bargaining. During negotiations, the bargaining teams from both sides may have to engage in intraorganizational bargaining—that is, confer with their constituents over changes in bargaining positions. Management negotiators may have to convince management to change its position on an issue—for instance, to agree to a higher wage settlement. Union negotiators must eventually convince their members to accept the negotiated contract, so they must be sensitive to the demands of the membership, as well as realistic. When the membership votes on the proposed package, it will be strongly influenced by the opinions of the union negotiators.

Preparation for Bargaining

Prior to the bargaining session, management and union negotiators need to develop the strategies and proposals they will use.

Management Strategies. For negotiations with the union, management needs to complete four different tasks:

1. Preparation of specific proposals for changes in contract language
2. Determination of the general size of the economic package that the company anticipates offering during the negotiations
3. Preparation of statistical displays and supportive data that the company will use during negotiations
4. Preparation of a bargaining book for use by company negotiators; this is a compilation of information on issues that will be discussed, giving an analysis of the effect of each clause, its use in other companies, and other facts[44]

The relative cost of pension contributions, pay increases, health benefits, and other bargaining provisions should be determined prior to negotiations. Other costs should also be considered. For instance, management might ask itself, "What is the cost—in our ability to do our job—of union demands for changes in grievance and discipline procedures or transfer and promotion provisions?" The goal is to be as well prepared as possible by considering the implications and ramifications of the issues that will be discussed and by being able to present a strong argument for the position taken.

Union Strategies. Like management, unions need to prepare for negotiations by collecting information. Because collective bargaining is the major means by which a union can convince its members that it is effective and valuable, this is a critical activity. Unions collect information in at least these areas:

- The financial situation of the company and its ability to pay
- The attitude of management toward various issues, as reflected in past negotiations or inferred from negotiations in similar companies
- The attitudes and desires of the employees

The first two areas give the union an idea of what demands management is likely to accept. The third area is sometimes overlooked. It involves awareness of the preferences of the union membership—for instance, the union might ask, "Is a pension increase preferred over increased vacation or holiday benefits?" Membership preferences will vary with the characteristics of the workers. Younger workers are more likely to prefer more holidays, shorter workweeks, and limited overtime, whereas older workers are more likely interested in pension plans, benefits, and overtime. The union can determine these preferences by using questionnaires and meetings to survey its members.

Unions also gather information from parties outside the immediate environment. Locals often receive from their national or headquarters unions input concerning the settlement patterns of other locals. The national may pressure a local to advance the larger aims of the union, even if those matters are not central to a particular office or plant. Interunion rivalries, whether labeled "orbits of coercive comparison" or "keeping up with the Joneses," may serve as a catalyst for demands as well. In these conflicts, gains achieved by one union challenge other unions to attain comparable or superior outcomes.

 NEGOTIATING THE AGREEMENT

Once a union is certified as the representative of a bargaining unit, it becomes the only party that can negotiate an agreement with the employer for all members of that work unit, whether they are union members or not. Technically, however, individuals within the unit can still negotiate with the employer personal deals that give them more than the other members receive, particularly if the agreement is silent on this issue.

The union serves as a critical link between employees and employer. It is responsible to its members to negotiate for what they want, and it has the duty to represent all employees fairly. The quality of its bargaining is an important measure of union effectiveness.

Negotiating Committees

The employer and the union select their own representatives for the negotiating committee. Neither party is required to consider the wishes of the other. For example, management negotiators cannot refuse to bargain with representatives of the union because they dislike them or do not think they are appropriate.

Union negotiating teams typically include representatives of the union local—often the president and other executive staff members. In addition, the national union may send a negotiating specialist, who is likely to be a labor lawyer, to work with the team. The negotiators selected by the union do not have to be members of the union or employees of the company. The general goal is to balance skill and experience in bargaining with knowledge and information about the specific situation.

At the local level, when a single bargaining unit is negotiating a contract, the company is usually represented by the manager and members of the labor relations or human resource staff. Finance and production managers may also be involved. When the negotiations are critical, either because the bargaining unit is large or because the effect on the company is great, specialists such as labor lawyers may be included on the team.

In national negotiations, top industrial relations or human resource executives frequently head a team of specialists from corporate headquarters and perhaps managers from critical divisions or plants within the company. Again, the goal is to have expertise along with specific knowledge about critical situations.

The Negotiating Structure

Most contracts are negotiated by a single union and a single employer. In some situations, however, different arrangements can be agreed on. When a single union negotiates with several similar companies—for instance, firms in the construction industry or supermarkets—the employers may bargain as a group. At the local level, this is called *multiemployer bargaining;* at the national level, it is referred to as *industrywide bargaining.* Industrywide bargaining occurs in the railroad, coal, wallpaper, and men's suits industries. When several unions bargain jointly with a single employer, they engage in *coordinated bargaining.* Although not as common as the multiemployer and industrywide bargaining, coordinated bargaining appears to be increasing, especially in the public sector. One consequence of coordinated and industrywide bargaining is often *pattern settlements,* where similar wage rates are imposed on the companies whose employees are represented by the same union within a given industry.

In the contract construction industry, a *wide-area and multicraft bargaining* structure arose in response to the unionized employers' need to be more price competitive and to have fewer strikes, and in response to the unions' desire to gain more control at the national level. Consequently, the bargaining is done on a regional (geographic) rather than local basis. In addition, it covers several construction crafts simultaneously instead of one. The common contract negotiations resulting from wide-area and multicraft bargaining help lessen the opportunity for unions to *whipsaw* the employer. Whipsawing occurs when one contract settlement is used as a precedent for the next, which then forces the employer to get all contracts settled in order to have all the employees working. As a result of whipsawing, an employer frequently agrees to more favorable settlements on all contracts, regardless of the conditions and merits of each one, just to get all employees back to work.[45]

Issues for Negotiation

The issues that can be discussed in collective bargaining sessions are specified by the Labor-Management Relations Act. This act has established three categories of issues for negotiation: mandatory, permissive, and prohibited.[46]

Employers and employee representatives (unions) are obligated to meet and discuss "wages, hours, and other terms and conditions of employment." These are the *mandatory issues.* These critical elements in the bargaining process include the issues that may affect management's ability to run the company efficiently or may clash with the union's desire to protect jobs and workers' standing in their jobs.

Permissive issues are those not specifically related to the nature of the job but still of concern to both parties. For example, decisions about price, product design, and new jobs may be subject to bargaining if the parties agree to it. Permissive issues usually develop when both parties see that mutual discussion and agreement will be beneficial, which may be more likely when a cooperative relationship exists between union and management. Management and union negotiators cannot refuse to agree on a contract if they fail to settle a permissive issue.[47]

Prohibited issues are those concerning illegal or outlawed activities, such as the demand that an employer use only union-produced goods or, where it is illegal, that it employ only union members. Such issues may not be discussed in collective bargaining sessions.

Direct Compensation. Wage conflicts are a leading cause of strikes. Difficulties arise here because a wage increase is a direct cost to the employer, whereas a wage decrease is a direct cost to the employee. As discussed in Chapters 12 and 13, rates of pay are influenced by a variety of issues, including the going rate in an industry, the employer's ability to pay, the cost of living, and productivity. All these subjects are often debated and discussed in negotiations.

Indirect Compensation. Because the cost of indirect compensation now runs as high as 40 percent of the total cost of wages, it is a major concern in collective bargaining. Benefit provisions are very difficult to remove once they are in place, so management tends to be cautious about agreeing to them. Some commonly negotiated forms of indirect compensation are: pensions, paid vacations, paid holidays, sick leave, health care and life insurance, dismissal or severance pay, and supplemental unemployment benefits.

Hours of Employment. Although organizations are already required by federal labor law to pay overtime for work beyond forty hours a week, unions continually try to reduce the number of hours worked each week. Negotiations may focus on including the lunch hour in the eight-hour-day requirement, or on providing overtime after any eight-hour shift rather than after a forty-hour workweek.

Institutional Issues. Some issues are not directly related to jobs but are nevertheless important to both employees and management. Institutional issues that affect the security and success of both parties include the following:

- *Union Security:* About two-thirds of the major labor contracts stipulate that employees must join the union after being hired into its bargaining unit. However, twenty states that traditionally have had low levels of unionization have passed right-to-work laws outlawing union membership as a condition of employment.
- *Checkoff:* Unions have attempted to arrange for payment of dues through deduction from employees' paychecks. By law, employees must agree in writing to a dues checkoff. A large majority of union contracts contain a provision for this agreement.
- *Strikes:* The employer may insist that the union agree not to strike during the life of the contract, typically when a cost-of-living clause has been included. The agreement may be unconditional, allowing no strikes at all, or it may limit strikes to specific circumstances.
- *Managerial Prerogatives:* More than half the agreements today stipulate that certain activities are the right of management. In addition, management in most companies argues that it has "residual rights"—that all rights not specifically limited by the agreement belong to management.

Administrative Issues. Administrative issues concern the treatment of employees at work. These issues include the following:

- *Breaks and Cleanup Time:* Some contracts specify the time and length of coffee breaks and meal breaks for employees. In addition, jobs requiring cleanup may have a portion of the work period set aside for this procedure.

- *Job Security:* Job security is perhaps the issue of most concern to employees and unions. Employers are concerned with a restriction of their ability to lay off employees. Changes in technology or attempts to subcontract work impinge on job security. A typical union response to technological change was that of the International Longshoremen's Association in the late 1960s to the introduction of containerized shipping. The union operated exclusive hiring halls, developed complex work rules, and negotiated a guaranteed annual income for its members. Job security continues to be a primary issue for ship loaders and unloaders, telephone workers, and most other blue-collar workers.

- *Seniority:* Length of service is used as a criterion for many human resource decisions in most collective agreements. Layoffs are usually determined by seniority. "Last hired, first fired" is a common situation. Seniority is also important in transfer and promotion decisions. The method of calculating seniority is usually specified in order to clarify the relative seniority of employees.

- *Discharge and Discipline:* As described in Chapter 3, termination and discipline are tough issues, and, even when an agreement addresses these problems, many grievances are filed concerning the way they are handled.

- *Safety and Health:* Although the Occupational Safety and Health Act specifically deals with worker safety and health, some contracts have provisions specifying that the company will provide safety equipment, first aid, physical examinations, accident investigations, and safety committees. Hazardous work may be covered by special provisions and pay rates. Often, the agreement will contain a general statement that the employer is responsible for the safety of the workers, so that the union can use the grievance process when any safety issues arise.

- *Production Standards:* The level of productivity or performance of employees is a concern of both management and the union. Management is concerned with efficiency, and the union is concerned with the fairness and reasonableness of management's demands. Increasingly, both are concerned about total quality and quality of work life.

- *Grievance Procedures:* The contract usually outlines a process for settling disputes that may arise during its administration.

- *Training:* The design and administration of training and development programs and the procedure for selecting employees for training may also be bargaining issues. This is particularly important when the company is pursuing a strategy of total quality management.

- *Duration of the Agreement:* Agreements can last for one year or longer, with the most common period being three years.

CONFLICT RESOLUTION

Although the desired outcome of collective bargaining is agreement on the conditions of employment, on many occasions, negotiators are unable to reach such an agreement at the bargaining table. In these situations, several alternatives are used to break the deadlock. The most dramatic response is a strike or lockout; indirect responses are also used, and third-party interventions such as mediation and arbitration are common as well.

Strikes and Lockouts

When the union is unable to get management to agree to a demand it believes is critical, it may tell employees to refuse to work at the company. This is called a *strike.* When management refuses to allow employees to work, the situation is called a *lockout.*[48]

In order to strike, the union usually holds a vote to gain members' approval. Strong membership support for a strike strengthens the union negotiators' position. If the strike takes place, union members picket the employer, informing the public about the existence of a labor dispute and preferably, from the union's point of view, convincing it to avoid this company during the strike. Union members commonly refuse to cross the picket line of another striking union, which gives added support to the striking union.

Employers usually attempt to continue operations while a strike is in effect. They either run the company with supervisory personnel and people not in the bargaining unit, or hire replacements for the striking employees. At the conclusion of the strike, employers will be expected to (a) reinstate strikers in all the positions that remain unfilled, unless they have substantial business reasons for doing otherwise, and (b) establish a preferential hiring list for displaced strikers to facilitate their recall as new openings occur.

The success of a strike depends on its ability to cause economic hardship to the employer. Severe hardship usually causes the employer to concede to the union's demands.[49] Thus, from the union's point of view, the cost of the company's lack of production must be high. The union, therefore, actively tries to prevent replacement employees from working. Although it appears that the company can legally hire replacements, the union reacts strongly to the employment of scabs, as these workers are called, and the replacement employees may be a cause of increasingly belligerent labor relations. The hiring of replacement workers has reached a level where companies are keeping them even after the strike is settled—if the strike is settled at all. This tactic has given employers even more power in a strike situation. Thus, the union movement seeks a law to prevent replacement workers from becoming permanent workers.

The timing of the strike is also often critical. The union attempts to hold negotiations just before the employer has a peak demand for its product or services, when a strike will have the maximum economic effect.

Although strikes have been on the decline (see Exhibit 16.4), they are costly to both the employer, who loses revenue, and employees, who lose income. If a strike is

■ *Exhibit 16.4*
Major Work Stoppages, 1947–1994

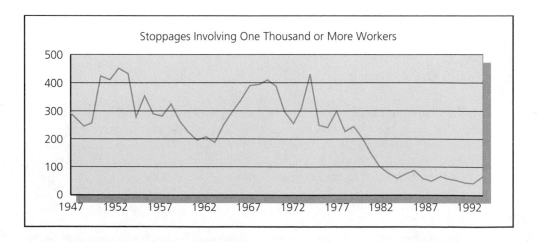

SOURCE: Adapted from "Strike Activity Up in 1994," *Bulletin to Management* (February 23, 1995): 61. Used by permission.

prolonged, the cost to employers will likely never be fully recovered by the benefits gained. In part because of this, employers seek to avoid strikes. Moreover, the public interest is generally not served by strikes. They are often an inconvenience and can have serious consequences for the economy as a whole.

Indirect Responses

Slowdown. Short of an actual strike, unions may invoke a slowdown, like the one described here:

> Until the resistance began at the Caterpillar plant, Lance Vaughan first installed a set of small hydraulic hoses on the huge off-highway trucks that he helps to assemble, and then a big outside hose. Now he installs the big one first, and reaches awkwardly around it to attach the others, losing production time in the process.
>
> This is not sabotage. The instructions furnished by Caterpillar's engineers specify the inefficient procedure, Mr. Vaughan says. Normally, he ignores such instructions and makes a note to himself to tell the engineers to fix the mistake. Now, he no longer speaks up. Withholding initiative, he works [according] "to the rules" furnished by the company.
>
> "I used to give the engineers ideas," said Mr. Vaughan, who is 38 and has worked at Caterpillar for nearly 20 years. "We showed them how to eliminate some hose clips and save money. And I recommended larger bolts that made assembly easier and faster, and were less likely to come loose."[50]

At Caterpillar, the slowdown was referred to as an "in-plant strategy." Regardless of the name, the result is the same: a reduction of work output, physically and mentally. Slowdowns can be more effective than actual strikes.

Primary Boycotts. Unions sometimes want to make the public more aware of their cause. As a consequence, they may engage in a *primary boycott.* For instance, a union that is striking a soda-bottling company may set up an informational picket line at grocery stores that sell the bottler's products. It has generally been ruled that as long as the picket line is directed at the bottling company, asking customers not to buy its soda, it constitutes a primary boycott and thus is legal. The picket line becomes illegal, however, when it tries to prevent customers from shopping at the grocery store. This action is called a *secondary boycott,* and it is illegal because it can harm an innocent third party—here, the grocery store.

Corporate Campaigns. In a *corporate campaign,* a union may ask the public and other unions to write letters to a company, asking it to change the way it bargains with the union.[51]

Mediation

Mediation is a procedure in which a neutral third party helps the union and management negotiators reach a voluntary agreement.[52] Having no power to impose a solution, the mediator attempts to facilitate the negotiations between union and management. The mediator may make suggestions and recommendations and perhaps add objectivity to the often emotional negotiations. To have any success at all, the mediator must have the trust and respect of both parties and have sufficient expertise and neutrality to convince the union and employer that she or he will be fair and equitable.

The U.S. government operates the Federal Mediation and Conciliation Service (FMCS) to make experienced mediators available to unions and companies. A program called Relationships by Objective is offered by the FMCS to eliminate the causes of recurrent impasses. It uses aspects of attitudinal structuring to increase the likelihood of a cooperative relationship between union and management.

Arbitration

Arbitration is a procedure in which a neutral third party studies the bargaining situation, listens to both parties and gathers information, and then makes a determination that is binding on the parties. The arbitrator, in effect, determines the conditions of the agreement.[53]

In *final-offer arbitration,* the arbitrator can choose between the final offer of the union and the final offer of the employer. The arbitrator cannot alter these offers but must select one as it stands. Since the arbitrator chooses the offer that appears most fair, and since losing the arbitration decision means settling for the other's offer, each side is pressured to make as good an offer as possible. By contrast, in conventional arbitration, the arbitrator is free to fashion any award deemed appropriate.

The arbitration process that deals with the contract terms and conditions is called *interest arbitration.* This type of arbitration is relatively infrequent in the private sector; it is more common in the public sector, where it becomes a necessary quid pro quo for foregoing the strike option.[54] Only about twenty states have compulsory interest arbitration procedures.

Once the contract impasse is removed, union and management have an agreement. Abiding by it is the essence of contract administration; however, at times, arbitration will again be necessary, namely when a grievance is filed. This type of arbitration is referred to as rights arbitration or *grievance arbitration.*

CONTRACT ADMINISTRATION

Once signed, the collective agreement becomes "the basic legislation governing the lives of the workers."[55] That is, the daily operation and activities in the organization are subject to the conditions of the agreement. Because of the difficulty of writing an unambiguous agreement anticipating all the situations that will occur over its life, disputes will inevitably occur over the contract's interpretation and application. The most common method of resolving these disputes is a grievance procedure. Virtually all agreements negotiated today provide for a grievance process to handle employee complaints.

Grievance Procedures

Basically, a grievance is a charge that the union-management contract has been violated.[56] A grievance may be filed by the union for employees, or by employers, although management rarely does so. The grievance process is designed to investigate the charges and to resolve the problem.

The following sources of grievances have been identified:

- Outright violation of the agreement
- Disagreement over facts
- Dispute over the meaning of the agreement
- Dispute over the method of applying the agreement
- Argument over the fairness or reasonableness of actions[57]

In resolving these sources of conflict, the grievance procedure should serve three separate groups: the employers and unions, by interpreting and adjusting the agreement as conditions require; the employees, by protecting their contractual rights and providing a channel of appeal; and society at large, by keeping industrial peace and reducing the number of disputes in the courts.

Grievance procedures typically involve several stages. The collective bargaining agreement specifies the maximum length of time that can elapse between the incident that is the subject of the dispute and the filing of a grievance on that incident. The most common grievance procedure, shown in Exhibit 16.5, involves four steps:

1. An employee who feels that the labor contract has been violated usually contacts the union steward, and together they discuss the problem with the supervisor involved. If the problem is simple and straightforward, it is often resolved at this level.
2. If agreement cannot be reached at the supervisor level, or if the employee is not satisfied, the complaint can enter the second step of the grievance procedure.

■ *Exhibit 16.5*
Typical Union-Management Grievance Procedure

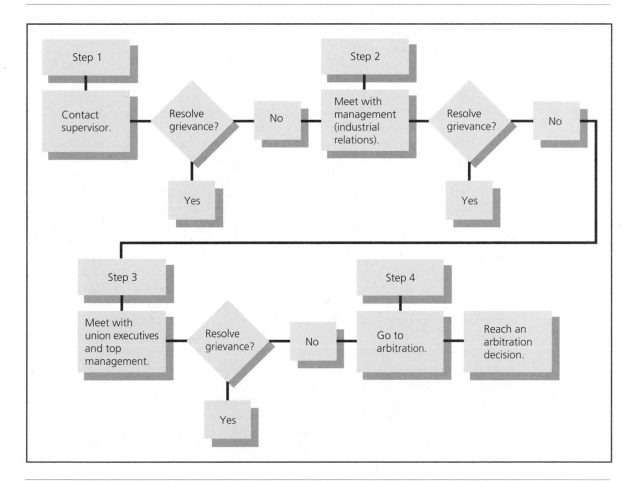

SOURCE: Prepared by William D. Todor, Professor of Human Resource Management, The Ohio State University.

Typically, a human resource representative of the company now seeks to resolve the grievance.

3. If the grievance is sufficiently important or difficult to resolve, it may be taken to the third step. Although contracts vary, they usually specify that top-level management and union executives be involved at this stage. These people have the authority to make the major decisions that may be required to resolve the grievance.

4. If a grievance cannot be resolved at the third step, an arbitrator will likely need to consider the case and reach a decision. The arbitrator is a neutral, mutually acceptable individual who may be appointed by the FMCS or some private agency. The arbitrator holds a hearing, reviews the evidence, and then rules on the grievance. The decision of the arbitrator is usually binding.

Since the cost of arbitration is shared by the union and employer, some incentive exists to settle the grievance before it goes to arbitration.[58] An added incentive in some cases is the requirement that the loser pay for the arbitration.[59] The expectation behind these incentives is that the parties will screen or evaluate grievances more carefully because pursuing a weak grievance to arbitration will be expensive.

Occasionally, the union will call a strike over a grievance in order to resolve it. This may happen when the issue at hand is so important that the union feels that it cannot wait for the slower arbitration process.[60] Such an "employee rights" strike may be legal; however, if the contract specifically forbids strikes during the tenure of the agreement, it is not legal and is called a *wildcat strike*. Wildcat strikes are not common; most grievances are settled through arbitration.

Grievance Issues

Grievances can be filed over any workplace issue that is subject to the collective agreement, or they can be filed over interpretation and implementation of the agreement itself. The most common type of grievance reaching the arbitration stage involves discipline and discharge, although many grievances are filed over other issues.

Absenteeism can be grounds for discharge, and a grievance procedure may be used to determine whether the absenteeism in question is excessive. Insubordination usually is either failure to do what the supervisor requests or the more serious problem of outright refusal to do it. If the supervisor's orders are clear and explicit and legal, and if the employee is warned of the consequences, discipline for refusal to respond is usually acceptable. The exception is when the employee feels that the work endangers health.

Because seniority is usually used to determine who is laid off, bumped from a job to make way for someone else, or rehired, its calculation is of great concern to employees. Seniority is also used as one of the criteria to determine eligibility for promotions and transfers, so management must be careful in this area in order to avoid complaints and grievances.

Compensation for time away from work, vacations, holidays, or sick leave is also a common source of grievances. Holidays cause problems because special pay arrangements often exist for people working on those days.

Wage and work schedules may also lead to grievances. Disagreements often arise over interpretation or application of the agreement relating to such issues as overtime pay, pay for reporting, and scheduling. Grievances have been filed over the exercise of management's rights—that is, its rights to introduce technological changes, use subcontractors (outsource), or change jobs in other ways. This type of behavior may also be the source of charges of unfair labor practices, since these activities may require collective bargaining.

The Taft-Hartley Act gives unions the right to file grievances on their own behalf if they feel their rights have been violated. It also gives unions access to information necessary to process the grievance or to make sure the agreement is not being violated. In addition, unions may file grievances for violations of union shop or checkoff provisions. On the other hand, employees have the right to present their *own* grievances on an individual basis (Taft-Hartley, Section 9(a)), and the employer can adjust that grievance without the union's presence. The only qualifying items are that adjustments cannot abrogate the collective agreement, and the union must be given an opportunity to participate in the grievance proceedings at some point prior to the adjustment.

Occasionally, other activities prompt grievances. Wildcat strikes or behavior that is considered to be a strike (e.g., mass absences from work) may result in a management grievance. The major focus of grievances, however, is in the administration of the conditions of the agreement.

 # WHAT UNIONS SHOULD DO

The topic of "the future role of the union" is generating a great deal of discussion and speculation.[61] Some foresee a halt to the decline in union membership in the private sector. This is expected to follow from a decline in the numbers entering the workforce and a subsequent tighter labor market; from more sophisticated and efficient organizing activities; from unions' rising appeal among less skilled workers; and from unions' ability and willingness to offer a broader array of consumer benefits and new forms of membership.[62] Others foresee a decline in union membership in the private sector, to 8 percent, by the 21st century. This is expected to follow from a continual growth of international competition and the service economy.

All this needs to be put in the perspective of the environment. The U.S. economy will continue to globalize, and firms will continue to have available for their hiring high-quality, low-wage workers. A decline in mass production will continue at the same time that the skill levels of the workforce increase. As Ray Marshall, former secretary of labor, says, "[E]conomic success will require new policies and high-performance systems more appropriate for a global, knowledge-intensive economic environment."[63] Although Marshall means this to describe the future of business, it could as easily be applied to the future of unions.[64]

Another perspective needs to be included here as well: The union movement will continue to be heterogenous. Differences will exist within the movement, with some unions, such as the UAW and the CWA, being more willing to enter into collaborative agreements and others less willing. Thus, we are likely to see several answers to the question "What should unions do?" Three particular activities we are likely to see include strategic involvement, board membership, and high-performance workplaces.

Strategic Involvement

Labor costs are critical to the success of many companies vis-à-vis their competitors. In many industries today, companies face possible bankruptcy because of high labor costs. Wage reductions reached between unions and management are helping to lower costs. During the 1980s, American Airlines, Greyhound, McDonnell Douglas, Boeing, and Ingersoll-Rand negotiated two-tier wage systems to help reduce total costs by reducing labor costs. Without these jointly negotiated systems, these companies may not have survived. Thus, a company's relationship with its union can be critical to its survival, and the better its relationship, the more likely the company is to gain a competitive advantage.[65]

Ford Motor Company has engaged in a program of more worker involvement and more cooperative labor relations with the United Auto Workers. The results of this program are higher product quality for Ford than for its competitors, and a marketing campaign centered on the slogan "Quality Is Job One." This program of more worker involvement gains competitive advantage through higher product quality and improved efficiencies. Similar results have been obtained at Eaton Corporation, Saturn, AT&T, Xerox, and the Mass Transportation Authority of Flint, Michigan. In these companies, gains in quality and efficiency have resulted from employee commitment associated with quality-circle programs. These companies have also experienced fewer grievances, reduced absenteeism and turnover, lower design costs, higher engineering productivity, and fewer costly changes in design cycles.

It is likely that we will continue to see this strategic involvement through at least the year 2000. This involvement will generally take a form similar to that at Saturn. It may, however, also take another form: workers actually taking over, or assuming part of the equity ownership of, the company. The workers at United, Southwest, and Northwest Airlines got a stake in the company for granting wage concessions. Watch for this trend of employees' giving up wage demands in exchange for ownership in the company and the hopes of job security.

Board Membership

A second trend occurring in collective bargaining is that of board membership. This has occurred at National Steel Corporation, Wheeling-Pittsburgh Steel Corporation, and the LTV Corporation. It is similar to the codetermination system of Germany. It is different, however, in that it results from union-management bargaining rather than federal mandate. Giving unions access to the board room is common in Europe, where the unions are stronger, but is still quite novel in the United States. It has generally only been entertained by troubled companies that have had to work closely with their unions to avert bankruptcy or liquidation.[66] Only the future will tell if nontroubled companies also elect to bring worker representation onto their boards.

High-Performance Workplaces

Global competition is increasing in the area of high quality and low cost, and U.S. firms want to compete on the same terms. Their success depends in large part on total quality management and the support of employees. Capturing this relationship is the trend toward "high-performance workplaces," as described in the feature "Positioning for the 21st Century: High-Performance Workplaces."

INTERNATIONAL CONCERNS

Mexico

In Mexico, unions have the right to organize workers at an operation, but only one union represents a given location, covering all employees at that location. When a strike is called, the workplace is closed until the strike is settled—picket lines are unknown. In most manufacturing operations, generally plant workers are unionized, first-line supervisors are sometimes unionized, and high-level supervisors are seldom unionized.[67]

Positioning for the 21st Century:
HIGH-PERFORMANCE WORKPLACES

Through workplace cooperation, employees are empowered to make meaningful decisions at L-S Electro-Galvanizing Company in Cleveland, according to Cal Tinsley, plant manager, and Thomas Zidek, process technician and president of Steelworkers Local 9126. The company, commonly referred to as L-SE, was created in 1985 as a joint venture between LTV Corporation and Sumitomi Metals of Japan.

With the agreement of the union, L-SE was designed to provide a work environment in which "respect, dignity, and cooperation were to be the way of life," Zidek explains. Adversarial relationships were typical in the steel industry at the time, Zidek notes, but workers still supported the new environment. Most of the individuals hired were laid-off steelworkers who realized they wanted something new for the future.

Before startup, workers received technical training as well as extensive training in problem-solving skills and how to deal with people. Workers then chose their positions based on the skills they brought to the company. That level of involvement continues at L-SE through problem-solving teams and committees on hiring, safety, gain sharing, skill-based pay, training, and customer concerns.

According to Tinsley, L-SE has tried to promote equality by eliminating traditional barriers between labor and management, whether they are physical or psychological. For example, there is no traditional personnel department at L-SE. Also, similar uniforms are worn by workers and managers, making it hard to distinguish between them, and the company has a common locker room, no assigned parking places, and no time clocks.

As part of the company's normal operations, employees hold weekly workshops that focus on quality, notes Zidek. "We are continuously improving our processes that way," he says. Moreover, he points out, employees have the power to stop production or shipments if quality is not high.

The most important innovation at L-SE, says Tinsley, is the creation of an environment where employees want to make participation work. The proof that it works, he says, is that L-SE has gained a reputation as the premium supplier of electro-galvanized material in the automotive industry.[68]

In case of a dispute, the burden of proof is always on the employer. Also, the labor law is part of Mexico's constitution, and workers are not allowed to renounce these rights. Therefore, any individual employment contracts or collective agreements that limit these rights are considered invalid.[69]

Since the advent of NAFTA, union organizations in the United States have seen relations with Mexico as a strategic opportunity and necessity. Many U.S. firms such as GE, Honeywell, and General Motors have increased operations in Mexico, and the U.S. unions need to have an effect where their jobs and workers are. They are doing this by providing support to the local unions in Mexico, such as the Authentic Workers Front, that are trying to organize the workers of these same companies. The U.S. union movement is also trying to work through NAFTA to help improve wages and working conditions in Mexico. NAFTA legislation empowers the secretaries of labor in Canada, the United States, and Mexico to impose fines on a country that fails to enforce its labor laws.[70]

Canada

Approximately one-third of the Canadian labor force is unionized. About three-fourths of the union members are affiliated with the Canadian Labor Congress (CLC). As in the United States, the union local is the basic local unit. The CLC is the dominant labor group at the federal level. Its political influence may be compared with that of the AFL-CIO.

The labor laws in Canada are similar to those in the United States, with noteworthy differences. For example, Canadian labor laws require frequent interventions by governmental bodies before a strike can take place. In the United States, such intervention is largely voluntary. For the Canadian union movement as a whole, the trend toward concessionary bargaining to avoid layoffs and plant closings appears to be less evident than it is in the United States.[71] At the same time, Canadian labor organizations affiliated with unions dominated by labor organizations in the United States are becoming increasingly autonomous. This trend was highlighted when the United Auto Workers in Canada became independent from the same union in the United States.

Germany

The belief that workers' interests are best served if employees have a direct say in the management of the company is called *Mitbestimmung* (codetermination). The original ideas about codetermination were conceived in Germany and are now spreading into many other European countries.

Codetermination means, for example, that unions are given seats on the boards of directors of corporations. In addition, managers are encouraged to consult with unions before making major organizational changes, whether they be mergers, investments, plant closings, or relocations. If management disagrees with the union position, management prevails. However, unions may veto subcontracts by the company, and they have access to all company records.

Since the defeat of German unions in the 1930s, the German labor movement has consisted of unions with unitary structures that are a synthesis of traditional elements of the socialist and Catholic labor movements. Although labor is dominated by social democracy, the Catholic influence on the development of such concepts as codetermination, social partnership, and capital formation for employees has become an integral part of the German trade unions' ideology. Trade unions in Germany are also organized on an industrial basis. The dominant labor organizations are seventeen trade unions affiliated with the DGB (Confederation of Trade Unions). The DGB sets the pattern in negotiating for most workers. The other trade union federations—the DBB (Association of Civil Servants), DAG (White Collar Association), and CGB (Christian Trade Unions)—lack significant bargaining power; hence, civil servants are not allowed to strike.

German employers are also organized and centralized. Several industries have employers' associations, often dominated by large-scale companies. The largest employers' umbrella organization is the BDA (Federation of German Employers' Association). The BDA coordinates various kinds of legally binding agreements for its members. For example, in 1978, it published a "taboo catalog" containing rules and provisions of the association designed to strengthen its bargaining power. It limited management compromise in bargaining; among its instructions was the mandate that Saturday, usually not a working day, should be a working day in order to maximize the use of labor and machinery. Although this instruction was reversed in 1984, it illustrates the strategy of the employers' association to establish common policies. The notable efficiency of German HR practices could be explained by the strong connection of the major partners to the labor relations system and the adherence of the German employees to discipline, rules, and regulations.[72]

Japan

The third sacred treasure of the Imperial House of Japan is the enterprise union. Unlike unions in the United States and Europe, which are organized horizontally and industrywide, almost all trade unions in Japan are formed on a company-by-company, or enterprise, basis. In 1978, as many as 70,868 labor unions could be found in Japan, with one existing in practically every company or plant, to conduct labor negotiations at that level. Enterprise unions today account for nearly 90 percent of all Japanese union organizations. Four principal industrywide federations of workers serve as coordinators, formulators of unified and reliable standards, and sources of information.

Although the enterprise concept received a fair amount of attention in the United States during the 1920s and 1930s, such unions collapsed, primarily as a result of excessive management involvement and the unions' narrow fields of interest. The success of the enterprise union in Japan is attributed to two major differences. The first is the allocation of financial responsibility between the enterprise union and the trade or regional organizations, which reflects a difference in the organizational roles of Japanese labor unions. In Western countries, where centralized union control and authority are predominant, the national union receives union dues, decides how they are to be used, and returns a portion to the local unions for expenses. In Japan, the enterprise union controls the dues, passing on 10 percent or, at most, 20 percent to the federation.[73]

As a result of the enterprise union's role, problems in labor-management relationships can be dealt with more directly, without necessarily involving an outside body. The "mixed" union representation of the organization's blue-collar workers and some of its white-collar workers also proves valuable in determining more representative concerns. As a result of greater union participation by employees of a given company, 15.7 percent of Japan's top managers have once been active labor union leaders. This should lead to better management understanding of the needs and interests of employees.

The second difference that accounts for the success of the enterprise union system in Japan is the greater company and national loyalty shown by each worker. Accordingly, workers do not look on the union solely as a negotiating body but use its structure to deal with such issues as industry and technical reforms, new plant and equipment investments, and matters of personnel and productivity development.

 SUMMARY

Line managers and HR professionals need to know as much as possible about unionization because the stakes are substantial. Employees are generally attracted to unionization because they are dissatisfied with work conditions and feel powerless to change these conditions. By correcting unsatisfactory work conditions, or by not allowing them to occur in the first place, organizations help prevent unions from becoming attractive. However, once a union-organizing campaign begins, a company cannot legally stop it without committing an unfair labor practice.

Historically, unions and management have operated as adversaries because many of their goals are in conflict, but because conflict is detrimental to both management and unions, effective labor relations have been established to reduce this conflict. Although cooperation is not widespread, it may be the style of union-management relations in the future. Its effects are particularly apparent in collective bargaining, contract negotiation, and grievance processing.

The quality of the union-management relationship can have a strong influence on contract negotiations. Labor and management each select a bargaining committee to negotiate the new agreement. The negotiations may be between a single union and a single company or multiple companies, or between multiple unions and a single company. Bargaining issues are mandatory, permissive, or prohibited. Mandatory issues must be discussed, permissive issues can be discussed if both parties agree to do so, and prohibited issues cannot be discussed. The issues can be grouped into wage, economic supplement, institutional, and administrative issues.

Almost all labor contracts outline procedures for handling employee complaints. The most common grievance is related to discipline and discharge, although wages, promotions, seniority, vacations, holidays, and management and union rights are also sources of complaints.

The effectiveness of collective bargaining and contract administration is usually assessed by measures of how well the process is working. Bargaining can be evaluated using measures such as the duration of negotiations, the frequency of strikes, the use of third-party intervention, and the need for government intervention. The effectiveness of the grievance process can be assessed by the number of grievances; the level in the grievance process at which settlement occurs; the frequency of strikes or slowdowns; the rates of absenteeism, turnover, and sabotage; and the need for government intervention.

Finally, as economic conditions in the world have changed substantially, so have union-management relations. Much more cooperation exists. Management sees cooperative relationships as instrumental in the implementation of quality-improvement strategies. Unions see cooperative relationships as instrumental in protecting the jobs and incomes of their members. And society as a whole sees cooperative relationships as necessary and appropriate in these times of intense global competition. Thus, with some exceptions, we are likely to see cooperative relationships well into the 21st century.

 Discussion Questions

1. How can the UAW and GM work together even more effectively than they are today?
2. Identify and discuss the conditions that make unionization attractive to employees. Are these conditions different today than they were fifty years ago?
3. What is a certification election? a decertification election?
4. What is the structure of unionization in the United States today?
5. What is a bargaining unit? Why is its formation important?
6. Why has there been a trend toward cooperation between unions and management?
7. What are the steps in a typical grievance procedure?
8. Distinguish unions' mandatory, permissive, and prohibited bargaining issues.
9. Distinguish mediation from arbitration. How does a grievance procedure differ from interest arbitration? What is final-offer arbitration?
10. What should unions do?
11. Describe high-performance workplaces and the union's role in them.
12. Compare and contrast union-management conditions in the United States, Mexico, and Canada.
13. What is codetermination? Would it work in the United States?

 In-Class Project

1. Answer the following for Lincoln Electric:
   a. What are the views of management at Lincoln Electric regarding union representation of their workers?
   b. Why does the management at Lincoln Electric hold these views?
   c. Why have the workers at Lincoln Electric not sought representation?
   d. What change could cause the workers at Lincoln Electric to seek union representation?
2. Answer the following for AAL:
   a. What are the views of management at AAL regarding union representation of their workers?
   b. Why does the management at AAL hold these views?
   c. Why have the workers at AAL not sought representation?
   d. What change could cause the workers at AAL to seek union representation?

✦ *Field Projects*

1. Interview a union official. Ask about his or her views on plant closings and employee rights. Then go to the library and find out what has been written about the topic.

2. Interview human resource managers on their views of unions. Visit union companies and nonunion companies. Also interview union members, nonunion members, and even union officers to learn their views on unions. Present your findings to the class.

Case Study:
THE UNION'S STRATEGIC CHOICE

 Maria Dennis sits back and thoughtfully reads through the list of strategies the union's committee gave her this morning. If her union is to rebuild the power it has lost over the past few years, it is time to take drastic action. If the union continues to decline as it has the last few years, it will not be able to represent the members who voted for it to be their exclusive bargaining representative.

Maria was elected two years ago, at her union's convention, to be the international president of the Newspaper Workers International Union (NWIU). At the time, she knew it would not be an easy job, and she eagerly looked forward to taking on a new challenge. But she had no idea just how difficult it would be to get the union back on its feet again.

The NWIU was founded in the late 1890s, made up of newspaper typographers who were responsible for such tasks as setting type on linotype machines, creating the layout of the newspaper, proofing the articles, and printing the newspaper. Members of the union typically completed a six-year apprenticeship, learning all the different tasks involved in the printing process. Before 1960, printing professionals were considered the elite of the industrial workforce. The craft demanded that typographers be literate at a time when even the middle and upper classes were not. Furthermore, printing was a highly skilled, highly paid craft.

Since the 1970s, however, the union has declined. Literacy is no longer a unique characteristic, and automation has led to a deskilling of the craft. The introduction of video display terminals, optical character recognition scanners, and computerized typesetting has eliminated substantial composing room work, and the demand for skilled union workers has been reduced. The union experienced its peak membership of 120,000 in 1965. During the 1970s, membership began a substantial decline, and in 1988, the total membership was only 40,000.

The reduced membership has resulted in other problems for the union. First, fewer members mean fewer dues, which are the union's main source of revenue. Consequently, the union is having some serious financial problems and is being forced to cut some of its services to members.

Second, the union is experiencing a significant loss in bargaining power with newspaper management. In the past, the printers were fairly secure in their jobs because there was a good demand in the labor market for individuals who could run the complicated printing equipment. But the recent switch to automation has eliminated many jobs and has also made it possible for employers to easily replace union employees. Anyone can be trained in a short time to use the new printing equipment. Therefore, if union members decide to strike for better wages, hours, and working conditions, management could easily, and legally, find replacements for them. In essence, the union is unable to fulfill its main mission, which is to collectively represent the employees who voted for it.

To solve the current crisis, Maria is considering five options:

- Implement an associate member plan through which any individual could join the union for a fee of $50 a year. Although these members would not be fully represented on the job, they would get an attractive package of benefits, such as low-cost home, health, and auto insurance.
- Attempt some cooperative labor-management relations programs, such as getting member representation on newspaper boards of directors or employee participation programs in the workplace.
- Put more effort into political action. For example, lobby for labor law reform or for new laws more favorable to unions. Initiate action that would result in harsher penalties against employers that practice illegal union-avoidance activities, such as threatening to move the business if a union is voted in or firing pro-union employees.
- Appeal to community leaders to speak out in favor of the union in order to improve public relations, to help recruit new members, and to encourage employers to bargain fairly when negotiating with the union.
- Search for another union with which the printing professionals might merge, thus increasing their membership, strengthening their finances, increasing their bargaining power, and obtaining economies of scale.

Maria realizes that each of these options could have both positive and negative results, and is unsure which strategy, if any, she should recommend for the union to pursue. In less than three hours, however, she will have to present the list to the council with her recommendations. ◉

Discussion Questions
1. What are the strengths and weaknesses of each strategy?
2. What strategies could be employed to get new bargaining units?
3. What other types of services could the union offer to its members?
4. What would be your final recommendation? Justify your response.

SOURCE: K. Stratton-Devine, University of Alberta.

Human Resource Information Systems and Assessment: Getting and Using the Facts

We operate the HR department so that we save the company more than we cost the company.

PAUL J. BEDDIA, Vice President of Human Resources
Lincoln Electric Company[1]

Managing Human Resources for the 21st Century for Boardroom Impact

What will it take to bring human resources out of the backroom and into the boardroom? In the age of information technology, a good HR department can make or break an organization. But information alone is not the answer. Creating a full partnership with line management will depend on HR's ability to provide true decision-support systems.

Decision-support systems represent the function that will redefine HR's role. To begin, you, as HR managers, must effectively weave total quality management into each aspect of every human resources function. Although TQM achieves the highest possible standards in business, the term too often is associated only with product output or end results, rather than an organization's overall approach to business. Therefore, the HR department has to break new ground by implementing TQM everywhere.

RETHINK YOUR CUSTOMERS

TQM affects all employee-related issues—from productivity, loyalty, and work ethic to overall well-being. HR provides services that greatly impact these elements, and it can directly influence a company's success or failure.

HR must be concerned not only with its own activities, but also with the organizations and vendors that the company entrusts its services to such as insurance companies, trainers and motivational speakers, and service bureaus, to name a few. Are you doing all you can to make sure these vendors have what they need to do their jobs? Insurance companies, for example, are vital to many organizations. Are you giving health-care providers timely and accurate information? Managing vendors as customers allows HR to serve its organization both in long-term strategy and in special situations.

Company departments should also be treated as customers. They rely heavily on HR to perform many functions that affect their own performance. Providing quality job candidates, filling open positions quickly, and providing timely and accurate attendance reports are just a few examples.

USE TECHNOLOGY WISELY

Weaving TQM into HR activities demands taking full advantage of today's computer technology. Automation has made it easier to be more effective and efficient. With effective HR management systems, you can provide prompt and reliable services. From timely and accurate government reports to speedy applicant screening and tracking, using technology to its fullest moves you one step closer to achieving maximum quality.

Software facilitates the accumulation of information, but it's the wise use of that information that determines HR's role in decision support. To facilitate this changing role, software companies offer integrated products that provide comprehensive information on employees, budgets, payroll, and position control. Effectively managing this information in terms of TQM brings HR into the long-term plans of an organization.[2]

The feature "Managing Human Resources for the 21st Century for Boardroom Impact" brings together many things. One is the importance of total quality. Another is the growing partnership role between HR professionals, line managers, and employees. The feature suggests that HR managers can extend this partnership all the way up to the boardroom. This feature also suggests that HR professionals should treat line managers as customers, and a major way to do this is through effective human resource information systems and the use of computer technology.

 ## HUMAN RESOURCE INFORMATION SYSTEMS AND ASSESSMENT

For many people, information is something they did not know or have and that can be used in the solution of a problem. Data can often be more basic, referring to numbers, people, or things. In this sense, data become information when accessed by people who need them and can use them in the solution of problems. When data and information are organized, systematic, and integrated, we refer to them as an information system. Computer technology enables organizations to combine their data and information in efficiently centralized locations, called databases, and then make them available for use by others regardless of their location. When these databases contain data and information for managing human resources, we call them human resource information systems (HRISs). An example of the type of data and information that can be stored on an HRIS is shown in Exhibit 17.1.

Assessment systems are organized approaches to measuring and evaluating the success of a human resource activity. Assessment systems enable HR professionals, line managers, and employees to use human resource data and information to determine whether human resources are being managed as effectively as possible.[3] This partnership is further described in the feature "Partnership in Human Resource Information Systems and Assessment."

Linking Human Resource Planning with Organizational Business Planning

With the power of computers, it becomes more feasible to relate human resource planning with the planning needs of the business. At Chevron Corporation in San Francisco, California, the HR group has been able to link HR planning more closely with business planning by decentralizing its HRIS to the business units. Each unit is different in terms of business needs, planning cycles, and degree of change, and decentralization allows it to use the system in a way that is comfortable for it. With greater comfort comes greater use of the system.[4]

Compensation. Computer technology and compensation data in an HRIS can be instrumental in managing total compensation and ensuring equity. In ledger format, human resource specialists can maintain the value (cost) of total compensation in several configurations. For example, total compensation can be computed for each employee, and the average for each position or department. In addition, specific components of total compensation can be calculated and used for projecting and establishing salary and benefits budgets for appropriate organization units. With job evaluation, the human resource department can determine whether compensable factors are being assigned monetary values systematically or randomly. This may serve as an initial step in minimizing inequities in compensation.[5]

Computer technology can accommodate the planning and administration of performance-based pay in the following ways: First, administration may be conducted by establishing a grid for a merit pay plan on a computer system and programming the computer to post the appropriate percentage increases. Second, budget planning is facilitated simply by manipulating the percentage values on the grid, automatically changing each individual's pay. As in total compensation, performance-based planning may be considered by department, position, or another meaningful unit. The resulting values may be equally useful to top management. Because time is a cost to the organization, the ability to analyze this information quickly represents a substantial cost efficiency.

Computer technology facilitates the management and manipulation of data that can be used to project salary structures, compa-ratios, "compensation cost-versus-amount-of-revenue-generated" ratios, the total cost of selected configurations of benefits packages, and the cost of compensation in the future under different rates of inflation. These

■ *Exhibit 17.1*

Primary Forms of Information Stored in a Human Resource Information System

General

Absenteeism	Applicant tracking
Attendance	Attitude surveys
Date of birth	Date of status
Department code	Dependents
Disciplinary actions	Emergency contact list
Employee number	Employment history
Grievance tracking	Hire date
Home address	Home telephone number
Job level	Job posting
Job title	Location
Office telephone number	Office address
Safety and OSHA	Performance appraisal rating
Job status (full-time, part-time, terminated)	Social Security number
Veteran status	Union code
Workers' compensation record	Work shift

Affirmative Action and EEOC

ADA status	Availability analysis
Citizenship	EEO code (professional, technical, etc.)
Gender	Job group within EEO code
Minority status	Workforce utilization analysis

Benefits

Accidental death and dismemberment coverage*	COBRA
Company credit union	Dental*
Flexible or cafeteria benefits plan*	Health plan coverage (family, single)*
Life insurance coverage*	Long-term disability coverage*
Marital Status	Stock plan option*
Savings bonds*	Vacation and sick leave
Tuition dollars refunded	
401(k) contribution*	*Employee and employer contribution

Compensation

Bonus pay	Job evaluation
Merit pay	Pay frequency (weekly, biweekly, monthly)
Payroll planning and implementation	Retiree pension obligations
Salary history	Salary level and range
Stock purchase plan	

Education

Field of degree	Highest degree earned
Skills profile (languages, training, licenses, etc.)	Training received (internal, external)
Year degree awarded	

Human Resource Planning

Candidate lists	Environmental scanning
Labor market analysis	Needs assessment
Recruitment source	Skills inventory
Succession planning	Supply assessment
Turnover analysis	

SOURCE: Adapted from E. P. Bloom, "Creating an Employee Information System," *Personnel Administrator* (November 1982): 68, by M. A. Huselid, Professor of Human Resource Management, Rutgers University, 1995.

Partnership in Human Resource Information Systems and Assessment

Line Managers	Human Resource Professionals	Employees
Provide accurate and current HR data to enable the linkage of HR data and business needs.	Link HR databases to the needs of the business.	Use computer-based HR activities to manage personal careers.
Help assess the quality of HR activities.	Develop a user-friendly HRIS.	Participate in organizational surveys.
Use on-line data in the daily management of employees.	Continually assess and improve HR activities.	Play an active role in assessing HR activities.
		Use computer-based HR activities to help solve organizational problems.

calculations may be made on the basis of an individual employee, a group, or the overall organization. Selected information may be further extracted to make summary reports and projections for areas other than the HR department, such as a budget sheet for the comptroller or the line manager.

Training and Development. Computer-based training (CBT) is now being used in several organizational settings. A great deal of training for airline pilots is conducted using CBT and flight simulators. However, although efficient, using CBT alone may not be the best way to train future pilots. SimuFlite Training International, a recent competitor to the long-established FlightSafety International, learned through trial and error—and customers' reactions—that CBT needs to be mixed with stand-up instructor training to be effective.[6]

At the Hudson Bay Company, a large Canadian retailer, CBT is being used to train new sales associates in everything from store procedures to customer service practices. CBT has replaced an intensive three-day training program that was all oral presentations by supervisors.

Because of its success, CBT is being used for training in many other areas, including

- Interviewing techniques
- Effective people management
- Retail method of inventory
- Retail marketing
- Sales promotion
- Professional selling skills
- Line-budget maintenance
- Check authorization
- Inventory systems
- Career planning
- Family budgeting[7]

Overall, the results indicate that CBT is more cost-effective than traditional training because students spend less time in the classroom and more time on the job being productive.

Total Quality Management. Getting total quality and then continuously improving depends on data, information, and assessment. A great deal of the data and information required is human resource in nature, so HR has to have the necessary material available—for example, who the best performers are, whether the firm is selecting the best applicants regarding math skills, or whether the firm is selecting people with the greatest potential to continually adapt. Even if the required data and information are not human resource related, HR has to be able to train employees to understand and utilize them—for example, HR has to train employees in the statistical process control described in Chapter 9. This provides some elementary tools in problem identification, solution development, and assessment and revision.

Testing. One area of computer technology that is receiving increased research attention among HR professionals is that of tailored or adaptive testing:

> A computer-assisted or adaptive test uses a multi-stage process to estimate a person's ability several times during the course of testing, and the selection of successive test items is based on those ability estimates. The person tested uses an interactive computer terminal to answer a test question. If the answer is correct, the next item will be more difficult; if not, an easier item follows. With each response, a revised and more reliable estimate is made of the person's ability. The test proceeds until the estimate reaches a specified level of reliability. Generally, the results are more reliable and require fewer items than a paper and pencil test.[8]

A few researchers have examined issues concerning the validity of computer-administered adaptive tests. One study compared the Arithmetic Reasoning and Word Knowledge subtests of the Armed Services Vocational Aptitude Battery (ASVAB) with computer-administered adaptive tests as predictors of performance in a training course for Air Force mechanics.[9] The study found that computer-administered adaptive tests that are one-third to one-half the length of conventional (i.e., paper-and-pencil) ASVAB tests could approximate the criterion-related validity coefficients of these conventional tests. These findings are even more impressive when one considers that adaptive tests administer different items to different individuals.

Others have pointed out that increased measurement accuracy is not the only benefit of computer-administered adaptive testing.[10] Additional benefits include reductions in testing time, fatigue, and boredom, as well as cost savings, in some cases, over conventional paper-and-pencil testing.[11] A study conducted within the U.S. Office of Personnel Management in Washington, D.C., placed the cost of adaptive testing at less than that of paper-and-pencil testing.[12] Moreover, a report prepared for the Canadian government estimated that, even considering the capital investment in computer equipment, computer-administered adaptive tests could show a savings over conventional paper-and-pencil tests in one year.[13]

Despite its potential benefits, computerized testing for making employment decisions has been the subject of numerous and significant court decisions,[14] and this legal scrutiny will likely continue.

Interviewing. Computers are also being used to reduce the first-impression biases inherent in job interviews. They present a structured interview directly to an applicant, without an interviewer present. Although computer-aided interviewing does not replace face-to-face interviewing, it complements it by providing a base of information about each applicant before the interviewer meets the applicant. This provides a first impression based on information that is job relevant rather than anecdotal.

Computer interviewing is also faster. An applicant can complete a one-hundred-question computer-aided interview in about twenty minutes. The same information would require a face-to-face interview of more than two hours. In addition, computer-aided interviewing provides an automatic record of answers so that they can be compared across applicants. More important, computer-aided interviews have been validated in a number of settings, including the manufacturing and service industries.[15]

Communicating with Employees through Surveys

Improving communication facilitates the transmission of employees' ideas into product improvements (as in quality circles) and organizational changes, and at the same time enhances employees' job involvement, participation, and sense of being in control. In addition, training programs can be established to improve supervisory communication.

Computer technology and data and information systems can also make it easier to conduct organizational surveys. Organizational surveys are systematic and scientific ways of gathering information for the purpose of assessing current conditions, seeking areas for improvements, and then developing programs to make the improvements. Weyerhaeuser and the Eaton Corporation have used surveys for these purposes (see Chapters 1 and 4).

What Do Surveys Measure? In many applications of human resource data, the data gathered are either measures of job performance itself or predictors of job performance, such as tests and background characteristics. But the human resource manager often needs other types of data. For example, to develop ways to improve employee performance, the human resource manager needs to measure how the employees perceive their environment, including the consequences of job performance, quality of feedback, and aspects of goal setting. It is equally necessary to gather data on employees' perceptions of quality of work life and of stress. With both kinds of data, objective and perceptual, the human resource manager can begin to make other changes for organizational improvement.

Employees also react to the environment and job qualities. Many of their reactions, which include physiological responses such as changes in blood pressure and heart rate, are symptoms of employee stress. Because one human resource management criterion is employee health, systematically gathering this type of information is important.

Thus, generally, organizational surveys can measure the following:

- Employee Perceptions: understanding of individual roles, role conflict, diversity, job qualities, and interpersonal qualities (such as those of the supervisor and group members)
- Employee Reactions: feelings (such as satisfaction) and physiological responses (such as heart rate and blood pressure)
- Employee Behaviors: performance, absenteeism, and turnover

How Is a Survey Conducted? The steps for a human resource manager—or an outside consultant or even a line manager, such as Jerry Laubenstein at AAL—to consider when conducting an organizational survey include planning carefully, collecting data, providing feedback, and ensuring employee participation.[16] Planning addresses each of the following:

- ◉ Specific employee perceptions and responses that should be measured
- ◉ Methods that will be used to collect the data, including observations, questionnaires, interviews, and personnel records
- ◉ Reliability and validity of the measures to be used
- ◉ People from whom the data will be collected—all employees, managerial employees only, a sample of employees, or only certain departments within the organization
- ◉ Timing of the survey and the way to make the survey part of a longer-term effort
- ◉ Types of analyses that will be made with the data
- ◉ Specific purposes of the data—for example, to determine the reasons for the organization's turnover problem

This last consideration is important, because by identifying the problem, the manager can determine which models or theories will be relevant to the survey. Knowing which one to use tells the manager what data are needed and what statistical techniques will be necessary to analyze the data.

The actual collection of data involves three things. First, it must be decided who will administer the survey—the line manager, someone from the human resource department, or someone from outside the organization. Second, it must be decided where, when, and in what size groups the data will be collected. All these considerations are influenced by the method used to gather the data. For example, if a questionnaire is used, larger groups are more feasible than if interviews are conducted. Finally, employee participation in the survey must be ensured. This can be done by gathering the data during company time and by providing feedback—for instance, by promising employees that the results of the survey will be made known to them.

As part of the feedback process, the data are analyzed according to the purposes and problems for which they were collected. The results of the analysis can then be presented by the human resource department to the line managers, who in turn discuss them with their employees. The feedback sessions can be used to develop solutions to any problems that are identified and to evaluate the effectiveness of programs that may already have been implemented on the basis of an earlier survey.

The extent to which employees actually participate in the development of solutions during the feedback process depends on the philosophy of top management. Organizations willing to survey their employees are also usually willing to invite their employees to help decide how to make things better. It is this willingness that allows organizational surveys to be used most effectively.

Legal Compliance

HRIS and computer technology can facilitate the easy storage and access of human resource records that are vital for organizations. To comply with federal equal employment laws, organizations must follow several requirements for keeping human resource records. Title VII of the 1964 Civil Rights Act says organizations must keep all employment records for at least six months. The Equal Pay Act and the Age Discrimination in Employment Act say organizations must keep records for three years—but three years is not always long enough. If an employee or a governmental agency lodges a charge against a firm, the firm should have all its records regarding the person making the complaint as well as records on all other employees in similar positions. Organizations also must keep records on seniority, benefits, and merit and incentive plans until at least one year after the plans end.

Organizations also have to fill out reports. Employers of one hundred or more workers must annually file EEO-1 reports to comply with equal employment opportunity laws. Multiestablishment employers need only file separate EEO-1 reports for each

Positioning for the 21st Century:
EMPLOYMENT POLICIES AUDIT

These headlines strike fear in employers:

- "$2 Million Settles Psychological Testing Suit" (reporting on a class action lawsuit against an employer for requiring a detailed preemployment psychological exam)
- "Salesman Wins Quarter Million for Wrongful Discharge"
- "Employee Seeks Punitive Damages under ADA"

How can an employer try to avoid these devastating results in employment litigation? One excellent avoidance technique is to undertake a comprehensive audit of all employment procedures, policies, and practices to ensure that all are in accord with the rapidly changing state and federal employment laws.

A comprehensive audit will allow employers to determine if they are complying with all applicable laws. Among other areas, an audit should consider the following:

- Has the employee handbook, manual, or policy been revised since the Family and Medical Leave Act became effective, to specifically set forth leave policies as required by federal regulations?
- Are all required notices posted in the workplace (e.g., "Sexual Harassment Is Illegal," state and federal wage and hour laws, state and federal OSHA guidelines, state and federal fair employment laws, and the Family and Medical Leave Act)?
- Do you have job descriptions, and, if so, have they been revised to set forth the essential tasks neces-

sary to do the jobs? (This is helpful in fully complying with the Americans with Disabilities Act.)
- Do you comply with the Immigration and Naturalization Service requirement to complete work authorization (I-9) forms for all employees?
- Have you complied with the state-mandated training requirements regarding the illegality of sexual harassment?
- Do you have a procedure to field complaints of sexual harassment in the workplace, is it effective, and does it protect the rights of the accused and the accuser?
- Where do you conduct your employment interviews? Are they accessible pursuant to the ADA?
- Does your employment manual have any provisions that are contrary to state or federal law in any way?
- Do you have an evaluation and discipline process that allows for accurate and thoroughly written documentation of employee performance?
- Is your hiring process subject to claims of discrimination because you have a narrow applicant pool?
- Have you implemented a policy of nondiscrimination in the workplace?

As this partial list indicates, an employment audit must be very comprehensive. It must analyze which laws are applicable to your business, and how your procedures, policies, and practices must be adapted to avoid lawsuits in the future. Because of the complexity of the issues, it is best to get advice from your lawyer and to work together to audit your employment practices.[17]

---

establishment employing fifty or more workers. Organizations with government contracts must fill out affirmative action reports that the Office of Federal Contract Compliance Programs sends. Government contractors required to fill out Standardized Affirmative Action Formats (SAAFs) for the OFCCP can propose the SAAF to cover all its establishment as long as its HR activities are the same for each establishment. Having safety and health records is a requirement of OSHA, and can also be part of a strategy to improve occupational safety and health.

In addition to providing the facts and figures needed for records and reports, HR data can help companies audit how well they are complying with the law. An HR department can audit the company's employment policies as they relate to all areas of managing human resources, as described in the feature "Positioning for the 21st Century: Employment Policies Audit."

ETHICAL CONCERNS

With computers and an HRIS, human resource departments can quickly generate confidential HR information in a variety of formats. Thus, many copies of confidential information may exist at any one time, increasing the likelihood that some may be misplaced or even stolen. As a result, file security is of concern. Today's computerized HRIS systems include access protectors that limit who can read or write to a file, and they can be designed to allow a single person or a group of individuals access or no access. Although these systems reduce the threat of file invasion, most contain a "back door," or secret entry, which, if discovered by an unauthorized user, may allow unauthorized access to files.

At the same time, computer technology is also being used to ensure that employee policies are implemented fairly. Expert systems such as those developed by HumanTek, a San Francisco, California, software company, guide managers with employee problems to solutions. By asking a series of questions, the computer steers the manager to organizational policies and precedents that relate to the specific performance problem. Some sophisticated programs even give managers advice. According to Walter Ratcliff, a HumanTek consultant, expert systems will be the best friend of tomorrow's manager. Rather than flipping through a human resource manual, a supervisor will turn on the computer for advice.

Computer technology is also being used to monitor the performance of employees. The Office of Technology Assessment in Washington, D.C., estimates that up to 10 million workers are regularly monitored at their computers:

> At hundreds of companies, the performance of data-entry clerks is judged by the speed of their computer-measured keystrokes. Directory-assistance operators at telephone companies are allotted 25 seconds or less to root out a number, however vague the request, and computers record their times.
>
> In supermarkets, computers measure the speed with which the checkout clerks sweep purchases over the optical scanners.
>
> In an office building in downtown St. Louis, customer-service representatives at Union Pacific Railroad offices who book shipments for companies that send their goods by rail work at the kind of pace that telephone operators and airline reservation agents do.
>
> "A customer calls in and says, 'I need two freezer cars to ship frozen french fries from American Falls, Idaho, to a warehouse in Kentucky,' " said Tracey Young, an official with the transportation and communication workers union. He said that computers track the origin, duration, and frequency of calls and that supervisors, secretly and at random, listen in.[18]

Employees who are monitored complain that their rights to privacy are being violated, and the company states that it needs the information in order to be competitive. The customer may claim the right to good service—and if computer monitoring is what it takes, then so be it, say the companies. The use of computer monitoring is an important employee rights issue that is likely to gain increased attention from its increased use, well into the 21st century.[19]

ASSESSMENT SYSTEMS FOR HUMAN RESOURCE MANAGEMENT

Assessment systems help the HR department to determine what its customers want, how well HR is doing, and what might be done to improve HR products and services. Thus, assessment systems are consistent with partnership.

The Human Resource Department

The human resource department can demonstrate its contribution to the organization in many ways. As HR departments seek to become partners with the rest of their organizations in providing strategic direction, they are being proactive in providing evidence of their contributions.

The contributions of HR departments can be grouped into two categories: doing the right things, and doing things right.[20] *Doing the right things* means doing the things that are needed to help make the organization successful. In essence, assessors ask if the department is helping the organization be more successful in areas such as competitiveness, profitability, adaptability, and strategy implementation. Is it helping line managers and employees contribute to the maximum of their potential?

Doing things right means doing the right things as efficiently as possible. Of course, the organization wants to hire the best people, but it wants to do so at the least possible cost for each hire. The HR department wants to facilitate the work of the line managers, but it wants to do so in a way that maximizes the benefit and minimizes the cost—as Paul Beddia suggests in the quote that opens this chapter.

HR contributions can be assessed by determining costs and benefits in dollars and cents, or by measuring timeliness. In other words, it can be assessed using quantitative measures. Whereas measures such as "the cost of each hire who stays three or more years" are very specific quantitative indicators, measures such as firm productivity or profitability (as discussed in Chapter 1) are very general quantitative indicators.

Assessment can also be done using qualitative measures. For instance, HR departments that want to focus more on the customer can ask the line managers, employees, and other constituents for their opinions of the quality of service the HR department is delivering.

Although it is easy to categorize these measures of assessment here, in reality, they are not always so clear-cut. For example, the HR department may measure the satisfaction of employees (with regard to any aspect of work that is related to the HR department) with a questionnaire. In a way, this assessment gathers qualitative information in a quantitative way.

Human Resource Planning

Without effective human resource planning, an organization may find itself with a plant or an office with no people to run it. On a broad level, then, human resource planning can be assessed on the basis of whether the organization has the people it needs at the right place, at the right time, at the right salary, and with the right skills and behaviors.

At more specific levels, human resource planning activities can be assessed by how effectively they, along with recruitment, attract new employees, deal with job loss, and adapt to the changing characteristics of the environment. In addition, human resource planning can be assessed by how well its forecasts—whether of specific personnel needs or of specific environmental trends—compare with reality. Other criteria for evaluating human resource planning include the following comparisons:

- Actual staffing levels against established staffing requirements
- Productivity levels against established goals
- Actual personnel flow rates against desired rates
- Programs implemented against action plans
- Program results against expected outcomes (e.g., improved applicant flows, reduced quit rates, and improved replacement ratios)

- Labor and program costs against budgets
- Program results (benefits) against program costs[21]

Job Design

Job design can be assessed in several ways. The first is through improvement in productivity. At UPS and Lincoln Electric, jobs have been redesigned through time-and-motion studies to improve efficiency. The success of these improvements can be measured in terms of the extent to which the worker is able to do more in less time, and thus be more productive.

If organizations choose to redesign jobs to enhance their skill variety, autonomy, significance, identity, and feedback, they can measure the success of the changes with indicators of these outcomes.[22] They should keep in mind that negative results for these indicators may not be evidence that the job redesign project did not work. They may simply mean that employees did not perceive any changes in the core job characteristics.

An abbreviated example of a survey used to assess a job redesign effort is shown in Exhibit 17.2. Line manager Jerry Laubenstein at AAL used this survey in his IPS unit, after making a systematic change in jobs. As a result, he discovered that not only are his employees feeling better, but they also have improved their productivity substantially.

The third way the efforts of job design can be assessed is through the rates of reported worker injury, particularly low-back pain and repetitive motion injuries. Because these injuries lead to reported absenteeism and more medical insurance claims and higher workers' compensation costs, companies are seeking ways to reduce them. One effective way to do so in many situations is through ergonomic redesign of the jobs. Although this may not change the core job dimensions, it may lead to less bending and lifting, less uncomfortable chairs, and better positioning of the computer screen. These changes may improve the safety of the workers, as well as their health.

Recruitment

The recruitment activity is supposed to attract the right people at the right time within legal limits, so that people and organizations can select each other in their best short- and long-run interests. Likewise, this is how recruitment should be assessed. Exhibit 17.3 shows specific criteria for assessing recruitment, grouped by the stages of the recruitment process in which they are most applicable.

Each method or source of recruitment can be valuated, or appraised, by looking at the short- and long-term costs of its benefits. Finally, the utility of each method can be determined by comparing the number of potentially qualified applicants hired by each method and by occupational group. The method resulting in the most qualified applicants at the lowest cost for each hire may be determined most effective in the short run.

Selection and Placement

If the organization can select and place applicants who perform well, organizational productivity will benefit. To make selection and placement decisions that will benefit organizational productivity, organizations must use predictors that are valid and legal. Organizations must also be concerned with the overall costs of the selection devices and weigh these against the benefits.[23] Utility analysis, described in Appendix A, is one approach to this assessment challenge.

■ *Exhibit 17.2*

Job Characteristics Questionnaire

Please use the scales below to describe the objective characteristics of your job. For each numbered item, enter a check mark in the blank which best describes the job.

1. How much *autonomy* is there in the job? That is, to what extent does a person decide *on his/her own* to go about doing the job?

```
_____ : _____ : _____ : _____ : _____ :
     (1)              (2)              (3)              (4)              (5)
  Very little                     Moderate autonomy                   Very much
```

2. How much *variety* is there in the job? That is, to what extent does a person have to do many different things on the job, using a variety of his/her skills and talents?

```
_____ : _____ : _____ : _____ : _____ :
     (1)              (2)              (3)              (4)              (5)
  Very little                      Moderate variety                   Very much
```

3. To what extent does the job involve doing a *"whole" and identifiable piece of work?* That is, does a person do a complete piece of work that has an obvious beginning and end? Or does he/she do only a small *part* of the job, which is completed by other people or by automatic machines?

```
_____ : _____ : _____ : _____ : _____ :
     (1)              (2)              (3)              (4)              (5)
 The person does                The person does a                The person does
only a tiny fraction             moderate sized                  the full piece of
 of the actual job               "chunk" of work                 work from start to
                                                                  finish
```

4. In general, how *significant or important* is the job? That is, are the results of work on the job likely to significantly affect the lives or well-being of other people?

```
_____ : _____ : _____ : _____ : _____ :
     (1)              (2)              (3)              (4)              (5)
  Not at all                       Moderately                  Highly significant
  significant                      significant
```

5. To what extent does *doing the job itself* provide a person with information about his/her work performance? That is, does the actual *work itself* provide clues about how well a person is doing—aside from any "feedback" obtained from co-workers or supervisors?

```
_____ : _____ : _____ : _____ : _____ :
     (1)              (2)              (3)              (4)              (5)
  Very little                        Moderate                     Very much
```

SOURCE: Based upon the *Job Characteristics Questionnaire,* in R. Hackman and G. R. Oldham, *Work Redesign* (Reading, MA: 1980).

Performance Appraisal

The best appraisal system is one that supports the formulation and implementation of an organization's strategy in a cost-effective manner. No rational manager is interested in rating accuracy or performance feedback for altruistic purposes alone.

In recent years, several studies have been undertaken to determine the utility of replacing a poorly designed performance appraisal system with one that provides valid feedback to workers.[24] For example, a city government had been using trait-

■ *Exhibit 17.3*

Some Criteria for Assessing Recruitment

Stage of Entry	Type of Criteria
Pre-entry	Total number of applicants Number of applicants from minority groups and female applicants Cost for each applicant Time to locate job applicants Time to process job applicants
Offers and hires	Offers extended by company Total number of qualified applicants Number of applicants from minority groups and female applicants Costs of acceptance versus rejection of applicants
Entry	Initial expectations of newcomers Choice of the organization by qualified applicants Cost and time of training new employees Salary levels required
Post-entry	Attitudes toward job, pay, benefits, supervision, and coworkers Organizational commitment Job performance Tenure of hires Absenteeism Referrals

based performance appraisals. In place of this system, the city was considering an output-based management-by-objectives system. Although the MBO process was intuitively appealing, managers were concerned about costs. The MBO system demanded thorough job analysis and regular updating of job descriptions, participative goal setting, and extensive documentation. The cost of doing these was estimated at $1,000 a person. By comparison, the trait-based appraisal process was relatively simple and took little time to complete, for a cost of only $100 a person. Five hundred managerial, technical, and professional employees would be evaluated with the new MBO system. These employees earned an average salary of $45,000 and stayed in their jobs an average of 8.6 years.

Research showed that the average validity for the MBO system should be .63 because the city manager and counsel members are all highly committed to the new appraisal process (see the Appendix for a discussion of validity scores). The validities of the trait-based system are much lower, estimated to be as low as –.15 and only as high as .15. Given these values, a utility analysis indicated that the current appraisal system may cost the city as much as $4.1 million in lost productivity, probably due to grievances, absenteeism, and lower motivation; at best, the trait system might yield gains in productivity valued at $4 million. By comparison, the MBO system, which includes goal setting, participation, and feedback, could be expected to yield productivity gains valued at $12 million.

Although utility analysis such as this can be quite convincing, it is erroneous to conclude that in this case the MBO system will actually produce an extra $8 to $16 million to spend. Since model parameters were only estimated, the actual gain in productivity may be more or less than predicted. However, the new system could be expected to have higher utility than the old system, and should yield substantial gains in productivity compared with the old system over the next several years.

Compensation

In assessing how effectively an organization administers its compensation program, the following major purposes of total compensation must be kept in mind:

- Attracting potentially qualified employees
- Motivating employees
- Retaining qualified employees
- Administering pay within legal constraints
- Attaining human resource plans and strategic business objectives

If an organization hopes to achieve these purposes, employees generally need to be satisfied with their pay. This means the pay levels should be extremely competitive, employees should perceive internal pay equity, and the compensation program should be properly administered.[25] It also means that compensation practices must adhere to the various state and federal wage and hour laws, including comparable worth considerations.

Consequently, an organization's total compensation can be assessed by comparing its pay levels with the pay levels of other organizations, by analyzing the validity of the organization's job evaluation method, by measuring employee perceptions of pay equity and performance-pay linkages, and by determining individual pay levels within jobs and across jobs.

Total compensation can also be assessed by measuring how well it helps attain strategic business objectives. As described in the first integrative case study at the end of the text, Lincoln Electric is a leader in small motors and arc welders and has a compensation system tied to the company's profits. This system has resulted in the average Lincoln worker's making as much as $80,000 a year. In addition to having a high motivation to produce, Lincoln workers rarely quit; their turnover rate is less than 1 percent. The result of Lincoln's compensation system is a cost-efficient competitive advantage that allows it to price its products below those of competitors yet maintain equal, if not better, quality.

Another objective measure that can be used to demonstrate compensation effectiveness is absenteeism. In times that call for lean manufacturing, total quality, and cost reduction, it is extremely important to have exactly the right number of employees—that is, just the number needed to run the operation assuming that everyone is there every day and on time—with precisely the right skills to perform the jobs as effectively as possible. Under this scenario, considerable savings can be gained by having perfect attendance. Thus, firms are seeking ways to get as close to this as possible.

The Engine Components Plant of Eaton Corporation in Saginaw, Michigan, used its compensation system for just this purpose. Under the leadership of the HR manager, Nick Blauwiekel, the plant said that each year, it would pay workers $100 for each successive year of perfect attendance. Thus, for instance, after five years, workers with continuous perfect attendance would receive $500 and would have received a total of $1,500. The result: following the program's installation in 1987, absenteeism quickly dropped from 5.5 percent to substantially less than 1.0 percent (see Exhibit 17.4).

Training and Development

Many ways of evaluating training and development programs have been proposed, including surveys to measure changes in productivity, attitudes (e.g., satisfaction with supervisor, satisfaction with diversity programs, satisfaction with job, stress, role conflict, and knowledge of work procedures), cost savings, benefits gains, and attitudes toward training.[26]

■ *Exhibit 17.4*
Absenteeism at Eaton's Engine Components Plant, 1987–1993

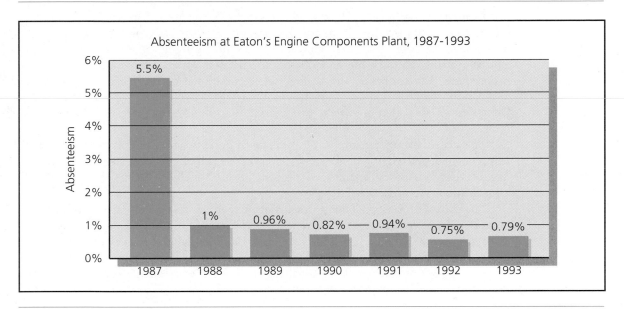

Evaluation Components. Most training experts agree that any evaluation should include at least four components:

- *Reaction to Training:* Did the trainees like the program? Was the instruction clear and helpful? Do the trainees believe that they learned the material?
- *Learning:* Did the trainees actually acquire the knowledge and skills that were taught? Can they talk about things they could not talk about before? Can they demonstrate appropriate behaviors in training (role-play)?
- *Behavior or Performance Change:* Can trainees now do things they could not do before (e.g., negotiate, or conduct an appraisal interview)? Can they demonstrate new behaviors on the job? Is performance on the job better?
- *Results:* Did the training produce tangible results in terms of productivity, cost savings, response time, quality, or quantity of job performance? Did the training program have utility?

The choice of criteria hinges on the level at which the training evaluation is to be conducted. For example, a short attitude survey could be used to assess the response of trainees to a course; it would not provide information on learning, behavior, and results.

If the objective is to assess what was learned, then paper-and-pencil tests can be used. It may also be possible to analyze responses to such training exercises as in-basket tests, role-plays, or case analyses.

Although testing for knowledge acquisition may indicate that learning has occurred, it will not reveal whether learning has been transferred to the job. To assess whether behavior or performance has changed, output measures, performance evaluation reports, and employee attitude surveys provide better information. For example, if employees report more positive attitudes toward supervisory communications after they complete an interpersonal skills program, it may be deduced (assuming other hypotheses can be ruled out) that the training resulted in the behavioral change.

Finally, bottom-line results might be assessed by examining output measures of the work group or unit.

Evaluation Designs. Evaluation designs help the manager determine if improvements have been made and if the training program caused the improvements. They also can help the manager evaluate (1) any human resource program to improve productivity and the quality of work life and (2) the effectiveness of any human resource activity. Combining data collection tools, such as organizational surveys, with knowledge of evaluation designs allows human resource departments to demonstrate their effectiveness—and that of specific programs and activities—to the rest of the organization.

The three major categories of evaluation designs are pre-experimental, quasi-experimental, and experimental (see Exhibit 17.5). Each offers advantages and disadvantages.[27] Data collection techniques that can be used include surveys, interviews, and organizational records.

The most rigorous evaluation designs are experimental designs, which include the pretest-posttest control group design and the Solomon four-group design. In both types of experimental design, individuals are randomly assigned to groups to be tested (identified as time 1 and time 2 in Exhibit 17.5) and not all groups receive a treatment (identified as X in Exhibit 17.5). Evaluation using an experimental design allows the training manager to be more confident that

- A change has taken place—for example, that employee productivity has increased
- The change is caused by the program or HR activity
- A similar change could be expected if the program were done again with other employees

■ *Exhibit 17.5*
Three Categories of Evaluation Design

Pre-Experimental	Quasi-Experimental	Experimental
1. One-shot case study design $\quad$ X $\qquad$ T_2	1. Time-series design $\quad T_1 T_2 T_3$ X $T_4 T_5 T_6$	1. Pretest-posttest control group design $\quad T_1$ $\qquad$ X $\qquad$ T_2 $\quad T_1$ $\qquad$ $\qquad$ T_2
2. One-group pretest-posttest design $\quad T_1$ $\qquad$ X $\qquad$ T_2	2. Nonequivalent control groups design $\quad T_1$ $\quad$ X $\qquad$ T_2 $\quad T_1$ $\qquad$ $\qquad$ T_2	2. Solomon four-group design $\quad T_1$ $\qquad$ X $\qquad$ T_2 $\quad T_1$ $\qquad$ $\qquad$ T_2 $\qquad$ $\quad$ X $\qquad$ T_2 $\qquad$ $\qquad$ $\qquad$ T_2

Note: X = Any Program Being Implemented to Produce Change; T_1 = Time 1; T_2 = Time 2; and so forth.
SOURCE: Based on I. Goldstein, *Training: Program Development and Evaluation,* 2nd ed. (Monterey, CA: Brooks/Cole Publishing Co., 1986), 157–67.

Organizations generally want all employees in a section trained, not just a few who are randomly selected. Consequently, they are more likely to use quasi-experimental design, which does not involve random selection. In both classes of quasi-experimental design shown in Exhibit 17.5, multiple measures (T_1, T_2, etc.) are taken. In the time-series design, several measures are taken before the treatment and several after. In the nonequivalent control groups design, two groups receive multiple measurement, but only one receives a treatment.

Again, although to a lesser extent than is true for experimental designs, quasi-experimental designs are time-consuming and constrained by the realities of organizations. Thus, pre-experimental designs look most attractive to companies. The two classes of pre-experimental design shown in Exhibit 17.5 are much simpler, far less costly, and far less time-consuming than the other designs. But with ease and low cost come less accuracy and confidence in measuring change that may have been the result of a training program—or any other program to produce change. However, these are the realities of organizations, and reflect the constraints and trade-offs HR professionals face daily.

Training and development practices also need to be assessed for the company going global. A sample of practices for such firms appears in Exhibit 17.6. Gaps between "is now" and "should be" might suggest initial areas for improvements.

Safety and Health

Companies trying to improve the safety and health of their environments often need to gather statistics on the frequency and severity of workplace accidents and diseases. For example, the five hundred-person Rosendin Electric company in San Jose, California, had severity and frequency rates that were soaring to worrisome levels.[28] Not surprisingly, workers' compensation costs were also soaring. Consequently, the benefits administrator teamed up with the safety director. Together, they decided to use CompWatch, a software program that tracks the type and total number of injuries. This enabled the firm to produce a great deal of information to help the HR department, line managers, and employees, in partnership, understand what was happening. An example of one type of data output the firm used (and still uses) is shown in Exhibit 17.7. In the first set of these data, Rosendin learned that 50 percent of its total claim costs were for back and eye-related injuries. The firm then decided to launch a safety campaign to increase awareness of the importance of safety regulations. It also streamlined claims processing, continued to track and pinpoint areas of concern, and developed safety programs.

The results of all this: the frequency of workers' compensation claims decreased 35 percent, the severity rate decreased 10 percent, and the money spent on claims decreased 27 percent. The dollar savings amounted to $350,000—not bad for a relatively small company. At an average manufacturing wage, including benefits, of around $18 an hour, this is almost the total annual payroll cost of ten additional employees. If the average annual sales value of Rosendin's products for each employee is $150,000, hiring those ten additional workers could provide the firm another $1.5 million a year. In addition, the firm now has the ability to continue tracking, monitoring, and improving its safety and health conditions.

Collective Bargaining

The effectiveness of the entire collective bargaining process and the union-management relationship can be measured by the extent to which each party attains its goals, but this approach has its difficulties. Because goals are incompatible in many cases and can

■ *Exhibit 17.6*
Training and Development Audit for Global Companies

Please describe the training and development practices of your division or business on two dimensions: *circle* the number describing what it "is now," and *square* the number describing what it "should be."

In our training and development (T&D) decisions . . .	Not at all	To a low extent	Somewhat	A great deal	Completely
1. The best T&D practices worldwide are used.	1	2	3	4	5
2. A global developmental perspective is used.	1	2	3	4	5
3. Opinions and views of several cultures are represented in T&D program design and delivery.	1	2	3	4	5
4. All levels of management are behind our efforts.	1	2	3	4	5
5. Employees from all parts of the world are considered for jobs all over the world.	1	2	3	4	5
6. International meetings are held with a purpose of learning from each other.	1	2	3	4	5
7. Formal and informal mechanisms exist so that managers worldwide can exchange ideas and learn from each other.	1	2	3	4	5
8. Global career paths are critical.	1	2	3	4	5
9. Cross-business and cross-division career paths are critical.	1	2	3	4	5
10. Global career development is in the hands of a corporate unit.	1	2	3	4	5
11. Promotion and compensation practices and policies reward the managers who develop globally.	1	2	3	4	5
12. Managers have a "career home" in a business or division rather than a geographic area.	1	2	3	4	5
13. Performance reviews, rewards, and incentives meet world-class standards.	1	2	3	4	5
14. The ways we do things are continually challenged.	1	2	3	4	5

SOURCE: Randall S. Schuler, Professor of Human Resource Management, New York University.

therefore lead to conflicting estimates of effectiveness, a more useful measure may be the quality of the system used to resolve conflict. Conflict is more apparent in the collective bargaining process, where failure to resolve the issues typically leads to strikes. Another measure of effectiveness is the success of the grievance process, or the ability to resolve issues developing from the bargaining agreement.

Effectiveness of Negotiations. Because the purpose of negotiations is to achieve an agreement, the agreement itself becomes an overall measure of bargaining effectiveness. A healthy and effective bargaining process encourages the discussion of issues and problems and their subsequent resolution at the bargaining table. In addition, the effort required to reach agreement is a measure of how well the process is working. Some indications of this effort are the duration of negotiations, the outcome of member ratification votes, the frequency and duration of strikes, the use of mediation and

■ *Exhibit 17.7*
Number of Claims by Body Part, January 1, 1993, to December 31, 1993

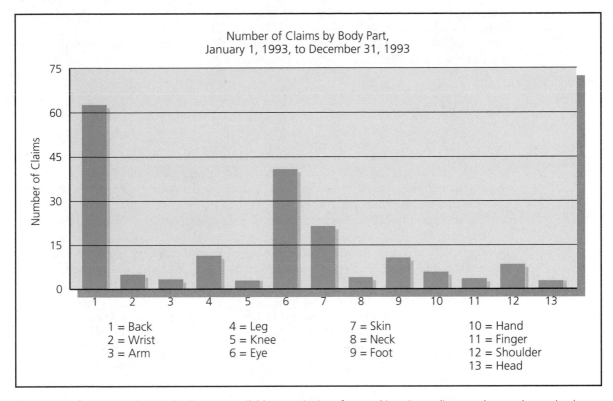

This is one of twenty-eight graphs that are available to assist in safety tracking. Rosendin uses the graphs to clearly illustrate where, when, and how injuries are occurring. During safety meetings, the HR staff uses these graphs, along with reports, to implement safety programs and design safety strategies.

SOURCE: Adapted from L. Johnson, "Preventing Injuries: The Big Payoff," *Personnel Journal* (April 1994): 64. Used by permission.

arbitration, the need for government intervention, and the quality of union-management relations (whether conflict or cooperation exists). Joint programs for productivity and quality-of-work-life improvements could be regarded as successes resulting from effective union-management relations.

Effectiveness of Grievance Procedures. How successful a grievance procedure is may be assessed from different perspectives. Management may view the number of grievances filed and the number settled in its favor as measures of effectiveness, with a small number filed or a large number settled in its favor indicating success. Unions may also consider these numbers, but from their point of view, a large number filed and a large number settled in their favor may indicate success.

An overall set of measures to gauge grievance procedure effectiveness may be related to the disagreements between managers and employees. Measures that might be included are frequency of grievances; the level in the grievance procedure at which grievances are usually settled; the frequency of strikes or slowdowns during the term of labor agreements; the rates of absenteeism, turnover, and sabotage; and the necessity for government intervention.

The success of arbitration is often judged by the acceptability of the decisions, the satisfaction of the parties, the degree of innovation, and the absence of bias in either direction. The effectiveness of any third-party intervention rests in part on how successfully strikes are avoided, because the motivation for such intervention is precisely to avert this extreme form of conflict resolution.

SUMMARY

For organizations to succeed today, they need to be managed systematically and scientifically. That is, they need to be managed with data, information, and assessment tools and techniques. In addition, a culture needs to be created to support the use of these tools and techniques, and skills must be developed among employees so that they are able to use these tools and techniques.

The success of the HR department in developing systems for collecting and using HR information and data depends on the partnership of line managers and employees working with HR professionals. Line managers must be willing to give data and information and then use it; employees need to be willing to learn how to use it and to change and adapt; and HR professionals must be willing to build HRISs that serve the needs of line managers and employees.

Through systematic approaches to assessment, these groups can carefully evaluate the organization's success in all its HR programs and activities. For example, many companies seek to determine how well they are doing in the area of job satisfaction, harassment, or diversity, by giving employees yearly confidential organizational surveys. The responses to these surveys can establish benchmarks that can in turn be used by assessment programs for continual improvements.

The HR data, information, and assessment systems built by organizations can be misused by firms and individuals. Consequently, HR professionals have a special responsibility to secure these systems, yet without limiting the systems' potential for helping the organizations to change conditions rapidly and correctly. The results of successfully accomplishing this balance of interests are beneficial for the organization and the individual.

Discussion Questions

1. What are the purposes of HR data, information, and assessment systems?
2. Describe how computer technology can help line managers fulfill their HR responsibilities.
3. Describe how computer technology can be used in the HR research process.
4. Should companies be limited in the amount of personnel information they can keep in an HRIS? Why or why not?

5. What are the key steps in conducting an organizational survey?
6. How can compensation systems be assessed?
7. How can the collective bargaining process be assessed?
8. What is the relationship between TQM, computer technology, and the HR department's efforts to be more focused on the customer?

In-Class Projects

1. Why would Lincoln Electric likely do an assessment of its HR activities?
2. For what HR activities does Lincoln Electric do assessment?
3. For what activities could or should Lincoln Electric do assessment, if it is not already?
4. Why would AAL likely do an assessment of its HR activities?

5. For what HR activities does AAL do assessment?
6. For what activities could or should AAL do assessment, if it is not already?

Note: These topics are not discussed specifically in the cases. Make your "best guesses" based on what you think effective firms are likely to be doing in assessing their human activities.

 ## Field Project

Visit a local company that has training programs for its employees. Ask a company representative to describe the methods used for evaluating their effectiveness.

Discuss with this person the various types of design the company could use, and record the responses you get. Share your findings with the class.

Case Study:

ALTERNATIVE PERSONNEL SELECTION STRATEGIES AT COMPUTEST

Note: To complete this case study, you may need to refer to Appendix A, where the types of validation strategies are discussed.

Fiscal 1985 was a landmark year of development and growth for CompuTest. As Jerome J. Rosner, president, indicated in a report to the stockholders, "Our company emerged to become a major force in the growing field of computerized psychological testing." It was a year that saw the company transform from 350 employees to over 460 employees. Although a number of employees were added to the marketing, sales, and research operations, the largest number were selected for clerical and administrative positions.

To date, the company has principally targeted its products (computerized psychological tests) at individual mental health practitioners, psychiatric hospitals, and other medical professionals. The company expects these specialized markets to continue to represent a substantial part of its revenue base through 1998. Thereafter, CompuTest expects its sources of revenue to shift as it aggressively enters the vast industrial market. In business and industry, thousands of psychological and ability tests are administered annually. In the past, these tests were given to employees and prospective employees by traditional paper-and-pencil methods—a long, cumbersome, and expensive process. As Paul Lefebre, the company's manager of personnel research states, "CompuTest's current and future testing products have the capability of revolutionizing the area of employee screening with new technologies never before available in the HR field."

One of the newest products developed for the industrial market is a comprehensive battery of computer-administered clerical tests. The company does not want to introduce these tests into the market before gathering evidence concerning their predictive effectiveness. Paul is searching for potential research sites to conduct a criterion-related validity study.

Lane Carpenter, the director of human resources, has told Jerome that many complaints are being raised about the quality of CompuTest's own clerical personnel being selected with the company's verbal ability test. Lane has informed Jerome that although 170 clerical and administrative personnel have been selected with this test, the company has not conducted a criterion-related validity study to evaluate its usefulness. Because of the com-

plaints and the need to select additional clerical personnel, Jerome has called a meeting with Lane and Paul.

Jerome: As you both are aware, we are facing a number of complaints about the quality and quantity of clerical job performance throughout our company. In addition, I would like to bring to your attention that we have projected a need of fifty additional clerical personnel in our current job categories by the end of 1998. This situation requires us to closely examine our current clerical selection procedure and possibly consider viable alternatives. Furthermore, I would like us to reconsider the performance appraisal form we are currently using to evaluate clerical personnel. Our performance appraisal system does not seem to incorporate some of the major duties or tasks that our clerical personnel are being asked to perform. Lane, you have expressed some concerns about the currently used verbal ability test for selecting clerical personnel.

Lane: Yes, I am concerned not only with how good this test is at screening potentially successful clerical personnel but also with how we would defend such a test if challenged in court. I assume you are aware that this test was developed and adopted only on the basis of a content-oriented validity study.

Jerome: Yes, Paul has informed me of the strategy used in developing the verbal ability test. Paul, you also mentioned in a previous discussion that we might be able to conduct another type of validity study for this test.

Paul: We currently have a sufficient number of clerical personnel with verbal ability test scores and performance ratings to conduct a criterion-related validity study. In addition, since we have just completed a comprehensive job analysis of all clerical positions and expected openings within the company, we have the capability of revising our clerical performance appraisal system to more accurately reflect the tasks our clerical employees perform.

Jerome: Does this job analysis also indicate the necessary abilities to effectively perform these tasks?

Paul: Yes, the job analysis clearly identified the required abilities. Furthermore, the job analysis indicated that although the major duties differed across some of our clerical jobs, the entry-level ability requirements for all our clerical jobs were similar.

Lane: If the ability requirements are similar across all clerical jobs, we might be able to conduct a criterion-related validity study for the verbal ability test with our current clerical employees.

Paul: That would be a definite possibility. It might also be helpful for us to consider validating our newly developed computerized clerical ability test battery. That is, we could gather some evidence for its predictive effectiveness in our own company before marketing it to industry. Of course, my department would have to determine which tests were appropriate or should be considered for a validity study here.

Jerome: Paul, that sounds like a good idea. If we are going to successfully market our computerized testing products to industry, we should also be willing to use them. An important question related to your suggestion is how our computer-administered clerical test battery would compare with our currently used verbal ability test. Would we be improving our predictions of who will turn out to be successful workers? If we decided to replace our current selection test with a battery of clerical tests, would it be cost-beneficial? Paul, I would very much appreciate your preparing a proposal for how we might go about validating our currently used verbal ability test and the computer-administered clerical test battery, and how we might compare these alternatives. ◉

Discussion Questions:

1. What is the difference between the test being developed on the basis of a content-oriented validity study and the one developed on the basis of a criterion-related validity study?

2. Does CompuTest first have to change its performance appraisal form before doing a criterion-related validity study?

3. On what basis will Paul go about determining the tests that should be included in the computerized clerical test battery?

4. How should Paul go about validating the firm's verbal ability test and the clerical test battery, and comparing them?

The Human Resource Department: Linking Human Resources with the Business

Capital, at one point, used to be a competitive advantage, but there's much more capital available and accessible now. Technology, at one point, was also a competitive advantage, but even that's become more available. And there was a time, particularly in the financial-services industry, when the half-life of products was very long. But now, you can't build a sustainable advantage on the type of products you offer. The only advantage that has endured is people.

JIM ALEF, Executive Vice President and Head of Human Resources, First Chicago Corporation[1]

Managing Human Resources for the 21st Century at Levi Strauss

Over the past few years, the Levi Strauss organization has linked its HR department and practices closely to the business:

HR participates in every major business decision, and every HR program directly supports a business goal. The payoff is enormous.

DONNA GOYA, Senior Vice President of Human Resources, Levi Strauss[2]

Instrumental in this approach has been the chairman and CEO, Robert B. Haas. Working with the employees, Haas and Goya have crafted a mission statement for human resources that emphasizes the importance of people and that guides the management of the firm's human resources. As a result, Goya says, "I really think that our senior directors do understand now that people can give you the competitive edge."[3] For the employees at Levi Strauss, this has meant empowerment. It is essential, says Goya, that all employees know where they fit into the organization and how they contribute to the broader vision and goals of the company. That may sound easy, but Levi Strauss is doing it with more than thirty thousand employees in 78 production, distribution, and finishing facilities throughout the world.

This insistence on linking the people to the business has also made the HR department more aware of the issues that line managers face daily: keeping employees excited about what they are doing and keeping their productivity high—so high that Levi Strauss continues to be a highly competitive manufacturer. This awareness has resulted in the development of several programs, including

- Management and awareness training organizationwide, to communicate the company's commitment to creating a comfortable work-and-family environment
- Flexible work hours to accommodate plant employees' needs to address family responsibilities
- A new time-off-with-pay program, to replace separate vacation, sick leave, and floating holiday plans
- Child care leave, expanded to cover care for other family members, including elders and significant others
- A corporate child care fund, to enhance the existing community services, ranging from infant day care to after-school programs, based on worker needs
- A child care voucher system for hourly employees working in field locations
- Elder care programs
- Expanded services to help employees in the field[4]

Developing and running these programs successfully is the work of a partnership of HR professionals, line managers, and staff. This partnership takes time and energy—and money—and is indicative of the company's level of commitment. At the San Francisco headquarters alone, one hundred people are employed in human resources, and another two hundred HR staffers work in various facilities around the United States and overseas.

The feature "Managing Human Resources for the 21st Century at Levi Strauss" highlights several things about HR management: (1) it contributes to the effectiveness of organizations; (2) it means developing effective policies and programs, aspiration statements, and a mission statement, and the HR practices that go with them; and (3) it can be very effective in the coordination and facilitation of an entire company's operation. Of course, Levi Strauss is doing much more in HR management, and other aspects of this function will be discussed throughout this chapter.

What is your impression of Levi Strauss? Do you think it is a good company? Is your opinion due in part to how well the firm manages its people? It appears that many people think Levi Strauss deals effectively with its employees; the firm gets thousands of student résumés annually. This phenomenon is due in large part to Levi Strauss's HR department. The HR department is important not only at Levi Strauss but at many organizations. Take a look at what is going on inside HR departments today and find out whether they offer a job for you.

 ## THE HUMAN RESOURCE DEPARTMENT

The *human resource department* is the group formally established by an organization to help manage the organization's people as effectively as possible for the good of the employees, the company, and society. As indicated in Chapter 1, the working partnership of HR staff, line managers, and employees is a major trend in business today. At times, this partnership extends outside the organization—for example, as the firm strives to forge better working relationships with its suppliers. It may also venture into local education facilities as the HR staff works with schools to prepare students for internships in the firm.

Today, a lot is happening in HR departments, in both small and large organizations. The HR department is being looked to anew as a key function that serves the firm's key stakeholders.[5]

 ## PURPOSES AND IMPORTANCE OF THE HUMAN RESOURCE DEPARTMENT

In 1991, IBM and the internationally recognized HR consulting firm Towers Perrin conducted a study of nearly three thousand senior HR managers and CEOs worldwide. Results indicated that a majority of HR managers saw the HR department as critical to the success of businesses in 1991, and even more expected it to be critical by the year 2000 (see Exhibit 18.1). The CEOs were only a bit less positive about this trend. Together, the two groups suggested that the 1990s would be a very dynamic time for HR departments and very different from past years:

> *I've been involved in the people business in one way or another for 35 years, and I'm having more fun today than I've ever had. . . . In the past, the HR function has been like a spare tire kept in the trunk. In an emergency, it's taken out, but as soon as the emergency's over, it's put away. Now I feel that we're a wheel running on the ground. We're not the HR we used to be, but in terms of partnering and helping our companies become competitive, we've only just begun. There are fun times ahead.*

CHARLES F. NIELSON, Vice President of Human Resources, Texas Instruments Incorporated[6]

The fun Nielsen talks about comes in part from performing a broad variety of activities. In addition, HR departments also play a broad variety of roles. How effectively they play all these roles depends on how effective the leader is, how well the department is staffed, and how the department is organized.

 ## THE MANY ROLES OF THE HUMAN RESOURCE DEPARTMENT

Effective firms in the highly competitive environments of today encourage their HR departments to play many roles. The more roles they play well, the more likely they will be to help improve the organization's productivity, enhance the quality of work life in the

■ *Exhibit 18.1*
Expectations of the Effect of the Human Resource Department on Business Success

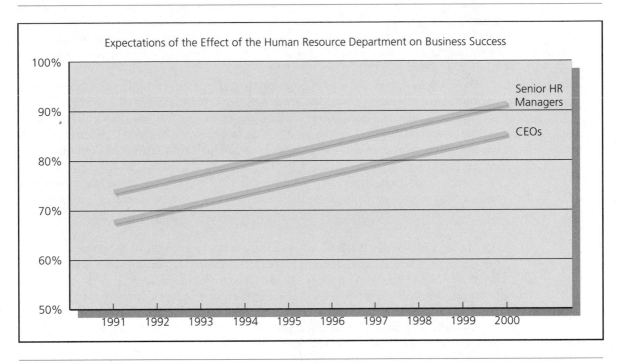

SOURCE: Used by permission. *Priorities for Competitive Advantage: A Worldwide Human Resource Study* (IBM/Towers Perrin: 1992): 27.

organization, comply with all the necessary laws and regulations related to managing human resources effectively, gain competitive advantage, and enhance workforce flexibility.

Business

Traditionally, HR departments had a relatively limited involvement in the total organization's affairs and goals. HR managers were often only concerned with making staffing plans, providing specific job training programs, or running annual performance appraisal programs (the results of which were sometimes put in the files, never to be used). They focused on the short-term—perhaps day-to-day—needs of human resources.

With the growing importance of human resources to the success of the firm (see Exhibit 18.1), HR managers and their departments are becoming more involved in the organization. They are getting to know the needs of the business—where it is going, where it should be going—and are helping it to meet those needs.[7] More typical today, then, is the following observation by Jim Alef, executive vice president and head of human resources, First Chicago Corporation:

"All of our HR programs serve the bank's mission. If they didn't, we wouldn't have them. In the last five years, we've become increasingly a part of the decision-making process at the bank," he says. "We assist with business strategy development by defining the HR implications of those strategies."

"It's much more rewarding," he adds, "to be a thinking participant on the front end of a decision, rather than someone who undoes the damage created by those decisions."[8]

Linking HR to the business is the newest role played by the HR department, and it may be the most important one. One consequence of this role is an increased involvement in the longer-term, strategic directions of the organization. A second consequence is a new emphasis on long-term activities in addition to the more typical medium- and short-term activities. Within these three distinct time horizons, HR departments are functioning at three levels: strategic, managerial, and operational.

Operational Level. At the operational (short-term) level, HR departments make staffing and recruitment plans, set up day-to-day monitoring systems, administer wage and salary programs, administer benefits packages, set up annual or less frequent appraisal systems, and set up day-to-day control systems. They also provide for specific job skill training and on-the-job training, fit individuals to specific jobs, and plan career moves.

As the department begins to perform within the business role, these operational-level HR activities also get linked to the business. For example, training programs are explicitly designed to provide specific employee skills needed by the business.

Managerial Level. At the managerial (medium-term) level, HR departments validate personnel selection criteria, develop recruitment marketing plans, establish new recruiting markets, set up five-year compensation plans for individuals, and set up benefits packages. They also form systems that relate current employment conditions and future business potential. They set up assessment centers, establish development programs for general management, participate in organizational development, foster self-development, identify career paths, and provide career development services.

Although these activities could be done in any HR department, when done in an HR department that is linked with the business, they take on three specific characteristics. The first is that the formulating process is different: for instance, before setting up an assessment center, the department begins with an assessment of what is needed by the business, and then identifies the types of leaders and managers needed to successfully drive the business. The second characteristic is that the content of the human resource activities begins to represent the views of all employees—managers and nonmanagers, workers inside and outside the human resource department. The third characteristic is that the implementation process is very interactive: the managers of human resources work closely with the managers of other areas. For example, John McMahon, corporate vice president of human resources for Stride Rite Corporation in Cambridge, Massachusetts, describes how his group worked with the information systems (IS) group to

> strengthen the information-systems department by creating state-of-the-art data architecture, introducing participative management, creating more effective end-user computing environments and establishing better business partnerships between IS employees and their internal customers. What we did, from an HR standpoint, was to work with the vice president of information systems on restructuring his organization. We assessed the bench strength of current IS employees and established a developmental plan to ensure that the department has the right skill mix. Then, we provided counseling on career management and managing change, we assisted the IS management team in their transition from a non-participatory to a participative management style, and we conducted a climate survey to help managers assess the effectiveness and employee satisfaction related to these changes.[9]

Strategic Level. At the strategic (long-term) level, HR departments get involved in broader decisions—those that provide overall direction and vision for the organization. Tim Harris, senior vice president of HR at Novell in San Jose, California, says, "Being a strategic partner means understanding the business direction of the company, including what the product is, what it's capable of doing, who the typical customers are and how the company is positioned competitively in the marketplace."[10]

By acting as a strategic business partner, the HR department can provide real value to top management. As Richard A. Zimmerman, CEO of Hershey Foods Corporation, says, "There was a time when the HR department was the last to know. Now, the first thing you do is call human resources and say, 'Can you help me do things properly?' "[11] This process of linking HR to the broader, longer-term needs of firms is the essence of *strategic human resource management.*[12]

Typically, strategic business needs arise from decisions such as what products and services to offer and on what basis to compete—quality, cost, or innovation, or for purposes of survival, growth, adaptability, and profitability. These decisions are associated with the formulation and implementation of the organization's strategy, so they are likely to reflect characteristics of the external and internal environments. The internal environment includes the nature of the business (i.e., manufacturing or service), top management's goals and values, organizational size, current and desired levels of profitability, and the technology, structure, and life cycle of the business. Characteristics in the external environment that affect organizational strategy include the basis on which competitive battles are being won in the industry (e.g., cost, quality, or innovation); the life cycle of the industry; social, legal, political, and cultural issues; economic conditions; the scope and degree of competition; labor pool attributes; and customers.

Together, these environmental aspects influence an organization's broader, longer-term, strategic needs and even its mission statement. In turn, the firm's aspiration statement (in essence, its HR philosophy), which indicates how the firm will manage its human resources, is closely linked with its mission statement. Both statements for Levi Strauss are shown in Exhibit 18.2.

Often, the significance of a mission statement lies in the process by which it is created. If the HR mission statement is created in a highly participatory process—that is, where all the employees, line managers, and HR staff are involved, and where public discussion brings clarity, understanding, and commitment—then the end result is not merely a piece of paper but a new atmosphere of partnership within the company. All those affected have a basis that they have created together, upon which they can evaluate the nature and quality of the practices that are developed. These types of HR mission statements become beacons of understanding and cooperation. They enable firms to develop a crucial consistency in HR philosophies, policies, and practices. This consistency in turn enables human resource management to have a positive influence on the bottom line of the organization.

Enabler

In reality, human resource programs succeed because line managers make them succeed. The HR department's bread-and-butter job, therefore, is to enable line managers to make things happen. Thus, in traditional activities—such as selecting, interviewing, training, evaluating, rewarding, counseling, promoting, and firing—the HR department is basically providing a service to line managers. In addition, the department administers direct and indirect compensation programs. It also assists line managers by providing information about, and interpretation of, equal employment opportunity legislation and safety and health standards.

To fulfill these responsibilities, the HR department must be accessible, or it will lose touch with the line managers' needs. The HR staff should be as close as possible to the employees. Being accessible and providing services and products to others (customers) is a trend called customerization.

■ *Exhibit 18.2*
Aspiration and Mission Statements for Levi Strauss

ASPIRATION STATEMENT

We all want a Company that our people are proud of and committed to, where all employees have an opportunity to contribute, learn, grow and advance based on merit, not politics or background. We want our people to feel respected, treated fairly, listened to and involved. Above all, we want satisfaction from accomplishments and friendships, balanced personal and professional lives, and to have fun in our endeavors.

When we describe the kind of LS&CO. we want in the future, what we are talking about is building on the foundation we have inherited: affirming the best of our Company's traditions, closing gaps that may exist between principles and practices, and updating some of our values to reflect contemporary circumstances.

What Type of Leadership Is Necessary to Make Our Aspirations a Reality?

New Behaviors: Leadership that exemplifies directness, openness to influence, commitment to the success of others, willingness to acknowledge our own contributions to problems, personal accountability, teamwork and trust. Not only must we model these behaviors, but we must coach others to adopt them.

Diversity: Leadership that values a diverse work force (age, sex, ethnic group, etc.) at all levels of the organization, diversity in experience, and a diversity in perspectives. We have committed to taking full advantage of the rich backgrounds and abilities of all our people and to promote a greater diversity in positions of influence. Differing points of view will be sought: diversity will be valued and honesty rewarded, not suppressed.

Recognition: Leadership that provides greater recognition—both financial and psychic—for individuals and teams that contribute to our success. Recognition must be given to all who contribute: those who create and innovate and also those who continually support the day-to-day business requirements.

Ethical Management Practices: Leadership that epitomizes the stated standards of ethical behavior. We must provide clarity about our expectations and must enforce these standards through the corporation.

Communications: Leadership that is clear about Company, unit, and individual goals and performance. People must know what is expected of them and receive timely, honest feedback on their performance and career aspirations.

Empowerment: Leadership that increases the authority and responsibility of those closest to our products and customers. By actively pushing responsibility, trust and recognition into the organization, we can harness and release the capabilities of all our people.

MISSION STATEMENT

The mission of Levi Strauss & Co. is to sustain profitable and responsible commercial success by marketing jeans and selected casual apparel under the Levi's brand.

We must balance goals of superior profitability and return on investment, leadership market positions, and superior products and service. We will conduct our business ethically and demonstrate leadership in satisfying our responsibilities to our communities and to society. Our work environment will be safe and productive and characterized by fair treatment, teamwork, open communications, personal accountability and opportunities for growth and development.

SOURCE: J. J. Laabs, "HR's Vital Role at Levi Strauss," *Personnel Journal* (December 1992): 38. Used by permission.

Customerization. Adding to the HR department's ability to gain strategic involvement are its knowledge of the business, its creative insights into how the organization can be more effective, and its familiarity with, and acceptance by, top management. More and more, these qualities are being found in departments that practice customerization. *Customerization* means the state of viewing everybody, whether inside or outside the organization, as a customer and then putting that customer first. For human resource departments, customers are typically other line and staff managers but increasingly include other organizations and nonmanagerial employees.

Essential to this philosophy is the realization that all HR departments produce and deliver products and have "customers."[13] So, too, is the realization that the products provided to satisfy the customer are determined with the customer. Together, in partnership, the customer and HR representatives determine what is best for the situation. This is exactly what happens at Levi Strauss under the leadership of Donna Goya.

Another important part of customerization is *benchmarking*. Benchmarking is a structured approach for going outside an organization to study and adapt the best outside practices to complement internal operations with creative, new ideas. Learning about the practices used by competitors and other companies usually challenges "business-as-usual" methods.[14]

Monitoring

Although the HR department may delegate much of the implementation of its activities to line managers, it is still responsible for seeing that its programs are implemented fairly and consistently—that is, monitoring their outcomes. This is especially true today because of fair employment legislation. Various state and federal regulations are making increasingly sophisticated demands on organizations. Responses to these regulations are best made by a central group supplied with accurate information, the needed expertise, and the support of top management.

Expertise is also needed for implementing human resource activities such as employee benefits administration. Since HR management experts are costly, organizations hire as few as possible and centralize them. Their knowledge and skills then filter to other areas of the organization.

In organizations with several locations and several divisions or units, tension often exists between the need to decentralize—or "flatten"—expertise and the need to centralize it. A major trend in this role of monitoring and coordinating development is the use of computer technology and human resource information systems (described in Chapter 17).

Innovator

An ever-expanding role for the HR department includes providing up-to-date applications of current techniques and developing and exploring innovative approaches to human resource problems and concerns. Benchmarking helps in this role.

Today, organizations are asking their human resource departments for innovative approaches and solutions to improve productivity and the quality of work life while complying with the law in an environment of high uncertainty, energy conservation, and intense international competition. They are also demanding approaches and solutions that can be justified in dollars and cents. Past approaches do not always make the cut in this environment; innovation is no longer a luxury—it is a necessity.[15]

Adapter

It is increasingly necessary for organizations to adapt new technologies, structures, processes, cultures, and procedures to meet the demands of stiffer competition. Organizations look to the human resource department for the skills to facilitate organizational change and to maintain organizational flexibility and adaptability. One consequence of this adapter role is the need to be more focused on the future. For example, as the external environment and business strategies change, new skills and competencies are needed. To ensure that the right skills and competencies are available at the appropriate time, HR departments must anticipate change. Having a mind-set of continuous change and continuous education, as Motorola has, fosters a flexible and adaptable workforce. The HR department can be the role model of change and adaptability.

Flexible Role Model. Human resource departments face the same demands as their organizations. They must continually streamline their operations. Not waiting for mandated cutbacks, they review and evaluate expenses and implement incremental changes to become, and stay, lean. Flexible HR departments aggressively seek to be perceived as "bureaucracy busters," setting an example for other staff functions and line organizations.[16]

 ## ROLES FOR THE HUMAN RESOURCE LEADER

For the HR department to perform all these roles effectively, it needs to have a very special leader. The leader not only must be knowledgeable in HR activities but also must be well versed in topics such as mergers and acquisitions, productivity, and total quality efforts. He or she also must be familiar with the needs of the business and able to work side by side with line management as a partner. Being part of the management team means assuming some new key roles, which are illustrated in Exhibit 18.3.

 ## ROLES FOR THE HUMAN RESOURCE STAFF

As the HR leader begins to play many of the roles listed in Exhibit 18.3, staff members must recognize this and adapt accordingly. After all, the leader is playing these roles because of the need to form a better link to the business, to be more effective, and to establish a partnership with the employees and the line managers. Just as the department and its leader must change, so must the staff members. Although they may not play the same roles to the same depth as their leader, the staff members still need to know the business, facilitate change, be conscious of costs and benefits, and work with line managers (although this is probably more true for the generalist than for the specialist). The HR staff is active at the operational level and the managerial level, whereas most of the leader's time is spent at the strategic level and some at the managerial level.

 ## STAFFING THE HUMAN RESOURCE DEPARTMENT

The top human resource leaders and staff members are often expected to be capable administrators, functional experts, business consultants, and problem solvers with global awareness. Management expects the HR staff "to have it all." Administrative skills are essential for efficiency. Specialized expertise is important, particularly in combination with business knowledge and perspective. In flexible organizations, problem-solving and consulting skills are vital in guiding and supporting new management practices.

In effective organizations, managers like the HR staff to work closely with them in solving people-related business challenges. Although line managers may best understand their own people, many desire the more distant perspective of HR staff in handling problems. As the HR staff actively builds working relationships with line management, the managers will find it easier to work with them as partners.

How effectively an organization's human resources are managed depends in large part on the knowledge, skills, and abilities of the people in the human resource department, particularly the HR leader, HR generalists, and HR specialists—collectively referred to as HR professionals.

■ *Exhibit 18.3*
Key Roles for the HR Leader

Key Role	What Is Expected on the Job
Businessperson	Shows concern for bottom line Understands how money gets made, lost, and spent Knows the market and what the business is Has a long-term vision of where the business is headed
Shaper of change in accordance with the business	Can execute change in strategy Can create sense of urgency Can think conceptually and articulate thoughts Has a sense of purpose—a steadfast focus, a definite value system
Consultant to organization and partner to line management	Has the ability to build commitment into action Responds to organizational needs Recognizes the importance of teamwork Is capable of building relationships
Strategy and business planner	Knows the plan of top executives Is involved in the strategy formulation of the executive committee—is not an afterthought Develops and sells own plans and ideas—is able to get needed resources Has a three- to five-year focus
Talent manager	Sees the movement from an emphasis on strictly the numbers or bodies needed, to the type of talent and skills needed in the organization Sees the emphasis on talent needed for executing future strategies as opposed to today's needs Is capable of educating line managers Knows high-potential people and anticipates their concerns—for example, who is bright but bored
HR asset manager and cost controller	Initiates—does not wait for others to call attention to the need for action Can educate and sell line managers Can creatively measure effectiveness in own areas of responsibility and other areas of the organization Can use automation effectively

SOURCE: Adapted from "How to Develop HR Professionals for Today's Business Environment," *HR Reporter* (August 1987): 6–7. Used by permission.

The Human Resource Leader

The most effective person who can head the HR department is an outstanding performer in the organization, with both HR management expertise and line management experience:

> In essence, to be a true professional in many areas of HR management, individuals virtually have to have an advanced degree in the subject and spend full time in that field. Areas like compensation have become incredibly complicated because of their close connection to strategic, legal, financial, and tax matters. . . . [But] with the exception of technical specialists, HR managers need to spend a significant amount of time in line management positions. It is not enough for senior HR managers to have worked in different areas of the HR function; they must have had some line business experience so that they have a first-hand familiarity with the business operations.[17]

Line experience gives the HR leader an understanding of the needs of the business and the needs of the department's customers. To prepare potential HR leaders, the HR department's staff should rotate through various line positions over several years. Short of actually serving as a line manager, such individuals could serve as special assistants to line managers or head up a special task force for a companywide project.

The Growing Job Description of the Human Resource Leader. To effectively play the roles described in Exhibit 18.3, the HR leader in a highly competitive environment needs the following knowledge, skills, and abilities (competencies):[18]

- Problem-solving skills
- Business knowledge and organization sensitivity
- Knowledge of compensation techniques that reinforce business plans
- Strategic and conceptual skills
- Knowledge of succession-planning and career-planning systems
- Acknowledged leadership skills
- The ability to analyze data and plan from them
- Computer literacy
- Competence in HR functional areas
- Awareness of financial effects, particularly in areas such as pension costs, health care, and compensation

Some firms are now adopting procedures to identify competencies for their HR staff:

At Weyerhaeuser each major division, led by its human resources director, is responsible for developing a list of specific, required competencies. Of course, overlaps occur among major divisions. The HR directors help generate a slate of competencies based on their interviews with the "customers"—others in the organization—and HR professionals, and on their own requirements. The corporation is also aiming to predict future HR issues as a basis for updating human resources strategies and developing future competency requirements for HR staff.[19]

The systematic preparation of a job description that captures all the required competencies helps firms, like Weyerhaeuser, that want to select their HR leaders from outside the organization. Exhibit 18.4 shows just how extensive this set of responsibilities can be for the senior HR leader in today's organization.[20] Exhibit 18.5 shows some ways companies can train their HR professionals to gain these competencies.

Human Resource Generalists

Line management positions are one source for human resource generalists. A brief tour by a line manager in an HR staff position, usually as a generalist, conveys the knowledge, language, needs, and requirements of the line in a particularly relevant way. As a result, the HR department can more effectively fill its roles.

Another source of generalist talent is nonmanagerial positions. Like line managers, nonmanagerial employees have information about employee needs and attitudes. These generalists should possess many of the same qualities as human resource specialists, but they will usually not have as much expertise in human resources. After serving as nonmanagerial generalists, their next job might be to manage a human resource activity or even one of the firm's field locations. Whereas the former may result in specialization, the latter is likely to result in a broadening of experience.

Human Resource Specialists

Human resource specialists should have skills related to a particular specialty, an awareness of the relationship of that specialty to other HR activities, and a knowledge of where the specialized activity fits in the organization. Since specialists may work at almost any human resource activity, qualified applicants can come from specialized programs in law, organizational and industrial psychology, labor and industrial relations, HR manage-

■ *Exhibit 18.4*
Job Description for Senior Vice President of Human Resources

POSITION PROFILE

This position represents the personnel point of view in the strategic and operational direction of the business. The incumbent is expected to provide, with the support and concurrence of the president, a philosophy and guiding principles for managing the human resources of the company. Authority is limited to the protection of the company's interests in relation to laws and regulations pertaining to personnel. The position directly affects all functions and areas of the company in matters of morale, management practices, employee well-being, compensation, benefits, structure, and development. The incumbent is expected to affect these matters positively through his or her personal influence and professional credibility rather than vested authority.

This position requires an incumbent with broad managerial and professional knowledge and experience. From the managerial standpoint, the human resource group comprises ten interrelated yet disparate functional areas: personnel relations, compensation, benefits, training, organizational development, recruiting, personnel administration, field personnel services, communications, and home office personnel services. The current staff consists of 75 people, including 42 professionals. The incumbent also has functional responsibility for personnel services to four distribution centers. Budget administration responsibilities approximate $29.7 million.

On the professional side, with the exception of the directors of compensation and staffing and of human resource development and the managers of benefits and of media projects, virtually all staff members have been developed inside the company. Technical and professional direction and training rest with the incumbent. The incumbent is expected to provide the company with systems, programs, and processes that effectively support business goals and organizational values. The company's principal executives rely on the incumbent's personal experience, skills, and resources to bring the company to current state-of-the-art status.

Critical competency requirements include preventive labor relations, personnel and labor law, compensation practices, benefits practices, training and organizational development practices, and employee involvement processes. The company's widespread training needs are especially important at this time. The incumbent must have highly developed consulting and communication skills.

Although the incumbent is not expected to create or invent systems and programs, he or she is expected to introduce successful new practices and to adapt them to the company's particular needs. The incumbent must be able to judge when to act and when not to act with patience and persistence. He or she must be able and willing to modify actions to gain agreement and consensus. The incumbent must be able to place the priorities of the company over those of the personnel function. At the same time, the incumbent is expected to be a strong advocate for employee interests and well-being.

SOURCE: Adapted from material used by the search firm Kenny, Kindler, Hunt & Howe of New York, NY, from *The Changing Human Resources Function* (New York: Conference Board, 1990): 15.

ment, counseling, organizational development, and medical and health science. In addition, specialists are needed in the newer areas of total quality management, service technologies, behavioral performance improvement systems, organizational change and design, and information systems.

The HRIS Manager. An emerging trend is to see the specialist who manages the HRIS as playing a strategic rather than technical role. This new role asks the HRIS manager to be concerned not with how efficiently the department can store and retrieve data and information but with how the HRIS manager can be a strategic partner and manage organizational change.[21]

Typically, when organizations create an HRIS, they develop a need to have a specialist manage the area. The HRIS can become a separate unit within the HR department, with its own manager. Over the years, the role of this leader has changed from that of a project manager to that of a systems manager and now that of a strategic change partner. A nice

■ *Exhibit 18.5*

Training and Development Activities for Human Resource Managers

BUSINESSPERSON

- Participates in courses on finance for nonfinancial executives as well as marketing courses
- Seeks exposure to marketing organization
- Participates in task forces, business planning teams, acquisition and divestiture teams

SHAPER OF CHANGE

- Participates in team-building exercises
- Engages in formalized mentor relationships
- Researches the change process

CONSULTANT AND PARTNER TO LINE MANAGERS

- Does volunteer work in professional organizations, health care coalitions, charities, or company consortiums
- Coaches and evaluates performance
- Pairs junior with senior staffers and consults with internal staff

STRATEGY FORMULATOR AND IMPLEMENTOR

- Learns content of business strategy
- Becomes knowledgeable in the strategies of all the businesses or divisions
- Describes the human resource implications of these various strategies

TALENT MANAGER

- Talks constantly to all line managers
- Monitors what the competition is doing
- Attends conferences to develop a network

ASSET MANAGER AND COST CONTROLLER

- Takes courses in finance and accounting
- Reads journal articles on utility analysis
- Confers with those in the finance and accounting departments

SOURCE: Adapted from *HR Reporter* (July 1987): 3–4. Used by permission.

description of these changes appears in the feature "Positioning for the 21st Century: Change for the HRIS."

The role changes for the HRIS manager have paralleled those for the HR manager. Not surprisingly, they have also produced the same need for new competencies. Today's HRIS manager needs to be aware of the global environment and of the organization's needs to be global and act local. HR information and data systems can enable the organization to operate as a global organization and at the same time be sensitive to local conditions and needs. An HRIS can enable managers worldwide to tap into a database giving information about candidates to run an operation in a distant country, without their even knowing the candidates. It also requires managers to become concerned with issues of information security.

Positioning for the 21st Century:
CHANGE FOR THE HRIS

Having a human resource information system (HRIS) manager within the organization was a relatively new concept in the early 1970s. The role of this position was largely to capture basic personnel data on homegrown systems. The automation of employee files, basic head-count reports, and such information as equal employment opportunity compliances represented the HRIS mission and guided internal development projects. As packaged mainframe-based systems became readily available, the capacity and functional capabilities of the HRIS expanded. The HRIS manager's role shifted from that of a *project manager* (responsible for internal systems development) to that of a *systems manager* (responsible for centralized processing of reports, data integrity, and other administrative functions). Then came the microcomputer revolution of the 1980s, which permitted decentralized access, shared processing, data ownership at the source, and the extension of HRIS data and processes to new constituencies. This revolution turned many HRIS managers into consultants.

Now a new era is at hand, as the human resource function and its systems support have become strategic partners in managing change. With this evolutionary stage, as with the others, comes the need for HRIS managers to learn new skills and competencies in order to remain assets to their organizations.[22]

With increases in regulatory requirements and the levels of expertise needed to deal with complex HR activities, some organizations have moved away from generalists and now rely more on specialists. However, under pressure to serve the customer better, other organizations are finding they still need generalists. Both are valuable, and both reflect the HR profession's drive to meet ever-increasing standards of excellence.

Information Security. According to Marc Tanzer, president of BCI/Information Security in Portland, Maine, "When corporate spies want confidential information, they often infiltrate HR departments first. A well-structured information-security program can keep spies from obtaining your company's secrets."[23] The names of employees, where they work, and what they do can be valuable information to other companies, especially competitors. Such information can be used to plan recruiting efforts to lure these people from their current employment. Organizations that value openness and access to information are especially vulnerable to this threat. Yet, if companies are to empower people, they often need to be open and allow access to information. Companies such as Tandem Computers in Cupertino, California, handle this concern by

- Creating an awareness among managers and employees that others could gain access to company information and data
- Tightening up telephone security so that callers need to identify themselves and the right screening questions are asked
- Weeding out bogus job candidates—that is, those who are only going through the motions in order to gain access to information
- Adding more restrictions in confidentiality agreements; for example, when individuals join the firm, they can be asked to sign agreements not to reveal company secrets to others at any time, even if they leave
- Classifying information and restricting access to it to a need-to-know basis

Not only can these programs limit the leakage of corporate information but also they can prevent unauthorized people from obtaining personal information about individual employees—not a trivial concern in today's atmosphere of rising employee violence and credit card scams.

Some say that restricting the type and amount of information collected reduces the potential for invasion of privacy. This solution has to be balanced against the HR department's need for information for its various programs. Family-friendly activities such as drug and alcohol abuse programs cannot take place without a sound database. Nor can the organization's numerous legal obligations be fulfilled without an effective HRIS. Some balance must be struck, the latest security must be used, and the environment must be continually scanned for the latest computer hacking scams—the best defense is a good offense.

✹ PROFESSIONALISM IN HUMAN RESOURCE MANAGEMENT

Like any profession, HR management follows a code of ethics and has an accreditation institute and certification procedures. All professions share the code of ethics that human resource management follows:

◉ Practitioners must regard the obligation to implement public objectives and protect the public interest as more important than blind loyalty to an employer's preferences.
◉ In daily practice, professionals must thoroughly understand the problems assigned and must undertake whatever study and research are required to ensure continuing competence and the best of professional attention.
◉ Practitioners must maintain a high standard of personal honesty and integrity in every phase of daily practice.
◉ Professionals must give thoughtful consideration to the personal interest, welfare, and dignity of all employees who are affected by their prescriptions, recommendations, and actions.
◉ Professionals must make sure that the organizations that represent them maintain a high regard and respect for the public interest and that they never overlook the importance of the personal interests and dignity of employees.[24]

Ethical Issues

Increasingly, HR professionals are becoming involved in ethical issues. Some of the most serious issues center around differences in the way people are treated because of favoritism or a relationship to top management. In a 1991 survey conducted by the Society for Human Resource Management (SHRM) and the Commerce Case Clearing House (CCCH), HR professionals identified more than forty ethical incidents, events, and situations relevant to HR activities. The ten most serious ethical situations are shown in Exhibit 18.6.

In the SHRM-CCCH study, the professionals surveyed agreed that workplace ethics require people to be judged solely on job performance:

> Ethics requires managers to eliminate such things as favoritism, friendship, sex bias, race bias, or age bias from promotion and pay decisions (it is, of course, also *unlawful* to take sex, race, or age into account).
>
> Is ethics a "bottom line" issue? It becomes one when we consider that by acting in an ethical manner, companies will, in fact, hire, reward and retain the best people. This will, in turn, help assure that the company has the best work force possible to achieve its business goals.[25]

Other ethical issues do not always affect the bottom line in the way favoritism versus employee performance does. By adopting a definition of workplace ethics that centers on

■ *Exhibit 18.6*
The Ten Most Serious Ethical Situations Reported by Human Resource Managers

Situation	Percentage*
Hiring, training, or promotion based on favoritism (friendships or family relationships)	30.7
Differences in pay, discipline, promotion, and so forth due to friendships with top management	30.7
Sexual harassment	28.4
Sex discrimination in promotion	26.9
Inconsistent use of discipline for managerial and nonmanagerial personnel	26.9
Failure to maintain confidentiality	26.4
Sex discrimination in compensation	25.8
Use of nonperformance factors in appraisals	23.5
Arrangements with vendors or consulting agencies leading to personal gain	23.1
Sex discrimination in recruitment or hiring	22.6

*Percentage responding with 4 or 5 on five-point scale measuring degree of seriousness, with 5 meaning a very great degree of seriousness.
SOURCE: Adapted from the *1991 SHRM/CCCH Survey* (Chicago: Commerce Case Clearing House, June 26, 1991): 1.

job performance, however, HR professionals will be in a better position to persuade others in the organization that making ethical behavior a priority will produce beneficial results.

Encouraging Ethical Behavior

To assume that a single policy can be devised to ensure that everyone in the organization always behaves ethically and legally is unrealistic. Nevertheless, business ethics can be improved in a number of ways. A good starting point is for top management to examine such management practices as reward systems, managerial style, and decision-making processes. In some organizations, the reward system promotes unethical behavior by encouraging the achievement of organizational goals at almost any cost. Because of HR's traditional involvement in reward systems, HR has a natural role in encouraging ethical behavior here. But in the spirit of partnership, encouraging ethical behavior is a responsibility of all parties—the employees, line managers, and HR professionals. A result of this partnership might be the creation of an easy-to-use hot line and standards book offering guidance on issues of ethical behavior. An example of such a program is is described in the feature "Managing Human Resources for the 21st Century at Eaton Corporation."

Professional Certification

The Society for Human Resource Management has established the Human Resource Certification Institute to certify human resource professionals.[26] The institute has the following purposes:

- To recognize individuals who have demonstrated expertise in particular fields
- To raise and maintain professional standards
- To identify a body of knowledge as a guide to practitioners, consultants, educators, and researchers
- To help employers identify qualified applicants
- To provide an overview of the field as a guide to self-development

The certification institute has two levels of accreditation: basic and senior. The basic accreditation is the professional in human resources. This designation requires an

Managing Human Resources for the 21st Century at Eaton Corporation

If employees of Eaton Corporation have to make an ethical decision at work and are unsure of how to proceed, they should first turn to management at their facility to discuss the problem. If that does not seem appropriate, the people at Eaton Center in Cleveland can help. In the following actual Ethics Line case, a foreman at an Eaton plant called the Line to discuss a situation after reading the *Eaton Standards of Ethical Business Conduct* booklet.

The foreman hired a machinist who proved to be very talented and an asset to the plant. When the machinist interviewed, he mentioned that he occasionally moonlighted with company ABC on specialty machining projects. It turned out that company ABC is a major supplier to this particular Eaton facility. The foreman became concerned that he had created a conflict-of-interest situation. When he called the Ethics Line and discussed the situation with one of the four corporate executives who answer the Line, they decided there was only a slim chance for conflict of interest. The foreman called ABC, and they agreed that the machinist would never work on an Eaton order while moonlighting at ABC.

Eaton employees are encouraged to turn to their local human resource manager or facility manager in situations where they feel it may be inappropriate to discuss a particular ethics issue with their supervisor. Ethics problems are often difficult to resolve. That is why the proper steps to resolve ethics problems are spelled out at the back of the fourteen-page *Standards* booklet. In brief, they are:

• Get all the facts.
• Ask yourself, "What specifically am I being asked to do?"
• Clarify your responsibility.
• Ask yourself, "Is it fair?"
• Discuss the problem with your supervisor.

In unusual cases where it may not be appropriate to seek help from local resources, U.S. employees have the option of calling the toll-free Ethics Line. All Ethics Line cases are given a number and a code name so that the caller can remain anonymous. Callers can speak to someone on weekdays from 8:00 A.M. to 5:00 P.M. eastern standard time, or leave a message on an answering machine at other times.[27]

examination covering the general body of knowledge and four years of professional experience. A bachelor's degree in HR management or social sciences counts for two years of professional experience. The senior level accreditation is the senior professional in human resources. This accreditation requires a minimum of eight years of experience, with the three most recent years including policy development responsibilities. All professionals receiving accreditation will be listed in the *Register of Accredited Personnel and Human Resource Professionals.*[28]

Careers in Human Resource Management

Numerous career possibilities exist in human resources. Human resource specialists can pursue their fields of specialization within a company and still sell some of their time to external organizations as consultants. Generalists can remain in human resources and also occasionally serve on companywide task forces for special issues such as downsizing or capital improvement projects. Generalists are likely to be from three ranks: career HR professionals with degrees in business or psychology, former line managers who have switched fields, and line managers on a required tour of duty. As human resources becomes more heavily valued by organizations, required tours of duty by line managers will become more frequent. Finally, as U.S. organizations become more global, opportunities for careers in international HR management will increase.[29]

ORGANIZING THE HUMAN RESOURCE DEPARTMENT

In organizing the HR department, two major questions need to be addressed:

1. Where are the HR decisions made?
2. What level of investment will the company make?

The first question has to do with the advantages and disadvantages of centralized and decentralized organizations. The second question has to do with budgets and compensation.

Centralization versus Decentralization

Centralization means structuring the organization so that essential decision making and policy formulation are conducted at one location (at headquarters); decentralization means structuring the organization so that essential decision making and policy formulation are conducted at several locations (in various divisions or departments of the organization).

How HR departments are organized differs widely from one company to another not only because of the differing requirements of various industries but also because of differing philosophies, cultures, and strategic plans of individual organizations. For instance, compare the centralized structure of Merck with the decentralized structure of TRW.

At Merck, large, specialized corporate staffs formulate and design human resource strategies and activities. These are then communicated to the small HR staffs of operating units for implementation. High levels of consistency and congruence with corporate goals are thus attained. At TRW, small corporate staffs only manage HR systems for executives and only act as advisers to operating units. This organization tends to operate with a wider divergence in practices and a greater flexibility in addressing local concerns.[30]

The organizational structures used by Merck and TRW are very appropriate for their respective types of businesses. TRW, a high-technology company with a diverse array of businesses, cannot use the consistent, stable approach to HR that Merck, with a more singular product focus, is able to employ.[31]

Because of today's rapidly changing and highly competitive business environment, the trend seems to be toward greater decentralization. This entails a greater delegation of responsibilities to lower HR levels and to the operating units and line managers themselves. Along with this is a trend toward less formalization of policies—that is, fewer rules that are seen as bureaucratic hurdles. Human resource departments and their organizations thus have greater flexibility to cope with the continually changing environment. Diminished bureaucratization can also lead to a greater openness in approaches to problems.

Some activities, such as fair employment practices and compensation matters, may have to be centralized because of legal requirements and for the sake of consistency. Nevertheless, the general trend is for less formalization and less centralization. Thus, we see firms such as Levi Strauss developing broad policy statements. Their local units then develop HR practices that are tailored to specific needs and yet consistent with overall company philosophy.

The Budget

The amount of money that organizations allocate to their HR departments generally rises yearly. In 1994, the average costs allocated to the human resource department for each employee was $696. Not surprisingly, department expenditures for each employee decrease steadily with company size. Firms with fewer than 250 employees recorded a median expenditure of $1,162 for each employee in 1993, compared with $1,031 for each employee in companies with 250 to 499 employees; $650 among employers with 500 to 999 employees; $542 in organizations with 1,000 to 2,499 workers; and $323 in firms with 2,500 or more employees.[32]

For all firms, the median ratio of HR department staff members to workers in 1994 was 1.1 to 100. Among firms with fewer than 250 employees, the median ratio was 1.7 staff for every 100 workers, and among companies with 250 to 499 employees it was 1.2 for every 100 employees. The ratio was substantially lower in organizations with 500 to 2,499 employees, at 0.8 for every 100 workers, and lowest among employers with 2,500 or more workers, at 0.6 for every 100 employees.[33]

Compensation of HR Staff

Human resource management is becoming very attractive as a field of employment. The results of a 1994 compensation survey, by types of jobs in a human resource department, are shown in Exhibit 18.7. In that survey, salaries were generally higher for individuals in larger organizations, for those with more experience, and for those with more education. In addition, salaries were higher in the Northeast. In other surveys, the senior HR senior, sometimes called senior vice-president, was the highest paid individual in the survey, earning an average of more than $350,000, including salary plus cash bonus and profit sharing.[34]

Reengineering and Outsourcing

Reengineering the HR department basically means reconsidering what the department is doing to see whether it can do it better and more effectively.[35] Customerization is consistent with this process because it asks, "What are we doing for our customers, what do they want, and how can we fill in the gaps between what they get and what they want?" Reengineering goes much further. It seeks to examine all the parts of the department, asking, "What is the purpose of this group, what does it do and how does it do it, and can it improve the way it does things? As in customerization, benchmarking can be used to ensure that, in the interest of continual improvement, the best available HR practices and activities are obtained.

Partnership is often a result of reengineering. The end product of such an endeavor is often a more effective department that better serves and involves employees. Consequently, reengineering is likely to grow in significance during the late 1990s.[36]

Another result of reengineering may be the decision to outsource some HR activities. The reengineering process should identify what counts; what adds value; and what can best be done by someone else—particularly another firm that specializes in supplying HR activities, such as pension plan administration. Novell, like many other companies, decided that some of its responsibilities were better left to outside vendors. According to Theresa Dadone, director of compensation and benefits for Novell:

> It wasn't long ago that employees had to come to HR and request a loan from their 401(k) plan. They had to talk to an HR person and fill out papers. A committee then had to review the request and decide whether or not to grant the loan. Well, that's not in keeping with customer service. That's treating our employees like children. So, we outsourced that responsibility. There's now a toll-free number for employees to call so they don't have to involve HR in their personal finances. We're out of the loop ... that isn't where our value is. Our value is in helping employees understand the plan.

Educational assistance is another responsibility that's been outsourced. Employees used to have to come to HR and request approval of a course and receive reimbursement. Today, an outside agency takes care of it. Employees don't have to come begging to HR, hat in hand, to process something. We now spend our time helping employees understand the benefits of educational assistance and how it can serve them in their personal and professional lives.[37]

 ## GLOBALIZATION

The globalization of world markets is inevitable. More and more firms are moving operations outside their domestic borders. The 1980s and 1990s in particular have seen dramatic changes in international trade and business. Once-safe markets are now fierce battlegrounds where firms aggressively fight for their share against both foreign and domestic competitors. It is, therefore, not surprising to find that in an increasing number of firms, a large proportion of the workforce is located in other countries. As a consequence, HR departments and their professionals have to be familiar with concerns and aspects of operating across countries and cultures.

Globalization is forcing managers to grapple with complex issues as they seek to gain or sustain a competitive advantage. Faced with unprecedented levels of foreign competition at home and abroad, firms are beginning to recognize that not only is operating an international business high on the list of priorities for top management, but so are finding and nurturing the human resources required to implement an international or global strategy. Thus, the process of globalization is affecting the activities HR departments can provide. It is also influencing the entire structure and operation of those departments.

HR departments can play a critical role in the globalization process by helping their companies evaluate the human resource prospects and possibilities involved in moving to different regions of the world. For example, the HR department of Novell helped its senior management decide to establish a technical center in Australia. According to Tim Harris, Novell's HR head:

> We were debating between establishing the center in Australia or Singapore. We have to evaluate local employment laws, the cost and availability of housing and what it would cost to recruit and relocate the multilingual employees needed to staff the center. We also researched tax issues, the competitive salary structure, medical facilities and the health-care system. There's a myriad of decisions in which HR must participate to go back to the business unit and say: "This is what you should do, this is what it will cost, and this is how long it will take to get the new business or division up and running."[38]

The effect of globalization on HR departments is being felt all over the world. A recent study of HR activities and departments worldwide identified the nature of this virtual transformation, as shown in Exhibit 18.8.

Across Countries

The complexities of operating in different countries and of employing people of different nationalities, not the functions performed, are the main issues that differentiate domestic and international HR management. Many companies underestimate these complexities, and some evidence suggests that business failures in the international arena are often linked to poor management of human resources:

> The primary causes of failure in multinational ventures stem from a lack of understanding of the essential differences in managing human resources, at all levels, in foreign environments. Certain management philosophies and techniques have proved successful in the domestic

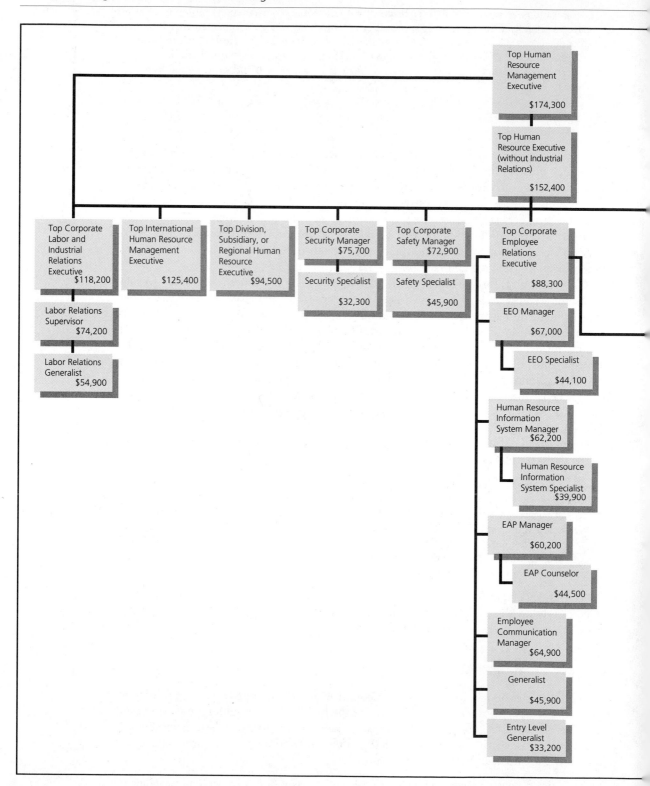

Note: Earnings equal salaries plus reported bonuses.
SOURCE: "Human Resource Compensation" *Bulletin to Management* (August 11, 1994): 252–53. Based on data provided by the Society for Human Resource Management and William M. Mercer, Inc. Used by permission of the Bureau of National Affairs, Washington, DC.

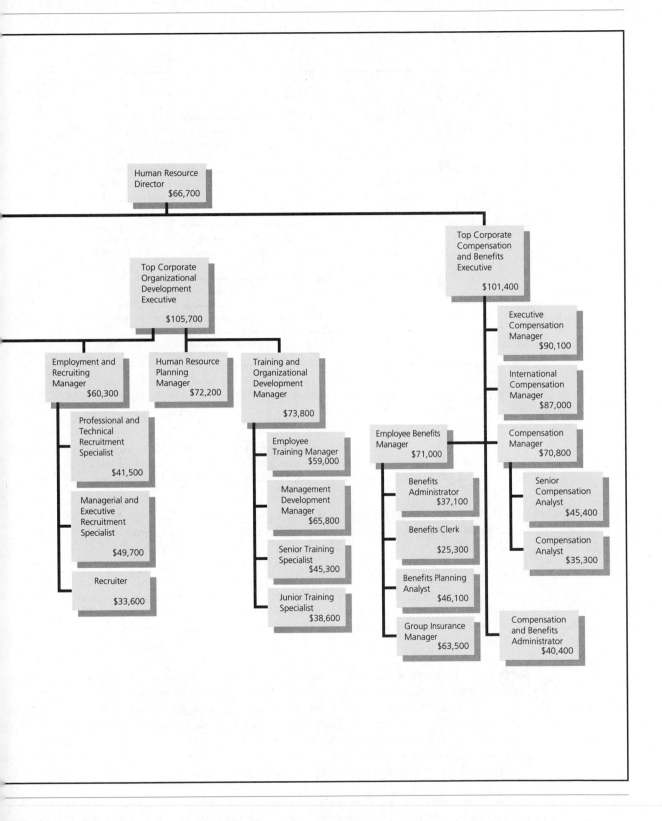

Human Resource Director
$66,700

Top Corporate Organizational Development Executive
$105,700

Top Corporate Compensation and Benefits Executive
$101,400

Employment and Recruiting Manager
$60,300

Human Resource Planning Manager
$72,200

Training and Organizational Development Manager
$73,800

Executive Compensation Manager
$90,100

International Compensation Manager
$87,000

Compensation Manager
$70,800

Professional and Technical Recruitment Specialist
$41,500

Employee Training Manager
$59,000

Employee Benefits Manager
$71,000

Managerial and Executive Recruitment Specialist
$49,700

Management Development Manager
$65,800

Benefits Administrator
$37,100

Senior Compensation Analyst
$45,400

Recruiter
$33,600

Senior Training Specialist
$45,300

Benefits Clerk
$25,300

Compensation Analyst
$35,300

Junior Training Specialist
$38,600

Benefits Planning Analyst
$46,100

Group Insurance Manager
$63,500

Compensation and Benefits Administrator
$40,400

■ *Exhibit 18.8*
A Model of the Human Resource Department's Transformation

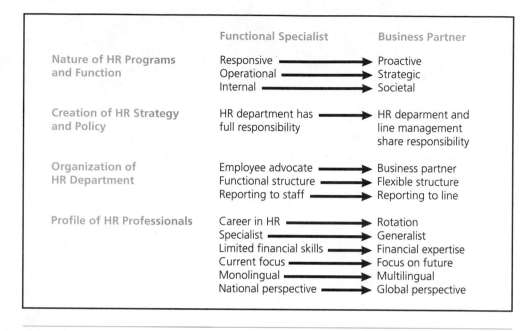

	Functional Specialist	Business Partner
Nature of HR Programs and Function	Responsive ⟶	Proactive
	Operational ⟶	Strategic
	Internal ⟶	Societal
Creation of HR Strategy and Policy	HR department has full responsibility ⟶	HR deparment and line management share responsibility
Organization of HR Department	Employee advocate ⟶	Business partner
	Functional structure ⟶	Flexible structure
	Reporting to staff ⟶	Reporting to line
Profile of HR Professionals	Career in HR ⟶	Rotation
	Specialist ⟶	Generalist
	Limited financial skills ⟶	Financial expertise
	Current focus ⟶	Focus on future
	Monolingual ⟶	Multilingual
	National perspective ⟶	Global perspective

SOURCE: Adapted from *Priorities for Competitive Advantage: A Worldwide Human Resource Study* (IBM/Towers Perrin, 1992): 6. Used by permission.

environment: their application in a foreign environment too often leads to frustration, failure, and underachievement. These "human" considerations are as important as the financial and marketing criteria upon which so many decisions to undertake multinational ventures depend.[39]

Increasingly, domestic HR is taking on an international flavor as the workforce becomes more and more diverse. But several issues differentiate international HR from domestic HR.

More Functions and Activities. To operate in an international environment, the HR department must engage in a number of activities that would not be necessary in a domestic environment: international taxation, international relocation and orientation, administrative services for expatriates, host-government relations, and language translation services.

Broader Perspective. Domestic managers generally administer programs for a single national group of employees who are covered by a uniform compensation policy and who are taxed by one government. International managers face the problem of designing and administering programs for more than one national group of employees, and they must therefore take a more global view of issues. This is exactly what is being done at the international pharmaceutical company whose activities are described in the feature "Managing Human Resources for the 21st Century at Baxter."

More Involvement in Employees' Lives. A greater degree of involvement in employees' personal lives is necessary for the selection, training, and effective management of expatriate employees. The international HR department needs to ensure that the

Managing Human Resources for the 21st Century at Baxter

Baxter International Incorporated is approaching its growing international business with the same people awareness that it used to successfully manage its merger with American Hospital Supply Corporation. "We do business in 100 countries, and over one-third of our revenue comes from overseas," says Anthony J. Rucci, senior vice president of human resources. "And that percentage is growing. As a result, we've made managing diversity a long range corporate goal."

"We define 'diversity' differently than most companies," says Rucci. "We look at it as 'what does it mean to do business in different countries around the world,' not just as 'how will we work with women and minorities?'

"As global marketers, we need to be sensitive to different cultural values around the world. As an example, we often think of Germany's culture as not that different from ours. But when we marketed our disposable surgical drapes and gowns in Germany, they just didn't sell. Why? Because in Germany there's a cultural norm against throwing things away. So a concept that made a lot of sense in the U.S. couldn't be translated there. We've learned from these experiences that we can't anticipate everything. To function well globally we are going to have to have a diverse range of opinion within our own company.

"We are approaching this with the same seriousness we used to implement our merger, and with many of the same values and techniques. We have established three corporate task forces to work on the diversity issue. Each addresses one of these issues:

- How should senior management send a visible commitment to this issue?
- *Awareness and training:* How can we broaden our company's perspective? How extensive and how deep should the training be?

- How do we identify, promote, and develop a more diverse pool of talent globally?

"Each of the top 27 officers of the company serves on one of these task forces—9 staff officers and 18 line officers. I'm on the third one myself. What we're looking for is five or six actionable things to do so that five years from now we really do have a more diverse work force. One of the things we're starting to do now is rotate managers in our foreign subsidiaries more actively with our U.S. people. We're bringing more European managers here, as well as rotating them within Europe. And we're sending more U.S. people overseas. With the European market opening up in 1992, we think this is even more important.

"Aside from the task force activities, we're giving the process an extra push by building diversity goals into our compensation and performance appraisal systems. Like everything else, we've made sure there's commitment from the top. One of the CEO's major objectives (one of four or five) is to promote work force diversity. Each of the top 100 officers, including the CEO, has a major portion of his or her bonus dependent on meeting diversity objectives. These objectives vary depending on the person's job, but every manager has at least one.

"We're not where we want to be yet. But we are making progress. As our people get more experience with diverse cultures, they are gaining more awareness. I think we've progressed to the point where at least people 'know they don't know.' They know that in another culture, they have to challenge everything they think is the right way to get something done. They know they can't rely on their intuition the way they used to be able to do at home."[40]

---

expatriate employee understands housing arrangements, health care, and all aspects of the compensation package provided for the assignment.

More Risk Exposure. Frequently, the human and financial consequences of failure are more severe in the international arena than in domestic business. For example, expatriate failure (the premature return of an expatriate from an international assignment) is a persistent, high-cost problem for international companies.

Another aspect of risk exposure that is relevant to international HR is terrorism. Major multinational companies must now routinely consider this element when planning international meetings and assignments.

More External Influences. Other forces that influence the international arena are the type of host government, the state of its economy, and business practices that may differ substantially from those of the originating country. A host government can, for example, dictate hiring procedures, as was the case in the late 1970s in Malaysia. The government required that foreign firms comply with what became known as the 30:30:30 Rule—that is, that 30 percent of employees must be indigenous Malays, 30 percent Chinese Malays, and 30 percent Indian Malays, at all levels of the organization, with monthly statistics to corroborate this breakdown.

◈ SUMMARY

Because of the increasing complexity of human resource management, nearly all companies have established an HR department. Not all these departments perform all the possible HR activities. A department's activities—and the way it performs them— depend greatly on the roles the department plays in the organization. Companies that are most concerned with HR management allow their departments to perform the business role as well as the roles of enabler, monitor, innovator, and adapter. When this occurs, the departments are able to link their activities to the business and demonstrate their value to their organization by showing how their activities influence productivity, quality of work life, competitive advantage, adaptability, and legal compliance—all goals associated with the organization's several stakeholders (shown in Exhibit 1.2).

For each human resource activity, departments can choose from many human resource practices. For example, in performance-based pay, human resource departments may choose to use a merit pay plan or a profit-sharing plan. Therefore, human resource departments need to be familiar with all the human resource activities and practices and must know which ones to use depending on the needs of the business. They also need to be staffed with individuals who know and appreciate the business and who understand the goals and roles of human resource management in organizations.

Furthermore, human resource professionals need to understand the issues of globalization. By going global, companies create many additional challenges for the HR department, what with radically differing employment laws in countries around the world to say nothing of subtle and not-so-subtle cultural differences. The knowledge needed to deal with these challenges can be gained through understanding the environments in which firms operate today.

Successful firms in today's highly competitive environments have found that it pays to have everyone involved in human resource management. Employees, line managers, and HR professionals have to work together if their firm is to manage its human resources effectively.

Discussion Questions

1. How does Levi Strauss link its HR department to the needs of the business?

2. Why is the HR department seen as critical to the success of organizations? Do line managers and HR managers agree with this view?

3. What roles can the human resource department play in an organization? How are its basic activities related to these roles?

4. What types of HR issues are faced at the operational, managerial, and strategic levels?

5. What can HR departments gain from customerization?

6. What are the roles for the HR leader and the HR staff?

7. Distinguish between generalists and specialists.

8. Why are some human resource management departments centralized and others decentralized?

 ## In-Class Projects

1. Describe the following for Lincoln Electric:
   a. The role the HR department appears to play
   b. The degree of partnership in managing human resources
   c. The backgrounds and qualifications of those in HR

2. Describe the following for AAL:
   a. The role the HR department appears to play
   b. The degree of partnership in managing human resources
   c. The backgrounds and qualifications of those in HR

Note: These topics are not discussed specifically in the case studies, but you should be able to make some good guesses based on your knowledge of what effective firms are likely to be doing. Many comments in the case studies can help you here.

 ## Field Project

Make appointments and visit local companies or colleges to interview a line manager and the human resource manager about their views of the HR department in the organization. Do these interviews separately. The human resource manager can probably arrange the interview with a line manager. Interview your working parents, other relatives, or friends to solicit their opinions of HR management and of the role it plays in their companies.

Case Study:

BRINGING THE HUMAN RESOURCE DEPARTMENT TO THE BUSINESS: PARTNERSHIP IN MANAGING HUMAN RESOURCES

 Mike Mitchell left the Bank of Montreal to become vice president of human resources at the North American branch of the Swiss Bank Corporation (SBC), a $110 billion universal bank, in autumn 1993. It was a move up for him in terms of status, responsibility, monetary compensation, and challenge. Of these, the challenge was the most intriguing to Mike. Being in his midthirties, he saw this as a perfect time to take a risk in his career. He realized that if he succeeded, he would establish a prototype that could be marketed to other firms. In addition, success could lead to further career opportunities—and challenges. Although he had a general idea of what he wanted to accomplish and had gotten verbal support from his superiors—the senior vice president of human resources and the president of SBC, North America—the details of exactly what he was going to do and how he was going to do it had yet to unfold.

In 1992, the parent company of SBC, headquartered in Basel, Switzerland, decided it needed a clearer statement of its intentions to focus its energies and resources, in light of growing international competition. Accordingly, it crafted a vision statement to the effect that the bank was going to better serve its customers with high-quality products that addressed the customers' needs rather than just the needs of the institution. (See Exhibit) Although the North American operation was relatively autonomous, it was still expected to embrace this vision. The details of the vision's implementation, however, were in local hands. For human resources, those hands became Mike's.

Although Mike had spent some time in human resources at the Bank of Montreal in New York, the bulk of his work experience was as an entrepreneur in Montreal, Canada. This experience had influenced his thinking the most. Thus, when he came to SBC, his self-image was that of a businessperson who happened to be working in human resources. In part because of this image, his stay at the Bank of Montreal had been brief: human resources was still a bit too conservative for his style. Too many of his ideas "just couldn't be done." In interviewing, the top managers at SBC had warned him of the same general environment. He thus knew he would have to go slowly to change almost one thousand employees, including his own department's ten employees, but he really did not know what this change would involve. He knew that his goal, his challenge was to reposition and customerize the HR department at SBC. He knew that this was necessary to connect the HR department to the business. ◉

Discussion Questions

1. Who are the customers of Mike and his HR staff?
2. Will the line managers cooperate with Mike and his staff? What will it take to see that they do? What would be reasons for their resisting a partnership with the HR department?
3. Develop a matrix with projects, dates, milestones, and people involved (i.e., HR managers, line managers, and employees) for Mike and his staff.

SOURCE: Randall S. Schuler, New York University.

◼ *Exhibit*
Human Resource Mission Statement for The Swiss Bank Corporation

Our mission is to

◉ Provide quality, innovative, and sensitive human resource products and services that meaningfully support the needs and vitality of our organization and its employees
◉ Create a business strategy for our function that challenges the limitations of the HR practice and provides the potential for us to become a successful business enterprise in our own right
◉ Be the best at who we are and what we do

Case Study:

A BROADER VIEW SEIZES MORE OPPORTUNITIES

 Don English, corporate vice president in charge of human resources, is now finally able to take a pause from the ongoing "firefighting" he has been engaged in since he came to Bancroft ten years ago. Like many of his colleagues in other firms, Don acquired his knowledge of human resource management as much from doing it as from formal education.

Because of his workload, Don tended to keep pretty narrowly focused, and he rarely read HR journals or attended professional conferences. However, recently, things have been easing up. He has been able to recruit and train almost all the division managers in charge of human resources. It is Don's intention that the newly trained division managers will put out most of the company's fires, and he will be freed to look at the big picture. And he has been doing more reading than ever before. Of course, Don has not been totally out of touch with the rest of the world or the growing importance of HR management planning. When he started filling the slots for division HR managers, he made sure that it was a learning experience for him. Don always required job candidates to prepare a one-hour talk on the state of research and practice in different areas of personnel—for example, selection, appraisal, compensation, and training. He would even invite MBA candidates who had no course work in HR to come in and relate their field of interest to human resource management.

Don is planning to become the chief executive officer of Bancroft or some other firm of similar or larger size, within the next five to seven years. He thinks he can achieve this if he remains in human resources and does an outstanding job. He will have to be outstanding by all standards, both internal and external to the firm. From his interviews during the past three years, Don knows that it is imperative to move human resources in a strategic direction while doing the best possible job with the "nuts-and-bolts" operational activities.

During a moment of reflection, Don begins to scribble a diagram on his large white desk pad. In the middle is Bancroft, a well-established clothing manufacturer. To its left are its suppliers and to its right are its customers. In his head are all the human resource practices he is so familiar with. He has a hunch that there must be a way to use the firm's expertise in performance appraisal and training to help Bancroft be more effective. Bancroft has been learning tremendously from a five-year drive to improve quality, but during the past year, quality gains have slowed. Bancroft must continue to improve its quality in order to gain and sustain a competitive advantage, but large gains in internal quality are becoming more and more difficult as Bancroft climbs the learning curve. Don wonders, how can he help Bancroft experience the excitement of seeing large gains in quality improvement again?

Don circles the list of suppliers and begins to formulate a plan that will improve his chances of becoming CEO. He now seeks your advice in exactly what to do and how to go about doing it. ◉

Discussion Questions

1. Is it reasonable for Don and the rest of Bancroft management to think about the suppliers of Bancroft as a source of competitive advantage?

2. Should Don go directly to Bancroft's suppliers and talk to them, or should he work with others in his company such as the person in charge of purchasing or even the CEO?

3. Can Don become a CEO by being effective in human resources?

SOURCE: Randall S. Schuler, New York University.

Role-Play: Don English

You are Don English, corporate vice president of human resources at Bancroft. You have decided to visit Paul Schaller, the CEO of one of your suppliers, Softstyle. Although this is definitely not the way things have been done in the garment industry before, you want to do things differently. After all, you do want to improve things, and you want to be the first to do so. Actually, you think that getting better supplies is critical to your success in moving Bancroft's line of men's sportswear upscale.

Paul is uncertain about your visit. Yes, you have told him about your ideas over the phone, but all this is very new to him as well as to the industry. Nevertheless, he is one of the five suppliers of cloth pieces to your Men's Sports Division.

You want to improve the quality and timeliness of Softstyle's shipments to you. Because of your experience at Bancroft, you think that by working on Softstyle's human resource practices, you can improve the business. Of course, it would help your rapport with Paul if you conveyed an understanding of his business, what your ideas would cost, and what benefits (or lack thereof) he could garner from your approach.

You are now being invited by Paul to sit down in his office. He only has a few minutes to listen to your presentation.

 Role Play: Paul Schaller

You are Paul Schaller, CEO of Softstyle, a supplier of cloth pieces to the garment industry. Bancroft is a valued, long-term customer and you know them rather well. You also know that they want to move their Men's Sportswear upscale. This means, among other things, better quality fabrics, faster response time vis-à-vis customer demands, and a better understanding of the needs of the customer.

Don English, corporate vice president of Bancroft, arranged for an appointment to discuss some ideas with you about moving their business upscale. You are not entirely sure who he is and what he wants to discuss. Nevertheless, Bancroft is a customer and you want to continue having their business. Consequently, you told him you would be more than happy to give him ten minutes.

Please welcome Don into your office.

INTEGRATIVE CASE STUDIES

All across the United States, millions of Americans buy a variety of insurance products each year. They buy them from insurers like Metropolitan Life Insurance Company and Prudential Insurance Company of America, the so-called commercial insurers, and from Aid Association for Lutherans (AAL) and Knights of Columbus, the so-called fraternal benefit societies. Unlike commercial insurers, the approximately two-hundred fraternal benefit societies, which are exempt from certain taxes, serve up a mix of financial products, good works, member services, and sometimes social activities. Generally founded at the turn of the twentieth century by immigrants to provide for each other in tough times, the groups were among the first to offer insurance to working-class people. Although the societies account for less than 2 percent of the new life insurance policies written each year, they sell life insurance and annuities—and sometimes health insurance, disability insurance, and mutual funds—to about 10 million Americans.

A key concern for anyone when buying life insurance is a company's financial soundness. In this regard, fraternal societies appear to be ahead of the pack. Policyholders have suffered no losses in recent memory, says a spokesman for A. M. Best, an independent agency that reviews and rates the insurance industry on the basis of overall performance and financial strength. But a few societies have merged because of declining membership. Of the forty-two fraternals rated by the agency, thirty fall in the top six of its fifteen rating categories, and the six largest fraternals, after which size drops off considerably, are in that upper tier. The largest of these is Aid Association for Lutherans.[1]

AID ASSOCIATION FOR LUTHERANS

AAL provides fraternal benefits and financial security for Lutherans and their families. Individuals who purchase financial products from AAL also become members of AAL and join one of over eighty-six hundred local volunteer service chapters called branches. Through the volunteer efforts of 1.6 million members,

branches are provided opportunities to help themselves, their churches, and their communities. Members also receive free educational materials on family and health topics. AAL also offers scholarship opportunities for members as well as grants to help Lutheran congregations and institutions. In total, nearly $62 million was spent on AAL's fraternal outreach in 1994.

AAL's financial product's include individual life, disability income, and long-term care insurance, and annuity products. Its subsidiary company, AAL Capital Management Corporation, offers mutual funds to AAL's members. The AAL Member Credit Union is an affiliate that offers members federally insured savings accounts, a credit card, and various types of loans and home mortgages.

AAL assets under management are over $12 billion. Total annual premium income is over $1.5 billion. AAL is among the top 2 percent of all U.S. life insurers and is the nation's largest fraternal benefit society in terms of assets and ordinary life insurance in force. AAL also maintains an A+ rating from A. M. Best, a AAA rating from Duff and Phelps Corporation, and a AAA rating from Standard and Poor's Corporation, all the highest possible.

AAL markets its products and services in all fifty states and the District of Columbia through a sales staff of over twenty-four hundred. Corporate headquarters are located in Appleton, Wisconsin, where over fourteen hundred are employed. (*Note:* Staffing numbers throughout this case study are in terms of full-time equivalents. [FTEs.] Since a sizable number of regular part-time workers are retained, the actual number of people employed is greater than stated.)

ORGANIZATIONAL CHANGE AT AAL

A major organizational change, dubbed Renewal and Transformation, officially began at AAL in December 1985 with the engagement of Roy Walters and Associates as consultants for a diagnostic process. But the beginnings of this change effort can be traced back to the early 1980s.[2]

Some seeds were planted during several very successful product introductions in 1982. The focus and energy level of the organization at that time was exciting, even though managers were up to their ears trying to keep up with business owing to the phenomenal success of the organization's universal life product. Company leaders remember saying AAL should have one of these situations every two years or so, for the energizing effects it had on them and the organization.

With the introduction of these new products, AAL also ushered in a new awareness of the shrinking margins in financial services and its need to rein in expenses in order to stay competitive. In addition, the organization's president and CEO had announced his upcoming retirement, and its new president, Richard L. Gunderson, came in September 1985 from another life insurance organization. Studies of the insurance industry convinced Gunderson that the association had to cut costs by over $50 million over the next five years to stay competitive. The question on the minds of some senior managers was; "What choices can be made now to position AAL for the future?" Organizational change or transformation became the answer.

Positive Dissatisfaction

The change effort was difficult in part because AAL was *not* in crisis. The good news was that this gave the organization time to change and adjust; the bad news was that it made it difficult for employees to motivate themselves to go through the effort of change. Many of the concerns mentioned were like clouds out at the distant horizon; sales, financial, and fraternal results were continuing to grow, and seemingly nothing in the status quo pointed to the need for fundamental change. As AAL's consultant Bob Janson pointed out, what employees did need to discover and tap was the sense of what he termed *positive dissatisfaction* within the organization—the feeling that even if AAL was doing well, it had an even higher potential.

Diagnosing AAL's Strengths and Weaknesses

The first task of the change effort was an organizational diagnosis to seek out this positive dissatisfaction. A team of twelve managers was trained in a structured interview process, then went out and conducted over two hundred interviews in a diagonal slice of the home office and field. The team asked people what AAL's strengths and weaknesses were in ten categories; control, culture, management, style, marketing, mission, historic strengths, productivity, quality, structure, and technology.

Those team interviews were a great experience; people in the organization did share their hopes and dreams for what AAL could become and their frustrations that the organization was not working as effectively as it could to reach those dreams. People identified many strengths on which to build: AAL's members and market, financial strength, fraternal focus and reputation, dedicated employees—both home office and field. But as the team reported to a larger management group in May 1986, some areas needed attention. The consultant has since said that he had never seen an organization so "ripe" for change.

Defining AAL's Vision

Working in parallel with the diagnosing team, one hundred of AAL's managers developed a vision statement for the organization.[3] The result was viewed as a reaffirmation of what AAL had become and what it stood for. It reads as follows: "AAL, the leader in fraternalism, brings Lutheran people together to pursue quality living through financial security, volunteer action and help for others."

Identifying the Gaps

So, six months from the start of the transformation process, AAL had both a vision statement and a current snapshot of the organization; when the two were compared, the gaps that needed to be addressed came into clearer focus. The organization was set to launch its efforts to close these gaps in order to position itself even more strongly for the future. The working theme at that time was "Touch tomorrow today."

Closing the Gaps

The first gaps to be addressed were in the areas of organizational structure, management style, and marketing strategy. Efforts to study and recommend ways to close the gaps between AAL's current situation and its vision in these three areas were launched anew, still employing participative methods. For example, for the structure study, a team of six managers was charged to develop alternative proposals for restructuring the organization through the two management levels below the president. Recommendations were developed by the team, with input from a larger circle of managers, then finally delivered to the president. He chose to reorganize AAL using many of the concepts recommended, and the new organization was put into place late in November 1986. The reorganization was significant: twenty-five of the top twenty-six positions in the organization had changes in responsibility, including significant changes in senior management.

The efforts in other areas continue to this day. A new marketing strategy was completed in the fall of 1988. Work has progressed at defining a more precise vision of desired management style and having managers assess themselves (and employees assess them) against that vision. AAL has also produced a technology strategy in response to a gap-closing need, and is now wrestling with ways to address productivity and quality variables in a more direct way.

Organizational Change Results

AAL's corporate restructuring, just by its nature, has been the most visible result. Frankly, after restructuring at the top of the organization was over, it was hard to convince employees that the change process was not complete.

In response to AAL's expense challenges, the organization also achieved its downsizing goal of 250 positions by 1990. This was primarily accomplished through an early retirement window offered in 1986, as well as through attrition.

Structure and personnel changes can always be disrupting, but were especially so in this organization. Not only was AAL a part of a very stable industry, it was also one of the largest employers in a relatively small community, with very low turnover. One key element of the change process was the guarantee of continued employment that was built into the change effort. As Robert H. Waterman, author of *In Search of Excellence,* says, "stability in motion" must be maintained throughout renewal. AAL strives to give its managers and employees the freedom and courage to reorganize and try new ways of work, by placing a safety net underneath them. Employees whose positions are eliminated during the change process, or who turn out to have a mismatch of skills for new ways of work, become members of a program. The program helps assess skills, finds temporary work assignments, offers support, and looks for internal placements, field transfers, or voluntary outplacements.

For a sharper focus on the planning and implementing of teams within a key service area of AAL, let us look at the transition of the Insurance Product Services Department, set against the backdrop of this larger change effort.

PLANNING AND IMPLEMENTING TEAMS IN THE IPS DEPARTMENT

The Insurance Product Services (IPS) Department at AAL provides all services related to the individual life, long-term care, and disability income insurance product lines, from the initial underwriting of contracts to the ultimate handling of claims. IPS consists of about 426 employees, about 30 percent of the home office employees.

Planning Phase 1: Identifying the Need

The desire for a new organizational design for IPS had its roots in the corporate change study and subsequent corporate reorganization called Renewal and Transformation. As a result, the change efforts of IPS management were fully supported by Dick Gunderson and top management in the spirit of corporate renewal, and IPS management had the freedom to restructure the department without periodic presentations and approvals.

The major concerns that came out of the corporate change study regarding the "old" insurance product services environment were as follows:

- The old environment was not truly focused on the customer, because of its functional rather than wholistic approach to service.
- Most decisions were made very high in a hierarchial organization with as many as six levels of supervision. As a result, decisions were made some distance from the problems, which decreased timeliness. They were also made by people other than those who knew the most about the problems, which reduced the quality of the decisions.
- The skills and abilities of people were underutilized, and many jobs tended to be boring because of their narrow scope.
- Productivity was viewed from a functional perspective rather than from an integrated perspective.
- Recent marketing successes had caused significant growth in staff and related expenses. Top management felt that it was *excessive* growth.

Related to the last point, the change of IPS was addressed in an environment that called for downsizing the corporate staff by 250 over a five-year period. Corporate staff numbered 1,556 on January 1, 1987.

As part of the corporate change action, a new IPS department head was put in place in December 1986. This new leader, Jerome H. Laubenstein, a former marketing executive, was noted for his participative style. He was given the charge to "regionalize" the IPS service function in an effort to get closer to the customer and to address the corporate downsizing goal as it related to the significant growth experienced by IPS in recent years.

Laubenstein brought in a new senior-level departmental management team in January 1987. This team consisted of five individuals to manage five geographic service regions. These people were selected for their active management style, creativity, and demonstrated willingness to take calculated risks (a contrast to the way they were selected in the risk-averse former culture). They were also selected because of their management strengths and highly participative management style. Technical insurance knowledge, though desirable, was not felt to be essential.

Planning Phase 2: Setting Broad Parameters.

The second week after selection, the new IPS management team came together in an off-site retreat to address the approach to be used for redesigning the department. The first step was to develop a vision for the new IPS organization. The result was a simple statement— "Regionalization plus 'one-team' processing"—and included the following list of "desired outcomes":

- A "customer-driven" organization. Customers were identified as field staff and members. Being customer driven was perceived to include
  —Listening to the customer for wants and needs
  —Being responsive and pro-active to customers wants and needs
  —Acknowledging that the customer's problem is the provider's problem
  —Seeing the provider as a problem solver rather than an order taker
  —Informing and educating the customer
  —Using customer-informed measures on how IPS is meeting customer needs
- A strong "team" relationship with the field staff and internal support units. The need for "networking" was heavily stressed.
- A "flat" organization with fewer levels of supervision and fewer staff.
- "One-stop" processing as fully as possible to avoid the delays and lack of ownership associated with an assembly line approach.
- A quality management team that would model participative management, more involvement of employees in deciding how work was to be accomplished, and more decision-making authority for employees in carrying out their day-to-day assignments.

A very simple mission statement was also established for the new organization: "To enable the agent, the primary customer, to do an even better job of serving the policyholder, the ultimate customer."

Planning Phase 3: Designing and Developing

The design process did not begin with the self-managing team concept as a goal. It did, however, begin with a strong desire to obtain the employees' appreciation for restructuring. Therefore, a major first task of the new departmental management team was to communicate the reasons for pursuing a change in work design to every employee in the department. The reasons for change really were restatements of what individuals had related to the corporate change interview teams.

Communication. Because AAL had no facility to bring the entire IPS staff (484 people) together at one time, the first attempt at communication to all employees was through the existing functional management structure in the department. The IPS managers were asked to conduct unit meetings, explaining the reasons for and parameters around which a new organization would be developed. Information and support materials were provided to facilitate communication. This approach met with limited success.

More Communication. A second effort was structured around large-group meetings, with approximately one

hundred employees in each group. Dick Gunderson and Jerry Laubenstein also participated. This attempt met with more success. Periodic unit meetings, led by the new regional managers, were continued. A departmental newsletter was also established. The newsletter was distributed to all IPS employees to provide continuing communication as the redesign progressed through the planning and implementation stages. Good, solid communication cannot be overemphasized in a restructuring process such as AAL experienced.

Design Teams. Because the new management team was committed to a highly participative team style of management, it involved a significant cross section of employees in the departmental redesign. Ten teams, with a total of approximately 125 employees, were appointed from lists of employees nominated by managers, supervisors, and employees. Team members came from all levels within the organization. The teams and their charges were as follows:

- *Three Structure Teams:* Independently propose a new departmental structure, taking into account several "givens" such as regional organization, and a maximum of three levels of supervision.
- *One Physical Resource Team:* Address the physical resource issues that need to be dealt with in any reorganization.
- *One Management Style Team:* Address management style and propose a culture in which employees can grow and perform in the spirit of service excellence.
- *One Management Information Team:* Evaluate the types of management information needed to lead the operation.
- *One Field Input Team:* Gain agent (customer) input on IPS's electronic data processing (EDP) support services.
- *One EDP Resource Team:* Look at the effect of this change on IPS's, EDP support services. IPS was a highly mechanized operation, and as a result, the effect was significant.
- *One Operations Team:* Look after ongoing operations during the renewal effort.
- *One Celebration Team:* Plan and administer appropriate and timely celebration events to highlight specific milestones and successes along the way.

The results produced by these teams in just three weeks were phenomenal—and were achieved while employees continued to handle normal work activities.

Role Clarification. During planning phase 3, management had to clearly articulate the role of teams within a participative management decision-making process, especially when proposals required modification or rejection. Employees tended to confuse the various teams' roles of providing input, with management's accountability for making decisions. Managers, on the other hand, had to remember to explain why team decisions were modified or rejected. It probably would have been better to label the approach high involvement rather than participative management. Doing so may have avoided some misunderstandings.

Decision Making and Implementation

Two of the three structure teams submitted organizational proposals that closely parallel IPS's current design. These proposals, together with input from a variety of sources including a literature search that produced the self-managing team concept, provided the direction for the organizational model. The next step was to contact some proponents of sociotechnical management. As a result, it was recognized that to attain the desired outcomes and accomplish its mission, the department had to move away from a hierarchically arranged, functional, and highly specialized structure that extensively used rules, records, reports, and precedents. Instead, it had to move toward a flat, full-service, self-managing, self-regulating service team structure that placed decision making closer to the transaction and to the customer. Management then created a tentative model of the new organization. This model was worked with all employees, using the nominal group process, in an attempt to get their input on potential pitfalls.

Once the organizational concept was finalized, the number of service teams needed to serve IPS's customers was determined by modeling service activity by region. The goal was to have as many teams (i.e., customer contacts) as could be supported by existing staff capabilities. IPS concluded that the "critical mass" of knowledge and skills currently available in the department could support sixteen service teams. Managers were then selected to lead these teams.

Implementation. The next step was to develop an implementation plan. Implementation teams were named, again using a significant cross section of employees. The teams were charged to do everything necessary to ready the department for a physical move to the new organizational structure. The EDP resource, physical resource, and celebration teams were continued, and additional teams were formed around service functions of the "old" organization. They were to address the disbursement of the three functions of the insurance services: life, medical, and disability.

Employee assignments. Now, the new management team addressed the issue of employee assignments. After an initial "reallocation" of employees was agreed on, employees were given the opportunity to request a change in tentative team assignment. However, because it was necessary to balance the existing knowledge among the teams, changes in assignments were not made

unless exceptional reasons existed. This "assignment issue" was perhaps one of the biggest and least anticipated social issues of the renewal effort. Not since high school had most of these adults had their social choices removed—choices of colleagues, work location, and work environment. As these new "groups" moved through the group formation stages of "forming, storming, norming, and performing," they spent much time and energy in the storming and norming stages.

Security The period of organizational change—including downsizing—was trying for many employees, even though all were guaranteed employment (not positions). It was especially so for supervisors and managers. The organizational redesign reduced supervisory positions from sixty-two to twenty-two. By the end of 1987, 57.5 full-time equivalent positions were eliminated. To reduce the negative effect of these changes, stress management sessions were made available to all employees through the medical department. Several hundred employees took advantage of this opportunity. A course on managing change was made available to management through a local technical institute. A career-counseling service was offered to employees whose jobs were eliminated. And the existing corporate Employee Placement Program was strengthened to help employees cope with the loss of positions (not employment) that resulted from the total corporate renewal effort.

The Move. The physical move from a functional structure to one centered around self-managing teams was made in August 1987. This was one of the first opportunities to demonstrate the power of team problem solving. IPS's building services and space management units estimated it would take three to five months to move the department's 484 employees and associated equipment. IPS management could not live with that time frame. The physical resource implementation team, led by its adviser, a newly appointed and creative regional manager, together with the building services people, synergistically arrived at an alternative, which was to move people but not workstations. This required employees to accept inadequacies in their new workstations until those stations could be modified at a later date. The organization's space management staffers also had to accept something less than a "clean" move. The only change in equipment would be the provision of computer terminals at workstations where they had not been required earlier. Employees moved themselves by packing their belongings in boxes, putting the boxes on their chairs, and wheeling both to their new workstations. This was something never before done. An incentive was provided: The move began at noon on a Friday. As soon as the unit was moved, employees would have the rest of the day off. The move was completed in less than two hours. Terminals caught up the following Tuesday.

Self-Managing Work Teams at IPS

Teams within teams. The IPS organizational team design has four significant aspects:

- It is a regional organization, with each region providing all services to its designated customers. (These service regions parallel the existing field distribution and management regions.)
- Each region has four service teams, with each service team providing almost all services to a specific group of agencies. Under the old system, a few services were handled by such a small staff that it was difficult to spread them to service teams in the early stages of restructuring. The number of employees sufficient to constitute an adequate "critical mass" to permit disbursement was a major point of discussion. Management tended to be more inclined to take risks than were staff in this area.
- Each service team was initially structured to have three self-managing work teams within it—one around the underwriting and issue functions; another around service functions such as loans, terminations, dividends, preauthorized check handling; and the third around the claims functions. The goal is to move to more wholistic self-managing teams by encouraging the integration of the three functional teams.
- Finally, IPS had a cadre of functional specialists with responsibility for establishing functional policy and for monitoring the appropriate administration of policy across the regions and teams. These specialists are currently organized by line of business and report to the regional managers.

Self-Managed Teams Defined. The focal point of IPS's current organization is clearly the self-managing work team. The self-managing work team *concept,* as found in the organization's literature search and adopted by AAL, is as follows:

- Self-managing work teams are semiautonomous groups of workers who share the responsibility for carrying out a significant piece of work and who run their own operations with almost no supervision. Each group has the authority and the technical, interpersonal, and managerial skills to make decisions about how the work should be done.
- Each team is accountable as a group for processing all the work for which it is responsible. Members plan, do, and control their work. The team decides who will do what work, and assigns members to tasks. The group has control over scheduling and coordinating its own work, formulating vacation schedules, monitoring quality, solving technical problems, and improving work methods. Employees have both responsibility and accountability for quantity, quality, and costs. The team meets regularly to discuss goals; to

identify, analyze, and solve work-related problems, and to provide improvement ideas.
- Employees typically possess a variety of skills and are encouraged to develop new skills to increase their flexibility. Workers typically learn second and third jobs. The team is responsible for motivating, training, coaching, and developing its members. Team members train each other or arrange for their own training.
- The team is also responsible for employee evaluation and discipline. The group, as a whole, reviews overall team performance, evaluates individual members, and handles problems such as absenteeism and poor performance. Teams need to be skilled in handling the social system as well. This means being able to celebrate their success, recognize each other's efforts, thank each other for help, and in general reinforce positive behavior. As teams mature, they hire new members or do the final selection of new team members.
- Reward systems typically reward teamwork as well as the individual's acquisition of skills and the individual's performance. For example, the team's results may determine the size of the compensation resource pool available to be distributed as increases or bonuses, or both. The team then determines how that pool is allocated to individual team members.

Some aspects of the self-managing work team concept have not been implemented at AAL. For example, peer appraisal is achieved by anonymous input, not direct input, and significant performance problems continue to be turned over to managers for disciplinary action.

Benefits of the Self-Managing Team Concept

Six intrinsic elements of the self-managing team concept that are motivators:

- Variety and challenge
- Elbow room for decision making
- Feedback and learning
- Mutual support and respect
- Wholeness and meaning
- Room to grow; a bright future

With respect to these motivators, Marvin Weisbord, in his book *Productive Workplaces: Organizing and Managing for Dignity, Meaning, and Community,* says, "The first three must be optimal—not too much, which adds to stress and anxiety, nor too little, which produces stultifying tedium. The second trio are open ended. No one can have too much respect, growing room, or 'wholeness'—meaning a view of both the origin and the customer's use of your work." All this assumes that in place are the "satisfiers," a list of six conditions of employment: fair and adequate pay, job security, benefits, safety, health, and due process. As Weisbord comments, "Only in workplaces embodying both lists can the century-old dreams of labor-management cooperation ever come true." The six motivators can be met far more effectively through the self-managing team structure than through the traditional multilevel hierarchical management structure that focuses on one person, one task.

Joseph H. Boyett and Henry P. Conn suggest in their book *Maximum Performance Management: How to Manage and Compensate People to Meet World Competition,* that excellence is a function of the knowledge and skills, motives and abilities of employees. They also suggest that we cannot directly change the internal traits and characteristics employees bring to the job and thus are stuck with them. They further suggest that we can, however, adjust the work environment to compensate for weaknesses in these attributes. The three leverages they propose for doing this are

- Information
  —Shared values and business strategies
  —Linked missions and goals
  —Measures and feedback
  —Identification of critical behaviors
- Consequences
  —Social reinforcement
  —Contingent awards
  —Pay for performance (a variable portion up to 40 percent of total compensation)
- Involvement
  —Nonvoluntary
  —Management-directed teams
  —Cross-functional task forces

AAL's self-managing team approach supported by its pay-for-performance compensation system, which is anchored to team measures and results, takes full advantage of these areas of leverage far better and with far less effort than can be done in a traditional hierarchical structure.

Manager's Role in the Self-Managing Team Environment

The move to self-managing teams required a redefinition of the role of the team manager. This leader is still responsible and accountable for the bottom-line results of the team, but these results are attained differently. In the new work environment, the creative abilities of all team members are used, not just those of the manager.

The redefined role requires managers to

- set direction by creating and focusing the team's efforts toward a common vision;
- coach and counsel, and ensure and support the development of team members;
- lead the team in problem solving;

- make sure the team has needed information and resources; and
- encourage the team to make its own decisions on operating problems.

The new role requires managers to manage through "boundaries" or "parameters" rather than by directive. Key challenges are the need to create a motivating work environment and to remove barriers for team members. The latter is accomplished by managing relationships between teams and between the team and other areas of the organization.

Although the role of the manager in a self-managing team environment differs from the role of a manager in the traditional environment, research has shown that the profile of outstanding managers is very similar regardless of the environment. Successful managers are visionaries, use a participative management style, and can deal with ambiguity and a lack of structure. They share information and responsibility with employees and are committed both to the work and to the individuals on their teams. And they deliver results.

Key Support Systems

Pay-for-Applied-Services for Individuals and Teams. Pay-for-Applied-Services (PAS) is the compensation system designed to support IPS's self-managing work teams. It offers maximum flexibility to meet the unique job design needs of each team.

One significant challenge during the development of PAS was to integrate it into a corporate culture firmly entrenched in the Hay system of job evaluation. This task was uniquely and creatively accomplished by a team including individuals from the service areas and corporate compensation services.

Within IPS, individual position descriptions have been replaced by a team job description and individual personal assignments. Each personal assignment is a listing of the services an individual performs to support the needs of the team and to support her or his own career interests. Employees have identified approximately 165 services that are being performed within the department.

Compensation is delivered through four components. The first is valued services. As new services are learned and applied, their values are added to the employee's ongoing compensation. The values of individual services are determined using the know-how portion of the Hay system. A matrix has been constructed using Hay know-how values. One axis of the matrix is absolute values representing the minimum AAL would be willing to pay for a service if it were a stand-alone service. The other axis of the matrix is incremental values. The more an individual learns with the same base know-how value, the less additional learning is worth.

The second component of pay delivery is the team incentive. Incentive dollars are tied to productivity measures. Allocation is based on a team's contribution to productivity. Distributions to individuals within the team are based on the individuals' support of the team. Incentive dollars are distributed quarterly.

The third component is a market adjustment feature. To remain competitive within the marketplace and among comparable jobs within the organization, IPS considers market adjustments annually. These adjustments may be made to either the matrix or the incentive "pot." When adjustments are made to the matrix, the values of individual personal assignments are recalculated. Where appropriate, immediate adjustments are made to pay.

The fourth component is an individual-incentive program, in which IPS recognizes outstanding achievement by individual employees. This lump-sum incentive is paid once a year only to employees who are already paid at market value. It is worth as much as 6 percent of an individual's compensation.

This new compensation system encourages cross training, enhances team flexibility, and encourages team performance, but still permits compensation dollars to be managed and controlled. It was implemented on April 1, 1989, and underwent a degree of modification in 1991 to bring it into closer synchronization with a new incentive compensation plan introduced to the rest of the organization that year.

Training for Self-Managing Work Teams. A comprehensive training program continues to be developed for all employees working in a sociotechnical management environment within the organization. The entire process of program design and delivery to all employees was completed in 1990. The topics covered include

- *Teams' Roles:* Typical supervisory responsibilities that teams may take on in their own self-management are
  —Planning and scheduling time schedules
  —Securing and allocating resources
  —Scheduling and coordinating work
  —Setting standards and rotating assignments
  —Providing performance data
  —Recruiting, selecting, and firing
  —Disciplining and rewarding
  —Celebrating successes
  —Motivating and training
  —Coaching and developing
  —Solving problems and resolving conflicts
  Management allocates these tasks to team members as the team is ready for them. A part of the preparation for this passing of responsibilities includes training and development relevant to each team's needs.
- *Team Managers' role:* Service team managers must play a stronger coaching and counseling role than do

traditional managers. They find themselves being facilitators, empowerers, and consultants, responsible for "managing the culture." Therefore, the training program developed for managers pays special attention to the development of these skills.

Performance Appraisal

- *Peer (Individual) Appraisal:* Self-managing work teams require a new concept in performance appraisals. Members of the team use an anonymous peer appraisal concept. In addition, teams "certify" their members' skill levels.
- *Group (Team) Appraisal:* Teams are expected to function as teams and not just groups of individuals. Team members receive training in the skill areas required to enable this. The individual's *ability* to function as a team member is evaluated as part of the training process. The *team's* actual *behavior* in this area is assessed by managers. The team's progress is assessed by the team itself, against the standards and goals that contribute to bonus results.

SUCCESSES AND CHALLENGES OF CHANGE AND SELF-MANAGED TEAMS IN THE IPS DEPARTMENT

External Visibility

The concept of a self-managing work team initially found only a modest level of credibility within the rest of the AAL organization because, in the minds of many, it still had to be proven. The attention given IPS's efforts helped support the validity of this concept. Examples include an article about IPS's efforts by John P. Hoerr in the July 10, 1989, issue of *Business Week;* several references by Tom Peters in his syndicated newspaper column; several other references in other national and local publications; requests for and subsequent site visits by many organizations; and invitations to make presentations about the team concept from organizations such as the Association for Quality and Participation and the Work in America Institute. Subsequently, demonstrated improvements in productivity and customer satisfaction made it more difficult to criticize the concept. However, the one soft spot that plagued IPS for some time was overall employee satisfaction. This was probably most affected by the introduction of an incentive compensation system with pay at risk while the rest of the organization remained on the traditional merit system.

Employee Successes and Challenges

Employee reactions to the redesigned organization are monitored by a number of approaches. First, monthly employee feedback sessions are sponsored and hosted by the department head. Employees are randomly selected from throughout the department and offered the opportunity to air their concerns, ask questions, and suggest changes. This approach is also used by regional managers.

In addition, in July 1987, a survey instrument was introduced to monitor employee attitude as IPS implemented the new design. The survey continues to be used on a periodic basis. Results are evaluated on a regional and service team level as well as on a departmental level. Employee attitude goals are established for service teams and actual results versus goals are used in evaluating managers' overall performance. The first reading was taken in July 1987, just prior to the physical move. The second was taken in October 1987, shortly after the physical move, followed by the third in May 1988, the fourth in September 1989 following the introduction of the Pay-for-Applied-Services compensation system, and the last in August 1990. A few comparative readings from the old organization were available from several years before. Some results are shown in Exhibit 1.

The significant effect of *change* can be noted in the overall satisfaction of employees. A very stable, "comfortably staffed" functional organization in 1983 resulted in a relatively high level of overall satisfaction. Surprisingly, the design stage and, not so surprisingly, the implementation stage of the new design resulted in a significant deterioration in overall employee satisfaction even though employees were heavily involved in developing and implementing the design. However, employees, for the most part, still respond that they would not want to go back to the old structure and organization, even though they dislike some things about the new system.

The Tough Spots. Two specific problem areas identified by the survey were:

(1) lack of *advance* training for the new roles and duties employees were being asked to assume and

(2) employees' inability to measure how well they were doing in their new roles.

The first area, the training issue, was an enormous challenge for both management and employees. Enlarging jobs put a tremendous strain on training capabilities during the early stages of transformation. That, together with not having a compensation system in place to support the cross-training concept, may have led to low employee morale owing to a lack of adequate incentives. It is understandable that employees did not feel very good about this aspect of the renewal effort. The second area, moving from individual standards to measuring and rewarding individuals on the basis of team results, is a difficult change for some to accept in a culture in which individuality has been lauded and many prefer to be fully in control of their own destiny.

In addition, the approach used to assign employees to new work teams significantly unbalanced the existing social system. This was further compounded in January 1989 when the department moved from a five-region structure to a four-region structure to parallel a similar move in the field distribution system.

Another major effect on employees satisfaction was the installation of a new compensation system that puts a part of their compensation at risk based on performance.

The aggregation of these changes has lowered employees' overall satisfaction level. It is doubtful that the negative effect of change can be avoided, but it is possible to avoid drawing the change out over an extended period of time. In IPS's case, the design was begun in January 1987 and the last piece, the compen-

■ *Exhibit 1*
Employee Satisfaction Survey Results

	1983	July 1987	October 1987	May 1988	September 1989	August 1990	August 1991
				Percentage Agreeing			
Overall satisfaction, employees. . .	70%	56%	47%	41%	51%	58%	65%
Are encouraged to innovate	—	58%	73%	69%	66%	70%	69%
Receive adequate training	—	60%	49%	51%	57%	58%	58%
Are permitted to use judgement	—	81%	90%	88%	89%	89%	88%
Enjoy good communication between the field staff and headquarters	30%	58%	66%	58%	54%	66%	68%
Are familiar with measures for doing a good job	—	64%	38%	42%	45%	52%	57%

sation program, was implemented in 1989 and 1991. This is probably an excessive time frame.

Nevertheless, changes has had some really positive results in the IPS Department. For example, communication between employees and customers has improved. Employees now feel challenged to innovate. And employees feel free to use their own rather than a supervisor's judgement. IPS also has a very large number of employees who favor the new compensation system because it has increased their ability to influence their earnings.

One noteworthy result is a gain in productivity (which is addressed later in this case study). An additional, "nice-to-see," result is the rapidity with which the organization is moving from the concept of three functional self-managing work teams within a service team to that of a more integrated, functionally inclusive self-managing team. This evaluation is a longer-range design goal that is being realized much sooner than anticipated.

Customer Successes and Challenges

Perhaps the most visible success thus far is the favorable effect the new self-managed design is having on IPS's customers, the field staff. Input gathered from them, as part of a field renewal effort and reported in March 1988, indicated that the field staff felt that the new IPS organization was one of the four best things about AAL. A survey instrument was implemented to measure the satisfaction of the field staff, and the results are shown in Exhibit 2.

An improvement in customer attitude between August 1985 and March 1988 was probably primarily related to (1) the promise of better service, (2) the pairing of specific service teams with specific customers (agencies), (3) field visits where members of service teams would attend agency meetings, and (4) an experimental partnership program in which specific IPS employees would work with specific agents. A slight dete-

rioration in October 1988 was probably somewhat related to the establishment of higher expectations and to field renewal activity that was taking place. Speed, for example, showed a fairly significant deterioration in level of satisfaction when, in fact, IPS was providing better service than earlier in the renewal process. Other "anecdotal evidences" of customer satisfaction are numerous letters and other communications about how pleased individuals are with the support they are getting from their home office service team; flowers, candy, and other treats received by service teams from their field customers; and customer-hosted celebrations for successful sales results.

Looking at "Percentage Disagreeing" results for the customer satisfaction survey, rather than "Percentage Agreeing" results, suggest an even better outcome:

Percentage Disagreeing

Overall, IPS...	September 1989	September 1990	September 1991
Understands the field staff	19%	12%	13%
Wants to help the field staff	2%	2%	2%
Will respond	4%	5%	2%
Responds with satisfactory speed	14%	8%	13%
Responds with accuracy	6%	2%	4%

Productivity Successes and Challenges

Very tangible productivity gains have been realized. IPS Department was initially rightsized by eliminating fifty-nine positions (12 percent of the workforce), resulting in a savings of over $1 million in salaries and benefits. Additional reallocation of employee resources has since occurred. On the other hand, business processing has

Exhibit 2
Customer Satisfaction Survey Results

Overall, IPS...	Percentage Agreeing					
	August 1985	September 1987	October 1988	September 1989	September 1990	October 1991
Understands the field staff	27%	47%	45%	48%	57%	60%
Wants to help the field staff	—	83%	78%	79%	84%	89%
Will respond	—*	84%	82%	85%	85%	89%
Responds with satisfactory speed	61%	68%	61%	65%	77%	73%
Responds with accuracy	76%	79%	74%	77%	85%	84%

*No survey data are available, but this area was the focus of a high number of complaints from the field staff.

continued to increase. A macro productivity model developed to monitor IPS's progress shows a cumulative productivity increase of approximately 29 percent through 1990. This means that if IPS had been operating at the same standard of productivity as in 1985 and 1986, it would have required about 120 more positions than it had at the end of 1990.

IPS anticipates additional productivity gains as cross training progresses and teams mature. However, the amount of time and energy it takes to cross train while continuing to process business should not be underestimated. A significant commitment of time and resources is required.

Future Design Changes

The first phases of the sociotechnical design was implemented in IPS in August 1987. A review of the original design decisions, in view of the knowledge gained from a little over a year of operation, took place in December 1988. As a consequence, IPS implemented several modifications to the organization in March 1989 and introduced the individual-incentive modification (PAS) to the compensation system in 1991.

First, the department moved from a five-region to a four-region design to match a similar change that was made in the alignment of its field distribution organization effective January 1989. Second, it moved the reporting relationship between specialists and service team managers to one between specialists and regional managers. This was done to recognize that specialists have a departmental role, not a service team role, and thus are a part of the departmental management team. IPS later reorganized the specialists by line of business, with each regional manager taking responsibility for one major area. Third, IPS moved from sixteen service team managers to fifteen, further broadening the spans of control of the managers. This was possible because of the progress made in the self-managing capabilities of employees.

This "fine-tuning" of the organization resulted in employee reassignments and as a result was followed by some deterioration in the morale of employees who were looking for stability.

CEO Diagnostic Intervention

IPS contracted with the Center for Effective Organizations (CEO), University of Southern California, in October 1992, to learn how to better understand the effect of IPS structure and support systems on team performance and employee satisfaction. The department felt that it needed to understand the employee concerns voiced in the November 1991 corporate employee survey, and needed to address those concerns. Also, it had been five years since IPS had been reorganized into teams, and it was time to reassess the department's

direction. IPS selected CEO to do the research because it would be a neutral third party, was an internationally known organization in the study of teams and teamwork, and employed some of the leading thinkers on compensation, particularly skill-based pay.

As IPS began its research in the fall of 1992, it had four key objectives:

- Assess the current status and design of the team-based IPS organization.
- Specifically address the issue of why improvements in employee morale lagged improvements in productivity and customer satisfaction.
- Suggest possible innovations in IPS's team-based design, which could be implemented and tested for their influence on the effectiveness of teams and the department as a whole.
- Assist with the design, implementation, and assessment of innovations related to new ways of doing business that were planned for at least some of the work teams.

Here is what IPS learned from a year of intensive self-scrutiny:

- Despite its hypothesis that employee quality of work life (QWL) lagged improvements in productivity and customer satisfaction, QWL for IPS employees was in fact above average compared with that for employees in other organizations.
- IPS's efforts at empowerment were effective, but room for continued progress remained.
- Employee QWL was not strongly related to either productivity or customer satisfaction. In other words, changes in employee QWL were not likely to have major effects on either productivity or customer satisfaction. This was a surprising finding, but is consistent with findings from other CEO research into the relationship of QWL to organizational performance.
- The need for communication was strong.
- Overall satisfaction with pay was high, but not all employees agreed with AAL's compensation system or the philosophy behind it. Most employees demonstrated a good understanding of the PAS compensation system (base pay, team incentives, and individual incentives) and the corporate Success Share incentive program. However, they indicated some dissatisfaction with nonannuitized incentive compensation (they would prefer annual base salary increases over annual bonuses), and felt that the compensation system does not effectively reward good performers.
- The visibility of the service team director was low; the supervisory style of the manager was not related to the team's performance. Most employees reported that they did not see their managers frequently and would appreciate more contact. A second finding on this issue was that management style had no correlation to

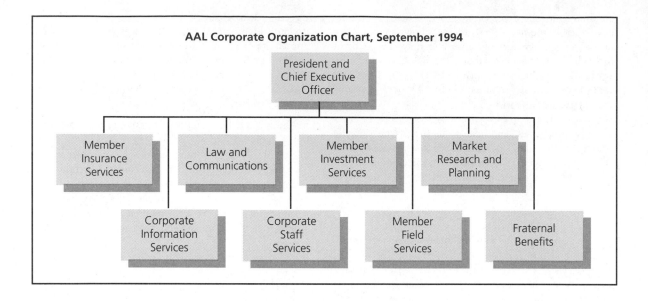

team results in employee QWL, productivity, or customer satisfaction.

These findings led IPS to convene the department management team (regional managers, service team directors, and lead specialists) so that it could communicate the issues to them and involve them in developing a work plan for addressing areas for improvement. The work of fine-tuning the organization based on the CEO findings was begun in August 1993.

SUMMARY

The primary driving forces for the redesign of IPS were a desire to get closer to the customer, a desire to enlarge jobs and empower employees, and a need to right-size staff levels. The organizational concept used to accomplish the task was the self-managing work team. Although early results indicate customers are more satisfied, and corporate productivity goals are being met, employee satisfaction goals are not being fully achieved. The transition from traditional hierarchical management to sociotechnical management has not been without a lot of pain for all involved. Thus, IPS management is heavily involved in the change process even though it has been going on for several years.

The greatest value of restructuring is probably derived from undergoing the *process* of organizational diagnosis, establishing a vision, and *participatively* discovering the gaps between the results of the diagnosis and the vision and creating the organizational response. Also, creating positive dissatisfaction is healthy when it helps unfreeze employee attitudes so that they will permit change to occur. This process is preferably led by top management example; in AAL's case, it took place through the

corporate change that preceded the IPS effort. IPS's managers suggest that it is impossible to overcommunicate to employees as the process unfolds, that affected employees must participate, and that the effect of change on employees cannot be underestimated. It is helpful if support systems are implemented concurrently with the renewal efforts and, if at all possible, it is probably best to implement all aspects of the change at one time to avoid prolonged organizational instability and the associated suppression of employee morale.

Thus, the keys for success include

- *Participation:* Employee involvement at all levels will help ensure employee acceptance and the best results. The more brainpower applied to the problem, the better the chance that the emerging solution will be successful.
- *Vision:* A clear energizing vision must be created to gain the commitment of staff and to motivate them through times of pain.
- *Commitment:* The commitment of top management and the support of other key corporate staff, such as human resource management, are critical. Employees have to know that their efforts are part of a larger strategy.
- *Patience:* If the focus is on short-term results, the effort will probably not achieve the ultimate vision. If the goal is to avoid all pain in the organization, it is probably unachievable. Change brings pain, but pain disappears with newfound stability.
- *Time:* Implementation and cultural change take time. Although some immediate benefits will occur, the ultimate payoff may not be realized for several years.

If these conditions are not present, success is unlikely.

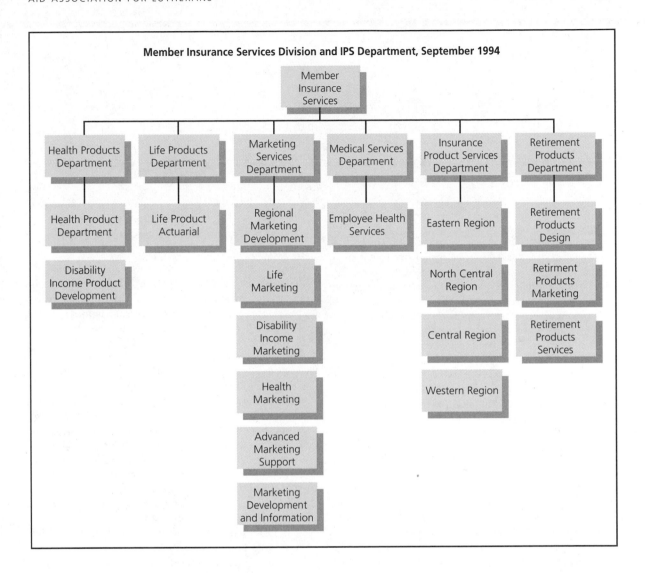

Member Insurance Services Division and IPS Department, September 1994

References

Boyett, J. H., and H. P. Conn. *Maximum Performance Management: How to manage and Compensate People to Meet World Competition. Glenbridge Publishing Ltd., 1988.*

Caudron, S. "Team Staffing Requires New HR Role." *Personnel Journal* (May 1994): 88–94.

Hoerr, J. "The Payoff from Teamwork." *Business Week* (July 10, 1989): 56–62.

Weisbord, M. R. *Productive Workplaces: Organizing and Managing for Dignity, Meaning, and Community.* Jossey-Bass, 1987.

Wellins, R. S., W. C. Byham, and J. M. Wilson. *Empowered Teams.* Jossey-Bass, 1991.

SOURCE: J. H. Laubenstein et al., Insurance Product Services Department, Aid Association for Lutherans. Used by permission.

The Lincoln Electric Company

People are our most valuable asset. They must feel secure, important, challenged, in control of their destiny, confident in their leadership, be responsive to common goals, believe they are being treated fairly, have easy access to authority and open lines of communication in all possible directions. Perhaps the most important task Lincoln employees face today is that of establishing an example for others in the Lincoln organization in other parts of the world. We need to maximize the benefits of cooperation and teamwork, fusing high technology with human talent, so that we here in the USA and all of our subsidiary and joint venture operations will be in a position to realize our full potential.

George Willis, former CEO
The Lincoln Electric Company

The Lincoln Electric Company is the world's largest manufacturer of arc-welding products and a leading producer of industrial electric motors. The firm employs 3,000 workers in 2 U.S. factories near Cleveland and an equal number in 11 factories located in other countries. This does not include the field sales force of more than 200. The company's U.S. market share (for arc-welding products) is estimated at more than 40 percent.

The Lincoln incentive management plan has been well known for many years. Many college management texts make reference to the Lincoln plan as a model for achieving higher worker productivity. Certainly, the firm has been successful according to the usual measures.

James F. Lincoln died in 1965 and there was some concern, even among employees, that the management system would fall into disarray, that profits would decline, and that year-end bonuses might be discontinued. Quite the contrary, 24 years after Lincoln's death, the company appears as strong as ever. Each year, except the recession years 1982 and 1983, has seen high profits and bonuses. Employee morale and productivity remain very good. Employee turnover is almost nonexistent except for retirements. Lincoln's market share is stable. The historically high stock dividends continue.

A HISTORICAL SKETCH

In 1895, after being "frozen out" of the depression-ravaged Elliott-Lincoln Company, a maker of Lincoln-designed electric motors, John C. Lincoln took out his second patent and began to manufacture his improved motor. He opened his new business, unincorporated, with $200 he had earned redesigning a motor for young Herbert Henry Dow, who later founded the Dow Chemical Company.

Started during an economic depression and cursed by a major fire after only one year in business, the company grew, but hardly prospered, through its first quarter century. In 1906, John C. Lincoln incorporated the business and moved from his one-room, fourth-floor factory to a new three-story building he erected in east Cleveland. He expanded his work force to 30 and sales grew to over $50,000 a year. John preferred being an engineer and inventor rather than a manager, though, and it was to be left to another Lincoln to manage the company through its years of success.

In 1907, after a bout with typhoid fever forced him from Ohio State University in his senior year, James F. Lincoln, John's younger brother, joined the fledgling company. In 1914 he became active head of the firm, with the titles of General Manager and Vice President. John remained president of the company for some years but became more involved in other business ventures and in his work as an inventor.

One of James Lincoln's early actions was to ask the employees to elect representatives to a committee which would advise him on company operations. This "Advisory Board" has met with the chief executive officer every two weeks since that time. This was only the first of a series of innovative personnel policies which have, over the years, distinguished Lincoln Electric from its contemporaries.

The first year the Advisory Board was in existence, working hours were reduced from 55 per week, then standard, to 50 hours a week. In 1915, the company gave each employee a paid-up life insurance policy. A welding school, which continues today, was begun in 1917. In 1918, an employee bonus plan was attempted. It was not continued, but the idea was to resurface later.

The Lincoln Electric Employees' Association was formed in 1919 to provide health benefits and social activities. This organization continues today and has assumed several additional functions over the years. In 1923, a piecework pay system was in effect, employees got two weeks paid vacation each year, and wages were adjusted for changes in the Consumer Price Index. Approximately 30 percent of the common stock was set aside for key employees in 1914. A stock purchase plan for all employees was begun in 1925.

The Board of Directors voted to start a suggestion system in 1929. The program is still in effect, but cash awards, a part of the early program, were discontinued several years ago. Now, suggestions are rewarded by additional "points," which affect year-end bonuses.

The legendary Lincoln bonus plan was proposed by the Advisory Board and accepted on a trial basis in 1934. The first annual bonus amounted to about 25 percent of wages. There has been a bonus every year since then. The bonus plan has been a cornerstone of the Lincoln management system and recent bonuses have approximated annual wages.

By 1944, Lincoln employees enjoyed a pension plan, a policy of promotion from within, and continuous employment. Base pay rates were determined by formal job evaluation and a merit rating system was in effect.

In the prologue of James F. Lincoln's last book, Charles G. Herbruck writes regarding the foregoing personnel innovations: "They were not to buy good behavior. They were not efforts to increase profits. They were not antidotes to labor difficulties. They did not constitute a 'do-gooder' program. They were expression of mutual respect for each person's importance to the job to be done. All of them reflect the leadership of James Lincoln, under who they were nurtured and propagated."

During World War II, Lincoln prospered as never before. By the start of the war, the company was the world's largest manufacturer of arc-welding products. Sales of about $4,000,000 in 1934 grew to $24,000,000 by 1941. Productivity per employee more than doubled during the same period. The Navy's Price Review Board challenged the high profits. And the Internal Revenue Service questioned the tax deductibility of employee bonuses, arguing they were not "ordinary and necessary" costs of doing business. But the forceful and articulate James Lincoln was able to overcome the objections.

Certainly since 1935 and probably for several years before that, Lincoln productivity has been well above the average for similar companies. The company claims levels of productivity more than twice those for other manufacturers from 1945 onward. Information available from outside sources tends to support these claims.

COMPANY PHILOSOPHY

James F. Lincoln was the son of a Congregational minister, and Christian principles were at the center of his business philosophy. The confidence that he had in the efficacy of Christ's teachings is illustrated by the following remark taken from one of his books:

> The Christian ethic should control our acts. If it did control our acts, the savings in cost of distribution would be tremendous. Advertising would be a contact of the expert consultant with the customer, in order to give the customer the best product available when all of the customer's needs are considered. Competition then would be in improving the quality of products and increasing efficiency in producing and distributing them; not in deception, as is now too customary. Pricing would reflect efficiency of production; it would not be a selling dodge that the customer may well be sorry he accepted. It would be proper for all concerned and rewarding for the ability used in producing the product.

There is no indication that Lincoln attempted to evangelize his employees or customers—or the general public for that matter. Neither the former chairman of the board and chief executive, George Willis, nor the present one, Donald F. Hastings, mention the Christian gospel in their recent speeches and interviews. The company motto, "The actual is limited, the possible is immense," is prominently displayed, but there is no display of religious slogans, and there is no company chapel.

Attitude toward the Customer

James Lincoln saw the customer's needs as the *raison d'etre* for every company. "When any company has achieved success so that it is attractive as an investment," he wrote, "all money usually needed for expansion is supplied by the customer in retained earnings. It is obvious that the customer's interests, not the stockholder's, should come first." In 1947 he said, "Care should be taken. . .not to rivet attention on profit. Between 'How much do I get?' and 'How do I make this better, cheaper, more useful?' the difference is fundamental and decisive." Willis, too, ranks the customer as management's most important constituency. This is reflected in Lincoln's policy to "at all times price on the basis of cost and at all times keep pressure on our cost. . . ." Lincoln's goal, often stated, is "to build a better and better product at a lower and lower price." "It is obvious," James Lincoln said, "that the customer's interests should be the first goal of industry."

Attitude toward Stockholders

Stockholders are given last priority at Lincoln. This is a continuation of James Lincoln's philosophy: "The last group to be considered is the stockholders who own stock because they think it will be more profitable than investing money in any other way." Concerning division of the largess produced by incentive management, he wrote, "The absentee stockholder also will get his share, even if undeserved, out of the greatly increased profit that the efficiency produces."

Attitude toward Unionism

There has never been a serious effort to organize Lincoln employees. While James Lincoln criticized the labor movement for "selfishly attempting to better its position at the expense of the people it must serve," he still had kind words for union members. He excused abuses of union power as "the natural reactions of human beings to the abuses to which management has subjected them." Lincoln's idea of the correct relationship between workers and managers is shown by this comment: "Labor and management are properly not warring camps; they are parts of one organization in which they must and should cooperate fully and happily."

Beliefs and Assumptions about Employees

If fulfilling customer needs is the desired goal of business, then employee performance and productivity are the means by which this goal can best be achieved. It is the Lincoln attitude toward employees, reflected in the following comments by James Lincoln, which is credited by many with creating the success the company has experienced:

The greatest fear of the worker, which is the same as the greatest fear of the industrialist in operating a company, is the lack of income. . . . The industrial manager is very conscious of his company's need of uninterrupted income. He is completely oblivious, evidently, of the fact that the worker has the same need.

He is just as eager as any manager is to be part of a team that is properly organized and working for the advancement of our economy. . . . He has no desire to make profits for those who do not hold up their end in production, as is true of absentee stockholders and inactive people in the company.

If money is to be used as an incentive, the program must provide that what is paid to the worker is what he has earned. The earnings of each must be in accordance with accomplishment.

Status is of great importance in all human relationships. The greatest incentive that money has, usually, is that it is a symbol of success. . . . The resulting status is the real incentive. . . . Money alone can be an incentive to the miser only.

There must be complete honesty and understanding between the hourly worker and management if high efficiency is to be obtained.

LINCOLN'S BUSINESS

Arc-welding has been the standard joining method in shipbuilding for decades. It is the predominant way of connecting steel in the construction industry. Most industrial plants have their own welding shops for maintenance and construction. Manufacturers of tractors and all kinds of heavy equipment use arc-welding extensively in the manufacturing process. Many hobbyists have their own welding machines and use them for making metal items such as patio furniture and barbecue pits. The popularity of welded sculpture as an art form is growing.

While advances in welding technology have been frequent, arc-welding products, in the main, have hardly changed. Lincoln's Innershield process is a notable exception. This process, described later, lowers welding cost and improves quality and speed in many applications. The most widely-used Lincoln electrode, the Fleetweld 5P, has been virtually the same since the 1930s. The most popular engine-driven welder in the world, the Lincoln SA-200, has been a gray-colored assembly including a four-cylinder continental "Red Seal" engine and a 200 ampere direct-current generator with two current-control knobs for at least four decades. A 1989 model SA-200 even weighs almost the same as the 1950 model, and it certainly is little changed in appearance.

The company's share of the U.S. arc-welding products market appears to have been about 40 percent for many years. The welding products market has grown somewhat faster than the level of industry in general. The market is highly price-competitive, with variations in prices of standard items normally amounting to only a percent or two. Lincoln's products are sold directly by its engineering-oriented sales force and indirectly through its distributor organization. Advertising expenditures amount to less than three-fourths of a percent of sales. Research and development expenditures typically range from $10 million to $12 million, considerably more than competitors.

The other major welding process, flame-welding, has not been competitive with arc-welding since the 1930s. However, plasma-arc-welding, a relatively new process which uses a conducting stream of super-heated gas (plasma) to confine the welding current to a small area, has made some inroads, especially in metal tubing manufacturing, in recent years. Major advances in technology which will produce an alternative superior to arc-welding within the next decade or so appear unlikely. Also, it seems likely that changes in the machines and techniques used in arc-welding will be evolutionary rather than revolutionary.

Products

The company is primarily engaged in the manufacture and sale of arc-welding products—electric welding machines and metal electrodes. Lincoln also produces electric motors ranging from one-half horsepower to 200 horsepower. Motors constitute about 8 to 10 percent of total sales. Several million dollars has recently been invested in automated equipment that will double Lincoln's manufacturing capacity for 1/2 to 20 horsepower electric motors.

The electric welding machines, some consisting of a transformer or motor and generator arrangement powered by commercial electricity and others consisting of an internal combustion engine and generator, are designed to produce 30 to 1,500 amperes of electrical power. This electrical current is used to melt a consumable metal electrode with the molten metal being transferred in super hot spray to the metal joint being welded. Very high temperatures and hot sparks are produced, and operators usually must wear special eye and face protection and leather gloves, often along with leather aprons and sleeves.

Lincoln and its competitors now market a wide range of general purpose and specialty electrodes for welding mild steel, aluminum, cast iron, and stainless and special steels. Most of these electrodes are designed to meet the standards of the American Welding Society, a trade association. They are thus essentially the same as to size and composition from one manufacturer to another. Every electrode manufacturer has a limited number of unique products, but these typically constitute only a small percentage of total sales.

Welding electrodes are of two basic types: (1) Coated "stick" electrodes, usually 14 inches long and smaller than a pencil in diameter, which are held in a special insulated holder by the operator, who must manipulate the electrode in order to maintain a proper arc-width and pattern of deposition of the metal being transferred. Stick electrodes are packaged in 6- to 50-pound boxes. (2) Coiled wired, ranging in diameter from .035″ to 0.219″, which is designed to be fed continuously to the welding arc through a "gun" held by the operator or positioned by automatic positioning equipment. The wire is packaged in coils, reels, and drums weighing 14 to 1,000 pounds and may be solid or flux-cored.

Manufacturing Processes

The main plant is in Euclid, Ohio, a suburb on Cleveland's east side. The layout of this plant is shown in Exhibit 1. There are no warehouses. Materials flow from the half-mile long dock on the north side of the plant through the production lines to a very limited storage and loading area on the south side. Materials used on

■ *Exhibit 1*
Main Factory Layout

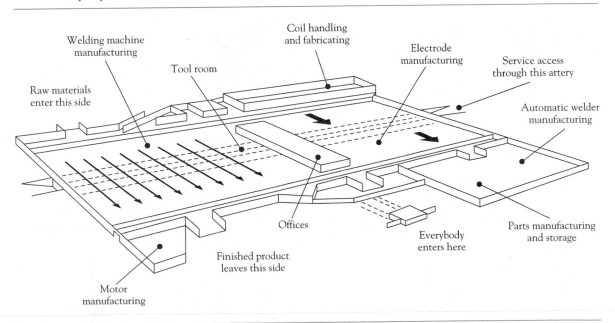

each work station are stored as close as possible to the work station. The administrative offices, near the center of the factory, are entirely functional. A corridor below the main level provides access to the factory floor from the main entrance near the center of the plant. *Fortune* magazine recently declared the Euclid facility one of America's 10 best-managed factories, and compared it with a General Electric plant also on the list: "Stepping into GE's spanking new dishwasher plant, an awed supplier said, is like stepping 'into the Hyatt Regency.' By comparison, stepping into Lincoln Electric's 33-year-old, cavernous, dimly lit factory is like stumbling into a dingy big-city YMCA. It's only when one starts looking at how these factories do things that similarities become apparent. They have found ways to merge design with manufacturing, build in quality, make wise choices about automation, get close to customers, and handle their work forces." A new Lincoln plant, in Mentor, Ohio, houses some of the electrode production operations, which were moved from the main plant.

Electrode manufacturing is highly capital intensive. Metal rods purchased from steel producers are drawn down to smaller diameters, cut to length and coated with pressed-powder "flux" for stick electrodes or plated with copper (for conductivity) and put into coils or spools for wire. Lincoln's Innershield wire is hollow and filled with a material similar to that used to coat stick electrodes. As mentioned earlier, this represented a major innovation in welding technology when it was introduced. The company is highly secretive about its electrode production processes, and outsiders are not given access to the details of those processes.

Lincoln welding machines and electric motors are made on a series of assembly lines. Gasoline and diesel engines are purchased partially assembled but practically all other components are made from basic industrial products, e.g., steel bars and sheets and bar copper conductor wire.

Individual components, such as gasoline tanks for engine-driven welders and steel shafts for motors and generators, are made by numerous small "factories within a factory." The shaft for a certain generator, for example, is made from raw steel bar by one operator who uses five large machines, all running continuously. A saw cuts the bar to length, a digital lathe machines different sections to varying diameters, a special milling machine cuts a slot for the keyway, and so forth, until a finished shaft is produced. The operator moves the shafts from machine to machine and makes necessary adjustments.

Another operator punches, shapes, and paints sheet-metal cowling parts. One assembles steel laminations onto a rotor shaft, then winds, insulates, and tests the rotors. Finished components are moved by crane operators to the nearby assembly lines.

Worker Performance and Attitudes

Exceptional worker performance at Lincoln is a matter of record. The typical Lincoln employee earns about twice as much as other factory workers in the Cleveland area. Yet the company's labor cost per sales dollar in 1989, 26 cents, is well below industry averages. Worker turnover is practically nonexistent except for retirements and departures by new employees.

Sales per Lincoln factory employee currently exceed $150,000. An observer at the factory quickly sees why this figure is so high. Each worker is proceeding busily and thoughtfully about the task at hand. There is no idle chatter. Most workers take no coffee breaks. Many operate several machines and make a substantial component unaided. The supervisors are busy with planning and record keeping duties and hardly glance at the people they "supervise." The manufacturing procedures appear efficient—no unnecessary steps, no wasted motions, no wasted materials. Finished components move smoothly to subsequent work stations.

Appendix A includes summaries of interviews with employees.

ORGANIZATION STRUCTURE

Lincoln has never allowed development of a formal organization chart. The objective of this policy is to insure maximum flexibility. An open door policy is practiced throughout the company, and personnel are encouraged to take problems to the persons most capable of resolving them. Once, Harvard Business School researchers prepared an organization chart reflecting the implied relationships at Lincoln. The chart became available within the company, and present management feels that had a disruptive effect. Therefore, no organizational chart appears in this report.

Perhaps because of the quality and enthusiasm of the Lincoln workforce, routine supervision is almost nonexistent. A typical production foreman, for example, supervises as many as 100 workers, a span-of-control which does not allow more than infrequent worker-supervisor interaction.

Position titles and traditional flows of authority do imply something of an organizational structure, however. For example, the Vice-President, Sales, and the Vice-President, Electrode Division, report to the President, as do various staff assistants such as the Personnel Director and the Director of Purchasing. Using such implied relationships, it has been determined that production workers have two or, at most, three levels of supervision between themselves and the President.

PERSONNEL POLICIES

As mentioned earlier, it is Lincoln's remarkable personnel practices which are credited by many with the company's success.

Recruitment and Selection

Every job opening is advertised internally on company bulletin boards and any employee can apply for any job so advertised. External hiring is permitted only for entry level positions. Selection for these jobs is done on the basis of personal interviews—there is no aptitude or psychological testing. Not even a high school diploma is required—except for engineering and sales positions, which are filled by graduate engineers. A committee consisting of vice presidents and supervisors interviews candidates initially cleared by the Personnel Department. Final selection is made by the supervisor who has a job opening. Out of over 3,500 applicants interviewed by the Personnel Department during a recent period fewer than 300 were hired.

Job Security

In 1958 Lincoln formalized its guaranteed continuous employment policy, which had already been in effect for many years. There have been no layoffs since World War II. Since 1958, every worker with over two year's longevity has been guaranteed at least 30 hours per week, 49 weeks per year.

The policy has never been so severely tested as during the 1981–83 recession. As a manufacturer of capital goods, Lincoln's business is highly cyclical. In previous recessions the company was able to avoid major sales declines. However, sales plummeted 32 percent in 1982 and another 16 percent the next year. Few companies could withstand such a revenue collapse and remain profitable. Yet, Lincoln not only earned profits, but no employee was laid off and year-end incentive bonuses continued. To weather the storm, management cut most of the nonsalaried workers back to 30 hours a week for varying periods of time. Many employees were reassigned and the total workforce was slightly reduced through normal attrition and restricted hiring. Many employees grumbled at their unexpected misfortune, probably to the surprise and dismay of some Lincoln managers. However, sales and profits—and employee bonuses—soon rebounded and all was well again.

Performance Evaluations

Each supervisor formally evaluates subordinates twice a year using the cards shown in Exhibit 2. The employee performance criteria, "quality," "dependability," "ideas and cooperation," and "output," are considered to be independent of each other. Marks on the cards are converted to numerical scores which are forced to average 100 for each evaluating supervisor. Individual merit rating scores normally range from 80 to 110. Any score over 110 requires a special letter to top management. These scores (over 110) are not considered in computing the required 100 point average for each evaluating supervisor. Suggestions for improvements often result in recommendations for exceptionally high performance scores. Supervisors discuss individual performance marks with the employees concerned. Each warranty claim is traced to the individual employee whose work caused the defect. The employee's performance score may be reduced, or the worker may be required to repay the cost of servicing the warranty claim by working without pay.

Compensation

Basic wage levels for jobs at Lincoln are determined by a wage survey of similar jobs in the Cleveland area. These rates are adjusted quarterly in accordance with changes in the Cleveland area wage index. Insofar as possible, base wage rates are translated into piece rates. Practically all production workers and many others—for example, some forklift operators—are paid by piece rate. Once established, piece rates are never changed unless a substantive change in the way a job is done results from a source other than the worker doing the job.

In December of each year, a portion of annual profits is distributed to employees as bonuses. Incentive bonuses since 1934 have averaged about 90 percent of annual wages and somewhat more than after-tax profits. Even for the recession years 1982 and 1983, bonuses had averaged $13,998 and $8,557, respectively. Individual bonuses are proportional to merit-rating scores. For example, assume the amount set aside for bonuses is 80 percent of total wages paid to eligible employees. A person whose performance score is 95 will receive a bonus of 76 percent (0.80 × 0.95) of annual wages.

Vacations

The company is shut down for two weeks in August and two weeks during the Christmas season. Vacations are taken during these periods. For employees with over 25 years of service, a fifth week of vacation may be taken at a time acceptable to superiors.

Work Assignment

Management has authority to transfer workers and to switch between overtime and short time as required. Supervisors have undisputed authority to assign specific parts to individual workmen, who may have their own preferences due to variations in piece rates. During the 1982–1983 recession, 50 factory workers volunteered to join sales teams and fanned out across the country to sell a new welder designed for automobile body shops and small machine shops. The result—$10 million in sales and a hot new product.

Employee Participation in Decision Making

Thinking of participative management usually evokes a vision of a relaxed, nonauthoritarian atmosphere. This is not the case at Lincoln. Formal authority is quite strong. "We're very authoritarian around here," says Willis.

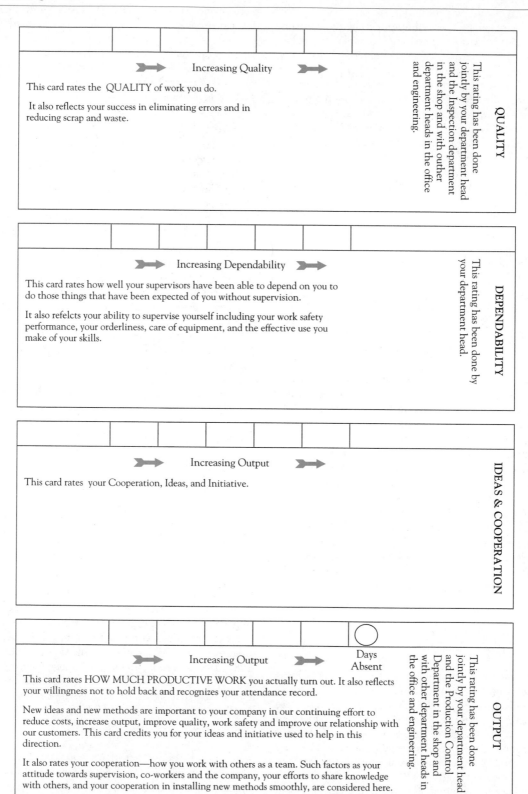

This card rates the QUALITY of work you do.

It also reflects your success in eliminating errors and in reducing scrap and waste.

Increasing Quality

QUALITY

This rating has been done jointly by your department head and the Inspection department in the shop and with outher department heads in the office and engineering.

Increasing Dependability

This card rates how well your supervisors have been able to depend on you to do those things that have been expected of you without supervision.

It also refelcts your ability to supervise yourself including your work safety performance, your orderliness, care of equipment, and the effective use you make of your skills.

DEPENDABILITY

This rating has been done by your department head.

Increasing Output

This card rates your Cooperation, Ideas, and Initiative.

IDEAS & COOPERATION

Increasing Output

Days Absent

This card rates HOW MUCH PRODUCTIVE WORK you actually turn out. It also reflects your willingness not to hold back and recognizes your attendance record.

New ideas and new methods are important to your company in our continuing effort to reduce costs, increase output, improve quality, work safety and improve our relationship with our customers. This card credits you for your ideas and initiative used to help in this direction.

It also rates your cooperation—how you work with others as a team. Such factors as your attitude towards supervision, co-workers and the company, your efforts to share knowledge with others, and your cooperation in installing new methods smoothly, are considered here.

OUTPUT

This rating has been done jointly by your department head and the Production Control Department in the shop and with other department heads in the office and engineering.

James F. Lincoln placed a good deal of stress on protecting management's authority. "Management in all successful departments of industry must have complete power," he said, "Management is the coach who must be obeyed. The men, however, are the players who alone can win the game." Despite this attitude, there are several ways in which employees participate in management at Lincoln.

Richard Sabo, Assistant to the Chief Executive Officer, relates job enlargement/enrichment to participation. He said, "The most important participative technique that we use is giving more responsibility to employees. We give a high school graduate more responsibility than other companies give their foremen." Management puts limits on the degree of participation which is allowed, however. In Sabo's words: "When you use 'participation,' put quotes around it. Because we believe that each person should participate only in those decisions he is most knowledgeable about. I don't think production employees should control the decisions of the chairman. They don't know as much as he does about the decisions he is involved in."

The Advisory Board, elected by the workers, meets with the Chairman and the President every two weeks to discuss ways of improving operations. As noted earlier, this board has been in existence since 1914 and has contributed to many innovations. The incentive bonuses, for example, were first recommended by this committee. Every employee has access to Advisory Board members, and answers to all Advisory Board suggestions are promised by the following meeting. Both Willis and Hastings are quick to point out, though, that the Advisory Board only recommends actions. "They do not have direct authority," Willis says, "and when they bring up something that management thinks is not to the benefit of the company, it will be rejected."

Under the early suggestion program, employees were awarded one-half of the first year's savings attributable to their suggestions. Now, however, the value of suggestions is reflected in performance evaluation scores, which determine individual incentive bonus amounts.

Training and Education

Production workers are given a short period of on-the-job training and then placed on a piecework pay system. Lincoln does not pay for off-site education, unless very specific company needs are identified. The idea behind this latter policy, according to Sabo, is that everyone cannot take advantage of such a program, and it is unfair to expend company funds for an advantage to which there is unequal access. Recruits for sales jobs, already college graduates, are given on-the-job training in the plant followed by a period of work and training at one of the regional sales offices.

Fringe Benefits and Executive Perquisites

A medical plan and a company-paid retirement program have been in effect for many years. A plant cafeteria, operated on a break-even basis, serves meals at about 60 percent of usual costs. The Employees' Association, to which the company does not contribute, provides disability insurance and social and athletic activities. The employees stock ownership program has resulted in employee ownership of about 50 percent of the common stock. Under this program, each employee with more than two years of service may purchase stock in the corporation. The price of these shares is established at book value. Stock purchased through this plan may be held by employees only. Dividends and voting rights are the same as for stock which is owned outside the plan. Approximately 75 percent of the employees own Lincoln stock.

As to executive perquisites, there are none—crowded, austere offices, no executive washrooms or lunchrooms, and no reserved parking spaces. Even the top executives pay for their own meals and eat in the employee cafeteria. On one recent day, Willis arrived at work late due to a breakfast speaking engagement and had to park far away from the factory entrance.

FINANCIAL POLICIES

James F. Lincoln felt strongly that financing for company growth should come from within the company—through initial cash investment by the founders, through retention of earnings, and through stock purchases by those who work in the business. He saw the following advantages of this approach:

1. Ownership of stock by employees strengthens team spirit. "If they are mutually anxious to make it succeed, the future of the company is bright."
2. Ownership of stock provides individual incentive because employees feel that they will benefit from company profitability.
3. "Ownership is educational." Owners-employees "will know how profits are made and lost; how success is won and lost. . . . There are few socialists in the list of stockholders of the nation's industries."
4. "Capital available from within controls expansion." Unwarranted expansion would not occur, Lincoln believed, under his financing plan.
5. "The greatest advantage would be the development of the individual worker. Under the incentive of ownership, he would become a greater man."
6. "Stock ownership is one of the steps that can be taken that will make the worker feel that there is less of a gulf between him and the boss. . . . Stock ownership will help the worker to recognize his responsibility in the game and the importance of victory."

Until 1980, Lincoln Electric borrowed no money. Even now, the company's liabilities consist mainly of accounts payable and short-term accruals.

The unusual pricing policy at Lincoln is succinctly stated by Willis: "At all times price on the basis of cost and at all times keep pressure on our cost." This policy resulted in the price for the most popular welding electrode then in use going from 16 cents a pound in 1929 to 4.7 cents in 1938. More recently, the SA-200 Welder, Lincoln's largest selling portable machine, decreased in price from 1958 through 1965. According to Dr. C. Jackson Grayson of the American Productivity Center in Houston, Texas, Lincoln's prices increased only one-fifth as fast as the Consumer Price Index from 1934 to about 1970. This resulted in a welding products market in which Lincoln became the undisputed price leader for the products it manufactures. Not even the major Japanese manufacturers, such as Nippon Steel for welding electrodes and Osaka Transformer for welding machines, were able to penetrate this market.

Substantial cash balances are accumulated each year preparatory to paying the year-end bonuses. The money is invested in short-term U.S. government securities and certificates of deposit until needed. Financial statements are shown in Exhibit 3. Exhibit 4 shows how company revenue was distributed in the late 1980s.

HOW WELL DOES LINCOLN SERVE ITS STAKEHOLDERS?

Lincoln Electric differs from most other companies in the importance it assigns to each of the groups it serves. Willis identifies these groups, in the order of priority ascribed to them, as (1) customers, (2) employees, and (3) stockholders.

Certainly the firm's customers have fared well over the years. Lincoln prices for welding machines and welding electrodes are acknowledged to be the lowest in the marketplace. Quality has consistently been high. The cost of field failures for Lincoln products was recently determined to be a remarkable 0.04 percent of revenues. The "Fleetweld" electrodes and SA-200 welders have been the standard in the pipeline and refinery construction industry, where price is hardly a criterion, for decades. A Lincoln distributor in Monroe, Louisiana, says that he has sold several hundred of the popular AC-225 welders, which are warranted for one year, but has never handled a warranty claim.

Perhaps best-served of all management constituencies have been the employees. Not the least of their benefits, of course, are the year-end bonuses, which effectively double an already average compensation level. The foregoing description of the personnel program and the comments in Appendix A further illustrate the desirability of a Lincoln job.

While stockholders were relegated to an inferior status by James F. Lincoln, they have done very well indeed. Recent dividends have exceeded $11 a share and earnings per share have approached $30. In January 1980, the price of restricted stock, committed to employees, was $117 a share. By 1989, the stated value, at which the company will repurchase the stock if tendered, was $201. A check with the New York office of Merrill Lynch, Pierce, Fenner and Smith at that time revealed an estimated price on Lincoln stock of $270 a share, with none being offered for sale. Technically, this price applies only to the unrestricted stock owned by the Lincoln family, a few other major holders, and employees who have purchased it on the open market. Risk associated with Lincoln stock, a major determinant of stock value, is minimal because of the small amount of debt in the capital structure, because of an extremely stable earnings record, and because of Lincoln's practice of purchasing the restricted stock whenever employees offer it for sale.

A CONCLUDING COMMENT

It is easy to believe that the reason for Lincoln's success is the excellent attitude of the employees and their willingness to work harder, faster, and more intelligently than other industrial workers. However, Sabo suggests that appropriate credit be given to Lincoln executives, whom he credits with carrying out the following policies:

1. Management has limited research, development, and manufacturing to a standard product line designed to meet the major needs of the welding industry.
2. New products must be reviewed by manufacturing and all producing costs verified before being approved by management.
3. Purchasing is challenged to not only procure materials at the lowest cost, but also to work closely with engineering and manufacturing to assure that the latest innovations are implemented.
4. Manufacturing supervision and all personnel are held accountable for reduction of scrap, energy conservation, and maintenance of product quality.
5. Production control, material handling, and methods engineering are closely supervised by top management.
6. Management has made cost reduction a way of life at Lincoln, and definite programs are established in many areas, including traffic and shipping, where tremendous savings can result.
7. Management has established a sales department that is technically trained to reduce customer welding costs. This sales approach and other real customer services have eliminated nonessential frills and resulted in long-term benefits to all concerned.

◼ *Exhibit 3*

Condensed Comparative Financial Statements ($000,000)*

Balance Sheets

	1979	1980	1981	1982	1983	1984	1985	1986	1987
Assets									
Cash	2	1	4	1	2	4	2	1	7
Bonds & CDs	38	47	63	72	78	57	55	45	41
N/R & A/R	42	42	42	26	31	34	38	36	43
Inventories	38	36	46	38	31	37	34	26	40
Prepayments	1	3	4	5	5	5	7	8	7
Total CA	121	129	157	143	146	138	135	116	137
Other assets**	24	24	26	30	30	29	29	33	40
Land	1	1	1	1	1	1	1	1	1
Net buildings	22	23	25	23	22	21	20	18	17
Net M&E	21	25	27	27	27	28	27	29	33
Total FA	44	49	53	51	50	50	48	48	50
Total assets	189	202	236	224	227	217	213	197	227
Claims									
A/P	17	16	15	12	16	15	13	11	20
Accrued wages	1	2	5	4	3	4	5	5	4
Accrued taxes	10	6	15	5	7	4	–6	5	9
Accrued div.	6	6	7	7	7	6	7	6	7
Total CL	33	29	42	28	33	30	31	27	40
LT debt		4	5	6	8	10	11	8	8
Total debt	33	33	47	34	41	40	42	35	48
Common stock	4	3	1	2	0	0	0	0	2
Ret. earnings	152	167	189	188	186	176	171	161	177
Total SH equity	156	170	190	190	186	176	171	161	179
Total claims	189	202	236	224	227	217	213	197	227

Income Statements

	1979	1980	1981	1982	1983	1984	1985	1986	1987
Net sales	374	387	450	311	263	322	333	318	368
Other income	11	14	18	18	13	12	11	8	9
Income	385	401	469	329	277	334	344	326	377
CGS	244	261	293	213	180	223	221	216	239
Selling, G&A***	41	46	51	45	45	47	48	49	51
Incentive bonus	44	43	56	37	22	33	38	33	39
IBT	56	51	69	35	30	31	36	27	48
Income taxes	26	23	31	16	13	14	16	12	21
Net income****	30	28	37	19	17	17	20	15	27

*Column totals may not check and amounts less than $500,000 (0.5) are shown as zero, due to rounding.
**Includes investment in foreign subsidiaries, $29 million in 1987.
***Includes pension expense and payroll taxes on incentive bonus.
****See end of case for financial statements for 1992, 1993 and 1994.

8. Management has encouraged education, technical publishing, and long-range programs that have resulted in industry growth, thereby assuring market potential for the Lincoln Electric Company.

Sabo writes, "It is in a very real sense a personal and group experience in faith—a belief that together we can achieve results which alone would not be possible. It is not a perfect system and it is not easy. It requires tremendous dedication and hard work. However, it does work and the results are worth the effort."

SOURCE: Arthur Sharplin, McNeese State University. Used by permission

■ *Exhibit 4*
Revenue Distribution

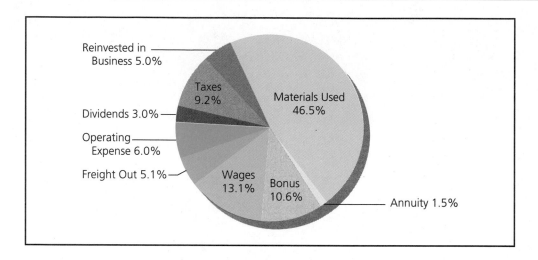

APPENDIX A: EMPLOYEE INTERVIEWS

Typical questions and answers from employee interviews are presented below. In order to maintain each employee's personal privacy, fictitious names are given to the interviewees.

Interview 1

Betty Stewart, a 52-year-old high school graduate who had been with Lincoln 13 years and who was working as a cost accounting clerk at the time of the interview.

Q: What jobs have you held here besides the one you have now?

A: I worked in payroll for a while, and then this job came open and I took it.

Q: How much money did you make last year, including your bonus?

A: I would say roughly around $25,000, but I was off for back surgery for a while.

Q: You weren't paid while you were off for back surgery?

A: No.

Q: Did the Employees' Association help out?

A: Yes. The company doesn't furnish that, though. We pay $8 a month into the Employee Association. I think my check from them was $130.00 a week.

Q: How was your performance rating last year?

A: It was around 100 points, but I lost some points for attendance for my back problem.

Q: How did you get your job at Lincoln?

A: I was bored silly where I was working, and I had heard that Lincoln kept their people busy. So I applied and got the job the next day.

Q: Do you think you make more money than similar workers in Cleveland?

A: I know I do.

Q: What have you done with your money?

A: We have purchased a better home. Also, my son is going to the University of Chicago, which costs $13,000 a year. I buy the Lincoln stock which is offered each year, and I have a little bit of gold.

Q: Have you ever visited with any of the senior executives, like Mr. Willis or Mr. Hastings?

A: I have known Mr. Willis for a long time.

Q: Does he call you by name?

A: Yes. In fact he was very instrumental in my going to the doctor that I am going to with my back. He knows the director of the clinic.

Q: Do you know Mr. Hastings?

A: I know him to speak to him, and he always speaks, always. But I have known Mr. Willis for a good many years. When I did Plant Two accounting I did not understand how the plant operated. Of course you are not allowed in Plant Two, because that's the Electrode Division. I told my boss about the problem one day and the next thing I knew Mr. Willis came by and said, "Come on, Betty, we're going to Plant Two." He spent an hour and a half showing me the plant.

Q: Do you think Lincoln employees produce more than those in other companies?

A: I think with the incentive program the way that it is, if you want to work and achieve, then you will do it. If you don't want to work and achieve, you will not do it no matter where you are. Just because you are merit rated and have a bonus, if you really don't want to work hard, then you're not going to. You will accept your 90 points or 92 or 85 because, even with that you make more money than people on the outside.

Q: Do you think Lincoln employees will ever join a union?

A: I don't know why they would.

Q: So you say that money is a very major advantage?

A: Money is a major advantage, but it's not just the money. It's the fact that having the incentive, you do wish to work a little harder. I'm sure that there are a lot of men here who, if they worked some other place, would not work as hard as they do here. Not that they are overworked—I don't mean that—but I'm sure they wouldn't push.

Q: is there anything that you would like to add?

A: I do like working here. I am better off being pushed mentally. In another company if you pushed too hard you would feel a little bit of pressure, and someone might say, "Hey, slow down; don't try so hard." But here you are encouraged, not discouraged.

Interview 2

Ed Sanderson, a 23-year-old high school graduate who had been with Lincoln four years and who was a machine operator in the Electrode Division at the time of the interview.

Q: How did you happen to get this job?

A: My wife was pregnant, and I was making three bucks an hour and one day I came here and applied. That was it. I kept calling to let them know I was still interested.

Q: Roughly what were your earnings last year including your bonus?

A: $45,000.

Q: What have you done with your money since you have been here?

A: Well, we've lived pretty well and we bought a condominium.

Q: Have you paid for the condominium?

A: No, but I could.

Q: Have you bought your Lincoln stock this year?

A: No, I haven't bought any Lincoln stock yet.

Q: Do you get the feeling that the executives here are pretty well thought of?

A: I think they are. To get where they are today, they had to really work.

Q: Wouldn't that be true anywhere?

A: I think more so here because seniority really doesn't mean anything. If you work with a guy who has 20

years here, and you have two months and you're doing a better job, you will get advanced before he will.

Q: Are you paid on a piece rate basis?

A: My gang does. There are nine of us who make the bare electrode, and the whole group gets paid based on how much electrode we make.

Q: Do you think you work harder than workers in other factories in the Cleveland area?

A: Yes, I would say I probably work harder.

Q: Do you think it hurts anybody?

A: No, a little hard work never hurts anybody.

Q: If you could choose, do you think you would be as happy earning a little less money and being able to slow down a little?

A: No, it doesn't bother me. If it bothered me, I wouldn't do it.

Q: Why do you think Lincoln employees produce more than workers in other plants?

A: That's the way the company is set up. The more you put out, the more you're going to make.

Q: Do you think it's the piece rate and bonus together?

A: I don't think people would work here if they didn't know that they would be rewarded at the end of the year.

Q: Do you think Lincoln employees will ever join a union?

A: No.

Q: What are the major advantages of working for Lincoln?

A: Money.

Q: Are there any other advantages?

A: Yes, we don't have a union shop. I don't think I could work in a union shop.

Q: Do you think you are a career man with Lincoln at this time?

A: Yes.

Interview 3

Roger Lewis, a 23-year-old Purdue graduate in mechanical engineering who had been in the Lincoln sales program for 15 months and who was working in the Cleveland sales office at the time of the interview.

Q: How did you get your job at Lincoln?

A: I saw that Lincoln was interviewing on campus at Purdue, and I went by. I later came to Cleveland for a plant tour and was offered a job.

Q: Do you know any of the senior executives? Would they know you by name?

A: Yes, I know all of them—Mr. Hastings, Mr. Willis, Mr. Sabo.

Q: Do you think Lincoln salesmen work harder than those in other companies?

A: Yes. I don't think there are many salesmen for other companies who are putting in 50- to 60-hour weeks.

Everybody here works harder. You can go out in the plant, or you can go upstairs, and there's nobody sitting around.

Q: Do you see any real disadvantage of working at Lincoln?

A: I don't know if it's a disadvantage but Lincoln is a spartan company, a very thrifty company. I like that. The sales offices are functional, not fancy.

Q: Why do you think Lincoln employees have such high productivity?

A: Piecework has a lot to do with it. Lincoln is smaller than many plants, too; you can stand in one place and see the materials come in one side and the product go out the other. You feel a part of the company. The chance to get ahead is important, too. They have a strict policy of promoting from within, so you know you have a chance. I think in a lot of other places you may not get as fair a shake as you do here. The sales offices are on a smaller scale, too. I like that. I tell someone that we have two people in the Baltimore office, and they say "You've got to be kidding." It's smaller and more personal. Pay is the most important thing. I have heard that this is the highest paying factory in the world.

Interview 4

Jimmy Roberts, a 47-year-old high school graduate, who had been with Lincoln 17 years and who was working as a multiple-drill press operator at the time of the interview.

Q: What jobs have you had at Lincoln?

A: I started out cleaning the men's locker room in 1967. After about a year I got a job in the flux department, where we make the coating for welding rods. I worked there for seven or eight years and then got my present job.

Q: Do you make one particular part?

A: No, there are a variety of parts I make—at least 25.

Q: Each one has a different piece rate attached to it?

A: Yes.

Q: Are some piece rates better than others?

A: Yes.

Q: How do you determine which ones you are going to do?

A: You don't. Your supervisor assigns them.

Q: How much money did you make last year?

A: $53,000.

Q: Have you ever received any kind of award or citation?

A: No.

Q: Was your rating ever over 110?

A: Yes. For the past five years, probably, I made over 110 points.

Q: Is there any attempt to let the others know. . .?

A: The kind of points I get? No.

Q: Do you know what they are making?

A: No. There are some who might not be too happy with their points and they might make it known. The majority, though, do not make it a point of telling other employees.

Q: Would you be just as happy earning a little less money and working a little slower?

A: I don't think I would—not at this point. I have done piecework all these years, and the fast pace doesn't really bother me.

Q: Why do you think Lincoln productivity is so high?

A: The incentive thing—the bonus distribution. I think that would be the main reason. The pay check you get every two weeks is important too.

Q: Do you think Lincoln employees would ever join a union?

A: I don't think so. I have never heard anyone mention it.

Q: What is the most important advantage of working here?

A: Amount of money you make. I don't think I could make this type of money anywhere else, especially with only a high school education.

Q: As a black person, do you feel that Lincoln discriminates in any way against blacks?

A: No. I don't think any more so than any other job. Naturally, there is a certain amount of discrimination, regardless of where you are.

Interview 5

Joe Tranhan, 58-year-old high school graduate who had been with Lincoln 39 years and who was employed as a working supervisor in the tool room at the time of the interview.

Q: Roughly what was your pay last year?

A: Over $56,000; salary, bonus, stock dividends.

Q: How much was your bonus?

A: About $26,000.

Q: Have you ever gotten a special award of any kind?

A: Not really.

Q: What have you done with your money?

A: My house is paid for—and my two cars. I also have some bonds and the Lincoln stock.

Q: What do you think of the executives at Lincoln?

A: They're really top notch.

Q: What is the major disadvantage of working at Lincoln Electric?

A: I don't know of any disadvantage at all.

Q: Do you think you produce more than most people in similar jobs with other companies?

A: I do believe that.

Q: Why is that? Why do you believe that?

A: We are on the incentive system. Everything we do, we try to improve to make a better product with a minimum of outlay. We try to improve the bonus.

Q: Would you be just as happy making a little less money and not working quite so hard?

A: I don't think so.

Q: Do you think Lincoln employees would ever join a union?

A: I don't think they would ever consider it.

Q: What is the most important advantage of working at Lincoln?

A: Compensation.

Q: Tell me something about Mr. James Lincoln, who died in 1965.

A: You are talking about Jimmy Sr. He always strolled through the shop in his shirt sleeves. Big fellow. Always looked distinguished. Gray hair. Friendly sort of guy. I was a member of the advisory board one year. He was there each time.

Q: Did he strike you as really caring?

A: I think he always cared for people.

Q: Did you get any sensation of a religious nature from him?

A: No, not really.

Q: And religion is not part of the program now?

A: No.

Q: Do you think Mr. Lincoln was a very intelligent man, or was he just a nice guy?

A: I would say he was pretty well educated. A great talker—always right off the top of his head. He knew what he was talking about all the time.

Q: When were bonuses for beneficial suggestions done away with?

A: About 18 years ago.

Q: Did that hurt very much?

A: I don't think so, because suggestions are still rewarded through the merit rating system.

Q: Is there anything you would like to add?

A: It's a good place to work. The union kind of ties other places down. At other places, electricians only do electrical work, carpenters only do carpenter work. At Lincoln Electric we all pitch in and do whatever needs to be done.

Q: So a major advantage is not having a union?

A: That's right.

CONSOLIDATED STATEMENT OF INCOME

(Dollars in thousands except per share data)

	Year Ended December 31		
	1994	1993	1992
Net sales	$906,604	$845,999	$853,007
Cost of goods sold	556,259	532,795	553,103
Gross profit	350,345	313,204	299,904
Distribution cost/selling, general & administrative expenses	261,681	277,003	299,195
Restructuring charges (income) – Note C	(2,735)	70,079	23,897
Operating income (loss)	91,399	(33,878)	(23,188)
Other income (expense):			
Interest income	1,442	1,627	3,061
Other income	3,067	2,922	4,433
Interest expense	(15,740)	(17,621)	(18,736)
	(11,231)	(13,072)	(11,242)
Income (loss) before income taxes and cumulative effect of accounting change	80,168	(46,950)	(34,430)
Income taxes (benefit) – Note E	32,160	(6,414)	11,370
Income (loss) before cumulative effect of accounting change	48,008	(40,536)	(45,800)
Cumulative effect to January 1, 1993 of change in method of accounting for income taxes – Note A		2,468	
Net income (loss)	$ 48,008	$ (38,068)	$ (45,800)
Per share:			
Income (loss) before cumulative effect of accounting change	4.38	(3.74)	(4.24)
Cumulative effect of accounting change		.23	
Net income (loss)	$ 4.38	$ (3.51)	$ (4.24)

See notes to consolidated financial statements.

To Our Shareholders:

Each of you is aware that your company faced enormous challenges in 1993. Those challenges required a focused, creative and positive leadership approach on the part of your management team. As I write this, first quarter 1994 results indicate that the domestic economy is continuing its upward surge. Because of the many tough decisions we had to make in 1993, we are now poised to take advantage of an improved economic climate. Even though much of my personal time has been devoted to overseeing the situation in Europe, excellent results are being achieved in the U.S.A. and Canada.

During 1993, a thorough strategic assessment of our foreign operations led to the conclusion that Lincoln Electric lacked the necessary financial resources to continue to support twenty-one manufacturing sites. We did not have the luxury of time to keep those plants operating while working to increase our sales and profitability. As a result, with the endorsement of our financial community, the Board of Directors approved management's recommendation to restructure operations in Europe, Latin America and Japan.

The restructuring included closing the Messer Lincoln operations in Germany; reducing employment throughout Lincoln Norweld, which operates plants in England, France, the Netherlands, Spain and Norway; and closing manufacturing plants in Venezuela, Brazil and Japan. The result was a workforce reduction totaling some 770 employees worldwide. We are not abandoning these markets by any means. Rather, the restructuring will allow us to retain and increase sales while relieving us of the high costs associated with excess manufacturing capacity. Now that the restructuring has been accomplished, we operate fifteen plants in ten countries. This capacity will be adequate to supply the inventory needed to support our customers and an increasingly aggressive marketing strategy. We are internationally recognized for outstanding products and service, and we have been certified to the international quality standard ISO-9002.

It was not easy for Lincoln Electric to eliminate manufacturing capacity and jobs. However, I must point out that the overseas companies were given repeated opportunities to turn their performance around. In all fairness, no one anticipated the depth of the recession that continues to devastate Europe, and particularly Germany. But we could not in good conscience, risk both the continuous erosion of shareholder value and the jobs of our dedicated U.S. employees, by retaining unprofitable manufacturing operations.

For the second year in the history of this company, it was necessary to take restructuring charges that resulted in a consolidated loss. The restructuring charge totaled $70,100,000 ($40,900,000 after tax), and contributed to a consolidated net loss for 1993 of $38,100,000, compared to a $45,800,000 consolidated loss in 1992.

In 1993 our U.S. and Canadian operations achieved outstanding results with increased levels of sales and profitability and a significant gain in market share. We made a huge step forward by concentrating on the "Top Line" to meet one of our major goals — manufacturing and selling $2.1 million worth of product from our Ohio company each billing day from June 1 through the end of the year. Our Canadian company also made significant contributions with a 38 percent increase in sales. The bottom line automatically moved into greater profitability.

These impressive gains were not made without sacrifice. Lincoln manufacturing people voluntarily deferred 614 weeks of vacation, worked holidays, and many employees worked a seven day week schedule to fill the steady stream of orders brought in by the sales department as we capitalized on an emerging domestic economy that we felt was being largely ignored by our major competitors.

This remarkable achievement would never have been possible without the expert management of your President and Chief Operating Officer Frederick W. Mackenbach. His leadership consistently inspired our employees and management team alike. The U.S. company's extraordinary performance encouraged the Board of Directors to approve a gross bonus of $55 million, and to continue the regular quarterly dividend payment throughout the year. As you know, the usual course of action for a company reporting a consolidated loss is to cut or defer bonuses and dividends. That these were paid is a tribute to our Board and their steadfast belief in the long range, proven benefits of the Incentive Management System.

Thinking in the long term is critical to our progress in a world that too often seems to demand instant solutions to complex problems. Your Chairman, your Board, and your management team are determined to resist that impulse. Currently, Lincoln people around the world are working diligently to formulate a Strategic Plan that will carry this company into the next century. An important element of this business plan will be our new state-of-the-art motor manufacturing facility, which is on schedule. Furthermore, we have strengthened our international leadership with the addition of executives experienced in global management to our Board and to key management posts.

While your company is indeed emerging from a very challenging period in its history, we project excellent results for 1994, with strong sales, increased profits, and the benefits of those developments accruing to shareholders, customers and employees. As the year proceeds, we will be looking forward to our Centennial in 1995. I am confident that you and I will enjoy celebrating that event together.

Sincerely,

Donald F. Hastings
*Chairman and
Chief Executive Officer*

Mission and Values Statement

World's Leader in Welding and Cutting Products • Premier Manufacturer of Industrial Motors

The mission of The Lincoln Electric Company is to earn and retain global leadership as a total quality supplier of superior products and services.

Our Core Values

As a responsible and successful company in partnership with our customers, distributors, employees, shareholders, suppliers and our host communities, we pledge ourselves to conduct our business in accordance with these core values:

• Respond to our customers' needs and expectations with quality, integrity and value

• Recognize people as our most valuable asset

• Maintain and expand the Lincoln Incentive Management philosophy

• Practice prudent and responsible financial management

• Strive continually to be environmentally responsible

• Support communities where we operate and industries in which we participate

To Realize Our Mission and Support Our Core Values, We Have Established the Following Goals:

Respond to Our Customers' Needs and Expectations With Quality, Integrity and Value

- Assure value through innovative, functional and reliable products and services in all the markets we serve around the world.
- Exceed global standards for products and service quality.
- Provide our customers with personalized technical support that helps them achieve improvements in cost reduction, productivity and quality.
- Lead the industry in aggressive application of advanced technology to meet customer requirements.
- Invest constantly in creative research and development dedicated to maintaining our position of market leadership.
- Achieve and maintain the leading market share position in our major markets around the world.

Recognize People As Our Most Valuable Asset

- Maintain a safe, clean and healthy environment for our employees.
- Promote employee training, education and development, and broaden skills through multi-departmental and international assignments.
- Maintain an affirmative action program and provide all employees with opportunities for advancement commensurate with their abilities and performance regardless of race, religion, national origin, sex, age or disability.
- Maintain an environment that fosters ethical behavior, mutual trust, equal opportunity, open communication, personal growth and creativity.
- Demand integrity, discipline and professional conduct from our employees in every aspect of our business and conduct our operations ethically and in accordance with the law.
- Reward employees through recognition, "pay for performance," and by sharing our profits with incentive bonus compensation based on extraordinary achievement.

Maintain and Expand the Lincoln Incentive Management Philosophy

Promote dynamic teamwork and incentive as the most profitable and cost-effective way of achieving:

- A committed work ethic and positive employee attitudes throughout the Company.
- High quality, low-cost manufacturing.
- Efficient and innovative engineering.
- Customer-oriented operation and administration.
- A dedicated and knowledgeable sales and service force.
- A total organization responsive to the needs of our worldwide customers.

Practice Prudent and Responsible Financial Management

- Establish attainable goals, strategic planning and accountability for results that enhance shareholder value.
- Promote the process of employee involvement in cost reductions and quality improvements.
- Recognize profit as the resource that enables our Company to serve our customers.

Strive Continually To Be Environmentally Responsible

- Continue to pursue the most environmentally sound operating practices, processes and products to protect the global environment.
- Maintain a clean and healthy environment in our host communities.

Support Communities Where We Operate and Industries In Which We Participate

- Invest prudently in social, cultural, educational and charitable activities.
- Contribute to the industries we serve and society as a whole by continuing our leadership role in professional organizations and education.
- Encourage and support appropriate employee involvement in community activities.

LINCOLN ELECTRIC

APPENDIX A

Statistics for Human Resource Management:
Positioning for the 21st Century

Throughout, this book refers to numerous research studies, which provide documentation for its assertions. Readers who wish to learn more about the studies cited are encouraged to consult the original sources, listed in the notes for each chapter. Much of this literature requires some basic familiarity with the statistics and research methods used in human resource management. This appendix describes some of the basic concepts needed to understand the original research reports. Although this appendix uses examples relevant to selection and placement (described in chapter 8), the basic concepts described here also apply to research on most other topics.

 ## MEASUREMENT

Regardless of the method or site used to study human resource issues, researchers need to be concerned about the reliability and validity of measurement devices. *Reliability* refers to the consistency of measurement and *validity* relates to the truth or accuracy of measurement. Both are expressed by a *correlation coefficient* (denoted by the symbol *r*).

Correlation Coefficient

A correlation coefficient expresses the degree of linear relationship between two sets of scores. A positive correlation exists when high values on one measure (e.g., a job knowledge test) are associated with high scores on another measure (e.g., overall ratings of job performance). A negative correlation exists when high scores on one measure are associated with low scores on another measure. The range of possible correlation coefficients is from +1 (a perfect positive correlation coefficient) to −1 (a perfect negative correlation coefficient). Several linear relationships represented by plotting actual data are shown in Exhibit A.1.

The correlation between scores on a predictor (x) and a criterion (y) is typically expressed for a sample as r_{xy}. If we did not have a sample but were able to compute our correlation on the population of interest, we would express the correlation as ρ_{xy} (ρ is the Greek letter *rho*). In almost all cases, researchers do not have access to the entire population. Therefore, they must estimate the population correlation coefficient based on data from a sample of the population. For instance, an organization may desire to know the correlation between a test for computer programming ability (scores on a predictor, x) and job performance (scores on a performance appraisal rating form, y) for all its computer programmers, but decides it cannot afford to test all computer programmers (i.e., the population of interest). Instead, the organization may select a

■ *Exhibit A.1*

Scatterplots Indicating Possible Relationships between Selection Test Scores and Job Performance Scores

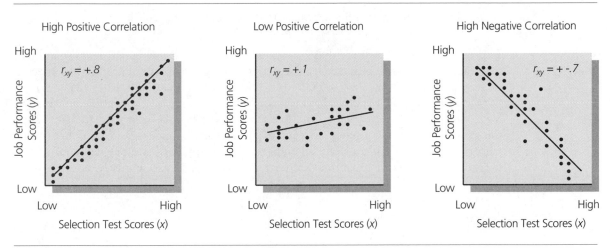

sample of computer programmers and estimate the correlation coefficient in the population (ρ_{xy}) based on the observed correlation in the sample (r_{xy}).

For each scatterplot in Exhibit A.1, a solid line represents the pattern of data points. Each line is described by an equation, which takes the general form for a straight line: y = a + bx, where *a* is the point at which the line intercepts the *y*-axis and *b* is the slope of the line. Such equations, called *prediction equations,* allow researchers to estimate values of *y* (the criterion) from their knowledge of *x* (the predictor). For example, we may conduct a study to determine the correlation between sales performance (i.e., dollar sales volume) and number of years of sales experience, for a group of salespeople. Once we have developed a prediction equation, we can then estimate how well a sales applicant might perform on the job.[1] The equation might read,

$$\text{Dollar Sales per Month} = \$50,290 + \$2,000 \times \text{Years of Sales Experience}$$

Using this equation, we would predict that a salesperson with ten years of experience will generate $70,290 a month in sales. A new salesperson with only one year of experience will be expected to generate only $52,290 a month in sales.

As you might expect, decision makers often employ more than one predictor in their equations. For example, organizations often use multiple predictors when making selection and placement decisions. Similar to that of the single-predictor approach, the purpose of multiple prediction is to estimate a criterion (*y*) from a linear combination of predictor variables: $y = a + b_1x_1 + b_2x_2 + \ldots + b_mx_m$). Such equations are called *multiple-prediction equations* or *multiple-regression equations.* The *b*s are the regression weights applied to the predictor measures. The relationship between the predictors and the criterion score is referred to as the *multiple-correlation coefficient* (denoted by the symbol *R*).[2]

For example, suppose a manager believed that sales were a function of years of experience, education, and shyness (scored 0 for people who are not very shy to 7 for people who are very shy). To determine whether the manager's intuition was correct, we might conduct a research study. Information on each of these predictors could be collected, along with sales performance, or criterion, data. A multiple-regression equation such as the following could be generated:

Dollar Sales per Month = \$25,000 + (\$1,500 × Years of Experience) + (\$500 × Years of Schooling) − (\$25 × Score on Shyness)

This equation would indicate that a salesperson who scored low on shyness (1) and had ten years of experience plus a college degree (sixteen years of schooling) will be expected to generate \$47,975 in sales [\$25,000 + (\$1,500 × 10) + (\$1,500 × 16) − (25 × 1)].

Multiple regression analysis has been used to determine how to combine information from multiple selection devices. Multiple regression has also been used to assess such things as the effects of rater and ratee characteristics (e.g., sex, experience, prior performance rating, and rate of pay) on performance appraisal and pay decisions and to measure the effects of organizational characteristics (e.g., size, industry, and sales) on human resource planning and policies.

Reliability

If a measure such as a selection test is to be useful, it must yield reliable results. As pointed out in chapter 8, the reliability of a measure can be defined and interpreted in several ways. Each of these methods is based on the notion that observed scores (x) comprise true scores (T) plus some error (E) or $x = T + E$ where T is the expected score if there were no error in measurement.[3] To the extent that observed scores on a test are correlated with true scores, a test is said to be reliable. That is, if observed and true scores could be obtained for every individual who took a personnel selection test, the squared correlation between observed and true scores in the population is (ρ^2_x) would be called the reliability coefficient for that selection test.

One means of estimating reliability is *test-retest reliability* (ρ_{xx}). This method is based on testing a sample of individuals twice with the same measure and then correlating the results to produce a reliability estimate.

Another means of estimating the reliability of a measure is to correlate scores on alternate forms of the measure. *Alternate test forms* are any two test forms that have been constructed in an effort to make them parallel; their observed score means, variances (i.e., measures of the spread of scores about the means), and correlations with other measures may be equal or very similar.[4] They are also intended to be similar in content.

A problem with test-retest reliability and alternate forms reliability is the necessity of testing twice. In contrast, *internal consistency reliability* is estimated based on only one administration of a measure. The most common method, *coefficient* α (alpha), yields a *split-half reliability* estimate. That is, the measure (e.g., a test) is divided into two parts, which are considered alternate forms of each other, and the relationship between these two parts is an estimate of the measure's reliability.

Researchers are interested in assessing the reliability of measures based on one or more of these methods because reliability is a necessary condition for determining validity. The reliability of a measure sets a limit on how highly the measure can correlate with another measure, because it is very unlikely that a measure will correlate more strongly with a different measure than with itself.

Estimating Population Coefficients

If we were able to assess the relationship between a predictor and a criterion in a population of interest with no measurement error, then we would have computed the true correlation coefficient for the population, ρ_{xy}. Because we almost never have the population available and almost always have measurement error, our observed correlation coefficients underestimate the population coefficients. That is, predictor and criterion unreliability are statistical artifacts that lower predictor-criterion relationships.

Two other statistical artifacts that obscure true relationships are sampling error and range restriction. A *sampling error* is an inaccuracy resulting from the use of a sample that is smaller than the population when computing the validity coefficient. A *range restriction* is a correlation or validity coefficient computed between the predictor and criterion scores for a restricted group of individuals. For example, suppose you were interested in determining the correlation between height and weight. if you had data that reflected the entire range of human variability, the correlation would be fairly substantial. However, if you studied only retired adult men, the correlation would be artificially low owing to the restricted range of heights and weights represented in your sample.

Formulas have been developed to remove the effects of predictor unreliability, criterion unreliability, and range restriction, and for determining sampling error variance. Researchers can use these correction formulas to remove the influence of statistical artifacts and, consequently, obtain a better idea of the predictor-criterion relationship in the relevant population. A number of studies have examined the effects of variations in sample size, range restriction, and reliability on the size and variability of observed validity coefficients. These studies have improved our understanding of how observed validity coefficients are affected by measurement error and statistical artifacts.

Validity

As defined in the American Psychological Association's *Principles for the Validation and Use of Personnel Selection Procedures,* validity is the degree to which inferences from scores on tests or assessments are supported by evidence. This means that validity refers to the inferences made from the use of a measure, not to the measure itself. Two common strategies used to justify the inferences made from scores on measures are criterion-related validation and content-oriented validation.

Criterion-Related Validation. *Criterion-related validation* empirically assesses how well a predictor measure forecasts a criterion measure. Usually, predictor measures are scores on one or more selection "tests" (e.g., a score from an interview or a score to reflect the amount of experience), and criteria measures represent job performance (e.g., dollar sales per year or supervisory ratings of performance). Two types of criterion-related validation strategies are concurrent validation and predictive validation. These are shown in Exhibit A.2.

Concurrent validation evaluates the relationship between a predictor and a criterion for all participants in the study at the same time. For example, the HR department could use this strategy to determine the correlation between years of experience and job performance. The department would collect from each person in the study information about years of experience and performance scores. All persons in the study would have to be working in similar jobs, generally in the same job family or classification. Then, a correlation would be computed between the predictor scores and criterion scores.

The steps in determining predictive validity are similar, except that the predictor is measured sometime before the criterion is measured. Thus, *predictive validity* is determined by measuring an existing group of employees on a predictor and then later gathering their criterion measures.

The classic example of a predictive validation analysis is AT&T's Management Progress Study.[6] In that study, researchers at AT&T administered an assessment center to 422 male employees. Then, they stored the scores from the assessment center and waited.

■ *Exhibit A.2*
Criterion-Related Validation Strategies

Concurrent Study

Time 1	Time 1	Time 1
Test (predictor) scores are gathered.	Criterion scores are gathered.	The correlation between scores on predictor measures (x) and criterion measures (y), r_{xy}, is calculated.

Predictive Study

Time 1	Time 2	Time 2
Test (predictor) scores are gathered.	Criterion scores are gathered.	The correlation between scores on predictor measures (x) and criterion measures (y), r_{xy}, is calculated.

After eight years, they correlated the assessment center scores with measures of how far the same individuals progressed in AT&T's management hierarchy. For a group of college graduates, the predictions were highly accurate; a correlation of .71 was obtained between the assessment center predictions and the level of management achieved.

Content-oriented Validation. On many occasions, employers are not able to obtain sufficient empirical data for a criterion-related study. Consequently, other methods of validation are useful. One of the most viable is *content-oriented validation*. It differs from a criterion-related strategy in that it uses subjective judgments and logic as the basis for arguing that a predictor is likely to be effective in forecasting a criterion. To employ a content validation strategy, one must know the duties of the actual job. As discussed in chapter 6, information about job tasks and duties can be obtained using one or more job analysis procedures. Once the duties are known, then logic is used to argue that a predictor is relevant to performance in the job. For example, if a job analysis showed that word processing duties were a substantial portion of a job, then you might logically conclude that a test of word processing skills would be a valid predictor of job performance. For this type of validation, the most important data are job analysis results.

Validity Generalization

Since the mid-1900s, hundreds of criterion-related validation studies have been conducted in organizations, to determine the predictive effectiveness of HR measures (e.g., ability tests) for selecting and placing individuals. Often, the validity coefficients for the same or a similar predictor-criterion relationship differed substantially from one setting to another. Although researchers were aware that these differences were affected by range restriction, predictor unreliability, criterion unreliability, and sampling error, only recently were corrections for these statistical artifacts integrated into systematic procedures for estimating to what degree true validity estimates for the same predictor-criterion relationship generalize across settings.

A series of studies has applied validity generalization procedures to validity coefficient data for clerical jobs, computer programming jobs, petroleum industry jobs, and so on.[7] In general, these investigations showed that the effects of range restriction, predictor unreliability, criterion unreliability, and sample size accounted for much of the observed variance in validity coefficients for the same or similar test-criterion relationship within an occupation (i.e., a job grouping or job family). Thus, the estimated true (corrected) validity coefficients were higher and less variable than the observed (uncorrected) validity.

The implications of these findings are that inferences (predictions) from scores on selection tests can be transported across situations for similar jobs. That is, if two similar jobs exist in two parts of an organization, a given selection test may have approximately the same validity coefficients for both jobs. If validity generalization can be successfully argued, an organization can save a great deal of time and money developing valid, job-related predictors when the inferences from a predictor for a job have already been established.

The concept of validity generalization, or *meta-analysis,* has also been applied to other areas of HR research.[8] Such research has led to a better understanding of the effectiveness of interventions such as training programs, goal-setting programs, and performance measurement (appraisal) programs.

Cross-Validation

HR researchers are also interested in how stable their prediction equations are across samples. Cross-validation studies address this concern. For the prediction equations developed by researchers to be of any practical use, they must produce consistent results. *Cross-validation* is a procedure for determining how much capitalization on chance has affected the prediction equation, (or *regression weights*). In the case of HR selection research, for example, one is interested in how well the regression weights estimated in a sample of job incumbents will predict the criterion value of new job applicants not tested in the sample.

Traditional or empirical cross-validation typically involves holding out some of the data from the initial sample and then applying the equation developed in the initial sample to the holdout sample to evaluate the equation's stability. In general, this procedure is less precise than one using a formula for estimating the stability of regression equations. The reason for this is that in formula-based estimates, all the available information (the total sample) is used at once in estimating the original weights.[9]

 ## UTILITY ANALYSIS

Armed with tools to determine the reliability and validity of measurement devices, researchers have become concerned about demonstrating the usefulness of the methods and procedures they use. This is particularly important when human resource activities and programs are vying for scarce financial resources. To justify funding, human resource activities must be cost-effective. The process used to assess the costs and benefits of human resource programs is called *utility analysis.* Although it is not yet used by many organizations, utility analysis helps human resource managers compare the economic consequences of two alternative HR practices. For example, you might compare the consequences of relying on a single interview to select people into a job, versus giving applicants a written ability test. Or you might compare the economic consequences of a three-week off-site training session versus a six-month on-the-job approach to training.[10]

In HR selection, most applications of utility analysis are premised on the assumption that supervisors can estimate the dollar values associated with performance at the 50th percentile, the 85th percentile, and the 15th percentile. This is called the *standard deviation (SD_y)* of the performance in dollars. Studies have been conducted in which supervisors have provided estimates of the SD_y for such jobs as sales manager, computer programmer, insurance counselor, and entry-level park ranger. The research indicates that the SD_y usually ranges from 16 to 70 percent of wages, with values most often being in the 40 to 60 percent range. This means that an estimate of the SD_y for a job paying $40,000 a year typically ranges from $16,000 to $24,000.

Utility analysis also considers other variables (e.g., the number of employees, tax rates, and the validity coefficient of the selection device) that affect the value or utility of a selection process. The following equation, which incorporates these economic concepts, can be employed when comparing two alternative selection procedures or other human resource options:

$$\Delta U = N_s \sum_{t=1}^{T} \{[1/(1 + i)^t] SD_y (1 + V)(1 - TAX)(\hat{\rho}_1 - \hat{\rho}_2)z_s\} - \{(C_1 - C_2)(1 - TAX)\}$$

where

ΔU = The total estimated dollar value of replacing one selection procedure (1) with another procedure (2) after variable costs, taxes, and discounting
N_s = The number of employees selected
T = The number of future time periods
t = The time period in which a productivity increase occurs
i = The discount rate
SD_y = The standard deviation of job performance in dollars
V = The proportion of SD_y represented by variable costs
TAX = The organization's applicable tax rate
$\hat{\rho}_1$ = The estimated population validity coefficient between scores on one selection procedure and the criterion
$\hat{\rho}_2$ = The estimated population validity coefficient between scores on an alternative selection procedure and scores on the criterion
z_s = The mean standard score on the selection procedure of those selected (this is assumed to be equal in this equation for each selection procedure)
C_1 = The total cost of the first selection procedure
C_2 = the total cost of the alternative selection procedure[11]

For illustration, let us employ a portion of the utility analysis information collected at a large international manufacturing company, which we will call company A. Company A undertook a utility analysis to obtain an estimate of the economic effect of its current procedure for selecting sales managers as compared with that of its previous program. The current procedure is a managerial assessment center. Although the assessment center had been in operation for seven years at the time of the utility analysis, a value of 4 years was used because this was the average tenure (T) for the 29 sales managers (N_s) who had been selected from a pool of 132 candidates. A primary objective of the utility analysis was to compare the estimated dollar value of selecting these managers using the assessment center with what the economic gain would have been if the managers had been selected by an interviewing program.

The values −.05 for V and .49 for TAX were provided by the accounting and tax departments, respectively. V was the proportion of dollar sales volume compared with operating costs. Its value was negative because a positive relationship existed between combined operating costs (e.g., salaries, benefits, supplies, and automobile operations) and sales volume. The value for i, .18, was based on an examination of corporate financial documentation. The accounting department also provided the figure for C_1 (the total cost of the assessment center), \$263,636. Based on 29 selected individuals, the cost of selecting one district sales manager was computed to be about \$9,091. The estimated total cost to select 29 sales managers by the previous one-day interviewing program (C_2) was \$50,485.

The estimated population validity coefficient for the assessment center, $\hat{\rho}_1$, was obtained by correlating five assessment dimension scores (i.e., scores for planning and organizing, decision making, stress tolerance, sensitivity, and persuasiveness) with an overall performance rating. The multiple correlation between the measures was .61. Next, the cross-validated multiple correlation for the population was calculated, using the appropriate formulas. The resulting value, .41 was corrected for range restriction and criterion reliability to yield an estimated value of .59 for $\hat{\rho}_1$.

Because company A had not conducted a criterion-related validity study for the interviewing selection program, a value was obtained from the validity generalization literature; the resulting of $\hat{\rho}_2$ for the interviewing program was .16. In addition, the standard score on the predictor, (z_s) was determined to be .872. This value was assumed to be the same for both the assessment center and the interviewing program.

The final, and traditionally the most difficult, component to estimate in the equation was SD_y. This expression is an index of the variability of job performance in dollars in the relevant population. The relevant population for evaluating a selection procedure is the applicant group exposed to that procedure. When evaluating the economic utility of organizational interventions, however, the relevant group is current employees. Because the intervention at company A would be applied to current employees, the appropriate value of SD_y was for this group. Thus, if SD_y were estimated from the applicant group, it could be an overestimate. Consequently, the approximate value for a sales manager, \$30,000, was used for SD_y.

Placing all these values into the utility analysis equation gave approximately \$316,460 as the estimated present value, over four years, to the organization from the use of the assessment center in place of an interviewing program to select 29 sales managers. Although the cost of the interviewing program was only about one-fifth that of the assessment center, the estimated dollar gain from use of the assessment center instead of the interviewing program was substantial. This result was primarily due to the greater predictive effectiveness (i.e., higher validity coefficient) of the assessment center.

Despite the potential usefulness of utility analysis, very few firms have adopted its procedures. Several circumstances may explain this failure. First, practices tends to lag theory. Because utility analysis is rather new, it may not yet have filtered down to organizations. Second, opponents of utility analysis question the viability of measuring the standard deviation of performance by using managerial estimates. However, this concern may be alleviated by a new utility approach that does not require the direct estimation of SD_y.[12] Finally, as noted in Chapter 8, validation studies have not been conducted as often as they should be. Without information regarding the validity of selection, training, safety, or absenteeism programs, utility analysis cannot be conducted.

Notes

CHAPTER 1

1. W. Zellner, R. Hof, R. Brandt, S. Baker and D. Greising, "Go-Go Goliaths," *Business Week* (February 13, 1995): 64–70; R. S. Teitelbaum, "Southwest Airlines: Where Service Flies Right," *Fortune* (August 24, 1994): 115–16; K. Labich, "Is Herb Kelleher America's Best," *Fortune* (May 2, 1994): 44–52; W. G. Lee, "A Conversation with Herb Kelleher," *Organizational Dynamics* (Autumn 1994): 64–74.

2. Based on numerous conversations between 1990 and 1995 with William R. Maki, director of human resources, Weyerhaeuser Company; internal company documents; and J. F. Bolt, *Executive Development: A Strategy for Corporate Competitiveness* (New York: Harper & Row Publishers, 1989).

3. J. F. Welch, "A Matter of Exchange Rates," *Wall Street Journal* (June 21, 1994): p. 23.

4. S. Sherman, "Are You as Good as the Best in the World?" *Fortune* (December 13, 1993): 95–96.

5. C. A. Bartlett and S. Ghosal, "What Is a Global Manager?" *Harvard Business Review* (September–October 1992): 131.

6. S. Caudron, "HR Leaders Brainstorm," *Personnel Journal* (August 1994): 54.

7. "Change in the Global Economy: An Interview with Rosabeth Moss Kanter," *European Management Journal* (March 1994): 1–9; J. Pfeffer, *Competitive Advantage through People: Unleashing the Power of the Work Force* (Boston: Harvard Business School Press, 1994); T. A. Stewart, "Your Company's Most Valuable Asset: Intellectual Capital," *Fortune* (October 3, 1994): 68–74.

8. A. Farnham, "America's Most Admired Company," *Fortune* (February 7, 1994): 50–87; M. Galen, D. Greising, and S. Anderson, "How Business Is Linking Hands in the Inner Cities," *Business Week* (September 26, 1994): 81, 83.

9. L. C. Thurow, *Head to Head* (New York: William Morrow & Co., 1992), 45.

10. A. S. Tsui, "Personnel Department Effectiveness: A Tripartite Approach," *Industrial Relations* (1984) 23: 184–97; W. F. Cascio, *Costing Human Resources: The Financial Impact of Behavior in Organizations,* 3rd ed. (Boston: PWS-Kent, 1991); R. A. Guzzo, R. D. Jette, and R. A. Katzell, "The Effects of Psychologically Based Intervention Programs on Worker Productivity: A Meta Analysis," *Personnel Psychology* (1985) 38: 275–91; N. Nicholson and S. O. Brenner, "Dimensions of Perceived Organisational Performance: Tests of a Model," *Applied Psychology: An International Review* (1994): 89–108.

11. G. E. Fryzell and J. Wang, "The Fortune Corporation 'Reputation' Index: Reputation for What?" *Journal of Management* (1994) 20: 1–14.

12. Chauvin and Guthrie, *Working Mother.*

13. See M. E. Porter, *Competitive Strategy* (New York: Free Press, 1985); M. E. Porter, *Competitive Advantage* (New York: Free Press, 1985.

14. Sherman, "Are You As Good As The Best?"

15. Ibid.

16. *Reinventing the CEO* (New York: Korn/Ferry International and Columbia University, 1989): 1.

17. *Priorities for Competitive Advantage* (New York: IBM and Towers, Perrin, 1992).

18. R. S. Schuler, "World Class HR Departments: Six Critical Issues," *Accounting and Business Review* (January 1994): 43–72.

19. *Harley-Davidson, Inc., Annual Report, 1992,* 10.

20. L. D. Lerner and G. E. Fryzell, "CEO Stakeholder Attitudes and Corporate Social Activity in the Fortune 500," *Business and Society* (April 1994): 58–81; R. E. Freeman, *Strategic Management: A Stakeholder Approach* (Boston: Pitman, 1984); D. J. Wood, "Corporate Social Performance Revisited," *Academy of Management Review* 16 (1991): 691–718; J. H. Dobrzynski, "Tales from the Boardroom Wars," *Business Week* (June 6, 1994): 71–72; G. T. Savage et al., "Strategies for Assessing and Managing Organizational Stakeholders," *Academy of Management Executives* 2 (1991): 61–75.

21. L. Therrien, "Plumper Profits Ahead," *Business Week* (January 10, 1994): 78; Z. Schiller, "No Rust on This Market," *Business Week* (January 10, 1994): 73; K. Kerwin, "Value Will Keep Detroit Moving," *Business Week* (January 10, 1994): 71; J. Weber, "Lean, Mean, And . . . Healthier?" *Business Week* (January 10, 1994): 76; C. Arnst, "The End of the End for 'Big Iron,' " *Business Week* (January 10, 1994): 81.

22. C. Farrell, "Is the Japanese Dynamo Losing Juice?" *Business Week* (June 27, 1994): 44.

23. S. Nasar, "The American Economy, Back on Top," *New York Times* (February 27, 1994): p. F1, col. 6; Kerwin, "Value Will Keep Detroit Moving," 71–108.

24. *High Performance Work Practices and Firm Performance* (U.S. Department of Labor: Washington, DC, 1993).

25. G. S. Hansen and B. Wernerfelt, "Determinants of Firm Performance: Relative Importance of Economic and Organizational Factors," *Strategic Journal of Management* (1989): 399–411.

26. J. P. MacDuffie and J. Krafcik, "Integrating Technology and Human Resources for High-Performance

Manufacturing," in *Transforming Organizations,* ed. T. Kochan and M. Useem (New York: Oxford University Press, 1992), 210–26. See also J. B. Arthur, "Effects of Human Resource Systems on Manufacturing Performance and Turnover," *Academy of Management Journal* 37 (1994): 670–87.

27. J. Bennet, "Chrysler and Nissan Top Auto Production Survey," *New York Times* (June 24, 1994): p. D5.

28. J. Hater, "Executive Commentary," *Executive* (May 1994): 48–50.

29. J. Huey, "The New Post-Heroic Leadership," *Fortune* (February 21, 1994): 42–50.

30. M. A. Huselid, "Human Resource Management Practices, Productivity, Turnover, and Firm Performance," *SHRM Report* (New Brunswick, NJ: Rutgers University, New Brunswick, N.J. 1994), as cited in *High Performance Work Practices.*

31. R. Levering and M. Moskowitz, *The One Hundred Best Companies to Work for in America* (New York: Doubleday, 1993); annual return data on publicly traded companies in the 1993 *One Hundred Best* (sixty-three firms), the 1994 *One Hundred Best* (sixty-two firms), and the Frank Russell 3,000—the three thousand largest companies in America (with each firm weighed equally, not by capital) was provided by Oliver Buckley of BARRA; Cascio, *Costing Human Resource: The Financial Impact of Behavior in Organizations;* G. R. Jones and P. M. Wright, "An Economic Approach to Conceptualizing the Utility of Human Resource Management Practices," in *Research in Personnel and Human Resource Management,* ed. K. Rowland and G. Ferris (1992).

32. M. Huselid, "The Impact of Human Resource Management Practices on Turnover, Productivity and Corporate Financial Performance." *Academy of Management Journal,* (1995):635–72. See also D. Dravetz, *The Human Resources Revolution* (San Francisco: Jossey-Bass, 1988); C. Ichniowski, "Human Resource Management Systems and the Performance of U.S. Manufacturing Businesses" (NBER working paper no. 3449, September 1990).

33. D. Denison, *Corporate Culture and Organizational Effectiveness* (New York: John Wiley & Sons, 1990); E. E. Lawler III et al., *Employee Involvement and Total Quality Management* (San Francisco: Jossey-Bass, 1992).

34. J. D. Olian and S. L. Rynes, "Making Total Quality Work: Aligning Organizational Processes, Performance Measures, and Stakeholders," *Human Resource Management* (fall 1991): 303–34; A. Parasuraman, L. L. Berry, and V. A. Zeithaml, "Perceived Service Quality as a Customer-Based Performance Measure: An Empirical Examination of Organizational Barriers Using an Extended Service Quality Model," *Human Resource Management* (Fall 1991): 335–64.

35. J. L. Heskett, W. R. Sasser, Jr., and C. L. W. Hart (1990). *Service Breakthroughs: Changing the Rules of the Game.* New York: Macmillan.

36. Olian and Rynes, "Making Total Quality Work"; Parasuraman, Berry, and Zeithaml, "Perceived Service Quality."

37. J. Carlzon. As quoted in C. Grönroos, *Service Management and Marketing.* Lexington, MA: Lexington Books, 1990, p. xv.

38. J. W. Wiley, "Customer Satisfaction: A Supportive Work Environment and Its Financial Cost," *Human Resource Planning* (1991): 117–28.

39. D. Ulrich, "Strategic and Human Resource Planning: Linking Customers and Employees," *Human Resource Planning* (1992): 47–62; M. A. Verespej, "How the Best Got Better," *Industry Week* (March 7, 1994): 27–28.

40. Teitelbaum, "Southwest Airlines."

41. C. Grönroos, *Service Management and Marketing* (Lexington, MA: D. C. Heath, 1990); J. Campbell Quick, "Crafting an Organizational Culture: Herb's Hand at Southwest Airlines," *Organizational Dynamics* (autumn 1992): 45–56; L. L. Berry and A. Parasuraman, "Prescriptions for a Service Quality Revolution in America," *Organizational Dynamics* (spring 1992): 5–15.

42. B. Schneider and D. E. Bowen, "The Service Organization: Human Resources Management Is Crucial," *Organizational Dynamics* (fall 1992): 39–52; D. E. Bowen and E. E. Lawler III, "Total Quality-Oriented Human Resources Management," *Organizational Dynamics* (spring 1992): 29–43.

43. See the entire special issue of *Academy of Management Review* (July 1994) featuring several articles on total quality management.

44. General Accounting Office, "Management Practices: U.S. Companies Improve Performance through Quality Efforts," GAO/NSIAD-91-190 (1991). Eleven companies reported data on market share, nine reported return on assets, and eight reported return on sales. The Baldrige finalists are not necessarily representative of all the firms that adopted the identifying work practices.

45. M. Magnet, "The Truth about the American Worker," *Fortune* (May 4, 1992): 50.

46. E. E. Lawler III, *The Ultimate Advantage: Creating the High Involvement Organization* (San Francisco: Jossey-Bass, 1992); E. E. Lawler III, S. A. Mohrman, and G. E. Ledford, *Employee Involvement in America: An Assessment of Practices and Results* (San Francisco: Jossey-Bass, 1992).

47. N. Alster, "What Flexible Workers Can Do," *Fortune* (February 13, 1989): 62–66; Magnet, "The Truth About the American Worker"; Thurow, *Head to Head.*

48. R. B. Freeman, *Working under Different Rules* (New York: Russell Sage Foundation, 1994).

50. Northwestern Life Insurance Co., *Employee Burnout: America's Newest Epidemic* (Minneapolis: NWNL, 1992); D. L. Nelson, J. C. Quick, and J. D. Quick, "Corporate Warfare: Preventing Combat Stress and Battle Fatigue," *Organizational Dynamics* (1989): 65–79.

50. R. S. DeFrank and J. E. Pliner, "Job Security, Job Loss, and Outplacement: Implications for Stress and Stress Management," in *Work Stress: Health Care Systems in the Workplace,* ed. J. C. Quick et al. (New York: Praeger Scientific, 1987), 195–219.

51. F. Rose, "Job-Cutting Medicine Fails to Remedy Productivity Ills at Many Companies," *Wall Street Journal* (June 7, 1994): p. A5.

52. "An Overview," in *Readings in Personnel and Human Resource Management,* 3rd ed., ed. R. S. Schuler, S. A. Youngblood, and V. L. Huber (St. Paul: West

Publishing Co., 1988); J. Ledvinka and V. G. Scarpello, *Federal Regulation of Personnel and Human Resource Management,* 2nd ed. (Boston: PWS-Kent, 1991).

53. J. W. Meyer and B. Rowan, "Institutionalized Organizations: Formal Structure as Myth and Ceremony," *American Journal of Sociology* (1977): 340–63; W. R. Scott, "The Adolescence of Institutional Theory," *Administrative Scientific Quarterly* (1987): 493–511; and L. G. Zucker, "Institutional Theories of Organization," *Annual Review of Sociology* (1987): 443–64.

54. E. E. Lawler III, "The New Plant Approach: A Second Generation Approach," *Organizational Dynamics* (Summer 1991): 5–14.

55. B. Cohen, "Corporate Responsibility for Social Change," interview in *Prevention: The Critical Need,* ed. J. Pransky (Springfield, MO: Burrell Foundation, 1991); J. J. Laabs, "Ben & Jerry's Caring Capitalism," *Personnel Journal* (November 1992): 50–57. See also S. Caudron, "Volunteer Efforts Offer Low-Cost Training Options," *Personnel Journal* (June 1994): 38–44.

56. *Ben and Jerry's Homemade Annual Report, 1992.*

57. L. L. Drey, "Making a Difference: Ice Cream Meets Charity in Harlem," *New York Times* (February 21, 1993): p. F13.

58. A. Halcrow, "Ben and Jerry's," *Personnel Journal* (January 1992): 59.

59. S. Greengard and C. M. Solomon, "The Fire This Time?" *Personnel Journal* (February 1994): 60–67.

60. J. J. Laabs, "Disney Helps Keep Kids in School," *Personnel Journal* (November 1992): 58–68.

61. "Training at Waste Management," *HR Reporter* (April 1991): 1–3. Reprinted with the permission of the publisher, Buroff Publications, 1350 Connecticut Ave. NW, Washington, DC 20036.

62. "NASA: Supplier Teamwork," *HR Reporter* (January 1992): 1–3; W. Zellner, E. Schine, and J. E. Ellis, "Turning Rivals into Teams," *Business Week Enterprise 1993,* 222–24.

63. J. N. Baron, P. Devereaux Jennings, and F. R. Dobbin, "Mission Control? The Development of Personnel Systems in U.S. Industry," *American Sociological Review* (August 1988): 497–514; J. N. Baron, F. R. Dobbin, and P. D. Jennings, "War and Peace: The Evolution of Modern Personnel Administration in U.S. Industry," *American Journal of Sociology* (92): 350–83.

64. B. Rice, "The Hawthorne Defect: Persistence of a Flawed Theory," *Psychology Today* (February 1982): 70–74; F. J. Roethlisberger, *The Elusive Phenomena* (Cambridge: Harvard University Press, 1977); F. J. Roethlisberger, W. J. Dickson, and H. A. Wright, *Management and the Worker* (Cambridge: Harvard University Press, 1939; E. Mayo, *The Human Problems of an Industrial Civilization* (Cambridge: Harvard University Press, 1933); I. C. Barnard, *The Functions of the Executive* (Cambridge: Harvard University Press, 1938); A. Bolton, "The Hawthorne Studies: Relay Assembly Participants Remember" (unpublished dissertation, Nova University, 1985); G. Greenwood, A. Bolton, and A. Greenwood, "Hawthorne a Half Century Later: Relay Assembly Participants Remember," *Journal of Management* (1983): 217–31; S. J. Carroll

and R. S. Schuler, "Professional HRM: Changing Functions and Problems," in *Human Resource Management in the 1980s,* ed. Carroll and Schuler (Washington, DC: Bureau of National Affairs, 1983).

65. G. S. Becker, *Human Capital* (New York: National Bureau for Economic Research, 1964).

66. R. S. Schuler and I. C. MacMillan, "Gaining a Competitive Advantage through Human Resource Management Practices," *Human Resource Management* (fall 1984): 241–56; P. M. Wright and G. C. McMahan, "Theoretical Perspectives for Strategic Human Resource Management," *Journal of Management* 18 (2): 295–320.

67. D. Ulrich, "Organizational Capability as a Competitive Advantage: Human Resource Professionals as Strategic Partners," *Human Resource Planning* (1987): 169–84; D. Ulrich and D. Lake, *Organizational Capability: Competing from the Inside Out* (Somerset, NJ: John Wiley & Sons, 1990).

68. B. Presley Noble, "Retooling the 'People Skills' of Corporate America," *New York Times* (May 22, 1994): p. F8.

69. M. E. McGill and J. W. Slocum, Jr., "Unlearning the Organization," *Organizational Dynamics* (autumn 1993): 67–81.

70. P. Oster et al., "The Fast Track Leads Overseas," *Business Week* (November 1993): 64–68; J. A. Byrne et al., "Borderless Management: Companies Strive to Become Truly Stateless," *Business Week* (May 23, 1994): 26–26; P. Dowling, R. S. Schuler, and D. Welch, *International Dimensions of Human Resource Management,* 2nd ed. (Belmont, CA: Wadsworth, 1994); C. M. Solomon, "Transplanting Corporate Cultures Globally," *Personnel Journal* (October 1993): 78–88.

71. S. E. Jackson et al., *Diversity in the Workplace: Human Resource Initiatives* (New York: Guilford Press, 1992).

72. L. Copeland, "Valuing Diversity, Part 2: Pioneers and Champions of Change," *Personnel Journal* (July 1988): 48–49.

73. A. Farnham, "America's Most Admired Company," *Fortune* (February 7, 1994): 50–52.

74. M. R. Weisbord, *Productive Workplaces* (San Francisco: Jossey-Bass, 1987); R. S. Wellins, W. C. Byham, and J. M. Wilson, *Empowered Teams* (San Francisco: Jossey-Bass, 1991).

75. S. E. Jackson and R. S. Schuler, "Understanding Human Resource Management in the Context of Organizations and Their Environments," *Annual Review of Psychology* (1995); P. Osterman, "How Common Is Workplace Transformation and How Can We Explain Who Adopts It? Results from a National Survey," *Industrial and Labor Relations Review* (1994).

76. R. S. Schuler, "Strategic Human Resources Management: Linking the People with the Strategic Needs of the Business," *Organizational Dynamics* (1992): 18–32; R. S. Schuler and S. E. Jackson, "Linking Competitive Strategies with Human Resource Management Practices," *Academy of Management Executive* (August 1987): 207–19; G. E. Ledford, Jr., J. R. Wendenhof, and J. T. Strahley, "Realizing a Corporate Philosophy," *Organizational Dynamics* (winter 1995): 5–19.

77. P. Cappelli and A. Crocker-Hefter, *Distinctive Human Resources Are the Core Competencies of Firms,* report no. R117Q00011-91 (Washington, DC: U.S. Department of Education, 1994); M. Hequet, "Worker Involvement Lights up Neon," *Training* (June 1994): 23–29.

78. Cappelli and Crocker-Hefter, *Distinctive Human Resources,* 7–10.

79. J. P. Begin, *Strategic Employment Policy: An Organizational Systems Perspective* (Englewood Cliffs, NJ: Prentice-Hall, 1991); J. E. Butler, G. R. Ferris, and N. K. Napier, *Strategy and Human Resources Management* (Cincinnati: South-Western Publishing Co., 1991).

80. For a full discussion of a competency-based perspective for aligning HR systems, see A. A. Lado and M. C. Wilson, "Human Resource Systems and Sustained Competitive Advantage: A Competency-Based Perspective," *Academy of Management Review* 19 (1994): 699–727.

81. F. Kofman and P. M. Senge, "Communities of Commitment: The Heart of Learning Organizations, *Organizational Dynamics* (autumn 1993): 5–23; D. Ulrich, M. Von Glinow, and T. Jick, "High-Impact Learning: Building and Diffusing Learning Capability," *Organizational Dynamics* (Autumn 1993): 52–66.

82. Advertisement, "An Open Letter to Sears Customers," *New York Times* (June 25, 1992): p. B2.

83. R. S. Schuler and J. W. Walker, "Human Resources Strategy: Focusing on Issues and Actions," *Organizational Dynamics* (Summer 1990): 4–19.

⊛ CHAPTER 2

1. L. Uchitelle, "U.S. Corporations Expanding Abroad at a Quicker Pace: Creating Jobs Overseas," *New York Times* (July 25, 1994): pp. A1, D2.

2. N. M. Tichy, "Revolutionize Your Company," *Fortune* (December 13, 1993): 114–18.

3. N. M. Tichy and S. Sherman, *Control Your Destiny or Someone Else Will* (New York: HarperBusiness, 1993).

4. J. R. Norman, "A Very Nimble Elephant," *Forbes* (October 10, 1994): 88–92.

5. A. P. Carnevale, *America and the New Economy: How New Competitive Standards Are Radically Changing American Workplaces* (San Francisco: Jossey-Bass, 1991).

6. For an extensive review of the research relevant to the important context variables for human resource management, see S. E. Jackson and R. S. Schuler, "Understanding Human Resource Management in the Context of Organizations and Their Environments," *Annual Review of Psychology* (1995): 237–64.

7. Uchitelle, "U.S. Corporations Expanding Abroad"; R. Norton, "Strategies for the New Export Boom," *Fortune* (August 22, 1994): 125–30; "Top Fifty U.S. Industrial Exporters," *Fortune* (August 22, 1994): 132; "The Year of Mixed Results," *Fortune* (August 22, 1994): 181–82; "The One Hundred Largest Diversified Service Companies," *Fortune* (August 22, 1994): 183–207.

8. W. B. Johnston, "Global Workforce 2000: The New World Labor Market," *Harvard Business Review* (March–April 1991): 115–27.

9. C. Farrell et al., "It Won't Take Your Breath Away, but...the Economy Is Posed for Modest, Steady Growth This Year," *Business Week* (January 10, 1994): 60–66.

10. *Business Week* (December 21, 1992): 29.

11. Johnston, "Global Workforce 2000."

12. D. Harbrecht, G. Smith, and S. Baker, "The Mexican Worker," *Business Week* (April 19, 1993): 84–130.

13. U.S. Department of Education, National Center for Education Statistics, *Digest of Education Statistics* (Washington, DC, 1989), table 341, pp. 386–87.

14. P. J. Dowling, R. S. Schuler, and D. Welch, *International Dimensions of Human Resource Management,* 2nd ed. (Belmont, CA: Wadsworth, 1994).

15. "Business Week/Harris Executive Poll: Cautious Optimism in the Corner Office," *Business Week* (February 10, 1994): 67.

16. P. Oster et al., "The Fast Track Leads Overseas," *Business Week* (November 1, 1993): 64–68.

17. R. L. Tung, "Managing Cross-National and Intra-National Diversity," *Human Resource Management* (Winter 1993): 461–77.

18. See Johnston, "Global Workforce 2000."

19. F. A. Maljers, "Inside Unilever: The Evolving Transnational Company," *Harvard Business Review* (September–October 1992): 46–51.

20. K. Miller, "Dwindling Supply of Engineers Brings a Sense of Desperation to Auto Makers," *Wall Street Journal* (June 7, 1994): p. B3.

21. C. Yang, "An Immigrant-Worker Scheme Comes Under Fire," *Business Week* (November 8, 1993): 40.

22. Ibid.

23. A. Pollack, "Japan Faces the Unthinkable: A Shortage of Engineers," *New York Times* (January 2, 1994): p. F4.

24. T. Peters, *Thriving on Chaos* (New York: Alfred Knopf, 1987), 123.

25. F. Kinsman, "Now You See It, Now You Don't," *Human Resources* (spring 1994): 35–37; "Virtual Office Redefines Workplace," *Bulletin to Management* (May 19, 1994): 160.

26. *Source:* "Helping Two Companies Form a Third," *Personnel Journal* (January 1994): 63. Used by permission.

27. J. A. Byrne, R. Brandt, and O. Port, "The Virtual Corporation," *Business Week* (February 8, 1993): 98–103; S. Tully, "The Modular Corporation," *Fortune* (February 8, 1993): 106.

28. M. G. Duerr, "International Business Management: Its Four Tasks," *Conference Board Record* (1986): 43.

29. Dowling, Schuler, and Welch, *International Dimensions.*

30. C. M. Solomon, "Transplanting Corporate Cultures Globally," *Personnel Journal* (October 1993): 80–88.

31. Ibid.

32. J. R. Fulkerson and R. S. Schuler, "Managing Worldwide Diversity at Pepsi-Cola International," in S. E. Jackson, ed., *Diversity in the Workplace: Human Resource Initiatives* (New York: Guilford Press, 1992).

33. J. A. Byrne et al., "Borderless Management: Companies Strive to Become Truly Stateless," *Business Week* (May 23, 1994): 24. Also see Solomon, "Transplanting Corporate Cultures Globally."

34. *Source:* "Pepsi's Expectations," *HR Reporter* (July 1987): 4–5. Used by permission of *HR Reporter,* © 1987.

35. Fulkerson and Schuler, "Managing Worldwide Diversity at Pepsi-Cola International."

36. M. Erez, "Towards a Model of Cross-Cultural I/O Psychology," in H. C. Triandis, M. D. Dunnette, and L. M. Hough, eds., *Handbook of Industrial and Organizational Psychology,* vol. 4 (Palo Alto, CA: Consulting Psychologists, 1994), 559–608; M. Erez and P. C. Earley, *Culture, Self-Identity, and Work* (New York: Oxford University Press, 1993).

37. P. R. Harris and R. T. Moran, *Managing Cultural Differences* (Houston: Gulf, 1979); R. S. Bhagat and S. J. McQuaid, "Role of Subjective Culture in Organizations: A Review and Directions for Future Research," *Journal of Applied Psychology* 67 (1982): 653–85.

38. Dowling, Schuler, and Welch, *International Dimensions.*

39. Ibid.

40. G. Hofstede, *Culture's Consequences* (Beverly Hills, CA: Sage, 1980); G. Hofstede, *Cultures and Organizations* (London: McGraw-Hill, 1991); G. Hofstede, "Cultural Constraints in Management Theories," *Academy of Management Executives* 7 (1993): 81.

41. See J. A. Chatman and K. A. Jehn, "Assessing the Relationship between Industry Characteristics and Organizational Culture: How Different Can You Be?" *Academy of Management Journal* 37 (1994): 522–53.

42. J. Huey, "Waking Up to the New Economy," *Fortune* (June 27, 1994): 36–46.

43. D. E. Bowen and B. Schneider, "Services Marketing and Management: Implications for Organizational Behavior," *Research in Organizational Behavior* 10 (1988): 43–80.

44. B. Schneider, J. K. Wheeler, and J. F. Cox, "A Passion for Service: Using Content Analysis to Explicate Service Climate Themes," *Journal of Applied Psychology* 777 (1992): 705–16.

45. D. E. Bowen, "Managing Customers as Human Resources in Service Organizations," *Human Resource Management* 23 (1986): 371–83; P. K. Mills and J. H. Morris, "Clients as 'Partial' Employees of Service Organizations: Role Development in Client Participation," *Academy of Management Review* 11 (1986): 726–35.

46. S. E. Jackson, R. S. Schuler, and J. C. Rivero, "Organizational Characteristics as Predictors of Personnel Practices," *Personnel Psychology* 42 (1989): 727.

47. A. Davis-Blake and B. Uzzi, "Determinants of Employment Externalization: A Study of Temporary Workers and Independent Contractors," *Administrative Science Quarterly* 38 (1993): 195–223; J. T. Delaney, D. Lewin, and C. Ichniowski, *Human Resource Policies and Practices in American Firms* (Washington, DC:

U.S. Government Printing Office, 1989); J. P. Guthrie and J. D. Olian, "Does Context Affect Staffing Decisions? The Case of General Managers," *Personnel Psychology* 44 (1991): 263–92; S. E. Jackson, "Organizational Practices for Preventing Burnout," In A. S. Sethi and R. S. Schuler, eds., *Handbook of Organizational Stress Coping Strategies* (Cambridge, MA: Ballinger, 1984); S. E. Jackson and R. S. Schuler, "Human Resource Management Practices in Service-Based Organizations: A Role Theory Perspective," *Advances in Services Marketing and Management* 1 (1992): 123–57; D. E. Terpstra and E. J. Rozell, "The Relationship of Staffing Practices to Organizational Level Measures of Performance," *Personnel Psychology* 46 (1993): 27–48; J. H. Reynierse and J. B. Harker, "Employee and Customer Perceptions of Service in Banks: Teller and Customer Service Representative Ratings," *Human Resource Planning* 15 (1992): 31–46; M. J. Burke, C. C. Borucki, and A. E. Hurley, "Reconceptualizing Psychological Climate in a Retail Service Environment: A Multiple-Stakeholder Perspective," *Journal of Applied Psychology* 77 (1992): 717–29; B. Schneider, J. K. Wheeler, and J. F. Cox, "A Passion for Service: Using Content Analysis to Explicate Service Climate Themes," *Journal of Applied Psychology* 77 (1992): 705–16.

48. See Jackson, Schuler, and Rivero, "Organizational Characteristics as Predictors."

49. D. E. Bowen, G. E. Ledford, and B. R. Nathan, "Hiring for the Organization, Not the Job," *Academy of Management Executive* 5 (1991): 35–51.

50. O. Port, "The Responsive Factory," *Business Week/Enterprise 1993,* 48; P. S. Adler, *Technology and the Future of Work* (New York: Oxford University Press, 1992).

51. J. P. Womack, D. T. Jones, and D. Roos, "How Lean Production Can Change the World," *New York Times Magazine* (September 23, 1990): 20–24, 34, 38; A. Taylor III, "New Lessons from Japan's Carmakers," *Fortune* (October 22, 1990): 165–66.

52. S. Zuboff, *In the Age of the Smart Machine: The Future of Work and Power* (New York: Basic Books, 1988). See also B. Garson, *The Electronic Sweatshop* (New York: Simon & Schuster, 1988); P. B. Doeringer, *Turbulence in the American Workplace* (New York: Oxford University Press, 1991); S. E. Forrer and Z. B. Leibowitz, *Using Computers in Human Resources* (San Francisco: Jossey-Bass, 1991); U. E. Gattiker, *Technology Management in Organizations* (Newbury Park, CA: Sage, 1990); A. Majchrzak, *The Human Side of Factory Automation: Managerial and Human Resource Strategies for Making Automation Succeed* (San Francisco: Jossey-Bass, 1988); P. S. Goodman et al., *Technology and Organization* (San Francisco: Jossey-Bass, 1990).

53. M. J. Piore and C. F. Sabel, *The Second Industrial Divide: Possibilities for Prosperity* (New York: Basic Books 1984); P. F. Drucker, *Post-Capitalist Society* (New York: HarperBusiness, 1993); see also Jackson, Schuler, and Rivero, "Organizational Characteristics as Predictors."

54. See Jackson, Schuler, and Rivero, "Organizational Characteristics as Predictors."

55. Huey, "Waking Up to the New Economy," 46.

56. Huey, "Waking Up to the New Economy."

57. J. Main, "The Winning Organization," *Fortune* (September 26, 1988): 50–56; J. A. Byrne, "The Horizontal Corporation," *Business Week* (December 20, 1993): 76–81.

58. S. Caminiti, "Can The Limited Fix Itself?" *Fortune* (October 17, 1994): 161–70; A. Kupfer, "Managing Now for the 1990s," *Fortune* (September 26, 1988): 44–47.

59. D. H. Whittaker, *Managing Innovation: A Study of British and Japanese Factories* (Cambridge: Cambridge University Press, 1990).

60. Kupfer, "Managing Now for the 1990s."

61. J. F. Coates, J. Jarratt, and J. B. Mahaffie, "Future Work," *The Futurist* (May–June 1991).

62. Ibid.

63. Ibid.

64. W. H. Miller, "Employers Wrestle with 'Dumb' Kids," *Industry Week* (July 4, 1988): 47.

65. B. Nussbaum, "Needed: Human Capital," *Business Week* (September 19, 1988): 100; A. P. Carnevale, L. J. Gainer, and A. S. Meltzer, *Workplace Basics: The Essential Skills Employers Want* (San Francisco: Jossey-Bass, 1990); A. P. Carnevale, L. J. Gainer, and E. Schulz, *Training the Technical Work Force* (San Francisco: Jossey-Bass, 1990).

66. N. J. Perry, "School Reform: Big Pain, Little Gain," *Fortune* (November 29, 1993): 130–38.

67. N. Ramsey, "What Companies are Doing," *Fortune* (November 29, 1993): 142–62.

68. L. S. Richman, "The New Worker Elite," *Fortune* (August 22, 1994): 56–66; C. Lee and R. Zemke, "The Search for Spirit in the Workplace," *Training* (June 1993): 21–28; Coates, Jarratt, and Mahaffie, "Future Work"; J. F. Coates, J. Jarratt, and J. B. Mahaffie, *Future Work: Seven Critical Forces Reshaping Work and the Work Force in North America* (San Francisco: Jossey-Bass, 1990).

69. R. Glier, "The Math Gap," *Profiles* (August 1993): 58.

70. S. A. Snell and J. W. Dean, Jr., "Integrated Manufacturing and Human Resource Management: A Human Capital Perspective," *Academy of Management Journal* 35 (1992): 467–504.

71. *Source:* R. Glier, "The Math Gap," *Profiles* (August 1993): 58. Used by permission.

72. B. Paik Sunoo, "Birkenstock Braces to Fight the Competition," *Personnel Journal* (August 1994): 68–75; J. E. Ellis and C. Del Valle, "Tall Order for Small Businesses," *Business Week* (April 19, 1993): 114–18; J. Gordon, "Into the Dark," *Training* (July 1993): 21–30; W. Woods, "The Jobs Americans Hold," *Fortune* (July 12, 1993): 33–41; L. S. Richman, "Jobs That Are Growing and Slowing," *Fortune* (July 12, 1993): 52–55.

73. M. Gerstein and H. Reisman, "Strategic Selection: Matching Executives to Business Conditions," *Sloan Management Review* (winter 1983).

74. J. N. Baron, F. R. Dobbin, and P. D. Jennings, "War and Peace: The Evolution of Modern Personnel Administration in U.S. Industry," *American Journal of Sociology* 92 (1986): 350–83; F. R. Dobbin et al., "The Expansion of Due Process in Organizations," in L. G. Zucker, ed., *Institutional Patterns and Organizations: Culture and Environment* (Cambridge, MA: Ballinger,

1988), 71–98; B. Gerhart and G. T. Milkovich, "Organizational Differences in Managerial Compensation and Financial Performance," *Academy of Management Journal* 33 (1990): 663–91; E. E. Lawler III, S. A. Mohrman, and G. E. Ledford, *Employee Involvement and Total Quality Management: Practices and Results in* Fortune *1000 Companies* (San Francisco: Jossey-Bass, 1992); W. Mellow, "Employer Size and Wages," *Review of Economic Statistics* 64 (1982): 495–501; L. M. Saari et al., "A Survey of Management Training and Education Practices in U.S. Companies," *Personnel Psychology* 41 (1988): 731–43.

75. D. Filipowski, "HR Remains a Challenge," *Personnel Journal* (December 1993): 51.

76. " 'Downsize Once and Move on from There,' " *Business Atlanta* (Atlanta: Argus, December 1993).

77. J. Child, *Organization* (New York: Harper & Row, 1977).

78. W. A. Randolph and G. G. Dess, "The Congruence Perspective of Organization Design: A Conceptual Model and Multivariate Research Approach," *Academy of Management Review* 9 (1984): 114–27.

79. J. W. Slocum et al., "Business Strategy and the Management of Plateaued Employees," *Academy of Management Journal* 28 (1985): 113–54.

80. P. Cappelli and A. Crocker-Hefter, "Distinctive Human Resources *Are* the Core Competencies of Firms," report no. R117 Q00011-91 (Washington, DC: U.S. Department of Education, 1994).

81. R. Jacob, "The Search for the Organization of Tomorrow," *Fortune* (May 18, 1992): 95.

82. S. M. Davis and P. R. Lawrence, *Matrix* (Reading, MA: Addison-Wesley, 1977).

83. D. Anfuso, "Novell Idea: A Map for Mergers," *Personnel Journal* (March 1994): 48–55.

84. "Doing Mergers by the Book Aids Growth," *Personnel Journal* (January 1994): 59.

85. A. F. Buono and J. L. Bowditch, *The Human Side of Mergers and Acquisitions: Managing Collisions between People, Cultures, and Organizations* (San Francisco: Jossey-Bass, 1989).

86. R. Reich, *The Work of Nations: Preparing Ourselves for 21st-Century Capitalism* (New York: Vintage Books, 1992).

87. J. A. Byrne, "Congratulations. You're Moving to a New Pepperoni," *Business Week* (December 20, 1993): 80; R. S. Wellins, W. C. Byham, and G. R. Dixon, *Inside Teams: How Twenty World-Class Organizations Are Winning through Teamwork* (San Francisco: Jossey-Bass, 1994).

88. R. J. Klimoski and R. G. Jones, "Suppose We Took Staffing for Effective Group Decision Making Seriously?" in R. A. Guzzo and E. Salas, eds., *Team Decision Making Effectiveness in Organizations* (San Francisco: Jossey-Bass, 1994).

89. J. A. Byrne, "The Horizontal Corporation," *Business Week* (December 20, 1993): 76–81.

90. Ibid., 78–79.

91. Ibid. See also B. Dumaine, "The Trouble with Teams," *Fortune* (September 5, 1994): 86–92; N. Steckler and N. Fondas, "Building Team Leader Effectiveness: A Diagnostic Tool," *Organizational Dynamics* (winter 1995): 20–35; S. Caminiti, "What Team Leaders Need to Know," *Fortune* (February 20, 1995): 93–100.

92. M. Hammer and J. Champy, *Reengineering the Corporation: A Manifesto for Business Revolution* (New York: HarperBusiness, 1993).

93. T. A. Stewart, "Reengineering: The Hot New Managing Tool," *Fortune* (August 23, 1993): 41–48; M. Hammer and J. Champy, "The Promise of Reengineering," *Fortune* (May 3, 1993): 94–97; "Reengineering Requires Communication," *Bulletin to Management* (June 30, 1994): 201.

94. S. Ghoshal and C. A. Bartlett, "The Multinational Corporation as an Interorganizational Network," *Academy of Management Review* 15 (1990): 603–25; A.V. Phatak, *International Dimensions of Management* (Boston: PWS-Kent, 1992).

95. S. J. Kobrin, "Multinational Strategy and International Human Resource Management Policy" (paper, Wharton School, University of Pennsylvania, 1992).

96. Dowling, Schuler, and Welch, *International Dimensions;* T. A. Kochan, R. Batt, and L. Dyer, "International Human Resource Studies: A Framework for Future Research in Research Frontiers," in D. Lewin, O. S. Mitchell, and P. D. Sherer, eds., *Industrial Relations and Human Resources* (Madison, WI: Industrial Relations Research Association, 1992); A. Laurent, "A Cross-Cultural Puzzle of International Human Resource Management," *Human Resource Management* 25 (1986): 91–102.

97. R. S. Schuler et al., "Formation of an International Joint Venture: Davidson Instrument Panel," *Human Resource Planning* 14 (1991): 51–59; R. S. Schuler and E. van Sluijs, "Davidson-Marley BV: Establishing and Operating an International Joint Venture," *European Management Journal* 10 (1992): 428–37; J. W. Slocum and D. Lei, "Designing Global Strategic Alliances: Integrating Cultural and Economic Factors," in G. P. Huber and W. H. Glick, *Organizational Change and Redesign: Ideas and Insights for Improving Performance* (New York: Oxford University Press, 1993).

98. L. Baird and I. Meshoulam, "Managing the Two Fits of Strategic Human Resource Management," *Academy of Management Review* 13 (1988): 116–28.

99. M. Gerstein and H. Reisman, "Strategic Selection: Matching Executives to Business Conditions," *Sloan Management Review* 24 (1983): 33–49.

100. G. R. Ferris, D. A. Schellenberg, and R. F. Zammuto, "Human Resource Management Strategies in Declining Industries," *Human Resource Management* 23 (1984): 381–94; A. D. Szilagyi, Jr., and D. M. Schweiger, "Matching Managers to Strategies: A Review and Suggested Framework," *Academy of Management Review* 9 (1984): 626–37; C. A. Lengnick-Hall and M. L. Lengnick-Hall, "Strategic Human Resources Management: A Review of the Literature and a Proposed Topology," *Academy of Management Review* 13 (1988): 454–70.

101. R. S. Schuler and S. E. Jackson, "Linking Competitive Strategy and Human Resource Management Practices," *Academy of Management Executive* 3 (1987): 207–19.

102. R. Kuttner, "Talking Marriage and Thinking One-Night Stand," *Business Week* (October 18, 1993): 16; P. B. Doeringer et al., *Turbulence in the American Workplace* (New York: Oxford University Press, 1991).

103. See Jackson, Schuler, and Rivero, "Organizational Characteristics as Predictors"; G. T. Milkovich, B. Gerhart, and J. Hannon, "The Effects of Research and Development Intensity on Managerial Compensation in Large Organizations," *Journal of High Technology Management Research* 2 (1991): 133–50; S. R. Peck, "Exploring the Link between Organizational Strategy and the Employment Relationship: The Role of Human Resources Policies," *Journal of Management Studies* 31 (1994).

104. R. D. Hof, "From Dinosaur to Gazelle," *Business Week/Reinventing America 1992,* 65.

105. K. Labich, "Is Herb Kelleher America's Best CEO?" *Fortune* (May 2, 1994): 44–52.

106. Ibid., 50. See also R. Mitchell and M. Oneal, "Managing by Values," *Business Week* (August 1, 1994): 46–52.

107. S. Sherman, "How Will We Live with the Tumult?" *Fortune* (December 13, 1993): 123–25.

108. *Source:* G. Flynn, "HR in Mexico: What You Should Know," *Personnel Journal* (August 1994): 38. Used by permission.

109. B. Kogut, "An Evolutionary Perspective on the NAFTA," in L. Eden, ed., *Multinationals in North America* (Calgary: University of Calgary Press, 1994), 117–42; A. Winsor, *The Complete Guide to Doing Business in Mexico* (New York: AMACOM, 1994); S. Baker, G. Smith, and E. Weiner, "The Mexican Worker," *Business Week* (April 19, 1993): 84–92; A. R. Meyerson, "The Booming, Bulging Tex-Mex Border," *New York Times* (August 7, 1994): sec. 3, pp. 1, 6.

✵ CHAPTER 3

1. M. Loeb, "Empowerment that Pays Off," *Fortune* (March 20, 1995): 146.

2. D. Anfuso, "Peer Review Wards Off Unions and Lawsuits," *Personnel Journal* (January 1994): 64.

3. D. Anfuso, "Coors Taps Employee Judgment," *Personnel Journal* (February 1994): 56.

4. J. Greenberg, "Looking Fair vs. Being Fair: Managing Impressions of Organizational Justice," in B. M. Staw and L. L. Cummings, eds., *Research in Organizational Behavior,* vol. 12 (Greenwich, CT: JAI Press, 1990), 111–57.

5. R. Levering, *A Great Place to Work* (New York: Random House, 1988).

6. For good reviews of research on these topics, see T. R. Tyler and E. A. Lind, "A Relational Model of Authority in Groups," *Advances in Experimental Social Psychology* 25 (1992): 115–91; R. Cropanzano, ed., *Justice in the Workplace: Approach-*

ing Fairness in Human Resource Management (Hillsdale, NJ: Lawrence Erlbaum Associates, Publishers, 1993); B. H. Sheppard, R. J. Lewicki, and J. W. Minton, *Organizational Justice: The Search for Fairness in the Workplace* (New York: Lexington Books, 1992).

7. K. James, "The Social Context of Organizational Justice: Cultural, Intergroup, and Structural Effects on Justice Behaviors and Perceptions," in Cropanzano, *Justice in the Workplace.*

8. M. P. Miceli, "Justice and Pay System Satisfaction," in Cropanzano, *Justice in the Workplace;* R. L. Heneman, D. B. Greenberger, and S. Strasser, "The Relationship between Pay-for-Performance Perceptions and Pay Satisfaction," *Personnel Psychology* 41: 745–61; M. P. Miceli et al., "Predictors and Outcomes of Reactions to Pay-for-Performance Plans," *Journal of Applied Psychology* 76: 508–21.

9. J. A. Byrne, "The Flap Over Executive Pay." *Business Week,* (May 6, 1991): 90–96.

10. James, "Social Context of Organizational Justice"; H. C. Triandis, "Cross- Cultural Industrial and Organizational Psychology," in H. C. Triandis, M. D. Dunnette, and L. M. Hough, eds., *Handbook of Industrial and Organizational Psychology,* vol. 4 (Palo Alto, CA: Consulting Psychologists Press, 1994), 103–72. H. C. Triandis, "The Self and Social Behavior in Differing Cultural Contexts," *Psychological Review* 96 (1989): 506–20; Y. Kashima et al., "Universalism in Lay Conceptions of Distributive Justice: A Cross-Cultural Examination," *International Journal of Psychology* 23 (1988): 51–64; K. Leung and M. H. Bond, "How Chinese and Americans Reward Task-Related Contributions: A Preliminary Study," *Psychologia* 25 (1982): 32–39; K. Leung and M. H. Bond, "The Impact of Cultural Collectivism on Reward Allocation," *Journal of Personality and Social Psychology* 47 (1984): 793–804.

11. Cropanzano, *Justice in the Workplace;* Sheppard, Lewicki, and Minton, *Organizational Justice;* Tyler and Lind, "A Relational Model of Authority in Groups."

12. See C. E. Rusbult et al., "Impact of Exchange Variables on Exit, Voice, Loyalty and Neglect: An Integrative Model of Responses to Declining Job Satisfaction," *Academy of Management Journal* 31: 599–627.

13. R. B. Freeman and J. L. Medoff, *What Do Unions Do?* (New York: Basic Books, 1984).

14. T. R. Tyler and R. Schuller, "A Relational Model of Authority in Work Organizations: The Psychology of Procedural Justice" (manuscript, American Bar Foundation, 1990).

15. D. B. McFarlin and P. D. Sweeney, "Distributive and Procedural Justice as Predictors of Satisfaction with Personal and Organizational Outcomes," *Academy of Management Journal* 35 (1992): 626–37; Tyler and Schuller, "A Relational Model of Authority in Work Organizations"; E. A. Lind, R. Kanfer, and P. C. Earley, "Voice, Control, and Procedural Justice: Instrumental and Noninstrumental Concerns in Fairness Judgments," *Journal of Personality and Social Psychology* 59 (1990): 952–59.

16. J. Greenberg, "Employee Theft as a Reaction to Underpayment Inequity: The Hidden Cost of Pay Cuts," *Journal of Applied Psychology* 75 (1990): 561–68.

17. See also Freeman and Medoff, *What Do Unions Do?;* D. G. Spencer, "Employee Voice and Employee Retention," *Academy of Management Journal* 29 (1986): 488–502; S. Alexander and M. Ruderman, "The Role of Procedural and Distributive Justice in Organizational Behavior," *Social Justice Research* 1 (1987): 117–98; G. E. Fryxell and M. E. Gordon, "Workplace Justice and Job Satisfaction as Predictors of Satisfaction with Union and Management," *Academy of Management Journal* 32 (1989): 851–66.

18. R. H. Moorman, "Relationship between Organizational Justice and Organizational Citizenship Behaviors: Do Fairness Perceptions Influence Employee Citizenship?" *Journal of Applied Psychology* 76, no. 6 (1991): 845–55.

19. M. P. Miceli and J. P. Near, *Blowing the Whistle: The Organizational and Legal Implications for Companies and Employees* (New York: Lexington Books, 1992).

20. J. Greenberg, "The Social Side of Fairness: Interpersonal and Informational Classes of Organizational Justice," in Cropanzano, *Justice in the Workplace.*

21. "Arbitration Provisions in Union Agreements in 1949," *Monthly Labor Review* 70 (1950): 160–65.

22. See M. E. Gordon and G. E. Fryxell, "The Role of Interpersonal Justice in Organizational Grievance Systems," in Cropanzano, *Justice in the Workplace.*

23. C. Ichniowski and D. Lewin, "Characteristics of Grievance Procedures: Evidence from Nonunion, Union, and Double-Breasted Businesses," in B. B. Dennis, ed., *Proceedings of the Fortieth Annual Meeting* (Madison, WI: Industrial Relations Research Association, 1988), 415–24; J. T. Delaney, D. Lewin, and C. Ichniowski, *Human Resource Policies and Practices in American Firms,* BLMR 137 (Washington, DC: Department of Labor, Bureau of Labor-Management Relations and Cooperative Programs).

24. D. W. Ewing, "Who Wants Employee Rights?" *Harvard Business Review* 49 (November–December 1971): 22–35.

25. J. T. Delaney and P. Feuille, "Grievance and Arbitration Procedures among Nonunion Employers" (paper presented at the Forty-Fourth Annual Meeting of the Industrial Relations Research Association, New Orleans, 1992), in J. F. Burton, Jr., ed., *Proceedings of the Forty-Fourth Annual Meeting* (Madison, WI: Industrial Relations Research Association).

26. D. J. Mesch and D. R. Dalton, "Unexpected Consequences of Improving Workplace Justice: A Six-Year Time Series Assessment," *Academy of Management Journal* 35 (1992): 1099–1114. See also Miceli and Near, *Blowing the Whistle.*

27. B. S. Klaas and A. DeNisi, "Managerial Reactions to Employee Dissent: The Impact of Grievance Activity on Performance Ratings," *Academy of Management Journal* 14 (1989): 445–58; D. Lewin, "Dispute Resolution in the Nonunion Firm: A Theoretical and Empirical Analysis," *Journal of Conflict Resolution* 31 (1987): 465–502; R. B. Peterson, "The Union and

Nonunion Grievance System," in *Research Frontiers in Industrial Relations and Human Resources,* ed. D. Lewin, O. S. Mitchell, and P. D. Sherer (Madison, WI: Industrial Relations Research Association, 1992), 131–64; R. B. Peterson and D. Lewin, "The Nonunion Grievance Procedure: A Viable System of Due Process?" *Employee Responsibilities and Rights Journal* no. 3, 1: 1–18.

28. D. Anfuso, "Coors Taps Employee Judgment," *Personnel Journal* (February 1994): 50–59.

29. M. E. Gordon and R. L. Bowlby, "Reactance and Intentionality Attributions as Determinants of the Intent to File a Grievance," *Personnel Psychology* 42 (1989): 309–29; D. W. Ewing, *Justice on the Job: Resolving Grievances in the Nonunion Workplace* (Boston: Harvard Business School Press, 1989); B. S. Klaas, "Determinants of Grievance Activity and the Grievance System's Impact on Employee Behavior: An Integrative Perspective," *Academy of Management Review* 14, no. 3 (1989): 445–58; D. Lewin and R. B. Peterson, *The Modern Grievance Procedure in the United States* (Westport, CT: Quorum Books, 1988).

30. W. L. F. Felstiner, R. L. Abel, and A. Sarat, "The Emergence and Transformation of Disputes: Naming, Blaming, Claiming. . . ," *Law and Society Review* 15 (1980): 631–54.

31. P. Feuille and J. T. Delaney, "The Individual Pursuit of Organizational Justice: Grievance Procedures in Nonunion Workplaces," *Research in Personnel and Human Resources Management* 10 (1992): 187–232.

32. Institute for Legal Studies, University of Wisconsin, cited in A. H. Ringleb, R. E. Meiners, and F. L. Edwards, *Managing in the Legal Environment* (Minneapolis: West Publishing Co., 1993).

33. A. F. Westin and A. G. Feliu, *Resolving Employment Disputes without Litigation* (Washington, DC: Bureau of National Affairs, 1988).

34. "Current Trends and Developments in EEO" (communication of the New York City Chamber of Commerce, 1994).

35. "Record Number of EEOC Charges Filed in Fiscal Year 1993," *Fair Employment Practices Guidelines* (January 27, 1994): 9.

36. This discussion is based mostly on Ringleb, Meiners, and Edwards, *Managing in the Legal Environment.* Useful overviews also appear in W. F. Cascio, *Applied Psychology in Personnel Management,* 3rd ed., chap. 2 (1987) Englewood Cliffs, N.J.: Prentice-Hall; R. D. Arvey and R. H. Faley, *Fairness in Selecting Employees,* 2nd ed. (Reading, MA: Addison-Wesley Publishing Co., 1988); and A. Gutman, *Law and Personnel Practices* (Newbury Park, CA: Sage Publications, 1993).

37. P. E. Varca and P. Pattison, "Evidentiary Standards in Employment Discrimination: A View toward the Future," *Personnel Psychology* 46 (1993): 239.

38. *Source:* B. Smith, *HR Focus* (February 1992): 1, 6. Used by permission.

39. "Firing Proves Costly," *Bulletin to Management* (May 13, 1993): 145.

40. "Record Settlement Breaks 'Glass Ceiling,' " *Fair Employment Practices Guidelines* (July 1992): 1–2.

41. R. Smothers, "$105 Million Poorer Now, Chain Mends Race Policies," *New York Times* (January 31, 1993): P. L16.

42. Adapted from "Alternative Ways to Resolve Disputes," *Fair Employment Practices Guidelines* (August 26, 1992): 4–5.

43. For more information, see M. E. Gold, *An Introduction to the Law of Employment Discrimination* (Ithaca, NY: ILR Press and Cornell University, 1993); M. D. Levin-Epstein, *Primer of Equal Employment Opportunity* (Washington, DC: Bureau of National Affairs, 1987); J. Ledvinka and V. G. Scarpello, *Federal Regulation of Personnel and Human Resource Management,* 2nd ed. (Boston: PWS Kent, 1991).

44. "A Question of Ethics," *Bulletin to Management* (July 9, 1992): 211.

45. L. Nathans Spiro, "The Angry Voices at Kidder," *Business Week* (February 1, 1994): 60–63.

46. "EEOC Proposes Harassment Guidelines," *Fair Employment Practices Guidelines* (July 29, 1993): 87.

47. "Reasonable Woman Standard Gains Ground," *Fair Employment Practices Guidelines* (June 25, 1993): 4.

48. *What Is Harassment?* (brochure of the Northern States Power Co. St. Paul, MN: Company Publication:) 1993 p. 1.

49. T. Segal and Z. Schiller, "Six Experts Suggest Ways to Negotiate the Minefield," *Business Week* (October 28, 1991): 33; D. E. Terpstra and D. D. Baker, "Outcomes of Federal Court Decisions on Sexual Harassment," *Academy of Management Journal* 35 (1992): 181–90; B. A. Gutek, A. G. Cohen, and A. M. Konrad, "Predicting Social-Sexual Behavior at Work: A Contact Hypothesis," *Academy of Management Journal* 33: 560–77; "Reasonable Woman Standard Gains Ground"; B. Southard Murphy, W. E. Barlow, and D. D. Hatch, "Court Broadens Scope of Sexual Harassment Law," *Personnel Journal* (April 1990): 24–31; J. K. Frierson, "Reduce the Costs of Sexual Harassment," *Personnel Journal* (November 1989): 79–85.

50. A. B. Fisher, "Sexual Harassment: What to Do," *Fortune* (August 23, 1993): 84–88.

51. *Source:* C. Sims, "GE Whistle-Blower Is Awarded $13.4 Million," *New York Times* (December 5, 1992): 35.

52. J. D. Aram and P. F. Salipante, "An Evaluation of Organizational Due Process in the Resolution of Employee/Employer Conflict," *Academy of Management Review* 2 (1977): 197–204; B. H. Sheppard, R. J. Lewicki, and J. W. Minton, *Organizational Justice: The Search for Fairness in the Workplace* (New York: Lexington/Macmillan, 1992).

53. "Firing," *Fair Employment Practices Guidelines* 241 (1985): 3. See also "Discrimination Denied," *Bulletin to Management* (June 13, 1985): 3.

54. C. Roberson, *Hire Right/Fire Right: A Manager's Guide to Employment Practices that Avoid Lawsuits* (New York: McGraw-Hill, 1992). See also D. L. Beacon and A. Gomez III, "How to Prevent Wrongful Termination Lawsuits," *Personnel* (February 1988): 70–72: D. A. Bradshaw and B. C. Stikker, "Wrongful Termination: Keeping the Right to Fire at-Will," *Personnel Journal* (September 1986): 45–47; B. S. Murphy, W. E. Barlow, and D. Hatch, "Constructive Discharge," *Personnel Journal* (October 1986): 30–31; "RIFS, Exit Incentives, and the ADEA," *Fair Employment Practices Guidelines* 273, no. 4; "Wrongful Discharge," *Fair Employment Practices Guidelines* 275, no. 6;

M. R. Buckley and W. Weitzel, "Employing at Will," *Personnel Administrator* (August 1988): 78–82; M. Manley, "The Competitors Within," *Inc.* (September 1988): 137–38; B. Aaron, "Employee Voice: A Legal Perspective," *California Management Review* (spring 1992): 124–38; S. A. Youngblood and L. Bierman, "Due Process and Employment-at-Will: A Legal and Behavioral Analysis," in *Research in Personnel and Human Resources Management,* ed. K. M. Rowland and G. R. Ferris (Greenwich, CT: JAI Press, 1985), 185–230.

55. T. J. Wiencek, "Privacy in the Workplace: A Guide for Human Resource Professionals," *Fair Employment Practices Guidelines* (December 10, 1993): 4.

56. J. E. Jackson and W. T. Schantz, "A New Frontier in Wrongful Discharge," *Personnel Journal* (January 1991): 101–4.

57. L. Smith "What the Boss Knows about You," *Fortune* (August 9, 1993): 88–93.

58. W. L. Holstein, "From Rare to Routine." *New York Times,* (November 28, 1993): section 3, p. 11.

59. For a full discussion, see T. L. Jones, *The Americans with Disabilities Act: A Review of Best Practices.* (New York: American Management Association, 1993).

60. For a comprehensive discussion of the difficult issues raised by AIDS in the workplace, see W. F. Banta, *AIDS in the Workplace: Legal Questions and Practical Answers* (New York: Lexington Books, 1992).

61. W. Wood, F. Y. Wong, and J. G. Chachere, "Effects of Media Violence on Viewers' Aggression in Unconstrained Social Interaction," *Psychological Bulletin* 109 (1991): 371–83; F. S. Andison, "TV Violence and Viewer Aggression: A Cumulation of Study Results," *Public Opinion Quarterly* 41 (1977): 314–31.

62. H. F. Bensimon, "Violence in the Workplace," *Training and Development Journal* (January 1994): 27–32; M. Braverman, "Violence: The Newest Worry on the Job," *New York Times* (December 12, 1993): 11; O. M. Kurland, "Workplace Violence," *Risk Management* 40 (1993): 76–77; D. J. Peterson and D. Massengill, "The Negligent Hiring Doctrine—A Growing Dilemma for Employers," *Employee Relations Law Journal* 15 (1989–90): 419–32; J. Rappaport and K. Holden, "Prevention of Violence: The Case for a Nonspecific Social Policy," in J. R. Hays, T. K. Roberts, and K. S. Solway, eds., *Violence and the Violence Individual* (N. p., 1981): 409–40; "A Post Office Tragedy: The Shooting at Royal Oak." *Report of the Committee on Post Office and Civil Service,* United States House of Representatives, 1992; J. E. Rigdon, "Companies See More Workplace Violence," *Wall Street Journal* (April 12, 1994): B1.

63. "E-Mail Raises Privacy Questions," *Bulletin to Management* (February 25, 1993): 64.

64. P. T. Kilborn, "Workers Using Computers Find a Supervisor Inside," *New York Times* (December 23, 1990): 1, 18L. Also see "Surveillance and Searches: Reducing the Risks," *Bulletin to Management* (November 7, 1991): 345; *Federal Government Information Technology: Electronic Surveillance and Civil Liberties* (Washington, D.C.: Office of Technology Assessment, OTA-CIT-293, October 1985); *The Electronic Supervisor: New Technology, New Tensions,* OTA-CIT-333 (Washington, DC: U.S. Government Printing Office, Sept. 1987); G. Rifkin, "Do Employees Have a Right to Electronic Privacy?" *New York Times* (December 8, 1991): F8. Used by permission.

65. M. Janofsky, "Drug Use and Workers' Rights," *New York Times* (December 28, 1993): D1.

66. P. J. Dowling, R. S. Schuler, and D. E. Welch, *International Dimensions of Human Resource Management* (Belmont, CA: Wadsworth, 1994).

67. B. J. Tepper, "Investigaton of General and Program-Specific Attitudes Toward Corporate Drug-Testing Policies," *Journal of Applied Psychology* 79 (1994): 392–401.

68. J. Schaubroeck, D. R. May and F. W. Brown, "Procedural Justice Explanations and Employee Reactions to Economic Hardship: A Field Experiment," *Journal of Applied Psychology* 79 (1994): 455–60; "Two Legal Challenges to Drug Testing," *Fair Employment Practices Guidelines* (February 1993): 2.

✧ CHAPTER 4

1. J. F. Welch, "A Master Class in Radical Change," *Fortune* (December 13, 1993): 83. See also S. S. Rao, "The Painful Remaking of Ameritech," *Training* (July 1994): 45–53; Howard et at., *Diagnosis for Organizational Change: Methods and Models* (New York: Guilford Press, 1994).

2. *Source:* Based on information in M. J. Plevel et al., "AT&T Global Business Communications Systems: Linking HR with Business Strategy," *Organizational Dynamics* (Winter 1994): 59–72.

3. R. Jacob, "TQM: More than a Dying Fad?" *Fortune* (October 18, 1993): 66–72; see also C. H. Deutsch, "U.S. Industry's Unfinished Struggle," *New York Times* (February 21, 1988): sec. 3, pp. 1, 6–7; "How Not to Get the Malcolm Baldrige Award and Still Come Out the Winner: The L. L. Bean Story," *NYNEX In-House Publications,* 10–12; L. Dusky, "Bright Ideas: Anatomy of a Corporate Revolution," *Working Woman* (July 1990): 58–63; A. Halcrow, "Northern Telecom Employees on Tour," *Personnel Journal* (November 1989): 39–41.

4. D. A. Garvin, "How the Baldrige Award Really Works," *Harvard Business Review* (November–December 1991): 80–95. See also W. E. Deming, *Quality, Productivity, and Competitive Position* (Cambridge: MIT Center for Advanced Engineering Study, 1992); W. E. Deming, *Out of Crisis* (Cambridge: MIT Press, 1986), 23–24; J. M. Juran, *Juran on Quality by Design* (New York: Free Press, 1992).

5. V. A. Zeithaml, A. Parasuraman, and L. L. Berry, *Delivering Quality Service* (New York: Free Press, 1990).

6. R. S. Schuler and D. L. Harris, *Managing Quality* (Reading, MA: Addison-Wesley, 1992), 32.

7. Deming, *Quality, Productivity, and Competitive Position,* 23–24.

8. Garvin, "How the Baldrige Award Really Works."

9. M. G. Brown, *The Pocket Guide to the Baldrige Award Criteria* (New York: Quality Resources, 1994).

10. J. Main, "The Winning Organization," *Fortune* (September 26, 1988): 51.

11. B. Filipczak, "Ericsson General Electric, the Evolution of Empowerment," *Training* (September 1993): 21–27; A. Bryant, "On the Cheap, and Yet Flying High," *New York Times,* (July 15, 1993): p. D1; E. E. Lawler III, S. A. Mohrman, and G. E. Ledford, *Employee Involvement and Total Quality Management: Practices and Results in* Fortune *1000 Companies* (San Francisco: Jossey-Bass, 1992).

12. "Giving Quality Programs a Boost," *Bulletin to Management* (July 22, 1993): 225. For reviews of research on this topic, see J. L. Cotton, *Employee Involvement: Methods for Improving Performance and Work Attitudes* (Newbury Park, CA: Sage, 1993), 16; E. A. Locke and D. M. Schweiger, "Participation in Decision-Making: One More Look," *Organizational Behavior* 1 (1979): 265–339.

13. C. Bovier, "Teamwork: The Heart of an Airline," *Training* (June 1993): 53–58.

14. S. Caudron, "How HR Drives TQM," *Personnel Journal* (August 1993): 48B.

15. J. F. Bolt, *Executive Development* (New York: Harper & Row, 1989), 140.

16. For a discussion of suggestions as a communication tool, see Japan Human Relations Association, ed., *Kaizen Teian 1: Developing Systems for Continuous Improvement through Employee Suggestions,* English ed. (Cambridge, MA: Productivity Press, 1992), 22.

17. *Source:* Based on a series of discussions and interviews by Randall S. Schuler with Nickolas L. Blauwiekel, division manager of human resources for the Automotive and Appliance Controls Operations Division of the Eaton Corporation, and with Jon R. Wendenhof, director of industrial relations for the Eaton Corporation during July 1993 and March 1995.

18. S. Phillips, "Change Alters Paths to Improvement," *Personnel Journal* (April 1994): 65–73.

19. Plevel et al., "AT&T Global Business Communications Systems."

20. S. Caudron, "How Xerox Won the Baldrige," *Personnel Journal* (April 1991): 98–102.

21. J. A. Byrne, "The Pain of Downsizing," *Business Week* (May 9, 1994): 60–69.

22. Ibid.

23. B. O'Reilly, "The New Deal: What Companies and Employees Owe One Another," *Fortune* (June 13, 1994): 44–52.

24. P. Stuart, "New Internal Jobs Found for Displaced Employees," *Personnel Journal* (August 1992): 50–56; E. Faltermayer, "Is This Layoff Necessary?" *Fortune* (June 1, 1992): 71–86.

25. R. L. Knowdell, E. Branstead, and M. Moravec, *From Downsizing to Recovery—Strategic Transition Options for Organizations and Individuals* (Palo Alto, CA: CPP Books, 1994); G. E. Prussia, A. J. Kinicki, and J. S. Bracker, "Psychological and Behavioral Consequences of Job Loss: A Covariance Structure Analysis Using Weiner's (1985) Attribution Model," *Journal of Applied Psychology* 78 (1993): 382–94; B. P. Noble, "At Work: Questioning Productivity Beliefs," *New York Times* (July 10, 1994): p. F21; Faltermayer, "Is This Layoff Necessary?"; L. A. Isabella, "Downsizing: Survivors' Assessments," *Business Horizons* (May–June 1989): 35–41; C. R. Leana and J. M. Ivancevich, "Involuntary Job Loss: Institutional Interventions and a Research Agenda," *Academy of Management Review* 2 (1989): 301–12; C. R. Leana and D. C. Feldman, *Coping with Job Loss: How Individuals, Organizations, and Communities Respond to Layoffs* (New York: Lexington Books, 1992); C. R. Leana and D. C. Feldman, "Individual Responses to Job Loss: Perceptions, Reactions, and Coping Behaviors," *Journal of Management* 3 (1988): 375–89; D. Krackhardt and L. W. Porter, "When Friends Leave: A Structural Analysis of the Relationship between Turnover and Stayers' Attitudes," *Administrative Science Quarterly* 30 (1985): 242–61.

26. C. R. Leana and D. C. Feldman, "When Mergers Force Layoffs: Some Lessons about Managing the Human Resource Problems," *Human Resource Planning* 1989 12, no. 2: 123–40; K. S. Cameron, S. J. Freeman, and A. K. Mishra, "Best Practices in White Collar Downsizing: Managing Contradictions," *Academy of Management Executive* 1991 5, no. 3: 57–73; W. F. Cascio, "Downsizing: What Do We Know? What Have We Learned?" *Academy of Management Executive* 1993 7, no. 1: 95–104.

27. D. M. Schweiger, J. M. Ivancevich, and F. R. Power, "Executive Actions for Managing Human Resources Before and After Acquisition," *Academy of Management Executive* 1986 1, no. 2: 127–38.

28. J. B. Treece, "Doing It Right, Till the Last Whistle," *Business Week* (April 6, 1992): 58–59.

29. *Source:* J. Meissner, "How HR Can Help Lay Off Employees in a Dignified Way," *Personnel Journal* (November 1993): 66. Used by permission.

30. "Employers Seldom Warn Workers about Layoffs," *Bulletin to Management* (August 26, 1993): 265; B. P. Noble, "Straddling the Law on Layoffs," *New York Times* (February 28, 1993): p. F37.

31. Treece, "Doing It Right"; D. L. Worrell, W. N. Davidson III, and V. M. Sharma, "Layoff Announcements and Stockholder Wealth," *Academy of Management Journal* 34, no. 3 (1991): 662–78; P. D. Johnston, "Personnel Planning for a Plant Shutdown," *Personnel Journal* (August 1981): 53–57.

32. T. Rendero, "Outplacement Practices," *Personnel* (July–August 1980): 4–11; B. H. Millen, "Providing Assistance to Displaced Workers," *Monthly Labor Review* (May 1979): 17–22; "Outplacement Assistance," *Personnel Journal* (April 1981): 250; M. Elleinis, "Tips for Employers Shopping Around for a New Plant Site," *AMA Forum* (July 1982): 34; "Plant Closings: Problems and Panaceas," *Management Review* (July 1982): 55–57; M. Harris, "A Lifetime at IBM Gets a Little Shorter for Some," *Business Week* (September 29, 1986): 40; J. Main, "Look Who Needs Outplacement," *Fortune* (October 9, 1989): 85–92.

33. M. Kohli et al., eds., *Time for Retirement: Comparative Studies of Early Exit from the Labor Force* (New York: Cambridge University Press, 1992), 34.

34. S. E. Jackson et al., *Working through Diversity: Human Resources Initiatives* (New York: Guilford Press, 1992); S. Caudron, "U.S. West Finds Strength in Diver-

sity," *Personnel Journal* (March 1992): 40–44. See also F. Rice, "How to Make Diversity Pay," *Fortune* (August 8, 1994): 78–86.

35. B. P. Foster, "Workforce Diversity and Business," *Training and Development Journal* (April 1988): 59.

36. Towers, Perrin, and Hudson Institute, *Workforce 2000: Competing in a Seller's Market: Is Corporate America Prepared?* (Valhalla, NY: Towers, Perrin, 1990).

37. S. G. Butruille, "Corporate Caretaking," *Training and Development Journal* (April 1990): 49–55.

38. J. Fierman, "Why Women Still Don't Hit the Top," *Fortune* (July 30, 1990): 40–62. See also J. M. Brett and A. H. Reilly, "All the Right Stuff: A Comparison of Female and Male Managers' Career Progression," *Journal of Applied Psychology* 77 (1992): 251–60; E. A. Fagenson, ed., *Women in Management,* vol. 4, *Women and Work* (Newbury Park, CA: Sage, 1993).

39. A. Edwards, "Special Report: Cultural Diversity in Today's Corporation," *Working Woman* (January 1991): 60.

40. "Welcome to the Woman-Friendly Company Where Talent Is Valued and Rewarded," *Business Week* (August 6, 1990): 48–50.

41. Edwards, "Special Report."

42. "Race in the Workplace: Is Affirmative Action Working?" *Business Week* (July 8, 1991): 50–63.

43. S. S. Fugita and D. J. O'Brien, *Japanese American Ethnicity: The Persistence of the Community* (Seattle: University of Washington Press, 1991).

44. J. S. Hirsch, "Older Workers Chafe under Young Managers," *Wall Street Journal* (February 26, 1990): pp. B1, B6.

45. G. H. Elder, Jr., "Age Differentiation and the Life Course," *Annual Review of Sociology* 1 (1975): 165–90; S. R. Rhodes, "Age-Related Differences in Work Attitudes and Behavior: A Review and Conceptual Analysis," *Psychological Bulletin* 93 (1983): 328–67; "Work Attitudes: Study Reveals Generation Gap," *Bulletin to Management* (October 2, 1986): 326.

46. Edwards, "Special Report."

47. J. Nelson-Horchler, "Demographics Deliver a Warning," *Industry Week* (April 18, 1988): 58.

48. L. Copeland, "Valuing Diversity, Part 2: Pioneers and Champions of Change," *Personnel* (July, 1988): 48.

49. Ibid.

50. A. Morrison, R. P. White, and E. Van Velsnor, "Executive Women: Substance Plus Style," *Psychology Today* (August 1987): 18–21, 24–26.

51. S. E. Jackson, ed., *Diversity in the Workplace: Human Resource Initiatives* (New York: Guilford Press, 1993); J. D. Goodchilds, ed., *Psychological Perspectives on Human Diversity in America: Master Lectures* (Washington, DC: American Psychological Association, 1991); J. P. Fernandez, *Managing a Diverse Workforce: Regaining the Competitive Edge* (Lexington, MA: Lexington Books, 1991); D. Jamieson and J. O'Mara, *Managing Workforce 2000: Gaining the Diversity Advantage* (San Francisco: Jossey-Bass, 1991); L. I. Kessler, *Managing Diversity in an Equal Opportunity Workplace* (Washington, DC: National Foundation for the Study of Employment Policy, 1990); S. B. Thiederman, *Bridging Cultural Barriers for Corporate Success* (Lexington, MA: Lexington Books,

1991); R. R. Thomas, Jr., *Beyond Race and Gender: Unleashing the Power of Your Total Workforce by Managing Diversity* (New York: AMACOM, 1991).

52. T. Cox, Jr., *Cultural Diversity in Organizations: Theory, Research, and Practice* (San Francisco: Berrett-Koehler Publishers, 1993), 216–18.

53. K. Myers, "Cracking the Glass Ceiling," *Information Week* (August 27, 1990): 38–41; G. N. Powell, "Upgrading Management Opportunities for Women," *HR Magazine* (November 1990): 67–70; D. T. Hall, "Moving Beyond the 'Mommy Track': An Organization Change Approach," *Personnel* (December 1989): 23–29; E. Ehrlich, "The Mommy Track," *Business Week* (March 20, 1989): 126–34; F. N. Schwartz, "Management Women and the New Facts of Life," *Harvard Business Review* (January–February 1989): 65–76.

54. Information provided by J. Hunt, Merck and Company, as part of an MBA project, New York University, Fall 1990.

55. Information provided by M. Penso, Prudential Insurance Company.

56. This discussion is based on S. E. Jackson, "Stepping into the Future: Guidelines for Action," in Jackson, *Diversity in the Workplace.* For more information, see Fernandez, *Managing a Diverse Workforce;* C. D. Fyock, *America's Workforce Is Coming of Age* (Lexington, MA: Lexington Books, 1990); M. Loden and J. B. Rosener, *Workforce America! Managing Employee Diversity as a Vital Resource* (Homewood, IL: Business One Irwin, 1991); A. M. Morrison, *The New Leaders: Guidelines on Leadership Diversity in America* (San Francisco: Jossey-Bass, 1992); S. B. Thiederman, *Bridging Cultural Barriers for Corporate Success* (Lexington, MA: Lexington Books, 1991); Thomas, *Beyond Race and Gender.*

57. G. Hamel and C. K. Prahalad, *Competing for the Future* (Boston: Harvard Business School Press, 1994); J. Huey, "The New Post-Heroic Leadership," *Fortune* (February 21, 1994): 42–50.

58. Huey, "New Post-Heroic Leadership."

59. Based on Bolt, *Executive Development.*

60. For a full discussion, see Howard, *Diagnosis for Organizational Change.*

61. B. J. Smith, J. W. Boroski, and G. E. Davis, "Human Resource Planning," *Human Resource Management* (spring–summer 1992): 81–94; J. W. Walker, "The Ultimate Human Resource Planning: Integrating the Human Resource Function with the Business," in *Handbook of Human Resource Management,* ed. G. R. Ferris (Oxford, England: Blackwell, 1995); K. S. McKinlay and A. McKinlay, *Strategy and the Human Resource* (Oxford, England: Blackwell, 1993); S. E. Jackson and R. S. Schuler, "Human Resource Planning: Challenges for Industrial/Organizational Psychologists," *American Psychologist* (February 1990): 223–39; M. London, E. S. Bassman, and J. P. Fernandez, eds., *Human Resource Forecasting and Strategy Development: Guidelines for Analyzing and Fulfilling Organizational Needs* (Westport, CT: Quorum Books, 1990); E. H. Burack, "Linking Corporate Business and Human Resource Planning: Strategic Issues and Concerns," *Human Resource Planning* 8 (1985): 133–46; D. Ulrich, "Strategic Human Resource Plan-

ning," in *Readings in Personnel and Human Resource Management,* 3rd ed., ed. R. S. Schuler, S. A. Youngblood, and V. L. Huber (St. Paul: West Publishing Co., 1988), 57–71.

62. R. S. Schuler and J. W. Walker, "Human Resources Strategy: Focusing on Issues and Actions," *Organizational Dynamics* (Summer 1990): 5–19; N. L. Bloom, "HRM's Planning Pays Off: Down-to-Earth Strategies for Your System's Success," *Personnel Journal* (April 1988): 66–70; E. H. Burack, "A Strategic Planning and Operational Agenda for Human Resources," *Human Resource Planning* 11, no. 2 (1988): 63–69; L. Dyer, "Strategic Human Resources Management and Planning," in *Research in Personnel and Human Resource Management* (Greenwich, CT: JAI Press, 1985), 1–30; G. L. Manis and M. S. Leibman, "Integrating Human Resource and Business Planning," *Personnel Administrator* (March 1988): 32–38; G. Milkovich, L. Dyer, and T. Mahoney, "The State of Practice and Research in Human Resource Planning," in *Human Resource Management in the 1980s,* ed. S. J. Carroll and R. S. Schuler (Washington, DC: Bureau of National Affairs, 1983).

63. C. Mackey, "Human Resource Planning: A Four-Phased Approach," *Management Review* (May 1981): 17–22. For an extensive description of each of these phases, see B. J. Smith, J. W. Boroski, and G. E. Davis, "Human Resource Planning," *Human Resource Management* (Spring–Summer 1992): 81–93; S. Caudron, "Contingent Work Force Spurs HR Planning," *Personnel Journal* (July 1994): 52–59; E. H. Burack, "A Strategic Planning Operational Agenda for Human Resources," *Human Resource Planning* 11, no. 2 (1988): 63–68; L. Dyer, "Studying Human Resource Strategy: An Approach and an Agenda," *Industrial and Labor Relations Review* 23 (1984): 156–69; L. Dyer and N. D. Heyer, "Human Resource Planning at IBM," *Human Resource Planning* 7, no. 3 (1984): 111–26; "Manpower Planning and Corporate Objectives: Two Points of View," *Management Review* (August 1981): 55–61; A. O. Manzini, "Integrating Human Resource Planning and Development: The Unification of Strategic, Operational and Human Resource Planning Systems," *Human Resource Planning* 11, no. 2 (1988): 79–94; G. S. Odiorne, "Developing a Human Resource Strategy," *Personnel Journal* (July 1981): 534–36; J. A. Sheridan, "The Relatedness of Change: A Comprehensive Approach to Human Resource Planning for the Eighties," *Human Resource Planning* (1979): 123–33; N. M. Tichy and C. K. Barnett, "Profiles in Change: Revitalizing the Automotive Industry," *Human Resource Management* (Winter 1985): 467–502.

64. M. J. Feuer, R. J. Niehaus, and J. A. Sheridan, "Human Resource Forecasting: A Survey of Practice and Potential," *Human Resource Planning* (1988): 85–97.

65. For a description of managerial estimates, see J. W. Walker, *Human Resource Planning* (New York: McGraw-Hill, 1980).

66. For a more extensive discussion of group techniques, including the nominal group technique, see A. C. Delbecq, A. H. Van de Ven, and D. H. Gustafson, *Group Technique for Program Planning* (Glenview, IL: Scott, Foresman, 1977); D. H. Gustafson et al., "A Comparative Study of Differences in Subjective Like-

lihood Estimates Made by Individuals, Interacting Groups, Delphi Groups and Nominal Groups," *Organizational Behavior and Human Performance* 9 (1973): 280–91; J. K. Murnigham, "Group Decision Making: What Strategy Should You Use?" *Management Review* (February 1981): 56–60.

67. H. Kahalas et al., "Human Resource Planning Activities in U.S. Firms," *Human Resource Planning* 3 (1980): 53–66. A few firms also use more complex statistical procedures, including simple and multiple linear regression. See D. M. Atwater et al., "An Application of Integrated Human Resource Planning Supply-Demand Model," *Human Resource Planning* 5 (1982): 1–15; E. P. Bloom, "Creating an Employee Information System," *Personnel Administrator* (November 1982): 67–75; Milkovich, Dyer, and Mahoney, "State of Practice"; G. Milkovich and T. Mahoney, "Human Resources Planning and PAIR Policy," in *PAIR Handbook,* vol. 4, ed. D. Yoder and H. Heneman (Berea, OH: American Society of Personnel Administration, 1976).

68. London, Bassman, and Fernandez, *Human Resource Forecasting*"; S. E. Forrer and Z. B. Leibowitz, *Using Computers in Human Resources: How to Select and Make the Best Use of Automated HR Systems* (San Francisco: Jossey-Bass, 1991); N. Scarborough and T. W. Zimmerer, "Human Resources Forecasting: Why and Where to Begin," *Personnel Administrator* (May 1982): 55–61.

69. Unilever, *Innovator* (quarterly, winter 1994); R. J. Sahl, "Succession Planning Drives Plant Turnaround," *Personnel Journal* (September 1992): 67–70; J. Fraze, "Succession Planning Should Be a Priority for HR Professionals," *American Society for Personnel Administration/Resource* (June 1988): 4; G. L. McManis and M. S. Leibman, "Succession Planners," *Personnel Administrator* (August 1988): 24–30.

70. T. P. Bechet and W. R. Maki, "Modeling and Forecasting: Focusing on People as a Strategic Resource," *Human Resource Planning* (1987): 209–19; J. Carnazza, *Succession Replacement Planning: Programs and Practices* (New York: Center for Research in Career Development, Columbia Business School, 1982). A few firms also use more complex ways to estimate supply, including a transition matrix or the Markov matrix. See Dyer, "Strategic Human Resources"; S. H. Zanksi and M. W. Maret, "A Markov Application to Manpower Supply Planning," *Journal of the Operational Research Society* 31 (1980): 1095–102; G. Milkovich and F. Krzystofiak, "Simulation and Affirmative Action Planning," *Human Resource Planning* (1979): 71–80; P. S. Bender, W. D. Northup, and J. F. Shapiro, "Practical Modeling for Resource Management," *Harvard Business Review* (March–April 1981): 163–75; Atwater et al., "An Application"; Bloom, "Creating an Employee Information System"; Milkovich, Dyer, and Mahoney, "State of Practice"; London, Bassman, and Fernandez, *Human Resource Forecasting;* Forrer and Leibowitz, *Using Computers in Human Resources;* Scarborough and Zimmerer, "Human Resources Forecasting."

71. London, Bassman, and Fernandez, *Human Resource Forecasting;* Forrer and Leibowitz, *Using Computers in Human Resources;* Scarborough and Zimmerer, "Human Resources Forecasting."

✦ CHAPTER 5

1. K. Labich, "Is Herb Kelleher America's Best CEO?" *Fortune* (May 2, 1994): 45–52.

2. C. Wiley, "Incentive Plan Pushes Production," *Personnel Journal* (August 1993): 86–91.

3. P. S. Adler, "Time-and-Motion Regained," *Harvard Business Review* (January–February 1993): 97–108.

4. L. S. Richman, "The New Worker Elite," *Fortune* (August 22, 1994): 56–66.

5. S. Caudron, "Are Self-Directed Teams Right for Your Company?" *Personnel Journal* (December 1993): 76. See also "Special Report: The New World of Work," *Business Week* (October 17, 1994): 76–102.

6. This discussion is an adaptation of the taxonomy presented in M. A. Campion and P. W. Thayer, "Job Design: Approaches, Outcomes and Trade-Offs," *Organizational Dynamics* (winter 1987): 66–79.

7. F. W. Taylor, "The Principles of Scientific Management," in *Scientific Management* (New York: Harper, 1947), 36.

8. W. C. Howell, "Human Factors in the Workplace," in M. D. Dunnette and L. M. Hough (eds.), *The Handbook of Industrial-Organizational Psychology,* vol. 2 (Palo Alto, CA: Consulting Psychologists Press, 1991): 209–70.

9. Eastman Kodak Company, *Ergonomic Design for People at Work,* vol. 2 (New York: Van Nostrand Reinhold, 1986); D. P. Levin, "The Graying Factory," *New York Times* (February 20, 1994): sec. 3, p. 1; N. L. Breuer, "Resources Can Relieve ADA Fears," *Personnel Management* (September 1993): 131–42; J. J. Laabs, "Individuals with Disabilities Augment Marriott's Work Force," *Personnel Journal* (September 1994): 46–53; P. Froiland, "Managing the Walking Wounded," *Training* (August 1993): 39.

10. Levin, "The Graying Factory," sec. 3, pp. 1, 6.

11. J. R. Hackman and G. R. Oldham, *Work Redesign* (Reading, MA: Addison-Wesley, 1980).

12. Y. Fried and G. R. Ferris, "The Dimensionality of Job Characteristics: Some Neglected Issues," *Journal of Applied Psychology* (August 1988): 419–26; D. Ilgen and J. Hollenbeck, "The Structure of Work," in M. D. Dunnette and L. M. Hough (eds.) *Handbook of Industrial-Organizational Psychology, vol. 2* (Palo Alto, CA: Consulting Psychologists Press, 1991): 186–88.

13. R. W. Griffin, "Effects of Work Redesign on Employee Perceptions, Attitudes, and Behaviors: A Long-Term Investigation," *Academy of Management Journal* 34 (1991): 425–35.

14. B. T. Loher et al., "A Meta-Analysis of the Relation of Job Characteristics to Job Satisfaction," *Journal of Applied Psychology* 70 (1985): 280–89; L. R. Berlinger, W. H. Glick, and R. C. Rodgers, "Job Enrichment and Performance Improvement," in J. P. Campbell and R. J. Campbell, eds., *Productivity in Organizations* (San Francisco: Jossey-Bass, 1988): 219–254; Y. Fried, "Meta-Analytic Comparison of the Job Diagnostic Survey and Job Characteristics Inventory as Correlates of Work Satisfaction and Performance," *Journal of Applied Psychology* 76 (1991): 690–97.

15. J. R. Hackman and G. R. Oldham, "Development of the Job Diagnostic Survey," *Journal of Applied Psychology* 60 (1975): 159–70. B. Gerhart, "How Important Are Dispositional Factors as Determinants of Job Satisfaction? Implications for Job Design and Other Personnel Programs," *Journal of Applied Psychology* 72 (1987): 366–73.

16. J. Kerr, "The Best Small Companies to Work for in America," *Inc.* (July 1993): 63.

17. Ibid.

18. A. Erdman, "How to Keep That Family Feeling," *Fortune* (April 6, 1992): 95; S. Neumeier, "Vans," *Fortune* (March 9, 1992): 63.

19. Provided by the Weyerhaeuser Company.

20. *Source:* Adapted from "Team Zebra Changes Kodak's Stripes," *Personnel Journal* (January 1994): 57. Used by permission. See also D. Anfuso, "Xerox Partners with the Union to Regain Market Share," *Personnel Journal* (August 1994): 46–53; D. Anfuso, "Kodak Employees Bring a Department into the Black," *Personnel Journal* (September 1994): 104–12.

21. Adapted from S. T. Johnson, "Work Teams: What's Ahead in Work Design and Rewards Management," *Compensation and Benefits Review* (March–April 1993): 37.

22. "The Problem with Teams: Individuals and Organizations," *HR Reporter* (April 1993): 3–6.

23. "Fine-Tuning for Better Teamwork," *Bulletin to Management* (March 10, 1994): 80; S. Caudron, "Diversity Ignites Effective Work Teams," *Personnel Journal* (September 1994): 54–63.

24. "Teamwork: Convenience or Survival?" *Solutions* (February 1994): 42; M. J. Ferrero, "Self-Directed Work Teams Untax the IRS," *Personnel Journal* (July 1994): 66–71; "Teams: Every Team Is a 'Force of Ones,'" *HR Reporter* (June 1994): 1–3; C. Lee, "Open-Book Management," *Training* (July 1994): 21–27; R. Henkoff, "S. C. Johnson and Son: When to Take on the Giants," *Fortune* (May 30, 1994): 111–12; B. Dumaine, "The Trouble with Teams," *Fortune* (September 5, 1994): 86–92.

25. B. Dumaine, "Payoff from the New Management," *Fortune* (December 13, 1993): 103–110.

26. Laabs, "Individuals with Disabilities."

27. Based on the end-of-text case, "Organizational Change: Planning and Implementing Teams at AAL and IPS."

28. "More Employers Are Providing Flexibility through Job Restructuring," *Personnel Journal* (March 1994): 16. See also C. M. Solomon, "Job Sharing: One Job, Double Headache?" *Personnel Journal* (September 1994): 88–96. Another trend here is for organizations to eliminate the traditional notion of job and to select for the organization-person fit, not the job-person fit; W. Bridges, "The End of the Job," *Fortune* (September 19, 1994): 62–74.

29. C. M. Solomon, "HR Is Solving Shift-Work Problems," *Personnel Journal* (August 1993): 36–48.

30. D. Filipowski, "Perspectives: Problems Are Common among Shift Workers," *Personnel Journal* (August 1993): 34.

31. B. Geber, "The Flexible Work Force," *Training* (December 1993): 23–30; J. J. Laabs, "Partnerships Benefit a Grower and Its Workers," *Personnel Journal* (June 1993): 44–52.

32. J. Pickard, "The Pros and Cons of Annual Hour Programs," *Personnel Journal* (April 1992): 92–97; J. Barton, "Choosing to Work at Night: A Moderating Influence on Individual Tolerance to Shift Work," *Journal of Applied Psychology* 79 (1994): 449–54.

33. For more information about how organizations are responding to family issues, see S. Zedeck, ed., *Work, Families, and Organizations* (San Francisco: Jossey-Bass, 1992); F. J. Crosby, *Juggling* (New York: Free Press, 1991).

34. D. Kroll, "Telecommuting: A Revealing Peek Inside Some of the Industry's First Electronic Cottages," *Management Review* (November 1984): 18–23; S. Caudron, "Working at Home Pays Off," *Personnel Journal* (November 1992): 40–49; "Virtual Office Redefines Workplace," *Bulletin to Management* (May 19, 1994): 160; S. Greengard, "Making the Virtual Office a Reality," *Personnel Journal* (September 1994): 66–79.

35. "Drawbacks of Telecommuting," *Bulletin to Management* (May 20, 1993): 153; "Ask the Experts: Managing Telecommuters," *Fair Employment Practices Guidelines* (June 10, 1993): 8; J. Kugelmass, *Telecommuting and Flex-Time: A Manager's Guide to Flexible Work Arrangements* (New York: Lexington Books, 1994), 211–12.

36. H. R. Northrup and J. A. Larson, *Impact of the American Telegraph & Telephone-Equal Employment Opportunity Consent Decree* (Philadelphia: University of Pennsylvania Press, 1979).

37. *Source:* Adapted from "Allergic to Latex," *Bulletin to Management* (October 22, 1992): 331. Used by permission.

38. P. T. Kilborn, "Big Change Likely as Law Bans Bias toward Disabled," *New York Times* (July 19, 1992): pp. 1, 24; "Employers' ADA Responses—Concerned but Waiting," *Fair Employment Practices* (July 30, 1992): 87. See also "Discrimination Charges Filed under ADA," *Bulletin to Management* (June 2, 1994): 172–73.

39. Kilborn, "Big Change Likely." See also *Fair Employment Practices Guidelines* (November 18, 1993): 136; J. G. Frierson, "A Fifty-Question Self-Audit on ADA Compliance," *Employee Relations Today* (summer 1992): 151–65; "ADA: Understanding the Americans with Disabilities Act," *Bulletin to Management* (April 15, 1993): 1–8.

40. L. Uchitelle, "A Call for Easing Labor-Management Tension," *New York Times* (May 30, 1994): 33.

CHAPTER 6

1. S. Caudron, "Master the Compensation Maze," *Personnel Journal* (June 1993): 64D; see also C. Roush, "Aetna's Heavy Ax," *Business Week* (February 14, 1994): 32.

2. Aetna Life and Casualty Company, *Our Vision and Our Values* (internal company document, Hartford, CT, 1994).

3. Ibid.

4. R. J. Harvey, "Job Analysis," in *Handbook of Industrial Organizational Psychology,* 2nd ed. M. D. Dunnette and L. M. Hough (Palo Alto, CA: Consulting Psychologists Press, 1991). Other definitions of job analysis are found in S. E. Bemis, A. H. Belenky, and D. A. Sodner, *Job Analysis* (Washington, DC: BNA Books, 1983); E. J. McCormick, "Job and Task Analysis," in *Handbook of Industrial and Organizational Psychology,* ed. M. D. Dunnette (Chicago: Rand McNally, 1976), 651–96; E. J. McCormick, *Job Analysis: Methods and Applications* (New York: AMACOM, 1979); C. P. Sparks, "Job Analysis," in *Personnel Management,* ed. K. M. Rowland and G. R. Ferris (Boston: Allyn & Bacon, 1982), 78–100; and C. P. Sparks, "Job Analysis," in *Readings in Personnel and Human Resource Management,* 3rd ed., ed. R. S. Schuler, S. A. Youngblood, and V. Huber (St. Paul: West Publishing Co., 1988). In these sources, job analysis is the process of determining, by structured or unstructured methods, the characteristics of work, often according to a set of prescribed dimensions, for the purpose of producing job descriptions *and* job specifications.

5. For more discussion of the purposes of job analysis, see J. I. Sanchez et al., "Reshaping Job Analysis to Meet Emerging Business Needs" (paper presented at the Academy of Management meetings, Atlanta, GA, August 1993); R. A. Ash and E. L. Levine, "A Framework for Evaluating Job Analysis Methods," *Personnel* (November–December 1980): 39–53; S. Gael, *Job Analysis: A Guide to Assessing Work Activities* (San Francisco: Jossey-Bass, 1983); P. C. Grant, "What Use Is a Job Description?" *Personnel Journal* (February 1988): 45–53; Sparks, "Job Analysis."

6. R. D. Arvey, "Sex Bias in Job Evaluation Procedures," *Personnel Psychology* 39 (1986): 315–35; M. K. Mount and R. A. Ellis, "Investigation of Bias in Job Evaluation Rating of Comparable Worth Study Participants," *Personnel Psychology* (1987); 85–96; D. P. Schwab and R. Grams, "Sex-Related Errors in Job Evaluation: A 'Real World' Test," *Journal of Applied Psychology* (1986): 533–39.

7. Equal Employment Opportunity Commission, "Uniform Guidelines on Employee Selection Procedures," *Federal Register* 43 (1978): 38290-38315; J. Ledvinka and V. G. Scarpello, *Federal Regulation of Personnel and Human Resource Management,* 2nd ed. (Boston: Kent Publishing, 1991).

8. Grant, "What Use Is a Job Description?" 45–53; *How to Analyze Jobs* (Stanford, CT: Bureau of Law & Business, 1982); V. L. Huber, "Job Descriptions," in *Cases in Personnel/Human Resources Management,* ed. E. Stevens (Plano, TX: BPI, 1986), 278–86; M. A. Jones, "Job Descriptions Made Easy," *Personnel Journal* (May 1982): 31–34; R. J. Plachy, "Writing Job Descriptions That Get Results," *Personnel* (October 1987): 56–63.

9. "Uniform Guidelines on Employee Selection Procedures," *Federal Register* 43, 38290-38315; D. E. Thompson and T. A. Thompson, "Court Standards for Job Analysis in Test Validation," *Personnel Psychology* 35 (1982): 865–74.

10. The essence of the Civil Rights Act of 1991 and various court decisions is that employment decisions should be made on the basis of whether the individual will be able to perform the job. To determine this, organizations should conduct job analysis to help them determine what skills, knowledge, and abilities individuals need to perform their jobs. Once this is known, selection procedures can be developed. Chapter 8 expands on the job relatedness of selection procedures.

11. See R. A. Swanson, *Analysis for Improving Performance: Tools for Diagnosing Organizations and Documenting Workplace Expertise* (San Francisco: Berrett-Koehler Publishers, 1994); "Objective Employee Appraisals and Discrimination Cases," *Fair Employment Practices* (December 6, 1990): 145–46; R. J. Nobile, "The Law of Performance Appraisals," *Personnel* (January 1991): 7.

12. "Job Analyses and Job Descriptions under ADA," *Fair Employment Practices* (April 22, 1993): 45.

13. F. J. Landy and J. Vasey, "Job Analysis: The Composition of SME Samples," *Personnel Psychology* 44 (1991): 27–50.

14. Ibid.

15. R. D. Arvey, "Sex Bias in Job Evaluation Procedures," *Personnel Psychology* 39 (1986): 315–35; A. P. O'Reilly, "Skill Requirements: Supervisor-Subordinate Conflict," *Personnel Psychology* 26 (spring 1973): 75–80.

16. B. Schneider and A. M. Konz, "Strategic Job Analysis," *Human Resource Management* 28 (1989): 51–63.

17. For full discussions of these and other techniques, see S. Gael, ed., *The Job Analysis Handbook for Business, Industry, and Government* (New York: Wiley, 1988).

18. R. H. Hayes and R. Jaikumar, "Manufacturing's Crisis: New Technologies, Obsolete Organizations," *Harvard Business Review* (September–October 1988): 77–85.

19. E. E. Adam, Jr., and R. J. Ebert, *Production and Operations Management* (Englewood Cliffs, NJ: Prentice-Hall, 1986); V. L. Huber and N. L. Hyer, "The Human Factor in Cellular Manufacturing," *Journal of Operations Management* 5 (1985): 213–28; B. W. Nieble, *Motion and Time Study* (Homewood, IL: Richard D. Irwin, 1976); W. J. Stevenson, *Production/Operations Management* (Homewood, IL: Richard D. Irwin, 1986).

20. McCormick, *Job Analysis.*

21. F. Luthans, R. M. Hodgetts, and S. A. Rosenkrantz, *Real Managers* (Cambridge, MA: Ballinger Publishing, 1988); N. Fondas, "A Behavioral Job Description for Managers," *Organizational Dynamics* (Summer 1992): 47–58.

22. S. A. Fine, "Functional Job Analysis: An Approach to a Technology for Manpower Planning," *Personnel Journal* (November 1974): 813–18. See also S. A. Fine, *Functional Job Analysis Scales: A Desk Aid* (Milwaukee: Sidney A. Fine, 1989); S. A. Fine and W. Wiley, *An Introduction to Functional Job Analysis* (Washington, DC: Upjohn, 1971); U.S. Department of Labor, *Dictionary of Occupational Titles,* 4th ed. (Washington, DC, 1991); S. A. Fine, "Functional Job Analysis," in *Job Analysis Handbook,* ed. Gael, 1019–35.

23. U.S. Department of Labor, Employment and Training Administration, *The New Database of Occupational Titles for the Twenty-First Century,* final report of the Advisory Panel for the Dictionary of Occupational Titles (Washington, DC, 1993).

24. McCormick, "Job and Task Analysis."

25. E. J. McCormick, P. R. Jeanneret, and R. C. Mecham, "A Study of Job Characteristics and Job Dimensions as Based on the *Position Analysis Questionnaire,*" *Journal of Applied Psychology* 56 (1972): 347–67.

26. N. G. Peterson, "America 2000 and SCANS Report: Implications for Industrial Psychology" (paper presented at the Conference of the Society for Industrial and Organizational Psychology, Montreal, Canada, 1992).

27. R. Korte, "The National Job Analysis Study: Validation of the SCANS Taxonomy" (paper presented at the Conference of the Society for Industrial and Organizational Psychology, Nashville, TN, 1994).

28. *Goals 2000: Educate America Act,* Public Law 103-227, Cong., sess. (1994).

29. U.S. Department of Labor, *New Database of Occupational Titles.*

30. *Source:* This feature is excerpted and adapted from W. J. Camara, "Skill Standards, Assessment, and Certification: One-Stop Shopping for Employers?" *The Industrial-Organizational Psychologist* 32 (1994): 41–49. Used with permission.

31. E. J. McCormick and J. Tiffin, *Industrial Psychology,* 6th ed. (Englewood Cliffs, NJ: Prentice-Hall, 1974), 53. Adapted and reprinted by permission of Prentice-Hall, Inc. The *Position Analysis Questionnaire (PAQ)* is copyrighted by the Purdue Research Foundation. The *PAQ* and related materials are available through the University Book Store, 360 West State St., West Lafayette, IN 47906. Further information regarding the *PAQ* is available through PAQ Services, Inc., P.O. Box 3337, Logan, UT 84321. Computer processing of *PAQ* data is available through the PAQ Data Processing Division at that address.

32. E. J. McCormick and D. R. Ilgen, *Industrial Psychology* (Englewood Cliffs, NJ: Prentice-Hall, 1980).

33. For discussion of the *PAQ,* see E. T. Cornelius III, A. S. DeNisi, and A. G. Blencoe, "Expert and Naive Raters Using the *PAQ:* Does it Matter?" *Personnel Psychology* (autumn 1984): 453–64; E. J. McCormick, A. S. DeNisi, and B. Shaw, "Use of the *Position Analysis Questionnaire* for Establishing Job Component Validity of Tests," *Journal of Applied Psychology* 64 (1979): 51–56.

34. R. J. Harvey et al., "Dimensionality of the *Job Element Inventory,* A Simplified Worker-Oriented Job Analysis Questionnaire," *Journal of Applied Psychology* 73 (1988): 639–46.

35. J. I. Sanchez and S. L. Fraser, "On the Choice of Scales for Task Analysis," *Journal of Applied Psychology* 77 (1992): 545–53; M. A. Wilson and R. J. Harvey, "The Value of Relative Time-Spent Ratings in Task-Oriented Job Analysis," *Journal of Business and Psychology* 4 (1990): 453–61.

36. S. Gael, *Job Analysis: A Guide to Assessing Work Activities* (San Francisco: Jossey-Bass, 1983).

37. Based on information provided to the author by Psychological Services, Inc., Glendale, CA, 1995.

38. J. C. Flanagan, "The Critical Incident Technique," *Psychological Bulletin* 51 (1954): 327–58.

39. See Harvey, "Job Analysis."

40. M. A. Wilson, "An Expert System for Abilities-Oriented Job Analysis: Are Computers Equivalent to Paper-and-Pencil Methods?" in R. J. Harvey, "Measurement Issues in Job Analysis: New Approaches to Old Problems" (symposium presented at the sixth annual conference of the Society for Industrial and Organizational Psychology, St. Louis, 1991).

41. R. J. Vance, M. D. Coovert, and A. Colella, "An Expert System for Job Analysis: An Evaluation" (paper presented at the third annual meeting of the Society for Industrial and Organizational Psychology, Dallas, 1988).

42. I. L. Goldstein, *Training in Organizations: Needs Assessment, Development, and Evaluation* (Pacific Grove, CA: Brooks/Cole Publishing Co., 1993).

43. W. W. Tornow and P. R. Pinto, "The Development of a Managerial Job Taxonomy: A System for Describing, Classifying, and Evaluating Executive Positions," *Journal of Applied Psychology* 61 (1976): 410–18. See also W. F. Cascio, *Applied Psychology in Personnel Management,* 2nd ed. (Reston, VA: Reston, 1982), 61.

44. B. E. Dowell and K. N. Wexley, "Development of a Work Behavior Taxonomy for First Line Supervisors," *Journal of Applied Psychology* 63 (1978): 563–72.

45. For excellent descriptions of issues related to job families or classes, see M. K. Garwood, L. E. Anderson, and B. J. Greengart, "Determining Job Groups: Application of Hierarchical Agglomerative Cluster Analysis in Different Job Analysis Situations," *Personnel Psychology* (1991): 743–62; J. Hogan, "Structure of Physical Performance in Occupational Tasks," *Journal of Applied Psychology* (1991): 495–507; K. Pearlman, "Job Families: A Review and Discussion of Their Implications for Personnel Selection," *Psychological Bulletin* 87 (1980): 1–27.

46. D. Hofrichter, "Broadbanding: A 'Second Generation' Approach," *Compensation and Benefits Review* (September–October 1993): 53–58.

47. W. Bridges, "The End of the Job," *Fortune* (September 19, 1994): 62.

48. *Source:* Excerpted and adapted from M. Moravec and R. Tucker, "Job Descriptions for the 21st Century," *Personnel Journal* (June 1992): 37. Used by permission.

49. *Source:* Adapted from "Reengineering the Organization," *Bulletin to Management* (November 11, 1993): 360. Used by permission.

50. "Reengineering the Organization," *Bulletin to Management* (November 11, 1993): 360. See M. Hammer and J. Champy, *Reengineering the Corporation: A Manifesto for Business Revolution* (New York: HarperCollins, 1993).

51. J. Shervington, "Return of the Handicapped to Employment," *Australian Occupational Therapy Journal* 30 (1983): 20; M. D. Shinnick and D. L. Gerber, "A Common Language for Analyzing Work," *Journal of Systems Management* (April 1985): 8–13; Y. Yokomizo, *Research Reports* (Waseda, Japan: Waseda University Press, 1982).

52. This section on Japan is adapted in large part from M. S. O'Conner, "Report on Japanese Employee Relations Practices and Their Relation to Worker Productivity" (prepared for a study mission to Japan, November 8–23, 1983). M. S. O'Conner's permission to reproduce this material is appreciated. See also K. J. Duff, "Japanese and American Labor Law: Structural Similarities and Substantive Differences," *Employee Relations Law Journal* (Spring 1984): 629–41; R. Marsland and M. Beer, "The Evolution of Japanese Management: Lessons for U.S. Managers," *Organizational Dynamics* (Winter 1983): 49–67; and E. Zussman, "Learning from the Japanese: Management in a Resource-Scarce World," *Organizational Dynamics* (Winter 1983): 68–76.

 CHAPTER 7

1. *Harley-Davidson, Inc., Annual Report, 1992,* 10; *Harley-Davidson, Inc., Annual Report, 1993,* 10. See also K. Kelly and L. Miller, "The Rumble Heard Round the World: Harleys," *Business Week* (May 24, 1993): 58–60.

2. P. Elmer-Dewitt, "Mine, All Mine," *Time* (June 5, 1995): 69–76. "Microsoft: Bill Gates's Baby Is on Top of the World. Can It Stay There?" *Business Week* (February 24, 1992): 60–65; R. Brandt, J. Flynn, and A. Cortese, "Microsoft Hits the Gas: It's Bidding to Lead the Info Highway Pack," *Business Week* (March 21, 1994): 34–35; A. Farnham, "America's Most Admired Company," *Fortune* (February 7, 1994): 50–89; D. Coupland, "Microserfs: Seven Days in the Life of Young Microsoft," *Wired* (January 1994): 87–95.

3. "Employer Recruitment Practices," *Personnel* (May 1988): 63–65; B. Schneider and N. Schmitt, *Staffing Organizations,* 2nd ed. (Glenview, IL: Foresman,

1986); J. A. Breaugh, *Recruitment: Science and Practice* (Boston: PWS-Kent, 1992).

4. Breaugh, *Recruitment;* M. F. Cook, ed., *The AMA Handbook for Employee Recruitment and Retention* (New York: AMACOM, 1992); M. S. Taylor and C. M. Giannantonio, "Forming, Adapting, and Terminating the Employment Relationship: A Review of the Literature from Individual, Organizational, and Interactionist Perspectives," *Journal of Management* 19 (1993): 461–515. See also S. L. Rynes, "Recruitment, Job Choice, and Post-Hire Consequences: A Call for New Research Directions," in *Handbook of Industrial and Organizational Psychology,* vol. 2, ed. M. D. Dunnette and L. M. Hough (Palo Alto, CA: Consulting Psychologists Press, 1991), 399–444.

5. Rynes, "Recruitment, Job Choice, and Post-Hire Consequences," D. Arthur, *Recruiting, Interviewing, Selecting and Orienting New Employees,* 2nd ed. (New

York: AMACOM, 1991); S. E. Jackson et al., "Some Differences Make a Difference: Individual Dissimilarity and Group Heterogeneity as Correlates of Recruitment, Promotions, and Turnover," *Journal of Applied Psychology* (1991): 675–89; Schneider and Schmitt, *Staffing Organizations.*

6. *Source:* Based on P. Cappelli and A. Crocker-Hefter, *Distinctive Human Resources Are the Core Competencies of Firms,* report no. RQ00011-91 (Washington, DC: U.S. Department of Education, 1994).

7. P. Froiland, "Managing the Walking Wounded," *Training* (August 1993): 36–39; J. J. Laabs, "HR's Vital Role at Levi Strauss," *Personnel Journal* (December 1992): 34–46.

8. *Source:* Adapted from A. Halcrow, "Optima Winners," *Personnel Journal* (January 1992): 57. Used by permission.

9. R. S. Schuler, "Repositioning the Human Resource Function: Transformation or Demise?" *Academy of Management Executive* 4, no. 3 (1990): 49–59.

10. N. C. Tompkins, "GTE Managers on the Move," *Personnel Journal* (August 1992): 86–91.

11. L. N. Spiro et al., "The Flight of the Managers," *Business Week* (February 22, 1993): 78–81.

12. S. Caudron, "Change Keeps TQM Programs Thriving," *Personnel Journal* (October 1993): 104–9.

13. G. Flander and M. Moravec, "Out of Chaos, Opportunity," *Personnel Journal* (March 1994): 83–87; J. R. Garcia, "Job Posting for Professional Staff," *Personnel Journal* (March 1981): 189–92; G. A. Wallrop, "Job Posting for Nonexempt Employees: A Sample Program," *Personnel Journal* (October 1981): 796–98; L. S. Kleiman and K. J. Clark, "An Effective Job Posting System," *Personnel Journal* (February 1984): 20–25.

14. W. Glueck, *Personnel: A Diagnostic Approach* (Plano, TX: Business Publications, 1982).

15. R. Stoops, "Employee Referral Programs: Part I," *Personnel Journal* (February 1981): 98; R. Stoops, "Employee Referral Programs: Part II," *Personnel Journal* (March 1981): 172–73.

16. For a detailed discussion of these errors in recruiting decisions, see S. Rubenfeld and M. Crino, "Are Employment Agencies Jeopardizing Your Selection Process?" *Personnel* (September–October 1981): 70–78.

17. For information about sources in recruiting salespeople, see S. L. Martin and N. S. Raju, "Determining Cutoff Scores That Optimize Utility: A Recognition of Recruiting Costs," *Journal of Applied Psychology* 77 (1992): 15–23.

18. P. J. Decker and E. T. Cornelius, "A Note on Recruiting Sources and Job Survival Rates," *Journal of Applied Psychology* 64 (1974): 463–64; D. P. Schwab, "Recruiting and Organizational Participation," in *Personnel Management,* ed. K. M. Rowland and G. R. Ferris (Boston: Allyn & Bacon, 1982), 103–28.

19. S. L. Rynes and A. E. Barber, "Applicant Attraction Strategies: An Organizational Perspective," *Academy of Management Review* (1990): 286–310; R. E. Herman, *Keeping Good People: Strategies for Solving the Dilemma of the Decade* (New York: McGraw-Hill, 1991); K. G. Connolly and P. M. Connolly, *Competing for Employees: Proven Marketing Strategies for Hiring and Keeping Exceptional People* (Lexington, MA:

Lexington Books, 1991): C. L. Cooper and I. T. Robertson, eds., *International Review of Industrial and Organizational Psychology 1991,* vol. 6 (New York: John Wiley & Sons, 1991); S. L. Rynes, R. D. Bretz, Jr., and B. Gerhart, "The Importance of Recruitment in Job Choice: A Different Way of Looking," *Personnel Psychology* 44 (1991): 487–521; J. M. Grant and T. S. Bateman, "An Experimental Test of the Impact of Drug-Testing Programs on Potential Job Applicants' Attitudes and Intentions," *Journal of Applied Psychology* (1990): 127–31; K. R. Murphy, G. C. Thornton III, and D. H. Reynolds, "College Students' Attitudes toward Employee Drug Testing Programs," *Personnel Psychology* 43 (1990): 615–31; T. J. Hutton, "Increasing the Odds for Successful Searches," *Personnel Journal* (September 1987): 140–52; M. S. Taylor and T. J. Bergmann, "Organizational Recruitment Activities and Applicants' Reactions at Different Stages of the Recruitment Process," *Personnel Psychology* (summer 1987): 265–85.

20. For a detailed discussion of these errors in recruiting decisions, see Rubenfeld and Crino, "Are Employment Agencies Jeopardizing Your Selection Process?"

21. J. A. Byrne, "Can Tom and Gerry Find a Big Cheese for Big Blue?" *Business Week* (February 22, 1993): 39–40.

22. Spiro et al., "Flight of the Managers."

23. J. A. Byrne, "Dream Jobs All Over," *Business Week* (April 4, 1994): 34–36.

24. B. J. Feder, "Companies Find Rewards in Hiring G. E. Executives," *New York Times* (March 9, 1992): pp. D1, D4.

25. J. Chuang, "Temps Drive Workplace Competition," *Personnel Journal* (August 1994): 32; J. E. Struve, "Making the Most of Temporary Workers," *Personnel Journal* (November 1991): 43–46; S. Diesenhouse, "A Temp Firm with a Difference," *New York Times* (December 26, 1993): p. F3; J. Fierman, "The Contingency Work Force," *Fortune* (January 24, 1994): 30–36; D. C. Feldman and H. I. Doerpinghaus, "Missing Persons No Longer: Managing Part-Time Workers in the '90s," *Organizational Dynamics* (summer 1992): 59–72; "Employment Law and Temporary Workers," *Bulletin to Management* (September 2, 1993): 280.

26. This form of recruiting is not without problems; see N. Jones-Parker and R. H. Perry, eds., *The Executive Search Collaboration: A Guide for Human Resource Professionals and Their Search Firms* (Westport, CT: Quorum Books, 1990); B. Lozano, "The Invisible Work Force: Transforming American Business with Outside and Home-Based Workers (New York: Free Press, 1989); B. Meier, "Some 'Worker Leasing' Programs Defraud Insurers and Employers," *New York Times* (March 20, 1992): D1; D. C. Feldman, "Reconceptualizing the Nature and Consequences of Part-Time Work," *Academy of Management Review* (1990): 103–12; D. R. Dalton and D. J. Mesch, "The Impact of Flexible Scheduling on Employee Attendance and Turnover," *Administrative Science Quarterly* 35 (1990): 370–87.

27. *New York Times* (March 15, 1992): p. E3.

28. J. Bredwell, "The Use of Broadcast Advertising for Recruitment," *Personnel Administrator* (February 1981): 45–49; R. Stoops, "Radio Recruitment Adver-

tising, Part II," *Personnel Journal* (July 1981): 532; "Affirmative Action in the 1980's: What Can We Expect?" *Management Review* (May 1981): 4–5; R. Stoops, "Television Advertising," *Personnel Journal* (November 1981): 838; R. Stoops, "Reader Survey Supports Market Approach to Recruitment," *Personnel Journal* (March 1984): 22–24.

29. S. Peters, "HR Helps Mirage Resorts Manage Change," *Personnel Journal* (June 1994): 22–30.

30. R. Stoops, "Recruitment Ads That Get Results," *Personnel Journal* (April 1984): 24–26; R. Siedlecki, "Creating a Direct Mail Recruitment Program," *Personnel Journal* (April 1983): 304–7; B. S. Hodes, "Planning for Recruitment Advertising: Part I," *Personnel Journal* (May 1983): 380–84; J. P. Bucalo, "Good Advertising Can Be More Effective than Other Tools," *Personnel Administrator* (November 1983): 73–78.

31. *Wall Street Journal* (February 8, 1983): 35.

32. P. Kruger, "For Job Seekers, On-Line Options," *New York Times* (August 28, 1994): p. F21.

33. *Source:* "Tips for Hiring Techies," *Fortune* (August 22, 1994): 66. Used by permission. See also L. S. Richman, "The New Worker Elite," *Fortune* (August 22, 1994): 56–66.

34. D. M. Schweiger, J. M. Ivancevich, and F. R. Power, "Executive Actions for Managing Human Resources Before and After Acquisitions," *Academy of Management Executive* (May 1987): 127–38.

35. B. Paik Sunoo and J. J. Laabs, "Winning Strategies for Outsourcing Contracts," *Personnel Journal* (March 1994): 69–78; J. S. Lord, "Contract Recruiting: Coming of Age," *Personnel Administrator* (November 1987): 49–53; see also L. Carroll, "Strategies to Make Outplacement an INHOUSE Program," *HR Focus* (September 1993): 12–13.

36. Fierman, "The Contingency Work Force." 30. See also S. Caudron, "Contingent Work Force Spurs HR Planning," *Personnel Journal* (July 1994): 52–60.

37. W. P. Barnett and A. S. Miner, "Standing on the Shoulders of Others: Career Interdependence in Job Mobility," *Administrative Science Quarterly* 37 (1992): 262–81.

38. "Interim Professionals . . . Are Corporations Ready to Put Them to Work?" *HR Reporter* (March 1993): 1–4.

39. "Two New Hi-Tech Tools," *HR Reporter* (March 1993): 2–4.

40. "Ask the Experts—Recruiting Older Workers," *Fair Employment Practices Guidelines* (May 10, 1993): 8.

41. D. Gunsch, "Comprehensive College Strategy Strengthens NCR's Recruitment," *Personnel Journal* (September 1993): 58–62. Also see B. Smith, "Pinkerton Keeps Its Eye on Recruitment," *HR Focus* (September 1993): 1, 6.

42. R. D. Gatewood, M. A. Gowan, and G. J. Lautenschlager, "Corporate Image, Recruitment Image, and Initial Choice Decisions," *Academy of Management Journal* 36 (1993): 414–27.

43. C. R. Williams, C. E. Labig, Jr., and T. H. Stone, "Recruitment Sources and Posthire Outcomes for Job Applicants and New Hires: A Test of Two Hypotheses," *Journal of Applied Psychology* 78 (1993): 163–72.

44. A. M. Saks, "A Psychological Process Investigation for the Effects of Recruitment Source and Organization Information on Job Survival," *Journal of Organizational Behavior* 15 (1994): 225–44.

45. C. Rosenfield, "Job Seeking Methods Used by American Workers," *Monthly Labor Review* (August 1975): 39–42; D. P. Schwab, "Organizational Recruiting and the Decision to Participate," in *Personnel Management,* ed. K. M. Rowland and G. R. Ferris (Boston: Allyn & Bacon, 1982); D. Schwab, S. L. Rynes, and R. J. Aldag, "Theories and Research in Job Search and Choice," in *Research in Personnel and Human Resource Management* (Greenwich, CT: JAI Press, 1987), 136–37; M. S. Taylor and D. W. Schmidt, "A Process-Oriented Investigation of Recruitment Source Effectiveness," *Personnel Psychology* 36 (1983): 343–54.

46. D. B. Turban and T. W. Dougherty, "Influences of Campus Recruiting Applicant Attraction to Firms," *Academy of Management Journal* 35 (1992): 739–65.

47. S. D. Maurer, V. Howe, and T. W. Lee, "Organizational Recruiting as Marketing Management: An Interdisciplinary Study of Engineering Graduates," *Personnel Psychology* 45 (1992): 807–33.

48. *Source:* Based on S. L. Rynes, R. D. Bretz, Jr., and B. Gerhart, "The Importance of Recruitment in Job Choice: A Different Way of Looking," *Personnel Psychology* 44 (1991): 487–521. See also R. J. Vandenberg and V. Scarpello, "The Matching Model: An Examination of the Processes Underlying Realistic Job Previews," *Journal of Applied Psychology* 75, no. 1: 60–67; S. Rynes and B. Gerhart, "Interviewer Assessments of Applicant 'Fit': An Exploratory Investigation," *Personnel Psychology* 43 (1990): 13–35; J. P. Wanous, "Installing a Realistic Job Preview: Ten Tough Choices," *Personnel Psychology* 42 (1989): 117–34; J. P. Kirnan, J. A. Farley, and K. F. Geisinger, "The Relationship between Recruiting Source, Applicant Quality, and Hire Performance: An Analysis by Sex, Ethnicity, and Age," *Personnel Psychology* 42 (1989): 293–308; R. A. Dean and J. P. Wanous, "Effects of Realistic Job Previews on Hiring Bank Tellers," *Journal of Applied Psychology* (February 1984): 61–68; B. M. Meglino and A. S. DeNisi, "Realistic Job Previews: Some Thoughts on Their More Effective Use in Managing the Flow of Human Resources," *Human Resource Planning* 10, no. 3 (1987): 157–67; B. M. Meglino et al., "Effects of Realistic Job Previews: A Comparison Using an Enhancement and Reduction Preview," *Journal of Applied Psychology* (May 1988): 259–66.

49. J. O. Crites, *Vocational Psychology* (New York: McGraw-Hill, 1969); J. P. Wanous, *Organizational Entry: Recruitment, Selection, and Socialization of Newcomers* (Reading, MA: Addison-Wesley, 1980); K. G. Wheeler and T. M. Mahoney, "The Expectancy Model in the Analysis of Occupational Preference and Occupational Choice," *Journal of Vocational Behavior* 19 (1981): 113–22.

50. Schwab, Rynes, and Aldag, "Theories and Research," 129–66.

51. G. T. Milkovich and J. Newman, *Compensation* (Plano, TX: BPI, 1984); Schwab, Rynes, and Aldag, "Theories and Research," 129–66.

52. A. E. Barber and M. V. Roehling, "Job Postings and the Decision to Interview: A Verbal Protocol Analysis," *Journal of Applied Psychology* 78 (1993): 845–56; T. A. Judge and R. D. Bretz, Jr., "Effects of Work Values on Job Choice Decisions," *Journal of Applied Psychology* 77 (1992): 261–71. See also S. Shellen-

barger, "Work-Force Study Finds Loyalty Is Weak, Divisions of Race and Gender are Deep," *Wall Street Journal* (September 3, 1993): pp. B1, B8.

53. C. E. Jergenson, "Job Preference: What Makes a Job Good or Bad?" *Journal of Applied Psychology* 63 (1978): 267–76; B. Major and E. Konar, "An Investigation of Sex Differences in Pay in Higher Education and Their Possible Cause," *Academy of Management Journal* 4 (1986): 777–92; Schwab, Rynes, and Aldag, "Theories and Research," 129–66.

54. R. D. Bretz, Jr., J. W. Boudreau, and T. A. Judge, "Job Search Behavior of Employed Managers," *Personnel Psychology* 47 (1994): 275–301.

55. Jergenson, "Job Preference"; Schwab, Rynes, and Aldag, "Theories and Research"; S. L. Rynes, H. Heneman III, and D. P. Schwab, "Individual Reactions to Organizational Recruiting: A Review," *Personnel Psychology* 33 (1980): 529–42.

56. J. P. Wanous et al., "The Effects of Met Expectations on Newcomer Attitudes and Behaviors: A Review and Meta-Analysis," *Journal of Applied Psychology* 77 (1992): 288–97.

57. From D. Arvey and J. G. Campion, "The Employment Interview: A Summary and Review of the Recent Literature," *Personnel Psychology* 35 (1982): 281–322. See also J. A. Breaugh, "Realistic Job Previews: A Critical Appraisal and Future Research Directions," *Academy of Management Review* (October 1983): 612–23; Dean and Wanous, "Hiring Bank Tellers"; M. D. Hakel, "Employment Interviewing," in *Personnel Management*, ed. K. M. Rowland and G. R. Ferris (Boston: Allyn & Bacon, 1982), 153–54; Meglino and DeNisi, "Realistic Job Previews"; B. M. Meglino et al., "Effects of Realistic Job Previews"; G. N. Powell, "Effects of Job Attributes and Recruiting Practices on Applicant Decision: A Comparison," *Personnel Psychology* (winter 1984): 721–32; S. L. Rynes and H. E. Miller, "Recruiter and Job Influences on Candidates for Employment," *Journal of Applied Psychology* (February 1983): 147–56.

58. Meglino and Denisi, "Realistic Job Previews." See also S. M. Colarelli, "Methods of Communications and Mediating Processes in Realistic Job Previews," *Journal of Applied Psychology* (1984): 633–42.

59. R. Koenig, "Toyota Takes Pains and Time Filling Jobs at Its Kentucky Plant," *Wall Street Journal* (December 1, 1987): 1.

60. M. J. Aamodt and D. L. Peggans, "Rejecting Applicants with Tact," *Personnel Administrator* (April 1988): 58–60; B. Adair and D. Pollen, "No! No! A Thousand Times No!" *Washington Post* (September 25, 1985): 5.

61. "Truth in Hiring Gains Importance," *Bulletin to Management* (July 28, 1994): 5; M. R. Buckley, D. B. Fedor, and D. S. Marvin, "Ethical Considerations in the Recruiting Process: A Preliminary Investigation and Identification of Research Opportunities," *Human Resource Management Review* (in press).

62. *Federal Express Corporation Annual Report, 1992*, 48. See also A. Halcrow, "Federal Express," *Personnel Journal* (January 1992): 52; D. Filipowski, "How Federal Express Makes Your Package Its Most Important," *Personnel Journal* (February 1992): 40–46.

63. R. D. Dickson, "The Business of Equal Opportunity," *Harvard Business Review* (January–February 1992):

46–53; W. Guzzardi, "A Fresh View of Affirmative Action," *Fortune* (September 23, 1991): 210–13; R. Turner, *The Past and Future of Affirmative Action: A Guide for Human Resource Professionals and Corporate Counsel* (Westport, CT: Quorum Books/ Greenwood Press, 1990); S. Carter, *Reflections of an Affirmative Action Baby* (New York: Basic Books, 1991); A. J. Jones, Jr., *Affirmative Talk, Affirmative Action: A Comparative Study of the Politics of Affirmative Action* (Westport, CT: Praeger Publishers, 1991); D. P. Twomey, *Equal Employment Opportunity Law*, 3rd ed. (Cincinnati: Southwestern 1994).

64. D. A. Kravitz and J. Platania, "Attitudes and Beliefs about Affirmative Action: Effects of Target and of Respondent Sex and Ethnicity," *Journal of Applied Psychology* 78 (1993): 928–38.

65. The steps in utilization and availability analysis are based on eight-factor analysis. For a description, see R. H. Faley and L. S. Kleiman, "Misconceptions and Realities in the Implementation of Equal Employment Opportunity," in *Readings in Personnel and Human Resource Management*, 3rd ed., ed. R. S. Schuler, S. A. Youngblood, and V. L. Huber (St. Paul: West Publishing Co., 1988); Biddle & Associates, 903 Enterprise Dr., Suite 1, Sacramento, CA 95825.

66. P. M. Perry, "ADA Missteps," *Training* (October 1994): 84–91; J. J. Laabs, "The ADA: Tough Subject, Straight Answers," *Personnel Journal* (February 1994): 25–30; "Small Business Prepares for ADA," *Fair Employment Practices* (January 13, 1994): 6; L. Reynolds, "ADA Complaints Are Not What Experts Predicted," *HR Focus* (November 1993): 1, 6; C. Yang and S. Anderson, "Business Has to Find a New Meaning for 'Fairness,' " *Business Week* (April 12, 1993): 72; A. Bryant, "Can One Person Make a Difference? 'The Woman Who Sued State Farm and Won,' " *New York Times* (April 30, 1992): p. D4.

67. S. Marshall, "$157 Million Ends Sex Bias Suit," *USA Today* (April 29, 1992): 14; "Record Settlement Breaks 'Glass Ceiling,' " *Fair Employment Practices Guidelines* (July 1992): 1, 2.

68. U.S. Department of Labor, *A Report on the Glass Ceiling Initiative* (Washington, DC, 1991).

69. Ibid.

70. J. P. Fields, *Women and the Corporate Ladders: Corporate Linkage Project* (Wellesley, MA: Wellesley College Center for Research on Women, July 31, 1984).

71. S. D. Clayton and F. J. Crosby, *Justice, Gender and Affirmative Action* (Ann Arbor, MI: University of Michigan Press, 1992); M. E. Turner and A. R. Pratkanis, eds., "*Affirmative Action*", A special issue of the journal, *Basic and Applied Social Psychology* 15 (1994); M. E. Heilman, "Affirmative Action: Some Unintended Consequences for Working Women," in *Research in Organizational Behavior*, ed. L. L. Cummings and B. M. Staw (Greenwich, CT: JAI Press, 1994); M. E. Heilman, C. J. Block, and J. A. Lucas, "Presumed Incompetent? Stigmatization and Affirmative Action Efforts," *Journal of Applied Psychology* 77 (1992): 536–44. C. Yang, M. Mallory and A. Cuneo, "A 'Race-Neutral' Helping Hand?" *Business Week* (February 27, 1995): 120–121.

72. A. Pollack, "Japanese Graduates Finding Few Jobs," *New York Times* (June 25, 1994): D39; B. R. Schlender, "Japan's White Collar Blues," *Fortune* (March 21,

1994): 97–98, 101–2, 104; A. Pollack, "Japan Finds Ways to Save Tradition of Lifetime Jobs," *New York Times* (November 28, 1993): 1, 20; E. Fingleton, "Jobs for Life," *Fortune* (March 20, 1995): 119–125.

73. V. Puick, "White Collar Human Resource Management in Large Japanese Manufacturing Firms," *Human Resource Management* 20, no. 2: 264; "Learning from Japan," *Business Week* (January 27, 1992): 52–60.

74. G. Flynn, "HR in Mexico: What You Should Know," *Personnel Journal* (August 1994): 34. This entire discussion of Mexico is based on this article.

75. Ibid.
76. Ibid.
77. Ibid.
78. Ibid.
79. Ibid.
80. F. Dany and V. Torchy, "Recruitment and Selection in Europe: Policies, Practices and Methods," in *Policy and Practice in European Human Resource Management,* ed. C. Brewster and A. Hegewisch (New York: Routledge, 1994), 68–88; and P. R. Sparrow and J. M. Hiltrop, *European Human Resource Management in Transition* (London: Prentice Hall, 1994).

 CHAPTER 8

1. "The Starbuck's Enterprise Shifts into Warp Speed," *Business Week* (October 24, 1994): 76.

2. P. Sellers, "Coke Gets off Its Can in Europe," *Fortune* (August 13, 1990): 68–76.

3. P. Sellers, "Pepsi Opens a Second Front," *Fortune* (August 8, 1994): 70–75.

4. R. S. Schuler, J. R. Fulkerson, and P. J. Dowling, "Strategic Performance Measurement and Management in Multinational Corporations," *Human Resource Management* (fall 1991): 365–92.

5. "Something to Get Worked up About: Bottlers Concerned About Reorganization of Pepsi-Cola Co.," *Beverage World* (November 1992): 6.

6. P. Cappelli and A. Crocker-Hefter, *Distinctive Human Resources Are the Core Competencies of Firms,* report no. R117 Q00011-91 (Washington, DC: U.S. Department of Education, 1994).

7. For recent detailed treatment, see F. L. Schmidt, D. S. Ones, and J. E. Hunter, "Personnel Selection," *Annual Review of Psychology* 43 (1992): 627–70; A. Tziner, *Organization Staffing and Work Adjustments* (Westport, CT: Praeger, 1990): N. Schmitt and I. Robertson, "Personnel Selection," *Annual Review of Psychology* 41 (1990): 289–319; N. Schmitt et al., eds., *Personnel Selection in Organizations* (San Francisco: Jossey-Bass, 1993); B. Schneider and N. Schmitt, *Staffing Organizations,* 2nd ed. (Prospect Heights, IL: Waveland, 1992); H. H. Heneman III and R. L. Heneman, *Staffing Organizations* (Middleton, WI: Mendota House, 1994); D. E. Bowen, G. E. Ledford, Jr., and B. R. Nathan, "Hiring for the Organization, Not the Job," *Academy of Management Executive* 5, no. 4 (1991): 35–51; D. F. Caldwell and C. A. O'Reilly III, "Measuring Person-Job Fit with a Profile-Comparison Process," *Journal of Applied Psychology* 75, no. 6 (1990): 648–57; C. A. O'Reilly III, J. Chatman, and D. F. Caldwell, "People and Organizational Culture: A Profile Comparison Approach to Assessing Person-Organization Fit," *Academy of Management Journal* 34, no. 3 (1991): 487–516; M. A. M. Fricko and T. A. Beehr, "A Longitudinal Investigation of Interest Congruence and Gender Concentration as Predictors of Job Satisfaction," *Personnel Psychology* 45 (1992): 99–117; R. D. Arvey and R. H. Faley, *Fairness in Selecting Employees* (Reading, MA: Addison-Wesley, 1988); M. D. Hakel, "Personnel Selection and Placement," *Annual Review of Psychology* 37 (1986): 351–80.

8. S. M. Colarelli and T. A. Beehr, "Selection Out: Firings, Layoffs, and Retirement," in *Personnel Selection in Organizations,* ed. N. Schmitt et al., 341–84.

9. See Bowen, Ledford, and Nathan, "Hiring for the Organization."

10. D. E. Terpstra and E. J. Rozell, "The Relationship of Staffing Practices to Organizational Level Measures of Performance," *Personnel Psychology* 46 (1993): 27–48.

11. C. C. Snow and S. A. Snell, "Staffing as Strategy," in *Personnel Selection in Organizations,* ed. N. Schmitt et al., 448–78.

12. M. London, "What Every Personnel Director Should Know about Management Promotion Decisions," *Personnel Journal* (October 1978): 551.

13. A. K. Gupta, "Contingency Linkages between Strategy and General Manager Characteristics: A Conceptual Examination." *Academy of Management Review* 9 (1984): 399–412; A. K. Gupta and V. Govindarajan, "Business Unit Strategy, Managerial Characteristics, and Business Unit Effectiveness at Strategy Implementation," *Academy of Management Journal* 27 (1983): 25–41.

14. C. Fombrun, "An Interview with Reginald Jones," *Organizational Dynamics* (Winter 1982): 46.

15. Gupta, "Contingency Linkages;" A. K. Gupta and V. Govindarajan, "Build, Hold, Harvest: Converting Strategic Intentions into Reality," *Journal of Business Strategy* 4 (1984): 34–37; D. C. Hambrick and P. A. Mason, "Upper Echelons: The Organization as a Reflection of Its Top Management," *Academy of Management Review* 9 (1984): 193–206; J. D. Olian and S. L. Rynes, "Organizational Staffing: Integrating Practice with Strategy," *Industrial Relations* 23 (1984): 170–83; A. D. Szilagyi and D. M. Schweiger, "Matching Managers to Strategies: A Review and Suggested Framework," *Academy of Management Review* 9 (1984): 626–37.

16. S. D. Friedman, "Succession Systems in Large Corporations: Characteristics and Correlates of Performance," *Human Resource Management* 25 (1986): 191–213; J. P. Kotter, "How Leaders Grow Leaders," *Across the Board* (1988): 38–42.

17. *Source:* Adapted from R. Sobotka, "Workers Are a Small Firm's Most Valuable Asset," *Cleveland Plain Dealer* (March 24, 1994): p. C4.

18. S. L. Rynes, "Who's Selecting Whom? Effects of Selection Practices on Applicant Attitudes and Behavior,"

in *Personnel Selection in Organizations,* ed. N. Schmitt et al., 242.

19. *Source:* Adapted from "Study Using Testers Reveals Age Bias in Hiring Is Prevalent," *Fair Employment Practices Guidelines* (June 10, 1994): 6. Used by permission.

20. For excellent reviews of this literature, see Rynes, "Who's Selecting Whom?"; S. L. Rynes, "Recruitment, Job Choice, and Post-Hire Consequences: A Call for New Research Directions," in *Handbook of Industrial and Organizational Psychology,* vol. 2, ed. M. D. Dunnette and L. M. Hough (Palo Alto, CA: Consulting Psychologists Press, 1991), 399–444.

21. See R. D. Arvey and P. R. Sackett, "Fairness in Selection: Current Developments and Perspectives," in *Personnel Selection in Organizations,* ed. N. Schmitt et al., 171–202; S. W. Gilliland, "Effects of Procedural and Distributive Justice on Reactions to a Selection System," *Journal of Applied Psychology* 79 (1994): 691–701.

22. R. Stoffey et al., "Relationships between Perceived Fairness of Selection and Perceptions of the Organization" (paper presented at the meeting of the Society for Industrial and Organizational Psychology, St. Louis, MO); J. W. Smither et al., "Applicant Reactions to Selection Procedures," *Personnel Psychology* 46 (1993): 49–76; J. Schwarzwald, M. Koslowsky, and B. Shalit, "A Field Study of Employees' Attitudes and Behaviors after Promotion Decisions," *Journal of Applied Psychology* 77 (1992): 511–14; R. D. Bretz, Jr., and T. A. Judge, "The Role of Human Resource Systems in Job Applicant Decision Processes," *Journal of Management* 20 (1994): 531–51.

23. See Rynes, "Who's Selecting Whom?"

24. See Arvey and Sackett, "Fairness in Selection."

25. "Women in Management: A Waiting Game," *Wall Street Journal* (March 29, 1994).

26. For a detailed review of what is known about this very special selection process, see G. P. Hollenbeck, *CEO Selection: A Street-Smart Review* (Greensboro, NC: Center for Creative Leadership, 1994).

27. J. A. Chatman, "Matching People and Organizations: Selection and Socialization in Public Accounting Firms," *Administrative Science Quarterly* 36 (1991): 459–84.

28. D. C. Hambrick et al., "Preparing Today's Leaders for Tomorrow's Realities," *Personnel* 66 (1989): 22–26.

29. M. A. Campion, E. D. Pursell, and B. K. Brown, "Structured Interviewing: Raising the Psychometric Properties of the Employment Interview," *Personnel Psychology* (spring 1988): 25–42; A. I. Huffcutt and W. Arthur, Jr., "Hunter and Hunter (1948) Revisited: Interview Validity for Entry-Level Jobs," *Journal of Applied Psychology* 79 (1994): 184–90.

30. I. L. Goldstein, S. Zedeck, and B. Schneider, "An Exploration of the Job Analysis–Content Validity Process," in *Personnel Selection in Organizations,* ed. N. Schmitt et al., 3–34.

31. W. F. Cascio, "Assessing the Utility of Selection Decisions: Theoretical and Practical Considerations," in *Personnel Selection in Organizations,* N. Schmitt et al.; J. W. Boudreau, "Economic Considerations in Estimating the Utility of Human Resource Productivity Improvement Programs," *Personnel Psychology* 36 (1983): 551–57; J. W. Boudreau, "Utility Analysis for

Decisions in Human Resource Management," in *Handbook of Industrial and Organizational Psychology,* ed. Dunnette and Hough; K. M. Murphy, "When Your Top Choice Turns You Down: The Effect of Rejected Offers on the Utility of Selection Tests," *Psychological Bulletin* 99 (1986): 133–38.

32. J. Zeidner and C. D. Johnson, *The Economic Benefits of Predicting Job Performance,* vol. 1, *Selection Utility,* vol. 2, *Classification Efficiency,* vol. 3, *Estimating the Gains of Alternative Policies* (Westport, CT: Praeger, 1991); W. F. Cascio, "Reconciling Economic and Social Objectives in Personnel Selection: Impact of Alternative Decision Rules," *New Approaches to Employee Management: Fairness in Employee Selection* 1 (1992): 61–86; M. E. Baehr et al., "Proactively Balancing the Validity and Legal Compliance of Personal Background Measures in Personnel Management," *Journal of Business and Psychology* 8 (spring 1994): 345–54; C. M. Solomon, "Testing Is Not at Odds with Diversity Efforts," *Personnel Journal* (March 1993): 100–4; S. E. Maxwell and R. D. Arvey, "The Search for Predictors with High Validity and Low Adverse Impact: Compatible or Incompatible Goals?" *Journal of Applied Psychology* 78 (1993): 433–37.

33. G. Dessler, "Value-Based Hiring Builds Commitment," *Personnel Journal* (November 1993): 98–102.

34. For more detailed reviews, see Heneman and Heneman, *Staffing Organizations;* C. P. Hansen and C. A. Kelley, eds., *A Handbook of Psychological Assessment in Business* (Westport, CT: Quorum Books, 1991).

35. D. G. Lawrence et al., "Design and Use of Weighted Application Blanks," *Personnel Administrator* (March 1982): 53–57, 101.

36. For a fuller discussion, see M. D. Mumford and G. S. Stokes, "Developmental Determinants of Individual Action: Theory and Practice in Applying Background Measures," in *Handbook of Industrial and Organizational Psychology,* ed. Dunnette and Hough, 61–138.

37. C. J. Russell et al., "Predictive Validity of Biodata Items Generated from Retrospective Life Experience Essays," *Journal of Applied Psychology* 75, no. 5 (1990): 569–80; H. R. Rothstein et al., "Biographical Data in Employment Selection: Can Validities Be Made Generalizable?" *Journal of Applied Psychology* 75, no. 2 (1990): 175–84; M. A. McDaniel, "Biographical Constructs for Predicting Employee Suitability," *Journal of Applied Psychology* 74, no. 6 (1989): 964–70; A. Childs and R. J. Klimoski, "Successfully Predicting Career Success: An Application of the Biographical Inventory," *Journal of Applied Psychology* (February 1988): 3–8.

38. A. F. Snell et al, "Adolescent Life Experiences as Predictors of Occupational Attainment," *Journal of Applied Psychology* 79 (1994): 131–41; G. Stokes, M. Mumford, and W. Owens, eds., *Biodata Handbook: Theory, Research, and Use of Biographical Information for Selection and Performance Prediction* (Palo Alto, CA: Consulting Psychologists Press, 1994).

39. A. T. Dalessio and T. A. Silverhart, "Combining Biodata Test and Interview Information: Predicting Decisions and Performance Criteria," *Personnel Psychology* 47 (1994): 303–19.

40. P. M. Muchinsky, "The Use of Reference Reports in Personnel Selection: A Review and Evaluation," *Journal of Occupational Psychology* 52 (1979): 287–97;

P. M. Muchinsky, "Vocational Behavior and Career Development, 1982: A Review," *Journal of Vocational Behavior* 23 (1983): 123–78.

41. "Background Checks," *Fair Employment Practices Guidelines* 266 (1987): 1.

42. *Source:* "Ask the Experts—Investigating Applicant Fraud," *Fair Employment Practices Guidelines* (April 10, 1993): 8. Copyrighted material reprinted with permission of *Fair Employment Practices Guidelines* and the Bureau of Business Practice, 24 Rope Ferry Rd., Waterford, CT 06386.

43. E. A. Fleishman and M. K. Quaintance, *Taxonomies of Human Performance* (New York: Academic Press, 1984).

44. B. Schneider and N. Schmitt, *Staffing Organizations* (Glenview, IL: Scott-Foresman, 1986); N. Schmitt and R. J. Klimoski, *Research Methods in Human Resources Management* (Cincinnati: South-Western, 1991); J. C. Hogan, "Physical Abilities," in *Handbook of Industrial and Organizational Psychology,* ed. Dunnette and Hough, 753–831; R. M. Guion, "Personnel Assessment, Selection, and Placement," in *Handbook of Industrial and Organizational Psychology,* ed. Dunnette and Hough, 327–98.

45. C. Sparks, "Paper and Pencil Measures of Potential," in *Perspectives of Employee Staffing and Selection,* ed. Dreher and Sackett, 349–67.

46. R. T. Hogan, "Personality and Personality Measurement," in *Handbook of Industrial and Organizational Psychology,* ed. Dunnette and Hough, 873–890.

47. M. R. Barrick and M. K. Mount, "The Big Five Personality Dimensions and Job Performance: A Meta-Analysis," *Personnel Psychology* 44 (1991): 1–26; D. V. Day and S. B. Silverman, "Personality and Job Performance: Evidence of Incremental Validity," *Personnel Psychology* 42 (1989): 25–36; T. Newton and T. Keenan, "Further Analyses of the Dispositional Argument in Organizational Behavior," *Journal of Applied Psychology* 76 (1991): 781–87; P. Warr and M. Conner, "Job Competence and Cognition," *Research in Organizational Behavior* 14 (1992): 91–127; R. P. Tett, D. N. Jackson, and M. Rothstein, "Personality Measures as Predictors of Job Performance: A Meta-Analytic Review," *Personnel Psychology* 44 (1991): 703–42.

48. See Barrick and Mount, "The Big Five Personality Dimensions and Job Performance."

49. L. M. Hough et al., "Criterion-Related Validities of Personality Constructs and the Effects of Response Distortion on Those Validities," *Journal of Applied Psychology* 75 (1990): 581–95. See also Barrick and Mount, "The Big Five Personality Dimensions and Job Performance."

50. M. R. Barrick and M. K. Mount, "Autonomy as a Moderator of the Relationships between the Big Five Personality Dimensions and Job Performance," *Journal of Applied Psychology* 78 (1993): 111–18.

51. F. E. Inbau, "Shoring up Eroding Options," *Security Management* 33 (1989): 53–58; G. Meinsma, "Thou Shalt Not Steal," *Security Management* 29 (1987): 35–37.

52. U.S. Congress, *The Use of Integrity Tests for Preemployment Screening,* report no. OTA-SET-442 (Washington, DC, 1990).

53. K. R. Murphy, *Honesty in the Workplace* (Pacific Grove, CA: Brooks/Cole Publishing Co., 1993); D. S. Ones, C. Viswesvaran, and F. L. Schmidt, "Comprehensive Meta-Analysis of Integrity Test Validities: Findings and Implications for Personnel Selection and Theories of Job Performance," *Journal of Applied Psychology* 78 (1993): 679–703; W. J. Camara and D. L. Schneider, "Integrity Tests: Facts and Unresolved Issues," *American Psychologist* 49 (1994): 112–19; J. M. Collins and F. L. Schmidt, "Personality, Integrity, and White Collar Crime: A Construct Validity Study," *Personnel Psychology* 46 (1993): 295–311; L. R. Burris, "Integrity Testing for Personnel Selection: An Update," *Personnel Psychology* 42 (1989): 491–529; J. W. Jones, ed., *Preemployment Honesty Testing: Current Research and Future Directions* (Westport, CT: Quorum Books, 1991); P. R. Sackett and M. M. Harris, "Honesty Testing for Personnel Selection: A Review and Critique," *Personnel Psychology* 37 (1984): 221–46.

54. E. F. Stone, D. L. Stone, and D. Hyatt, "Personnel Selection Procedures and Invasion of Privacy," in R. M. Guion, chair, *Privacy in Organizations: Personnel Selection, Physical Environment, and Legal Issues* (symposium presented at the Fourth Annual Conference of the Society for Industrial and Organizational Psychology, Boston, 1989).

55. H. J. Bernardin and D. K. Cooke, "Validity of an Honesty Test in Predicting Theft among Convenience Store Employees," *Academy of Management Journal* 36 (1993): 1097–1108; T. F. O'Boyle, "More Honest Tests Used to Gauge Workers' Morale," *Wall Street Journal* (July 11, 1985): 27.

56. L. J. Hogan, "Interests and Competencies: A Strategy for Personnel Selection," in *Readings in Personnel and Human Resource Management,* 3rd ed., ed. R. S. Schuler, S. A. Youngblood, and V. L. Huber (St. Paul: West Publishing Co., 1988), 484–95.

57. See R. Dawis, "Vocational Interests, Values, and Preferences," in *Handbook of Industrial and Organizational Psychology,* ed. Dunnette and Hough, 833–72.

58. *Source:* Adapted from "Retailer Hit with $2M Settlement," *HR Focus* (November 1993): 12.

59. For an extensive review of and guide to these tests, see L. P. Plumke, "A Short Guide to the Development of Work Sample and Performance Tests," 2nd ed. (Washington, DC: U.S. Office of Personnel Management, February 1980). Note the interchangeability of the terms *work sample* and *performance test.*

60. R. J. Campbell, "Use of an Assessment Center as an Aid in Management Selection," *Personnel Psychology* 46 (1993): 691–99; A. Howard and D. W. Bray, *Managerial Lives in Transition: Advancing Age and Changing Times* (New York: Guilford Press, 1988); J. R. Kauffman et al., "The Construct Validity of Assessment Centre Performance Dimensions," *International Journal of Selection and Assessment* 1 (1993): 213–23.

61. G. C. Thornton, *Assessment Centers in Human Resource Management* (Reading, MA: Addison-Wesley, 1992); S. B. Parry, "How to Validate an Assessment Tool," *Training* (April 1993): 37–42; S. J. Motowidlo, M. D. Dunnette, and G. W. Carter, "An Alternative Selection Procedure: The Low-Fidelity Simulation"

Journal of Applied Psychology 75, no. 6 (1990): 640–47; W. Arthur, Jr., G. V. Barrett, and D. Doverspike, "Validation of an Information-Processing-Based Test Battery for the Prediction of Handling Accidents among Petroleum-Product Transport Drivers," *Journal of Applied Psychology* 75, no. 6 (1990): 621–28; J. S. Schippmann, E. P. Prien, and J. A. Katz, "Reliability and Validity of In-Basket Performance Measures," *Personnel Psychology* 43 (1990): 837–59; J. S. Shippman, G. L. Hughes, and E. P. Prien, "Raise Assessment Center Standards," *Personnel Journal* (July 1988): 69–79.

62. *Source:* Adapted from J. Kirksey and R. A. Zawacki, "Assessment Center Helps Find Team-Oriented Candidates," *Personnel Journal* (May 1994): 92. Used by permission.

63. For the LGD, see M. M. Petty, "A Multivariate Analysis of the Effects of Experience and Training upon Performance in a Leaderless Group Discussion," *Personnel Psychology* 27 (1974): 271–82. For business games, see B. M. Bass and G. V. Barnett, *People, Work, and Organizations,* 2nd ed. (Boston, Allyn & Bacon, 1981).

64. B. B. Gaugler et al., "Meta-analysis of Assessment Center Validity," *Journal of Applied Psychology* 72 (1987): 493–511; R. Klimoski and M. Brickner, "Why Do Assessment Centers Work? The Puzzle of Assessment Center Validity," *Personnel Psychology* 40 (1987): 243–60; A. Tziner and S. Dolan, "Validity of an Assessment Center for Identifying Female Officers in the Military," *Journal of Applied Psychology* 67 (1982): 728–36.

65. A. J. Kinicki et al., "Interviewer Predictions of Applicant Qualifications and Interviewer Validity: Aggregate and Individual Analyses," *Journal of Applied Psychology* 75 (1990): 477–86; C. L. Martin and D. H. Nagao, "Some Effects of Computerized Interviewing on Job Applicant Responses," *Journal of Applied Psychology* 74, no. 1 (1989): 72–80; W. L. Tullar, "Relational Control in the Employment Interview," *Journal of Applied Psychology* 74, no. 6 (1989): 971–77; A. Peek Phillips and R. L. Dipboye, "Correlational Tests of Predictions from a Process Model of the Interview," *Journal of Applied Psychology* 74, no. 1 (1989): 41–52; T. H. Macan and R. L. Dipboye, "The Relationship of Interviewers' Preinterview Impressions to Selection and Recruitment Outcomes," *Personnel Psychology* 43 (1990): 745–68; M. M. Harris, "Reconsidering the Employment Interview: A Review of Recent Literature and Suggestions for Future Research," *Personnel Psychology* 42 (1989): 691–726; R. A. Fear and R. J. Chiron, *The Evaluation Interview,* 4th ed. (New York: McGraw-Hill, 1990); A. H. Eagly et al., "What Is Beautiful Is Good, But. . . : A Meta-Analytic Review of Research on the Physical Attractiveness Stereotype," *Psychological Bulletin* 110, no. 1 (1991): 109–28; M. E. Heilman et al., "Has Anything Changed? Current Characterizations of Men, Women and Managers," *Journal of Applied Psychology* 74, no. 6 (1989): 935–42; M. S. Singer and C. Sewell, "Applicant Age and Selection Interview Decisions: Effect of Information Exposure on Age Discrimination in Personnel Selection," *Personnel Psychology* 42 (1989): 135–54; M. A. Hitt and S. H. Barr, "Manage-rial Selection Decision Models: Examination of Configural Cue Processing," *Journal of Applied Psychology* 74, no. 1 (1989): 53–61; B. R. Nathan and N. Tippins, "The Consequences of Halo 'Error' in Performance Ratings: A Field Study of the Moderating Effect of Halo on Test Validation Results," *Journal of Applied Psychology* 75, no. 3 (1990): 290–96; M. E. Heilman, J. C. Rivero, and J. F. Brett, "Skirting the Competence Issue: Effects of Sex-Based Preferential Selection on Task Choices of Women and Men," *Journal of Applied Psychology* 76, no. 1 (1991): 99–105; D. Arthur, *Recruiting, Interviewing, Selecting and Orienting New Employees,* 2nd ed. (New York: AMACOM, 1991); A. Feingold, "Good-Looking People Are Not What We Think," *Psychological Bulletin* 111, no. 2 (1992): 304–41; R. D. Arvey et al., "Interview Validity for Selecting Sales Clerks," *Personnel Psychology* (spring 1987): 1–12; T. W. Dougherty, R. J. Ebert, and J. C. Callendar, "Policy Capturing in the Employment Interview," *Journal of Applied Psychology* (February 1986): 9–15; G. P. Latham and L. M. Saari, "Do People Do What They Say? Further Studies on the Situational Interview," *Journal of Applied Psychology* (November 1984): 569–73; S. D. Maurer and C. Fay, "Effect of Situational Interviews and Training on Interview Rating Agreement: An Experimental Analysis," *Personnel Psychology* (summer 1988): 329–44; S. M. Raza and B. N. Carpenter, "A Model of Hiring Decisions in Real Employment Interviews," *Journal of Applied Psychology* (November 1987): 596–603; D. D. Rodgers, "Personnel Computing: Computer-Aided Interviewing Overcomes First Impressions," *Personnel Journal* (April 1987): 148–52.

66. *Source:* Adapted from "Computerized Interviews: A Wave of the Future?" *Bulletin to Management* (May 26, 1994): 167.

67. S. J. Motowidlo et al., "Studies of the Structured Behavioral Interview," *Journal of Applied Psychology* 77 (1992): 571–87; M. A. Campion, E. D. Pursell, and B. K. Brown, "Structured Interviewing: Raising the Psychometric Properties of the Employment Interview," *Personnel Psychology* 41 (1988): 25–42; M. A. McDaniel et al., "The Validity of Employment Interviews: A Comprehensive Review and Meta-Analysis," *Journal of Applied Psychology* 79 (1994): 599–616; Huffcutt and Arthur, "Hunter and Hunter (1984) Revisited."

68. T. Lin, G. H. Dobbins, and J. Farh, "A Field Study of Race and Age Similarity Effects on Interview Ratings in Conventional and Situational Interviews," *Journal of Applied Psychology* 77 (1992): 363–71.

69. "Expert Opinion—Interviewing Skills: Using Past Performance to Predict the Future," *Fair Employment Practices Guidelines* (May 25, 1993): 8. Copyrighted material reprinted with permission of *Fair Employment Practices Guidelines* and the Bureau of Business Practice, 24 Rope Ferry Rd., Waterford, CT 06386.

70. Ibid.

71. Ibid.

72. H. J. Bernardin and R. W. Beatty, *Performance Appraisal: Assessing Human Behavior at Work* (Boston: Kent, 1984), 258–60; W. C. Borman, "Format and Training Effects on Rating Accuracy Using Behavior

Scales," *Journal of Applied Psychology* 3 (1979): 103–15.

73. M. H. Peak, "Are Your Ready for ADA?" *Fair Employment Practices Guidelines* (August 1991): 14.

74. E. A. Fleishman, "Some New Frontiers in Personnel Selection Research," *Personnel Psychology* 41, no. 4 (1988): 679–702; E. A. Fleishman, *The Structure and Management of Physical Abilities* (Englewood Cliffs, NJ: Prentice-Hall, 1964); D. L. Gebhardt and C. E. Crump, *Joint Mobility Evaluation Manual for Entry Level Natural Gas Industrial Jobs* (Bethesda, MD: Advanced Research Resources Organization, 1983); D. L. Gebhardt, D. C. Meyers, and E. A. Fleishman, "Development of a Job-Related Medical Evaluation System," *San Bernardino County Medical Standard News* 1 (1984): 1–2; D. C. Meyers, M. C. Jennings, and E. A. Fleishman, *Development of Job-Related Medical Standards and Physical Tests for Court Security Officers,* ARRO final report no. 3062/r81-3 (Bethesda, MD: Advanced Research Resources Organization, 1981).

75. Olian, "New Approaches to Employment Screening," in *Readings in Personnel and Human Resource Management,* ed. Schuler, Youngblood, and Huber, 206–16.

76. R. R. Faden and N. E. Kass, "Genetic Screening Technology: Ethical Issues in Access to Tests by Employers and Health Insurance Companies," *Journal of Social Issues* 49 (1993): 75–88.

77. R. Cropanzano and K. James, "Some Methodological Considerations for the Behavioral Genetic Analysis of Work Attitudes," *Journal of Applied Psychology* 75, no. 4 (1990): 433–39; Office of Technology and Assessment, *The Role of Genetic Testing in the Prevention of Occupational Disease* (Washington, DC, 1983); Z. Haranyi and R. Hutton, *Genetic Prophecy: Beyond the Double Helix* (New York: Bantam Books, 1981).

78. "New Guide Examines State Drug Testing Laws," *Bulletin to Management* (September 15, 1994): 289; I. A. Lipman, "Fight Drugs with Workplace Tests," *New York Times* (July 18, 1993): p. F15; W. L. Holstein, "Finding a Better Way to Test for Drugs," *New York Times* (November 28, 1993): p. F11; "Employee Drug Abuse," *Bulletin to Management* (March 15, 1992): 71; J. Normand, S. D. Salyards, and J. J. Mahoney, "An Evaluation of Preemployment Drug Testing," *Journal of Applied Psychology* 75, no. 6 (1990): 629–39.

79. "Drug Policy Pointers," *Bulletin to Management* (January 7, 1988): 8. © 1988. Used by permission. See also M. A. Konovsky and R. Cropanzano, "Perceived Fairness of Employee Drug Testing as a Predictor of Employee Attitudes and Job Performance," *Journal of Applied Psychology* 76, no. 5 (1991): 698–707; "Drug Testing: Conference Policy Pointers," *Bulletin to Management* (August 7, 1986): 261–62. For more information, see B. Heshizer and J. P. Muczyk, "Drug Testing at the Workplace: Balancing Individual, Organizational and Societal Rights," *Labor Law Journal* (June 1988): 342–57; P. L. Hunsaker and C. M. Pavett, "Drug Abuse in the Brokerage Industry," *Personnel* (July 1988): 54–58; M. F. Masters, G. Ferris, and S. L. Ratcliff, "Practices and Attitudes of Substance Abuse

Testing," *Personnel Administrator* (July 1988): 72–78; J. P. Muczyk and B. P. Heshizer, "Mandatory Drug Testing: Managing the Latest Pandora's Box," *Business Horizons* (March–April 1988): 14; M. Rothman, "Random Drug Testing in the Workplace: Implications for Human Resource Management," *Business Horizons* (March–April 1988): 23; W. H. Wagel, "A Drug-Screening Policy That Safeguards Employees' Rights," *Personnel* (February 1988): 10–11.

80. "The AIDS Epidemic and Business," *Business Week* (March 23, 1987): 122; "AIDS Focus: Employee Rights and On-Site Education," *Bulletin to Management* 10 (March 1988): 74.

81. Arvey and Sackett, "Fairness in Selection"; P. E. Varca and P. Pattison, "Evidentiary Standards in Employment Discrimination: A View toward the Future," *Personnel Psychology* 46 (1993): 239–58.

82. "Americans with Disabilities Act Final Regulations," *Fair Employment Practices* (August 15, 1991); B. P. Noble, "As Seen from a Wheelchair," *New York Times* (January 26, 1992): p. F25, J. West, ed., *The Americans with Disabilities Act: From Policy to Practice* (New York: Milbank Memorial Fund, 1991).

83. Equal Employment Opportunity Commission, *"Americans with Disabilities Act,"* Technical Assistance Manual on Employment Provisions (Title I) (Washington, DC, 1992). See also R. Klimoski and S. Palmer, "The ADA and the Hiring Process in Organizations," *Consulting Psychology Journal: Practice and Research* (in press); P. M. Perry, "ADA Missteps (and How to Avoid Them)," *Training* (October 1994): 84–91.

84. T. Adler, "APA, Two Other Groups to Revise Test Standards," *APA Monitor* (September 1993): 24.

85. For the most recent information about relevant changes in the *Standards* and the *Principles,* consult current issues of the SIOP's newsletter, *The Industrial-Organizational Psychologist.* For information about the SIOP and its newsletter, contact the SIOP Administrative Office at 657 East Golf Rd., Suite 309, Arlington Heights, IL 60005.

86. R. D. Arvey and R. H. Faley, *Fairness in Selecting Employees* (Reading, MA: Addison-Wesley, 1988); R. A. Baysinger, "Disparate Treatment and Disparate Impact Theories of Discrimination," in *Readings in Personnel and Human Resource Management,* ed. Schuler, Youngblood, and Huber, 162–77; P. M. Podsakoff, M. L. Williams, and W. E. Scott, Jr., "Myths of Employee Selection Systems," in *Readings in Personnel and Human Resource Management,* ed. Schuler, Youngblood, and Huber, 178–92.

87. "Go Ahead for AA Data Disclosure," *Fair Employment Practices Guidelines* (October 29, 1987): 129. See also R. E. Biddle, *"Ward's Cove Packing v. Atonio Redefines EEO Analyses," Personnel Journal* (June 1990): 56, 59–62, 64–65.

88. J. Ledvinka and V. G. Scarpello, *Federal Regulations in Personnel and Human Resource Management* (Boston: PWS-Kent, 1990); Baysinger, "Disparate Treatment and Disparate Impact Theories"; V. L. Huber, G. B. Northcraft, and M. A. Neale, "Foibles and Fallacies in Organizational Staffing Decisions," in *Readings in Personnel and Human Resource Management,* ed. Schuler, Youngblood, and Huber.

89. Heneman and Heneman, *Staffing Organizations*.

90. Arvey and Faley, *Fairness in Selecting Employees*.

91. P. J. Dowling and R. S. Schuler, *International Dimensions of Human Resource Management* (Boston: PWS-Kent, 1990).

92. C. M. Solomon, "Staff Selection Impacts Global Success," *Personnel Journal* (January 1994): 88–101; M. A. Conway, "Reducing Expatriate Failure Rates," *Personnel Administrator* (July 1984): 31–38; J. S. Lublin, "More Spouses Receive Help in Job Searches When Executives Take Positions Overseas," *Wall Street Journal* (January 26, 1984); J. D. Heller, "Criteria for Selecting an International Manager," *Personnel* (May–June 1980): 47–55; R. L. Tung, *The New Expatriates* (Cambridge, MA: Ballinger, 1988); K. D. Stuart, "Teens Play a Role in Moves Overseas," *Personnel Journal* (March 1992): 72–77; A. K. Gupta and V. Govindarajan, "Knowledge Flows and the Structure of Control within Multinational Corporations," *Academy of Management Review* 16, no. 4 (1991): 768–92; C. A. Bartlett and S. Ghoshal, "What Is a Global Manager?" *Harvard Business Review* (September–October 1992): 132; Solomon, "Staff Selection Impacts Global Success."

93. B. R. Schlender, "Matsushita Shows How to Go Global," *Fortune* (July 11, 1994): 159–66.

94. M. E. Mendenhall, E. Dunbar, and G. R. Oddou, "Expatriate Selection, Training and Career-Pathing: A Review and Critique," *Human Resource Management* (Fall 1987): 331; M. Jelinek and N. J. Adler, "Women: World-Class Managers for Global Competition," *Executive* (February 1988): 11–20; P. Dowling and R. S. Schuler, *International Human Resource Management* (Boston: PWS-Kent, 1990); J. S. Black, M. Mendenhall, and G. Oddou, "Toward a Comprehensive Model of International Adjustment: An Integration of Multiple Theoretical Perspectives," *Academy of Management Review* 16, no. 2 (1991): 291–317; H. B. Gregersen and J. S. Black, "Antecedents to Commitment to a Parent Company and a Foreign Operation," *Academy of Management Journal* 35, (1992): 65–90.

95. "Age Bias in Germany," *Fair Employment Practices Guidelines* (December 17, 1992): 145.

96. D. Briscoe, *International Human Resource Management* (Boston: Allyn & Bacon, 1994). Used by permission of the author as adapted here.

CHAPTER 9

1. Internal company documents provided by Coca-Cola. See also J. Huey, "The World's Best Brand," *Fortune* (May 31, 1993): 44–54; and N. Nash, "Coke's Great Romanian Adventure," *New York Times* (February 26, 1995): sec. 3, 1.

2. *Source:* This feature is based on several sources, including B. Saporito, "And the Winner Is Still . . . Wal-Mart," *Fortune* (May 2, 1994): 62–70; W. C. Symonds, "Invasion of the Retail Snatchers," *Business Week* (May 9, 1994): 72, 74; S. Walton, "Sam Walton in His Own Words," *Fortune* (June 29, 1992): 98–106; B. Saporito, "A Week aboard the Wal-Mart Express," *Fortune* (August 24, 1993): 77–84; V. Johnston and H. Moore, "Pride Drives Wal-Mart to Service Excellence," *HR Magazine* (October 1991): 79–82; J. Huey, "America's Most Successful Merchant," *Fortune* (September 23, 1991): 46–59; T. C. Hayes, "Wal-Mart's Late Founder Still Stirs Stockholders," *New York Times* (June 6, 1992): 39.

    By no means is Wal-Mart without fault or criticism. For some commentary on this, particularly on its alleged hiring of low-wage Chinese workers for products made in China while running its "Made in America" campaign, see T. C. Hayes, "Wal-Mart Disputes Report on Labor," *New York Times* (December 24, 1992): pp. D1, D4. For some discussions on Wal-Mart's movements into areas that bring competition to towns, see B. J. Feder, "Messages for Mom and Pop: There's Life after Wal-Mart," *New York Times* (October 24, 1993): p. F4.

3. For some extensive treatments of this topic, see J. K. Ford et al., *Improving Training Effectiveness in Work Organizations* (Hillsdale, NJ: LEA, 1994); I. L. Goldstein, *Training in Organizations*, 3rd ed. (Pacific Grove, CA: Brooks/Cole, 1993); I. L. Goldstein et al., *Training and Development in Organizations* (San Francisco: Jossey-Bass, 1989); J. W. Pfeiffer, ed., *The 1991 Annual: Developing Human Resources* (San Diego: University Associates, 1991); L. A. Ferman et al., eds., *New Developments in Worker Training: A Legacy for the 1990s* (Madison, WI: Industrial Relations Research Association, 1990); R. R. Sims, *An Experimental Learning Approach to Employee Training Systems* (Westport, CT: Quorum Books, 1990); M. Silberman, *Active Training* (Lexington, MA: Lexington Books, 1990); J. E. Morrison, ed., *Training for Performance* (New York: John Wiley & Sons, 1991); M. London, *Managing the Training Enterprise: High-Quality, Cost-Effective Employee Training in Organizations* (San Francisco: Jossey-Bass, 1989); A. P. Carnevale, L. J. Gainer, and J. Villet, *Training America: The Organization and Strategic Role of Training* (San Francisco: Jossey-Bass, 1990); L. Nadler and Z. Nadler, eds., *The Handbook of Human Resource Development* (New York: John Wiley & Sons, 1990); M. Silver, *Competent to Manage: Approaches to Management Training and Development* (New York: Routledge, 1991); S. I. Tannenbaum and G. Yukl, "Training and Development in Work Organizations," *Annual Review of Psychology* 43 (1992): 399–441; W. R. Scott, and J. W. Meyer, "The Rise of Training Programs in Firms and Agencies: An Institutional Perspective," *Research in Organizational Behavior* 13 (1991): 297–326; R. E. Snow and J. Swanson, "Instructional Psychology: Aptitude, Adaptation, and Assessment," *Annual Review of Psychology* 43 (1992): 583–626; R. A. Noe and J. K. Ford, "Emerging Issues and New Directions for Training Research," *Research in Personnel and Human Resource Management* 10 (1992): 345–84; G. Mitchell, *The Trainer's Handbook:*

The AMA Guide to Effective Training, 2nd ed. (New York: AMACOM, 1993); G. M. Piskurich, ed. (New York: McGraw-Hill, 1992).

4. R. R. Ritti, *The Ropes to Skip and the Ropes to Know: Studies in Organizational Behavior,* 2nd ed. (Columbus, OH: Grid Publishing, 1982).

5. D. C. Feldman, "Socialization, Resocialization, and Training: Reframing the Research Agenda," in Goldstein et al., *Training and Development in Organizations,* 376–416.

6. J. Van Ahn, "The Voice of Experience," *Personnel* (January 1991): 17; J. P. Meyer et al., "Organizational Commitment and Job Performance: It's the Nature of the Commitment That Counts," *Journal of Applied Psychology* (1989): 152–56; G. H. Ironson et al., "Construction of a Job in General Scale: A Comparison of Global, Composite, and Specific Measures," *Journal of Applied Psychology* (1989): 193–200; J. E. Mathieu, "A Cross-Level Nonrecursive Model of the Antecedents of Organizational Commitment and Satisfaction," *Journal of Applied Psychology* (1991): 607–18; M. Tait, M. Y. Padgett, and T. T. Baldwin, "Job and Life Satisfaction: A Reevaluation of the Strength of the Relationship and Gender Effects as a Function of the Date of the Study," *Journal of Applied Psychology* (1989): 502–7; R. Pascale, "Fitting New Employees into the Company Culture," *Fortune* (May 28, 1984): 28–40.

7. R. E. Ganger, "HRIS Logs on to Strategic Training," *Personnel Journal* (August 1991): 50–54; B. J. Martin, P. J. Harrison, and G. Ingram, "Strategies for Training New Managers," *Personnel Journal* (November 1991): 114–17; T. R. Horton, "Training: A Key to Productivity Growth," *Management Review* (September 1983): 2–3.

8. "1994 Industry Report," *Training* (October 1994): 29–64; B. Filipczak, "Looking Past the Numbers," *Training* (October 1994): 67–81.

9. For a description of how to assess the economic utility of training, see W. F. Cascio, "Using Utility Analysis to Assess Training Outcomes," in Goldstein et al., *Training and Development in Organizations.*

10. K. Kelly and P. Burrows, "Motorola: Training for the Millennium," *Business Week* (March 28, 1994): 158–61.

11. B. Dumaine, "Those Highflying PepsiCo Managers," *Fortune* (April 10, 1989): 78–79.

12. R. Henkoff, "Companies That Train Best," *Fortune* (March 22, 1993): 62–75; R. Henkoff, "Inside Andersen's Army of Advice," (October 4, 1993): 62. For more on Motorola training, see Kelly and Burrows, "Motorola," 158–62; J. J. Laabs, "Hotels Train to Help Japanese Guests," *Personnel Journal* (September 1994): 28–35.

13. J. P. MacDuffie and T. A. Kochan, "Do U.S. Firms Underinvest in Human Resources? Determinants of Training in the World Auto Industry," *Industrial Relations* (September 1993).

14. P. Froiland, "Who's Getting Trained? *Training* (October 1993): 53–65.

15. J. Cuther-Gershenfeld et al., *The Scope and Implications of Private Employer-Specific Training Initiatives in Michigan: A Case Study Analysis* (East Lansing, MI: Social Science Research Bureau, Michigan State University, 1991).

16. G. T. Chao et al., "Organizational Socialization: Its Content and Consequences," *Journal of Applied Psychology* 79 (1994): 730–43; E. W. Morrison, "Newcomer Information Seeking: Exploring Types, Modes, Sources, and Outcomes," *Academy of Management Journal* 36 (1993): 557–89; C. Ostroff and S. W. J. Kozlowski, "Organizational Socialization as a Learning Process: The Role of Information Acquisition," *Personnel Psychology* 45 (1992): 849–74.

17. T. J. Maurer and B. A. Tarulli, "Investigation of Perceived Environment, Perceived Outcome, and Person Variables in Relationship to Voluntary Development Activity by Employees," *Journal of Applied Psychology* 79 (1994): 3–14. See also L. A. Hill, *Becoming a Manager: Mastery of a New Identity* (Cambridge, MA: Harvard Business School Press, 1992).

18. Used by permission of Siemens, Siemens, USA, New Brunswick, NJ.

19. R. Henkoff, "Finding, Training and Keeping the Best Service Workers," *Fortune* (October 3, 1994): 110–22; "Pul-eeze! Will Somebody Help Me?" *Time* (February 1987): 49.

20. W. Finn, "No Train, No Gain," *Personnel Journal* (September 1991): 95, 98; T. J. Von der Embse, "Choosing a Management Development Programs: A Decision Model, *Personnel Journal* (October 1973): 908; W. McGehee and P. W. Thayer, *Training in Business and Industry* (New York: Wiley, 1961); M. L. Moore and P. Dutton, "Training Needs Analysis."

21. L. Saari et al., "A Survey of Management Training and Education Practices in U.S. Companies," *Personnel Psychology* 41 (1988): 731–45.

22. W. F. Joyce and J. W. Slocum, "Climates in Organizations," in *Organizational Behavior,* ed. S. Kerr (San Francisco: Grid, 1979); W. F. Joyce and J. Slocum, "Climate Discrepancy: Refining the Concepts of Psychological and Organizational Climates," *Human Relations* 35 (1982): 951–72; B. Schneider, "Organizational Climates: An Essay," *Personnel Psychology* 28 (1975): 447–79; B. Schneider, "Organizational Climates: Individual Preferences and Organizational Realities Revisited," *Journal of Applied Psychology* 60 (1975): 459–65; B. Schneider and A. E. Reichers, "On the Etiology of Climates," *Personnel Psychology* 36 (1983): 19–40.

23. For a discussion of ethical corporate culture, see F. J. Aguilar, *Managing Corporate Ethics* (Oxford: Oxford Business, 1994).

24. R. W. Rogers and W. C. Byham, "Diagnosing Organization Cultures for Realignment," in *Diagnosis for Organizational Change: Methods and Models,* ed. A. Howard et al. (New York: Guilford Press, 1994); K. Fisher, "Diagnostic Issues for Work Teams," in *Diagnosis for Organizational Change,* ed. A. Howard et al.

25. K. Blanton, "Working Together: Exploring Diversity in the Workplace," *Boston Globe Special Section* (March 7, 1994): 1, 15–16. See also S. Caudron, "Training Can Damage Diversity Efforts," *Personnel Journal* (April 1993): 51–62; "1993 SHRM/CCH Survey: Diversity Management Is a Culture Change, Not

Just Training," part II, *Human Resources Management* (May 26, 1993).

26. B. Z. Posner and W. H. Schmidt, "Values of American Managers: Then and Now," *HR Focus* (March 1992): 13.

27. "Ethics Exams: Focus for Too Few?" *Bulletin to Management* (February 19, 1987): 64; R. W. Goodard, "Are You an Ethical Manager?" *Personnel Journal* (March 1988): 38–47; "Policy Guide," *Bulletin to Management* (December 18, 1986): 420; "Values and Ethics," *HR Reporter* (March 1987): 3.

28. Posner and Schmidt, "Values of American Managers."

29. *Source:* Based on P. Cappelli and A. Crocker-Hefter, *Distinctive Human Resources Are the Core Competencies of Firms,* report no. R117Q00011-91 (Washington, DC: U.S. Department of Education, 1994).

30. J. Lynch and D. Orne, "The Next Elite: Manufacturing Supermanagers," *Management Review* (April 1985): 49.

31. J. W. Walker, "Training and Development," in *Human Resource Management in the 1980s,* ed. R. S. Schuler and S. Carroll (Washington, DC: Bureau of National Affairs, 1983); I. L. Goldstein, *Training: Program Development and Evaluation* (Monterey, CA: Brooks/Cole, 1986); Wexley and Latham, *Developing and Training.*

32. For more discussion of the advantages and disadvantages of basic assessment techniques, see I. L. Goldstein, "Training in Work Organizations," in *Handbook of Industrial and Organizational Psychology,* vol. 2, 507–620.

33. L. A. Berger, "A DEW Line for Training and Development: The Needs Analysis Survey," *Personnel Administrator* (November 1976): 51–55.

34. H. Holzer et al., "Are Training Subsidies for Firms Effective? The Michigan Experience," *Industrial and Labor Relations Review* (1994).

35. P. Stuart, "New Directions in Training Individuals," *Personnel Journal* (September 1992): 86–99.

36. D. Anfuso, "Self-Directed Skills Building Drives Quality," *Personnel Journal* (April 1994): 84–93; R. B. McAfee and P. J. Champagne, "Employee Development: Discovering Who Needs What," *Personnel Administrator* (February 1988): 92–93.

37. "Waste Management: Building an Ethical Culture," *HR Reporter* (April 1991): 1–3.

38. Latham, "Human Resource Training and Development."

39. *Source:* D. Anfuso, *Self-Directed Skills Building Drives Quality,*" *Personnel Journal* (April 1994): 84–93. Used by permission.

40. C. Berryman-Fink, "Male and Female Managers' View of the Communication Skills and Training Needs of Women in Management," *Public Personnel Management* 14 (1985): 307–14; Latham, "Human Resource Training and Development"; F. D. Tucker, "A Study of Training Needs of Older Workers: Implications for Human Resources Development Planning," *Public Personnel Management* 14 (1985): 85–95.

41. M. E. Gist, A. G. Bavetta, and C. K. Stevens, "Transfer Training Method: Its Influence on Skill Generalization, Skill Repetition, and Performance Level," *Personnel Psychology* 43 (1990): 501–23; N. Schmitt, J. R. Schneider, and S. A. Cohen, "Factors Affecting Validity of a Regionally Administered Assessment Center," *Personnel Psychology* 43 (1990): 1–12; M. J. Kruger and G. D. May, "Two Techniques to Ensure That Training Programs Remain Effective," *Personnel Journal* (October 1985): 70–75; E. E. Lawler III, "Education Management Style and Organizational Effectiveness," *Personnel Psychology* (spring 1985): 1–17; M. London and S. Stumpf, "Individual and Organizational Career Development in Changing Times," in *Career Development in Organizations,* ed. D. T. Hahl (San Francisco: Jossey-Bass, 1986).

42. J. J. Laabs, "Kinney Narrows the Gender Gap," *Personnel Journal* (August 1994): 83–88; J. Main, "The Executive Yearn to Learn," *Fortune* (May 3, 1982): 234–48; M. M. Starcevich and J. A. Sykes, "Internal Advanced Management Programs for Executive Development," *Personnel Administrator* (June 1982): 27–28.

43. D. C. Feldman, *Managing Careers in Organizations* (Glenview, IL: Scott, Foresman, 1988); M. W. McCall, M. M. Lombardo, and A. M. Morrison, *The Lessons of Experience: How Successful Executives Develop on the Job* (Lexington, MA: Lexington Books, 1988); C. D. McCauley et al., "Assessing the Developmental Components of Managerial Jobs," *Journal of Applied Psychology* 79 (1994): 544–60.

44. P. J. Ohlott, M. N. Ruderman, and C. D. McCauley, "Gender Differences in Managers' Developmental Job Experiences," *Academy of Management Journal* 37 (1994): 46–67.

45. L. Nadler and Z. Nadler, *Designing Training Programs: The Critical Events Model* (Houston, TX: Gulf Publishing Co., 1994).

46. "Medtronic Expects Managers to Value Differences," *HR Reporter* (February 1993): 3.

47. M. E. Gist, C. Schwoerer, and B. Rosen, "Effects of Alternative Training Methods on Self-Efficacy and Performance in Computer Software Training," *Journal of Applied Psychology* 74 (1989): 884–91; "AMA Designs Training Program for Use on Personal Computers," *AMA Forum* (December 1983): 29–30; W. C. Heck, "Computer-Based Training—The Choice Is Yours," *Personnel Administrator* (February 1985): 39–46; V. L. Huber and G. Gray, "Channeling New Technology to Improve Training," *Personnel Administrator* (February 1985): 49–57; G. Kearsley, *Computer-Based Training: A Guide to Selection and Implementation* (Reading, MA: Addison-Wesley, 1983); S. Schwade, "Is It Time to Consider Computer Based Training?" *Personnel Administrator* (February 1985): 25–35.

48. K. Kraiger, J. K. Ford, and E. Salas, "Application of Cognitive, Skill-Based, and Affective Theories of Learning Outcomes to New Methods of Training Evaluation," *Journal of Applied Psychology* 78 (1993): 311–28.

49. "Orientation Goals: Better Learning, Reduced Turnover," *Bulletin to Management* (May 9, 1985): 1–2.

50. C. H. Deutsch, "Vocational Schools in a Comeback," *New York Times* (July 21, 1991): p. F21.

51. "Employee Development Drives Growth," *Personnel Journal* (January 1993): 61; J. J. Laabs, "Business

Growth Driven by Staff Development," *Personnel Journal* (April 1993): 120–35.

52. S. Gordon, *Systematic Training Program Design: Maximizing Effectiveness and Minimizing Liability* (Englewood Cliffs, NJ: Prentice-Hall, 1994).

53. L. S. Richman, "The New Worker Elite," *Fortune* (August 22, 1994): 56–66.

54. S. Caudron, "Volunteer Efforts Offer Low-Cost Training Options," *Personnel Journal* (June 1994): 38–44; V. Larson, "Program Challenges Top Executives," *Personnel Journal* (May 1994): 54–62; J. Bennet, "Team Spirit Is New Message at Olds," *New York Times* (June 23, 1994): pp. D1, D15; K. Johnson, "Corporate Conscience: Insurer Gives Retreat a Social Mission," *New York Times* (July 2, 1994): 24. See also T. T. Baldwin, "Effects of Alternative Modeling Strategies on Outcomes of Interpersonal-Skills Training," *Journal of Applied Psychology* 77 (1992): 147–54.

55. *Source:* Adapted from "Experiential Board Games— More Relevant Than Rock Climbing," *HR Reporter* (November 1993): 5.

56. "How Does Disney Do It?" *Personnel Journal* (December 1989): 50–57; S. Toy and C. Green, "Roy Disney's Adventures in Tomorrowland," *Business Week* (August 5, 1985): 66–67; G. E. Willigan, "The Value-Adding CFO: An Interview with Disney's Gary Wilson," *Harvard Business Review* (January–February 1990): 85–93; S. Greenhouse, "Playing Disney in the Parisian Fields," *New York Times* (February 17, 1991): 1, 6; J. J. Laabs, "Disney Helps Keep Kids in School," *Personnel Journal* (November 1992): 58–68; "Disney," *Personnel Journal* (January 1992): 58.

57. J. Barling and R. Beattie, "Self-Efficacy Beliefs and Sales Performance," *Journal of Organizational Behavior Management* 5 (1983): 41–51; A. Bandura, "Self-Efficacy: Toward a Unifying Theory of Behavioral Change," *Psychological Review* 84 (1977): 191–215.

58. H. W. Marsh, G. E. Richards, and J. Barnes, "Multidimensional Self-Concepts: The Effects of Participation in an Outward Bound Program," *Journal of Personality and Social Psychology* 50 (1986): 195–204; H. W. Marsh, G. E. Richards, and J. Barnes, "A Long-Term Follow-up of the Effects of Participation in an Outward Bound Program, *"Personality and Social Psychology Bulletin* 12 (1987): 465–92.

59. Goldstein, *Training;* B. M. Bass and J. A. Vaughan, *Training in Industry: The Management of Learning* (Belmont, CA: Wadsworth, 1966), 88.

60. L. A. Ferman et al., *Worker Training: A Legacy for the 1990s* (Madison, WI: Industrial Relations Research Association, 1990); A. P. Carnevale, L. J. Gainer, and A. S. Meltzer, *Workplace Basics Training Manual* (San Francisco: Jossey-Bass, 1990); T. T. Baldwin, R. J. Magjuka, and B. T. Loher, "The Perils of Participation: Effects of Choice of Training on Trainee Motivation and Learning," *Personnel Psychology* 44 (1991): 51–65; A. P. Carnevale, L. J. Gainer, and E. Schulz, *Training the Technical Work Force* (San Francisco: Jossey-Bass, 1990); Goldstein, *Training.*

61. Bureau of National Affairs, "Planning the Training Program," *Personnel Management, BNA Policy and Practice Series* 41 (Washington, DC, 1975), 205; see also Bass and Vaughan, *Training in Industry,* 89–90;

J. M. Geddes, "Germany Profits by Apprentice System," *Wall Street Journal* (September 15, 1981): 33.

62. S. Overman, "Apprenticeships Smooth School to Work Transitions," *HR Magazine* (December 1990): 40–43; K. Matthes, "Apprenticeships Can Support the 'Forgotten Youth,' " *HR Focus* (December 1991): 19; "Focus at Ford Is Education for the Sake of Education," *GED on TV* (July–August 1993): 3; E. Kiester, "Germany Prepares Kids for Good Jobs; We Are Preparing Ours for Wendy's," *Smithsonian* (March 1993): 44–55.

63. M. W. McCall, Jr., M. M. Lombardo, and A. M. Morrison, *The Lessons of Experience: How Successful Executives Develop on the Job* (Lexington, MA: Lexington Books, 1989); T. Delone, "What Do Middle Managers Really Want from First-Line Supervisors?" *Supervisory Management* (September 1977): 8–12; W. E. Sasser, Jr., and F. S. Leonard, "Let First Level Supervisors Do Their Job," *Harvard Business Review* (March–April 1980): 113–21; L. R. Sheeran and D. Fenn, "The Mentor System," *Inc.* (June 1987): 138–42; Woodlands Group, "Management Development Roles: Coach, Sponsor, and Mentor," *Personnel Journal* (November 1980): 918–21.

64. R. F. Morrison and J. Adams, eds., *Contemporary Career Development Issues* (Hillsdale, NJ: Lawrence Erlbaum Associates, 1991); A. Saltzman, *Down-Shifting: Reinventing Success—on a Slower Track* (New York: Harper Collins, 1991); S. L. Willis and S. S. Dubin, eds., *Maintaining Professional Competence: Approaches to Career Enhancement, Vitality and Success throughout a Work Life* (San Francisco: Jossey-Bass, 1990); J. A. Schneer and F. Reitman, "Effects of Employment Gaps on the Careers of M.B.A.'s: More Damaging for Men than for Women? *Academy of Management Journal* 33 (1990): 391–406; J. H. Greenhaus, S. Parasuraman, and W. M. Wormley, "Effects of Race on Organizational Experiences, Job Performance Evaluations and Career Outcomes," *Academy of Management Journal* 33 (1990): 64–86; N. Nicholson and M. West, *Managerial Job Change: Men and Women in Transition* (Cambridge: University of Cambridge Press, 1988); S. J. M. Freeman, *Managing Lives: Corporate Women and Social Change* (Amherst, MA: University of Massachusetts Press, 1990).

65. S. Bartlett, "Our Intrepid Reporter Wheels and Deals Currencies," *Business Week* (February 1, 1988): 70–71; N. Madlin, "Computer-Based Training Comes of Age," *Personnel* (November 1987): 64–65.

66. "B-School Faculty Quality Training," *Fortune* (January 13, 1992): 14. See also W. Wiggenhorn, "Motorola U: When Training Becomes an Education," *Harvard Business Review* (July–August 1990): 71–83.

67. J. Bolt, *Executive Development* (New York: Harper & Row, 1989); A. A. Vicere and K. R. Graham, "Crafting Competitiveness: Toward a New Paradigm for Executive Development," *Human Resource Planning* 13 (1990): 281–96; J. K. Berry, "Linking Management Development to Business Strategies," *Training and Development Journal* (August 1990): 20–22.

68. G. S. Odiorne and G. A. Rummler, *Training and Development: A Guide for Professionals* (Chicago: Commerce Clearing House, 1988); D. Torrence, "How

Video Can Help," *Training and Development Journal* (December 1985): 122–30; M. Piedmont, "Put Computer Software Training $$$ to Better Use," *HR Focus* (November 1991): 13.

69. G. C. Thornton III and J. N. Cleveland, "Developing Managerial Talent through Simulation," *American Psychologist* (February 1990): 190–99; G. Waddell, "Simulations: Balancing the Pros and Cons," *Training and Development Journal* (January 1982): 75–80.

70. For an excellent discussion of assessment centers, see G. C. Thornton III, *Assessment Centers* (Reading, MA: Addison-Wesley, 1992); V. R. Boehm, "Assessment Centers and Management Development," in *Personnel Management,* ed. K. M. Rowland and G. Ferris (Boston: Allyn & Bacon, 1982), 327–62; R. B. Finkle, "Managerial Assessment Centers," in *Handbook of Industrial and Organizational Psychology,* ed. M. D. Dunnette (Chicago: Rand McNally, 1976), 861–88; I. T. Robertson and S. Downs, "Work-Sample Tests of Trainability: A Meta-Analysis, *Journal of Applied Psychology* 74 (1989): 402–10; V. J. Marsick and K. Watkins, *Informal and Incidental Learning in the Workplace* (New York: Routledge, 1991).

71. S. Carey, "These Days More Managers Play Games, Some Made in Japan, as a Part of Training," *Wall Street Journal* (October 7, 1982): 35.

72. J. P. Campbell et al., *Managerial Behavior, Performance, and Effectiveness* (New York: McGraw-Hill, 1970); B. Mezoff, "Human Relations Training: The Tailored Approach," *Personnel* (March–April 1981): 21–27.

73. "Downward Bound," *Fortune* (August 15, 1988): 83.

74. L. W. Hellervich, J. F. Hazucha, and R. J. Schneider, "Behavior Change: Models, Methods, and a Review of Evidence," in *Handbook of Industrial and Organizational Psychology,* vol. 3.

75. V. L. Huber, "A Comparison of Goal Setting and Pay as Learning Incentives," *Psychological Reports* 56 (1985): 223–35; V. L. Huber, "Interplay between Goal Setting and Promises of Pay-for-Performance on Individual and Group Performance: An Operant Interpretation," *Journal of Organizational Behavior Management* 7 (1986): 45–64.

76. Latham, "Human Resource Training and Development"; C. A. Frayne, *Reducing Employee Absenteeism through Self-Management Training: A Research-Based Analysis and Guide* (Westport, CT: Quorum Books, 1991); A. Bandura, "Self Efficacy Mechanisms in Human Agency," *American Psychologist* 37 (1982): 122–47; A. Bandura, *Social Foundations of Thought and Action* (Englewood Cliffs, NJ: Prentice-Hall, 1986); M. E. Gist, "Self Efficacy: Implications for Organizational Behavior and Human Resource Management," *Academy of Management Review* 12 (1987): 472–85; M. E. Gist, C. Schwoerer, and B. Rosen, "Modeling versus Nonmodeling: The Impact of Self Efficacy and Performance in Computer Training for Managers," *Personnel Psychology* (1989); Latham, "Human Resource Training and Development."

77. J. K. Harrison, "Individual and Combined Effects of Behavior Modeling and the Cultural Assimilator in Cross-Cultural Management Training," *Journal of Applied Psychology* 77 (1992): 952–62.

78. S. J. Ashford and A. S. Tsui, "Self-Regulation for Managerial Effectiveness: The Role of Active Feedback Seeking," *Academy of Management Journal* 34 (1991): 251–80; S. I. Tannenbaum et al., "Meeting Trainees' Expectations: The Influence of Training Fulfillment on the Development of Commitment, Self-Efficacy and Motivation," *Journal of Applied Psychology* 76 (1991): 759–69; M. E. Gist, "The Influence of Training Method on Self-Efficacy and Idea Generation among Managers," *Personnel Psychology* 42 (1989): 787–805; Bandura, "Self Efficacy Mechanisms"; Bandura, *Social Foundations.*

79. Huber, "Interplay between Goal Setting and Promises of Pay-for-Performance"; J. D. Eyring, D. Steele Johnson, and D. J. Francis, "A Cross-Level Units-of-Analysis Approach to Individual Differences in Skill Acquisition," *Journal of Applied Psychology* 78 (1993): 805–14; P. C. Earley, "Self or Group? Cultural Effects of Training on Self-Efficacy and Performance," *Administrative Science Quarterly* 39 (1994): 89–117.

80. V. L. Huber, G. P. Latham, and E. A. Locke, "The Management of Impressions through Goal Setting," in *Impression Management in the Organization,* ed. R. A. Giacalone and P. Rosenfield (Hillsdale, NJ: Erlbaum, 1989); D. R. Ilgen, C. D. Fisher, and M. S. Taylor, "Consequences of Individual Feedback on Behavior in Organizations," *Journal of Applied Psychology* 64 (1979): 349–71; E. A. Locke, "Effects of Knowledge of Results, Feedback in Relation to Standards, and Goals on Reaction-Time Performance," *American Journal of Psychology* 81 (1968): 566–75.

81. P. Hogan, M. Hakel, and P. Decker, "Effects of Trainee-Generated vs. Trainer-Provided Rule Codes on Generalization in Behavioral Modeling Training," *Journal of Applied Psychology* 71 (1986): 469–73.

82. J. E. Driskell, C. Copper, and A. Moran, "Does Mental Practice Enhance Performance?" *Journal of Applied Psychology* 79 (1994): 481–92.

83. W. Honig, *Operant Behavior* (New York: Appleton-Century-Crofts, 1966); Huber, "Interplay between Goal Setting and Promises of Pay-for-Performance"; J. S. Russel, K. Wexley, and J. Hunter, "Questioning the Effectiveness of Behavior Modeling Training in an Industrial Setting," *Personnel Psychology* 34 (1984): 465–82.

84. C. Frayne and G. P. Latham, "The Application of Social Learning Theory to Employee Self-Management of Attendance," *Journal of Applied Psychology* 72 (1987): 387–92; Latham, "Human Resource Training and Development."

85. "A Comparison of Goal Setting and Pay"; V. L. Huber, E. Locke, and G. Latham, *Goal Setting: A Motivational Technique That Works* (Englewood Cliffs, NJ: Prentice-Hall, 1984).

86. *Source:* Based on R. Kanfer and P. L. Ackerman, "Motivation and Cognitive Abilities: An Integrative/Aptitude-Treatment Interactive Approach to Skill Acquisition," *Journal of Applied Psychology* 74 (1989): 657–90.

87. J. Fierman, "Shaking the Blue-Collar Blues," *Fortune* (April 22, 1991): 209–10, 214–18; S. R. Siegel, "Improving the Effectiveness of Management Development Programs," *Personnel Journal* (October 1981): 770–73.

88. "Personal Supervisory Liability," *Fair Employment Practices Guidelines* (May 25, 1993): 5–6; "Teaching Tolerance in the Workplace," *Fair Employment Practices Guidelines* (February 10, 1994): 3–5; B. P. Noble, "An Employee-Rights Minefield," *New York Times* (May 30, 1993): p. F25.

89. "The Job Training Partnership Act," *Bulletin to Management* (April 23, 1992): 124–25; J. J. Laabs, "How Federally Funded Training Helps Business," *Personnel Journal* (March 1992): 35–37; S. B. Garland, "Ninety Days to Learn to Scrub? Sure, if Uncle Sam's Paying," *Business Week* (January 20, 1992): 70–73. Changes may be made to the Job Training Partnership Act, enacted as the Reemployment Act. For details, see B. Geber, "Can the Federal Job-Training System Be Rebuilt?" *Training* (September 1994): 31–35.

90. J. W. Walker, "Managing Human Resources in Flat, Lean and Flexible Organizations: Trends for the 1990s," *Human Resource Planning* 11 (1988): 124–32.

91. J. Fulkerson and R. S. Schuler, "Managing Worldwide Diversity at Pepsi-Cola International," in *Working through Diversity: Human Resources Initiatives,* ed. S. E. Jackson (New York: Guilford Publications, 1992), 248–78; P. Sellers, "Pepsi Opens a Second Front," *Fortune* (August 8, 1994): 71–76.

92. *Source:* Adapted from J. J. Laabs, "How Gillette Grooms Global Talent," *Personnel Journal* (August 1993): 65–76. Used by permission.

93. A. Rahim, "A Model for Developing Kay Expatriate Executives," *Personnel Journal* (April 1983): 315.

94. See note 63. See also M. Forsberg, "Cultural Training Improves with Asian Clients," *Personnel Journal* (May 1993): 80–89.

95. *Developing Effective Global Managers for the 1990s* (New York: Business International, 1991), 38.

96. C. G. Howard, "How Best to Integrate Expatriate Managers in the Domestic Organization," *Personnel Administrator* (July 1982): 27–33; A. Kupfer, "How to Be a Global Manager," *Fortune* (March 14, 1988): 52–58; M. E. Mendenhall, E. Dunbar, and G. R. Oddou, "Expatriate Selection, Training and Career-Pathing: A Review and Critique," *Human Resource Management* 26 (fall 1987): 331–45; F. Rice, "Should You Work for a Foreigner?" *Fortune* (August 1, 1988): 123–34; N. Shahzad, "The American Expatriate Manager," *Personnel Administrator* (July 1984): 23–28.

97. J. C. Roberts, "Section 401(k) and the Expatriate Employee," *Personnel Administrator* (July 1984): 18–21. For related issues, see R. L. Tung, *The New Expatriates* (Boston, Ballinger, 1988).

◆ CHAPTER 10

1. G. E. Forward et al., "Mentofacturing: A Vision for American Industrial Excellence," *Academy of Management Executive* 5 (1991): 32–44.

2. *Source:* This feature is drawn from L. Brokaw, "The Mystery-Shopper Questionnaire," *Inc.* (June 1991): 94–97. For more information see *Au Bon Pain 1993 Annual Report;* K. Mullins, *Smith Barney Report, Au Bon Pain* (New York: Smith Barney, August 16, 1994.)

3. H. S. Feild and W. H. Holley, "The Relationship of Performance Appraisal System Characteristics to Verdicts in Selected Employment Discrimination Cases," *Academy of Management Journal* 25 (1982): 392–406; D. L. De Vries et al., *Performance Appraisal on the Line* (Greensboro, NC: Center for Creative Leadership, 1986).

4. R. L. Cardy and G. H. Dobbins, *Performance Appraisal: Alternative Perspectives* (Cincinnati: South Western Publishing Co., 1994); "The Power of Performance Appraisals," *Bulletin to Management* (February 10, 1994): 48; J. A. Austin and P. Villanova, "The Criterion Problem: 1917–1992," *Journal of Applied Psychology* 77 (1992): 1–35; J. N. Cleveland, K. R. Murphy, and R. E. Williams, "Multiple Uses of Performance Appraisal: Prevalence and Correlates," *Journal of Applied Psychology* 74 (February 1989); K. R. Murphy and J. N. Cleveland, *Performance Appraisal: An Organizational Perspective* (Boston: Allyn & Bacon, 1991).

5. N. Napier and G. P. Latham, "Outcome Expectancies of People Who Conduct Performance Appraisal," *Personnel Psychology* (1986): 827–37; C. E. Schneier, "Implementing Performance Management and Recognition and Rewards (PMRR) Systems at the Strategic Level: A Line Management Driven Effort," *Human Resource Planning* (1989): 205–20.

6. M. Rozek, "Can You Spot a Peak Performer?" *Personnel Journal* (June 1991): 77–78.

7. P. Sellers, "Pepsi Opens a Second Front," *Fortune* (August 8, 1994): 71–76; J. Fulkerson and R. S. Schuler, "Managing Worldwide Diversity at Pepsi-Cola International," in *Diversity in the Workplace: Human Resources Initiatives,* ed. S. E. Jackson (New York: Guilford Publications, 1992).

8. "You Don't Say: Performance Management Isn't Perfect," *Personnel Journal* (March 1994): 19; J. E. Butler, G. R. Ferris, and N. K. Napier, *Strategy and Human Resource Management* (Cincinnati: South Western Publishing, 1991); R. D. Pritchard, *Measuring and Improving Organizational Productivity: A Practical Guide* (New York: Praeger, 1990); R. D. Pritchard et al., "The Evaluation of an Integrated Approach to Measuring Organizational Productivity," *Personnel Psychology* 42 (1989): 69–115; S. B. MacKenzie, P. M. Podsakoff, and R. Fetter, "Organizational Citizenship Behavior and Objective Productivity as Determinants of Managerial Evaluations of Salesperson's Performance," *Organizational Behavior and Human Decision Processes* 50 (1991): 123–50; J. Hogan and R. Hogan, "How to Measure Employee Reliability," *Journal of Applied Psychology* 47, no. 2 (1989): 273–79; T.

McDonald, "The Effect of Dimension Content on Observation and Ratings of Job Performance," *Organizational Behavior and Human Decision Processes* 48 (1991): 252–71; B. M. Staw and R. D. Boettger, "Task Revision: A Neglected Form of Work Performance," *Academy of Management Journal* 33, no. 3 (1990): 534–59; J. A. Weekley and J. A. Gier, "Ceilings in the Reliability and Validity of Performance Ratings: The Case of Expert Raters," *Academy of Management Journal* 32, no. 1 (1989): 213–22.

9. For a practical guide to performance appraisal, see R. T. Sachs, *Productive Performance Appraisals* (New York: AMACOM, 1992).

10. The importance of this is further emphasized by the ADA; see "Problem of the Month: Performance Appraisals and the ADA," *Fair Employment Practices Guidelines* (September 1992): 3–5.

11. D. I. Rosen, "Appraisals Can Make-or-Break-Your Court Case," *Personnel Journal* (November 1992): 113–18.

12. H. J. Bernardin and W. F. Cascio, "Performance Appraisal and the Law," in *Readings in Personnel and Human Resource Management,* 3d ed., ed. R. S. Schuler, S. A. Youngblood, and V. L. Huber (St. Paul, West Publishing Co., 1988), 239; G. V. Barrett and M. C. Kernan, "Performance Appraisal and Terminations: A Review of Court Decisions since *Brito v. Zia* with Implications for Personnel Practices," *Personnel Journal* (autumn 1987): 489.

13. D. W. Organ, *Organizational Citizenship Behavior: The Good Soldier Syndrome* (Lexington, MA: Heath, 1988); D. W. Organ, "The Motivational Basis of Organizational Citizenship Behavior," *Research in Organizational Behavior* 12 (1990): 43–72.

14. W. C. Borman and S. J. Motowidlo, "Expanding the Criterion Domain to Include Elements of Contextual Performance," in *Personnel Selection in Organizations,* ed. N. Schmitt et al. (San Francisco: Jossey-Bass, 1993), 71–99.

15. J. P. Campbell et al., "A Theory of Performance," in *Personnel Selection in Organizations,* ed. Schmitt et al., 35–70.

16. A. M. Mohrman, S. M. Resnick-West, and E. E. Lawler III, *Designing Performance Appraisal Systems* (San Francisco: Jossey-Bass, 1989), 119–20; R. Johnson and R. D. Bretz, Jr., *Research and Applications of the Processes of Performance Appraisal: An Annotated Bibliography of Recent Literature, 1981–1989* (Monticello, IL: Vance Bibliographies, 1991).

17. P. O. Kingstrom and L. E. Mainstone, "An Investigation of Rater Ratee Acquaintance and Rater Bias," *Academy of Management Journal* 28 (1985): 641–53; K. R. Murphy, "Dimensions of Job Performance," in *Testing: Theoretical and Applied Perspectives,* ed. R. Dillion (New York: Praeger, 1992).

18. Murphy and Cleveland, *Performance Appraisal.*

19. H. J. Bernardin and J. Abbot, "Predicting (and Preventing) Differences between Self and Supervisory Appraisals," *Personnel Administrator* (June 1985): 151–57; A. S. Tsui and C. A. O'Reilly III, "Beyond Simple Demographic Effects: The Importance of Relational Demography in Superior-Subordinate Dyads," *Academy of Management Journal* 32, no. 2

(1989): 402–23; B. B. Gaugler and A. S. Rudolph, "The Influence of Assessee Performance Variation on Assessor's Judgments," *Personnel Psychology* 45 (1992): 77–98; W. C. Borman et al., "Models of Supervisory Job Performance Ratings," *Journal of Applied Psychology* 76, no. 6 (1991): 863–72; R. A. Jako and K. R. Murphy, "Distributional Ratings, Judgment Decomposition, and Their Impact on Interrater Agreement and Rating Accuracy," *Journal of Applied Psychology* 75, no. 5 (1990): 500–505; S. J. Ashford, "Self-Assessments in Organizations: A Literature Review and Integrative Model," *Research in Organizational Behavior* 11 (1989): 133–74; T. H. Shore, L. M. Shore, and G. C. Thornton III, "Construct Validity of Self- and Peer Evaluations of Performance Dimensions in an Assessment Center," *Journal of Applied Psychology* 77, no. 1 (1992): 42–54; S. Fox, Z. Ben-Nahum, and Y. Yinon, "Perceived Similarity and Accuracy of Peer Ratings," *Journal of Applied Psychology* 74, no. 5 (1989): 781–86; L. K. Trevino and B. Victor, "Peer Reporting of Unethical Behavior: A Social Context Perspective," *Academy of Management Journal* 35, no. 1 (1992): 38–64; J. L. Farh, G. H. Dobbins, and B. S. Cheng, "Cultural Relativity in Action: A Comparison of Self-Ratings Made by Chinese and U.S. Workers," *Personnel Psychology* 44 (1991): 129–47.

20. J. L. Farh and J. Werbel, "Effects of Purpose of the Appraisal and Expectation of Validation on Self Appraisal Leniency," *Journal of Applied Psychology* 71 (1986): 527–29; R. P. Steel and N. K. Ovalle, "Self Appraisal Based on Supervisory Feedback," *Personnel Psychology* 37 (1984): 667–85; P. R. Sackett, C. L. Z. DuBois, and A. W. Noe, "Tokenism in Performance Evaluation: The Effects of Work Group Representation on Male-Female and White-Black Differences in Performance Ratings," *Journal of Applied Psychology* 76, no. 2 (1991): 263–67; D. A. Waldman and B. J. Avolio, "Race Effects in Performance Evaluations: Controlling for Ability, Education and Experience," *Journal of Applied Psychology* 76, no. 6 (1991): 897–901; P. R. Sackett and C. L. Z. DuBois, "Rater-Ratee Race Effects on Performance Evaluation: Challenging Meta-Analytic Conclusions," *Journal of Applied Psychology* 76, no. 6 (1991): 873–77; E. D. Pulakos et al., "Examination of Race and Sex Effects on Performance Ratings," *Journal of Applied Psychology* 74, no. 5 (1989): 770–80; B. S. Klaas and A. S. DeNisi, "Managerial Reactions to Employee Dissent: The Impact of Grievance Activity on Performance Ratings," *Academy of Management Journal* 32, no. 4 (1989): 705–17; J. W. Smither, H. Collins, and R. Buda, "When Ratee Satisfaction Influences Performance Evaluations: A Case of Illusory Correlation," *Journal of Applied Psychology* 74, no. 4 (1989): 599–605.

21. "Measuring Performance: Employee Initiated Reviews," *Inc.* (July 1991): 80. See also P. Lanza, "Team Appraisals," *Personnel Journal* (March 1985): 50; J. D. Coombe, "Peer Review: The Emerging Successful Application," *Employee Relations Law Journal* (spring 1984): 659–71; J. S. Kane and E. E. Lawler III, "Methods of Peer Assessment," *Psychological Bulletin* 3

(1978): 555–86; G. M. McEvoy, P. F. Buller, and S. R. Roghaar, "A Jury of One's Peers," *Personnel Administrator* (May 1988): 94–98; L. Reibstein, "More Firms Use Peer Review Panel to Resolve Employee's Grievances," *Wall Street Journal* (December 3, 1986): 25; J. Zigon, "Making Performance Appraisal Work for Teams," *Training* (June 1994): 58–63.

22. Shore, Shore, and Thornton, "Construct Validity of Self- and Peer Evaluations"; R. Saavedra and S. K. Kwun, "Peer Evaluation in Self-Managing Work Groups," *Journal of Applied Psychology* 78 (1993): 450–62.

23. *Source:* Based on J. L. Farh, G. H. Dobbins, and B. S. Cheng, "Cultural Relativity in Action: A Comparison of Self-Ratings Made by Chinese and U.S. Workers," *Personnel Psychology* 44 (1991): 129–47.

24. Discussions between company officials and V. L. Huber. See also C. A. Norman and R. A. Zawacki, "Team Appraisals—Team Approach," *Personnel Journal* (September 1991): 101–4; J. Fitz-Enz and J. Rodgers, "Get Quality Performance from Professional Staff," *Personnel Journal* (May 1991): 22–24; L. Thornburg, "Performance Measures That Work," *HR Magazine* (May 1991): 35–38; T. Slater, "Get It Right the First Time," *Personnel Journal* (September 1991): 35–40.

25. Bernardin and Abbott, "Predicting Differences."

26. *HR Focus* 71, no. 3; "Upward Appraisals Rate Highly," *Bulletin to Management* (March 31, 1994): 104.

27. D. Antonioni, "The Effects of Feedback Accountability on Upward Appraisal Ratings," *Personnel Psychology* 47 (1994): 349–360.

28. T. L. Griffith, "Teaching Big Brother to Be a Team Player: Computer Monitoring and Quality," *Academy of Management Executive* 7 (1993): 73–80.

29. 'Workplace Monitoring: The End of Employee Privacy?" *Bulletin to Management* (August 18, 1994): 258.

30. *Conditions of Work Digest: Worker's Privacy* (Albany, NY: ILO Publication Center, 49 Sheridan Ave., Albany, NY 12210, [518] 436-9686).

31. R. J. Greene, "A '90s Model for Performance Management," *HR Magazine* (April 1991): 62–65.

32. *Source:* Adapted from "Electronic Employee Monitoring," *Fair Employment Practices Guidelines* (June 25, 1993): 8. Used by permission. See also J. J. Laabs, "Surveillance: Tool or Trap?" *Personnel Journal* (June 1992): 96–104; A. Gabor, *New York Times* (January 26, 1992): 1, 6; R. D. Gatewood and A. B. Carroll, "Assessment of Ethical Performance of Organization Members: A Conceptual Framework," *Academy of Management Review* 16, no. 4 (1991): 667–90; R. G. Eccles, "The Performance Measurement Manifesto," *Harvard Business Review* (January–February 1991): 131–37.

33. W. F. Cascio and H. J. Bernardin, "Implications of Performance Appraisal Litigation for Personnel Decisions," *Personnel Psychology* 34 (1981): 211–26.

34. R. Jacobs and S. W. J. Kozlowski, "A Closer Look at Halo Error in Performance Ratings," *Academy of Management Journal* (March 1985): 201–12; L. M. King, J. E. Hunter, and F. L. Schmidt, "Halo in a Multi-Dimensional Forced Choice Performance Evaluation Scale," *Journal of Applied Psychology* 65 (1980): 507–16.

35. K. N. Wexley and G. P. Latham, *Improving Productivity through Performance Appraisal* (Reading, MA: Addison-Wesley, 1981).

36. In some forms of BARS, the anchors are stated as expected behaviors (e.g., "Could be expected to develop loan documentation accurately"). When expected behaviors are included, the BARS is more appropriately labeled a BES—Behavioral Expectation Scale. For further discussion, see F. J. Landy and J. L. Farh, "Performance Rating," *Psychological Bulletin* (January 1980): 72–107; K. R. Murphy and J. I. Constans, "Behavioral Anchors as a Source of Bias in Rating," *Journal of Applied Psychology* (November 1987): 573; S. Zedeck, "Behavioral Based Performance Appraisals," *Aging and Work* 4 (1981): 89–100.

37. H. J. Bernardin and R. W. Beatty, *Performance Appraisal: Assessing Human Behavior at Work* (Boston: Kent, 1984); F. J. Landy and J. L. Farh, *The Measurement of Work Performance: Methods, Theory and Applications* (New York: Academic Press, 1983).

38. J. Fierman, "The Death and Rebirth of the Salesman," *Fortune* (July 25, 1994): 80–91; G. P. Latham and K. N. Wexley, "Behavioral Observation Scales for Performance Appraisal Purposes," *Personnel Psychology* 30 (1977): 255–68.

39. T. H. Poister and G. Streib, "Management Tools in Government: Trends over the Past Decade," *Public Administration Review* 44 (1984): 215–23; S. R. Ruth and W. W. Brooks, "Who's Using MBO in Management?" *Journal of Systems Management* (1982): 1–17.

40. E. A. Locke and G. P. Latham, *A Theory of Goal Setting and Task Performance* (Englewood Cliffs, NJ: Prentice-Hall, 1990); J. R. Hollenbeck, C. R. Williams, and H. J. Klein, "Am Empirical Examination of the Antecedents of Commitment to Difficult Goals," *Journal of Applied Psychology* 74, no. 1 (1989): 18–23; P. C. Earley, T. Connolly, and G. Ekegren, "Goals, Strategy Development and Task Performance: Some Limits on the Efficacy of Goal Setting," *Journal of Applied Psychology* 74, no. 1 (1989): 24–33; R. E. Wood and E. A. Locke, "Goal Setting and Strategy Effects on Complex Tasks," *Research in Organizational Behavior* 12 (1990): 73–109; C. E. Shalley, "Effects of Productivity Goals, Creativity Goals, and Personal Discretion on Individual Creativity," *Journal of Applied Psychology* 76, no. 2 (1991): 179–85; S. Siero et al., "Modification of Driving Behavior in a Large Transport Organization: A Field Experiment," *Journal of Applied Psychology* 74, no. 3 (1989): 417–23; T. R. Mitchell and W. S. Silver, "Individual and Group Goals When Workers Are Interdependent: Effects on Task Strategies and Performance," *Journal of Applied Psychology* 75, no. 2 (1990): 185–93; R. Rodgers and J. E. Hunter, "Impact of Management by Objectives on Organizational Productivity," *Journal of Applied Psychology* 76, no. 2 (1991): 322–36; P. C. Earley et al., "Impact of Process and Outcome Feedback on the Relation of Goal Setting to Task Performance," *Academy of Management Journal* 33, no. 1 (1990): 87–105; M. Erez and R. Arad, "Participative Goal-Setting: Social, Motivational, and Cognitive Factors," *Journal of Applied Psychology* (November

1986): 591; J. R. Hollenbeck and H. J. Klein, "Goal Commitment and the Goal-Setting Process: Problems, Prospects, and Proposals for Future Research," *Journal of Applied Psychology* (May 1987): 212; R. E. Wood, A. J. Mento, and E. A. Locke, "Task Complexity as a Moderator of Goal Effects: A Meta-Analysis," *Journal of Applied Psychology* (August 1987): 416; G. S. Odiorne, *MBO II: A System of Managerial Leadership for the 80s* (Belmont, CA: Pitman Publishers, 1986).

41. For a comprehensive review, see R. Rodgers and J. E. Hunter, "Impact of Management by Objectives on Organizational Productivity," 316–22. For an application of this, see A. Hadjian, "Why to Go for Stretch Targets," *Fortune* (November 14, 1994): 145–54.

42. See note 41.

43. J. Zigon, "Making Performance Appraisal Work for Teams;" J. J. Carlyle and T. F. Ellison, "Developing Performance Standards," in *Performance Appraisal,* ed. Bernardin and Beatty, 343–47.

44. L. Hugh, "Development of the Accomplishment Record Method of Selecting and Promoting Professionals," *Journal of Applied Psychology* 69 (1984): 135–46.

45. J. E. Santora, "Rating the Boss at Chrysler," *Personnel Journal* (May 1992): 38–45; A. Taylor III, "Will Success Spoil Chrysler?" *Fortune* (January 10, 1994): 88–92; "Chrysler's Neon: Is This the Small Car Detroit Couldn't Build?" *Business Week* (May 3, 1993): 116–26; J. Bennet, "The Designers Who Saved Chrysler," *New York Times* (January 30, 1994): sec. 3, pp. 1, 6.

46. Santora, "Rating the Boss at Chrysler."

47. Ibid., 42.

48. Ibid., 45. See also Taylor, "Will Success Spoil Chrysler?"

49. B. B. Gaugler et al., "Meta-Analysis of Assessment Center Validity," *Journal of Applied Psychology* 72 (1987): 493–511; R. Klimoski and M. Brickner, "Why Do Assessment Centers Work? The Puzzle of Assessment Center Validity," *Personnel Psychology* 40 (1987): 243–60; A. Tziner and S. Dolan, "Validity of an Assessment Center for Identifying Female Officers in the Military," *Journal of Applied Psychology* 67 (1982): 728–36; S. B. Parry, "How to Validate an Assessment Tool," *Training* (April 1993): 37–42.

50. A. S. DeNisi and K. Williams, "Cognitive Approaches to Performance Appraisal," in *Research in Personnel and Human Resource Management,* ed. G. R. Ferris and K. M. Rowland (Greenwich, CT: JAI Press, 1988), 109–56; A. S. DeNisi, T. P. Cafferty, and B. M. Meglino, "A Cognitive View of the Appraisal Process: A Model and Research Propositions," *Organizational Behavior and Human Performance* 33 (1984): 360–96.

51. J. N. Cleveland and K. R. Murphy, "Analyzing Performance Appraisal as Goal-Directed Behavior," *Research in Personnel and Human Resource Management* 10 (1992): 121–85; T. A. Judge and G. R. Ferris, "Social Context of Performance Evaluation Decisions," *Academy of Management Journal* 36 (1993): 80–105.

52. DeNisi and Williams, "Cognitive Approaches to Performance Appraisal"; D. R. Ilgen and J. M. Feldman, "Performance Appraisal: A Process Focus," in *Re-*

search in Organizational Behavior, ed. B. Staw and L. Cummings (Greenwich, CT: JAI Press, 1983), 141–97.

53. K. R. Murphy, R. A. Jako, and R. L. Anhalt, "Nature and Consequences of Halo Error: A Critical Analysis," *Journal of Applied Psychology* 78 (1993): 218–25; C. E. Lance, J. A. LaPointe, and A. M. Stewart, "A Test of the Context Dependency of Three Causal Models of Halo Rater Error," *Journal of Applied Psychology* 79 (1994): 332–40; W. K. Balzer and L. M. Sulsky, "Halo and Performance Appraisal Research: A Critical Examination," *Journal of Applied Psychology* 77 (1992): 975–85; B. E. Becker and R. L. Cardy, "Influence of Halo Error on Appraisal Effectiveness: A Conceptual and Empirical Reconsideration," *Journal of Applied Psychology* (November 1986): 662; R. L. Cardy and G. H. Dobbins, "Affect and Appraisal Accuracy: Liking as an Integral Dimension in Evaluating Performance," *Journal of Applied Psychology* (November 1986): 672; M. E. Heilman and M. H. Stopeck, "Being Attractive, Advantage or Disadvantage: Performance-Based Evaluations and Recommended Personnel Actions as a Function of Appearance, Sex and Job Type," *Organizational Behavior and Human Decision Processes* 35 (1985): 202–15; K. Kraiger and J. K. Ford, "A Meta-Analysis of Ratee Race Effects in Performance Ratings," *Journal of Applied Psychology* (February 1985): 56–65; K. N. Wexley and E. D. Pulakos, "The Effects of Perceptual Congruence and Sex on Subordinates: Performance Appraisals of Their Managers," *Academy of Management Journal* (December 1983): 666–76.

54. G. Northcraft and G. Wolf, "Dollars, Sense, and Sunk Costs: A Life Cycle Model of Resource Allocation," *Academy of Management Review* 9 (1984): 225–34.

55. M. Bazerman, *Judgment in Managerial Decision Making* (New York: Wiley, 1986); Bazerman, Beekun, and Schoorman, "Performance Evaluation in a Dynamic Context," 873–76; Huber, "Comparison of the Effects of Specific and General Performance Standards"; G. B. Northcraft, M. A. Neale, and V. L. Huber, "The Effects of Cognitive Bias and Social Influence on Human Resources Management Decisions," in *Research in Personnel and Human Resource Management,* ed. G. Ferris and K. M. Rowland (Greenwich, CT: JAI Press, 1988), 157–89; Northcraft and Wolf, "Dollars, Sense, and Sunk Costs."

56. R. L. Dipboye, "Some Neglected Variables in Research on Discrimination in Appraisals," *Academy of Management Review* (January 1985): 118–25; M. R. Edwards and J. R. Sproull, "Rating the Raters Improves Performance Appraisals," *Personnel Administrator* (August 1983): 77–82; J. L. Gibson, J. J. Ivancevich, and J. H. Donnelly, *Organizations: Behavior, Structure, Processes,* 3d ed. (Dallas: Business Publications, 1979), 361; B. R. Nathan and R. A. Alexander, "The Role of Inferential Accuracy in Performance Rating," *Academy of Management Review* (January 1985): 109–17; R. M. McIntyre, D. E. Smith, and C. E. Hassett, "Accuracy of Performance Ratings As Affected by Rater Training and Perceived Purpose of Rating," *Journal of Applied Psychology* (February 1984): 147–56.

57. T. J. Maurer, J. K. Palmer, and D. K. Ashe, "Diaries, Checklists, Evaluations, and Contrast Effects in Mea-

surement of Behavior," *Journal of Applied Psychology* 78 (1993): 226–31; H. J. Bernardin and M. R. Buckley, "Strategies in Rater Training," *Academy of Management Review* 6 (1981): 205–12.

58. P. H. Lewis, "A Way to Rate Employee Performance More Effectively," *New York Times* (December 19, 1993): p. F10.

59. Henderson, *Performance Appraisal.* See also D. T. Stamoulis and N. M. A. Hauenstein, "Rater Training and Rating Accuracy: Training for Dimensional Accuracy versus Training for Ratee Differentiation," *Journal of Applied Psychology* 78 (1993): 994–1003; L. M. Sulsky and D. V. Day, "Frame-of-Reference Training and Cognitive Categorization: An Empirical Investigation of Rater Memory Issues," *Journal of Applied Psychology* 77 (1992): 501–10.

60. Murphy and Cleveland, *Performance Appraisal,* 190–210; C. G. Banks and K. R. Murphy, "Toward Narrow-

ing the Research-Practice Gap in Performance Appraisal," *Personnel Psychology* 38 (1985): 335–45; Northcraft, Neale, and Huber, "The Effects of Cognitive Bias and Social Influence."

61. K. R. Murphy, "Difficulties in the Statistical Control of Halo," *Journal of Applied Psychology* 67 (1982): 161–64; L. Hirshhord, *Meaning in the New Team Environment* (Reading, MA: Addison-Wesley, 1991); Murphy and Cleveland, *Performance Appraisal.*

62. R. F. Martell and M. R. Borg, "A Comparison of the Behavioral Rating Accuracy of Groups and Individuals," *Journal of Applied Psychology* 78 (1993): 43–50.

63. "A New Focus on Achievement," *Personnel Journal* (February 1991): 73–75.

❖ CHAPTER 11

1. J. F. Welch, "A Master Class in Radical Change," *Fortune* (December 13, 1993): 83.

2. *Source:* This feature is based on J. September, "Mrs. Fields' Secret Weapon," *Personnel Journal* (September 1991): 56–58; A. Prendergast, "Learning to Let Go," *Working Woman* (January 1992): 42, 44–45.

3. R. W. Beatty and C. E. Schneier, "Strategic Performance Appraisal Issues," in *Readings in Personnel and Human Resource Management,* ed. R. S. Schuler, S. A. Youngblood, and V. L. Huber (St. Paul: West Publishing Co., 1988), 256–66; J. N. Cleveland, K. R. Murphy, and R. E. Williams, "Multiple Uses of Performance Appraisal: Prevalence and Correlates," *Journal of Applied Psychology* 74, no. 1 (1989): 130–35; R. D. Pritchard, *Measuring and Improving Organizational Productivity: A Practice Guide* (New York: Praeger, 1990).

4. "A New Focus on Achievement," *Personnel Journal* (February 1991): 73–75.

5. P. Villanova and H. J. Bernardin, "Impression Management in the Context of Performance Appraisal," in *Impression Management in the Organization,* ed. R. A. Giacalone and P. Rosenfeld (Hillsdale, NJ: Lawrence Erlbaum, 1989), 299–314.

6. C. O. Longnecker, H. Sims, and D. Gioia, "Behind the Mask: The Politics of Employee Appraisal," *Academy of Management Executive* 1 (1987): 183–93; H. J. Bernardin and P. Villanova, "Performance Appraisal," in *Generalizing from Laboratory to Field Settings,* ed E. A. Locke (Lexington, MA: Heath/Lexington, 1986), 43–67.

7. M. Beer, "Performance Appraisal: Dilemmas and Possibilities," *Organizational Dynamics* (winter 1981): 26; A. Zander, "Research on Self-Esteem, Feedback and Threats to Self-Esteem," in *Performance Appraisals: Effects on Employees and Their Performance,* ed. A. Zander (New York: Foundation for Research in Human Behavior, 1963).

8. M. Ross and G. J. O. Fletcher, "Attribution and Social Perception," in *Handbook of Social Psychology,* 3rd

ed., vol. II, ed. G. Lindzey and E. Aronson (New York: Random House, 1985), 73–122.

9. M. Hequet, "Giving Good Feedback," *Training* (September 1994): 72–77; R. S. Schuler, "Taking the Pain out of the Performance Appraisal Interview," *Supervisory Management* (August 1981): 8–13; K. S. Teel, "Performance Appraisals: Current Trends, Persistent Progress," *Personnel Journal* (April 1980): 296–301.

10. C. Hymowitz, "Bosses: Don't Be Nasty (and Other Tips for Reviewing Worker Performance)," *Wall Street Journal* (January 17, 1985): 35.

11. D. R. Ilgen, C. D. Fisher, and M. S. Taylor, "Consequences of Individual Feedback on Behavior in Organizations," *Journal of Applied Psychology* 64 (1979): 349–71; D. R. Ilgen and C. F. Moore, "Types and Choices of Performance Feedback," *Journal of Applied Psychology* (August 1987): 401; B. L. Davis and M. K. Mount, "Design and Use of Performance Appraisal Feedback System," *Personnel Administrator* (March 1984): 91–107; B. C. Florin-Thuma and J. W. Boudreau, "Performance Feedback Utility in Managerial Decision Processes," *Personnel Journal* (winter 1987): 693; T. R. Mitchell, M. Rothman, and R. C. Liden, "Effects of Normative Information on Task Performance," *Journal of Applied Psychology* (February 1985): 66–71; J. L. Pearce and L. W. Porter, "Employee Responses to Formal Performance Appraisal Feedback," *Journal of Applied Psychology* (May 1986): 211.

12. L. Smith, "The Executive's New Coach," *Fortune* (December 27, 1993): 126. See also "Out with Appraisals, In with Feedback," *Training* (August 1993): 10–11; B. O'Reilly, "360 Degree Feedback Can Change Your Life," *Fortune* (October 17, 1994): 93–100; E. Van Velsor and J. B. Leslie, *Feedback to Managers, Vol. II: A Review and Comparison of Sixteen Multi-Rater Feedback Instruments,* report no. 150 (Greensboro, NC: Center for Creative Leadership, 1991).

13. J. Greenberg, "The Distributive Justice of Organizational Performance Evaluation," in *Research in Negotiations in Organizations,* ed. M. Bazerman, R.

Lewicki, and B. Sheppard (Greenwich, CT: JAI Press, 1986), 25–41; J. Greenberg, "Using Diaries to Promote Procedural Justice in Performance Appraisal," *Social Justice Review* (1987): 20–37.

14. *Source:* Adapted from "Performance Management in the Round," *Bulletin to Management* (August 12, 1993): 256. Used by permission.

15. D. Jamieson and J. O'Mara, *Managing Workforce 2000* (San Francisco: Jossey-Bass, 1991), 125–26.

16. "Starting Fresh at Neiman-Marcus," *HR Reporter* (April 1988): 1–2.

17. G. Bylinski, "Turning R&D into Real Products," *Fortune* (May 2, 1990): 72–77.

18. For a discussion of these characteristics for an effective appraisal interview, see Beer, "Performance Appraisal," 34–35; *Bulletin to Management* (October 18, 1984): 2, 7; P. Wylie and M. Grothe, *Problem Employees: How to Improve their Performance* (Belmont, CA: Pitman Learning, 1981).

19. Smith, "The Executive's New Coach," 126.

20. R. Rodgers, J. E. Hunter, and D. L. Rogers, "Influence of Top Management Commitment on Management Program Success," *Journal of Applied Psychology* 78 (1993): 151–55; R. Rodgers and J. E. Hunter, "Impact of Management by Objectives on Organizational Productivity," *Journal of Applied Psychology* 76 (1991): 322–36.

21. *Source:* Based on W. F. Giles and K. W. Mossholder, "Employee Reactions to Contextual and Session Components of Performance Appraisal," *Journal of Applied Psychology* 75 (1990): 371–77.

22. S. W. Gilliland and R. S. Landis, "Quality and Quantity Goals in a Complex Decision Task: Strategies and Outcomes," *Journal of Applied Psychology* 77 (1992): 672–81; P. M. Wright et al., "Productivity and Extra-Role Behavior: The Effects of Goals and Incentives on Spontaneous Helping," *Journal of Applied Psychology* 78 (1993): 374–81; E. W. Morrison and R. J. Bies, "Impression Management in the Feedback-Seeking Process: A Literature Review and Research Agenda," *Academy of Management Review* 16 (1991): 522–41; J. R. Larson, Jr., "The Dynamic Interplay between Employees' Feedback-Seeking Strategies and Supervisors' Delivery of Performance Feedback," *Academy of Management Review,* 14 (1989): 408–22; T. E. Becker and R. J. Klimoski, "A Field Study of the Relationship between the Organizational Feedback Environment and Performance," *Personnel Psychology* 42 (1989): 343–78; Giles and Mossholder, "Employee Reactions"; R. A. Baron, "Countering the Effects of Destructive Criticism: The Relative Efficacy of Four Interventions," *Journal of Applied Psychology* 75 (1990): 235–45; B. R. Nathan, A. M. Mohrman, Jr., and J. Milliman, "Interpersonal Relations as a Context for the Effects of Appraisal Interviews on Performance and Satisfaction: A Longitudinal Study," *Academy of Management Journal* 34 (1991): 352–69.

23. This section is adapted in part from R. F. Mager and P. Pipe, *Analyzing Performance Problems, or "You Really Oughta Wanna"* (Belmont, CA: Fearon Pittman, 1970).

24. M. J. Markinko and W. L. Garner, "Learned Helplessness: An Alternative Explanation for Performance Deficits," *Academy of Management Review* 1 (1982): 195–204; M. E. Kanfer and F. H. Kanfer, "The Role of Goal Acceptance on Goal Setting and Task Performance," *Academy of Management Review* (July 1983): 454–63; S. E. Jackson and R. S. Schuler, "A Meta-Analysis and Conceptual Critique of Research on Role Ambiguity and Role Conflict in Work Settings," *Organizational Behavior and Human Decision Processes* 36 (1985): 16–78; J. L. Pearce and L. W. Porter, "Employee Responses to Formal Performance Appraisal Feedback," *Journal of Applied Psychology* (May 1986): 211.

25. H. H. Kelly, "Attribution in Social Interaction," in E. Jones et al., (eds.), *Attribution: Perceiving the Causes of Behavior* (Morristown, N.J.: General Learning Press, 1972).

26. V. L. Huber, P. Podsakoff, and W. Todor, "An Investigation of Biasing Factors in the Attributions of Subordinates and Their Supervisors," *Journal of Business Research* 4 (1986): 83–97.

27. C. Carr, "The Ingredients of Good Performance," *Training* (August 1993): 51–54; P. Froiland, "Reproducing Star Performers," *Training* (September 1993): 33–37; L. F. McGee, "Keeping up the Good Work," *Personnel Administrator* (June 1988): 68–72; S. O'Neal and M. Palladino, "Revamp Ineffective Performance Management," *Personnel Journal* (February 1992): 93–102; M. H. Yarborough, "Warning! Negative Influences at Work," *HR Focus* (September 1993): 23.

28. E F. Huse, *Management,* 2nd ed. (St. Paul: West Publishing Co., 1982), 390–91.

29. A. Bandura, *Principles of Behavior Modification* (New York: Holt, Rinehart & Winston, 1969); W. Nord, "Beyond the Teaching Machine: The Neglected Area of Operant Conditioning in the Theory and Practice of Management," *Organizational Behavior and Human Performance* 4 (November 1969): 375–401; R. Beatty and C. Schneier, "A Case for Positive Reinforcement," *Business Horizons* 2 (April 1975): 57–66; H. Wiard, "Why Manage Behavior? A Case for Positive Reinforcement," *Human Resources Management* 11 (summer 1972): 15–21.

30. E. Feeney, "At Emery Air Freight: Positive Reinforcement Boosts Performance," *Organizational Dynamics* 1 (Winter 1973): 41–50.

31. Ibid., 47–48.

32. Ibid., 42.

33. W. C. Hamner, "Reinforcement Theory and Contingency Management in Organizational Settings," in *Organizational Behavior and Management: A Contingency Approach,* ed. H. Tosi and W. C. Hamner (Chicago: St. Clair Press, 1974), 86–111.

34. Ibid.

35. R. D. Arvey, G. A. Davis, and S. M. Nelson, "Use of Discipline in an Organization: A Field Study," *Journal of Applied Psychology* (August 1984): 448–60; J. Brockner and J. Guare, "Improving the Performance of Low Self-Esteem Individuals: An Attributional Approach," *Academy of Management Journal* (December 1983): 642–56; D. N. Campbell, R. L. Fleming, and R. C. Grote, "Discipline without Punishment at Last," *Harvard Business Review* (July–August 1985): 162–

78; D. Cameron, "The When, Why and How of Discipline," *Personnel Journal* (July 1984): 37–39.

36. D. A. Nadler and E. E. Lawler III, "Motivation—A Diagnostic Approach," in *Perspectives on Behavior in Organizations,* ed. J. R. Hackman, E. E. Lawler III, and L. W. Porter (New York: McGraw-Hill, 1977).

37. Campbell, Fleming, and Grote, "Discipline without Punishment at Last."

38. "Alcohol Misuse Prevention Programs: Department of Transportation Final Rules," *Bulletin to Management* (March 24, 1994): 1–7; "Productivity and Performance EAP-Improved," *Bulletin to Management* (July 23, 1987): 1; D. Masi and S. J. Freidland, "EAP Actions and Options," *Personnel Journal* (June 1988): 61–67.

39. *Source:* This feature is adapted from S. Feldman, "Today's EAPs Make the Grade," *Bulletin to Management* (February 1991): 3. Used by permission of the Bureau of National Affairs. See also W. F. Scanlon, *Alcoholism and Drug Abuse in the Workplace* (Westport, CT: Praeger, 1991); D. Klinger and N. O'Neill, *Workplace Drug Abuse and AIDS: A Guide to Human Resource Management Policy and Practice* (Westport, CT: Quorum Books, 1991); A. J. Gelenberg and S. C. Schoonover, *The Practitioner's Guide to Psychoactive Drugs* (New York: Plenum Medical Books, 1991); W. F. Banta and F. Tennant, Jr., *Complete Handbook for Combating Substance Abuse in the Workplace* (Lexington, MA: Lexington Books, 1989); R. Thompson, Jr., *Substance Abuse and Employee Rehabilitation* (Washington, DC: BNA Books, 1990); K. B. O'Hara and T. E. Backer, *Organizational Change and Drug-Free Workplaces: Templates for Success* (Westport, CT: Quorum Books, 1991).

40. C. Frayne and G. P. Latham, "The Application of Social Learning Theory to Employee Self-Management of Attendance," *Journal of Applied Psychology* 72 (1987): 387–92; F. H. Kanfer, "Self-Management Methods," in *Helping People Change: A Textbook of Methods,* ed. P. Karoly and A. Goldstein (New York: Pergamon Press, 1980), 334–89; P. Karoly and F. H. Kanfer, *Self-Management and Behavior Change: From Theory to Practice* (New York: Pergamon Press, 1986).

41. Manz, Keating, and Donnellon, "Preparing an Organizational Change.

42. S. Caudron, "Working at Home Pays Off," *Personnel Journal* (November 1992): 40–49; C. A. Frayne, *Reducing Employee Absenteeism through Self-Management Training: A Research-Based Analysis and Guide* (Westport, CT: Quorum Books, 1991).

43. L. K. Trevino, "The Social Effects of Punishment in Organizations: A Justice Perspective," *Academy of Management Review* 17 (1992): 647–76; R. Bennett and L. L. Cummings, "The Effects of Schedule and Intensity of Aversive Outcomes on Performance: A Multitheoretical Perspective," *Human Performance* 4 (1991): 155–69; J. M. Beyer and H. M. Trice, "A Field Study of the Use and Perceived Effects of Discipline in Controlling Work Performance," *Academy of Management Journal* 27 (1984): 743–64; R. D. Arvey, G. A. Davis, and S. M. Nelson, "Use of Discipline in an Organization: A Field Study," *Journal of Applied*

Psychology 69 (1984): 448–60; R. D. Arvey and J. M. Ivancevich, "Punishment in Organizations: A Review, Propositions, and Research Suggestions," *Academy of Management Review* 5 (1980): 123–32; R. D. Arvey and A. P. Jones, "The Use of Discipline in Organizational Settings: A Framework for Future Research," *Research in Organizational Behavior* 7 (1985): 367–408; R. A. Baron, "Negative Effects of Destructive Criticism: Impact on Conflict, Self-Efficacy, and Task Performance," *Journal of Applied Psychology* 73 (1988): 199–207; R. A. Baron, "Countering the Effects of Destructive Criticism: The Relative Efficacy of Four Interventions," *Journal of Applied Psychology* 75 (1990): 235–45; J. R. Redeker, *Discipline: Policies and Procedures* (Washington, DC: Bureau of National Affairs, 1984); M. E. Schnake, "Vicarious Punishment in a Work Setting," *Journal of Applied Psychology* 71 (1986): 343–45; H. P. Sims, "Further Thoughts on Punishment in Organizations," *Academy of Management Review* 5 (1980): 133–38.

44. P. Wylie and M. Grothe, *Problem Employees: How to Improve Their Performance* (Belmont, CA: Pittman Learning, 1981).

45. K. Johnson, "You're Fired! See You Out of Court," *New York Times* (March 29, 1995): B1, 4.

46. J. R. Fulkerson and R. S. Schuler, "Managing Worldwide Diversity at Pepsi-Cola International," in *Working through Diversity: Human Resources Initiatives,* ed. S. E. Jackson (New York: Guilford Publications, 1992), 248–78; R. S. Schuler, J. R. Fulkerson, and P. J. Dowling, "Strategic Performance Measurement and Management in Multinational Corporations," *Human Resource Management* (Fall 1991): 365–92.

47. J. Sargent, "Performance Appraisal 'American Style': Where It Came from and Its Possibilities Overseas" (working paper, University of Washington, September 1991); A. Nimgade, "American Management as Viewed by International Professionals," *Business Horizons* (November–December 1989): 98–105.

48. N. Adler, *International Dimensions of Organizational Behavior,* 2nd ed. (Boston: PWS-Kent, 1991); W. H. Newman, "Cultural Assumptions Underlying U.S. Management Concepts," in *Management in an International Context* (New York: Harper & Row, 1972).

49. P. Drucker, *Management: Tasks, Responsibilities and Practices* (New York: Harper & Row, 1973), 424–25.

50. R. Steers, Y. K. Shin, and G. Ungson, *The Chaebol: Korea's New Industrial Might* (Reading, PA: Harper & Row, 1990), 121–22.

51. V. L. Huber et al., "Cognitive Similarity and Cultural Dissimilarity: Effects on Performance Appraisal and Compensation Decisions of Chinese and Americans" (working paper, University of Washington, 1991).

52. S. Carroll, "Asian HRM Philosophies and Systems: Can They Meet Our Changing HRM Needs?" in *Readings in Personnel and Human Resource Management,* ed. Schuler, Youngblood, and Huber, 442–55.

53. W. Ouchi, *The M-Form Society* (Reading, MA: Addison-Wesley, 1984).

54. T. Mroczkowski and M. Hanaoka, "Continuity and Change in Japanese Management," *California Management Review* (Winter 1989): 39–52.

⊛ CHAPTER 12

1. R. Henkoff, "Service Is Everybody's Business," *Fortune* (June 27, 1994): 50.

2. *Source:* Based on P. V. LeBlanch, "Skill-Based Pay Case Number Two: Northern Telecom," *Compensation and Benefits Review* (March–April 1991): 39–56. See also G. E. Ledford, Jr., "Three Case Studies on Skill-Based Pay: An Overview," *Compensation and Benefits Review* (March–April 1991): 11–23; G. E. Ledford, Jr., W. R. Tyler, and W. B. Dixey, "Skill-Based Pay Case Number Three: Honeywell Ammunition Assembly Plant," *Compensation and Benefits Review* (March–April 1991): 57–77.

3. A. Farnham, "How to Nurture Creative Sparks," *Fortune* (January 10, 1994): 98. See also R. E. Sibson, *Compensation,* rev. ed. (New York: AMACOM, 1990); G. T. Milkovich and J. M. Newman, *Compensation,* 4th ed. (Homewood, IL: Irwin, 1993) D. B. Balkin and L. R. Gomez-Mejia eds., *New Perspectives on Compensation* (Englewood Cliffs, NJ: Prentice-Hall, 1987). The use of divisions is practical because it is then easier to discuss compensation. This is just one way to divide up the components of compensation. For an alternative, see R. I. Henderson, "Designing a Reward System for Today's Employee," *Business* (July–September 1982): 2–12.

4. L. S. Richman, "CEOs to Workers: Help Not Wanted," *Fortune* (July 12, 1993): 42–43; R. Jacob, "The Economy: Girding for Worse," *Fortune* (October 18, 1993): 10; "Employees' Views on Work," *Bulletin to Management* (September 16, 1993): 289.

5. J. Fierman, "When Will You Get a Raise?" *Fortune* (July 12, 1993): 34–36.

6. A. B. Krueger, "The Determinants of Queues for Federal Jobs," *Industrial and Labor Relations Review* 41 (1988): 567–81; H. J. Holzer, "Wages, Employer Costs, and Employee Performance in the Firm," *Industrial and Labor Relations Review* 43 (1990): 147S–64S; J. M. Barron, J. Bishop, and W. C. Dunkelberg, "Employer Search: The Interviewing and Hiring of New Employees," *Review of Economics and Statistics* 67 (1985): 43–52; C. Brown and J. Medoff, "The Employer Size-Wage Effect," *Journal of Political Economy* 97 (1989): 1027–53; D. M. Cable and T. A. Judge, "Pay Preferences and Job Search Decisions: A Person-Organization Fit Perspective," *Personnel Psychology* 47 (1994): 339–48.

7. R. G. Ehrenberg and R. S. Smith, *Modern Labor Economics* (Homewood, IL: Irwin, 1988); S. J. Motowidlo, "Predicting Sales Turnover from Pay Satisfaction and Expectation," *Journal of Applied Psychology* 68 (1983): 484–89.

8. L. M. Kahn and P. D. Sherer, "Contingent Pay and Managerial Performance," *Industrial and Labor Relations Review* 43 (1990): 107S–20S; M. L. Weitzman and D. L. Kruse, "Profit Sharing and Productivity," in *Paying for Productivity,* ed. A. S. Blinder (Washington, DC: Brookings Institute, 1990); R. A. Guzzo, R. D. Jette, and R. A. Katzell, "The Effects of Psychologically Based Intervention Programs on Worker Productivity: A Meta-Analysis," *Personnel Psychology* 38 (1985): 275–91; R. T. Kaufman, "The Effects of Improshare on Productivity" (proceedings of the forty-third annual meeting of the Industrial Relations Research Association, 1990); J. A. Wagner III, P. Rubin, and T. J. Callahan, "Incentive Payment and Non-managerial Productivity: An Interrupted Time Series Analysis of Magnitude and Trend," *Organizational Behavior and Human Decision Processes* 42 (1988): 47–74.

9. L. R. Gomez-Mejia and D. B. Balkin, *Compensation, Organizational Strategy, and Firm Performance* (Cincinnati: Southwestern Publishing, 1992); L. R. Gomez-Mejia and T. M. Welbourne, "Strategic Design of Executive Compensation Programs," in *Compensation and Benefits,* ed. L. R. Gomez-Mejia (Washington, DC: Bureau of National Affairs, 1989); L. R. Gomez-Mejia and T. M. Welbourne, "Compensation Strategy: An Overview and Future Steps," *Human Resource Planning* (1990): 173–89.

10. For detailed coverage of these and related issues, see M. L. Rock and L. A. Berger, *The Compensation Handbook: A State-of-the-Art Guide to Compensation Strategy and Design* (New York: McGraw-Hill, 1991); G. T. Milkovich and J. M. Newman, *Compensation,* 4th ed. (Homewood, IL: Irwin, 1993); J. R. Schuster and P. K. Zingheim, *The New Pay: Linking Employee and Organizational Performance* (New York: Lexington Books, 1992); B. Gerhart and G. T. Milkovich, "Employee Compensation: Research and Practice," *Handbook of Industrial and Organizational Psychology,* ed. M. D. Dunnette and L. M. Hough (Palo Alto, CA: Consulting Psychologists Press, 1992), 481–569; R. I. Henderson, *Compensation Management,* 6th ed. (Englewood Cliffs, NJ: Prentice-Hall, 1994).

11. L. S. Richman, "The New Work Force Builds Itself," *Fortune* (June 27, 1994): 70.

12. For excellent reviews of strategic compensation, see E. E. Lawler III, *Strategic Pay: Aligning Organizational Strategies and Pay Systems* (San Francisco: Jossey-Bass, 1990); E. E. Lawler III and G. D. Jenkins, Jr., "Strategic Reward Systems," in *Handbook of Industrial and Organizational Psychology,* vol. 3, ed. Dunnette and Hough; F. K. Foulkes, *Executive Compensation: A Strategic Guide for the 1990s* (Boston: Harvard Business School Press, 1991); C. L. Weber and S. L. Rynes, "Effects of Compensation Strategy on Job Pay Decisions," *Academy of Management Journal* 34 (1991): 86–109; Rock and Berger, *The Compensation Handbook;* Gomez-Mejia and Balkin, *Compensation, Organizational Strategy, and Firm Performance;* R. G. Ehrenberg, ed., *Do Compensation Policies Matter?* (Ithaca, NY: ILR Press, 1990). For a discussion of approaches to HR strategy, see J. E. Butler, G. R. Ferris, and D. S. Cook, "Exploring Some Critical Dimensions of Strategic Human Resource Management," in *Readings in Personnel and Human Resource Management,* ed. R. S. Schuler, S. A. Youngblood, and V. L. Huber (St. Paul: West Publishing Co., 1988), 3–13; E. E. Lawler III, *Pay and Organi-*

zational Development (Reading, MA: Addison-Wesley, 1981); L. Dyer, "Strategic Human Resource Management and Planning," in Research in Personnel and Human Resources Management, ed. K. Rowland and G. Ferris (Greenwich, CT: JAI Press, 1985), 1–30.

13. G. T. Milkovich, "A Strategic Perspective on Compensation Management," in Research in Personnel and Human Resources Management, ed. Rowland and Ferris; M. J. Wallace, Jr., and C. H. Fay, Compensation Theory and Practice (Boston: PWS-Kent, 1988); S. Carroll, "Business Strategies and Compensation Systems," in New Perspectives on Compensation, ed. Balkin and Gomez-Mejia; B. Gerhart and G. T. Milkovich, "Organizational Differences in Managerial Compensation and Financial Performance," Academy of Management Journal 33 (1990): 663–91.

14. R. L. Heneman, "Merit Pay Research," in Research in Personnel and Human Resources Management, ed. Rowland and Ferris, 203–65; J. M. Newman, "Selecting Incentive Plans to Complement Organizational Strategy," in New Perspectives on Compensation, ed. Balkin and Gomez-Mejia, 214–25; R. M. Steers and G. R. Ungson, "Strategic Issues in Executive Compensation Decisions," in New Perspectives on Compensation, ed. Balkin and Gomez-Mejia, 294–309; G. T. Milkovich, "A Strategic Perspective on Compensation Management," in Research in Personnel and Human Resources Management, ed. Rowland and Ferris, 263–88; Wallace and Fay, Compensation Theory and Practice.

15. P. Burstein, R. M. Bricher, and R. L. Einwohner, "Policy Alternatives and Political Change: Work, Family, and Gender on the Congressional Agenda," American Sociological Review 60 (1995): 67–83.

16. Source: Excerpted and adapted from E. W. Morrison and J. M. Herlihy, "Becoming the Best Place to Work: Managing Diversity at American Express Travel Related Services," in Diversity in the Workplace: Human Resources Initiatives, ed. S. E. Jackson et al. (New York: Guilford Press, 1992).

17. See Henderson, Compensation Management: Rewarding Performance, for a comprehensive summary of major legislation affecting pay.

18. A. Bernstein, C. Del Valle, and M. McNamee, "A Higher Minimum Wage: Minimal Damage?" Business Week (March 22, 1993): 92–93; S. Nasar, "Two Economists Catch Clinton's Eye by Bucking Common Wisdom," New York Times (August 22, 1993): 67; "Crackdown on Child Labor Violations," Fair Employment Practices Guidelines 299 (June 6, 1990); "FLSA Amendments of 1989: Higher Federal Minimum Wage, Plus New Training Wage," Bulletin to Management (December 28, 1989): 1–3; B. S. Murphy, W. E. Barlow, and D. D. Hatch, "A News Report for Personnel Professionals: Subminimum Training Wages Available," Personnel Journal (June 1990): 19.

19. C. Yang and C. Del Valle, "In a Sweat over Sweatshops," Business Week (April 4, 1994): 40; "Youth Employment: Child Labor Limitations Reviewed," Bulletin to Management (May 19, 1994): 153.

20. "White-Collar Exemptions under FLSA," Bulletin to Management Datagraph (February 13, 1992): 44–45; "Ask the Experts—Questions and Answers on Classifying White-Collar Employees as Exempt from Over-time Regulations," Fair Employment Practices Guidelines (April 10, 1994): 8.

21. Source: Adapted from "Record Settlement under Fair Labor Standards Act," Bulletin to Management (August 12, 1993): 249. Used by permission.

22. T. Linesenmayer, "Comparable Worth Abroad: Mixed Evidence," Wall Street Journal (May 27, 1986): 26.

23. Source: Adapted from "Pay Equity Makes Good Business Sense," Fair Employment Practices (August 30, 1990): 103. Used by permission. See also A. Bernstein, "What's Dragging Productivity Down? Women's Low Wages," Business Week (November 27, 1989): 171; "Comparable Worth Policies That Work: The Minnesota Case," Urban Institute/Policy and Research Report (summer 1990): 10–12; G. J. Meng, "All the Parts of Comparable Worth," Personnel Journal (November 1990): 99–104; P. England, Comparable Worth: Theories and Evidence (Hawthorne, NY: Aldine de Gruyter, 1992); C. Wells, Corporations and Criminal Responsibility (New York: Oxford University Press, 1993); J. A. Jacobs, "Women's Entry into Management: Trends in Earnings, Authority, and Values among Salaried Managers," Administrative Science Quarterly 37 (1992): 282–301; L. A. Jackson, P. D. Gardner, and L. A. Sullivan, "Explaining Gender Differences in Self-Pay Expectations: Social Comparison Standards and Perceptions of Fair Pay," Journal of Applied Psychology 77 (1992): 651–63.

24. See note 14.

25. H. C. Bentiam, "Union–Non-Union Wage Differential Revisited," Journal of Labor Research 8 (1987): 381; D. Lewin, "Public Sector Labor Relations: A Review Essay," in Public Sector Labor Relations: An Analysis and Readings, ed. D. Lewin, P. Feuill, and T. Kochan (Glen Ridge, NJ: Thomas Horton & Daughters, 1977), 166–84; R. Flanagan, R. Smith, and R. G. Ehrenberg, Labor Economics and Labor Relations (Glenview, IL: Scott Foresman, 1984).

26. M. Bowers and R. Roderick, "Two-Tiered Pay Systems: The Good, the Bad and the Debatable," Personnel Administrator 32 (1987): 101–12; Towers, Perrin, Forster, and Crosby, Survey of Company Experiences with Two-Tier Wage Systems (Washington, DC: Towers, Perrin, Forster, & Crosby, 1986).

27. R. Freeman and J. Medoff, What Do Unions Do? (New York: Basic Books, 1984); T. A. Kochan, H. C. Katz, and R. B. McKersie, The Transformation of American Industrial Relations (New York: Basic Books, 1986).

28. R. S. Schuler and I. C. MacMillan, "Gaining Competitive Advantage through Human Resource Management Practices," in Readings in Personnel and Human Resource Management, ed. Schuler, Youngblood, and Huber, 14–23.

29. D. B. Balkin and L. R. Gomez-Mejia, "Entrepreneurial Compensation," in Readings in Personnel and Human Resource Management, ed. Schuler, Youngblood, and Huber, 14–23; D. B. Balkin and L. R. Gomez-Mejia, "The Strategic Use of Short-Term and Long-Term Pay Incentives in the High Technology Industry," in New Perspectives on Compensation, ed. Balkin and Gomez-Mejia, 237–49.

30. G. T. Milkovich, "A Strategic Perspective on Compensation Management," in Research in Personnel and

Human Resources Management, ed. Rowland and Ferris, 263–88.

31. J. Kerr and J. W. Slocum, Jr., "Managing Corporate Culture through Reward Systems," *Executive* (May 1987): 99–108; J. Kerr and J. W. Slocum, Jr., "Linking Reward Systems and Organizational Cultures," in *Readings in Personnel and Human Resource Management,* ed. Schuler, Youngblood, and Huber, 297–311.

32. D. Jamieson and J. O'Mara, *Managing Workforce 2000: Gaining the Diversity Advantage* (San Francisco: Jossey-Bass, 1991), 108.

33. V. L. Huber et al., "Cognitive Similarity and Cultural Dissimilarity: Effects on Performance Appraisal and Compensation Decisions of Chinese Americans" (working paper, University of Washington, 1990).

34. R. S. Schuler, "Managing Resource Management Choices and Organizational Strategy," in *Readings in Personnel and Human Resource Management,* ed. Schuler, Youngblood, and Huber, 24–39; E. E. Lawler III and J. A. Drexler, "The Corporate Entrepreneur" (working paper, Center for Effective Organizations, University of Southern California, 1984); E. E. Lawler III, "The Strategic Design of Reward Systems," in *Readings in Personnel and Human Resource Management,* ed. Schuler, Youngblood, and Huber, 253–69.

35. Jamieson and O'Mara, *Managing Workforce 2000.*

36. "Aligning Compensation with Quality," *Bulletin to Management* (April 1, 1993): 97.

37. D. M. Cowherd and D. I. Levine, "Product Quality and Pay Equity between Lower-Level and Top Management: An Investigation of Distributive Justice Theory," *Administrative Science Quarterly* 37 (1992): 302–20. See also J. Pfeffer and N. Langton, "The Effect of Wage Dispersion on Satisfaction, Productivity, and Working Collaboratively: Evidence from College and University Faculty," *Administrative Science Quarterly* 38 (1993): 382–407.

38. For other definitions, see Milkovich and Newman, *Compensation.*

39. E. R. Livernash, "Internal Wage Structure," in *New Concepts in Wage Determination,* ed. G. W. Taylor and F. C. Pierson (New York: McGraw-Hill, 1957), 143–72; P. Cappelli and W. F. Cascio, "Why Some Jobs Command Wage Premiums: A Test of Career Tournament and Internal Labor Market Hypotheses," *Academy of Management Journal* 34 (1991): 848–68; S. R. Rynes, C. L. Weber, and G. T. Milkovich, "Effects of Market Survey Rates, Job Evaluation, and Job Gender on Job Pay," *Journal of Applied Psychology* 74 (1989): 114–23; D. Gleicher and L. Stevans, *A Classical Approach to Occupational Wage Rates* (Westport, CT: Praeger, 1991).

40. G. T. Milkovich and J. M. Newman, in *Compensation* (Homewood, IL: Irwin, 1993).

41. Ibid., 121.

42. R. Sneigar, "The Comparability of Job Evaluation Methods in Supplying Approximately Similar Classifications in Rating One Job Series," *Personnel Psychology* (summer 1983): 371–80.

43. D. Doverspike, "An Internal Bias Analysis of a Job Evaluation Instrument," *Journal of Applied Psychology* (November 1984): 648–50; S. L. Fraser, S. F. Cronshaw, and R. A. Alexander, "Generalizability Analysis of a Point Method Job Evaluation Instrument: A Field Study," *Journal of Applied Psychology* (November 1984): 643–47.

44. A. J. Candrilli and R. D. Armagast, "The Case for Effective Point Factor Job Evaluation, Viewpoint Two," *Compensation and Benefits Review* (1990): 49–54.

45. W. Bridges, "The End of the Job," *Fortune* (September 19, 1994): 52–74; H. Murlis and D. Fitt, "Job Evaluation in a Changing World," *Personnel Management* (May 1991): 39–43.

46. N. Gupta et al., "Survey-Based Prescriptions for Skill-Based Pay," *ACA Journal* (fall 1992): 48–58; M. Rowland, "It's What You Can Do That Counts," *New York Times* (June 6, 1993): p. F17; M. Rowland, "For Each New Skill, More Money," *New York Times* (June 13, 1993): p. F16.

47. Ledford, "Three Case Studies on Skill-Based Pay"; H. Tosi and L. Tosi, "What Managers Need to Know about Knowledge-Based Pay," *Organizational Dynamics* (winter 1986): 52–64.

48. *Bulletin to Management* (January 14, 1988): 10.

49. Milkovich and Newman, *Compensation.*

50. J. Domat-Connell, "Labor Market Definition and Salary Survey Selection: A New Look at the Foundation of Compensation Program Design," *Compensation and Benefits Review* (March–April 1994): 38–46.

51. C. Viswesvaran and M. R. Barrick, "Decision-Making Effects on Compensation Surveys: Implications for Market Wages," *Journal of Applied Psychology* 77 (1992): 588–97.

52. Ledford, Tyler, and Dixey, "Skill-Based Pay Case Number Three."

53. D. W. Belcher and T. J. Atchison, *Compensation Administration,* 2nd ed. (Englewood Cliffs, NJ: Prentice-Hall, 1987); J. Franklin, "For Technical Professionals: Pay for Skills and Pay for Performance," *Personnel* (May 1988): 20–28; J. C. Kail, "Compensating Scientists and Engineers," in *New Perspectives on Compensation,* ed. Balkin and Gomez-Mejia, 278–81; G. T. Milkovich, "Compensation Systems in High-Technology Companies," in *New Perspectives on Compensation,* ed. Balkin and Gomez-Mejia, 269–77; Milkovich and Newman, *Compensation;* C. F. Schultz, "Compensating the Sales Professional," in *New Perspectives on Compensation,* ed. Balkin and Gomez-Mejia, 250–57.

54. R. I. Henderson, *Compensation Management* (Reston, VA: Reston Publishing, 1985).

55. Ledford, Tyler, and Dixey, "Skill-Based Pay Case Number Three."

56. *Source:* Based on C. L. Weber and S. L. Rynes, "Effects of Compensation Strategy on Job Pay Decisions," *Academy of Management Journal* 34 (1991): 86–109.

57. "Employee Involvement in Compensation Plans," *Bulletin to Management Datagraph* (May 19, 1994): 156–57.

58. J. R. Schuster and P. Z. Zingheim, *The New-Pay: Linking Employee and Organizational Performance* (New York: Lexington Books, 1992).

59. M. Zippo, "Roundup," *Personnel* (September–October 1980): 43–45.

60. E. E. Lawler III, *Pay and Organizational Development* (Reading, MA: Addison-Wesley, 1981).

61. B. S. Murphy, W. E. Barlow, and D. D. Hatch, "Manager's Newsfront," *Personnel Journal* (December 1992): 22.

62. M. P. Miceli and M. C. Lane, "Antecedents of Pay Satisfaction: A Review and Extension," *Research in Personnel and Human Resource Management* 9 (1991): 235–309; P. Capelli and P. D. Sherer, "Satisfaction, Market Wages, and Labor Relations: An Airline Study," *Industrial Relations* 27 (1988): 56–73; H. G. Heneman III, "Pay Satisfaction," in *Research in Personnel and Human Resources Management,* vol. 3, ed. Rowland and Ferris, 115–39; N. Weiner, "Determinants and Behavioral Consequences of Pay Satisfaction: A Comparison of Two Models," *Personnel Psychology* 33 (1980): 741–57; V. Scarpello, V. L. Huber, and R. J. Vanderberg, "Compensation Satisfaction: Its Measurement and Dimensionality," *Journal of Applied Psychology* (May 1988): 163–71; R. W. Rice, S. M. Phillips, and D. B. McFarlin, "Multiple Discrepancies and Pay Satisfaction," *Journal of Applied Psychology* 75 (1990): 386–93.

63. L. A. Witt and L. G. Nye, "Gender and the Relationship between Perceived Fairness of Pay or Promotion and Job Satisfaction," *Journal of Applied Psychology* 77 (1992): 910–17.

64. "Labor Letter," *Wall Street Journal* (July 17, 1990): 1.

65. "Executive Pay: Compensation at the Top Is Out of Control—Here's How to Reform It," *Business Week* (March 30, 1992): 52–57; G. S. Crystal, *In Search of Excess: The Overcompensation of American Executives* (New York: Norton, 1992); G. Colvin, "How to Pay the CEO Right," *Fortune* (April 6, 1992): 61–69; A. Franham, "The Trust Gap," *Fortune* (December 4, 1990): 56–58.

66. I. T. Kay and R. F. Robinson, "Misguided Attacks on Executive Pay Hurt Shareholders," *Compensation and Benefits Review* (January–February 1994): 25–37; "Executive Pay: It Doesn't Add Up," *Business Week* (April 26, 1993): 122; A. E. Serwer, "Payday! Payday!" *Fortune* (June 14, 1993): 102–111.

67. A "properly administered" compensation program has several qualities of total compensation, including that the job evaluation process is valid, pay structures are fairly and objectively derived, pay is administered in a nondiscriminatory way, compensation policies are communicated so as to be understood, administrative costs are contained, the program has sufficient motivational value, and the program is supported by top management. For a discussion of these, see R. E. Azevedo and J. M. Beaton, "Costing the Pay Package: A Realistic Approach," in *New Perspectives on Compensation,* ed. Balkin and Gomez-Mejia, 143–50; S. B. Henrici, "A Tool for Salary Administrators: Standard Salary Accounting," *Personnel* (September–October 1980): 14–23; J. C.

Horn, "Bigger Pay for Better Work," *Psychology Today* (July 1987): 54–57.

68. The following materials are adapted from P. Dowling, R. S. Schuler, and D. Welch, *International Dimensions of Human Resource Management* (Belmont, CA: Wadsworth, 1994), 117–35. See also three excellent articles: "Compensating Your Overseas Executives, Part 1," *Compensation Review* (May–June 1990); "Part 2" (July–August 1990); "Part 3" (January–February 1991). And see also K. I. Kim, H. J. Park, and N. Suzuki, "Reward Allocations in the United States, Japan, and Korea: A Comparison of Individualistic and Collectivistic Cultures," *Academy of Management Journal* 33 (1990): 188–98; A. R. Thomann, "Flex-Base Addresses Pay Problems," *Personnel Journal* (February 1992): 51–52, 55.

69. C. Reynolds, "High Motivation and Low Cost through Innovative International Compensation" (Proceedings of the fortieth national conference of the ASPA, Boston, 1989).

70. See B. W. Teague, *Compensating Key Personnel Overseas* (New York: Conference Board, 1972), for a discussion of the concept of keeping the expatriate "whole."

71. This discussion of the balance sheet approach is based on C. Reynolds, "Compensation of Overseas Personnel," in *Handbook of Human Resources Administration,* 2nd ed., ed. J. J. Famularo (New York: McGraw-Hill, 1986). Although the balance sheet approach is the one most typically cited, other forms are used to pay expatriates. These include negotiation, localization, lump sum, and cafeteria. For a discussion, see C. Reynolds, *Compensation Basics for North American Expatriates* (Scottsdale, AZ: ACA, 1994).

72. *HR Reporter Update* (February 1987): 2.

73. V. Pucik, "Strategic HRM in Multinational Corporations," in *Strategic Management of Multinational Corporations,* ed. H. V. Wortzel and L. H. Wortzel (New York: John Wiley, 1985), 430.

74. *HR Reporter Update* 3 (January 1987): 5.

75. M. S. O'Connor, *Report on Japanese Employee Relation Practices and Their Relationship to Worker Productivity* (report prepared for a study mission to Japan, November 8–23, 1980). M. S. O'Connor's permission to reproduce this material is appreciated. See also *Employment and Employment Policy* (Tokyo: Japan Institute of Labor, 1988); D. I. Levine, "What Do Wages Buy?" *Administrative Science Quarterly* 38 (1993): 462–83.

76. The section on Mexico is adapted from G. Flynn, "HR in Mexico: What You Should Know," *Personnel Journal* (August 1994): 34; G. Koretz, "Economic Trends: The Stretch in Mexican Wages," *Business Week* (October 31, 1994): 33.

❖ CHAPTER 13

1. Personal correspondence with Randall Schuler, March 30, 1994.

2. *Source:* Based on C. Wiley, "Incentive Plan Pushes Production," *Personnel Journal* (August 1993): 86–92; K. Chilton, "Lincoln Electric's Incentive System: Can It Be

Transferred Overseas?" *Harvard Business Review* (November–December 1993): 21–30.

3. B. L. Hopkins and T. C. Mawhinney, *Pay for Performance: History, Controversy and Evidence* (Binghamton, NY: Haworth Press, 1992).

4. E. E. Lawler III, G. E. Ledford, Jr, and S. A. Mohrman, *Employee Involvement in America* (Houston, TX: American Productivity & Quality Center, 1989); C. O'Dell, *People, Performance and Pay* (Houston, TX: American Productivity Center, 1987); "Pay-for-Performance Plans Become More Popular," *Personnel Journal* (February 1994): 22.

5. E. E. Lawler III and D. Jenkins, "Strategic Reward Systems," in *Handbook of Industrial and Organizational Psychology*, vol. 3, ed. M. D. Dunnette and L. M. Hough (Palo Alto, CA: Consulting Psychologists Press, 1992).

6. H. Gleckman et al., "Bonus Pay: Buzzword or Bonanza?" *Business Week* (November 14, 1994): 62–64.

7. J. Greenwald, "Workers: Risks and Rewards," *Time* (April 15, 1991): 42.

8. "Compensation," in *Readings in Personnel and Human Resource Management*, ed. R. S. Schuler, S. A. Youngblood, and V. L. Huber (St. Paul: West Publishing Co., 1988), 291–97; J. Kerr and J. W. Slocum, Jr., "Linking Reward Systems and Organizational Culture," in *Readings in Personnel and Human Resource Management*, ed. Schuler, Youngblood, and Huber, 297–308.

9. M. J. Wallace and C. H. Fay, *Compensation Theory and Practice*, 3rd ed. (Boston: PWS-Kent, 1995); J. M. Newman and D. J. Fisher, "Strategic Impact Merit Pay," *Compensation and Benefits Review* (July–August 1992): 38–45.

10. W. Wilson, "Video Training and Testing Supports Customer Service Goals," *Personnel Journal* (June 1994): 48–51; J. E. Santora, "Dupont Builds Stakeholders," *Personnel Journal* (December 1989): 72–75; R. P. McNutt, "Achievement Pays Off at Dupont," *Personnel* (June 1990): 5–10.

11. See Gleckman et al., "Bonus Pay.

12. C. Babski, "Turning Glass into Art—and Profits, Too," *New York Times* (June 5, 1988): p. F4.

13. R. I. Henderson, *Compensation Management: Rewarding Performance* (Englewood Cliffs, NJ: Prentice-Hall, 1989), 298; J. C. Kail, "Compensating Scientists and Engineers," in *Current Trends in Compensation Research and Practice*, ed. D B. Balkin and L. R. Gomez-Mejia (Englewood Cliffs, NJ: Prentice-Hall, 1987), 278–81.

14. "Clarified Carrots," *HR Reporter* (May 1987). Personal correspondence with Richard Goodwin.

15. A. Morrison, M. N. Ruderman, and M. Hughes-James, *Making Diversity Happen: Controversies and Solutions* (Greensboro, NC: Center for Creative Leadership, 1993), 11.

16. E. E. Lawler III, *Strategic Pay* (San Francisco: Jossey-Bass, 1990).

17. "Compensation: Growth Bonuses," *Inc.* (February 1988): 100.

18. N. H. Mackworth, "High Incentives versus Hot and Humid Atmospheres in a Physical Effort Task," *British Journal of Psychology* (1947): 90–102; P. M. Podsakoff, M. L. Williams, and W. E. Scott, Jr., "Myths of Employee Selection Systems," in *Readings in Personnel and Human Resource Management*, ed. Schuler, Youngblood, and Huber, 178–92.

19. L. C. Cumming, "Linking Pay to Performance," *Personnel Administrator* (May 1988): 47–52; T. Rollins, "Pay for Performance: Is It Worth the Trouble?" *Personnel Administrator* (May 1988): 42–46.

20. A. Peers, "Wide Gaps in Wall Street Bonuses Spark Bitterness and Waves of Job Hopping," *Wall Street Journal* (February 9, 1994): pp. C1, C10; D. Filipowski, "Perspectives: Is Pay Linked to Performance?" *Personnel Journal* (May 1991): 39.

21. A. Kohn, "Why Incentive Plans Cannot Work," *Harvard Business Review* (September–October 1993): 54–63; P. M. Podsakoff, C. N. Greene, and J. M. McFillen, "Obstacles to the Effective Use of Reward Systems," in *Readings in Personnel and Human Resource Management*, ed. Schuler, Youngblood, and Huber, 275–90; T. R. Hinkin, P. M. Podsakoff, and C. A. Schriesheim, "The Mediation of Performance-Contingent Compensation by Supervisors in Work Organizations: A Reinforcement Perspective," in *New Perspectives on Compensation*, ed. D. B. Balkin and L. R. Gomez-Mejia (Englewood Cliffs, NJ: Prentice-Hall, 1987), 196–210; R. K. Miller, "Discrimination Is a Virtue," *Newsweek* (July 21, 1980): 15.

22. S. Tully, "Your Paycheck Gets Exciting," *Fortune* (November 1, 1994): 83–98.

23. P. M. Wright et al., "Productivity and Extra-Role Behavior: The Effects of Goals and Incentives on Spontaneous Helping," *Journal of Applied Psychology* 78 (1993): 374–81.

24. J. Fierman, "The Perilous New World of Fair Pay," *Fortune* (June 13, 1994): 58–59.

25. See Lawler and Jenkins, "Strategic Reward Systems."

26. B. Gerhart and G. T. Milkovich, "Organizational Differences in Managerial Compensation and Financial Performance," *Academy of Management Review* 33 (1990): 663–91.

27. K. M. Evans, "On-the-Job Lotteries: A Low-Cost Incentive That Sparks Higher Productivity," *Personnel* (April 1988): 20–26; "Recognizing Reward Programs," *Personnel Journal* (December 1986): 66–78; W. S. Humphrey, *Managing for Innovation: Leading Technical People* (Englewood Cliffs, NJ: Prentice-Hall, 1987), 128–33; M. Magnus, "First Interstate Banks on Compensation Redesign to Beat Competition," *Personnel Journal* (September 1987): 106–8.

28. Gerhart and Milkovich, "Organizational Differences."

29. T. L. Ross and L. Hatcher, "Gainsharing Drives Quality Improvement," *Personnel Journal* (November 1992): 81–89.

30. Bureau of National Affairs, *Change Pay Practices: New Developments in Employee Compensation* (Washington, DC: 1988).

31. Association of Machinists and Aerospace Workers.

32. R. B. Hill, "A Two-Component Approach to Compensation," *Personnel Journal* (May 1993): 154–61; M. J. Wallace, *Rewards and Renewal: America's Search for Competitive Advantage through Alternative Pay Strategies* (Scottsdale, AZ: American Compensation Association, 1990); Wallace and Fay, *Compensation Theory and Practice.*

33. Tully, "Your Paycheck Gets Exciting," 83–98; "Compensation Practices: Incentives on the Rise," *Bulletin to Management* (February 17, 1994): 49; Wallace, *Rewards and Renewal.*

34. *Source:* Based on K. A. Brown and V. L. Huber, "Lowering Floors and Raising Ceilings: A Longitudinal Assessment of the Effects of an Earnings-at-Risk Plan

on Pay Satisfaction," *Personnel Psychology* 45 (June 1992): 297–312.

35. K. A. Brown and V. L. Huber, "Lowering Floors and Raising Ceilings: A Longitudinal Assessment of the Effects of an Earnings-at-Risk Plan on Pay Satisfaction," *Personnel Psychology* 45 (June 1992): 279–311.

36. J. M. Newman, "Selecting Incentive Plans to Complement Organizational Strategy," in *Current Trends in Compensation Research and Practice*, ed. Balkin and Gomez-Mejia, 14–24.

37. J. Kerr, "Diversification Strategies and Managerial Rewards: An Empirical Study," *Academy of Management Journal* 28 (1985): 155–79; G. T. Milkovich and J. M. Newman, *Compensation* (Homewood, IL: BPI-Irwin, 1990); E. E. Lawler III, *Pay and Organizational Development* (Reading, MA: Addison-Wesley, 1981).

38. Hinking, Podsakoff, and Schriesheim, "Mediation of Performance Contingent Compensation," in *New Perspectives on Compensation*, ed. Balkin and Gomez-Mejia, 196–210; Milkovich and Newman, *Compensation*, 337.

39. C. Peck, *Pay and Performance: The Interaction of Compensation and Performance Appraisal* (New York: Conference Board, 1984); C. Peck, *Variable Pay: New Performance Rewards* (New York: Conference Board, 1990).

40. R. Heneman, "Merit Pay Research," in *Research in Personnel and Human Resource Management*, vol. 8, ed. K. Rowland and G. Ferris (1990), 204–63; R. Heneman, *Pay for Performance: Exploring the Merit System* (New York: Pergamon Press, 1984).

41. Filipowski, "Perspectives," 39.

42. L. R. Gomez-Mejia and D. B. Balkin, "Merit Pay Perspectives," in *Current Trends in Compensation Research and Practice*, ed. Balkin and Gomez-Mejia, 159–61; H. A. Levine, "Performance Appraisals at Work," *Personnel* 62 (1986): 63–71.

43. C. Peck, *Variable Pay*, 4.

44. Filipowski, "Perspectives."

45. Henderson, *Compensation Management*, 298.

46. "Pay-for-Performance Plans Become More Popular," 22; Sibson and Company, press release (Princeton, NJ, September 5, 1989), p. C.

47. G. S. Crystal, "How Much CEOs Really Make," *Fortune* (June 17, 1991): 72–80; M. C. Jensen and K. J. Murphy, "CEO Incentives—It's Not How Much You Pay, but How," *Harvard Business Review* (May–June 1990): 138–49; H. Fox and C. Peck, *Top Executive Compensation*, report no. 875 (New York: Conference Board, 1986); C. Peck, *Variable Pay*, 6.

48. *Source:* Adapted from C. Wiley, "Incentive Plan Pushes Production," *Personnel Journal* (August 1993): 91.

49. J. Birnbaum, "Recognition Programs Are Widespread," *HR News* (November 1991): 2.

50. D. W. Belcher and T. J. Atchison, *Compensation Administration*, 2nd ed. (Englewood Cliffs, NJ: Prentice-Hall, 1977); Henderson, *Compensation Management;* Milkovich and Newman, *Compensation*.

51. R. Lenzner, "Merrill at the Half-Trillion Mark," *Forbes* (April 26, 1993): 42–43; L. N. Spiro, "Raging Bull: The Trimmer New Look of Merrill Lynch," *Business Week* (November 25, 1991): 218–21.

52. J. S. Lublin, "Looking Good," *Wall Street Journal* (April 13, 1994): p. R1.

53. Jensen and Murphy, "CEO Incentives."

54. E. E. Lawler III and S. G. Cohen, "Designing Pay Systems for Teams," *ACA Journal* (autumn 1992): 6–18; C. Meyer, "How the Right Measures Help Teams Excel," *Harvard Business Review* (May–June 1994): 95–103; J. Huret, "Paying for Team Results," *HR Magazine* (May 1991): 39–43; T. Stambaugh, "An Incentive Pay Success Story," *Personnel Journal* (April 1992): 48–54.

55. Huret, "Paying for Team Results."

56. G. P. Latham and V. L. Huber, "Schedules of Reinforcement: Lessons from the Past, Issues for the Future," *Journal of Organizational Behavior Management* (in press).

57. Lawler and Cohen, "Designing Pay Systems for Teams," 6–16.

58. R. I. Henderson, *Compensation Management: Rewarding Performance* (Reston, VA: Reston Publishing, 1985).

59. Bureau of National Affairs, "Incentive Pay Schemes Seen as a Result of Economic Employee Relation Change," *BNA Daily Report* (October 9, 1984), 1; Milkovich and Newman, *Compensation;* G. W. Florkowski, "The Organizational Impact of Profit Sharing," *The Academy of Management Review* (October 1987): 622–636.

60. J. Labate, "Deal Those Workers In," *Fortune* (April 19, 1993).

61. *Source:* Based on and adapted from S. Caudron, "Master the Compensation Maze," *Personnel Journal* (June 1993): 641. Used by permission.

62. "Productivity Boosters in Employee-Owned Firms," *Bulletin to Management* (May 5, 1994): 137; "Profit Sharing Plans Scarce but Successful," *Bulletin to Management* (June 2, 1994): 169; L. Uchitelle, "Good Jobs in Hard Times," *New York Times* (October 3, 1993): 1, 6; K. Matthes, "Greetings from Hallmark," *HR Focus* (August 1993): 12–13; Labate, "Deal Those Workers In," 63; S. Greengard, "Leveraging a Low-Wage Work Force," *Personnel Journal* (January 1995): 90–102.

63. Henderson, *Compensation*.

64. Peck, *Variable Pay*, 6.

65. B. E. Moore and T. L. Ross, *The Scanlon Way to Improved Productivity: A Practical Guide* (New York: Wiley, 1978); R. J. Schulhof, "Five Years with a Scanlon Plan," *Personnel Administrator* (June 1979): 55–63; L. S. Tyler and B. Fisher, "The Scanlon Concept: A Philosophy As Much as a System," *Personnel Administrator* (July 1983): 33–37.

66. *Changing Pay Practice: A BNA Special Report* (Washington, DC, 1988), 68.

67. I. Sager, G. McWilliams, and R. D. Hof, "IBM Leans on Its Sales Force," *Business Week* (February 7, 1994): 110; B. Graham-Moore and T. Ross, *Productivity Gainsharing* (Englewood Cliffs, NJ: Prentice-Hall, 1983); R. J. Bullock and E. E. Lawler III, "Gainsharing: A Few Questions and Fewer Answers," *Human Resource Management* 23 (1984): 23–40.

68. Wallace, *Rewards and Renewal*, 41.

69. Huret, "Paying for Team Results," 41.

70. "Work Redesign, Empowerment Touted," *Bulletin to Management* (August 4, 1994): 248.

71. J. Fierman, "The Perilous New World of Fair Play," *Fortune* (June 13, 1994): 57–64; Wallace, *Rewards and Renewal*, 14–16.

72. S. Baker, "Why Steel Is Looking Sexy," *Business Week* (April 4, 1994): 106–8; "Incentive Compensation," *Fortune* (December 19, 1988): 50–58.

73. C. F. Schultz, "Compensating the Sales Professional," in *New Perspectives on Compensation,* ed. Balkin and Gomez-Mejia, 250–58.

74. Sager, McWilliams, and Hof, "IBM Leans on Its Sales Force," 110.

75. T. Goss, R. Pascale, and A. Athos, "The Reinvention Roller Coaster: Risking the Present for a Powerful Future," *Harvard Business Review* (November–December 1993): 97–108.

76. F. Schwadel, "Chain Finds Incentives a Hard Sell," *Wall Street Journal* (July 5, 1990): 3. See also C. H. Deutsch, "Avon Keeps Ringing, but Wall Street Won't Answer," *New York Times* (July 15, 1990): p. F7.

77. B. Filipczak, "Why No One Likes Your Incentive Program," *Training* (August 1993): 19–25.

78. B. Dumaine, "A Knockout Year," *Fortune* (July 25, 1994): 94–103; J. A. Byrne, L. Bongiorno, and R. Grover, "That Eye-Popping Executive Pay: Is Anybody Worth This Much?" *Business Week* (April 25, 1994): 52–58; J. A. Byrne, "Their Cup Runneth Over—Again," *Business Week* (March 28, 1994): 26–27; Crystal, "How Much CEOs Really Make," 72–80.

79. J. R. Deckop, "Top Executive Compensation and the Pay-for-Performance Issue," in *New Perspectives on Compensation,* ed. Balkin and Gomez-Mejia, 285–93.

80. J. Weber, "Offering Employees Stock Options They Can't Refuse," *Business Week* (October 7, 1991): 34; J. R. Blasi and D. L. Kruse, *The New Owners: The Mass Emergence of Employee Ownership in Public Companies and What It Means to American Business* (New York: HarperCollins, 1991); K. J. Klein, "Employee Stock Ownership and Employee Attitudes: A Test of Three Models," *Journal of Applied Psychology* 72 (1987): 319–32; M. Quarrey, J. Blasi, and C. Rosen, *Taking Stock: Employee Ownership at Work* (Cambridge, MA: Ballinger Publication Co., 1986), 66.

81. T. A. Steward, "The Trouble with Stock Options," *Fortune* (January 1, 1990): 93–95.

82. See "Looking Good," p. R2.

83. J. A. Lopez, "A Better Way?" *Wall Street Journal* (April 13, 1994): p. R6.

84. J. Bennet, "Bonus Triples for Chrysler Chairman," *New York Times* (March 18, 1994): p. D4; L. Rorimer, "Put More Incentive in Incentive Pay," *New York Times* (January 16, 1994): p. F11.

85. J. D. McMillan and C. Young, "Sweetening the Compensation Package," *HR Magazine* (October 1990): 36–39.

86. P. Chingos, "Executive Compensation in the 1990s: The Challenges Ahead," *Compensation and Benefits Review* (November–December 1990): 20–31; M. J. Mandel, "Those Fat Bonuses Don't Seem to Boost Performance," *Business Week* (January 8, 1990): 26; B. A. Stertz, "Chrysler Urges Its One Hundred Top Executives to Bet More of Their Pay on Firm's Fate," *Wall Street Journal* (April 2, 1990): p. A4; G. S. Crystal, "Incentive Pay That Doesn't Work," *Fortune* (August 28, 1989): 101, 104; G. S. Crystal, "Rendering Long-Term Incentives Less Risky for Executives," *Personnel* (September 1988): 80–84; M. A. Mazer, "An End to Stock Appreciation Rights?" *Personnel Journal* (November 1990): 53–57; G. S. Crystal, "Handling Underwater Stock Option Grants," *Personnel* (February 1988): 12–15; M. A. Mazer, "Benefits: Are Stock Option Plans Still Viable?" *Personnel Journal* (July 1988): 48–50.

87. "Microsoft: Bill Gates's Baby Is on Top of the World. Can It Stay There?" *Business Week* (February 24, 1992): 60–65.

88. "Incentives: The ABCs of Phantom Stock," *Inc.* (May 1991): 100–102.

89. J. McMillen, K. Allen, and R. Salwen, "Private Companies Offer Long-Term Incentives," *HR Magazine* (June 1991): 63–66.

90. See also K. E. Foster, "Does Executive Pay Make Sense?" *Business Horizons* (September–October 1981): 47–58; "Pay at the Top Mirrors Inflation," *Business Week* (May 11, 1981): 58–59; "Surge in Executive Job Contracts," *Dunn's Business Month* (October 1981): 86–88; D. B. Thompson, "Are CEOs Worth What They're Paid?" *Industry Week* (May 4, 1981): 65–74.

91. The following material is adapted from P. Dowling, R. S. Schuler, and D. Welch, *International Dimensions of Human Resource Management,* 2nd ed. (Belmont, CA: Wadsworth, 1994); A. V. Phatak, R. Chandram, and R. A. Ajayi, "International Executive Compensation," in *New Perspectives on Compensation,* ed. Balkin and Gomez-Mejia, 315–27.

92. Phatak, Chandram, and Ajayi, "International Executive Compensation," in *New Perspectives on Compensation,* ed. Balkin and Gomez-Mejia, 315–27; B. J. Springer, "1992: The Impact on Compensation and Benefits in the European Community," *Compensation and Benefits Review* (July–August 1989): 20–27.

93. M. J. Bishko, "Compensating Your Overseas Executives, Part 1: Strategies for the 1990s," *Compensation and Benefits Review* (May–June 1990): 33–43; M. J. Bishko, "Compensating Your Overseas Executives, Part 2: Europe 1992," *Compensation and Benefits Review* (July–August 1990): 25–35.

94. H. J. Ruff and G. I. Jackson, "Methodological Problems in International Comparisons of the Cost of Living," *Journal of International Business Studies* 5 (1974): 57–67.

95. G. Flynn, "HR in Mexico: What You Should Know," *Personnel Journal* (August 1994): 44.

✦ CHAPTER 14

1. J. Holusha, "Du Pont Sets a Charge of $5 Billion," *New York Times* (January 5, 1993): p. D4.

2. *Source:* Adapted from G. Kramon, "Rockwell's Point Man in the Health Care Campaign," *New York Times* (April 7, 1991): p. C5. See also J. Galbraith, "Positioning Human Resource As a Value-Adding Function: The Case of Rockwell International," *Human Resource Management* (winter 1992): 287–300; V. Byrd,

"The Nimble Giants," *Business Week* (March 28, 1994): 64–78; N. J. Perry, "Rockwell International: Getting Out of Rocket Science," *Fortune* (April 4, 1994): 101–2; L. Uchitelle, "Offer by Northrop for Grumman Tops Martin Marietta Bid," *New York Times* (March 11, 1994): pp. A1, D4.

3. "Employee Benefits—March 1994," *Bulletin to Management Datagraph* (July 14, 1994): 220–21; "Benefits in Small Firms," *Bulletin to Management Datagraph* (March 24, 1994): 92–93.

4. "Americans on Benefits: Keep Them Coming," *HR Reporter* (February 1991): 4–5.

5. T. Chauran, "Benefits Communication," *Personnel Journal* (January 1989): 70–77.

6. T. J. Bergmann and M. A. Bergmann, "How Important Are Fringe Benefits to Employees?" *Personnel* (December 1987): 59–64; R. M. McCaffery, *Employee Benefit Programs: A Total Compensation Perspective* (Boston: PWS-Kent, 1988).

7. "Employer-Based Health Coverage Declining," *Bulletin to Management Datagraph* (June 23, 1994): 196–97; M. Hequet, "The People Squeeze in Health Care," *Training* (July 1994): 35–39; M. D. Fefer, "Tailored Health Plans Take Off," *Fortune* (June 27, 1994): 12; B. P. Noble, "Surprise: Bigger Isn't Always Better," *New York Times* (June 19, 1994): p. F21.

8. S. Caudron, "Health-Care Reform: Act Now or Pay Later," *Personnel Journal* (March 1994): 57–67; M. Porter, E. Teisberg, and G. Brown, "Innovation: Medicine's Best Cost-Cutter," *New York Times* (February 27, 1994): p. F11; "Health Care Cost Sharing: Coating the Pill," *Bulletin to Management* (March 10, 1994): 73.

9. M. L. Williams and G. F. Dreher, "Compensation System Attributes and Applicant Pool Characteristics," *Academy of Management Journal* 35 (1992): 571–95.

10. M. Rowland, "A Farewell to Paternalism," *New York Times* (March 8, 1992): p. F16.

11. J. E. Santora, "Employee Team Designs Flexible Benefits Program," *Personnel Journal* (April 1994): 30–39; "Americans on Benefits," 4–5; McCaffery, *Employee Benefits Programs,* 14–30.

12. F. Foulkes, *Personnel Policies in Large Nonunion Companies* (Englewood Cliffs, NJ: Prentice-Hall, 1980), 209–29.

13. A. Bernstein, "The Mommy Backlash," *Business Week* (August 10, 1992): 42.

14. "Permissible Pregnancy Practices," *Fair Employment Practices Guidelines* (December 1, 1983): 3. The Pregnancy Disability Amendment also has other provisions; for a description of them, see S. R. Zacur and W. Greenwood, "The Pregnancy Disability Amendment: What the Law Provides, Part II," *Personnel Administrator* (March 1982): 55–58.

15. *Source:* B. P. Noble, "Interpreting the Family Leave Act," *New York Times* (August 1, 1993): p. F24. See also D. Gunsch, "The Family Leave Act: A Financial Burden?" *Personnel Journal* (September 1993): 48–57; "Companies Willing to Stretch Employees Still Further," *HR Reporter* (March 1993): 5–6.

16. Ibid.

17. E. Galinsky, D. E. Friedman, and C. A. Hernandez, *The Corporate Reference Guide to Work-Family Programs* (New York: Families & Work Institute, 1991).

18. C. Del Valle, "Harsh Medicine for Ailing Pension Plans," *Business Week* (September 19, 1994): 91–94; M. Rowland, "An Unseen Trap in Pension Funds," *New York Times* (August 28, 1994): p. F13; R. D. Hylton, "Don't Panic about Your Pension—Yet," *Fortune* (April 18, 1994): 121–28; "ERISA's Effects on Pension Plan Administration," *Bulletin to Management* (August 9, 1984): 1–2; K. D. Gill, ed., *ERISA: The Law and the Code,* 1985 ed. (Washington, DC: Bureau of National Affairs, 1985); B. J. Coleman, *Primer on Employee Retirement Income Security Act* (Washington, DC: Bureau of National Affairs, 1985).

19. McCaffery, *Employee Benefit Programs;* "ERISA's Effects on Pension Plan Administration"; Coleman, *Primer on Employee Retirement Income Security Act;* Gill, *ERISA.*

20. J. A. LoCicero, "How to Cope with the Multi-Employer Pension Plan Amendments Act of 1980," *Personnel Administrator* (May 1981): 51–54, 68; J. A. LoCicero, "Multi-Employer Pension Plans: A Time Bomb for Employers?" *Personnel Journal* (November 1980): 922–24, 932.

21. J. Case, "ESOPs: Dead or Alive?" *Inc.* (June 1988): 94–100; P. Nulty, "What a Difference Owner-Bosses Make," *Fortune* (April 25, 1988): 97–104.

22. *Source:* "The Real Strengths of Employee Stockownership," *Business Week* (July 15, 1991): 156. Also see A. Bryant, "Betting the Farm On the Company Stock," *New York Times* (April 16, 1995): Sec 3, 1, 7.

23. M. Rowland, "A Pension Perk with a Lot of Strings," *New York Times* (September 25, 1994): p. F13; M. Rowland, "Red Flag on Pensions at Nonprofits," *New York Times* (October 2, 1994): p. F13; D. Schwartz, "The Last Word on Section 89," *Personnel Journal* (January 1989): 48–57; R. E. Johnson and S. J. Velleman, "Section 89: Close the New Pandora's Box," *Personnel Journal* (November 1988): 70–78; J. Ortman, "Section 89: Why You Should Act Now," *Personnel Journal* (November 1988): 78–79.

24. "Social Security and Employees," *Bulletin to Management* (February 17, 1994): 52–53; "Changes in the Social Security Law," *Bulletin to Management* (January 14, 1988): 12; B. Keller, "Another Stab at Pension Reform," *New York Times* (July 15, 1984): 1; R. C. Murphy and R. E. Wallace, "New Directions for the Social Security System," *Personnel Journal* (February 1983): 138–41.

25. *Bulletin to Management* (December 19, 1991): 396–98; B. DeClark, "Cutting Unemployment Insurance Costs," *Personnel Journal* (November 1983): 868–72; McCaffery, *Employee Benefits Programs;* B. S. Murphy, W. E. Barlow, and D. D. Hatch, "Unemployment Compensation and Religious Beliefs," *Personnel Journal* (June 1987): 36–43; L. Uchitelle, "Jobless Insurance System Aids Reduced Number of Workers," *New York Times* (July 26, 1988): 1.

26. M. D. Fefer, "Taking Control of Your Workers' Comp Costs," *Fortune* (October 3, 1994): 131–36; "Workers' Compensation: Total Disability Benefits," *Bulletin to Management* (May 19, 1988): 156–57.

27. *Source:* Adapted from J. J. Laabs, "Steelcase Slashes Workers' Comp Costs," *Personnel Journal* (February 1993): 72–87. See also "Workers' Comp Strategy Saves $4 Million Yearly," *Personnel Journal* (January 1993): 55.

28. *Managing Workers' Compensation Costs* (William M. Mercer Co., 1991); A. Tramposh, *Avoiding the Cracks: A Guide to the Workers' Compensation System* (New York: Praeger, 1991).

29. "Injured Workers: Cost-Cutting Rehabilitation Option," *Bulletin to Management* (October 15, 1987): 330, 335; M. W. Fitzgerald, "How to Take On Workers' Compensation and Win," *Personnel Journal* (July 1991): 31–33.

30. McCaffery, *Employment Benefits Programs,* 130–31.

31. Hylton, "Don't Panic about Your Pension—Yet"; P. F. Drucker, "Reckoning with the Pension Fund Revolution," *Harvard Business Review* (March–April 1991): 106–14.

32. Hylton, "Don't Panic about Your Pension—Yet," 121–28; B. Leonard, "Agency Protects Pan Am Pension Benefits," *HR News* (September 1991): pp. A1, A10.

33. Martin E. Segal Co., *Pension Issues: A Fifty Year History and Outlook,* newsletter 33, no. 3 (February 1990); T. F. Duzak, "Defined Benefit and Defined Contribution Plans: A Labor Perspective," in *Economic Survival in Retirement* (New York: Salisbury Publishing, 1990), 69; U.S. Department of Labor, Bureau of Labor Statistics, *Employee Benefits in Medium and Large Firms, 1989* (Washington, DC, June 1990).

34. C. H. Farnsworth, "Experiment in Worker Ownership Shows a Profit," *New York Times* (August 14, 1993): pp. L33, L46; "New Developments in Global Stock Plans," *HR Focus* (November 1992): 19; L. Wayne, "Pension Changes Raising Concerns," *New York Times* (August 29, 1994): p. D1.

35. A. Shanker, "Where We Stand," *New York Times* (August 28, 1994): p. E7; "Employee Benefits Update," *Bulletin to Management* (August 25, 1994): 272.

36. "CEOs Seek Help on Health Costs," *Fortune* (June 3, 1991): 12.

37. M. Freudenheim, "H.M.O.'s That Offer Choice Are Gaining in Popularity," *New York Times* (February 7, 1994): pp. A1, D3; M. Freudenheim, "Health on a Budget," *New York Times* (September 2, 1991): p. D1.

38. B. J. Feder, "Deere Sees a Future in Health Care," *New York Times* (July 1, 1994): p. D1; J. J. Laabs, "Deere's HMO Turns Crisis into Profit," *Personnel Journal* (October 1992): 82–89.

39. McCaffery, *Employee Benefits Programs,* 130–31.

40. P. Kerr, "Betting the Farm on Managed Care," *New York Times* (June 27, 1993): 1, 6.

41. "An Incentive a Day Can Keep Doctor Bills at Bay," *Business Week* (April 29, 1991): 22.

42. S. Caudron, "The Wellness Pay Off," *Personnel Journal* (July 1990): 55–60; "How Healthy Are Corporate Fitness Programs?" *The Physician and Sports Medicine* (March 1989). Also contact Wellness Councils of America (WELCOA), 1823 Harney St., Suite 201, Omaha, NE 68102, (402)444-1711.

43. "Wellness Plans and the Disabilities Act," *Bulletin to Management* (May 27, 1993): 168.

44. C. M. Steele and R. A. Josephs, "Alcohol Myopia: Its Prized and Dangerous Effects," *American Psychologist* (August 1990): 921–33; P. M. Roman, ed., *Alcohol Problem Intervention in the Workplace: Employee Assistance Programs and Strategic Alternatives* (Westport, CT: Quorum Books, 1990); W. J. Sonnenstuhl and H. M. Trice, *Strategies for Employee Assistance Programs: The Crucial Balance* (Ithaca, NY: ILR Press, 1990).

45. McCaffery, *Employee Benefits Programs.*

46. G. Latham and N. Napier, "Practical Ways to Increase Employee Attendance," in *Absenteeism: New Approaches to Understanding, Measuring and Managing Employee Absence,* ed. P. Goodman and R. Atkins (San Francisco: Jossey-Bass, 1984); R. Steers and S. Rhodes, "Major Influences on Employee Attendance: A Process Model," *Journal of Applied Psychology* 63 (1978): 391–407.

47. D. Scott and S. Markham, "Absenteeism Control Methods: A Survey of Practices and Results," *Personnel Administrator* 27 (1982): 73–86.

48. C. R. Deitsch and D. A. Dilts, "Getting Absent Employees Back on the Job: The Case of General Motors," *Business Horizons* (Fall 1981): 52–58.

49. J. Chadwick-Jones, N. Nicholson, and C. Brown, *Social Psychology of Absenteeism* (New York: Praeger, 1982).

50. S. Zedeck, ed., *Work, Families, and Organizations* (San Francisco: Jossey-Bass, 1992).

51. E. E. Kossek and V. Nichol, "The Effects of On-Site Child Care on Employee Attitudes and Performance," *Personnel Psychology* 45 (1992): 485–509.

52. A. Halcrow, "Optimas Reflects Changes in HR," *Personnel Journal* (January 1994): 50; C. M. Solomon, "Work/Family's Failing Grade: Why Today's Initiatives Aren't Enough," *Personnel Journal* (May 1994): 72–83.

53. J. Fierman, "Are Companies Less Family-Friendly?" *Fortune* (March 21, 1994): 64–67.

54. Kossek and Nichol, "The Effects of On-Site Child Care," 485–509; McCaffery, *Employee Benefits Programs,* 172–73; M. B. Scott, "How Companies Help with Family Care," *Employee Benefit Plan Review* (May 1990): 12.

55. *Source:* Adapted from "Life Is Enriched at Lotus Development," *Personnel Journal* (January 1994): 62. Used by permission.

56. D. Jamieson and J. O'Mara, *Managing Workforce 2000,* 148–49; "International Foundation of Employee Benefits Plans," *Nontraditional Benefits for the Work Force of 2000: A Special Report* (Brookfield, MA: IFEBP, 1990).

57. *Source:* Adapted from "Listening: An Action-Driver at Allstate," *HR Reporter* (November 1992): 1–3. Used by permission.

58. C. M. Loder, "Merck and Co. Breaks New Ground for Employee Child Care Centers," *Star Ledger* (May 1990): 12; "Companies Cited for Supporting Working Mothers," *HR Focus* (December 1991): 13; S. J. Goff, M. K. Mount, and R. L. Jamison, "Employer Supported Child Care, Work/Family Conflict, and Absenteeism: A Field Study," *Personnel Psychology* 43 (1990): 793–809; S. Zedeck and K. L. Mosier, "Work in the Family and Employing Organization," *American Psychologist* (February 1990): 240–51; S. Scarr, D. Phillips, and K. McCartney, "Working Mothers and Their Families," *American Psychologist* (November 1989): 1402–9; E. E. Kossek, "Diversity in Child Care Assistance Needs: Employee Problems, Preferences,

and Work-Related Outcomes," *Personnel Psychology* 43 (1990): 769–91; E. E. Kossek, *Childcare and Challenges for Employers* (Horsham, Australia: LRP Publications, 1991); S. L. Grover, "Predicting the Perceived Fairness of Parental Leave Policies," *Journal of Applied Psychology* 76 (1991): 247–55.

59. J. J. Laabs, "How Campbell Manages Its Rural Health Care Dollars," *Personnel Journal* (May 1992): 74–81; "Campbell Soup Co.," *Personnel Journal* (January 1992): 56.

60. E. Smith, "First Interstate Finds an Eldercare Solution," *HR Magazine* (July 1991): 152; A. E. Scharlach, B. F. Lowe, and E. L. Schneider, *Elder Care and the Work Force* (Lexington, MA: Lexington Books, 1991); L. Crawford, *Dependent Care and the Employee Benefits Package* (Westport, CT: Quorum Books, 1990).

61. International Foundation of Employee Benefits Plans, *Nontraditional Benefits for the Work Force of 2000: A Special Research Report.*

62. "The Perspectives of Childless Employees," *Bulletin to Management* (May 5, 1994): 144.

63. D. J. Jefferson, "Gay Employees Win Benefits for Partners at More Corporations," *Wall Street Journal* (March 18, 1994): pp. A1, A2.

64. "Lotus Opens a Door for Gay Partners," *Business Week* (November 4, 1991): 80–81. See also D. Anfuso, "Soul-Searching Sustains Values at Lotus Development," *Personnel Journal* (June 1994): 54–61; M. Rowland, "Hurdles for Unmarried Partners," *New York Times* (May 22, 1994): p. F15.

65. J. J. Laabs, "Smooth Moves," *Personnel Journal* (February 1994): 68–76; G. Flynn, "Relocation Has a New Look," *Personnel Journal* (February 1995): 48–60.

66. J. Reese, "Mortgage Help as a Job Benefit," *Fortune* (June 3, 1991): 13; "Housing Aid—Benefit of the 90s?" *Bulletin to Management* (September 5, 1991): 280; *Employer-Assisted Housing Programs* (Lincolnshire, IL: Hewitt Associates, 1991).

67. K. P. Shapiro and J. A. Sherman, "Employee Attitudes Benefit Plan Designs," *Personnel Journal* (July 1987): 49–53; A. Barber, R. B. Dunham, and R. A. Formisano, "The Impact of Flexible Benefits on Employee Satisfaction: A Field Study," *Personnel Psychology* 45 (1992): 55–75; C. A. Baker, "Flex Your Benefits," *Personnel Journal* (May 1988): 54–60.

68. R. Brookler, "HR in Growing Companies," *Personnel Journal* (November 1992): 802.

69. J. E. Santora, "Employee Team Designs Flexible Benefits Program," *Personnel Journal* (April 1994): 30–

39; R. Brookler, "HR in Growing Companies," *Personnel Journal* (November 1992): 802.

70. See *1994 Hay/Huggins Benefits Report.*

71. "Employees Would Change Benefits if Possible," *Bulletin to Management* (August 15, 1985): 1–2. Reprinted by permission from *Bulletin to Management.* © 1985 by the Bureau of National Affairs, Washington, DC.

72. "Benefit Communication: Looking at the Voice Response Option," *HR Reporter* (November 1993): 1–5.

73. "Cost, Communication, and Compliance Concerns," *Bulletin to Management* (March 21, 1985): 7; "Pay Off," *Wall Street Journal* (July 8, 1982): 1; R. Foltz, "Communiqué," *Personnel Administrator* (May 1981): 8; R. M. McCaffery, "Employee Benefits: Beyond the Fringe?" *Personnel Administrator* (May 1981): 26–30; T. F. Casey, "One-to-One Communication of Employee Benefits," *Personnel Journal* (August 1982): 572–74; "Employee Benefits: Attitudes and Reactions," *Bulletin to Management* (April 11, 1985): 1.

74. E. Faltermayer, "Getting Health Alliances Right," *Fortune* (May 16, 1994): 82–88; S. Caudron, "Health-Care Reform: Act Now or Pay Later," *Personnel Journal* (March 1994): 57–67; "Employers, Employees Have Different Views on Paying for Health Care Reform," *HR Reporter* (April 1994): 1–3; "Health Care Cost Sharing: Coating the Pill," *Bulletin to Management* (March 10, 1994): 73–74; M. Porter, E. Teisberg, and G. Brown, "Innovation: Medicine's Best Cost-Cutter," *New York Times* (February 27, 1994): p. F11.

75. This section is adapted from G. Flynn, "HR in Mexico: What You Should Know," *Personnel Journal* (August 1994): 34–44. See also A. Winsor, *The Complete Guide to Doing Business in Mexico* (New York: AMACOM, 1994).

76. "Tips to Succeed South of the Border," *Bulletin to Management* (April 28, 1994): 129–30. For more discussion on pensions in Latin America, see J. Brooke, "Quiet Revolution in Latin Pensions," *New York Times* (September 10, 1994): 37.

77. Flynn, "HR in Mexico."

78. G. Smith, S. Baker, and W. Glasgall, "Mexico: Will Economic Reform Survive the Turmoil?" *Business Week* (April 11, 1994): 24–27; S. Baker, G. Smith, and E. Weiner, "The Mexican Worker," *Business Week* (April 19, 1993): 84–92.

79. S. Dolan and R. S. Schuler, *Human Resource Management* (Toronto: Nelson, 1994).

✸ CHAPTER 15

1. *Ben and Jerry's Homemade Incorporated Annual Report, 1992, 1993,* and *1994.*

2. Source: *Ben and Jerry's Homemade Incorporated Annual Report, 1992, 1993,* and *1994.*

3. L. Johnson, "Preventing Injuries: The Big Payoff," *Personnel Journal* (April 1994): 61–64; R. S. Schuler, "Occupational Health in Organizations: A Measure of Personnel Effectiveness," in *Readings in Personnel and Human Resource Management,* 2nd ed., ed. R. S.

Schuler and S. A. Youngblood (St. Paul, MN: West Publishing Co., 1984). See also D. R. Ilgen, "Health Issues at Work: Opportunities for Industrial/Organizational Psychology," *American Psychologist* (February 1990): 273–83.

4. J. A. Kinney, "Why Did Paul Die?" *Newsweek* (September 10, 1990): 11. See also B. J. Feder, "A Spreading Pain, and Cries for Justice," *New York Times* (June 5, 1994): sec. 3, pp. 1, 6.

5. T. F. O'Boyle, "Fear and Stress in the Office Take Toll," *Wall Street Journal* (November 6, 1990): pp. B1, B2. See also Bureau of Labor Statistics, *Shifting Work Force Spawns New Set of Hazardous Occupations,* summary report no. 94-8 (Washington, DC: Bureau of Labor Statistics Office of Safety, Health Conditions, [202]606-6304).

6. K. Matthes, "A Prescription for Healthier Offices," *HR Focus* (April 1992): 4–5; "Indoor Air Issues Confront Employers," *Bulletin to Management* (October 22, 1992): 329.

7. J. Nordheimer, "Pressures of Costs Driving Some Contractors to Stress Worker Safety," *New York Times* (August 21, 1993): 25.

8. M. D. Fefer, "Taking Control of Your Workers' Comp Costs," *Fortune* (October 3, 1994): 131–36.

9. "Back Injuries," *Bulletin to Management* (January 9, 1992): 396; "Sprains and Strains Lead Workplace Injuries," *Bulletin to Management* (May 26, 1994): 164–65; "Occupational Injuries and Illnesses," *Bulletin to Management* (January 12, 1995): 12–13.

10. "Workplace Fatalities," *Bulletin to Management* (September 1, 1994): 276–77; L. Reynolds, "Labor Secretary Calls for 'Time Out' in OSHA Battle," *HR Focus* (August 1993): 4; "Occupational Injuries and Illnesses," *Bulletin to Management* (January 6, 1994): 4–5.

11. B. Saporito, "The Most Dangerous Jobs in America," *Fortune* (May 31, 1993): 131–40; "Occupational Injuries and Illnesses," *Bulletin to Management* (January 6, 1994): 4–6.

12. Nordheimer, "Pressures of Costs Drive Some Contractors to Stress Worker Safety," 25.

13. These estimates should be regarded as conservative because they do not include the costs due to stress and to a low quality of working life.

14. "OSHA: Reforms and Penalties," *Bulletin to Management* (January 28, 1993): 25; D. Foust, "Stepping into the Middle of OSHA's Muddle," *Business Week* (August 2, 1993): 53; "OSHA Penalties Fall in Fiscal 1993," *Bulletin to Management* (April 21, 1994): 124–25; "Safety and Health Highlights," *Bulletin to Management* (August 11, 1994): 250, 255.

15. "On the Safety and Health Scene," *Bulletin to Management* (April 2, 1987): 105.

16. B. Meir, "Use of Right-to-Know Rules Is Increasing Public's Scrutiny of Chemical Companies," *Wall Street Journal* (May 23, 1985): 10; "OSHA's Final Labelling Standard," *Bulletin to Management* (December 1, 1983): 1.

17. P. A. Susser, "Update on Hazard Communication," *Personnel Administrator* (October 1985): 57–61; M. G. Miner, "Legal Concerns Facing Human Resource Managers: An Overview," in *Readings in Personnel and Human Resource Management,* 3rd ed., ed. R. S. Schuler, S A. Youngblood, and V. L. Huber; "Hazard Communication Training: Compliance Cues," *Bulletin to Management* (March 13, 1986): 81.

18. *Wall Street Journal* (October 2, 1984): 1; "State Right-to-Know Laws: Toxic Substances," *Bulletin to Management* (November 2, 1984): 4–5; "Worker Right to Know," *Chemical Work* (April 18, 1984): 38–44.

19. M. Novit, "Mental Distress: Possible Implications for the Future," *Personnel Administrator* (August 1982): 47–54. The Civil Rights Act of 1871, section 1983, enforces the Fourteenth Amendment, providing for "equal protection of the laws," and prohibits employment discrimination on the basis of race, color, national origin, religion, sex, or age.

20. Determining responsibility is sometimes difficult because determining cause-and-effect relationships is difficult, especially since reactions such as asbestosis or hypertension take a long time to develop or occur only in some people working under the same conditions as others. For a discussion, see A. D. Marcus, "Fearful of Future, Plaintiffs Are Suing Firms for What Hasn't Happened Yet," *Wall Street Journal* (July 11, 1990): pp. B1, B8.

21. "Cutting Workers' Compensation Costs," *Bulletin to Management* (April 22, 1993): 122.

22. "Workplace Torts," *Bulletin to Management* (October 1, 1992): 213. © 1992 by the Bureau of National Affairs, (800)372-1033. Reprinted by permission.

23. D. Frum, "Oh My Aching . . . You Name It," *Forbes* (April 26, 1993): 53. See also A. Farnham, "Back Ache," *Fortune* (December 14, 1992): 132–40.

24. O'Boyle, "Fear and Stress in the Office Take Toll," 2.

25. Personal correspondence with Donald Brush, President, Bearings Division, Barden Corporation, March 8, 1989.

26. B. Filipczak, "Armed and Dangerous at Work," *Training* (July 1993): 39–43; "Workplace Violence: When Dissatisfaction Turns to Fury," *HR Reporter* (March 1994): 1–5. See also "Workplace Violence: An Array of Potential Legal Repercussions?" *Fair Employment Practices Guidelines* (August 25, 1994): 6–8.

27. *Source:* Adapted from "Preventing Workplace Violence," *Bulletin to Management* (June 10, 1993): 177. © 1993 by the Bureau of National Affairs, (800)372-1033. Reprinted by permission.

28. C. S. Weaver, "Understanding Occupational Disease," *Personnel Journal* (June 1989): 86–94.

29. Ibid.

30. C. L. Wang, "Occupational Skin Disease Continues to Plague Industry," *Monthly Labor Review* (February 1979): 17–22.

31. K. R. Pelletier, "The Hidden Hazards of the Modern Office," *New York Times* (September 8, 1985): p. F3; J. Hyatt, "Hazardous Effects of VDT Legislation," *Inc.* (March 1985): 27; W. L. Weis, "No Smoking," *Personnel Journal* (September 1984): 53–58; "VDT Study: Safety Charges, Design Changes," *Bulletin to Management* (July 21, 1983): 285; "Office Hazard: Factory Environment Can Boomerang," *Impact* (June 22, 1983): 1.

32. "Charges of Emotional Distress: A Growing Trend," *Fair Employment Practices Guidelines* 284 (1989): 1–4. See also a set of references identifying and discussing each preference or interest listed here, in R. S. Schuler, "Definition and Conceptualization of Stress in Organizations," *Organizational Behavior and Human Performance* 23 (1980): 184–215; R. S. Schuler, "An Integrative Transactional Process Model of Stress in Organizations," *Journal of Occupational Behavior* 3 (1982): 3–19.

33. A. B. Shostak, *Blue Collar Stress* (Reading, MA: Addison-Wesley, 1980).

34. R. C. Kessler, J. B. Turner, and J. S. House, "Unemployment and Health in a Community Sample," *Journal*

of Health and Social Behavior 28 (1987): 51–59; R. C. Kessler, J. B. Turner, and J. S. House, "Intervening Processes in the Relationship between Unemployment and Health," Psychological Medicine 17 (1987): 949–61; R. D. Caplan et al., "Job Seeking, Reemployment and Mental Health: A Randomized Field Experiment in Coping with Job Loss," Journal of Applied Psychology 74 (1989): 759–69; S. J. Ashford, C. Lee, and P. Bobko, "Content, Causes, and Consequences of Job Insecurity: A Theory-Based Measure and Substantive Test," Academy of Management Journal 32 (1989): 803–29; S. E. Markham and G. H. McKee, "Declining Organizational Size and Increasing Unemployment Rates: Predicting Employee Absenteeism from Within- and Between-Plant Perspectives," Academy of Management Journal 34 (1991): 952–65; P. Cappelli, "Examining Managerial Displacement," Academy of Management Journal 35 (1992): 203–17; R. H. Price, "Psychological Impact of Job Loss on Individuals and Families," Current Directions (American Psychological Society, 1992).

35. S. Cohen and G. M. Williamson, "Stress and Infectious Disease in Humans," Psychological Bulletin 109 (1991): 5–24; S. R. Barley and D. B. Knight, "Toward a Cultural Theory of Stress Complaints," Research in Organizational Behavior 14 (1992): 1–48; R. Martin and T. D. Wall, "Attentional Demand and Cost Responsibility as Stressors in Shopfloor Jobs," Academy of Management Journal 32 (1989): 69–86; C. A. Higgins and L. E. Duxbury, "Work-Family Conflict in the Dual-Career Family," Organizational Behavior and Human Decision Processes 51 (1992): 51–75; S. Parasuraman et al., "Work and Family Variables as Mediators of the Relationship between Wives' Employment and Husbands' Well-Being," Academy of Management Journal 32 (1989): 185–201; B. A. Gutek, S. Searle, and L. Klepa, "Rational versus Gender Role Explanations for Work-Family Conflict," Journal of Applied Psychology 76 (1991): 560–68; L. E. Duxbury and C. A. Higgins, "Gender Differences in Work-Family Conflict," Journal of Applied Psychology 76 (1991): 60–74; K. J. Williams et al., "Multiple Role Juggling and Daily Mood States in Working Mothers: An Experience Sampling Study," Journal of Applied Psychology 76 (1991): 664–74; M. F. Frone, M. Russell, and M. L. Cooper, "Antecedents and Outcomes of Work-Family Conflict: Testing a Model of the Work-Family Interface," Journal of Applied Psychology 77 (1992): 65–78.

36. M. Frankenhaeuser and B. Gardell, "Underload and Overload in Working Life: Outline of Multidisciplinary Approach," Journal of Human Stress 2 (1976): 36–45; M. Pesci, "Stress Management: Separating Myth from Reality," Personnel Administrator (January 1982): 57–67. But even if individuals are under heavy workloads and stress, they may not necessarily want to eliminate them; see R. Richlefs, "Many Executives Complain of Stress, but Few Want Less-Pressured Jobs," Wall Street Journal (September 29, 1982): 35.

37. Hyatt, "Hazardous Effects of VDT Legislation," 27; Pelletier, "Hidden Hazards of the Modern Office," p. F3; R. Sutton and A. Rafaeli, "Characteristics of Work Stations as Potential Occupational Stressors,"

Academy of Management Journal 30 (June 1987): 260–76; "VDT Study," 27; Weis, "No Smoking," 53–58.

38. M. Friedman and R. Roseman, Type A Behavior and Your Heart (New York: Alfred A. Knopf, 1974).

39. S. E. Jackson and R. S. Schuler, "Preventing Employee Burnout," Personnel (March–April 1983): 58–68; B. Dumaine, "Cool Cures for Burnout," Fortune (June 20, 1986): 78–84.

40. H. J. Hilaski, "Understanding Statistics on Occupational Illnesses," Monthly Labor Review (March 1981): 25–29; R. A. Reber, J. A. Wallin, and J. S. Chhokar, "Reducing Industrial Accidents: A Behavioral Experiment," Industrial Relations (winter 1984): 119–25.

41. "Safety: A Quick Pay-Off, a Long-Term Commitment," HR Reporter (October 1990): 6. See also R. Pater, "Safety Leadership Cuts Costs," HR Magazine (November 1990): 46–47.

42. S. Dolan and R. S. Schuler, Human Resource Management Canada (Toronto: Nelson, 1993).

43. D. P. Levin, "The Graying Factor," New York Times (February 20, 1994): sec. III, pp. 1, 3. For extensive discussion of office space and physical design issues, see L. Altman, "Some Who Use VDTs Miscarried, Study Says," New York Times (June 5, 1988): 22; "Reproductive Hazards—How Employers Are Responding," Fair Employment Practices Guidelines (October 29, 1987): 132; R. S. Schuler, L. R. Ritzman, and V. Davis, "Merging Prescriptive and Behavioral Approaches for Office Layout," Production and Inventory Management Journal 3 (1981): 131–42.

44. "National ASPA Conference Highlights," Bulletin to Management (July 28, 1988): 239. See also J. R. Hollenbeck, D. R. Ilgen, and S. M. Crampton, "Lower Back Disability in Occupational Settings: A Review of the Literature from a Human Resource Management View," Personnel Psychology 45 (1992): 247–78.

45. "Personnel Shop Talk," Bulletin to Management (April 25, 1994): 266.

46. J. Komaki, K. D. Barwick, and L. Scott, "Pinpointing and Reinforcing Safe Performance in a Food Manufacturing Plant," Journal of Applied Psychology 63 (1978): 434–45.

47. H. M. Taylor, "Occupational Health Management-by-Objectives," Personnel (January–February 1980): 58–64.

48. M. Williams, "Ten Minutes Work for Twelve Hours Pay? What's the Catch?" Wall Street Journal (October 12, 1983): 19.

49. J. Olian, "New Approaches to Employment Screening," in Readings in Personnel and Human Resource Management, 3rd ed., ed. Schuler, Youngblood, and Huber.

50. J. C. Erfurt, A. Foote, and M. A. Heirich, "The Cost-Effectiveness of Worksite Wellness Programs for Hypertension Control, Weight Loss, Smoking Cessation and Exercise," Personnel Psychology 45 (1992): 5–27; D. L. Bebhardt and C. E. Crump, "Employee Fitness and Wellness Programs in the Workplace," American Psychologist (February 1990): 262–72.

51. "Fetal Protection Policy Struck Down," Fair Employment Practices Guidelines (May 1991): 1–2; "Fetal Protection Ruling," Fair Employment Practices Guide-

lines (March 28, 1991): 31; S. Wermiel, "Justices Bar 'Fetal Protection' Policies," *Wall Street Journal* (March 21, 1991): p. B1; C. Trost, "Workplace Debate," *Wall Street Journal* (October 8, 1990): 1; B. Meier, "Companies Wrestle with Threats to Workers' Reproductive Health," *Wall Street Journal* (February 5, 1987): 25; Altman, "Some Who Use VDT's Miscarried," 22; "Reproductive Hazards," 132.

52. *Source:* Adapted from "Solutions to Workplace Stress," *Bulletin to Management* (February 11, 1993): 48. © 1993 by the Bureau of National Affairs. Reprinted by permission. For more on employee burnout see *Employee Burnout: Causes and Cures, Part 2,* NWNL, P.O. Box 20, Minneapolis, MN 55440, (612)342-7137; S. E. Jackson and R. S. Schuler, "Preventing Employee Burnout," *Personnel* (March–April 1983): 58–68; B. Dumaine, "Cool Cures for Burnout," *Fortune* (June 20, 1986): 78–84.

53. S. B. Garland, "A New Chief Has OSHA Growing Again," *Business Week* (August 20, 1990): 57; P. T. Kilborn, "Who Decides Who Works at Jobs Imperiling Fetuses?" *New York Times* (September 2, 1990): pp. A1, A12; R. Winslow, "Air Polluted by Carbon Monoxide Poses Risk to Heart Patients, Study Shows," *Wall Street Journal* (September 4, 1990): p. B4; R. Winslow, "Safety Group Cites Fatalities Linked to Work," *Wall Street Journal* (August 31, 1990): p. B8; C. Trost, "Business and Women Anxiously Watch Suit on 'Fetal Protection'" *Wall Street Journal* (October 8, 1990): 1.

54. Erfurt, Foote, and Heirich, "Cost-Effectiveness of Worksite Wellness Programs," 5–27.

55. F. B. James, "Study Lays Groundwork for Tying Health Costs to Workers' Behavior," *Wall Street Journal* (April 14, 1987): 37.

56. M. Rowland, "Matching Life-Styles to Benefits," *New York Times* (March 1, 1992).

 CHAPTER 16

1. D. Woodruff, "At Saturn, What Workers Want Is . . . Fewer Defects," *Business Week* (December 2, 1991): 117–18. As of October 1994, Richard G. LeFauve was given the additional responsibilities of running GM's entire domestic small-car operation. His challenge now is to ensure that Saturn's successes are transferred elsewhere.

2. *Source:* Adapted from D. Woodruff, "At Saturn, What Workers Want Is . . . Fewer Defects," *Business Week* (December 2, 1991): 117–18.

3. "Highlights of GM/UAW Agreement," *Bulletin to Management* (October 11, 1990): 321. Information for the feature was also taken from J. Zalusky, "Variable Pay: Labor Seeks Security, Not Bonuses," *Business Week* (January 1991): 13; C. Brown and M. Reich, "When Does Union-Management Cooperation Work? A Look at NUMMI and GM—Van Nuys," *California Management Review* (summer 1989): 27–44; Roger B. Smith, CEO of General Motors, "The U.S. Must Do What GM Has Done," interview in *Fortune* (February 13, 1989): 70–73; G. A. Patterson, "GM's New Contract with UAW May Be Ratified Sunday," *Wall Street Journal* (September 28, 1990): p. A11; D. Woodruff, "It Looks As If the UAW Is Drawing a Bead on GM," *Business Week* (August 20, 1990): 38; D. Woodruff, "The UAW Veers Closer to Reality," *Business Week* (October 1, 1990): 33; W. Zellner, "Suddenly, the UAW Is Raising Its Voice at GM," *Business Week* (November 6, 1989): 96, 100; W. Zellner, "All the Ingredients for Disaster Are There," *Business Week* (April 16, 1990): 20–29.

4. D. Woodruff, "Saturn: Labor's Love Lost?" *Business Week* (February 8, 1993): 122–23.

5. "The Changing Situation of Workers and Their Unions," *Report of the AFL-CIO Evolution of Work Committee* (February 1985), 18–19; P. Jarley and J. Fiorito, "Associate Membership: Unionism or Consumerism?" *Industrial and Labor Relations Review* (January 1990): 209–24.

6. For a more extensive discussion of unionization and the entire union-management relationship, see G. Strauss, D. G. Gallagher, and J. Fiorito, *The State of the Unions* (Madison, WI: Industrial Relations Research Association, University of Wisconsin, 1991); P. C. Weiler, *Governing the Workplace* (Cambridge, MA: Harvard University Press, 1990); H. J. Anderson, *Primer of Labor Relations,* 21st ed. (Washington, DC: Bureau of National Affairs, 1980); B. W. Justice, *Unions, Workers, and the Law* (Washington, DC: Bureau of National Affairs, 1983).

7. For an overview and in-depth discussion of collective bargaining, see L. Balliet, *Survey of Labor Relations* (Washington, DC: Bureau of National Affairs, 1981): J. A. Fossum, "Union-Management Relations," in *Personnel Management,* ed. K. M. Rowland and G. R. Ferris (Boston, MA: Allyn & Bacon, 1982), 420–60; J. A. Fossum, "Labor Relations," in *Human Resource Management in the 1980s,* ed. S. J. Carroll and R. S. Schuler (Washington, DC: Bureau of National Affairs, 1983); R. B. Freeman and J. L. Medoff, *What Do Unions Do?* (New York: Basic Books, 1984); R. J. Donovan, "Bringing America into the 1980s," *American Psychologist* (April 1984): 429–31.

8. A good discussion of earlier contributions to labor law can be found in B. E. Kaufman, *The Origins and Evolution of the Field of Industrial Relations* (Ithaca, NY: ILR Press, 1993). See also D. P. Twomey, *Labor Law and Legislation,* 6th ed. (Cincinnati, OH: Southwestern, 1990); R. C. Trussell, ed., *U.S. Labor and Employment Laws* (Washington, DC: Bureau of National Affairs, Cambridge University Press, 1987).

9. L. Balliet, *Survey of Labor Relations* (Washington, DC: Bureau of National Affairs, 1981).

10. Twomey, *Labor Law and Legislation.*

11. J. Barling, E. K. Kelloway, and E. H. Bremermann, "Preemployment Predictors of Union Attitudes: The Role of Family Socialization and Work Beliefs," *Journal of Applied Psychology* 75, no. 5 (1991): 725–31; S.

Mellor, "The Relationship between Membership Decline and Union Commitment: A Field Study of Local Unions in Crisis," *Journal of Applied Psychology* 75, no. 3 (1990): 258–67; C. Fullagar and J. Barling, "A Longitudinal Test of a Model of the Antecedents and Consequences of Union Loyalty," *Journal of Applied Psychology* 74, no. 2 (1989): 213–27; S. P. Deshpande and J. Fiorito, "Specific and General Beliefs in Union Voting Models," *Academy of Management Journal* 32, no. 4 (1989): 883–97; G. E. Fryxell and M. E. Gordon, "Workplace Justice and Job Satisfaction as Predictors of Satisfaction with Union and Management," *Academy of Management Journal* 32, no. 4 (1989): 851–66.

12. E. H. Schein, *Organizational Psychology* (Englewood Cliffs, NJ: Prentice-Hall, 1965).

13. J. G. Getman, S. B. Goldberg, and J. B. Herman, *Union Representation Elections: Law and Reality* (New York: Russell Sage Foundation, 1976); "Employee Survey: Unionization and Attitude Measure," *Bulletin to Management* (April 24, 1986): 133–34.

14. A. Ritter, "Are Unions Worth the Bargain?" *Personnel* (February 1990): 12–14; J. M. Brett, "Behavioral Research on Unions and Union-Management Systems," *Research in Organizational Behavior,* vol. 2, ed. B. M. Staw and L. L. Cummings (Greenwich, CT: JAI Press, 1980); J. M. Brett, "Why Employees Want Unions," *Organizational Dynamics* 8 (1980): 47–59.

15. S. A. Youngblood et al., "The Impact of Work Attachment, Instrumentality Beliefs, Perceived Labor Union Image, and Subjective Norms on Union Voting Intentions and Union Membership," *Academy of Management Journal* (1984): 576–90.

16. T. A. Kochan, *Collective Bargaining and Industrial Relations* (Homewood, IL: Irwin, 1980); J. LeLouarn, *Proceedings of the 32nd Annual Meeting of the Industrial Relations Research Association* (1979), 72–82.

17. "Union Membership and Earnings," *Bulletin to Management Datagraph* (March 2, 1995).

18. "More Women Leading Unions," *Fair Employment Practices Guidelines* (November 22, 1990): 141; J. G. Kilgour, "The Odds on White-Collar Organizing," *Personnel* (August 1990): 29–34; S. R. Premeaux et al., "Managing Tomorrow's Unionized Workers," *Personnel* (July 1989): 61–64; M. L. Colosi and W. A. Krupman, "Nurses: Supervisory Status or Union Solidarity?" *Personnel* (September 1989): 13–18; "Professionals Not Ready for Union Organizing," *Bulletin to Management* (October 26, 1989): 337–38.

19. *Source:* Based on J. Barling, E. K. Kelloway, and E. H. Bremermann, "Preemployment Predictors of Union Attitudes: The Role of Family Socialization and Work Beliefs," *Journal of Applied Psychology* 75, no. 5 (1991): 725–31.

20. C. Gifford, *Directory of U.S. Labor Organizations, 1990–1991 Edition* (Washington, DC: Bureau of National Affairs, 1990).

21. Getman, Goldberg, and Herman, *Union Representation Elections.*

22. Balliet, *Survey of Labor Relations,* 72–105.

23. Getman, Goldberg, and Herman, *Union Representation Elections,* 1. For a discussion of possible changes here, see B. P. Noble, "At the Labor Board, New Vigor," *New York Times* (September 4, 1994): p. F21.

24. Balliet, *Survey of Labor Relations,* 72–105.

25. For an extensive discussion of the organizing campaign, see J. A. Fossum, "Union-Management Relations," in *Personnel Management,* ed. Rowland and Ferris; W. E. Fulmer, "Step by Step through a Union Campaign," *Harvard Business Review* (July–August 1981): 94–102.

26. "Dealing with Organizing: Do's and Don'ts," *Bulletin to Management* (March 7, 1985): 8.

27. J. Hoerr, "The Strange Bedfellows Backing Workplace Reform," *Business Week* (April 20, 1990): 57. See also R. Koenig, "Quality Circles Are Vulnerable to Union Tests," *Wall Street Journal* (March 28, 1990): p. B1; L. E. Hazzard, "A Union Says Yes to Attendance," *Personnel Journal* (November 1990): 47–49.

28. Twomey, *Labor Law and Legislation,* 134.

29. Getman, Goldberg, and Herman, *Union Representation Elections,* 72.

30. "Union Win Rate in 1991," *Bulletin to Management* (March 26, 1992): 92–93.

31. "Do Union Contracts Conflict with ADA?" *Bulletin to Management* (December 19, 1991): 400.

32. Brett, "Behavioral Research on Unions," 200.

33. See N. Herrick, *Joint Management and Employee Participation: Labor and Management at the Crossroads* (San Francisco: Jossey-Bass, 1990); Brett, "Behavioral Research on Unions"; Brett, "Why Employees Want Unions," 45–59.

34. D. Q. Mills, *The New Competitors* (New York: Free Press, 1985), 225–42; M. Schuster, "The Impact of Union-Management Cooperation on Productivity and Employment," *Industrial and Labor Relations Review* (April 1983): 415–30; H. C. Katz, T. A. Kochan, and K. R. Gobeille, "Industrial Relations Performance, Economic Performance, and QWL Programs: An Interplant Analysis," *Industrial and Labor Relations Review* (October 1983): 3–17.

35. B. P. Noble, "More Than Labor Amity at AT&T," *New York Times* (March 14, 1993): p. F25. See also Chap. 6 in J. Pfeffer, *Competitive Advantage through People* (Boston: Harvard Business School Press, 1994).

36. See note 27.

37. T. Hayes, "Saving 3,727 GM Jobs in Texas," *New York Times* (March 1, 1992): p. F10.

38. J. A. Fossum, *Labor Relations: Development, Structure, Process,* 4th ed. (Plano, TX: Business Publications, 1988).

39. A. Blum, "Collective Bargaining: Ritual or Reality?" *Harvard Business Review* (November–December 1961): 64.

40. M. H. Bazerman, *Judgment in Managerial Decision Making* (New York: Wiley, 1986); M. H. Bazerman and J. S. Carroll, "Negotiator Cognition," in *Research in Organizational Behavior,* vol. 9, ed. Cummings and Staw; M. H. Bazerman, T. Magliozzi, and M. A. Neale, "The Acquisition of an Integrative Response in a Competitive Market," *Organizational Behavior and Human Decision Processes* 34 (1985): 294–313.

41. K. Jennings and E. Traynman, "Two-Tier Plans," *Personnel Journal* (March 1988): 56–58.

42. Sloan and Witney, *Labor Relations.*

43. Fossum, "Labor Relations," in *Human Resource Management in the 1980s,* ed. Carroll and Schuler, 395–96.

44. Sloan and Witney, *Labor Relations,* 59.

45. P. Hartman and W. Franke, "The Changing Bargaining Structure in Construction: Wide-Area and Multicraft Bargaining," *Industrial and Labor Relations Review* (January 1980): 170–84.

46. Hartman and Franke, "The Changing Bargaining Structure in Construction."

47. Fossum, *Labor Relations.*

48. L. Reynolds, "Management-Labor Tensions Spell Union Busting," *Personnel* (March 1991): 7–10; "Teamsters Hope Democracy Brings New Membership," *Personnel* (March 1991): 1–2; B. Schiffman, "Tougher Tactics to Keep Out Unions," *New York Times* (March 3, 1991): p. F8; "Lockout and Shutdowns," *Labor Relations Reporter* (Washington, DC: Bureau of National Affairs, 1985), 688–91.

49. D. Mitchell, "A Note on Strike Propensities and Wage Developments," *Industrial Relations* 20 (1981): 123–27; J. Kennan, "Pareto Optimality and the Economics of Strike Duration," *Journal of Labor Research* 1 (1980): 77–94.

50. L. Uchitelle, "Labor Draws the Line in Decatur," *New York Times* (June 13, 1993): sec. 3, pp. 1, 6; L. Uchitelle, "Strikes: They Don't Make 'Em Like They Used To," *New York Times* (August 21, 1994): p. E3.

51. J. Tasini, "For the Unions, a New Weapon," *New York Times Magazine* (June 12, 1988): 24–25, 69–71; C. Perry, *Union Corporate Campaigns* (Philadelphia: Wharton Industrial Relations Center, 1987).

52. S. Briggs, "Labor/Management Conflict and the Role of the Neutral," in *Personnel and Human Resource Management,* 3rd ed., ed. R. S. Schuler, S. A. Youngblood, and V. L. Huber (St. Paul, MN: West Publishing Co., 1988).

53. "Judgment Day for Arbitrators," *Business Week* (April 19, 1982): 66; R. Johnson, "Interest Arbitration Examined," *Personnel Administrator* (January 1983): 53–59, 73; P. Compton-Forbes, "Interest Arbitration Hasn't Worked Well in the Public Sector," *Personnel Administrator* (February 1984): 99–104.

54. Johnson, "Interest Arbitration Examined"; "Collective Bargaining through Diplomacy," *Bulletin to Management* (January 25, 1990): 32.

55. R. L. Blevins, "Maximizing Company Rights under the Contract," *Personnel Administrator* (June 1984): 75–82; D. A. Hawver, "Plan before Negotiating . . . and Increase Your Power of Persuasion," *Management Review* (February 1984): 46–48; R. J. Colon, "Grievances Hinge on Poor Contract Language," *Personnel Journal* (September 1990): 32–36.

56. S. Slichter, J. Healy, and E. Livernash, *The Impact of Collective Bargaining on Management* (Washington, DC: Brookings Institution, 1960), 694.

57. See note 68, pp. 694–96.

58. J. N. Draznin, "Labor Relations," *Personnel Journal* (July 1981): 528; J. N. Draznin, "Labor Relations," *Personnel Journal* (August 1980): 625; B. A. Jacobs, "Don't Take 'No' for an Answer," *Industry Week* (January 26, 1981): 38–43; Kochan, *Collective Bargaining and Industrial Relations,* 385–86; I. Paster,

"Collective Bargaining: Warnings for the Novice Negotiator," *Personnel Journal* (March 1981): 203–6; M. H. Bazerman and M. A. Neale, *Negotiating Rationally* (New York: Free Press, 1992).

59. B. Skeleton and P. Marett, "Loser Pays Arbitration," *Labor Law Journal* (May 1979): 302–9.

60. G. Bolander, "Fair Representation: Not Just a Union Problem," *Personnel Administrator* (March 1980): 39.

61. J. Hoerr, "What Should Unions Do?" *Harvard Business Review* (May–June 1991): 30–45.

62. C. McDonald, "U.S. Union Membership in Future Decades: A Trade Unionist's Perspective," *Industrial Relations* (winter 1992): 13–30; A. Gladstone et al., eds., *Labour Relations in a Changing Environment* (New York: Walter de Gruyter, 1992); M. Bognanno and M. Kleiner, "Introduction: Labor Market Institutions and the Future Role of Unions," *Industrial Relations* (winter 1992): 1–12.

63. R. Marshall, "The Future Role of Government in Industrial Relations," *Industrial Relations* (winter 1992): 31–49.

64. J. Reid, Jr., "Future Unions," *Industrial Relations* (winter 1992): 122–36.

65. T. A. Kochan and P. Osterman, *The Mutual Gains Enterprise: Forging a Winning Partnership among Labor, Management, and Government* (Boston: Harvard Business School Press, 1994); T. A. Kochan, R. B. McKersie, and P. Cappelli, "Strategic Choice and Industrial Relations Theory," *Industrial Relations* (winter 1984): 16–38; T. A. Kochan and J. Chalykoff, "Human Resource Management and Business Life Cycles: Some Preliminary Propositions" (paper presented at the UCLA Conference on Human Resources and Industrial Relations in High Technology Firms, June 21, 1985); Mills, *New Competitors,* 243–71.

66. A. L. Cowan, "Steel Pact Lets Union Name a Board Member," *New York Times* (August 1, 1993): p. L34.

67. G. Flynn, "HR in Mexico: What You Should Know," *Personnel Journal* (August 1994): 34.

68. *Source:* Adapted from "High Performance Workplaces," *Bulletin to Management* (August 5, 1993): 248. Reprinted by permission of the Bureau of National Affairs, (800)372-1033.

69. S. Dolan and R. S. Schuler, *Human Resource Management* (Toronto: Nelson, 1994); G. Smith, S. Baker and W. Glasgall, "Mexico: Will Economic Reform Survive the Turmoil?" *Business Week* (April 11, 1994): 24–27; S. Baker, G. Smith, and E. Weiner, "The Mexican Worker," *Business Week* (April 19, 1993): 84–92.

70. A. R. Myerson, "Big Labor's Strategic Raid in Mexico," *New York Times* (September 12, 1994): pp. D1, D4.

71. D. J. Schneider, "Canadian and U.S. Brands of Unionism Have Distinctly Different Nationalities," *Management Review* (October 1983): 31–32.

72. J. M. Markham, "German Workers Watch the Clock," *New York Times* (May 13, 1994); P. Revzin, "Swedes Gain Leisure, Not Jobs, by Cutting Hours," *Wall Street Journal* (January 7, 1985): 10.

73. M. S. O'Connor, *Report on Japanese Employee Relations Practices and Their Relation to Worker Productivity* (report prepared for a study mission to Japan, November 8–23, 1980).

CHAPTER 17

1. Randall Schuler's interview with Paul J. Beddia, Cleveland, Ohio, March 30, 1994.
2. *Source:* Adapted from D. Harriger, "Use TQM to Reengineer Human Resources," *HR Focus* (April 1993): 17. Used by permission of American Management Association.
3. M. Kavanagh, H. G. Guental, and S. I. Tannenbaum, *Human Resource Management Information Systems* (Boston: PWS-Kent, 1990); A. J. Walker, *Handbook of Human Resource Information Systems* (New York: McGraw-Hill, 1993); V. R. Ceriello, *Human Resource Management Systems: Strategies, Tactics, and Techniques* (Lexington, MA: Lexington Books, 1991).
4. J. F. Stright, Jr., "Strategic Goals Guide HRMS Development," *Personnel Journal* (September 1993): 68–79; E. E. Kossek et al., "Waiting for Innovation in the Human Resources Department: Godot Implements a Human Resource Information System," *Human Resource Management* 33 (spring 1994): 135–59.
5. "Choosing a New HRIS to Meet Unique and Demanding Business Requirements," *Solutions* (January 1994): 10–11; K. Barnes, "Small Business Productivity Power," *Solutions* (January 1994): 14; J. J. Laabs, "OLIVER: A Twist on Communication," *Personnel Journal* (September 1991): 79–82; "Compensation Advances into a New Decade: Report on 1990 ACA National Conference," *Bulletin to Management* (November 1, 1990); "Computer Use Rising in HR Departments," *Bulletin to Management* (June 15, 1989); R. J. Sahl, "Get It Together! Integrating the HR Department," *Personnel* (February 1989): 39–45.
6. C. Bovier, "How a High-Tech Training System Crashed and Burned," *Training* (August 1993): 26–29.
7. K. Allan, "Computer Courses Ensure Uniform Training," *Personnel Journal* (June 1993): 68. See also "Data Base Helps Employees Learn from Experiences," *Personnel Journal* (January 1993): 57; B. C. Herniter, E. Carmel, and J. Nunamaker, Jr., "Computers Improve the Efficiency of the Negotiation Process," *Personnel Journal* (April 1993): 93–99.
8. M. J. Burke, "Computerized Psychological Testing," in *Personnel Selection,* ed. N. Schmitt and W. C. Borman (San Francisco: Jossey-Bass, 1993). For summaries of research related to adaptive testing by computer, see D. J. Weiss, "Improving Measurement Quality and Efficiency with Adaptive Testing," *Applied Psychological Measurement* 6 (1982): 473–92.
9. J. B. Sympson, D. J. Weiss, and M. J. Ree, *Predictive Validity of Conventional and Adaptive Tests in an Air Force Training Environment,* report no. AFHRL 81-40 (Brooks Air Force Base, TX: Manpower & Personnel Division, Air Force Human Relations Laboratory).
10. C. L. Hulin, F. Drasgow, and C. K. Parsons, *Item Response Theory: Application to Psychological Measurement* (Homewood, IL: Dorsey, 1983).
11. For a critique of the espoused benefits and problems associated with not only adaptive testing but also computerized psychological testing in general, see M. J. Burke and J. Normand, "Computerized Psychological Testing: An Overview and Critique," *Professional Psychology* 3 (1987): 42–51.
12. V. W. Urry, "Tailored Testing: A Successful Application of Latent Trait Theory," *Journal of Educational Measurement* 14 (1977): 181–96.
13. D. R. Budgell, "Preliminary Analysis of the Feasibility of Computerized Adaptive Testing and Item Banking in the Public Service" (unpublished report, Public Service Commission, Ottawa, Ontario, Canada, 1982).
14. L. S. Kleiman and R. H. Faley, "The Implications of Professional and Legal Guidelines for Court Decisions Involving Criterion-Related Validity: A Review and Analysis," *Personnel Psychology* 38 (1985): 803–33. See also the January 1987 issue of *Personnel Administrator* for a series of articles on how recent court decisions have affected management policy.
15. R. S. Schuler and V. L. Huber, *Personnel and Human Resource Management,* 5th ed. (St. Paul: West Publishing Co., 1993), 259-60.
16. R. B. Dunham and F. J. Smith, *Organization Surveys* (Glenview, IL: Scott, Foresman, 1979), 91–97. See also W. H. Read, "Gathering Opinions On-Line," *HR Magazine* (January 1991): 51–53; E. E. Kossek and S. C. Zonia, "Assessing Diversity Climate: A Field Study of Reactions to Employer Efforts to Promote Diversity," *Journal of Organizational Behavior* 14 (1993): 61–81.
17. *Source:* Adapted from M. S. Berry, "Ask the Experts—Employment Policies Audit Helps to Avoid Employee Lawsuits," *Fair Employment Practices Guidelines* (January 10, 1994): 8. See also P. Rosenfield and J. E. Edwards, "Automated System Assesses Equal Opportunity," *Personnel Journal* (September 1994): 99–103.
18. P. T. Kilborn, "Workers Using Computers Find a Supervisor Inside," *New York Times* (December 23, 1990): 1, 18L. See also "Surveillance and Searches: Reducing the Risks," *Bulletin to Management* (November 7, 1991): 345; *Federal Government Information Technology: Electronic Surveillance and Civil Liberties,* report no. OTA-CIT-293 (Washington, DC: Office of Technology Assessment, October 1985); *The Electronic Supervisor: New Technology, New Tensions,* report no. OTA-CIT-333 (Washington, DC: September 1987).
19. See note 18. See also N. J. Beutell and A. J. Walker, "HR Information Systems," in *Managing HR in the Information Age,* by R. S. Schuler (Washington, DC: BNA Books, 1991), 167–203.
20. M. E. Cashman and J. C. McElroy, "Evaluating the HR Function," *HR Magazine* (January 1991): 70–73; M. Mercer, *Turning Your Human Resources Department into a Profit Center* (New York: American Management Association, 1989); B. R. Ellig, "Controlling HR Costs," *Personnel* (April 1990): 20–23; W. F. Cascio, *Costing Human Resources: The Financial Impact of Behavior in Organizations,* 3rd ed. (Boston: PWS-Kent, 1991); D. Ulrich, "Assessing Human Resource Effectiveness: Stakeholder, Utility and Relationship Approaches," *Human Resource Planning* 12, no. 4

(1989): 301–16; L. Dyer, *Human Resource Management: Evolving Roles and Responsibilities* (Washington, DC: BNA Books, 1988), 187–227; J. Fitz-Enz, *Human Values Management: The Value-Adding Human Resource Management Strategy for the 1990s* (San Francisco: Jossey-Bass, 1990); A. S. Tsui, "A Multiple-Constituency Model of Effectiveness: An Empirical Examination at the Human Resource Sub-unit Level," *Administrative Science Quarterly* 35 (1990): 458–83.

21. H. L. Dahl and K. S. Morgan, "Return on Investment in Human Resources" (unpublished manuscript, Upjohn Co., 1982).

22. R. Hackman and G. R. Oldham, *Work Redesign* (Reading, MA: 1980).

23. J. W. Boudreau, "Utility Analysis for Decisions in Human Resource Management," in *Handbook of Industrial and Organizational Psychology,* 2nd ed., ed. M. D. Dunnettee and L. M. Hough (Palo Alto, CA: Consulting Psychologists Press, 1991), 621–746; J. W. Boudreau and S. L. Rynes, "Role of Recruitment in Staffing Utility Analysis," *Journal of Applied Psychology* (May 1985): 354–66; D. F. Caldwell and W. A. Spivey, "The Relationship between Recruiting Source and Employee Success: An Analysis by Race," *Personnel Psychology* (spring 1983): 67–72; D. Dennis, "Are Recruitment Efforts Designed to Fail?" *Personnel Journal* (September 1984): 60–67; P. Farish, "Cost per Hire," *Personnel Administrator* (January 1985): 16; D. A. Levinson, "Needed: Revamped Recruiting Services," *Personnel* (July 1988): 50–52; M. London and S. A. Stumpf, "Effects of Candidate Characteristics on Management Promotion Decisions: An Experimental Study," *Personnel Psychology* (Summer 1983): 241–60; Taylor and Schmidt.

24. F. J. Landy and J. L. Farr, *The Measurement of Work Performance: Methods, Theory and Applications* (San Diego, CA: Academic Press, 1983); Murphy and Cleveland, *Performance Appraisal: An Organizational Perspective.*

25. A "properly administered" compensation program implies several qualities of total compensation: the job evaluation process is valid; pay is administered in a nondiscriminatory way; compensation policies are communicated to be understood; the administrative costs are contained; the compensation has sufficient motivational value; and the compensation is supported by top management.

26. For an extensive description of training and development assessment, see J. Fitz-Enz, "Yes . . . You Can Weigh Training's Value," *Training* (July 1994): 54–58; M. J. Burke and R. R. Day, "A Cumulative Study of the Effectiveness of Managerial Training," *Journal of Applied Psychology* (1986): 232–45; "Cost-Effective Training Techniques," *Bulletin to Management* (August 21, 1986): 284; H. E. Fisher and R. Weinberg, "Make Training Accountable: Assess Its Impact," *Personnel Journal* (January 1988): 73–75; J. Fitz-Enz, "Proving the Value of Training," *Personnel* (March 1988): 17–23; J. K. Ford and S. P. Wroten, "Introducing New Methods for Conducting Training Evaluation and for Linking Training Evaluation to Program Redesign," *Personnel Psychology* (Winter 1984): 651–66.

27. I. Goldstein, *Training: Program Development and Evaluation,* 2nd ed. (Monterey, CA: Brooks/Cole Publishing Co., 1986), 58a.

28. L. Johnson, "Preventing Injuries: The Big Payoff," *Personnel Journal* (April 1994): 61–64.

 CHAPTER 18

1. S. Caudron, "HR Leaders Brainstorm," *Personnel Journal* (August 1994): 54.

2. J. J. Laabs, "HR's Vital Role at Levi Strauss," *Personnel Journal* (December 1992): 34.

3. Ibid., 35.

4. Ibid., 43. See also A. Halcrow, "A Day in the Life of Levi Strauss," *Personnel Journal* (November 1988): 14–15.

5. B. P. Noble, "Retooling the 'People Skills' of Corporate America," *New York Times* (May 22, 1994): p. F8; "Present and Future Human Resources Challenges: American Management Association's Sixty-Fifth Annual HR Conference," *Bulletin to Management* (May 26, 1994): 1.

6. Caudron, "HR Leaders Brainstorm," 61.

7. R. S. Schuler, "Strategic Human Resource Management: Linking the People with the Strategic Needs of the Business," *Organizational Dynamics* (Summer 1992): 18–32.

8. S. Caudron, "Strategic HR at First Chicago," *Personnel Journal* (November 1991): 56. See also P. Stuart, "HR and Operations Work Together at Texas Instruments," *Personnel Journal* (April 1992): 64–68.

9. Caudron, "HR Leaders Brainstorm," 56.

10. See note 9, p. 54.

11. S. Lawrence, "Voice of HR Experience," *Personnel Journal* (April 1989): 64. For an extensive description of HR's new role at AT&T, see D. Anfuso, "AT&T Connects HR and Business Leaders for Success," *Personnel Journal* (December 1994): 84–94.

12. See note 11.

13. "Customers for Keeps: Training Strategies," *Bulletin to Management* (March 31, 1988): 8. See also R. L. Desatnik, *Managing to Keep the Customers* (San Francisco: Jossey-Bass, 1987).

14. P. Hawken, "The Employee as Customer," *Inc.* (November 1987): 21–22; A. Halcrow, "Operation Phoenix: The Business of Human Resources," *Personnel Journal* (September 1987): 92–109; R. S. Schuler and S. E. Jackson, "Customerizing the HR Department," *Personnel Journal* (June 1988): 36–44; R. N. Bramson, "The Secret Weapon in the War for Customers," *HR Magazine* (January 1991): 65–68.

15. S. Caudron, "Team Staffing Requires New HR Role," *Personnel Journal* (May 1994): 88–94; E. E. Lawler III and J. R. Galbraith, "Staff Organizations: New Direc-

tions," in *Organizing for the Future: New Approaches to Managing Complex Organizations* (San Francisco: Jossey-Bass, 1995).

16. J. Walker, "Managing Human Resources in Flat, Lean and Flexible Organizations: Trends for the 1990's," *Human Resource Planning* 11 (1988): 129.

17. E. E. Lawler III, "Human Resource Management: Meeting the Challenge," *Personnel* (January 1988): 25. See also R. E. Walton and P. R. Lawrence, eds., *HRM Trends and Challenges* (Cambridge, MA: Harvard Business School Press, 1985); W. H. Wagel and H. Z. Levine, "HR '90: Challenges and Opportunities," *Personnel* (June 1990): 18–21.

18. "Roundtable Report," *HR Reporter* (December 1988): 3–6.

19. J. Walker, "What's New in HR Development?" *Personnel* (July 1990): 41.

20. C. M. Solomon, "Managing the HR Function," *Personnel Journal* (June 1994): 62–76.

21. J. Fasqualetto, "New Competencies Define the HRIS Manager's Future Role," *Personnel Journal* (January 1993): 91–99.

22. *Source:* Adapted from J. Fasqualetto, "New Competencies Define the HRIS Manager's Future Role," *Personnel Journal* (January 1993): 2. Used by permission.

23. M. Tanzer, "Keep Spies Out of Your Company," *Personnel Journal* (May 1993): 45–51. See also T. Hunter, "How Client/Server Is Reshaping the HRIS," *Personnel Journal* (July 1992): 38–46; J. J. Laabs, "Electronic Campus Captures Apple's Corporate Memory," *Personnel Journal* (November 1993): 104–9.

24. S. H. Applebaum, "The Personnel Professional and Organization Development: Conflict and Synthesis," *Personnel Administrator* (July 1980): 57–61; F. R. Edney, "The Greening of the Profession," *Personnel Administrator* (July 1980): 27–30, 42; F. R. Edney, "Playing on the Team," *Personnel Journal* (August 1981): 598–600; L. B. Prewitt, "The Emerging Field of Human Resources Management," *Personnel Administrator* (May 1982): 81–87.

25. S H. Applebaum, *1991 SHRM/CCCH Survey* (June 26, 1991); M. T. Brown, *Working Ethics: Strategies for Decision Making and Organizational Responsibility* (San Francisco: Jossey-Bass, 1990); L. L. Nash, *Good Intentions Aside: A Manager's Guide to Resolving Ethical Problems* (Boston, MA: Harvard Business School Press, 1990); L. T. Hosmer, *The Ethics of Management* (Homewood, IL: Irwin, 1991).

26. *Certification Information Handbook,* (Alexandria, VA: HR Certification Institute, 1994); D. Yoder and H. Heneman, Jr., *PAIR Jobs, Qualifications, and Careers: ASPA Handbook of Personnel and Industrial Rela-*

tions (Washington, DC: Bureau of National Affairs, 1978), 18; W. M. Hoffman, R. Frederick, and E. W. Petry, Jr., eds. *The Ethics of Organizational Transformation: Mergers, Takeovers and Corporate Restructuring* (New York: Quorum Books, 1989).

27. *Source:* Adapted from "Ethics Line, Standards Booklet Are Ethical Answer Resources," *Eaton Today* (August 1994): 3. Used by permission.

28. W. W. Turnow, "The Codifications Project and Its Importance to Professionalism," *Personnel Administrator* (June 1984): 84–100; C. Haigley, "Professionalism in Personnel," *Personnel Administrator* (June 1984): 103–6. Also contact the Human Research Certification Institute directly by calling the Society for Human Resource Management at (800)331-2772.

29. R. Henson, "Globalization: A Human Resource Mandate," *Solutions* (January 1994): 62–63.

30. J. Walker, "Human Resources Roles for the '90's," *Human Resource Planning* 12 (1989): 55.

31. S. Carroll, "HRM Roles and Structures in the Information Age," in *HRM in the Information Age,* ed. R. S. Schuler (Washington, DC: Society for Human Resource Management and Bureau of National Affairs, 1991).

32. *Human Resource Compensation Survey* (Dearfield, IL: William M. Mercer, Inc., 1993); "Human Resource Compensation Survey," *Bulletin to Management* (July 22, 1993): 228–29; "Human Resources Activities, Budgets and Staffs, 1993–94" (Society for Human Resource Management and Bureau of National Affairs survey no. 59), *Bulletin to Management* (June 30, 1994).

33. "Human Resource Effectiveness Explored," *Bulletin to Management* (July 7, 1994): 216.

34. "The $350,000 HR Director," *Personnel Journal* (June 1993): 18.

35. T. A. Stewart, "Re-engineering: The Hot New Management Tool," *Fortune* (August 23, 1993): 41–48; M. Hammer and J. Champy, *Re-engineering the Corporation* (New York: Harper-Collins, 1993); C. M. Solomon, "Working Smarter: How HR Can Help," *Personnel Journal* (June 1993): 54–64.

36. See note 35.

37. Caudron, "HR Leaders Brainstorm," 59–60.

38. C. M. Solomon, "Managing the Baby-Busters," *Personnel Journal* (March 1992): 56.

39. Caudron, "HR Leaders Brainstorm," 57.

40. P. J. Dowling, R. S. Schuler, and D. Welch, *International Dimensions of Human Resource Management,* 2nd ed. (Belmont, CA: Wadsworth, 1994).

41. *Source:* Adapted from "Giving and Getting Respect at Baxter," *HR Reporter* (April 1992): 7. Used by permission.

⬥ INTEGRATIVE CASE: AID ASSOCIATION FOR LUTHERANS

1. S. Scherreik, "Off the Beaten Path in the Insurance Field," *New York Times* (December 25, 1993): p. L45.

2. J. Hoerr, "Work Teams Can Rev-Up Paper-Pushers, Too," *Business Week* (November 28, 1988): 64–72.

3. This vision statement later became the organization's mission statement.

✤ APPENDIX A

1. For a summary of the conditions under which each type of correlation coefficient is used, refer to M. J. Allen and W. M. Yen, *Introduction to Measurement Theory* (Monterey, CA: Brooks/Cole, 1979), 36–41.

2. G. V. Glass and J. C. Stanley, *Statistical Methods in Education and Psychology* (Englewood Cliffs, NJ: Prentice-Hall, 1970).

3. F. M. Lord and M. R. Novick, *Statistical Theories of Mental Test Scores* (Reading, MA: Addison-Wesley, 1968).

4. E. E. Ghiselli, J. P. Campbell, and S. Zedeck, *Measurement Theory for the Behavioral Sciences* (San Francisco: Freeman, 1981).

5. P. Bobko, "An Analysis of Correlations Corrected for Attenuation and Range Restriction," *Journal of Applied Psychology* 68 (1983): 584–89; R. Lee, R. Miller, and W. Graham, "Corrections for Restriction of Range and Attenuation in Criterion-Related Validation Studies," *Journal of Applied Psychology* 67 (1982): 637–39.

6. A. Howard, "College Experience and Managerial Performance," *Journal of Applied Psychology* 53 (1968): 530–52. For a discussion of the AT&T Management Progress Study, as well as an overview of assessment centers, see A. Howard, "An Assessment of Assessment Centers," *Academy of Management Journal* 17, no. 71 (1974): 115–34. See also A. Howard and D. W. Bray, *Managerial Lives in Transition: Advancing Age and Changing Times* (New York: Guilford, 1988).

7. For a review of validity generalization research, see M. J. Burke, "A Review of Validity Generalization Models and Procedures," in *Readings in Personnel and Human Resource Management,* 3rd ed., ed. R. S. Schuler, S. A. Youngblood, and V. L. Huber (St. Paul, MN: West Publishing Co., 1988). See also F. L. Schmidt and J. E. Hunter, "Development of a General Solution to the Problem of Validity Generalization," *Journal of Applied Psychology* 62 (1977): 529–40. Alternative validity generalization procedures have been presented in J. C. Callender and H. G. Osburn, "Development and Test of a New Model for Validity Generali-

zation," *Journal of Applied Psychology* 65 (1980): 543–58; N. S. Raju and M. J. Burke, "Two New Procedures for Studying Validity Generalization," *Journal of Applied Psychology* 68 (1982): 382–95.

8. G. V. Glass coined the term *meta-analysis* to refer to the statistical analysis of the findings of many individual studies, in "Primary, Secondary, and Meta-Analysis of Research," *Educational Researcher* 5 (1976): 3–8. Numerous articles and books have been written on the subject of meta-analysis (of which validity generalization can be considered a subset); two original and frequently cited texts in this area are G. V. Glass, B. McGaw, and M. L. Smith, *Meta-Analysis in Social Research* (Beverly Hills, CA: Sage, 1981), and J. E. Hunter, F. L. Schmidt, and G. Jackson, *Meta-Analysis: Cumulating Research Findings across Settings* (Beverly Hills, CA: Sage, 1982).

9. P. Cattlin, "Estimations of the Predictive Power of a Regression Model," *Journal of Applied Psychology* 65 (1980): 407–14; J. G. Claudy, "Multiple Regression and Validity Estimation in One Sample," *Applied Psychological Measurement* 2 (1978): 595–607; K. R. Murphy, "Cost-Benefit Considerations in Choosing among Cross-Validation Methods," *Personnel Psychology* 37 (1984): 15–22.

10. W. Cascio, *Costing Human Resource Management,* 3rd ed. (Boston, PWS-Kent, 1991); G. R. Jones and P. M. Wright, "An Economic Approach to Conceptualizing the Utility of Human Resource Management Practices," in *Research in Personnel and Human Resource Management,* 10th ed., ed. K. Rowland and G. Ferris (1992), 271–99.

11. A study that employed this full equation and provides useful information for estimating economic components as well as true validity coefficients is presented in M. J. Burke and J. T. Frederick, "A Comparison of Economic Utility Estimates for Alternative *SD,* Estimation Procedures," *Journal of Applied Psychology* 71 (1986): 334–39.

12. N. S. Raju, M. J. Burke, and J. Normand, "A New Approach for Utility Analysis," *Journal of Applied Psychology* 75, no. 1 (1990): 3–12.

NAME INDEX

SUBJECT AND COMPANY INDEX